Volume II of
The Austrian Army in the Seven Years War

With the support of the Austrian Army Museum
(Heeresgeschichtliches Museum), Vienna

Christopher Duffy

THE EMPEROR PRESS

© 2008 Emperor's Press

All rights reserved. No part of this publicationmay be reproduced, stored in a retrieval system, or transmitted, in any form, or by any means, electronic, mechanical, photocopying, recording, or otherwise, without the prior written permission of the author.

Original edition; Published in 2008

ISBN 1-883476-30-5

Printed and bound in the United States of America

Book Layout by Bitter Books

The Emperor's Press
6000A West Irving Park Road
Chicago, Illinois 60634 U.S.A.
(773) 794 1804
www.emperorspress.com

Table of Contents

	List of Maps	4
	Introduction	8
Chapter I	1756	11
Chapter II	1757	41
Chapter III	1758	92
Chapter IV	1759	153
Chapter V	1760	213
Chapter VI	1761	308
Chapter VII	The War in the Balance, Winter 1761/2	328
Chapter VIII	1762	335
Chapter IX	Peace	392
Appendix 1	The Theatre of War	400
Appendix 2	Leading Personalities	420
Appendix 3	List of Regiments	428
	Notes	458
	Bibliography	470
	Index	477

Maps

The Theatre of Operations	6 & 398
Lobositz, 1 October 1756	20
The expedition to Saxony, October 1756	30
Browne and the Saxons, 11-14 October 1756	32
The Prussians invade Bohemia, April 1757	40
Prague, 6 May 1757	44
Kolin, 18 June 1757	50
The pursuit after Kolin, June-July 1757	54
The confrontation at Eckartsberg, August 1757	60
Hadik Visits Berlin: October 1757	68
Breslau, 22 November 1757	72
Leuthen, 5 December 1757	82
The enemies of Prussia—axes of operations	96
The march to relieve Olmütz, June - July 1758	102
Gundersdorf, 28 June, and Domstadtl, 30 June 1758	106
The defence of Olmütz, May - July 1758	112
Frederick's retreat to Bohemia, July - August 1758	118
To Hochkirch, October 1758	126
The Austrians converge on Hochkirch, 14 October 1758	130
Hochkirch, the battle	134
Before and after Kunersdorf: Austrians, Russians, and Prussians, July-September 1759	160
Kunersdorf, 12 August 1759	164
Kunersdorf, the crisis	168
First Torgau, 8 September 1759	185
Löthain (Korbitz) 21 September 1759	186
Pretzsch, 29 October 1759	192
Maxen 20 November 1759	198
Maxen, the main assault	202
Dresden and Lusatia, June-July 1760	222
The siege of Dresden, July 1760	224
The scene of operations around Dresden, 1756-1760	226
Landeshut, 23 June 1760	234
The storm of the Alte Festung, Glatz, 26 July 1760	242
Before and after Liegnitz, August 1760	248
Liegnitz, the Austrian Plan	250

Liegnitz, 15 August 1760	252
The Silesian Hills, August-September 1760	262
Lacy Visits Berlin: October 1760	264
Berlin, 7-8 October 1760	266
Strehla overall, 20 August 1760	272
The Dürren-Berg at Strehla	274
Hülsen is evicted from Döbien, 2 October 1760	277
Wittenberg, 10-13 October 1760	278
Before Torgau, October-November 1760	280
Torgau, 3 November 1760, the Prussian approach	286
Torgau overall, 3 November 1760	288
Torgau, the fatal counterattack of Arenberg's infantry	291
Torgau, the counterattack against the Prussian breakthrough	292
Torgau, O'Donnell against Holstein	293
Torgau, Zieten is contained	294
Torgau, night, the Prussian junction and the Austrian retreat	299
Loudon and the Russians in Silesia, 1761	314
The positions at Bunzelwitz, August-September 1761	318
Loudon storms Schweidnitz, 1 October 1761	324
Teplitz, 2 August 1762	338
Adelsbach, 6 July 1762	342
The campaign in Silesia and north Bohemia, 1762, schematic	344
Daun's successive positions in Silesia, July 1762	348
Burkersdorf, 20/21 July 1762	352
The scene of operations in Silesia and north Bohemia, 1762	360
Reichenbach, 16 August 1762	364
The Jauernicker Fort at Schweidnitz, August-October 1762	370
Hadik's offensive in Saxony, September - October 1762	376
Freiberg overall, 29 October 1762	380
Freiberg, the battle of the woods	384
The Central and Eastern Border Passes	412

The Theatre of Operations

INTRODUCTION

The rise of a militarised Prussia, and ultimately of a Prussianised Germany, forms a recognisable theme in European history from 1740 until the German catastrophe of 1945. Already in the middle of the eighteenth century the great and gracious Habsburg Empress Maria Theresa and her chief minister Count Kaunitz had a clear sense of what kind of public enemy was ascending in northern Europe, and the present work is a record of their striving to confront this threat between the years 1756 and 1763 in what has become known as 'The Seven Years War'.

Maria Theresa and Kaunitz fell short of the specific objectives which they had set before themselves, but it is likely that they put back the aggrandisement of Prussia by one or more generations, and their efforts in any event helped indirectly to create that Central European cultural community which outlived the Habsburg Empire itself and extends far beyond the boundaries of present-day Austria.

My first volume, *Instrument of War* (Chicago 2000) set out the background in terms of the territorial and cultural base, the human, material and financial resources, and the institutions and policies. All that is an important part of the story, but it is not the whole story. It pains me to be at variance with my good friend Michael Hochedlinger, a scholar-archivist in the tradition of Arneth, Brabant, Allmayer-Beck and Broucek, but I have to disagree with him when he can write: 'Campaign and battle history, is not only old-fashioned and likely to arouse deep-rooted prejudices against a discipline that still has to struggle to find a place in the sun; in addition the older narrative history has largely and in considerable detail exhausted the study of campaigns and battles' ['Bella gerant allii..? On the state of Early Modern Military History in Austria,' *Austrian History Yearbook*, XXX, Minneapolis 1999, 24].

On the contrary, the study of even the most familiar battles and campaigns is literally inexhaustible, being always open to re-interpretation in the light of unsuspected sources and new perspectives, a process which French historians term *la nouvelle histoire bataille*. For the Austrian military commitment in the Seven Years War there exists not even a basic chronicle (a want deplored by Theodor von Bernhardi as long ago as 1881), let alone an exploration of the vocabulary, grammar and logic of the Austrian way of war at that time, all of which deserve our best attentions. 'The art of war is of vital importance to the state. It is a matter of life and death. A road leading to safety and ruin. Hence it is a subject of enquiry which can on no account be neglected' (Sun Tzu).

Only by reviewing events in their proper sequence does it emerge that over the generations the study of 'The Background of Napoleonic Warfare' has remained bookish and francocentric. The story of the Seven Years War in Central Europe has been left entirely out of account, and yet it was there that the Austrians (followed closely by the Prussians) broke with the former rigidity of the armies of monarchial Europe, and not just foreshadowed but put into actual effect initiatives that are normally associated with the campaigns of the Revolution and Napoleon.

For a much neded survey of the war on the continent as a whole I recommend Franz Szabo's *The Seven Years War in Europe 1756-1763*. Professor Szabo takes a generally more benevolent view of Kaunitz's mentality and doings than you will find in my pages.

In my striving I hope I have not neglected the oldest of all duties of an historian, which is to tell a tale. In this case the amount of detail which can be retrieved from the memoirs, diaries and documents is immense, and bears comparison with that available for the Napoleonic Wars. It is therefore with confidence that I can invite readers to put themselves on easy terms with Maria Theresa, Browne, Daun,

Lacy, Loudon and Kaunitz (well, on consideration perhaps not with Kaunitz). These people will make good company, and help us to answer what is even now the most important question which can be asked of any institution or activity, namely 'who is in charge?'

There are episodes that would be worthy of note in any age. Among those that clamour for attention I just adduce Brentano's little battle at Adelsbach in 1762, when he turned back a thrust of Prussians and Russians, and sent King Frederick packing amid hails of howitzer shells and rocks his Hungarians were tumbling down from a hilltop.

This work was longer in the writing than I care to tell, and I owe much to the patience and constant encouragement of my publisher. I am deeply indebted to Dean West and the late Jim Mitchell, fellow members of the Seven Years War Association, who did so much to put the manuscript in a state fit for printing.

The term 'Austrians' is applied in the same loose way that was current in the period, to embrace all who were in the Habsburg service. Likewise the word 'Croats' takes in many peoples who in later times would be careful to define themselves as Serbs. The suffix 'von' is generally omitted, except in compound names, like 'Losy von Losenau.'

For the deployment of forces and key commanders in combat, please refer to the text and supporting maps. These are based on the manuscript accounts and maps of the time, which are much more reliable guides than conventional orders of battle, which were so often overtaken by events.

For further detail on the campaigns of 1757 please see the author's *The Wild Goose and the Eagle. A Life of Marshal von Browne 1705-1757*, London 1964; *Prussia's Glory. Rossbach and Leuthen 1757*, Chicago, 2003, and the forthcoming *Austria Saved. Prague and Kolin 1757*.

In memory of Jim Mitchell, true gentleman and scholar.

The ranks of field officers ran as follows:

British	Austrian	Prussian
Major General	*Generalfeldwachtmeister (GFWM.)*	*General-Major (GM.)*
Lieutenant General	*Feldmarschalllieutenant (FML.)*	*General-Lieutenant (GL.)*
General (full)	*Feldzeugmeister (FZM.)* (infantry)	*General der Infanterie (G.d.I)*
	General der Cavallerie (GdC.)	*General der Cavallerie (G.d.C.)*

*Wenzel Anton Count Kaunitz-Rietberg,
architect of Austria's grand strategy in the Seven Years War*

I
1756

To War

The first shot of the Seven Years War in Europe was fired on 3 September 1756. The Prussians were invading Saxony, and one of their columns was approaching the rock castle of Stolpen, in the hills to the east of Dresden. Lieutenant Colonel Charles-Emanuel Warnery was leading with a party of hussars. He presented himself at the gate, and by brandishing his pair of heavy horse pistols he made the guards open the door. He rode across the bridges which spanned the three ditches, and emerged in the central courtyard, which was surrounded by tall buildings. He was alone, except for his trumpeter and one of his officers. He ordered the trumpeter to blow *Appel*, whereupon the garrison of seventy-one men began to spill into the courtyard, and the commandant, Major General Liebenau, stuck his head out of a window and asked by what leave Warnery had entered his castle. In this emergency Warnery could think of nothing better to do than to fire one of his pistols at Liebenau, who fell back wounded.

The second shot of the war went off by accident, when Warnery waved his other pistol at the Saxon troops, who were taking up their weapons. The double shock broke the nerve of the garrison, which surrendered without putting up a fight.

Frederick II (later 'The Great' to his admirers) of Prussia had broken the public peace of Europe in a spectacular way, and he unwittingly conjured up what he most feared, which was to cause the great powers of the continent to league against him. The contest was going to last seven years, and it put in question the survival of Prussia as a militaristic state, capable of threatening its neighbours. We must pause for a little explanation.

Frederick had come to the throne of Brandenburg-Prussia in 1740, and he had the best army in the world at his disposal. He put it to almost immediate use by invading the rich northern Austrian province of Silesia, which covers a sizeable area of present-day Poland. The ramshackle Austrian monarchy was in no state to resist the aggression, and it took all the efforts of its young ruler, Maria Theresa, to hold the rest of her vast domains together in 1741.

Maria Theresa could not reconcile herself to the verdict of the two Silesian Wars (1740-2 and 1744-5), which left Frederick in possession of Silesia. She and her advisers now began the slow process of transforming the Habsburg body politic into something which was capable of surviving into the new age. From 1749 they addressed themselves to the finances and the administration. It was just as important to mend and improve the army, and for this they looked to *FM.* Leopold Daun for the infantry and cavalry, and to Joseph Wenzel Prince Liechtenstein for the artillery. The work was given a new purpose and direction by Wenzel Anton Count Kaunitz, who became foreign minister (*Staatscanzler*) in 1753. Kaunitz believed that it was not only possible to win back Silesia by force of arms, but to so humble Prussia as to put it beyond the power of Frederick and his successors to challenge the ascendancy of the House of Habsburg in Central Europe.

Maria Theresa and Kaunitz were moved by complementary but disparate impulses. Highly intelligent, and ultimately to be reckoned among the most successful of the reforming monarchs of her age, the Empress was also alive to her status and obligations as the eldest daughter of the House of Habsburg, generations of which had been sustained by their attachment to the Catholic Church, and more recently by an almost bourgeois way of family life. Cosiness, austerity and grandeur came together at her court in a combination which struck foreign visitors as unique. For Maria Theresa, warm, impulsive and emotional, her people and her soldiers were a family writ large, and in this middle period of her reign she was torn between her perceived duty to rescue her beloved Silesians from Prussian rule, and her growing knowledge of what the effort might cost her troops and the rest of her subjects.

For Kaunitz, the ability to set aside emotion in matters of state was one of the faculties which raised him above the rest of humanity. Eccentric to extreme in his manners, he brought a cold brilliance to forwarding his career and his policies, and as a pioneer of what became known as the 'Enlightenment' he believed that the world was susceptible to rational exploration. Kaunitz was confident that he had it in his power to identify a state's interests, such as those which bound Russia to Austria, but brought Austria and Prussia into 'violent' collision. It seemed to him that a man of elevated perception (like himself) could therefore govern foreign policy in a dispassionate way. In comparison, managing war was an intellectually inferior activity, something like understanding and winding up the mechanism of a clock, 'and hence when we direct the military machine towards an objective, it is just a question of imparting movement in a physical sense.'[1]

By the summer of 1756 the work of transforming the Habsburg state was far from complete, and it could scarcely have been otherwise. Hardly seven years had been devoted to the task, whereas the groundwork of Prussian military strength had been laid as early as 1653. The core lands of the Habsburg monarchy comprised a great block which extended in the one direction from the Swiss border to Transylvania, and in the other from the Elbe and the Oder to central Italy and the Adriatic. Separated geographically from the rest, the Austrian Netherlands stretched from the Ardennes to the Channel coast. There was no commonality of race, language, religion, law or social and economic development, and the lands could be governed at all only with the consent of powerful established interests. Maria Theresa tested the tolerance of the magnates as far as she dared, but their power imposed limits on the human and financial resources she could draw from her realms, and obstruction and faction were to be found in all branches of civil and military affairs. The spirit of 'democracy' (as it was termed sarcastically at the time) was carried into the highest counsels by Maria Theresa's consort Francis Stephen, who, although not of the Habsburg blood, inevitably shared a measure of authority with her in the Habsburg lands, and owned a degree of moral and legal power in the German states as the elected Emperor of Germany. It was the influence of Francis Stephen which maintained in high position such undeserving individuals as his brother Prince Charles of Lorraine in 1757, and Field Marshal Serbelloni from the middle until almost the end of the war.

The army had a particular place in Maria Theresa's regard, as the means of defending or recovering her territories, and as the one institution which in one form or another represented every land of the monarchy. Here too the progress of reform was uneven. The material in general was much improved, and the opening actions of the war were to demonstrate that the artillery had become probably the finest in Europe. Field Marshal Daun had established a greater uniformity of drill and discipline through the regular infantry and cavalry, and the foot soldiers were to show themselves tenacious and reliable. Much was still to be done. The regular cavalry had improved in absolute terms, but that of the Prussians (very bad in the early 1740s) was now better still, and, scandal of scandals, the Prussian hussars were going to outclass the 'authentic' Hungarian version. The changes as they affected the Croatian light infantry were an unsatisfactory compromise, for they had deprived the Croats of something of their warrior virtues, without endowing them with the solidity of the 'German' infantry. Altogether the Austrians were in danger of losing the edge in irregular warfare which they had enjoyed as recently as the 1740s.

Staff work was amateurish, and professional curiosity among the body of officers was not always easy to find. *FM.* Browne noted in June 1756 that Frederick and his officers knew more about the geography of the northern Habsburg provinces than did the Austrians themselves, and 'it is safe to say that our regimental officers have never got into the habit exploring the lie of the land in the locations where they are quartered, and that is something you must do if you are to orientate yourself when the need arises.'[2] More fundamentally the Habsburgs had not yet developed an ethos of devotion to army and state such as had been cultivated in Prussia. So it was that traditions of officer service scarcely existed outside the nobility of the southern Austrian Netherlands, the southeastern Austrian Alpine provinces and Hungary, or certain families of Irish émigrés and the German *Reich*.

Kaunitz admitted to just one weakness in himself, and that was that he found it difficult to keep more than one matter in his head at a time. Perhaps this failing accounts for the mismatch between Austria's respective states of diplomatic and military preparedness in the summer of 1756. Kaunitz was bent on war with Prussia. It was nevertheless clear to him that such a war could be won only if Prussia could be brought under attack from three directions, by the Russians from the east, by the Austrians from the south, and by the French from the west.

What is called the 'Diplomatic Revolution,' or in the more explicit French '*Le Renversement des Alliances*,' was the business of weaning Habsburg Austria and Bourbon France from generations of hostility, and bringing the two powers together in an understanding against Prussia. In Vienna Kaunitz had succeeded in winning over Maria Theresa and most of his astonished colleagues, but in France his converts had been limited to King Louis XV and his mistress the Pompadour. All the same the support of France was well worth having, for that kingdom was the most powerful state in Europe, and the clients of the French included Sweden, Bavaria, Saxony and the prince bishops of the Rhineland. The French liked to think that their influence extended to Prussia as well, and they therefore considered themselves betrayed when the Prussians and British concluded a deal (the Convention of Westminster, 16 January 1756) which provided for the security of Hanover, which belonged to King George II of Britain in his capacity as Elector of Hanover.

Kaunitz at last had his opening, and on 1 May 1756 the representatives of France and Austria signed a defensive alliance (the First Treaty of Versailles), in which they undertook to support each other with 25,000 troops or a cash equivalent if either came under attack from a third power. The French were nevertheless unwilling to engage themselves any further.

Austria's alliance with Russia dated back to an agreement of 1726, and it was now sustained by Empress Elizabeth and her shifting constellations of ministers, who believed that Frederick had ambitions to gain the ascendancy in northern Europe. In the case of Elizabeth the determination was reinforced by her regard for Maria Theresa, and by her dislike of Frederick, who had written rude poems about her.

On 22 May 1756 Kaunitz actually had to send word to the Russians to put off their attack until the next year, for he still did not have an active military alliance with France. A few days later he learned that the Austrian army was in any case in no condition to open war (below). On 26 July and again on 22 August the Prussian envoy Klinggräffen asked the Austrians to explain their mobilisation, which was in fact lagging behind that of the Prussians, and Kaunitz had to put him off by vague assurances.

On 24 August Kaunitz reported to Maria Theresa the first potentially hostile act, for the Prussians had detained 439 cavalry remounts which the Austrians had bought in northern Germany. By any reckoning these were critical days in the history of the House of Habsburg-Lorraine, and yet it was behaving with extraordinary insouciance. Francis Stephen had set out on 20 August for an extended hunting holiday at Holitsch on the Moravian-Hungarian borders, and Maria Theresa followed him the next day. The Emperor was amused when, on 2 September, the warning came from the Austrian ambassador in Dresden, Count Sternberg, that Saxony was about to be invaded by the Prussians. *FML.* Buccow arrived a little later with the same tale, which added to the merriment, and Francis Stephen was still laughing when he drove through the forest in the cool of the evening. On

3 September the Imperial party was diverted by the sight of the cuirassier regiments of Birkenfeld and Lucchesi, which were on the march from Hungary, and 'after we dined we hunted with beaters and there was a repeat of yesterday's pantomime.'[3] News arrived on the same day that Prussian troops had crossed the Saxon border on 29 August. Maria Theresa left for Vienna on 4 September, but Francis Stephen lingered at Holitsch until the 19th.

Frederick had been aware that a league of some kind was being conjured up against him, and an official of the court of Bayreuth (which had family links with the House of Hohenzollern) later explained in conversation that 'the certainty of this great plot had been confirmed to him by the secretary to Count Puebla, the Austrian minister plenipotentiary in Berlin.' He had been passing on copies of the correspondence with Kaunitz in Vienna.[4]

Conceivably the secretary was a double agent, who had been briefed to provoke the king into action. Certainly nothing could have better suited the present purposes of Kaunitz. By turning into Saxony, rather than immediately into the Habsburg provinces of Bohemia and Moravia, Frederick had given the Austrians some needful days in which to press ahead with uninhibited military preparations. Better still, at least from the diplomatic point of view, Saxony was not only innocent of complicity in the plots, but was the home of Luther and renowned in Germany as the birthplace of the Reformation. The moral authority of Francis Stephen as Emperor of Germany could now be brought into play to summon up the support of the *Kaisertreu* elements of the *Reich*, whether Protestant or Catholic.

How well was Austria prepared to fight its war? The answer was not very well at all, and the reason was the disparity between the aggressive nature of Kaunitz's foreign policy and the backward state of the Austrian military machine. Rumours of war had been circulating two years before, and as 1756 wore on even the junior officers noted how 'we girded our loins accordingly, but ever so slowly... we began to rummage our house for our weapons when the enemy was already in full battle gear at our gates.'[5]

Someone in a high military position (his identity is still unknown) at last shared his concerns with Maria Theresa's cabinet secretary Ignaz Koch. On 16 May Koch had given Maria Theresa an extended memorandum which showed how unready Austria was to wage war. He pointed out that the number of men available for the field was much less than had been supposed. Proper military understandings should be reached with the French and Russians, and meanwhile such troops as were available should be concentrated in Bohemia and Moravia at the beginning of August. Something must also be done to provide them with field artillery, nearly all of which was still in depot in Vienna.[6]

Up to now Kaunitz had not given much consideration to the matter. 'As a political animal he had invariably acted on the basis of purely political considerations. From the beginning he had paid surprisingly little attention to the military tasks which had been set by his great design.'[7] Kaunitz learned of the paper in a conversation with Koch on 24 May. The cabinet secretary retrieved his document from Maria Theresa and passed it to Kaunitz on the 26th, apologising for its appearance: 'Her Majesty can read my poor handwriting without any trouble; I do not know whether Your Excellency will be able to do the same.'[8]

Kaunitz was now at least aware of what had to be done, and he became a prominent member of a *Rüstungscommission* (mobilisation committee) which sat from 8 July to manage the transition to a war footing. Even now he judged that politics spoke for letting Prussia take some kind of a lead in military initiatives, and he was certainly correct, but the consequent delays, together with oversights on the part of the *Hofkriegsrath* (the main body of military administration) left Austria ill-prepared to face hostilities.

Austria's backwardness was partly a question of numbers. If every unit had been recruited up to its full peacetime establishment, the army would have amounted to 156,750 regular troops, together with 46,740 Croats who would be liable for military service in batches of one-third at a time. On 22 July *FM.* Wilhelm Reinhard Neipperg, as Vice-President and moving force of the *Hofkriegsrath*, estimated that it would be possible to mobilise only 45,320 regular infantry, 12,000 Croats, 14,400 cuirassiers and dragoons, and 3,000 hussars, or a total of just short of 75,000 troops, to which we should add the 1,620 artillerymen who were actually mustered. By the end of August the authorities had succeeded in bringing together no more than 32,456 troops in Bohemia, and 22,606 in Moravia, or rather over 55,000 in all, including those 1,620 gunners.

In peacetime the troops and the cavalry horses were quartered where they could best be accommodated and fed, and not where they were most needed for a war against Prussia. About one-third of the infantry was to be found in Bohemia and Moravia, which was useful, but only about 9 per cent of the regular cavalry, for 70 per cent of that arm was quartered in Hungary and distant Transylvania. Within the kingdoms and provinces many of the troops were dispersed in penny packets in villages and farmsteads, since no importance was attached to keeping even the basic units of the squadron and company together. The process of mobilisation could be counted as beginning only on 18 June, and then in a discreet way, when orders went out to concentrate the cavalry in two camps near the western borders of Hungary.

The trains of transport for moving the artillery, ammunition, equipment and provisions had to be created anew to meet every war. That was the common practice of the time, but it was all the more important to collect the carts and draught animals at the first inkling of trouble. The contracts for the artillery horses were placed only on 24 July. By 31 August most of the pieces had still not arrived, and the Prussians were already marching through Saxony. *FM*. Browne had to send an urgent *Pro Memoria* to explain what his forces in Bohemia still needed to wage war. He could spare no artillery for the companion army in Moravia, and the first instalment of pieces for his own army had arrived at Kolin only the day before, and consisted of just forty 3-pounder regimental pieces, six 6-pounders, and four 7-pounder howitzers, which was ninety-eight pieces short of the proper complement. The train of forty or fifty sheet metal pontoons was still languishing in Vienna, and Browne would have only 400,000 small-arms cartridges in reserve, after he had issued the initial allowance of twenty-four rounds for each weapon.

Browne's paper was read out at a military conference on 3 September, and Maria Theresa was outraged at the bureaucratic inertia which was revealed. 'I simply cannot understand why there is no sign of the artillery trains,' she noted in the margin, 'something urgent must be done.'[9] She ordered forty pieces to be sent immediately, and if necessary from Vienna, if they were not available from the Bohemian depot at Moldathein. 'Theresa now opened the gates of her stables and gave up her own horses to forward the cannon. The Austrian and Bohemian nobles competed to imitate her in the great example she had set… and so the pieces were transported at a quite unexpected speed.'[10]

By contrast, sensible and reasonably prompt measures had already been taken to provide the remounts to raise the regiments of horse up to their proper strength. The contractor Altvatter had been bringing in strings of animals from north-west Germany (the breeding ground par excellence of the heavy cavalry horse), though as late as 25 July it was thought inadvisable for him to take his normal route through Prussian territory, lest any kind of detour should betoken hostile intent. Nine hundred horses were bought on home ground in Bohemia and Moravia, and the regiments were given the freedom to purchase whatever remounts they still needed.

Some of the most important talks in Vienna related to the business of feeding the army and its animals. On 8 and 9 July it was agreed that the priority must be to buy up the hay, oats and other cereals in the exposed areas of Bohemia north of the Elbe, before they could be snapped up by the Prussians. On 30 July the chief commissary Franz Ludwig Salburg was able to report that the noble assemblies (*Stände*) of Moravia had agreed to provide the necessary flour, grain and hay to sustain the forces in that province for the next four months, and that similar arrangements had been made in Bohemia.

On the matter of field command, Maria

Maximilan Ulysses Count Browne, focus of hopes in the first period of the war (Military Academy, Wiener Neustadt)

Theresa listened to her innermost circle of military advisers, and appointed *FZM.* Piccolomini and *FM.* Browne to lead the gathering forces. Aeneas Anton Prince Piccolomini d'Arragona was destined for the local command in Moravia. He was the last of his branch of a famous and ancient military family, and he was a straight-dealing and tough-minded man who inspired awe and confidence among his troops

FM. Maxmilian Ulysses Browne was described as being 'brimming over with courage and ambition. He is masterly in his planning, and carries out his designs with bravery and foresight. He is inventive, certainly, but perhaps a little facile in putting forward proposals if he knows that he will not be the man who will have to carry them out, or suspects that they will not be accepted in the first place. For all of that Your Majesty has in him an excellent general, and all the more because he is respected by the enemy, and is loved by the ordinary soldiers.'[11] Maria Theresa already held Browne in high personal regard, and on 4 August he was placed in formal command of the field army now gathering in Bohemia, together with overall authority over Piccolomini's forces in Moravia.

The family of Browne was now in its second and third generations of service to the Habsburgs, and was connected by marriage with the Lacys, another of the Norman-Irish families of County Limerick. Maximilan Ulysses had conducted a skilful holding action in the face of Frederick's first aggression, in 1740-1. He had turned the tide against the Spanish in north Italy in 1746, and carried the fight into Provence in the following winter. In 1752 Browne was made commanding general of Bohemia, and he schooled his troops to a high degree of proficiency in the new tactics. In August 1754, as a newly-promoted field marshal, he gathered his regiments in the largest of all the pre-war encampments at Kolin, and put them through their paces under the eyes of Their Imperial Majesties. The manoeuvres were of a novel 'contested' kind, resembling real combat, and led to some fatalities when the native Austrians happened to meet Hungarians.

Browne was a hard man, but his rapport with his troops was remarkable in the Austrian service at the time, and it came from his love of theatrical gesture, his willingness to share all the hardships of the field, and the trust he put in his army. He put together his notions of military obligation in a set of directions ('*Verhaltungspuncte*') which he first circulated in Italy in 1746, and which he distributed again in Bohemia in September 1756. Here we read: 'Duty is not just a question of carrying out orders to the letter. On the contrary, every officer in authority must make his own judgement of time and circumstances, and in the lack of higher orders he must act on his own initiative and do whatever will promote the Imperial service. Whoever does this, if only a private soldier, shows that he knows what military honour is about, and deserves to be promoted and rewarded.'[12]

In all of this Browne was guided by a strong sense of destiny, for he believed that he was living through a life as foretold by a Carthusian monk of Rome, whom he met while he was a pupil at the Clementinum in Prague in 1719.[13]

On 19 June, the day after the first move towards mobilisation, the *Hofkriegsrath* ordered Browne to be on the alert for the gathering of forces in Silesia. Browne replied on the 24th that it was difficult to obtain reliable information, but he knew that the Prussians had it in their power to be deep inside Bohemia in a matter of days.[14] On 29 July a military conference in Vienna approved Browne's contingency plan to move the troops from the mobilisation camp at Kolin to Königgrätz in north-east Bohemia. The choice of Königgrätz was sensible, in the light of what was known to the Austrians at that time. Concentrated there, the main Austrian forces could not only guard the meeting point of all three routes from Silesia to north-east Bohemia, but also support Piccolomini by acting against the flank of any Prussian advance directly south by way of Moravia against Vienna. It was true that in 1744 the Prussians had actually invaded to the west, up the axis of the Elbe towards Prague, but that route seemed to be closed off by the neutral buffer state of Saxony.

THE GENESIS OF THE PIRNA EXPEDITION

Kaunitz wrote to Browne on 25 August, to keep him up to date with the latest diplomatic exchanges, which were pointing to war. Browne answered three days later, and mentioned that he was concerned about the threateningly large forces that the Prussians were now building up around Magdeburg and Halle, in other words well to the west of the gathering in Silesia, which up to now had seemed to pose the main danger. On the next day, the 29th, the Prussians irrupted across the borders of Saxony on a wide frontage. Frederick intended to eliminate one of the supposed partners in the hostile league in a single blow, and he hoped to find proof of Saxon complicity when he ransacked the archives in Dresden. Frederick was mistaken, and he had made a political blunder of the first order. However the military advantages were great, for he could now exact recruits, cattle, fodder and cash from Saxony at will, and he had opened up Bohemia to invasion from the north-west.

Frederick was confident that the Saxon army would soon be in his power. The Saxons had evaded the first Prussian lunge into the electorate, but instead of escaping into Bohemia while there was still time, they had bottled themselves up in the celebrated camp of Pirna, which lay between Dresden and the Bohemian border. The little fortresses of Pirna and Königstein secured the northern and southern ends of the position; the long western flank was studded with batteries, earthworks, abattis and the steep Gottleube valley, while the rear was bordered by the precipitous sandstone gorge of the Elbe and was absolutely impregnable. But the very strength of the camp made it into something of a prison, and by 10 September it was under close blockade from all sides. The 19,000 Saxon troops were thrown entirely on their own resources, and their provisions and fodder would not last beyond four weeks.

The strategy agreed so recently in Vienna had been overtaken by events, and on 1 September Browne wrote to Kaunitz to explain that he must now march directly from Kolin to confront the enemy in the border hills of north-west Bohemia, and that Piccolomini would have to move from Moravia to guard north-east Bohemia in his place.

Augustus was one of those dual-hatted sovereigns of eighteenth-century Europe, being at the same time Friedrich August II as Elector of Saxony, and King Augustus III of Poland. He was now a de facto ally of the Austrians, and on the face of it he deserved support. However the plight of the little Saxon army, stranded on the plateau of Pirna, presented Vienna and Browne with some nice problems.

The provisions in Pirna would have run out even more quickly, if a corps of 10,000 Austrians had simply reinforced the Saxons in their camp, as was now being proposed. More dangerous still was another Saxon scheme, whereby the main Austrian army would march into Saxony —and run the risk of being destroyed if the Saxon generals and ministers suddenly made a deal with the Prussians. It was a physical impossibility for the Austrians to get supplies to Pirna over the hill tracks of the border, or along the Elbe. 'I put all of this in some detail before the Saxon officers who had been sent to me,' explained Browne on 7 September, 'and indicated at the same time how their retreat could best be secured. I am firmly convinced that their best course would be for their forces to fall back into Bohemia, and so avert their impending fate.'[15]

Browne got his troops at Kolin ready to march, while at the same time he fed detachments to the Saxon border to guard the exits from the hills, to calm the panic-stricken landowners, and generally do what they could to keep up contact with the Saxon army. A first instalment of 3,000 elite troops set out under the command of *GFWM*. Wied on 3 September. *GFWM*. Prince Löwenstein left with an increment of 1,000 cavalry on the 7th, and on the evening of that day the Saxon lieutenant colonel Riedesel reached Browne at Kolin. It seemed to Riedesel that the Austrians were ready to move, 'but everything is conducted with such secrecy that it is difficult for me to learn anything, and particularly because I am only getting to know people.'[16]

The campaigning season was already far advanced, and Frederick, who had unfinished business with the Saxons, had no intention of

The castle of Tetschen

invading Bohemia in force. He thought it enough to send detachments a short distance into the kingdom, just to secure the rear of his blockading forces around Pirna. On the night of 22/23 September the Prussian lieutenant colonel Strozzi attacked the castle, or rather palace of **Tetschen**, which crowned a low rock table on a bend of the Elbe. It took just a few shots from his battalion pieces to persuade the garrison of seventy-three men to surrender. The Prussians built a bridge of twenty-four pontoons where the valley widened once more further upstream at Aussig, but upriver again the narrows were commanded by the grim little stronghold of **Schreckenstein**, which was a proper castle, and overlooked the Elbe from a crag of black basalt on the east bank. Here Browne's compatriot Colonel Peter MacElligot had a force of 400 Croats, who repulsed a storm on 27 September. The Croats proceeded to plague the Prussians so effectively that the pontoon bridge at Aussig became unusable, and it was taken apart on Frederick's instructions two days later.

On 14 September Browne's army finally set out from Kolin. The field marshal was riding ahead, and on the 16th he reached Lobositz, on the west bank of the Elbe just short of the border hills. The ground had some interesting possibilities, but it was vulnerable to an outflanking move further to the west from the direction of Teplitz, which persuaded him to bring up his army on the 20th only as far as Budin, where it could occupy a long continuous ridge that descended smoothly to the levels of the winding river Eger, which formed a natural outer ditch. The plain beyond was rimmed by an irregular row of volcanic peaks and domes. These were the sinister heights of the Mittel-Gebirge which had a way of taking on a curious misty bluish-green in the daylight, and

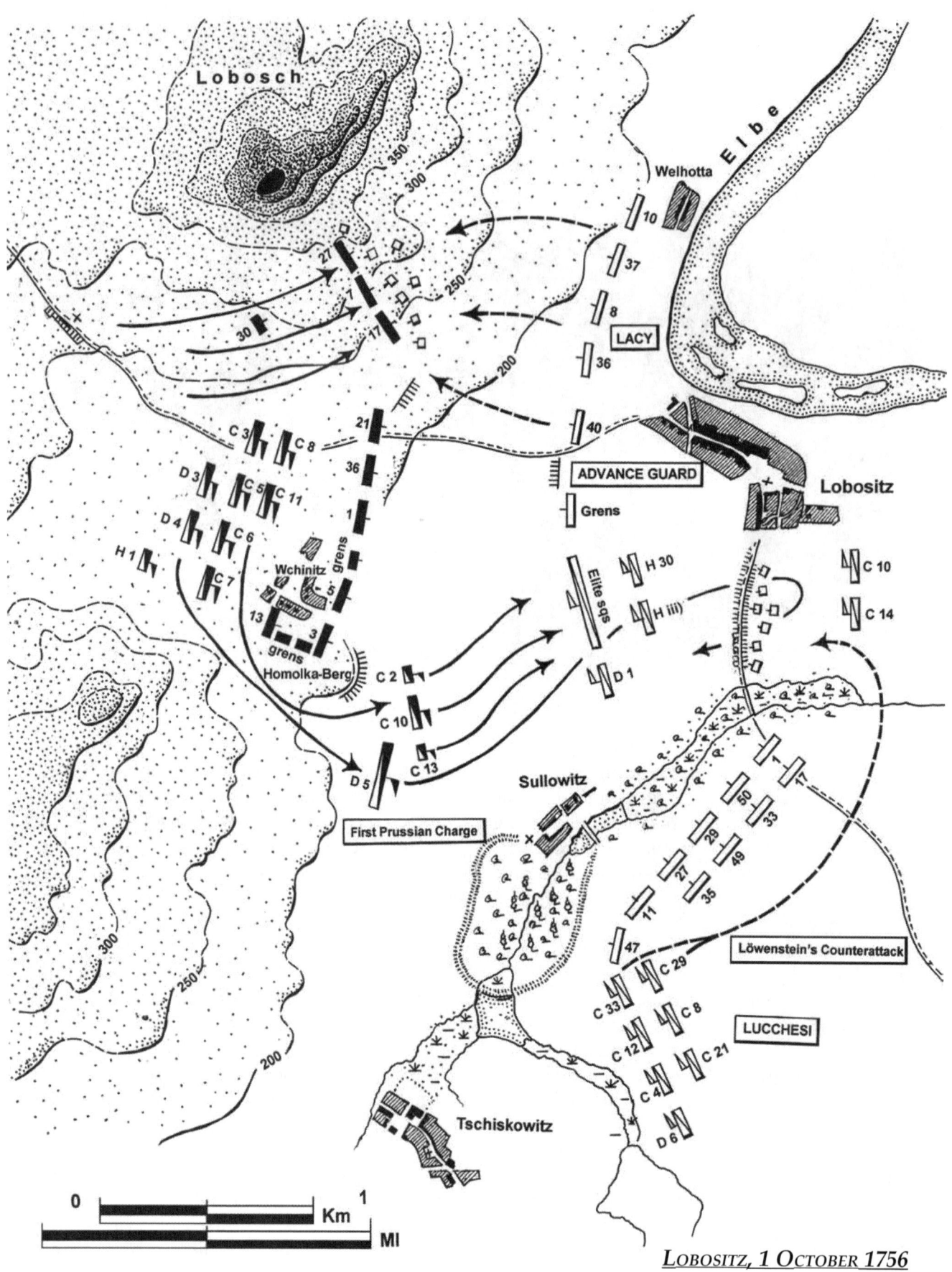

Lobositz, 1 October 1756

darkening gradually to a toothy silhouette against the sunsets.

The Colonel Comte de Lameth, one of the French military attachés, commented that 'all the cavalry and infantry are in an excellent state, despite the long marches that most of the regiments have made. The officers and soldiers are likewise all full of enthusiasm, and have complete trust in their chief. He deserves that confidence in every respect, though, as things stand at the moment, I do wish he were in a better state of health'.[17] The final remark was ominous, for Browne was afflicted with a lung disease, and this, together with the burdens of high command had prevented him from getting more than two hours' sleep at a stretch.

Browne was sustained by nervous energy, and by an inspiration which had been brought to him by a French officer of the Saxon Leibgarde, Major de Martagne (nicknamed *Le Roué*). Instead of using the established routes into Saxony west of the Elbe, where there were certain to be Prussian forces in strength, Martagne proposed that the Austrians should send a flying column through the virtually trackless hills to the east of the Elbe, and emerge on the river bank facing the Saxon camp. The Saxon army would make a simultaneous passage of the river to join the Austrians, and escape together with them into Bohemia.

On 21 September Martagne embarked on a perilous journey to Pirna, carrying Browne's fully worked-out plan. The field marshal selected his senior officers 'regardless of their seniority or rank, but solely according to the abilities and skills which I know they possess.' He again ignored convention by deciding to lead the expeditionary force in person, even though it was certain to be far smaller than was thought fitting for a field marshal's command.[18]

Browne waited with growing anxiety until, on 28 September, Martagne's peasant guide returned with an enthusiastic response from the Saxon prime minister, Heinrich Count Brühl. He assured Browne that the Saxons would be able to assemble a bridge of boats and pass the Elbe on the night of 11/12 October. Arrived on the east bank, a short push would carry them through the weak Prussian outposts at Schandau and enable them to reach the Austrians on the morning of the 12th.

Browne wrote at once to confirm the arrangements. He sent Colonel Lacy with a detachment of 4,000 troops down the Elbe, to serve as a nucleus for the flying corps, which he would reinforce in a surreptitious way. The main army's part in the great design would be to keep the attention of the Prussians fixed on the western bank of the Elbe, and to this end it would advance to Lobositz on the 30th, and then push down the axis of the river as far as Aussig, while extending its left wing as far as Teplitz.

Neither Browne nor Frederick suspected that they were shortly to meet head on. The king wished merely to stabilise affairs on his Bohemian flank for the winter. He had dispatched *FM*. Keith with an *armée d'observation* to join the corps of Prince Ferdinand of Brunswick on the border. Keith arrived on 19 September, but he was unable to put an end to the skirmishing (which sent Croatian bullets whistling around the ears of the Prussians in Aussig), or to provide Frederick with any firm intelligence about the enemy. The impatient Frederick reached Keith's camp at Johnsdorf on 28 September, and two days later the whole Prussian army of 28,000 men was winding across the Paschkopole, the volcanic saddle which formed the last pass of the Mittel-Gebirge short of the Bohemian plain.

On the same 28 September the Austrian army struck camp, crossed the Eger at Budin and Doxan, and after an easy march arranged itself in a new position on the northernmost edge of the plain just in front of the little town of Lobositz. Browne drew up Colonel Lacy from Leitmeritz, and was delighted to be joined by an old friend and fellow spirit, the fiery *GdC*. Joseph Count Lucchesi d'Averna. Browne learned that the Prussians were advancing in force, and 'I at once advanced two thousand Croats to the hills and vineyards above Lobositz, and issued the necessary supplementary orders to the army to stand firm if it came under attack, for there was certain to be a major action the next day, if the enemy continued their advance from Welmina. Meanwhile the Prussian army marched on, and towards half past one in the morning it encountered the outposts of the hussars and Croats. This gave rise to some skirmishing, which however ceased after one hour.'[19]

LOBOSITZ, 1 OCTOBER 1756

a) Austrians
33,354: 25,682 infantry, 7,672 cavalry; 94 pieces
Losses: 2,863: 422 killed, 1,719 wounded, 722 prisoners
b) Prussians
c. 28,000: 17,500 infantry, 10,500 cavalry, 98 pieces
Losses: 2,873: 727 killed, 1,879 wounded, 240 prisoners, 27 deserters

The battle of Lobositz was not big, by the standards of the war that followed, but it was a very important action, since it formed the first major test of the new Austrian army. The operational setting was unusual. Frederick had not expected to fight at all. Browne was fighting because he had no alternative, and he could hope at best for a negative success. An outright victory would merely push the Prussians back towards Pirna, and run counter to his larger purpose, which was to save the Saxons; at the same time he could not afford an outright defeat, because that would cost him Leitmeritz and the line of the Eger, and so deprive him of the base from which he must mount his rescue expedition.

In terms of numbers the forces were equally balanced, since the arithmetical superiority of the Austrians consisted largely in their Croatian light infantry, while the Prussians had the advantage in their cavalry and in particular their heavy artillery. The Austrians were generally in a much better physical state, being fed and rested, whereas the Prussians had executed a series of prolonged and difficult marches, and had spent a wretched night under the open sky.

No other battlefield of the Seven Years War, and few sites in other conflicts, have ever brought together so many features in a confined space. The least striking element was a plain which extended around the town of Lobositz. Seemingly devoid of tactical possibilities, the ground served Browne's purpose of springing what was in effect a giant ambush. For a start, a sunken road running for about 600 metres south from Lobositz offered concealment for a body of Banalist Croats (or grenadiers and Hungarian infantry according to Prussian accounts), who were ordered to lie flat on their stomachs. The cuirassier regiments of Stampach [C10] and Cordua [C14] were standing to the rear in support.

The sunken road gave out by a tiny chapel, and was prolonged as a low causeway which crossed the swampy channels of the Morellen-Bach, which Browne chose as protection for the centre and left wing of his main line of battle. In the subsequent action the Prussians never penetrated far beyond the outer channel, which they described as 'a ditch six feet wide, very deep and muddy'.[20] To the south again, the outlying village of Sullowitz and the walled park spanning the upper Morellen-Bach helped to conceal the Austrian forces massed behind, and the rumour later spread in the Prussian army that the ditches thereabouts were relics of battles which the Austrians had fought against the Swedes in the Thirty Years War. All of them had been Austrian victories, which was supposed to have encouraged Browne to make his stand in the same location.[21]

The position faced the outlying heights of the Bohemian Mittel-Gebirge, and the remaining space between the main army and the rising ground was only lightly held, almost certainly because Browne did not wish to fight with the obstacles of the sunken road and the Morellen-Bach to his back. In front of the sunken road itself Browne deployed a screen which consisted of a body of foot grenadiers, twelve squadrons of carabiniers and mounted dragoons, and the Erzherzog Joseph Dragoons [D1]. Two feeble hussar regiments, those of Baranyay [H30] and Hadik [Hiii)], were waiting in reserve, under orders to fall on the flank of the Prussian cavalry, should it choose to attack.

Browne made no attempt to occupy the mound of the Homolka-Berg, most likely because any forces there would have been difficult to support. The penalty was to present the Prussians with a site which lay within distant but effective artillery range of Sullowitz and the Morellen-Bach.

Everything reviewed so far relates to the centre and the left wing of the Austrian army. The topography on the right (northern) wing enabled Browne to position forces on the deep flank of any Prussian advance along the main road. A bend of the Elbe gave this wing absolute security against any kind of turning movement. More usefully still, the ground to the north of the highway rose with increasing steepness to form the volcanic cone of the Lobosch Hill. The slopes were terraced into vineyards, and the plots were divided one from the other by dry stone walls of black rock, or ditches which were deep enough to conceal a man who was standing to his full height. The great dome was surmounted by a sheer-sided plug of black basalt.

The Lobosch was held by 2,000 Croats, and the terrain suited their tactics to perfection. Grenadiers and five regiments of fusiliers were standing between the Lobosch and the bend of the Elbe, ready to lend support as necessary.

Overnight the Prussians had traversed the Paschkopole narrows and marched down the valley as far as Welmina, where Frederick allowed the troops a little rest. At first light on 1 October the king rode out with a small but select party—his brother and heir Crown Prince August Wilhelm of Prussia, *FM*. Keith, and the lieutenant generals the Prince of Brunswick and the Duke of Bevern. By August Wilhelm's account 'everything was quiet, not a single

The Lobosch hill from the Homolka mound, with the houses of Wchinitz on the right.

musket shot, and to all appearances the plain was empty. Just here and there you could see a few figures on horseback, which I took to be generals on reconnaissance.'[22] The unproductive view seemed to confirm the opinion of the chief of staff, *GL.* Schmettau, who had seen lanterns flickering in the plain overnight, then diminishing gradually in number, from which he concluded that the Austrian army had retreated, and had left only a screen about Lobositz.

Frederick went back to hasten the advance, which brought about the first encounter, which developed on the Lobosch Hill from about 6.30 in the morning. The second battalion of the regiment of Blanckensee [30] and the regiments of Alt-Kleist [27], Braunschweig-Bevern [7] and Manteuffel [17] were all drawn into the combat against the Croats, and they had to extend up the slopes so as to give the rest of the infantry more space to deploy. 'As our army... approached the vineyards, the Croats and infantry behind the rocks deluged us with a frightful rain of bullets, then slung their muskets and scampered up the hill like cats.'[23] The Croats rallied under the ample cover and proceeded to engage the Prussian left wing in a prolonged fire-fight.

The sounds of musketry reached the Homolka mound, on which Frederick and his suite had emerged after a few cannon shot had cleared the Austrian outposts from the hamlet of Wchinitz. The view was as unrewarding as ever, for the morning mist (typical of those

The Homolka mound as seen from the plain of the Morellen-Bach. Two typical peaks of the Mittel-Gebirge rise in the background. (Photographs taken in the middle 1990s.)

parts) was hanging about, 'and most of the Austrian army, and the cavalry in particular, was hidden so skilfully behind rises in the ground and the village of Sullowitz that all we could see of the latter was a few squadrons of German horse and a scattering of hussars.'[24]

The fact that the enemy had failed to dispute the exit from the valley could only have confirmed Frederick in the belief that the Austrians, whoever they were, did not intend to stand their ground. Meanwhile the Prussian army was deploying in three lines across the valley, and the heavy artillery began to mass in three locations—one battery on each side of the highway, and a further battery immediately under Frederick's nose on the Homolka (probably four 24-pounders, four 12-pounders and a number of howitzers).

The Prussian pieces opened up at about 7.30, and the sound stunned both armies and carried down the gorge of the Elbe as far as Pirna, which told the beleaguered Saxons that something serious was afoot. Down in the plain the screen of Austrian cavalry was swimming in and out of view, and with admirable control its officers shuffled and re-shuffled their squadrons into chequers, lines and other formations so as to throw the gunners off their aim. The casualties were nevertheless heavy. The popular *FML.* Alois Count Radicati had a leg carried away, and was borne off mortally wounded. Among *GFWM.* Hadik's small force of hussars five men and forty-one horses were brought down by the fire.

Browne brought a dozen battery cannon into position to the west of Lobositz, and they answered with devastating effect. The Prussian regiments crowded into the valley floor were hit particularly hard, and a soldier of the regiment of Itzenplitz [13] noted how his comrades turned pale and emptied their flasks of spirits. 'My God! How those chunks of iron whistled over our heads, plunged into the earth just to our front or rear and threw stones and clods high into the air, or pitched among us and snatched away the men from the ranks as easily as if they had been wisps of straw!'[25]

Prince August Wilhelm had rejoined his royal brother, and asked to know his thoughts.

'" This won't cause much trouble," he said, "it's just a rearguard action. They have crossed the bridge [at Leitmeritz], and see, their hussars are covering the retreat." Unfortunately I believed him, and as a result I made the mistake of advising him to send ten or so squadrons to take the hussars in flank'.[26]

Frederick ordered *GL.* Kyau to take a number of squadrons into the plain and attack whatever he found there. Kyau detached eight squadrons of cuirassiers (the Garde du Corps [C13], the Gensd'armes [C10] and two squadrons of Prinz von Preussen [C2]) and led them around the right flank of the infantry to the foot of the Homolka. The eight available squadrons of the elite Bayreuth Dragoons [D5, more of a brigade than a regiment] were told off in support, and Frederick ordered the attack to proceed.

The cavalry was the cream of the Prussian mounted arm, and the Austrians let it advance without opposition, 'but after they had lured the enemy close enough, not only did they open up a heavy fire against the flank from the village of Sullowitz, but all the Hungarian infantry (probably Croats), up to now hidden in the sunken roads and ditches in the plain, came to life all of a sudden… and shot into both the front and flank of the cavalry, supported by a horrible fire of cannon.'[27] The squadron of Garde du Corps therefore veered sharply to its left, and there was no help at hand from the Bayreuth regiment, for 'our dragoons caught sight of a large number of bearskins, belonging to their (i.e. Austrian mounted) grenadiers, in the hollows at Sullowitz, and hung back from the attack.'[28]

Colonel Joseph Prince Lobkowitz of the Stampach Cuirassiers [C10] saw his opportunity, and swung his regiment into the exposed right flank of the Garde du Corps. The Prussians were led by Lieutenant Colonel Blumenthal, distinctive in his metal helmet. 'A cannon shot from Sullowitz hit the leg of his horse, and bowled it over in such a way that he was thrown onto his knees in front of the Austrian cuirassiers. They all hacked away at him, and his helmet showed twenty-two sword cuts.'[29] He was retrieved by his troopers, but his wounds were mortal.

The Bayreuth Dragoons came up in time to prevent a massacre, and the struggling mass of cavalry made towards the sunken road, where the Banalist Croats gave way to right and left. Colonel Joseph Lobkowitz now became separated from his men, and tried to escape across the front of the Prussians. 'Everyone set up a cry: "An Austrian, an Austrian!" But we were all so jammed together that nobody could get out of the press quickly enough to catch him. However the corporal on the left wing of the Garde du Corps had a horse which was nimble enough to break free. He caught the prince in front of our standard and gave him a cut over the head. Lieutenant von Wackenitz, who was later a famous general, had been positioned a few paces to the right. He now rode out, seized the horse of the prince by the reins, and declared: "Prince, you are now my prisoner!"'[30] The Prussians described their prize as 'a fine lad, lively and intelligent.'[31]

By now the Prussian cavalry had ventured beyond further support, and it was being shot up from Lobositz and the main Austrian army, as well as from Sullowitz. Kyau ordered a trumpeter to blow *Appel*, and the cuirassiers and dragoons streamed back towards the Homolka. It was a standing rule of the Prussian cavalry that the rearward regiments must attack without hesitation, if the leading ones were in trouble, and now all the remaining forty-three squadrons poured through the intervals in the infantry and joined Kyau's men under the Homolka. *FM*. Gessler was nominally in control, but he bore a grudge against Frederick for a reprimand, and he just 'went along with the battle, a riding stick in his hand, not bothering about anything except to put himself in the way of danger.'[32]

The entire Prussian cavalry surged across the plain, braving the cross-fire of artillery and musketry. The squadrons on the far left penetrated almost as far as Lobositz town before they were driven back by fire. On the right, the Garde du Corps, Colonel Seydlitz's Rochow Cuirassiers [C8] and other dauntless horsemen went splashing into the Morellen-Bach under the eyes of the main force of Austrian infantry, while the great mass of cavalry in the centre was pressed into the funnel of open ground between the bog and Lobositz. The Austrian Erzherzog Joseph Dragoons [D1] were outmatched, and it was probably then that the hard-fighting Cordua Cuirassiers [C14] lost two of their standards.

Browne had ridden towards the right flank of the army, and now sent word to *GdC*. Lucchesi to render help from the main force of the cavalry on the left wing, which was standing behind the upper Morellen-Bach and was as yet unengaged. Lucchesi at once despatched *GFWM*. Christian Philipp Prince of Löwenstein-Wertheim with the six squadrons of the Ansbach Cuirassiers [C33] and two of the Brettlach Cuirassiers [C29]. The Prussians were already across the sunken road, and 'we arrived at a time when the Erhzherzog Joseph Dragoons were already returning in the greatest confusion. At seeing this Prince Löwenstein had a fit of rage and called out to them that they had to stand, but it did no good.'[33]

The newcomers arrived to join the Stampach Cuirassiers, who were still in good order, in spite of the loss of Prince Lobkowitz, and the three regiments now carried out a joint attack which decided the issue. Many years afterwards Lieutenant Colonel Mohr remembered how, as a young standard-bearer, he had seen Löwenstein wheel his squadron to the left, attach himself to the first rank with drawn sword, 'whereupon we crossed the sunken road and flew at the enemy on our sweating horses.' The two bodies came to a halt, belabouring one another with their swords, until the Prussians finally gave way. Not a shot had been fired in the combat.[34]

One of the Prussian infantryman had watched the battle from the valley, 'and what a rattling and flashing there was as they hacked away! But it lasted scarcely a quarter of an hour before our cavalry, beaten by the Austrians, were pursued almost under the muzzles of our cannon. Then we had the sorry sight of horses which were dragging their riders along by the stirrup, and others trailing their guts behind them'.[35] The legendary Prussians turned out to be mortals like the rest of humanity, and 'once their squadrons were opened up the only thought of the troopers was to flee, cowards as they were.'[36]

The Cordua Cuirassiers had meanwhile rallied, and now joined in the pursuit, as did *GFWM*. Hadik with his much-depleted hussars, who cut down the wounded or dismounted Prussian cavalrymen without mercy. 'In this last engagement one of the Hadik Hussars took a standard, and as his horse had been shot, he tried to bring it back on foot. But the enemy cut him over the head and tore the standard from his hands.'[37]

While the main body of the Prussian cavalry fell back, the squadrons of their right were still struggling in the meadows of the Morellen-Bach. According to an officer of the Garde du Corps 'many of the horses lacked the strength to heave themselves up from the swampy hollow to the high bank; I remember seeing one of our Schönaich Cuirassiers [C9] lying dead in the ranks of the Austrian infantry; many of the cuirassiers got stuck in the mud on the far bank, and lost a good many dead and wounded in the process.'[38] Only the intervention of the Prussian Székely Hussars [H1] saved Colonel Seydlitz from being counted among them.

The initiative was passing to the Austrians, and Frederick was now aware that he was facing an entire army, and at a time when his own troops were running out of ammunition. During the cavalry fight the Austrian *GFWM*. Wied detached some 2,000 regulars from the reinforced advance guard to climb the eastern slopes of the Lobosch and support the Croats, who had been battling on the hill all this time.

The Lobosch from the south-west. The bushes in the photograph have obliterated the terraced vineyards which were still visible on the lower slopes in the 1960s.

The troops were led by Colonel Lacy, and consisted of two battalions of Joseph Esterházy [37], one battalion of Lacy's own regiment of Jung-Colloredo [40] and six companies of grenadiers.

The Prussians too had been feeding reinforcements into the combat on the Lobosch. The second battalion of Itzenplitz [13\ was disengaged from the valley, where the soldiers had been at the mercy of the Austrian cannon shot, and 'now we imagined that we were going back to camp and all the danger was past. We tripped cheerfully up through the steep vineyards, filled our hats full of fine red grapes, and sat down and ate to our hearts' content.'[39] They were disabused soon enough when they were thrown into the battle on the hill. The regiment of Alt-Kleist, a battalion of Münchow [36] and finally the second battalion of Hülsen [21] came alongside them on the hill, and this effort reduced the Prussian infantry to a single line. By now the Prusssian cavalry had attacked twice over, and was incapable of doing any more. Early in the afternoon Frederick gave up the battle for lost, and he secreted himself in the hamlet of Wchinitz, which huddled to the rear of the Homolka.

The decision came about half an hour later, and was precipitated by an attempt on the part of the Austrians to evict the battalion of Münchow from the steep slopes towards the top of the hill. The Prussians had kept up the fight so far by breaking into dispersed order, and exchanging shots with the Austrians amid the rocks, bushes and vines, but even this resource now failed them. 'Our lads had exhausted their ammunition, and the cartridges of their dead and wounded comrades had been used up as well…"Boys," the Duke of Bevern shouted at them, "shoot, for God's sake, shoot and move forward!" The soldiers replied that they were out of ammunition. "What," yelled the duke back, "haven't you got bayonets? Skewer the dogs dead!" On the instant the lads fell blindly on the enemy, thrust their bayonets into their ribs, and some of them reversed their muskets and smashed them over the enemy heads.'[40]

Browne states that it took him three-quarters of an hour to ride from one end of the line to the other. He was on his way to his left wing when he looked back and saw that the Prussians were attacking once more on the Lobosch, and that they had heavy guns firing uphill in enfilade. He ordered the three right-flanking regiments of the main army, those of Kaiser [1], Kollowrat [17] and Nicolaus Esterházy [33] to make for the Lobosch. For the rest, he had to put his trust in the officers on the spot. 'The Austrian regiment of Jung-Colloredo, which Count Lacy had formed and drilled, and commanded on this day, fought very well; if the others had done the same, the victory might have been with the [Austrian] enemy.'[41] The Colloredo regiment was literally marching backwards, while presenting a front of fire and bayonets to the Prussians. Lacy was however incapacitated by a musket shot in the wrist, and Browne describes the other officers as just standing at the head of their troops, waiting to get themselves killed.[42]

On the Prussian side the battle was being directed by Prince Ferdinand of Brunswick, now that Frederick had abdicated control. The advance of the Prussian left wing carried the infantry down the Lobosch in what appeared to be a flood of blue. By the account of Captain Arnim of the regiment of Bevern it is clear that many of the Prussian officers had lost contact with their own units, but (unlike their Austrian counterparts) they had been happy to take charge of whatever troops they encountered, and to lead them into the fight. Now the Croats and the Austrians abandoned the hill, and were chased as far as the Elbe to the right of the village of Welhotta. Arnim liked to think that some of them fell over the steep bank out of pure terror.[43]

The impetus of the new Prussian advance was lost in a standing fire-fight outside Lobositz town, and during the pause the Austrians were able to retrieve their heavy guns from the highway, and draw back the troops who were being squeezed between the Prussians and the Elbe. The Austrians were firing to considerable effect from windows and holes in the roofs, and 'words cannot describe what now transpired, when smoke and fumes ascended from Lobositz amid a crashing and thundering which befitted the Last Judgement. The senses were numbed by the continuous resounding of field music of every description, the shouts of the officers and the bellowing of their adjutants, and the cries and shrieks of all those thousands of wretched and smashed half-dead victims of that day.'[44]

The Duke of Bevern managed to break the new deadlock by borrowing some howitzers from Prince Ferdinand and setting the most exposed houses of Lobositz on fire. The whole of the Austrian right wing was now in danger of breaking up, and Browne resorted to some urgent measures.

A dull thunder of drums announced what seemed to be an Austrian counterattack across the plain from Sullowitz, and a number of battalions debouched from the north-western exit, only to draw back again, apparently responding to howitzer fire from the Homolka which set the village alight. Only afterwards did the Prussians realise how completely they had been deceived, and Frederick spoke of Browne's trick with unreserved admiration. 'What this general did was to take some brigades from his intact left wing and advance them through Sullowitz. While the attention of the Prussians was thus diverted, he reassembled his right wing, which had fled from Lobositz in dire disorder. That done, he pulled back the first troops to behind Sullowitz.'[45]

Browne slid the two lines of his main army to the right across the lower Morellen-Bach, then northwards until the heads of the columns approached the Elbe behind Lobositz. The movement can best be compared with that of a sliding door. The Prussians meanwhile pushed into the burning town. They were appalled by the screams which came from the helpless Austrian wounded, and discovered 'hundreds of half-consumed corpses lying in the flames; it would have been inhuman not to have shuddered at the horrific sight.'[46] When they emerged on the far side of Lobositz the Prussians were stopped short by the intact lines of Browne's army which now faced them. Then, quite suddenly, the action came to an end at three in the afternoon.

With the night came a thunderstorm and heavy rain, which extinguished the fires in Lobositz, and drenched the two armies. The Austrians retrieved a number of Prussian wounded along with their own, and buried a number of the Prussian dead, but early the next morning Browne ordered the army to fall back to its old camp behind the Eger at Budin. It was galling to have to leave the ground to the enemy, but a retreat was in any case inevitable, since the army had been issued with bread and fodder for just two days, and the baggage and all the rest of the supplies had been left behind in Budin.

The possession of the field gave the tactical victory to the Prussians, and the presence of the Prussian army so near to Leitmeritz was almost certainly one of the considerations which forced Browne to reduce the size of the flying column which was assigned to relieve the Saxons. However the losses of the rival armies were almost identical, at nearly 2,900 each, and in every other respect the Austrians had gained a clear moral advantage, as their enemies were willing to concede.

A saying went around Frederick's army, 'they are no longer the same old Austrians.'[47] The Prussians had seen for themselves that the Austrians had 'done everything in the character of good soldiers; their dispositions were excellent, and from general to the lowliest musketeer they had all done their duty to the letter. We may deduce their fine discipline from the fact that when they were shot down their dead lay by complete files, indeed by entire platoons.'[48] Altogether the infantry had 'a much improved look about them, more order and a finer stock of men.'[49]

'Compared with its former state, the Austrian cavalry was better mounted, dressed and drilled,'[50] and 'the Austrian cuirassier regiment of Cordua distinguished itself particularly through its courage, and earned the highest praise of the Prussians, albeit at a price which reduced it to a small handful of men.'[51] The Austrian artillery had never shot so fast.

Frederick had been shaken so badly that it was late at night before he could be persuaded that he had not been beaten, and he was thrown into a new consternation by the cannon shot

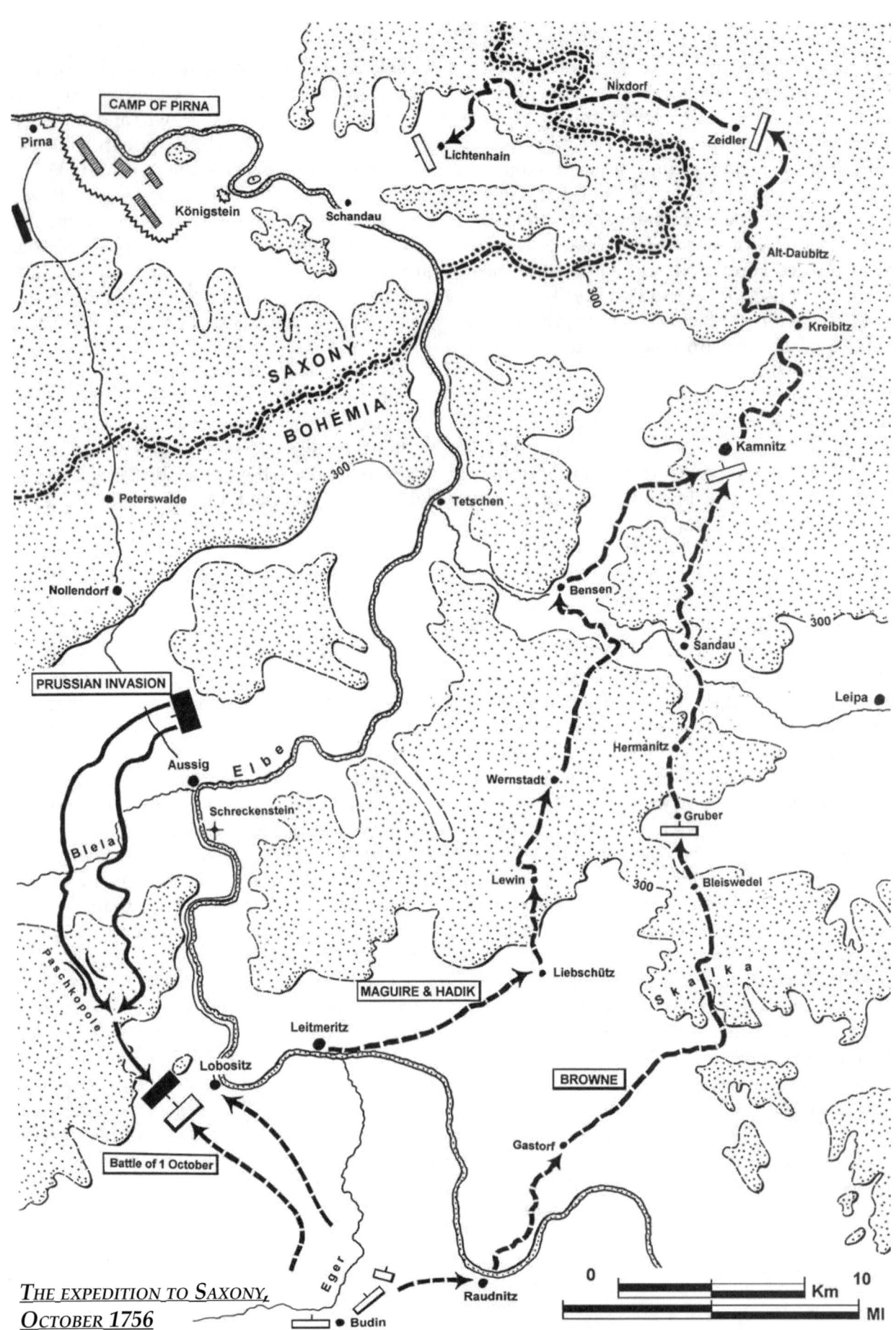

(aimed with malice at the Prussian camp) which signalled the Austrian retreat. He wrote to *FM.* Schwerin, 'they have more tricks at their disposal than ever before; believe me, unless we can bring a mass of cannon against them it will cost us a great number of men to beat them down.'[52] Captain Henckel von Donnersmarck noted how well Browne had concealed his numbers and deployment. His infantry lay flat on the ground until the time came for it to stand up; he first presented his cavalry on a narrow front, and then, when the Prussian horse attacked, he shot it up in the flanks from concealed batteries and destroyed it.[53]

Above all, Lobositz had affirmed the work of military reform. 'On this occasion Frederick did not meet the kind of Austrians he had beaten in four previous battles. He was not facing a Neipperg, or a blustering Prince Charles of Lorraine, but the veteran warrior Browne, a man whose talents and experience had made him the hero of his age. Here also the king encountered an artillery which Prince Liechtenstein had brought to perfection at his own expense, and an army which had trained itself in the arts of war over the ten years of peace, while striving to acquire the methods of its former conquerors, and form itself on their discipline.'[54]

All of these are testimonies of the Prussians. On her side Maria Theresa ordered every soldier to be rewarded with a silver florin, and, learning that Browne had lost two horses in the battle, she sent him two of the finest and most reliable beasts from her stable.

THE EXPEDITION TO RELIEVE PIRNA, 7-19 OCTOBER 1756

'I become uneasy when I don't know where Browne is. It would be just like him to reappear all of a sudden at the last place you could imagine' (Frederick to *GL.* Manstein, Tetschen, 25 September 1756).[55]

Browne could not ignore the presence of the Prussian army, so close at hand beyond the Eger. The battle of Lobositz had nevertheless bought him some time, and he entrusted his friend *GdC.* Lucchesi with the responsibility of holding the attention of the Prussians on this side of the Elbe, while Browne in person took his flying column to the east bank and marched to rescue the Saxons. Frederick was taken in completely, and he writes about having interviewed an exceptionally intelligent deserter, who convinced him that the Austrians intended 'nothing more than to dispute the line of the Eger.'[56]

The flying column consisted of the infantry regiments of Browne [36], Baden-Durlach [27] and Kollowrat [17], twelve companies of grenadiers, 200 assorted dragoons and 400 hussars under *GFWM.* Hadik, 1,200 Carlstädter Croats under Colonel Franz Vela, and sixteen pieces of artillery. The whole, excluding the gunners, numbered 5,239 regular infantry, 1,020 dragoons and hussars and 1,200 Croats, making a grand total of 7,459 troops.

The Austrians crossed the Elbe on 7 and 8 October. The major generals Maguire and Hadik passed at Leitmeritz, and followed a westerly route by way of Lewin, Wernstadt and Bensen. Behind this screen the main force crossed upstream at Raudnitz, and marched further to the east. Considered as a whole, the Austrian routes ran from south to north, and therefore across the grain of the country, where the cultivated valleys alternated with rows of wooded heights.

Browne at first climbed steadily to the small rounded plateau of Skalka. From there the fields fell away to the roofs of Bleiswedel immediately in front, but already the horizon was lined with the dark humps of the border hills with Saxony. Passing the volcanic cone of the Ronov to their left, the Austrians descended first to Gruber, and then, after a gentle climb through Hermanitz, down again to the broad and agreeable valley of Sandau. From there a short but taxing march brought them on 9 September to Kamnitz, where Browne was rejoined by Maguire and Hadik. Morale was high, and so far not a man had deserted.

North from Kamnitz the Austrians entered the highlands proper, and almost all of the tent carts were left behind in Kamnitz, 'so that we can march more easily.'[57] Browne was in the lead with the grenadiers as they trudged through

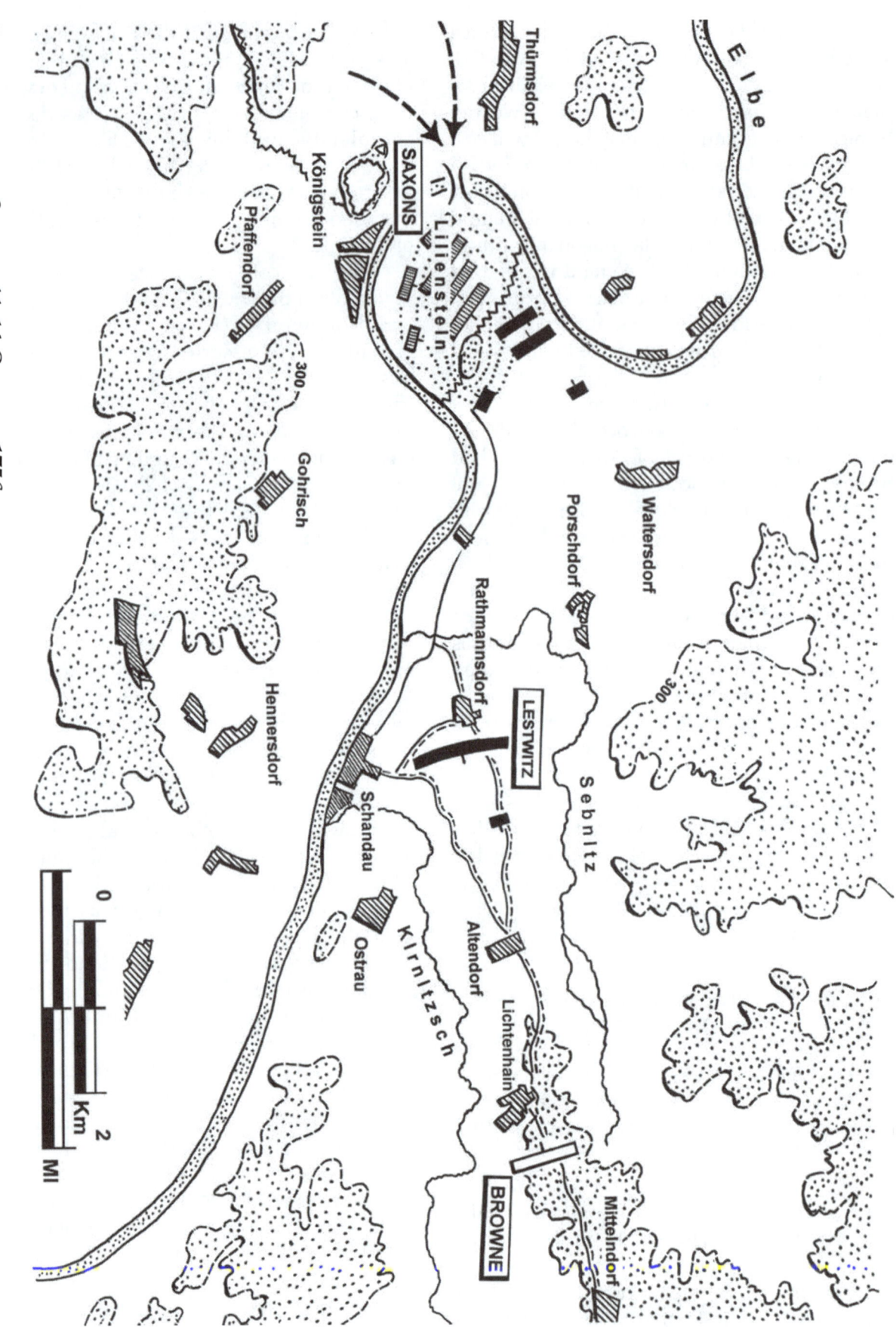
BROWNE AND THE SAXONS, 11-14 OCTOBER 1756

a dripping forest of beech, oak, ash and fir. The infantry were marching in three files, with their muskets reversed against the rain, and the officers rode to the side of the track to avoid splattering the troops with mud. Not until the coming of the Romantic age would men learn to enjoy the wild scenery of these parts, and the picturesque cabins with their walls of squared logs, and gable ends of fantastic arrangements of wooden shingles. The Austrians of 1756 pressed on unheeding through quaint little Kreibitz, and after ten hours of unrelieved marching they threw themselves down at Zeider. Browne was coughing up blood, and after one such march he sank into an exhausted sleep. 'His brave comrades in arms crowded about him, took off their own coats and competed in a spirit of noble concern as to who would be fortunate enough to be the one to cover that loyal and beloved father of the army with his clothing.'[58]

The eleventh of October promised to be the decisive day of the enterprise. The Austrians were now among the highest border hills, and they made their way between bulging slabs of sandstone, among which sprouted an incongruously elegant vegetation of fern, birch and delicate grasses. They then turned west into Saxony, and the column struck towards the Elbe down the winding valley of the Kirnitzsch-Bach. Browne had already committed his corps well inside Saxon territory by the time a message reached him from the Saxon prime minister, Count Brühl, asking him to put off his attack by twenty-four hours, until the evening of the 12th, for the Saxons were encountering difficulties in crossing to the right bank of the river. Browne commented that 'a delay of this nature inevitably caused a considerable upset, because everything hung upon surprise and exact timing.'[59]

The root of the problem lay in the run-down state of the Saxon forces: 'the whole army knows that the pontoon company here in Saxony consists of just the officers, a sergeant, a corporal and four pontoneers; all the others are in Poland.'[60] The intended crossing place was at Thürmsdorf, just downstream from Königstein, which was close to the intended junction with the Austrians, and from where the crossing could be made under the protection of the fortress guns. Unfortunately the pontoons of sheet copper were in bad repair and stored downstream at Pirna. The Saxons had to turn to river barges instead, and on successive nights (8/9 and 9/10 October) they tried to haul the clumsy craft upstream. On each occasion Prussian cannon took the barges under fire from the heights at Wilstädel, and the bargemen abandoned their boats and fled, 'even though we went to the length of presenting our swords and bayonets at their backs.'[61]

The Prussians had assumed that Browne was still at Budin, six or seven conventional marches away, and if the field marshal had been informed of the delay a few hours earlier he could have hung back out of sight in the border hills. As it was, he now had shown his hand to no purpose. At noon on 11 October the leading Austrian patrols encountered an outpost of the Prussian Puttkamer Hussars [H4] at Lichtenhain. Their leader was Lieutenant Colonel Warnery (the same who had fired the first shot of the war). He fell back with his main force to Mittelndorf, and sent word to *GM.* Meyerinck, the commander of the six battalions down by the Elbe at Schandau. Meyernick had the reputation of an *Eisenfresser* (man who chews on iron) as the governor of Berlin in peacetime, but since then he had been living high off the hog at Schandau, guzzling salmon, trout and game at the expense of the Saxons, and it was only with difficulty that he could be persuaded to move his forces up the valley to confront the Austrians.

Meyerinck took up a good position with his flanks anchored on the Sebnitz and Kirnitzsch streams, but six rounds of cannon were enough to reduce him to panic and evoke the morale-inspiring cry of 'What shall we do now?' The 3,000 Prussians abandoned the village of Altendorf and returned to the Elbe at Schandau, where they dug themselves in among the woods at the exit of the Kirnitzsch valley. If Browne's troops had all been fresh and at hand, if he had had full information of the Prussian numbers and positions, and if the operation had not been planned from the beginning as a joint enterprise with the Saxons, he might now have been able to break through to the bank of the Elbe opposite Königstein.

On 12 October Browne's main force was standing east of Mittelndorf, while his light troops pushed on to Altendorf and skirmished with the Prussians. From his viewpoint at Mittelndorf the field marshal could see the Königstein 'as clearly as you can make out Vienna from the hill at Schönbrunn,'[62] but the day passed without any signs of movement from the Saxons. At nine in the evening a Saxon nobleman arrived in the guise of a peasant, and delivered a letter from Brühl which not only asked for the enterprise to be put off for a further day, but left the initiative entirely to the Austrians, who were requested to attack if possible on the following morning, while the Saxons postponed their own attack until half past six in the evening.

At six in the morning of 13 October Browne was encouraged by a noisy exchange of Saxon and Prussian cannon fire, accompanied by musketry, and he put his forces in readiness to attack. He stood them down again when the firing ceased all of a sudden, which was most sinister. He waited 'as impatiently as the Jews for the coming of the Messiah,'[63] but the continuing silence was broken only by desultory cannon shots, and the rain which poured relentlessly until four in the afternoon. About an hour later Browne received another message from Brühl, the third of its kind, begging for a postponement until the morning of the 14th. This time Browne replied directly to the Saxon commander Field Marshal Count Rutowsky. He reminded him of everything he had done on behalf of the Saxons, but promised to wait until nine the next morning to see if the Saxons would break through, 'in which case I will do everything possible to lend help, and attack the enemy who are standing in front of me.'[64] What had been happening down by the Elbe?

On the evening of 12 October the Saxons had finally succeeded in throwing a bridge of

Saxon gunners lazing in the Sonnenstein castle shortly before the war (Bernardo Bellotto)

forty-two pontoons (brought overland from Pirna) to the right bank of the Elbe from a point just above Thürmsdorf. They began to cross an hour before midnight. The men and horses were hungry and exhausted. They had first to negotiate the steep paths down to the river, wait their turn to file across the single bridge, then face a climb up the dark, stony and slippery tracks of the Lilienstein on the far side. The troops had gobbled down their final ration of bread as soon as it had been issued, and they were now reduced to foraging for cabbage stalks among the fields.

When the passage had been completed, at three in the afternoon of the 13th, the Saxons had attempted to gather up their pontoons to the right bank, only to see them break loose and drift downstream. Before the day was out the Prussians had occupied the abandoned camp and a party of their Jäger had seized Thürmsdorf, which left only Königstein in the hands of the Saxons on the left bank. Their main army was now committed irretrievably to the right bank, where it was bottled up in a peninsula formed by a loop of the Elbe gorge. Most of the troops were jammed in conditions of acute misery along a short stretch of plateau and sloping river bank. The centre of the peninsula was occupied by the great, flat-topped sandstone crag of the Lilienstein, and beyond that the Saxons had managed to deploy seven battalions of grenadiers.

Between the grenadiers and Browne's leading troops at Lichtenhain there extended six miles of tangled country, and two fast-assembling corps of Prussians. The Saxons were confronting *GM*. Forcade and a respectable corps of eight battalions and three squadrons, which could put up an obstinate resistance along the abattis of the Walthersdorf ridge. If the Saxons penetrated thus far, they would have to rely on the help of the Austrians to overcome the six-and-a-half battalions of *GL*. Lestwitz, who had entrenched himself on the far side of Rathmannsdorf to face the Austrians.

On the afternoon of 14 October Field Marshal Rutowsky convened a council of war at the foot of the Lilienstein, and the dispirited Saxon commanders agreed unanimously that they must seek a capitulation with the Prussians. To attempt to force a way through to the Austrians would 'not be fighting, but leading our troops to a massacre.'[65]

The Saxons concluded their capitulation, or rather outright surrender, on 16 October. King Augustus III was allowed to leave for Warsaw, but otherwise the Saxons delivered themselves completely to the exiguous mercy of the Prussians. The Saxon troops were brought back across the Elbe, regiment by regiment, and between 17 and 19 October the entire army of about 18,000 men was sworn forcibly into the Prussian service.

On the morning of the 14th Prussian deserters had brought Browne the news that they were under orders to cease hostilities against the Saxons. Even now Browne was unwilling to abandon his de facto allies to their fate, and at great risk to his corps he held his positions into the afternoon. So far the troops had put up with 'every hardship calculated to try human patience and resolution,'[66] but to risk them for no good purpose would have been irresponsible. At three in the afternoon, having delayed his departure by six hours, he began the retreat.

Browne decided to make his first march to Hinter-Hermsdorf, as offering a shorter route than the way by which he had come. He had not gone far before he encountered a difficult abattis, and the Prussian lieutenant colonel Warnery was soon on his heels with nearly four hundred hussars. *GFWM*. Hadik was covering the retreat with a body of five hundred hussars and two companies of Croatian grenadiers. East of Lichtenhain Warnery managed to catch the Croats at a disadvantage just one hundred paces short of a wood. 'The Carlstädter [grenadiers] were assailed by Prussian horse, and on account of their lack of training they had forgotten to fix bayonets. For the same reason they delivered a general salvo against the Prussian cavalry, and this double mistake rendered them powerless to offer any resistance. They had to give way, and they were cut down. The Banalist grenadiers on the other hand had fixed their bayonets, and by levelling their muskets and holding their aim they managed to deter the enemy.'[67]

Browne marched without further

disturbance across the Bohemian border to Schönlinde, where he arrived at five in the afternoon of 15 October. The French volunteer Colonel de Lameth wrote to his minister of war: 'We were full of joy and hope when we set out from here, but we returned utterly downcast. It must be the consequence of having spent eight days without baggage, with hardly anything to eat, constantly exposed to the rain and cold— and all for nothing. I came out of it feeling half dead, never having been able to shift my clothes since we departed, but I know would have been unaware of my tribulations if we had brought it off.'[68]

Browne reached Kamnitz on 16 October, Politz on the 17th, Gastorf on the 18th, and on the 19th he crossed the Elbe at Raudnitz and regained the camp at Budin. He had lost 186 men, 82 of whom had been killed (probably nearly all of them at Lichtenhain), one had died from other causes, and 103 had deserted. Kaunitz admired the kind of spirit he found in Browne, and he wrote to him from Vienna: 'Sir, I congratulate you from the bottom of my heart on your successful and glorious return. Your prospects could not be better!'[69]

Browne cast his mind back to his raid on the King of Naples at Velletri in 1744, and concluded that the recent enterprise had been attended with more risk, for his enemies on this occasion were no longer the Spanish and Neapolitans but the vigilant Prussians.[70] If any blame can be attached to Browne on the present occasion, it must be on account of his unwillingness to press on with his advance on 11 October, before the element of surprise disappeared entirely. His hesitations came from the fact that he could put so little trust in the Saxons. He wrote to Kaunitz that the outcome came from 'the carelessness and irresolution of those gentlemen. I had always

The Lilienstein as seen from the Königstein fortress

suspected something of the sort, and now it cost us the fruit of our sacrifices on the day of Lobositz, and all the efforts and resources we had put forth on their behalf.'[71]

During Browne's expedition the main forces of the Austrian and Prussian armies remained in their respective camps of Budin and Lobositz. The same did not apply to the light troops, and especially those of the Austrians, and on 18 October, in one of the many small actions, Colonel MacElligot and 500 Croats surprised the Prussian hussar regiment of Székely in **Tetschen** town and drove it into the castle. He was aided by Lieutenant Colonel Loudon of the Ottochaner Croats, who had already made an impression on Browne through his enterprise and bravery.

Browne had scarcely returned to Budin before he decided on a strategy to 'dispute the ground as far as the rules of war will permit.'[72] Loudon was now at Kamnitz, barring the valleys on the right bank of the Elbe to the enemy foraging parties. The newly promoted *GFWM*. Lacy was leading more than 2,000 men towards Jung-Bunzlau and Gabel to secure the country further to the east, while on 22 October *GFWM*. Althann marched up the Eger valley to the west to deny the Circle of Saaz.

The control of territory had always figured largely in Browne's calculations, for he knew that it was more economical to starve an army into retreat than to beat it in open battle. On 23 October Browne learned that the Prussians had just retired from their camp at Lobositz. Hadik followed in the enemy tracks, and he was able to establish that the enemy had all recoiled across the border on the 28th.

The Austrian army was 'still in excellent shape, and highly motivated, which is particularly fortunate now that the weather is deteriorating. There has hardly been a day since the battle of Lobositz when we have not had enemy prisoners and deserters coming in, in addition to all the numbers we have killed or wounded.'[73] Browne could now post a security cordon towards Saxony and Silesia, and distribute his troops in winter quarters.

PICCOLOMINI AGAINST SCHWERIN IN NORTH-EAST BOHEMIA

By invading Saxony, the Prussians had forced Browne to move his main concentration of forces from Kolin to north-west Bohemia. This left a void in the north-east, and he accordingly got *FZM*. Piccolomini to move his corps from Moravia to Königgrätz, where it could guard one of the most important avenues in the kingdom.

Piccolomini's Prussian counterpart was that enterprising veteran *FM*. Schwerin, who decided that the best way to protect Prussian Silesia was to carry the war into Bohemia. On 15 September Piccolomini was nevertheless able to anticipate him at Königgrätz. The Austrian position was strong, but it left the country to the west of the upper Elbe completely to Schwerin's Prussians, who were much better behaved than their counterparts in Saxony, and were able to attract large numbers of Bohemian peasants to sell provisions in their camp. Browne was greatly displeased.

Piccolomini and Schwerin might have been brothers. Their forces were almost equally balanced (Piccolomini's 29,260; Schwerin's 25,700), and they were both courteous, aged gentlemen of impeccable standards of behaviour. Schwerin blamed his master Frederick for having embarked on what seemed an unnecessary war, and he wrote to Piccolomini of his desire for peace. Piccolomini got into the habit of reading some of the letters aloud to his own officers. 'May the Lord of Hosts incline the hearts of our sovereigns to peace,' wrote Schwerin in a typical passage, 'and avert from oppressed humanity that blood-bath which will otherwise engulf nation after nation.'[74] On 24 September Schwerin went so far as to propose a meeting at which they could concert measures to bring their sovereigns together. He was probably sincere, but Maria Theresa's suspicions were aroused, and Kaunitz wrote to Piccolomini on the 28th to forbid any interview of the kind.

Having achieved his modest objectives, Schwerin began a leisurely retreat on 12 October, and he finally disappeared into the County of Glatz at the end of the month.

1756, An Assessment

Where did the balance of loss and gain lie at the end of the year? It would be a pardonable exaggeration to call the advantages which Frederick derived from the conquest of Saxony as 'inestimable,' for some of them can be given a numerical value, namely a 150-kilometre deep buffer zone to the south-west of his heartland, and material resources which he plundered during the course of the war to a final worth of an estimated 70,000,000 taler. However these were assets which proved their full worth only as the war went on, and the fact that the war was to be prolonged beyond a single campaign was proof of an immediate strategic failure.

Prussia's open breach of the peace played into the hands of Kaunitz, who was able to draw Russia, Sweden and France into an active military alliance (below). The cruel and misguided enlisting of the captive Saxon army did the Prussians more harm than good, for many of the Saxons were deserting by entire units by the spring of 1757, and the others remained as a source of dangerous instability. Above all, by turning into Saxony, and keeping so many of his troops locked up in the blockade of Pirna, Frederick missed the opportunity to strike deep into Austrian territory when Maria Theresa's forces were in no condition to meet a powerful attack. Browne concluded that the king's behaviour was 'quite incomprehensible… it seemed to me to be in no way that of a great captain, and rather calculated to make a great stir than to tend to solid advantages. This is the usual danger with people who act by caprice, without system, and without regard for the rules of war.'[75]

As early as 21 October, when Brown had only just returned from Budin, reinforcements were on their way from the Austrian Netherlands, the Russians were reported to be on the move, and there were hopes of something good from France, 'in such a way that there is reason to believe that early next year the King of Prussia can be made the object of a powerful offensive war, so that, with the help of allies, large diversions can be made into the Prussian states from different directions.'[76]

The diplomatic initiative lay entirely with the Austrians. In St. Petersburg the ambassador Nicolaus Esterhazy had the responsibility of engaging Russia in the new war, and it now turned out to be little more than a question of settling the practical details. By the Treaty of St. Petersburg (11 January 1757) Empress Elizabeth acceded to the first, or defensive Austro-French Treaty of Versailles (1 May 1756). A confidential treaty was concluded on 2 February 1757, and set out the nature of the military effort. One of the clauses became of particular importance to the commanders in the field, for military attachés (the first of the kind) were assigned to the respective headquarters, and were given a voice in councils of war.

Austria's new connection with France gave Kaunitz a diplomatic bridgehead into Sweden, and on 21 March 1757 a treaty brought that kingdom into the alliance. Sweden's immediate interest was to win back the parts of Pomerania (on the German coast of the Baltic) which had been lost to Prussia by an earlier generation, but the Swedes were willing to engage only 20,000 troops to the operations against Prussia. However even that modest force could prove a useful diversion, and the link with Sweden as a Protestant power had an important political worth, for it helped the Austrians to represent that they were not engaged in a war of religion. The same was true of those German states of Germany which supported the *Reichsexecution* which was pronounced on 17 January against the Marquis of Brandenburg (Frederick's title as a German sovereign), for having broken the public peace of Germany. A *Reichsarmee* was now put together to put the sentence into effect.

It proved much more difficult to induce the French to extend their obligations beyond those contained in the defensive First Treaty of Versailles. France had little to gain directly from reducing the power of Prussia and restoring Silesia and Glatz to Maria Theresa, and, now that hostilities had opened in North America, Austria had no interest at all in promoting the war of the French against the British. All the gain would therefore seem to have been on Austria's side, when her representative finally persuaded the French to sign the Second Treaty of Versailles (1 May 1757). King Louis bound himself to support Maria Theresa until she had regained her lost lands. To that end he would put 105,000 troops into the field against Prussia, and subsidise Austria to the tune of 12,000,000 florins per annum, as well as making large payments to Sweden and the friendly German states.

On paper Austria reciprocated only by promising to cede to France a strip of territory along the southern borders of the Austrian Netherlands, and by handing over the rest to Louis' son-in-law the Infant Don Philip, the transfers to take place only after Frederick had been duly humbled and forced to give up Silesia and Glatz.

The land war in Europe certainly turned out badly for France, and it suited French public opinion (and French historians) to put the blame on Louis XV and his circle for having subordinated the interests of his subjects to those of Maria Theresa. That was to ignore the compromise as actually reached in 1757, which extended beyond the terms set down at Versailles. The story is complicated, but in essentials Kaunitz had to acquiesce in the ambition of the French to put Hanover under direct military occupation. Hanover was not just another of the Protestant states of Germany, but the personal possession of King George II of Britain in his capacity as Elector. The French were weak at sea, but to all appearances very strong on land, and the conquest of Hanover would have been a hard blow against British commercial and strategic interests, and to the authority of the Protestant Succession in Britain.

Kaunitz had to give up his efforts to dissuade the French from their course, and by May 1757 the breach between Austria and Britain was nearly complete. Events were to show how little effort France put into supporting Austria by her armies, and how much into the ambition of subjugating Hanover, which in turn became the focus of a league of Protestant German states.

The fact remained that by the early summer of 1757 Austria was linked by active alliances or pledges or support with Russia, France, Sweden and three score of the states of Germany. Diplomacy had for the moment reached its limits, and the rest would have to be determined by the sword.

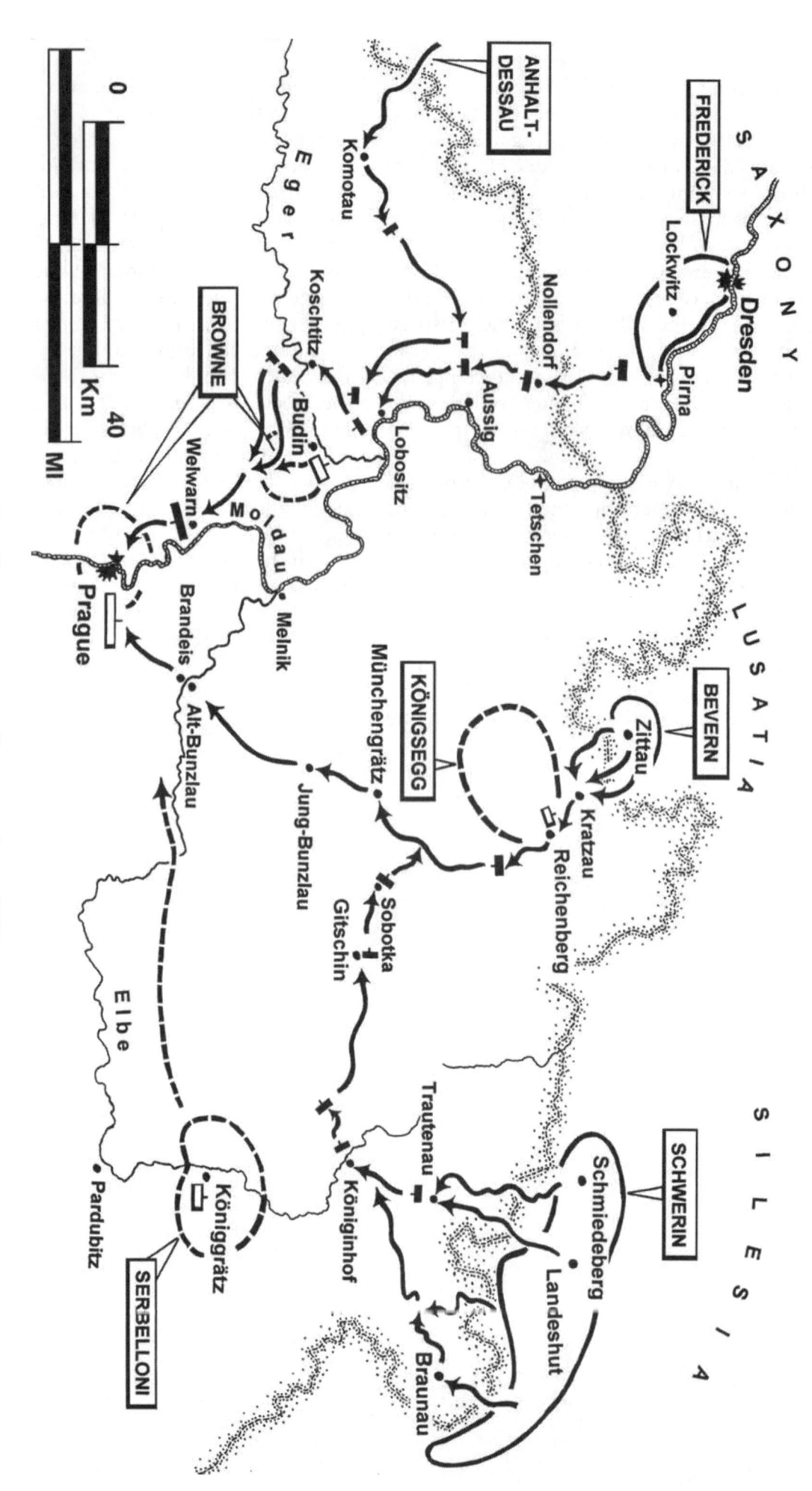

The Prussians Invade Bohemia, April 1757

II
1757

THE CRISIS OF SPRING 1757

Early in February 1757 Browne's health improved, and he was able to travel to Vienna to take part in the debates on the forthcoming campaign. *FM.* Daun was urging a concentration in Moravia, *FM.* Neipperg something similar in Bohemia; Emperor Francis Stephen wished to attack into the Voigtland in western Saxony, while his brother Prince Charles favoured an advance through Lusatia in eastern Saxony. At various times Browne advocated a thrust against one or other of the enemy flanks, either through the Voigtland towards Leipzig, or into Silesia.

All sense of urgency drained from the Austrian councils. Nothing positive could be determined until the intentions of the allies became clear, and Browne himself became preoccupied with questions of supply. For the time being he worked out plans to concentrate the army in eight forward camps, but he assured the conferences that he would not move the troops before the need arose.

The army was disturbed by rumours that Browne was to be moved aside in favour of Prince Charles, and their fears were realised when Charles was proclaimed commander of the forces in Bohemia. Maria Theresa would have much preferred to see Browne at the head, but she gave way to Francis Stephen and Neipperg. Browne declared that he would serve willingly under the new chief, and he rejected the unworkable suggestion that he should have a share in directing the army.

Browne set out for Bohemia in the middle of March. Responsibility for the forces for the time being was entirely his own, for Prince Charles was detained in Vienna by a sore foot, and just sent his luxurious field baggage on to Prague. Browne reached the Bohemian capital on 21 March, and found little that seemed worthy of his attention. The Prussians were heaping up great magazines of provisions in Silesia, but everywhere along the border hills they were constructing abattis, redoubts and entrenchments with meticulous care, and their *FM.* Keith agreed to hold an exchange of prisoners at the end of April. All of this indicated to Browne that the Prussians envisaged no major operations before that date at the earliest. He happened to be on good terms with the old Scottish warrior, and sent Keith a crate of English beer with his best wishes.

Warnings of aggressive Prussian designs were certainly pouring in from all sides, but the sources did not seem particularly trustworthy, and Friedrich Christian the Electoral Prince of Saxony, who had already been the author of a number of fanciful reports, seemed to have excelled himself when he furnished Browne with a complete plan of operations, whereby Frederick would launch 160,000 men into Bohemia by five avenues.[1]

Browne contented himself with a few measures of basic security. *FZM.* Königsegg took command of the troops in the Circle of Bunzlau in north-central Bohemia, and by 6 April *FML.* the Duke of Arenberg had concentrated eight regiments of infantry and three of cavalry on the upper Eger in north-east Bohemia, to counter any move on the part of the up to 18,000 troops which Prince Moritz of Anhalt-Dessau had assembled near Zwickau in the Voigtland.

The sixth of April, the day indicated by the Electoral Prince for the great invasion, passed without incident. Four infantry regiments and four cavalry regiments were ready at Prague to march when necessary, and Browne was still disinclined to place the army under canvas or to begin to consume the precious magazines. To all appearances Frederick would stay with his main army about Dresden, 'to be able to turn in whatever direction the torrent of our forces will burst upon him'.[2]

Towards the middle of April some unusual concentrations of Prussian transport at last seemed to lend some colour to the rumours of an imminent invasion, and Browne undertook an extensive inspection of the borders. He travelled first to the Circle of Königgrätz in north-east Bohemia, and found that the dour *GdC.* Serbelloni had made sensible arrangements for the defence. He made his way westwards through the outposts of *FML.* Maguire, and reconnoitred the Prussian positions about Zittau. Browne was pleased with what he saw, and expressed the hope that the enemy might be foolish enough to try to attack in that quarter.

Browne was back in Prague on the evening of 19 April, and found awaiting him a report from Serbelloni that Prussian troops had crossed into north-east Bohemia and reached Braunau and Trautenau. Browne at once ordered five battalions to join Serbelloni, but he was otherwise still inclined to wait on events. A little later came the news that the cordon along the north-west border was also under threat.

By 23 April there was no escaping the fact that Prussian troops were invading Bohemia in great force, and almost exactly as the Electoral Prince of Saxony had foretold. The right wing of more than 19,000 troops under Moritz of Anhalt-Dessau was marching by way of Komotau and Brüx towards Frederick's main army of 40,000, which had taken the familiar invasion route closer to the Elbe by way of Peterswalde. To the east, Maguire's outposts were being pushed back by a corps of 20,000 men under the Duke of Bevern, who was advancing from Zittau on Reichenberg. *FM.* Schwerin had been entrusted with the left wing, and was directing 34,000 troops from Silesia by several channels into north-east Bohemia. The Austrians had altogether 114,000 men in Bohemia, but the units were so scattered that Browne could bring together no more than 60,000 troops to confront the enemy. The infantry and 'German' cavalry were confused and exhausted by the precipitate marches, while the hussars were disintegrating in the face of their much-improved Prussian counterparts.

There was no single explanation as to why Browne had been caught so completely off his guard. His optimism had been sustained for week after week, but it was now dissolving in emotional and physical collapse. His enemies asserted that his head had been turned by the praise which had been heaped on him in Vienna, but the sudden reversal was more probably occasioned by the advance of his lung disease. In addition Browne had fallen into ways of thinking which rendered him particularly vulnerable. He had come to regard Bohemians of all kinds as stupid and materialistic, and he ceased to regard them as useful sources of information. He placed no more credibility in the reports of his junior outpost commanders, who had seemed to form an altogether exaggerated opinion of the King of Prussia.[3]

Reichenberg, 21 April 1757

a) Austrians
15,000: 12,300 infantry, 2,700 cavalry; 26 pieces
Losses: 874; 87 killed, 311 wounded, 476 missing or prisoners
b) Prussians
14,550: 11,450 infantry, 3,100 cavalry, 12 heavy pieces
Losses: 655; 193 killed, 462 wounded

At five on the afternoon of 21 April Browne learned that Serbelloni had fallen back to a camp behind the confluence of the Adler and the upper Elbe at Königgrätz, abandoning all the ground between there and the border to the enemy. Worse still, he had sent his personal baggage back to Pardubitz, which was good as telling the troops that he was bent on retreating still further.

Vague but ominous news was coming from Reichenberg, where *FZM.* Königsegg had assembled 15,000 troops on the upper reaches of the Lausitzer Neisse. The Austrians were strong in terms of numbers, and they were also strongly emplaced, with their two flanks resting on steep and heavily-wooded heights—the right on the Iser-Gebirge to the east, and the left on the Jeschken-Gebirge on the west. A line of entrenchments covered the right and centre of the intervening plain, and the Austrian cavalry was concentrated on the remaining gap which extended for more than half a mile to the

Jeschken-Gebirge.

On the same 21 April the outnumbered Duke of Bevern attacked with great determination. The Liechtenstein Dragoons [D6] put up a brave fight against three regiments of their Prussian counterparts, but the Austrian infantry seems to have been in a state of shock and demoralisation, for the troops on the Jeschken-Gebirge flank disappeared into the woods, and the others fell back from the earthworks in the face of the advancing Prussians. Königsegg had to abandon the whole position.

For days Browne could ascertain little except the bare fact that Königsegg had been beaten, and that according to orders he was making for Jung-Bunzlau on the upper Iser, where there was one of those precious magazines. Maguire had meanwhile been holding seven regiments of foot and three of horse at Gabel, and ought to have been in a position to intervene against the exposed right flank of Bevern's advance into Bohemia. He was nevertheless deterred by a screen of hussars which Bevern extended along the Lausitzer-Neisse, and he fell back through Gabel and ultimately joined Königsegg on his retreat.

The scattered Austrian troops were marching up to sixteen hours a day to reach the assembly points, and Königsegg was confronted with a new crisis when Schwerin dodged around Serbelloni's position and hastened up from the east to anticipate the Austrians at Jung-Bunzlau. Königsegg escaped the trap by forcing his troops through another of the exhausting night marches, and put himself beyond immediate danger by crossing the upper Elbe to Brandeis. The way was now clear for Bevern and Schwerin to join on the Iser at Jung-Bunzlau on 27 April.

The retreat on Prague

The Prussian forces were now coalescing into two great armies, poised within a few short marches of Prague. However the Austrians were still well placed to hold them apart. Königsegg had a respectable 25,000 men at Brandeis, and he now had the task of holding the line of the upper Elbe against the combined forces of Schwerin and Bevern, while Browne turned to deal with the nearly 60,000 troops of Frederick's army which were now advancing up the west bank of the Elbe.

On the morning of 26 April the main Austrian army under the command of Browne entered the familiar camping ground on the heights above Budin. Frederick had moved down to the plain of Lobositz, and Browne could make out part of the enemy right wing from his viewpoint in the village of Martinowez. The king had by now almost certainly been joined by the corps of Anhalt-Dessau, but Arenberg was hurrying to reach Browne from the upper Eger, and the field marshal had hopes of beating the enemy before they could reach Prague.

Browne had to evacuate the position at Budin sooner than he expected, for the Prussians had made a speedy crossing of the Eger several miles upstream, and on 27 April the Austrian army drew back some eight miles to Welwarn, the better to cover Prague. A cloud of dust hanging in the air to the west indicated that the enemy were once more circling around the left flank, and Arenberg with the troops from the upper Eger had to make a wide detour by way of Schlan to avoid being cut off.

At first light on the 28th Browne rode out to view the Prussian movements. He had been determined to hold the position at Welwarn, but the opinion among the generals seems to have been against him, and his standing had been weakened by the events of the campaign and his status as no more than interim commander. A cannon shot signalled the army to march off in six columns, soon to be reduced to one for the difficult passage of the valleys of Minkowitz. The new camp was planted on the heights of Tursko, and early on the morning of 29 April Browne assembled a council of war. He grasped that the two prongs of the Prussian advance could not be considered in isolation, and that if the king and Schwerin were permitted to advance any further they would soon be separated only by the narrow tongue of land between the Moldau and the Elbe.

Browne urged the company to stake everything on attacking Frederick, but although Arenberg had reached Tursko the day before, which brought the Austrian numbers to probably more than 30,000, the army was still

Prague, 6 May 1757

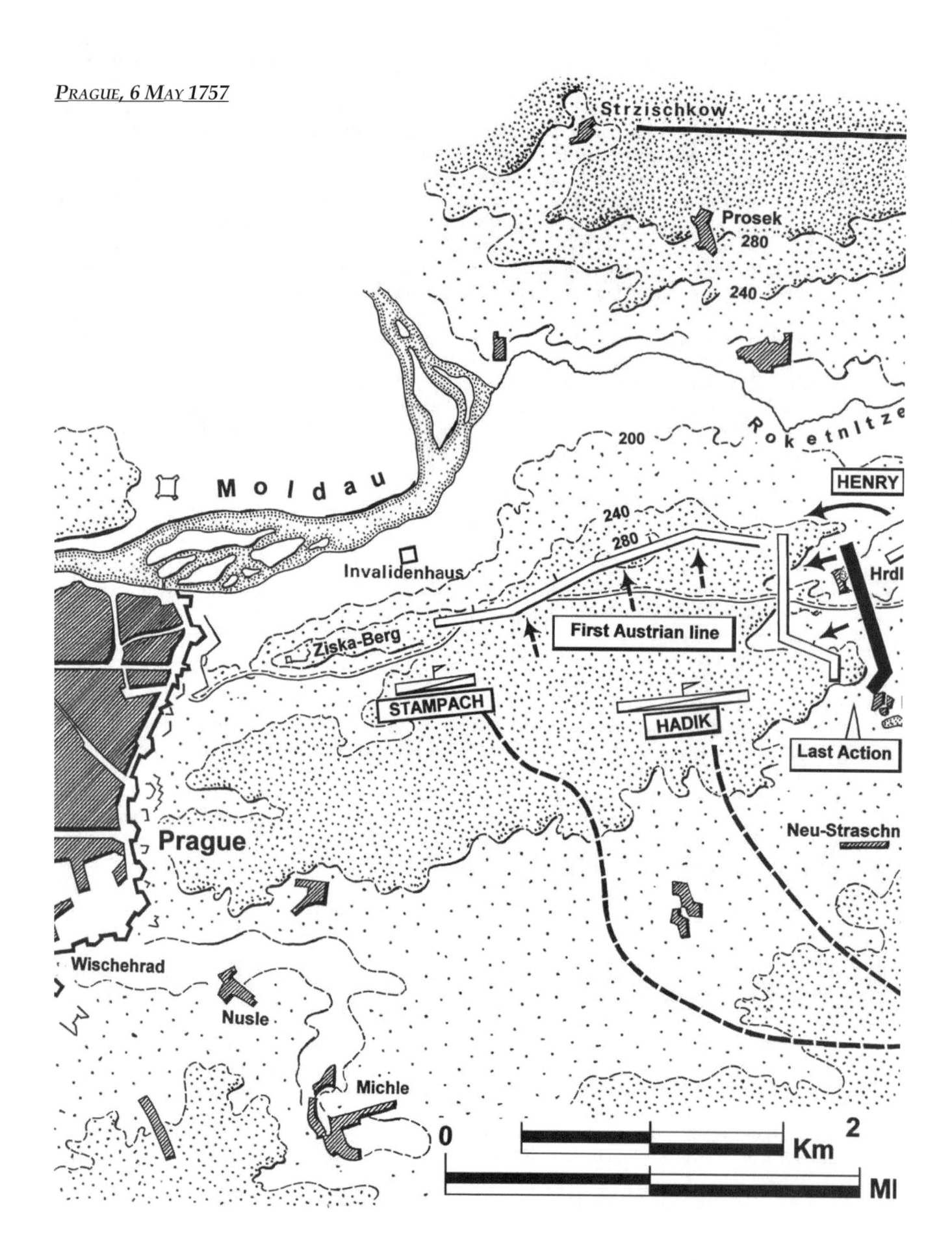

Strzischkow
Prosek 280
240
Moldau
Roketnitze
200
240
280
Invalidenhaus
Ziska-Berg
First Austrian line
HENRY
Hrdl
STAMPACH
HADIK
Last Action
Neu-Straschn
Prague
Wischehrad
Nusle
Michle

0 — 2 Km
MI

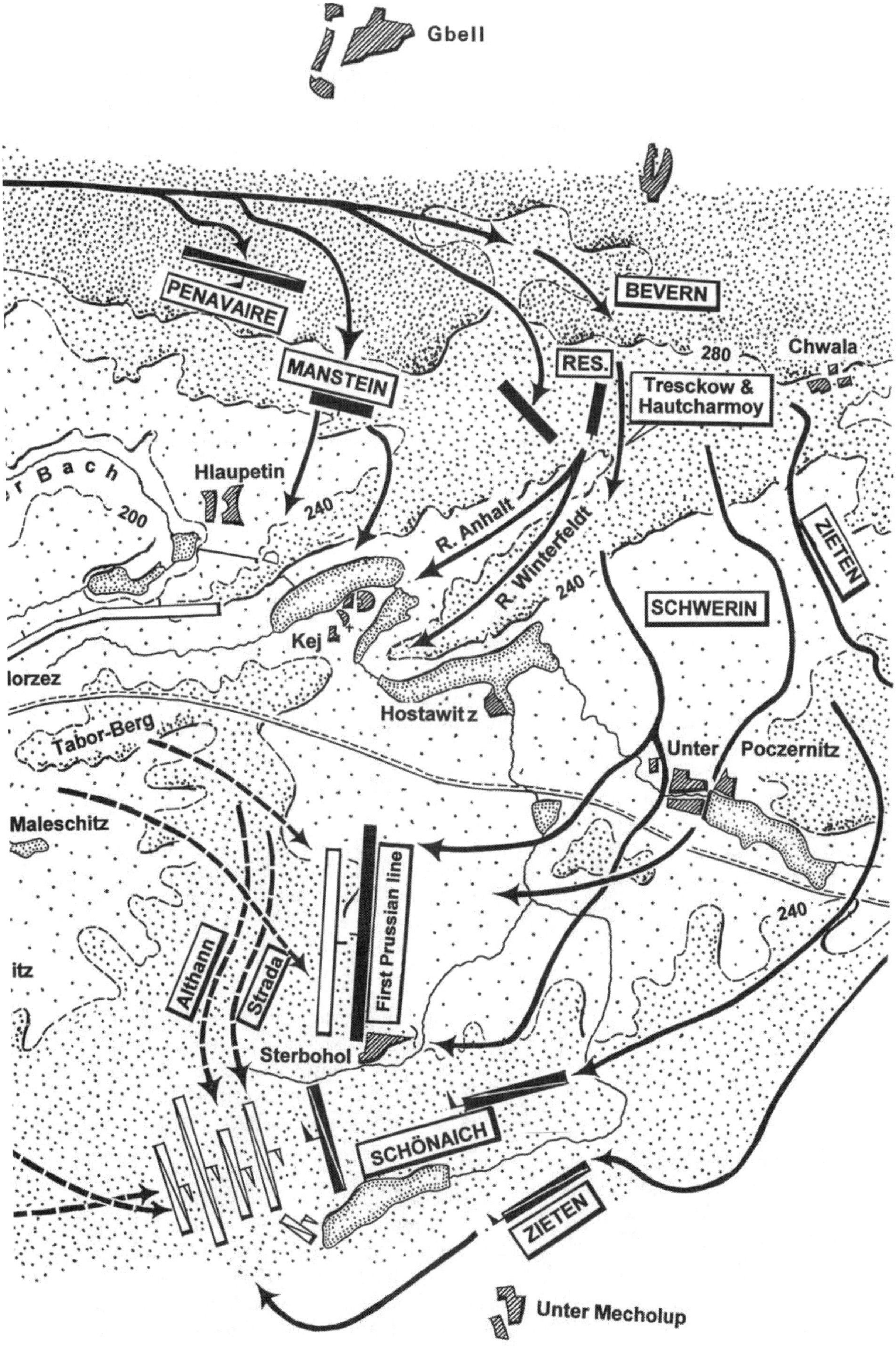

Gbell
PENAVAIRE
MANSTEIN
BEVERN
RES.
Tresckow & Hautcharmoy
280
Chwala
r Bach
Hlaupetin
200
240
R. Anhalt
R. Winterfeldt
240
ZIETEN
SCHWERIN
Kej
lorzez
Hostawitz
Tabor-Berg
Unter
Poczernitz
Maleschitz
First Prussian line
240
itz
Althann
Strada
Sterbohol
SCHÖNAICH
ZIETEN
Unter Mecholup

much weaker than the king's, and the generals spoke out for retreating to Tuchomirschitz, scarcely five miles from the ramparts of Prague. Browne had to give way, and his standing was undermined still further because Prince Charles was at last coming to join the army. On the road to Prague the prince had been alarmed to encounter refugees fleeing with their goods, and at Tuchomirschitz on the 30th he found Browne in what he described as a tearful and thoroughly pitiable state.[4]

Once more the generals met in council. Browne declared that the Austrians must fall on the enemy when they were passing through the narrows to the north, but on seeing that the others were unconvinced he turned to Charles and begged him to give him just 4,000 men with which to attack. Charles believed that Browne was almost out of his wits, and he did what he could to calm him down. Against Browne's unyielding opposition, the generals determined to cross the Moldau and take up station on the far (i.e. eastern) side of Prague.

The decision of the council was put into effect on 1 May. Charles led the right wing of the army through the city of Prague and across the Moldau by the ancient Carlsbrücke, while Browne formed the left wing into column and made for a bridge of boats which had been thrown across the river downstream. The march lay through difficult country, and the hussars and Croats of the rearguard still had to complete the passage of the narrows at Tuchomirschitz when twenty squadrons of Prussian hussars threatened to ride them down. Browne brought up six cannon and the grenadiers and carabiniers of the rearguard to give covering fire, and the Croats and hussars were able to cross the intervening ground safely. Browne had clearly lost none of his facility in handling troops, and the passage of the river was completed without further disturbance.

The arguments at headquarters continued through the day. Prince Charles, over the objections of Browne, resolved to withdraw Königsegg from the line of the upper Elbe, and thus removed the final obstacle to the junction of Frederick and Schwerin. On 2 May Charles proposed to abandon Prague altogether and fall back into central Bohemia. This time Browne had the generals on his side, for they all agreed that it was most important to hold the capital, and that a further retreat would shatter the morale of the troops. Charles accepted the voice of the council, but nothing could persuade him to send Königsegg back to the upper Elbe to block Schwerin's approach.

At four in the afternoon heavy firing was heard from the direction of Brandeis, and it transpired that Colonel MacElligot and his Croats had come under strong attack and been forced to abandon the last Austrian foothold on this reach of the upper Elbe. On 5 May came news that Frederick's army had crossed the Moldau to the north of Prague, and was marching eastwards to join Schwerin, who had just passed the Elbe at Brandeis. Towards four in the afternoon Browne rode from the camp, and somewhere between Gbell and Winortz he came across a commanding position from where the Austrians could even now assail one of the enemy armies before it could unite with the other. He had discovered the last opportunity to fight at an advantage, but Charles insisted that the army must do battle where it stood.

Prague, 6 May 1757

a) Austrians
c. 60,000: 45,400 infantry, 10,400 'German' cavalry, 2,100 hussars, 2,000 Croats, 60 pieces
Losses: up to 14,000, including 4,275 prisoners
b) Prussians
c. 65,000: 47,000 infantry, 17,000 horse, 210 pieces
Losses: 14,287

The chosen battle line of the Austrian army faced north, and extended for some two miles over the open rolling plateau to the east of Prague. The whole front overlooked the wide valley of the Roketnitzer-Bach, with the left leaning on the rocky Ziska-Berg above Prague, while the right reached to a complex of lakes and wooded headlands around the village of Kej. The ground would serve well enough for a defensive battle, and Browne set to work to make of it what he could. Entrenchments were dug out of the stony soil at various points along the heights, and Browne paid particular attention to a narrow and isolated ridge in front of Kej, which could be considered the key to the right flank. By the morning of 6 May the works were sufficiently advanced to receive twenty-seven pieces of heavy artillery, and an entrenchment had been dug across the ridge with the flanks resting on two stretches of the winding Roketnitzer-Bach.

In the evening of the 5th there were already signs of the confusions which marked the next day's battle. The Prussian movements could be seen clearly from the outposts, yet when Charles inspected the regiments after dinner he found that many men and horses were missing from the cavalry. He asked the reason, and was told that a ticket of leave had allowed 325 of the best men of each regiment, unarmed, and dressed in their working smocks, to take unsaddled horses to Prague to fetch bread and fodder. The muddle was going to cost Charles 5,000 out of the 60,000 men under his command.

At three in the morning of 6 May reports of Prussian movements brought Charles to the outposts at Prosek. He at once ordered the army to assemble outside its camp on the Kolin road, and he hastened back to his headquarters in Maleschitz, where he told Browne that he was putting him in charge of the right wing.

Roundshot were falling through the mist among the outposts of the hussars and German cavalry, and powerful enemy forces were observed to be approaching from the direction of Brandeis, which indicated that Schwerin's corps was arriving on the scene. Soon afterwards the outposts at Prosek were driven in by further columns advancing from the north-west, and these in turn were obviously those of Frederick's army. At first light the Austrians could see that the far side of the valley of the Roketnitzer-Bach was covered with the united forces of the king and Schwerin, marching to their left in two beautifully-formed columns with a large force of cavalry in the lead.

The Austrian ranks dissolved when the army was ordered to prepare breakfast. The Prussians had stopped as well, and it seemed safe enough to call the army to morning service. Mass was still being celebrated when adjutants rode up to order the regiments to advance into line of battle along the rim of the valley a few hundred paces to the north. The kettles were left steaming over the fires, and every single man was called upon to extend the front. The infantry were ranged in three ranks instead of the habitual four, and Browne insisted that nobody was to be left behind to guard or strike the tents. When the arrangements were nearly complete, Prince Charles and Browne rode along the entire front from left to right.

By seven in the morning the whole Prussian army was again marching to the east across the Austrian front. All eyes were on the movement, and, before the enemy trailed out of sight behind a fold of land, the battery on the ridge near Kej had the time to throw a few shots at the cavalry at the head, which forced them and the blue columns behind to veer out of the fire.

Browne now grasped that the enemy were bent on gaining the unguarded right rear of the Austrian position, where the slopes were far less steep than those facing north. When the Prussians reappeared the change of direction was clear, for their infantry were now marching across the plain of the upper Roketnitzer-Bach, and would soon be able to form up at right angles to the existing Austrian deployment. The leading cavalry had already passed Unter-Poczernitz and were defiling at a short trot along a causeway. Browne, who was then probably standing on the ridge to the north of Kej, sent the Dutch colonel Cullen to *GdC*. Lucchesi with the order to throw the cavalry of the Austrian right wing into the attack before the enemy had time to form in line of battle. Lucchesi promptly marched the whole of his wing along the eastern edge of the plateau to a position beyond Sterbohol, more than a mile to the south, so interposing himself in the path of the approaching enemy.

Lucchesi's move had inevitably left a gap between his new position and the infantry of the Austrian right wing. Browne left the first line along the heights to the north, but directed the regiments of the second line in a great fan-like movement to form an entirely new line along the eastern edge of the plateau, and so ward off the Prussian thrust to the rear.

One of Browne's adjutants galloped along

the line crying *'Grenadiers heraus!'*. Forty companies of these elite troops at once marched off to form to the left of Lucchesi's cavalry. Immediate support for Lucchesi arrived in the shape of the second line of the cavalry of the left wing under *GdC*. Stampach, and in a short time a total of more than one hundred squadrons were assembling south-west of Sterbohol. The benefit of interior lines, together with Browne's quick responses, now promised to turn the balance of advantage in favour of the Austrians.

All this time the Prussian left wing under Schwerin was labouring across the causeways and meadows of the upper Roketnitzer-Bach. Only a few pieces had passed through the hamlet of Unter-Poczernitz before the narrow street became jammed with heavy artillery, and for a time the battalion pieces were strung out motionless along the road behind.

Finally at about 9.30 in the morning fourteen Prussian battalions began a somewhat ragged advance towards the swarming plateau. Frederick came up and showed some anxiety at the lack of order, but Schwerin was glad to see the troops on the move when time was so short. Almost at the same moment the few pieces which the Prussians had been able to bring with them began to throw shot and shell against Lucchesi's cavalry, and bowled over a few horses. Browne rode up sword in hand, to restore order and confidence, and the Austrian troopers repulsed a determined charge which the Prussian cavalry launched a little later.

Turning back towards the infantry, Browne had two 12-pounder cannon brought up speedily from the reserve, and placed them beside two battalion 3-pounders on the low swell of the Homole-Berg behind Sterbohol. Eight further battalion pieces had been distributed among the grenadiers below, and soon the whole available artillery of the Austrian right wing was blowing gales of canister through the advancing enemy ranks. The Austrians were now deriving tangible benefit from the work which Prince Liechtenstein had put into reforming the artillery before the war.

Browne was regaining the initiative, and he now led all the infantry at his disposal down the gentle slope at a measured step. The enemy troops opened fire at long range, but the Austrians maintained their unhurried march, and disdained to reply until they could discharge their volleys in the face of the enemy. They then rushed forward with sabre and bayonet.

The Prussian grenadiers on the left of Schwerin's line broke in disorder, but the remaining fusiliers gathered around their colours and pressed on a little more under the urgent calls of their officers. At that critical moment *GL*. Winterfeldt was hit in the neck by a ball and fell stunned from the saddle, and the troops behind him took to their heels. Numbers of the Prussian wounded, probably Catholics from the County of Glatz, cared so little for the fight that they offered their loaded muskets to the Austrians for use against their former comrades.

Schwerin had helped to throw his cavalry into their first charge, but with mounting anxiety he was now riding back towards his routed infantry. He snatched up the colour of the second battalion of his own regiment and led the men forward again. He had covered only a few yards before five canister shot tore through his body, and he sank to the ground, dead. His horrified troops now gave way entirely.

The last glimpse we have of Browne in action comes from Captain Szent-Ivány of the Hungarian volunteers, who was buffeted from behind by a horse. 'Thinking it must be one of that swarm of volunteers who plagued the army at that time, I was on the point of saying something rude to the rider. You can imagine my astonishment when I recognised him as Field Marshal Browne...who was simply crying out "Bravo, grenadiers, bravo!"'.[5] Heavy fire was already being exchanged with the intact Prussian second line, and it must have been just moments later that a cannon shot shattered one of Browne's legs above the foot, and threw him heavily to the ground. Those nearest him cut away the blood-filled boot, and did what they could to stem the flow until surgeons could arrive.

Browne's soldiers swept on, now burning for revenge, yet no longer with any leadership or direction. They captured the village of Sterbohol, together with a number of colours and eleven or twelve pieces, but the advance of the grenadiers came gradually to a halt in a savage fire-fight. The fusiliers were still streaming up to their support when the Austrian line staggered under the impact of fresh masses of Prussian infantry, this time coming against their left rear.

Szent-Ivány's encounter confirms the impression that Browne had become too heavily involved in the detailed business of combat, and had lost sight of the larger picture. Moreover, the further he had advanced with his troops down the slope, the more a gentle spur, projecting from the plateau, denied him a view of what was happening further to the north. Frederick chose this time to throw a number of densely-packed lines of infantry into a wide gap that had opened between Kej and the men under Browne's immediate command. Browne had indeed ordered up *FZM.* Kheul to take up position there with the eleven battalions of the left wing of the second line, but the troops had first to traverse the marshy hollow near Hrdlorzez and the tent lines of the camp, and the movement stopped altogether on instructions from Prince Charles. *FML.* Clerici, who had set off with three of the battalions, was astonished to find that none of the others were following him, and it was altogether too late when Charles changed his mind and finally got Kheul to move. The Prussians were now entering the gap in force, and they proceeded to tear apart the two halves of the Austrian army.

The Austrian high command collapsed altogether when Prince Charles was overcome by a violent pain in the throat and rode from the field without saying a word. He reached the village of Nusle, where he received some attention, but he still had no idea where he was, and he was carried on to Prague. Nothing was heard from Lucchesi and the other generals except an endless cry of '*Drauf los!*'

Browne's grenadiers were fighting on, completely ignorant of the catastrophe which was developing to their north, and they were stranded completely when the Austrian cavalry to the south of Sterbohol collapsed all of a sudden.. A second Prussian cavalry attack had met with no more success than the first, but even as *Appel* was blown to recall the victorious Austrian troopers, a cloud of dust enveloped the entire scene. Wild rumours had already spread among the Austrians by the time the enemy presented themselves a third time. Pistols crackled from the hussars who were leading the Prussian charge, at which the first line of the Austrian cavalry turned tail and dashed into the second line, which also fled at a gallop, without knowing really why. Nothing could persuade the heavy cavalrymen to turn about and face the hussars they normally despised as mounted bandits.

The Austrian grenadiers continued to hold their ground until it dawned on them that the missiles rushing overhead from the back came not from supporting troops, but from Prussian battalions and artillery which had gained their left flank and rear. Fighting furiously, the Austrian regiments covering the northern edge of the plateau were meanwhile being forced back towards the gates of Prague, where the press of fugitives was such that Prince Charles found it impossible to return to the field after he regained his senses. All the time the Prussians were driving with irresistible force into the widening gap between the two Austrian wings. Just in time the badly-wounded Browne was escorted back to the city, but 15,000 of the infantry and cavalry on the right were cut off completely from the army and had to retreat south to Beneschau.

The evening found the main force of the Austrian infantry and artillery ranged along the ramparts of Prague, while the cavalry assembled in the principal squares. As a matter of form Frederick sent one of his adjutants with a violently-worded summons to surrender. He was brought before Browne, who had sufficient strength to send him on his way again. There were more than 30,000 troops in the city, and Charles himself considered that it would be a disgrace to '*l'honneur germanique*' if he failed to hold the same place which far fewer Frenchmen had defended so well in 1742.

Elaborate plans for breaking out of the encircling Prussians were worked out in consultation with Browne, but towards the end of May the Austrians learned through a daring

KOLIN, 18 JUNE 1757

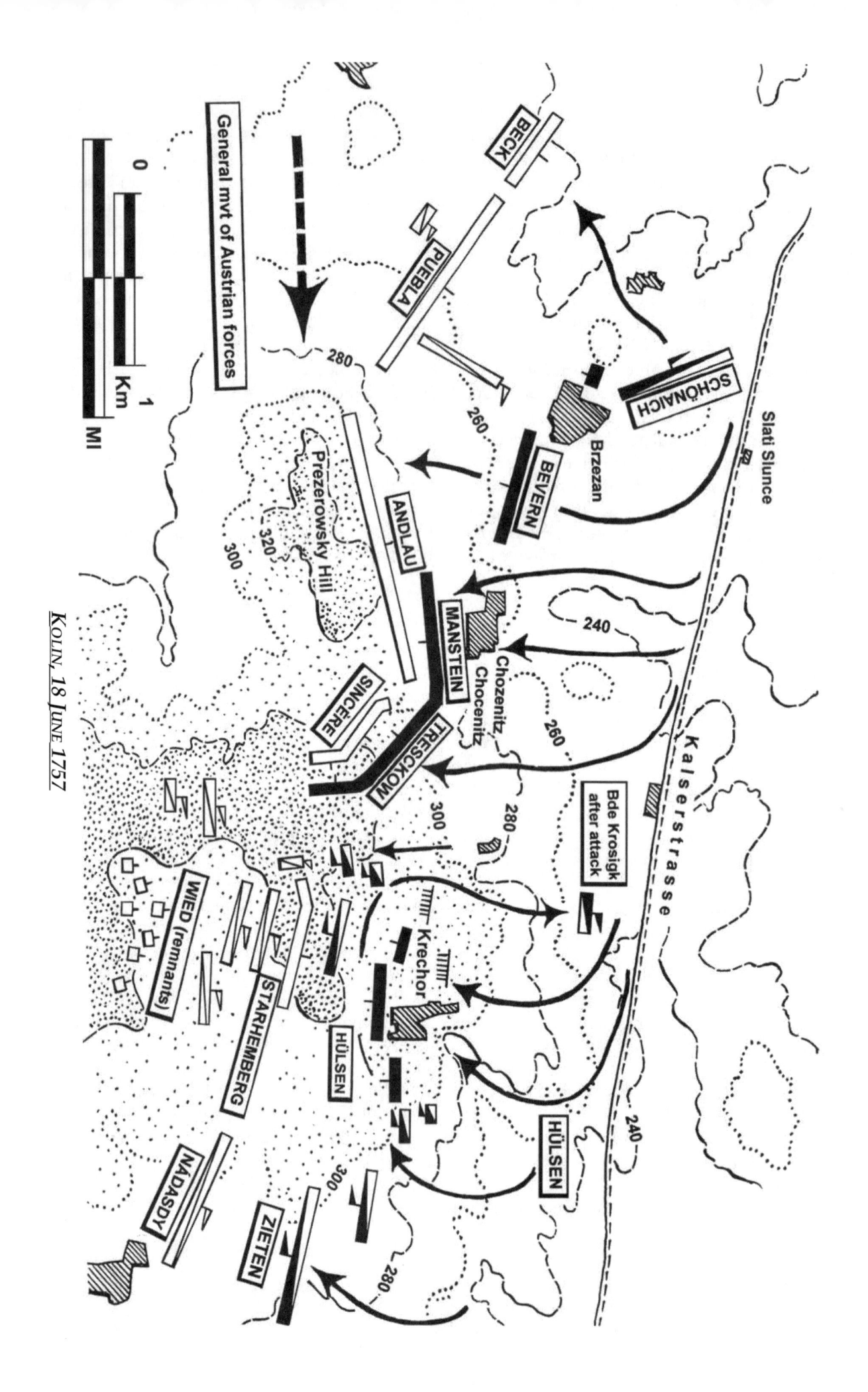

courier that a conference in Vienna had decided that the defenders could do far more good by holding down substantial Prussian forces in front of the city, and so give greater freedom of action to a new field army which *FM*. Daun was putting together from Serbelloni's corps and the fugitives who had escaped to Beneschau.

The morale of the garrison was suffering from successive misfortunes. A sortie led by *GFWM*. Materni had cost the Austrians more than 600 men, and Charles rejected a plan advanced by Browne for destroying the weak corps of *FM*. Keith on the left bank of the Moldau, at a time when the enemy communications across the river were interrupted by a flood. The spirits of the defenders were at last restored by a sortie which Colonel Loudon and Browne's elder son Colonel Philipp launched at midnight on 2/3 June. They took the defenders of some of Keith's outworks completely by surprise, and the Austrians were able to drag three cannon back to Prague.

The situation of the Prussians before Prague became unsustainable. A bombardment of the city proved more noisy than effective, and the Prussian cavalry had to forage further and further afield. Frederick was forced to send detachment after detachment to observe the 54,000 troops which Daun assembled on the upper Elbe, and on 13 June the king himself set out to take command of the Prussian field army, leaving only a small force to contain Prague.

On 19 June trains of baggage and artillery were seen to be leaving the Prussian camp before the city, and a little later came the report that on the day before Frederick had attacked Daun near Kolin, and suffered a terrible defeat.

KOLIN, 18 JUNE 1757

a) Austrians
52,750 (with gunners): 30,000 regular infantry, 1,700 cavalry, 4,000 Croats, 145 pieces
Losses: c. 9,250, nearly all casualties, 5 colours and 1 standard
b) Prussians
34,500: 19,500 infantry, 14,000 cavalry, 90 pieces
Losses: 13,792: including 4,083 prisoners, most of whom were wounded, 22 colours, 45 pieces

The new war was being fought with extraordinary energy, and so much had happened already that a brief recapitulation will perhaps be useful. In April 1757 the Austrians had been caught off their guard (for the second time in the conflict) when the Prussians undertook a full-blooded invasion of Bohemia. The Austrian commander Browne was a brilliant and inspirational soldier, but his judgement was clouded by ill-health, and before long he had to defer in command to the irresponsible Prince Charles of Lorraine, brother of the Emperor. Early in May the multiple Prussian columns were allowed to coalesce in front of Prague, and the subsequent battle (6 May) was a hard-fought but tactically decisive victory for the Prussians, and by the end of the day Charles, the badly-wounded Browne and over 30,000 of their troops had been compelled to seek shelter behind the city ramparts. The rest of their army was scattered to the winds.

It was small wonder that the Prussians now considered themselves unbeatable, and that some of Frederick's own officers became uneasy at the thought of the 'universal monarchy' which now seemed to be within their master's grasp. Matters had been going so badly for the Austrians even before the battle that Kaunitz found it necessary to set out for the theatre of operations from Vienna on 5 May. The great battle had been fought and lost before he could reach Prague, and after conferring with *FM*. Daun the *Staatscanzler* was back in Vienna on 11 May, bursting in on a conference in boots and riding dress (for dramatic effect) to render a first report on the crisis which was threatening to overturn the dynasty.

Maria Theresa and her advisers now had to turn their attention to matters as fundamental as mobilising the resources of the state, restoring discipline and morale in the remaining forces, and persuading the allies that Austria was still in the war. They entrusted the task of putting together a new field army to Daun, who had won Maria Theresa's confidence during the recent reforms, and was bound to her by close ties of friendship. He gathered his forces in east-central Bohemia, mainly from the troops who had escaped from the field of battle, and from the corps of the sluggish *GdC.* Serbelloni, who had not stirred from Königgrätz during the invasion. For a time Daun was free to gather in the reinforcements and drill the troops in his typically painstaking way, but affairs suddenly became more urgent when, on 9 June, he learned that the provisions in Prague would run out eleven days later. He was now under orders to break through to relieve the city, whatever the risks, and he began his westward march on 12 June.

GL. the Duke of Bevern had meanwhile done his best to hold Daun at a distance while Frederick proceeded to bombard Prague. The king did not have a battle in mind when he left to join Bevern with a reinforcement of four battalions and sixteen squadrons. He assumed that the city would be able to hold out until the end of July, and he intended nothing more than to expand the Prussian foraging areas by pushing Daun further to the east. He had just reached the end of his first day's march when he learned from Bevern that a whole Austrian army was on the advance.

Frederick and Bevern joined on 14 June, and by the afternoon of the 16th reinforcements brought their combined army to about 34,000 men, which was well short of the total force available to the king in Bohemia, but enough, so he believed, to give him the advantage over the Austrians. Daun was therefore disappointed in his hopes of eliminating Bevern before he was reinforced, and on 15 June he made a cautious march to the position of Krcynow, just three miles from the Prussian army. He deployed his troops facing west on the rounded hills which overlooked the Beczvarka stream. The position was tactically strong, but so was that of the enemy on the far side, and Daun was still pondering how he might manoeuvre his way to Prague when, late in the afternoon of 17 June, the king snatched the initiative from him.

Frederick had decided to break the deadlock by moving north to take up the Kaiserstrasse (Imperial Highway), and then push along it to the east to turn Daun's right flank. Daun countered the first move by rearranging his forces. He designated the division of Wied as the mobile *corps de reserve*, and retained it for the moment in the original position above the Beczvarka. By the early morning of 18 June the rest of the army had been extended at right-angles in a new north-facing position along a frontage of three miles. The infantry were concentrated in two groups—on the Pobor height in the west (divisions of Puebla and Sincere), and the high and breezy Prezerowsky Hill to the east (divisions of Andlau and Starhemberg). The greater part of the cavalry were deployed across the saddle between the two hills, a departure from the conventional battle arrays, in which the horse were stationed on the two flanks. Later in the morning the light corps of *GdC.* Franz Leopold Nádasdy arrived on the scene after a forced march, and was emplaced by Daun on the Krechor Hill well to the east.

In essence the Austrians were now standing on a smooth and undulating ridge which sloped gradually to the Kaiserstrasse. The ground was an extension of the fertile plain of the upper Elbe, and at this season the year supported a growth of wheat and rye. Daun had not been given the time to prepare artificial defences, and there was little to remark in the shape of existing obstacles, except a couple of steep and narrow little valleys which cut perpendicularly into the ridge, together with the churchyard wall at Krechor, the ancient earthwork (the so-called 'Schwedenschanze') which extended to the west of the village, and an oak wood a little way down the reverse slope. Krechor itself was lightly built, and the other place names indicated little more than complexes of farm buildings. In compensation the defenders had open fields of view and fire, and their cannon shot could exert their full grazing effect down the smooth slopes, which were nevertheless steep enough to sap the stamina of the attackers, who in addition would have to labour through the crops in the heat of this cloudless day.

The sun was already very hot in the middle of the morning, by when the Prussian army had emerged from the Beczvarka valley and marched east along the Kaiserstrasse before coming to a halt. Frederick was taking in what he could see of the Austrian deployment from the inn of Slati Slunce ('Golden Sun') which rose beside the road, and was formulating his plan. His scheme was basically the one he applied at Prague, namely, to turn the Austrian right flank and roll up the enemy array from east to west. In this case:

1. *GL.* Zieten was to take the lead with his fifty-odd squadrons of hussars, and push back the newly-arrived Austrian corps (Nádasdy's) on the far right, so that it did not interfere with the unfolding of events
2. The main attack was to be spearheaded by a strong advance guard under the command of *GL.* Hülsen, who would climb to the ridge in the vicinity of Krechor
3. The left wing of the main army, as the principal striking force, would climb in Hülsen's steps and develop the attack westwards along the ridge
4. The right wing of the main army was to be held back, or 'refused,' in the classic style of the 'oblique order,' to help to fix the unengaged forces of the Austrians, and to provide the king with an ultimate reserve

At Prague the Prussian left wing under Schwerin had cut in sharply against the enemy from its original line of march, and thus become entangled with the Austrians too early, with literally fatal consequences for him and many of his troops. In the present case Frederick hoped that the battle would unfold cleanly, with Hülsen gaining the ridge with little difficulty, and the army's refused wing standing clear of the fighting.

Daun and his suite were trying to divine what the Prussians would do next. The basic problem (which the Austrians would confront again at Leuthen) was that they could not be certain whether the impending move would be a simple continuation of the normal jockeying for advantage in the campaign, or a prelude to an actual attack. Daun called on the advice of a comparatively junior officer, Major Franz Vettesz of the regiment of Erzherzog Carl [2], who was renowned through the army for the sharpness of his tactical eye. He told Daun that he had little doubt but that Frederick was bent on a battle, and that he would try to roll up the Austrian army from its right.

Daun was convinced by this reasoning, and in retrospect that moment can probably be seen as the decisive episode of the battle. Shortly after 1.30 in the afternoon the Prussian army took up arms and resumed its march. The light horse of Zieten and Nádasdy had been skirmishing since the morning, and now a full-scale private war broke out to the east of the field, continuing for the rest of the afternoon with little reference to the great battle which was unfolding to the west.

Meanwhile Frederick's grand scheme was unravelling piece by piece. The king and Hülsen seem to have expected that the advance guard would have an altogether uncontested march to the ridge at Krechor. However Nádasdy had emplaced 500 Banalist Croats and some of their minuscule 1-pounder cannon in the village. It was a small force compared with the others which were gathering on the field, but Frederick and Hülsen responded disproportionately, by throwing the advance guard into a full-blooded attack, supported by three grenadier battalions from the main force. It was perhaps then that Daun took the spyglass from his eye and exclaimed: 'My God, I think the king is going to lose today!'[6] Meanwhile the rest of the Prussian army remained strung out motionless along the Kaiserstrasse, exposed to the long-range fire from the Austrian artillery on the ridge.

The first phase of the battle took on its distinctive shape from about two in the afternoon. Alerted by Major Vettesz, Daun fed successive reinforcements to take up the fight for the ridge in the neighbourhood of Krechor—first a batch of ten companies of grenadiers, followed by the *corps de reserve* under *FML.* Wied from above the Beczvarka valley and an initial twelve cannon from the artillery reserve. Other divisions followed in succession, so that the army shifted bodily to the right and enabled Daun to establish a near-continuous line along the ridge as far as Krechor.

Towards the middle of the afternoon virtually nothing remained of the king's plan of battle, for the Prussian army, instead of following in Hülsen's tracks to Krechor, was now being cast into an attack directly against the ridge along a broad front. Frederick himself was

The pursuit after Kolin, June-July 1757

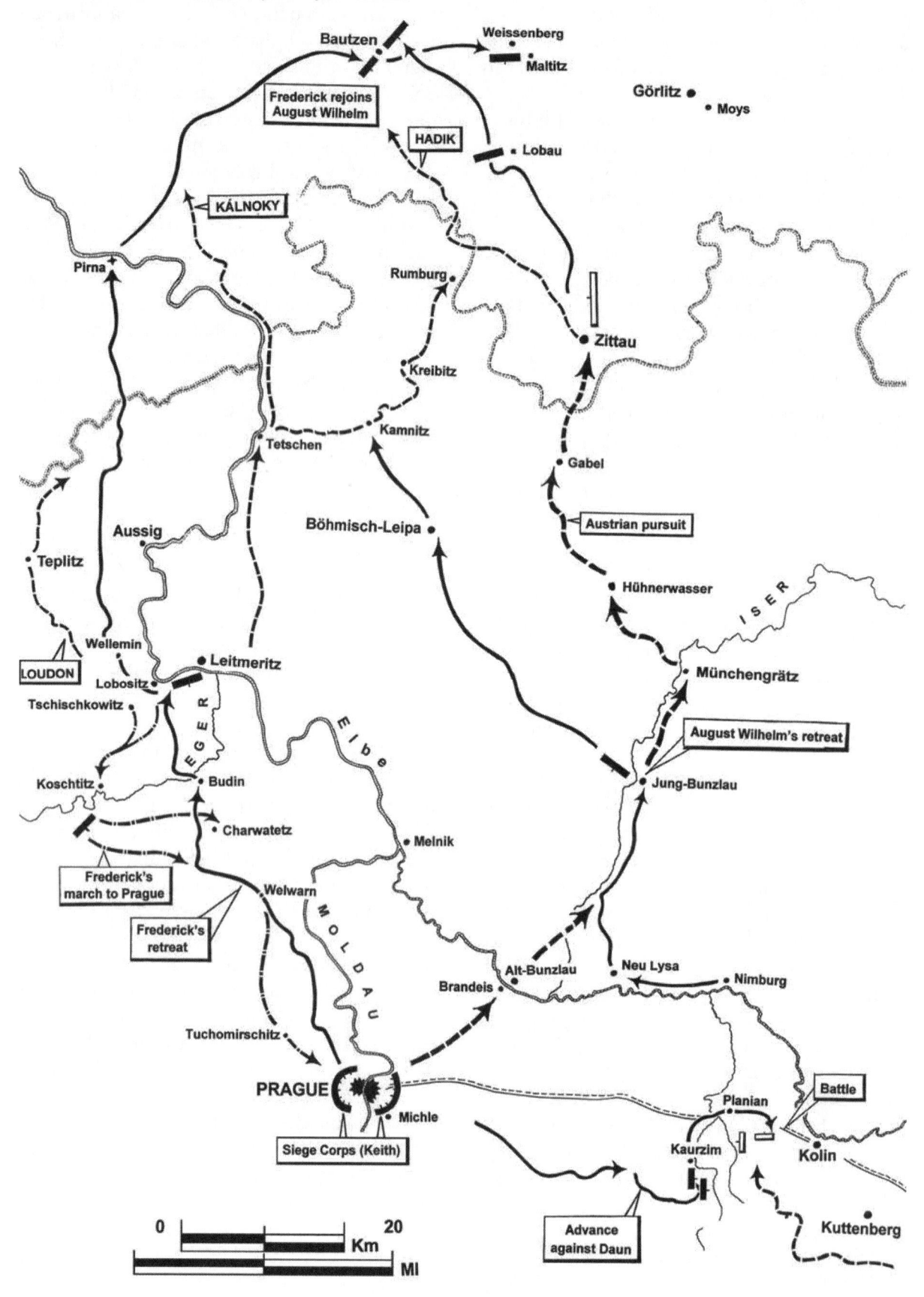

responsible for ordering his second in command, General Prince Moritz of Anhalt-Dessau, to throw *GL.* Tresckow into the assault with the main body of the centre. Moritz was appalled, but he had to obey. In the general battle which now developed the Prussian left and centre were repeatedly driven back from the ridge about Krechor, while the right wing under Bevern, which should have been 'refused,' was plagued by misunderstandings which led to five of its battalions being drawn into an attack on the Prezerowsky Hill.

The second phase of the battle may termed 'the combat of the cauldron,' and opened when Wied's *corps de reserve* succumbed to over-enthusiasm, and threw itself into a counter-attack from the crest just to the west of Krechor. In those days of linear tactics it was always dangerous for units or formations to advance from the main line of battle without proper support—the Austrians were to make the same mistake at Torgau in 1760, and now at Kolin the *corps de reserve* laid itself open to an attack by the three regiments of the Prussian cavalry brigade of *GM.* Krosigk, which cut into its right flank. Krosigk was mortally wounded in the charge, but Colonel Friedrich Wilhelm Seydlitz of the Rochow Cuirassiers [C8] was able to renew the momentum, and the infantry of the Prussian centre began to exploit into the gap in the Austrian line.

Towards six in the afternoon the attention of both Frederick and Daun concentrated on the potentially decisive battle which had thus developed on the summit of the Krechor Hill. The Austrians were forming an improvised and irregular line around the sides of the cauldron, while Frederick was drawing on the commands of Hülsen, Tresckow and Bevern to throw more and more forces into the pot, until, at the time of the supreme effort, altogether fourteen Prussian battalions were concentrated against the western side of the cauldron.

About twenty regiments of Austrian infantry and horse and the allied Saxon chevaulegers were caught up in the struggle to contain the breakthrough. Out of the many units which distinguished themselves, two in particular stand out. On the western side of the cauldron the fusilier regiment of Botta [12] stood firm under the inspired leadership of Colonel Franz Ulrich Prince Kinsky, who commandeered an ammunition cart at pistol point to enable his men to keep on fighting. From the eastern side, the de Ligne Dragoons [D31] precipitated a general counterattack by the Austrian and Saxon cavalry which ultimately broke the resistance of the Prussian infantry inside the cauldron.

By nine in the evening the exhausted and battered Prussians had disengaged along the whole extent of their battle lines, having lost about 46 per cent of their effectives. The Austrians did not pursue. They too were weary and short of ammunition, and Daun, his officers and his troops were not yet able to adjust themselves to something that was entirely new in their experience, which was victory over the King of Prussia.

On 20 June the Prussians were retreating from their lines and batteries in front of Prague (below), and all the ground between there and Kolin was abandoned to the Austrians. Frederick had displayed over-optimism and a lack of self-discipline in the way he managed the battle. Many of his regiments had fought doggedly, but the same was true of many of the Austrian units, and in addition Liechtenstein's new artillery had been given an opportunity to display its mobility and destructive power to the full. Daun's enemies claimed that at one stage he had given up the battle for lost, but the accusation is almost certainly false. On the contrary he kept the field as a whole under calm review, and the facility with which the Austrian commanders conducted their grand lateral movement to the east contrasts strikingly with the piecemeal and fragmentary nature of the Prussian attacks.

The outcome of the battle of Kolin was of far-reaching political, moral and symbolic importance. It put a term to whatever plans Frederick might have harboured for further aggrandisement at the expense of Austria, and it was seen as a defeat for the entire avowedly Protestant party in Germany. Daun promoted Vettesz to lieutenant colonel, and singled him out to take the news to Vienna. He arrived on 20 June, and two days later Maria Theresa took the opportunity to promulgate the establishment of the Military Order which bore her name. In its history the cross of the *Militärischer-Maria Theresien-Orden* was to be earned by many of the new nobility of service which became the most loyal support of Habsburg rule until that dynasty's end. Kolin was, in Maria Theresa's words, truly the 'Birthday of the Monarchy.'

Prague is free of the Prussians
First light on 20 June confirmed to the Austrians in Prague that the enemy had suffered a reverse of the first order. The Prussian forces to the east of the Moldau were in full retreat across the battlefield of 6 May. On the west bank, FM. Keith was responsible for taking away all the heavy artillery and the transportable sick and wounded, and (to the surprise of the Austrians) he showed no immediate signs of abandoning his siege lines. Prince Charles decided to attack with 24,000 of his infantry, 3,000 Croats and all the available cavalry. The force was to debouch from the city in three main columns, but it took so long to bring the troops through the streets, then out through the gates and to deploy them on the far side, that the assault could not begin until three in the afternoon.

The Prussians abandoned the remaining siege works in some confusion, and put up a fight only at some ready-made strongpoints along their line of retreat. An outflanking move on the part of the Austrians compelled the enemy to leave the walled Imperial park called the *Stern* ('Star'), and the Prussians left the area 'strewn with the bodies of their grenadiers, killed by the great volume of the Austrian canister fire and by the musketry of the Croats'.[7]

Colonel Loudon was commissioned to continue the pursuit with his mobile column of 2,000 Croats and 600 hussars, while the Austrian regulars returned to Prague as had been arranged. Over the following days Loudon harried Keith's Prussians as they retreated towards the Mittel-Gebirge. He mobilised 3,000 armed peasants to fell the trees and break up the roads along the Prussian path of retreat, while his Croats and hussars mopped up rearguards and laggards. On 22 June the Croats caught up with a transport of Prussian wounded at Welmina, just short of the Paschkopole Pass. The escort (one hundred men of the former Saxon regiment of Prinz Ferdinand) put up no effective opposition when the Croats stormed in from all sides, but according to Prussian legend GM. Christoph Hermann Manstein, who had been wounded at Kolin, was bayoneted to death after defending himself to the utmost. By Loudon's account 'General Manstein had surrendered upon parole, but then made his escort fire on the Croats. The Croats hacked him in pieces together with the escort. Very few were spared, but his son was numbered among them'.[8]

On the same day the army of Prince Charles made a triple feu de joie from the ramparts of Prague. Daun held celebrations of his own in his old camp at Krychnow, hard by the site of his almost incredible victory, and he now set his troops on the march to Prague. Daun rode ahead to confer with Charles, whose army emerged from the city on the 24th. There was a tricky issue of command to be resolved, and it seemed to a French observer that the field marshal was 'not at all inclined to hasten the union of the two armies. Prince Charles, on the other hand, appears to desire it very much indeed, and keeps on pressing for it… The field marshal hopes to spin out time until he has the impatiently-awaited news of the result of his intrigues in Vienna'.[9]

On 30 June the armies finally joined on the upper Elbe at Brandeis with a strength of 67,424 troops. Detachments amounting to a further 11,600 infantry and 9,000 horse were chasing the Prussians to the east of the Elbe, while Loudon's light corps was continuing its destructive work to the west.

The tents, kettles and so on had arrived on 28 June, which was earlier than had been expected, and Baron Netolitzky was doing what he could to bring up the necessary provisions and fodder. It took longer to decide who was in charge. At his first meeting with Charles on 23 June, Daun had accepted a reversal of roles without apparent demur. In fact everything still hung upon what was decided in Vienna, where Daun enjoyed the support of 'some ladies close to the Empress'.[10] Daun had sent Lieutenant

Colonel Vettesz to take the news of Kolin to the capital, as we have seen, but whatever impression was made by that excellent man it was destroyed by Maria Theresa's impulsive response to a letter carried by Lieutenant Schoger, who had been dispatched by Charles to tell of his little victory over the retreating Prussians on 20 June. If Vettesz was Daun's favourite aide-de-camp, Schoger was the son of Charles's groom, and he owed everything to the Prince. The Empress exclaimed that she could now do something to make up to Charles for all the injustices he had suffered. Her word was taken to signify the formal appointment of Charles as commander of the united forces in Bohemia. 'This imprudent step made a bad impression on many people, and she herself later regretted it very much; but the great lady is good-natured, she has a particular affection for her brother-in-law, and she can be easily won over to do something for good friends'.[11]

As far as Daun could establish, he was to remain with Charles *ad latus*, rather in the style of the mortally-stricken Browne. The French brigadier-general de Montazet noticed that Charles himself felt humiliated: 'The plan of the court was to give the direction of the army to the field marshal, and adorn His Royal Highness with the title of general commanding. You may imagine the effect on the feelings... of a prince who is by nature proud, and has a high opinion of himself. I was able to detect as much from the bitterness which crept into some personal conversations which I had with him. It is true that the field marshal keeps up the show of being subordinate to His Royal Highness, but that is only for public consumption and to keep up appearances... Before I finish I must outline the respective positions of the prince and the field marshal. The first has always been dogged by misfortune... he would like to make use of the forces which are nominally under his command, but it comes to exercising that command he succumbs to doubt and fear... The field marshal on his side is an extraordinarily brave man—of that there can be no doubt, but by disposition he is slow and timid... he has, moreover, been loaded with honours and good things, and he fears to compromise the reputation which he has won by his victory.[12]

The gifted, charismatic, and ultimately unfortunate Browne already belonged to history. His wound, his chest complaint and his gallant failure had left him barely alive when Daun came to see him in Prague on 23 June. Speaking with difficulty, Browne assured the field marshal of his esteem, and gave his best riding horse to the man 'against whom, by ordinary human reckoning, he ought to have felt the deepest resentment'.[13] Browne died at six in the morning of 6 July. 'He was a brave man,' commented Frederick, 'and, I believe, their best general'.[14]

The king sank into a prolonged lassitude. He divided his forces (contrary to one of his own cardinal principles), and assumed command of Keith's army of 34,000 men, which had been retreating down the west bank of the Elbe. The other grouping, of 33,800 troops, consisted of the rest of the siege corps and the force which had been beaten at Kolin. It remained to the east of the Elbe, and was commanded by the king's brother Prince August Wilhelm, a gentle soul who had never exercised independent command. Frederick's overall strategy was nothing more dynamic than to eat northern Bohemia bare of provisions, then take off to fight the French, the *Reichsarmee* or the Swedes as soon as they came within reach.

Reinforcements gave Prince Charles a more than two-fold advantage over the luckless August Wilhelm east of the Elbe, and in a conference in Vienna on 24 June Kaunitz argued that nothing was more important than to exploit the recent success. Every day counted. He was unable to transmit his sense of urgency to Maria Theresa, Francis Stephen or the other conference ministers, and Prince Charles was instead told to proceed with great caution. As a further drag on operations, the army was put under strict orders not to go foraging or to take anything from the peasants.

The first and very modest offensive movement on the part of the united army was delayed until 1 July, when it crossed the upper Elbe from Brandeis. Only on the 4th did the Austrians push north up the cultivated valley of the Iser to Benatek. August Wilhelm was given all the time he needed to slip away from Jung-

Bunzlau, and on the 7th he consolidated himself at Böhmisch-Leipa, among the southern spurs of the Mittel-Gebirge. His front was covered by the Poltzen stream and a deep ravine. 'It is a devilish country,' commented Montazet, 'where an army of forty thousand men can check a force of a hundred thousand.'[15]

The Austrians advanced cautiously up the east bank of the Iser. They reached Kosmanos on the 5 July, and on the 6th they arrived opposite Münchengrätz, which had been the capital of Wallenstein's private empire in the Thirty Years War. On the 8th they crossed the little river and moved upstream to Swijan, which set them on the most direct path for Reichenberg and Silesia.

So far Prince Charles had lost scarcely a man to enemy activity, but at last Maria Theresa lost patience with the slow pace of affairs, and on 9 July she penned a note which reminded him 'that the time will come when I must commit my army to breaking through somewhere or other, if I am not to be condemned to an endless, difficult and dangerous war. This is, moreover, the only way to avert the carping of my allies, who will say that my victorious and greatly superior army just sat still, instead of getting on with operations.'[16] The influence of Kaunitz may be deduced from the reference to foreign opinion, and the aggressive tone of the whole.

THE STORM OF GABEL, 14-15 JULY 1757

On 13 July the army left the densely-settled region of the upper Iser, and pushed north-west through an immense forest of fir to an isolated clearing at Hühnerwasser. It had not escaped the Austrians' attention that the Prussian depot at Böhmisch-Leipa had its line of supply line running from the depot of Zittau in Lusatia, in other words across the axis of the direction of the Austrian advance. The enemy line of communications therefore lay open to attack, and the way-station at Gabel offered a particularly tempting target.

On 14 July the main Austrian force advanced to Niemes, as if to approach Böhmisch-Leipa head on. However *FML.* Maguire was already marching directly for Gabel by way of Wartenberg with a striking force of sixteen grenadier companies, the Hungarian infantry regiment of Haller [31], 1,500 assorted fusiliers, a complement of hussars and twenty-eight pieces of artillery. The neighbourhood of Gabel, a little walled town in a hollow, was familiar to him from the time he had spent there in the previous winter,[17] and he accordingly detached *GFWM.* Wulffen to close off the path of retreat with seven of the grenadier companies, 300 fusiliers and 220 hussars

Unknown to the Austrians, the Prussian major general Puttkamer was returning from Böhmisch-Leipa to Zittau with a large convoy of empty provision waggons, and he was close to Gabel when he ran into Wulffen's force approaching from the direction of Brims. The two parties opened an artillery duel, in the course of which a Prussian ammunition cart exploded in the middle of the enemy column and caused considerable damage. Puttkamer threw himself into Gabel with his escort of two battalions, and left 200 waggons to the enemy. The unexpected arrival of Puttkamer and his people brought the Prussian force in Gabel to about 2,000 men, and the Austrians now had a big fight on their hands.

Maguire brought his main body around to the north side of the town, and opened fire against the Zittau Gate with his little train of medium artillery (probably two 12-pounder cannon and two howitzers). The shot and shell had some effect on the outer door, but could not reach the inner door or the strong barricade which the Prussians had piled up behind. Maguire detached Major Ernst Baron Normann to complete the work with four companies of grenadiers and a party of regimental pioneers with their axes. The pioneers hacked through the damaged outer door, and the artillery reinforced their efforts against the inner door. The Prussians concentrated their fire on the gap which was being opened, and an Austrian officer 'flattened himself against the wall, and took the grenadiers by the arm to force them inside. One of the grenadiers seized him by the scruff of the neck and threw him into the street, where he was killed on the spot.'[18]

The grenadiers finally penetrated in sufficient strength to be able to swarm over the barricade and seize the nearest houses. For a time the attention of the Prussians had been diverted by a demonstration against the southern gate, but now they devoted their whole attention to the break-in. It was difficult to feed reinforcements to the grenadiers across the barricade, and at ten at night Major Normann had to recognise that most of his men were casualties, and that he was losing control in the smoke-filled streets. Normann reported as much to Maguire, who ordered him to retreat through the gate. 'The successive orders brought to me by... First Lieutenant von Qualem, who kept on urging me to set fire to the town, but I answered him every time by pointing out that the place belonged to Her Imperial and Royal Majesty, and was having a bad enough time anyway without my setting it on fire. More relevant still, I knew for certain that in any case the town was going to surrender on the next day, for I had had all the water conduits dug up, and not a drop was getting through.'[19]

Part of the Austrian reserve corps arrived overnight, and at noon on 15 July the Austrians opened fire with three new batteries to the south of the town. Within three hours the wall had been breached in several places, and the defence collapsed in circumstances of some confusion. A number of deserters scampered to freedom through the gaps, and it was alleged that during the negotiations Puttkamer had tried to let himself down from the wall by a rope, but was captured by the Croats.[20]

After some parleying Puttkamer, sixty-seven officers and 1,887 men gave themselves up as prisoners of war. The Prussian general's excuse was that he had run out of ammunition, however 'the officers and soldiers are loud in their complaints against Puttkamer, for they complain that they had plenty of powder.'[21] On the next day a Prussian major explained that the 'main reason why they had been forced to surrender was because they ran out of water, as the supplies had been cut off right at the start, when the Austrian grenadiers seized the suburbs'.[22] This was the work of Normann, as we have seen.

Brigadier General de Montazet could not understand why the Prussians had failed to act in their usual decisive style, for they had neither reinforced Gabel, or abandoned it in good time. He had assumed that Frederick had been in command, but in fact the king was still with Keith's former siege corps at Leitmeritz, totally isolated from the army at Böhmisch-Leipa. He had left his trusted confidant, *GL.* Winterfeldt, to serve as August Wilhelm's right-hand man, not understanding that Winterfeldt had never recovered fully from the wound he had sustained at Prague. The Prussians would now have to take urgent measures if they were to cross the highlands and reach Lusatia in Saxony ahead of the Austrians. The most direct route thither was a perfectly respectable road which ran due north, but the peasants persuaded the Prussians that the enemy had got there before them and lined the way with cannon. Winterfeldt in his prime would have investigated the story in person, but a short-sighted officer was sent to reconnoitre the road instead. 'He went only as far as the castle at Birkwein, from where he saw cattle grazing at a considerable distance. He mistook them for artillery.'[23]

The result was that the army of August Wilhelm swung out of the direct path into the steep and heavily forested hills to the west, following the same tracks which had been taken by Browne when he marched to relieve the Saxons at Pirna. The Austrian generals Hadik, Beck and Morocz could not have asked for finer prey for their fast-moving light troops. On 18 July *GFWM.* Beck wreaked havoc among the train of pontoons and baggage waggons on the winding paths from Manitz to Kreibitz, and on the following day *FML.* Hadik and four battalions of Croats captured the iron ovens of the field bakery on the Kaltenberg. The heads of the Prussian columns were now descending into Lusatia, but thousands of troops had already deserted, and over the last few days the losses in men and materials had been equivalent to those in a major battle.

The main Austrian force had made direct for Zittau, which was the site of August Wilhelm's principal supply depot, and which, in Austrian hands, would give Charles and Daun a prime base for operations beyond the border hills. The leading Austrian troops placed Zittau under a loose blockade on 19 July, and by

The Confrontation at Eckartsberg, August 1757

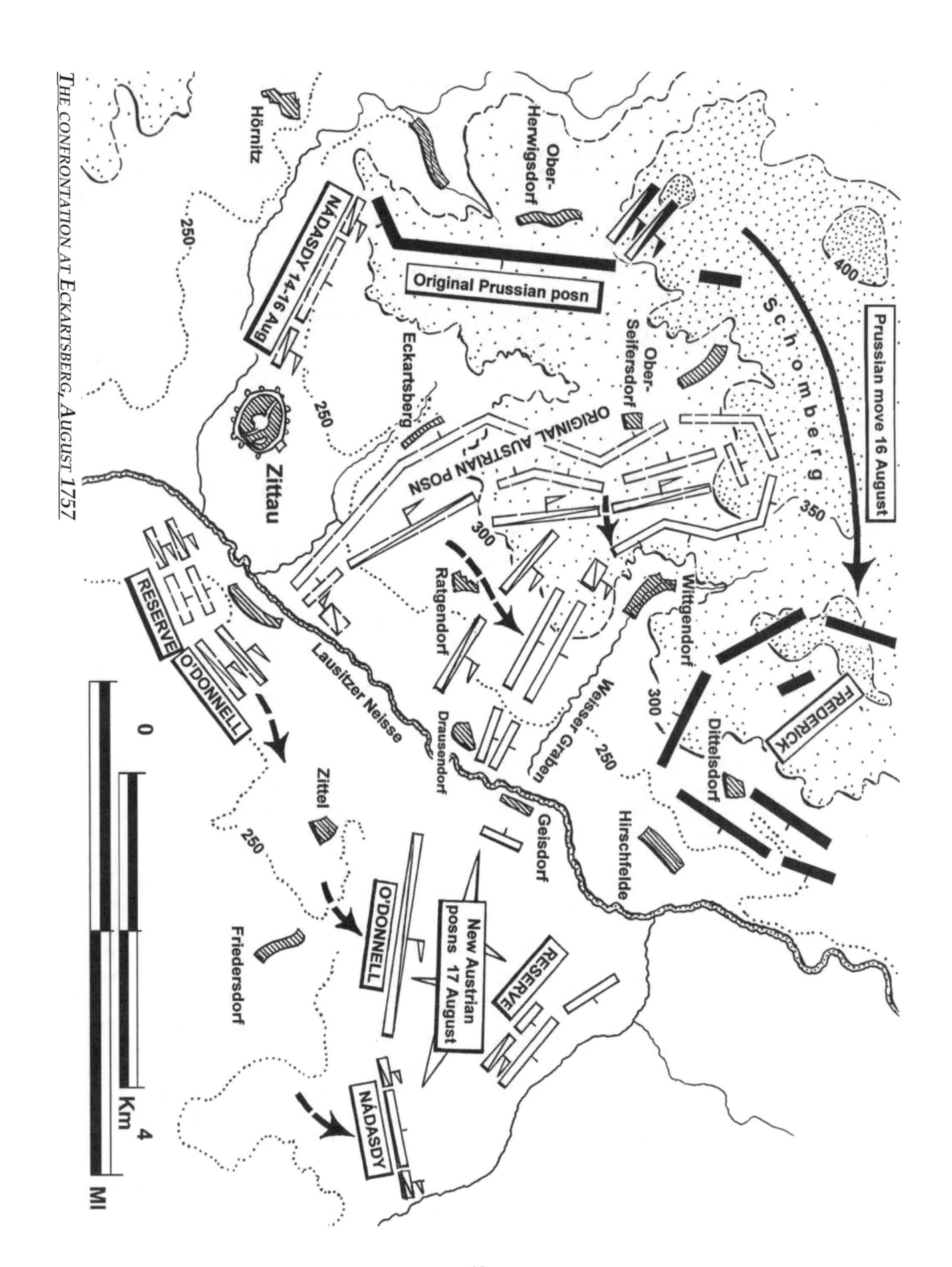

the 22nd, when the pillars of dust from the depleted Prussian columns were seen approaching from the west, the Austrians were emplaced in blocking positions on the heights which dominated the access to the town. Daun was already examining the batteries which had been established thereabouts, and one of the French attachés reported that 'we are getting ready to bombard this place and set it on fire, if confirmation comes that the townspeople have taken up arms for the Prussians.'[24]

ZITTAU IN FLAMES, 23 JULY 1757

Gabel had been little more than a walled village. Zittau was the leading commercial town of Saxony, after Leipzig, producing cloth, beer and paper, and it stood on a nodal point of communications between Bohemia and the north German plain. In July 1757 its immediate importance for the rival forces lay in the thousands of barrels of flour which the Prussians had assembled there with great effort over the last few months. Its tactical strength was however negligible, for the medieval wall stood twelve feet high at the most, and was far too lengthy to be defended by the Prussian colonel Diericke and his garrison, which amounted to the equivalent of five battalions.

At this stage of the war the Austrian army was still unversed in the technical business of siege warfare. The French were the acknowledged masters of that science, but they made their influence felt only towards the end of 1757, and now, in front of Zittau, Charles and Daun decided to reduce the town by the crudest possible means, a generalised bombardment. A first overnight attempt having produced little effect, the Austrians opened fire at eleven in the morning of 23 July with thirty-two cannon and ten howitzers, firing a variety of red hot shot, shells and incendiary carcasses. 'The orders were carried out so well that, in less than one and a half hours, eleven locations were ablaze, and these were now taken under a heavy cannon fire to prevent the flames from being put out.'[25]

Early in the afternoon the Austrians assaulted the Frauen Tor, and were beaten off. The battalion of the regiment of Andlau [57] lost thirteen killed and fifty-one wounded in the attempt, and 'an Irish officer by the name of Butler, having seen one of his soldiers beheaded, commented by way of jest: "next morning the poor devil will have a bit of a surprise when he wakes up and finds that he has no head!"'[26] The joke was not very good, but the attack proved to be effective after all. Colonel Diericke was hastening towards the threatened gate when he encountered the men of the grenadier battalion of Bähr streaming back into the town. They were ex-Saxon soldiers, enlisted by force in the Prussian army, and they carried their muskets muzzle-downwards as a sign that they were no longer willing to fight. The contagion spread among the garrison, and most of the troops escaped over the walls and into the country. The Austrians were now able to burst into the town from the Frauen Tor, and Diericke was left to surrender with a mere seventeen officers and twenty other ranks.

Lieutenant Gorani commanded one of the fifteen detachments which were sent around the town to extinguish the flames and prevent looting. He was fortunate enough to have been assigned to a quarter which was relatively unscathed, and a grateful Luthern pastor invited him to dine with his family, along with his curate.. 'They sang songs around the table, the most delightful I have ever heard. When the dinner was over the evening was rounded off by a duet between the young clergyman, who was something of a poet and musician, and the pastor's eldest daughter who was to about to marry him.'[27]

Elsewhere the damage was immense: 'What a shocking vision! We had succeeded in reducing to ashes a fine, perfectly well-built town, and, what is more annoying still, the home to some of the prettiest girls you could imagine. We found all this out the next day when the fire, which had lasted more than twenty-four hours, finally permitted us to tour the sad remains of a place which had ceased to exist. It was dangerous to walk about, on account of the masonry which was still collapsing, and a really grim experience to enter the cellars and discover whole families which had suffocated to death, and infants lying dead at their mothers' breasts[28]… in one of those cellars we found fifty-seven bodies, among which were those of an entire family of husband and wife along with their nine children[29]... their contortions and features showed every sign of a prolonged and excruciating death.'[30]

The capture of Zittau crowned an unheroic but ultimately successful operation, which had achieved its declared aims, that of manoeuvring the enemy army out of Bohemia without having to fight a battle, and that of establishing a foothold north of the border hills. The Austrians now had a long but secure line of communication which reached up by way of Jung-Bunzlau and the Iser valley, and among the ruins of Zittau they found large intact stores of ammunition, and enough flour to feed 40,000 men for three weeks.

Stalemate in Lusatia, July-August 1757

The momentum, such as it was, that the Austrians had derived from their victory at Kolin, was now dissipated in the six weeks of high summer which they spent immobile in their camp north of Zittau. The positions faced west, and ran from the Lausitzer Neisse and the village of Eckartsberg and then up an open ridge to the commanding Schomberg on the right. There was a wide field of fire to the front and to the right flank, and to the south the devastated town of Zittau could be seen in its hollow below the steep border hills.

August Wilhelm gave up all hope of regaining Zittau, and fell back towards Löbau on the night of 24/25 July. The 80,000 Austrians nevertheless remained in the camp at Eckartsberg, because Daun did not want to leave the head of his wonderful new line of communications from Bohemia, and by 27 August Montazet could still detect no disposition to move: 'It is not because I believe that the Austrian troops are not very good. On the contrary they are excellent, and particularly the infantry. What I have seen of them has impressed me greatly. The same testimony comes from hyper-critical foreigners who have witnessed them in action a number of times, and are unstinting in their praise. But they have almost no proper generals, no general staff, and there reigns a general disorder. In fact the machine moves by force of habit, without conscious thought. There is no fellow-feeling, and I believe that a combined operation of any kind is pretty well beyond their capacity, from the lack of men capable of putting it into effect. As to a sense of honour... I am convinced that there is far more of it among the Austrian soldiers than the Prussians, but the latter have a precision and an agility which will give them the victory whenever the combat is a question of manoeuvre, rather than bearing down the enemy by sheer weight of numbers.'[31]

Away from the divided counsels and the clumsy great army at Eckartsberg, Colonel Franz Baron Jahnus was ranging about Silesia with a corps of 4,000 Croats. The Prussian *GM.* Kreytzen gathered the equivalent of six battalions from the garrisons in an attempt to track him down, and late on 13 August the Prussians fancied that they had found an opportunity to fall on him to the east of **Landeshut**. Darkness fell before Kreytzen was able to deploy for the attack, and he accordingly arranged his troops in an oblong formation for the night. Jahnus had learned from his patrols what the Prussians had in mind, and to keep the enemy amused he detached Colonel Nematz and fifty Peterwardeiner Croats to snipe at the flanks of their position, which caused confusion among the horse lines, and persuaded the Prussians to fire on one another in the darkness.

Jahnus arranged his main force on the Buch-Berg, with Captain Laskupich holding a wood over to his right with a battalion of Warasdiner, and the rest of the Peterwardeiner positioned close to Landeshut town. Early on 14 August the leading Prussian units (the grenadier battalions of Kreytzen and Diezelsky) drove Laskupich from the wood after one and a half hours of skirmishing—an easy success which had the effect of drawing the whole Prussian force into an attack up the Buch-Berg in a single line. A very hot fire-fight now developed, and, according to Jahnus, the Prussians advanced in the face of the Austrian canister fire and pressed his men back into a zone of bushes. 'As the wind was blowing towards me I could not at first detect the results of our canister, but on seeing the enemy hesitate and then prepare to come on again, I made my troops break ranks and charge with bayonets and sabres and to the accompaniment of loud cries.' This occasioned a general confusion among the enemy, who gave way to right and left.[32]

The Prussian losses amounted to 1,367 officers and men, and the survivors fled to Schweidnitz. The Croats had sustained just seventeen dead and eighteen wounded, and in the damp meadows at the bottom of the hill they discovered one 4-pounder and three 3-pounders, including a piece which had been lost to the Prussians at Prague in 1744.

The brilliant little action at Landeshut offered a welcome contrast to the stagnation in Lusatia, and Charles wrote generously to Maria Theresa that 'this happy event is attended with some remarkable circumstances, in that a handful of Croats were facing regulars who were double their strength and equipped lavishly with cannon. Through good leadership and pure courage the Croats nevertheless went after them sabre in hand, and proceeded to break their morale, overcome them and put them to flight.'[33]

The idleness of the Austrian main force at Eckartsberg appears reprehensible. If, however, the object of military operations is to achieve what is least welcome to the enemy, then Charles and Daun could scarcely have done better than they did, by hanging around indecisively by the exit from the border hills near Zittau. Frederick needed to have his hands free to face the French and the *Reichsarmee*, but the loss of Gabel and Zittau and the plight of August Wilhelm gave him no alternative but to leave Prince Moritz of Anhalt-Dessau in charge of affairs to the west of the Elbe, and to go to Lusatia in person. The king reached the crestfallen army of August Wilhelm at Bautzen on 29 July, and humiliated his younger brother in terms so savage that the man literally lost the will to live.

Frederick's temper was not improved by the two weeks he had to spend immobile in the neighbourhood of Bautzen, waiting for provisions to replace those which had been lost at Gabel and Zittau. His troops and convoys were being harassed endlessly by the Croats. He was angry to think that Daun's heavy thought processes had managed to grasp the advantages of the Austrian situation, and how Prince Charles must be at his ease, eating, drinking, laughing and telling lies. 'Oh, would it not be delightful to get our hands around the throats of that arrogant and haughty tribe! It would be to the benefit of mankind, as well as a happy outcome, if we were to humiliate those barbaric tyrants, those enemies of every kind of liberty, who respect good faith only as far as it serves their advantage!'[34]

By 15 August Frederick had his rations of bread loaded up, and he set off with 50,600 troops and seventy-two heavy pieces to deal what he hoped would be a decisive blow. Early on the afternoon of the 16th he approached the Austrian camp from the north, and just after three he rode to a view point on the heights west of Dittelsdorf, from where he hoped to direct his assault. He arrived to the north-east, or right-rear, of the enemy camp, which had been facing west ever since the Austrians had blocked August Wilhelm's path to Zittau. The ground in front of the king fell away to a low saddle, then rose to the extremity of the Austrian right wing on the Schomberg—a prospect which was distinctly uninviting. However the 'Austrian' ridge sloped markedly down to the south, and it merged with the plain of Zittau in the neighbourhood of the village of **Wittgendorf**, with its distinctive onion-dome church tower. It was there that Frederick decided to stage his attack.

Frederick was already too late. At two in the afternoon alarm shots had rung out in the enemy camp, and the enemy were now putting one of the contingency plans into effect. 'All the efforts of the king were in vain... Prince Charles traversed in a circle and matched his every manoeuvre.'[35] The Austrians were shuffling their main army by its right to a staked-out position which reached all the way from the salient on the Schomberg south-east to the Lausitzer-Neisse near Drausendorf, in other words occupying the originally open rear of the camp. Twenty-one bridges were already in position across the little river, and to guard against any move on the far bank the Austrians shifted their *corps de reserve*, that blessed creation of Daun, to the far side.

The immediate danger was that of a breakthrough in the centre of the hastily-occupied main position, and at four in the afternoon Frederick sought to clear the way by sending the free battalion of Le Noble and four pieces down the gentle slope to Wittgendorf, which now became the key ground of the whole confrontation. Two companies of Austrian grenadiers arrived first. They had to recoil in front of the superior Prussian forces, but they held fast in the western part of the village, where they could exploit the massive churchyard wall which dominated the steep grassy banks of the Weisser-Graben rivulet. The first battalion of the Prussian regiment of Prinz Ferdinand [34] had to fall back in the face of the Austrian artillery, and this small but decisive action ended with the Prussians being held at bay. 'We maintained our fire until evening, to drive back the picquets which the king seemed determined to advance. We could see him... riding about his camp on a great grey horse, giving orders here there and everywhere.'[36]

Altogether the Austrians had nearly 350 pieces ready to fire, and their more than 100,000 troops were keen to fight. A drenching rain set in towards noon on 17 August, making the ground so slippery that movement became almost impossible, and Charles ordered the tents to be brought up to the combat positions to give the men some shelter. 'Our generals were equipped lavishly with telescopes, and seemed to wish to project themselves into the enemy camp... It was fine to see how the lights in our camp extended all the way from the hill (Schomberg) to the corps of Nádasdy. Our lines were crescent-shaped, and seemed to curve around all the way to the Prussian positions.'[37] Nádasdy's troops, just mentioned, had joined the *corps de reserve* on the far bank of the Neisse.

On the night of 19/20 August figures could be seen flitting in the Prussian camp fires, and by the morning the enemy had gone. The immediate reason why Frederick had abandoned his challenge was that his army had run out of bread, and he needed to fall back to his magazine at Bautzen. More compellingly still, he had concluded that nothing would force the Austrians to fight, and that he must take himself off to central Germany to confront the French and the *Reichsarmee*. The king rode away, and left the Duke of Bevern in command of the 45,000 men in Lusatia, with the commission to deny access to Brandenburg from the south, and to cover the way to Silesia.

The end of August found Prince Charles and Daun still at Eckartsberg, and arguing as to how many troops they should send to Silesia. Daun was for moving the entire army into the province, while Charles believed that it would be unwise to send anything more than a detachment, as long as there seemed to be any threat to Bohemia. The root of the problem lay in the continuing divisions in the high command. There were generals like Nádasdy who refused to obey orders from Daun unless they were also signed by Charles, while others took the contrary course. Kaunitz told the French ambassador that the most obvious remedy, that of removing Charles, was unthinkable now that Emperor Francis Stephen had declared 'that he would regard the recall of his brother as a personal affront.'[38]

The Austrian main army now amounted to a massive 112,000 troops, comprising 90,000 regular infantry and horse, and some 22,000 Croats and hussars. However the prospect of action had come and gone in the middle of August, and demoralisation was setting in. 'Over these last three days thirty-nine men have deserted from the regiment of Batthyány [34], thirty-two from that of Erzherzog Carl [2] and thirty-seven from Haller [31]. You should note that the Hungarians are devoted to their horses, and don't like to serve in the infantry. They desert and sign up as hussars with the king of Prussia.'[39]

The great host finally left the camp of Eckartsberg on the rainy 2 September, but did not so much pursue the heavily-outnumbered Bevern, as permit itself to be sucked a short distance down the Lausitzer Neisse in the path of his retreat. Bevern had ceded just a dozen miles of Silesia, and took up a fresh position in the neighbourhood of Görlitz, thus denying the Austrians the main lateral route across the northern theatre of war. His positions on the left (west) bank of the Neisse reached out to the Landeskrone (420 m) and were particularly strong, and the Austrians would probably have been content to keep their distance if they had not espied an opportunity on the right bank of the Neisse, where the battle-shocked Lieutenant General Winterfeldt commanded an isolated force.

Moys, 7 September 1757
a) Austrians
32,549
Losses: 1577: 177 killed, 1,313 wounded, 87 missing
b) Prussians
c. 13,300
Losses: 1,856, 7 colours, 5 pieces

For the first time in this war the Austrian high command conceived a good offensive plan, and put it into effect with secrecy and speed. Prince Charles grasped that a well-concerted attack could not only exploit the vulnerable position of Winterfeldt's corps on the eastern bank of the Lausitzer Neisse, but also take at a disadvantage the small forces which Winterfeldt had stationed at the salient of his position on the Jäckelsberg (also known as the Holtzberg and the Height of Kunna).

The initial shock was to be delivered by a concentrated mass of forty-two grenadier companies, backed by the twenty-one fusilier battalions of the *corps de reserve*, which had reverted to the command of *FML.* Arenberg, after *GFWM.* Colloredo had parted company with his horse. There was talk in the army that the fall had not been 'quite heavy enough to justify a general from staying behind when an action was about to be fought.'[40] The standard formation was to be in battalion columns, each stacked up three battalions deep—two such columns for the grenadiers, and seven for the *corps de reserve*. Ten heavy guns were assigned to the grenadiers, and six to the *corps de reserve*.

The flanks of the striking force were to be covered by bodies of light troops, namely *GFWM.* Draskovich with the Banal Croats on the left, and *GdC.* Nádasdy with three battalions of Croats and three regiments of hussars to the right. The veteran *GFWM.* Wöllwarth was to give support as necessary with the three regiments of the right wing of the regular cavalry.

The *corps de reserve* joined Nádasdy's corps at nightfall on 6 September, and the combined force got on the move early the next morning. The Austrians were unaware that the enemy had built a redoubt atop the Jäckelsberg, but they had two elements of surprise on their side—the wooded and broken ground which concealed their advance, and the fact that the attack would arrive towards the end of the morning, which was unusually late for such enterprises.

The two Prussian grenadier battalions (Benckendorff and Dieringshofen) on the hill were indeed caught off their guard, but they fought back so vigorously that they stopped the Austrian grenadiers half-way up the slope, and gained time for Winterfeldt to send successive reinforcements, first the grenadier battalion of Anhalt, and then the regiments of Manteuffel [17] and Tresckow [32]. Major Franz de Piza could see that the leading Austrian grenadiers were inclined to lie flat on the ground or run away, whereupon 'General Nádasdy came up and told us that it was essential to take the work. I enjoined the grenadiers not to lose time firing, but rely on the bayonet... I was the first to reach the ditch of the earthwork which, unknown to us, was sited on the hill. I threw myself down into the ditch, followed by my grenadiers, and then, seizing the muzzles of two muskets, I had myself pushed up to the parapet. I heaved the two grenadiers up behind me, and they in turn helped the others up. When I had fifteen or sixteen with me, I rushed forward with the bayonet to prevent the enemy from hauling away their cannon. They abandoned the pieces, together with three colours which were taken by the troops coming up behind.'[41] The grenadiers were joined by Draskovich and his Croats, who had been ascending the hill from the left.

Once again the attack ran out of momentum, and this time because the grenadiers dispersed to ransack the tents or chase the enemy The Prussian reinforcements were well on their way, and so, luckily for the Austrians, were the fusiliers of Arenberg's *corps de reserve*. The two sets of forces were climbing the hill from opposite sides, each unaware of the other's existence until they collided at the top, which gave rise to one of the very few authenticated cases of close-quarter combat in this period. For a time the troops were crowded together as closely as the audience in the pit of an opera house, and Captain the Prince de Ligne describes how 'it was impossible to get our bearings in the smoke. Several times I found myself right in front of the Prussians, who were giving and receiving bayonet thrusts as they fell back. I had several soldiers of my company wounded in this way. So many men were being killed by my neighbours and by my idiots in the fourth rank that it was absolutely essential to stop the random firing, but my senior officers could not be everywhere, on account of the pits, kitchens and tents which obstructed the old camp site. Some of oldest companions had been killed, and nearly all my officers wounded. I kept yelling out 'Shoulder your muskets!' but if ten or a dozen heard me, the thirteenth did not—he would fire, and all the others would start firing again.'[42]

The enemy at last gave ground, and the struggling mob fell back down the 'Prussian' side of the hill to the village of Moys. The Prussian major general Kannacher was captured in the mêlée, and told the Austrians that he had seen Winterfeldt shot from his horse.

The Austrians had won the battle in the centre against the Prussian grenadiers and reinforcements, while Nádasdy with his Croats and hussars countered a threat which had been building up against the now-vulnerable attacking force in the shape of *GL.* Zieten with the thirty-five squadrons and eight battalions of the Prussian left wing. If things had turned out badly, old *GFWM.* Wöllwarth would have intervened with the three cavalry regiments of the Austrian right (the Sachsen-Gotha Dragoons [D28], the Alt-Modena Cuirassiers [Ciii]] and one of the Saxon chevaulegers). He records 'our cavalry wanted to get to grips with the enemy, but we were under orders not to... become involved in a general engagement, but just to dislodge Winterfeldt's corps from the Kunna hill. This did not prevent our cavalry being exposed to a lively fire of cannon and howitzers for a good hour, though no great damage was done, on account of the soft ground. A 6-pounder shot and a howitzer shell landed immediately in front of my horse's hooves.'[43]

Prince Karl of Bevern had assumed the acting command of the enemy, and at one in the afternoon he disengaged his corps. The Austrians had attained their objective, and did not pursue. Meanwhile on the western bank of the river Daun had advanced the little corps of *GFWM.* Beck to Leschwitz and prevented the Duke of Bevern himself from sending more substantial reinforcements to the east bank. At midnight the Austrian regulars withdrew from the Jäckelsberg, and were relieved there by the Croats of Draskovich. 'It very much devalued our conquest to see it handed over to people like that.'[44]

Winterfeldt died of his wounds on 8 September. Both sides acknowledged that he had left his life as a hero, and that with his defeat and death the war had turned a corner. For the Austrians the action at Moys marked the time from which their army began true offensive operations.[45] In the tight community of the Prussian officer corps Winterfeldt had been counted as a leading member of a self-consciously hard-nosed school of leadership, which derived from the tradition of Prince Leopold of Anhalt-Dessau (the 'old Dessauer'), and which was at odds with the more humane outlook of Schwerin, Prince Henry of Prussia, the Duke of Bevern and their associates. Among the latter Winterfeldt had been mistrusted for the influence he had exercised over the king, and for his alleged ambition to found a universal Protestant monarchy. Many years later the son of a Prussian veteran wrote that the clash at Moys had terminated the first phase of the conflict, 'in that it put an end to the man (Winterfeldt) who had conceived the war, or who had been at the least its standard bearer.'[46]

On Bevern's heels into Silesia, September - November 1757

On the night of 10/11 September the Duke of Bevern abandoned his camp, marched around to the north of the Austrian positions and made for Silesia. He thereby transferred the theatre of operations to that rich province, the recovery of which was one of the main reasons why the Austrians had gone to war. The stakes were raised accordingly. The Austrians should still have gained the heart of Silesia before him, since they had at their disposal the main lateral route, which ran roughly parallel with the border hills, and enabled them to reach Lauban on 12 September, Löwenberg on the 14th, Pilgramsdorf on the 16th, and Jauer on the 18th. They nevertheless remained at Jauer on the 19th, for etiquette demanded that they must celebrate the victory of their Russian allies at Gross-Jägersdorf (30 August), and in such a way Bevern was able to anticipate them at the major road junction at Liegnitz, and plant himself behind the little river Weidelach, which was swollen by recent rains.

On 26 September the Austrians evicted the Prussian from their outposts at **Barschdorf**, by bringing the wretched village under the concentric fire of ten batteries, and on the misty night which followed Bevern evacuated his main position and marched down the Katzbach towards the Oder. He had once again broken free, and this time he was plainly seeking to deny the Austrians the great prize of Breslau, the capital of Silesia. If the Austrians had got on the move without delay, they could even then have isolated the weakly-guarded city, as Montazet pointed out: 'Everything has been agreed and approved by our chiefs, but we are progressing so feebly that I believe that the enemy will get to Breslau before us, and will be able to deny us the passage of the Oder… I have to tell you that my pain and disgust exceed anything I can possibly convey.'[47]

When the Austrians finally came within sight of Breslau, on 2 October, they found that Bevern was already there, and that he was digging himself into a strong position among the villages behind the marshy-banked Lohe stream. He had reached the Oder, crossed to the right bank, marched upstream, re-crossed at Breslau and emerged in time to greet the Austrians. He had all the facilities of the place at his disposal, while the Austrians were exposed to all the hardships of the open field.

The lull which superved lasted until 22 November, which was longer still than the great sit-down at Eckartsberg. But, away from the clogging, faction-ridden army, the honour of Austrian arms was meanwhile upheld by two particularly bold enterprises.

HADIK'S RAID ON BERLIN, 11-23 OCTOBER 1757

In the middle of September *FML*. Andreas Hadik was in charge of the light troops screening the 14,000-strong corps of *FZM*. Marschall, who had remained in eastern Saxony to watch out for Frederick, and to keep the main army in touch with the doings of the French and the *Reichsarmee*. Overweight and heavily married, Hadik did not appear to be a natural commander of light forces, but he was a hard rider and an effective leader, and his attention to detail (he had once thought of studying for the priesthood) made him his own chief of staff.

On 17 September Hadik jumped at an offer which was held out to him by Prince Charles, that of raiding on a grand scale into Brandenburg, which was the heartland of the Prussian monarchy. Kaunitz told the French ambassador that 'we flatter ourselves that this expedition, although of brief duration, will throw the king of Prussia's civil and military economy into a fair measure of disorder. It could also force him to detach troops from Saxony to go to the help of the capital.'[47]

The raiding force proper consisted of a balanced and fast-moving force of 3,400 hussars, Croats, regular cavalry and infantry, and a train of two 3-pounders and four 6-pounders. In addition the reliable *GFWM*. Kleefeld was to line the Röder and the Schwarze Elster with 1,870 troops to cover the left flank of the corps as it raced for Berlin. Hadik would cut himself free of the line of communication, both for the sake of speed, and because he intended to make direct for Berlin by way of the boggy and sandy Spreewald, away from the conventional axes of operations along the Elbe and the Oder. Once in enemy territory the troops were to live off requisitions, and, having no tents, they must bivouac in the open.

HADIK VISITS BERLIN: OCTOBER 1757

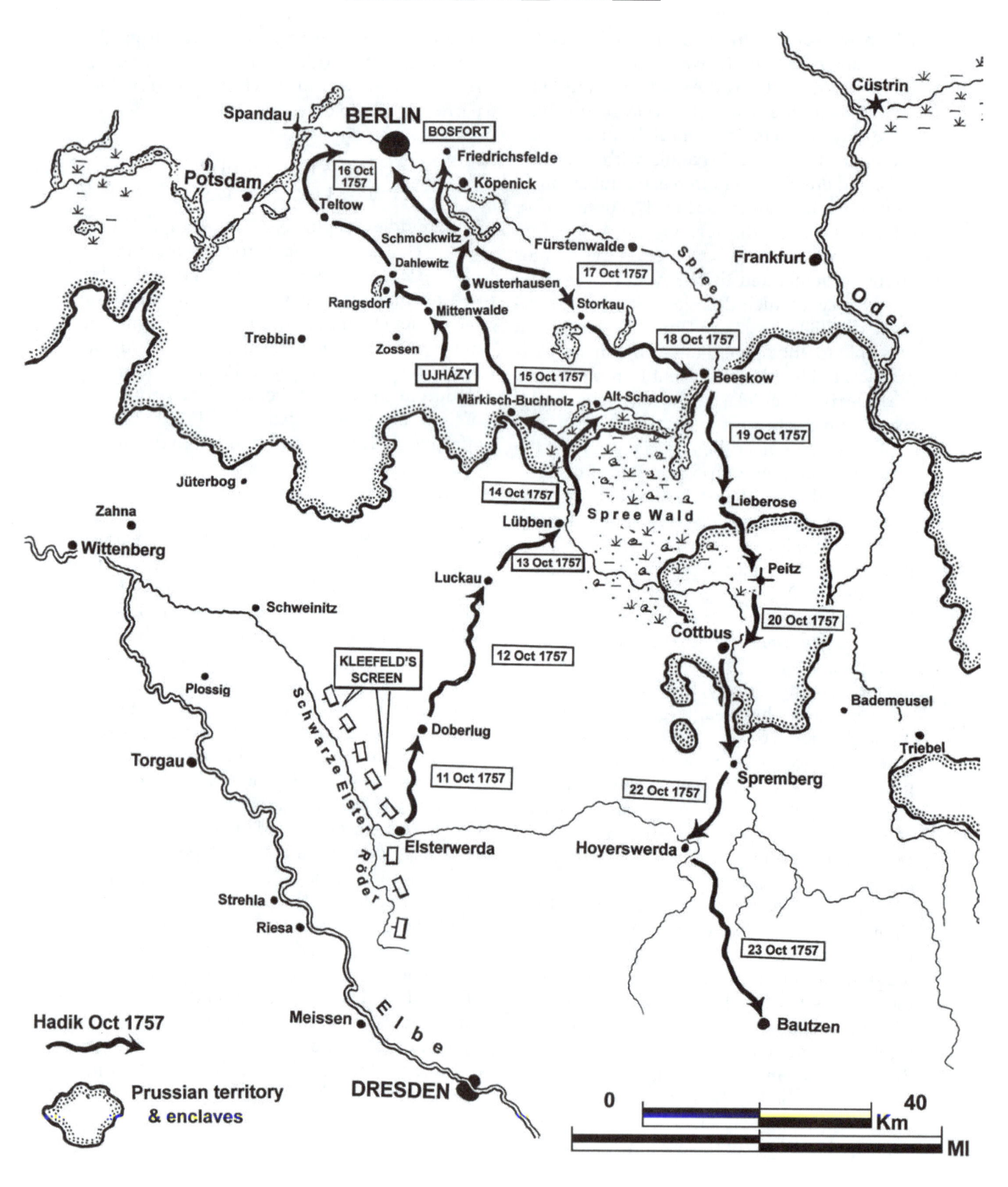

Speed and self-sufficiency also dictated the tactics: 'If we encounter the enemy, the cavalry is to act with determination, and not allow itself to receive the charge. During the combat the cavalry will station small parties out on the flanks of the two wings, and, if circumstances allow, detach the third rank so as to work around to the enemy flanks and rear. The other two ranks continue to act in close order, and we must always retain a reserve. The infantry will advance boldly, and not open fire unless it finds itself in an advantageous position to do so, in which case it must keep up a continuous fire at will. After the Croats have fired, their third rank will go over to the attack with drawn swords, while observing the proper intervals.'[48]

At the same time Hadik compiled a most detailed list of economic and political targets, which included the arms works at Alt-Schadow on the upper Spree, and the Arsenal, factories, depots and records in Berlin. Prominent members of the mercantile community and civil administration were to be taken away prisoner.

The expedition set out from Elsterwerda on 11 October, and marched initially through Saxon territory, reaching Doberlug on that day, Luckau on the 12th, and Lübben on the 13th. The next day Hadik entered Brandenburg and proceeded to launch a series of feints to right and left. Colonel Ujházy, who had been left at Luckau with 300 hussars, made N.N.W. by way of Mittenwalde to reach the road from Potsdam to Berlin. Hadik spread reports that he himself was marching for Frankfurt-an-der-Oder, well to the east, and on the 15th Major Bosfort peeled off to the right, crossed the Spree near Köpenick, and took up the highway from Frankfurt to the capital. On the 14th Hadik marched with the main force through the Spreewald to Märkisch-Buchholz, and Lieutenant Colonel Vécsey turned aside to the foundry at Alt-Schadow, where his men spent a busy day smashing foundry moulds, commandeering 1,211 rounds of mortar bombs, howitzer shells and cannon shot, and breaking up nearly 19,000 more. Strict discipline was being observed throughout, and no harm was done to the civil population.

By the evening of 15 October the Austrians were approaching Berlin from three directions: Ujházy from the south-west, Bosfort along the Frankfurt highway beyond the Spree, and Hadik arriving at Wusterhausen to the south-east. On the 16th Hadik struck at Berlin. To have marched directly across the open country from Wusterhausen would have revealed how few men he had with him, and so he turned to the right into the cover of the royal hunting forest and came out on the far side within reach of the Schlesisches Tor, which was where the defensible Excise Wall met the Spree above Berlin (for these locations, please see the map of Lacy's strike at Berlin in 1760, page 266).

Hadik's situation was perilous. The Excise Wall in front of him was proof against his light artillery, a Prussian relieving force was certain to be on its way, and the governor of Berlin, *GL.* Rochow, had recovered from his surprise and had 4,000 troops at his disposal, including the garrison regiment of Lange [Gar7], which was of better quality than most of its kind; Colonel Tesmar now arrived on the scene with six of its companies, and he was in time to bar the Schlesisches Tor, and raise the nearby drawbridge which led to the right (northern) bank of the Spree.

The city authorities made no reply to Hadik's first summons, and so he felt justified in bringing the gate and the bridge under simultaneous attack. The *Alter Feuerwerker* Georg Joseph Thun aimed the two 3-pounders against the raised drawbridge, and by a fluke or extraordinarily accurate shooting he parted a chain and the raised portion crashed down, which permitted two companies of Hadik's grenadiers to storm across with levelled bayonets and chase the enemy from the suburbs on the far side of the Spree, leaving fourteen of the Prussians dead.

Meanwhile two of the 6-pounders smashed open the Schlesisches Tor, and Hadik advanced inside with 700 of his Croats, 300 hussars and 400 German horse. He found himself in the largely open space which extended from the inside of the Excise Wall to the built-up area of the city. The enemy were coming at him from the inner side of the Cottbuser Tor with a force he put at nearly two battalions: 'I let them approach as close as I wanted, then sent the cavalry and hussars against them at an all-out gallop with drawn swords and sabres, while I advanced Colonel Baron v. Ried and his Croats to take them in flank at bayonet point. The attacks arrived simultaneously, and, in spite of coming under heavy fire, our troops did so well that not a single one of the enemy escaped. They were all shot dead, cut down or made prisoners, and we took six colours in the process. The three to five hundred men standing in reserve behind the Cottbuser Tor now took to their heels; they were overhauled by our cavalry, and, apart from a few who got away, they were all captured or cut down.'[49]

Rochow retreated towards the citadel of Spandau with his remaining troops, and sent word to Hadik that the Austrians would encounter no further opposition. The Austrian casualties amounted to less than forty, but included the much-regretted *GFWM*. Baboczay, who was mortally wounded. Over the years he had resisted all the blandishments of Frederick, who wanted him for the Prussian service, and it was ironic that he should now die in Berlin under very different circumstances.

Hadik was now aware that the corps of Prince Moritz of Anhalt-Dessau was on the way from Torgau by forced marches. He had to abandon his elaborate programme of demolitions, confiscations and kidnappings, and hastened to make terms with the city fathers, who now agreed to make over a contribution of 500,000 taler, with 10,000 on top as a consolation for the troops for not being allowed to plunder the place. To make sure that Berlin was indeed spared, Hadik kept his forces outside the Excise Wall and put the gates under guard. By legend, at least, 'after everything was agreed, General Hadik asked the council to deliver two dozen pairs of ladies' gloves, stamped with the city coat of arms, so that he could make a present of them to his Empress. The money and the gloves were duly brought to him, and he then beat a hasty retreat.'[50] Hadik used to go to great lengths to secure agreeable presents for his wife, on occasion from as far away as Paris, which gives some credibility to the story of the Empress's gloves.

At ten at night the Austrians were on the move. Fourteen confiscated coaches were groaning with whatever cash the Berliners had been able to raise at such short notice, and the rest was made up in paper monetary instruments. Hadik chose a return route which took him to the east of the Spreewald—both to lay fresh areas of Brandenburg under contribution, and to put as much space as possible between himself and the Prussian field forces which were now streaming towards him. He reached Storkow on 17 October after a continuous march of fifty kilometres, then Beeskow on the upper Spree on the 18th, Lieberose on the 19th, and Cottbus on the 20th. Even so he had been cutting his margins fine. The leading troops of the Prussian relief columns arrived at Berlin on the evening of the 17th, and during the whole march Hadik was under threat from enemy forces cutting in from the west against his path of retreat. Colonel Ujházy was guarding this flank with 300 men, and lost up to twenty of his people in one of the skirmishes.

Finally on 21 October Hadik was able to give his troops some rest. He reached Hoyerswerda on the 22nd, and the next day he reunited with the main body of Marschall's corps at Bautzen.

Hadik's excellently-managed expedition had thrown Frederick's strategy into disorder, and created opportunities for Soubise, Hildburghausen and the allied forces in central Germany. Maria Theresa was delighted at the control which Hadik had exercised throughout, and the fact that he had not taken the opportunity to enrich himself. She made him an ex gratia payment of 3,000 ducats which Hadik, as a poor family man, was glad to have. It is uncertain whether the Empress ever received her gloves.

THE SIEGE AND STORM OF SCHWEIDNITZ, 26 OCTOBER - 12 NOVEMBER 1757

a) Austrians and auxiliaries
43,000, with covering forces; siege train of c 59 heavy cannon and 10 mortars
Losses: nearly 3,000, including 1,200 killed or wounded, of which 448 were in the assault on 12 November
b) Prussians
c. 6000, with c. 180 pieces
Losses: the entire garrison

Prince Charles and Field Marshal Daun were aware that Frederick must be somewhere far away to the west, confronting the French and the *Reichsarmee*, and, while they were making up their minds whether to attack Bevern at Breslau, they agreed that they could do something to strengthen their position in Silesia. This was to reduce the isolated fortress of Schweidnitz, which stood in the plain within sight of the border hills, and at the head of routes which led from north-east Bohemia to Lower Silesia. Once in the possession of the Austrians, Schweidnitz would offer them a direct line of communication from Bohemia, and an alternative to their existing supply route, which described a long and vulnerable dog's leg up the Iser valley and over the hills to Zittau in Lusatia, and then east into Silesia.

Frederick had been alive to the strategic significance of this piece of ground, and shortly before the war he had transformed Schweidnitz into a fortress. He had shrunk from the cost of surrounding the town with a continuous rampart *à la Vauban*, and so he devised a completely new principle, that of a ring fortress, in which the weight of the defence rested on detached works standing into the country, in this case five forts and five intermediate redoubts, with the fortification of the town consisting of a simple wall. The most famous attack and defence of a ring fortress was to be at Verdun in 1916, but it all began at Schweidnitz late in 1757.

The first of the Austrians to arrive before Schweidnitz were those of the corps of *GdC*. Franz Nádasdy, who placed it under a light blockade on 30 September. The arrival of a contingent of Württemberg auxiliaries and the Austrian *corps de reserve* brought the would-be besiegers to a strength of 43,000, and on 24 October they sealed the place off completely. The incompetence of the Austrians in siege warfare now displayed itself again. For a start there was no map of the new fortress to be found anywhere, though one was rumoured to be in the possession of a captain of the regiment of Botta. It was always going to take a long time to bring up the train of siege artillery from Vienna, but, when it was supposed to have been on its way for eight or ten days, the cannon and mortars were discovered to be still in the capital. *FM*. Neipperg, in his capacity as commandant of Vienna, had forgotten to issue the necessary orders, 'which is scarcely credible, since the season was already far advanced and it was almost too late to undertake a siege. Everything therefore indicated that not a moment was to be lost. Kaunitz as the leading minister had some harsh words to say on the subject, but the damage was done.'[51]

On both technical and political grounds the direction of the siege was entrusted to a French expert, Brigadier General Riverson. Maria Theresa assured Prince Charles that Riverson brought together 'a becoming modesty with consummate knowledge and experience,'[52] though the choice was inevitably taken as a slight on the Austrian engineers.

The attack opened in a cautious enough way, with the digging of a first parallel on the night of 26/27 October, but time was so precious that the usual rules of siegecraft did not answer the present circumstances, and the Austrian high command decided on the desperate expedient of assaulting the ring of forts across open ground. The targets were three works to the south-west of the town, the Garten star fort, the diamond-shaped intermediate Garten-Redoute, and the Bögen star fort. Each assault was to be spearheaded by three companies of grenadiers, with a reinforced battalion of fusiliers in support. Additional battalions of fusiliers were told off to advance through the intervals between the works, so as to counter any Prussian reinforcements which might come up from the town. The attackers were supposed to surge forward at eleven on the night of 11/12 November, but the signal rounds from the thirteen mortars did not go off at the same time, which meant that the assaulting columns arrived in succession—first at the Garten-Redoute, then at the Garten-Fort, and last of all at the Bögen-Fort (for the location of these works please see the map of the Austrian storm of Schweidnitz in 1761, page 324. The connecting lines shown there had not been built at the time of the storm in 1757).

At the **Garten-Redoute** the defenders were

Breslau, 22 November 1757

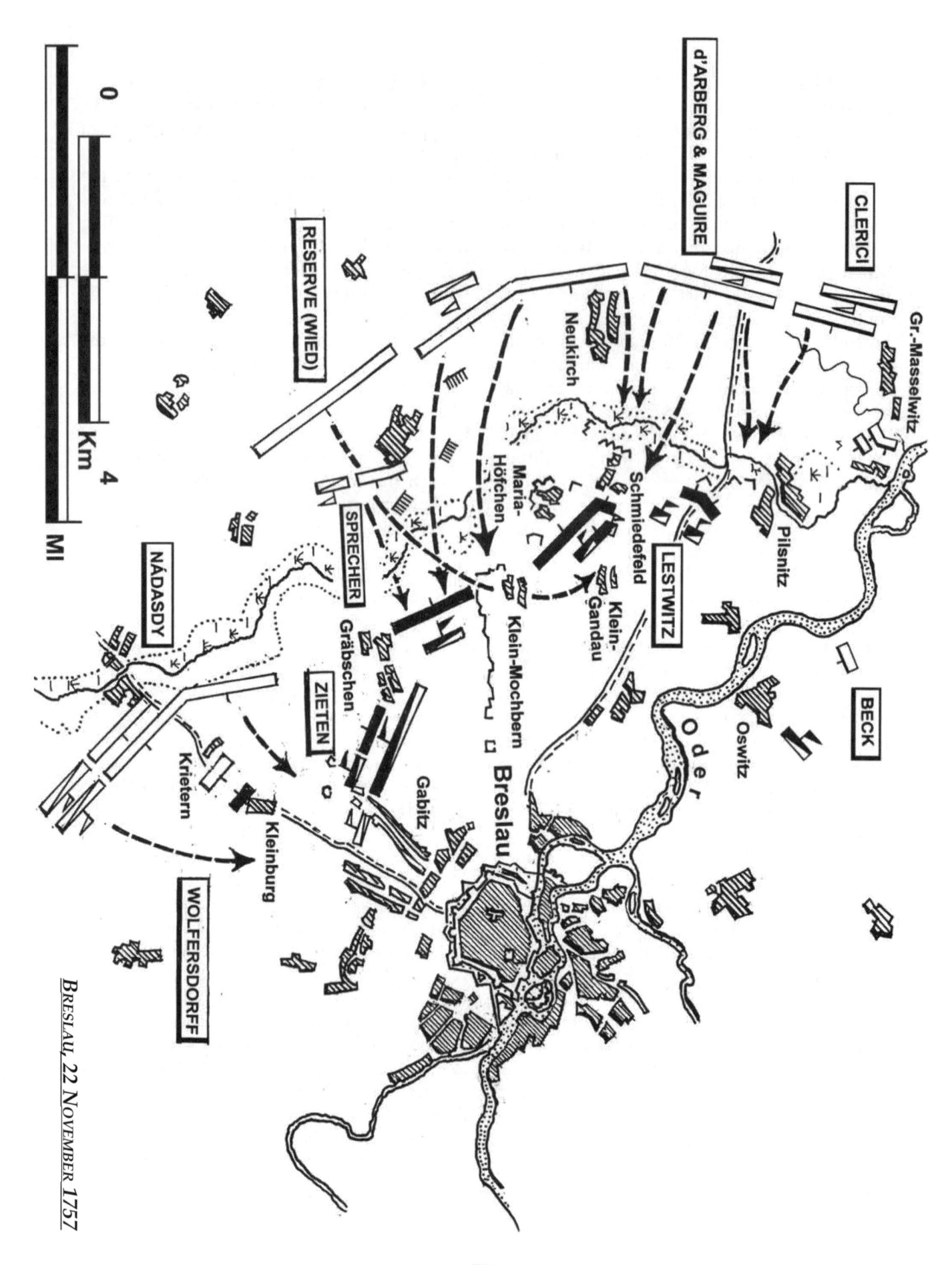

taken completely off their guard, and it did not take the Austrians long to swarm inside and turn the eight cannon against the town wall. At the altogether more substantial **Garten-Fort** the 350 defenders lured the Austrians on by beating *chamade*, as if they desired to surrender, and then opened up against the advancing grenadiers. The Austrian commander, Major Johann Rhédy, continues the story in the usual retiring style of candidates for the Military Order of Maria Theresa: 'Instead of surrendering, the enemy greeted me with a frightful fire of canister, cannon shot, incendiary carcasses, muskets, bombs and shells. In addition the glacis of the fort was stuffed with fougasses, which exploded continuously like an earthquake, and pretty well engulfed and covered me with debris. The ranks of the surviving grenadiers were thinned out by the darkness of the night, the ascending clouds of sulphurous smoke, and the explosions and the rain of rubbish as just described. But… with a calm courage I did everything in my power to hearten the troops I still had with me, to restore the scattered men to order, and to fulfil the duty before me. My example of steadfastness worked so well on the others that I was able to press on through wreckage, across trenches, and seize the crest of the glacis and all the various outworks. I traversed the outer ditch, in the face of a desperate resistance with spiked clubs and pikes, and proceeded to smash through whole rows of palisades and *chevaux de frise*, and turned the cannon in the outworks around against the enemy, or broke up their carriages.'[53]

Colonel Franz Guasco brought up a battalion of the regiment of Luzan [48], which carried the assault into the inner ditch, but the main rampart behind proved to be an insurmountable obstacle. The success of the whole enterprise now depended on what happened at the **Bögen-Fort**. Here the assaulting troops approached unobserved, probably because the defenders were distracted by the commotion at the other two works. While a company of the Württemberg grenadiers made for the salient (and were repulsed), the two companies of Austrian grenadiers (those of the regiments of Heinrich Daun [45] and Leopold Pálffy [19] arrived at the rear of the fort, and eight of them set about uprooting the palisades so as to open the way for a rush over the drawbridge which spanned the ditch. The scheme went awry when a Prussian sentry opened fire, and the drawbridge (contrary to expectations) proved to be raised. Following a contingency plan, Major De Vins led the Leopold Pálffy grenadiers and some of those of Heinrich Daun to one of the lateral faces, and with the help of the few ladders at their disposal the grenadiers were able to negotiate both sets of ditches and ramparts, and De Vins decanted himself inside the fort with the twelve leading grenadiers. The Prussians retreated into the casemates, and De Vins was able to invite Captain Joseph Rummel to ascend the inner rampart with the rest of the grenadiers. Rummel was very fat, and it was considered amazing that he was able to make the climb at all.[54]

There were farcical scenes in the ditch outside when Lieutenant Colonel Maximilan August Zorn von Plobsheim arrived with the supporting battalion of fusiliers, in this case that of the regiment of Leopold Daun [59]. He reached the foot of the main rampart, 'but the men who assigned to carry the ladders had come under heavy fire and thrown them away. I therefore encouraged the men to stick their bayonets into the wall and climb on one anothers' shoulders… a lengthy procedure, as you can well imagine. I ran two hundred paces back along the ditch and shouldered two ladders. In the darkness of the night Colonel Amadei tried to snatch them from me, until I enlightened him. I brought up the ladders, planted them on the spot, and climbed to the top of the work.'[55] Zorn von Plobsheim discovered that he could have spared himself the trouble, for the grenadiers were already inside the fort, and he therefore re-deployed his battalion to the rear of the fort to beat off any counterattacks. It was an exposed position, and his men suffered heavily under the fire from the town.

The Austrian grenadiers and technical officers now set about combing the casemates and the countermine galleries to root out isolated parties of Prussians and defuze the charges, which was a nerve-wracking business. With the Garten-Redoute and the Bögen-Fort now in their possession, the engineers advanced the captured trenches to the captured works; heavy cannon were brought up at the same time, and at first light on 23 November the gunners were able to open fire against the unprotected town wall.

Nádasdy followed the instructions of Prince Charles to demand that Major General Sers must surrender his garrison as prisoners of war. Later in the day Sers gave himself up along with two other major generals, 5,968 officers and men, 180 pieces of artillery, a military chest of 333,600 taler, and enough rations to feed 80,000 men for two months. The only concession which Nádasdy allowed was to permit the garrison to march out with the honours of war. The Württemberg contingent did full justice to the occasion by turning out in full parade order, complete with white gaiters. One of the Württemberg officers noted that 'as they marched past the Prussians noticed our corps in particular, and paid us the complement of saying that it was a pity that such splendid men were drawn up alongside such shabby ones.'[56]

Prince Charles and Daun now had their line of communication running directly from Bohemia, and they could bring up heavy guns along with Nádasdy's corps and the *corps de reserve* for something of consequence against Breslau.

BRESLAU AND THE END OF BEVERN, 22 NOVEMBER 1757

a) Austrians
c. 83,000, of which 60,400 regular infantry and 12,000 'German' horse, about 120 heavy pieces
Losses: 5,854: 692 killed, 4,703 wounded, 459 missing
b) Prussians
38,400: 20,700 infantry, 7,700 cavalry, 80 pieces
Losses: c. 6,350: c. 800 killed, 5,500 wounded

Maria Theresa and Kaunitz were bringing heavy pressure to bear on the Austrian high command to finish with Bevern at Breslau, but opinion among the generals remained as divided as ever. The Empress was unwilling to tell the commanders categorically that they must fight, but she made it clear that she was disappointed. Councils of war on 14, 15 and 18 October brought no resolution, and a month passed before the generals were virtually forced to make up their minds. On 12 November news arrived that Frederick had beaten the French and the *Reichsarmee* at Rossbach on the 5th (below), and so gained the freedom to turn back against the Austrians. A little later there came a letter in which Maria Theresa reminded Prince Charles 'that the more or less favourable outcome of this campaign will determine the character of the forthcoming peace, and thus the welfare and security of my hereditary house.'[57]

In a crucial meeting on 18 November Daun finally threw his weight behind the more aggressive party, which was enough to sway the argument. On the next day Nádasdy arrived with 28,500 of the troops from Schweidnitz, and the siege train followed on the 20th, which gave the army an unprecedented weight of heavy artillery

The prepared defences of the Duke of Bevern extended for about seven miles in an arc to the west and south-west of Breslau. The right (northern) flank rested on the Oder by Gross-Masselwitz, and the nearby woods had been felled into an abattis. The woods gave way to the more open plain at Pilsnitz, where four redoubts guarded the highway coming from the west. The generally west-facing line continued by way of the entrenched village of Schmiedefeld to those of Maria-Höfchen and Klein-Mochbern, which could be considered as the corner stones of the position as a whole. Flèches and breastworks were thrown up between the villages, and the Lohe stream did service as an outer ditch. The nearby meadows were unusually dry, on account of the recent dry weather, instead of lying under water as they normally were at this season, but the Lohe and marshy banks still presented an obstacle to artillery and formed bodies of troops.

From Klein-Mochbern the defences extended eastwards along a low ridge as a nearly continuous line of entrenchments almost as far as the suburbs of the fortified city of Breslau, which offered a secure flank to the Prussian left wing under *GL*. Zieten. Some rather clever manoeuvres by the Austrians nevertheless persuaded the Prussians to abandon this part of their position and come forward into the country. When Nádasdy arrived with his corps on the 19th, he was directed to the upper Lohe, which was enough to induce Bevern to advance Zieten's wing from the line of entrenchments. On the 21st Nádasdy pushed a detachment across the Lohe and threw the free battalion of Angelelli from the village of Krietern, and won enough ground to enable him to construct four bridges. This seemed to betoken a thrust directly up the highway from the south, and Bevern accordingly reinforced Zieten's far left, at the cost of weakening the Prussian main position.

The meticulous *GFWM*. Lacy devised a plan for an elaborate set-piece attack for the 22nd, and it was an operation which had more in common with an offensive in the First World War than any other battle in this conflict. Nádasdy was to maintain his threat against the Prussian left wing, so pinning it down for the benefit of the Austrian centre, which was to deliver the main attack on the sector between Gräbschen and Schmiedefeld, taking in the fortified villages of Klein-Mochbern and Maria-Höfchen. Over to the north, the Austrian left wing was to beat its way through the defences of Pilsnitz, while the roving corps of *GFWM*. Beck would engage the two Prussian battalions in the Oswitzer Wald on the far side of the Oder.

The attack opened in the foggy mid-morning of 22 November. On the right Nádasdy fulfilled his not particularly heroic role in a not particularly heroic way. He already had his bridgehead on the far bank of the Lohe, and was now able to deploy his entire corps on that side along an impressive frontage of three miles. The ground was flat but seamed with ditches, and although both Nádasdy and Zieten were both renowned as dashing leaders of light troops, they now sparred in the same inconclusive style as they had done at Kolin. The one episode of importance did not redound to the credit of the Austrians. The Prussian free battalion of Angelelli, having lost Krietern on the 21st, now stood its ground at Kleinburg in the face of sixteen grenadier companies and three battalions under the command of *GFWM*. Joseph Wolfersdorff, 'who was not exactly the luckiest of our commanders.'[58] The Prussians fed in reinforcements, and the combat ended with the Austrians in full retreat and leaving thirteen pieces behind them.

The main weight of the Austrian attack was falling on the centre. The Austrians had planted nine batteries of heavy guns overnight, and eight of them were assigned to soften up the enemy by a preparatory fire. The first of the cannon opened towards 9.45 in the morning, and the rest joined in as the vapours dispersed over the following hour. Major Franz de Piza had prospected the relevant course of the Lohe, and discovered a stretch where the stream formed a single channel, and where there was enough space on the far bank for the Austrians to form a bridgehead under the cover of rising ground.

While the cannonade was still thundering, Colonel Spallard of the engineers had the Lohe spanned by seven pontoon bridges for the infantry, and a fascine crossing for the cavalry upstream. *FML*. Salomon Sprecher was in overall command of the assault in this sector, and he sent his corps of elite troops across the stream by two instalments—his thirty-five companies of foot grenadiers, then the twelve companies of carabiniers and mounted grenadiers under *GFWM*. Christian Philipp Prince Löwenstein.

There were no fortifications immediately to the front, but the Austrians were soon assailed by the Prussian lieutenant general Pennavaire and his four regiments of cuirassiers. The foot grenadiers beat off the first lunge with musketry and canister, and gained time for Löwenstein's horse to reach the bridgehead. The Austrians deliberately let the Prussian force come on, and when it stuck in the heavy ground they lashed it with canister.

Captain the Prince de Ligne was with his Netherlanders when they approached the bridges under a furious Prussian cannonade 'which carried away a good many of our men during the passage. It was raining shot. One of our bridgeheads was secured by fifteen grenadiers of our regiment who had returned from hospital the day before, even though they were still crippled by the wounds they had received at Moys… It was a fine sight when we deployed into battle formation on the far side of the bridge.'[59] The Prussian infantry could not sustain the weight of the reinforced attack, and towards 1.30 in the afternoon the bluecoats abandoned the village of Gräbschen.

Further to the north the battalion of Prinz Heinrich [35] had been making a stand at Klein-Mochbern at the angle of the original fortified position, and the troops maintained their spirits by singing the new and very popular 'Prussian grenadier' songs to words by the poet Gleim. Cavalry were not supposed to attack dug-in infantry and artillery, but the impetuous *GdC.* Lucchesi swept over the nearby lines with the three regiments of the right wing of the Austrian horse, and his Erzherzog Joseph Dragoons [D1] captured seven officers, one hundred men and two guns in the village.

The fighting on the Austrian left centre had a different character, for the fortified village of Schmiedefeld lay only just beyond the stream, and the Prussian lieutenant general Lestwitz was able to bring the crossings under near point-blank fire. The Hungarian infantry regiment of Joseph Esterházy [37] halted in front of the place in some disarray. Lieutenant Colonel Philipp de Souhay claims that he was able to keep the companion regiment of Nicolaus Esterházy [33] in better order, and that he now yelled out: '"Nicolaus and Joseph Esterházy, you are of the same nation, and twin regiments... you must do your duty for the honour of the nation!" The great fortification at Schmiedefeld was now attacked and conquered, along with ten heavy cannon and a 24-pounder howitzer.'[60]

In fact the reduction of both Klein-Mochbern and Schmiedefeld was hastened by the brilliant handling of the thirteen battalions of the *corps de reserve* by *FML.* Friedrich Georg Wied, who had wheeled to the left on the 'Prussian' side of the Lohe, and come at the two villages from the rear. Later in the afternoon he forced the Prussians to abandon their compact and strong positions at Pilsnitz, which had so far defied the efforts of the twenty-two battalions of the Austrian left wing.

By nightfall the Prussians were in full retreat on Breslau, and 'when the battle was over a general cry of *Vivat Maria Theresia!* was to be heard over the field, and the army gave a general and spontaneous feu de joie.'[61] Good leadership had brought forth 'all the inherent composure and courage of our troops.'[62] They had lost not far short of 6,000 of their number, 'but it must be counted an extraordinary dispensation and blessing of God that it did not cost us three times as much blood to dislodge the enemy from that camp of theirs, strong by nature through all those ditches and cuttings, with a river running in front and a multitude of bogs, marshes and ponds, not to mention the eight weeks of work which the enemy had put into fortifying it.'[63]

With hindsight the Austrian casualties were disproportionately damaging, for Austrian army would have to fight the King of Prussia two weeks later. 'The recent action at Breslau cost us a number of able officers killed, and others who were wounded too badly to do further service with their regiments. The time was too short for us to be able to repair the damage and settle down.'[64] The Prince de Ligne had his own reasons for regret. 'On the eve of the battle of Breslau I won four or five hundred ducats from General Wrbna, a certain Count Dessweffy and three other officers. I lost two thousand to Rodeny, Thomassoly, Gablosson and Blanckenstein... The next day I asked how the various gentlemen had fared. Those who were in debt to me had been killed; the others were in the best of health.'[65]

Among the Prussians the physical defeat was accompanied by a total collapse of will. The Duke of Bevern assigned Breslau to the keeping of *GL.* Lestwitz and a garrison of 3,840 men. Bevern fell back with the rest of his disintegrating army to the far bank of the Oder, and on 24 November he ran into a party of Beck's Croats and was taken prisoner. He gave out that he had lost his way on reconnaissance, though it was believed widely that he had preferred to be taken prisoner rather than render account to his king.

Lestwitz had put up a good fight in the battle, but he had suffered painful wounds, and was convinced that Breslau was now indefensible. On 25 November he was still engaged in negotiations with the Austrians when his troops disbanded, many of them staggering about the streets under the influence of alcohol supplied by the Catholic clergy. The capitulation looked good on paper, but it signified nothing in practice. The men deserted to the Austrians or scattered over the countryside, and just 151 soldiers stood by their officers and NCOs when the column marched out early on the 26th.

The triumph of the Austrians was to be so short-lived that the battle of the 22nd remains the least-known of the big actions of the Seven Years War, and it is easy to forget that the Austrians now held the mastery of the greater part of Silesia along with its capital. When they first crossed the Queiss on 12 September they had nailed up proclamations whereby Maria Theresa promised to treat the land as once more part of her domains, and that she intended no harm to well-intentioned subjects. 'The Prussian eagle has been snatched down, and the Imperial eagle set up in its place;'[66] 'wherever we have come with the army we have found the nobles, the townspeople and the peasants at home, and giving us everywhere a warm welcome, though observing a certain restraint, just in case events even now took a different turn.'[67]

In Breslau the Austrians were paying due regard to Protestant sensibilities, and it was no coincidence that the guard of the city was entrusted to the Calvinist *FML*. Sprecher and the Lutheran *GFWM*. Wolfersdorff. The Protestant clergy were loud in their professions of rediscovered loyalty, and the Catholic Bishop of Breslau, Gotthard Count Schaffgotsch, was in fact something of an embarrassment, for he was a man of notoriously immoral life and an appointee of Frederick's. As a matter of form he intoned the Te Deum at the High Mass that was celebrated in the cathedral on 26 November in the presence of Prince Charles and the generals, but he was then banished to a remote corner of his diocese and ordered to resign his functions to a Vicar General, who was to be chosen from the faithful clergy.

THE AUSTRIANS WITH THE *REICHSARMEE* AND THE BATTLE OF ROSSBACH, SUMMER, AUTUMN EARLY WINTER 1757

On 22 November 1757, the day of the battle of Breslau, the Prussian royal army was at Bautzen, enjoying a respite on its headlong march from Saxony to recover Silesia. By rights Frederick should have been held fast by the combined forces of the French and the *Reich* in the heart of Germany. How had matters transpired otherwise? The explanation lies in the deplorable campaign of Rossbach. Austrian forces were involved only marginally, but some of the details claim our attention.

In the second half of March 1757 Marshal d'Estrées entered Germany at the head of an army of 105,000 troops. On the face of it the French were fulfilling their defensive treaty obligations to Austria, and early in April they overran the Prussian enclaves on the lower Rhine. However an important divergence of interest between the allies had already become apparent. These concerned the electorate of Hanover, which to the Austrian way of thinking was an avenue by which the French could reach the theatre of war in Saxony, and where the transit could best be obtained by peaceful negotiation. For the French, on the other hand, Hanover was an objective in its own right, in view of the variety of connections with Britain, and under pressure from Versailles the Austrians now demanded that the Hanoverians must not only repair and open the communications between the Weser and the Elbe, and supply the French on the way, but evacuate the fortress of Hameln and confine their own troops to quarters. George II rejected the terms as intolerable, and commissioned his second son, William Augustus Duke of Cumberland, to take command of an 'Army of Observation,' a force of 45,000 troops assembled from the Hanoverian army and contingents from neighbouring states.

There was an end to all hopes of securing the neutrality of Hanover and its associates among the small Protestant states of north Germany, and Kaunitz had undergone (or allowed himself to undergo) a major diplomatic reverse. The full military penalties were revealed only in the next year, and in the short term the French attained what seemed to be a decisive success. D'Estrées crossed the Weser in the middle of July, and on the 26th he beat the Army of Observation at **Hastenbeck** (Austrian regiments from the Netherlands taking a part). The Duke of Cumberland abandoned Hanover and retreated all the way to the Stade, where he was trapped in the peninsula formed by the lower reaches of the Elbe and the Weser. On 10 September d'Estrées' successor Richelieu forced the enemy into the Convention of Kloster-Zeven, whereby the Army of Observation was disbanded.

When further and very considerable contingents of French entered Germany in the high summer, it was less from strategic calculation than from Louis XV's instinct to display his personal commitment to the Austrian alliance. Under the impact of the Austrian defeat at Prague (6 May) Louis resolved to send an additional 40,000 troops across the Rhine, of which 15,000 were to reinforce Marshal Richelieu, and 25,000 under the Prince of Soubise to act more directly by marching to join the newly-summoned *Reichsarmee*.

The *Reichsarmee* was in no respects 'the German Army,' but an ad hoc creation, which had been called into being periodically since the 1680s to defend the interests of the Empire against a common enemy. Altogether 25,000 of these Germans actually went on campaign in 1757. As a broad generalisation, the better units were those supplied as formed bodies by individual sovereigns; the worst were cobbled together from a host of small or tiny contingents as furnished by the Circles (*Creise*), which were the loose administrative groupings of states within the *Reich*.

In 1757 the components of the *Reichsarmee* had only just been thrown together, and were in every need of encouragement and fine words. They received the reverse from their commander, Joseph Friedrich Prince of Sachsen-Hildburghausen. He was at the same time the sovereign of a minor state of western Saxony, and a field marshal in the Austrian service, and he had once been regarded as a virtual reincarnation of the celebrated Prince Eugene of Savoy, to the extent that the Habsburgs had settled him in the Belvedere Palace in Vienna, and married him off to *der edle Ritter*'s hideous and greedy niece.

Hildburghausen was now called upon to manage an army which was less of an armed force than an expression of the wild diversity of the German Empire. The Austrian *GdC*. Franz Joseph Brettlach wrote after the campaign that 'he is detested by the officers and the men alike, and I cannot think of a single prince or general of the Circles who would wish to serve under him any longer. He has, moreover, not the slightest concern for the ordinary soldiers. He tires them out for no purpose whatsoever, and lets them go without bread for seven days at a time. This must be laid entirely to his account, and his lack of foresight proceeds largely from his extreme sloth, for he is entirely out of sorts if he cannot spare ten hours out of the twenty-four in bed.'[68]

Hildburghausen first met the commander of the French forces, Lieutenant General Charles de Rohan, Prince de Soubise, at Erfurt on 29 August. Soubise too was a man of princely house who had attained his present command through the highest patronage, in this case that of Madame de Pompadour. Neither then, nor later, was it established who had overall command of the joint forces, and it was probably from self-knowledge that each man considered the other incapable of commanding an army.

Hildburghausen never discovered how completely he was being betrayed in Versailles and Vienna. Louis XV had been genuinely dedicated to assisting Maria Theresa in her time of need. Her immediate crisis was surmounted by Daun's victory at Kolin, and in any case not all the members of the ministry shared the commitment of their king. On 21 October the war minister Paulmy wrote to Soubise that the French, who had been joining in the pursuit of the Prussians in Saxony, must now pull back and consolidate on the line of the Saale. They would then be in a position to take up winter quarters behind the river, and secure the southern flank of the army of Richelieu, which was now in possession of Hanover.

In the opinion of Kaunitz it was politically useful to have the *Reichsarmee* brought together, 'but we would be very much mistaken if we were to place the slightest reliance on it in direct military operations against Prussia.'[69] By way of the French ambassador he actually encouraged Soubise to raise difficulties concerning questions of supply, so that army would be unable to move at all when the time came.[70] Vienna refused outright to send much-needed pontoons and gunners, and the direct Austrian presence with the force was confined to two regiments of cuirassiers (Brettlach [C29] and Trautmannsdorff [C21]), two of hussars (Splényi [Hii]) and

Széchenyi [H32]), and 3,500 Croats under the newly-promoted *GFWM*. Loudon, or about 4,500 troops in all.

Frederick could spare just 25,000 troops to form an army under his personal command, with which he hoped to bring the allies to battle. He had to be ready at any time to confront his other enemies, and he was unwilling to commit himself much further west than Erfurt in Thuringia. Soubise for his part shrank from exposing his forces in the open plain of Leipzig, for they were weak in cavalry, and the result was a near-bloodless campaign of lunge and counter-lunge which extended into October. On the 19th Lieutenant General the Duc de Broglie arrived on the theatre of operations with 20,000 troops from Richelieu's army, which brought the combined forces to about 50,000 men. Frederick had already given up hope of forcing a decision, and he had taken off to anticipate the Austrian raiding corps (that of Hadik) which had been making for Berlin.

The allies were tempted forward, and on 25 October Hildburghausen summoned the Prussian garrison in Leipzig to surrender. Frederick was on his way back, in fact only a single march distant, and the allies recoiled first to the line of the Saale, and then to a camp at Mücheln. The king was bringing his scattered forces together once more, and assembled them at Rossbach just to the east of the allied position. Soubise and Hildburghausen alternated between panic and over-confidence, and the latter happened to prevail when they resolved the take their greatly superior forces on a flanking move around to the south of the Prussian camp

Rossbach, 5 November 1757

a) French
c. 30,000, 32 heavy pieces
Losses: c. 7,000

b) *Reichsarmee*
c. 9,900 at most
Losses: officially 2,335

c) Austrians
c. 3,850, the Splényi Hussars absent
Losses: 462

d) Prussians
22,200, 18 heavy pieces
Losses: 549

The winter night fell quickly, and *GdC*. Franz Johann Brettlach relates how 'all the generals stayed the whole night… in the open air by my regiment. Prince Soubise often came over to us, and repeatedly debated what we ought to do, whether we should attack the enemy camp or not.'[71] At ten in the morning of 5 November the combined army set out on its chosen route, corresponding with a smooth ridge which ran east above Pettstädt, and descended in gentle spurs between Lunstädt and Reichardtswerben. Through a complicated series of checks, delays and catchings-up the original arrangement of three columns became four, and the Austrian and German cavalry at the head parted company with the infantry labouring behind. There would have been no advance guard at all if the Széchenyi Hussars had not arrived in response to a vaguely-worded order from Hildburghausen.

GFWM. Anton Széchenyi rode up to ask Hildburghausen for further instructions, but the prince merely replied '"I have more important things to think about than the hussars. Just get on with the march!"'[72] A little later the Prussian army packed up its camp and disappeared behind a parallel ridge running to the north. Hildburghausen concluded that the enemy were on the run, and without further hesitation he gestured for the army to plunge into the pursuit.

A trusted Hungarian volunteer from the Dutch service, Captain Zarnocsay, rode to the crest of the further ridge and saw the whole of the royal Prussian army advancing towards him in battle array. It was clear that the enemy had swung out of their line of 'retreat' in the dead ground and were now approaching to take the allied columns head-on. He sped back to deliver his findings to Hildburghausen, who retorted '"You hussars are all the same—useless! A waste of the Empress's rations!'.[73]

A line of eighteen Prussian pieces appeared on the ridge and opened fire at 3.15 in the afternoon. Incomprehensibly, the combined army held on its course until, at 3.30, the twelve hundred Austrian cuirassiers at the head faced the onrush of a first line of fifteen squadrons of Prussian cuirassiers and dragoons. Colonel August Marchese Voghera, as commander of the '*Schmeisser*' (the Brettlach Cuirassiers) saluted the officer leading the Prussian attack and wheeled his troopers into line, while the Trautmannsdorff Cuirassiers to their right-rear had to fight as best they could in columns of squadrons.

The Austrian cuirassiers hacked away at the Prussians, bringing them to a halt, and were joined by ten squadrons of the French reserve corps. The combat lasted for altogether half an hour before G.M. Seydlitz brought the eighteen squadrons of the Prussian second line into action and swept the allies away.

While Seydlitz reassembled his victorious cavalry beyond Tagewerben, the Prussian infantry came on in a great line against the tightly-packed foot soldiers of the allies, still mostly in column of march. 'The day before the French infantry had been all for skewering the enemy with the bayonet, but now the terrible fire made them change their minds all of a sudden. The solitary brigade of Piémont... advanced to within thirty paces of the enemy, but it wilted under the hostile fire, and turned about. At this the whole of the first and second line fled, and it was hopeless to try to get the troops to halt and re-form.'[74]

Seydlitz's cavalry dealt the coup de grace by coming on again and falling on the right flank of the columns of infantry. A total massacre was averted by the arrival of darkness, by a fine stand which was put up by the regiment of Blau-Würzburg and the battalion of Hesse-Darmstadt, and by the timely intervention of the light corps of Saint-Germain and Loudon's 500 Croats and 300 hussars. Saint-Germain and Loudon had been working together for a number of days, and on the dreadful 5 November they had been posted on the heights to the west of the field to screen the march of the combined army.

The routed troops fled south towards the Unstrut. The fastest and luckiest men crowded across the narrow bridge at Freyburg, while the others crossed by boat or drowned. The combined army proceeded to break apart on the days after the battle, for Soubise ignored a rendezvous with Hildburghausen and took his French up the right bank of the Unstrut to seek refuge with the intact corps of Richelieu. Hildburghausen assembled what he could of his troops, and made direct for the Thüringer-Wald by way of Weimar and Saalfeld. The Brettlach and Trautmannsdorff Cuirassiers did their best to cover the disintegrating army. They were now isolated from their sources of cash and supplies, and they were forced to raise what they could from the territories of Sachsen-Gotha and Bayreuth, which occasioned outraged protests from the reigning princes.

By the middle of December the authorities in Vienna were able to make some sense of what was happening in the *Reich*. The Splényi and Széchenyi Hussars were accordingly instructed to remain in Germany to offer some security against Prussian raids, while the cuirassiers and the excellent *Reich* regiment of Blau-Würzburg were ordered to march for Eger in western Bohemia.

Loudon, Széchenyi, the brothers Brettlach and their Croats, hussars and cuirassiers had all acquitted themselves well as representatives of the Austrian service with the combined army. Hildburghausen had been appointed to his command as much on political as military grounds. He can be considered an Austrian general only in a qualified way, and he was not an exponent of any school of Austrian generalship. He sensed that he was being betrayed in Vienna, but he would still have been shocked to know that Kaunitz considered him and his army as dispensable.

If the Austrian responsibility for the combined army's rout is limited, the consequences for Austrian war-making can hardly be overstated, and at the strategic level they equalled or surpassed even those of the battle of Leuthen one month later. George II drew so much heart from the news that he refused the ratify the Convention of Kloster-Zeven, on the grounds that the Duke of Cumberland had not been entitled to dispose of the Hessian corps, which stood in British pay. George entrusted the command of the Hanoverian army to an exceptionally able Prussian lieutenant general, Prince Ferdinand of Brunswick, who before the end of the year undertook a fulminating offensive against the French in their winter quarters in Germany.

Henceforth the Austrians failed to gain even indirect military support from their ally in the war against Prussia, and to that extent the work of the Diplomatic Revolution was undone.

To Leuthen,
23 November—4 December 1757

As early as 18 November Prince Charles had heard that Frederick was on the march from Saxony. Two days later came news that the king was not far from Bautzen in Lusatia, which was important information, for it suggested that the royal army had not turned up the Elbe into Bohemia, but was approaching Silesia by the route which led under the border hills. On the 22nd the Austrians beat the Duke of Bevern out of his position in front of Breslau and on the 24th they entered the city.

Many officers in the victorious army believed that the Austrians would now pursue and destroy the remains of Bevern's army without delay,[75] but one of the fastest-rising major generals in the army, Franz Moritz Lacy, urged that the Austrians should bear in mind that Frederick was on his way, and that they should confront him along the Katzbach to the west of Breslau. At first glance the little river appeared to be scarcely more than an ambitious field ditch, as it flowed from the hills by way of Liegnitz to meet the Oder just below Parchwitz, but the swift current, the low but steep banks, and the extensive water meadows could be used to advantage by a defending army, as the Austrians were going to prove in 1760.

Instead of any of this, the army settled into Bevern's old camp just outside Breslau, and the Prussian deserters began to return to their colours. In fairness to Prince Charles and Daun it must be said that business of supply had been taken out of the hands of the experienced *General-Kriegs-Commissarius* Franz Ludwig Count Salburg, and lodged instead with the supreme organ of civil administration, the *Directorium*, which was unfamiliar with this specialised work. 'The inevitable result was an initial crisis in our military system... to the disadvantage and obstruction of operations in the field.'[76]

Meanwhile detachments were being posted over the landscape, which was a sure sign of indecision. The more substantial among many others were the garrisons in Schweidnitz, Breslau and Liegnitz, and the 3,500-strong corps of *GFWM*. Beck on the far side of the Oder. However no more than 500 troops were guarding the wooden bridge where the highway approaching Breslau from the west crossed the Katzbach at Parchwitz. Prince Charles and Daun had not grasped that Frederick was in a state of desperation, prepared to run any risk to evict the Austrians from Lower Silesia.

On 28 November Frederick seized the crossing at Parchwitz, and the security of the line of the Katzbach was now compromised. *GL.* Zieten had been rounding up the survivors of the beaten army from Breslau, and on 2 December he led them to the king at Parchwitz, together with a train of heavy artillery from the fortress of Glogau. The combined force stood at 39,000 troops, and through a unique display of public emotion Frederick was able to convince his men that the salvation of the Prussian homeland depended on beating the Austrians in front of Breslau.

On the same fateful 2 December Charles assembled the generals in Breslau to determine a course of action. There is no first-hand account of the debate, and the version which has passed into history was penned by a junior officer, Captain Jacob Cogniazzo, who has *GdC.* Lucchesi exciting the vanity of Charles and persuading him to give battle.[77] On this occasion Cogniazzo is almost certainly wrong. Charles wrote to Maria Theresa the next day that he put the Prussian strength at 40,000 (which was only a slight exaggeration), 'as for us, we have 50,000 at the most capable of doing service... the regiments of horse are so feeble that some can scarcely put together three squadrons apiece, and they have made detachments... to God knows where. It is the same story with the infantry, and most of the men they send to the hospitals do not get better. The hussars are in the same state. It means that Your Majesty has plenty of troops on paper, but scarcely two thirds of them are fit to serve.'[78]

Neither here nor anywhere else in the correspondence of Prince Charles at this time is

Leuthen, 5 December 1757

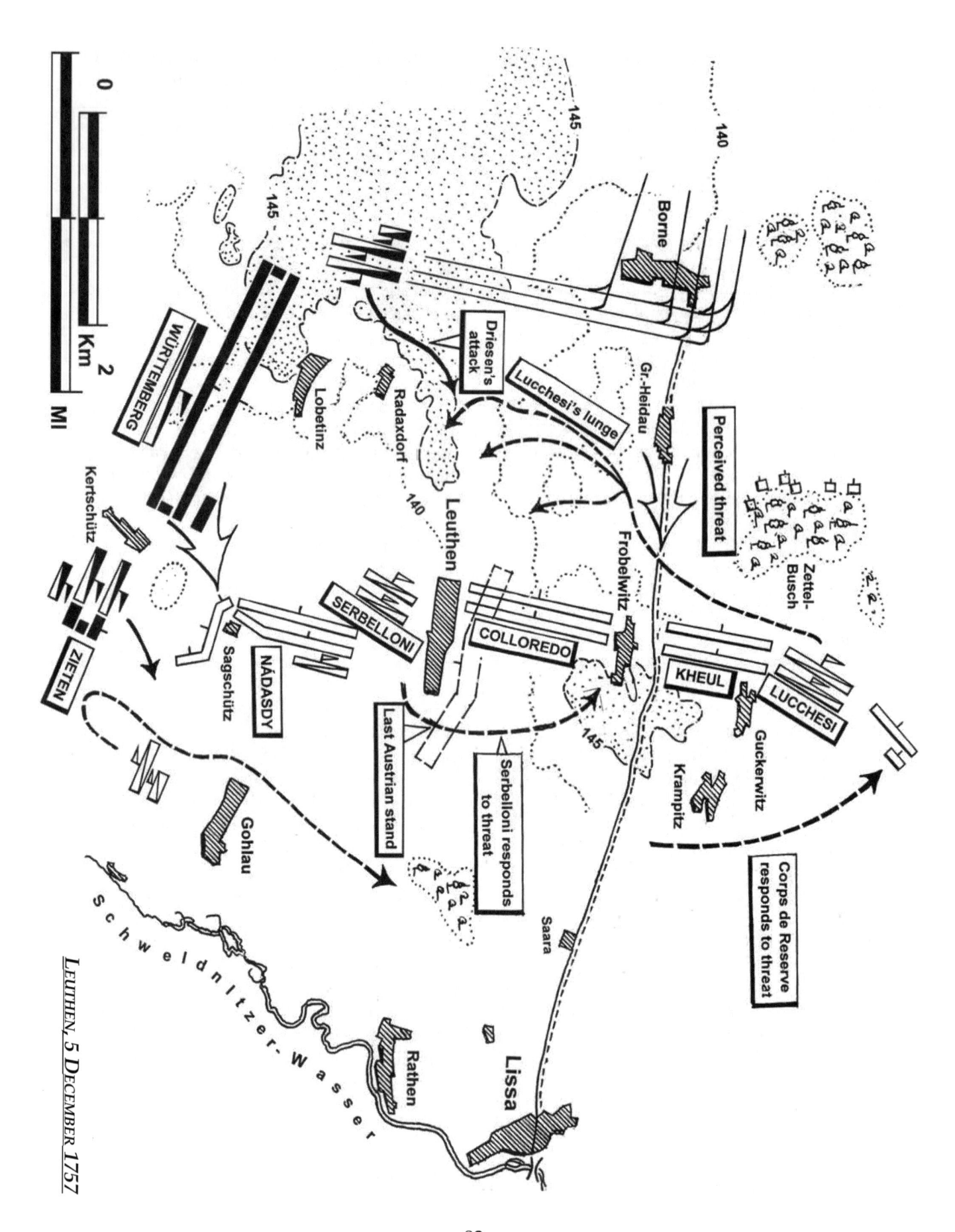

there anything to suggest that the army was committed to anything more than manoeuvring for advantageous winter quarters in Silesia. This could best be secured by advancing the army to check the Prussians on the Katzbach, as Lacy had advocated after the last battle. The Prussians already had a bridgehead at Parchwitz, and Frederick now seemed intent on laying siege to the walled town of Liegnitz just twenty kilometres upstream. Charles ordered 1,000 infantry to be sent to the threatened town, to strengthen the 2,000 troops already there. The reinforcement arrived at five in the morning of 3 December, and later in the day Charles must have been confirmed in his judgement when he received a letter from Maria Theresa which emphasised how important it was to hold Liegnitz as a strongpoint for the winter quarters.[79] Meanwhile the army made ready to march from Breslau.

The Saxon lieutenant general Georg Nostitz rode ahead with three regiments of his chevaulegers towards the walled village of Neumarkt, where the Austrians had their main field bakery. The *Generalquartiermeister* Franz Guasco was simultaneously prospecting sites for a camp. The morning of the 3rd was foggy, which left him time to reconnoitre the country only as far as Neumarkt, and he ordered his assistants to stake out the lines on the Pfaffendorfer-Berg, a low swell of ground just short of the town.

The Austrian army wound out of the camp in front of Breslau on the morning of 4 December. Since the advance to the Katzbach was a matter of urgency, the troops carried three day's rations of bread in their haversacks, and the heavy baggage and most of the heavy pieces were left behind. The planned march to Guasco's camp was on the longish side, at twenty or so miles, and the progress was delayed by the heavy rain, and the need to cross the double obstacles of the Lohe and the Schweidnitzer-Wasser (Weistritz).

Unknown to Prince Charles, Frederick was moving towards him with the entire Prussian army. The king led the way with a fighting advance guard, and descended with overwhelming force on Neumarkt, where he had the gate blown in by dismounted hussars. Six hundred Croats made good their escape to the Pfaffendorfer-Berg, but they were left in the lurch by the two regiments of hussars which should have been supporting them, and 300 of their number were killed or captured. The survivors were received by the three regiments of Saxon light horse west of Borne. Frederick had therefore anticipated the enemy on Guasco's camp site, where the lines were already staked out, and inside Neumarkt the Prussians discovered the Austrian baking ovens, together with 80,000 rations of bread which had been prepared for the army of Prince Charles.

At noon Charles in person had scarcely reached the western side of the Schweidnitzer-Wasser at Lissa when he learned that the Prussians were on the way, and that they had taken Neumarkt along with the field bakery and many of the covering force. The report was confirmed by the 'Croats who were coming back with blood streaming from their heads… altogether this first reverse was taken as a bad omen for our army, and the generals were in evident perplexity as to whether to continue with the advance.'[80]

The high command once more resorted to half measures. The heavy guns had been left irretrievably behind the Lohe, and yet Charles hastened the march of the columns across the only advantageous tactical barrier available to him, namely the Schweidnitzer-Wasser, which now stood across his path of retreat in the event of a reverse. The army hastened over the country on the far side, separated by the river from its tents and light baggage.

The last units (the Württemberg auxiliaries) streamed in until eleven at night. The regiments were deployed haphazardly over a wide frontage as they arrived, and the troops bivouacked on a light covering of snow without tents, straw, firewood or hot food. Prince Charles wrote hurriedly to Maria Theresa: 'We trust that the Almighty has been working for our good today. If it comes to another battle tomorrow, which seems more likely than not, for the two armies are so close, I hold to the firm belief that He will once more bless your Imperial Majesty's arms, and thus prepare the way for a successful end to the campaign.'[81]

Leuthen, 5 December 1757

a) Austrians, auxiliaries and Saxons
49-55,000
Losses from all causes: c. 23,190: c. 19,830 Austrians and Würzburgers, 2,250 Württembergers, 630 Bavarians, 479 Saxons
b) Prussians
c. 39,000: 29,900 infantry, 9,800 cavalry, 71 heavy pieces
Losses: 6,382 casualties (1,175 killed, 5,207 wounded) and a small number of prisoners

The ground where the Austrians were going to fight was forced upon them by circumstances. It was an arable plain, interspersed with hamlets and scattered woodlands. The only significant obstacles to movement were presented by the marshes to the north of Nippern and the nearby block of the Zettel-Busch, by the woods behind Leuthen village (the contiguous Leuthener-Busch and Rathener-Busch), and the ditches and coppices near Sagschütz in the south. Almost completely flat at first sight, the terrain rose to a number of small mounds to the west and south of Leuthen; there was a swell in the ground between Borne and Lobetinz down the western side of the field, and the little village of Sagschütz crowned the low ridge of the Kiefern-Berg towards the south-eastern extremity.

The regiment of Roth-Würzburg was loopholing the churchyard wall at Leuthen: otherwise the Austrians had not had the opportunity to prepare the field. To derive any advantage from the insignificant features of the ground demanded an intimate knowledge of the country, and this belonged exclusively to the Prussians, who had made the area around Leuthen the scene of the annual autumn manoeuvres of their Lower Silesian regiments.

Before the frosty daylight on 5 November the king pushed down the axis of the Breslau highway with an advance guard consisting of his combined hussars, twelve battalions of infantry and ten 12-pounder cannon. To the east of Borne stood two lines of allied light horse under the command of Nostitz and *FML.* Emmerich Morocz. The Austrian hussar regiments of Nádasdy [H11] and Dessewffy [H34] were supposed to withdraw under pressure through the three regiments of Saxon chevaulegers which were standing to their rear, but Nostitz and Morocz had failed to allow for the speed and strength of the Prussian onset, and both the hussars and the Saxons were thrown back by a combined frontal and right-flanking assault by thirty-five enemy squadrons.

The chevaulegers were overhauled when they tried to escape through Borne and across the nearby ditches, and many of their number were taken prisoner. The Prussian hussars maintained their headlong progress through Gross-Heidau before they were called back, and one of them split the skull of an Austrian cuirassier just thirty paces from the nearest house of Leuthen. The way was clear for Frederick move forward and make a close reconnaissance. It was now a day of brilliant sunshine, which set off the snow-covered ground against the intense blue of the winter sky, and from the Schön-Berg he claimed (with some exaggeration) that he could have counted the enemy forces man by man.

The Austrian army advanced from its bivouacs to a westward-facing battle line which was extraordinarily long. It extended for an initial four miles from Nippern on the right to the neighbourhood of Sagschütz in the south, and the available heavy artillery was positioned in four widely-separated sites along the front. The *GdCs.* Lucchesi and Serbelloni commanded the respective right and left wings of cavalry, and the main body of infantry was deployed in the centre on either side of the village of Leuthen. The all-important *corps de reserve*, consisting of eight battalions under *FML.* the Duke of Arenberg, was placed behind the right wing. The *corps de reserve* had been one of the keys of victory at Kolin, and instrumental in frustrating the Prussian turning movement at Eckartsberg, and now, as then, it offered the Austrians the means of confronting unexpected turns of events.

The other potential battle-winner was the corps of the popular hero *GdC.* Franz Nádasdy-Fogaras, which had expanded into a miniature army of thirty-three battalions and twenty-one squadrons. This force was now deployed on the far left (south) of the main army, and its left wing was bent back in a kind of hook which extended along the Kiefern-Berg ridge as far as the woods behind Schriegwitz.

Nádasdy's corps had originally formed a third line behind the main body, and there had been some discussion as to whether it should be arrayed at right angles, as a south-facing line pivoting on Leuthen, which would have given the Austrians a compact position and enabled them to exploit the obstacle-value of the woods and bogs which extended from behind the village to the Schweidnitzer-Wasser. Instead the corps prolonged the already lengthy axis of the main army still further to the south, in the hope of blocking any attempt by Frederick to outflank the host in that direction. Moreover the army's infantry was now deployed in three ranks as a matter of routine. The Austrians had abandoned the original four-rank line of battle at Kolin through tactical necessity, and they had probably adopted the three-rank line as the norm from 21 October, when the last batch of reinforcements had left the main army for the siege of Schweidnitz. Now at Leuthen their army was drawn up 'with that combination of gigantic length and inadequate depth that was needed to ensure that we were going to be beaten.'[82]

After the battle Prince Charles blamed Nádasdy for a significant detail of the deployment, namely for having positioned his two contingents of German auxiliaries—ten battalions of Bavarians and thirteen of Württembergers—on the inherently vulnerable left flank of his corps. The Bavarian troops were Catholics, but they had been recruited in haste, and were actually less reliable than the Lutheran Württembergers, who by the time of the battle had been brought into a state of disciplined obedience by their officers.

Towards eight in the morning the defeated Austrian hussars and Saxon light horse fell back towards the main army, and a couple of hours later the Prussian army marched in a densely-packed formation of column of wings through and around the village of Borne, then executed a number of deliberately complicated movement on far side. The Austrian right (northern) wing appeared to be the most threatened, and according to the Austrian official account GdC. Lucchesi made repeated requests for support. Prince Charles and Daun hesitated to release the *corps de reserve*, 'because they wished to be more certain of the enemy purpose,'[83] but finally towards noon the eight battalions of the reserve were redeployed on both sides of Nippern to prolong the northern flank of the army. They were followed shortly by a substantial part of the cavalry of the left wing (brigades of Hohenzollern and Ludwig Starhemberg). After the battle Frederick asked GFWM. Beck how the Austrians allowed themselves to be beaten so completely. Beck just replied '"We expected to be attacked on our right wing, and we made our arrangements accordingly." "How was that possible?" answered the king. "A patrol against our left wing would have identified my intentions soon enough."'[84]

The Prussian army now set itself in motion 'by lines,' not against the Austrian right wing, but off to the south, in other words, as the Austrians saw it, from right to left across the front of their army. The direction of the movement was now unmistakable, even if it is probable that some of the units were out of sight for some of the time. Prince Charles comments that 'after a series of marches and counter-marches, the enemy all of a sudden marched off to their right along the row of heights with an extraordinary speed, and in such a way that for a moment we believed that they were marching for Canth to cut us off from Schweidnitz.'[85] Thus the movement happened to play on the lively fears of the Austrian high command for the communications with Bohemia, while the threat of an imminent attack appeared to recede. The Austrians were caught unawares by what happened next.

The Prussian columns turned sharply to their left, behind Lobetinz, and early in the afternoon Frederick formed a heavy concentration of infantry to deal a hammer blow at the far southern end of the enemy line in front of Sagschütz. The rest of the infantry were coming up to the left in staggered formation, while GL. Zieten was moving out on the Prussian right flank with a wing of cavalry. Batteries of the murderous heavy-barrelled 12-pounder *Brummers* were being advanced with extraordinary speed, ready to move from one battery site to another in support of the attack.

Nádasdy's Württembergers were arrayed

along the top of the ridge of the Kiefern-Berg, which had some defensive potential, but one of their staff officers, Colonel Friedrich Nicolai, had accompanied the Prussian manoeuvres at Leuthen before the war, and knew that the ground which extended to the front was not a bog, as Nádasdy supposed, 'but dry, and passable by all arms. About one in the afternoon General Nádasdy came up to the Württemberg troops on the left wing. Major General von Romann communicated this news to him, and it was confirmed to him by a number of officers who were sent out to look at the ground. He had to recognise that the left flank of the army was therefore without support, and he rode off immediately, declaring that these circumstances demanded that more heavy artillery must be sent to that flank.'[86]

The pieces never arrived. The Württemberg battalion of Röder put up something of a fight, but was overwhelmed with heavy casualties, and all the rest of the auxiliaries, Württembergers and Bavarians, took to their heels. Three battalions of Nádasdy's Austrian infantry (Maguire [46], Haller [31] and Johann Pálffy [39]) gave way under the pounding of a mass of Prussian artillery which had been assembled on the low Juden-Berg. Nádasdy sought to throw his cavalry against the right flank of his old rival Zieten, but he was beaten back by six battalions of supporting Prussian infantry which had been deployed there against this eventuality. The six battalions pressed on, and unseated the left flank of the infantry which Nádasdy was attempting to rally behind the Gohlauer-Graben.

Nádasdy's foot soldiers would probably have been cut down there and then if Zieten's horse had not been checked by repeated counterattacks on the part of the allied cavalry, which culminated in an epic combat by *FML*. Johann O'Donnell and his Jung-Modena [D13] and Sachsen-Gotha [D28] Dragoons against the Prussian Garde du Corps and Gensd'armes. O'Donnell ended up surrounded by the Prussians. 'I hacked away at the first enemy I encountered. I had it in mind to break through by brute force, and although I took a sword cut in the head I managed to break free. I would have escaped capture altogether if my wound had not rendered me so feeble and powerless that I could scarcely stay on my horse, which had received a similar wound.'[87] Nádasdy's cavalry now had to fall back behind the protection of the Rathener-Busch, and the right wing of the Prussian horse now had a free run against the Württembergers and Bavarians as they fled towards Leuthen.

Prince Charles now began to order reinforcements to march south with the greatest possible speed. The *corps de reserve* had the furthest to go, since it had moved north to Nippern earlier in the day, but it now came down at a run and contrived to be the first of the infantry to make a stand against the Prussians south of Leuthen. Since the direction of the attack had declared itself so clearly, Prince Charles and Daun set about building an entire south-facing line, which eventually reached a frontage of 1,800 paces and extended on both sides of the village. The units arrived piecemeal and out of breath, and encountered scenes of already considerable disorder. The men of the battalion of Erzherzog Carl [2] saw blue-coated infantry swarming towards them, 'and under the impression that they were Prussians... they made ready to receive them with a good platoon fire. By good fortune somebody set up a cry of "Württembergers!" and the misunderstanding was overcome. They opened up intervals between the divisions and let the fugitives pass through without hindrance.'[88]

At 3.30 in the afternoon the Prussians threw themselves at the mass of Austrians which had assembled along the new axis. There was now fierce resistance to the south of Leuthen, where the Austrian infantry, standing in places up to two hundred deep, were supported by the Austrian heavy artillery, which for the first time had been gathered in force and was firing from a slight elevation to the north of the village. The Austrians gave ground only when Frederick brought up two batteries of 12-pounders to the Butter-Berg and took the Austrians in enfilade.

At Leuthen itself the Prussians had first to break into the enclosed farmyards, and then crack the inner core of resistance at the church, which was surrounded by a low cemetery wall of rough brown stone, with small round towers at the corners. Here the regiment of Roth-Würzburg proved that German troops were good at more than running away. After repeated repulses the Prussians finally broke in at the eastern gate and by a breach they had shot in the southern wall. Just four Würzburg officers and thirty-four of their men escaped over the rear wall, carrying one of their colours with them.

By four in the afternoon the Prussians had cleared the village, only to be checked in a new standing fire-fight with the Austrians, who were standing their ground to the north. All the Prussian battalions had been committed to the action, and the only unengaged forces on either side were the cavalry commands of *GdC*. Lucchesi and of the Prussian lieutenant generals Driesen and Prince Friedrich Eugen of Württemberg (fighting against his compatriots).

Lucchesi had been one of Browne's circle. He shared the late field marshal's fiery and charismatic style, and in the style of his friend he now sought to turn the tide of his last battle by a bold counterattack. At Leuthen he still had his first line of cavalry at his disposal, together with reinforcements from Serbelloni, and he brought his squadrons down in a great sweep to the south, intending to fall on the left wing of the Prussian infantry battling near Leuthen. Georg Wilhelm Driesen, a former student of theology, was watching and calculating from his viewpoint on the Sophien-Berg, one of the low eminences which stretched to the west of the field. He could see both Lucchesi's march, and his own immediate command of thirty squadrons waiting in dead ground, and when he judged that the moment had come he threw his troopers at the right flank of Lucchesi's force as it progressed across his front.

Lucchesi sought to wheel hard left to get behind the protection of the Austrian infantry, but the Benedict Daun Dragoons [D31] and the Erzherzog Leopold [C3] and Serbelloni Cuirassiers [C12] had no choice but to form front against the enemy in the decisive moments before the impact. The savage hand-to-hand fighting turned decisively to the advantage of the Prussians when Friedrich Eugen of Württemberg intervened with thirty squadrons of Frederick's former advance guard. Lucchesi was beheaded by a cannon shot, and the Austrian cavalry, intermingled with the victorious Prussians, bore down on the Austrian infantry behind Leuthen.

The battle was lost beyond redemption. By the windmill north of Leuthen the Austrian gunners and the regiment of Baden-Baden [23] were engulfed almost in their entirety, and the salvation of the rest of the army lay in escaping across the Schweidnitzer-Wasser to the east of the battlefield. Even now the Austrians were not overtaken by the same kind of panic and disintegration which had affected the allies at Rossbach. Scratch groups of forces were putting up determined rearguard actions, and Nádasdy succeeded in holding back Zieten at a time when the troops of the main army were crowding across the bridges at Lissa, Rathen and Stabelwitz. Nádasdy then followed with his corps. The action ended with an exchanges of fire across the river.

At ten at night Charles and Daun met in a hurried and ill-tempered conference at Neukirch. The immediate fear was that the army might become trapped in the corridor of land between the Schweidnitzer-Wasser and the Lohe, and they decided that the troops must withdraw across the Lohe before the night was out. The resulting order talked in ambiguous terms about returning to the 'old camp,' and 'nobody knew whether this was the first camp after the battle (of Breslau) or the second, some troops remained between the two rivers, being taken prisoner the next morning.'[89]

The Austrians and their auxiliaries had lost more than 23,000 men from all causes, and Breslau and all the rest of Lower Silesia were now at risk. Who had been to blame? Emperor Francis Stephen and his circle were anxious at all costs to preserve the reputation of Prince Charles, and scapegoats were all too easy to find. In both his official and private relations Charles emphasised that Nádasdy had ignored what had been agreed among the commanders, and placed the thoroughly unreliable Bavarians and Württembergers in a key position.[90] Maria Theresa hastened to fall in with this version of events.

Nádasdy cannot escape some responsibility for deploying the Germans where he did, but many of the circumstances of the battle on his wing were omitted from the official relations. Among the Germans the Württemberg battalion of Röder had put up more than a nominal resistance, and the more astute commentators noted that 'just think of some Austrian grenadier battalions—the cream of out troops—being put in their place. They might have got off a few dozen rounds more, but in the end they would have gone under to the same attack.'[91]

Nádasdy then brought his remaining forces into the battle time and time again, and one of Zieten's biographers was compelled to write 'how remarkable it is, that the Austrian relations have nothing to say about the opening battle of their cavalry with that of Zieten, which in fact went fairly well.'[92] Just as little credit was given to Nádasdy's work in covering the escape of the army across the bridges.

GdC. Lucchesi had not survived to answer the grave charges that were laid to his account, of having raised a false alarm on the right wing, and having urged the army to give battle in the first place. A typical anecdote claims that 'it is scarcely possible to exaggerate the contempt which our Austrian generals showed for the Prussian army on the eve of the battle. *GdC.* Lucchesi openly called it a "cloud of gnats." When Count Serbelloni... heard later that the head of his rival Lucchesi had been carried away by a cannon shot, he gave vent to the comment "yes, and now one of these gnats has stung him"'[93]

If Lucchesi was indeed bemused by Frederick's deceptions, the blame must be shared among the high command. When Marainville reviewed the various mistakes, he gave first place to the choice of the ground, and then to the failure to support the advanced troops with infantry and artillery after the style of Frederick. The result was that 'our generals were totally ignorant of the movements of the Prussian army, and talked of them as... if it were something three or four marches away. The king of Prussia, on the other hand, drove in our light troops right back to our army, and was therefore as well informed of our positions as we were.[94]

It is possible to detect further shortcomings, this time of a technical nature: the half-hearted measures which led to the Austrians fighting on the defensive without the usual advantages of a well-chosen and prepared position; the inordinately strung-out line of battle; the dispersion and relative immobility of the Austrian artillery; the inadequate quantity of the powder in the musket cartridges.[95]

In his diaries the well-informed head of the Imperial household, Johann Joseph Count Khevenhüller-Metsch, took due note of all the faults and errors of judgement, 'but the root of all the evil and the radical flaw is to be found in our internal constitution. We have two people in charge, the Emperor and the Empress.'[96] The outcome was a lack of direction and co-ordination, and a culture of favouritism which could place a man like Prince Charles at the head of an army.

Among all the horrors the one undeniable consolation was that the Austrians at the regimental level had fought with the greatest tenacity, as was conceded by Frederick, his suite and the officers of his army.[97] Maria Theresa wrote to Charles that she was glad to hear that her troops had not been led astray by the bad example of the auxiliaries, 'but had fought with an heroic steadfastness, and with their blood had earned to the full the praise of all right-thinking military men.'[98]

AFTER LEUTHEN:
THE RETREAT AND THE DEFENCE OF BRESLAU AND LIEGNITZ, 6-28 DECEMBER 1757

On the morning after the terrible battle the surviving regimental officers assembled what they could of their men on the eastern side of the Lohe. The troops who remained on the western bank were being rounded up by the enemy, while fugitives of every kind surged through the gates of Breslau. 'Just imagine a cloudburst descending from the hills with thunder and lightning, and flooding the valleys at the foot... in the same way we saw those countless troops flowing under our eyes... Every street became a river of men, and every lane a torrent.'[99]

It was still dark when Captain de Ligne reached Gräbschen, 'where I saw the prince and the field marshal plunged into the deepest gloom. One seemed to be saying: "I can't believe it!" and the other, "I told you so!"'... But little by little the troops began to come together, and the least-battered regiments began to assume a recognisable state. There was talk of marching to Schweidnitz.'[100] That place was stocked with provisions, and from there the army would have a secure communication with Bohemia. The garrison of Breslau, now swollen by reinforcements and runaways from the battle, was abandoned to its own devices.

Zieten did not press the Austrians very hard, but still managed to take 400 waggons on 6 December, along with the much-needed rations of bread, and a further 2,000 carts and more than 1,700 troops on the 7th. All the time the Austrians were struggling through the snows and rains towards the border hills and mountains. At last on 13 December the Austrians were able to halt under the heights, and for the next two days they drew their supplies from nearby Schweidnitz. Scarcely 16,000 of their regular troops remained.

The Prussian pursuers had been reinforced to 17,000 men, and they had an aggressive new commander in *GL.* Fouqué, but they were checked by the Austrian rearguard under the capable *GdC.* Buccow, who extended a security cordon along the Peile and the Schweidnitzer-Wasser, gathered up abandoned artillery pieces together with 1,100 sick and wounded, and contrived to send two convoys of cattle and flour into Schweidnitz, to replace the provisions which had been consumed by the army.[101] On 19 December a short march brought the Austrians to the neighbourhood of Landeshut, where the troops crowded into the scanty villages and farmhouses, or sought shelter in the woods. On the 20th the remains of the army began to pass under the gallows hill at Schwarzwasser, which marked the Bohemian border, and marched on to Schurz, 'where the Jesuits have a gloomy castle which overlooks the little hollow at Bernstadt.'[102]

At Leuthen the Austrians had sustained their greatest single reverse in the course of the war. They were shortly to lose nearly as many men in Breslau, and in a way which Prince Charles and Daun could have avoided.

The first news of the defeat at Leuthen had reached Maria Theresa on the morning of 9 December. The impact was all the more shocking because the battle had terminated nearly six months of unbroken Austrian success. 'The Empress wept incessantly and was almost beyond consolation. But she betook herself at once to the chapel, where she offered up prayers amid her tears.'[103] After she had recovered a little she was able to say, 'it's true, the King of Prussia is my enemy, yet I have to admire him for the courage and speed with which he restores his affairs. But my men behaved like grenadiers.'[104]

Maria Theresa entered into an intense round of meetings with her ministers. They had to ask themselves whether the alliance had suffered fatal damage, and whether Austrian could continue the war. Her most immediate concerns were with the fortunes of her forces in Silesia, and in particular the troops who were bottled up in Breslau. She feared that Frederick would lay immediate siege to the place, and she could only hope that Charles and Daun must have known what they were doing when they piled so many troops into the city and left it surrounded by the enemy.[105]

The governor of Breslau *FML.* Salomon Sprecher v. Bernegg, seemed to be doubly qualified for his post, as a Protestant in charge of a largely Protestant city, and a determined commander of grenadiers in the recent victory over the Duke of Bevern. On 7 December he reviewed his resources and liabilities. He had about 18,000 troops in all, including the 3,500-strong light corps of *GFWM.* Beck which Charles had ordered into the city from the right bank of the Oder. The numbers appeared impressive, but they included about 2,300 Croats and many thousands of sick and wounded.

The defences dated from before the time Vauban had refined the art of fortification. The ramparts were of unrevetted earth, devoid even of palisades, and the security of Breslau depended on keeping the water in the ditch free of ice, as was pointed out by Lieutenant Colonel d'Ayme of the French corps of engineers.[106] He was also concerned about the inadequate cover for the magazines and the artillery 'laboratories' (where the charges for the pieces were made up). On 14 December the Prussian fire caused a first explosion which wrecked the Sand-Tor and the nearby Sand-Bastion. On the afternoon of the 16th a Prussian mortar bomb penetrated the magazine of 300 barrels of gunpowder in the Taschen-Bastion opposite the Ohlau Suburb, and a secondary explosion tore a hundred-foot wide breach and filled the ditch with earth and rubble. The Prussians opened a trench opposite the ravaged sector on the following night.

Sprecher had assumed that the mass of troops had been left in Breslau to help the Austrian field army to rally nearby, and that he would shortly be relieved. On the 17th, however, a message got through to him from Prince Charles, and he learned for the first time that the army was retreating to the Bohemian border, and that he, Sprecher, must now conform with the instructions he had been given. No such orders had been passed on to him, and it was evident that there was no hope of Breslau being relieved.

On 18 December Sprecher asked the Prussians what terms were on offer. They replied that nothing short of surrender as prisoners of war would serve, and that the Austrians must conform within twenty-four hours. The unspoken alternative was storm and massacre. Towards evening Sprecher assembled his senior officers. *GFWM.* Philipp Levin Beck, 'a little man with an acute and penetrating gaze,'[107] proposed issuing emergency rations to all the available troops, and breaking through the enemy blockade on the far side of the Oder to escape by way of Poland. Sprecher and his second in command Wolfersdorff supported the project, but when the votes were collated there was a clear mandate to seek fresh terms of surrender. Sprecher explained afterwards that the consensus was reached in view of all the relevant considerations, and especially the fact that the able-bodied men were confined to no more than 6,893 'German' troops and 2,279 Croats, who would not be able to keep the ditch free of ice even if they had no other duties.

On 19 December Sprecher had to deny Beck's request to break out with at least the Croats and the 200 hussars, 'for the rest of the garrison would otherwise be subject to harsh terms.'[108] On the next day the Austrians ratified a capitulation whereby they would surrender with all the due honours, and be taken into captivity as prisoners of war. On the 21st all the officers and men capable of walking now made their way out of the Schweidnitzer-Tor to sounding music, deposited their arms on the meadows on the meadows outside, and returned by way of the Nicolai-Tor to their places of confinement in the city. Frederick and his party stood perilously close to the route, and his secretary admitted that 'both the officers and men of the Austrian regiments make a much better impression than ever before… though they are still defective in many respects.'[109]

The consternation in Vienna was great, and the public condemned Sprecher as a Protestant traitor. The senior officers were duly exchanged for their Prussian counterparts, and it was fortunate for them that Maria Theresa suspended judgement until all the circumstances of the affair could be established. Prince Charles and Daun claimed that Breslau had been perfectly tenable, and that Sprecher had shown a lack of resolution by calling so frequently on the advice of his generals—a most curious charge when we consider its source. Informed military opinion decided otherwise. On 21 June 1758 a first commission reported that there was no need for formal proceedings, and on 5 September the *Hofkriegsrath* announced that Sprecher and his associates were free of the threat of court martial. They were reassigned to the army with full enjoyment of their ranks, and it was desirable that, 'in order to silence any reproaches concerning what happened, a perpetual and universal silence on the subject should be… imposed.'[110]

The loss of Breslau was more damaging to the honour of Charles and Daun than the defeat at Leuthen, for they had abandoned Sprecher morally as well as operationally, and they had brought their integrity into question as well as their judgement. If a criticism of Sprecher was to be made, it came not from this tainted authority but indirectly from the example of Colonel Ferdinand Friedrich Bülow, who commanded the 2,700 troops in **Liegnitz**, which was another of the forsaken Austrian garrisons in Silesia. Bülow was a Curlander by birth, and 'a man of a quite different stamp from most of our generals, being likeable, engaging, fair-minded and generous. He had the gift of making himself obeyed and loved at the same time, for we went to great lengths to avoid displeasing him.'[111]

Bülow had little in the material way on which to base his defence, for the fortifications of Liegnitz consisted only of a medieval wall and improvised outworks, and the Katzbach and its inundations had frozen over. Everything had to depend on a show of defiance. He rejected a Prussian summons on 23 December, and then set about burning the suburbs to clear a field of fire and distributing his troops among the works. Lieutenant Gorani was typically entertained to lunch, then told to defend a redoubt outside the Breslauer-Tor, 'under the most positive orders to have myself and my men cut to pieces rather than surrender.'[112]

FM. Prince Moritz of Anhalt-Dessau had arrived on the scene with a siege corps of 10,000 troops, but an artillery duel told him that the Austrians were still bent on holding out, and the picks of the Prussian workers could make no impression on the hard-frozen ground. The Prussians now delivered a summons which was phrased much more politely than their first.

On 28 December Bülow signed a capitulation whereby his garrison was allowed to march free. In his own words 'I had always insisted on nothing short of a free evacuation with all the honours of war, and formed the resolution to hold out to the last man. The enemy noted that I was not to be moved on those points, and thus I finally obtained those terms which… in the circumstances of that time, were most consonant with the interests of the Imperial service.'[113]

Ferdinand Friedrich Baron Bülow.

His resolute defence of Liegnitz in the winter of 1757/8 stood in contrast with the blunders which let thousands of troops fall into captivity at Breslau.

(Military Academy, Wiener Neustadt)

III
1758

Daun and the Rebuilding of the Army

1757, the year of battles, had seen the collision of armies which had been schooled intensively in the preceding peace, or rather the period of armed truce. The reinvigorated Austrian monarchy had been brought to the edge of dissolution when the Prussians invaded Bohemia in the spring of 1757. The Austrian victory at Kolin not only came as a heaven-sent reprieve, but provided the foundation on which the Austrians were able to regain Bohemia, and claw their way into the heart of Silesia. On 5 December 1757, long after the close of any conventional campaigning, the devastating defeat at Leuthen threw into the balance everything that had so far been won.

The Austrian *GFWM*. Philipp Wöllwarth was old in war, but in his opinion 'this campaign was one of the hardest ever fought. Not only were many men lost in the course of the five battles and the siege of Schweidnitz, but many others fell ill, died of disease or deserted over the cold winter following.'[1] The work of destruction continued for months. The last of the Austrian troops to leave Silesia were the former defenders of Liegnitz, who made for Bohemia at the turn of the year. The soldiers were too paralysed with the cold to be able to look after themselves, and whenever the column reached an overnight stop the officers inspected their troops and rubbed the frozen hands, ears and noses of their men to restore the circulation. Arriving at their quarters in Bohemia, the troops found the huts already full of sick. The malady was a 'spotted Hungarian fever' which spread through the armies in their cramped billets throughout Central Europe. It devastated the Württembergers, who were now released to go home, and just 2,000 of them survived to reach Stuttgart in April 1758.

When everything was taken into account, the Austrian army had suffered a diminution of about 40,000 men[2], or about half the effectives in the theatre of war. The money spent to make good the losses in men and materiel amounted to 9,584, 117 florins, or almost exactly one-third of the entire income of the state for 1758.[3]

The army had been damaged at every level. A number of units had been effectively destroyed by their losses at Leuthen, headed by the infantry regiments of Baden-Durlach ([27] 91 per cent), Neipperg ([7] 80 per cent), Carl Lothringen ([3] 75 per cent) and Wallis ([11] 73 per cent).

Individuals of no particular merit were now commissioned en masse to fill the gaps among the officers. By late 1761, when Kaunitz embarked on his notorious reduction of the army, these unworthy people had acquired enough seniority to be sheltered from the cuts, and Lacy complained that 'the pity is that this misfortune has befallen just those officers who have been raised or promoted to their various ranks through selection, and by having shown proof of their courage, ability and merits.'[4] Even then a number of the regiments were still trying to sort out their accounts, which had been thrown into chaos by the loss of their paperwork at Leuthen.

The snowy border hills saved the Austrians from what would otherwise have been the consequence of a rout as big as Leuthen, namely an invasion of their homeland. Before she could think of restoring her army, and before even she could be entirely certain that she could continue the war, Maria Theresa had a brief period of grace in which she could address the issues of command.

Some of the appointments were settled readily enough. The Prince of Zweibrücken, (a lieutenant general in the French service) was chosen to replace Hildburghausen with the *Reichsarmee*. The respected veteran *FZM*.

Marschall was put forward by Maria Theresa in person to command the fortress of Olmütz, which was the northern gateway to Vienna, and the newly-promoted *GFWM*. Lacy took up the post of *Generalquartiermeister*, or chief of staff, 'an office which he put on a completely new and improved footing.'[5]

After the battle of Leuthen the Emperor Francis Stephen went to great lengths to guard the good name of his brother Prince Charles of Lorraine, but it was not long before the eyes of Maria Theresa were opened. Her first reservations were confirmed by critical messages from her French and Russian allies, and by the report of *FZM*. Ferdinand Philipp Harsch, who was sent to discover the truth from trustworthy officers in the army.

Prince Charles returned to Vienna on 7 January 1758, and for a time kept himself in a decent seclusion, 'but as that gentleman is fortunate enough not to allow setbacks to get the better of him, he soon forgot what had happened, and showed himself as cheerful and relaxed as it if he had come back from the campaign as a victor crowned with laurels.'[6] It never occurred to him that he ought to step aside, and Francis Stephen was finally compelled to write a *Reflequesion particulier pour vous seul et à bruler ensuit*, pointing out that it was in his own best interests to lay aside the command. There was no response.

On 16 January Maria Theresa had to write to Charles in words that were drafted by Kaunitz. She explained that great damage was being done by the criticisms that were being levelled at him at home and abroad. 'Nothing could be more unfair, certainly, but since we cannot direct the opinions of mankind as we would wish, we have to resort to the only measure which can change them. This is to go to the root of the problem, and, however painful it is to me, I must deny myself the pleasure of seeing you any longer in command of my armies.'[7] Charles now wrote a dignified letter of resignation, which Maria Theresa hoped would be accompanied by an equally seemly silence, but he continued to behave as if nothing had happened. 'Time and time again representations had been made to her concerning his weak character, and now she was driven to recognise that the accusations were only too true.'[8]

GdC. Franz Count Nádasdy-Fogaras, the *papa moustache* of the Netherlanders, the darling son of the Hungarian nation, was linked too conveniently with the defeat at Leuthen to be spared the role of scapegoat. Daun was no friend of his, and now the interests of the house of Habsburg-Lorraine demanded that Prince Charles should not go to the sacrificial altar alone. 'The deserving Nádasdy had the same standing among the Austrian troops as did Zieten among the Prussians. He was now driven from the army by vexation, cabals and intrigue.'[9]

For the sake of decorum both Charles and Nádasdy were decorated with the *Grosskreuz* at the first investiture of the Military Order of Maria Theresa. They then went their ways. Charles remained for a time in Vienna, then left to begin a long and successful career as governor of the Austrian Netherlands. Nádasdy returned to his native land, and did as valuable service as ever, this time by promoting the enlistment of Hungarians and Croats for the war.

There was no obvious successor to the supreme command. The gifted Lacy had only just been advanced to *GFWM*. and chief of staff, and was not yet in contention. Hadik's name was associated too directly with the leadership of light forces, as were those of the considerably more junior Loudon, Jahnus, Beck and Brentano. In her dilemma Maria Theresa asked Brigadier General Montazet to extend her invitation to Marshal d'Estrées, who had beaten the Hanoverians at Hastenbeck. Kaunitz was appalled, and on 4 January he hastened to instruct Count Starhemberg, his ambassador in Paris, to tell the French that Maria Theresa had in mind only a gesture of friendship to King Louis, and that they should not think that the Austrians were incapable of commanding their own armies. On the 14th Kaunitz was able to write to Starhemberg that the choice had fallen on *FM*. Leopold Daun (1705-66).

Leopold's inheritance was a mixed blessing. His father *FM*. Philipp Wirich Daun was a hero of olden times, having defended Turin most gloriously in 1706, and conquered Naples for the Emperor. He also left the family fortunes in disorder. Leopold had to make his way through his own efforts, and in the course of the War of

Leopold Joseph Maria Count Daun

the Austrian Succession he earned the respect of his soldiers by his personal courage and his concern for their welfare, and the trust of his superiors through his intelligence and attention to detail. He was the right-hand man of the veteran *FM*. Traun in the successful campaign against Frederick in Bohemia in 1744, and another old war-horse, *FM*. Khevenhüller, singled him out as the man to re-make the Austrian army.

Daun never promoted his interests better than when he married the widowed Josepha Countess Nostitz on 4 March 1745. The match occasioned some surprise, because Josepha had been in deep mourning for her late husband, and because both partners 'when no longer of the age when love is spiced with mystery.'[10] However Daun's finances were now repaired, and, more significantly, he had a direct *entrée* to the Imperial circle, for Josepha was the daughter of Maria Theresa's much-loved nanny Charlotte Countess Fuchs ('*die Fuchsin*,' vixen). With this backing, and through the commendation of his military superiors, Daun was entrusted with the task of reforming the army after the last war. He established the first Austrian codes of military service, with everything which that implied in the form of drills and discipline, he founded Europe's premier officer academy at Wiener Neustadt, and he began to bring the troops together for annual autumn manoeuvres—all of which made the army into something which was capable of measuring swords with the Prussians. In 1753 he was invested with the Order of the Golden Fleece, the highest honour in the gift of the Habsburgs, and he was promoted field marshal in the following year.

On 21 January 1758 Leopold Daun took the place of Prince Charles as commander for the coming campaign. The reasons for his elevation were not immediately apparent, for Kaunitz was not ranked among his partisans, and the field marshal had lost much of the popular esteem he enjoyed immediately after his victory at Kolin. However Maria Theresa never forgot what she owed him for what he did on that day, and his new appointment not only gave him the full direction of the forces in the field, but the authority he needed to continue the work of repair and reform. He was a 'safe pair of hands,' in the English phrase.

The labour had begun in Daun's absence at a conference on 14 December 1757. The *Hofkriegsrath* reorganised the regimental structures on the 22nd, and a further conference on 4 January addressed important practical details concerning recruitment, remounts and the procurement of uniforms. Maria Theresa made certain that the impetus did not flag, and among the most productive outcomes were the establishment of a 'garrison' battalion for each regiment of infantry and a 'depot' squadron for each regiment of cavalry. These new units received, trained and forwarded recruits, and accommodated troops who had recovered from wounds or sickness but would otherwise have been 'lost in the system.' A new form of short-term military service, by 'capitulation,' now brought in a higher standard of recruits, many of whom were advanced in turn to NCOs.

The reviving spirits affected not only the troops with the army. Six thousand prisoners were exchanged by way of cartel, and Captain Boisgelin, a French volunteer, noted that in addition 'men are escaping back by every possible means. At Königgrätz I saw three hundred of them from the regiment of Wied [28] alone, and they will re-constitute it for the field. Many of the prisoners enlisted in the King of Prussia's free battalions for the chance of getting back here, and they are arriving with every regiment daily.'[11]

Despite themselves, Boisgelin and the other French observers were impressed by what they were seeing. The thirty companies of grenadiers assembled at Skalitz were 'very fine indeed.'[12] The cavalry was being brought rapidly up to strength, and by early May the horses were reported to be 'in good condition, and, according to all the cavalry officers, the remounts are the best the Empress had received for a long time. The recruits are excellent, and large numbers of the "old moustaches" are also evident.'[13]

Daun returned to the army in Bohemia on 12 March, and put the generals and the troops alike through their paces in the camps which were formed at Skalitz, Leitomischl and Gewitz before the start of active operations. The French were forced to admire 'the discipline and good order which, frankly, are more easily to inculcate among these people than among ours. Everything was on a good footing last year, but we have to admit that it is even better now, and that applies to everyone from the officers to the rank and file.'[14]

In February *GFWM*. Lacy had taken on the responsibility of creating a General Staff, the first of its kind in the Austrian service, and one of the first in Europe. He selected and trained officers for the work of drawing up maps, prospecting routes and guiding columns. 'I had still to recover from my wound [sustained at Lobositz]. Moreover the theoretical base was itself new, and I had to get the system to work quickly and accurately, which raised a host of difficulties. In spite of all that, everything was ready by April 1758.'[15] At the same time Lacy set up units of Staff Infantry, Dragoons and Pioneers who not only supported the officers, but relieved the ordinary infantry of tasks like guarding transport and clearing obstructions. The effects were apparent as soon as the campaign began, for 'the army can carry out a march of three *Meilen* [about 14 miles] more speedily and easily than a march of one last year.'[16]

After its poorish showing at Leuthen, the Austrian artillery was provided with the means of giving a much better account of itself. The companies of trained gunners (*Büchsenmeister*) were augmented by six to the number of thirty, while the gradual formation of the specialised *Artillerie-Füsiliere* in 1758-9 reduced another of the drains on the infantry, and provided skilled help when it came to the donkey work of serving the guns. In the course of 1758 the train of field

THE ENEMIES OF PRUSSIA—AXES OF OPERATIONS

artillery was brought up to 418 cannon, not including the howitzers, which set a standard for the rest of Europe.

The Wider War

For a long time it was not clear to what use the renewed Austrian army might be put. Indeed at the turn of the year, when the process of restoration had scarcely begun, the Franco-Austrian alliance had been staggering under the dual blows of Rossbach and Leuthen. On 29 December Maria Theresa had prepared a letter to King Louis which raised the possibility, however remote, of having to bring the war to an end by a disadvantageous peace. The letter was never sent. Kaunitz touched on this moment of despair in the course of a conversation with Nils Bark, the Swedish ambassador, on 16 January. He explained that confidence was reviving, for the army would be reconstituted, and a long view indicated that the means at Frederick's disposal did not stand comparison with those of the allies. The king 'had not gained so much as a foot of ground in the dominions of the Empress Queen, whereas she was in possession of Schweidnitz, and thus of the entry to Silesia, which was the most important of his possessions. Count Kaunitz added that the king had lost a number of his other states, and that his resources had diminished accordingly. In the light of all these considerations he asked me to represent to my court that… there was every reason to believe that courage and unity would carry the alliance to its objectives.'[17]

As they concerned Austria, Kaunitz set out these objectives for the benefit of Maria Theresa in a lengthy *tour d'horizon* on 28 April. The least desirable outcome of the war would see the Austrian army destroyed, the enemy invading the Hereditary Lands, and more territory lost to the King of Prussia. Towards the other end of the scale was a full transfer of Prussian territory and the exaction of indemnities as defined by the allies in their treaties. Best of all would be to gain all these advantages, without Austria having to yield the Netherlands to the Bourbons. Kaunitz finally looked beyond the end of the war and urged that Austria must hold to France. It was true that France was being held back by internal weaknesses, but the goodwill of the French promoted peace for the Austrians in the Netherlands, Italy, the *Reich* and along the borders with Turkey.[18]

No plan of campaign existed as such, for on 29 January a conference had established the principle to 'hold to a sound and sagacious defensive, until the operations of the allied armies make another strategy preferable.'[19]

What help might be forthcoming from the various allies? In 1757 the Swedes had agreed to advance with 20,000 troops from their trans-Baltic bridgehead in western Pomerania. Their attack was a feeble affair, and as soon as he was free of the Russians (below) the Prussian field Marshal Lehwaldt built up a force of 29,000 troops and went over to the counter-offensive at the end of October. He recovered the strongpoints of Demmin and Anclam, crossed the border river of the Peene, and penned up the Swedes around the fortress-port of Stralsund. Kaunitz was not discouraged, for he believed that the Swedes would have a useful diversionary role to play in 1758, helped by a new French subsidy.

Austria's connection with France was admittedly under some stress, for the French were four million florins in arrears with their promised subsidies, and in February and March their confidence was dealt a new blow when the reanimated Army of Observation (the forces of Hanover and a number of other north German Protestant states) bundled the French troops out of their winter quarters and back across the Rhine. British gold supported the Army of Observation, and with the British apparently gaining the upper hand in North America the London government was unlikely to agree to a treaty of neutrality between Hanover and France, 'and not least because Pitt had his hand on the tiller. What we have seen of him so far indicates that he is not the kind of man who lives from hand to mouth, but goes to work in a systematic way, and knows how to direct their policies towards a single goal.'[20]

Kaunitz nevertheless hoped that the French would still assemble powerful new forces in Germany in the course of the summer, and that they would at least prevent the Hanoverians from sending help to Frederick. It was more realistic to expect something useful from the east. In 1757 Kaunitz's expectations of the Russians had been low. Their promised invasion of East Prussia was slow to get under way, and when Field Marshal Apraksin beat Lehwaldt at Gross-Jägersdorf on 30 August his victory was attributed to luck. For no compelling reason the Russians then retreated all the way to Memel in the far northern corner of East Prussia.

Early in 1758 the new Russian commander Fermor undertook an offensive (as unexpected in its way as that of Ferdinand of Brunswick in Germany) which overran East Prussia without resistance. Kaunitz came to see that a Russian threat to the Oder might now weigh heavily in Frederick's calculations. 'No belligerent power is more happily placed than that of the Russians. Now that they hold all East Prussia and the course of the Vistula it is far easier for them to continue the war, and to push their operations into the heart of the enemy lands.'[21]

The Loss of Schweidnitz, 1-18 April 1758

With the approach of spring the 'sound and sagacious' defensive left the initiative entirely to the Prussians. Despite the importance which Kaunitz attached to Schweidnitz, no serious thought was given to saving that place, which was Austria's only outpost in the Silesian plain. The governor was the brave and vigilant *FML.* Franz Ludwig Count Thürheim, who had a sizeable but sickly garrison which had been left behind during the general Austrian retreat from Silesia in December. The siege that follows sits chronologically in 1758, but is best regarded as one of the penalties for the defeat at Leuthen.

Two thousand of the defenders had already fallen ill by the time the Prussians opened the siege proper on the night of 1/2 April, when they dug a parallel only five hundred paces from the Galgen-Fort, to the north-east of the town. The Austrian infantry was in no state to put up a vigorous defence of the perimeter of detached works, and Thürheim based his defence almost entirely on his artillery, which he placed to take the siege approaches in enfilade. He had one such concentration in the Wasser-Fort to the east, and a battery of four pieces in open ground to the north of the Jauernicker-Fleche. According to the Prussian gunner Tempelhof 'our work accordingly went very slowly and cost us a lot of men. I was at the siegeworks myself, and often bore witness to the panic that ensued when a shot from the Wasser-Fort fell among the labourers. Nothing is better calculated to deprive soldiers of the will to work or fight than coming under flanking and enfilading fire... it just takes one shot in every hundred to hit, and it will make an impression a hundred times greater than a shot arriving from the front.'[22]

On 13 April the Prussians opened up with all their batteries, and Thürheim withdrew his artillery to the town ramparts and resumed his duel from there. He had abandoned the Galgen-Fleche on the evening of 10 April, and at three in the morning of the 16th three Prussian battalions escaladed the Galgen-Fort, with scarcely a show of resistance from the 153 defenders. The Prussians had now gained a long sector of the outworks, and Thürheim at once ordered the beating of *chamade*.

The Prussian lieutenant general Tresckow insisted on the same harsh terms as Nádasdy had exacted from the Prussian garrison in 1757, and on 18 April the Austrians marched out of the Striegauer-Tor and laid down their arms. The Prussians took into captivity 4,912 officers and men, including the many sick.

Some Austrian officers were inclined to judge Thürheim harshly, for having run through his gunpowder too quickly, but Vienna took no proceedings against him. He had been weak in able-bodied infantry, and had contrived to hold out beyond 15 April, which was the date by when Daun had promised that the whole Austrian army would arrive to relieve him.

Frederick's Invasion of Moravia, April-July 1758

Daun had set off from Vienna early on 9 March, 'after he had, after his praiseworthy Christian habit, gone to Mass.'[23] He arrived at Königgrätz in north-east Bohemia three days later. His army had a paper strength of 63,000, but the number of men fit for action was scarcely one-third of that number, and his task was to continue the work of restoration until Austria's allies made their presence felt on the enemy flanks.

The directions from Vienna conveyed no particular sense of urgency, since Frederick would now have to take the Russians into account, and it was thought unlikely that he would stray too far from the threatened line of the Oder.[24] The king had the danger from the Russians only too well in mind, but he drew entirely different conclusions from those mapped out for him in Vienna. He estimated the time available to him before the Russians reached the theatre of war, and found that nothing would suit him better than to force the Austrian army into a battle. A new invasion of Bohemia was unlikely to serve, because Daun had plenty of space at his disposal, and would merely recoil out of reach. A strike from a base further east into Moravia held out much more promise, for it would put Vienna under threat, and compel the enemy to fight somewhere in the great plain of the river March. The hills which separated Silesia from Moravia were the lowest along the whole border region, and he wrote to his brother Prince Henry 'if I march directly on Olmütz, the enemy will come up to defend it, and then we will have a battle on ground which will not be of their choosing.'[25]

Almost unregarded in the Austrian calculations, the defence of Moravia had been left to the 8,800 or so troops of *FML.* Charles Marquis de Ville de Camon, who was an impudent and witty Lorrainer, and high in the favour of Francis Stephen. De Ville had his informants in Silesia, 'and they were not of the stupid populace, but men of landed substance, and some of them soldiers.' At the beginning of march he learned from them that Frederick would besiege Schweidnitz as soon as the weather permitted, and then proceed to invade Moravia and attack Olmütz. 'I reported all of this to the *Hofkriegsrath*, but was told in reply that they knew the intentions of the King of Prussia better than I did, and that I must be content with that.'[26]

On 24 April de Ville discovered that the Prussians were assembling at Neisse, and that an invasion of Austrian Silesia and Moravia was imminent. Daun was on the alert, but he suspected that Fritz intended to draw the Austrians away from the invasion route from Glatz into north-east Bohemia. Still uncertain as to the enemy designs, Daun brought his troops together in the camp of Skalitz on the 29th, which happened to be the same day that Frederick crossed into Austrian Silesia with 55,000 men. That little province was located indefensibly on the 'Prussian' side of the hills, and de Ville fell back over the snowy highlands to the heart of Moravia.

After a tiring climb from the Mohra river the Prussians reached a broad tract of undulating tableland, and on 2 May they emerged on the brow which overlooked the wide corridor of flat ground which lay to the south—the watery levels of Olmütz and the Hanna, and the contiguous and fertile Marchfeld which extended towards the Danube below Vienna. Two days later the Prussian advance guard forced de Ville away from Olmütz, and there remained nothing between them and Vienna except de Ville's rattled troopers, the decayed town ramparts and the citadel of Brünn, and the Danube.

Meanwhile northern and central Moravia stood open to the Prussians, who engaged in misdeeds which were shocking to the sensibilities of the time. They did at least four civilians to death. They deposited turds in the churches and took cattle from their rightful owners. They plundered the monastery of Sternberg of its stocks of beer and wine, they burned the villages of Bobiowitz and Topplan to the ground, they sacked the town of Tobitschau and meted out the same treatment to the hamlet of Bärn, where the Kyau Cuirassiers [C12] threatened to nail the ears of the people to their tables.[27]

It was sixteen years since the Prussians had come so close to the capital, where richer plunder by far was at hand, and Lacy predicted 'that there will be some upset to the round of pleasures in Vienna and the groups of friends who like to take the air in the Prater.[28] Francis Stephen was more annoyed than concerned, for he was being called away from his beloved theatre, and on 6 May the Empress still believed that Vienna stood in no immediate danger. The departure of 9,000 Saxons for the French army had been delayed, five or six thousand recruits were on their way, as were three battalions of Tuscan infantry, all of which, together with the standing garrison, would shortly concentrate 20,000 men for the defence of the capital. Maria Theresa resisted all pressure to take off with the court to the safety of Innsbruck in the Tyrol or Graz in Styria, declaring that she would not move until the Prussians were before the ramparts.

Maria Theresa's resolution was soon put to a new test. On 13 May Prussian columns in the strength of three battalions and thirty-three squadrons descended on de Ville at Prödlitz. When he had thrown the troops into Olmütz (above) he had reduced his force to 4,500 men, all cavalry, but he was able to extricate himself in time and fall back on Brünn. Honours would have been considered even if some of de Ville's troopers had not been accused of plundering their own baggage and scampering off in the direction of Vienna.

The Prussians had been carrying out nothing more than a foraging expedition writ large, but fugitives from the fight spread reports that de Ville had been routed and that the way to Vienna was open. The capital was gripped by a panic greater still than in the first alarm, and an outraged Maria Theresa demanded that de Ville and his senior officers must render account. He was unabashed, and expressed the hope that Their Imperial Majesties would not be led astray by clouds of dust and the carping people who knew nothing of the military trade.[29]

Frederick estimated that his irruption into Moravia had gained him the advantage of nine days over Daun. The main Austrian army, still in the process of being re-made, was assembling more than sixty miles to the west at Skalitz in Bohemia, and was separated from the plain of the March by a wide zone of craggy and heavily-forested hills—the worn-down remnants of an ancient mountain range. Still not entirely certain that he was not being lured towards Moravia by design, Daun prosecuted a first march on 3 May from Skalitz to Leitomischl, just short of the Moravian border. He knew that the Prussians had got to Moravia before him, but at least he had secured the important magazine at Leitomischl, and he formed an excellent camp where he could continue to gather and train the recruits.

The combatant strength of the army had still reached only about 23,000 men, and the work of feeling out the enemy had to be left to detachments. Out in front, the *GFWM*s. Loudon and Jahnus led 5,000 troops through the hills to explore and torment the Prussian communications. Back in Bohemia, another 8,000 men under *FZM*. Harsch stood guard at Nachod and Trautenau, lest the Prussians should after all strike in force from the County of Glatz into north-east Bohemia. In all of this Daun leaned heavily on the advice of his new *General-Quartiermeister GFWM*. Lacy, who dissuaded him from plunging into Moravia with an army which was still coming together. Lacy advised that the Austrians should wait until they could strike at Frederick's communications with Silesia, or take advantage of the fact that the Prussian forces investing Olmütz would be split by the river March.[30]

So far the Austrians had taken it for granted that the fortress-town of Olmütz—strongly-built, amply provisioned and well garrisoned— would be able to withstand any conceivable attack. Daun first began to harbour doubts on this point on the evening of 9 May, when news came to him that reinforcements and a full siege train of sixty cannon and twenty mortars was on its way from Neisse. On the 15th Maria Theresa wrote to him that circumstances now demanded 'that a battle must be risked in the near future, whether or not Olmütz comes under siege; otherwise my army will have to be withdrawn to the Danube.'[31] Lacy's preferred strategy of waiting and pouncing was now under threat.

At least it was by now clear that Frederick was committed to a full-scale campaign in Moravia, and Daun felt justified in calling up *FZM*. Harsch with the greater part of the corps which had been covering the avenues into north-east Bohemia. On the 19th Daun rode out to Loudon's position on the fine wooded hills above Konitz, and surveyed the Prussian deployments in the plain around Olmütz. Directly to the east the spires and ramparts of the town rose above the shining sheet of the inundation. On the low hill on the near side a Prussian corps (*FM*. Keith) was maintaining a close blockade. Away to Daun's left another corps (Prince Moritz of Anhalt-Dessau) was sited by the low mound of Littau on the highway from Bohemia; to the right, or south, Frederick's main army was positioned on the edge of the plain near Prossnitz, guarding the highway to Brünn and Vienna. The enemy were thinly spread, though still superior in numbers.

After a stay of nearly three weeks Daun's army left the camp of Leitomischl on 23 May, and made an easy march across open country to Zwittau. After an overnight halt the Austrians moved to a camp north-west of Gewitsch, in a broad fertile plain in the shelter of the wooded hills. The second march had been taxing, in the great heat, but the French observers allowed that the staff work could not have been bettered. 'Bridges had been thrown across all the little streams so that the infantry could cross on full divisional [i.e. two-platoon] frontages without breaking off files... The tents are carried on pack horses and are set up before they arrive. The columns are guided across country by the officers of the General Staff... these officers are immediately at hand whenever the general wants to know something or issue orders.' The Pioneers cleared obstructions from the chosen routes, while another of the new formations, the Staff Infantry Regiment, guarded the baggage and kept it in order.'[32] All of this was Lacy's work, and a telling comparison is to be made with the events of June 1866, when the Austrian North Army, marching across the same hills but in the opposite direction, arrived on the upper Elbe in a state of disorganisation and exhaustion.

Now in May 1758 recruits and re-convalescents were arriving with Daun all the time, which brought his combatant strength to about 40,000 troops, and the training continued without let. 'One day the field marshal wished to test his army, and had the troops rush to arms upon an imaginary alarm. It might have seemed like play-acting, but it was important to know how the army would respond. In less than half an hour the cavalry were saddled up, the infantry under arms, and the whole army ready to do whatever might have been demanded of it. The field marshal was looking on from the top of a hill, and appeared delighted.'[33]

Frederick summed up the state of affairs very well. 'The enemy will choose one or two courses—either want to hem us in and cramp our supplies, or march to the relief of the town. If we come together too soon we will be giving up too much ground, so that their light forces will be able to deprive us totally of our fodder and provisions[34]... they have their big scum, who screen their manoeuvres, and their little scum—swarms and swarms of them by little packages—who prevent our patrols from penetrating the woods and nests of criminals where those brigands hide out.'[35]

On the night of 7/8 June the 'big scum' *GFWM.* Loudon surprised the Möhring Hussars [H3] in their post at **Klein-Senitz**, and his 300 hussars and 300 Croats put the whole regiment to flight.[36]

As a representative of the 'little scum,' Lieutenant Colonel Carl Ludwig Lanjus led a party of 1,100 Croats and hussars across the northern plateau and on 8 June attacked the Prussian free battalions of Le Noble and Salenmon, which were escorting a convoy of empty waggons back to Neisse. The 1,000 Prussians made a stand on a height east of **Deutsch-Lodnitz**, but were then chased in a state of increasing disorder from one hill to another and through the village of Siebenhöfen, losing in the process three of their cannon and about 500 men. This highly successful action helped to inspire the altogether bigger ambush which was staged towards the end of the month (below), and encouraged Vienna, in its highly volatile mood, to believe that Frederick had shot his bolt.

All of that was well and good, but Daun knew that he must sooner or later lead his army to the relief of Olmütz, and that he must first put his troops to the enormous tactical risk of debouching from the wooded hills into the plain of the upper March in the immediate presence of the enemy. The reconnaissances were complete, the routes had been mapped out by Lacy, the security was absolute, and now everything hung on the speed and precision of the forced march from Gewitsch.

To prevent a second Leuthen, or worse, *GdC.* Buccow had been given overall command of the troops on 'Loudon's' sector to the north around Konitz, and was reinforced by two regiments of infantry and two of cavalry to enable him to take the Prussians in the rear, if

THE MARCH TO RELIEVE OLMÜTZ, JUNE - JULY 1758

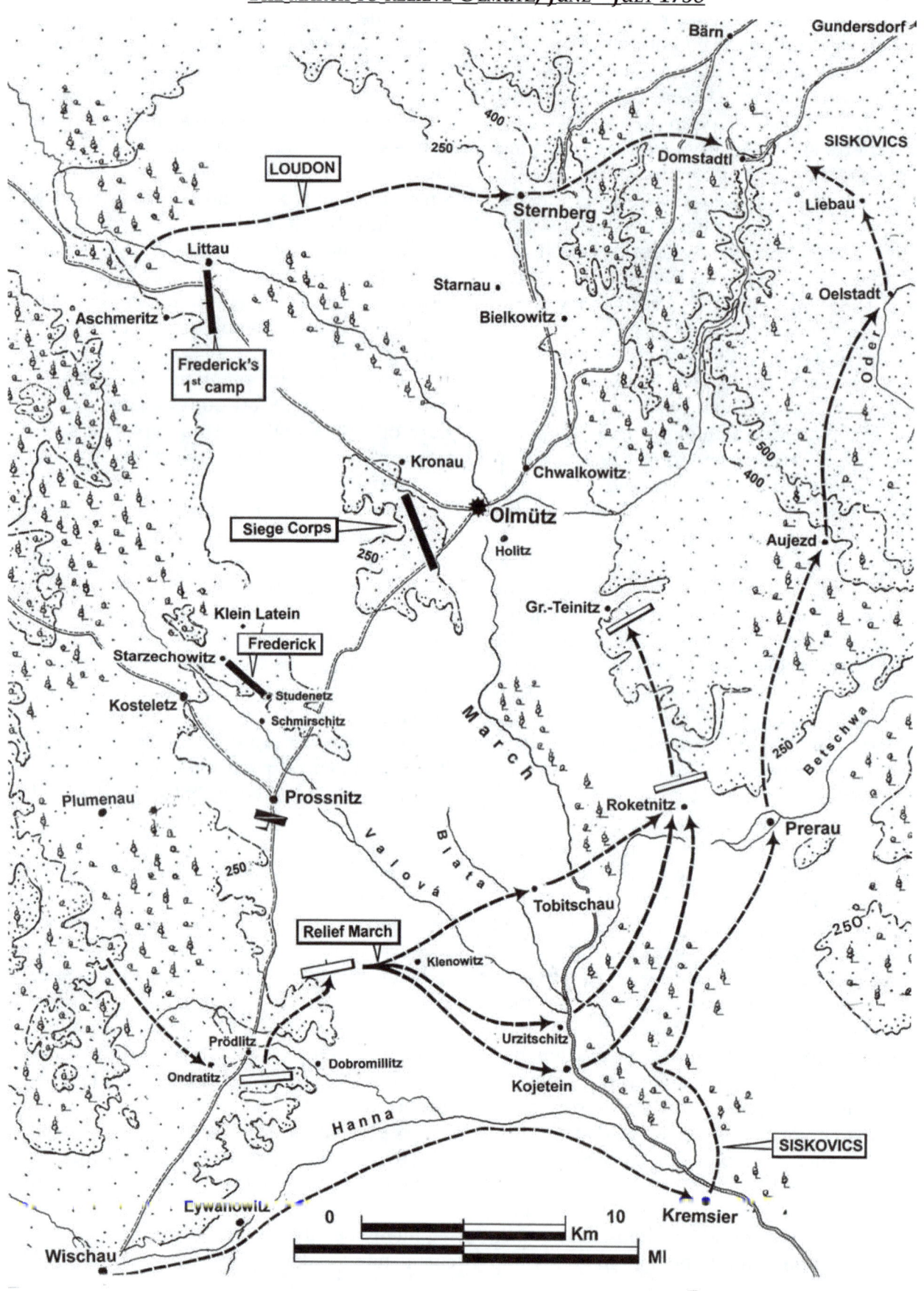

the king tried to strike at Daun while he was emerging from the woods.

Late in the rainy evening of 15 June the army received orders to make ready to march the next day. The four columns took off at first light on the 16th, climbed the muddy tracks which led through the woods beyond Usborno, and struggled across the broad tableland beyond. The troops made slow progress in these adverse conditions, and Daun had to order them to bivouac for the night on the high open ridge of Protiwanow.

Early on the 16th the columns made for the black forests which stretched across the eastern horizon, and within a few hours the regiments were hastening through a wild country of steep ridges and deep valleys, all set in a dense growth of oak, beech and larch. The two northerly columns were in particular danger, for they were separated from the others by impassable ravines, and they passed close to the Prussian outposts, and notably the garrison in the hill town of Plumenau, where the slab-like castle of the Liechtensteins and the windows of the houses were in clear view.

Lacy led the combined grenadiers to the exits from the woods at dawn, and he was joined later in the day by Daun in person. Over to the right, de Ville's cavalry was posted along the line of the little river Hanna, as had been arranged. Prussian hussars were foraging across the plain, but showed no signs of alarm, and the royal army remained all unsuspecting in its positions north of Prossnitz. Daun now marched into the open ground at the head of the carabiniers and mounted grenadiers, and occupied the site of his intended camp in force (a lesson probably learned from the debacle at Neumarkt on 4 November the previous year). When everything had been secured, the four columns of the main army, which had halted at the edge of the woods, were ordered to take up their positions.

The new camp straddled the highway to Olmütz, and faced north along one of those wave-like Moravian ridges which would be familiar to anyone who has seen the heights of Pratzen at Austerlitz. The left wing rested on the woods at Ondratitz, and the right reached into the plain as far as Dobramillitz, where a redoubt was built to cover the open flank.

The next day was crowned by a brilliant action on the far side of the March beyond Olmütz. The Prussian blockading forces east of the river were spread thinly, and Daun learned that the posts at Gross-Wisternitz and Holitz invited attack. He sanctioned a large mounted raid from de Ville's command, and early on the 17th Colonel Count Stainville and a fast-moving force (the Löwenstein Chevaulegers [D31], the Dessewffy Hussars [H34] and a pulk of Saxon-Polish uhlans) surprised eight squadrons of the Bayreuth Dragoons [D5] at **Gross-Wisternitz**, and cut down or captured the greater part of them. This was the cue for several hundred Croats and dragoons to sally from Olmütz and burn the abandoned tents and baggage. At the same time *GFWM*. Saint-Ignon advanced from Prerau with another striking forces (the Württemberg Dragoons [D38], the Saxon Prinz Karl Chevaulegers and a number of Croats) and attacked **Holitz**, evicting the free battalion of Rapin and the remaining two squadrons of the Bayreuth Dragoons.

The successes at Gross-Wisternitz and Holitz were more than usually gratifying, for the super-large regiment of Bayreuth was the foremost mounted unit of the Prussian army, next to the Rochow (Seydlitz) Cuirassiers, and had been responsible for destroying the Austrian infantry at the battle of Hohenfriedeberg in 1745. Now it had been surprised in broad daylight and lost ten officers and 458 men. The newly-constituted Löwenstein Chevaulegers had received their blooding, and carried off the silver drums of the Bayreuth regiment as their trophies. They would have taken the ten standards as well, if 'by a very strange chance'[37] they had not been left with the regimental commander at a nearby village.

Meanwhile the outposts of the rival armies were in immediate contact west if the river March, and the two commanders carried out reconnaissances every day. Both forces were sited equally strongly, with their western wings reaching out to the forested hills, and the eastern extending towards the fertile levels of the March. Everything seemed set for a battle on the scale of Prague, Kolin or Leuthen, but on this occasion somewhere in the corridor of ground between the woods and the river. Montazet believed that Daun's troops would be equal to what might be demanded of them. 'I must distance myself from what is believed all too readily in Europe, that the Empress's army was destroyed in the last battle [Leuthen]. It is not true, and I have been astonished to see its present state, well clad, well recruited, well equipped, and the cavalry in a splendid state.'[38]

Montazet had been observing Daun in his quarters at Eywanowitz, but he was unable to detect what the man had in mind: 'our leader is a prudent and wise general who communicates his projects to no one. I have found that he has very good cause.'[39] On the 26th Daun had been penning a letter to Maria Theresa when a message got through to him from *FZM*. Marschall in Olmütz, suggesting that a manoeuvre on the eastern side of the March would be of the most use to him. Daun resolved on the instant to risk losing his communications, and commit himself to the relief of Olmütz with the main force of his army on the far side of the river.

Without having to give prior notice, Daun sounded the alarm on the afternoon of 27 June, and shuffled the army in eight columns northeast to the 'camp of Dobramillitz,' which extended from the highway to Klenowitz and the Capellen-Berg. 'I am enchanted at the order with which the army marched,' commented Montazet, 'at no less by its strength, for I saw at least 50,000 combatants under arms.'[40] The move had been calculated to bring the army closer to the intended crossings of the March, while seeming to augment the direct challenge to Frederick on the near side of the river. To reinforce that impression Daun put on a great show of activity, knowing that every move would be seen by the king or reported to him.

At ten on the night of 30 June the army was ordered to break camp. When the process was complete the troops were given two hours' rest, then set in motion. The destination had not been revealed to the regimental officers, but it was immediately evident that the army was not moving against the Prussians to the front, but off to the right in the direction of the river March.

Early on 1 July the three main columns began to cross the multiple water barrier on a frontage of tfive miles from Kojetein downstream to Tobitschau—an elaborate business, for the centre and left-hand columns had to pass the Valová and Blata tributaries as well as the main river, with its branches and islands. The cavalrymen had to dismount to lead their horses down the marshy banks to the fords, while some at least of the infantry crossed by four bridges of pontoons which had been sent down from Kremsier on the 26th. Lacy attended to all of these details.

On the far side of the river the columns marched along the dykes which crossed the polder landscape, and towards noon they began to arrive on the higher ground at Roketnitz, and were given their first respite. It was clear that the army had got away from the camp of Dobramillitz undetected by the Prussians, and during the halt at Roketnitz the first report arrived that the light troops far to the north had destroyed a great convoy which was destined for the enemy in front of Olmütz. The news was made known to the troops before they once more set themselves in march on the afternoon of this glorious day. 'The heat was crushing, yet that is something you can endure quite happily, as long as you believe you are marching against the enemy.'[41]

The army was now making north across firm and high ground, and it continued unopposed on its way until it reached Gross-Teinitz towards nine in the evening, having covered about twenty-five miles and crossed a river in twenty-one hours of continual movement. 'The march was so arranged that the army was steered clear of the highway, and even of the known and frequented roads. Each division and each column… was assigned the particular route which would bring it to a point where the army as a whole would come together again. The regiments appeared in the greatest possible strength, and every combatant was under arms. Order, discipline and subordination had at last been established, and were maintained during this march and the rest of the campaign, as also among the baggage train which followed the army. This mobility, this harmony and this reorganisation of our military forces combined to give us what we needed to carry out successful initiatives.'[42]

The fortress-town of Olmütz and the batteries, trenches and camp of the Prussian siege corps were in full view before darkness descended and rain fell in torrents. First light on 2 July showed that the enemy had gone and that Olmütz was free. This happy outcome was the combined effect of Daun's brilliant march, the blow which Loudon and Siskovics had carried out against the Prussian line of communication, and Marschall's dogged defence of Olmütz.

THE GREAT AMBUSH: GUNDERSDORF, 28 JUNE, AND DOMSTADTL, 30 JUNE 1758

The scheme

Eighteenth-century sieges were hungry creatures, and the attack on Olmütz in 1758 was particularly expensive for Frederick. He had known that Olmütz was strong, but he had not expected that the Austrian army would hang back and deny him his battle. Meanwhile he was committed to a sit-down siege which not only consumed bombs and heavy shot at an inordinate rate, but also compelled his detachments to fire musket cartridges by their hundreds of thousands against the Austrian light forces which plagued the outposts.

On 26 June a great train of up to 4,000 carts set out for the siege army from Troppau under the escort of six battalions of fusiliers, two of grenadiers, three battalions-worth of recruits and reconvalescents, and 1,000 horsemen. The commander was Colonel Mosel, 'a man of determination and experience,'[43] and *GL*. Zieten was detailed to meet and if necessary reinforce the convoy from the troops around Olmütz. The precautions were by no means extravagant, since the Moravian peasants kept the roving Austrian detachments informed of everything the Prussians were doing. 'They have some sort of scheme afoot,' said Frederick, 'and no doubt they want to strike at the great convoy which is on the way for me. It is up to me to make sure it arrives safe and sound, for it is carrying something out of the ordinary.'[44]

From his headquarters at Konitz *GdC*. Adolph Nicolaus Buccow commanded the Austrian troops in the hinterland. He was aware of every detail of the convoy, from its intended departure to its assigned route, and he suggested to Daun that it would make an excellent target. The field marshal accordingly devised a scheme on a grand scale. Buccow was to play a part, by advancing his main body south-east to Ptin and Plumenau and sitting on the right flank of the Prussian field army. With Frederick thus pinned down, two striking forces were to converge in a pincer movement from the west and east. These comprised:

The Western Force

Buccow was to detach *GFWM*. Loudon with four battalions, one dragoon regiment, one regiment of hussars and 600 Croats, with orders to join the command of Colonel Lanjus (280 grenadiers, 340 hussars and 600 Croats) which had gone ahead to Reigersdorf. The joint force was then to attack the convoy from the west.

The Eastern Force

GFWM. Siskovics was detached from Daun's main army with one grenadier battalion, two battalions of fusiliers and four companies of carabiniers. He was to execute an anti-clockwise and altogether longer march by way of Prerau (where he would pick up 1,200 horse and 1,000 Croats under *GFWM*. Saint-Ignon), and approach the route of the convoy from the east.

Loudon's Opening Attack at Gundersdorf, 28 June

Loudon set out from Neuschloss on the evening of 26 June, and marched overnight to reach Sternberg, at the foot of the border plateau. The great convoy had begun to wind up the opposite side of the watershed on the 26th, but its march was 'very slow and difficult.'[45] Allowing for a length of eighteen two-foot paces for the normal cart and its four horses, and two more paces for the gaps between the carts, the convoy would have occupied something like thirty miles of route in ideal conditions. The conditions were not ideal, for rain was falling, and the road was already churned up by the Prussian military transport. On that day only one-third of the convoy arrived at the first overnight stop in the neighbourhood of Bautsch, and the rest was still

Gundersdorf, 28 June, and Domstadtl, 30 June 1758

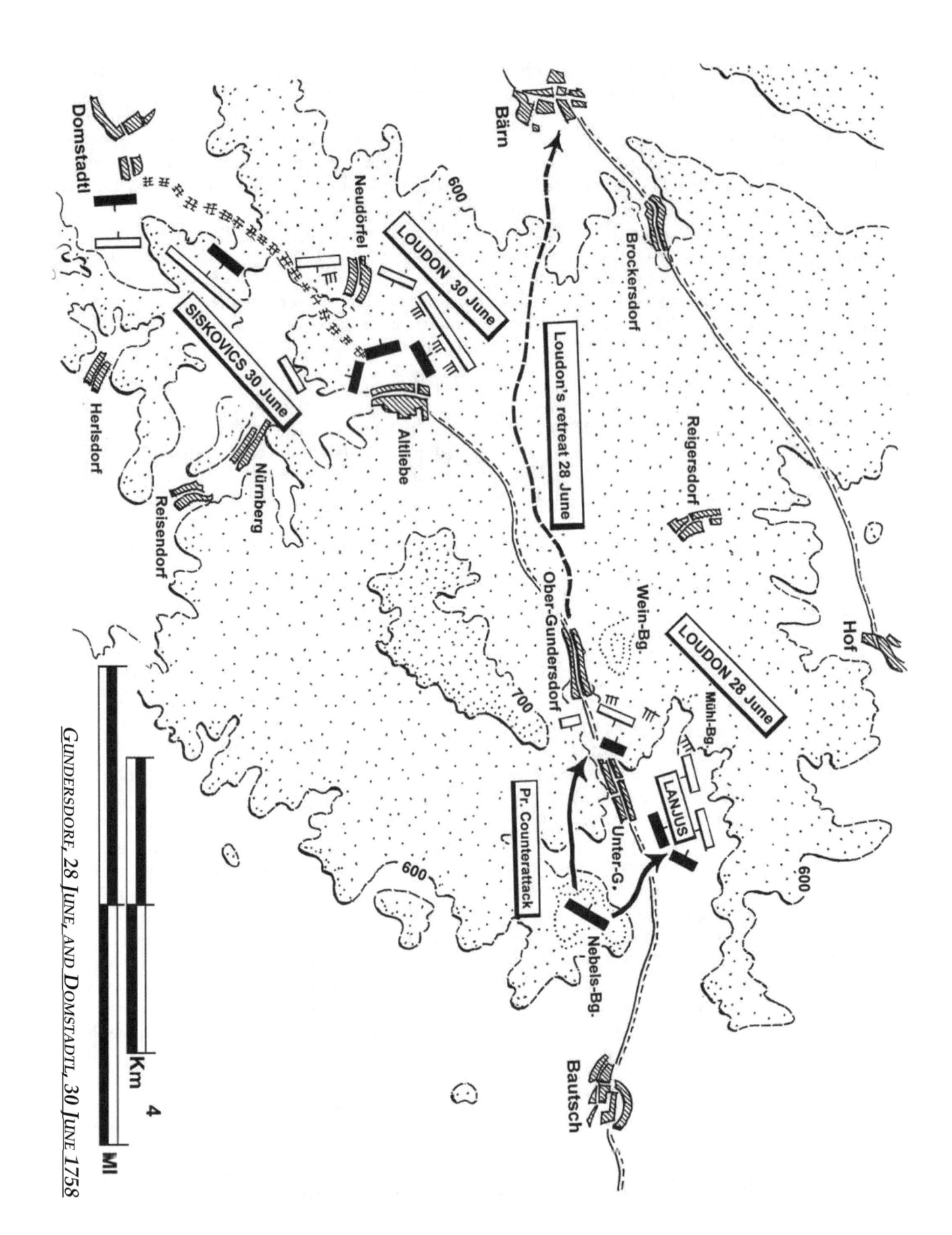

labouring up from Troppau.

All the same Loudon took alarm when he was told that the convoy had progressed as far as it had, and that the Prussian lieutenant general Markgraf Karl of Brandenburg-Schwedt was on the way to join it with 4,000 troops from the camp in front of Olmütz (actually just Colonel Paul Werner with an initial reinforcement of one grenadier battalion, 300 hussars and 200 dragoons). Nothing had been heard from Siskovics, and Loudon executed a forced march over the plateau, and reached the vicinity of Domstadtl in the evening of the 27th. He resolved to attack the convoy when it was still well short of Olmütz, so as to avoid the danger of being caught between the powerful escort and the reinforcements which were now approaching from the plain.

As a guard against the reinforcements, Loudon left Major Goes with 300 hussars and 300 Croats at Domstadtl, and ordered his remaining forces to their feet at midnight. This was the third forced march in succession, and Loudon hastened ahead of his tiring troops with an advance detachment to intercept the route of the enemy at Ober-Gundersdorf. The road through the lush valley was hemmed in on both sides by hills which sloped smoothly and steeply to the village—a typically straggling affair of log huts. There was no sign of Siskovics on the far side of the valley, but Loudon could not delay, for his scouts reported that the head of the convoy had already entered the village, 'upon which I rode forward a little and came in contact with the enemy, taking three prisoners.'[46]

Loudon brought up his main force to the high ground north of the valley, and opened an immediate attack. At the same time Captain Rouvroy positioned three batteries of artillery on the bald hills which dominated the western exit of Unter-Gundersdorf, and from this site he forced the escort's leading unit (the first battalion of Jung-Kreytzen [28]) to retreat to the battalion of Alt-Billerbeck Grenadiers to the south of the road. Harried by the Croats, and pursued by the cannon shot, the Prussians fell back along the southern ridge as far as the wooded Nebels-Berg.

While Colonel Mosel rallied his escort on the Nebels-Berg, the Croats discovered something of more compelling interest in the village. 'The bloody encounter with the Austrians had thrown a panic into the Prussian convoy. A whole crowd of conscripted-peasant drivers cut the traces and fled with the teams towards Troppau as fast as they could[47] ... in the convoy which we had just taken there were a large number of barrels bearing the inscription *Flintensteine*, musket flints. A number of Croats took it into their heads to tackle them with swords and bayonets, and succeeded in opening a number of them [actually four], and there immediately streamed forth a rain of four- and eight-groschen pieces.'[48] The waggons were now in the nominal charge of Captain Anton Kovatshovitz of the Warasdiner St. Georger Croats, who was powerless to prevent his men from helping themselves to the cash. Years later he expressed his surprise at being overlooked for promotion, and the *Hofkriegsrath* overruled his protest with the warning that he was being 'held to a more seemly conduct.'[49]

Loudon had meanwhile drawn the command of Colonel Lanjus (above) down to his left (eastern) flank, which extended his total deployment to a very thinly-spread two miles. The Austrians had stirred up a hornets' nest, and their new left flank came under a determined attack from three Prussian battalions advancing north from the Nebels-Berg, and two further battalions which Colonel Mosel summoned up from the rearguard. The Prussians pushed Lanjus from the hill (the Mühl-Berg, 642 m.), and once in possession of this commanding ground they were able to plant their own artillery and beat off five counterattacks on the part of Loudon's infantry. The Prussians crowned their success when their left-flanking battalion (Alt-Billerbeck Grenadiers) seized the third of Rouvroy's batteries in a hand-to-hand fight.

After more than three hours of combat Loudon had been defeated with the loss of more than 450 troops (52 killed, 104 wounded, 339 missing or captured), and in the middle of the afternoon his position became altogether untenable when a powerful Prussian reinforcement arrived at Domstadtl from the camp before Olmütz. This was *GL.* Zieten, who

*Joseph Count Siskovics, distinguished leader, trainer and public servant
(Military Academy, Wiener Neustadt)*

had gathered up Colonel Werner's detachment on the way, and was coming to the help of the convoy with five battalions and twelve squadrons. Loudon believed that in spite of everything he would still have won the day 'if I did not also fear coming under attack from the rear.'[50]

Loudon recoiled to Bärn, and the moment he arrived he learned that Siskovics had reached Altstadt. 'I told him by way of answer that if he were still minded to attack the enemy convoy I would do everything I could to support him, but that I believed it was already too late, since the enemy general Zieten was already on the way with a considerable force, and was supposed to be already at Altliebe.'[51] Why had Loudon's partner arrived so late on the scene?

The march of Siskovics and Zieten's further progress

The formidable *GFWM.* Joseph Siskovics, although a native Hungarian, was devoid of all experience of *der kleine Krieg*, and had made his reputation with the Hungarian line infantry. Jacob Cogniazzo, who knew him from his service with the regiment of Erzherzog Carl [2], describes him as 'a magnificent drillmaster, and he owed to this gift his unusual good fortune to be promoted out of turn from captain of grenadiers to major, and a couple of days after that to leap all the way to colonel commandant of the regiment of Haller [31]. Lieutenant Colonel Rebentisch, who also fancied himself as a drillmaster, was so put out that he left our service and enlisted with the Prussians.'[52] The most recent promotion of Siskovics, to *GFWM.*, was nevertheless a direct result of his bravery at Kolin, and now in Moravia it is difficult to see how he could have arrived to support Loudon any earlier than he did.

The route assigned to Siskovics was much longer than Loudon's, but for reasons of security he could set out from his camp at Kralitz only at the same time as Loudon marched from Neuschloss, namely on the evening of the 26th, and he spent most of the 27th being led astray by his guides among the woods of the March plain. He reached Prerau only late in the day, but on the 28th he succeeded in making up most of the time when he executed a remarkable forced march which brought him into the hills only just short of Loudon's fight.

Meanwhile the Prussian convoy stretched over miles of road, and many of the carts at the head had been abandoned by their drivers or wrecked. Rather than press on at once to the plain of Olmütz, Zieten therefore devoted 29 June to putting the convoy in order and leading it up from the Gundersdorf valley and to a fine open country which offered views as far east as the Carpathians; he then descended gradually to the hollow at Altliebe, from where a steep but very short climb brought him to another forward slope, where the head of the column assembled for the final stage of the journey by way of Domstadtl to the plain on the following day. Zieten had been undisturbed, and he could be forgiven for thinking that the worst of the danger was over.

Loudon's troops had been put through three forced marches and a costly little action, and they and their chief passed the 29th at Bärn in a state of some dejection. Their ranks had been thinned by casualties and sickness, they had shot away most of their ammunition, and they were running short of rations for man and horse. Loudon was in communication with Siskovics before the day was out, and the two commanders were able to concert a plan of attack for the next day. Inevitably it was Siskovics with his relatively fresh troops who would have to take the initiative.

In retrospect Siskovics believed that it was fortunate that he had not alarmed the enemy by arriving sooner than he did, for the Prussians had devoted a whole day to sorting themselves out, and 'in such a way Siskovics gained the time to emplace himself in ambush, and carry out a second and decisive attack the next day as agreed with General Loudon.'[53] Siskovics was now able to take up a position to the east of the Prussian route, allow the convoy to make a start on its way, and then fall on its left flank and bring it to a halt. When the convoy was hopelessly jammed, Loudon's troops, who by then would have recovered somewhat from their exertions, would attack from the west and complete the work of destruction.

In detail, Siskovics planned to arrange his forces along the summit of a continuous ridge which ran parallel the Prussian route as it made the gradual descent of a couple of miles from Neudörfel to Domstadtl. His deployment took advantage of two tracts of woodland which extended along the crest 1,000 yards from the road. The left-hand, or southern wood, was to be stuffed with Warasdiner Croats, the Hungarian infantry regiment of Haller [31], and the Saxon Prinz Karl Chevaulegers, with a body of Austrian grenadiers in the rear and a battery of artillery on either flank—two light pieces and two 6-pounders over to the right, and the regimental 3-pounders of Haller to the left. Parties of dragoons, hussars and Saxon-Polish uhlans were to secure the right flank of the whole force, while small bodies of infantry occupied the right-hand wood. Meanwhile the troops remained tucked away in the woods well out of sight of the Prussians.

The joint attack, 30 June

At nine in the morning of the 30th Colonel Carl Nauendorff sent word that the head of the Prussian column had set out, and Siskovics brought his troops forward into their ambush positions. For a while he let the unsuspecting enemy pass on their way, and then opened fire at 10.30. By a Prussian account, 'General Zieten's cavalry were marching by squadrons with wide intervals to the right of the road, because the ground on that side was mostly level; the infantry were marching to the left. The head of the column reached the narrows at Domstadtl without any sign of the enemy, but scarcely had about 120 carts passed through than the enemy appeared on the heights on the left-hand side and at once opened a heavy fire of artillery at the village entrance. They shot a number of horses dead, and the convoy came to a halt.'[54]

GL. Zieten reacted in a manner that would do credit in a military exercise today, by throwing all his available forces into a counterattack. Two hundred Puttkamer Hussars [H4] and three and a half battalions advanced unhesitatingly up the slope. They did not halt to fire (their muskets were in any case unusable in the rain), and they chased the Croats through the wood. The thinly-spread Austrian forces were in danger of breaking apart, but Colonel Nauendorff had perceived the danger, and sent Lieutenant Colonel Voit and one hundred Löwenstein Chevaulegers [D31] crashing into the enemy left flank.[55] Out of breath, and out of rank and file, the Prussians were rolled up and broken, and the intervention of Voit's little force precipitated a general rout in which the enemy left all their colours, five cannon, six officers and three hundred men in the hands of the Austrians.

Zieten turned back up the road towards Neudörfel, and sent another one and a half battalions into an attack against the woods. This last show of defiance was short lived, for the Austrian horse threatened to take the Prussians in their right flank, and by the end of the day all Zieten's attempts to organise a counterattack had collapsed.

Meanwhile Loudon had arrayed his force in front of Bärn, ready to attack the convoy from the west. He wrote dismissively concerning the opening of Siskovics' action that 'the attack having been nothing more than a cannonade, I had no means of knowing whether or not it had turned out well.'[56] Towards noon musketry could be heard as well, and Loudon launched a general attack. Details concerning this part of the action are scanty, but it is clear that Loudon formed his infantry into two groups on his left, and directed them against Altliebe and Neudörfel.

Major Tom Caldwell led the grenadiers of the detachment of Colonel Lanjus, which formed a kind of second line, but he took the opportunity to insert his men in a gap which opened in the first line, between the regiments of Kollowrat [17] and Alt-Wolfenbüttel [29] 'and from there I sped forward with my unsupported grenadiers, making for a height from where some enemy cannon were doing us a great deal of damage. I came to within eighty paces of the muzzles before giving two volleys. I was wounded in the foot, but we hastened up the hill with fixed bayonets, came at the enemy in the flank and forced them to give way, leaving two cannon which had caused some disorder in our left wing.'[57]

The Nádasdy Hussars [H11] and the Zweibrücken Dragoons [D39] kept pace out to Loudon's right, and threw back repeated attacks on the part of the numerically superior Prussian cavalry (Schmettau and Kyau Cuirassiers [Cs 4, 12], and the Werner and Zieten Hussars [Hs 6, 2].

In the afternoon the two Austrian attacks, those of Siskovics and Loudon, converged on Altliebe. Some 1,000 of the Prussian carts were strung out motionless on the road leading down past Neudörfel to Domstadtl. Another 2,000 vehicles had not so much as set out from Altliebe, and had been leaguered up by *GM*. Puttkamer in a defensible *Wagenburg* in a saucer-like depression set into high ground to the south-west of Altliebe. Altogether eight and a half battalions of the escort were drawn in to form a protective semi-circle. The Prussians were jammed so closely together that they formed an excellent target for the Austrian cannon, and 'through the skill of the artillery captain Rouvroy the pieces were served so well that every shot scored a hit.' 'They... shot the horses dead, blew up the ammunition waggons and plunged everything into the most frightful disorder.'[58]

By the nature of things the Prussians had to fight where they had been positioned around the semi-circle, whereas the Austrians were able to concentrate their attacks on individual sectors, and (at least by his own estimation) the decisive break-in was made by Lieutenant Colonel Franz Carl Riesse, who got into the flank with his Warasdiner St. Georger Croats, while the regiments of Kollowrat [17], Alt-Wolfenbüttel [29] and Starhemberg [24] attacked frontally, 'upon which the enemy... fell back in

The destruction of the Prussian Wagenburg *at Domstadtl.*
The beleaguered fortress of Olmütz is at the top left-hand corner.

The Defence of Olmütz, May - July 1758

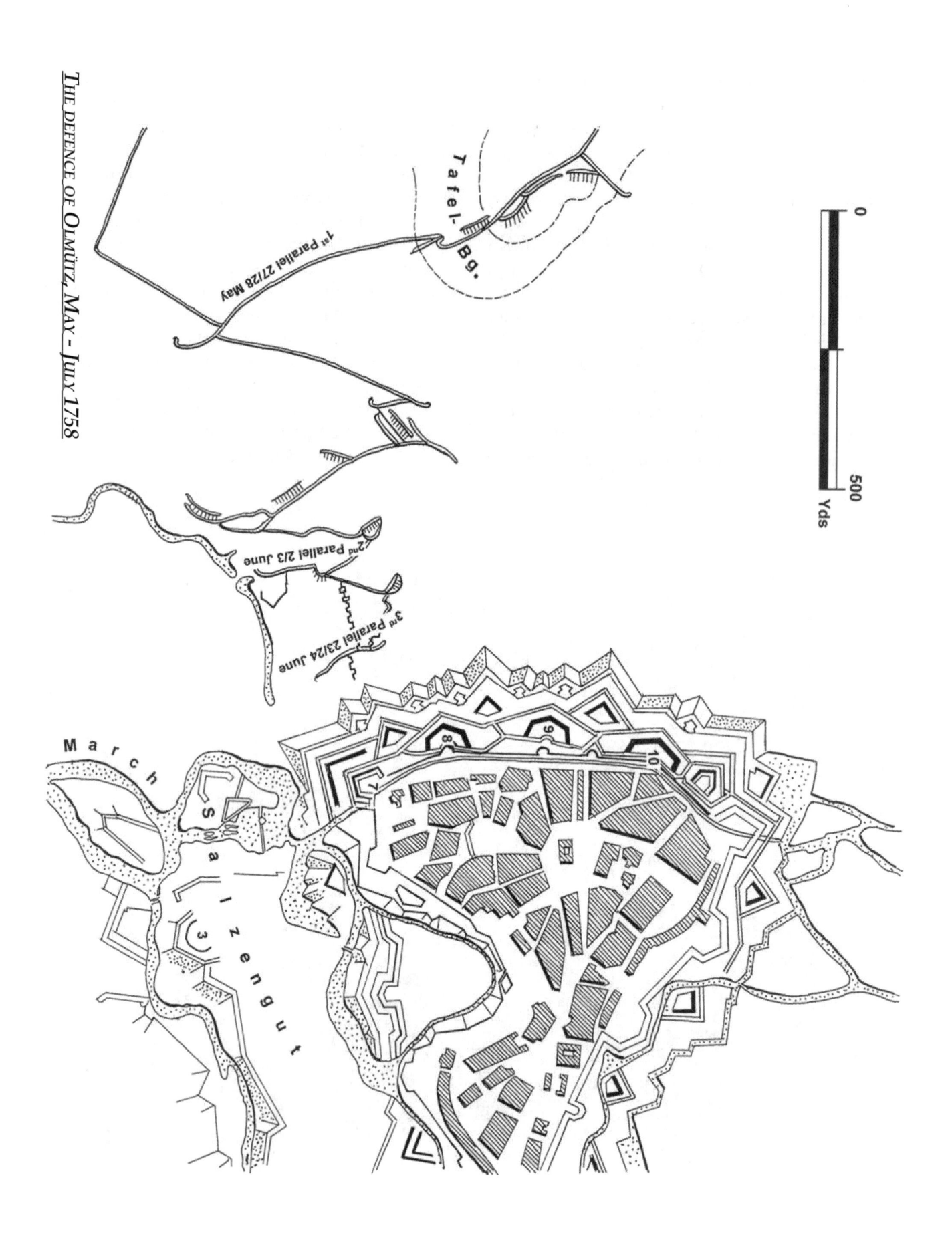

considerable confusion and abandoned the convoy.'⁵⁹

Probably the last of the Prussian units to stand its ground was the battalion of Prinz Ferdinand [34], composed of scantily-trained cantonal recruits from Ruppin in Brandenburg, who (as was the way with new soldiers) did not know when it was sensible to run away: 'Never did Spartans or Roman veterans fight for their fatherland with more composure than these blooming youths of seventeen or twenty years. Determined to hold out until the last breath, they most of them followed their leader Captain Pirch in taking their laurels with them into the grave. Out of 900 just 65 were taken prisoners. A few wounded returned to Troppau, but all the rest lay dead in the files which had been assigned to them.'⁶⁰

The fight for the *Wagenburg* had lasted two hours, and by the late afternoon the Austrians commanded the whole ground between Altliebe and Domstadtl, and the surviving Prussian forces were split in two and retreating to the opposite sides of the plateau. The right wing of Siskovics set out to chase the Prussians who were to the north of the plateau, but Zieten was able to break contact and reach Troppau, where by 2 July he had assembled fugitives to the number of 3,000 infantry and 1,200 cavalry.

To the south, General Krockow commanded the troops at the head of the column. The concussions and the smoke told him that the convoy to his rear was coming under a destructive attack, and when everything fell silent he knew that it was too late for him to intervene. He pressed on to Olmütz with the remains of eight battalions, six squadrons of cuirassiers and a force of 500 hussars.

At a cost to themselves of a little more than 600 troops, the Austrians had killed, wounded or taken 58 Prussian officers and 2,328 men. Three thousand laden waggons were heaped up in the unimaginable wreckage of the *Wagenburg* at Altliebe, or stood abandoned on the road to the south. It would have been physically impossible for the Austrians to move the vehicles, even if they had not been in an extremity of exhaustion, and so they had to destroy the convoy on the spot. The set fire to the carts, blew up the gunpowder and the loaded bombs and shells, and threw the flour to the wind or burnt it in its barrels. The only worthwhile booty had been taken at Gundersdorf two days before, and a young officer of the regiment of Andlau [57] reports that 'since the Croats, being light troops, had no horses with which to carry goods, they exchanged the cash for something more portable, and changed it for gold at a rate of thirty, forty and finally up to fifty silver crowns for a ducat. Our colonel [Otto Heinrich Rath], who had with him four horses and more than three hundred golden ducats, made a fortune and bought an estate in his own country with the profits'.⁶¹

Taken in association with Daun's relief march to Olmütz, the great ambush made Frederick's position in Moravia untenable, and contributed to throwing him onto the strategic defensive for the rest of the war. The scale of the ambush had been gigantic, and bears comparison with the attacks by the Vietminh on the French convoys in Indo-China in the early 1950s. The Austrian cavalry and artillery had acquitted themselves particularly well, and essential contributions to the outcome had been made by Buccow, who was seized with the original inspiration, and by Daun, who fitted the operation into the larger scheme of campaign. Of the commanders on the spot, posterity has given all the credit to Loudon. Siskovics had done at least as much, but a Prussian cuirassier commented shrewdly that 'as is always the case, it was one name, Loudon's, which became fashionable. General Gessler used to say: "When somebody has won a reputation, he becomes the one who has done everything." He is the man of the moment, like Hercules in ancient times, and takes the credit for the work of perhaps a dozen people altogether.'⁶²

Loudon's conduct gives us an inkling of his future behaviour in high command. His enterprising spirit was to win Glatz and Schweidnitz for the Austrians in 1760 and 1761; his headlong and unsupported attack on 28 June was going to find a close parallel at Liegnitz (1760); his dejection and immobility on the 29th foreshadowed much longer episodes of the same later in the war.

The defence of Olmütz, 28 May - 2 July 1758

a) Austrians
8,713: 8,206 effective infantry, 200 dragoons, 100 hussars, 7 engineers, 158 gunners, 42 miners
Artillery: 324 pieces, including 110 12-pounders and heavier, 6 howitzers, 41 mortars, 20 pierriers, 50 coehorn mortars
Expenditure of ammunition: 58,200 shot, 6,100 bombs and shells, 2,700 pierrier loads, 538 fire balls, 51,664 rampart piece rounds, 472,462 musket cartridges
Losses: Garrison: 206 killed, 581 wounded. Townspeople: 11 killed, 12 wounded

b) Prussians
Siege corps c 8,000, but of greatly fluctuating strength
Artillery: maximum pieces in action (15 June) 31 cannon, 16 mortars, 14 howitzers
Expenditure of ammunition (as observed by Austrians): 103,532 shot, 25,622 bombs and howitzer shells, 700 pierrier loads
Losses: Total unknown, but included 143 prisoners, and 426 deserters to the garrison

In Frederick's scheme for 1758 he hoped, by laying siege to the Moravian fortress-town of Olmütz, to force Daun's army into a battle which would remove the Austrians from the strategic map for the rest of the year. By the middle of May, however, it was clear that Daun was unwilling to be drawn into a confrontation on anything but his own terms, and that the reduction of Olmütz was becoming an objective for the Prussians in its own right.

Olmütz was a strong, modern and well-found fortress. It stood on the right (west) bank of the river March on the most direct avenue from Prussian territory to Vienna, and between 1742 and 1757 it had been remodelled and extended by Bechade de Rochepine (now *GFWM.*). He had taken full advantage of the potentialities of the site, for the river not only covered the eastern side of the fortress, but could be used to fill the ditches at will, and to spread an extensive inundation across the northern approaches to prevent the enemy digging trenches. 'You don't need eight... feet of water to make an inundation: half a foot is more than enough to render an attack difficult, if not impossible.'[63]

Rochepine was free to give full attention to the western side of the fortress, which gave onto dry ground and the low Tafel-Berg 600 yards away. Along this sector he retained the medieval town wall as a continuous interior rampart, and in front of three of the little towers he placed spacious detached bastions (counterguards) with casemated (covered-in) gun positions. Ravelins were sited between the counterguards, and a well-designed covered way and permanent countermines defended the access to the ditch. The brick retaining walls (scarps) of the works stood twenty-four feet high, and were four feet thick at the top, and eight at the bottom. The only identifiable weakness was that the outer wall (counterscarp) of the ditch was too low, and that (inevitably) the fortifications had only just been built: 'every kind of new work, whether of masonry or earth, is much easier to wreck than older ones, where the masonry has had time to harden and the earth to settle properly. In this respect the fortifications of Olmütz are actually much weaker than if they had been built fifteen or twenty years earlier.'[64]

As seen from above, the three crucial western fronts extended along a straight line, which was considered the best means of bringing a cross-fire to bear against an enemy. In addition a low-lying and unassuming work (No. 3) on the Salzergut island in the March was sited to take enemy trenches in enfilade just when they were nearing the fortress.

Maria Theresa had intervened in person to appoint old *FZM*. Ernst Dietrich Count Marschall v. Biberstein as commandant at the beginning of the year.[65] Marschall was a Thuringian Lutheran in his middle sixties, and he was wizened, stooped and battered from a lifetime of military service. He already wore a silver plate to cover a hole in his head before he was appointed to command the fortress of Maastricht, which he proceeded to defend with great distinction from 6 April 1748 until the close of the War of the Austrian Succession. Now at Olmütz his technical skills and his knowledge of mankind more than made up for his physical frailties.

Rochepine was now engaged actively in the preparations for defending Olmütz, and it is curious to find that Marschall acknowledged him publicly as chief engineer only after the siege began. Upon that, writes Rochepine, 'he embraced me… most tenderly. He asked me to put the essential points respecting the defence in writing, and that he would like to have them in French, so as not to lose time in translating them into German.'[66] Possibly Marschall's preference for chief engineer would have been Captain Nicolaus Steinmetz of the Netherlands engineers, who was recalled from the *Reichsarmee* to Olmütz at his special request.

Marschall had no reservations concerning his chief gunner, the native Norwegian Colonel Adolph Nicolaus Alfson. Marschall testified afterwards that he could not render sufficient praise for Alfson's skill and energy, 'and in particular for the useful and necessary example he gave both to the young men of his corps and to the garrison as a whole.'[67]

It was fortunate that Marschall and Rochepine recognised so early that Olmütz was likely to come under attack. Before the end of January they had defined the most urgent needs, and begun their battle against inertia to stock the fortress with provisions and materiel of every kind. They had to invoke special powers to force the lordships to deliver what they had promised, but Rochepine had more success when he told the municipality (*Magistrat*) to make sure that all the citizens who chose to stay in Olmütz had sufficient private stocks of food, and that the town must organise a proper system for fighting fires.[68]

On 1 May *FML.* de Ville broke contact with the Prussians who were pouring into Moravia, and arrived at Olmütz to make over reinforcements to Marschall, as ordered by the *Hofkriegsrath*. The troops in question comprised the regiment of Simbschen [53], one battalion of Preysach [39], two battalions of Warasdiner Croats, 200 dragoons, 100 hussars, and 1,500 men of the auxiliary regiment of Kur-Bayern, who were persuaded with some difficulty to join the garrison rather than continue their march to the quarters which had been assigned to them in Upper Austria. De Ville claims that in addition he bolstered up Marschall's confidence when it had been flagging, though that seems unlikely.

The first Prussian hussars made their appearance on 5 May, and two days later the enemy began to form their bridges and camps around the fortress. Not long before the river March had been at its lowest level in living memory, but the inundation was working so well that the water already reached towards the stop of the sluices.

On the 15th the Prussians advanced a battalion of infantry and three cannon over the Tafel-Berg and the Galgen-Berg, as cover for a reconnaissance by a party of generals and engineers, 'but their first reception by our cannon was pretty hot. Firing at a range of 2,700 paces the third shot was fortunate to knock over an hussar and his horse.'[69] Frederick could see the work which the Austrians had put into spreading the inundation, strengthening the fortifications, and demolishing the outlying houses to clear fields of fire, and on the 19th he began to worry about the outcome of his adventure in Moravia.

On 20 May the Prussians planted fascines and gabions for their lines of circumvallation and countervallation. This was the signal for Marschall to establish garrisons in Kloster Hradisch and the villages of Hattschein, Rebschein, Pablowitz and Chwalkowitz; from these bases his Croats, dragoons and hussars were able to keep open his communications on the eastern side of the March.

When the mist lifted on the morning of 28 May the Austrians saw that the enemy had constructed a first siege parallel and a battery on the Tafel-Berg, which signified the formal opening of the siege. Marschall writes that 'from this day on I kept up a fire with my cannon on the enemy. Little real damage could be done, because the targets were on an elevated site, but the experience offered good training to the young gunners, because they got to know their pieces and their effect. Likewise the soldiers helping with the guns acquired the necessary skills.'[70]

The siege was now taking on its particular character. The main body of Field Marshal Keith's siege corps was concentrated on the west bank of the March, while the blockade on the eastern side was so casual that many Prussian officers ordered their meals from the town.[71] On 5 May Marschall had sent a party of hussars to Daun to convey a cipher for correspondence, and thereafter the two were in almost daily contact through messengers. Captain Carl Huff, who was probably the most trusted of Daun's adjutants, was able to make the return journey four times.[72] Another of the arrivals was Colonel Ernst Friedrich Giannini, who was not an engineer by profession, but who had a feel for staff work and topography, and had known Olmütz in time of peace, all of which persuaded Daun to accept his offer to attempt the journey. He arrived on 17 May, after an arduous three-day trek on foot, and delivered a letter from *FM.* Neipperg, together with a technical paper from the *Hofkriegsrath.*[73]

Now that his young gunners were blooded, Marschall moderated the fire of his artillery, and as long as the enemy remained at a distance he was content to reply mainly through his bombardiers, who made some very accurate shooting with their mortars. On 3 June 'a bomb from one of my batteries landed in an enemy battery, exploding up to 300 bombs, ruining several cannon and killing as many as two officers and thirty men.'[74] Another hit on the 14th touched off an estimated 100 mortar bombs and howitzer shells.

Episodes of this kind aggravated the friction at Prussian headquarters. Frederick picked his engineers in the same erratic way as a medieval prince might choose a court jester, and the king treated them in much the same way. His current favourite was Colonel Giovanni Balbi, a hideous creature from Genoa, who had directed the recent sieges of Breslau and Schweidnitz. For the present attack Balbi decided to base his attack on the Tafel-Berg, for a sunken road across the top could be adapted as a first parallel, and from there the gunners could see almost two-thirds of the scarps of the fortifications. However the range was on the long side, at 600 yards, and very little effect could be distinguished. Frederick railed at his engineers, 'those two-footed animals... my fucking engineers have made the opening of the trenches into a farce, and landed me in the mess I am now in... double-dyed buggers.'[75] Balbi bleated that he was in despair to find that 'despite all the care and effort I have put forth, Your Majesty should still manifest his displeasure at us, and the work being carried out under my direction.'[76]

Frederick now imposed his will on the conduct of the siege, and established a battery to the south-east of the Tafel-Berg which (according to measurements taken by the Prince de Ligne afterwards) was actually further from the targets that the original battery on the hill. However significant reinforcements of troops and heavy artillery were arriving from Silesia, and early on 30 May the enemy opened up from all their batteries with a total of thirty pieces. The fire was now beginning to take effect, and Marschall threatened to hang anyone, military or civilian, who spoke a word about surrendering. He had just learned that de Ville had intercepted a peasant lad called Kolleck, who had confessed 'after sharp interrogation' that a Prussian officer with a star on his uniform had given him messages to carry to two townsmen, the alderman Franz Piehalleck, and one Wessely, who was a dealer in spirits. The information rang 'all the more true, because the confession had been wrung from him with great effort, especially as it concerned the alderman.'[77] Marschall at once instituted a search, but the two traitors had disappeared. The townspeople gave him no further cause to suspect their loyalty.

On the night of 2/3 June the besiegers made their second parallel, about half-way between the Tafel-Berg and the fortress. By the night of 4/5 June the enemy were close enough to justify a major sortie, which was launched by Major Simbschen with 200 grenadiers, 200 fusiliers and working party of 150 men. They filled in some lengths of sap, killed or wounded about 100 of the enemy, and brought in 22 prisoners along with 30 or so willing deserters. *GFWM.* Draskovich led the second and last sortie of the kind, on the night of 12/13 June, when 560 men broke into the Prussian batteries from two sides. The loss of the Austrians amounted to 137, which was a heavy price, but they succeeded in spiking eighteen of the cannon and mortars.

Thereafter the sallies were confined to short-range raids by small groups of men. At the same time small improvised arrow-shaped earthworks were built down the glacis, sited in such a way to plague the enemy saps by fire. The progress of the trench attack was put back by up to six days, but there was nothing the Austrians could do to prevent the besiegers from completing two new batteries behind their second parallel. The Prussians were unable to dismount two particularly troublesome 24-pounders, which were firing from casemated protection in Bastion No. 8, but the adjacent Bastion No. 7 was suffering badly. Howitzer shells were tearing chunks out of the fresh masonry, and on 23 June a nasty breach began to open in one of the shoulder angles. It widened day by day in spite of every effort on the part of the defenders, who tried to clear the rubble and fill the gap with wine casks filled with earth.

Marschall had already sent word to Daun that the losses in troops and specialised officers were beginning to tell on the garrison, and on 10 June or early on the 11th seventeen technicians were able to get into the fortress. They were followed on the night of 21/22 June by a whole corps under the command of the excellent *GFWM*. Ferdinand Friedrich Bülow, comprising 1,366 veteran infantry, the engineer major Stockhaus and 24 gunners. This Bülow was the same who had defended Liegnitz in 1757.

There was scarcely time for the reinforcements to be assigned to their posts before the Prussians opened a third parallel on 24 June, and began to worm their way forward by covered sap. Marschall made every preparation for a last-ditch stand. By 1 July the besiegers had advanced their saps to within practicable assaulting distance of the covered way, and this day brought a redoubling of the Prussian fire, together with a report that Frederick in person was on the march to Olmütz with 12,000 men of his field army.

Marschall believed that a storm was imminent, and at midnight on 1/2 July he joined his troops, who were standing under arms on the ramparts. A few moments later Austrian patrols reported that the enemy were abandoning their trenches. Marschall at once sent out 300 grenadiers who verified the fact, and captured an adjutant and a few stragglers. The Prussians had left behind just five 6-pounder coehorn mortars and one cannon, together with a single soldier, who had been wounded in the knee, and was now dragging himself along and trying to spike the touch-holes. The Austrians were much impressed.

In the hills to the north, the wreckage of the great Prussian convoy was still smouldering at Altliebe. In the plain of the March, Daun's army was only a few hours short of Olmütz. But the fact that the fortress had survived until its final deliverance was due to old Marschall, its defender. One of the relieving force noted his trembling voice and head when he showed his liberators the wide ditch he had built behind the threatened sector, fully resolved to die in its defence.[78]

Marschall had nothing to say in his own praise, but he detailed at some length to Maria Theresa what he owed to his officers and garrison, to the clergy and to the townspeople. Afterwards the Empress ennobled fifteen of the citizens who had been the most active in the effort.

Frederick escapes to Bohemia, 2 July - 9 August 1758

Military history has few parallels for what Daun had accomplished since the spring of 1758, when he created an army in the course of a campaign, recruiting it not just in terms of numbers, but in morale (after a near-terminal defeat), and by completing a ten-year programme of reform. Brigadier General Montazet presented the judgement of the professional soldier: 'It is impossible to praise too highly the resolute, prudent and skilful way this general has manoeuvred since the opening of the campaign, and especially on this occasion [the relief of Olmütz]. It is also important to render justice to the army. It is full of dedication, and everyone, from the highest officer to the ordinary soldier, carries out his duty to the utmost of his powers.'[79]

Daun's standing was at its apogee, and Maria Theresa saw in him 'the one general worthy to hold the supreme command, and on this account she rejected the representations which were even now being made to have him share authority with Prince Charles.'[80]

Frederick's conduct after his failure at Olmütz nevertheless helps to explain why the eighteenth century found so much to admire in a well-judged retreat. The time and effort he had expended in Moravia had surpassed his self-imposed limits, and he now had the courage to stand aside from his losses and open a new chapter in the campaign. The Russians as yet posed no immediate danger to Silesia, and rather than take his army on the short but extremely dangerous route back over the plateau to the north, the king determined to strike across the tangled country to the west and arrive in northeast Bohemia, where he could eat the country out of provisions, search for new opportunities to bring Daun to battle, and then make for Silesia in his own good time.

By marching his army around to the east of Olmütz, Daun had inevitably left the way to the west open. All the same the terrain of the Moravian-Bohemian borders offered the Austrian light troops excellent ground for catching the enemy at a disadvantage, and not least because the Prussians were marching by two columns—Frederick and his main army by way of Konitz, Mährisch-Trübau and Zwittau,

FREDERICK'S RETREAT TO BOHEMIA, JULY - AUGUST 1758

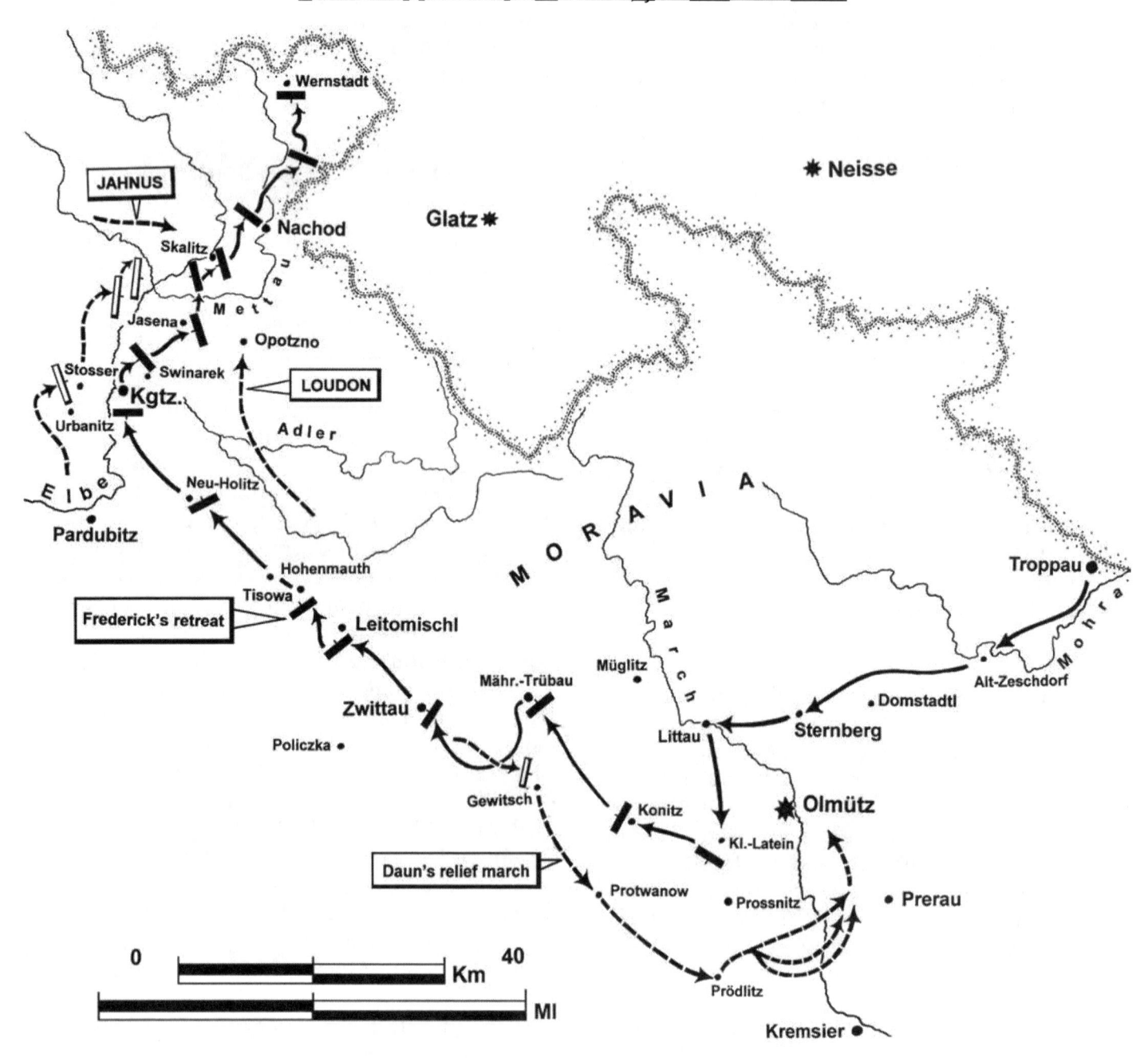

and Keith with the heavy ordnance and the former siege corps along a more northerly axis through Littau.

It was already evident on 2 July that the Prussians were moving on Bohemia, and Daun entrusted the pursuit to his light detachments, which together amounted to 24,000 troops. While Loudon snapped at Keith's heels, *GdC*. Buccow tried to obstruct the progress of the royal army, and on 5 July he positioned his Croats on the Schönhengst Pass (556 m.), a saddle in the massive forested wall which rose just beyond Mährisch-Trübau. Frederick viewed the barrier of felled trees, suspected (wrongly) that there were heavier forces lurking behind, and dodged around the obstacle by taking his army on a southerly circuit to reach Zwittau. These forced marches ought to have favoured desertion in such a difficult country, but the king 'had so thoroughly dispersed the less reliable regiments among the Pomeranians and the Prussians that scarcely a single man could escape.'[81] On the 6th the royal army reached Leitomischl, and subjected it to a comprehensive sack.

Daun and the main Austrian army crossed to the western side of the March only on 4 July, in other words two days after the enemy had removed themselves from the neighbourhood of Olmütz. In contrast the Prussians were showing revived energy. On 7 July the third division of Keith's former siege corps smashed through a force of grenadiers and carabiniers which Lacy had thrown in his path at Krönau, and on the 12th the final lumbering convoy passed safely past Neu-Holitz, defying all the efforts of Loudon, Siskovics and Saint-Ignon.

These days also saw the failure of another bold initiative on the part of Buccow. He had abandoned his largely unproductive attacks on the Prussian columns, and hastened ahead to Königgrätz, the nodal point of communications in north-east Bohemia, which he knew must be the ultimate enemy objective. Buccow's force, together with the detachments already in Bohemia (those of Jahnus, Kálnoky, Esterházy and Harsch) amounted to 6-7,000 men, which was not much to stand in the way of the whole of the Prussian army, but he put 500 labourers to work to divert the upper Elbe and the Adler to form a great inundation, and sent an urgent request to Daun for a consignment of artillery, to come to him by way of Chrudim and Pardubitz. Daun received the message on 9 July, but decided that the Prussians had already stolen too far ahead to enable the guns to arrive in time. Buccow was also disappointed in his inundation, which might have embarrassed a formal siege, but was too shallow to stop the leading troops of Frederick's army from splashing through the water and fording the Adler just to the east of Königgrätz on 11 July.

Buccow's position was turned, and on the following night he fell back to Chlumetz. Daun rarely had anything good to say of his subordinates, and he now wrote to Maria Theresa to express his disappointment. He had to admit that Buccow had escaped just in time to avoid being cut off, but Jahnus 'takes things all too easily and no longer shows any real enthusiasm'; Kálnoky was full of pretensions, while 'Harsch would be good as commandant of Prague, and for paperwork, but he is no kind of warrior.'[82]

On 14 July Frederick reunited all the Prussian forces along the northern bank of the Adler, and the 'Moravian' phase of the campaign of 1758 was definitively over. The Prussians had extricated themselves neatly from around Olmütz, survived the passage westward across the Moravian-Bohemian borders at a time when they had lost all communication with their homeland, and they were now ensconced on one of the classic avenues of the theatre of war, with a short (c. 40 miles) if dangerous communication north-east to Silesia and the County of Glatz.

On 16 July Maria Theresa wrote to Daun to assure him that she approved his new scheme of operations. He was intending to re-insert the Austrian army north of the border hills by way of the passage of Jung-Bunzlau and Zittau into Lusatia, from where he would have freedom of movement between the Elbe and the middle Oder, and in particular to reach out to the Russians when they emerged on the theatre of war.

Daun still had the immediate task of levering the Prussians out of north-east Bohemia. He had some 70,000 troops to Frederick's 40,000,

Adolph Nicolaus Baron Buccow, a tough and resourceful individual, as was proved again and again in the course of the war. He was wounded badly at Torgau but returned to service (Military Academy, Wiener Neustadt)

but if it came to a big battle all the advantage would lie with the enemy 'on account of their well-drilled troops, and we cannot compare with them in that respect. War is a curse, certainly, but Bohemia can sustain it much better than Moravia, for there is a big difference between the two lands.'[83]

Daun proceeded to apply two indirect means of coercion. The first was to set out light troops on either side of the Prussian line of communication. While Jahnus closed in from the west, Loudon (newly promoted to *FML.*) hovered in the hills about Opotzno, and threatened the Prussian supply line from the east. Then, on 17 and 18 July Daun brought the main force of the Austrians across the Elbe at Pardubitz, and began a process of edging up the right (western) bank. He hoped that the constant pressure from this direction would not only unseat the Prussian army from its positions east of the river, but deny Frederick any possibility of reaching Lusatia by way of Bohemia.

Frederick sought in vain to identify any weakness in Daun's deployment, and on 29 July he abandoned Königgrätz and the line of the Adler, and recoiled to a new camp extending between Jasena and Königslhota. On the 30th Daun prolonged his sideways shuffle to the north, and threatened to outflank Frederick's last tenable water barrier on the other side of the river, namely the Mettau stream. The manoeuvre succeeded in forcing the king back to a position between Skalitz and Jesenitz.

Maria Theresa was becoming impatient,[84] but Daun had his defenders, and one of them was Sir Andrew Mitchell, the British envoy to the King of Prussia. He observed that 'Marshal Daun seems to stick fast to his plan of risking nothing, and, I am sorry to say, he acquits himself like a wise general.'[85] In Daun's own circle Lacy remarked on the short memories of the critics in Vienna, who only recently had been in a state of alarm for their city.[86]

On 2 August a last sideways shift brought the Austrians to a position between Czaslawez and Salnei, which promoted Frederick to fall back behind Skalitz. On the morning of the 4th Daun rode out on reconnaissance to explore the possibility of attacking the Prussians. Their position proved to be too strong, and in the afternoon the enemy retreated out of his reach. The two armies parted company on 9 August, when Frederick made off to fight the Russians, and Daun marched back to take up the road to Lusatia. Bohemia, like Moravia, was now free of the enemy.

To Saxony, Late August 1758

The contending forces which had been massed in far north-east Bohemia suddenly broke apart in the second week of August. Frederick took off with 11,000 troops for his urgent business with the Russians, and left Markgraf Karl of Brandenburg-Schwedt with 33,000 men to cover Silesia. On the Austrian side *FZM.* Harsch (despite Daun's misgivings) took over the guard of north-east Bohemia with 15,000 troops, while the main force (now 70,000 men) looped back through Bohemia to make for the northern plain by way of Zittau in Lusatia.

Daun set out from Jaromiersch on 9 August, and on the 17th he planted himself in the camp at Zittau, from where he had faced the enemy in a tense confrontation exactly one year before. He wrote from there to Maria Theresa to propose turning to the west, so as to act with the *Reichsarmee* to liberate Saxony from the forces of Frederick's brother Prince Henry of Prussia. The Empress and Kaunitz agreed, for they were already thinking along the same lines.[87]

The Austrians were sacrificing the opportunity to act in concert with the Russians and crush Frederick between them. However it was entirely in keeping with the conventional military thinking of the eighteenth century to give priority to geographical and logistic advantages, and to regard one's most powerful ally, in this case the Russians, as a counterweight rather than a partner in the destruction of an enemy.

If it would be unhistorical to condemn the new 'Saxon' strategy of the Austrians outright, there is little to be said for the half-hearted way in which Daun put it into effect. As was only sensible, he left *FZM.* Prince Christoph of Baden-Durlach with some 16,000 troops at Zittau, so as to guard the army's rear and its line of

*The genial Friedrich Michael Prince of Zweibrücken-Birkenfeld,
commander of the Reichsarmee in the middle years of the war
(Military Academy, Wiener Neustadt)*

communication from Bohemia. It was however no more than an empty gesture to send *FML.* Loudon and 7,000 light troops raiding down the Spree into Prussian Lower Lusatia. On 25 August Loudon captured the tiny fortress of **Peitz** from its garrison of militia, and planted himself at Cottbus as a base for his raiding parties. Lieutenant Geissler of the Nádasdy Hussars [H11] was able to make contact with the Russians, while Lieutenant Colonel Palasty of the Esterházy Hussars [H24] plundered in the western suburbs of Frankfurt, but enterprises of this kind were too feeble to constitute an effective diversion against Berlin, or to lend any real encouragement to the Russians.

Free of any interference from the Austrians, Frederick had set off from Landeshut with 11,000 troops, and on 21 August he reached the 26,000 men of Lieutenant *GL.* Dohna on the Oder. Over the previous week the Russian *Generalanshef* Fermor had dragged his cumbersome army into the Neumark of Brandenburg, and was now bombarding Cüstrin, a little fortress which stood at the confluence of the Wartha and the Oder just over eighty kilometres from Berlin.

Frederick forced the Russians to raise the siege, crossed the Oder downstream, and on 25 August brought Fermor to battle at **Zorndorf**. The encounter was indecisive but exceptionally bloody. Maria Theresa commented that 'the courage shown by the Russians surpasses all belief; the two armies must have been virtually wiped out.'[88]

On 1 September the Russians fell back in good order to Landsberg, their forward supply base on the Warthe, which was still only a couple of marches distant from the Oder. Frederick's success had been of the most slender kind, but he could not afford to linger any more in this part of the world, and on 2 September he turned back west to settle with the Austrians.

Daun was 120 kilometres away at Görlitz when the Russians and Prussians fought at Zorndorf, and this great distance not only precluded him from giving even indirect help to his allies, but resulted in the Austrians receiving the news of the outcome in a tardy and garbled form. Daun set out for the Elbe on 26 August, and a slow westward march brought him to the river at the beginning of September.

THE *REICHSARMEE* AND THE AUSTRIANS, SPRING AND HIGH SUMMER 1758

By transferring the scene of his operations into Moravia so early in the season, Frederick had left something of a vacuum in north-west Bohemia and Saxony. On the Prussian side the king's place was taken by his brother Prince Henry, who took command (in fact his first independent command) on 3 March, and had some 27,000 troops at his disposal in Saxony. Inside Germany the *Reichsarmee* was being recruited and re-equipped with surprising speed after the battering it had sustained in 1757. Prince Hildburghausen resigned the command in January 1758, and on 28 April Friedrich Michael Prince (*Pfalzgraf*) Zweibrücken-Birkenfeld took charge of the troops who were gathering around Bamberg. Still only thirty-five years of age, Zweibrücken was a tall, affable individual who had already accumulated considerable experience with the French in the War of the Austrian Succession. He had become a French lieutenant general in 1746, and by the spring of 1758 he was field marshal in the services of both Austria and the *Reich*.

Maria Theresa assured Zweibrücken that 'as far as the *Reichstruppen* are concerned, I will do everything in my power to avoid any accusation that I am employing them solely for the defence of my own lands.'[89] In fact the *Reichsarmee* was being used in Austrian interests, for in the wider scheme of things the Germans were being used to help to compensate for the absence of the main Austrian field army under Daun, which was drawn into Moravia to counter the great Prussian invasion. In the second half of May the *Reichsarmee* marched east into Bohemia, and encamped to the number of some 26,500 troops behind the Eger. The Austrian forces remaining in that part of the world consisted of 27,650 men under *GdC.* Serbelloni, who was once more plaguing his generals by his 'peasant pride... his miserable Italian artifices, his pedantic trickery.'[90]

Prussian detachments were already launching a series of spoiling attacks into the *Reich* and Bohemia—the precursors of many of the same early in the following years. The most serious of the kind was undertaken in late May

123

and early June by *GL.* Driesen with up to 4,000 troops. The Prussians returned to the charge in the third week of June, but this time were met by a mixed force under the command of the Austrian *GFWM.* Gabriel Luzinsky, who commanded the Splényi Hussars [Hii)], supported by volunteers of the *Reichsarmee*, and beat off an attack by an estimated 4,000 Prussians at **Asch**, on the 19th. The Austrians praised 'the courage and composure with which the troops of the Empire fought on this occasion.'[91]

The only enterprise of note by the friendly forces also had the character of a raid. The author was *GdC.* Hadik, who commanded an advance corps of ten battalions and eleven squadrons stationed ahead of the Eger line. His target was the walled town of **Pirna** and the adjacent castle of **Sonnenstein** by the Elbe only nine miles above Dresden. He intended to take the defenders by surprise, remove the artillery, ammunition and supplies, and wreck the fortifications. A number of Croats and hussars would then occupy the ruins, under orders to fall back in the face of superior forces.

Hadik set off with a mixed force of some 3,500 Austrian troops from Teplitz, marched north-east under the border hills, then struck across the highlands to arrive at Krietschwitz, within tactical striking distance of his objectives, at ten in the morning of 5 June. Hadik's plans were typically elaborate. When they worked well, they worked very well indeed, and when they did not they tended to fall apart in a complicated way. On the present occasion the decisive break-ins were to be made by two columns:

Left-hand (W.) column:

GFWM. Prince Sulkowsky, c. 700 grenadiers, fusiliers and Croats, to work around to the west of the town, arrive on the northern side facing the river and break in from there.

Right-hand (E.) column:

GFWM. Campitelli, c. 1270 grenadiers, Hungarian fusiliers and Croats, to reach the Elbe at Cunnersdorf, progress along the river bank, pass under the Sonnstein and break into the town by the Schitt-Tor on the northern side, and then come at the Sonnenstein from the rear.

Hadik with the follow-up forces would advance, and penetrate the town from the south.

It went badly from the start. Sulkowsky had been foisted on Hadik by higher authority, and the prince repaid Hadik's mistrust to the full. His guide was the loyal and thoroughly reliable Saxon gardener Johann Christian Hähnl, but Sulkowsky claimed to recognise him as a double agent. In the darkness the progress fell further and further behind, amid argument and recriminations, and the confusions were augmented when the Hungarian infantry regiment of Gyulai [51] wandered over from Campitelli's column and joined Sulkowsky's by mistake. By Sulkowsky's account 'the day began to dawn when we reached the suburb of Pirna, and after we had been led astray for a quarter of an hour… it was so light that the grenadier captain Ressler took out a letter and was able to read it. We were then by the archway of the fortress… and we heard quite distinctly the cry of *Wer da?* which the sentries give out every quarter of an hour.'[92] Sulkowsky called off the enterprise, and Hadik was astonished to encounter him on his way back.

With the disappearance of his 773 Hungarian fusiliers Campitelli had lost his main striking force. He reached his assigned attacking position thirty minutes after midnight, but he was greatly-under strength, and detecting no sign of Sulkowsky (who was supposed to initiate the attack), he ordered the retreat. The Prussian garrison was unaware that it had ever been under threat.

Hadik's entire force fell back over the border. In the earnest investigations which followed the key question was put to Hähnl: 'Why did you take the column on so long and roundabout a route?' 'I can affirm with a good conscience that… on the contrary I led it along the most direct path, and the reason why the march went so slowly was that the troops were not made to march in an orderly and regular fashion, but allowed to proceed at a leisurely pace and with frequent halts. I am perfectly confident that even at an ordinary pace it would have taken one and a quarter hours at the most to arrive at the Elbe-Tor [of Pirna] from Krietschwitz, instead of which we came to a stop at least four or five times, and on each occasion for a good half an hour. I can call on the testimony of the general adjutant Lieutenant Mohr, who went back several times to beg the prince to march in a proper and suitable fashion.'[93]

Hadik rightly trusted his Saxon gardener more than his Polish prince, and Sulkowsky was suspended from duty. Later in the war Sulkowsky was found to be implicated in scandalously fraudulent dealings.

All of this time the main forces of the Austrians and the *Reichsarmee* remained out of harm's way behind the Eger, During the period of waiting the Prince of Zweibrücken got the better of Serbelloni in a matter of some technical interest. The conventional order of battle assigned the *Reichsarmee* to the left wing, and the Austrians, as the senior partners, to the right, which reminded Zweibrücken of an episode in the war of the Austrian Succession when the French had singled out the Dutch contingent for attack. There was a distinct relationship with the battle tactics of the King of Prussia, who in almost of all his battles had adopted 'the oblique order, whereby he holds one of the enemy wings in check by various manoeuvres, and meanwhile overwhelms the other by his full force. For that reason I thought it dangerous to have all the Austrian troops positioned on one side, and all the *Reichstruppen* on the other.'[94] The obstinate Serbelloni refused to be swayed, upon which Zweibrücken submitted the matter to Maria Theresa, and the *Hofkriegsrath,* (doubtless at her request) ordered Serbelloni to station Austrian cavalry and foot on both wings.

The joint forces encamped in this way for the first time at Teplitz, beyond the Eger, on 30 July. Prince Henry had already decided to evacuate western Saxony, and to mask his retreat he had dispatched Major General Asseburg to fall on the fieldworks of *GFWM.* Kleefeld at **Sebastiansberg** on 31 July. A five-hour fight ended with the Prussians beaten off with a loss of 238 men.

It was not until the middle of August that the main forces of Zweibrücken and Serbelloni moved across the border into Saxony, which was their first offensive action of any kind.

Prince Henry had 30,000 troops at the most available for the open field, and towards the end of the month he decided that even his new positions were untenable against the enemy forces moving against him on both sides of the Elbe, and that he must fall back behind the steep, wooded ravine of the Müglitz, which offered him his last defence short of Dresden.

Hadik was back near the **Sonnenstein** on 4 September, this time having marched his twelve battalions and thirteen squadrons from Berggiesshübel to cover the siege of the isolated garrison under Colonel Grape. Three batteries opened fire at first light on the 5th, and later in the day Grape asked for terms. He surrendered himself and his 1,483 troops as prisoners of war. There had been no casemated protection in the place, the magazines were located in wooden structures, and the parapets were of splintery stone. 'All the same the commandant had the advantage of three rock-hewn ditches, of which the one nearest the fortress was of astounding depth. He could have awaited the completion of the siege approaches, which would have enabled him to hold out a further eight days, and gained more favourable terms.'[95]

TO HOCHKIRCH,
1 SEPTEMBER - 13 OCTOBER 1758

If Daun moved fast he could still make a great deal out of the passing opportunities in Saxony, for which the Austrians had sacrificed their co-operation with the Russians. Prince Henry and the 21,000 troops under his immediate command were situated unenviably in the hills south of Dresden. He was outnumbered almost two to one by the forces which faced him, namely Zweibrücken's 18,500 *Reichstruppen* and 20,860 Austrians. Henry now also had to reckon with Daun and his army of 57,000 troops, who were poised within close bridging distance of the Elbe downstream near Meissen, from where they could gain the west bank of the Elbe and come against the Prussian rear.

Daun spent 2 and 3 September waiting on the eastern bank of the Elbe, in other words consuming two or more days of the putative fifteen which had been given him by Frederick's march against the Russians. He was disturbed by the first contradictory reports of the battle of Zorndorf, which reached him on 31 August, and he now wanted Zweibrücken to attack Prince Henry south of Dresden, so that the Austrians could cross the Elbe at Meissen unopposed. Lacy arrived with Daun's plan on 1 September, but if Zweibrücken had any wish to comply, he lost it on the same day, when he learned that Prince Henry had fallen back from the camp of Sedlitz to behind the Müglitz valley (below).

Daun's scheme collapsed altogether when he received mistaken reports from Loudon, which put Frederick much further along the road back to Saxony than he really was. Daun gave up the idea of crossing the Elbe below Dresden, and instead marched his army upriver past the city to Radeberg on 4 September, and to Stolpen on the 5th.

If the first grand manoeuvre against Henry had collapsed, the royal brother Frederick had still to arrive from the eastern theatre, and the allied forces were now at least on a level with one another on the respective banks of the Elbe above Dresden. Zweibrücken was able to occupy the whole of the historic camp of Pirna, after the castle of Sonnenstein had surrendered on 5 September (above). On the eastern side of the Elbe, Daun's army was ensconced behind the Weissnitz stream among the basalt crags of Stolpen, 'one of the strongest [positions] in Saxony, covered by steep slopes, ponds, bogs, woods and sunken roads.'[96] The two sets of forces communicated by means of a pontoon bridge which was built from Stadt Wehlen on the east bank to the camp of Pirna, and Daun and Zweibrücken were in daily contact.

Daun, the victor of Kolin, the saviour of Olmütz, now received a letter in which Maria Theresa began to display anger and impatience at the pace of his operations. She could not understand why he had found it impossible to cross the Elbe at Meissen at the beginning of the month. She was now open to the reproaches of her allies, both for having allowed Frederick to fall on the unsupported Russians, and for having achieved so little against Prince Henry, who was outnumbered so vastly by the Austrians and the *Reichsarmee*. For these reasons it was vital 'to go straight for the enemy by one means or other in the course of the present campaign.'[97]

Conscious of the pressure that was bearing upon him, Daun returned to the notion of bringing Henry under a joint attack. Zweibrücken's main force was to assail Henry's

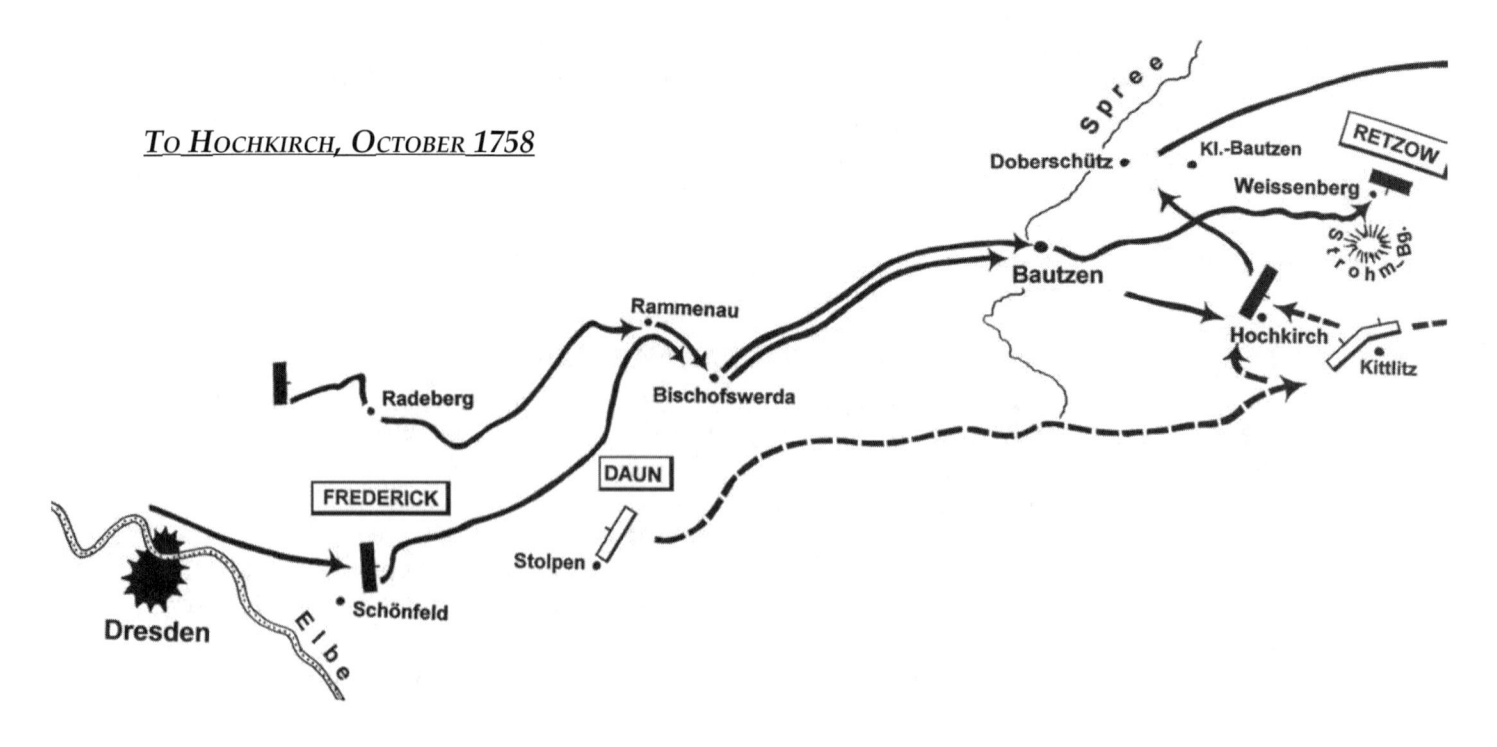

To Hochkirch, October 1758

position behind the Müglitz in multiple columns, while the corps of Hadik worked around to the west and fell upon the enemy right flank in the neighbourhood of Maxen. On the eastern side of the Elbe, the 10,000-strong corps of Loudon had arrived on the scene, and was now to lunge through the forested Dresdener Heide as if to attack the Neustadt of Dresden. With the attention of the Prussians thus distracted, Daun would bring the main Austrian army across the Elbe to the west bank above Dresden, by the mouth of the Lockwitz stream. The effect would be to bring Henry under attack from three sides—by Zweibrücken across the Müglitz from the south, by Hadik from the west, and by Daun from his rear.

The grand scheme was supposed to be put into effect on the night of 9/10 September, but was put off until the following night because Zweibrücken pleaded that it was impossible for his forces to be ready on time. It was already too late, for Daun had used up all his term of grace, and by the 10th Frederick had brought up 15 or 16,000 troops from the Oder, reunited with his covering force from Silesia, and was now scarcely one march distant from the Elbe with a combined army of 43,000 troops. At 11.30 that morning Daun asked Montazet to call on him at his headquarters at Stolpen. The Frenchman discovered him in the company of *GdC.* Carl O'Donnell, the Intendant Baron Netolitzky, *FML.* Lacy the chief of staff, and the Russian military attaché Colonel Springer.

Daun gave Montazet the alarming news from Loudon that Frederick's army or at least a large Prussian corps had arrived at Gross-Dobritz and would be able to reach Dresden on the 11th. As the debate developed, Montazet saw that he and Lacy were alone in desiring the strike against Prince Henry to go ahead. Daun and all the others were concerned about the Austrians being sandwiched between Henry and Frederick, and O'Donnell let slip the revealing phrase that in spite of the frustrations 'the important thing is to conserve the army of the Empress.' Daun had in addition lost all faith in the support of the *Reichsarmee*, and the meeting ended with the decision to call off the attack.[98]

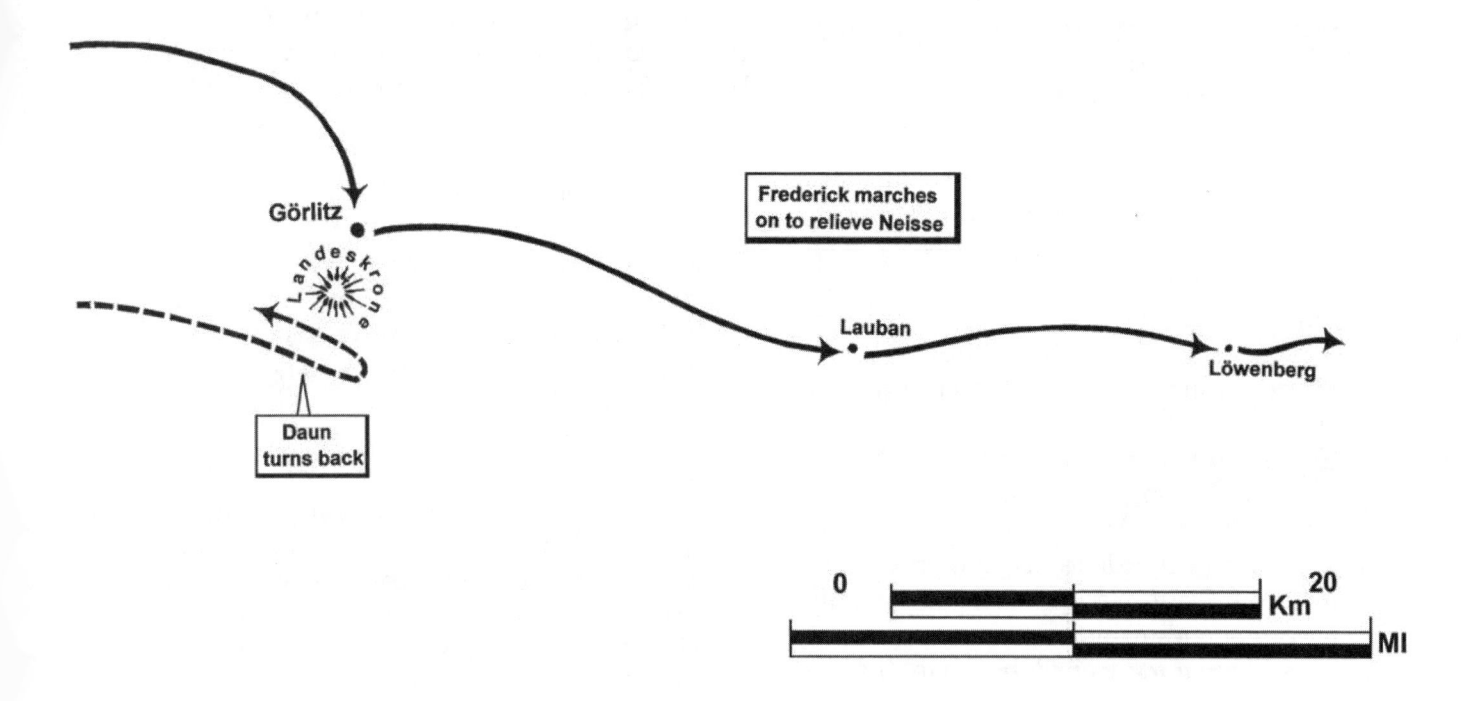

Daun's reputation with his army had suffered its first serious blow. The regimental officers believed that the operation had been abandoned for no better reason than to stage a review for Count Haugwitz, the Austrian chief minister of internal affairs, who in the event scarcely bothered to look at the troops who were being paraded for him.[99] The Prince of Zweibrücken gave out that he was furious at the debacle, and that he would have liked to remove himself with 24,000 troops to go campaigning with the Russians.[100]

Daun offered his own explanations to Maria Theresa. 'The blow failed on account of the arrival of the king, the misleading report of Loudon—the man on whom I had placed the greatest reliance—and the delay of twenty-fours before the combined army [of Zweibrücken] could have taken part. The enterprise would have succeeded if I had been a man attended with greater good fortune, and more deserving of the divine assistance. I begged the Prince of Zweibrücken to join in without this delay of twenty-four hours, but it was hopeless, because I am dogged by bad luck which set at nought all my zeal and sense of urgency, and renders me useless for the service of Your Majesty.'[101]

When Vienna now reviewed the friendly forces, it found that:

The combined forces of Zweibrücken west of the Elbe amounted to 40,000 troops.
Daun and the main army of 57,000 Austrians (including Loudon's corps) were on the east side of the river in the neighbourhood of Stolpen.
Baden-Durlach's corps of 15,800 men was guarding Daun's flank towards Silesia, and the line of communication coming up from central Bohemia by way of Zittau.
FZM. Harsch (15,250) was stationed at Königgrätz, the entry to north-east Bohemia, with *FML.* de Ville's corps of 17,000 was hovering on the Silesian-Moravian borders.

Both sides began to look east as the means of breaking the deadlock around Dresden. Maria Theresa and Kaunitz authorised Daun to send a flying corps to join the Russians, or even to go to meet them with his entire army. In any case they commissioned Harsch to lay siege to Neisse in south-east Silesia. His background was in engineering, and he had long been keen on this project.

Frederick was also searching for ways to restore his freedom of movement, for his army was jammed on the east bank of the Elbe between the Neustadt of Dresden and Daun's position at Struppen. If Daun was unassailable frontally, he was vulnerable in his line of communication, which still ran north from Bohemia to Zittau in Upper Lusatia, then west around the foot of the hills to Stolpen. The first sign of a threat to this sensitive flank materialised in the shape of a Prussian advance guard of 9,000 troops under *GL.* Retzow, whom Frederick sent marching east. Retzow reached Bautzen on 29 September, and on 2 October he pushed a detachment to Weissenberg near Hochkirch, which presented a direct challenge to the corps of Baden-Durlach (above) at Löbau, The camp at Stolpen was in danger of having its supplies cut off, and Daun and his generals decided that they must abandon their position after a month's residence, and move to protect their link with Bohemia. The retreat seemed like a further episode in an endless chapter of frustrations, and the Austrians had no inkling that the move was to give them battle and victory.

On the night of 5/6 October Daun's army slipped away from the camp of Stolpen in two columns. It was a technically difficult march, which had to be executed in darkness and across broken country, but Lacy's staff work was admirable, and the main body was well on its way to the new camp between Crostau and Cunewalde before the Prussians noticed on the 6th that Daun had departed. Frederick sent the free battalions of Angelelli and du Verger by way of Bischofswerda to reach the road beyond Nieder-Putzkau. Just short of their destination these gentry were attacked by the Austrian rearguard (the Kaiser and Esterházy Hussars [Hs 2, 24] under the command of *GFWM.* Emmerich Esterházy).[102] The Prussians lost altogether 324 men, and Frederick himself was nearly captured in the scramble.

Daun resumed his eastward march on 7 October, and planted is army in a sprawling camp which extended from the heavily-wooded Kuppritzer-Berg (an outlying ridge of the border hills) to the right wing on gently-sloping ground by Kittlitz. Durlach's corps was sited out to the right at Reichenbach, and the Austrian deployment as a whole not only gave direct cover to the line of communication leading up from Zittau, but placed the Austrians on the important lateral route which extended to Saxony in the west and Silesia in the east.

The Austrian army now stood within striking distance of the corps of *GL.* Retzow, positioned at Weissenberg just four miles to the north, and Daun planned to attack from two sides on the morning of 9 October, with the right wing of the main army advancing from the south, and Durlach approaching from the east. The operation was countermanded on the evening of the 8th, because Durlach was not ready. It was a familiar story, and Daun wrote to Maria Theresa that 'it is impossible, Most Gracious Lady, to do anything with the generals. A state of affairs which I find most depressing and unfortunate.'[103] There was no time to revive the project, for Frederick was now on the scene with his main army.

On the morning of 10 October the king advanced his 30,000 troops along the axis of the highway from Bautzen; he halted at Hochkirch to wait for the dense fog to clear, and trusted that Retzow would carry out a particular commission to emplace his corps (now 10,000 troops) on the smooth knob of the Strohm-Berg, a commanding height opposite Daun's right wing. In the event Retzow delayed his advance until Frederick was within supporting distance, and the delay gave time for *GFWM*. Siskovics to rush four battalions of grenadiers and a number of heavy cannon to reinforce the Croats who had been holding this isolated position. The fog lifted at eleven in the morning, and showed Frederick that the Austrians were ensconced on this key terrain.

Daun was now able to wheel his right wing so that its flank rested on the Strohm-Berg. From there his camp extended south-west in a straggling alignment to the ridge of the Kuppritzer-Berg. Frederick deployed his army three miles to the north-west on a roughly parallel alignment. He was not over-concerned with the tactical niceties, for he intended to stay at Hochkirch only until a convoy of bread arrived from Bautzen and he could resume his eastward progress. Meanwhile the civilian traffic passed along the highway, escorted by the troops of the rival armies, who handed the vehicles to each others' safekeeping as they passed through the outpost zone.

It appeared to Kaunitz that the Austrians had once more forfeited the initiative to Frederick, who seemed to be able to move at will between Saxony and Silesia, and had somehow learned of the Austrian designs on Neisse even before they had been settled in Vienna.[104] Kaunitz summoned an emergency conference, and on 13 October Maria Theresa wrote to Daun in the most urgent terms that something decisive was needed to keep France in the alliance, and to restore the goodwill of the Russian generals.[105] The next day, 14 October, was the eve of the Empress-Queen's patron saint Theresa, and Daun was going to honour it in a quite unexpected way.

HOCHKIRCH, 14 OCTOBER 1758

a) Austrians
Main army: c. 60,000; c 46,000 regular and Croatian infantry; c. 14,000 cavalry
Corps of Baden-Durlach: 18,000.
Total of pieces: 240, including forty-four 12-pounders and howitzers with the main army, and six 12-pounders and howitzers with Baden-Durlach
Losses: 7,579 (excluding Croats and gunners); 6,663 infantry, 916 German cavalry and hussars
b) Prussians
Main army: up to 30,000
Corps of Retzow: c. 10,000
Total of pieces: 200, including 140 heavy
Losses: 9,097, with 104 pieces

Positions and plans

Frederick had placed his army in a long, shallow deployment which faced generally east, and was designed to take advantage of the frontal obstacle presented by a brook which descended to the north in a deepening little valley by way of Kuppritz and Niethen. Five regiments of infantry and four regiments of cuirassiers were therefore ranged about 800 yards to the west of the stream along the axis of the path from Hochkirch north to Rodewitz (the headquarters).

The area around Rodewitz was a close-set country of small fields, hollows and patches of woodland, and Frederick thought it necessary to place his left wing (eight battalions of grenadiers, one of fusiliers, and some Jäger) on the far, or eastern side of the stream, where the ground swelled between the valley near Rodewitz and the hollow of Lauske. This wing formed a distinct right-angle, with east- and south-facing fronts, and just in front of the latter the Prussians built a battery and stuffed it with heavy cannon.

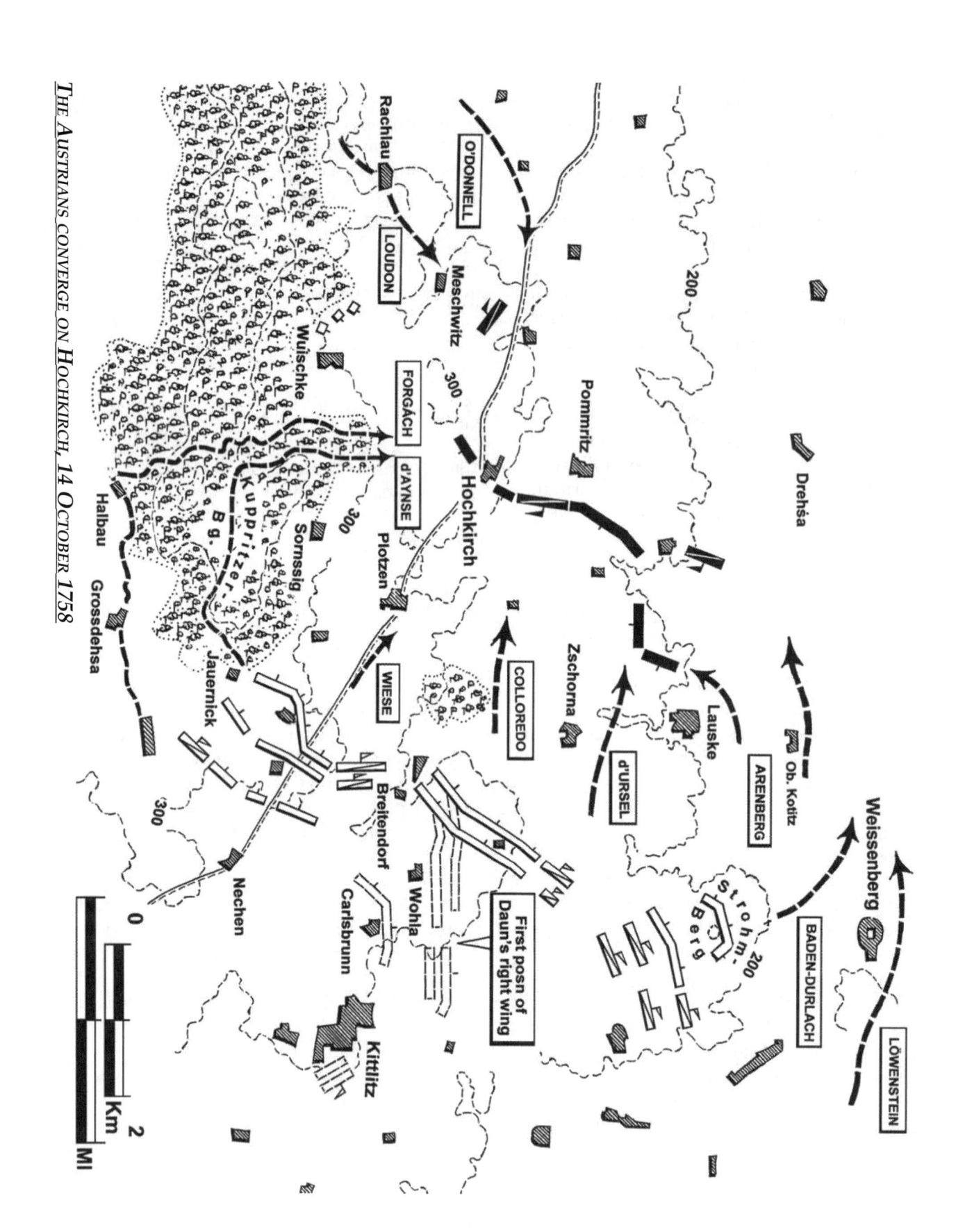

The Austrians converge on Hochkirch, 14 October 1758

The matching right (southern) wing of the army was emplaced on the hill of Hochkirch, a village of narrow streets, dominated by a splendid new Lutheran church with a tall and elegant onion-dome tower that could be seen for miles around. The two battalions of the regiment of Markgraf Karl [19] were stationed in the village, and Jäger garrisoned the churchyard, where an outlying palisade gave added strength to the substantial surrounding wall. This flank of the army was closed up by a large entrenched battery with a smaller earthwork on either side.

The ground to the south of the fieldworks was deceptively open, and descended smoothly into a broad hollow before it rose through the pinewoods of the Kuppritzer-Berg (known as the Czorneboh to the Slavonic Sorbs who lived thereabouts.) The irregular margin of the forest lay generally about one mile from Hochkirch. However a tongue of woodland between Wuischke and Sornssig offered the enemy the facility of a covered approach to within a few hundred yards, and, more dangerously still, the greater part of the hollow was invisible from the earthworks, which were sited too far back from the edge of Hochkirch hill to take the low ground under view. All the security of the Prussian right flank therefore rested on two free battalions (Angelelli and du Verger), which were posted on the far side of a birch wood which overlooked the path from Wuischke.

Daun decided that he must attack. He knew that all ranks of the army were in the mood, and he detected that the enemy had become overconfident and careless, as he verified in the course of a reconnaissance on 11 October. The Prussians were indeed fortifying their southern flank at Hochkirch, but Daun had concluded that the whole of their army could be rolled up from there.[106]

It can hardly be emphasised strongly enough that the form of attack was entirely novel, namely by means of independent, converging columns, a form of grand tactics which influenced the Austrian way of making war until the 1790s. Lacy as chief of staff devised the scheme as a whole, though an important contribution to the detail was made by Colonel Charles Amadei, who writes that he had been 'entrusted with the chief attack, and in a conference or meeting beforehand I proposed … to assault in columns, as giving a greater chance of success.'[107] He was probably harking back to the action at Moys (7 September 1757) when columns were employed to attack the Jäckelsberg.

In general terms, Daun intended to bring his main force over the Kuppritzer-Berg and destroy the Prussian right wing in the neighbourhood of Hochkirch. Two columns (Forgách and d'Aynse) were to make directly from the woods and attack Hochkirch from the south. Although he did not put it down on paper, it was clear from the Prussian accounts that the fortifications and churchyard were to be infiltrated by trusted soldiers, who would persuade the Prussians that they were deserters, and so facilitate the assault of the two main columns, which would come at the enemy from the flank and rear and press the initial attack with bayonet and sabre.[108] A further attack was to be delivered by the Austrian left (columns of O'Donnell and Loudon) which would reach the highway to the west of Hochkirch, and assault from that side. The Netherlandish regiment of de Ligne [38] had the particular task of evicting the free battalions who were assumed to be guarding the highway, and for the sake of speed they were ordered to leave their colours with the baggage. The men were affronted, but Captain the Prince de Ligne persuaded them that 'it was doing us a great deal of honour to treat us like grenadiers, who do not carry colours. If we wanted colours, we would take those of the enemy.'[109] For convenience the columns of O'Donnell, Loudon, Forgách and d'Aynse will together be termed 'Main Attacks' in the description which follows.

Further columns (Wiese, Colloredo, d'Ursel, Arenberg) were to present themselves opposite the east-facing front of the Prussian camp, to fix the attention of the enemy, and then exploit the success of the main attack. In the narrative these activities will be called 'Subordinate Attacks.' The entirely separate corps under the Prince of Baden-Durlach would move to the Strohm-Berg to the east of the field, and prevent the corps of Retzow from intervening in the battle. Durlach's responsibility will be termed the 'Holding Operation.' Finally the Prince of Löwenstein was to operate in the far north beyond the Löbauer-Wasser and (although this was not spelt out) possibly cut in behind the defeated Prussians.

Every passing hour increased the risk that Frederick might discover the weakness of the Prussian right wing, but the Austrians could not open their attack before they had cleared the paths for their columns over the Kuppritzer-Berg, and for that reason the enterprise was postponed from 12 to 13 October, and again from the 13th to the 14th. However the Austrian high command had limitless reserves of guile, and now put into effect an elaborate programme of hoaxes. Lacy prevailed on a Walloon soldier called Alexander to desert and act as a spy, but 'not entirely trusting him, he made him believe that our left wing had furnished itself so densely with obstacles that our army could not get through them, even if wanted to exit the camp on that side ... Our picquets fired blank rounds after Alexander, who carried the bogus information to the king, which contributed greatly to his false security.'[110] On the evening of the 13th the Croats were deployed in a chain along the edge of the forest, to prevent any genuine deserters from reaching the enemy, and 'the tents remained standing in the Austrian camp, and the usual watch fires were tended assiduously. A crowd of workers were assigned to fell trees for an abattis the whole night long, which they did amid singing and constant calling-out.'[111]

Over in the Prussian camp the field chaplain Carl Daniel Küster spoke with a number of officers who shared his sense of unease, and he finally settled down in a peasant hut fifty paces from the great church. 'Meanwhile it became dark, and the watches lit their fires. The result was at once festive and dismal, for in the damp weather the whole area of the two camps lay under what seemed a cloud-covered sky,

The Prussians surprised at Hochkirch (Menzel)

through which the stars glimmered only faintly.'[112]

The main Austrian striking force had set off from its camp after nightfall, and was now making its way in four columns over the bosky ridge of the Kuppritzer-Berg. The tents were kept standing, two men from every company remained behind to feed the fires, and two drummers and one fifer from each regiment to make the regular calls. The first and second columns stumbled through the murky night, but Lacy's staff work had made due allowance for the slow progress, and all the units reached their appointed places in good time. The troops of the southern columns had less far to go, and 'before the attack we remained motionless under arms, without talking, without daring to smoke, from ten in the evening of the 13th until five in the morning of the 14th. We were so close to the enemy that we could hear them chatting, gambling, and dancing in a number of tents which had been set up by the sutlers. We muttered amongst ourselves, "It won't be long before we make you dance and play to another tune."'[113]

The clock in the church tower struck five, and the forest disgorged the columns of the main attack. 'They had scarcely marched more than a quarter of an hour before they heard a musket shot. It was followed by two others, and finally by the fire of an entire outpost, which now had a clear view of the heads of columns, and gave the alarms by shouts which soon resounded along the front of the enemy army.'[114] The musketry swelled into a roar, and 'the Austrians seemed to spring from the earth amid the colours of the Prussians in the heart of their camp! Several hundred troops had their throats cut before they could open their eyes; others sprang half-naked to their weapons.'[115] A thick fog rose at almost the exact moment of the assault, and it was rendered still more dense by the smoke from the guns and the burning straw roofs of Hochkirch, which reduced visibility to a dozen yards. It seemed to each of the Austrian columns, and to each component of the column, that it was having to fight the battle all by itself. As far as the accounts of the participants can be reconciled, they are represented by the narrative which follows

The Main Attack

The Opening Phase

First Column. *GdC*. Carl O'Donnell
4 bn, 20 sq. *GFWM*. d'Ayasasa in support with 16 elite companies of carabiniers and mounted grenadiers

Column of *FML*. Loudon
5-6,000 troops, mostly Croats, reinforced by c. 5 battalions, 2 regiments of cuirassiers, 3 of dragoons and 3 of hussars

O'Donnell's division was ordered to fall on the defences of Hochkirch from the rear (west), and it reached its attacking position after a gruelling march of a dozen hours. The advance guard was commanded by *GFWM*. Philipp George Browne, elder son of the late field marshal. He was one of the most promising of the younger generals, and he now deployed the component two regiments of infantry (de Ligne [38] and Browne [36]) in the neighbourhood of Steindörfel, and pushed east towards Hochkirch along the axis of the highway.

Approaching the area of brushwood near the Locksmiths' Inn (*Schlosserschenke*) the Austrians were met by an outburst of fire, which felled Colonel Joseph Browne (younger brother of Philipp Georg) with a wound to the head. Captain the Prince de Ligne, as acting commander of the family regiment, was now left to his own devices, and advanced his Walloon infantrymen on a broad front to clear the brushwood. The enemy proved not to be the Prussian free battalions as had been supposed, but the Zieten Red Hussars [H2], who made a fighting retreat towards Hochkirch, firing their carbines and pistols. The column continued its advance to the immediate neighbourhood of the village, where the right-hand battalion of the de Ligne regiment overran the camp of one of the Prussian grenadier battalions. The men emerged from their tents half dressed, but maintained a heavy and lethal fire as they fell back.

By now the columns of O'Donnell and Loudon were converging in the smoke and darkness, and de Ligne heard what seemed to be the sound of Prussian cavalry approaching at a trot to his right. 'What resistance could I have

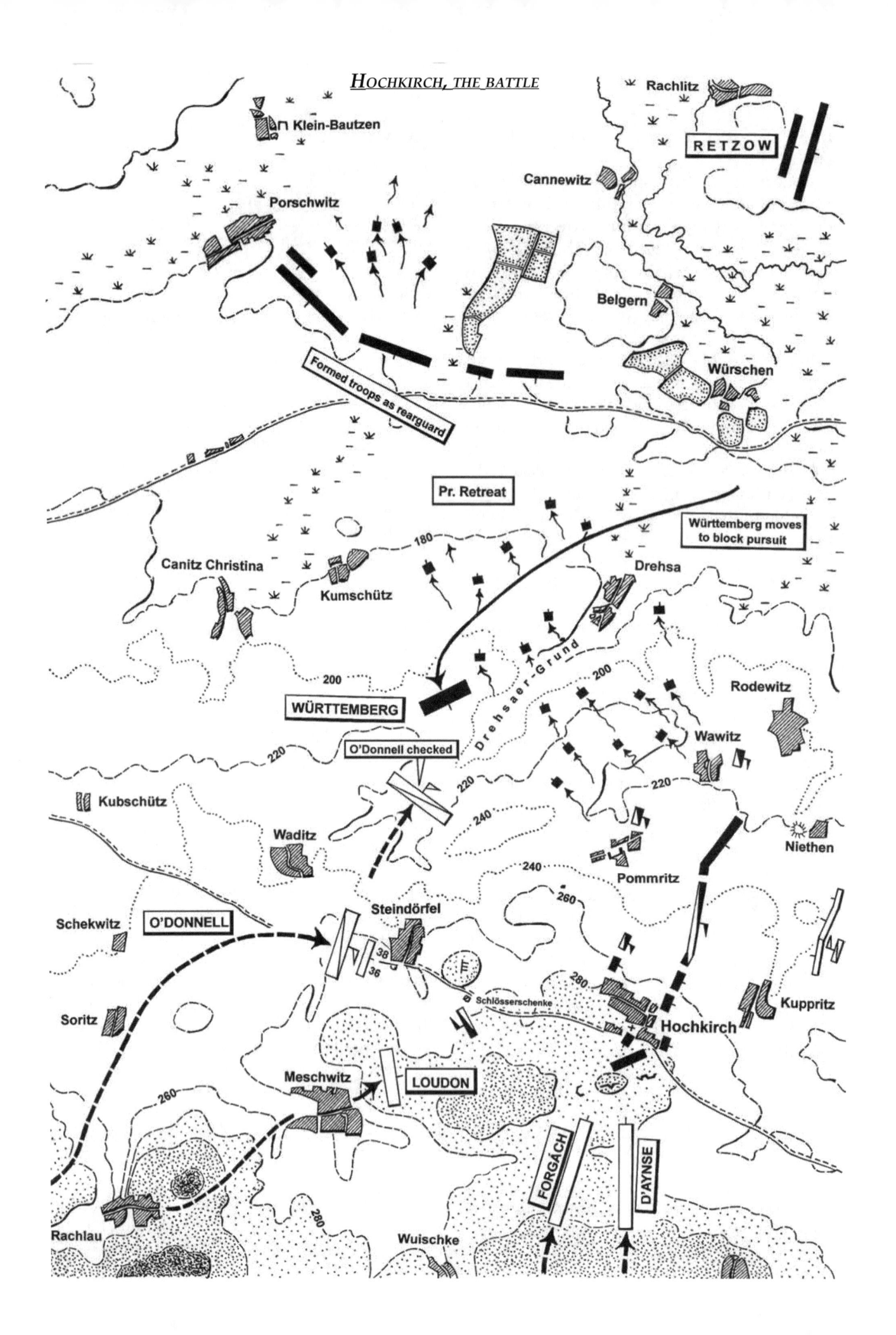

HOCHKIRCH, THE BATTLE

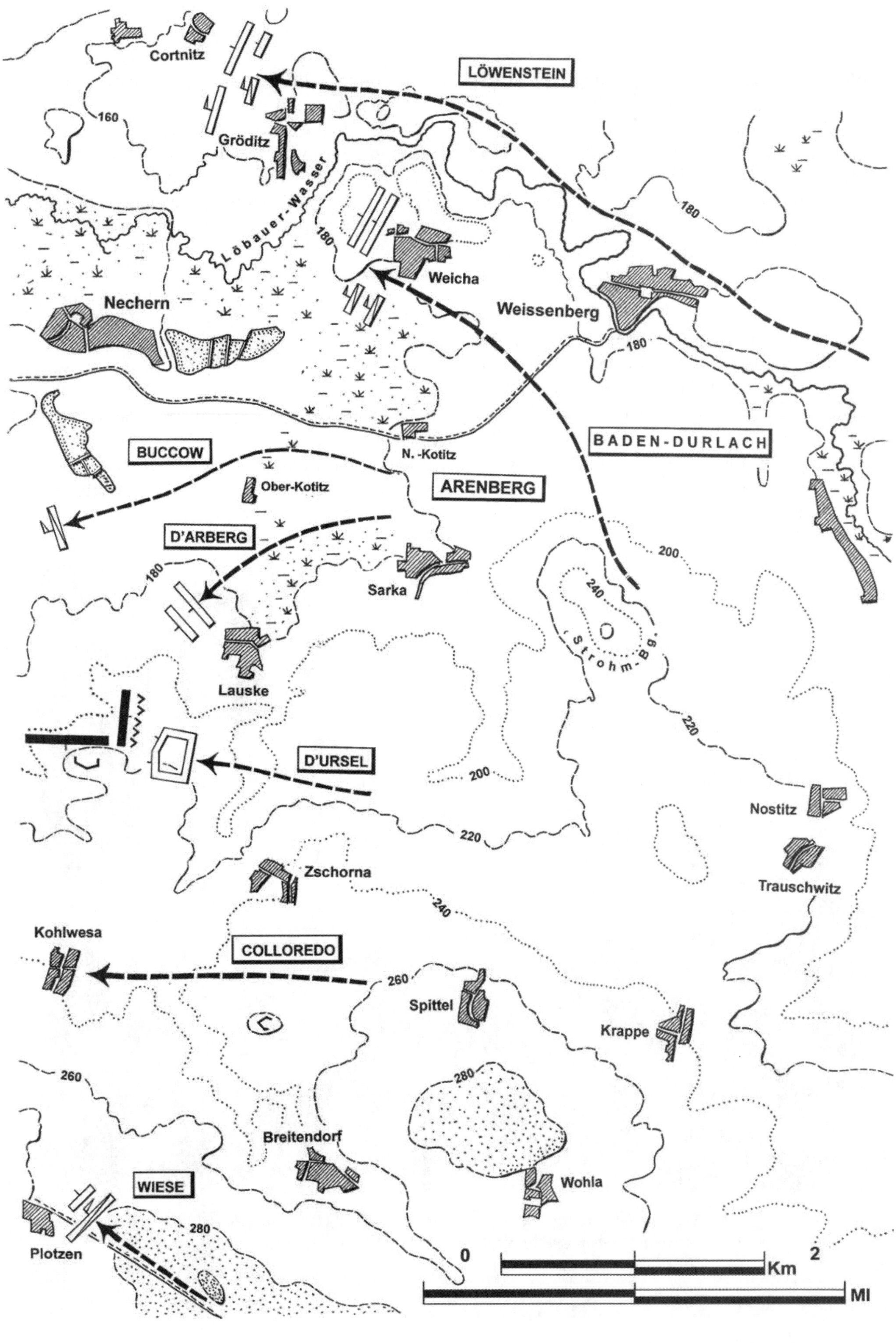
Cortnitz
LÖWENSTEIN
160
Gröditz
Löbauer-Wasser
180
180
Weicha
Nechern
Weissenberg
180
BUCCOW
N.-Kotitz
BADEN-DURLACH
Ober-Kotitz
ARENBERG
D'ARBERG
180
Sarka
200
240
Strohm-Bg.
Lauske
220
D'URSEL
200
220
Nostitz
Zschorna
Trauschwitz
240
Kohlwesa
COLLOREDO
260
Spittel
Krappe
260
280
Breitendorf
WIESE
Wohla
280
Plotzen
0
2
Km
MI

offered? However I gave the command *"Fertig!"* ("Ready!") to all my battalion, just made up of recruits. I was astonished at how calm and obedient they turned out to be. They did not let off a single round.'[116] The newcomers proved to be two regiments of horse from the companion column.

Second Column.
FML. Forgách
4 grenadier battalions, 6 infantry regiments

While O'Donnell and Loudon came at the Prussian defences in front of Hochkirch from the rear and right flank, the second Austrian column had to climb the full height of Hochkirch hill and attack the nearest fortification. They were spearheaded by the Hungarian infantry regiment of Erzherzog Carl [2], which had a fine reputation. 'And yet everything began badly. The regiment did not know what to do… for it was torn between responding to enemy fire, and advancing sabre in hand as had been ordered. The outcome was a horrible confusion. The cries of the Hungarians and of the enemy who were being taken by surprise, and the horror of the night, illuminated only by the musket shots, had something really terrifying about it.'[117]

Time was being lost in trying to re-form the regiment into a proper line by its sub-units, but Major Jekey 'rejected this military pedantry, and told the officers they must bring the men together in rank and file… it didn't matter whether they belonged to the grenadier corps or other battalions… This was in fact the shortest, indeed the only way to form a well closed-up line without loss of time.'[118] Second Lieutenant Dezier and sixty volunteers of Erzherzog Carl

The Austrians break into the tent lines at Hochkirch (Hyacinth de Pegna, part of a series which was possibly commissioned by Daun, Austrian Army Museum)

were now able to break into the closest fieldwork, whereupon the Prussian commander, a captain, escaped by vaulting the rearward face of the fortification on horseback.

The four battalions of grenadiers exploited the success by pressing on through Hochkirch village to the far end, where they were rejoined by the Netherlandish regiment of Los Rios [9], which had been directed around the side of the village (probably the west) by Forgách, and arrived still in column.

Third Column. *FML.* d'Aynse
4 grenadier battalions, four fusilier battalions

Out of all the columns of the main attack, the command of d'Aynse arrived closest to its goal without being disturbed. The projecting belt of woodland (above) gave complete cover to within 600 yards of the great redoubt, and from there it was guided by Major Johann Peter Baron Beaulieu de Marconnay of the General Staff, who had crept forward to find a way through the chain of Prussian sentries, and was able to lead the entire column to within one hundred paces of the battery.

The Prussian lieutenant Barsewisch was told afterwards that the officer of the watch had admitted a group of Austrian 'deserters' and 'allowed them to stand with the garrison around the fire, where they warmed themselves and chatted about their experiences. Our soldiers believed that they were under no kind of threat, and it seems that many of them were sitting or lying by the fire. But now the Austrians responded to an agreed signal and rushed to the weapons of the Prussian detachment and snatched them up. The first man to do so fired his musket, which was the sign for the five battalions which were lying flat on the earth close by.'[119]

The opening of this assault was nevertheless overtaken by something of a disaster. The super-large Italian regiment of Clerici [44] took the lead at the special request of its commander, Colonel Franz Valentiniani. 'With typical brutality he brandished his sword, declaring "I'll use it to skewer any coward who turns his back on the enemy."'[120] The Italians and Mediterranean riff-raff who made up the column displayed no lack of courage, but they were beaten off with a loss of 267 killed, wounded and missing, Valentiniani himself being mortally wounded. The Hungarian infantry regiment of Joseph Esterházy [37] was next in line. It collapsed and ran, following the example of its commander, Colonel Gottlieb Weiss, who made himself scarce upon the first cannon shot. He demanded urgent medical attention, but was seen later in the day in Löbau, regaling himself with beef and pork, washed down with wine.[121]

If is not clear how the redoubt was finally taken. The Prussian gunner officer Tempelhof had been stationed in the smaller work just to the east with two light 24-pounder cannon and the grenadier battalion of Plotho. A little earlier he had discharged his guns into the fog, without eliciting any response, and concluded that the firing thereabouts was occasioned by skirmishing between the outposts. 'But the firing came nearer, and so I traversed the cannon to bear on the location where the enemy must be, and got off a few more rounds. We were answered by a salvo from several battalions, which had already approached to within a couple of hundred paces. The battalion of Plotho began to fire in its turn, and I fired so rapidly that I must have discharged about fifteen rounds before I was struck to the ground all of a sudden and lay there totally stunned. My first thought was that I had been hit by a musket ball, because the blood was pouring over my face. But when I tried to get up I saw the battery behind me full of Austrian grenadiers, who had come up from behind through the tents, and I established afterwards that somebody had given me a blow over the head with a musket butt and thrown me to the earth. The battalion of Plotho was now under attack from all sides, and I witnessed an infantry combat which was more murderous than you could imagine. There was no more question of shooting, for the men did not have the space to load, and instead they concentrated on murdering each with bayonet and musket butt.'[122]

The battalion of Plotho was beaten down. The reference to Austrian grenadiers advancing through the lines of tents suggests that both the great redoubt and Tempelhof's redoubt were captured by the middle elements of the second or third columns.

Hochkirch church, with the celebrated tower. The Blutgasse leads off to the right.

The Austrians now encountered a further knot of resistance in the village churchyard. This ready-made redoubt was defended by an initial party of Jäger and fifty men of the second battalion of the regiment of Markgraf Karl [19] under First Lieutenant von der Marwitz, who beat off an assault by fifty Austrian grenadiers who had been led to their destination by a spy. In a second attack forty Austrian grenadiers actually penetrated by the back gate before they were evicted, and this effort left Marwitz shot in the chest and leaning mortally wounded against the churchyard wall. His sacrifice won time for Major Simon v. Langen to arrive with the rest of the battalion and take over the defence.

The Battle in and around Hochkirch

The Imperial collection in Vienna has a painting by the Bohemian artist Johann Christian Brand, *Die Schlacht bei Hochkirch*, which depicts the village in flames, and conveys further details of the developing battle. Austrian gunners and infantry have now turned around some of the cannon in the captured fieldworks and are firing them at their former owners (a point confirmed by the cannon shot embedded in the church today). The Prussians are lining the southern wall of the churchyard and are throwing grenades or howitzer shells, while Austrian grenadiers outside are returning the compliment. To the rear of the village multitudes of blue-coated Prussians are fleeing like ants.

The Prussian counterattacks made the fighting around Hochkirch more ferocious still. *GL.* Zieten launched the first of the kind with three regiments in the immediate neighbourhood, namely his own regiment of hussars [H2], the Czettritz Dragoons [D4] (encamped along the Bautzen highway) and the Normann Dragoons [D1]. A number of Austrian dragoons fled through the files of the Transylvanian regiment of Haller [31], and Prussian hussars, who were in close pursuit, hacked away at the infantrymen until Colonel Rhédy rallied his troops and drove them off.[123] Loudon now arrived on the scene, and the hussars were in turn pressed back on their own infantry by three squadrons of the Austrian Gelhay Cuirassiers [Ci].

Zieten's efforts gave some respite to the Prussian infantry in the village, and they advanced some way up a narrow lane which was literally running with blood (the present Blutgasse). The Austrians in their turn crowded around the churchyard wall and fought the Prussians in the alleys hand to hand. 'Our [Austrian} grenadiers were looking out for the 'Brasscaps,' as they called the Prussians, while the Prussians were making for the bearskins of the Austrians, so that they could identify each other and cut each other's throats. The soldiers were fighting in a blind fury, cutting or pointing with their swords, thrusting with their bayonets, or striking out with their musket butts, without caring overmuch whether the shots, cuts or blows landed on friend or foe. The men were just laying about themselves in self-defence, and in the hope of somehow breaking out of the appalling crush.'[123]

The Austrians now brought up pieces from the captured fieldworks to clear their advance down the lane, and *Feldprediger* Küster remembers 'that was a pretty hot three-quarters of an hour. You should bear in mind that a single copper canister holds fifty to one hundred iron balls of two to six ounces weight, and the enemy in addition loaded little chunks of hacked-about iron down the muzzles, so you may imagine just how many brave warriors were wounded or killed when just one cannon emitted a spray of such missiles. The enemy were at the same time enfilading us with 6-and 12-pounder cannon shot, so that it is a wonder that anyone had a limb that remained intact. On top of all that howitzer shells often came down among us in high trajectory. These were particularly murderous, because they squashed heads and shoulders when they landed, and smashed the feet when they exploded on the ground. Many of the soldiers who had been killed by the fire could fall to the ground only when the press became less acute.[125]

For a time the Prussians fed their reinforcements of infantry piecemeal into the battle. The Prussian field marshal James Keith organised a first push by the formidable *Donner und Blitzen* regiment of Itzenplitz [13], and the troops progressed two-thirds of the way up the lane before they were laid low by Austrian artillery firing canister from the far end. Keith

Joseph Count Murray de Melgum warded off one of the dangerous Prussian counterattacks at Hochkirch. He was one of the few Scots remaining in the Austrian service at the time. (Military Academy, Wiener Neustadt)

rode up in person to observe the fortunes of the next attack, by the regiment of Prinz von Preussen [18], and he was shot dead from his horse just twenty paces from the horrified Carl Daniel Küster. The *Feldprediger* tried to reach him, but was thrown back by the survivors of Prinz von Preussen who came crashing out of the village under a hail of bullets.

A second Prussian field marshal, the crude and energetic Prince Moritz of Anhalt-Dessau, arrived on the scene to direct a general counterattack by all the available infantry (about fourteen battalions), and this concerted effort succeeded in clearing the village and bringing some relief to the churchyard. On the Austrian side, Colonel Joseph Murray de Melgum brought up his regiment of Los Rios [9] on the initiative of *GFWM*. Tillier, who ordered him to get to the great battery before it could be retaken by the enemy. Murray reached the work in the nick of time, and found that it was being held for the Austrians by a handful of grenadiers and thirty-odd fusiliers from a variety of regiments.[126]

In such a way the Austrians were able to form a new line facing the village, and when the enemy emerged they were greeted with musketry and fire from the cannon in the battery. In the fog Moritz received a salvo from Austrian grenadiers at a range of twenty paces, and was shot through and through. He was still alive, and spent a brief period as the prisoner of the Austrian hussar cornet Tombowitz before he was rescued by a party of Prussian hussars.

The ground to the west of Hochkirch gave the Prussians much more space to deploy for their counterattacks, and it was here that Frederick in person came close to turning the course of the battle. His infantry was drawn from the unengaged Prussian centre, and comprised some of the finest units in the army, namely the regiments of Wedel [29] and Bornstedt [20], the Grenadier-Garde Battalion [6], and the second and third battalions of the Garde [15]. These fearsome people pressed south over the Löbau highway, and they were seconded by renewed attacks on the part of Zieten's cavalry, which was reinforced by the fresh elite regiments of the Leib-Carabiniers [C11] and the Garde du Corps [C13].

The Austrian cavalry in this part of the field were taken by surprise, and a number of the Austrian battalions were caught up some scrappy and desperate fighting. The Prince de Ligne found himself in command of a group of Croats, two hundred grenadiers and two battalions of his Walloon infantry, and Loudon told him to lodge his troops in the little quarries thereabouts. Dense bushes gave the men further cover as the confused fighting swirled about them. It was difficult to distinguish friend from foe, and a shot from an Austrian cannon passed uncomfortably close to Loudon and de Ligne.

The regiment of Erzherzog Carl [2] was caught up in the new battle, which indicates that the counterattack by the Prussian cavalry must have reached as far as the second Austrian column south of Hochkirch. Lieutenant Colonel Oross makes special mention of one of his subalterns, Second Lieutenant Tessedik, who 'urged his men forward again, and ended up fighting sword in hand until he was laid low by a serious wound in the head.'[127]

The exhausted Prussian cavalry came under the fire of a number of pieces which Loudon had placed near Neudörfel, and they fell back to the north, carrying with them three standards and several hundred prisoners as trophies. Major Joseph Graffenstein of the Nádasdy Hussars [H11], at the head of Loudon's corps, took the opportunity to fall on the Garde du Corps [C13], and managed to retrieve some of the cavalry's honour by recovering one standard, and rescuing four officers and a large number of men, and the Prussian regiment was 'so badly beaten up that more than one hundred of its men stuck in the ponds and bogs thereabouts.'[128] The Löwenstein (formerly de Ligne) Dragoons [D31] had seen their commander Colonel Thiennes, a hero of Kolin, killed by the pistol of the commander of the Prussian Gensd'armes, and they exacted a terrible revenge.

It was now daylight, and the fog was lifting. The retreat of the Prussian cavalry, just described, left Frederick's infantry engaged in a standing firefight to the west of Hochkirch. Some of the Prussian soldiers had fired up to 120 rounds each, for waggons had arrived with extra ammunition, but the Austrians were favoured by rising ground and the cover of the trees, and Lieutenant Barsewisch testifies that 'the shots which came from the woods were well aimed, and most of them hit our officers and soldiers in the head or chest. Major Haugwitz had his left arm shot through just by His Majesty. The king's horse, standing close by me, sustained a bullet in the neck... Our brigadier, the valiant Prince William (Franz) of Brunswick crashed dead to the ground immediately in front of our battalion, drilled by a bullet. His horse, a pure white grey... galloped off and careered up and down between the Austrian line and ours, without finding a refuge, which was very sad to see. Where the beast

Hochkirch from the north. The road is a continuation of the Blutgasse.

ended up I cannot tell.'[129]

The Austrians had nevertheless lost almost everything they had gained inside the village, and their hold on the approaches was still being threatened by Frederick and his obstinate infantry. Daun was in need of inspiration, and this was supplied by his chief of staff, *FML. Lacy*, who looked to *GFWM.* d'Ayasasa's body of elite cavalry. The first line had been engaged in holding ground under a heavy fire of artillery and musketry, and had lost 150 men in the process[130], but the second line of five companies (from the O'Donnell, Serbelloni, Ansbach and Buccow Cuirassiers [Cs 14, 12 , 33, ii]) and the Zweibrücken Dragoons [D39]) was intact. Lacy in person ordered up three of the companies, and at 8.30 in the morning he brought them in a devastating charge against the right flank of the Prussian infantry. It was the kind of attack which Lucchesi had sought to achieve at Leuthen. Now at Hochkirch Major Ravizza was in the lead with the O'Donnell Carabiniers, followed by those of Ansbach and Buccow, and his company took seven of the eight colours which fell into the hands of the Austrian horsemen as they hacked into the powerless Prussian infantry, who had at last run out of ammunition.

Brigadier Montazet had helped Lacy to persuade Daun to consent to the attack. He had ignored all the warning to change his blue French officer's coat for the Austrian white, and now 'typically brave, enthusiastic and curious, he got a little too near some cuirassiers whom he wished to attend more closely to their duty; they slashed his nose, and the more he said he was a French general, the more they hewed away at him.'[131] He recovered well from his wound, and it was reckoned that his formerly bent nose had benefited by being trimmed.

All the time the second battalion of the Prussian regiment of Markgraf Karl [19] had been holding the churchyard against repeated attacks. The defeat of Frederick's infantry left the defenders without support, and Major Simon Langen gathered the last knot of survivors at the back (northern) gate, and tried to break out of the alley which led to the Blutgasse. A few men made good their escape, but Langen was brought down with eleven wounds. The Austrians retrieved him from the carnage, treated him like the hero he was and restored him to the Prussians, but he died one week later in the keeping of the Prussians at Bautzen.

The troops of the Prussian right wing and centre, most of them in considerable disarray, made off to the north, screened by *GM.* Saldern with the fresh regiment of Alt-Braunschweig [5] and three further battalions. The cavalry of O'Donnell and Loudon had mauled the Prussian horse, but did not continue their pursuit into the infantry, and Saldern (a famous drillmaster) made his troops execute a zig-zag retreat which made it difficult for the Austrian gunners and bombardiers to find the range.

Intermediate Forces
4th Column, *GFWM.* Wiese
600 attached infantry, 2 dragoon regiments
Central Column, *FML.* Colloredo
6 infantry regiments, 1 cuirassier regiment

These bodies served to fill some of the space of three miles which extended between the Main Attack (above) to the left, and the Subordinate attack (below) to the right. They took no significant part in the battle, and Brand's painting shows them lurking on the right-hand side of his view.

Subordinate Attacks (i.e. right wing under *FZM.* Arenberg)
2nd Column, *FML.* d'Ursel
9 bn
1st Column, *FML.* d'Arberg
14 bn, supported by the cavalry division of *GdC.* Buccow, 5 cuirassier regiments, 2 hussar regiments

The commanders of the right wing were under orders to advance their columns to their attacking positions in the early morning, but then to delay the assault until the left wing's battle at Hochkirch was fairly under way. Their objective was the angular position of the isolated Prussian left (northern) wing, as it stood on the hill south of Lauske, rising between the little wooded ravines of Lauske and Niethen. By the time the action opened on this sector the Prussians had sent so many reinforcements towards Hochkirch that their forces here were reduced to six weak battalions of grenadiers. As some compensation their south-facing front was protected by an entrenched battery of thirty-seven cannon.

At midnight the Duc d'Ursel set the second (left-hand) column in march. On arriving at his forming-up position north of Zschorna he advanced the Netherlands regiment of Sachsen-Gotha [30] to an outlying valley, where the two battalions were screened by a row of bushes which lined the western side like a hedge: 'I posted the artillery some distance to the rear, and brought it up piece by piece so that the enemy would not hear it.'[132]

At seven in the morning word came from Arenberg to open the attack. Having been told that Prussian hussars were in the vicinity, the Duc d'Ursel had formed his nine battalions into a square, which was a most peculiar formation for offensive purposes. The engineer Debrout had reconnoitred the ground carefully, but when the attack finally opened the regiment of Sachsen-Gotha, at the head of the square in battalion column, veered too far to the left and arrived under the guns of the monster Prussian battery. The regiment was wrecked by canister, and d'Ursel called off the whole attack.

Further north, the powerful corps of *FML.* d'Arberg had been waiting to open its attack from the Strohm-Berg (he is to be distinguished from the overall commander on this wing, *FZM.* Arenberg). He advanced at eight in the morning, but was checked by the Prussian grenadier battalions of Kleist and Unruh [St. Gb, 2] which had moved north to block the new Austrian threat. D'Arberg renewed his attack, this time with the help of seven battalions of reinforcements from the corps of Baden-Durlach (below). The two Prussian grenadier battalions were unable to escape in time to the main body of the Prussian left wing, and were taken in flank and rear by the O'Donnell Cuirassiers [C14], who crossed four ditches and a stretch of boggy ground to get at them.[133] Forty Austrian volunteer cavalrymen now drove into the great Prussian battery from the rear, while d'Ursel's division came to life once more and attacked from the valley of Lauske.

Comprehensively assailed from all sides, the Prussian grenadiers and gunners abandoned their position, leaving the tents and cannon in place.

The Prussian Escape and the End of the Battle

By about eight in the morning the Prussian army had been beaten out of all its prepared defences and almost the whole extent of its camp. Frederick rallied his troops along a line north-eat of Pommritz, and then directed them along a general path of retreat across the bushy valley of the Drehsaer-Grund. The Austrians were closing in on all sides except the north, and they had the opportunity to change the king's defeat into an annihilation.

The former advance guards of the rival armies, the corps of the Prussian lieutenant general Retzow (14 bn, 40 sq), and the Austrian *FZM.* Christoph Markgraf of Baden-Durlach, had fallen back well to the north-east of the scene of the battle. On the map, at least, the Austrian forces on this side had the potential to block Frederick's path of escape by coming at it from the rear. The instructions, however, did not extend that far, and in the event Baden-Durlach was content to occupy the high ground at Weicha, and send *FML.* Angern with seven battalions (above) to help Arenberg in his attack on the strongly-emplaced Prussian left wing north of Hochkirch. North of the Lobauer-Wasser, the corps of Prince Löwenstein pushed around to the north of Weissenberg and finally halted between Groditz and Cortnitz. He had been unable to pin down the opposing corps of Retzow, and the Prussian was free to detach Lieutenant General Friedrich Eugen of Württemberg with four battalions and fifteen squadrons to help the king's army, now crowding towards the potential death-trap of the Drehsa valley.

Württemberg hastened across the front of the victorious Austrians and managed to reach the heights which overlooked the valley of Drehsa from the west. His battalions and his light artillery were enough to repulse an attempt by O'Donnell and the left wing of the Austrian horse to thrust down the valley from Steindörfel and Waditz. The threat to the retreat of the Prussians from their western flank, as well as their eastern, was now effectively nullified.

The only damage inflicted on the Prussians was early in the afternoon, when Major Brunyan with 600-odd dragoons and hussars and 150 Liccaner Croats overtook a convoy of Prussian baggage on its way to Baruth and the Spree. He wrecked up to 200 of the carts, and set free several hundred Austrian prisoners, most of them wounded, who had been captured early in the battle.[134]

A party of Slavonian hussars surrounded the Prussian lieutenant Cunno von der Hagen, who was escorting the wounded Field Marshal Moritz of Anhalt-Dessau to Bautzen. 'The first officer on the scene, a cornet of the Slavonians, was all for shooting and plundering us, and it took all my efforts to cover the prince against the sabres which were raised against him. It would still have been no good if I had not been fortunate enough to find a captain of the Slavonians [Baron Veldner]. I begged him to rescue the prince from those evil-minded enemies, and he behaved like an honest man, defending us pistol in hand against his own men.'[135]

A little later the whole party was overtaken by a mass of Prussian hussars. Von der Hagen claims that he in turn now saved the Austrian captain, but another account has Veldner presenting his pistol at Moritz and saying "I must now shoot Your Highness on the spot, unless you get your men to stop, and renew your parole."[136] Moritz pledged his word of honour, for the second or third time that day, and was carried on to Bautzen.

At 9.30 in the morning Daun ordered his forces to halt, 'since it was not advisable to pursue the enemy in our state of disorder. The enemy were in any case almost as strong as we were, and had the advantage of their good order and powers of recovery. We cannot compare with them in those respects; that is something that still demands a great deal of work, for our officers are altogether too sleepy and lacking in ambition and zeal. However the most important consideration was that the troops had shot off all their cartridges, and the artillery had exhausted its ammunition reserve… The fire had been maintained with great intensity for four and a half hours, with great efforts being put forth by the attack and the defence alike.'[137]

The Austrians sent a few cannon shot in the direction of Frederick's army, and in the afternoon they returned to their camp, leaving only the carabiniers and the mounted grenadiers and the intact corps of *FML*. Colloredo to clear the field. Lieutenant Gorani emphasised 'that we must always render justice where it is due. Field Marshal Daun now gave fresh proofs of his humanity, for he took the greatest care of the Prussian wounded, who were treated in the same way as ours. All the officers of our army at once gave up their horses and carriages to transport them to the hospitals.' Gorani himself was one of the twenty-six officers assigned to supervise the burial of the dead. 'Each of us had thirty soldiers and a hundred or so peasants under our orders. We collected the dead in heaps of twelve to fifteen at a time, and beside each of the piles we made a ditch, then threw the bodies inside and covered them with quick lime. We recorded the numbers of the Prussian and friendly dead in our notebooks.'[138]

The Prussians had lost more than 9,000 officers and men from all causes, including the high number of four generals and one field marshal (Keith) killed, and one field marshal (Moritz of Anhalt-Dessau) wounded and captured. They left to the Austrians the impressive number of 104 artillery pieces.

The losses of the Austrians probably amounted to rather over 8,000, including those among the Croats and the artillery. The highest unit losses among the infantry were sustained by the regiments of Clerici (267), Nicolaus Esterházy (264) and Carl Lothringen (258), and among the cavalry by the Darmstadt Dragoons (133), the Zweibrücken Dragoons (125) and the Gelhay Cuirassiers (89).

The bodies of the senior officers were brought into the cathedral-like interior of Hochkirch church. Daun entered the building, and drew Lacy's attention to a form which was lying on a wheelbarrow and covered by a red Croatian cloak. 'Lacy approached the corpse, and attentively regarding it, exclaimed with great emotion, "Alas! 'tis my father's best friend, 'tis Keith! … a Croat made his appearance, dressed in the marshal's uniform, and having across his breast the yellow riband of the Prussian order of the Black Eagle. Daun demanded of him how he came by those spoils. "I took them," answered the Croat, from the man who lies yonder, whom I killed and stripped. I have given him in return my cloak." The corpse was scarcely in the least disfigured, or bloody; not was it without some difficulty, and after considerable search, that the wound which he had received, was discoverable. A musket-ball had penetrated his side or flank, but the orifice was scarcely perceptible, and only marked by a small purple spot.'[139]

None of the Austrian field officers had been killed, but the loss of Field Marshal Browne's second son, Colonel Joseph, was felt severely. He showed every sign of recovering from the wound he had received at the outset of the action, but declined all of a sudden and died on 29 April 1759, 'one of the most skilful, brave and intelligent officers of our time. By universal consent the Empress and the state sustained with his death a loss which will not easily be made good.'[140]

Assessments

After such an achievement, it is striking to find that a number of Austrian officers viewed the happenings as a chapter of lost opportunities. According to the Prince de Ligne 'we should have completed the battle, instead of writing about it ... True, we took more than one hundred pieces of cannon and many colours. But, I repeat, we should have taken their army as well. We were just too surprised at having brought off our surprise.'[141]

Searching for the underlying causes, another regimental officer, Jakob Cogniazzo, identified the difficulty of concerting the action of the widely-separated corps.[142] On this point the Prince Hildburghausen (who had set himself up as a commentator on strategy from Vienna), adds that it was 'impossible for the generals who led the various attacks to penetrate what the field marshal had in mind, because the orders he gave were so obscure and imprecise.'[143] Arenberg had been told little more than to open his attack after the main army had assailed Hochkirch village, while Baden-Durlach could hardly have imagined from the *Disposition* that he was intended to act as a *corps de chasse*.

Although they did not grasp it, these critics were touching on the fundamental mis-match between the new grand tactics and the way the army was structured. Hitherto the generals had been accustomed to going into battle in long continuous lines, and been assured on support on at least one flank. Now they were being called upon to act as leaders of independent bodies, and in 1758 it was probably asking too much of them to plunge into what seemed a tactical void. The necessary confidence and cohesion would have been provided if the army had been reorganised into standing formations, such as the divisions as now being explored by the French, and advocated in the course of the war in various forms by Lacy and *GFWM*. Wartensleben. Nothing of the kind appeared among the Austrians until 1799, and meanwhile the regiments were being re-shuffled among the formations by the constantly-changing orders of battle, as dictated by the relative seniority of the units and the generals.

Daun's disappointment came from the fact that he had failed to annihilate the enemy. He interpreted the shortfall in personal terms, writing in confidence to Maria Theresa that the cavalry had behaved very badly, and that the grenadiers had performed below their best. Even Loudon was 'not what he used to be' (in fact he was falling ill), 'and if Durlach, Arenberg and Löwenstein had done everything that was so clearly and expressly asked of them, the enemy would have lost much more heavily, and would not been able to retreat in the way they did. In general the sad fact is that I can place so little reliance on the generals. They are willing enough, but they lack the necessary perception. I cannot be everywhere, and thus all our operations are cumbersome and attended with risk, and especially when faced with enemies like these, who have good trained generals, and serve under the eyes of their master. It is the same with their other officers, all of which makes a great contrast with our people. They, on the other hand, know that they are acting under the gaze of an exacting master upon whom their fate in this world entirely depends.'

There were just a few exceptions. On two occasions Daun almost believed that the battle had been lost, but the cavalry had been rallied through the efforts of O'Donnell, Stampa, Saint-Ignon and Caraccioli, and 'in Lacy and Tillier Your Majesty has two individuals who are worth at least six or eight of the others, and I must hasten to recommend them to Your Majesty's grace, having been beyond doubt those who contributed the most to yesterday's victory. Without them I would have been entirely without support.'[144]

When every regret had been duly registered, the fact remained that Daun had taken the foremost soldier of the age totally by surprise, and had beaten him completely from his camp. Immediately after the battle the field marshal laid out a piece of paper on a boulder of rough stone and scribbled a few lines for his senior adjutant Major Georg Sigmund Rothschütz to carry the news to the capital with all possible speed.

In Vienna 'today is the 15th, the feast day of St. Theresa, and the Almighty has honoured it in the most glorious fashion.' The gala in Schönbrunn had followed its accustomed course, except that the sermon had lasted unusually long. Maria Theresa and Francis Stephen had lunched at the great table while the ambassadors and the high nobility were regaled in the Grosse Galerie. The evening had closed with a reception, 'but scarcely had the Empress retired when, towards 8.30 postillions rode into Schönbrunn with sounding trumpets. Everyone naturally ran together, for the accustomed notice had not been given... Finally the general adjutant Baron von Rothschütz mounted the stairs and delivered the wonderful message of yesterday's magnificent victory.'[145] Maria Theresa sent word to her children in their various rooms, and they began to assemble in various states of disarray in her apartment. 'They had just congratulated her on the occasion of her name day, and now

Cajetan Count Stampa helped to rally the panicking cavalry at Hochkirch, and distinguished himself at Torgau and Teplitz (Military Academy, Wiener Neustadt)

they renewed their good wishes on account of the triumph.'[146]

On 18 October *GFWM*. Tillier arrived to the sound of twenty-four postillions, and made over the captured colours and standards together with the field marshal's formal relation. Four days later Maria Theresa and Francis Stephen attended the Te Deum in St. Stephen's cathedral, 'and in the evening there was a show in the Schönbrunn, together with two new ballets, the first representing the salvation of Europe, and the second an impromptu entertainment on a military theme… The theatre was decked out like a festive camp, with a statue of victory planted at the end. The artistes wore red and white costumes in the Roman style, and danced a ballet to the accompaniment of trumpets and drums.'[147]

After the battle
Within a week it was becoming clear what the experience signified for the Austrian army, and how much advantage Daun was likely to gain from his victory.

Maria Theresa did not stint her gratitude to the field marshal at the first news of the outcome, for her trust in him had been repaid, and the reproaches of her allies would now fall silent.[148] Daun's more detailed report of 15 October revealed the shortcomings among the regiments and the officers. Maria Theresa decided not to initiate any immediate proceedings, lest they should tarnish the victory and the courage which had been shown by the rest of the army, but she was resolved 'that in future I shall cease to regard matters so indulgently, and instead invoke the full severity and the letter of the articles of war to call to account all parties which fail in their duty, whether entire regiments or individuals. Promotions will be judged accordingly.'[149] She was as good as her word, and shortcomings and scandals of every kind were brought to light over the following years.

The Austrians stayed in their old camp at Kittlitz for two days after the battle, and Frederick's instincts told him that they did not know how to exploit their victory. The king had taken up position in front of Bautzen, and showed no inclination to move when Daun at last advanced to Wurschen, which was as close as the field marshal dared to approach. Frederick had his army fully in hand, and on the 20th he was reinforced by troops from Saxony. Lacy compared him to a dogged prize-fighter who was indifferent to the battering he had received, or 'to a phoenix which comes to life again from its ashes; no sooner do we shoot it down when we have to take another shot at it.'[150] A week after the triumph Daun reported to Maria Theresa that the situation was one of stalemate. He foresaw no reasonable prospect of liberating Saxony during the present campaign, and hoped at best to hold his footing in Lusatia through the winter.

For a time Daun forgot, or lost his faith in, the design for this phase of the campaign, which had been to entice Frederick away from Dresden by attacking Neisse in the far corner of Silesia. The siege corps of *FZM*. Harsch was now indeed emplaced before Neisse (below), and Frederick decided that he must march east to save it. After dark on 25 October he skirted around the northern flank of the Austrian camp, and by the next morning he was well on his way to Görlitz. The Austrians took up the chase with their most mobile forces (the Kaiser and Esterházy Hussars [Hs 2,24], the carabiniers and mounted grenadiers, and the *corps de reserve* under Baden-Durlach). Frederick was too quick for them. He got to Görlitz first, and the Prussian horse counterattacked so effectively that the Austrian hussars and elite cavalry had about fifty men killed and wounded and no less than 426 taken prisoner. Montazet (still nursing his truncated nose) commented that Frederick was not a military genius, 'but he has an army which allows him to commit mistake after mistake, because it repairs itself so readily. That is his strength, and that is what makes him feared by Europe.'[151]

Daun marched only as far as Jauernick. He was aware that the Prussians were on the highway, whereas the Austrians would have to continue along 'difficult and primitive roads.'[152] In any case Frederick was unwittingly falling in with the underlying Austrian plan, which was to draw him to the far end of Silesia. The only substantial force which Daun was now willing to commit in that direction was a corps of 12,000 troops under *FML*. Wied, who left the army on

28 October with orders to make for Neisse by forced marches along side roads. The risky business of snapping at Frederick's heels along the highway was left to a mixed corps (sixteen battalions and thirty-seven squadrons) under the command of the enterprising *FML*. Loudon, now recovered from his illness. With Frederick thus encouraged on his way, the main Austrian army could return to the Elbe and reduce Dresden at leisure.

Daun put the scheme to his generals on 29 October, and they endorsed the proposal without hesitation. He informed Vienna of what he had in mind, and Kaunitz replied that he could assure him 'with the greatest sincerity, that nothing has ever inspired me with such lively and heartfelt pleasure than this great and intelligently-conceived plan.'[153]

The Prussian army left Görlitz at two in the morning of 30 October, and Loudon at once took up the pursuit. He followed the Prussians as far as Jauer in Silesia, which he reached on 5 November, and he did his work so well that for many days yet Frederick was convinced that the whole of the Austrian army must be close behind.

Harsch and his Siege of Neisse, October - November 1758

FZM. Ferdinand Philipp Count Harsch was a bookish individual, despised on that account by Daun, but he was also an unusual phenomenon in the Austrian service, as being an officer who understood the sciences of siegecraft and fortification. For almost the whole of the campaigning season he had been left idle in charge of a corps which guarded the passage into north-east Bohemia by way of Königgrätz, and he had made use of his enforced leisure to devise a scheme for an attack on Neisse, the most isolated of the major front-line fortresses of Prussian Silesia.

At last, late in September, he was authorised to go ahead, because his project now fitted in with the larger scheme of campaign. He now had under his command a very substantial force of 40,500 troops, including a Bavarian auxiliary corps of 4,585 men. The French ambassador exclaimed 'how surprised I have been by the appearance of this new army, composed of garrison battalions, Bavarians and troops from Tuscany. It goes to show that this power has inexhaustible reserves of men.'[154] Harsch was given first-rate technical assistance by Jean-Baptiste Gribeauval de Vaquette, who had been taken from the French service into the Austrian with the rank of *GFWM*., and together they put more creative effort into the enterprise than their masters probably thought it deserved.

Neisse was well furnished with ammunition, and had an adequate garrison of 5,000 troops under *GL*. Tresckow. The main part of the town lay on the right bank of the river Neisse, and was enclosed by a bastioned enceinte and multiple lines of envelopes. The key to the position was however the modern star-shaped Fort Preussen, which was sited on a commanding hill on the left bank, and whose ditches and covered ways were planted with a 'forest of palisades.'[155]

The Austrians formed their investment at the beginning of October, but the authorities in Vienna delayed the march of the siege train so as to await the outcome of Daun's confrontation with Frederick, and the artillery opened fire only on the 26th. To make up for the lost time Gribeauval and Harsch did everything they could to hasten the march of the siege, and on the night of 28/29 October they established their first parallel only about 350 yards from the covered way of Fort Preussen. In the darkness the Prussians overestimated the range, and in spite of a storm of fire the Austrians escaped with only two wounded, 'which indicates that Count Harsch was... blamed wrongly for having begun the siege too late.[156]

On the 30th Harsch learned that the Prussian army had reached Görlitz on its way east into Silesia. Daun had promised that *FML*. Wied would come with reinforcements, but by 5 November there was still no news of him, and two days later Harsch abandoned the siege. Tresckow took the opportunity to make a sortie, and snapped up almost all of the Austrian ammunition and a whole battalion of the Bavarian auxiliaries.

Wied and the reinforcements from Daun

finally joined Harsch on 7 November, when he was retreating to Moravia, and on the same day Frederick in person reached Neisse with a strong escort of cavalry. Harsch had given up his siege not a moment too soon, but he had been unpopular with the public ever since the Second Silesian War, and without any interests to support him in the army or at court he became the scapegoat for everything which had gone wrong. Gribeauval was better informed, and pointed out that the operation had failed 'by reason of the delays and muddles in Vienna.'[157] Harsch had undoubtedly achieved the wider strategic aim of pulling Frederick away from Saxony, and it remained to be seen whether Daun would avail himself of the opportunity which had been created for him.

Failure before Dresden, November 1758

Daun had thrown bridges across the Lausitzer Neisse at Görlitz, to give the impression that he was going to follow Frederick into Silesia. Instead, early on 4 November, his army made off west towards the Elbe. The troops were glad to be on the move, and marched so speedily that they reached Bautzen on the first night, Harta on 5 November and the familiar craggy country west of Stolpen on the 6th. The Prussians in and about Dresden were unaware that the Austrian army was in the neighbourhood until they saw the long lines of camp fires extending across the heights of Dittersbach.

Daun had hatched an elaborate scheme to take advantage of the state of affairs in Saxony, where the Prussian forces (weakened by the departure of Prince Henry to reinforce Frederick) were split in two, with *GL.* Carl Christoph Schmettau (6 battalions) holding Dresden, and *GL.* Itzenplitz (14-15,000 troops) to the south defending the line of the Müglitz against Zweibrücken's *Reichsarmee*. To divert the attention of Itzenplitz from Dresden, the allied forces were to execute a march out to the west, with the main body of the *Reichsarmee* moving from Berggiesshübel to Freiberg, while *FML.* Hadik's Austrians (8 battalions, 5 squadrons) lunged from Freiberg to Nossen on the Mulde, and dispatched an advance guard to threaten the Prussian line of communication up the Elbe.

With Itzenplitz thus alarmed for his western flank and rear, Daun would make for the Elbe at Pratzschnitz and Pillnitz, cross the pontoon bridges which were being guarded for him by Lieutenant General Rosenfeld's detachment of the *Reichsarmee* (12 battalions, 4 squadrons), and finally advance between Itzenplitz and Dresden by way of the Lockwitz valley. A last refinement of the plan provided for bribing Schmettau to surrender Dresden, though it is not entirely certain whether he took up the offer.

It all went wrong. Zweibrücken and Hadik reached their destinations on 6 November, but Itzenplitz did the opposite of what was being planned for him, for he fell back to the camp of Kesseldorf east of Dresden, from where he could support the city at will. Schmettau, whatever his private intentions might have been, was now deprived of any reasonable excuse to surrender.

On the morning of 7 November the Austrian columns made for the bridges which were held ready for them on the Elbe above Dresden. Daun intended to bring his 12,000 leading troops cross the river and against Dresden in the way just described, but the march was delayed by fog, and seven hours elapsed between the time the cavalry passed at one in the afternoon, and the last of the infantry arrived in position at eight in the evening. Itzenplitz moved closer to Dresden, ready to reinforce as necessary.

The French captain de Viomenil wrote to his masters that he found the Austrian delays incomprehensible, and that he could not understand why Daun had not at once thrust between the Prussian field forces and the city. His dispatch was intercepted by the Austrians, opened, deciphered, re-sealed with the skills of centuries of practice, and duly sent on its way. Daun could not take the young man to task without revealing the Austrian skulduggery, and had to be content with noting the mistakes which de Viomenil had made in his timings, numbers and geography.[158]

On the following day Daun made a detailed reconnaissance of the approaches to Dresden, and at one in the afternoon of 9 November the army took up arms in its camp at Lockwitz and advanced against the city on a broad front. Prussian Jäger and free battalions were now roaming in the great walled enclosure of the Grosser Garten, which projected beyond the suburbs of the Altstadt like an outwork. Daun lacked the heavy artillery and other requisites for a siege, and was content to deploy his army in the vicinity of the house at Nöthnitz, where 'a learned man of that country [Count Bünau von Nöthnitz], had a magnificent library.'[159]

FML. Angern was told off to assault the Grosser Garten with just four battalions of the right wing (Carl Lothringen [3], Hildburghausen [8], de Ligne [38] and Gaisruck [42]). They arrived outside the south-eastern wall after a march of two and a half hours, and were greeted by the fire of the Prussian Jäger. The Prince de Ligne opened the way by battering down the gate with his pioneers, and advancing into the park with four hundred men. He had to fire a number of cannon shot to discourage a free battalion which had come up to help the Jäger. Some of the fine statues in the garden now became casualties. Thereafter he encountered no opposition, and Angern marched the rest of his force up the central avenue. Itzenplitz decided that he could no longer remain on the west bank of the Elbe, and crossed to the east bank, some of his troops by way of the city and the Augustusbrücke, and the rest by a bridge of boats below Dresden, and he left Schmettau in Dresden with a reinforced garrison of nine battalions of line infantry, two free battalions, five hundred reconvalescents and a number of squadrons of the Belling Hussars [H9].

Schmettau was now committed to at least a show of defiance. He knew that the Austrians might try to bring up troops and field artillery under cover of the tall and substantially-built houses of the suburbs. At four in the morning of 10 November, without any notice to the population, the Prussian artillery opened fire with howitzer shells, red-hot shot and incendiary carcasses against the suburbs to the south-east east of the walled city. The conflagration destroyed 286 houses, and the British envoy Sir Andrew Mitchell reported that it was beyond his powers to convey 'the horror of the night, nor the terror and confusion it struck in the poor inhabitants, as the whole town seemed to be environed with flames. I mounted one of the steeples, from whence I saw the most melancholy prospect: the poor frightened inhabitants running from the burning suburbs with the wretched remains of their furniture towards the Great Garden, and the whole circuit of the town appeared to be in flames, ruins and smoke.'[160]

There was no sanctuary to be found in the park, for the six hundred Austrian troops holding out there were being assailed by hot and cold shot and incessant sorties. Lieutenant Gorani found himself 'twice during the night and at dawn in the middle of flames, wreckage, the dead and the dying without having a scratch upon me, though there were several bloodstains on my coat.' Both coat and hat showed a number of bullet holes and sword cuts, though he had no idea how he had come by them. The explanation probably lay with his commander, Lieutenant Colonel Count de Navarro, 'although Spanish by nation, he had taken to table and good wine like the Germans, as you learn to howl when you run with wolves.' At the first lull he invited his officers to dine with him. 'We consumed great quantities of food, together with much splendid wine from all the countries of the globe; nor were liqueurs neglected. Our commander set us the example, and we as good comrades could only follow.'[161]

Daun held his army back in the camp of Nöthnitz and contemplated the city across the burning suburbs. He now put all his trust in two enterprises which were launched against the enemy deep rear, by Hadik's corps of Austrians against the depot at Torgau down the Elbe, and by the *Reichsarmee* against the city of Leipzig. Daun hoped that he could thereby establish secure quarters for the winter in western Saxony, behind a line extending from Leipzig by way of Freiberg to Pirna.

In the event Hadik abandoned the attack on Torgau, after the Prussian commandant Colonel Grolman beat off his first assault, and Major General Wedel hastened to the relief with a detachment which had been facing the Swedes in Pomerania. The expedition against Leipzig was postponed from the 10th to the 11th, and from the 11th to the 12th, and finally given up altogether, whereupon Zweibrücken withdrew the *Reichsarmee* to Chemnitz and made ready to enter winter quarters.

It was extraordinary that the schemes of the Austrians and Zweibrücken had collapsed well before Frederick was in a position to affect the outcome. Having relieved distant Neisse, the king turned back towards Saxony only on 9 November. He and his cavalry entered Dresden on the 20th, by when the Austrians had long decamped from Nöthnitz.

Even before news came that Zweibrücken had failed at Leipzpig, Daun decided in principle to retreat to Bohemia. On 16 November the army fell back to a temporary position between Pirna on the Elbe and Berggiesshübel in the hills to the west. The cold was already acute, and the Austrians waited only until they had demolished the little fortress of Sonnenstein before they marched for winter quarters in Bohemia on the 21st.

West of the Elbe the security cordon was formed by the commands of the *FML*s. d'Arberg (based at Eger), Forgách (Kaaden) and Loudon (Teplitz); to the east of the river *FML*. Beck secured the hills towards Saxony, while *FML*. Kálnoky guarded the avenues in front of Königgrätz. Beyond the borders Saxony was left in a state of devastation.[162]

Frederick exulted in the way the year had ended. The enemy had certainly brought off a surprise at Hochkirch, but they had then failed in front of Neisse, Dresden, Torgau and Leipzig. Lacy wrote to a friend: 'You are quite right. We ended up in exactly the situation you feared. By trying to take on too much at the same time we came away with nothing.'[163] In Vienna Frederick's recovery was admired all the more because his defeat at Hochkirch had been followed so soon by the news of the death of his beloved sister Wilhelmina.[164]

Daun had remained as fertile as ever in strategic expedients, and had created magnificent opportunities for himself against Prince Henry outside Dresden early in September, against Frederick immediately after Hochkirch, and back at Dresden against Schmettau in November. What he lacked on all of these occasions was the will to drive forward to a successful conclusion. It seemed that nothing short of a threat to the heart of the monarchy, as in Bohemia in June 1757, or in Moravia one year later, could move this cautious commander to the effort which was demanded.

Daun had just completed his longest period in independent command, and his style of generalship did not alter fundamentally until the end of the war. The overwhelming impression at the time and in the judgement of historians is one of extreme caution, and there is certainly a case to be made for regarding this circumspection as indicating shortcomings in a man who was entrusted with the supreme command. But the picture as it stands is incomplete.

In King Frederick the field marshal Daun confronted the foremost soldier of his age, who possessed dictatorial power over the Prussian army and state, a body politic which was set on firmer foundations than was the Habsburg monarchy in the 1750s. In contrast Daun lacked support where he might reasonably have expected to find it. A perceptive officer commented that in the Austrian service a commanding general 'does not have the power to regulate the whole military machine, to master it or to give it the necessary impulse ... nor can he change existing practices, or introduce new ones, as he would wish. The reason is that he has first to combat and identify all too many internal enemies and prevailing fads, and in particular the powerful opponents to be found among the leading ministers and the noble assemblies. All of this absorbs the time which he ought to be devoting to the external enemy.'[165]

If anything, Daun's distrust of his generals grew in the course of the war, and he ultimately retained full confidence only in the Netherlander *FML*. Joseph Carl Count d'Ayasasa, whom he dispatched on confidential missions to Vienna. His cause in the capital was also sustained by his wife, the Countess Josepha Theresa. 'She is always in the circle of the Empress, and exploits this favour and ease of access with great skill to promote the interests of her husband.'[166]

Daun's own correspondence with Maria Theresa was intimate and idiosyncratic. It set down in a wandering and globular hand, devoid of punctuation, and drifted from German to French and back again as he found an idea easier to express in one or the other. The phonetic spelling enables us to hear the voice of the field marshal himself, soft and mincing compared with the Prussian military speech, thus:

Daun	Standard German	English
allergnedichste	*allergnädigste*	most gracious
beherich	*behörig*	fitting, suitable
eysserlich	*äusserlich*	outwardly
folgents	*folgends*	accordingly
kinfftich	*künftig*	future
Krich	*Krieg*	war
Leidte	*Leute*	people, soldiers
lengstens	*längstens*	at the latest
ruhich	*ruhig*	quiet, leisurely
teitlich	*deutlich*	clearly, directly

The hesitations and the sense of gloomy isolation were undoubtedly components of Daun's make-up, but they were far from being the whole. Daun was a thoroughgoing professional, his personal courage was never in doubt, and his composure was legendary. Pietro Verri was astonished at the field marshal's relaxed and discursive conversation in company, which never touched on war.'[167]

Frederick termed his rival variously as '*die dicke Excellenz von Kolin*,' or '*die grosse Perücke*,' and made fun of the blessed sword and hat which the Pope was supposed to have presented to him. In private the king expressed the greatest admiration for Daun's generalship, and he later advised his generals not to launch all-out attacks against the kind of positions which had been taken up by the Austrians in the Seven Years War. 'It is very probable that the Austrian generals will adhere to the method of Field Marshal Daun (which is undoubtedly the best), and that in the next conflict they will be as careful to position themselves as strongly as they did in the war under consideration.'[168]

Even that testimony did not go far enough, for Daun did not hesitate to strike when the favourable opportunity offered, as at Moys, Hochkirch, Maxen and Liegnitz, and on all of those occasions he was striving to destroy the enemy outright, and not just unseat them from a patch of ground.

In 1758 Daun had at least succeeded in transferring the theatre of war to the north of the border hills, and it was to remain there, apart from occasional Prussian incursions, until the peace. Was he now the man who would be capable of carrying the war to the enemy in their own land? The field marshal himself sensed that he was not, and on 17 November he wrote to Maria Theresa's cabinet secretary to offer his resignation: 'the sad ending of this campaign, and the little which I accomplished in the course of it, offer only too much proof to Your Majesty that dedication and loyalty are not enough in themselves for the good of Your service... I am therefore not a man fitted for the command of the army, and you must look to somebody else—someone more capable, more fortunate, and who will get on better with the ministers and the allies.'[169]

The letter hinted that relations between Daun and Kaunitz were poor, and Kaunitz for his part doubted whether the field marshal was fit to stay in command. However Maria Theresa was bound by her sense of obligation to 'the most precious treasure of her house,'[170] and she answered that Daun must remain in charge. Kaunitz could not have expected otherwise, and all that he could reasonably do now was to seek to repair Daun's broken self-confidence. 'Thank God, I know enough not to judge men by events. If I thought that any failings in the campaign could have been attributed to you, I would not have concealed it. If I thought that the Empress could entrust her arms to better hands than yours, I would say so, even if you were my brother.'[171]

IV
1759

GRAND STRATEGIES

1759 was to be the fourth year of the war, but, extraordinarily, the first in which the Austrians worked out a plan of campaign in concert with friends. In 1756 and again in 1757 the Austrians were anticipated by Frederick while they were still in the process of forming active military alliances. For 1758 the Austrians had formulated no plans as such, preferring to wait until their allies had begun to make their presence felt in the war. Deprived of Austrian help, the Russians had battled bloodily and indecisively with Frederick at Zorndorf on 25 August, and then fallen back into Poland after it became clear that Daun's ambitions lay in the direction of Saxony,

On the western theatre Prince Ferdinand of Brunswick had driven the French behind the Rhine earlier in that year. In these circumstances Maria Theresa and Kaunitz had been pressing altogether too hard when they insisted that the French must fulfil something like their full treaty obligations, by dispatching an auxiliary corps of 24,000 French troops to join the Austrians in Bohemia. In effect Maria Theresa was relying on her personal credit with Louis XV, who undertook to send the reinforcement, and damned himself thereby in the French historiography of the war.[1]

It was perhaps fortunate for the alliance that Ferdinand of Brunswick proceeded to beat the French on the western side of the Rhine, at Krefeld on 23 June 1758. The Austrian demands were now patently untenable, and Maria Theresa wrote directly to Soubise to halt the march of the auxiliaries. The foreign minister Cardinal Bernis congratulated the Austrian ambassador. 'How fortunate you are... to be a subject of the Empress!... I have gone about proclaiming at the top of my voice her virtues of generosity, magnanimity and friendship. The king is deeply touched, and I am reduced to tears.'[2]

Before the campaigning season was over the French had won their way back across the Rhine, and defeated one of Ferdinand's detachments at Sandershausen on 9 October 1758, but it was clear that the French were now preoccupied with the contest against the Hanoverians and their British-funded associates. More realistic counsels prevailed in Vienna towards the end of the year, and the process was aided by the fall of Bernis, who had lost confidence in himself and the outcome of the war. Maria Theresa told the Swedish ambassador that at first she had been disturbed by the departure of Bernis, 'who had been the chief instrument in upholding the system of alliance between her and France.' But she was then mightily reassured by the conduct of Choiseul, his replacement, 'whose way of thinking had always inspired her with confidence... this state of affairs set her fears at rest, and gave every hope that there would not be the slightest change in the relationship.'[3]

The Duc de Choiseul was the new title of the man who had been familiar to the Austrians as Étienne-Francois de Stainville, Comte de Choiseul, who had been the highly-regarded French ambassador in Vienna since 1757, and who arrived in Paris on 29 November 1758 to take the place of Bernis. Kaunitz told Maria Theresa that Choiseul was in addition a born Lorrainer and the son of a father who had been in the Austrian service. All of that was without precedent, 'and cannot fail to make a great sensation at all the other courts, and in France itself.'[4] Another of Austria's friends at the Court of Versailles, however embarrassing it might be, was Louis' mistress the Pompadour, and Maria Theresa found it expedient to send her a diamond-encrusted miniature of her Imperial likeness, with a covering letter from Kaunitz.

The re-negotiated terms of the alliance were

*Johann Anton Count Tillier, the busy go-between of the Austrian high command.
His illness and death in 1761 cut short a promising career.
(Military Academy, Wiener Neustadt)*

set out in secret treaties on 31 December 1758. They took as their basis the first, or defensive Treaty of Versailles of 1 May 1756. Louis undertook to do everything in his power to promote the return of Silesia and Glatz to Maria Theresa, but their restitution was no longer held as a precondition of peace. Louis was still bound to support the Austrians by a corps of 24,000 auxiliary troops, but in fact the obligation was commuted to a monthly subsidy of 288,000 florins, which was the equivalent of a useful 3,456,000 per annum. The French undertook to keep 100,000 troops in Germany, though in the nature of things they were likely to be employed not against the Prussians, but against the Hanoverians and their supporters.

Thanks largely to Austria's links with France, the ruling circles in Sweden were still committed to the war against Prussia. The maps however showed that the Prussians had forced a passage over the Recknitz and were lodged in Swedish Pomerania, which endangered Stralsund and threatened to paralyse the operations of the Swedish forces. Moreover the Austrian officers, who had returned from captivity on exchange, related that in Berlin and Breslau they had heard the Prussians speaking of the Swedish army with total contempt.[5] The course of the war was to show that Lacy was the only Austrian general who made a serious attempt to conduct joint operations with these allies

While Empress Elizabeth still breathed, Austria could be assured of the steadfast support of Russia, which seemed to be proof even against such an affront as had been offered in August last, when Daun had turned his back on Fermor, and left him to fight the Prussians without support.

It remained to be seen how these differing dispositions and capabilities could be reconciled in common plans of campaign for 1759. Daun offered his first thoughts on the subject on 20 December 1758. He pointed out that Frederick had survived with the assistance of the quality of his army, the military character of his government, and his personal talents. However the Prussians were not invincible, for the king had made mistakes, his armies had been beaten several times, and he owed a great deal to readily-identifiable advantages like the command of the Elbe and the Oder, and the help of his system of fortresses and magazines, which had so far enabled him to exploit the geographical separation of his enemies, and deal with them one at a time.[6]

For the next campaign, explained Daun, the allies ought therefore to bring together two large groupings of armies, one in Saxony, and the other on the Oder in Silesia, each of them large enough to withstand the most powerful force the Prussians could bring against it. The grouping in Saxony should be formed of 100,000 troops, namely 30-40,000 Austrians, 30-40,000 French (an unlikely happening), and the rest comprising *Reichstruppen* to guard the communications. On the eastern theatre the Austrians would assemble 100,000 men on the Oder, and 40-50,000 Russians should march to join them.

Daun's proposals formed the basis for the draft plan of operations which the Austrians sent to Paris and St. Petersburg on 22 December 1758. The Duc de Choiseul, as the new French foreign minister, was at first inclined to favour the Austrian strategy. He was nevertheless overborne by the marshals Belleisle and d'Estrées, who directed the French military machine, and who knew that they were going to have their hands full in coping with the Hanoverians and their partners.

Vienna already knew that the Russian Military Conference had set its heart on besieging Stettin in concert with the Swedes. The scheme had its merits, but it would leave the Austrians in Silesia exposed to the undivided attention of Frederick. *GFWM*. Tillier, 'a man of intelligence and a distinguished officer,'[7] was sent to St. Petersburg to reinforce the Austrian case, and in spite of 'that nonchalance with which affairs are conducted here'[8] he was able to report on 23 February that the negotiations were complete.

The Austro-Russian accord came close to Daun's plan. The Russians would still operate in Prussian Pomerania, but on a smaller scale, with 40,000 men advancing from the Vistula and renewing the siege of the little port of Colberg. A total force of 90,000 men, of whom 60,000 were regular infantry and cavalry, would assemble at Posen at the end of May, and set out on the same day (25 June) as the Austrians began their advance from Bohemia. The two armies were to meet on the Oder between Breslau and Glogau.

On 26 May the French military attaché Montazet presented himself to Maria Theresa and Francis Stephen at the hunting palace of Laxenburg, and learned what the Austrians had in mind for the Saxon theatre, now that no French contingent was to be present there. 'No further trust can be placed in the *Reichsarmee*, because it does nothing but retreat in front of the enemy. In effect it will now be eliminated from the map, and all the Austrians extracted from it are to form a new army of 30-35,000 exclusively Austrian troops. The command will be given to General Hadik, who is one of her best officers.' Hadik's army would be at the complete disposal of Daun, and had the immediate responsibility of observing Saxony and covering Bohemia.[9]

Setting out the pieces

The spring of 1759 was generally mild and early, though spells of heavy rain kept the roads in a muddy condition well into April. The main Austrian concentration of 42,000 troops spent an undisturbed winter in the area of Königgrätz in north-east Bohemia, as the most central position on the Austrian side of the border heights. Just to the front, the avenues towards Silesia were guarded by the various corps of the generals Harsch at Nachod (19,000), Beck at Braunau (7,000) and Loudon at Trautenau (10,000). By early March the army and the three advanced corps had built up to a total strength of 92,000 troops.

To the east, the corps in Austrian Silesia and Moravia (28,000) was commanded by *GdC*. de Ville. To the west, *GFWM*. Vela had 5,000 troops in the hills around Gabel, watching the entry from Upper Lusatia by way of Zittau. *FML*. Gemmingen and *FZM*. Arenberg (17,000) guarded the Bohemian-Saxon borders to the left of the Elbe, and to the west again *FM*. Serbelloni commanded the 20,000 Austrians who were still deployed with the 20,000 *Reichstruppen* in Franconia and Thuringia.

Altogether the Austrians could put more than 160,000 troops into the field for the new campaign. As for their condition, Francis Stephen observed 'that we are in a pretty good state, that is to say almost complete... so that with the grace of God we may hope affairs will turn out well.'[10]

Daun set out for the army on 26 March. On arriving at his first headquarters at Münchengrätz he was greeted with the news of a little victory which *FML*. Beck had contrived specifically to do him honour. On the same 26th he had attacked the unoffending detachment of Colonel Dieringshofen at **Greiffenberg**, just inside Silesia, and forced him to surrender with his 16 officers and 700 men, including the whole complement of his own grenadier battalion.

When the Prussians came across the borders it was not out of pique, but as part of an ambitious scheme of spoiling attacks which Frederick launched before the start of the campaigning season. In February Major General Wobersnow had advanced some 8,000 troops from Glogau to anticipate the Russians in western Poland. He wrecked the magazine in Posen, continued his work of destruction down the Warthe river, and ravaged the estates of Prince Sulkowsky.

The Austrian forces in north-west Bohemia and the adjacent *Reich* were spread thinly, in comparison with the concentration on the other side at Königgrätz, and Prince Henry of Prussia was able to break repeatedly across the weakly-held borders. These incursions had a variety of individual targets, tactical, economic or logistic, but they were all ultimately designed to undermine the Habsburg authority in the Empire, and disrupt Austrian or German preparations for the next campaign.

In the first enterprise of the kind the Prussian major general Knobloch broke into Thuringia with a reported 15,000 troops at the turn of February and March. Later in March Knobloch pushed up the Saale, drove an Austrian detachment from **Saalfeld** on the 26th, and broke through to the Sattel-Pass and Judenbach.

Henry's next project was a virtual invasion of Bohemia to the west of the Elbe. By now the corps of *FML*. Gemmingen in the Erz-Gebirge had been teased out into small detachments, and on 15 April the Prussians coursed through the abattis at Peterswalde, Passberg and Comotau in a strength of some 20,000 men. On that day *GFWM*. Reinhardt stood in the way of Lieutenant Colonel Belling's column at **Sebastiansberg** with a command of about 2,800 troops (one super-large battalion of Andlau [57], one battalion of Königsegg [16], and 1,000 hussars and Croats).

The Austrians stood their ground for a time behind fieldworks and an abattis, but the position collapsed when its right flank was turned, and Reinhardt was captured along with 1,500 of his men, three cannon and two colours. Still more trophies would have been lost if Colonel Count Königsegg had not recaptured a colour of his battalion, and if Lieutenant Gorani had not grabbed a colour of Andlau and galloped off, pursued in vain by several Death's Head Hussars.

Gemmingen rallied the scattered Austrian forces at Welwarn, less than twenty miles to the north of Prague. Colonel Johann Andreas Török and four hundred of his hussars saved the magazine at Saaz, before it could be destroyed completely by the 'Sebastiansberg' column, but there was nobody to cover the important depots nearer the Elbe. Not content with burning the stores at Aussig, Lobositz and Leitmeritz, the Prussians put the towns of Aussig, Leitmeritz and Budin under contribution, and *GM*. Wunsch burnt the whole of the last place down when he marched away on 19 April.

At the eastern end of the theatre of war de Ville was duelling with Frederick's particular friend, the fanatically Protestant *GL*. Fouqué. The Prussians irrupted into Austrian Silesia with 25,000 troops on 17 April. De Ville responded by a counter-strike into Prussian Silesia, and affairs took such a serious turn that Frederick had to bring back substantial reinforcements. De Ville fell back in his turn to Austrian Silesia, planted himself at Hermannstadt, and held the Prussians at bay until they retired across the border and broke up their concentration.

Early in April the troops of Daun's army had moved to new cantonments close to the border, and with the arrival of spring they marched on 2 May to the 'Camp of Schurz,' which extended up the agreeable valley of the upper Elbe to the north of Königgrätz. They stayed there for nearly two months, and Daun took the opportunity to drill the army and incorporate the recruits. The new soldiers were of unusually high quality, 'since more recruits had been enlisted in the Hereditary Lands at the end of the last campaign than were actually needed. Hence they have been able to select the best of them.'[11]

On 6 May Maria Theresa was able to write to Daun that *GFWM*. Tillier had returned from the Russians, this time with their detailed plan of operations, and that Daun should devise his plan of campaign accordingly. His first objective should however be to force Frederick to abandon the strong position he now occupied on the ridge just south of Landeshut in Silesia.[12]

Daun and his generals concluded that the best way to evict Frederick would be through indirect pressure, by advancing across hills and down the little river Queiss to Lauban, which sat on the border between Saxony and Silesia. Lauban was not a significant feature in itself, but Austrian forces emplaced there could obstruct the Prussian communications between those two lands, and could be supplied easily enough by way of Zittau. From the Queiss also the Austrians could stride north to reach the Russians on the Oder. Daun delayed his move until he could be certain that the Russians were fairly on their way through western Poland. Meanwhile he was content to drill his army, much to the frustration of Frederick, who wished to tempt him across the border and bring him to battle. 'Lacy has not come to reconnoitre us, and until I hear that man's name I can never persuade myself that the enemy really intend to come to these parts.'[13] Lacy had in fact been commissioned to see how affairs stood in Vienna and gain some positive instructions. He made his round of visits on 16 and 17 June, and discovered that Francis Stephen, Maria Theresa and *FM*. Neipperg had little real expectation of the Russians. Kaunitz alone maintained that something might be hoped from them.[14]

A couple of days later the Russian attaché General Springer brought Maria Theresa into a much more positive frame of mind, and she wrote to Daun on 21 June that the advance to the Queiss was still the best opening for operations, but this time with the more ambitious aim of drawing Frederick into a great battle.[15] Daun had been looking for guidelines, but he had not expected anything so categorical. He now had to put his misgivings behind him. 'The cork is drawn,' he replied to his Empress, 'and now we must empty the wine.'[16]

On 26 June Daun got his main army of 60,500 troops on the move to the west. He was aware that the Riesen-Gebirge projected into Bohemia in great lumpy spurs, and that he would need eight days just to work around the southern side of the massif to reach the upper Queiss, whereas Frederick could make an easy lateral movement to the same part of the world in just three marches. The Austrians reached Reichenberg on 3 July, then pushed along the muddy roads to arrive on the 6th at Marklissa on the upper Queiss. There was no sign of the enemy, and Daun had arrived on the edge of the northern lowlands, only about sixty miles from Carolath, where the Russians intended to cross the Oder. He could now give his army some rest, 'and it stands in great need of that commodity, as it has been pouring with rain for eight days past; and very cold too, for this is a mountainous country.'[17]

On 9 July, two hours before the Austrians were due to set out for the Oder, Daun learned that yet another Prussian spoiling action up the Warthe, this time by 40,000 troops under *GL*. Dohna, had forced the Russians to suspend their march. The way to the Russians was in any case now blocked by Frederick, who had been marching his 44,000 troops west from Landeshut, and redeployed them on the 10th in the 'Camp of Schmottseiffen.' He proceeded to entrench himself strongly on a crescent-shaped ridge, and planted batteries on the two north-westward facing horns. The country around was a lush landscape of grassy knolls and steep wooded ravines, and the camp was difficult for Daun to see, let alone take by assault.

The Austrians were still under an obligation to find a way to the Oder, and Daun now put together an elaborate scheme of diversions and manoeuvres. The main army would confront the king, and follow on his heels into Silesia if he abandoned the position of Schmottseiffen, meanwhile:

—the combined forces of *FZM*. Harsch and *GdC*. de Ville would press back the corps of Finck in southern Silesia and mount a threat to Frederick's rear;

—the important task of reaching out to the Russians was now entrusted to the corps of *GdC*. Hadik, who was on the march from the Elbe, and would be reinforced to a strength of 34,000 troops to make the dash to the Oder.

We shall follow the course of these two enterprises in turn.

Harsch and de Ville in southern Silesia

The great eastward diversion was to be put into effect by a powerful corps, or miniature army, of no less than 38,500 men, composed of 23,600 troops which had remained with Harsch in the old camp of Schurz, and the forces of de Ville already in confrontation with *GL*. Fouqué.

Harsch and de Ville were both full generals, and it only through the working of seniority that the scholarly, retiring Harsch was placed in command of the combined force. His position was ultimately untenable, for he had lost the confidence of Daun and the public, whereas his nominal subordinate de Ville was a brash, argumentative Lorrainer, and a protégé of the Emperor himself.

The Austrians came together in the valley of Trautenau in north-east Bohemia, and began the advance into Silesia on 16 July. Harsch was now bludgeoned into resigning, nominally on grounds of ill-health, and de Ville now had carte blanche for his bold scheme of turning Fouqué's eastern flank by a thrust deep into Silesia. On 20 July the Austrians resumed their march, this time under the command of de Ville.

The adventure began prosperously enough, but on 23 July the Prussians began to cut across de Ville's communications with Bohemia, and he found himself cut off at Freiburg. On the 27th the Austrians turned back towards the border, and *GFWM*. Jahnus tried to break open a passage for the corps at **Gottesberg** near Conradswaldau. He uncharacteristically spent a good five hours preparing a set-piece assault, and when he finally attacked he found it impossible to evict the Prussians from the commanding heights. On the next day Jahnus tried to batter a way through at **Friedland**, but was again beaten off, and the Austrians were reduced to finding a way back to Bohemia along forest tracks leading by way of Gersdorf and the difficult passage of Johannesberg.

GFWM. Wolfersdorff and 6,000 troops were still stranded on the original line of communication at **Goldenöls**, where Fouqué tried to trap them on the night of 31 July/1 August. Wolfersdorff learned of the coup in time, and made good his escape to Trautenau, albeit at the price of some disorder among his near-mutinous troops, who insulted him to his face. A whole battalion of the regiment of Toscana lost its way in the woods for two days before reaching safety. Thus closed a comprehensively horrible episode. Harsch had been put aside, de Ville had failed completely, and even Jahnus had performed well below his best.

Hadik and the western flank

Well before Daun had contrived his pincer movement to evict Frederick from his position at Schmottseiffen, Vienna had decided to cut the Austrian commitment to the *Reich* and make fresh forces available for the main theatre of war. *GdC*. Hadik was ordered to leave a minimal force with the *Reichsarmee*, and take off with 15,800 of the Austrians into Bohemia.

Hadik set out on 4 June, and ducked behind the screen of the Fichtel-Gebirge to reach the corridor of the Eger in north-west Bohemia. This choice of route saved him from serious disturbance by Prince Henry, and the only clashes were little affairs like the one at **Buchwalde** near Aussig on 8 July. 'We had one man dead, and two wounded; we do not know the enemy losses, but we heard them give vent to cries of *Ach!* and *Weh!* When daylight came we discovered a great deal of blood in various places, along with some hats and bayonets.'[18]

Hadik passed to the east bank of the Elbe at Leitmeritz on 15 and 16 July. Up to now his role had been the tame one of reinforcing Daun's army, but on the 20th he was told that he was to take command of an independent corps of 34,000 troops, assembled from his original force and the detachments of Gemmingen, Vela and Loudon. His initial task was to hold back Prince Henry, who was known to be on his way eastward with substantial forces from Saxony, 'and then to advance through Lower Lusatia to Sagan, from where he will undertake further operations as circumstances develop.'[19] The 'further operations,' as Daun informed Montazet, were to march 'towards Crossen on the lower Oder, as proof to the Russians that we are anxious to support them, and to spur them on to vigorous action.'[20]

Hadik assembled his augmented corps north of the border hills at Gross-Hennersdorf in Upper Lusatia, and on 24 July moved to Löbau to head off the march of Prince Henry, who was coming up from the west by way of Bautzen. On that day the Prussians surprised and evicted a small outpost which *FML.* Rudolph Pálffy had placed at Hochkirch. This was a very severe blow, for it indicated to the Austrians that Prince Henry had made good time and was present in force on the west flank of their intended march to join the Russians.

Daun did some rapid re-calculations. Hadik was now to devote all his intention to holding down Prince Henry. Loudon, standing out to the right at Rothenburg on the Lausitzer Neisse, was reinforced to some 19,200 troops with the task of reaching out to the Russians on the Oder. On 26 July a patrol of fifteen hussars returned to Loudon. These bold fellows had disguised themselves as their Prussian counterparts and succeeded in penetrating as far as Grünberg, where they learned that the Prussian lieutenant general Wedel, who had been charge of the corps facing the Russians, had been beaten on the 23rd in a pitched battle at **Paltzig** (also known as Kay or Züllichau). The way was now clear for the Russians to march to the Oder, and Daun hoped to retrieve something of his original plan.

Unknown to the Austrians, Prince Henry was speeding along the shortest path to the Oder. On 26 July a first march carried him from Königswartha to Tschelln, and on the 29th he reached Sagan, just thirty miles short of the river. Hadik and Loudon grasped that Henry had stolen a march on them, and inserted himself between them and the Russians. However it was still possible to find a way through to the allies along a more northerly route by way of Guben. The Oder downstream at Frankfurt appeared to be a suitable rendezvous, and Loudon was now to hasten thither, un-encumbered by his field bakery and train of

BEFORE AND AFTER KUNERSDORF: AUSTRIANS, RUSSIANS, AND PRUSSIANS, JULY-SEPTEMBER 1759

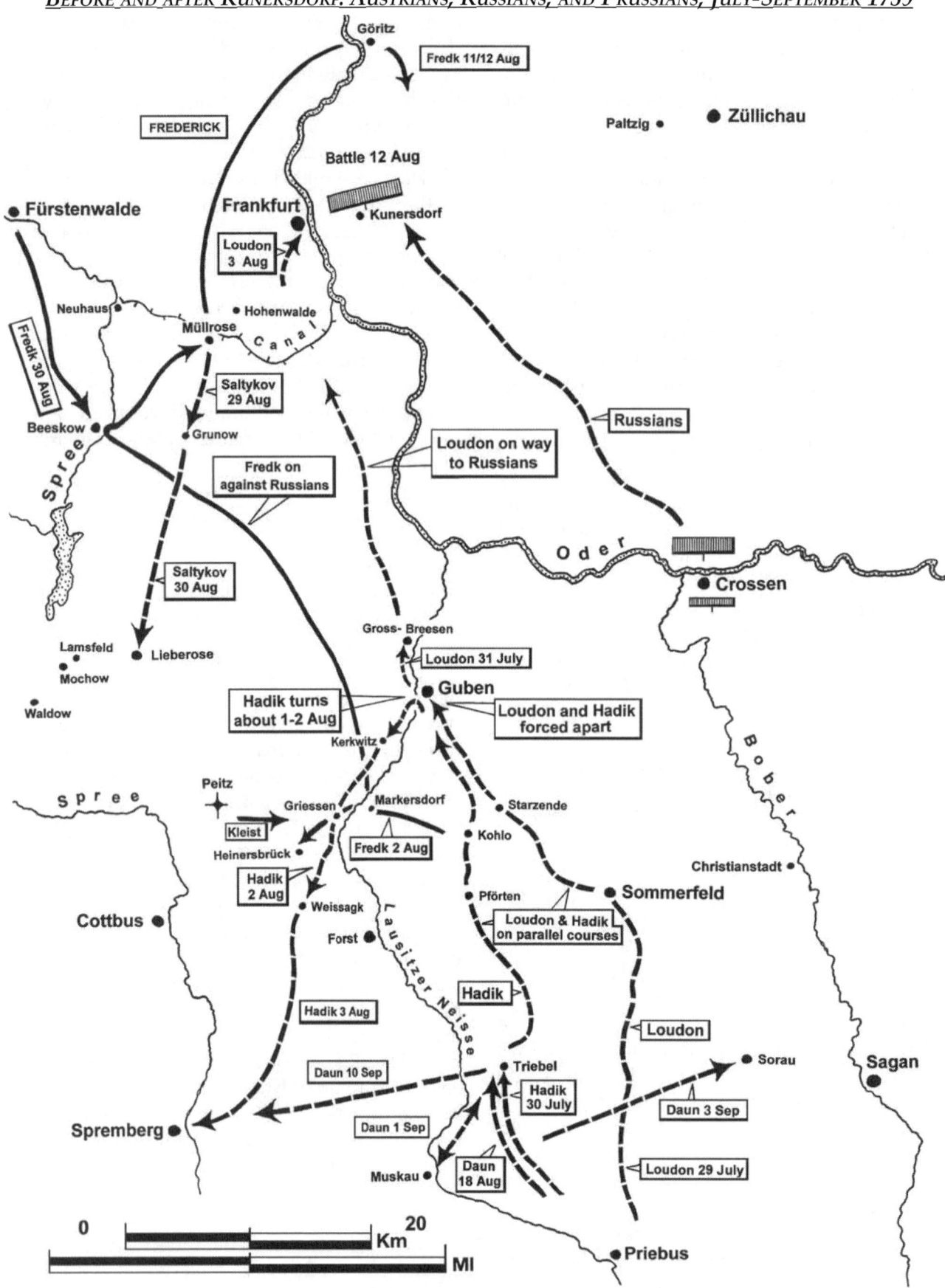

provisions, which were left in charge of Hadik, who would plant himself at Guben to cover the march.

The Oder was now emerging as the decisive theatre of the campaign, and Frederick was prompted to reverse the command of the two Prussian armies. Prince Henry was put in charge of the 40,000 troops who were still in the Camp of Schmottseiffen facing Daun, while the king took charge of Henry's former corps at Sagan, and drew on all his disposable forces to build up a body of 50,000 troops to confront the Russians.

To Kunersdorf. 29 July - 11 August 1759

It is time to summarise the course of events to date. The campaign of 1759 had been extraordinarily late in starting, for the Russians had been slow to gather their forces at Posen, and Daun was unwilling to venture into Silesia from the border hills. His first move, from the camp of Schurz around the rear of the Riesen-Gebirge to Upper Lusatia, had been blocked when Frederick took up his camp at Schmottseiffen, and refused to budge. Seeking to apply indirect pressure, Daun had ordered Harsch and de Ville to advance their combined forces against Fouqué in south central Silesia—an enterprise which ended with the Austrians being almost cut off from Bohemia and forced into an humiliating retreat.

Daun now pinned his expectations on the forces which were brought together by Hadik and Loudon in Lusatia, for they alone were in a position to reach out to the Russians, who had just beaten the Prussian corps of Wedel at Paltzig on 23 July, and were within a couple of marches of the Oder. Frederick gave his brother Henry the command of the forces which were facing Daun, while he himself made ready to meet the Russians. The French ambassador wrote from Vienna that 'we do not yet know when it [Frederick's new army] can be brought together, but as operations are being conducted at a great pace I am convinced... that it will come to a second battle before long, the outcome of which will be determine the outcome of the rest of the campaign, and perhaps the war itself.'[21]

A coherent sequence of events now led to the eve of the great victory of the allies at Kunersdorf, and the opportunity which it indeed presented of finishing the war. We shall follow the story as it affected the three groups of Austrian forces concerned, which were the main army under the command of Daun, and the two corps of Hadik and Loudon.

Daun's army

After three weeks spent motionless in the camp of Marklissa, facing the Prussians entrenched around Schmottseiffen, Daun believed that the time had come for some show of activity on his part, to prevent the enemy from concentrating all their forces against the Russians. The field marshal set off with the left wing of his army on 30 July. Captain Pietro Verri observed in fascination: 'The field marshal had in front of him four general adjutants and two wing adjutants, and immediate behind him a trumpeter, then an hussar of his suite, followed by a multitude of volunteers—the Duke of Braganza, Prince Louis of Württemberg, a son of Count Kaunitz, a Lobkowitz and a mob of other generals. A poor captain like me naturally came up behind with all the little people. Nobody knew where we were going... and all the pounding of hooves raised an enormous cloud of dust.'[22]

The movement concerned only the left wing already mentioned, or about 20,000 men out of the total of 53,000 troops, and the distance was a single march of some 15 miles to Lauban.

Prince Henry was impressed by none of this, and for the time being he would not move his 44,000 troops from the camp of Schmottseiffen. Daun was unwilling to venture any further down the Queiss, for he feared that he might then give Henry a free hand and lose contact with him altogether. The king's whereabouts were a total mystery, and the field marshal had given up all hope of achieving anything in Silesia until, on or about 7 August, he received the first indication that the Russians might at last cross the Oder.

Daun sent word to Loudon that he intended to set out for the river with part of his army, and he wrote in the same vein to Maria Theresa. She was delighted at the news, and replied that Daun ought to encourage any favourable dispositions among the Russian high command,

161

where there had been some important changes. Fermor had succumbed to his enemies in the army and at court, and on 30 June he reverted to the responsibility of a divisional commander, yielding his place to *Generalanshef* Petr Semenovich Saltykov. The new commander was a sixty year-old in the traditional Russian mould, fervent in his Orthodox religion, simple in his manners, genial to his officers and soldiers, and less spectacularly corrupt than most of his fellows. Maria Theresa now forwarded a beautiful ring and a sum of cash to reward him for having beaten the Prussians at Paltzig, 'and it is to be intimated to him and to General Fermor, that the present honours are just an indication of what will unfailingly follow, if I, as is to be hoped, will have reason to be pleased at their achievements. I will, moreover, represent their deeds to the Russian Empress in the best light.' Maria Theresa hoped that Russians and Austrians would work together in the same spirit as Prince Eugene of Savoy and the Duke of Marlborough fifty years before, and she was confident that Lacy and Loudon would be able to promote fellow-feeling, 'as both have an intimate knowledge of the Russian mentality.'[23]

When he took fresh stock of his own situation, Daun calculated that it would be possible to hold Prince Henry in check at Schmottseiffen by detachments, and that he could take the 25,000 troops of the left wing of the main army under his personal command, and march to operate with the Russians on the Oder. Daun set out from Lauban on 11 August. It was high summer, and the tall plumes of dust told Henry that considerable Austrian forces were moving down the Queiss.

Hadik and Loudon

Nearly two weeks before, the commands of Hadik and Loudon had marched with considerably greater urgency, for they were striding north to meet the Russians, while Frederick was bringing up his scratch army from Sagan in the south-east to welcome the Russians in his own way.

Unencumbered by a supply train, Loudon allowed his troops only brief pauses on the road. He set out from Priebus on 29 July, and marched by way of Sommerfeld, Starzende and Guben to reach Gross-Breesen, on the Frankfurt road, on the 31st. Hadik was coming up behind with his corps of 21,600 troops and the main provision convoy for both himself and Loudon. His pace was inevitably slow. He reached Priebus on 29 July, after a taxing march of sixteen hours, and the last of his troops arrived at Guben in a state of total exhaustion at six in the morning of 1 August.

Loudon and Hadik had been spurred into these efforts not only by reports that Prussians were across the Bober and closing in from the east, but through some unwelcome news from Saltykov, who was being forced by supply difficulties to make his intended passage of the Oder not at Crossen, as had been planned, but at Frankfurt. That town lay nearly twice as far from Guben than did Crossen, and by stipulating a rendezvous so far downstream, Saltykov made it far more difficult for Hadik to make up time and catch up with Loudon.

From the reports of deserters and prisoners Hadik deduced correctly that the enemy had decided to make the Austrians their immediate target rather than the Russians, and that he could best help Loudon and Saltykov by drawing Frederick on to himself.[24] Hadik reversed direction at Guben, and marched back south overnight on the night of 1/2 August. He was following the left (west) bank of the Lausitzer Neisse by way of Griessen, and after a brief halt the fighting component of the column reached Weissagk at five in the morning of the 2nd. A little later Hadik heard a few distant cannon shot, which seemed to merit little attention, and only later did he learn that his transport had been overtaken by a disaster.

The corps baggage had been escorted by Colonel Moser's battalion of Blau-Würzburg and 58 Alt-Modena Cuirrasiers [Ciii)], and for additional security Hadik had assigned the column a route over to the west by way of Kerkwitz and Heinersbrück. Owing to the sandy roads the carts failed to make the necessary progress, and found themselves at the mercy of Colonel Friedrich Wilhelm 'Green' Kleist, who was leading the advance of Frederick's army with his regiment of hussars and the Krockow Dragoons [D2]. He now passed the Neisse at **Markersdorf** and fell on the escort.

The Würzburgers maintained excellent order, and fought their way along the road for one and a half hours, until the Prussian dragoons cut ahead of them and opened fire with their 6-pounder horse artillery (the first time on which this new arm saw action). Two of the four pieces of the Würzburg artillery were dismounted, and the battalion was surrounded and forced to surrender. Only twenty of the men had been killed, but many more had been hacked about by swords. The sole survivor seems to have been Captain Baron Saint-Genois of the Alt-Modena Cuirassiers, who made his way on foot through the bogs.[25]

The misfortunes were far from being at an end. The ammunition carts and the regimental baggage at the tail of Hadik's own column were guarded by the powerful reserve under *FML.* Gemmingen, and should have been in no danger. However Austrian marauders were roaming about, shooting at deer and cattle, and the shots threw the column into a disgraceful panic. Ensign Postlob describes how an unknown officer 'uniformed in white and red and with a hat bordered with silver,' cried out that the enemy had broken into the train. 'On top of this the cavalry escort crashed through the baggage, and he himself saw how a number of the troopers slashed through the traces of the horses and beat the drivers unmercifully. Much of the baggage was lost thereby.'[26]

The confusion was compounded when Colonel Lanjus arrived on the scene with 2,000 Croats and Loudon's train of iron baking ovens and provision waggons laden with flour, which he had been trying to bring up in the opposite direction, from Forst to Guben. He now joined his light infantry to the light cavalry of *FML.* Rudolph Pálffy to cover the general retreat of the corps to Weissagk. On falling back through a wood Pálffy 'not only found a great deal of baggage standing motionless, but that some of the vehicles had been overturned, smashed and plundered. The hussars had not yet arrived, and I saw large numbers of the German cavalry and infantry crowding around and taking goods from the waggons.' A number of the officers of the Austrian cavalry now tried to make off with Pálffy's own horses and effects, and desisted only when one of his servants threatened them with a pistol.[27]

Every detail was more shaming than the last. Second Lieutenant Johann Thomas Dotsches of the artillery tried to save the abandoned ammunition carts, but was unable to persuade *FML.* Gemmingen and a party of cavalry to lend some help, and a colonel of horse even refused the invitation to help himself to cartridges for his men. Dotsches blew up one of the ammunition waggons, and was trying to unload another which had stuck fast when cuirassiers rode by, having thrown aside their breastplates, followed by hussars who were in a state of complete panic. Nobody was in a mood to listen to his appeals, and he had to blow up the second cart as well.

Hadik's command had lost 1,497 men, 198 horses, some 500 vehicles, Loudon's field dispensary, and great quantities of uniforms, weapons, equipment and documentation, the whole amounting to a cash value of 109,045 florins, quite apart from the loss of Loudon's field bakery and heavy provision train. The cost of the events of 2 August was greater still in terms of the campaign, for Loudon was not only devoid of all conceivable support from Hadik, but was thrown on the Russians for his supplies.

Frederick and his improvised 'Sagan' army now crossed the Neisse in the wake of Kleist's cavalry, and on 3 August Hadik fell back out of immediate reach of the Prussians to a strong position at Spremberg, where he could give his spent and shaken troops some rest. It was still possible to keep up communication with Loudon and the Russians, albeit by roundabout routes, and he learned from Saltykov that it would be helpful for him to operate against Frederick's flank and rear. For this purpose Hadik decided to position himself south of Frankfurt, and early on 12 August he began his march from Spremberg. In the middle of the morning he could see that a huge and persistent cloud of smoke was rising far to the north, and he knew that a great battle must be in progress.

For an explanation it is necessary to return to the doings of Loudon, whom we left on 2 August, when he was racing ahead of Hadik for his rendezvous with the Russians at Frankfurt. He reached the Oder immediately above the town at noon on the 3rd, and camped between

Kunersdorf, 12 August 1759

Frankfurt and Tzchetzchnow. Here he learned that his baking ovens, his provision train and his medical supplies had been lost in the debacle on the day before.

The Russians were on the far side of the river, and the two forces were linked by the standing bridge in Frankfurt town, and by a bridge of boats and a pontoon bridge which the Russians had thrown across the water. Communication in other senses was lacking. The Russians were unwilling to venture across the Oder, and they were divided among themselves. Loudon received their generals on the 'Austrian' bank on 4 August, and it at once transpired that he was at a number of disadvantages in his dealings with them. His corps amounted to 19,200 troops at the most, as opposed to the reinforcement of 45,000 which the Russians had been led to expect, and he could in no honesty guarantee that Daun would march the main Austrian army from the upper Neisse to join his allies. Far from helping to provision the Russians, Loudon had lost his own supply train, and the Russians now forbade him to take anything from the large magazine of provisions which had been captured in Frankfurt.

Loudon's corps was already acquiring a reputation for plundering, and there is no doubt that his troops now made free in Brandenburg at the expense of the civilian population. He later put up a number of naive defences. He claimed that his troops had been kept under strict discipline, and in any case the Russians were at fault for having set a bad example; he had never sent out parties to ransack properties for his personal profit, and he could only suggest that the robbers must have invoked his name in vain. All that he had taken for himself was a paltry 8,000 florins.[28]

Loudon became all the more dependent on the Russians when Frederick's army arrived in strength at Müllrose, south-west of Frankfurt, on 5 August, and the Austrians were forced out of self-preservation to join Saltykov's army on the east bank in the afternoon. The Russian generals, in their perverse way, now began to talk in much more confident terms. On the 10th they actually committed themselves to passing the Oder upstream at Crossen, as the Austrians had desired all along. It was too late, for news came in the evening that Frederick was moving towards the river below Frankfurt.

Kunersdorf, 12 August 1759

a) Austrians and Russians together
Total: c. 79,000, c. 66,000 regulars, c. 13,000 irregulars
Losses: 16,396 killed, wounded and missing
b) Austrians
Total: 18,500-19,200, including 5,186 Croats, number of pieces unknown
Losses: 2,215: 425 killed, 1,343 wounded, 447 missing
c) Russians
Total: c. 59,800: up to 43,000 regular infantry, 4,650 regular cavalry, 7,200 hussars and Cossacks, another 4,650 gunners and engineers, 200 pieces
Losses: 14,181 killed, wounded and missing
d) Prussians
c. 49,900: 35,000 infantry, 13,000 cavalry, 1,000 gunners, 160 heavy pieces, 126 battalion pieces
Losses: c. 18,625; c. 6,170 killed, 11,099 wounded, 1,356 prisoners or missing

Since the beginning of August it had been clear to Frederick how the manoeuvres of the rival armies must culminate. 'It will come to a battle near Frankfurt. I am doing all I can to force the march, but it is impossible to drag the infantry along any more quickly. It is a furious crisis, and we must do what we can to get out of it.'[29] On the 2nd he had cut through the middle of the Austrian reinforcements (above), leaving Loudon to join the Russians with less than half of the intended number. Frederick did his utmost to build up his own forces, by adding the scattered corps he found on the theatre to the 13,200 troops of Henry's former 'Sagan' army. He was inferior to the united forces of Saltykov and Loudon by 37 per cent overall, and a still daunting 17 per cent in regular troops. He counted on redressing the difference through speed, the inherent quality of the Prussian forces, and the inspiration of the moment.

Shortly after midnight of 11/12 August Saltykov learned that the Prussians were in the process of crossing to the near (east) bank of the Oder at Göritz, twelve miles downstream from Frankfurt. No attempt was made to dispute the passage. Saltykov was in no doubt that Frederick intended to attack him, and at first light he made a detailed tour of the friendly positions in the company of Loudon and the senior officers.

The Russians had arrived here, on the heathland to the east of Frankfurt, on 3 August, and Loudon had joined them five days later, which gave the allies plenty of time to acquaint themselves with the ground and prepare themselves for combat. The deployment extended for more than three miles along a ridge, whose general alignment ran from south-west to north-east. The names of the various eminences terminated in the German 'Berg,' or the plural form 'Berge,' which conjures up images of Alpine peaks. Their tactical importance, however, resided not in their altitudes, which were very modest, but in their relative commands over the surrounding terrain (the elevations in our maps are again given in metres). The ridge was interrupted by hillocks, and by little valleys of greater or lesser width, of which the most significant was the Kuh-Grund, a sunken path which originated at the north edge of Kunersdorf village, and wound through the ridge as a narrow and steep-sided valley up to forty feet deep. A similar depression, the Tiefer-Grund, left Kunersdorf near the entrance to the Kuh-Grund, but diverged further to the west.

The reedy marsh of the Hühner-Fliess and its channels ruled out the possibility of the Prussians attacking in any strength directly from the north. The ground on the other side of the ridge was wooded, but higher-lying and more accessible, and it was this circumstance which determined the way Saltykov and Loudon arranged their forces.

The narrowest and most exposed sector of the allied position was the north-eastern salient, the hillocks termed the Mühl-Berge. The defence was therefore entrusted to the powerful artillery (42 heavy pieces) and five super-large regiments (c. 12,500 men) of Prince Golitsyn's Observation Corps, a kind of private army which had been created by the Russian Master General of the Ordnance, Petr Ivanovich Shuvalov. The Russians were entrenched on the Mühl-Berge on all sides except one, which faced the Kuh-Grund.

The main body of the army was deployed in two lines along the remainder of the ridge. The troops had been hard at work cutting abattis and throwing up bastions and connecting curtains, and by the day of battle the allies were emplaced strongly along a frontage which faced generally to the south-east. Five batteries were positioned in the bastion-like fortification of the Grosser-Spitzberg salient, which projected from near the centre of the line. Saltykov was still more concerned for the security of the south-western extremity of the position, towards Frankfurt, for if the Prussians broke through there they would cut him off from Frankfurt and his last remaining line of communication up the Oder (he was already resigned to at least the temporary loss of the direct communication from Posen). The battery on the commanding Juden-Berge therefore counted as a key position, and the greater part of Loudon's force was retained on this sector in deep reserve, with the dragoons and the chevaulegers standing behind the Russian infantry, and the six regiments of fusiliers facing north on the rearward slopes of the Juden-Berge. Three of the battalions of Croats were told off to guard a redoubt which covered a new bridge across the Oder above Frankfurt.

Towards eight in the morning of 12 August the mist gave way to a burning day, and the allies could see that the Prussian army was in full movement. A force (8 battalions and 40 squadrons under GL. Finck) positioned itself on the low heights beyond the Hühner-Fliess to the north, as if waiting to cross the marshy levels and attack. For the moment no assault materialised from this direction, and the attention of the Russians was drawn increasingly to clouds of dust which were climbing from the woods to the east. Saltykov was disinclined to take countermeasures until the enemy intentions became clear, for 'we knew by experience that the king's usual way is to attack a flank, and to mask his real intentions by a variety of false attacks.'[30]

In fact Frederick's calculations were already going badly astray. Finck's move, just described, was intended primarily as a diversion, and the king had staked everything else on taking his main force on a march through the eastern woods and throwing it against the supposedly undefended 'rear' of the allies. He did not know that Saltykov's army had been all the time dug in and facing in that direction. Frederick's embarrassment was compounded when he discovered that the space for deploying his troops was constricted by Kunersdorf village, a marshy stream and a line of lakes (the Dorf-See, the Blanken-See and the Fauler-See) which together formed an obstruction which ran to the south-east perpendicularly from the ridge. Saltykov, on the other hand, now grasped that the threat to the Juden-Berge sector was less than he had feared, and he was able to draw on the right wing of his army, and especially the Austrians, as reinforcements for his embattled left.

Towards 11.30 in the morning the outlying Observation Corps on the Mühl-Berge espied Prussians in the trees six hundred paces away, and opened fire with its cannon and howitzers. In response the enemy brought a devastating cross fire of sixty or more heavy pieces to bear on the Russians from the outlying hillocks of the Walk-Berge, the Kloster-Berge and the Kleiner Spitz-Berg. After this pounding the nine battalions of the Prussian advance guard went into the assault at 12.30. The earthworks on the Mühl-Berge had been laid out in a rigidly geometrical way, and the advancing Prussians repeatedly disappeared into dead ground. The infantry of the Observation Corps was not of particularly high quality, since it had relied primarily on the power of its artillery, and now the exposed regiments on the Mühl-Berge gave way.

The survivors fell back across the open end of the position, and were received by the Russian Second Grenadier Regiment, and by the first of the Austrian reinforcements which Saltykov was now summoning from his unengaged right wing, namely the two composite grenadier battalions of Loudon's infantry. The Austrian grenadiers were under the acting command of Major Joseph De Vins, and they contrived to wrest back much of the Mühl-Berge from the enemy and capture or recover a number of trophies.

It was, however, impossible for the Russian and Austrian grenadiers to hold ground which the entire Observation Corps had proved incapable of defending. Finally overborne by weight of numbers, the Austrians and Russians were thrown back across the Kuh-Grund and the Tiefer-Weg, and carried away with them the two regiments (Nizhegorod and Belosersk) which had been moving up to support them. The allied position might have been rolled up altogether if a new flank had not been formed behind the Tiefer-Weg. This was the work of the Novgorod and St. Petersburg regiments from the Russian second line, and the Austrian regiment of Grün-Loudon Grenadiers which formed up to the right of the Russians. The Austrian commander Major Chevalier d'Alton supplies some of the details. 'At this moment *FML.* Campitelli came up to the front of our troops and asked if we were willing to attack and follow him. We all of us, officers and men, answered with a "*Ja!*" While we led the way, the whole of our line advanced so smartly that we not only fell upon the enemy, but drove them from where they were standing. Although I was shot wounded from my horse... I continued to command on foot, and we held our ground until our ammunition was running out and *FML.* Campitelli brought up reinforcements.'[31]

The green-clan desperados of the Loudon Grenadiers had indeed 'fought like lions,' as Campitelli exclaimed,[32] and had lost 24 officers and 472 men in the course of three-quarters of an hour of combat. The troops brought up by Campitelli were the Austrian fusiliers of the regiment of Baden-Baden [23], which took the place of Grün-Loudon on the right flank of the exposed line behind the Tiefer-Weg. The newcomers were hit just as badly. The regimental commander, Lieutenant Colonel Strasser von Waldegg, was wounded, and he had not only to beat off the enemy storming against the front but send a major to curb the enthusiasm of a Russian regiment, which was firing into the backs of his men through the dust and smoke.[33]

Frederick had meanwhile brought up the right wing of his main army to support his advance guard, together with some heavy cannon which the Prussians dragged with some difficulty from the Walk-Berge. By now 'the canister fire of the enemy [Prussian] cannon was much heavier in its way than the Russian musketry, not to mention the fire of the Prussian infantry, which swelled constantly and won the enemy more and more ground. We had against

Kunersdorf, the Crisis

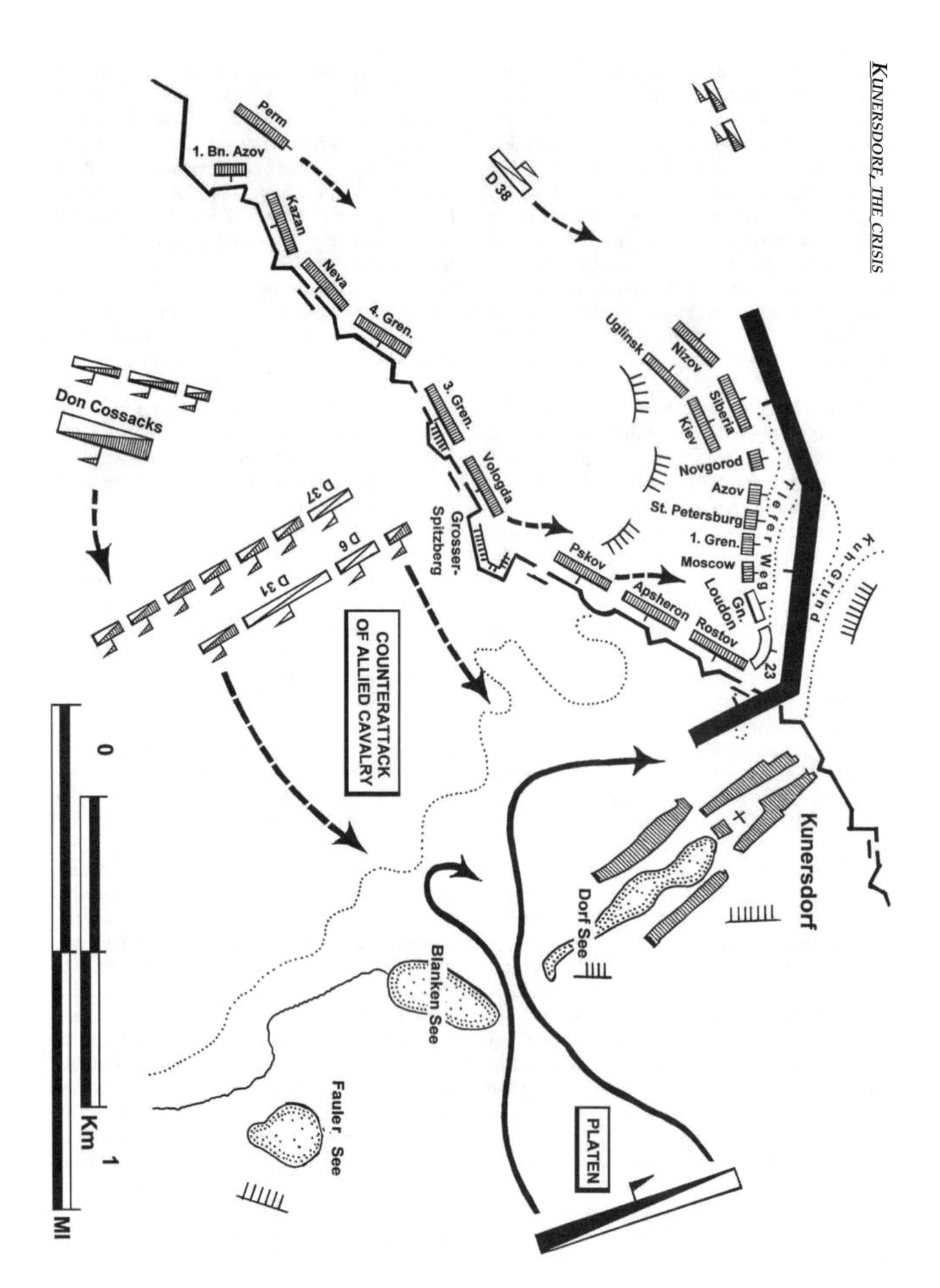

us the sun, the wind, the smoke and the extraordinarily dense dust which was thrown up from this sandy ground and prevented us from seeing more than three paces. The result was as useful to the enemy as it was disastrous for us, quite apart from the fact that the king was at the head of his troops, urging them on by his presence, his voice and his example... the state of affairs now began to appear critical... for more than half of the field together with some of the Russian cannon were in the hands of the enemy.'[34]

The Prussians were now battering away at the left allied flank from two directions, While the right-hand 'Austrian' salient held firm along the edge of the Tiefer-Grund, the Russians to their left underwent a hammering which bent them back into a hairpin bend which faced north across the Tiefer-Ground, and north-east over the marshes. The reason was that Finck had brought eight battalions struggling across the fringes of wetlands, and threw them into the attack at 3.45 in the afternoon to support the infantry of the main Prussian army. He was finally checked by four regiments of Russian infantry, which confronted him in a double line, and he found himself exposed to a battery of Austrian artillery which took up an enfilading position to the south-west.

The efforts of Finck's infantry were punctuated by piecemeal attacks on the part of bodies of Prussian cavalry, which were pushing along the cramped space between the ridge and the marshes. The first threat of the kind was presented by the Alt-Platen Dragoons [D8] and the Kleist Hussars [H1], which Frederick summoned up from behind his right wing. After a brief hand-to-hand combat they were driven back by eight squadrons of allied dragoons, comprising two regiments of Russians and the Austrian regiment of Kollowrat [D37].

The Russo-Austrian dragoons were in turn thrown back by the Belling Hussars [H9] and the free hussar squadron of Kleist, which were brought up by GL. Seydlitz in person. The Prussians advanced too far for their own good, for the impetus carried them into a devastating fire of the Russian infantry which was packed behind the Tiefer-Weg. Seydlitz pulled his men back, and shortly afterwards he was disabled by a canister ball which struck his sword hand, forcing him to leave the field in agony.

A pair of isolated probes terminated the efforts of the Prussian cavalry on this side. The short-sighted GL. Friedrich Eugen of Württemberg (brother of the 'Austrian' Louis) led a regiment of dragoons (probably Menicke [D3]) into the rear of General Berg's Russian infantry, and was driven off by the canister fire of regimental pieces.

The Prussian major general Puttkamer made a last effort with his regiment of White Hussars [H4]. He not only came under the same destructive fire as the others, but was counterattacked by what Captain Podgursky describes as Austrian hussars in light green dolmans, who can only have been those of the Nádasdy regiment [H11]. 'The turmoil increased with every second. Sabres and uniforms were stained by blood. The horses were driven mad, and leaped over the bloody corpses... You could see no more than a few feet about yourself, on account of the dust and smoke.'[35] Puttkamer reeled backwards, shot dead through the chest, and his hussars were driven away.

In contrast to the piecemeal Prussian attacks against the northern flank of the Tiefer-Grund position, Frederick built up a potentially decisive concentration of force in the middle of the afternoon against the Austrian infantry holding its right-hand salient, and against the entrenchments which ran back from there at an acute angle to the Grosser-Spitzberg, the grandiose name for the sandy hillock which was now the decisive ground of the battle. As long as the Russians were allowed to hold this feature their artillery would continue to enfilade the lines of entrenchments stretching on either side, and sweep the crossings of the line of ponds. If it were lost to the enemy, the Prussians would be able to gain the ridge and take all the other defences from the rear.

Frederick positioned a substantial part of his heavy artillery in three batteries (behind Kunersdorf village, at the southern end of the Dorf-See, and behind the Blanken-See) to take up the duel with the pieces on the Spitz-Berg, and he fed the left wing of his infantry through the smoking ruins of Kunersdorf to attack the entrenchments beyond. The Austrians' right-hand neighbours, the Rostov and Apsheron regiments, were smashed in a grisly manner (the Apsherons were later awarded the honour of wearing red breeches in memory of this day), but the line was prolonged as far as the Grosser-Spitzberg by the timely arrival of the regiments of Pskov and Vologda.

Pskov and Vologda in turn gave way at about five in the afternoon in the face of a final effort by the Prussian infantry. Frederick was present in person, but Saltykov countered by summoning up three regiments (Vyborg, Kazan and Perm) from the seemingly inexhaustible reserves on his far right flank. The Prussian troops had been 'marching through the sand under a crushing heat, dying of thirst, and capable only of dragging themselves along. It was always the same battalions which were fed into the action, while the enemy countered us with fresh troops.'[36]

The Prussian lieutenant general Platen now precipitated a sequence of events which completed the ruin of Frederick's army. As the surviving senior officer of horse, he took charge of the cavalry of the main army and the corps of Finck, and on his own authority he fed the troopers across the zone of ponds by way of the corridor of land between the Dorf-See and the Blanken-See. This was the first time that the Prussians had advanced in any force so far west along the foot of the entrenchments, and after he had gained sufficient ground he began to wheel against the Grosser-Spitzberg.

The Schorlemer Dragoons [D6], the leading regiment, were wiped out by the guns of the bastion. Still worse for the Prussians was the fact that they were now stranded to the west of the ponds, and had unwittingly offered their left flank to a great mass (more than sixty squadrons or squadron equivalents) of largely fresh Russo-Austrian cavalry which Loudon brought together in dead ground below the fortifications of the Grosser Spitz-Berg. The onset was going to have close parallels with Driesen's attack at Leuthen, only this time with the Prussians as the target.

The Austrian Löwenstein Chevaulegers [D31] and Liechtenstein Dragoons [D6] constituted the main force of the first line, flanked on either side by Russian cuirassiers. The Kollowrat Dragoons [D37] formed the left of the second line, with Russian cuirassiers and mounted grenadiers extending to their right. Major General Totleben's Don Cossacks and Russian hussars held themselves in the rear, ready to exploit any success, and *GFWM*. Bethlen's two regiments of Austrian hussars were also poised for the pursuit, though their exact place cannot be determined.

Precise details are difficult to find concerning the decisive episode of the battle—the ensuing half-hour of combat in which Loudon and his combined cavalry overcame Platen's horse on the ground south of the Grosser-Spitzberg. The dust hid the struggling squadrons from the Russian gunners, who rained down canister indiscriminately on the scene, but the encounter ended with the surviving Prussian cavalrymen fleeing between the ponds and riding down their own exhausted infantry. The cohesion of the Prussian units collapsed, most of the heavy guns were abandoned, and tens of thousands of beaten troops made for the flimsy bridges which spanned the channels of the wetlands to the north.

In a final clash the remnants of the Prussian cavalry wing of Schorlemer were driven from the northern slopes of the Mühl-Berge into the marshlands, and the Cossacks and the Russian hussars proceeded to capture large numbers of Prussians, mainly cavalrymen and gunners, along the road to Zolow, and at the crossings of the Hühner-Fliess at the Faulen-Brücke and the Stroh-Brücke. *GFWM*. Bethlen directed the Nádasdy and Kálnoky Hussars [Hs11,17] towards Trettin. Major Joseph Graffenstein of the Nádasdy regiment was chasing Prussian cuirassiers when he 'espied an officer in a blue uniform embroidered with gold. He was coming towards me from the direction of the enemy, and accompanied by four others. I awaited them in hiding, and was about to attack when the officer called out, and I made out *FZM*. [really *FML*.] Loudon, who had been rendered totally unrecognisable by the dust and smoke.'[37]

When Bethlen approached Trettin village he found the churchyard stuffed with Prussian infantry. 'I accordingly ordered half my men to dismount, and attacked the churchyard by brute force. The enemy had to abandon the village…

along with a number of heavy pieces which they had rescued from the action, but they now had to leave the guns in a sunken road between Trettin and the field of battle.'[38] Bethlen brought back 650 prisoners and deserters, 'and there would have been more if the Russian hussars had not snatched many of them from our men.'[39]

In so far as the battle of Kunersdorf had been lost by Prussian failings, it was due to miscalculations on the part of Frederick, and by demands which finally overtaxed his fine army. The outcome was also a positive victory for the Russians and Austrians, and remains a model of what is capable of being achieved by allies, and not just in the context of the Seven Years War. Saltykov had selected and prepared his positions admirably, and if we have to except the exposed Mühl-Berge, it is because the Observation Corps was a law unto itself. Saltykov had taken due note of the Prussian grand tactics, he refused to be panicked into any precipitate move which might have given Frederick an opening, and he made an excellent use of his reserves. As the combat developed, the Russian and Austrian units fought interchangeably, and Loudon (who overcame his dislike of Saltykov) combined the Russian and Austrian cavalry into a force which dealt the death blow to the Prussian army.

Loudon was delighted at the performance of his two battalions of combined grenadiers and of his own grenadier regiment of Grün-Loudon, which together helped to save the allies from collapse after the Mühl-Berge had been lost. The Baden-Baden fusiliers [23], fighting alongside the Russians, then had the credit of stabilising the line behind the Tiefer-Weg. The Austrian cavalry did well, and Loudon made special mention of Lieutenant Colonel Caraffa's mounted grenadiers, who had taken four pieces, and of the Löwenstein Chevaulegers [D31], who had captured two 12-pounders. The two regiments of hussars came into their own towards the end of the day, though almost nothing is heard of the Croats, for three of their battalions were guarding the bridge near Frankfurt, and the other two were probably hiding in the woods.

The losses of the Austrians bear out in general terms Loudon's assessment of the battle. The grand total came to more than 2,200, among whom the highest unit losses were sustained by the Grün-Loudon Grenadiers (496), the Baden-Baden fusiliers (465), and among the cavalry by the Löwenstein Chevaulegers.

Concerning what was due to Loudon in person, Daun was distinctly grudging in his recommendations to Maria Theresa. 'It is difficult to reward Loudon more than he has already been rewarded. I would advise Your Majesty not to be over-hasty, for graces are welcome whenever they come... If Your Majesty is absolutely set on some kind of recognition, I can think of nothing better than 2,000 or so ducats, which he will be able to put to very good use. I have to say that an immediate promotion to *FZM*. would be premature, for then Your Majesty would have nothing in reserve for a further occasion, not to mention that such an advance would make all the generals senior to him distinctly out of sorts.'[40]

THE MIRACLE OF THE HOUSE OF BRANDENBURG

From the middle of August until the middle of September 1759 the Prussian state endured a period of continual crisis. Kunersdorf was the greatest tactical victory achieved by any of the allied forces in the war, and it was potentially decisive in the strategic sense as well, for the Russians and Austrians were at the gates of the core area of the Brandenburg-Prussian state. The Prussians had just 3,000 troops of the royal army under command by the evening of the battle, and for a number of hours Frederick lost faith in the survival of his person, his army and his monarchy. By the end of the following day his officers had brought together 18,000 panic-stricken men at the rallying point of Reitwein on the left side of the Oder, but there were some 100,000 allied troops potentially capable of being brought against them in less than a week, namely Daun with the 23,000 of the left wing of the Austrian army to the south at Priebus, Hadik's 13,350 at Guben and Neuzelle, Beck's 9,000 at Sommerfeld, and the 62,000-strong victorious army of Saltykov and Loudon on the far side of the Oder on the reeking field at Kunersdorf.

This mass of forces, inarticulated though it

was, stood between Frederick and the only other Prussian concentrations of any consequence, those of Prince Henry (35-40,000) in the old camp of Schmottseiffen, and *GL.* Fouqué (18,000) at Landeshut. Henry was hemmed in between *GdC.* Buccow with the right wing (19,000) of the main Austrian army at Marklissa, and by the detachments of d'Aynse (3,400) at Lauban, and Maguire (6,100) at Görlitz. De Ville (12,000) was on the way from Bohemia to Marklissa, while Harsch (21,500) watched Fouqué from Trautenau.

Bernado Bellotto (nephew of Canaletto) spent the burning summer of 1759 painting townscapes of Vienna. One of his most familiar productions is his representation of the great courtyard of the Schönbrunn Palace at the moment when the formal news of the victory at Kunersdorf was carried to Maria Theresa. A crowd of two or three hundred is already gathered before the chapel wing, and spectators are lining the balcony above (which is actually a physical impossibility). Joseph Count Kinsky is being whisked past the central fountain in a light, yellow-lacquered carriage, and a troop of red-coated dragoons (probably of the Württemberg regiment [D38]) is coming up behind. Shortly before tidings of any kind had reached Vienna, Maria Theresa had written to Daun to impress upon him 'that the sooner the enemy is dealt a decisive blow, and our superiority put to proper use, the more we shall spare human blood, gold and danger.'[41]

The issues which seemed to stand forth in such clarity in Vienna were not so evident to some of the commanders in the theatre of operations. On 13 August, the day after the battle, the Russians were entirely preoccupied in clearing the field, and staging a great ceremony of victory on the Grosser-Spitzberg, and they could not be persuaded by Loudon into launching a serious pursuit. *GdC.* Hadik commanded the largest intact grouping of Austrian troops in the vicinity. His infantry set off from Forst at four in the morning of the 13th, and covered the eighteen miles north to Guben after ten hours of marching in extreme heat. In the evening he received a letter from Loudon which told him of the bloody battle, and how, 'in spite of everything, the almost unbelievable steadfastness of the Russians finally prevailed.' Saltykov now desired Hadik to march to Müllrose and establish himself there, to help to prevent the king falling back to cover Berlin, or joining Prince Henry.[42]

Hadik was on the road with his hussars and German cavalry at two hours after midnight on 14 August, and reached Müllrose at nine the same morning. He was separated only by the Friedrich-Wilhelms-Canal and a few miles from the southern flank of the Prussian army, which was rallying west of Frankfurt, but he was nonplussed by a series of contradictory messages which came to him from Saltykov. He appealed for clarification. He was told to stay where he was, and it 'was now enough for him [Saltykov] that I was so close to the army as to be virtually united.'[43]

Hadik's infantry came up to him at Müllrose at nine in the morning of 15 August, and he dispatched *FML.* Rudolph Pálffy with a mixed command to scout towards Fürstenwalde and Berlin. There was little to be seen of the enemy, but the handiwork of the Cossacks and Kalmyks was all too evident in the despoiled churches and the barbarities which were inflicted on the people.

On 15 August Loudon and the Russian regulars crossed to the left bank of the Oder above Frankfurt. They did so as much for sanitary as operational reasons, for by now the stench on the field of Kunersdorf was intolerable. The allies were losing time, and every day of grace was invaluable to Frederick, for it gave him the opportunity to gather his wits and re-make his army, and on the 17th and 18th he fell back to a blocking position on the Spree at Fürstenwalde. Even now the Prussians came under pressure only from the Austrians, and then only by detached corps.

Out on the eastern flank, *FML.* Beck at Sommerfeld learned that the Prussians had left a weak and exposed garrison in **Grünberg**, and he executed a forced march to arrive outside the town with a force of 2,600 horse and Croats on 18 August. The Land-Battalion of de Rege tried to break out, but was caught at Lawaldau by two squadrons of the Bethlen Hussars [H35] and was wiped out, losing 26 killed or wounded, and 513 taken prisoner.[44]

The descent on Grünberg had the unfortunate effect of carrying Beck well to one side of the potentially decisive country west of Frankfurt, where Loudon and Hadik were probing the positions of the Prussian royal army in a region of dense forests. Saltykov refused to lend the Austrians even so much as a small corps of Russian troops, which would at least have created the impression that Loudon had the whole of the Russian army behind him. Loudon instead made an unsupported reconnaissance on 18 August, and found that the Prussians were deployed most cunningly in concealed positions.[45]

Hadik to the south was still well placed to threaten the Prussian right flank and rear, and on the 16th he asked Saltykov for his blessing on a scheme to lever Frederick out of his position, by lunging towards Beeskow and sending detachments as if to threaten Berlin.[46] Saltykov approved Hadik's project in principle, as a welcome show of initiative. It was clear that he expected the same of the rest of the Austrians, but no such response was forthcoming. The reasons call for some explanation.

What Vienna meant by 'decisive' action was merely to establish the Russians in secure winter quarters in enemy territory. 'This can only be in Silesia and along the Oder. This must be our chief objective, for solid advantages are to be preferred to everything else.'[47] Daun's response was less than energetic. He had marched north from Rothenburg to Priebus on 13 August, and on the 18th he advanced to Triebel, where he was to remain inactive for the next three weeks. To judge affairs from a Napoleonic perspective what was needed now was a man who could see his way through the clutter of subordinate issues to what was of fundamental importance at this juncture, and one who had the decisive will to direct all his resolutions to that end. By that standard, at least, Daun qualified on neither account, but his 'shortcomings' were as much the product of the thinking of his time as of his own cautious and pessimistic temperament.

If he had no other intention than to concentrate all the available troops at his disposal, Daun could have brought together between 40 and 50,000 men, made up of the 23,000 troops of the left wing of the main Austrian army, together with the detachments of Loudon, Hadik and Beck. However Daun was not, or did not believe himself to be, at liberty to direct all the Austrian field forces in the direction of Frederick's field army and Berlin. To have attacked the Prussians immediately after the battle of Kunersdorf he would have had to execute five forced marches in succession.[48] Thereafter, quite apart from the difficulties attending co-operation with the Russians, Daun still had to keep an eye on the doings of Prince Henry, who was still lurking in the camp of Schmottseiffen, and might choose to intervene on behalf of his brother.

Disinclined to do anything dramatic on his own account, Daun concluded that the continuing prosperity of the campaign depended on whatever arrangements he could make with the Russians. The physical bravery of those people could not be denied, 'for they fight and win in spite of themselves. Their present and unalterable indecisiveness is therefore much to be regretted.'[49] From his reading of the mentality of their generals Daun reckoned that he could still encourage favourable dispositions by a suitable deployment of presents, 'not forgetting the secretariat, which is said to be all-influential.'[50]

Saltykov was delighted to receive a snuff box set with diamonds, but he was particularly pleased to be given 5,000 ducats in cash, as Daun had foreseen. Fermor affected a certain indifference, though the greed showed in his eyes, and he sent his surgeon to claim his present of 4,000 ducats in private. The sum of 6,400 ducats was distributed among the other generals. But nothing was capable of effecting a genuine change of heart in the Russian high command. The highly able French military attaché Brigadier the Marquis Marc-René de Montalembert arrived at headquarters on 20 August, and heard Saltykov declaring that he had done enough for the Austrians. All the Russians without exception were 'firmly convinced that the Court of Vienna has no concern about sparing them, and just wishes to load them with all the burden of the war.'[51]

Loudon and Hadik were the men who were best placed to judge the limits of Russian tolerance. *FML.* Lacy had arrived from Daun on

Joseph Count d'Ayasasa, leader of elite cavalry and Daun's most trusted confidant. (Military Academy, Wiener Neustadt)

15 August with a completely unpalatable plan of joint operations. *GFWM*. d'Ayasasa followed on the evening of the 19th with another scheme which would have been just as unacceptable, but Loudon and Hadik took him aside before he could deliver the proposals. Loudon told him that the least hint of the Russians being asked to pursue Frederick would induce them to re-cross the Oder. Hadik then took a great deal on himself by getting d'Ayasasa to represent that nothing more was demanded of Saltykov than 'that the Russian army, having suffered so much through its two victories, should march on to Guben to recover.' Daun would leave 30,000 troops on the Queiss to contain Prince Henry, and lead 50,000 in person against the king, and hold him in check until Dresden was reduced by the *Reichsarmee* and Austrian reinforcements, after which the Austrians and Russians would act together in Silesia. The details could be settled by a meeting of Saltykov and Daun in Guben.

Saltykov fell in with the scheme 'most cheerfully.'[52] In effect, at the prompting of Loudon, and with the connivance of d'Ayasasa, Hadik had worked out a compromise plan on his own authority, representing it to the Russians as that of Daun, and in turn to Daun as the Russian reply. Daun travelled to Guben on 22 August, and thanks to the hidden agency of Hadik he reached a complete agreement with Saltykov. The two armies would hold their present positions for up to two weeks, and Daun would supply the Russians with the bread and fodder they needed to stay on the western side of the Oder. As soon as they had learned that Dresden had fallen, the Austrians and Russians would set about reducing the Prussian fortresses in Silesia and consolidating themselves there.[53]

Day after day passed without the allies undertaking anything of consequence against Frederick, who was gathering his forces behind Fürstenwalde. Hadik's corps now amounted to a respectable 23,465 troops, and he repeatedly asked Saltykov by way of Loudon for leave to threaten Berlin. Each time Saltykov told him to stay at Müllrose, and Hadik therefore had to be content with operations of secondary importance. He had first turned his attention to the Friedrich-Wilhelms-Canal, which was at least of economic consequence, for it completed the link of the Elbe with the Oder by way of the Havel and the Spree, and 'the entire traffic of the East India Company to Breslau and Frankfurt is routed along this canal.'[54] In his scholarly way he took note of the inscriptions on the stretch west of Müllrose at Neuhaus, then blew up the locks between 19 and 22 August. The Russians were responsible for the stretch to the east, and exploded their demolitions on the 24th. Three days later one of Hadik's detachments browbeat the weak garrison holding the little fortress of Peitz into surrendering, which opened the most direct route to the Elster, if anyone might be inclined to exploit it.

Loudon's corps had still less freedom of action, being tied so closely to the Russians. Daun explained that he would have to stay with them indefinitely, for 'his presence with them is essential, as has been shown by the recent battle. He knows the language, and has won their trust, and will always carry more influence with them than any one else.'[55]

What Frederick termed a miraculous salvation (below) can be traced to some specific happenings. Running short of provisions, and fearing that he might still be left to face the king unsupported, Saltykov decided that he must shift his army south into the relatively untouched country closer to the Austrians. His first march, on 28 August, was a short move to Hohenwalde, which scarcely took him clear of his old camp at Lossow. On the 29th he turned abruptly to the south, reaching Grunow by way of Müllrose, and on the 30th he continued in the same direction as far as Lieberose.

The Russians, and Loudon with them, had therefore removed themselves from the direct axis between Frankfurt and Berlin, as Frederick noted with surprise and delight. In a celebrated letter he wrote to Prince Henry to announce 'the miracle of the House of Brandenburg. At a time when the enemy had passed the Oder, and could have finished the war by risking a second battle, they marched from Müllrose to Lieberose.'[56]

Frederick matched the sideways shuffle of the Russians by decamping from Fürstenwalde on 30 August and marching as far as Beeskow.

Hadik's corps was now sandwiched between the rival armies, and he was left wholly responsible for the security of the Russian left flank. Hadik reached Mochow, near Lamsfeld, on 30 August, which was a reasonably good position in itself, but left him exposed to the whole force of Frederick's reconstituted army, which crossed the Spree by several pontoon bridges and advanced against him at speed. Hadik fell back under heavy skirmishing, but Frederick was content to plant himself at Waldow.

These days were enlivened by encounters of a passably genial nature between the Austrians and the Russian irregular cavalry. Hadik had a visit of this kind on 3 September, when a Cossack brigadier arrived with 150 of his Cossacks and Kalmyks and offered to put on a show. The Kalmyks thereupon set up caps as targets on posts, and drilled them with arrows as they swept past at full gallop. Hadik invited the chief to his table, and he announced himself as Brigadier Krasnoshchekov ('Red-Cheeks,' of a famous or notorious family of Don Cossacks), 'a well built and well educated man of cheerful demeanour and a pleasing face.'

All the rest sat in a circle on the ground, eating with a surprising decorum, and becoming quietly drunk on wine and schnapps. One of the officers opened a copper box, and unwrapped cloths of green, red and white silk to show an image of a seated Oriental god, and explained their singularly practical theology: 'When it is too hot in summer, they smear the statue with butter or bacon fat, and leave it in the sun so that it becomes really hot, and force the god to give them cooler weather. When the weather turns too cold, they throw it into the water or bury it in the snow, and thus compel him to warm things up. Excessive rain is answered by flogging the statue and thus bringing fine weather.' The guests departed with much bowing and expressions of gratitude. The next day one of the Cossack officers came back to Hadik and presented him with a Turkish horse, two cows and twenty sheep.[57]

While Hadik was entertaining his picturesque guests at Lamsfeld, he did not forget that one of his tasks was to counter any movement of forces from Frederick's army to the theatre of war in Saxony, where the *Reichsarmee*'s siege of Dresden was under threat from a corps under the command of *GM.* Wunsch, who was advancing up the Elbe. On 2 September Hadik received a letter from the Prince of Zweibrücken, begging him for help. Hadik at once wrote to Saltykov and Daun, to ask them for permission to set off with his troops for Saxony. Daun was in full agreement, and the unpredictable Saltykov not only gave his blessing, but urged Hadik to make haste.

On the night of 4/5 September Hadik was able to make a clean break of contact with Frederick's army nearby at Waldow. He drove south-west in a succession of forced marches in his usual style, and his exhausted men staggered into the Neustadt of Dresden on the 9th. He was not a moment too soon, for the king had put together a reinforcement of 10,000 troops under Finck and sent them racing towards the Elbe almost on Hadik's heels.

Up on the border hills at Schmottseiffen, Prince Henry had been so isolated from his brother that he heard of the disaster at Kunersdorf only on 25 August. 'The dismal news... ran from rank to rank... the silence of the graveyard reigned in the tents, and over them the night spread its raven wings... But our hero was not a man to be overwhelmed by despondency or anxiety! Henry awoke!'[58] On 27 August Henry set off down the right (eastern) bank of the Bober with sixteen battalions and thirty squadrons, hoping to divert the attention of the Austrians from his brother. On the 29th he reached the familiar surroundings of Sagan, which was on a line with Daun's left flank. The field marshal responded on the next day, by falling back to Muskau, and summoning up Buccow to join him with the right wing to the army from Rothenburg.

The dilemma now facing the Austrians was that Frederick was about thirty miles away to the north-west, but Henry's axis of advance down the Bober only some twenty to the east, and Daun had to concentrate against one or the other. On 1 September Daun marched his reunited army to his old camp at Triebel, which gave a temporary comfort to Saltykov, but two days later he turned east and took up position at Sorau to confront Henry. The prince fell back up the Bober on 5 September, but Daun held his troops in the same position until the 9th. He had turned his back on Frederick, the Russians and the road to Berlin, and chosen to counter Prince Henry, who was an exceptionally clever opponent, commanding an intact army, and at least his equal in a war of position and manoeuvre. Montalembert concluded that Daun's conduct was beyond reproach, but knew that it would be impossible to convince the Russians, who believed that they had been abandoned.[59]

Belying his reputation for caution, Daun decamped from Sorau on the 9th, and marched by way of Triebel to Spremberg on the 10th. The move was but the first stage of an intended advance to fight the king or take Berlin. Frederick's hastily-reconstituted army needed another Brandenburg Miracle, if it was not to face a second and possibly terminal battle in less than a month, and such a wonder was now provided by Prince Henry.

After he had been balked on the lower reaches of the Bober, Henry recoiled upstream and encamped on 7 September at Löwenberg and Kunzendorf close under the border hills. Daun suspected that he had it in mind to join Fouqué at Landeshut, and execute a powerful diversionary attack into north-east Bohemia by way of Trautenau. The Austrians were unprepared for what Henry actually did, which was to lead them on a merry dance around Lusatia.

Quite unexpectedly Henry struck west against the line of communication and the complex of magazines which had supported the Austrian effort north of the hills over the last two summers. *GdC.* de Ville and his corps of 12,000 troops were responsible for guarding this vital route, which ran up from Bohemia to Zittau. On 9 September Henry's advance guard lunged west to Lauban, to the surprise and consternation of de Ville, who fell back behind the Lausitzer Neisse to Görlitz, where he met the corps of Beck. The combined force amounted to about 20,000 troops, but de Ville did not consider that he was out of harm's way, and in a single forced march he reached Bautzen on the 11th. De Ville's retreat, or rather flight, was damaging in itself. Worse still, in his alarm he had fallen back west, and the Prussians had the freedom to roam almost at will in the Austrian base area.

Colonel Conti repulsed a powerful raiding force from the main Austrian depot at Zittau on 10 September, but the enemy revenged themselves by destroying a number of smaller magazines, and the Möhring Hussars [H3] captured a convoy of 400 waggons which had been carrying flour from Gabel. Losses of this kind could be made good, but it was impossible for Daun to ignore the fact that Henry had now planted his main force in the neighbourhood of Görlitz, in other words directly on the Austrian line of communication.

The accumulation of bad news stopped Daun in his tracks at Spremberg. On 12 September he assembled his senior officers, and they reached the decision to abandon their march on Berlin and turn back to settle with Prince Henry. A strenuous march took the army south by way of Lohsa to Bautzen, where it arrived on the 13th. Daun confronted de Ville, told him that he was 'ill' and must leave the army. Montazet reported the change in Daun's fortunes, 'but I must say in confidence that what is worse is that he does not have a single general on whom he can rely. Until now the ones in highest repute and the most frequently employed were Harsch and de Ville, but just think of what they have done in the course of this campaign! Doesn't it make you shudder?... The field marshal has only two really able generals, as he has told me a hundred times: one is Lacy, and the other is Loudon.' The latter was out of reach with the Russians, and Montazet urged his political masters to do everything in their power to promote the rise of Lacy, as the one person capable of giving impetus to the Austrian military machine.[60]

Over the ten days from 13 September Daun remained immobile at Bautzen, in a distant confrontation with Henry's army twenty-five miles to the east at Görlitz. On the 14th Daun learned that Saltykov was still willing to fulfil his part of the plan settled at Guben, to the extent of laying siege to the fortress of Glogau on the Oder, as the northern gateway to Silesia, but he must be provided with siege artillery and a reinforcement of up to 15,000 troops. For the sake of good relations *FML*. Campitelli accordingly departed for the Russians on the 16th with five regiments of infantry and five or six of horse.

Daun was aware that he was in a state of strategic paralysis. He explained to Maria Theresa that there were about 25,000 Austrian troops with Loudon, including Campitelli's recent reinforcement; another 25,000 were with the *Reichsarmee*, which was a waste in some respects. Daun was left with a central core of 60-70,000 men, which was impressive by itself, but not enough to deal with concerted actions on the part of Henry and Frederick.

By 20 September Daun knew that he did not have to worry about the king, for he was now following Loudon and the Russians to the Oder. Henry was therefore devoid of support, and on the 23rd Daun advanced from Bautzen to seek him out. The first day's march came to a halt at Reichenbach, which was short of Görlitz town and within immediate view of the great dome of the Landeskrone, where the Austrians could see a large number of camp fires. They did not know that they had been lit by a small Prussian rearguard, and that Henry had just decamped from Görlitz unseen, and was already on his way to circumvent the left (northern) flank of Daun's army.

Henry's march was another master stroke, comparable in its way with his telling blow against the base area at Zittau. He crossed to the east bank of the Lausitzer Neisse, hurried north downriver as far as Rothenburg, recrossed there and struck west to Hoyerswerda on 25 September, having covered fifty miles in two days of consecutive marching.

GFWM. Vela was standing in Henry's path at **Hoyerswerda** with a little corps of about 2,500 troops. The Prussians scarcely checked in their stride, and by the end of the action Vela had fallen into the hands of the enemy along with 1,812 officers and three cannon. Only the hussars managed to escape.

The news of the destruction of Vela's corps reached Daun later on the 25th, and without giving his army any time to rest or cook, he put it through an about turn and marched it back west through a night of streaming rain. 'Near Markersdorf, a village of ill omen, we lost our way, became muddled up, collided with one another and got into arguments. We spent a most frightful night trying to find the right road... Finally on the 26th we reached Bautzen, some at noon, the others at six or seven in the evening.' Six thousand men were missing, having been totally lost, deserted or gone marauding.[61] Daun and Henry now made west for the Elbe on parallel courses. On 28 September the first forced march from Bautzen brought the Austrians to Hartha, south-west of Bischofswerda, and on the next day the army crossed the Elbe below Dresden.

Over the course of four weeks, in the course of the most complex series of manoeuvres by any army in the entire war, Henry had accomplished the Miracle of the House of Brandenburg by teasing the Austrian and Russian allies apart, and thus exploiting the manifold contradictions in their aims. They had been unable to make up their minds whether to finish off the king by a further great battle, gain fortresses and winter quarters in Silesia, or (increasingly tempting for the Austrians) to seize opportunities which seemed to be opening up in Saxony. In the event the great transfer of Austrian and Prussian forces to the Elbe late in September guaranteed that the Saxon theatre would become the principal theatre of war for the rest of the campaigning season. Loudon and 25,000 Austrian troops were however stranded with the Russians beyond any foreseeable recall, and we must now trace their via dolorosa.

Loudon, the Russians and the end of the campaign in the east

In August and September 1759 the allies had failed to terminate the war by a decisive stroke, when they had it in their power to do so. The opportunity never returned in that form, but they still had the means to end that year's campaigning with the balance of strategic advantage in their favour, by securing solid gains along the Elbe in Saxony, and along the Oder or its tributaries in Silesia.

A couple of good, tenable fortresses in the hands of the Russians would not only be useful in immediate operational terms, but could advance the next campaign by weeks or even months, by enabling the Russians to stay in Silesia over the winter, instead of having to retreat to quarters on the Vistula, and then walk all the way back the next summer.

The courts of St. Petersburg and Vienna settled independently on the fortress of Glogau as the best target. It was an easier place to crack than the modernised stronghold of Neisse. It was situated close to Brandenburg and to the main lateral lines of communication across the northern plain, and once it had fallen the enemy would lose their means of water transport to Breslau and the other fortresses up the Oder, and that place and the fortresses beyond would probably fall of themselves. Simultaneous orders went out to Saltykov and Daun on 29 August.

For the time being, at least, the combined pressure of the French and Austrian attachés (Montalembert and Finé) held Saltykov true to the purpose of besieging Glogau, and the Russian was further encouraged when *FML.* Campitelli reached him on the Bober at Christianstadt on 21 September with the substantial reinforcement from Daun's army.

Nobody was prepared for the energetic way Frederick responded to the threat to Glogau. The Russians were still toiling towards the fortress when the king put his 31,000 troops through a series of forced marches and on 23 September established himself at Neustädtl, at the end of the Katzen-Gebirge, a ridge which dominated the access to Glogau by the left (western) bank of the Oder. Loudon arrived with the allied advance guard later in the day, and found that the enemy were already in possession of this key terrain. Saltykov thereupon assembled the Russian generals and decided to withdraw the combined army to the right bank of the river. Loudon had been excluded from the council, 'and it cannot be denied that this distinguished fighting man was less suited for the role of courtier than the one of a warrior at the head of his army. His character, talents and dauntless spirit qualified him for the latter, but his manner and his noble heart, imbued with the spirit of truth and straight dealing, made him a stranger to intrigue.'[62]

The allied army passed to the far side of the Oder downstream from Glogau at Carolath on the night of 30 September/1 October. Frederick arrived close by with twenty squadrons of horse at seven in the morning, too late to disturb the passage. In the excitement Loudon had forgotten about two Ansbach cuirassiers who had been left on the western side, to protect the local population against marauders, but Frederick now sent the pair back to rejoin their master.

The king's display of good manners was the only agreeable incident which Loudon had to record at this tail end of the proceedings. He confided in Kaunitz that 'just after the victory of 12 August the Russians decided to abandon all offensive action for the rest of this campaign, and instead wait to see what we would do. Some of the more honest people in the Russian army told me over and over again that it was no use trying to get the Russians to go and attack the enemy. They knew it would just never happen.'[63]

Frederick had been feeding forces across the Oder to Glogau at will, and he now crossed with his main army and faced the allies across the swampy hollow of Bartsch. To prevent literal starvation among his men and horses Loudon sent out officers of the commissariat to requisition fodder and provisions in the Circle of Guhrau. These people discovered that the region had been devastated and thoroughly eaten-out by the Russians. A Polish Jew now agreed to provide the fodder by contract, but only on payment of half the cash in advance. The Austrian officers and soldiers were going unpaid, and Loudon was forced to apply to Count Sternberg, the Austrian ambassador in Warsaw, for a credit to the value of at least 30,000 florins to enable him to support his corps until the end of November and possibly beyond. These desperate measures indicated how completely Loudon was isolated from any support.

If the Russians postponed their departure for a few days, it was not out of regard for Loudon, but because Saltykov received an elaborate reprimand from the Russian Conference (roughly equivalent to a cabinet), which told him that he had diminished the honour of Russian arms by failing to exploit the victory at Kunersdorf, and that he had been wrong to hang on to Loudon's corps and to have misused it so signally. On 23 October the

Russians brought their weight in heavy artillery to bear in a useless bombardment of Herrnstadt, which was held by the Prussian free battalion of Collignon. This was the last action of the campaign in the east. On the next day Saltykov and Loudon began to fall back by mutual consent towards temporary quarters on the Warthe, to ease their critical problems of supply. So far they had succeeded in fixing Frederick on the right bank of the Oder, but the threat they presented to his army and his lands was now so diminished that the king re-crossed the river at Köben on 26 and 27 October, and made off west to settle accounts with Daun in Saxony, leaving only a small corps at Trachenberg.

Loudon and his generals settled on the desperate expedient of making for Austrian territory by way of Poland. On 2 November Loudon marched from Rawitsch for Zduny, and six days later the Austrians took the road for Austrian Silesia by way of Wieln, Czestochowa and Krakow. Never in the course of the war did Austrian forces operate so far to the east. Scarcely any arrangements could be made for food or shelter along the way, and Loudon was wrong to think that this roundabout route would spare him the attentions of the enemy. Colonel Bülow was on his tail with six squadrons of dragoons and three of hussars, and on 22 November he was able to capture some of the baggage in Czestochowa, two days after the main force had departed. On the 27th Loudon crossed into Austrian territory at Bielitz, and prosecuted a final exhausting march to Teschen, where he met a small corps under *FML.* Draskovich, who had come from Troppau to receive him.

The *Reichsarmee*, the Austrians and their offensive in Saxony, July–August 1759

The high summer of 1759 saw great concentrations of Austrians, Russians and Prussians heaped up in Lower Lusatia and along the Oder, which created opportunities for the *Reichsarmee* and its supporting Austrians in Saxony west of the Elbe, where the Prussians were now so depleted.

The Prince of Zweibrücken had been ill and out of sorts, and although he held the overall command of the of the *Reichsarmee*, he had left it to his director of operations *GdC*. Serbelloni to drill the troops of the *Reichsarmee* in his dour way and restore a modicum of discipline. The army then marched by short stages across the Thüringer-Wald, and its two columns reached Saalfeld and Erfurt on 26 July.

Now the *Reichsarmee* and the remaining Austrians managed to recover the greater part of Saxony from the enemy, and so helped to draw the main Austrian and Prussian armies back to the Elbe. This unlikely outcome was due partly to the fact that Prince Henry had gathered up most of the troops and marched east to confront Daun, but it was to the credit of the Austrian light forces, which raced across the northern plain well ahead of the two main columns of *Reichstruppen*.

Out on the left, *GFWM*. Ried came up with the Széchenyi Hussars [H32] and 1,200 Croats, and raided into the Bishopric of Halberstadt, which was one of the core provinces of Brandenburg-Prussia. The chief families had fled before Ried arrived, but he was still able to raise the equivalent of 30,000 florins in cash. On 21 July he pushed on to Halberstadt town, which had been abandoned by its garrison, and levied a mighty contribution of 80,000 taler, of which 25,000 was made over at once for the *Refraichissement* of his troops. Ried could not dwell overlong in this exposed position, and so he turned aside by way of Querfurt to the Saale, where there were further objects of interest.

On 1 August a tiny force consisting of a captain of horse and about thirty of Ried's hussars forced their way into the substantial Prussian town of Halle, and split up in search of plunder. 'In this place neither youth, maiden nor the lowliest day labourer were spared. The enemy pointed their carbines at the chests of whoever they encountered on the streets, and forced them to give up everything they had… they had equipped themselves comprehensively for this enterprise, and brought along such necessary implements as axes, cleavers and crowbars. If the householders did not open their doors immediately, they smashed their way in, presented their sabres at the throats of the inhabitants and threatened to cut them in pieces, if they did not at once open everything up and yield up their valuables and treasures.'[64]

Halle remained under Austrian occupation until 24 August. The commissary Kozchina von Freudenthal, an ennobled former lackey of Kaunitz, installed himself there and exacted contributions from the neighbouring villages at leisure. Little Reideburg had already been plundered so thoroughly that it could deliver only one-tenth of the 2,250 taler which were demanded, whereupon Kozchina had the place wrecked by a detachment of Mainz infantry.

While Ried's detachment functioned as a raiding force in enemy territory, the commands of the Austrian *GFWM*s. Kleefeld and Luzinsky were regarded by Zweibrücken as instruments for the liberation of Saxony. He first directed them towards the city of Leipzig on parallel courses, Kleefeld by way of Weimar and Naumburg, and Luzinsky further to the east through Jena and Zeitz. 'All of this was designed to leave the garrison of Leipzig uncertain and in the dark as to what we had in mind. In such a way we gained the time to put our designs into effect.'[65]

On 4 August Kleefeld presented himself before **Leipzig** and summoned the place to surrender. The four battalions of the Prussian garrison included a large number of ex-Saxon soldiers, who could not be trusted to defend the antiquated wall. On his side Zweibrücken 'would have liked to have taken the garrison prisoners of war, but he wished to spare the town the miseries of being taken by storm.'[66] *GM*. Hauss surrendered in return for a free evacuation to Wittenberg. About seven hundred Austrian prisoners and twenty Bohemian and Saxon civilian hostages regained their liberty, and when the garrison marched out on the 7th many of the Saxon soldiers took the opportunity to desert from the Prussian ranks.

If Leipzig counted as a political prize, the little Saxon fortress-town of **Torgau** was of more direct military importance, since it functioned as a forward base for Prussian operations in Saxony, and offered the enemy one of their most useful crossings of the Elbe. The Prince of Zweibrücken now reinforced Kleefeld by the Palatinate infantry regiment of Effern, and the combined Austro-German force presented itself in front of Torgau on 10 August.

An ill-tempered exchange of words set the mood for what was to follow. Kleefeld sent Major Keller to tell the Prussians, as Zweibrücken had instructed, that if the Prussians burnt the houses, the magazine or the bridges, 'the unfailing consequence would be that the town of Halle and the whole of their territory in our hands would go up in flames.'[67] The Prussian commander, Colonel Karl Friedrich Wolfersdorff had a garrison of only three battalions and a few hundred convalescents and invalids, but replied that he would set fire to the suburbs if Kleefeld came any nearer. Two battalions of Prussian reinforcements got into Torgau in the evening, and Marainville noted 'this could make this enterprise more difficult than is thought. The town has a double wall surrounded by wet ditches; there is a square-shaped fortification on the other side of the town, and the two are connected by a wooden bridge which rests on masonry piles.'[68]

More than two days of bloody infantry combat followed. The Liccaner and Oguliner Croats were sniping from the south-eastern suburbs and launched repeated assaults, while the Prussians beat back every one of the attacks and periodically irrupted in sorties. On 12 August the *Reichsfeldmarschallieutenant* Prince Carl of Stolberg arrived from the *Reichsarmee* with a reinforcement of two battalions, two regiments of cuirassiers and two 12-pounder cannon, and planted a battery on the dyke of the river bank immediately below the town, from where the besiegers could take the bridge under fire.

Moreover, by a Prussian account, 'overnight the Croats had brought up quantities of wood on the main road outside the Spittel-Tor, and used it to construct a blockhouse, from where they began fire with a little cannon against the town wall, causing some losses among the garrison.'[69] The Prussians tried to bring two cannon to bear against the annoying blockhouse, but these were immediately knocked out by the besiegers' main artillery.

On 14 August the parties agreed to a

capitulation on generous terms, whereby the Prussians were granted a free evacuation, together with their artillery and three days' of supplies for the march. Once the document was signed, Stolberg, Kleefeld and Luzinsky congratulated the Prussian commandant on his defence. Colonel Wolfersdorff replied that his king would get Torgau back soon enough, 'but His Highness [Stolberg] retorted that just now the king had been beaten by the Russians for the second time, losing everything he had in the battle, and that he was completely surrounded by the Austrians and Russians.'[70]

At eight in the morning of 15 August the garrison began to march out by way of the Elbe-Tor and so along the road to Wittenberg. When one of the regiments was marching past, the allied officers called out '"If you are a brave Saxon, if you are good Austrian or if you are of the *Reichsarmee*, you just have to step out. His Highness will protect you." At this the men of the garrison battalion of Grolman, who were mostly Saxons, or Austrian deserters, broke ranks in chaotic scenes. They hid themselves variously behind the ranks of Croats, behind the palisades, or under the bridge of the outer ditch, while whole units ran back towards the Elbe.'[71]

Kleefeld's next task was to take **Wittenberg**, the lowest of the fortress-towns along the Saxon stretch of the Elbe. He knew nothing of the defences, and he accordingly set out from Torgau to make a reconnaissance, escorted only by a small party of Croats, hussars and German cavalry. On the 21st the Prussian outposts were pushed back into the town, and Kleefeld viewed the place undisturbed. He had no artillery with him, but on an impulse he sent his adjutant into the town to summon *GM.* Horn to surrender. The Prussian commander (like Hauss in Leipzig) had no faith in his own soldiers, and he signed the capitulation before the day was out.

We left the main body of the *Reichsarmee* as it was still crawling from Franconia over the hills into Thuringia. The Prince of Zweibrücken wrote from Erfurt on 27 July 'as I now have reliable news that Prince Henry has fallen back over the Elbe, I will at once set myself in march. I will be at Weimar tomorrow, continue the advance into Electoral Saxony, and push my operations as activity as the circumstances allow.'[72] The *Reichstruppen* crossed the Saale at Naumburg on 5 August, passed uncomfortably close by the field of Rossbach, and arrived at Leipzig on the 8th. 'We found considerable stores of every kind, and the town in an extremely good state and overjoyed to see itself liberated from the Prussians.'[73]

The Capture of Dresden, August 1759

The final phase of the operations of this eventful year began to take shape, drawing more and more troops of the respective armies to the vicinity of Dresden. Six thousand Austrians under *GFWM*s. Brentano and Vela were already operating in the neighbourhood, and they were now assigned to Zweibrücken's command, so that he could act effectively against that city. Daun in addition dispatched *FML.* Maguire with a corps of about 5,500 troops. The total force nominally at Zweibrücken's disposal now stood at about 30,000 men, though not all of them were available for the impending operation against Dresden.

Zweibrücken set out from Leipzig for Dresden on 24 August. On the next day he and his suite passed by the castle of Nischwitz, a property of the Saxon prime minister Heinrich Count Brühl, whom Frederick regarded as a personal enemy. They could see for themselves how the Prussians had smashed the wooden panelling of the interior with axes, and chopped off the arms and legs of the statues in the park.

On 27 August Maguire arrived before Dresden, and found that the Prussians had evacuated the Neustadt, the part of the city which lay on the right (eastern) bank of the Elbe. The *Reichsarmee* reached Meissen at the same time, after four days of marching in great heat, and after a day's rest the troops reached the heights overlooking the Altstadt on the 29th.

In friendly hands, the fortified city of Dresden would offer the Austrians and the *Reichsarmee* a base for operations down the Elbe, and signify that they had regained the Saxon *Redidenz* of the Polish-Saxon royal family. All the same, it is not entirely clear why Daun now set such a high store on recovering Dresden that he was jeopardised his chances of acting jointly with the Russians to crush Frederick and the remnants of his army.

On the importance of recovering Saxony as a whole, Maria Theresa emphasised to Daun that the objective was 'all the more deserving of our attention… as it would deprive the enemy of huge resources in recruits and cash, present a standing threat to the Prussian *Residenz* of Berlin, and give complete cover on this side to my Hereditary Lands and the Empire.'[74] Daun's own opinions are difficult to establish. He could write to Maria Theresa that he was 'never in favour of operations in Saxony, because we would be working for other people and not on our own behalf, and although the land may be conquered cheaply enough, we would have to spend three times as much to keep it.'[75] Five days later, without recognising the contradiction, he mentioned that he would have been quite content with crowning his campaign by liberating Dresden and Saxony, if the Russian victories at Paltzig and Kunersdorf had not pulled him to the theatre of war in the east.[76]

Possibly the clue lies in the word 'cheaply,' which occurs in the first of Daun's letters, and matches some phrases in a communication from Daun to Maria Theresa on 21 August, namely 'that it is reported that we have a contact in the town which assures us that he will take care of the garrison. We simply have to show ourselves in front of the place with a corps and some artillery, and in that case it will just be a matter of days.'[77] The 'contacts' and 'treason' pointed to the Prussian commandant, *GL.* Karl Christoph Count Schmettau.

In fairness to Schmettau, it must be said that his recent conduct and his public statements offer the best evidence to the contrary. He had defended Dresden with great resolution in 1758, and now he stuffed the suburbs with incendiary materials and threatened to set them on fire if an enemy army came near. On 30 August Schmettau rejected the second of two offers from *GFWM.* Brentano, who promised him the Imperial favour and 118,000 taler if he would hand over the city. He told Brentano's intermediary, a merchant of Dresden, that if he dared to come back he would condemn him to imprisonment with hard labour.

At six in the evening of 30 August Schmettau's men duly set fire to the suburbs, 'a way of conducting war which is alien to civilised peoples, and practised only by the Prussian forces.'[78] In fact the besiegers probably had no intention of attacking from this side of the river, for their plan seems to have been to take the defences of the Altstadt under a carefully-aimed fire across the water from the Neustadt.[79] On 31 August a siege train from Prague was disembarked from the Elbe at Lockwitz, and the building of the batteries went ahead.

A curious truce prevailed between the outposts which faced one another across the Augustusbrücke in Dresden, and Schmettau met Maguire there on 2 September. He told the Austrian that he could surrender the Altstadt only on the most advantageous terms, namely a free evacuation for his garrison, with all the military chest, artillery and warlike stores. Zweibrücken at first found the demands unreasonable, but by the 4th he was willing to concede almost everything that Schmettau demanded. He was under pressure from Daun to finish with Dresden so that operations could proceed, the forces under his immediate orders were depleted by detachments to 7,000 infantry and 1,400 cavalry, and he knew (and Schmettau did not) that a relief force under *GM.* Wunsch was advancing to the relief, which put him into some 'painful dilemmas.'[80]

The besiegers and the besieged came to terms on the evening of 4 September, and Schmettau gained a free evacuation to Magdeburg for his garrison of 3,650 troops, together with all his funds and effects. It remains an open question why Schmettau was willing to surrender so quickly. Frederick was angry to learn what had happened. He banished Schmettau from his presence and never employed him again, but, significantly, he stopped short of arraigning him as a traitor.[81] Possibly he feared that to publicise any betrayal on this scale would create all too great a scandal. Possibly he bore in mind that he had written to Schmettau on 14 August, immediately after the defeat at Kunersdorf, authorising him to surrender Dresden if he could gain good terms.

On the morning of 5 September, and too late for their purposes, the Prussians in Dresden heard sounds of artillery and musketry from the direction of Grossenhain, and saw Austrian troops falling back towards the Neustadt. Some kind of attempt at relief was evidently in progress, but the work of gathering transport for the evacuation continued, and the garrison finally made its exit on the morning of the 8th. The ranks and files broke apart in the same style as at Leipzig and Torgau, and the deserters amounted to 870, including two ensigns who took their colours with them.

AGAINST WUNSCH, FINCK AND HENRY IN SAXONY, AUGUST - OCTOBER 1759

When the corps of *GM.* Wunsch arrived on the Elbe it was the first sign that Frederick too was feeding forces to the Saxon theatre. Wunsch had set out from Fürstenwalde on 20 August, and gathered up the former garrison of Torgau and other pockets of troops on his way, which brought his numbers up to 5-6,000 men. It was an inconsiderable force, but it was commanded by a tough and resourceful commander. His first ambition was to recover the recent enemy gains on the lower Elbe, and he began by presenting himself before **Wittenberg** on 27 August. The works were too extensive to be held for any length time by the small garrison, which consisted of the regiment of Baden-Durlach (270) and a few hundred Croats. The Austrian commander, Colonel Losy von Losenau, agreed to capitulate in return for a free evacuation to Leipzig, and duly marched out on the 28th. The Prince of Zweibrücken believed that Losy had behaved reasonably, and he expressed no immediate concern.

Colonel Wolfersdorff marched up the Elbe with the Prussian advance guard, and arrived outside **Torgau** on 30 August. Sterner measures were needed here, for the place was of genuine military importance, and was held by the resolute Austrian *GFWM*. Kleefeld, who commanded two battalions of the *Reichs* regiment of Chur Trier, one battalion each of the Liccaner and Oguliner Croats, and a mixed force of cuirassiers and hussars. Kleefeld rejected the first summons, whereupon Wunsch made active preparations for a storm, and rooted the Croats from the suburb.

The matter became serious when Prussian grenadiers began to line the glacis between the Spittel-Tor and the Becker-Tor, and the regiment of Hessen-Cassel brought up fascines and ladders for the assault. Rather than await the arrival of Wunsch and the main enemy force, Kleefeld hastened to make what terms he could. The garrison marched out to freedom on 31 August, but had to leave behind the contents of the magazine and all the ammunition and artillery. The Prussian casualties amounted to just eleven.

Wunsch made his way up the east bank of the Elbe to bring help to Dresden, now besieged by Zweibrücken and Maguire. He learned on the evening of 4 September that negotiations were already in train, and he marched overnight from Grossenhain in an attempt to break through to the Neustadt. Late in the morning of 5 September Wunsch pushed on by way of Trachau and Trachenberg, and forced Maguire's main force to retreat behind the ramparts of the Neustadt. No word had come from Schmettau (who had already surrendered), but reports from down the Elbe indicated that a powerful enemy force was moving against the Prussian base at Torgau. Without further delay Wunsch made an about turn, and hastened back down the Elbe to reach Torgau on 7 September.

Up to this time Wunsch had operated without the slightest hindrance from the Austrian *GFWM*. Saint-André, who responsible for holding the liberated areas of Saxony with a substantial part of the German and Austrian forces. He had known nothing of Wunsch's dash up the Elbe, for he had been led astray by a feint towards Leipzig, and it was 7 September before he could bring his 13-14,000 troops against Torgau, which had been regained by the Prussians in the way we have just seen.

The Prussian commandant of Torgau refused to be browbeaten into surrendering, and Saint-André's troops were still standing to the west of the town when Wunsch came out on 8 September to do battle

Torgau, 8 September 1759
(not to be confused with the great battle at the same place on 3 November 1760)
a) Austrians and *Reichstruppen*
Total: 13-14,000
Losses: casualties unknown: 596 prisoners
b) Prussians
Total: 4-5,000
Losses: 199: 36 killed, 163 wounded

Saint-André had drawn up his troops facing east towards Torgau, with his right (southern) wing extending to the Grosser Teich ('Big Pond'), and his left resting on the vine-covered ridge of the Ratsweinberg, which was held by *GFWM*. Ried's brigade of two battalions of Croats, with the combined grenadiers in support. At one in the afternoon Wunsch opened a sustained bombardment of the Ratsweinberg. The Prussian infantry then emerged from Torgau, formed up on a broad front two ranks deep, and drove the Croats back on the grenadiers, whereupon the Prussian colonel Wolfersdorff was now able to rush twelve cannon up to the ridge

Three squadrons of the Prussian Plettenberg Dragoons [D7] launched an all-out charge across the plain to the south, then turned back and galloped off, as if in panic. The Austrian and *Reichs* cavalry set after them, and did not grasp that the manoeuvre had been contrived to draw them under Wolfersdorff's fire, 'which inflicted heavy losses and threw them back in confusion. The Prussian dragoons meanwhile turned around again and now hacked into the enemy cavalry, and succeeded in taking prisoner 209 of the scattered enemy horse.'[82]

The combined infantry were now isolated, and the five squadrons of dragoons and hussars of the Prussian right wing now worked around to the north, and came at the terrified German infantry from the rear. With the exception of the battalion of Hessen-Darmstadt, the entire *Reichs* infantry fled in panic. The Austrians were saved from the same fate by their grenadiers and Croats, who had re-formed, and now fell back by stages as a covering force. The corps as a whole made back to Eilenburg, with Ried's Croats doing service as a rearguard.[83]

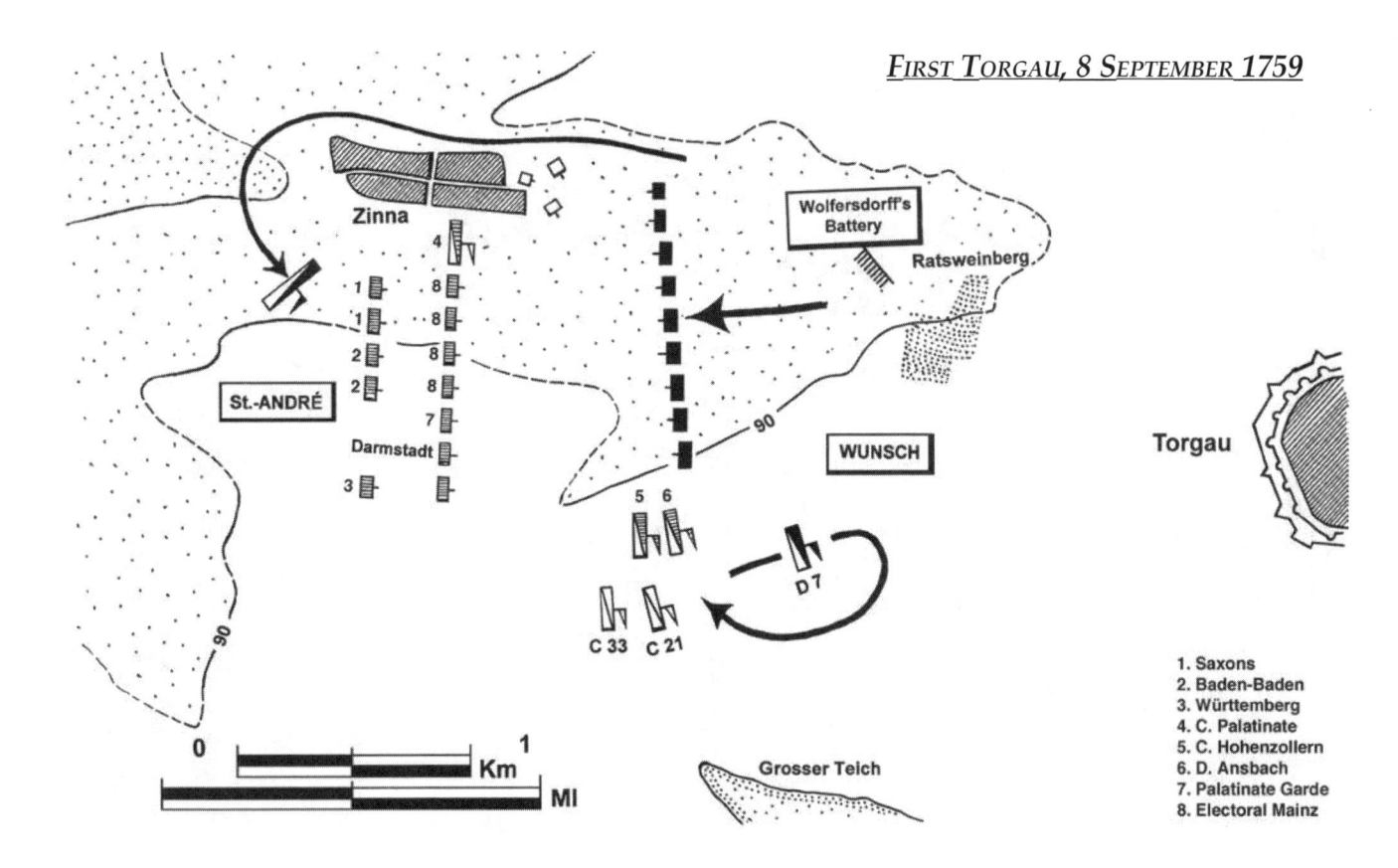

First Torgau, 8 September 1759

1. Saxons
2. Baden-Baden
3. Württemberg
4. C. Palatinate
5. C. Hohenzollern
6. D. Ansbach
7. Palatinate Garde
8. Electoral Mainz

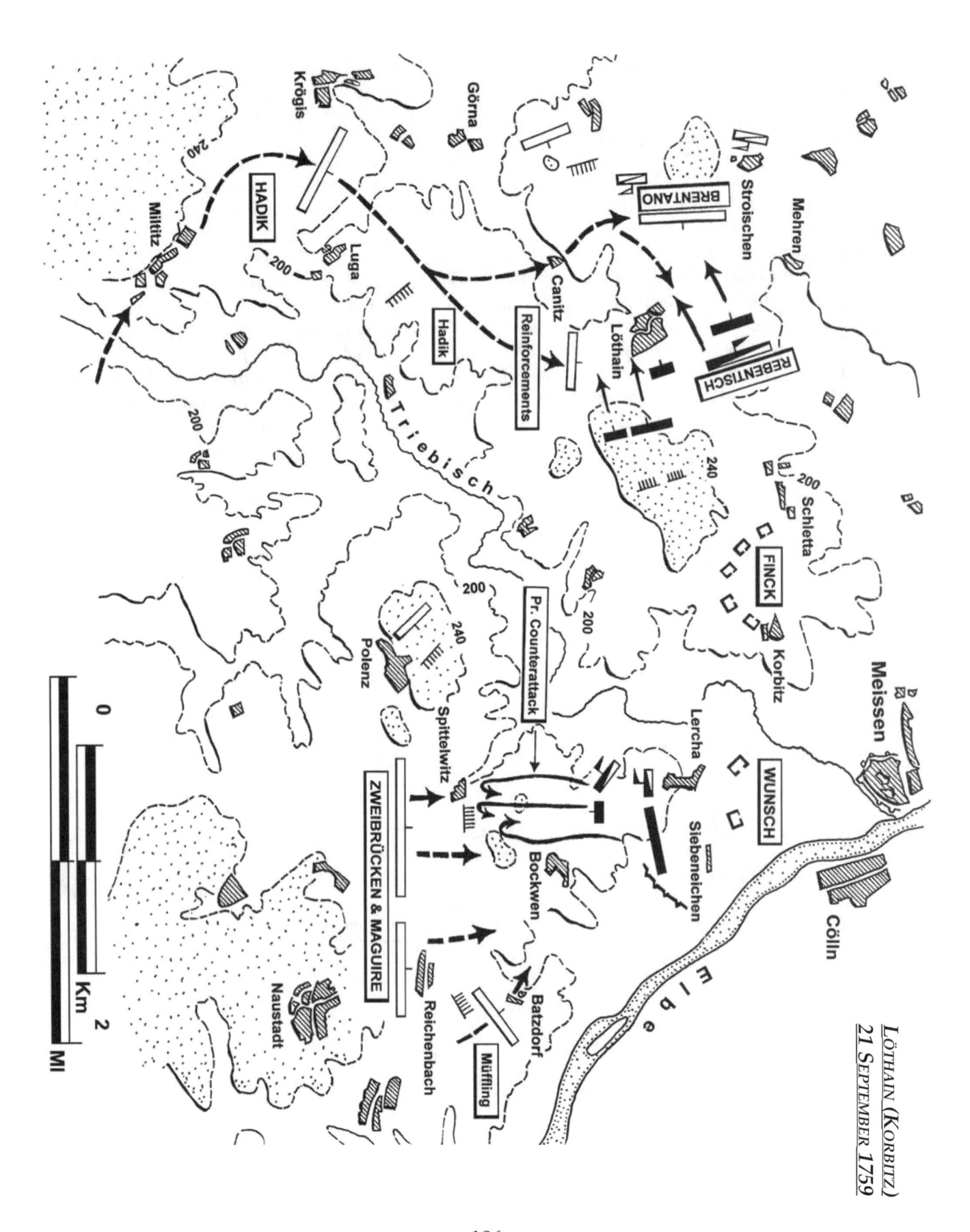

LÖTHAIN (KORBITZ)
21 SEPTEMBER 1759

In this brave and clever action Wunsch had contrived to beat an Austro-German force three times the size of his own. For Kaunitz it was a lesson which had been re-learned in a costly and humiliating way. He wrote to Maria Theresa that 'what has just happened to Saint-André's corps of 13,000 men offers further proof that we must never, for all eternity, leave troops to operate on campaign alongside those of the Holy Roman Empire.'[84]

Löthain (Korbitz), 21 September 1759

a) Combined forces of Austrians and *Reichsarmee*
v. approx. 30,300
Losses: 1,617

b) Corps right (east) of the Triebisch under Zweibrücken and Maguire
v. approx. 14,000
Losses: 203

c) Corps left (west) of the Triebisch under Hadik
16,293: 6,721 regular infantry, 5,286 German cavalry, 870 hussars, 3,416 Croats. All Austrians except for Hohenzollern Cuirassiers. 74 pieces
Losses: 1,414

d) Prussians
v. approx. 18,000, deployed on both sides of the Triebisch
Losses: c. 1,350. One standard and 10 pieces, all taken by Hadik's corps

While the momentum from the allied victory at Kunersdorf was being dissipated in the eastern part of the theatre of war, significant Prussian and Austrian reinforcements arrived on the Elbe in the second half of September, and indicated that a new confrontation was forming in the west.

On the allied side the first move was on the part of more than 14,000 troops under the command of GdC. Hadik, who was coming in answer to an appeal from the Prince of Zweibrücken, alarmed at the appearance of Wunsch on the Elbe. After a series of forced marches the corps of Hadik reached the Neustadt of Dresden on the night of 9/10 September. He was just in the nick of time, for Dresden was threatened not only by the corps of Wunsch, but by GL. Finck who had been detached by Frederick with 10,000 troops and was pounding along the roads just behind Hadik's reinforcement. On 10 September Hadik brought his troops across the Augustusbrücke and encamped them on the west bank in the classic position of the Plauenscher Grund.

By 11 September it was clear that Finck was falling back and that Dresden was out of immediate danger. However the two Prussian corps (those of Wunsch and Finck) still amounted to a formidable body, which now dominated most of the open country of Saxony, and the two *Reichs* battalions holding the isolated city of **Leipzig** surrendered to Wunsch on the 13th without firing a shot.

Daun confirmed that Hadik was to remain at Zweibrücken's disposal for the reconquest of Saxony, and his corps now acted as the advance guard of the combined Austrian and German forces. Hadik was disappointed in his hopes of being able to strike at Finck before the two Prussian bodies could unite, and on 19 September that general slipped down the west bank of the Triebisch to join Wunsch just outside Meissen.

Early in the morning of 20 September Zweibrücken, Serbelloni and Hadik rode out to Taubenheim to reconnoitre the Prussian positions. They found that the enemy had formed in two groups: Wunsch with an estimated 5-6,000 troops had moved to the near (eastern) side of the steep valley of the Triebisch, and established himself on the Plassen-Berg at Siebeneichen ('Seven Oaks'), in the triangle of land south of Meissen between the Triebisch and the Elbe; Finck with the main force was planted south-west of Meissen on the far (western) side of the gorge on the heights of Korbitz, where he had thrown up redoubts and batteries on the hills (up to 232.6 m) to the south of Schletta and Korbitz.

Serbelloni was director of operations, and gave verbal instructions for an attack to be undertaken early on the 21st. He assigned Maguire's corps and the *Reichsarmee* the secondary task of advancing by way of Naustadt to attack Wunsch, or at least shoot him up with their artillery. Hadik with the main striking force was to cross to the western side of the ravine upstream, then wheel to the north, and push or manoeuvre against Finck's right, throwing him back towards the Elbe at Meissen, where the bridge had been destroyed in 1757 and not replaced. 'To this the Prince [Zweibrücken] added that I was to run no risk whatsoever, but act according to circumstances.'[85]

Hadik's troops had the furthest to go, and they set off at three in the afternoon of 20 September through the rain which had been falling almost without a break since the middle of the month. The paths leading across the gorge of the Triebisch were deep in mud, and at 9.30 at night Hadik sent word to Serbelloni at Wilsdruff that he would be late arriving on the western side. Serbelloni's written reply came at six in the morning of the 21st. Hadik was to march on to Miltitz and Krögis, 'and do whatever is possible to get at the enemy, as has been agreed.'[86]

The Austrian infantry were only now struggling onto the heights at Miltitz, and the heavy artillery arrived only two hours later. Hadik judged that his men needed time to clean their dripping weapons, feed the horses, and prepare some food. He once again notified Serbelloni, and for a second time Serbelloni insisted that the operation must go ahead,

Between nine and ten in the morning of 21 September a lifting of the dense mist allowed Maguire's Austrians and the *Reichsarmee* to begin the subsidiary attack against Wunsch to the east of the Triebisch. The Prussians fell back from Naustadt, but made a stand closer to Meissen where the ground narrowed between the Triebisch and the Elbe. Maguire now detached *GFWM*. Müffling to execute a flanking move against the enemy left flank on the Elbe at Batzdorf. The Austrians duly stormed this village, and set fire to Bockwen behind with howitzer shells, but they were unable to drive any deeper into this compact position. Conversely a powerful Prussian counterattack was driven back just short of Spittelwitz. The fighting on this side of the Triebisch was now reduced to violent duels between the heavy artillery, with which all the parties were plentifully equipped.

Everything now hung on the progress of Hadik's operation on the western side of the Triebisch. He marched his troops northward through the fog from Miltitz, deployed them at eleven in the morning between Krögis and Luga, and advanced to meet the Prussians, who were holding the high ground behind Löthain. The position was crowned by a semi-circle of earthworks, behind which the Prussians could manoeuvre out of Hadik's sight, whereas the Austrian approach was obstructed by sunken roads and steep little valleys. An immediate head-on assault was out of the question, and early in the afternoon Hadik detached *GFWM*. Brentano across the ravine at Canitz with four battalions, six squadrons of German horse and the Palatinal Hussars [H36]. All the units were under-strength, and the hussars numbered only 283, which indicates how badly Hadik's corps had been depleted by its exhausting campaign. Brentano's task was to position himself on the height of Stroischen, keep an eye on the enemy, and, 'if the opportunity offers', attack the enemy camp in the rear above Löthain.[87] Brentano's 'opportunity' would come when Hadik's main force came at the Prussians from the front. Colonel Vecsey and his Croats meanwhile took up station at Canitz, to maintain the connection between the two bodies.

Hadik's calculations were thrown out by a particularly energetic Prussian response. The enemy commander Finck jumped to the mistaken conclusion that the Austrians were moving on Lommatzsch in order to cut him off from Torgau, and he countered in a most aggressive style by advancing *GM*. Rebentisch from his right wing with five battalions of grenadiers and one battalion of the crack regiment of Markgraf Karl [19], with three regiments of cavalry in support.

It seemed to the Austrians that this powerful force (7,000 troops) was making for Torgau, but it suddenly wheeled to its left north of Löthain, and advanced in three groups, of which the left-hand body was making for Löthain village itself. At two in the afternoon the Prussians came on with sounding music and thundering artillery, and south-east of Stroischen they encountered *GFWM*. Losy von Losenau's two battalions of Liccaner and Oguliner Croats, who fled 'in spite of all the efforts of this brave general.'[88]

Brentano was in danger of being cut off and destroyed, but the first impetus was checked by Colonel La Fontaine who counterattacked with a battalion of Warasdiners and two field pieces.

On his side, Hadik responded by sending a first instalment of reinforcements. The major generals Rehbach and Gourcy hastened up with the Schmerzing and Benedict Daun Cuirassiers (Cs 20,27) and Colonel Vecsey with the Széchenyi Hussars [H32], and together with the cavalry already with Brentano they threw themselves on the advancing Prussians.

The first infantry reinforcement consisted of the lone regiment of Marschall [18], under Colonel Christian Friedrich Baron Leubelfing. Losy's Croats had disappeared from the scene, but Leubelfing was determined to stand his ground, so as to cover the flank of the Austrian cavalry while it was battling against the Prussian horse. The last exchanges of musketry were delivered at a range of a few feet, and Leubelfing was finally induced to retreat when he saw a force of enemy hussars and infantry emerge from behind Stroischen and threaten his rear. By that time *Stuckjunker* Swoboda and the attached regimental gunners had fired 617 rounds, the ammunition of the infantry had run out, the regiment had lost 18 officers and 358 men, and its 261 files had been reduced to 101.[89]

At Hadik's orders the next surge of reinforcements was coming up from the main body, and consisted of the Hungarian infantry regiment of Gyulai [51], then the three battalions of grenadiers which made up the rest of the *corps de reserve*, and finally all the remainder of the regular infantry, 'which... advanced on its entire frontage to sounding music.'[90] This staggered progression left Gyulai, as the leading regiment, exposed to a mauling, but together with the battered regiment of Marschall it was rescued by the able *GFWM*. Joseph Prince Lobkowitz with the nearest cavalry at hand, namely his five companies of carabiniers together with the Alt-Modena Cuirassiers [Ciii)].

The Austrian horsemen threw themselves at the enemy infantry and cavalry, and afterwards the officers of the carabiniers competed to detail the grisly injuries they had sustained. Colonel Gabelkoffen received a bayonet thrust which he counted as the twenty-

Löthain. Looking east towards the high ground over which Rebentisch launched the great Prussian counterattack.

first of his career. Captain Franz Philipp Rüdt von Callenberg fell among the Prussian ranks, having been skewered no less than eleven times in the action (and contrived to escape the next night). Colonel Bergonzo Marquis Botta d'Adorno relates that he took a shot in the body and another in the arm, but managed to stay at the head of the Schmerzing Carabiniers. Both he and Colonel Ziegesar mention the interesting tactical detail that they broke the resistance of the Prussian cavalry not by cold steel, but by giving them a volley with their mousquetons (a kind of blunderbuss, firing buckshot).[91] The carabiniers then captured four cannon and a number of ammunition carts.

The Prussian squadrons rallied behind the infantry of Rebentisch, and made a new effort which hit the Austrian cavalry in the flank and regained the captured pieces. However the combat took a decisive turn when *FML.* Schallenberg and the major generals Podstadzky and Vitzthum arrived to support Lobkowitz with four squadrons of the Serbelloni Cuirassiers [C12] together with two squadrons each of the Brettlach Cuirassiers [C29] and the cuirasssier regiment of Hohenzollern (probably the best heavy mounted unit of the *Reichsarmee*). Captain Johann August Count Deym von Stritetz of the Serbelloni regiment claims that he put the idea into the heads of his seniors, and 'this determined attack worked particularly well because I was lucky enough to gain the enemy left flank with 135 of my men, force their seven squadrons to turn about, and overthrow them.'[92] The Austrians were now able to reclaim the guns they had lost, and capture five 12-pounders and a howitzer which the Prussians had abandoned in a sunken lane.

Under the pressure of the Austrian attacks Rebentisch began to withdraw his troops towards the semi-circle of earthworks. The battalion of Markgraf Karl helped to cover the general retreat, and 'an NCO noticed how the bold behaviour of Major Fischer of the enemy cuirassier regiment of Brettlach seemed to inspire the Austrian troopers with an especial ferocity. At every onset he rode at the head of the attacking force and urged them on to behave bravely. "We ought to get rid of that officer," he remarked to the lieutenant who was commanding beside him. "If he comes within my reach, then I can get him." In fact at the next attack... the enemy major came to within a short distance of the first Prussian rank, and in a trice the bold NCO ran forward a few paces, and struck the major over the head with his half-pike. This weapon is only a designation of rank, but it has a hook which enabled him to take the major by the shoulder and snatch him off his horse at the very moment when a well-aimed platoon fire dispersed his companions.'[93]

The Brettlach Cuirassiers in question were the two squadrons which had been brought up by Lobkowitz, and together with the three battalions of grenadiers they were now being advanced by *FML.* Gemmingen to attack the fortifications which lay behind the scene of the action. However the night closed in before the Austrians could exploit their success any further, and the artillery fell silent at seven in the evening, having fired without interruption for ten hours. The infantry battled blindly for three hours more among the orchards and barns.

In detail the Austrians had fought extremely well, and Hadik testified 'that infantry and cavalry have never acted better or more bravely than they did here.'[94] However the gains had been confined to the ground on which the action had been fought, and the limited and costly Austrian victory was turned into an operational defeat by Serbelloni's next actions.

On 22 September, the day after the combat, Hadik noted that the Prussian forces were still split, and that Wunsch was even now standing on the near side of the Triebisch with his back to the ravine. Serbelloni turned down the proposal of a new attack, and Hadik took the refusal as evidence of 'his insatiable hatred against me, which accordingly grew day by day.'[95]

On the 23rd the entire force marched back to its former camp at Wilsdruff, 'and thereby fell back in the face of an enemy who was trembling with the fear of being annihilated at any moment.'[96] Finally on the 27th the combined army recoiled to the ultra-secure position of the Plauenscher Grund just outside Dresden. Serbelloni later justified himself to the *Hofkriegsrath* by claiming that he had called off the strike because he had news that Prince Henry was on his way to the Elbe. However Serbelloni's statements at this period are riddled with contradictions, and it was on the 26th, not the 22nd, that intelligence came that Henry had defeated Vela at Hoyerswerda and was making for Saxony.

The action at Löthain was now seen not as a victory, but as a useless 'blood-bath,'[97] and on 27 September Maria Theresa's cabinet secretary Ignaz Koch wrote to Hadik that he had lost the favour of the Empress, and that he was suspended from duty. This was the doing of Serbelloni, who now reinforced his first accusation by a long report to the *Hofkriegsrath* which detailed Hadik's delays before the action, and the way he had fed in reinforcements piecemeal once combat had been joined.[98] On 13 November the *Hofkriegsrath* referred the matter to Daun and Zweibrücken for their adjudication.

Hadik was helped by the fact that his accuser, Serbelloni, was detested throughout the service. Friends rallied to his support, and *FML*. Stampa assured Hadik that 'there is every reason to hope that Your Excellency will shortly triumph over all the adverse blows which envy is directing at you… the whole army is of one mind with me, and shows the greatest sympathy with your fate.'[99] Maria Antonia, the Electoral Princess of Saxony, was well acquainted with all the leading personalities on the theatre of war, and wrote to Maria Theresa on 18 October that, whatever the rights and wrongs of the affair, Serbelloni had succeeded in poisoning the relationships among the Austrian generals.[100]

Hadik enters in his diary that on 22 November Daun wrote to him that the Empress 'knows very well that accusations are without foundation, and that you will very soon be informed that you are restored to your functions.'[101] The formal notification was sent on 1 December.

Meanwhile the continuing build-up of forces on the Elbe indicated that Saxony would become the scene of the final trials of strength in 1759. In late September the attention of King Frederick was still taken up by the Russians and Loudon in the far east of the theatre of war, but Prince Henry was on his way back to the Elbe, and Daun's first priority was to anticipate him at Dresden. The Austrians gained a precious lead, and on 29 September Daun was able to bring his army across the Elbe on three bridges of boats, just below Dresden, and arrange his troops at Kesselsdorf.

Daun established his headquarters in the city, where the young Italian officer Pietro Verri (writing for the entertainment of his readership) recorded the style of his military court. 'In addition to Prince Louis of Württemberg, the Duke of Braganza and other gentlemen of the highest distinction, the field marshal has bodyguards drawn from the hussars and Jäger, and a company of grenadiers at his lodgings— altogether as many troops as if the Emperor were present in person. The principle of subordination sets him above everybody else, and you may see royal princes reporting to him hat in hand, while he remains covered. War returns mankind to a state of nature: the strongest commands, while the others must seek his favour.' Verri claims to have seen Daun on a particularly hot day without hat or wig, and enjoying a huge cup of iced lemon sorbet, while the first gentlemen and leading gentlemen and officers stood about him. After the sorbet Daun addressed a carafe of Tokay, and at no stage thought of offering anything to anyone else.[105]

Over the short term Daun with his 60,000 troops had a marked superiority of force over the only Prussians on the theatre, namely *GL*. Finck with 15,000 at the most. Daun decided at once to leave the *Reichsarmee* outside Dresden, and march the Austrians down the west bank of the Elbe to drive back Finck and hold the line of the river against Henry.

The Austrians began their advance on 1 October. Finck slipped away on the following night, but then checked the Austrian advance guard along the Döllnitz stream on the foggy 3 October. The reason for his obstinacy became clear on the next day. Prince Henry, who was leading the next batch of reinforcements from the eastern theatre, had given up any ambition to get to Dresden before Daun. He instead crossed the Elbe twenty miles downstream at Torgau, and now marched smartly up the left

Pretzsch, 29 October 1759

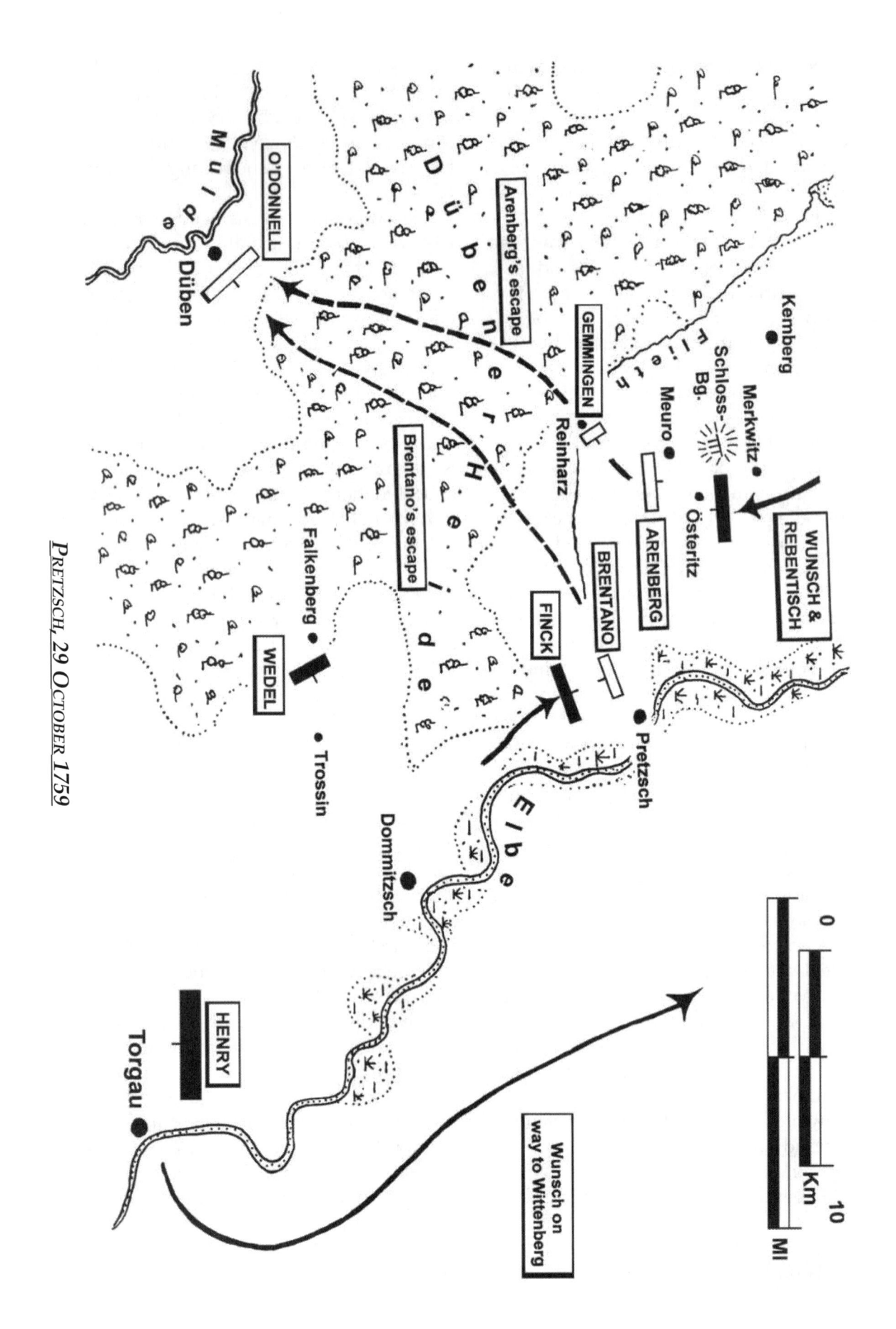

bank to join Finck behind the Döllnitz at Strehla on 4 October. Daun and Henry, two masters of the war of position and manoeuvre, were now pitted against one another in a fair contest of skills.

The combined Prussian force still amounted only to 40-45,000 men, but it had the advantage of Henry's expert knowledge of the theatre of war, which he employed to dig himself into the 'Camp of Strehla,' which was one of the last tenable pieces of ground short of the north German plain. From the Elbe behind Strehla the position ran westwards by way of the Dürren-Berg to the Windmühlen-Berg south-west of Laas. The ground sloped gently from the centre like a fortress glacis to the steep banks of the Döllnitz, while in front of his right wing Henry emplaced seven grenadier battalions, ten squadrons, and four heavy 12-pounders on the commanding Otten-Berg, which was fortified strongly, like the rest of the position.

Skirmishing fire crackled continuously along the Döllnitz, and Daun reckoned that the cost of a full-scale assault would be prohibitive. However *FML.* Lacy conducted a bold reconnaissance in the Prussian rear which convinced him that an attack was feasible after all. Everything was prepared for the blow on the 10th, and 'it was only due to bad advice that they changed their minds.'[103]

Daun instead resorted to indirect pressure, and dispatched *GdC.* Buccow with 15,000 troops to threaten Henry's right flank. By the 15 October Buccow was virtually across Henry's line of communication up the Elbe, and the prince stole away from his position at seven in the misty evening of the 16th.

Henry entrenched himself anew outside Torgau, and by 21 October the impetus was again in danger of being lost. Daun recommended Lacy and Loudon for promotion to *FZM.*, but as for 'Daun' (perhaps significantly referring to himself in the third person, 'he is no longer suitable… he has lost faith in himself, after all the recent misfortunes, which is a great defect for any one in command, and especially of an army like this.'[104] A few days earlier Maria Theresa had scribbled in the margin of one of Daun's letters 'what a sad situation! I can see no remedy, because the fault lies in the person.'[105] Now in Vienna a wag sent the *Feldmarschallin* a sleeping cap as a present for her husband, and the new French ambassador Choiseul-Praslin, who had been doing his best to bolster Daun's reputation in the courts of Europe, now found his task hopeless.[106]

It was time for another grand manoeuvre. On 22 October Daun shifted his army laterally from the Elbe at Belgern to Schildau, S.S.W. of Torgau, where he was better placed to form a threat against the flank of Henry's new position. The chief instrument was to be the former command of Buccow (above), which now built up to a strength of nearly 20,000 men and placed under the orders of *FZM.* Charles-Marie Duke of Arenberg. On 24 October Arenberg duly advanced to Dommitzch on the Elbe, athwart Henry's communications with Wittenberg.

Arenberg's position was almost directly in the rear of the main Prussian camp at Torgau, but Henry was determined not to allow himself to be manoeuvred out his position as tamely as had happened at Strehla, and he fell in with an ingenious scheme which was put to him by *GM.* Wunsch to bring Arenberg under a concerted attack. Wunsch was to slip across to the right (east) bank of the Elbe at Torgau with six battalions and ten squadrons, march down river, re-cross to the left bank at Wittenberg, establish contact with the detachment of *GM.* Rebentisch, and fall on Arenberg from the north. *GL.* Finck, an old comrade in arms, would advance directly from Henry's camp and attack simultaneously from the south, thus completing Arenberg's encirclement and destruction.

On 26 October Wunsch crossed the river at Torgau, according to the Prussian plan. On the same day the Prussian light troops contrived to capture one of Arenberg's adjutants, and 'what they found on him contributed not a little to what happened three days later, for they discovered the strength of our corps, and what it was lacking. They could see that the authorities had forgotten to give us ammunition, and they could also read all the field marshal's instructions.'[107] Wunsch passed the river again at Wittenberg on the 28th, and began the agreed march against Arenberg.

Pretzch, 29 October 1759

a) Austrians
14-16,000
Losses: casualties unknown; *GFWM*. Gemmingen captured along with 24 officers and 1,276 men, one piece and seven ammunition carts

b) Prussians.
The detachments of Wunsch and Rebentisch together amounted to c. 15,000
Losses: c 110

In technical terms the action at Pretzch could be termed a 'meeting' or 'encounter' battle, for it was precipitated by two offensive moves. Arenberg was marching at Daun's repeated orders on Wittenberg, while three Prussian corps were moving to destroy him—those of Wunsch and Rebentisch from the north, while Finck was assigned to fall on the Austrians from the south with ten battalions and twenty squadrons. As a finishing touch a further body from Henry's army, five battalions and seven squadrons under *GL.* Wedel, was to operate in the area of Falkenberg and Trossin to block any Austrian attempt to escape to the west.

By 29 October Arenberg had formed a reasonably accurate picture of the composition and likely deployment of the Prussian forces. He suspected rightly that the enemy detachment at Vogelsang (Finck's command) would assail him from the south, and he therefore reinforced *GFWM*. Brentano by the Serbelloni Cuirassiers [C12] and Saint-Ignon Dragoons [D31], and told him to hold the camp at Dommitzch for a couple of hours after the rest of the Austrian forces had marched off.

At first Arenberg was just as well informed concerning the enemy formations on the axis of his intended advance, which lay by way of Kemberg against Wittenberg. On the night of 28/29 October, however, he received a mistaken report from Colonel Bosfort to the effect that the Prussian major general Rebentisch was marching back west from Bitterfeld towards Leipzig. Arenberg therefore concluded that he would have to contend only with the 6,000-odd troops of *GM.* Wunsch. He could not entirely calm his fears that even this force might launch spoiling attacks against his flank or rear during the advance. However the situation was altogether worse than he suspected. Not only did he discount the presence of Rebentisch (three battalions, one regiment of dragoons and one of hussars) east of the Mulde, but he deprived himself of nine battalions and twenty squadrons under *GdC.* O'Donnell, whom he ordered to stay at Düben, to keep a watch out for Rebentisch, supposedly west of the Mulde.

Leaving Brentano behind in the camp of Dommitzch, Arenberg set the rest of his force in motion at three in the morning of 29 October. The advance guard negotiated the narrow passage of Pretzch, which lay between the Elbe and the woods of the Dübener-Heide, and at about nine it encountered the leading troops of both Wunsch and Rebentisch on the more open ground beyond. The Prussians were now equipped with horse artillery, and while the Austrian cavalrymen were seeking to deploy at Österitz they came under fire from a battery which Rebentisch rushed through Merkwitz to the Schloss-Berg. The covering Prussian dragoon regiment of Jung-Platen [D11] was soon reinforced by the Württemberg Dragoons [D12], and the rival infantry began to form—the Prussians in two lines to the south-east of Merkwitz, and the Austrians south of Meuro near the edge of the Dübener-Heide.

While Arenberg was engaged frontally against what now seemed to be very considerable forces, he learned of the increased threat to his rearguard under *GFWM*. Brentano, who had been left in the camp at Dommitzch, and was now engaged in the neighbourhood of Pretzsch with the corps of Finck, who had set off in a tardy pursuit. Arenberg was now caught between two fires, in the space of less than five miles between the Elbe and Meuro. His first instinct was to go to the help of Brentano, but the Prince de Ligne suggests that it was overtaken by the fear of being trapped by the combined Prussian forces. Arenberg assembled his generals, who urged him with one voice to extricate himself as soon as he could. De Ligne protested that they ought to stay and fight, but he was very young and still only a colonel..

Arenberg brought together the main body of his corps, and made good his escape across the heath south-south-west to Düben town, leaving all the rest of his forces to their fate. He owed his salvation to the former advance guard, under *FML*. Gemmingen, who was now told off to cover the retreat. Gemmingen had at his disposal just eight companies of grenadiers, one battalion of the fine regiment of Botta [12] and a single squadron of the Schmerzing Cuirassiers [C20].

The fat and dour Gemmingen made a stand in front of the woods, and tried to hold off the Prussians by artillery fire. It could not last for long, for the Prussians were closing in from two sides, and they brought him under a comprehensive attack before he could reach the relative safety of the trees: 'During the retreat our own cavalry rode over our grenadiers, and caused confusion. *FML.* Baron Gemmingen himself rode into the bog to the left of the bridge, and everyone who could not pass through the narrows was taken prisoner, including the said lieutenant general and Colonel Haller of the regiment of Colloredo (Jung-Colloredo [40]; actually Friedrich Haller von Hallerstein did not become colonel until 1763). The grenadiers broke completely apart when they were trying to cross the bridge, all mixed up with the Prussian dragoons and hussars.'[108]

The hussars in question were those of Colonel Gersdorff's Red regiment and three squadrons of the Möhring regiment [Hs7,3]. The bridge in question was probably the crossing of the Flieth rivulet at Reinharz. The hussars had ridden around the marsh and overrun the artillery at the bridge, and their triumph would have been complete if Captain Sigmund Worbeer had not brought together a scratch force of grenadiers and recovered two 6-pounders and two 3-pounders.

Brentano escaped a comparable disaster by warding off Finck in a well-managed little fight, and 'his Croats having abandoned two pieces of cannon during the action, Captain Baudéant of our Walloon dragoons dismounted his squadron and chased Finck's infantry away. His lieutenant, Herr Pfortzheim, regained the pieces, hitched them up to the horses of his dragoons and brought them back to his general.'[109] Finck gave up the chase in the difficult country of the Dübener-Heide, and Brentano arrived without further incident in Düben town, where he joined Arenberg and O'Donnell. Nothing is heard of the detachment of the Prussian lieutenant general Wedel, who was supposed to have blocked this kind of escape.

On 30 October, the day after the action, the reunited Austrian forces fell back south to Eilenburg, on the technical ground that the marshes and streams around Düben prevented them from placing any more than 8,000 troops in a proper order of battle.

The Prussians had formed a design in the new 'Austrian' style, by converging columns. They had failed to annihilate the Austrians in their entirety, as had been Prince Henry's intention, but Frederick was delighted at what had been done, and he lavished promotions and decorations on the most deserving officers.

On the Austrian side nobody except Gemmingen and Brentano had emerged with particular credit, and the Prince de Ligne was struck by the lack of concert which prevented the Austrians from bringing their 25,000 available troops, including those of O'Donnell, to bear against the 15,000 Prussians. In his report to Maria Theresa, Daun blamed Arenberg for having failed to march by the most direct path to Kemberg, as he had been told, whereby he could have beaten the enemy before Finck had time to come up on the Austrian rear. Arenberg's subsequent retreat to Düben was also contrary to orders, 'and O'Donnell induced the further retreat to Eilenburg. Both of them had lost their heads, as they are always liable to do in similar cases. They are much inclined to fits of depression, but when things are going well they become extremely brave, and especially the latter [O'Donnell]. I would ask Your Majesty to keep all of this to Yourself.' However just one squadron of the Schmerzing Cuirassiers had been with Gemmingen, 'and so the bad behaviour of this squadron should not reflect on the regiment as a whole.'[110]

The coming of Frederick and the retreat to Dresden, November 1759

For the Austrians, the inglorious episode of Pretzch was followed by days of retreat and humiliation. So completely had the moral ascendancy passed to the Prussians that, on 3 November, the news that Frederick was returning to the Saxon theatre was enough to persuade Daun that he must renounce any further ambition of ousting Henry from the camp of Torgau, and that he must fall back to cover Dresden and the Bohemian border.

On 4 November the Austrian army fell back from Oschatz, which had been the furthest point of its advance, and two days later Daun took up the tactically strong camp of Heynitz, which extended in front of the Triebisch. On the 8th *GL.* Hülsen arrived on the Oder with 16-17,000 troops of the royal army from the eastern theatre, which brought the Prussian forces in Saxony to about 60,000 men. The Austrians still had the advantage in numbers, if we add *FML.* Beck's corps (10,000) east of the Oder to the main army of 59,300 troops, but Frederick in person was expected in a few days, and Daun trembled for the future of Dresden. For the time being he seems to have discounted the *Reichsarmee* altogether for active operations in the field.

Prince Henry now intended to turn the Austrians out of Saxony altogether, by sending detachments around their open left flank to threaten their communications with Bohemia. The first blow of the kind was the work of Colonel Friedrich Wilhelm ('Green') Kleist and his Hussar Free Corps. On 16 November these rapacious gentlemen evicted four battalions of the *Reichsarmee* from Dippoldiswalde, which opened the way to the pass of Sebastiansberg, and over the next three days the Prussians ranged over the area of Bohemia on the far side. In tangible terms the most effective of their blows was to destroy the great riverside magazine at Aussig and exact a ransom of 50,000 taler from the town, but their other deeds were particularly calculated to spread terror and a sense of the impotence of Austrian arms.

Colonel Kleist in person reached the monastery of Osseg on the evening of the 17th, and found that some of his men had already made a good start by breaking open tombs in the search for valuables. On the next morning the monks laid before him a pathetic 1,000 florins, which fell well short of his demands, whereupon he summoned the whole community to appear in his presence, and selected eleven monks to leave with him as hostages. He left the monastery to the mercy of his men, who wrecked and desecrated the church, to the extent of smashing the very altar stones.

Kleist violated sanctuary of another kind at the spa of Teplitz, where he made prisoner eleven generals and more than one hundred officers who had been taking the 'cure.' The disgraced General Hadik lost horses and baggage to the value of 11,000 florins, and he would have been taken in person if he had not been already two hours into his journey from Teplitz to Prague. Hitherto the establishments at Teplitz, like those of Carlsbad, the Landecker Bad and the 'Warmbrunn' in Silesia had been open to ailing Prussian officers and soldiers on the production of passports, but now these niceties came to an end, and the *Hofkriegsrath* told Daun that the people abducted from Teplitz had been taken prisoner unlawfully, and that they were not bound by any paroles which they might have given to the enemy.[111]

Frederick reached Prince Henry's army on 13 November, and approved another enterprise which his brother had just set in train, this time in the shape of *GL.* Finck with a sizeable corps of 14,000 troops. The threat to the Austrian lifeline would now be more than a passing raid. Finck marched from Rosswein on the same 13 November, and after a prolonged exchange of artillery fire he pushed the corps of Brentano from Nossen, which gained the Prussians the most direct route to the road junction at Freiberg.

Daun was slow to recognise the specific threat which was now forming against his left flank and rear, but the continuing build-up of the Prussian forces and the coming of the king persuaded him to abandon the position at Heynitz on 14 November and fall back over the Triebisch towards Dresden. The troops at the rear of the Austrian column ran into desperate trouble when they were negotiating the steep valley of the Triebisch where it entered the Elbe at Meissen. The force in question, which consisted of one battalion of the regiment of Clerici [44] and troops from the former garrison of Dresden, had been delayed by a traffic jam of guns and carts in the town, which gave *GM.* Aschersleben time to bring the Austrians under attack by hussars, Jäger and the free battalion of Wunsch. The whitecoats were being shot up simultaneously by the artillery of *GM.* Diericke, and in their consternation they abandoned twelve regimental cannon and all their baggage. Daun had to point a pistol at the lieutenant colonel of Clerici (Francesco de Feretti) to get him to go back to Meissen and retrieve the guns, and one of his regimental officers testifies that 'never have I seen Field Marshal Daun so angry.'[112]

The Austrians lost more than 250 men in the debacle, and Montazet concluded that the breakdown of discipline had been symptomatic. 'I cannot conceal from you that the mood of the army makes me shudder. Everyone is disgusted and longs for the end of the campaign. The enemy march constantly at our heels, and we offer not the slightest resistance, which encourages them to attempt bold and ridiculous things. I cannot imagine how all this will end.'[113]

Not without further disorder the Austrians crossed the Weisseritz on 17 November, and formed what was almost their camp of last resort above the Plauenscher Grund, with their left on the Wind-Berg and the right extending to the suburbs of Dresden. This position too would become untenable if Finck established himself across the communications with Bohemia, as Daun now recognised.

Honour Restored— Maxen, 20 November 1759

a) Austrians and *Reichstruppen*
Total: c. 32,000
Losses: Austrian losses 915 casualties (303 killed, 612 wounded)

b) Reinforced Austrian *Corps de Reserve* under *GdC.* O'Donnell
Total: c 17,000

c) Corps of *GFWM.* Brentano
Total: c. 6,000

d) *Reichstruppen* and attached Austrians under *FML.* Prince Stolberg
Total: c 9,000

e) Prussians
c. 15,000; 11,000 infantry, 4,000 cavalry
Losses: The entire corps. The total taken into captivity comprised c. 13,750 officers and men, with 96 colours, 24 standards, 4 pairs of drums and all the artillery

GL. Finck struck due east from Freiberg, and on 16 November reached Dippoldiswalde on the main road from Dresden to Teplitz. On the 17th his advance guard occupied the plateau of Maxen, and the main force arrived there the next day, just in time to anticipate *GFWM.* Brentano with his force of 6,000 Austrians. Brentano brought up his troops as close as he could, and opened fire with his cannon, but the enemy were far too strong to be dislodged, and Brentano himself was nearly captured by the Prussian hussars.

Maxen lay directly in the rear of Daun's army, and from this position Finck could threaten the other main route from Dresden to Bohemia, the one which ran further east by way of Berggiesshübel and Nollendorf. If the Prussians were allowed to establish themselves in further strength the Austrians would be forced to abandon the open country of Saxony and possibly also the poorly-provisioned city of Dresden, and retreat into Bohemia by the only means then open to them, namely by crossing to the east bank of the Elbe and taking the difficult path over the border hills to Rumburg.

On 18 November Daun summoned a council of war. It transpired that Brentano was not nearly strong enough to be able to dislodge the enemy from their blocking position, and so Daun decided that he would take 20,000 troops of the main army under his personal command and go to Brentano's help.

The Austrians at once put together the nucleus of a striking force, composed of the *corps de reserve* under *FZM.* Sincère and reinforcements from the second line of the main army. Daun retained the overall direction, but on account of the high proportion of cavalry (42 squadrons, as opposed to 25 battalions of fusiliers and 5 of grenadiers) he devolved the tactical command to *GdC.* Carl O'Donnell.

The improvised corps set out from Rippien at seven in the morning of 19 November, and struggled south along the snowy route which threaded through the wooded hills by way of Karsdorf. While the artillery and the German cavalry fell behind, Colonel Franz Petrovsky scouted ahead with his Széchenyi Hussars [H32] and espied what he took to be a Prussian corps marching across his front to reinforce Maxen (in fact one regiment each of cuirassiers and dragoons and two battalions of grenadiers,

MAXEN
20 NOVEMBER 1759

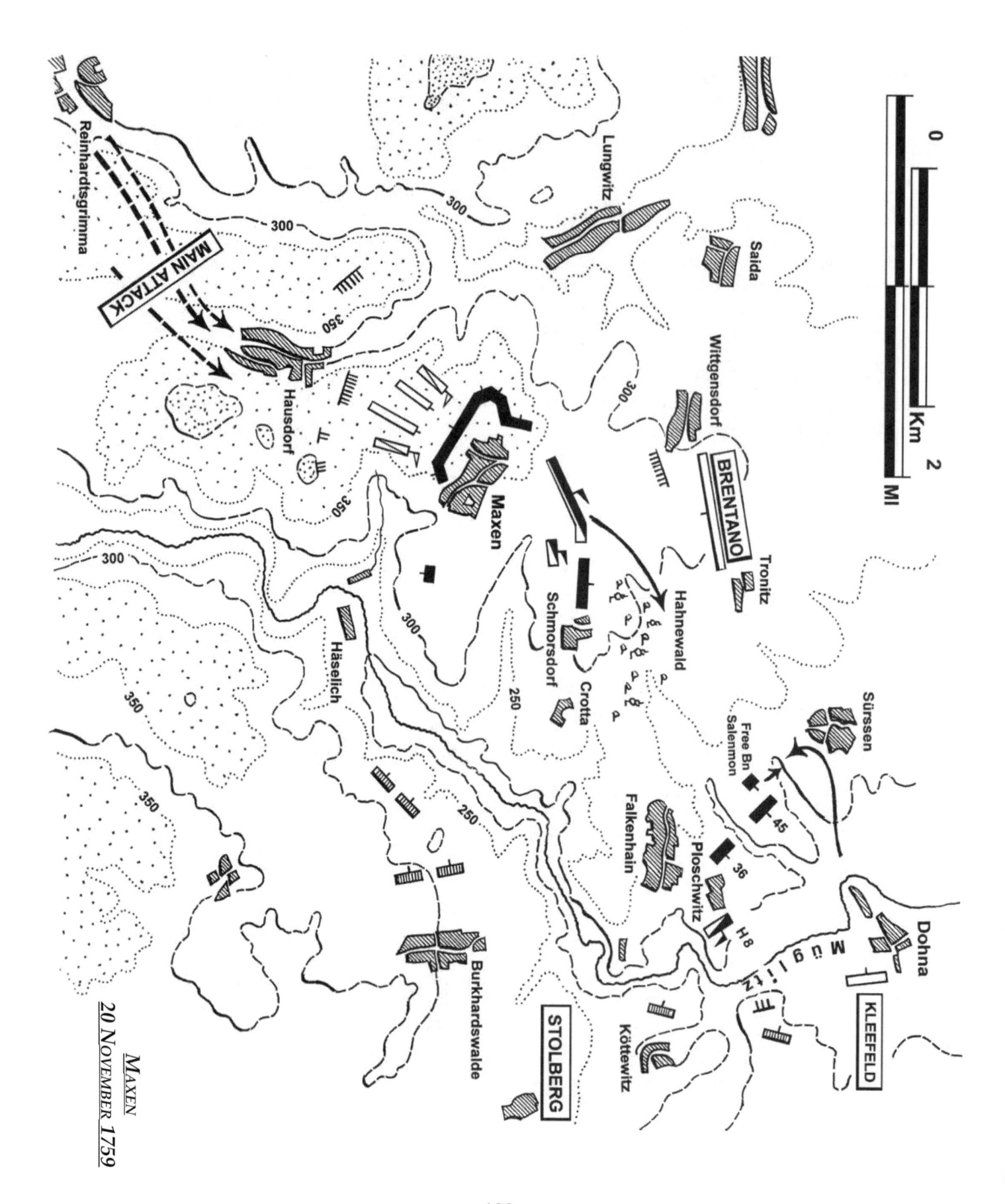

escorting a convoy of bread). Expectations of a battle were high, and Sincère passed along the ranks to remind the men of the military virtues, but the light faded before it was possible to bring the main force into action. Petrovsky had to be content with chasing the Prussians as far as the wall of Reinhardtsgrimma churchyard, and making off with two officers, fifteen men, six bread waggons and one ammunition cart.[113] The Austrians took up a position facing south, with their right on Malter and their left towards Oberläslich.

Nothing could yet be seen of Finck's position, which lay to the east beyond the woods at Maxen, but the delay gave time for *FML.* Lacy to put together a plan to attack the Prussians from three sides. 'Difficulties were raised. Lacy countered them by staking his reputation and head on the outcome. The arguments went on until the last moment, because nearly all the generals were against it. At last Lacy won over the field marshal, and he was able to set out dispositions every bit as good as those at Hochkirch.'[114]

Lacy's scheme was a simplified variant of the attack by columns and converging corps which had first been employed at the battle just mentioned. The main blow was to be struck by a force of 17,000 Austrians approaching the plateau of Maxen from the south-west; Daun accompanied the corps in person, but left the tactical command to O'Donnell (above), and the immediate direction of the infantry to *FZM.* Claudius Sincère, 'a brave man and a good drillmaster… but not so good when it comes to an independent command when he has to use his head. He then goes to pieces.'[115]

As for the tactics, 'the cavalry must never attack in a single body, but will adopt a chequer formation, and manoeuvre as the terrain indicates.'[116] 'The [grenadier] brigade of General Siskovics, which follows the cavalry, will upon sight of the enemy strive to occupy the high ground, bring up the artillery and facilitate the advance of the horse. The two following columns of infantry will conform, and deploy according to circumstances.'[117] The approach was to be conducted by the cavalry in column of squadrons, and by the infantry in column of battalions. The emphasis on the use of terrain is significant, as is the near-abandonment of traditional linear formations.

GFWM. Brentano, one of the most promising of the middle-ranking generals, was to advance his corps (c. 6,000) by way of Lockwitz and Kreischa and come at the plateau from the north. In Daun's words, 'I ordered General Brentano to approach the enemy with his corps through Lockwitz, and in such a way as to assault after I have opened the attack with the corps which I shall accompany in person.'[118]

Daun's record of his instructions for Stolberg is equally terse. 'It was agreed that the combined *Reichsarmee* will be detached to the high ground towards Dohna, with the purpose of cannonading the enemy from there.'[126] The *Reichstruppen* and the attached Austrian hussars and Croats under Pálffy, Kleefeld and Ried were to advance to the deep and heavily wooded ravine of the Müglitz, and (although it was not mentioned by Daun) also block any attempt by the Prussians to escape to the east.

The odds in favour of the allies were less clear than might be suggested by the balance of force on their side. They were acting by three separate corps, whereas Finck had the facility of interior lines. If the bare plateau of Maxen was beset on all sides by hollows and woods, which offered the allies the advantage of covered approaches, they could know little of Finck's position before they were committed to the attack. The snow had undergone a partial thaw on 19 November, but froze again in the extreme cold of the following night, which produced an icy surface which offered no purchase for the shoes of the men or the hooves of the cavalry horses. Many of Finck's units of infantry had been depleted at Kunersdorf and in subsequent actions, and had been filled up with allied prisoners of war and deserters, but his cavalry and artillery were powerful and in good condition. Finck's generals, and notably Wunsch, Gersdorff and Rebentisch, had done excellent service in the present campaign. Finck himself was one of Frederick's most trusted lieutenants, 'a second Turenne,'[120] to the extent of having taken over the command of the royal army immediately after Kunersdorf. The Austrian troops were eager to fight, but the generals were demoralised by the run of recent reverses.

The main force of the Austrians set out from the camp of Malter and Oberläslich at eight in the morning of 20 November. 'Every element received its instructions, which were clear and precise.'[121] Daun joined the columns when they were approaching the village of Reinhardtsgrimma, in the little valley of the Lockwitz stream. O'Donnell was riding at the head of the cavalry, and Sincère was leading the infantry. The four squadrons of the Széchenyi Hussars [H32] sounded the way, under the guidance of Captain Bechard of the General Staff. *GFWM*. Siskovics was in close support with his brigade of five battalions of combined grenadiers, 200 Croats and two companies of carabiniers.

Daun initiated the first action by sending the hussars and Croats and one of the battalions of grenadiers to clear Reinhardtsgrimma, where Prussian hussars and a battalion of infantry had seemed intent on making a stand. On the far side of the village the Austrians found a track which followed a valley up through uncharted woods in the direction of Maxen. All but a couple of generals now lost their nerve, but Daun and Lacy knew that they must fight, and they were helped at this critical moment by one of the officers of the General Staff.

Major Dominicus Sanctes Tomioti de Fabris, 'a native of Friuli, a man of intelligence,' was fretting at the delay. It was hopeless to look for a guide among the hostile Saxon villagers, but he found a captain of Croats who was willing to support him with his company. They pushed on and established that the path was clear of obstructions, and that there were no Jäger or other light troops lurking in the trees on either side. 'This oversight on the part of the Prussians led them to believe that the enemy must be badly deployed.' Leaving the Croats in a wood, Fabris prospected the ground beyond, where there was space to form twelve men abreast, albeit within cannon range of three hills. These heights were unoccupied, and 'upon examining the enemy he saw that everything in their camp was in uneasy movement, as if they were looking for a new position.' He observed also that there were two paths by which the Austrians could approach without being seen. 'Fabris left the Croats where he had gathered them, and returned to us at a fast gallop. He called out to the field marshal, "Sir, now's the moment. Come and see, and you will know that victory will be yours! I can lead a column within musket range without losing a man. Let Beaulieu lead the other, and his column will be just as secure. The enemy don't know what we are doing. I've seen everything! There is not a moment to lose!"'[122] The time was already noon on that winter day, and 'this report finally determined the field marshal to attack the enemy. The troops wanted nothing better than to fight, and their enthusiasm when they received the news was the best guarantee of success.'[123]

It would certainly have been within Finck's power to have checked the Austrians for a considerable time at the exit of the wood, but at the first indication of the enemy advance he judged that he could best deploy his limited forces in a tight perimeter around Maxen village. He ordered the three battalions originally facing the wood (Billerbeck and Benckendorff Grenadiers and a battalion of Zastrow [38]) to fall back to the hill of Hausdorf, and reinforced them there by a battalion of Grabow [47].

Siskovics emerged from the wood and dispatched his leading battalion of grenadiers to seize the hill to the right of the exit (418.3 m., S.E of Hausdorf). Daun rode up to the viewpoint, grasped its potential as a site for his artillery, and advanced an extra-large battery of eight 12-pounders to bring the Prussians under a flanking fire. Finck had already withdrawn two of these outlying battalions, and when the Austrian guns opened fire the remaining two (Grabow and Zastrow) fell back towards the main position, together with three squadrons of hussars.

Daun had now won the space to form up in the open ground which rose towards Maxen, and early in the afternoon the Austrians deployed in five columns:

1. Right-hand column of cavalry (14 sq: led by the Jung-Modena Dragoons [D13], and also comprising the Serbelloni, Brettlach and Schmerzing Cuirassisers [Cs12,29,20])

2. Somewhat in advance of the rest, the grenadier brigade (5 bn) of *GFWM*. Siskovics, with 200 Croats, the carabinier companies of the Serbelloni and Schmerzing regiments, and the 4 sq of the Splényi Hussars [Hii]

3. Right-hand column of fusiliers (*FML.* Dombasle: the regiment of Tillier [36], one battalion each of Angern and Marschall [49, 18], the regiment of Gyulai [51], one battalion of Clerici [44], and the regiment of de Ligne [38]. Total 9 bn)

4. Left-hand column of fusiliers (*FMLs.* d'Aynse and Plunkett: regiment of Wied [28], regiment of Harsch [50, three bn], and the regiments of Haller and Baden-Durlach [31, 27]. Total 9 bn)

5. Left-hand column of cavalry (*FML.* Stampach: cuirassier regiments of Stampach, Anhalt-Zerbst, Alt-Modena [Cs 10, 25, iii)]. Total 11 sq)

Finck had detached *GM.* Wunsch with five battalions and four squadrons of hussars to watch the gorge of the Müglitz at Dohna, but he formed the rest of his corps on two sides of the high ground which overlooked the saucer-like depression sheltering Maxen village. He had a general indication of the Austrian attacks from spies and scouts, and he arrayed three battalions of infantry and four regiments of horse along the axis of the Scheer-Berg, to confront Brentano when he emerged over the northern lip of the plateau. He consolidated his main body (9 bn) to face Daun in a tight right-angled deployment on the readily-defensible wave-like ridge of the Maxner-Berg. The Württemberg Dragoons [D12] and six squadrons of the Gersdorff Red Hussars [H8] were held back on the reverse slope towards Maxen village, and the lone grenadier battalion of Willemy secured the wooded Steinhübel mound out to the SSE.

The Prussians were well provided with heavy artillery, of which they placed two 12-pounders on the Scheer-Berg, and another two north of Maxen, which together would enable them to bring Brentano under a cross-fire. Confronting Daun, the Maxner-Berg was furnished with a battery of four 6-pounders; five 12-pounders and two howitzers were placed in a redoubt.

The action proper opened with a noisy artillery duel which was prolonged indecisively until the Austrians advanced their heavy guns

Maxen. The attack of the left wing of the Austrian cavalry.
(F.P.Findenegg, Austrian Army Museum)

MAXEN, THE MAIN ASSAULT

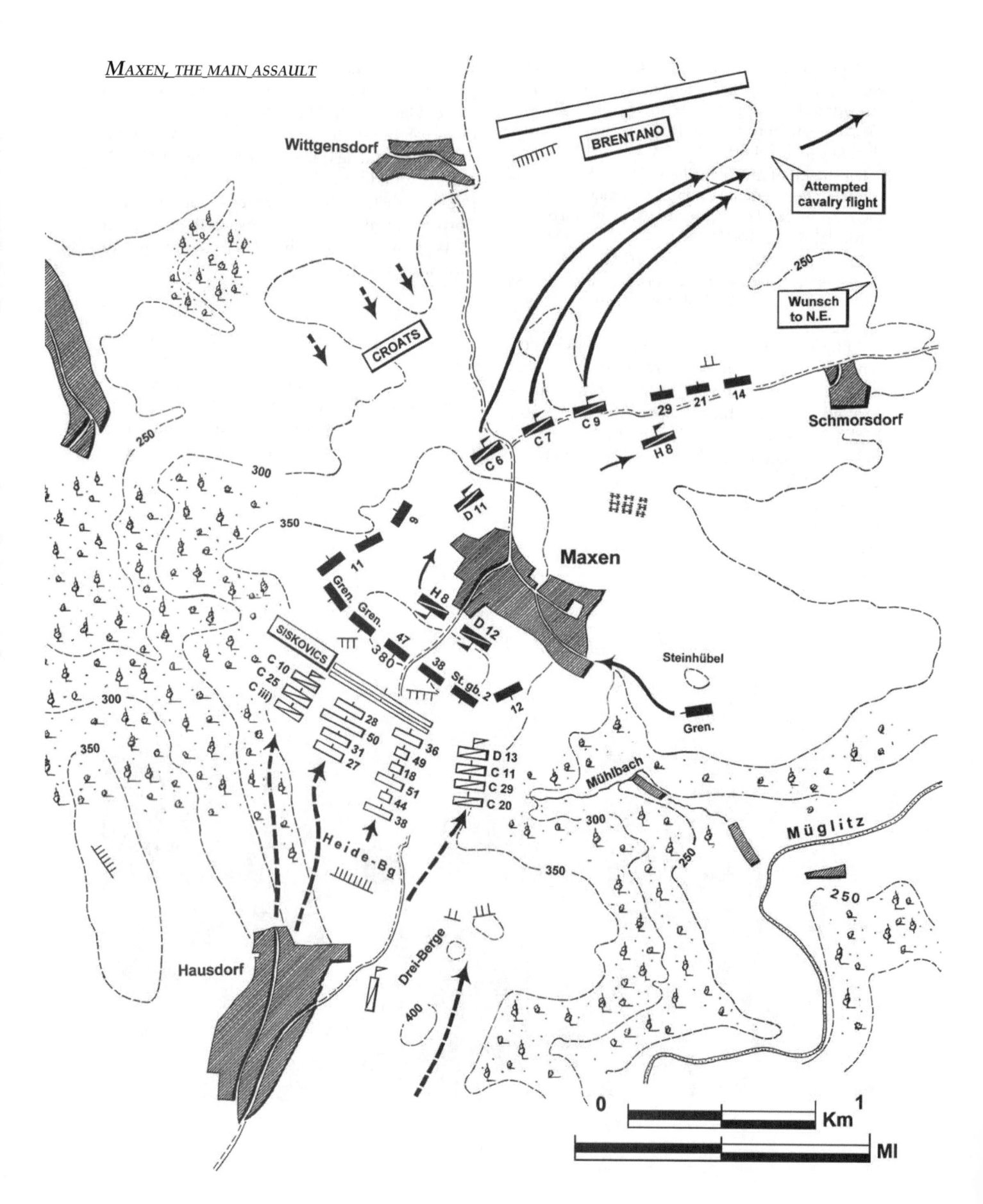

and howitzers to a row of new positions on the Drei-Berge, the Heide-Berg and Hill 396.8 N.W. of Hausdorf. From these sites the gunners and bombardiers were able to keep up a continuous fire over the heads of their advancing troops until the assault approached the crest of the Maxner-Berg. 'Our artillery… was so well served that it was not long before we could see disorder in the enemy line. Some of our batteries were slashing into the Prussians from their flank, which opened wide openings in their ranks and seemed to make them reel.'[124] Unseen by the Austrians, the overshoots wreaked destruction well into the Prussian rear, and the Gersdorff Hussars and the Württemberg Dragoons became so restless under the ordeal that *GM.* Gersdorff finally had to withdraw them behind Maxen. They were not safe even there, for many of the missiles carried clear over the village and landed in the hollow beyond, causing panic among the drivers and teams of the baggage train. In Maxen itself a number of the straw-thatched houses flared up when they were hit by the howitzer shells.

'Our fire,' reported Daun, 'was extraordinarily speedy, skilful, well-aimed and sustained. As soon as I observed the considerable damage in the enemy lines, I ordered the attack to proceed.'[125] The time was half past three in the afternoon. The opening assault was delivered by the grenadier brigade of Siskovics, which attacked in an initial formation of two lines, the first commanded by Colonel Marquis Botta, supported by a rearward line under Lieutenant Colonel Paul Seriman. Major Fabris showed the grenadiers the most expeditious way to descend the hollow in front of the Maxner-Berg, when he slid unceremoniously down the icy slope on his backside. The grenadiers followed his example, landed in heaps in the hollow, and began to climb the far side, where necessary by planting their muskets bayonet-first in the ground, and hauling themselves up. The Prussian grenadier battalions of Kleist, Billerbeck and Benckendorff rained down a terrible fire, which seems to have forced the leading grenadiers some way back down the slope, but the brigade was finally able to reach the crest on a broad frontage. While Botta's line had veered off to the right to meet a Prussian countermove (below), Seriman had taken the opportunity to incline to the left. The entire brigade therefore formed a single irregular line, and towards the centre of the array some of Seriman's companies took the redoubt by storm.

The right-flanking column of Austrian cavalry had to cross the hollow where it descended steeply towards the Mühl-Bach, and the Prince de Ligne deduced that the troopers must have been exceptionally eager to fight, since their horses were sliding and falling at every moment. Carl O'Donnell's younger brother, *GFWM.* Johann, was still in pain from the wound he had suffered at Leuthen, but he was careful to keep the leading regiment (the Jung-Modena Dragoons [D13]) in close support of the grenadiers, and he beat off a number of squadrons of the Gersdorff Hussars [H8], who descended in an attempt to get at the Austrian grenadiers (probably the move which caused Botta's line to make off to the right).

In the centre of the Austrian array, the right-hand column of fusiliers was commanded by *FML.* Dombasle, who urged forward his leading unit, the regiment of Tillier [36], under a heavy fire from the Prussian artillery. Dombasle fell from his horse, and was shortly afterwards bruised by a musket ball or canister shot, but the regiment pressed on to the crest, and delivered a succession of volleys at a range of scarcely thirty paces.

Another Netherlander, Major Jean-Pierre Beaulieu de Marconnay of the General staff, guided the left-hand column of fusiliers across the valley and up the particularly steep slope which was formed by the western end of the ridge. The attacking formations were closed on the far left by *FML.* Stampach's cavalry of the left wing, which was forced to make the ascent almost in single file.

The most violent fighting of the day took place in the immediate surroundings of Maxen village. The first of the Prussian units to break were the battalions of Grabow and Zastrow, which contained a large number of forcibly-enlisted Saxons, and had been hit very hard by the Austrian artillery earlier in the action. The Austrian breakthrough was probably the work of Lieutenant Colonel Seriman with the second line of Austrian grenadiers, which had come up on a line with the first (above), and was now executing a left-flanking attack to come at Maxen from the west, while the first line approached frontally from the south.

The panting Austrian grenadiers were now potentially vulnerable to the Württemberg Dragoons [D12], who were ideally placed to counterattack from their new position behind Maxen. They advanced through the village at a trot, and duly deployed to the south, but their commander Colonel Münchow was struck down by a mortal wound, and the demoralised troopers advanced no more than a few paces before they came to a halt. The fleeing battalions of Grabow and Zastrow threw the dragoons into a terminal confusion, and the whole mass fell back through the village.

The two Prussian battalions (Benckendorff and Finck) standing to the east of Maxen were now cut off and being shot up from their rear. Temporary relief came in the shape of the grenadier battalion of Willemy, which hastened up from its position on the outlying Steinhübel and marched up one of the narrow lanes which led past the village church. 'This battalion reached Maxen at exactly the same time as the Austrians threw themselves into the village with a great shout.'[126] The Willemy Grenadiers were beaten off by the Austrian grenadiers, most probably the Netherlanders commanded by Colonel de Ligne, who mentions that he wheeled his men by platoons, and fired a number of volleys which got rid of a body of Prussian troops who were bent on making a counterattack.

The defeat of the Prussians around Maxen village was completed by the Jung-Modena Dragoons [D13], who were guided up to the eastern extremity of the Maxner-Berg by Daun's trusted general adjutant Lieutenant Colonel Rothschütz. Two of their squadrons, commanded by Johann O'Donnell in person, now swept along the entire length of the feature,

Maxen. The slope (then covered with ice-encrusted snow) up which the right wing of the Austrian cavalry made its attack.

and at the far (western) end they broke the second battalion of the regiment of Rebentisch [11], together with another battalion (probably Schenckendorff [9]) which came to its support, and captured a total of five colours and ten pieces of artillery. The nearby dragoon regiment of Jung-Platen [D11] had suffered severely under the fire of artillery and musketry, and it fell back without attempting to intervene.

By now the corps of Brentano had emerged into view along the gentle northern edge of the plateau. Finck still had substantial unengaged forces facing in that direction, and he made the bold decision to throw the Gersdorff Hussars [H 8] and his three fresh regiments of cuirassiers against Brentano, and so gain time to deploy his three intact battalions of foot (Lehwaldt [14], Hülsen [21] and Knobloch [29]) against Daun.

The Prussian horsemen began their advance in good order, supported by pairs of 12-pounders firing from either flank, and threw back Brentano's four squadrons of the Saint-Ignon Dragoons [D31], who seem to have come forward to meet them. However the Prussians were already inclining to their right, in order to attack Brentano's infantry, which had formed between Wittgendorf and Tronitz, and after some eight hundred paces the charge degenerated into an outright flight to the east across Brentano's front. The collapse was occasioned by parties of Croats who had climbed the steep wooded slopes to the Prussians' left, by the fire of the artillery which Brentano had brought up to the low mound of the Sand-Berg, and by two regiments of cuirassiers who were sent by *FML*. Stampach at the news that Brentano was under threat. Colonel Lossgallner writes of the intervention of the Anhalt-Zerbst regiment [C25] that 'such moments determine the outcome.' He claims to have despised trophies in the form of prisoners and standards, 'and I did not permit a single man to ride from his file to pick up a standard from the ground, because I was well aware that every second counted.'[127] These inhibitions did not prevent his regiment from taking eight hundred prisoners.

All the time the thunder of artillery carried from the great ravine of the Müglitz to the east, where the five battalions of *GM*. Wunsch confronted the *Reichstruppen* and heavy artillery of *FML*. Prince Stolberg and three battalions of Croats commanded by *GFWM*. Kleefeld. The Croats had begun by evicting a Prussian outpost from atop the pointed Goldberg hill on the eastern side of the Müglitz. Kleefeld then directed his men through the village of Dohna, across the little Müglitz stream, and up the steep wooded slopes on the western side of the ravine towards Sürssen, probably hoping to turn the left flank of the enemy position. Stolberg brought his own troops to the eastern side above Dohna, and supported Kleefeld from there by the fire of his howitzers and 12-pounder cannon. However Wunsch was in a characteristically aggressive mood, and he drove the Croats back towards Sürssen by laying down a devastating fire of canister, and launching three of his battalions (regiment of Hessen-Cassel [45], free battalion of Salenmon) into a counter-attack. Kleefeld's Croats had nevertheless sealed off the avenue of escape by way of Dohna, and prevented Wunsch from rendering any help to his chief at Maxen.

GFWM. Ried meanwhile descended the upper Müglitz from Liebstadt with a further three battalions of Croats, together with the Sclavonian and Banalisten Hussars. He emerged on the closing scenes of the main action near Falkenhayn, where the advancing grenadiers of Siskovics at first mistook his hussars for Prussians.

The encirclement of the Prussians was completed by *FML*. Rudolph Pálffy with the Splényi and Hadik Hussars [Hs ii), iii)] who crossed the Müglitz well downstream at Gamig, reached the plain of Röhrsdorf, and finally cut in against the fleeing Prussians from the north. Pálffy had to wait four days before he could present Daun with trophies in the form of one standard and the two colours. 'The reason why I am sending it only now, is that the Splényi hussar who captured the standard was so ignorant that he took it into the village and kept it hidden. He has brought it in today, and so I have placed him under arrest on account of his mistake, and await your further orders.'[128] This seems very harsh.

As night fell, the rest of Finck's corps was virtually past redemption. It had been driven completely from the heights around Maxen,

*Maxen church from the west. The Prussian Willemy
grenadier battalion advanced up the lane in front.*

which Major Bärnkopp was now free to use as sites for the Austrian artillery. Prince Albert of Sachsen-Teschen was astonished at 'the speed with which the artillery supported and followed all the attacks, and over ground which only shortly before had seemed to condemn it to be stationary and useless. I saw with my own eyes how pieces of every calibre were being drawn at a gallop over those icy hills, and how men were dragging others at a run to join the infantry who were pursuing the enemy.'[129]

The only Prussian units which hung together were the remains of the battalion of Schenckendorff [9], falling back in square, and the three battalions under the command of GM. Lindstedt (Lehwaldt, Hülsen, Knobloch [14, 21, 29]) which held out for a time in the hamlet of Schmorsdorf and the neighbouring Hahnewald, and deterred the Austrian cavalry from overrunning the entire corps there and then. Even now Finck hoped that he could collect enough troops to escape to the south-west, but his major generals reported that they could find only 2,836 infantry under effective command. In these desperate circumstances the fiery Wunsch gained permission to try to break out to the east with twenty squadrons of dragoons and hussars, but his men were overtaken by events while they were still leading their horses down the steep little valleys towards the Müglitz.

Daun was busy far into the night. Amongst other things he had to order counter-measures to be taken against a Prussian corps which was reported to be approaching Dippoldiswalde. The precautions were sensible, for GL. Hülsen had been sent by his king to reinforce Finck by seven battalions and thirty-two squadrons. Fortunately the intervening Tharandter-Wald proved to be impenetrable in these wintry conditions, and Hülsen had to make an anti-clockwise detour. He was joined towards evening by the raiding corps of Colonel Kleist, on its return journey from Bohemia, which brought the Prussians up to a strength of 8-9,000 men, but the leading troops were able to progress only as far as Klingenberg before the march came to a halt for the night.

Otherwise Daun's time was entirely taken up with preparations to renew the fight on the next morning. His main force was now deployed over the Scheer-Berg near Schmorsdorf, and formed a continuous line with the corps of Brentano to the left. Over to the right, the grenadiers extended as far as Falkenhayn. The stocks of artillery and musket ammunition were meanwhile being replenished from the main army.

Daun snatched a couple of hours' rest in Maxen, and was back with his leading troops early on the 21st. 'Shortly before first light an outpost reported that a Prussian general [GM. Rebentisch] had presented himself with a trumpeter, and desired to speak to him. At this I sent FML. Lacy with the commission to tell him outright that I required the entire enemy corps to surrender as prisoners of war. In the case of refusal I would drive it into the Elbe.'[130] Lacy found that the Prussians were resigned to surrender in that way, and asked only to retain their effects. Lacy consented, for the request was reasonable, but he insisted that the dragoons and hussars under Wunsch must be included in the surrender, and the capitulation was signed on these terms in the village of Ploschwitz.

When the enemy laid down their arms the Austrians found them 'much stronger than we had thought. It was extraordinary to see more than 4,000 cavalrymen, making up thirty-five squadrons, almost all up to strength, proceed to dismount and yield up their arms. All of this was in the open field, which must been almost unique in history.'[131]

So full of doubt on campaign, Daun on the day of Maxen had acted with the same composure, judgement and resolution as he had displayed at Kolin. Just as in that battle, he made certain that he was in the best position to direct the action, and the Prince de Ligne testifies that 'for most of the engagement the field marshal was in front of my men, and whenever he set off it was to lead and encourage some body or other of troops, which put him in greater danger still.'[132] There was another reminder of Kolin in the willingness of Daun to follow the judgement of a much junior officer, in this case Major Fabris, in the other Major Vettesz. The normally cynical Pietro Verri observed Daun afterwards and wrote to a friend: 'The field

Daun receives Finck's surrender at Maxen. (Hyacinth de la Pegna, Austrian Army Museum)

marshal is a most interesting subject for a student of mankind. He was neither amazed by his victory nor carried away by his success. He received the prisoners in a courteous way, and sat down to a cold meal, in all of this acting like a true victor. Altogether I saw in him that moderation and self-control which indicates a great mind.'[133]

Lacy's plan of attack by columns and corps had worked much better than at Hochkirch, and not least because of the close co-operation between the officers of his General Staff and the individual field commanders. Daun reported to Maria Theresa that 'I keep Lacy with me on account of his facility with words, and the evidence which he still gives of his efforts, labours, intelligence and activity.' Lacy nevertheless wished to resign as Chief of Staff, 'and everything he does at the present time is done grudgingly, and in a perpetual bad temper... Otherwise I cannot praise too highly to Your Majesty the courage and good conduct displayed on this occasion by all the generals, officers and ordinary soldiers. I make special mention of the grenadiers and the artillery, and the latter behaved incomparably.'[134] All of this stands in striking contrast to the months of almost unrelieved failure and vacillation which had supervened with the high summer.

Major Leopold Prince Lobkowitz brought the news of the victory to Vienna on the 24th. 'The two Imperial Majesties came out into the Hall of Mirrors and admitted all present—foreigners and natives alike—to kiss hands and offer their congratulations.'[135]

Negatively, the victory frustrated 'all the king's mighty and well-conceived design... which was nothing less than to attack the Austrians on three sides, from Lockwitz by General Finck, from Rabenau, and then from Plauen... the king intended to cut off the Austrian communications with Bohemia by way of Peterswalde, as was already done by positioning Finck where he was, and thus compel the Austrian army to abandon Dresden, where there were provisions for only eight days.'[136]

It should be said in Frederick's favour that it was a dangerous part of the world in a military sense: not far away at Kulm in 1813 Napoleon lost a detached corps in somewhat similar circumstances.

Though it had been a tactically small action which had lasted only three hours and cost him less than 1,000 men, Daun had inflicted a staggering reverse on the enemy. In bare numbers the Prussian losses were the equivalent of those at Kolin, and exceeded those sustained at Hochkirch and even in the bloodbath at Zorndorf. The loss in quality was just as significant. Daun wrote to Maria Theresa that 'now we have another batch of people to exchange, but I am not at all sure that the enemy will not derive the greater profit. The reason is that Your Majesty has mostly replaced the losses among Your officers, whereas the enemy will be running short of theirs. Generals like Finck and Wunsch are among their best, and they have always commanded detached corps, whereas we can readily spare the generals who are in enemy hands. Again the regiments we have captured are some of the finest the Prussians have, made up mostly of veterans, and they would very much like to have them back. This is a matter which deserves careful consideration, and is not to be decided too quickly.'[137] The prisoners from Maxen were ultimately consigned to the Alpine provinces of south-eastern Austria, where they died by the thousand of disease, and after due 'consideration' the Austrians became more obstructive and difficult in the matter of exchanges in general.

Thus Frederick was deprived of Finck's detachment as effectively as if it had been killed outright. The losses were the equivalent to one-tenth of the officer corps of the entire Prussian army, while the gaps in the cavalry were so severe that Frederick had to recall the ten squadrons of dragoons which were doing service with Prince Ferdinand of Brunswick in western Germany. For the first time the king was brought face to face with a process of attrition which threatened him with ultimate defeat.

Early Winter in Dresden

The stroke at Maxen had been a body blow to the Prussians, which weakened them greatly over the long term, but for the near future it became only too clear that the rival armies would remain in confrontation outside Dresden for what threatened to be an exceptionally hard winter. In this literally killing cold Daun established a routine whereby the regiments alternated their component battalions every twenty-four hours, one of the battalions being placed under cover in buildings, while the other remained on duty in the positions. On Christmas Day the Austrians began to create 'barracks' of timber and sods to shelter the exposed troops, and simultaneously set about throwing up batteries and redoubts for the sake of tactical protection. Twenty years later a Prussian gunner found that the works were still in excellent condition.[138]

Daun also had to provide for the defence of Dresden itself, so that the city could hold out for ten or twelve days at the least if the army happened to be forced back. The needs were set out in an expert fashion by the leading French engineer and gunner Gribeauval, who was now doing service as an Austrian major general,[139] and by 26 October a programme of works had been agreed with the consent of the Saxon envoy Count Flemming, whose co-operation was needed if the Austrians were to raise the necessary materials, labour and transport from the part of Saxony still under their control. From Warsaw the Saxon prime minister Brühl objected that by making Dresden into a tenable fortress the Austrians would expose it to destruction, 'to judge by our experience of the Prussian way of conducting war.'[140] Kaunitz replied that the freedom of Dresden and Saxony as a whole depended on the Austrians having a secure base, and that Dresden was the only possible choice.[141]

Firmness with the Saxons was also needed if the army was to feed itself in this part of the world. The Prussians in Freiberg imposed a western limit on the area open to Austrian foraging, which was confined to the foothills of the Erz-Gebirge near Dresden. Daun explained to Maria Theresa, that he did not have the same freedom enjoyed by the enemy to raise provisions in Saxony by force,[142] and it was an indication of the steeling of hearts by this stage of the war that the Empress answered that his priority must be 'the maintenance of my army... no matter how hard that might be for the land.

In emergencies like these you are not to be deflected by all the cries, objections and complaints.'[143]

The euphoria among the Austrians dissipated within a matter of hours of the victory at Maxen, and without the stimulus of immediate action Daun sank back into his habitual melancholy. He did not know how long he could endure the daily reproaches which came to him from the Emperor, Kaunitz and Neipperg, 'who find everything so straightforward.' He would have liked the newly-promoted *FZM*. Loudon to take his place in Saxony for the winter, but such a move would have displaced Loudon's seniors Buccow, O'Donnell, Arenberg and Sincère, and there was nowhere else to send them.[144]

On 1 December the *Reichsarmee* left Berggiesshübel for its winter quarters along the Main in Franconia, taking the roundabout route by way of Bohemia rather than the direct path along the foot of the Erz-Gebirge, where they might have been trapped by the enemy. Daun was glad to be rid of those people, who had been consuming his precious provisions to no purpose. On the same day he approved an enterprise which, against all likelihood, gave the Austrian a victory which could be mentioned in the same breath as Maxen.

Meissen, 2-3 December 1759
a) Austrians
c. 6,000 in action
Losses: 187; 72 killed, 115 wounded
b) Prussians
c. 5,000
Losses: casualties unknown, 1,544 captured along with 9 pieces

For days the attention of Daun and Frederick had been taken up by the skirmishing and foraging across the tract of land between Dippoldiswalde and Dresden. Saxony to the east of the Elbe was a kind of strategic no man's land, where the opposing corps of the Prussian *GM*. Diericke and the Austrian *FML*. Beck were in a distant confrontation. The Prussians had been left in almost undisturbed possession of the Elbe itself, which enabled them to bring supplies of every kind up to their army. The road up the left (west) bank was still negotiable, even after the river had frozen solid, and Diericke laid timber across the ice downstream at Meissen to enable him to cross from one bank to the other.

At the end of November a brief thaw sent floes of ice racing down the Elbe, and Beck espied an opportunity to destroy the isolated cantonments of Diericke on the east bank. Daun gave his blessing to the scheme, and on 1 December *GFWM*. Pellegrini hastened to reinforce Beck with two battalions of grenadiers, four of fusiliers and five hundred carabiniers.

Overnight on 1/2 December the combined Austrian force advanced against the scattered Prussians, intending to sweep them up in their quarters before they could reach their boats and escape across the Elbe. At two in the morning the Austrians arrived between Weinbohla and Niederau, but the blow fell on thin air, for Diericke (as he later told Pellegrini) had learned of the design from an informant, and had gathered his troops into defensible positions closer to the crossing-point opposite Meissen.

Rather than attack the Prussians head-on in their main concentration at Zeschwitz, Beck executed a right-flanking move by way of Gröbern and Proschwitz to reach the Elbe further downstream at Buntsch and Zscheila. He was now placed to open fire with two howitzers and two 6-pounders when Diericke began to ferry his stranded troops to the west bank. The Austrians had to withdraw their artillery when the enemy brought six heavy pieces to bear against them from Meissen, but they were able to open fire on the moonlit night of 2/3 December, and managed to sink a number of the Prussian craft.

The Prussians managed to bring off most of their cavalry and heavy artillery, but the early hours of the 3rd found Diericke and three of his battalions (Anhalt-Bernburg [3], Kanitz [2] and Hauss [55]) still isolated on the east bank. Before daylight Diericke abandoned the steep little peaks of the Fürsten-Berge, and fell back to the village of Cölln and the Ratsweinberg hills which overlooked the crossing point. Beck deduced what was happening from a slackening in the fire, and now brought the shrinking Prussian bridgehead under a two-pronged attack from the south.

Colonel Riese and 1,000 Croats opened the way for the advance of four battalions of regulars under Pellegrini, while the decisive stroke was dealt by Colonel Zedtwitz who struck directly along the river bank towards Cölln. Zedtwitz placed a battalion of Croatian grenadiers in the lead, and brought up a battalion of the Banal Croats and the infantry regiment of Joseph Esterházy [37] in support on the left.

By the account of Zedtwitz the first assault carried the outlying houses of Cölln, but the enemy 'established themselves… once more in the centre of the village and on the vineyard hills. They fought on for a further hour from the houses and from behind the walls, ceding hardly an inch. I finally sent an officer and sixty men to take up position in the highest houses, from where they could shoot up the enemy in the vineyards and behind the walls. The Prussians began to give way, and were finally jammed together against the Elbe.'[145] Diericke asked for quarter, which Zedtwitz granted, and all the Prussians on this side of the river were taken prisoner.

1759—The Diplomatic and Military Outcome

The fight at Meissen was the last action of any consequence on the Saxon theatre, and the happy issue helped to colour perceptions of the balance as it existed at the end of that extraordinarily busy year. Viewed across the centuries, 1759 was notable for the succession of British victories over the French (Minden 1 August, the naval battles of Lagos on 17 August and Quiberon on 20 November, and the capture of Quebec on 18 September), and for the chapter of lost opportunities which made up the 'Miracle of the House of Brandenburg' after the Russo-Austrian triumph at Kunersdorf. The Russians still had East Prussia in their grasp and (to the embarrassment of their allies) indicated that they wished to retain it at any eventual peace settlement. However the French were forced to abandon Hesse after the battle of Minden, and in any event the time had long passed since French and Austrians had worked in direct co-operation.

Some kind of common effort between Austrians and Swedes was still a physical possibility, and a few days after the battle of Kunersdorf the French ambassador reported from Vienna that 'now that the king of Prussia has brought together all his forces on the Oder, this would be the favourable time for the Swedish army to emerge from its passivity and begin operations. We are already in the middle of the campaigning season and have still heard nothing about it... for the military world the Swedes do not exist. Kaunitz on his side has commented in the same vein, and sent a courier to the commander of their army to get him to move.'[146]

Only after the chastened Frederick had stripped the northern theatre of troops did the Swedish commander Lantingshausen venture into enemy territory, and the Swedes were still at Pasewalk when on 1 October they received a further invitation from the Austrians to co-operate in Saxony. Lantingshausen was disinclined to take any further risks, since he was short of fodder and had just 10,000 effectives under his command, and in November his little army fell back into Swedish Pomerania, abandoning the fortresses of Anklam and Demmin together with the islands of Wollin and Usedom at the mouth of the Oder.

As for the Austrian gains from the Prussians, it was true in the strictest sense that 'the city of Dresden and the stretch of land from there to the Bohemian border was all the profit we had to show... from this bloody campaign and the other three which preceded it.'[147] In other respects, however, the adjustments of balance between Austria, her allies and her enemy had worked to Maria Theresa's advantage.

Political relations with France were on the whole progressing well. The Duc de Choiseul had left the embassy in Vienna for Paris to take up the post of foreign minister, and at the end of 1758 the representatives of France and Austria had agreed on a sensible adjustment of the treaties of subsidy and support, as noted earlier. The secretary of the French embassy, Boyer, took over the management of affairs until the Comte de Choiseul-Praslin (cousin of the duke) arrived to take up his post on 28 June 1759. Kaunitz took a liking to the new man, and the feelings were reciprocated.

As the summer wore on the Austrians began to take alarm at the Duc de Choiseul's ambition to extricate France from the war with Britain, for this was a move which might bring about the collapse of the grand alliance. In the short term Choiseul hoped to manoeuvre himself into a favourable negotiating position by putting military pressure on the British, and at the end of July Maria Theresa informed Daun that the British were threatened with an invasion of their homeland and the loss of their king's Hanoverian lands, and that their credit and gold reserves were run down. In the event, the sequence of British victories then robbed the French of any advantage, and relieved Maria Theresa and Kaunitz of one of their anxieties.

Kaunitz was able to abate some of the urgency in Russia's claim to East Prussia by promising to recommend it to the French (which he never did), and by holding out the possibility of two-million florins' worth of compensation in case Frederick could not be forced to sign it away. Russia's other demand, for some kind of military performance to match their own efforts, remained a reproach to the Austrians until it was satisfied by the spectacular coups of 20-21 November and 2-3 December. No less importantly, Maxen and Meissen eliminated twelve regiments of Frederick's infantry and six regiments of horse, and contributed significantly to Prussia's total loss for that year of at least 50,000 troops, who could never be replaced by men of the same quality.

On 4 December Kaunitz learned that Prussia and Britain had put forward a joint proposal to convene a congress which would discuss terms for a general peace. He viewed the démarche as a confession of weakness on the part of his enemies, and one which justified Austria and her allies in prosecuting the war with all the more vigour. He calculated that a favourable but vague reply would put off the congress indefinitely, without incurring the odium of turning down the invitation outright, and that Frederick, who seemed to be nearing the limit of his human and material resources, would in all likelihood succumb to a concerted offensive on the part of the allies in 1760.

V

1760

THE NEW YEAR AND THE RISE OF LOUDON

The campaign of 1759 was being prolonged well into the new year, for the armies of Daun and Frederick were facing one another in southern Saxony. Daun kept his main force towards Dresden in the celebrated position above the Plauenscher Grund. Now that the Elbe was frozen, all the provisions had to come overland from Bohemia by way of the steep Peterswalde pass, 'and yet, by great efforts, the troops were kept supplied throughout the winter, and not just with bread and fodder, but provisions of every kind. For the whole season long trains of carts were moving endlessly even from the depths of Hungary, laden with assorted foodstuffs.'[1]

If life in the outposts was very hard for the troops on both sides, the Prussians were suffering proportionately more, since their only shelter was in overcrowded little villages, whereas the Austrians had the facility of the larger villages near Dresden and the city itself. Polite society had long deserted Dresden, which had a frozen and desolate look, but Daun established himself upriver at Pirna, and the attaché Montazet, who was something of a violinist, enlivened headquarters by inviting the Duke of Braganza to contribute his fine singing voice, with the generals Pellegrini and Carl O'Donnell accompanying on their flutes.

The Prussians launched no spoiling attacks to compare with the expeditions early in 1758 and 1759, and Daun was free to turn his mind to the debates concerning the next campaign. Maria Theresa had asked the leading men in the army and the state to put forward their ideas, and *FZM*. Lacy was probably the first person to commit himself to paper. He believed that the Austrians should hold back until the Russians were well on their way from the winter quarters, upon which both armies should concentrate their efforts in Silesia, with the Russians being given the straightforward task of reducing Breslau, while the Austrians turned their efforts against Schweidnitz.[2]

Loudon subjected Lacy's plan to searching criticisms. The proposed late start to the Austrian operations would set no kind of example to the Russians, and give Frederick time to establish himself impregnably, as in 1759, in the difficult country around Schmottseiffen on the borders of Lusatia and Lower Silesia. Instead the Austrians must act on the principle by compelling Frederick to split his forces 'through separate and widely-distant points of attack.' The Austrians would have an army in Saxony, and another operating in Upper Silesia. Loudon also opposed Lacy's plan of inviting a mass of 60,000 Russians to Silesia, for they would reduce the land to a desert. The best way to make use of the Russians would be to ask them to send a corps of 20-30,000 men to act under direct Austrian command.[3]

Kaunitz declared his support for Loudon's plan in a set of *Réflexions*. He saw the forthcoming campaign as 'in all probability the last of the war,' and believed that Loudon's scheme had the virtue of taking the initiative from Frederick before he had time to respond.[4]

FM. Liechtenstein pronounced in favour of Loudon and Kaunitz. Daun nailed his colours to no particular mast, but his own *Operations-Plan* corresponded with Loudon's principle of simultaneous offensives by a main army in Saxony, and by a combined force of Austrians and manageable Russians in Silesia.[5] The balance of debate was clearly moving in favour of Loudon and Kaunitz.

By 14 February Daun had fallen in completely with the *Réflexions*, and on 1 March a conference in Vienna consolidated the agreement. Specific proposals were sent to St.

Gideon Ernst Baron Loudon, wearing antique studio armour, probaly to assert ancient ancestry.

Petersburg on 10 March, and Lacy (who had attended the conference) described the scheme to Daun as 'very well conceived, perfectly detailed and wonderfully well reasoned.'[6]

There is no trace here of any resentment on the part of Lacy that Loudon's plan had been adopted rather than his own. Likewise Lacy betrayed no satisfaction when he learned that the Russians had decided against sending 20-30,000 of their infantry to Silesia, as the Austrians had requested, but were set on advancing their army en bloc to the Oder between Frankfurt and Glogau. Even now the essentials of the Austrian strategy held true. Maria Theresa was able to inform Daun on 21 April that she had turned to a contingency plan, whereby an Austrian corps was to assemble in Lusatia, and march from there straight to Lower Silesia to distract the attention of the enemy from the Russians. *FZM.* Loudon was designated commander of the corps, and Maria Theresa reckoned that the balance of forces was such that she could spare him at least 40,000 troops,[7] which gave the corps something of the weight of an army.

More important than the details of geography and numbers was the fact that Loudon was now the coming man. Gideon Ernst Loudon was born on 17 February 1717 to a Lutheran family of German descent, long settled in Livonia, which became part of the Russian Empire in 1721. With little formal education, and no fortune behind him, Loudon entered the Russian infantry regiment of Pskov in 1732. His nominal rank was that of 'cadet,' but to all intents and purposes he served as a private soldier and NCO in Russia's campaigns in Poland, and had advanced only to first lieutenant by the time the war with Turkey ended in 1740.

Early in 1744, in circumstances which are still obscure, King Frederick rejected Loudon's application to enter the Prussian service as a captain. Loudon betook himself to Austria, and Franz von der Trenck admitted him in the same rank to his *Panduren-Freicorps*. This body was acquiring a name for indiscipline and barbarity, and Loudon broke with Colonel Trenck after the battle of Soor (30 September 1745). After only a short intermission Loudon was appointed major with the regiment of Liccaner Croats on 1 May 1746, and in that year or the next married Clara von Hagen, the daughter of an ennobled official of the tobacco monopoly. Clara is described as having 'neither attractions of mind, nor of person... Sickly, uneducated, homely in her figure, she never appears in public, and her principal merit consists in the attachment she feels for her husband.'[8] It was probably through her influence that Loudon converted to Catholicism at about the time he was promoted to lieutenant colonel, in 1753.

In the capacity as a leader of light forces Loudon made an extraordinary impression in the early campaigns of the Seven Years War. He conducted the successful coups at Ostritz on 1 January 1757 and at Hirschfeld on 20 February of the same year, which helped to secure his promotion to colonel on 17 March. He was active in the pursuit of the Prussians after the liberation of Prague, and was advanced to *GFWM.* at the time of the Rossbach campaign. The Prussians captured the patent while it was still on its way to him from Vienna, and Frederick forwarded it to Loudon with his compliments.

Loudon consolidated his career in 1758. On 30 June he was largely responsible for the strike against the great Prussian convoy at Domstadtl. Daun prized him alongside Lacy as his foremost helpmate, and in 1759 Loudon's outstanding talents, as well as his familiarity with things Russian, fitted him eminently to command the Austrian corps which fought alongside the Russians in the campaign of Kunersdorf. The promotion to *FZM.* came during Loudon's subsequent retreat to Poland. He had earned the Great Cross of the Military Order of Maria Theresa in 1758, and on 5 March 1759 the Empress created him a baron (*Freiherr*) of the Hereditary Lands. A corrupt genealogist (one of the many of the kind) invented a noble Scottish ancestry for him in the form of a mythical third son of Sir Matthew Campbell of Loudon, an adherent of Mary Queen of Scots, and Gideon Ernst now took to signing his name 'Loudon' instead of the original 'Laudon.'

Loudon's standing with the public and the body of the army was unique. Giuseppe Gorani was with him for fifteen days as orderly officer, and testifies that 'out of all the Austrian generals, Brentano excepted, he was the one under whose orders we would most love to serve. Loudon was affable, he had a polite word for everyone, and at the same time he was capable of inspiring the deepest respect.'[9] He could earn the same regard from an intellectual of the status of Professor Gellert, who met him at Carlsbad in 1763. 'My first and best acquaintance was Loudon, a man of particular traits of character—serious, modest, inclined to melancholy (rather like me). He spoke little (again like me), but what he said was solid and true. His conversation touched not at all on his deeds, and little on war; he was an attentive listener, and his whole manner, and even his way of dressing betrayed the same pleasing simplicity and dignity that could be observed in his speech'.[10]

Loudon's rise had so far owed nothing to 'protection' of the kind he could observe among so many of the Austrian generals. In March 1760 Loudon wrote to Kaunitz that he had decided to gloss over the failure of a series of strikes by subordinates against the Prussian quarters in Upper Silesia on 15 March 'because this... business, even if it had turned out well, would have been of no great moment, and I am not unaware that a man of reasonably high birth like Draskovich [*FML.* Joseph Count Draskovich] will always find support.'[11]

Loudon was devoid of the social graces, and had no kind of commanding presence in civilian company. He was small in stature and slight in build, and at times there could be something forbidding in his craggy features: his complexion was dark and rough, his cheeks were haggard, and his light greyish-blue eyes were set deep beneath heavy russet brows. It was possible to harbour reservations even about his military capacities. He had risen fast to extremely high rank and honours after only brief independent command of regular forces. There was still something of the free-booting soldier of fortune about him, as was sensed by the men who were attracted to his command by the prospect of plunder. The alternating bursts of inspiration and spells of lassitude even now betrayed the Russian in him, as did (it must be admitted) the guile which lay beneath his rustic simplicity.

Considered objectively, the rise of Loudon therefore offers impressive proof that the Austrian service was indeed a 'career open to talents.' The contrary has always been taken to be the case, and it is perhaps worth asking the reasons why. There is an obvious appeal about a man who seems to have made his way entirely by his own efforts, and there was a supposed contrast immediately at hand in the person of Franz Moritz Lacy. This Austro-Irishman enjoyed the personal friendship of Maria Theresa, and later of her son Joseph II. Neat and composed in appearance, fluent in the very best German and French, Lacy had the 'figure, deportment and manners of a man of quality; but there is in them still more of the courtier and the gentleman, than of the soldier... Lacy is more respected at Vienna; Loudon is more dreaded at Berlin... If Lacy is more considered by the present age, in the circle where he moves; Loudon will probably fill a much higher place... in different times, and among foreign nations, when the little malignities, prejudices and partialities of the hour are buried in oblivion.'[12]

The picture is overdrawn and crude, and does a great injustice to Lacy, who in addition to his social and organisational talents was probably more of the fighting soldier than was Loudon, having been wounded six or seven times in the course of his fighting career, whereas Loudon was probably wounded no more than once. To some extent Loudon was a pawn in an altogether higher game that was now being played out between Daun and Kaunitz. The Chancellor saw in Loudon the instrument by which he could conduct his war with energy and success, and there is every reason to suppose that the notion of setting up an Austro-Russian corps in Silesia in 1760 was supported, and probably even devised, by Kaunitz as a means of giving his protégé a command independently of Daun.

With great skill Loudon was opening up a channel of communication direct to Kaunitz. He apologised for writing to him, 'for Your Highness must have your hands full with affairs of great moment,' but he had found the *Hofkriegsrath* to be slow and obstructive, and he asked Kaunitz to take his case to the Empress.[13] To this he added a request to be allowed liberty of action in his forthcoming campaign.[14] Kaunitz was able to give him the assurance he desired.

GdC. de Ville no longer counted as a potential rival for the command in the eastern theatre. He was now paying for the failure of his campaign in Upper Silesia in 1759, and perhaps also for his feud with the *Hofkriegsrath*. He was informed in January that there was a superfluity of officers of his rank, and that his services were not required for the coming campaign. De Ville went to Vienna to see his old patron Emperor Francis Stephen, who exclaimed '"What! Have they removed you from service? I didn't know anything about that.'[15] Francis Stephen intervened with Maria Theresa, but months passed without further news, and de Ville retired from active service with a pension of 2,000 florins from the Emperor.

Lacy was also in a bad way. The continuing operations in Saxony gave him no respite from his heavy labours as chief of staff, and, as he confided in Franz Liechtenstein, 'what I find most painful of all is the news which came to me from Riga yesterday, telling me that my dear mother left this world on 27 November last. I owe a great deal to her, and I loved her dearly, and it has hit me very hard.'[16]

The senior Liechtenstein, Prince Wenzel Anton, nevertheless wrote to Maria Theresa to support Loudon's plan of campaign, and tell her 'as a good and zealous patriot… that the factions in the army are supported from here [Vienna], and are greatly damaging to the service. It is important to excise this corrupt element from our military, without respect of individuals.'[17] When Lacy, the political innocent, came to Vienna in the spring he wrote to Daun that Liechtenstein regarded him 'as an enemy to Loudon. He is not the only one, for a number of other people have got the same idea into their heads. But I am not concerned in the slightest. Your Excellency knows how things stand, and I am content to proceed on my own straight way.'[18]

Lacy had every reason to believe that he could rely on the support of Daun, who wrote to reassure him that he could place all his trust in his friendship, 'not indeed on account of my beautiful eyes, but because it is for the good and best interests of our Most August Sovereign.'[19] Lacy did not know that his trust had already been betrayed. The *Hofkriegsrath* had informed him that although he had been promoted to FZM., he would be accorded only the pay due to his former rank as *FML*. This was a restriction which was being applied only to Lacy and fourteen or so of the most recently-promoted generals, and Lacy wrote to Daun that he wished to be assured that the retrenchment was at the express order of Maria Theresa; if that were the case, Lacy would not utter a further word. He closed his letter by touching on the extravagances of the court, and the contrasting them with another economy, this time at the expense of the wretched military invalids.[20]

Daun forwarded Lacy's letter to Maria Theresa, together with a similar complaint from Tillier: 'I must admit to Your Imperial Highness, that I have been sickened by the nasty little trick of Lacy and Tillier, and I would never have believed that the former was capable of such self-interest… but it is fitting that Your Majesty should know both the bad and good sides of her people… although he [Lacy] always does justice to Loudon, from time to time it is possible to

Franz Moritz Count Lacy, creator of the Austrian General Staff and victim of the intrigues of Kaunitz (Austrian Army Museum)

Joseph Count Draskovich. Remained part of Loudon's circle of generals in spite of alleged limitations. (Military Academy, Wiener Neustadt)

detect a touch of jealousy.'[21]

In his low state Lacy resigned the functions of chief of staff, and on 1 June took command of a corps of 16,800 Austrian and Saxon troops. Frederick soon recognised the change in the Austrian style of operations. After the war he told the Prince de Ligne that nobody in either history or modern times had rivalled Lacy in ability to move and position armies, 'and so it was that as long he was chief of staff... I was unable to gain the slightest advantage. Don't you remember the two campaigns of 1758 and 1759? You succeeded in everything you attempted. I kept asking "Will I ever be rid of that man?"... but then somebody replaced him. Now I could say "This might not turn out too badly for me; this might give me an opening." I looked for it, and I found it at Torgau.'[22]

As was usual in this war, operations opened on a small scale by clashes between the forward forces in the early spring. What was most unusual was that the Austrians were taking the initiative.

This time the Prussians were making their presence felt in the *Reich* only in the form of isolated detachments and raiding parties. In western Saxony *GFWM*. Kleefeld cut short Captain Franz Isaak Froideville's career of raiding in the Voigtland, when he trapped him against the Mulde at **Nieder-Mülsen** on 9 April. The Prussian infantry fought its way out, but Froideville was forced to surrender with 111 of his people. All the rest were cut down, except for the few who swam the river, and Kleefeld was able to restore 688 draught horses and 172 four-horse carts to their peasant owners.

In Saxony east of the Elbe *FML*. Beck, the recent victor of Meissen, determined to deal a further blow at the Prussian rear areas, this time at the expense of Major General Ernst Heinrich Czettritz, who had 1,600 cavalry scattered in apparently security across the plain in the neighbourhood of Kossdorf and Blumberg not far short of Torgau. Beck advanced with 3,200 men from the Neustadt of Dresden, and on 20 February beat up two squadrons of the Bayreuth Dragoons [D5] at **Kossdorf** and captured the Schmettau Cuirassiers' [C4] set of new uniforms in their pristine colours of straw, black and white. The cheerful Czettritz also fell into Austrian hands, along with a copy of Frederick's *General-Principia vom Kriege* (1753), which the king had issued to his generals under the most stringent conditions of safekeeping. The Austrians now gained an insight into Frederick's military thinking, and were very impressed by what they found. Daun read every page with great care and almost unreserved admiration, and only wished that the Austrians had it in them to wage war in the same way.

The only failure was on the part of Loudon's forces gathering in the east, where on 15 March their chief ordered a blow to be struck against the Prussian quarters at **Neustadt**, **Ober Glogau** and **Leobschütz** in Upper Silesia. The enemy were vigilant and quick on their feet, and were able to break contact before the main body of Austrians, five battalions of regulars under *FML*. Draskovich, arrived on the scene. Loudon put the chief blame on Draskovich, who was brave and enthusiastic, but unsuited for independent command, 'being totally devoid of judgement and reflection. He is every bit as lacking in discretion, and hence he reduces everything around him to confusion.'[23]

Loudon was every bit as disillusioned with the forces under his command, for in May they still fell far short of the numbers he believed he needed to counter the 50,000 troops which he reckoned that Fouqué and Prince Henry could bring against him in Silesia. In these circumstances Loudon concluded that he must scale down his ambitions and ask Daun for support. Daun had to write to Maria Theresa on 22 May that he was in no position to help, since he must match the 30-40,000 Prussian troops in Saxony with a comparable number of Austrians. He commented that Loudon was finding that 'the command of an army is by no means as easy as he once imagined it to be.'[24]

The root cause of all these sorry proceedings—Daun's delays in Saxony, and Loudon's vacillations in the east—lay in the uncertainty as to what the Russians were going to do. Maria Theresa recognised that the Austrians were in a weak bargaining position, 'for... the Russian court has nothing to fear from the enemy in the present war, and has already seized a concrete advantage through the conquest of East Prussia. I am the one who must seek Russian help and active co-operation, and not the other way around.'²⁵

All the same a suitable man might still do a great deal of good at the Russian headquarters, and on the advice of Lacy the field marshal chose the veteran *FML*. Thomas Plunkett instead of the gifted young staff officer *GFWM*. Jakob Nugent. Lacy explained that Plunkett was good with words, and 'as they are both Irishmen it means that Plunkett would be able to get on with Browne just as well as would Nugent.'²⁶ The Browne in question was the influential Russian general George (Yury Yurevich) Browne, a member of the celebrated Irish military family.

After he reached the Russian army Plunkett was able to report that the normally taciturn Saltykov became more accessible on hunting excursions, when a good opening gambit was to ask him about a wonderful time he had once spent in Paris. Lieutenant General Zakhar Chernyshev too repaid some cultivation, for he had a keen intellect and was extremely ambitious, and remembered how Daun had made him welcome during a spell on mission with the Austrians.

Meanwhile the months'-long confrontation between Daun and Frederick near Dresden came to an end on 25 and 26 April, when the Prussians abandoned Wilsdruff, the immense abattis in the Tharandter-Wald and the post at Freiberg, and fell back to a line which extended from Nossen on the Mulde to Meissen. Frederick commented 'here we are at the camp of Meissen, without those Austrian buggers even deigning to look at us.' The king was amused to learn that Daun had banished 400 prostitutes from Dresden, and (so the story went) drowned two of them in the Elbe. 'Now I wonder what the Pompadour will have to say about that!'²⁷

Daun moves to Silesia, June - July 1760

In everything except the calendar date Frederick's retreat from before Dresden should be counted as the last episode in the campaign of 1759. The main Austrian army opened the new campaigning season by leaving its quarters on 1 June 1760. At that time the friendly and hostile forces were deployed as follows:

a) Austrians

FM. Daun's main army by Dresden and the detachments out to the west at Dippoldiswalde and Freiberg: 52,400

FZM. Lacy's corps at Boxdorf, on the eastern side of the Elbe below Dresden: 16,800

FML. Beck's corps at Zittau: 6,500

FZM. Loudon's army on the Bohemian-Silesian borders: 49,400

Garrisons: 7,400, of whom *FML*. Maguire commanded 3,300 in Dresden

b) Associated Forces

Reichsarmee and supporting Austrians under *FM*. the Prince of Zweibrücken: 22,500, of whom 6,000 were detached under *GFWM*. Luzinsky at Saalfeld, leaving 16,500 to join the Austrians on the Elbe

Russian army: field establishment of 100,000

Swedish army 25 weak bn, 42 sq

c) Prussian Forces (nominal establishments: supernumeraries brought the true figures higher)

Frederick in Saxony: 44,500

GL. Fouqué in Silesia: 13,800

Prince Henry at Sagan: 31,800

GM. Jung-Stutterheim in Pomerania: 6,500

Having taken his troops out of quarters, Daun held to the west of the Elbe near Dresden, waiting for the *Reichsarmee* to relieve him in the position of Plauen. Meanwhile he kept himself ready to counter any move by Frederick in the direction of Silesia.

The king finally declared his hand on 15 June, when he brought the greater part of his army across the Elbe downstream at Meissen. Daun countered by moving the right wing of his army to the east bank, which set Lacy free to move from Boxdorf and array his troops between Bärnsdorf and Gross-Dittmannsdorf, athwart Frederick's most direct route to Silesia. The king hoped to destroy him by a surprise attack on 19 June, but Lacy recoiled out of his reach. 'I missed! How very sad! I really feel like going out and hanging myself… it's my bad luck, it pursues me everywhere. That Lacy got out of the way! I ought to have beaten him.'²⁸

The forces remained in essentially the same positions in the hills to the east of Dresden for the next twelve days. The Austrians meanwhile gained a theoretically greater freedom of action, for the 16,500 troops of the *Reichsarmee* reached the Plauen position on 22 June. All the Prussians had been committed to facing the Austrians, and so for once the *Reichsarmee* had been able to take the route north of the hills of the Bohemian border.

On 24 June Major Tom Caldwell arrived in the company of seven postmasters, blowing their horns, and brought the news that Loudon had attacked Fouqué at Landeshut at first light the day before, and destroyed his corps almost in its entirety (below). The Austrians at once conveyed these glad tidings to the enemy outposts, and the Prince de Ligne rode out to jeer at the Prussians.

On 28 June the Austrians were told that Frederick was digging himself in between Grossdöbritz and Grossenhain and showed no signs of moving. Daun was already under orders from Maria Theresa to join Loudon, but in the present circumstances he thought it best to keep Frederick in view, and feed reinforcements to Silesia by batches. These would give Loudon a total of 60,000 troops, which ought to be enough for his purposes.

Daun had judged Frederick's dilemma correctly, for if the king allowed himself to be detained any longer the whole position of the Prussians in Silesia would be in danger of collapse. Frederick made his first march in that direction on 2 July. Daun commissioned Lacy to shadow the enemy progress, and set off with the main army on the 3rd.

Frederick thought it worth his while to devote 4 July to yet another effort to rid himself of Lacy, his incubus. Lacy slipped away from Lichtenberg in the nick of time, and with the help of a brave rearguard action by the Kaiser Hussars [H2] he was able to retire across the Röder and establish himself behind the ponds, ravines and woods at Radeberg. The Prince de Ligne records that 'the general judged the time of our departure wonderfully... His *coup d'oeil* never served us so well.'[29]

Frederick and Daun were now marching east on roughly parallel courses. The Prussians were falling behind, and on 6 July, in an attempt to make up for lost time, Frederick got his troops on their feet at Kloster Marienstern, and drove them at a punishing rate across the Spree below Bautzen and on to camps on the right bank at Nieder-Gurig and Gleina. This was remembered as the most taxing of all the marches in all his wars, and 105 of his men perished of heat stroke, their vital organs cooked from the inside. All the effort was in vain. Daun had been making better time, and over more difficult country, by way of Bischofswerda, and on the 7th he made an undisputed crossing of the Neisse at Görlitz. He reported to Maria Theresa that 'such a march in this heat was most gruelling, but the stakes were high.'[30]

On the 8th Daun crossed the Queiss into Silesia, and could now establish direct contact with Loudon. The Austrians' velocity now told against them, for Frederick grasped that his army could now do an about turn and march back west to capture Dresden before Daun could possibly return to the Elbe. He also noted that the Austrian forces had become greatly teased out on their way to the east, which would give him yet a further chance to be rid of Lacy, who was now out of touch with Daun's army.

At daylight on 9 July the Prussians were in full march against Lacy with the intention of cutting him off from Dresden. Lacy took to the highway, and although the skirmishing lasted all day, he was able to reach Weissig with his corps tired but intact. On the 10th, and just ahead of the Prussians, Lacy was able to cross to the left (west) bank of the Elbe, partly by the Augustusbrücke, and partly by a bridge of boats to the Friedrichstadt. Lacy then swung to the south-east and took up position above Dresden between the Lockwitz and Müglitz streams. Lacy was under orders from Zweibrücken to post his 18,558 troops to hold this stretch of the Elbe against the substantial enemy force which had reached the opposite bank (the Duke of Holstein-Gottorp with ten battalions and thirty squadrons).

These events left the friendly forces facing in two directions—the *Reichsarmee* and its supporting Austrians looking north over the hollow of Plauen, and Lacy's Austrians guarding the Elbe above Dresden. On 12 July the extended

Dresden and Lusatia, June–July 1760

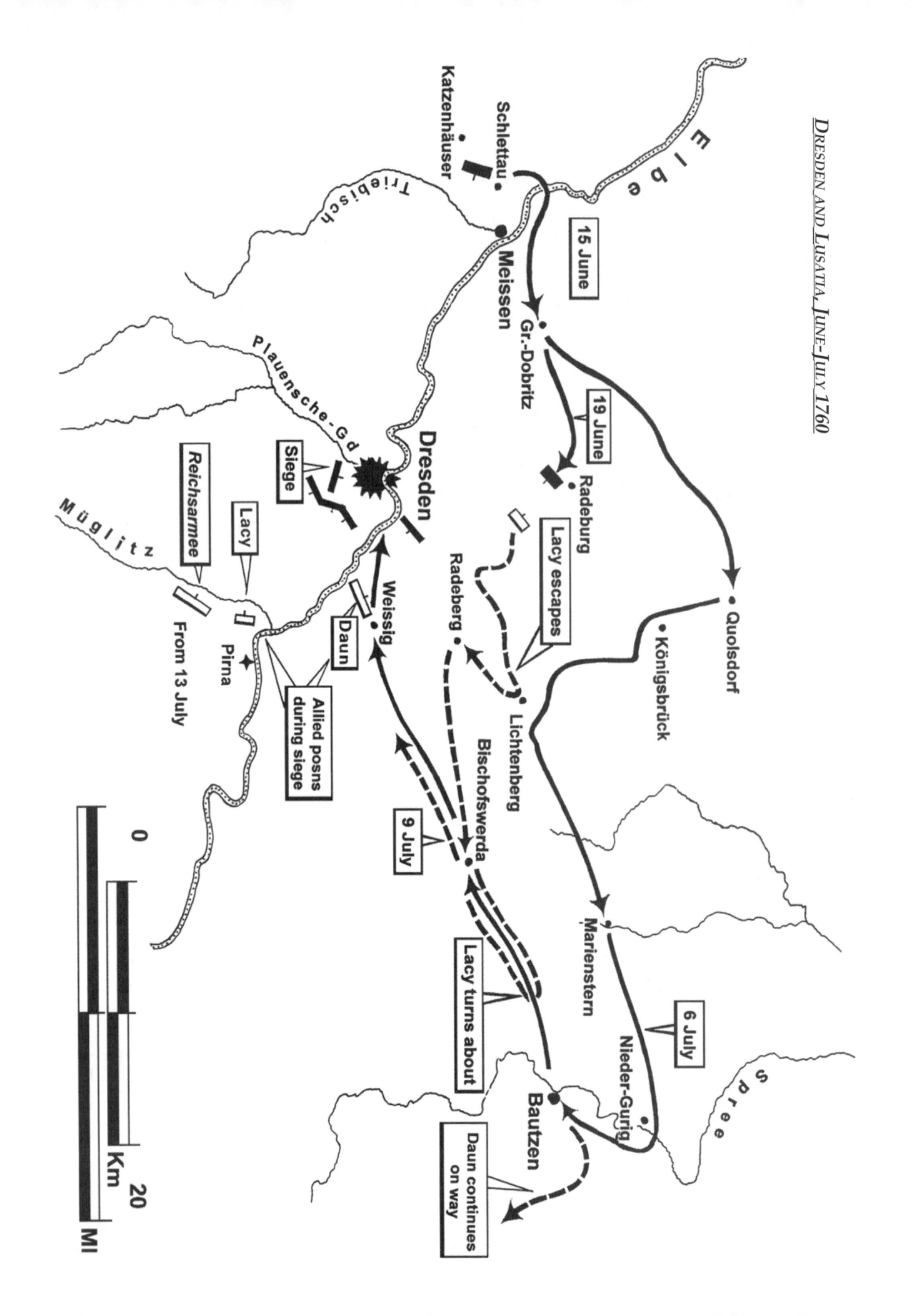

deployments became untenable. The aggressive *GL.* Hülsen, who had been left behind by Frederick in the old camp at Meissen, now lunged against the *Reichsarmee* to threaten its front and its left flank, while at the same time he gained the riverside meadows at Briesnitz just below Dresden, thus staking out a bridgehead for Frederick to cross to the left bank, should he return from the east.

GdC. Hadik was making his calculations, and arrived at some disturbing results. All of Lacy's troops were needed to hold the river above Dresden against the main Prussians army which was still at Weissig. Zweibrücken had just 16,505 combatants, which was very much less than the forces which had been available to Daun during the previous winter. Of those 16,505, one-third comprised the Austrians and Saxons, who were as good as the Prussians. The remaining two-thirds were made up of Circle troops of the Empire, 'put together from all kinds of little contingents, many of them from states which are not just unenthusiastic but positively hostile. Most of the troops are poorly drilled and undisciplined, many of them are Protestant, and—because their sovereigns are inimical to us—most of them have been furnished with incapable, careless and cowardly officers, and inexperienced and ignorant generals in whom we can place no trust.'[31]

In these circumstances Hadik advised Zweibrücken to place a strong garrison in Dresden, withdraw the rest of the *Reichsarmee* to join Lacy's corps two or three hours' march from the city, and wait for Daun to bring his army back from Silesia. All the generals of the *Reichsarmee* agreed, and so, with some reluctance, did *FML.* Maguire, the Austrian commandant of Dresden. Lacy signified his assent by letter.

Overnight on 12/13 July the *Reichsarmee* abandoned the position of Plauen, and deployed on the next day along the heights of Gross-Sedlitz. The ravine of the Müglitz gave the position immense tactical strength, and the Prince of Zweibrücken and his suite established themselves in full security in the baroque garden palace of Gross-Sedlitz, from where they had an excellent view of the events which now unfolded at Dresden.

Word arrived from *GdC.* Buccow that he had reached Görlitz on the 12th with a substantial reinforcement from the main Austrian army, and that *GFWM.* Ried had arrived at Bischofswerda with the advance guard. All the letters from Daun, however, indicated that he saw no need to move the rest of his army from its present position, just inside Silesia on the far side of the Queiss. For the time being, therefore, Dresden was left without support.

Crisis at Dresden, July 1760

With Daun and his troops so distant, and Zweibrücken and Lacy behind the Müglitz, it was left to Maguire to hold Dresden against the efforts of Frederick's Prussians. He now had under his command 14,170 troops of all kinds, with a preponderance of Austrians, and a total of 110 medium and heavy cannon (6-, 12- and 18-pounders), thirty howitzers (7- and 10-pounders) and six heavy mortars (45- and 60-pounders, stone weight).

FML. Johann Sigismund Maguire von Inniskillin was a stoutly-built Catholic Irishman, who had made his name as one of the reformers of the Croatian military borders. His solid qualities were complemented in a useful way by his right-hand men, the quick-witted and raffish Piedmontese brothers Guasco: *FML.* Franz directed the troops, while *GFWM.* Peter managed the local defence of the Neustadt.

Dresden was a city with fortifications, rather than a fortified city, and the styles of its defences were of architectural rather than military value. The less immediately-threatened Neustadt lay on the right (east) bank of the Elbe, and was connected with the main city by the stone Augustusbrücke. The Neustadt faced onto open country, and was defended by spacious (if not particularly well-maintained) bastions, curtains and outworks in the seventeenth-century German manner. On the other side of the river the churches, palaces and tall housing blocks of the Altstadt were crammed behind fortifications in the Renaissance style, with long curtains and hammer-headed bastions. Beyond the narrow ditch the fields of fire from the ramparts were restricted by the suburbs, and towards the south in particular, where the houses of the Pirna

The siege of Dresden, July 1760

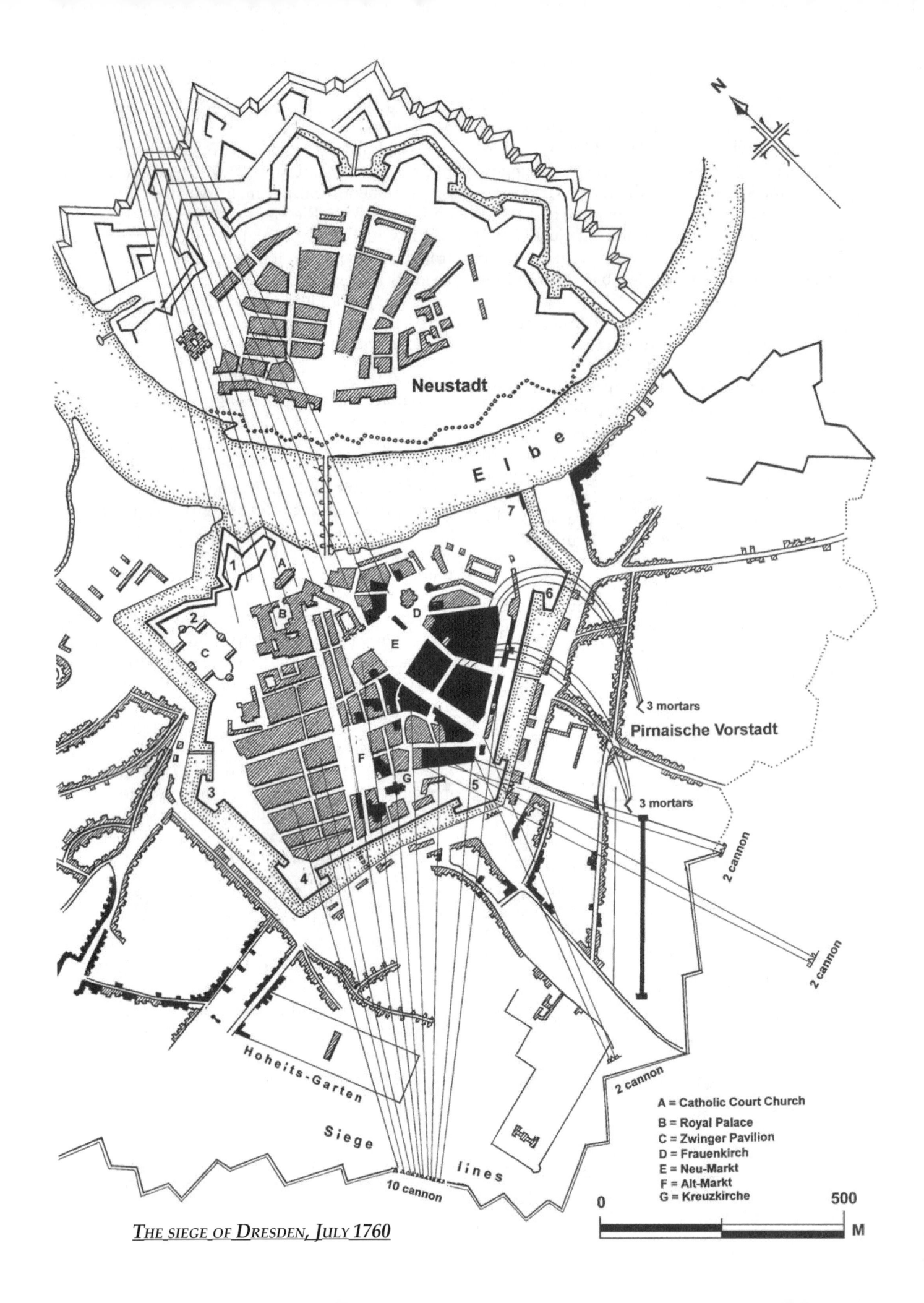

A = Catholic Court Church
B = Royal Palace
C = Zwinger Pavilion
D = Frauenkirch
E = Neu-Markt
F = Alt-Markt
G = Kreuzkirche

Suburb (Pirnaische Vorstadt) crowded to the counterscarp (outer edge) of the ditch.

On 13 July the Prussian royal army completed its crossing of the Elbe below Dresden, and Frederick moved the greater part of the combined forces around to the southern side of the city, thus interposing himself between Dresden and the *Reichsarmee* and the Austrians behind the Müglitz. Without further ceremony he threw his Jäger and the free battalion of Courbière into an attack on the walled park of the Grosser Garten, which extended in front of the Pirna Suburb. The enclosure was defended by Colonel Zedtwitz with six companies of the Banal Croats, who beat off the first assault, but they fell back on Maguire's orders when the Prussians came on again and attacked them in the flank with the support of eight cannon.

The Prussian lieutenant general Wedel now sent an officer to demand the surrender of Dresden. Maguire replied that 'General Wedel is somebody who is totally unknown to me. His Royal Majesty cannot be aware that I have the honour to command the Imperial and Royal garrison here, otherwise he, as a great commander, would not have supposed that an old and long-serving officer could do other than hold out to the last man, and await whatever His Majesty might have it in mind to do.'[32]

On the morning of 14 July the Jäger and Courbière's ruffians burst into the Pirna Suburb before the Croats could disengage, and a mass of intermingled friend and foe surged towards the Pirnäer-Tor. The guards were swept away in the crowd, and the Altstadt might have fallen there and then if Colonel Amadei, as acting brigadier, had not hastened up and saw that 'the gate had been completely abandoned, and that the enemy were already on the bridge which led to it, firing into the town with cannon and muskets. I therefore commandeered two assistant gunners, and with their help I personally raised and barred the drawbridge.'[33]

Finding the drawbridge raised, the Prussian light infantry spread out to right and left in the wreckage of the houses which lined the ditch. The Pirna Suburb had been devastated by the Prussian commandant Schmettau in 1758, and the gaping windows and stretches of ruined wall offered the Prussians excellent cover for sniping at the Austrians on the rampart. Amadei knew that a number of Croats had been stranded outside the gate during the scramble, and so he arranged to have ropes let down over the ramparts the next night and the fugitives hauled to safety.

Overnight on 14/15 July Colonel Joseph Maximilian Tillier reached Lacy from the main Austrian army, and told him that Daun had changed his mind and decided to march back to the Elbe. He counted on reaching the neighbourhood of Dresden on the 19th or 20th. Already on the evening of the 15th the garrison could see lines of camp fires on the heights of Weissig, and Maguire deduced correctly that *GFWM*. Ried had arrived at the head of Buccow's reinforcement. Brief contact was established near the Weisser Hirsch inn on the 16th, but Frederick was now alive to the importance of denying the eastern heights to Daun, and on the evening of the 17th the Prussians regained control of the post.

Meanwhile the king had brought the southern front of the Altstadt under direct attack. Although the Prussians had no siege cannon with them, they positioned their heavy field pieces in a number of well-chosen sites in the shelter of the suburbs. Their main point of attack was Bastion No. 5 (Jupiter) at the southernmost angle of the ramparts, and they set to work to build a breaching battery of 12-pounders against this target. Another battery was opened against the Pirnäer-Tor closer to the river, while cannon shot bounded along the whole length of the attacked front (Bastions Nos. 5 and 6 and the connecting curtain) from a ricochet battery sited behind the Hoheits-Garten to the west of the suburbs. A further battery in the Scheunen settlement on the far side of the Elbe carried its shot clear over the Neustadt and the river to land in the area of the royal Schloss and the Catholic Church.

All the time the troops on the ramparts were on the alert to beat off attempts at escalade on the part of the Prussian Jäger and free battalions. The defenders repulsed a first attack on the evening of the 17th, and after this alarm Maguire ordered all his batteries to fire one round every quarter of an hour, 'so that the nearby forces of relief, becoming aware of a sudden silence after

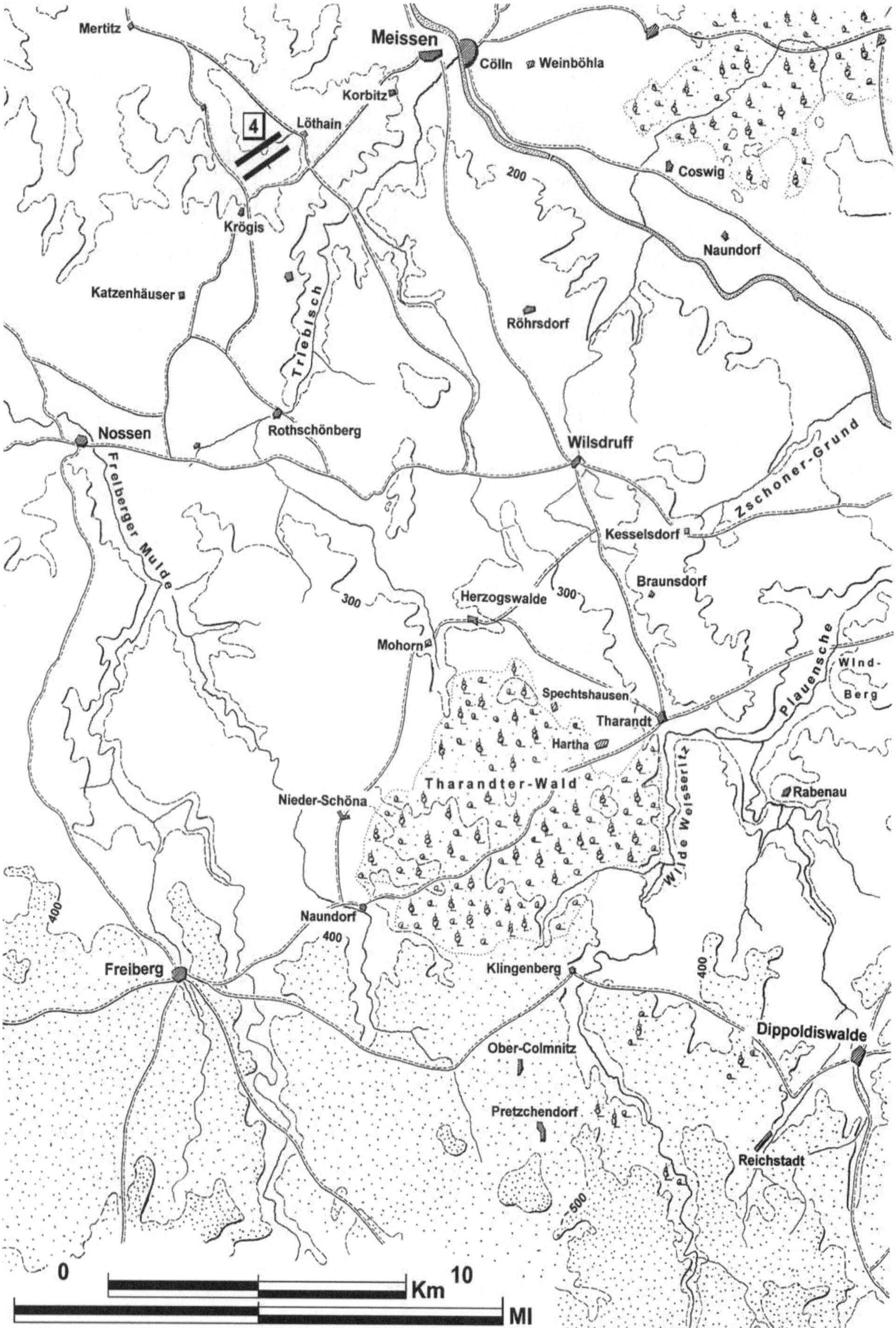
Mertitz
Meissen
Cölln
Weinböhla
Korbitz
4
Löthain
200
Coswig
Krögis
Naundorf
Katzenhäuser
Triebisch
Röhrsdorf
Nossen
Rothschönberg
Wilsdruff
Zschoner-Grund
Freiberger Mulde
Kesselsdorf
Braunsdorf
300
Herzogswalde
300
Mohorn
Plauensche
Wind-
Berg
Spechtshausen
Tharandt
Hartha
Wilde Weisseritz
Tharandter-Wald
Rabenau
Nieder-Schöna
400
Naundorf
400
Freiberg
Klingenberg
400
Dippoldiswalde
Ober-Colmnitz
Pretzchendorf
Reichstadt
500
0
10
Km
MI

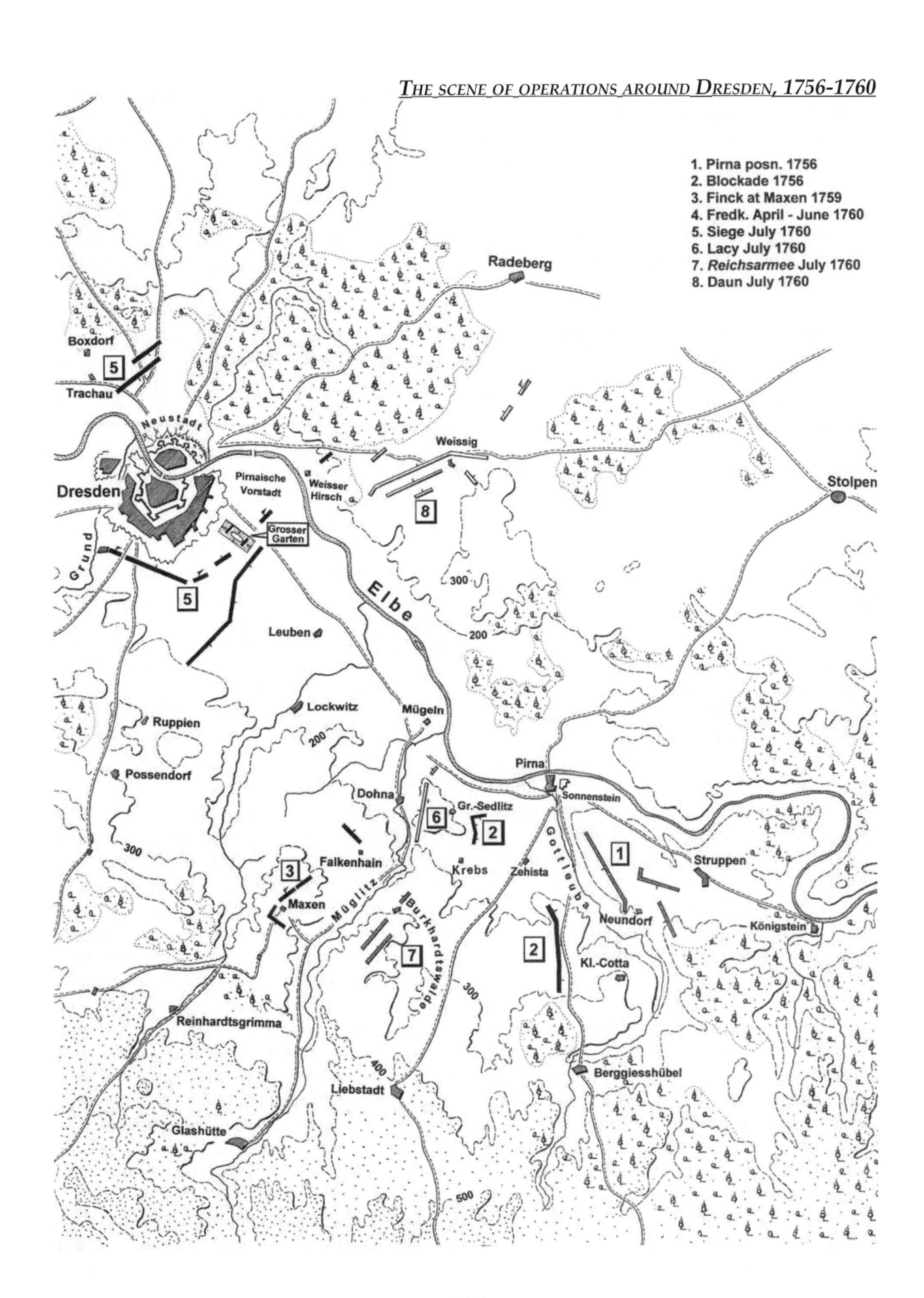

The scene of operations around Dresden, 1756-1760

1. Pirna posn. 1756
2. Blockade 1756
3. Finck at Maxen 1759
4. Fredk. April – June 1760
5. Siege July 1760
6. Lacy July 1760
7. *Reichsarmee* July 1760
8. Daun July 1760

a violent outburst of fire, might not suppose that the city had surrendered.'[34] The skirmishing continued across the ditch, 'and to get the better of the enemy Jäger... sixty-five volunteers were drawn from various regiments and issued with rifles; they were posted in the houses which adjoined the rampart, and the happy results were evident at once. The enemy Jäger were held down and our men were now better protected from their fire.'[35]

A new and critical phase of the siege opened at ten in the morning of 19 July. Mortars had reached the enemy camp by river, and the Prussians now opened a fire of bombs and incendiary carcasses against the Altstadt, and deluged Bastion No. 5 with bombs, howitzer shells and pierrier stones. The Austrians repulsed a new assault on the part of the enemy light troops, who had apparently wished to take advantage of the state of the ditch outside the Pirnäer-Tor, where it was partly filled with rubble. Scarcely had the escalade been beaten off than the fires in the city spread with startling speed.

One of the sources was the Kreuzkirche, which was surmounted by a curious wall-like tower of wood. The Prussians aimed five mortar bombs at the tower in succession, 'and the last one set it on fire. There was a good deal of woodwork inside, and so it blazed up within a few minutes. As it fell it crashed into the church, and set this on fire as well, so that this great building was reduced to ashes in a couple of hours.'[36]

The Prussians now aimed deliberately at the conflagrations, which added to the casualties among the soldiers who were fighting the fires, and by the afternoon the flames were rampaging out of control, for the pumps and wells were running dry, and a strong wind sprang up to fan the flames. The apartment of the book-loving Gottlieb Wilhelm Rabener was consumed at two in the afternoon. He himself had taken refuge across the river in the Neustadt, but he heard that 'the bombs had smashed through the vault under which we had stored all our effects, and had consumed everything. The cellar itself was plundered bare by the soldiers who were supposed to be putting out the fires. My servant, the very soul of loyalty, had stayed in the house until it began to collapse; he beat a dozen of those rogues out of the house, but he was finally overwhelmed by numbers and had to flee to me in the Neustadt.'[37]

Maguire's most lively concern was for the security of the ramparts, for the blaze caused by the collapse of the tower of the Kreuzkirche had spread to all the houses overlooking Bastion No. 5, and the flames were very close to the magazine. 'The danger was acute and there was no time to lose. The governor [Maguire] came running up accompanied by *FML.* [Franz] Guasco. Men were sent out to search everywhere for woollen coverings which could be soaked in water and thrown against the door of the magazine, which was being hosed down continually... thus was saved the magazine upon which the survival of the garrison and the town depended.'[38]

During the night Franz Guasco had to alert Maguire to a new peril, for the houses near the rampart of the Pirnäer-Tor were now on fire, and the flames were approaching the Arsenal and the Palais Brühl, through which ran the only access for the troops to the curtain. The efforts of Maguire and Guasco, together with a providential change in the wind, kept the fire temporarily at bay, but Maguire had to send word to the main army that Dresden was in danger of being reduced to a heap of ashes.

Urged on by messages from Lacy, Daun brought his army of relief by forced marches to the heights of Weissig on 18 July. He assembled his generals in council the next morning, and after a long debate the gathering concluded that it would be best to veer out of the direct path to Dresden, and instead cross to the left bank safely upstream at Pirna. Daun was out of touch with his advance guard under Ried, and, ridiculously, was not aware that the direct path to Dresden was reopened on the same day by a highly successful joint operation by Ried and the garrison of the Neustadt against the Weisser Hirsch. Daun postponed all operations on the part of the main army until 20 July, when he would attack the supposed positions of the Prussians.

Dresden, meanwhile, stood in as much danger from the Prussian artillery as ever, and its survival could not be guaranteed for more

*Johann Sigismund Count Maguire von Inniskillin,
stalwart defender of Dresden against Frederick in 1760
(Military Academy, Wiener Neustadt)*

than three hours at a time. No alleviation was brought by a costly sortie on the night of 19/20 July against the ricochet battery behind the Hoheits-Garden. The Austrians overran the battery for a time, but nobody had given any thought to how the nine cannon were to be brought back, smashed or spiked and so the effort was in vain.

The Prussians sustained the fire from their other batteries during that night and on the next day, and completed the destruction of 210 of the 740 houses of the Altstadt, or about one-third of that part of the city (marked black in our plan). The Pirnäer-Strasse, the Moritz-Strasse and the Kreuz-Gasse were aflame from end to end. Among the officers of Lacy's corps behind the Müglitz 'there was excellent conversation and excellent fare. In the distance one of the finest capitals in the world was burning... By noon everything was on fire. The field marshal [Daun] was a witness from his headquarters at Schönfeld, as was the Prince of Zweibrücken from his beautiful palace of Gross-Sedlitz. Pieces of cloth and paper were flying into our camp; it was a picture of total ruin. Pirna and the banks of the Elbe were crowded with desperate people who were ready to throw themselves into the river.'[39] The Neustadt offered no security, and in the course of the day further thousands of refugees fled from there to the fields and vineyards. 'It is very much to their credit,' commented Maguire, 'that in all their distress none of them complained or spoke about yielding the city.'[40]

At dusk the flames licked across the ramparts on the front of attack in the Altstadt, and set fire to the fascines which crowned the parapet. Maguire had to order his men to withdraw the cannon and pull back to the bastions on either side. The Austrians were not safe even there, and they had to tear away the fascines from the bastion flanks to prevent them too from catching fire.

At first light on the 20th Daun had led the best troops of his main army in their intended blow against the Weisser Hirsch, only to find that the Prussians had abandoned the position long before. Lacy still went ahead with a diversion which had been planned against Frederick's main army, and nearly brought the war to an end in the process. *GFWM*. Brentano (commanding the Esterházy Hussars [H24] and the Saxon-Polish Rudnicki Uhlans) evicted the Möhring Hussars [H3] from Leuben, and drove them briskly towards Frederick's headquarters on the Grüne Wiese. The guards fled and the king 'came out of his bedroom in his nightshirt, stood in the courtyard and set up an endless yell of "Save me! Hide me somewhere!"'[41] The Austrians were unaware of their opportunity, and fell back in good order when the Prussians came to their senses.

The twenty-first of July can be counted the last day of the siege proper. At first light the Prussians opened fire with their breaching battery of 12-pounders against the left face of Bastion No. 5. However the bombardment of the city fell away, and by the evening the joint efforts of the garrison and the remaining townspeople had succeeded in extinguishing the flames.

In the course of the day the Austrian main army descended from the heights of Weisser Hirsch to the plain outside the Neustadt, and proceeded to cast a bridge of boats to the Osterwiese just below Dresden, and another (unseen by the Prussians) immediately above the city to the Pirna Suburb. After nightfall *FML*. Ludwig Angern took ten grenadier companies, nine battalions and five squadrons to the left bank. His mission, as planned by the army's new chief of staff, *GFWM*. Jakob Nugent, was to capture the Prussian batteries in the suburbs.

Angern was unwilling to take guidance from Nugent, as the Irishman was junior to him. The troops were left without detailed directions, and they ended up stumbling blindly through the darkness in search of their objectives. It was only through chance that Major Lemède, leading his battalion of Carl Lothringen [3], captured a Prussian officer and forced him at sword point to lead him to the battery he was supposed to be attacking.[42] The battery in question was probably the 12-pounder breaching battery, where the Prussian regiment of Anhalt-Bernburg [3] provided the covering force while the pieces were being evacuated. The Austrians took the work from the rear, spiked the cannon and smashed the carriages. The Prussians lost altogether about 430 men, but the Austrians, many of whom were totally disorientated, left not far short of 600 in enemy hands. The irreplaceable Nugent was among the captives, and the British envoy Sir Andrew Mitchell describes him as 'a young gentleman of Ireland, who is much trusted and employed in the Austrian army, and who seems to deserve all the confidence they have in him.'[43]

On 25 July there were clear signs that the Prussians had abandoned all pretence at a siege, and had fallen back to blockading positions. In the process they converted the Grosser-Garten into an abattis, and, according to a Prussian lieutenant, 'the tall majestic trees, of venerable age and priceless rarity, which lined the magnificent avenues in the finest order, were now hacked down, and the garden… as a whole was converted in a matter of hours into an horrific wilderness.'[44] Marainville adds that the Prussians went on to smash the sculptures which had been taken for safekeeping into the pavilions in the park, and the work of destruction extended as far as the orange trees, 'which were hacked in pieces. I would not have believed such barbarities if I had not seen them, for conduct of this kind would have seemed unthinkable from one sovereign towards another.'[45]

Frederick kept his forces interposed between Dresden to the north, and the *Reichsarmee* and the corps of Lacy to the south, and for some days the city itself remained little more than a bridgehead for Daun on the left bank of the Elbe. But the king was now paying a heavy price for being tied down for so long in front of Dresden, for his communications stretched up the Elbe by way of Torgau and Meissen, and were vulnerable to the Austrian detachments which were ranging down the right bank. Convoys of barges were destroyed in this way on the 27th and the 28th. The loss did not compare with the ambush of the much larger land transport at Domstadtl in 1758, but it must have reminded Frederick of how little good he was doing in Saxony, when Silesia and Glatz were being left open to the ravages of Loudon.

Towards noon on the 28th news came to Maguire that Loudon had taken Glatz by storm. 'I had postillions ride around the ramparts with sounding trumpets, and the garrison call out *Vivat Maria Theresia!* so that the sound would carry to the enemy camp.' In the morning of the 29th he ordered the singing of the Te Deum in the Catholic churches, and in the afternoon a triple *feu de joie* was fired from the ramparts, the cannon being loaded with solid shot and aimed at the Prussians. 'Towards the evening we saw a great deal of baggage and some artillery being taken through the enemy camp by way of Plauen towards Pennrich.'[46]

First light on the 30th revealed that the Prussians had gone. In fourteen days of siege and blockade the Austrians and *Reichstruppen* in Dresden had lost 697 of their number, of whom 182 had been killed and 435 wounded, and 80 were missing. These losses do not include the heavy losses in Angern's force, which had come from the main army, and had suffered so badly in the sortie of 20/21 July. The garrison had fired off altogether 27,704 rounds of artillery, the largest single category being the 7,057 roundshot fired by the invaluable 18-pounders. In roundshot alone the weight of the missiles amounted to 246,521 pounds, and in howitzer shells and mortar bombs to 24,636 pounds (stone weight).

The defence of Dresden redounded to the credit of Maguire's firmness and judgement. He already wore the Grand Cross of the Military Order of Maria Theresa, and on 15 September he was promoted to *FZM*. Two of his compatriots had less cause to celebrate. Nugent was a prisoner of the Prussians, and the Austrians were deprived of the services of their new chief of staff. *FZM*. Lacy had relinquished that post only a short time before, and in the capacity of a corps commander he had performed brilliantly until he arrived near Dresden and came under the orders of Zweibrücken. He had little to reproach himself with even then, but (probably at the prompting of Kaunitz) Maria Theresa wrote to him to express her surprise 'that an officer of your zeal and prudence' had not opposed Zweibrücken's decision to retire behind the Müglitz.[47] Lacy set out the facts in detail in his reply,[48] but the Empress reminded him that he was in 'a peculiarly delicate situation. Behaviour which arouses no comment in somebody else, will draw more attention to you, as inclining certain people to believe that it proceeds more from considerations of politics and favouritism than from what is for the good of the service. You will see from the frankness, with which I write to you, that I have taken the present occasion to put you on your guard as a matter of urgency.'[49]

Loudon's progress

For a time Kaunitz had reason to fear that he might have made a bad investment in his protégé, *FZM.* Loudon. At the beginning of June Loudon had completed an unopposed advance from north-east Bohemia through the County of Glatz and taken up position at the edge of the Silesian plain. He was now overcome by doubts. He still had 38,000 troops under his direct command, out of his total force of 50,000 men, and had an overwhelming superiority (although he did not grasp it) over the 13,800 available to the Prussian lieutenant general Fouqué.

Logic was deserting Loudon, as well as resolution, for he wrote to Kaunitz on 5 June that it would be wrong to expose him to defeat 'before the Russian army and our main army have reached their assigned destinations.'[50] These words ran directly counter to the plan of campaign, which had been adopted at Loudon's urging, and supported by Kaunitz, namely for the Austrians to seize the initiative by taking early and aggressive action in Silesia. Again, Loudon wrote to his patron on 13 June 'that I can see not the slightest advantage in holding the post of Landeshut, whether from our point of view, or for facilitating the operations of the Russians.'[51] Four days later Fouqué pushed the detachment of *FML.* Gaisruck from the hills overlooking this important town and road junction, and, without perceiving the contradiction, Loudon now put all his effort into evicting the Prussians.

Loudon (as even his supporters admitted) found it difficult to keep a campaign as a whole in view. But it was a different question when something made him focus his attention on a specific objective. Loudon now left just 7,000 troops to keep the fortress of Glatz under blockade, and set out with the rest from Pischkowitz on 18 June. The advance guard reached Schwarzwaldau, east of Landeshut, on the 19th, and Loudon was able to establish that Fouqué was present with his entire corps, and that he had brought up heavy artillery from Schweidnitz to augment the guns emplaced on the hills. Early on 21 June, a day of depressing rain, Loudon decided that he must retreat to Glatz, but few hours later he made a detailed reconnaissance which convinced him that an attack on Fouqué was feasible after all.

Landeshut, 23 June 1760

a) Austrians
up to 35,000; c. 28,000 infantry, 7,000 cavalry, gunners unknown
Losses: 2,888 casualties; 774 killed, 2,144 wounded, missing and prisoners unknown

b) Prussians
11,427; 9,542 infantry, 1,885 cavalry, gunners unknown
Losses: c. 10,300; 1,917 killed, 8,299 prisoners (including nearly all the unknown numbers of wounded), all the artillery of the corps, 34 colours and 2 standards

The Prussians were standing along two ranges of sandstone heights which extended respectively to the east and south of the walled town of Landeshut:

The Eastern Heights: Doctor-Berg, Mummel-Berg, Buch-Berg, with the Thiemen-Berg with its star fort just to the rear

The Southern Heights: the Kirch-Berg on an outlying spur, then the Galgen-Berg, Gerichts-Berg, Hahn-Berg, Blasdörfer-Berg

Since 1759 the Prussians had been working hard to make this naturally formidable position stronger still, and the fortifications consisted of 'really solid works with blockhouses, palisades, storm poles, drawbridges and amazingly deep ditches. In addition nearly all the hills were interconnected by a line of communication.'[52] The greatest single weakness of the position was its great length, for the two sequences extended for more than a mile each, and the units were split up among the works and the interconnecting lines.

On the dismal afternoon of 22 June Loudon brought his generals together on the ridge of

Ziegenrücken, and explained his plan of attack for the next day. In essence he was going to overcome Fouqué's left (northern) wing by enveloping and frontal assaults by three groups of forces:

Two small infantry detachments of Lieutenant Colonel Luzzeni and *GFWM. Naselli*, who were to approach the Doctor-Berg from the north and north-east respectively

Three waves of infantry (*GFWM. Ellrichshausen. FMLs. Campitelli* and *Müffling*) destined to attack the Mummel-Berg and the Buch-Berg from the front (east)

Finally another powerful body, this time of cavalry (47 sq: *FML. Podstadzty, GFWM. Nauendorff*, Colonel *Kinsky*) were held in reserve on the right flank, ready to exploit any success

Meanwhile the outlying hills provided excellent sites for the twenty-two pieces of supporting artillery, deployed concentrically in five batteries.

On the far Austrian left (southern) flank, the commands of *FML. Wolfersdorff* and *GFWM. Saint-Ignon* (10 bn, 14 sq) were to execute a diversionary attack against the scattering of flèches on the isolated Blasdörfer-Berg. *FML. Gaisruck*'s two battalions of infantry were spread thinly along the axis of the Langer-Berg ridge to keep the Prussians on the Hahn-Berg and the Gerichts-Berg amused, and preserve the communication between the main attack by the Austrian right, and the subordinate attack by the Austrian left under Wolfersdorff and Saint-Ignon.

Late on 22 June the Austrians formed their lines in the dripping woodlands, which reached in places almost up to the Prussian defences. The rain gave way to fog, which offered further concealment, and at 1.45 in the earliest morning of the 23rd four howitzer shells burst in the air to give the signal for the attack. Major Joseph Frierenberger then opened fire against the **Doctor-Berg** with a battery of six heavy cannon and two howitzers, and through the murk he succeeded in dismounting four Prussian cannon in rapid succession, which was a remarkable technical achievement. Perhaps he had marked out the place for the wheels and trails of his carriages in advance.

This promising start was exploited by the leading elements of Naselli's infantry, namely the two battalions of the grenadier regiment of Grün-Loudon, 'raised principally from Prussian deserters.'[53] The renegades soon mastered the work on the Doctor-Berg, and on the rearward slopes they were assisted by forces from the cavalry reserve, in the shape of Colonel Joseph Kinsky and his 300 volunteer carabiniers, who raced ahead of the rest of Podstadzty's cavalry and broke the Prussian free battalion of Mellin which had been standing in support. The Prussian major Hoven collected the survivors and fell back to the star fort on the Thiemen-Berg. The Austrians had now gained the far left flank of Fouqué's position, and prepared the way for the attack by their main force of infantry against the works on the summits of the Mummel-Berg and the Buch-Berg, which formed the bulwarks of the enemy left centre.

Two battalions of grenadiers spearheaded the assault, one of them probably storming the **Mummel-Berg**, while Major De Vins led the other against the **Buch-Berg**, which he describes 'a considerable height… which, if taken by us, would enable us to dominate not only most of the rest of the camp, but also most of the other hills.' The battalion approached in column of companies. Nearer the work the two leading companies made off to either side to take the redoubt in the rear, 'by which it was taken on all sides, and assaulted by all the companies simultaneously and with such violence that it was taken in the face of the determined enemy resistance.'[54] Some details are added by the grenadier captain Worbeer of the regiment of Marschall, who talks of an initial repulse which caused twenty-nine casualties in his company. Together with a number of his grenadiers he penetrated by way of the ditch to the rear of the work and contrived to lower the drawbridge, which enabled him (as he claims) to be the first into the redoubt.[55] Wherever the credit lies, all accounts agree that the northern flank of Fouqué's position was now breaking open.

The fort on the rearward strongpoint of the **Thiemen-Berg** was now coming under attack from the small detachment of Lieutenant Colonel

LANDESHUT, 23 JUNE 1760

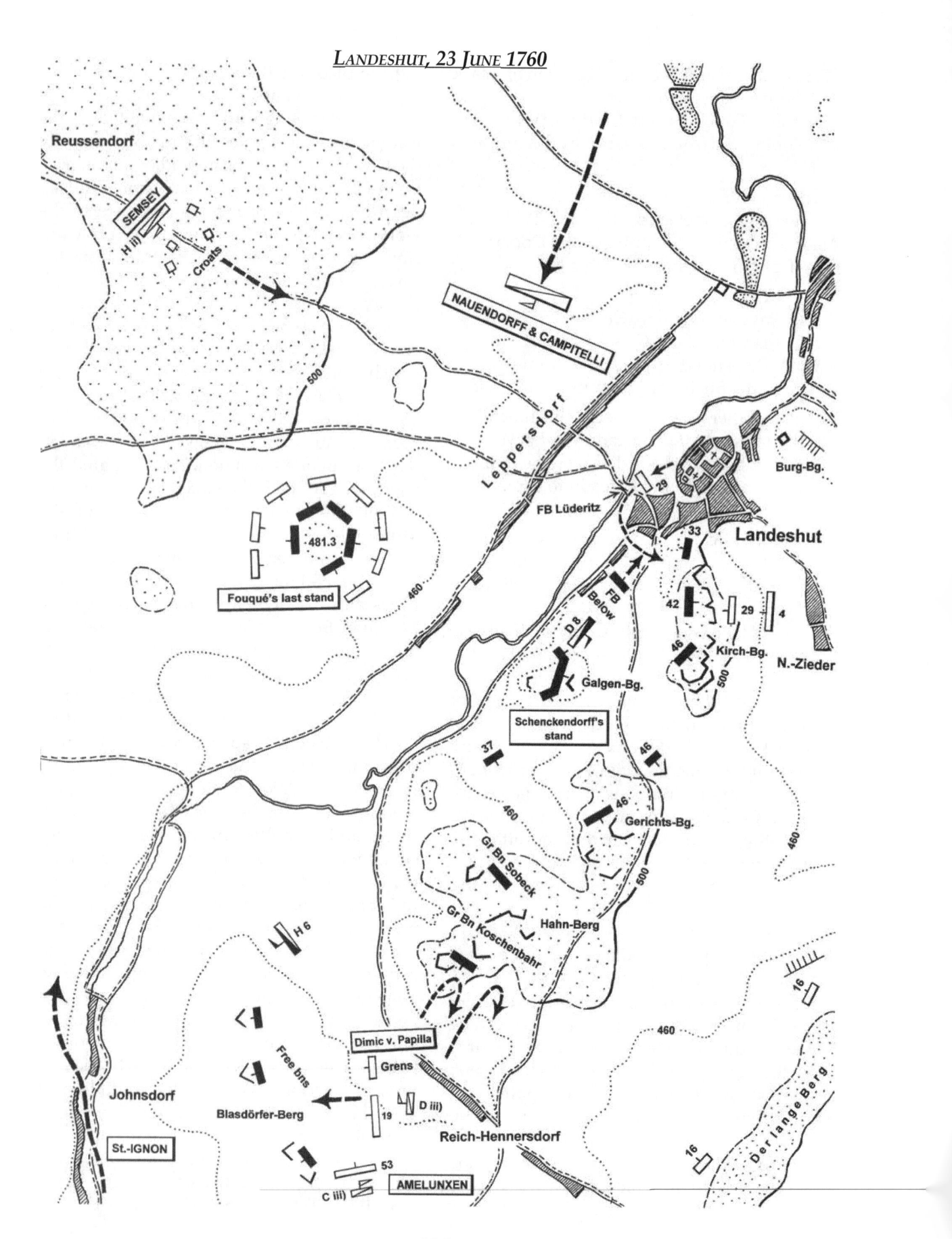

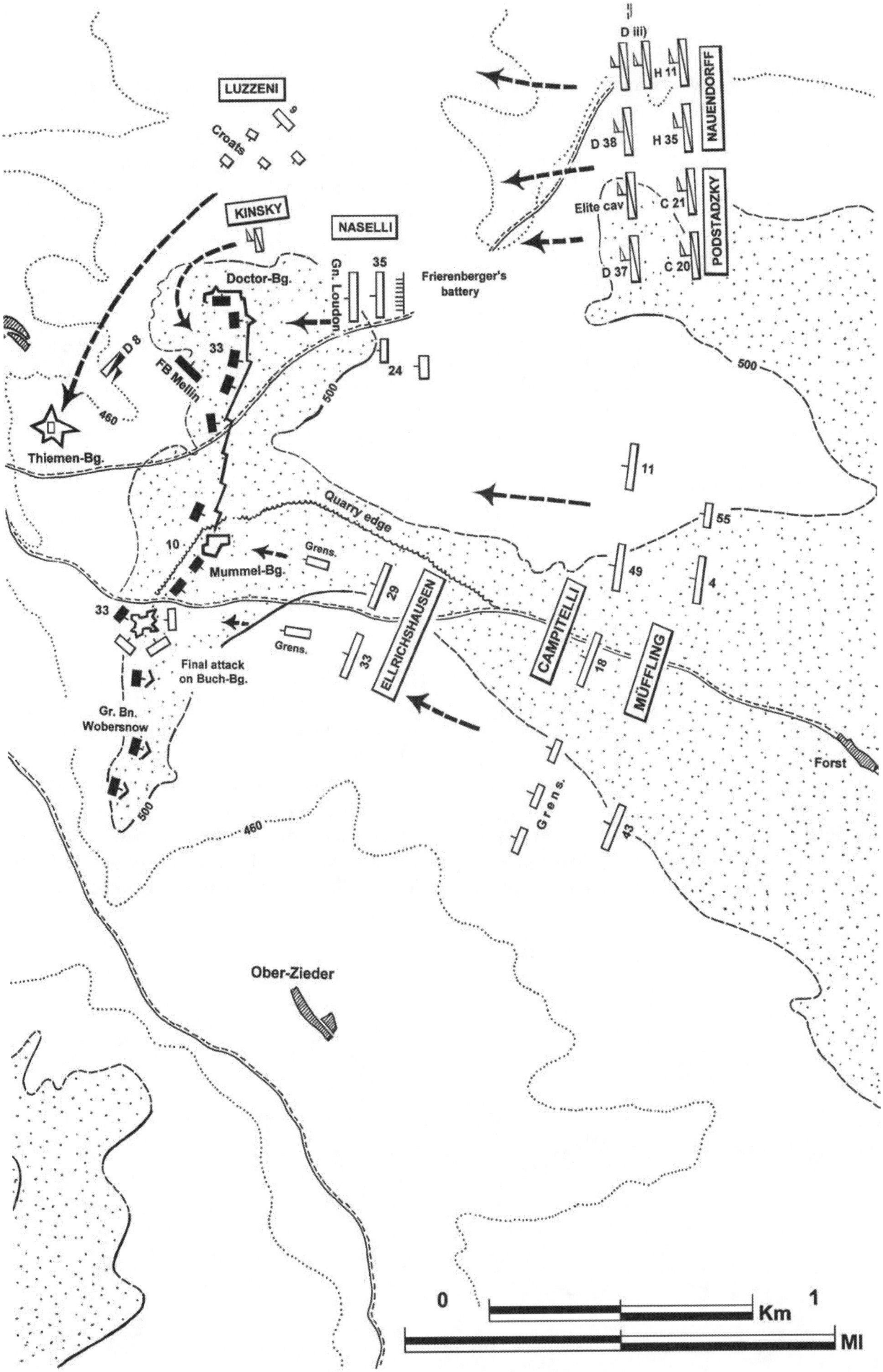

D iii)
H 11
NAUENDORFF
LUZZENI
Croats
D 38
H 35
KINSKY
NASELLI
Elite cav
C 21
PODSTADZKY
35
Gn. Loudon
Doctor-Bg.
Frierenberger's battery
D 37
C 20
D 8
33
FB Mellin
24
500
460
Thiemen-Bg.
11
Quarry edge
55
10
Mummel-Bg.
Grens.
49
4
29
ELLRICHSHAUSEN
CAMPITELLI
33
18
MÜFFLING
Grens.
33
Final attack on Buch-Bg.
Gr. Bn. Wobersnow
Forst
Grens.
43
500
460
Ober-Zieder
0
1
Km
MI

Luzzeni (the Liccaner, Ottocaner and Oguliner Croats, and one battalion of Los Rios [9]), while the main body of Loudon's right wing flooded over the collapsing Prussian defences in front. Major Joseph Graffenstein of the Nádasdy Hussars led the advance guard of Nauendorff's brigade of cavalry, which broke every attempt by the Prussians to re-form, while *GFWM.* Ellrichshausen with his infantry surmounted the heights and gave such vigorous support that 'this effort by itself contributed mightily to the success of the action; and, although he received a pretty dangerous wound in the head he remained in command all through the fight and kept up a relentless pursuit of the enemy with the grenadiers.'[56] Scattered companies of the regiment of Fouqué were left holding the line of earthworks which connected the Doctor-Berg and the Mummel-Berg, and this position was overcome in its turn by *FML.* Campitelli with the second line of Austrian infantry.

Now that the Mummel-Berg, the Buch-Berg and the Thiemen-Berg had fallen, the Austrians were free to push the few hundred yards downhill against the little **Burg-Berg** and Landeshut town. The grenadier captain Wilhelm Count Lacy relates that 'a Prussian captain had been ordered to come to the help of that work with a couple of hundred troops. The fog was very dense, and I had scarcely set off towards Landeshut with my hundred men than we encountered one another almost at the distance of bayonet-thrust. As soon as the enemy captain recognised my people, he called out for quarter and ordered his men to lay down their weapons. I seized him by the lapels, and, because his troops had taken up their muskets instead of throwing them down, my men presented their weapons and made a general discharge which killed and wounded a great many of them, whereupon the others fled in disorder.'[57]

While the main assault was prospering so well on the Austrian right, *FML.* Wolfersdorff ran into repeated difficulties with his subsidiary attack to the south. To make the best show he had divided his forces to assault the works on the **Blasdörfer-Berg** from two directions:

—a left-flanking force (Lieutenant Colonel Amelunxen: two battalions of Simbschen fusiliers [53], two squadrons of Alt-Modena Cuirassiers [Ciii)] making the long trek from the Faule-Brücke across swampy hollows to attack the flèches from the south

—a right-flanking force (Lieutenant Colonel Dimic von Papilla: one battalion of grenadiers, two battalions of Pálffy fusiliers [19], two squadrons of Althann Dragoons [Diii)]) to climb from the hollow of Reichhennersdorf to come at the Prussians from the east

Meanwhile *GFWM.* Saint-Ignon was to cross the Bober upstream to the left (west) bank and position his command (three battalions of Croats, two battalions of Preysach fusiliers [39], the Prince Albert Cuirassiers [C22] and the Pálffy

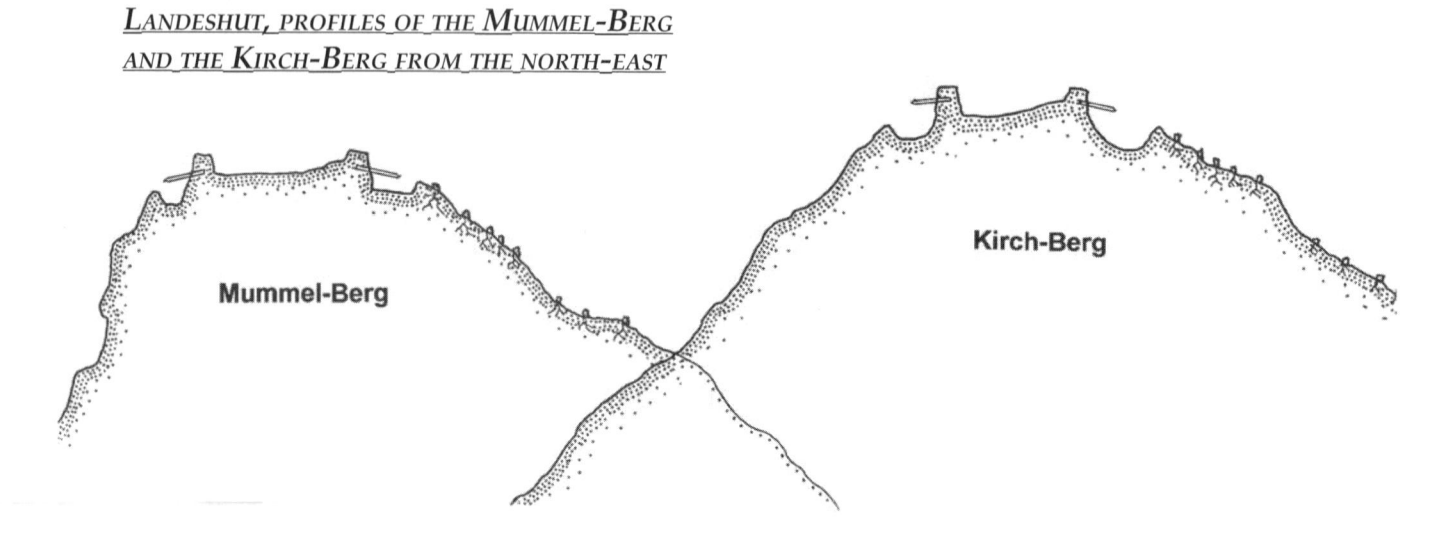

Landeshut, profiles of the Mummel-Berg and the Kirch-Berg from the north-east

Hussars [H16]) in the neighbourhood of Johnsdorf to cut off the Prussian retreat.

Wolfersdorff's troops were too few to make light work even of a diversionary attack, and they were faced with an uncommonly active enemy in the person of *GM*. Schenckendorff, who called down successive reinforcements from the right wing of Fouqué's main position. Three Prussian free battalions were already emplaced on the **Blasdörfer-Berg**, and with the help of the grenadier battalion of Sobeck they were able to beat off the first Austrian assaults. Dimic von Papilla finally succeeded in levering the Prussians by a deep flanking movement which he executed from the hollow of Reich-Hennersdorf under the cover of fog and darkness, and he and Amelunxen then turned their attention to the daunting Prussian position on the T-shaped **Hahn-Berg** ridge, on the southern flank of Fouqué's position proper. They threw back a further grenadier battalion, in this case that of Koschenbahr, but the enemy rallied with the help of two battalions of musketeers (Braun [37] and Bülow [46]), and the Prussians drove the Austrians back to Reich-Hennersdorf, taking two colours and a standard in the process. Wolfersdorff's lunge must be counted a success, in terms of the enemy units it diverted to the south, but the cost was disproportionately heavy.

It was now full daylight, and Fouqué, now that his two flanks were turned, was consolidating his defence around the craggy hillocks in the centre of his position. There was no room for the Prussian cavalry to do any good on this side of the Bober, and Fouqué ordered *GM*. Malachowsky to gather his fifteen squadrons and escape west by way of Reussendorf and Schmiedeberg.

The Prussian cavalry crossed the Bober above Landeshut, but found their way barred by a body of Austrian horse which had forded the little river downstream at Krausendorf and worked its way up the west bank. *GFWM*. Nauendorff was there with his twenty-seven squadrons of chevaulegers and hussars, and *GFWM*. Caramelli with the five squadrons of the Kollowrat Dragoons [D37], which he had brought up on his own initiative, suspecting that the enemy would be trying to get away.[58]

Malachowsky formed his cavalry into column and threw it at the Austrians, which gave rise to a running fight along the route of the intended escape. All but 900 of the Prussians were taken or killed, and Malachowsky himself captured after his horse was shot from under him. Among the trophies of the action the silver drums of the Alt-Platen Dragoons [D8] were captured by Captain Wilhelm Joseph Looz-Coswarem de Nyel of Kollowrat, who 'held the drummer's horse fast with his left hand, until his [the drummer's] regiment was totally destroyed, and the drummer hacked to pieces.'[59]

The rival infantry and artillery were meanwhile making ready for the final contests for the Kirch-Berg and the Galgen-Berg, which were the crags rising immediately to the south of Landeshut. The Austrians advanced fourteen heavy pieces to the Buch-Berg to bring these last redoubts under a frontal fire, and sited further batteries on the Burg-Berg and the northern end of the Langer-Berg to shoot up the Prussians from the two flanks.

Carl (Ludwig) Baron Ellrichshausen, highly-valued member of Loudon's team (Military Academy, Wiener Neustadt)

The Loudon fusiliers [IR 29] opened the final attack at six in the morning. Colonel Botta took four of the platoons on a right-flanking move by way of Landeshut town. He got the better of the free battalion of Lüderitz in a lively action by the stone bridge, and emerged by way of the Lutheran churchyard with the intention of coming at the fortifications of the **Kirch-Berg** by their northern flank. His progress was halted for a time when he was in turn assailed on his right flank by a battalion of Prussian volunteers (that of Below) which had been lurking in the enemy rear. Lieutenant Colonel Olivier Wallis meanwhile advanced the rest of the Loudon fusiliers up the short but steep slope from Zieder village. Wallis encountered a murderous fire, 'but I stood firm with my regiment, with the result that not only was Colonel Botta able to bring off his flank attack, but the regiment of Deutschmeister [4] (ordered by our general [Loudon] to march up from the line to support us) had the time to advance. Then the Deutschmeister and Loudon regiments climbed simultaneously to crown the hill and the fortifications, and drove the enemy from one piece of high ground after another.'[60]

Fouqué summoned Schenckendorff's command from the south, and rallied it with the remaining Prussian infantry on the low and conical **Galgen-Berg** just short of the meadows of the Bober. He rejected repeated invitations from Loudon to surrender, but he finally saw that his only chance of survival was to disengage, battalion by battalion, and make for the road to Schmiedeberg. Fouqué took off with the Below volunteers and one company of the regiment of Braun [37]. He waded the Bober above Landeshut, drove through the screen of Croats holding the houses on the far bank, and halted on one of the hills above Leppersdorf to wait for Schenckendorff to join him. Here he was overtaken by events.

According to Loudon it was Major Ripke of his general staff who first detected that the enemy were bent on making their escape, and who posted himself with an unspecified battalion and a number of squadrons on the heights of Schreibersdorf, which gave time for *GFWM*. Nauendorff to arrive on the scene with the Löwenstein and Sachsen-Gotha Chevaulegers [Ds31,28] and the Nádasdy and Bethlen Hussars [Hs11,35], so barring the way completely.

Some at least of the regimental commanders were acting on their own initiative, for Major Graffenstein describes how he arrived on the Galgen-Berg with the Nádasdy regiment, and saw what seemed to be two battalions of the enemy crossing the Bober. He spurred down the slope and captured up to thirty soldiers, who told him that Fouqué was just ahead with the others. The Nádasdy Hussars attacked the main body four times, but could make no impression, but 'I gave every unit I encountered the encouraging news that General Fouqué was here in person, and so at the fifth attack... the two battalions were finally overthrown.'[61]

By then the beleaguered Prussians were beset by all four regiments of Nauendorff's cavalry. The Prussians were fighting like madmen. 'Fouqué himself was badly wounded in the head, and he and his dead horse crashed to the ground. Several of his most valiant soldiers tried to save their commander, and fought on in a protective circle till they fell beside him. Fouqué received two further sabre cuts, in the arm and in the back, and an Austrian horseman was about to deal him the coup de grace when our hero was saved by the extraordinary loyalty of an ordinary groom, Trautschke by name, who threw himself on his master and received the blows that were intended for him.' Fouqué was rescued by Colonel Carl Voith von Salzburg of the Löwenstein Chevaulegers, who brought up his parade horse to have him carried away. 'He refused, saying "I would only ruin your fine saddlery." Voith replied, "no, it would gain enormously from being stained with the blood of a hero!"'[62]

Voit had Fouqué's wounds dressed by a surgeon of the corps of Beck, which was now arriving on the scene from Schmiedeberg. 'A certain officer, who was not worthy to undo the laces of Fouqué's shoes, was... churlish or shameless enough to taunt that worthy commander about the defeat of his corps. All the honourable officers who were present now took offence, and reproached him from his thoughtless words. "Let him be," said Fouqué, "you know how it goes in war: today it's my turn, tomorrow it's yours!'"[63]

The last troops to remain on the Galgen-Berg were those of the infantry regiment of Bülow [46] under the command of *GM.* Schenckendorff, who held his ground until he believed Fouqué was well on his way, and then tried to effect his escape. He was dismounted and captured before he could reach the Bober. His men forded the stream and beat their way through the swarming cavalry to the vicinity of Reussendorf, where they encountered 150 Croats and 300 Splényi Hussars [Hii)] under Major Semsey. These people were leading the advance of the corps of Beck, who had been summoned by Loudon to block any escape by Fouqué to the west.

The Prussians formed square and delivered a well-aimed fire, but were finally overcome by Semsey's Croats and hussars, who came at them from the front, and by Loudon's cavalry who arrived to take them in the flanks and rear. 'Overwhelmed by the general onslaught the men threw aside their muskets and called out "quarter!" But what a scene followed! Most of these brave, but now defenceless men now fell victim to the swords of our undisciplined warriors ... Some indeed tried to spare these helpless troops, but others, wild and unrestrained like their horses, thrust and hacked at all who came within reach of their swords.'[64]

Semsey reported that the victory was complete by eight in the morning.[65] Loudon's corps had a reputation for running out of control, and the final act was the sack of Landeshut, which left twelve of the townspeople dead and hundreds injured.

The campaign and battle of Landeshut exemplify Loudon's style of generalship with particular clarity. Out of close contact with the enemy, Loudon could be a pathetic creature, subject to paralysis, fits of panic, and almost hourly vacillations. There was a marked contrast with the ways of the purposeful Lacy, which sprang from constant and exact calculation.

When Loudon committed himself to action, it could be in an impulsive and unpredictable manner, but here his instincts were channelled by his excellent chief of staff *GFWM.* Ernst Friedrich Giannini. Like Lacy, Loudon was clever at moving his heavy guns forward to support his infantry, but there the resemblance in tactics came to an end. Whereas Lacy aimed his forces at the enemy by tightly-packed columns (Hochkirch, Maxen), Loudon at Landeshut swamped and overwhelmed his opponent by multiple lines advancing on broad frontages. Here, as at Kunersdorf, he tucked his cavalry away in a mass behind his right wing, ready to intervene with irresistible force to complete his victory. He was the first commander to exploit to the full the potential of Austria's new category of light horse, when he brigaded his fifteen squadrons of chevaulegers (Löwenstein and Sachsen-Gotha) together with two regiments of hussars (Nádasdy and Bethlen) to form a total of twenty-squadrons which were able to move at speed to block the escape of the Prussians.

Loudon had good reason to be pleased with the way his corps had behaved. Every provision of his plan had been carried out to the letter, and 'the troops fought with unsurpassable concert and courage. One unit would support the other without the slightest delay, as the enemy commander Fouqué was willing to testify in their praise... Lieutenant Colonel Rouvroy did particularly well, and not only managed the artillery most effectively, but supported me actively by word and deed. I freely admit that without his help and assistance it would have been difficult to attain so complete a victory.'[66] The last phrases reveal that generosity of spirit which attracted such devotion, and Loudon, Giannini, Rouvroy and the others were to remain part of a close-knit team.

Loudon's victory had a symbolic importance which made it something more than the elimination of just another enemy corps, like that of Finck at Maxen, or Diericke at Meissen. *GL.* Heinrich de la Motte Fouqué was the son of a Huguenot refugee, and had been able to give his hatred of the Catholic Church full expression in the course of the eighteen years (1742-60) he had ruled the fortress town and county of Glatz as governor, or rather as a virtual viceroy. He abolished the many feast days which had been enjoyed by the Catholic population, and his persecutions finally engendered a genuine religious martyr in the person of the priest Andreas Faulhaber, who was accused of assenting to a desertion plot. The seal of the confessional prevented Faulhaber from offering any kind of defence. Fouqué had him killed out of sight of the townspeople on 30 December 1757, then displayed him in a gibbet outside the Feld-Tor, where he remained until the place was liberated by the Austrians in 1760.

Fouqué had been a companion of Frederick since the 1730s, and after Winterfeldt had been killed in 1757 he was left as the king's sole confidant, entrusted with Frederick's innermost thoughts on statecraft and the conduct of war. Their correspondence was discovered among Fouqué's effects, and the Austrians learned that Frederick was now putting great faith in a great invasion of Hungary by the Turks. The king hoped that the Austrians would have to detach at least 60,000 men to counter the threat, which would give him the opportunity to invade Bohemia, while Fouqué entered Moravia 'to receive several thousand Tartars which would be sent by the Turks through Upper Hungary. Together with them he would spread devastation to the walls of Vienna.' From this the Austrians could deduce 'the extreme and godless nature of the king's intentions and plots.'[67]

Fouqué's restless and malignant spirit did not allow him to accept the comforts which he could have enjoyed in his time in Austrian captivity. His ceaseless complaints soon led to a deterioration in the conditions of officer prisoners as a whole, whether Prussian or Austrian, and exacerbated the bitterness of an already hard-fought war.

Loudon's siege and storm of Glatz, 21-26 July 1760

The Austrian plan of campaign for 1760, which was largely Loudon's own, was designed to assemble a mass of troops for offensive operations in Silesia. After his first hesitations Loudon had wiped out the main Prussian field corps on 23 June in the way we have just seen. The Austrians were already masters of the open country of the County of Glatz, and had gained the passages through the tangled Eulen-Gebirge to the Silesian plain by way of the passages of Silberberg and Wartha, and if they won the fortress-town of Glatz as well, they would have complete freedom to pass from north-east Bohemia to Lower Silesia.

Loudon had set his heart on reducing Glatz, over the objections of *FM.* Neipperg, the acting president of the *Hofkriegsrath*, who pointed to the dangers presented by the 'galleries and mines which riddled the rock, many of which had been driven by the engineer colonel Tello at my orders when… I commanded in Silesia.'[68] Loudon was adamant, for he made a detailed study of military topography (maps were his favourite reading), and he knew from men who had been working on the mines only recently that 'there are such wide intervals between them that you can march to the covered way by whole platoons without encountering a single one of them.'[69] Neipperg had to give way when, on 17 June, Their Imperial Majesties resolved 'quite positively' in favour of Loudon's enterprise.[70]

On 4 July Loudon set out from the scene of his victory at Landeshut, and after five days of continuous marching reached Eichholz (S.S.W of Liegnitz), which became his base for the next month. This was part of an agreed strategy whereby he would position himself deeper inside Lower Silesia. However the design on Glatz was far from being forgotten. On the 9th Daun in person met Loudon at Ottendorf, and as a result Loudon was to detach forces to build up a substantial force under *FML.* Draskovich, who was to lay siege to Glatz. Loudon wrote to his confidant Kaunitz a few days later 'that one of our main objectives at the present time is to support this siege. If the Russians approve the proposal which had been put to them, to besiege Breslau… I am confident that we will be able to deal the enemy as painful a blow as the one at Landeshut.'[71]

The main part of the fortress complex of Glatz lay on the left (west) side of the Silesian Neisse, and consisted of the small walled town, and the multiple ramparts of the Alte Festung which crowned the dominating hill to the north. A modern star fort, the Neue Festung, sprawled over the Schäfer-Berg on the far side of the river. The garrison of 3,200 troops was adequate in terms of numbers, but dangerously uneven in quality. Since 1757 the garrison regiment of Quadt von Wickeradt [Gar 8] had been forced to yield up 1,500 of its best men to the field army, and the gaps in its four battalions had been made up with deserters and forcibly-enlisted prisoners of war. The regiment of Fouqué [33] was just as untrustworthy, for it had been recruited in the County of Glatz, whose population for the most part detested their Prussian masters. The once-famous grenadier battalion of Nimschöffsky hardly came into the reckoning, for it was being reconstituted after the batterings it had received earlier in the war, which left the Magdeburg grenadier battalion of Unruh as the one fully effective unit in the garrison.

Now that Fouqué was a prisoner of the Austrians, the place was under the orders of the Piedmontese-born Lieutenant Colonel Barthomomaeus Marquis d'O, in his capacity as vice-commandant. D'O had served the Prussians since 1727. He had been wounded at Mollwitz, and he was now so swollen with dropsy that he could move or breathe only with difficulty. He was nevertheless a shrewd individual, valued by Fouqué for his management of military intelligence, and he was proof against a bribe which the Austrians now held out to him through *FML*. Caramelli. Loudon wrote to Kaunitz that d'O had refused to receive his countryman, 'but I have already learned through spies and deserters that the commandant is much concerned about the bad state of his troops, and particularly as he has few gunners in the place. The garrison is made up of thoroughly bad men, who are much inclined to mutiny, and show not the slightest enthusiasm for the defence. As for the townspeople, they long to be free of the Prussian yoke.'[72]

After weeks of blockade, *FML*. Joseph Casimir Draskovich signalled the opening of the formal attack when he dug a siege parallel to the north of the Alte Festung on the night of 20/21 July. The business was managed by the engineer captain Nikolaus Steinmetz, under the overall supervision of *GFWM*. Gribeauval. On the following night the Austrians began work on the batteries to accommodate the 114 pieces of heavy artillery which had been brought up from Brünn and Olmütz. On the third night of the siege, however, the Croats miscarried badly in an attempted coup de main against an outwork which ran for 300 yards along the ridge extending to the north of the Alte Festung. This relatively insignificant fortification had been held by just thirty-nine Prussian troops, and in their honour d'O renamed the work *der Kranich*, ('the Crane') after the fishing bird which was renowned for its vigilance.

The Austrians opened up with their artillery at first light on 26 July, and Loudon's trusted gunner Lieutenant Colonel Theodor Rouvroy concentrated the heaviest of his battering fire against the Schellenbauer half-bastion, which overlooked the town. At the same time the bombardiers wrought devastating damage by wrecking the wooden communication bridges between the works, and touching off explosions in the magazines in the Schellenbauer, the Böhmisches-Tor and the Kranich. The Prussian gunners abandoned their pieces, the infantry began to panic and desert, and Lieutenant Lettow was reduced to holding the Kranich with four men.

A large party of Austrian officers had been gathering in the left-hand section of the parallel, facing the Kranich. Loudon was there in person, together with Draskovich, Rouvroy, *GFWM*. Vogelsang and his adjutant Lieutenant Anton Ulrich Mylius, and two senior officers of the newly-founded *Sappeurs-Corps*—Major Joseph Bechardt and Captain Jacob Eghls. It was now seven in the morning. The harassing fire from the Kranich had fallen away, and deserters were making their way down towards the Austrians. Both Draskovich and Rouvroy afterwards claimed the credit for seeing an opportunity to take the work by storm. Loudon approved the enterprise, whereupon Vogelsang told young Mylius that this was the time to make himself a name.

Mylius took a party of fifty volunteers from the regiments of Andlau and Batthyány [57, 34], and formed them up to the left of the grenadiers of the regiment of Simbschen [53] and a further group of assorted grenadiers. The combined force climbed from the parallel, descended a gentle hollow, and rushed up the far slope and into the Kranich. They seized the flèche at the outer end of the work, and Mylius and his men pushed along the long communication line towards the Alte Festung. He records with some

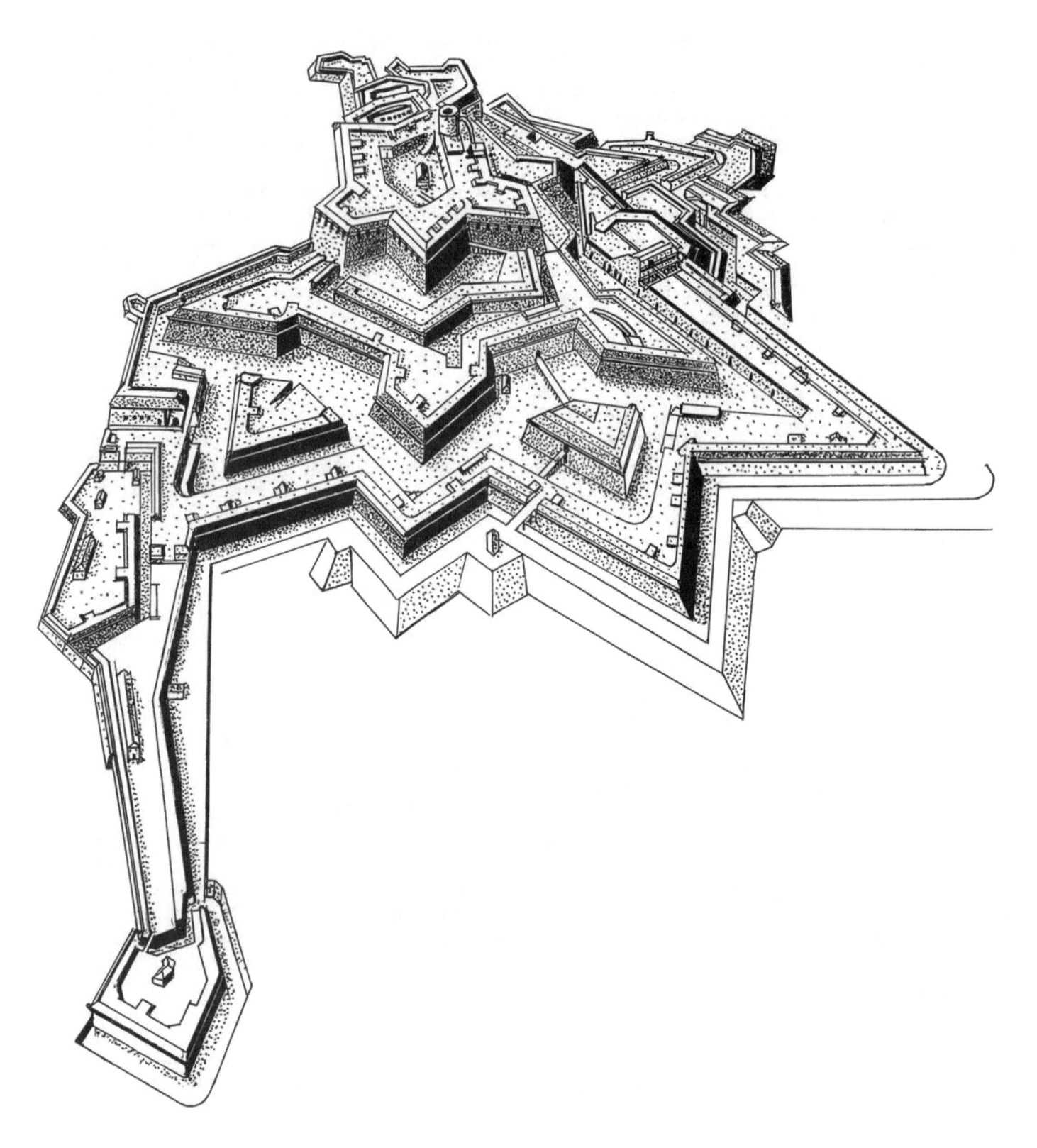

THE STORM OF THE ALTE FESTUNG, GLATZ, 26 JULY 1760
The donjon *crowning the hill is shown in its state as rebuilt after the war.
It is uncertain how far the Kranich was revetted in masonry in 1760.*

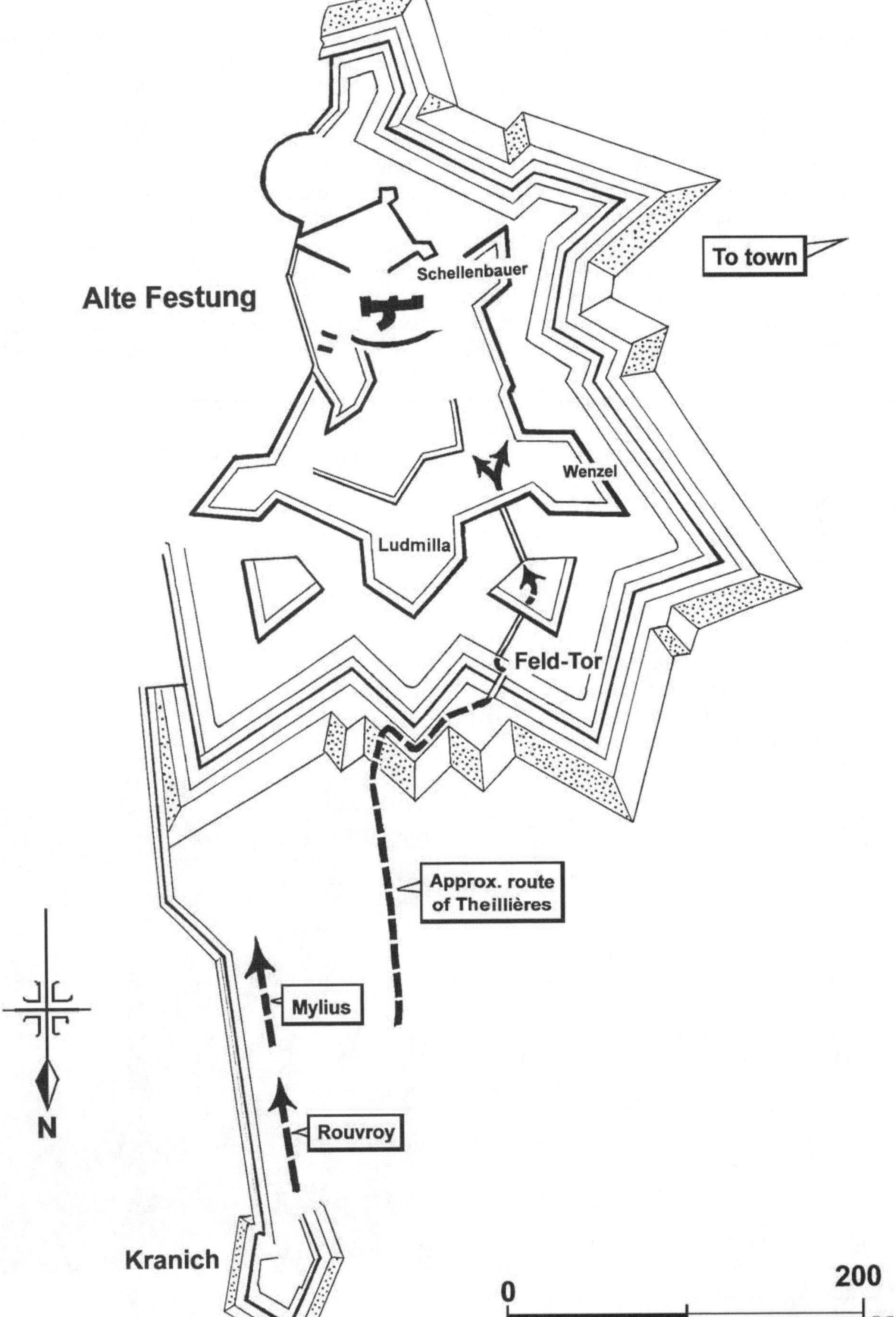

Alte Festung
Schellenbauer
To town
Wenzel
Ludmilla
Feld-Tor
Approx. route of Theillières
Mylius
Rouvroy
N
Kranich
0
200
M

annoyance that he was about to continue his advance and climb into the covered way when Lieutenant Colonel Rouvroy came up with a drummer to summon the fortress to surrender.[73]

The impetus was lost, and Rouvroy, his drummer and all the rest were taken off their guard by a fulminating counter-attack by a company of the Unruh grenadiers, who cleared the whole length of the Kranich and consolidated in the flèche. The lieutenant colonel of the regiment of Toscana, Franz Baron Theillières, happened to be close to the siege batteries at this moment, and he ordered the howitzers to lob shells into these Prussian heroes, who were packed together and made an excellent target. A corporal of the regiment of Salm [14] led a party forward at a run to see what was going on, and signalled that the Prussians were wavering under the ordeal. Major O'Donnell of the regiment of Angern [49] was present when Rouvroy proposed to Loudon that the time had come for another assault. 'Herr Loudon told him that he first wished to wait for General Harsch, upon which I took the liberty of saying that there was no time to lose, and that we must seize the opportunity. He finally gave way.'[74]

Major Bechard and a group of fifty volunteers advanced against the flèche and the communication, while Rouvroy and a similar party made for the covered way of the Alte Festung behind. The decisive blow was dealt by Lieutenant Colonel Theillières, who looked to the right from the parallel and noticed that a number of deserters were leaving the Alte Festung by the Feld-Tor. He at once commandeered 200 men from Captain Swoboda's section of the trench, ran with them up the glacis, jumped the palisade sword in hand, and continued to the right along the glacis to the Feld-Tor, where he found that the gates of both the envelope (outer rampart) and the main rampart had been left open.

The Prussian grenadiers saw that their only avenue of retreat was threatened, and made for the Feld-Tor in their turn. Vogelsang and Rouvroy were at their heels with a grenadier company of Toscana, a battalion of Andlau [57] and a number of volunteers, and a mob of intermingled Austrians and Prussians crashed through the outer gate, across the bridge to the ravelin, and finally across a further bridge and so through the gateway of the rampart and arrived in the interior of the Alte Festung. It was probably at that moment that a sixty year-old Catholic corporal of the regiment of Quadt, Philipp Scharff of Nassau, 'being well-affected to the Imperial and Royal Service, and wishing to facilitate the entry of the Austrian troops, had the drummer beat *Appel* (fall back!), whereupon the Prussian officers did their best to put a bullet through his head.'[75] A number of Prussian diehards kept up a heavy fire from the ramparts, but the forcibly-enlisted Austrian prisoners in the regiment of Quadt were throwing away their muskets and coming across in swarms to their old comrades, whereupon Colonel Quadt and Lieutenant Colonel Knobelsdorff beat *chamade* and yielded the entire Alte Festung, 'for no other reason than cowardice,' according to d'O.[76]

Glatz town from the Alte Festung

Theillières did not bother with formalities. 'A Prussian miner had already come to us, and without further ado I went with him to the principal mine, extracted the three narrow fuze hoses from the charge, and bent all my energies to extinguish the considerable conflagration which had broken out in the ditch by the mine entrances. The timbers had been catching fire, and so I had them thrown away, and I had carts brought up with water to make sure the fire was put out completely.'[77]

The Prussian reserve had been ordered up from the town to bring relief to the Alte Festung, but the troops turned back with cries of '*Herr Jesus!*' and other indications of alarm when they learned that the Austrians had already broken into the defences. The commandant Lieutenant Colonel d'O and his chief engineer, Colonel Wrede, a veteran of forty years' service, had been lagging behind, and they were stranded outside the town when the fugitives streamed down from the fortress, followed by Austrian grenadiers who now made them prisoner. Second Lieutenant Charles Hubert Henry had left his post in the parallel to see the happenings for himself, and describes the collapse of the Prussian resistance. He ran towards the town and 'found Baron Theillières… at the head of a couple of hundred men, who were helping each other up with their muskets to surmount a door behind which they had a good idea that some of the enemy were hiding. I kept on alone, turned to my left and crossed a bridge which led me straight to the town. There was nobody to be seen except a number of officers who were laying down their arms of their own accord. The first three I encountered wished to deliver their swords to me, but I told them that an officer of the general staff was coming up behind and would be delighted to receive them. And in fact it was not long before I saw Baron Theillières at the head of his detachment descend from the Alte Festung, and take up position in the square. A number of battalions followed, and very soon took the whole town under occupation.'[78] Probably mindful of the sack of Landeshut, Theillières at once posted standing patrols to prevent plunder, and placed the Arsenal, the records and the officers' effects under guard.

The check at Breslau, 30 July - 4 August 1769

Loudon's next target was Breslau, the fortified capital city of Silesia. Both Loudon and Vienna had feared that the Russians might reach the place first, and either provoke the garrison into offering a fanatical resistance, or storm the city and leave it waste. These concerns were allayed when the Austrian representatives at Russian headquarters reported that the Russians had still to assemble at Posen. However it was important to take advantage of the fact that Prince Henry and King Frederick were still absent from Silesia, and Loudon now moved with all possible speed.

The Austrian forces converged on Breslau from the south and west, and on 30 July Loudon brought the city under investment on both sides of the Oder. The contest was going to be a battle of wills, rather than of technical resources. Time was so short, and Loudon had moved so fast, that it had been impossible for him to bring the heavy ordnance from Glatz. A formal siege was therefore out of the question. On his side, the Prussian major general Bogislav Friedrich Tauentzien commanded some 5,600 troops, which would have been a respectable garrison for a modern and purpose-built fortress, but was not equal to putting up a sustained defence of the bulky earthen bastions and ramparts of the city.

On the evening of 31 July Loudon was given a first clue that he was dealing with a particularly tough individual when Tauentzien set the suburbs on fire to deny cover to the Austrians, and refused a first summons outright. All the same Loudon knew that the garrison was weak, and on 1 August he employed a threat of brute force 'in order to show how mischievously wrong he was to think of putting up a defence.'[79] He told Tauentzien that Breslau was 'just a commercial and trading city,' and that if he were so unreasonable as to try to hold out, the Austrians would be justified in reducing the place to a heap of ashes.[80] To reinforce his moral pressure, Loudon wrote separately to the civil authorities to inform them that he had forty-five mortars ready to hurl their bombs into the city.

Nothing was heard from the town fathers. Tauentzien's reply came in writing, and this forceful message was probably drafted by the dramatist Lessing, his secretary from 1760 to 1765. He pointed out that the Austrians themselves had regarded Breslau as a tenable fortress when they defended it against the Prussians after the battle of Leuthen, and now he and his garrison would hold out to the last drop of their blood, as befitted brave men.

As a substitute for his mortars, which were actually far away in Glatz, Loudon deployed his howitzers in three batteries, one in the Ohlau Suburb to the east, one between the villages of Neudorf and Gabitz to the south-west, and the third in front of the Nicolai Suburb. The fire opened at nine in the evening of 1 August, but ceased at midnight, by when the garrison had lost only four men killed and ten wounded. Loudon wrote to Kaunitz on the 2nd that his real intention had been to drive the enemy from the ramparts, and then take the place by storm. The assault was never put into effect, and on the same day Loudon sent a third summons into Breslau, which suggested that he might fall in with whatever terms Tauentzien would propose. Loudon hoped that his more conciliatory tone might produce some results, but this summons too was rejected.

Exterior events now supervened. The day had still not run its course when Loudon was told that the Russians had marched only as far as Zduny in Poland, and would need more than a week to arrive at Breslau. The allies, instead of being too close to Breslau for Austrian purposes, were therefore altogether too distant. Loudon therefore wrote to the Russians to ask them to send Lieutenant General Chernyshev in advance with up to 30,000 troops.

The other news concerned Prince Henry. Successive reports told him that he had marched from Glogau and across the Katzbach to Parchwitz, a name which bore evil memories of the campaign of Leuthen. Loudon then learned that Saltykov had agreed to release Chernyshev, but with no more than 12,000 troops, and without any pontoons to enable him to cross the Oder.

Loudon judged that it was impossible for him to stay any longer in front of Breslau. On 4 August he concentrated his forces and marched south-west towards Striegau, from where he hoped he could reach out to the main army under Daun, 'and force the king to a decisive action.'[81] Loudon's stroke against Breslau had been 'essentially a partisan raid *à la Trenck*, and was criticised by friend and foe alike. It was like one of those frightening meteors which spread panic but do no harm.'[82]

The massing of forces in Silesia and the Battle of Liegnitz, August 1760

Events now moved with such speed that within a matter of days nearly one quarter of a million troops—Austrians, Prussians and Russians—converged in central Silesia to bring about, in numerical terms, the crisis of the Seven Years War. The underlying reason was a change in the mechanics of the conflict. For campaign after campaign the rival forces had been distributed in such a way as to bring about a rough equilibrium of strength between the rival forces in what had become the two main theatres, in Saxony and in Silesia.

Now the balance was upset. Loudon had annihilated the greater part of the Prussian forces in Silesia at Landeshut on 23 June, and was threatening to gobble up the uncovered fortresses one by one. No less significantly the Russians, after repeated delays, were now making towards the central Silesian stretch of the Oder, and for the second time in the war had an opportunity to act in immediate concert with the Austrians. The mastery of Silesia might now lie with whatever party was able to mass the greater concentration of forces in this critical part of the world.

With his 37,000 men Prince Henry was superior in numbers to Loudon, but he would find it difficult to withstand Saltykov's 74,000 Russians, let alone any combination of Russians and Austrians, unless he received support from his brother Frederick with any disposable troops from the Saxon theatre. If the king indeed committed himself along the road to Silesia, Daun's priorities were to get to the province before him, join Loudon (thus bringing together an initial concentration of more than 90,000 Austrians) and bar Frederick's way to Henry. This considerable preponderance of forces would become well-nigh irresistible, if Daun could then proceed to the second stage of the concentration, that of operating with the Russians, which would group more than 165,000 allied troops in central Silesia.

On the stormy night of 29/30 July Frederick broke contact with the Austrians at Dresden and marched down the left bank of the Elbe. He left up to 12,000 troops to guard that side of the river, then crossed with the remaining 30,000 to the right bank below Meissen on 1 August. Two days later he marched east to Königsbrück, and the race to Silesia began in earnest.

Daun told off 25,000 Austrians and *Reichstruppen* to remain in Saxony, while he prepared the rest of the army for the march to Silesia. Daun and the main army would take advantage of the highway which led east from Dresden by way of Bautzen and Görlitz, while *FZM.* Lacy's mobile corps of 20,000 men was detailed to shadow Frederick in the usual way. It was disappointing to learn that Loudon would have to abandon the siege of Breslau, but at least Loudon would now be free to join Daun somewhere in south-western Silesia.

The opposing armies prosecuted their eastward marches through the same kind of appalling heat which had obtained one month earlier. Frederick drove his men without a single day's rest to reach Bunzlau in Silesia on 7 August. Taking the easier southern route, Daun reached Reichenbach on 4 August, Lauban inside Silesia on the 5th, and the celebrated old Prussian camp at Schmottseiffen on the 6th. Both armies needed rest urgently, and Daun was ready to cede a marginal lead to Frederick as long as his own troops were in a good condition to make the final bound to gain the tactical barrier of the Katzbach. River barriers are very difficult to defend over the long term, but this example now fitted better than some. 'The Katzbach rises in the mountains at Schönau, flows by way of Goldberg and Liegnitz and enters the Oder just below Parchwitz, opposite Leubus. It is really no more than a stream, which can be waded everywhere, but it is difficult for an army to cross, on account of its marshy and wooded banks... especially when it is defended by another army more than twice as strong.'[83]

Having abandoned his enterprise on Breslau, Loudon marched west to Neu-Sorgau on 6 August, and to Striegau on the 7th, just two marches short of the Katzbach. On that day a Russian hussar (who was looking for Loudon) ran into Daun's army, and reported that Major General Totleben and a detachment of Russian troops had already crossed the Oder from Leubus. Frederick's camp at Bunzlau was a little deeper into Silesia than was Daun's at Schmottseiffen, however the westward bend of the upper Katzbach worked in favour of the Austrians, and Daun cancelled any remaining Prussian advantages by getting his troops on the move first. At seven in the morning of 9 August Loudon arrived behind the Katzbach at Seichau, and by four in the afternoon the main Austrian army came up on his left, having crossed to the right bank of the stream just ahead of the Prussian advance guard, which was led by Frederick in person.

For the next three days Frederick ranged up and down the Katzbach, seeking an opportunity to slip past the Austrians and join his brother Henry in the heart of Silesia. At five in the morning of 10 August he set off down the left bank in an attempt to work around Daun's right flank. However the Austrians were on a high state of alert, and within minutes their columns were moving down the far bank. That morning was remembered for one of the great spectacles of the war, since the multiple columns of the Austrian and Prussian armies were marching on parallel courses on their respective sides of the Katzbach. The Austrians were observing their intervals exactly, for at any moments their units might have to wheel into fighting formation, and 'it is difficult to conceive of a more magnificent or entrancing sight than that of the orderly march of such a numerous, picked and combat-ready army.'[84]

On their way the Austrians had to ford the Wüthender ('raging') Neisse, but they marched with such precision and speed that by eleven in the morning they had gained a clear lead over the Prussians, and Frederick had to give up the race short of Liegnitz. The king decided to try his luck upstream, and at eleven at night of 11/12th August he broke camp and made for his intended crossing points between Kroitsch and Kopatsch. When he approached the stream he was surprised to see extensive camp fires stretching across the heights on the far side.

Lacy had in fact come up to join the main Austrian army, and now brought his artillery into action to sweep the crossings.

Not even the Austrian hosts could stretch themselves out indefinitely, and after his first repulse Frederick continued his march upstream and at first light on the 12th he found an unguarded crossing, at Niederau immediately above Goldberg. He passed unopposed. In this emergency the safest course for Lacy would have been to recoil to his right and consolidate on Daun's army, but he knew what was at stake in the campaign and instead rallied his shaken troops directly in front of the Prussians at Kolbnitz, so as to deny them the way to Jauer. In this vulnerable situation Lacy was saved by a rapid about-turn on the part of the main Austrian army, and towards the end of the day Frederick found that he was boxed in by Daun to his left as well as Lacy to his front.

At nine in the evening of 12 August Frederick began to march back to the left bank of the Katzbach. In the course of the next day all the troops of the main armies trailed back to their old positions—Frederick to his camp just above Liegnitz, and Daun, Lacy and Loudon to the wooded heights on the right bank. The only satisfaction which Frederick could derive from this episode came from the Möhring Hussars [H3], who had captured the personal baggage of Lacy at Goldberg. The king returned it to Lacy under the escort of a trumpeter, 'who was also under orders to bring back a most pretty and demure Tyrolean girl of Lacy's suite.'[85]

Daun had finally succeeded in out-marching Frederick to the heart of Silesia, and even now he was keeping the king's army (30,000) penned up on the west bank of the Katzbach with no

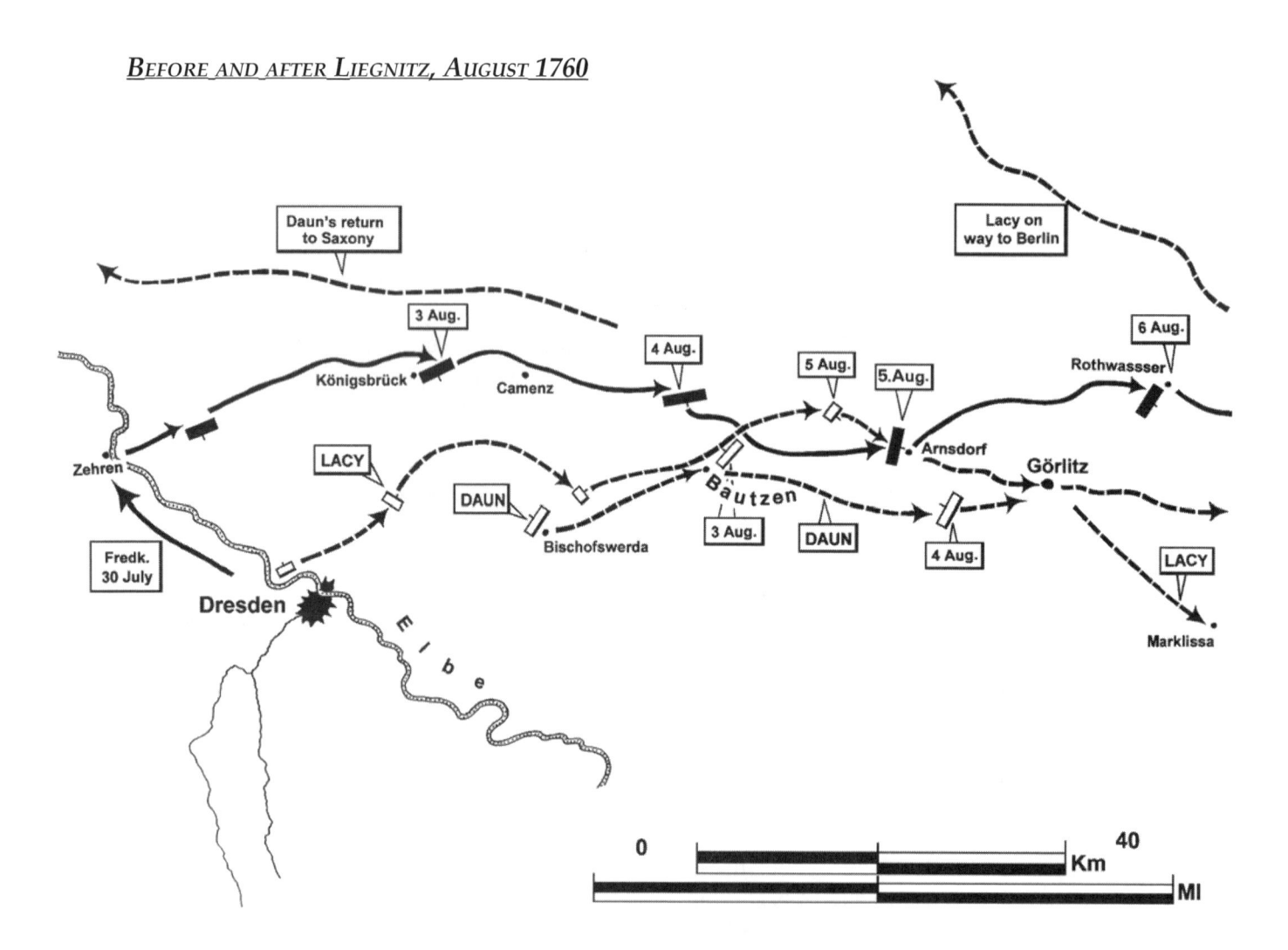

Before and after Liegnitz, August 1760

apparent prospect of breaking through to join Prince Henry (37,100) near Breslau. Towards the middle of the month, however, Daun could no longer resist the pressures that were forcing him to take more positive action.

The Russians were present in great force (74,000) only about twenty miles away beyond the Oder, and on 13 August Loudon travelled to Saltykov's headquarters to try to persuade him to cross to the left bank. All that Saltykov would agree for the moment was to send Lieutenant General Zakhar Chernyshev across the river with a reinforced corps of 20,000 men. The train of pontoons had still to reach the crossing point at Auras, and although Chernyshev crossed on the same day, it took ten hours for his corps to file across the single bridge of boats. Arrived on the left bank of the Oder, Chernyshev marched only as far as Gross-Biese, and halted there to await developments. Something more positive was needed to stir the Russian main army into movement.

The urgings from Vienna were more insistent still. Maria Theresa wrote to Daun that the continuing delays could be more damaging than a lost battle, 'whereas a single successful blow would guarantee the junction with the Russians, and establish the welfare of my house for the present and for the time to come... I am aware that the outcome of a battle is always uncertain, and so for your consolation I take the responsibility upon myself, and pledge my word in advance that not the slightest responsibility will fall upon you, whatever the outcome of the enterprise.'[86]

Whether he was going into action willingly or not, Daun cannot be accused of any lack of ambition in his consequent scheme of attack for

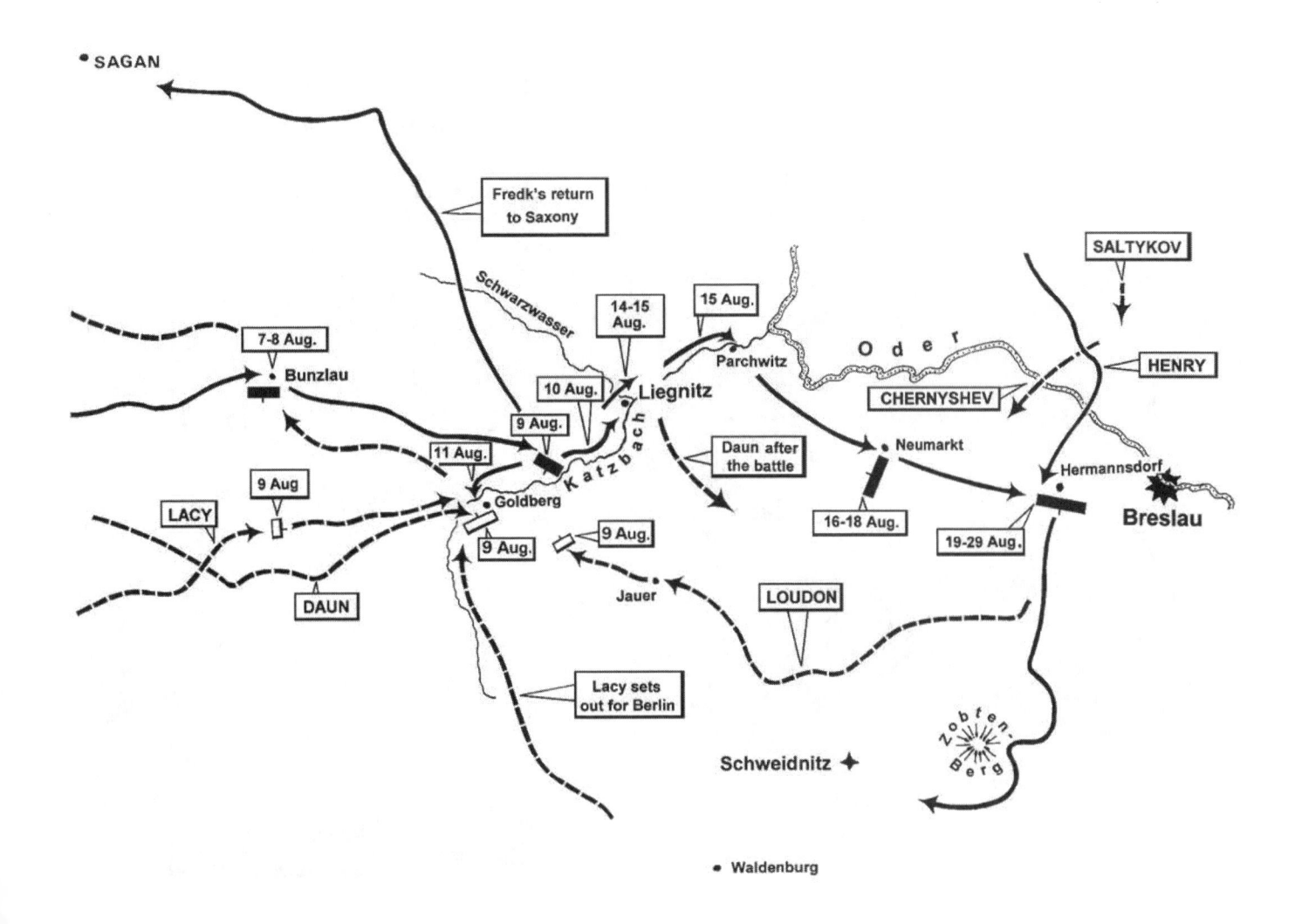

15 August, 'which aimed at nothing less than the complete destruction of the king and his army.'[87] In essence he planned to attack the Prussian army outside Liegnitz from three directions:

1. The main force would pass the Katzbach upstream at or near Dohnau, form an eastward-facing front, and attack the right wing of the royal army

2. Lacy was to cross the Katzbach upstream to Kroitsch, and march way of Lobendau to an attacking position behind the rear of the Prussian right

3. Loudon would cross the Katzbach downstream at the Furt-Mühle opposite Bienowitz, then march up the left bank to hold a blocking position on the high ground in the vicinity of Hummel and Pfaffen-Berg

Meanwhile a diversionary force (Beck and Wolfersdorff) would extend along the right bank of the Katzbach from Dohnau downstream 'to draw the... attention of the enemy upon themselves, but not to become embroiled before the Prussians are forced to give way.' Daun enjoined strict security, and forbade any shouting or smoking.[88]

All of these particulars were based on the reasonable assumption that Frederick would remain overnight in his densely-packed camp on the near side of Liegnitz. However the king had no intention of awaiting the Austrian onslaught, which he was sure was coming. He would instead fall back under cover of darkness to a new position on the far (north) side of the town, and then make a fourth attempt to cross the Katzbach, this time downstream and just short of the Oder at Parchwitz.

In the afternoon of 14 August Frederick settled down for a few hours of rest in his lodgings in a suburb of Liegnitz. He was awakened in the evening by a party of officers who brought before him an Austro-Irish lieutenant whose name is rendered variously as

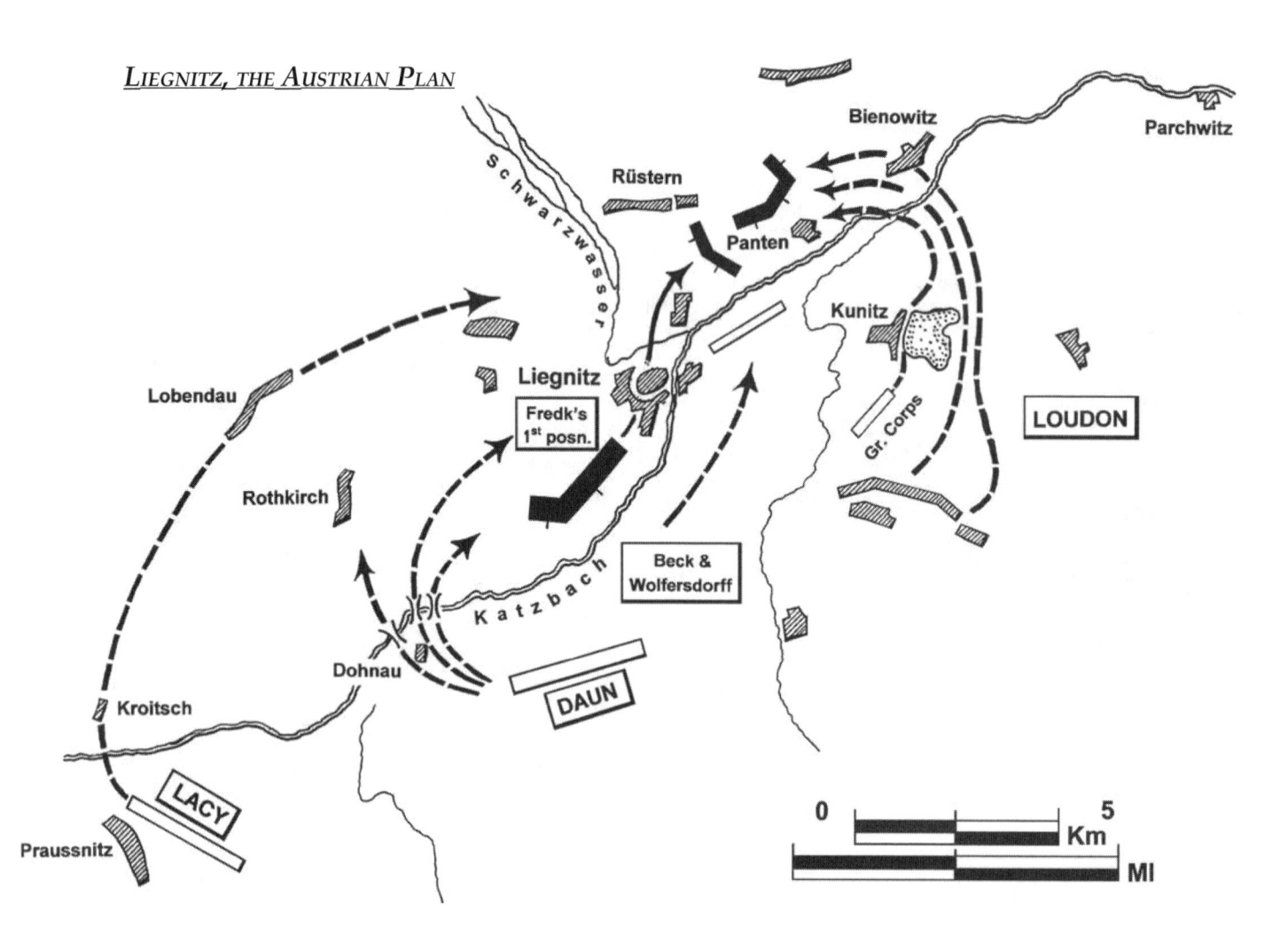

LIEGNITZ, THE AUSTRIAN PLAN

'Weidt,' 'Wiesse' or 'Wyse.' This person had been cashiered from the O'Donnell Cuirassiers, but 'under the pretence of piety' had managed to insinuate himself into the graces of Daun,[89] and continued to hang about the Austrian camp. Weidt, or whatever we ought to call him, was noisy and drunk, but the officers plied him with tea and water, and he eventually sobered up sufficiently to declare that the Prussians were about to be attacked by Daun and Lacy. Frederick knew that already, and was preparing to march,[90] and he found that Weidt knew nothing of any role which might have been assigned to Loudon, who had not attended the verbal briefing and who had received his instructions in writing. After the battle Frederick sent Weidt to Prince Ferdinand of Brunswick, and added the note that 'this recommendation is worth only the value you choose to put upon it.'[91]

Although it was high summer, the weather had turned cold and dark, and the armies were swept by a fine rain. Unseen by the Austrians, Frederick struck his camp at eight in the evening of 14 August, and marched through and around Liegnitz to his new position on a low, bushy plateau to the north-east of the town.

Liegnitz, 15 August 1760
a) Corps of Loudon
c. 24,000; 20,000 infantry, 4,400 cavalry, including the 5,673 elite infantry and cavalry of the *corps de reserve*. However Loudon put his forces actually engaged as 'scarcely 14,000 men under arms'
Losses: 8,498; 1,408 killed, 2,359 wounded, 4,731 prisoners and missing
b) Other Austrian forces
Main army under Daun: 33,900
Lacy's corps: c. 18,150
Detachments of Ried, Beck and Wolfersdorff: c. 16,000
c) Prussian forces engaged against Loudon
15,800; 11,600 infantry, 4,200 cavalry
Losses: c. 3,420; 637 killed, 2,535 wounded, c. 250 missing and prisoners, with ten colours and one standard
d) Other Prussian forces
c. 14,300

According to the *Disposition* Loudon was to take no more active role than to pass the Katzbach below Liegnitz and take up a position well to the rear of the supposed location of the Prussians—in other words to act as the 'anvil' to the 'hammers' of Daun and Lacy. His troops set off from Koischwitz in the drizzle between eight and ten in the evening of 14 August. The heads of columns had to cover only about three miles to arrive at the Katzbach, and marching north by way of Kunitz the corps reached the three bridges at the Furt-Mühle in the early hours of the 15th. The two battalions of the Green Loudon Grenadiers crossed the bridges and hastened along the winding path on the far side to secure the village of Bienowitz, which overlooked the water meadows. The Althann Dragoons [Diii)] were the first unit of the main force to make the passage, and together with the green-coated grenadiers they covered the crossing of the rest of the corps.

Arrived on the left bank of the Katzbach, Loudon detached *FML*. Nauendorff with the dragoons and the hussars to scout downstream towards Steinau and the Oder. However Loudon's main business lay upstream, for he intended to deploy to the north of Pfaffendorf, where a low plateau of hillocks offered a passably open space between the woodlands to the north, and the bushy levels which extended to the Katzbach in the south-east and the Schwarzwasser to the west.

Loudon had been told that a Prussian free battalion and two regiments of hussars were stationed on the ground in question, and towards three in the morning this intelligence seemed to be confirmed when the Grün-Loudon regiment ran into two hundred Zieten Hussars [H2] near Panten, and drove them back into the night and fog. Loudon had no reason to believe that there were particularly strong forces nearby, but the clash had underlined how important it was to get his corps into position, and he ordered his nearly 6,000-strong *corps de reserve* to march with all possible speed, leaving the rest of his corps to come up as best as it could. Loudon was unaware that Frederick's army, instead of awaiting its fate on the far side of Liegnitz, was springing to arms scarcely four hundred paces away.

The *corps de reserve* was skirting the woods out to Loudon's right (northern) flank, and by chance this direction of march brought it against

LIEGNITZ, 15 AUGUST 1760

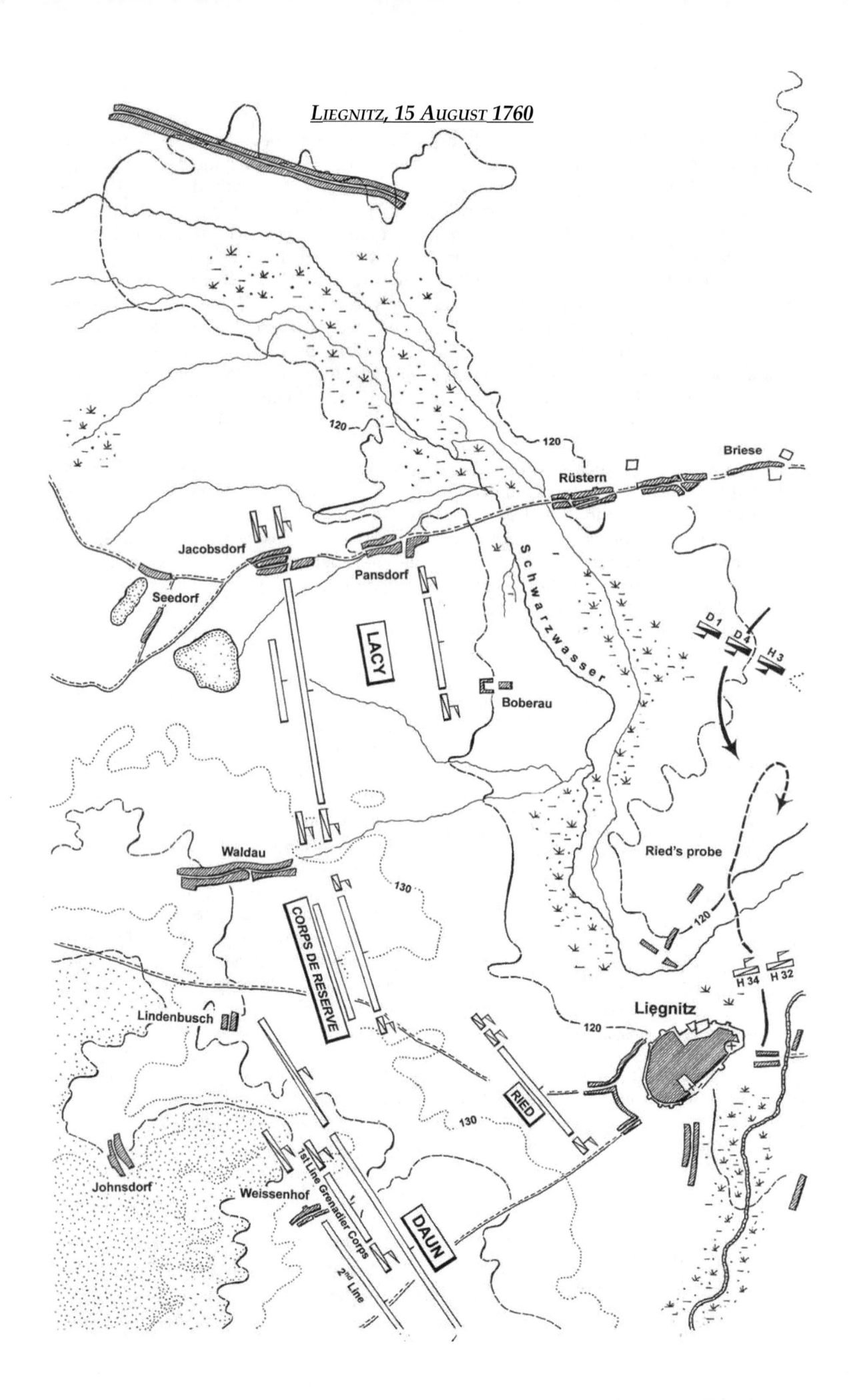

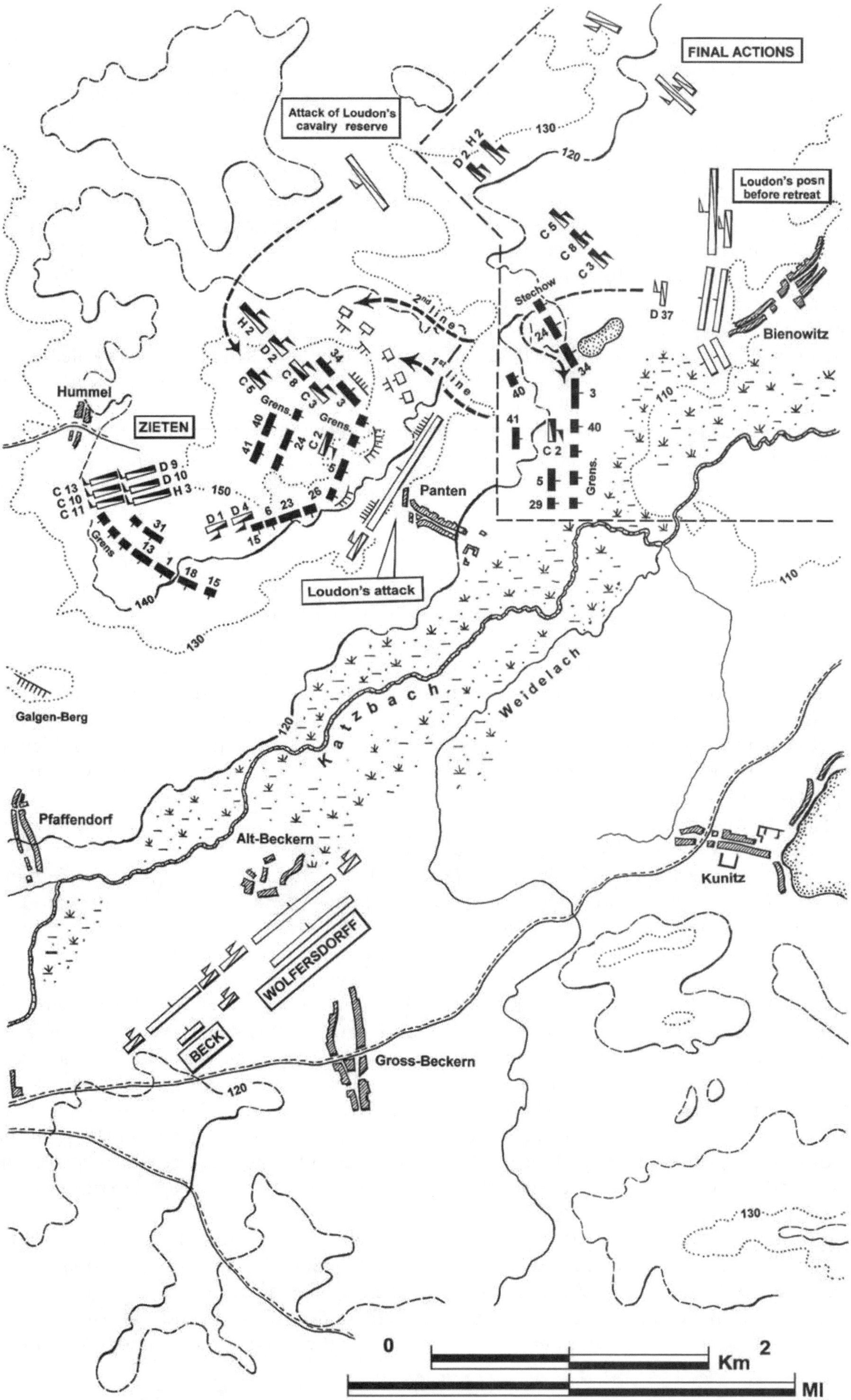

FINAL ACTIONS
Attack of Loudon's cavalry reserve
Loudon's posn before retreat
Stechow
D 37
Bienowitz
2nd line
1st line
Hummel
ZIETEN
Grens.
Panten
Loudon's attack
Galgen-Berg
Katzbach
Weidelach
Pfaffendorf
Alt-Beckern
WOLFERSDORFF
BECK
Gross-Beckern
Kunitz
0
Km 2
Ml

the rear of the Prussian Krockow Dragoons [D2] and the main body of the Zieten Hussars. The Austrians pressed home their first advantage, but they soon encountered altogether more considerable forces than were supposed to be in this locality, namely a line of Prussian infantry which shot them up in their right flank, and three full regiments of cuirassiers (Markgraf Friedrich, Seydlitz and Leibregiment [Cs 5, 8, 3]) which burst out of the darkness and drove them back towards Bienowitz.

Loudon had done well to approach the low plateau as speedily as he did; but he was still short of the hillocks when the first light of day showed him that 'they were occupied by strong forces of infantry and artillery. I could no longer fall back, and as I was confident that the main army and Lacy's corps would shortly reach the enemy as well, I had no alternative but to close with the Prussians.'[92] In their first onrush the foot grenadiers of the *corps de reserve* gained the high ground just to the north-west of Panten and captured a number of cannon, but even then the woods towards Hummel still concealed the great mass of the Prussian forces which were advancing against them.

In the event Frederick was able to form three brigades of infantry, with their attached batteries of light 12-pounder cannon, in a continuous line along the south-eastern edge of the plateau. There were two lines of infantry in support, and over to the right flank of this remarkably compact position General Zieten had three brigades (thirteen battalions) and six regiments of horse lining the south-western side of the plateau, facing the Schwarzwasser stream.

On their side the Austrian grenadiers found it difficult to shake themselves into coherent lines amid the bushes and thickets, and every time they tried to form three or four battalions abreast and push uphill, they were broken up again by musketry and blasts of canister from the devastating 12-pounders. One of the Prussian officers noted that 'an Austrian officer was riding in front of their line on a light brown horse. I had two Jäger in my platoon, and called out to them, "Jäger, shoot that colonel from his horse!" It took them scarcely two minutes for my two Jäger to mark him down and hit him, so that he fell from his horse and the riderless beast galloped off. I now commanded "Platoon! Make ready! Present! Fire!" The enemy showed no inclination to give way, and opened a lively fire as well. But we loaded more speedily, and in addition they had lost heavily to our first salvo and our muskets were longer-ranged than theirs (as I had already noted in the battle of Leuthen), and so the enemy took to their heels.'[93]

The Austrian artillery was also losing heavily, since most of the pieces were being smashed by roundshot, or were immobilised when their teams of horses were killed in their traces. For a time the grenadiers' right-hand battery continued to make good practice (one of its cannon killed six infantrymen of the regiment of Wedel [26] in a single discharge of canister), but its career came to an end when the Prussian brigade commander Saldern intervened in person, and offered ten taler to Bombardier Kretschmer if he succeeded in silencing the offending guns. 'The first howitzer shell fell just short, which made the Austrians fall back from their pieces, and we got time to fire another round. At this second attempt Kretschmer hit the Austrian ammunition cart. A man was standing on it, handing down the charges to the others. When the shell hit the cart it blew up, together with another nearby. Two gunners flew into the air, and eight others were mutilated and killed. Now the enemy abandoned their battery altogether.'[94]

In an attempt to save his grenadiers from complete destruction Loudon sought to bring his two lines of fusiliers into position on the right (northern) flank of the *corps de reserve*, but the only outcome was to feed these fresh forces into the grinder. By about half past four in the morning the Prussians were extending and thickening their line and erupting in a series of violent counterattacks. Those by their left were particularly effective, for the Anhalt-Bernburg regiment [3] was burning to make up for their disgrace at the siege of Dresden (above), while the Prussian cavalry managed to ride down the files of infantry (probably of the Austrian second line) which were marching up through the trees and mistook the approaching squadron for friends. This may be how the Seydlitz Cuirassiers were able to work behind the Austrian right wing and crash into the regiments of Toscana,

Waldeck [35] and Starhemberg [24], taking six colours and eleven cannon in the process. Loudon testifies that the Toscana regiment stood its ground with admirable firmness, but the Italians paid an appropriate price, and Bretton their colonel was killed.

By Loudon's account it was towards six in the morning that he grasped not only that he was facing the whole Prussian army, but that neither Daun nor Lacy was doing anything. He therefore began to withdraw the main body of his infantry towards the crossings near Bienowitz. A retreat in the immediate presence of the enemy was always a dangerous operation, and Loudon now had to look for help. *FML.* Nauendorff was trying to rejoin after prospecting down the Katzbach with his chevaulegers and hussars, but the 120 losses sustained by his command indicate that he was not engaged heavily. Any salvation must lie with the rest of the cavalry, which Loudon now concentrated on his right wing to screen the flank of the retreat. He then turned to Lieutenant Colonel Tom Caldwell and told him to go from regiment to regiment and order them to attack.

When the word came to the Prinz Albert Cuirassiers [C22] the captain lieutenant Wipper von Uschitz set off willingly enough, but when he looked behind him he found that he was being followed by only about forty of his troopers. Caldwell therefore brought up the *Leibescadron* of the Schmerzing Cuirassiers [C20] and threw the scratch force at the Prussians, 'so that almost all their troops, except those who sought safety in the woods, were cut down. It worked so well that when further enemy infantry tried to emerge from the woods and form up, they were forced to recoil, and fell back again without further ado. This was of great help to our own infantry in its retreat.'[95]

On receiving the same order *GFWM.* Belgiojoso had unhesitatingly committed the Kollowrat Dragoons [D37], and his blue-coated troopers not only rode down the grenadier battalion of Stechow, but ploughed through the exposed left wing of the musketeer regiment of

Liegnitz. The Katzbach meadows by Panten, looking upstream with the marshy meadows extending to the right

Prinz Ferdinand [34] and into the right flank of that of Anhalt-Bernburg [3]. In one of the most celebrated episodes of Prussian military history the Bernburgers pressed among the Austrian dragoons with the bayonet, and held them off until the Seydlitz Cuirassiers [C8] and the Krockow Dragoons [D2] could come to their help and push the enemy back towards Bienowitz. However the combined efforts of the Austrian cavalry had checked the Prussian infantry at a particularly opportune moment, and carried away the respectable total of ten captured colours.

In such a way, according to Loudon, the retreat was conducted 'with as much composure and order as was possible in the sight of such a superior enemy. I then occupied the heights at Bienowitz with my two grenadier battalions [of *Grün-Loudon*] and reassembled my artillery there through the agency of Colonel Rouvroy. I had the pieces open fire on the enemy, which deterred them from pursuing any further, and enabled us to retreat in an orderly manner.'[96]

While Loudon's main force had been making for the Furt-Mühle bridges near Bienowitz, there was a brush further upstream at Panten, where a party of Austrians tried to retrieve a number of abandoned cannon, and were chased out again by the Third Battalion of the Prussian Garde [15]. The encounter ended with the village being set on fire by the Prussian howitzers. Most probably the Austrian troops in question belonged to a brigade which is known to have been acting under the personal command of the chief of staff *GFWM*. Giannini, who kept up the fight until eight in the morning, and barely escaped being surrounded.[97]

This was the last episode in the unplanned and unsought-for battle between Loudon and Frederick. 'The troops who came back were in an almost worse state than those who remained on the field. They wept for the sorrows of their general, and had less thought for their own wounds than at his agony at having sacrificed, despite himself, those brave men whom he had always led to victory.'[98]

Daun's army had begun to march from its strung-out camp at about ten the previous night. The right wing had been instructed to set out first, regiment by regiment, and march to the left across the front of the army to the crossing points of the Katzbach near Dohnau. 'The stupidity of most of our generals, together with the weakness of most of the officers of our general staff when it came to manoeuvring troops—which ought to have been foreseen—upset an essentially simple procedure. The regiments of the right wing... ought to have awaited their turn, then marched to their front and turned to their left to follow on. Instead of this, they put themselves to the trouble of first marching all the way to the original station of the right wing.'[99]

In the darkness the four main columns lost their way and collided, and when at last they made their way to the crossing points 'the passage was dragged out still further, for the bridges were so narrow that scarcely four men could pass abreast.'[100]

The first troops across the Katzbach were the Croats and hussars of the divisions of Ried and Beck, who had expected to find themselves in almost immediate contact with the enemy. To their astonishment they discovered that the villages of Schimmelwitz and Schochwitz were empty, and that the Prussians had abandoned the camp site beyond. Daun did not receive the news until between two and three in the morning. He knew that Loudon would be in great danger if the Prussians were moving towards him and at once sent a warning, 'but unfortunately the officer was forced to take a long way round, and arrived late, by when he found that Loudon's corps was already engaged in a most lively hand-to-hand combat.'[101]

Daun hurried the rest of the army across the Katzbach, restored the troops to order on the far side, and pressed on towards Liegnitz in the hope of overhauling the Prussian rearguard and lending help to Loudon as might be necessary. The Austrians reached the site of the abandoned camp between four and five in the morning, but when it was light they could see that the entire Prussian army had already passed through Liegnitz and reached the far side of the marshy-banked Schwarzwasser stream. Some of the officers concluded that Frederick was trying to reach his magazines at Glogau by way of the Steinau road, 'but it was not long before we saw a heavy fire of musketry and cannon which was descending from the heights in the direction of Panten. We could no longer doubt that General Loudon's corps was engaged, which was confirmed by a report from General Ried, whose light troops had already pushed to the heights behind Pfaffendorf... We redoubled our pace, in the hope of sharing Loudon's ordeal, but it was too late.'[102]

Daun's detractors afterwards claimed that he should have plunged across the Schwarzwasser and thrown himself into the attack as soon as he saw the smoke. One of his party took up the challenge, and asked 'if you believe (as has been confirmed) that the field marshal had more than three hours to march before he could reach the enemy, how then can you conclude that he would have arrived in time? Is it realistic to expect that an army of 40,000 men together with its artillery, divided as it was into several columns, and not knowing the position of the enemy, could have crossed hills, ravines, narrows, woods and rivers, made its dispositions, and then open a simultaneous and forceful attack?'[103] Daun was about six miles from the scene of Loudon's action, which corresponds to the time just cited, and a strong westerly wind heightened the sense of distance by silencing the sounds of combat.

All of the Austrian plans had been based on the premise that Daun and Frederick would now be locked in battle on the near side of Liegnitz, and there had been no perceived need to investigate how the army might pass the Schwarzwasser beyond the town. Ried's light troops had already occupied Liegnitz, and were emerging on the far side of the rivulet by way of the single bridge, which was a lengthy process. Daun sent officers to prospect for crossings further upstream. They found that broad swampy meadows bordered the rivulet as far as Rüstern, and these too could be traversed (if at all) only after lengthy preparations.

The only forces which managed to carry the fight to the enemy were Ried's Széchenyi and Dessewffy Hussars [Hs 32, 34], who skirmished to within long range of a fast-augmenting line of Prussian troops who crowned the near edge of the plateau between Hummel and Pfaffendorf. Here Zieten's initial three brigades and forty-three squadrons were being reinforced by Frederick, who had broken off his pursuit of Loudon at the sight of Austrian hussars passing the Schwarzwasser. The Prussian Normann and Czettritz Dragoons [Ds1,4] and Möhring Hussars [H3] now emerged from the woods, and with the support of the massed 12-pounders they chased the intruders back over the Schwarzwasser.

The role assigned to Lacy had been to take his corps on a wide left-flanking move and hit the supposed position of the Prussians in the right rear. He set off from his camp at Praussnitz at nine in the evening of the 14th, passed the Katzbach without difficulty upstream to Kroitsch, and, after a delay experienced by his left-hand battalions on the far bank, he resumed his march. The roundabout route lay by way of Rothbrünnig and Lobedau, and it probably took Lacy five or more hours to cover the nine or ten miles to the isolated farm of the List-Vorwerk, where there was presumed to be an outpost of the main Prussian army. There was no sign of the enemy in this location, but clouds of smoke were rising silently about four miles to the east.

Lacking further information, Lacy formed his corps in line of battle in the agreed position near Waldau, in other words still on the right (west) side of the Schwarzwasser at a time when all the Prussians had already crossed to the left bank, and were hotly engaged with Loudon. The only element of Lacy's corps to reach the far bank was a party of dragoons and hussars, who discovered a ford above Rüstern and attacked the train of Frederick's personal baggage at Küchel. They were beaten off by Lieutenant Prittwitz and a flank grenadier company of the First Battalion of the Garde [15], who barricaded the village against them.

By the afternoon of the day of battle Loudon was back on the right bank of the Katzbach, licking his wounds, and Daun and Zieten were exchanging artillery fire across the Schwarzwasser. Frederick's priority even now was to find somewhere to cross the Katzbach and join Henry, and towards three the Austrians detected that the enemy were thinning out their forces on the plateau, and at four reliable news came that the Prussians were in full march for Parchwitz. Daun thereupon directed his army towards the Katzbach and the old camp on the right bank.

No other action in the Seven Years War, not even Leuthen, gave rise to such recriminations among the Austrians as did the battle of Liegnitz. The sense of a magnificent opportunity, which had been somehow bungled and thrown away, was compounded by the widely-shared belief that Daun and Lacy had made a deliberate sacrifice of Loudon, their supposed rival. At 8,500 men the losses in Loudon's corps were heavy, but an equally heavy blow in its way was dealt against relationships in the Austrian high command.

One of Daun's supporters (probably *GFWM*. Pellegrini) represented that 'it is well known that one day the ordinary people praise a general to the skies, and the next they detest him as a coward or traitor. But when a large element of the nobility here [Vienna] and the officers of the army cry out at the same time against the field marshal, it is a clear sign that there are ministers and generals who have joined together to destroy his reputation in the eyes of the sovereign, the soldiers and the people.' Loudon could not be a serious contender for the highest place, for the generals senior to him would resign en masse, and he had never exercised independent command of a large army against the king. It was easy for hotheads to demand bloody action, 'but a general who plays for time is more fitted to command against the king than one who fights battles for their own sake; this is a truth which has been justified time and time again by experience... he [the king] must be reduced little by little, and when he is close enough to the precipice he will throw himself over the edge of his own accord.'[104]

In his first chagrin and outrage Loudon literally rolled on the ground, or so Austrian deserters reported to Frederick. In any event Loudon hastened to write to his protector Kaunitz that 'if the main army and *FZM*. Lacy had reached the enemy at first light, as the *Disposition* laid down, we would have brought off a total victory. This is evident by the fact that although I had scarcely 14,000 men under arms, I nevertheless forced the enemy back twice over. All that was needed was for the other two attacks to be delivered as well, and then the enemy would have been unfailingly beaten.'[103] Loudon sent Lieutenant Colonel Erbach to Vienna to reinforce the message by word of mouth, and probably also to make the accusation of outright betrayal.

Kaunitz was reluctant to condemn Daun before the relevant facts were known, but the Viennese public declared itself solidly on Loudon's side, and ridiculed the field marshal in verses and caricatures. If Loudon looked to Kaunitz, Daun knew that he must rely on the goodwill of Maria Theresa. He explained to her that on Loudon's sector 'the action developed piecemeal, without orders after the style of a Croatian attack, and over broken ground where the enemy were already in place. The *Disposition* said nothing about attacking... but just to sound out what might be there, and not plunge blindly into a hole like that with the Katzbach at your back... I was a good two hours distant from him, and everything was over in less than an hour and a half.'[106] Daun likewise sent *GFWM*. Pellegrini to counter the influence of Loudon's supporters in Vienna.

Lieutenant Colonel Erbach returned to Loudon bearing three messages of consolation from Their Imperial Majesties, and a cautious reply from Kaunitz. He was aware how pained Loudon must feel, but he assured him that the Imperial pair and all the public were doing him full justice. Most of the people shared Loudon's belief that he had been left deliberately in the lurch, but Kaunitz had seen 'convincing proofs to the contrary, and when I put everything together it is clear that the only cause was indecision.'[107]

It was good for Loudon's fragile peace of mind that he was unaware of the damage he had inflicted on himself by his robust defence. While he consolidated himself in the esteem of the public and Francis Stephen, 'he was not so fortunate as regards the Empress. It was not so easy for her to forget that under the first impact of his disappointment he had virtually accused the field marshal of having abandoned him on purpose.'[108] Indeed the French ambassador Choiseul-Praslin discovered that Maria Theresa had accepted Daun's explanations in their entirety, and blamed Loudon for the defeat.[109]

Loudon himself continued to derive almost unalloyed satisfaction from the performance of his corps, where so many of his officers had shared his sense of initiative. Lieutenant Colonel Maguer objected to Lieutenant Colonel Caldwell's so readily commandeering the Life Squadron of the Schmerzing Cuirassiers [C20] for his counterattack, and Captain Bott for having agreed so readily. Major Count Clam overheard the argument, and intervened to say that they had been entirely in the right, 'because the general [Loudon] had made it known that if a subordinate officer perceived an advantage, he must seize it without further reference.'[110]

In an attempt to reach a balanced assessment of the battle of the whole, we have to take account of what the officers of the army thought at the time. A number of them condemned the scheme as over-complicated.[111] However Prince Albert of Sachsen-Teschen specifically disassociated himself from this opinion. In fact the plan of attack by converging forces was less elaborate than the one which had worked so well at Maxen, and less complicated still than the one attempted at Hochkirch.

As for mistakes in execution, we shall never be able to determine how conscientiously Loudon tried to put into effect the tasks which had been set before him, for the reason that his part in the battle plan had not been set down in detail in the *Disposition*. The Austrian shortcomings in reconnaissance, the transmission of information and in staff work are notable not just on account of their dire effects, but because they are so difficult to reconcile with the known strengths of the Austrian army at this period. It is still impossible to establish why the plentiful Austrian light troops lost contact with the Prussians so completely when Frederick was changing his position overnight, but perhaps the dismal performance of the staff can be explained by recent changes in personnel. Lacy had resigned from the staff to take command of a corps, and his respected successor Jakob Nugent was a prisoner of the Prussians, which left the management of the main army in the hands of *GFWM*. Siskovics, an extremely able general who nevertheless lacked staff experience. Loudon had an excellent chief of staff in the person of *GFWM*. Giannini, but he was at fault in allowing that gentleman to take command of an infantry brigade for the duration of the battle. Loudon should have congratulated him on his enthusiasm, but kept him close by him to make use of his particular talents.

Conversely Frederick had timed his move from his original camp extremely well, and thereby escaped the danger of being overwhelmed by the greatly superior Austrian forces, or trapped by the Schwarzwasser meadows and Loudon's forces when he tried to escape. Much of the devastation in Loudon's corps had been wrought by a new weapon in the Prussian armoury, or rather a new use of an old weapon, in the shape of the light 12-pounders. They had been introduced by Frederick before the war. They had been a disappointment in their intended role, being too feeble to meet the demands of medium artillery, but they were now employed to great effect in the role of super-heavy regimental artillery, discharging gales of whistling canister in the faces of the enemy.

In the operational context the Austrians were very mistaken to have crossed the Katzbach in the first place. All they needed to do to hold their advantage was to keep on their guard behind the little river, and match every move of Frederick on the far bank. That Daun was forced to act out of character, and against Austrian interests, was the result of the urging from Vienna (for which we should read 'Kaunitz') and the Russians. After the fight a Prussian officer looked about him and exclaimed: 'there are certainly up to three thousand dead on the field. I came across places where for every Prussian body there were six of seven of the Austrians. All of that is miraculous.'[112] In the setting of the campaign the Austrians lost more heavily still, for they had lost precious time in their effort to deny the king his way across the Katzbach.

The first confrontation in the Silesian Hills, August - September 1760

The smoke had scarcely cleared from the field before Frederick took off with half his army, and executed a forced march down the left bank of the Katzbach. By the evening of the day of battle he had crossed unopposed to the right bank at Parchwitz, and towards midnight he was joined by the rest of the army under General

Zieten, who had remained to collect the Prussian wounded and the abandoned weapons.

The nerve of the allies now gave way. Lieutenant General Chernyshev and his 20,000 Russians were standing almost in the king's path on the near bank of the Oder. In the course of 15 August they learned first that Loudon had been in action and had been beaten, and then that Frederick was at Parchwitz and that they themselves were in danger of being attacked with their backs to the Oder. Saltykov sent word to rejoin the main Russian army, and Chernyshev's troops accordingly filed back over their bridge to the right bank and retrieved their boats.

On the morning of the 16th news came to Daun that Chernyshev was out of his reach, and that Frederick was on the near side of the Katzbach. Daun now abandoned the purposes he had followed with admirable consistency until now, those of barring Frederick's way to Breslau and Prince Henry, and forging the eventual union with the Russians. Turning south-east, and therefore away from the Oder, Daun marched towards Schweidnitz and by the late evening he had formed his army in a cordon to the north of the Prussian-garrisoned fortress. The behaviour of the troops hints at a wider demoralisation. The Prince de Ligne comments: 'The spirit of plunder had taken hold of our soldiers to an unimaginable extent. In the course of the 14th, 15th and 16th they were responsible for some dreadful excesses. I imagine that the high command had its reasons for not restoring them to order, and that it was not altogether upset to see the ruin of a country... where it was extremely unlikely that we would now be taking up our winter quarters.'[113]

In a confidential letter to Kaunitz, his patron, Loudon prophesied correctly that Frederick would leave just 10-12,000 troops to observe the Russians on the far side of the Oder, and turn with the rest of the his army against the Austrians. 'All our gains might be limited to the County of Glatz, and we will have to be on our guard to keep even that.'[114]

On 17 August Daun arrayed his troops in the Camp of Conradswaldau to the north and north-west of Schweidnitz, facing in the one direction towards the fortress, and in the other towards Frederick's army, which had now formed up at Hermsdorf in front of Breslau. Daun was at a loss what to do next, now that he had drawn away from the Russians and given the king a free passage to Breslau. He sounded the opinions of his generals, but found that they were at cross-purposes. Maria Theresa wrote to him on the 22nd, explaining that it was still possible to join the Russians, at least by dispatching Loudon with 40,000 troops to lay a joint siege to Glogau on the lower Oder. The main Austrian army should meanwhile set about the siege of Schweidnitz, with the underlying purpose of drawing Frederick into a battle[115]— advice which could scarcely have been palatable to Daun at this time.

By recoiling into southern Silesia, Daun had already shown how little store he set by uniting with the Russians, and these people would have been amply justified in falling back into Poland. They were persuaded otherwise by the cantankerous old Austrian military attaché *FML*. Plunkett and his French counterpart Montalembert. Plunkett explained to Daun that it was neither possible nor desirable to bring this rapacious army across the Oder, but it might still be put to good use by carrying out a diversion on the lower Oder.[116] Plunkett's scheme happened to correspond with the intentions of Maria Theresa, who wished to see the Russians besiege Glogau, and it also appealed to Saltykov, who accepted it without hesitation.

On 24 August the 66,000 Russians moved from Kainowe west to Trachenberg, and on the following day to Herrnstadt, a double march which took them half-way to Glogau. Prince Henry could not mistake the Russians' intentions, but he was in no position to bar their way, for he was ordered by Frederick to leave nearly 14,000 men to observe Saltykov, and send the rest to join the royal army in its camp near Breslau.

Daun and Loudon agreed that the project which had just arrived from Vienna, namely to send the Austrian siege train and 40,000 troops against Glogau, was difficult and dangerous, but for the moment they could not bring themselves to tell that to the Russians outright. At this period they were in fact functioning as little more than intermediaries between Vienna and the Russian headquarters. The one positive outcome was to place the Russians within striking distance of Brandenburg, a circumstance which they would shortly exploit in a spectacular way.

Daun now had the initiative snatched from him by Frederick. On 27 August the Austrian observers on the conical Zobten-Berg espied lines of tents on the far side of Breslau, and concluded correctly that large reinforcements had reached the king from Prince Henry. Even now Frederick had only 49,950 troops to pit against the 92,120 Austrians, but he went on to establish and maintain his moral superiority by a series of outflanking moves that were designed to drive the Austrians away from Schweidnitz and into the border hills with Bohemia.

On 30 and 31 August the king moved around the Austrians's right (eastern) flank. Lacy frustrated him when he lunged against the Zobten-Berg, but the Prussians were able to arrive in the rear of the Camp of Conradswaldau, which was consequently untenable. Daun abandoned his blockade of Schweidnitz, and fell back towards the magnificent line of the Waldenburger-Gebirge in the south-west.

Frederick's attention was then drawn to the other Austrian flank, on the west, for Daun's communications from Bohemia ran north from Trautenau to the forward magazine at Landeshut, from where they ran at right-angles to the east. Frederick made his move on 11 September. This time it was Loudon who thwarted his design, by shifting his corps to the heights of Reichenau. Daun's force came up behind, and the rival armies ended jammed together in the hills. 'They [the Prussians] were within range of even our smallest-calibre cannon, and you could make out the soldiers' uniforms with no difficulty.'[117]

The running fight—Kunzendorf, Bögendorf and Hoch-Giersdorf, 17 September 1760

Daun was parrying the lunges from the enemy, and just as doggedly resisting the urgings from Kaunitz and Maria Theresa to strike back through actions that were *'vigoureusse et decisive.'*[118] By waiting as patiently as he did, the field marshal actually placed Frederick in a severe embarrassment. Fodder and water were running short for the Prussians in the plain, and the longer that Frederick was nailed down in southern Silesia, the greater was the danger to Brandenburg from the Russians, and to his forces in Saxony from the *Reichsarmee* and the Austrians. The king returned to the principle of finding a way around Daun's right (eastern) flank, now with the purpose of gaining the road which led south from Schweidnitz by way of Waldenburg to the Bohemian border at Friedland.

The Prussian army accordingly set out under cover of darkness and mist at 3:45 in the morning of 17 September. The immediate objective was the Limmel-Berg east of **Kunzendorf**, for if the Prussians seized this feature ahead of the Austrians they would be able to cut in close under Daun's right before he could devise countermeasures.

The danger was first perceived by *GdC*. Löwenstein's elite corps of carabiniers and mounted and foot grenadiers, posted between Oelse and Zirlau. Löwenstein ordered his cavalry to make for the Limmel-Berg, and two of his squadrons of carabiniers swept the Zieten Hussars [H2] from this key ground. The position was consolidated by a battalion of Croats and three battalions of fusiliers, and the Austrian light corps of *GFWM*. Ried, which had been in danger of being cut off at Arnsdorf, was now able to recoil out of immediate harm's way to Hoch-Giersdorf.

Frederick was forced to make a wider circuit than he had foreseen, but he was not to be deflected from his purpose, and he continued his march eastwards by way of Arnsdorf and Schönbrunn. The Austrians advanced their artillery to the edge of the hills, and kept the Prussian columns under fire as they marched across their front. The hammering went on until 7.30 in the evening, and by Frederick's account 'the noise, which they heard in Breslau, was so considerable that the officers of the garrison believed that a battle must be in progress. It was really only a march, but in previous times there had been battles in which fewer rounds were fired than on that day.'[119]

During all of this Frederick remained 'perfectly relaxed, even through everybody around him was trembling and giving vent to

The Silesian Hills, August–September 1760

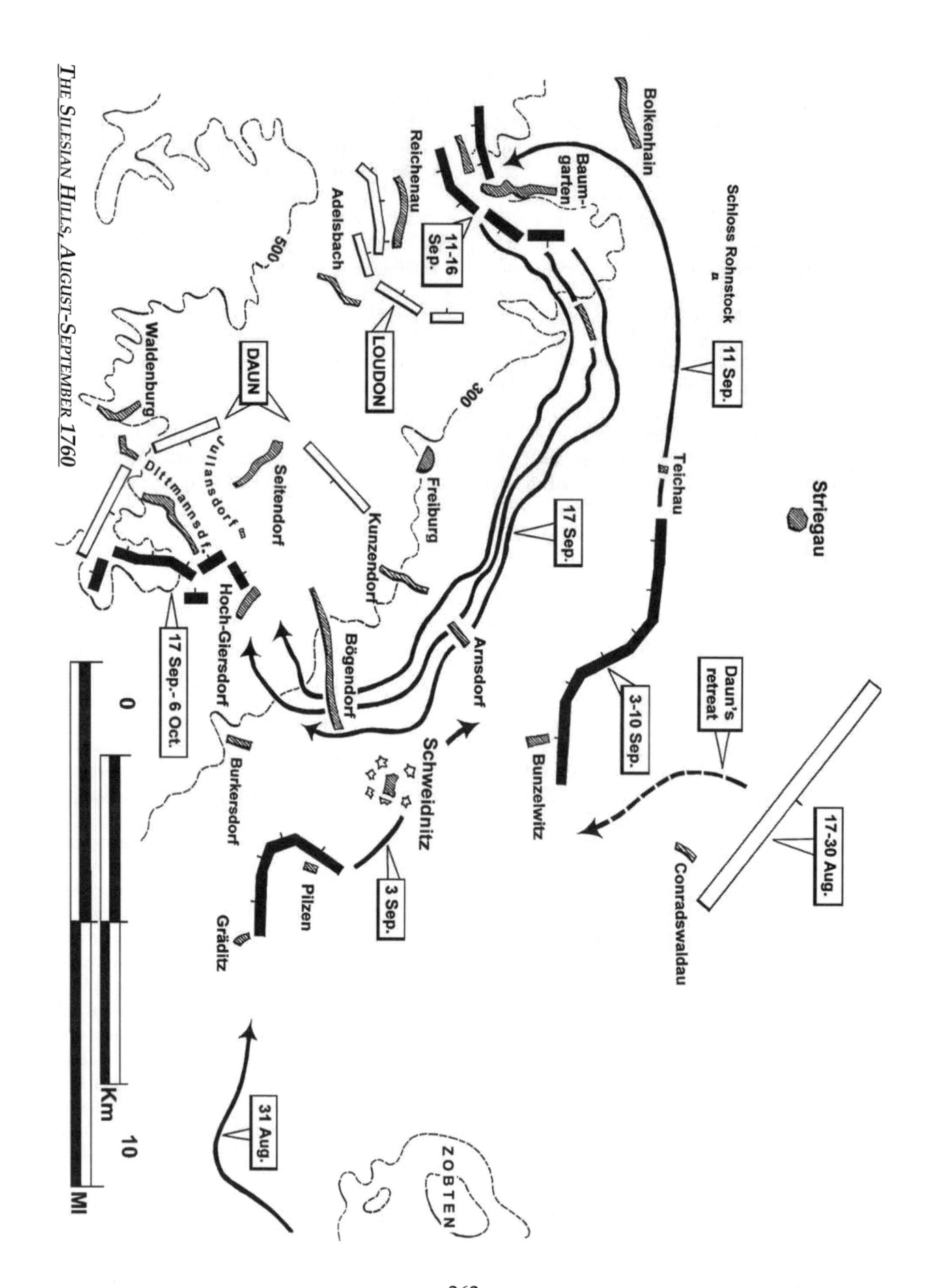

comments like "Gentlemen, stop your ears! Now we have to run the gauntlet!" On noticing this the king veered towards a nobleman's country house, which had an arched entrance, and would offer some concealment when they marched through… on emerging from the garden of the mansion, however, they were once more seen by the Austrians, who re-opened fire at him… not far away a sutler woman was hit, but he stayed cheerful and encouraged his suite to ride smartly and keep up with him.'[120]

GFWM. Joseph d'Ayasasa, who led the mounted element of Löwenstein's corps, was a commander who 'would have been acclaimed a great cavalryman in any service, and would have been an Austrian "Seydlitz" if someone like Frederick had been at the head of our army.'[121] His horsemen were shadowing the Prussian progress from a distance of 500 paces from the nearest column. His troopers were impatient to attack, and d'Aysasa himself 'saw the need for some real action at least once during the present campaign.'[122] He found his opportunity when the Prussians wheeled to the right just short of Schweidnitz and their cavalry reached the far side of the ravine at Bögendorf, thereby losing contact with the infantry, still strung out on the near side.

D'Ayasasa formed his command into two columns, and the Austrians broke through the first enemy line, smashing the first battalion of the regiment of Anhalt-Bernburg [3], and taking hundreds of prisoners and up to twenty-one cannon. He had reckoned without the new firepower at the disposal of the Prussian infantry. The enemy second line stood firm, helped by the batteries of light 12-pounders which now formed part of the complement of their brigades. D'Ayasasa's cavalry (like Loudon's infantry at Liegnitz) ran into an intensive fire of canister, and the Austrians were finally swept away by the Seydlitz and Prinz Heinrich Cuirassiers [Cs 8, 2]. D'Ayasasa lost about 190 men, and was able to bring off only 200 of the Prussians he had captured and just one of the enemy cannon. A number of Austrian infantrymen contrived to install themselves ahead of the enemy in the walled churchyard of **Bögendorf**, and shot up the Prussian cuirassiers in their turn, but a few rounds from the 12-pounders were enough to evict them, and the Prussians were able to continue on their way.

It was now about four in the afternoon, and the intermittent march had continued for almost twelve hours when the Prussian columns emerged on the far side of Bögendorf and inclined once more to their right to come at the exposed Austrian flank from the east. After his escape from Arnsdorf *GFWM*. Ried halted his troops on the commanding heights north of **Hoch-Giersdorf**, which now stood squarely in the path of the Prussians, seemingly bent on destroying him. He fell back yet again, and so the hill became the prize in a race between two brigades of Prussians approaching from the east, and the regiment of Tillier [36] and three battalions of grenadiers who had been sent by Daun to reinforce Ried.

The Tillier regiment arrived first. Colonel Ferraris was not far behind with the grenadiers, and they counterattacked to such effect that he broke the fusilier regiment of Prinz Heinrich [35] and captured twelve cannon and a number of colours. However three battalions of Prussians and a battery of horse artillery arrived on the scene, and the regiment of Tillier (which had already been in action at Kunzendorf) collapsed in panic and left the grenadiers in the lurch. 'Ferraris had been badly bruised, but he averted a still greater rout. Without his good management hardly anyone would have been retrieved.'[123]

All of this time Daun had been directing the main army to the right along the hill slopes to counter the Prussian move, and when he saw the action developing at Hoch-Giersdorf he made a final push to the hills at Seitendorf. This was enough. Frederick could not think of attacking him in this position, for his troops were exhausted by sixteen hours of marching, skirmishing and cannonading. The prolonged and indecisive fight had been costly to both sides, with the Prussians losing 982 men to the Austrians' 626.

On 18 September Frederick assailed Ried's position on the far Austrian right at Reussendorf and Neu-Reussendorf, but he was deterred from pushing home his attack by the great quantity of artillery which Daun brought up to his forward positions. This action only confirmed the verdict

Lacy Visits Berlin: October 1760

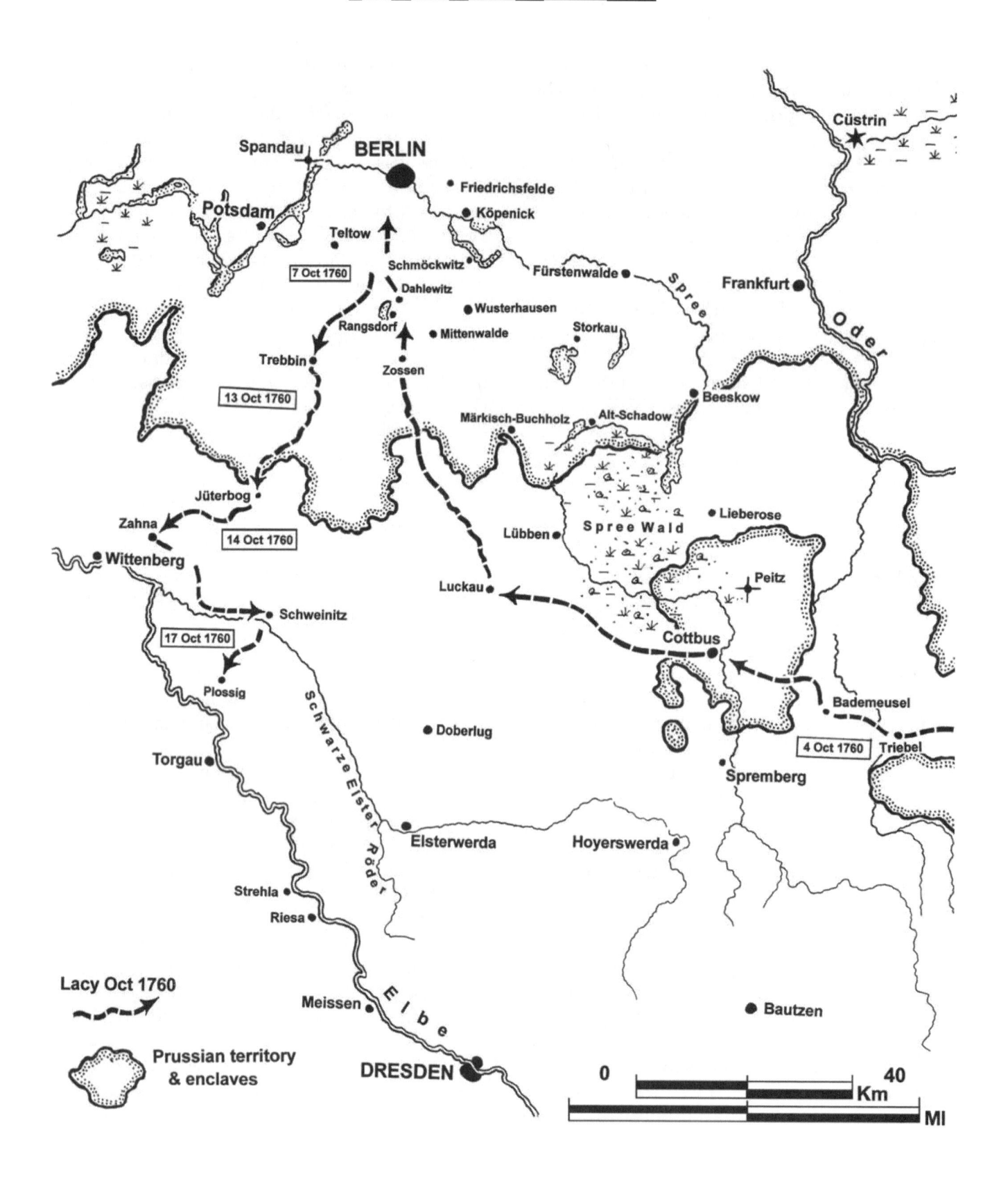

which had been delivered on the 17th, and both sides proceeded to dig in.

Kaunitz believed that something more positive was needed to end the campaign in a way that would influence affairs at the grand strategic level, where it was vital to persuade the allies to stay in the war for another year.[124] But it was at a lower level, where the strategic merged with the operational, that the time gained by Daun was like 'pure gold.' The *Reichsarmee* and the attached Austrians were driving the outnumbered Prussians from Saxony, while the Russians (free of the attentions of Frederick) were being enticed back from Poland. 'For these reasons the way that Daun was stringing affairs out was never less worthy of blame than now.'[125] The words were those of Jakob Cogniazzo, who could be unsparing in his criticisms of the field marshal.

Frederick calculated that as long as he was being held fast by 80,000 Austrians in Silesia he would be powerless to go to the help of his scattered forces elsewhere, which were facing 60,000 Russians to his rear, 40,000 *Reichstruppen* and Austrians in Saxony, and 15-16,000 Swedes in Pomerania. What he had achieved so far 'had no result beyond making Daun more cautious than ever. On each occasion he took up positions in the hills where he was totally unassailable. I did everything I reasonably could to draw him into some kind of decisive action, and contrive to turn his flank, but it proved impossible to tempt him out.'[126]

The Austrian and Russian ideas now coalesced in a remarkable way. Daun wrote to Maria Theresa on 22 September that he hoped that the Russians could be persuaded to remain in the field until the end of October, and advance down the Oder into Brandenburg, 'in which case I will at once detach 18,000 troops to carry out the expedition against Berlin, leaving it to them whether they wish to join in with a corps of 25,000 men.'[127] On the same day a courier reached Russian headquarters from St. Petersburg, bearing orders for the army to execute a powerful diversion of some kind.

Maria Theresa welcomed Daun's proposal, as breaking the current deadlock[128] and fitting in with a scheme which was being hatched in Vienna for an offensive in Saxony, whereby the *Reichsarmee* and the Austrians would take Torgau and Wittenberg, and perhaps even prolong their offensive in the direction of Berlin. The Prussian general Jung-Stutterheim would have to turn his 6,000 troops to meet this threat, which would give the Swedes an opportunity to detach 10,000 men against the capital from their force in Pomerania. No communication had yet been established between the Austrian and Swedish field forces, but this was almost the first time that the Swedes had been brought into the Austrian calculations, and the Swedish ambassador welcomed the chance to restore the reputation of Swedish arms, for now at last 'His Majesty's operations could make a weighty contribution to the efforts of the allies.'[129]

At ten in the night of 27 September Daun learned from *FML.* Plunkett that the Russians were in the process of sending an advance party under Major General Totleben against Berlin, and that Lieutenant General Chernyshev would follow with the main force. To Plunkett's astonishment, Fermor (now in acting command) had assured him that he would do everything in his power to make the blow an effective one. Early on the 28th Daun summoned Lacy and Loudon to headquarters, and 'there was total agreement that the best course would be to send a similar corps from here against Berlin without loss of time, lest the Russians should think we were doing nothing at all to support them.'[130]

The choice fell on Lacy with his 18,500 or so troops rather than Loudon's 25,000, since Lacy's corps at Lang-Waltersdorf was out of sight of the enemy, and its departure could be concealed for longer. The commission was certainly to Lacy's liking, for a strike against the military stores and industries in Berlin had formed part of his original plan of campaign.

LACY'S EXPEDITION AGAINST BERLIN, 28 SEPTEMBER - 17 OCTOBER 1760

For the second time in the war the Austrians were in a position to deal a blow against Berlin. The place counted for nothing as a location for making decisions (for that resided in Frederick's head), but it was an important centre of administration, it was the home of some of the king's closest associates, and together with

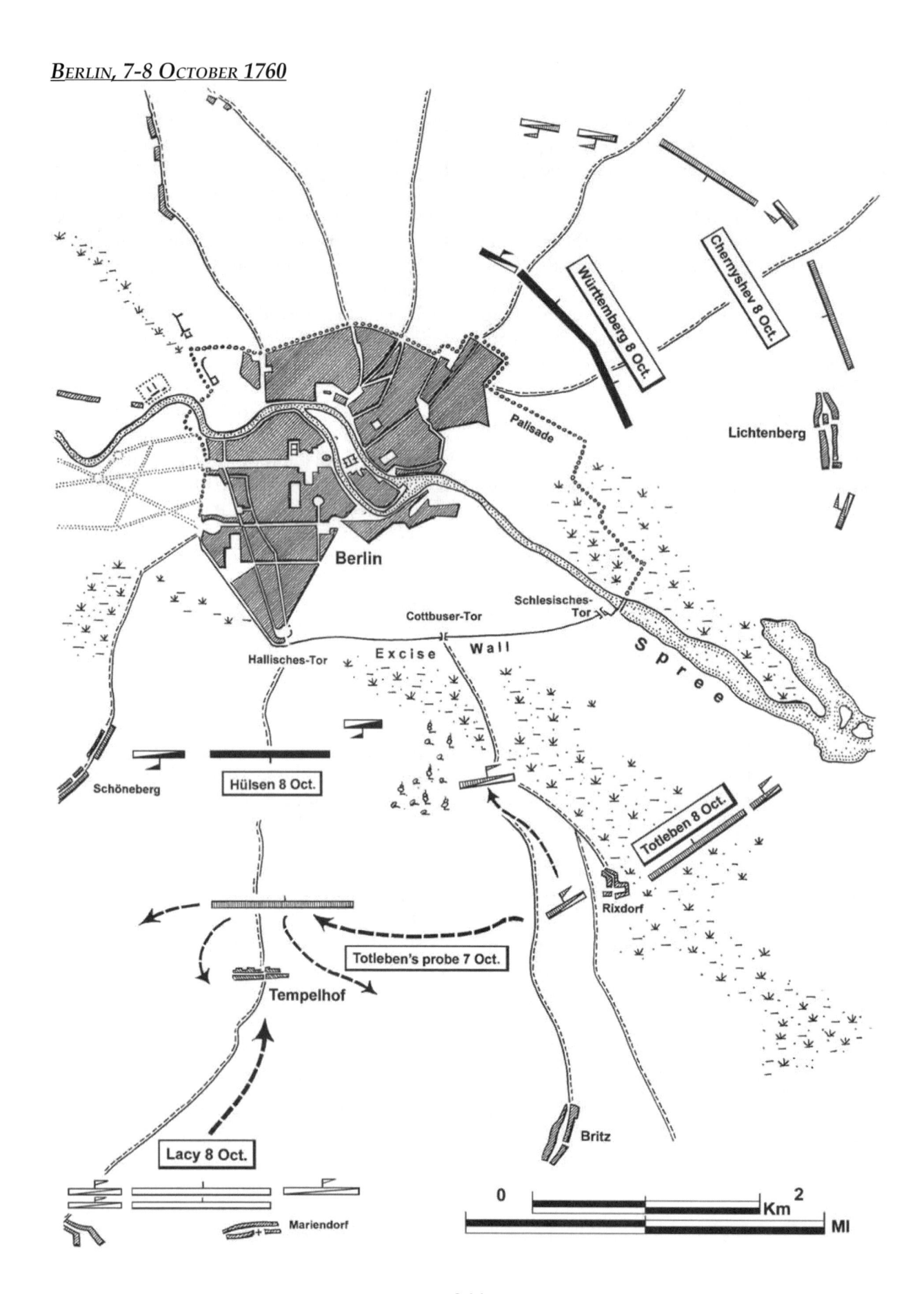

Berlin, 7-8 October 1760

Potsdam it housed the main manufactures and stores of weapons and military equipment of all kinds. As we have seen, the task was entrusted to *FZM.* Franz Moritz Lacy, who combined enterprise with a gift for precise calculation, and delighted in the kind of independent command which took him away from the gloom which reigned at Daun's headquarters. He had under his command seventeen battalions, seventeen companies of grenadiers, one company of Jäger, fifty squadrons of horse, and a respectable train of 63 pieces of artillery. Lacy therefore commanded a much bigger corps than the force which Hadik had brought against Berlin in 1757, but this time the Austrians were operating in support of Russian allies, which was going to complicate matters considerably.

The Russian army was already on its way down the left (west) bank of the Oder towards Frankfurt, and Fermor was about to detach an advance guard of 12,000 troops under the highly capable Lieutenant General Chernyshev, who was well known to the Austrians, and who now got word to Lacy that he had learned 'with in expressible' joy that he was moving on the city.[131]

Fermor, the temporary commander of the Russian army, was a man of unpredictable moods. What concerned the Austrians more was the character of Major General Eduard Totleben, the leader of Chernyshev's scouting force of 5,600 troops. In that age of military adventurers Totleben had acquired a more than usually shady reputation, having deserted the Dutch service, and contrived to 'lose' a great deal of money while recruiting on behalf of the Austrians in the *Reich*. Totleben had a son in the Prussian army, and the Austrians would have been even more concerned if they had known that he had contacts in merchant circles in Berlin. Proof of outright treason emerged later in the war.

Totleben (with Chernyshev in his wake) had a head start on Lacy. He set out from Schönau on 26 September, and by forced marches reached Guben on the 29th, Beeskow on the 30th, and took a route by way of Storkow and Wusterhausen around the south of Berlin to arrive outside the excise wall on 3 October, having covered almost 90 miles in just eight days. It was a creditable performance, and almost certainly speeded in the final stages by the knowledge that Lacy too was on the way. By four in the morning of 4 October Totleben nevertheless had to recognise that his first attempt on Berlin had failed, for his train of artillery was too light to have any effect on the improvised defences in front of the Halle and Cottbus gates, which beat off his attempts to break in.

When Totleben first arrived in front of Berlin the city had been held by just 1,500 troops. In the course of 4 October Lieutenant General Prince Friedrich Eugen of Württemberg arrived with 6,000 men who had been facing the Swedes. Over the west, the *Reichsarmee* and Austrians had beaten back Lieutenant General Hülsen to the right bank of the Elbe, which weakened the Prussian hold on that river, but put him in a better position to lend assistance to Berlin. His leading troops (6,000 men under Lieutenant General Kleist) arrived there on 7 October.

A great deal had therefore been going on before Lacy was able to influence affairs. The Austrian raiding corps had set out from Langen-Waltersdorf in Silesia on 28 September. Lacy detached the thoroughly reliable *GFWM.* Brentano with the Esterházy Hussars [H24], two pulks of Saxon-Polish uhlans and 400 German cavalry as a roving security against interference by Frederick, a danger which dictated a roundabout route. Marching through the hills and woods the Austrians arrived at Seydendorf on the same day, and on the 29th they reached Probsthayn and Johnsdorf, where the country began to open out. The 30th brought Lacy to Bunzlau. News of the destination spread among the soldiers, who were beside themselves with joy.[132] Lacy shared their impatience. He had got clean away from the scene of operations in Silesia, but he was chagrined at the delays in bringing up the provision carts, which had already set him back by two marches by 1 October. After an enforced wait at Bunzlau the troops were on the move again at four in the morning of the 2nd. Now the great heat and the sandy going exacted their toll, and the corps reached Freywalde in a state of collapse.

The Austrians got to Triebel on 3 October, and Cottbus on the 4th. The artillery was now being dragged by requisitioned farm horses and oxen, for the horses had foundered. The corps was now entering Prussian territory, and the Saxon-Polish uhlans were ravaging in the neighbourhood, in spite of every effort to rein them in.

Lacy could no longer tie himself to the pace of his infantry. He gathered up four regiments of horse, and rode with them to join Brentano at the advance guard. Their combined forty-three squadrons made all possible speed by way of Luckau and Zossen, and arrived before Berlin at ten in the morning of 7 October. It was an interesting moment, for the main body of Chernyshev's division had come up on the right (north) bank of the Spree and was skirmishing against the palisade which did service as an excise barrier on that side of Berlin, while on the near side Lacy found Totleben making a 'hellish fire' in that sandy and very Prussian-looking plain, where even the villages seemed to stand up like battalions.[133] Totleben was shooting at the Hallisches-Tor, but he desisted at the news that a Prussian column was approaching from Potsdam. It was in fact no more than a field bakery travelling under escort.

A more worthy element presented itself in the shape of a column of 6,000 troops (Kleist with the leading element of Hülsen's corps) advancing from Teltow. Lacy suggested a joint attack, and Totleben replied 'yes, we'll give it a try.'[134] Lacy brought up his cavalry on Totleben's left flank, but the joint advance progressed no more than a few hundred paces before Totleben commanded his Russians to halt, having contrived in the meantime to lose four of his unicorns (howitzers with long barrels). The Prussians were falling back, and Lacy took up the chase with 400 of his cavalry. Brentano recovered the unicorns, and the Austrians exchanged fire with the main body of Hülsen's corps before falling back.

A full-scale campaign appeared to be taking shape around Berlin. The successive reinforcements had brought the Prussian forces to between 14,000 and 17,000 men and Lieutenant General Prince Friedrich Eugen of Württemberg took charge of the whole.

The allies would shortly gather to a total strength of up to 34,000 troops. On 8 October Lieutenant General Panin joined Chernyshev to the north east of the city with the first division of Fermor's main army. That day was wild and wet, and the rain and the murk at first concealed from the Prussians the sight of Lacy's infantry arriving to join the rest of his corps south of Tempelhof. Lacy and Chernyshev were now planning to attack Berlin from their respective sides of the Spree on the 9th, and Lacy had every confidence that the Austrians would soon be in Berlin.

Lacy had brought with him a 'shopping list' of the kind that Hadik had carried in 1757, specifying as targets the *Zeughaus* (Arsenal), the *Lagerhaus* and other repositories of clothing and equipment, as well as the gunpowder and flour mills along the Spree and the artillery foundry, 'from where we will take away the chief foundryman, who is a famous Dutchman. We are to ruin the arms factories in Potsdam and seize the best workmen. In Potsdam itself we are to empty the map room, where there are to be found the plans of all the fortresses in Europe.'[135] The military and civilian records were certain to reveal much of interest, and Lacy intended to spirit away the heads of the government departments, the leading entrepreneurs, and Splitgerber the celebrated banker and arms contractor.

In view of the threat which was forming against them the Prussian generals decided to extricate all their troops except the original garrison, and make for the open country and Spandau by way of the unguarded north-western side of the city. Before daylight on 9 October, the day of the intended assault, Lacy learned that Hülsen's corps was retreating from its position in front of Berlin. Lacy ordered Brentano to send the Austrian grenadiers to occupy the high ground in front of the excise wall. 'A minute later I hastened up myself. I found that there were still Prussian picquets at the gates, but that on sighting our grenadiers the Russian dragoons and hussars were hastening to get to the gates first and place themselves in possession.' Lacy had just the time to occupy the Hallisches-Tor by one of his companies, and bring up two battalions in support.[136]

Only now did Lacy discover that Totleben

The Arsenal at Berlin

had been negotiating with the Prussian commandant, old Lieutenant General Rochow, to arrange the surrender of Berlin to the Russians on his own authority. They concluded their deal without reference to Lacy, and Totleben assured the Berliners that their freedoms and private property would be undisturbed, that he would admit no light troops to the city, only a minimum of the Russian regulars, and no Austrians at all. On their side the Berlin authorities agreed to pay a 'contribution' which, as negotiated down by the merchant Gotzkowsky, came to one and a half million taler, all of it to go to the Russians, with 65,875 taler on top for the Russian officers as a reward for their magnanimity. The Austrians had been left out of account altogether, and it soon transpired that Totleben had persuaded the city fathers that he alone was in a position to prevent them from being plundered by his Austrian allies. Lacy noted that the Russians on the far side of the Spree had made no attempt to bar the routes by which the enemy had escaped towards Spandau. 'Russians make themselves scarce whenever it is a question of having to fight. They are quick off the mark only when there is a prospect of pillage and booty... it is impossible to convey... just how much these people are swayed by their self-interest, confusion and ignorance. Unless I am very much mistaken we will never derive any real benefit from this connection.'[137]

Chernyshev had in fact been no party to any of this, and when he rode into Berlin with the furious Lacy he did what he could to mollify him. The Austrians were to keep guards at the Hallisches-Tor and the Potsdamer-Tor, and such of their troops who had already passed the excise wall were to remain in the Neustadt and the Friedrichsstadt. Chernyshev pointed out correctly that Vienna had promised all the proceeds of the capture of Berlin to the Russians (which had not been known to Lacy) as an incentive to them to advance, but to show his goodwill he diverted 50,000 taler of the contribution to Lacy as a sweetener for his troops.

Throughout 10 October the allies had Berlin in their undisputed possession. Drunken Russians were directed by their officers to the key establishments. Some damage was done to the artillery foundry, but the *Gold- und Silber Maufaktur* (which made the lace for the uniforms) and the military textile factory were spared as being privately owned, and the Russians went about the rest of their business in an ineffective way. They threw the weapons from the *Zeughaus* into the Spree (to be fished out later by the citizens), and patriotic Berliners saved arms and uniforms for their king by buying them back from the Russians at ridiculously low prices. A thunderous detonation from the *Zeughaus* signified only that the Russians had touched off a mortar in the courtyard, and their attempt to demolish the building came to an end when fifteen of their fellows blew themselves up when they were transporting the necessary gunpowder from the mill on the Spree below Berlin. Totleben's account nevertheless claims that the Russians by one means or another destroyed 57 pieces of artillery, 9,000 muskets, 4,000 carbines, 7,000 pairs of pistols, 9,765 cannon shot, 7,000 mortar bombs and 5,500 howitzer shells.[138]

Most of the Austrian troops were held back in and around Tempelhof, where Lacy had his headquarters. The troops already admitted to the suburbs were making the best of their opportunities. Colonel the Prince de Ligne lodged his grenadiers in the palaces, where 'they hung their cartridge pouches and their sabres from the bronze statues, the candelabra and the mirrors. They gave themselves airs and graces, but they took nothing and damaged nothing.'[139] However there is ample support for Totleben's claim that 'several thousand Austrians made their way into the city by force and claimed the whole of the Friedrichsstadt for their quarters. All the streets were full of them, so that I sent out more than 800 men to check all the robbing and plundering, and had to back them up by admitting Brigadier Benckendorff with a further regiment of infantry, together with all the mounted grenadiers. Finally, as they proceeded to assail and beat my guards, I had to open fire on them.'[140]

Lacy, 'who invariably showed himself a most bitter enemy to the Prussians,'[141] was glad to see that most of his colonels had the initiative to fit out their regiments by approaching the Russians and buying, or snatching, such items as lengths of cloth, belts and cartridge pouches.[142]

The Prince de Ligne was numbered among these enterprising gentlemen. He entered one of the great storehouses, and threw cloaks, leather gear and other good things out of a window to his drivers, who had drawn up a large cart outside.

To the west of Berlin the lakes around Potsdam and Spandau made the region 'a second Mantua.'[143] The Prussians had taken away the bridges, and they had placed a garrison in the citadel of Spandau, but otherwise the Austrians had a much freer hand than in Berlin. Lacy dispatched *GFWM*. Emmerich Esterházy to secure Potsdam with the Kaiser Hussars [H2] and two regiments of the Saxon-Polish uhlans. Esterházy exacted a contribution from Potsdam town, requisitioned the military clothing stored in the *Montirungskammer*, and wrecked as much as he could of the celebrated small arms factory of the *Splitgerber und Daum* combine. His men broke up the weapons, tools and lathes, and threw the brassware into the Havel along with more than 18,000 musket locks.

Esterházy set out guards on the exquisite pavilion of Sans Souci, and persuaded Franz Xaver Neffer, as supervisor of the royal palaces and gardens, to testify in the name of the staff of the Prussian court that 'the Austrian general Count Esterházy has left the royal palace here at Potsdam totally intact and undamaged. He has maintained the finest discipline and order, and shown all the respect due to the residence of a sovereign.'[144] That was simply untrue, for Esterházy appropriated a writing desk for Lacy, a flute for Carl O'Donnell, a pen for de Ligne, and for himself he took vases, table services, figurines and a large painting of a classical nude. Maria Theresa was scandalised when she heard of the theft, and ordered the painting and the pots to be restored to the king.

There was no protection of any kind for Charlottenburg, the royal palace just to the west of Berlin, which was at the mercy of the Cossacks and the Saxon-Polish uhlans. They ripped up wall hangings and paintings, splintered the doors, wainscoting and cabinets with their axes, and left the floors deep in the shards of chandeliers, mirrors and porcelain. The collection of Greek statuary which Frederick had bought from Cardinal Polignac was smashed so completely that it was impossible to think of putting it together again. All most deplorable, no doubt, but how mild, how very mild, compared with the destruction wreaked on Berlin in the Second World War.

By 11 October Lacy had news from Daun that Frederick and his army were on the march, which was the first indication of the general move of the main forces of the Prussians and Austrians to the Elbe, where they were to meet in bloody confrontation at Torgau on 3 November. Lacy told the Russians at once, and Field Marshal Saltykov, who had just resumed the command after a period of illness, needed no further prompting to order his forces back to the Oder at Frankfurt. The first of the Russians left Berlin in the afternoon, and all save Totleben's corps had departed by the morning of the 12th.

Lacy hoped that it might still be possible to operate in the heart of Brandenburg in association with the Swedes of General Lantingshausen, who were located somewhere to the north. On the 7th Lacy had dispatched a party of hussars to carry a message to them. There was no response to that feeler, or to a second party which Lacy sent after the first. In fact Lantingshausen was four marches away at Werbelow, near Pasewalk, with 17 battalions and 42 squadrons, and immobilised by hunger, sickness and losses in action. A lieutenant of the Kaiser Hussars delivered Lacy's invitation (probably the second) on 13 October. The Swedes were in no state to comply, and the Austrians were in any case already falling back from Berlin.

Lacy concluded that his corps could be of most use in the Saxon theatre, where the Prince of Zweibrücken had been waging a respectable campaign with the *Reichsarmee* and its attached Austrians, but needed help in his operation against Wittenberg. The Austrian infantry began to extricate itself from the Friedrichsstadt and the neighbourhood of Berlin on the evening of 11 October. Lacy lingered with five of his cavalry regiments until three in the afternoon of the 12th, hoping in vain to hear something from the Swedes. The last of the hussars fell back after nightfall, and on the 13th the reassembled corps reached Juterbog by way of Trebbin, as the first

Strehla overall, 20 August 1760

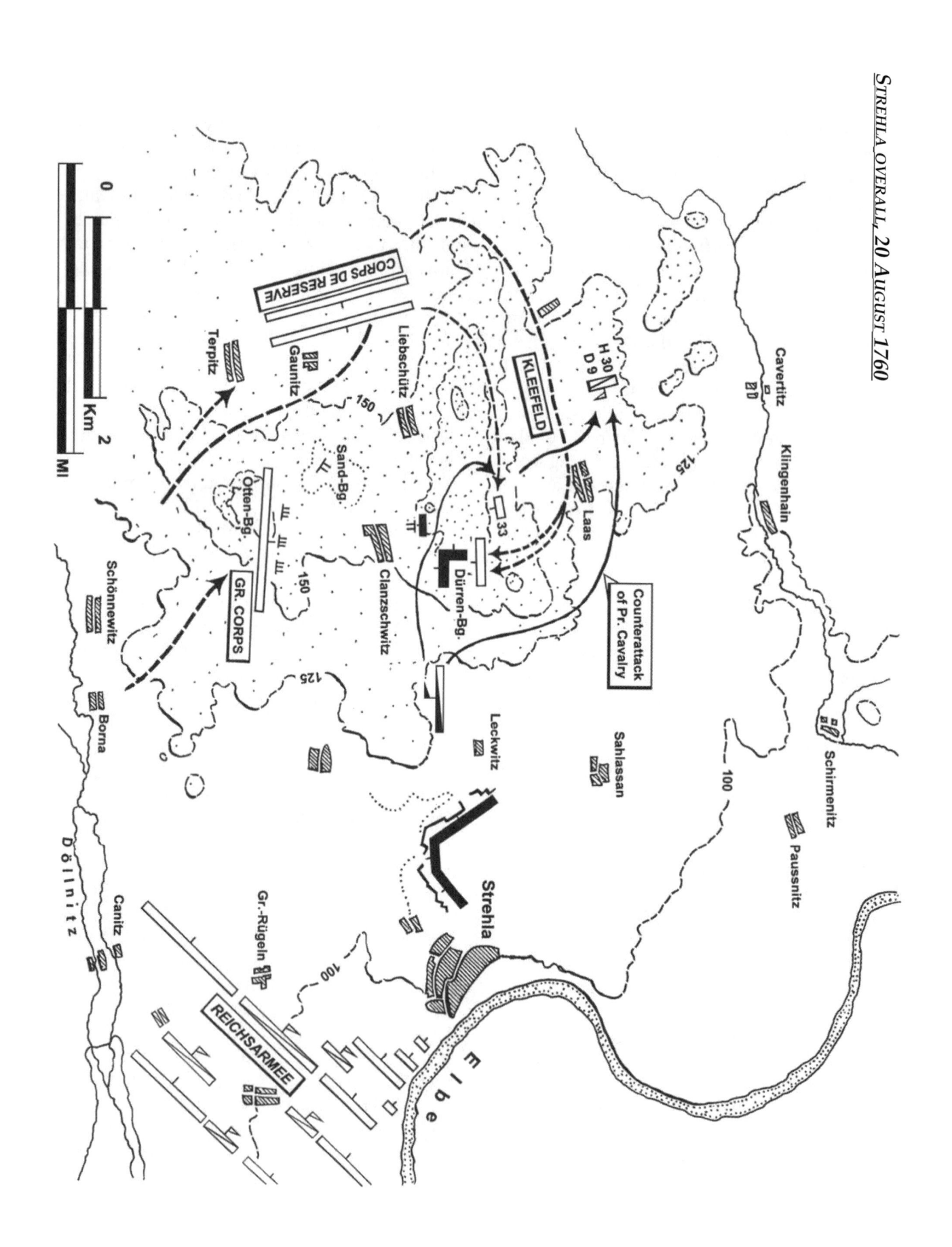

stage on the march to join Zweibrücken. These days offered the last opportunity for the Austrians to raise contributions in Prussian territory, and by the end of the expedition the sums amounted in all to 480 taler from Peitz and 4,775 from Cottbus and the vicinity (on the outward journey), and 42,000 in cash and promissory notes from Potsdam town, which together with the sums raised by hussars in the final days brought the total to 74,356 taler, or the equivalent of 111,534 florins.[145]

The corps reached Zahna on 14 October, and Lacy in person rode on to the Elbe, from where the sound of artillery had been heard. He found that Wittenberg had capitulated overnight, and that there was no longer any urgent need of his corps with the *Reichsarmee*. Lacy moved his corps to Plossig on the 17th, and the exhausted men could enjoy some rest, sheltered from the weather by the forests. They needed all the repose they could get, for on that day Lacy learned that the main Austrian and Prussian armies were on the march from Silesia.

The fact that the allies had lorded it in Berlin could not fail to make a sensation in Europe, and the exactions and booty had brought them some tangible gains. They ought to have been able to do a great deal more. An officer of the Prussian hussars noted that the allies in general did not press the enemy hard enough in this war, and among the instances he cited was the fact that 'the enemy forces which penetrated to Berlin and Potsdam only put on a show of ruining the arms factories and the other establishments.'[146] In any case the 'centre of gravity' of Frederick's state resided not in its materiel but in its troops, and here the failure of the allies was to have allowed Hülsen and Württemberg to escape from Berlin scot free.

In operational terms the main consequence of the blow at Berlin was to contribute to breaking the stalemate in Silesia, and draw Frederick and Daun over to the west. That part of the world was now the focus of the attention of the Austrians and the *Reichsarmee*, for, as Maria Theresa pointed out, 'we must do everything we can to maintain all Saxony on this (western) side of the Elbe for the winter, at least as far down as Torgau.'[147]

Tenuous Gain—The *Reichsarmee* and the Austrians in Saxony, August - October 1760

In the area of Dresden the campaign of 1759 had spilled over into the early weeks of 1760, and for months to come the operations in this corner of Saxony were dominated by the presence of the main forces of the Austrians and Prussians. At last, at the beginning of August, the scene of the confrontation of Daun and Frederick seemed to move definitively to Silesia, and the field marshal and the king left behind in Saxony only such troops as they could spare.

On 12 March Serbelloni had been promoted to field marshal, which gave the authorities a good excuse to move him from Saxony. On 3 May the command was invested in the Prince of Zweibrücken, who was at the very least a welcome replacement, and who kept the resourceful Austrian *GdC*. Andreas Hadik at his side. When they finally opened independent operations in August they had a superiority of more than two to one over the 12,000 troops of the veteran Prussian lieutenant general Johann Dietrich Hülsen, who could hope at best to dispute the Saxon Elbe step by step, cover Brandenburg from the south-west, and in general win time for his master on this theatre of war.

On 12 August Hadik had devised a plan 'whereby the army will advance to the left of the Elbe, evict the corps of Hülsen from Meissen by force or manoeuvre, or, failing that, shut him up in that position.'[148] By 16 August Hülsen's communications were under severe threat, and on the dark and rainy night that followed he slipped away undetected.

On the 18th Hülsen planted himself in another of the classic defensive positions of Saxony, one which Prince Henry had occupied in 1759, namely from the Elbe at Strehla westwards along the straggling heights to Leckwitz, with the wooded Dürren-Berg serving as the right-hand buttress of the camp. Here the old general learned of Frederick's victory at Liegnitz. He was so buoyed up that he was actually in the process of launching a surprise attack on the enemy flank when he discovered that the allies too were on the move.

Strehla, 20 August 1760

The enterprise was an affair by multiple columns in the new Austrian style, designed to draw Hülsen's attention to his south-facing front, and so leave his positions on the Dürren-Berg exposed to the main attack. The fixing role fell to the main body of the *Reichsarmee*, which was to march by way of Merzdorf and Canitz. The Prussian flank on the Dürren-Berg was to come under a concerted attack by

—*FML*. Guasco's Grenadier corps approaching the objective directly from the south, over the summit and eastern flank of the Otten-Berg (where there was an old Swedish earthwork) and on by way of Clanzschwitz

—*FML*. Prince Stolberg with the *corps de reserve* (8 bn and 10 sq) advancing due east

—*GFWM*. Kleefeld continuing around the Prussian flank as far as Laas, and coming at the Dürren-Berg from the north or rear

The allies set themselves in movement at 11 on the night of 19/20 August. The plan looked good on paper, but it failed to allow for the possibility of the vigilant and enterprising Hülsen's taking advantage of his interior lines to concentrate his forces, when the allies were most at risk of losing their orientation among the woods, hills and rocks to the north of the Dürren-Berg.

At first light Hülsen was busy reinforcing his right flank. On the threatened hill *GM*. Braun was therefore able to bring together not only his five battalions of grenadiers, but the regiment of Bevern [7] and three companies of that of Hauss [55] which had come from the main force. The Prussians now had the strength to form a three-sided defence of the Dürren-Berg. The west-facing flank came under a destructive fire from the guns which the *corps de reserve* brought up to the Liebschützer-Berg, but Braun had a north-facing line ready to greet Kleefeld's troops at close range when they emerged from the northern woods. At the same time he advanced the grenadier battalion of Burgsdorff with two heavy 12-pounders to the outlying Sittel-Berg, from where the gunners had a clear shot over Clanzschwitz against the Grenadier Corps. Guasco accordingly halted his massed grenadiers short of that village, and opened an unproductive artillery duel.

The Grenadier Corps was out of the reckoning, at least for the moment. The *corps de*

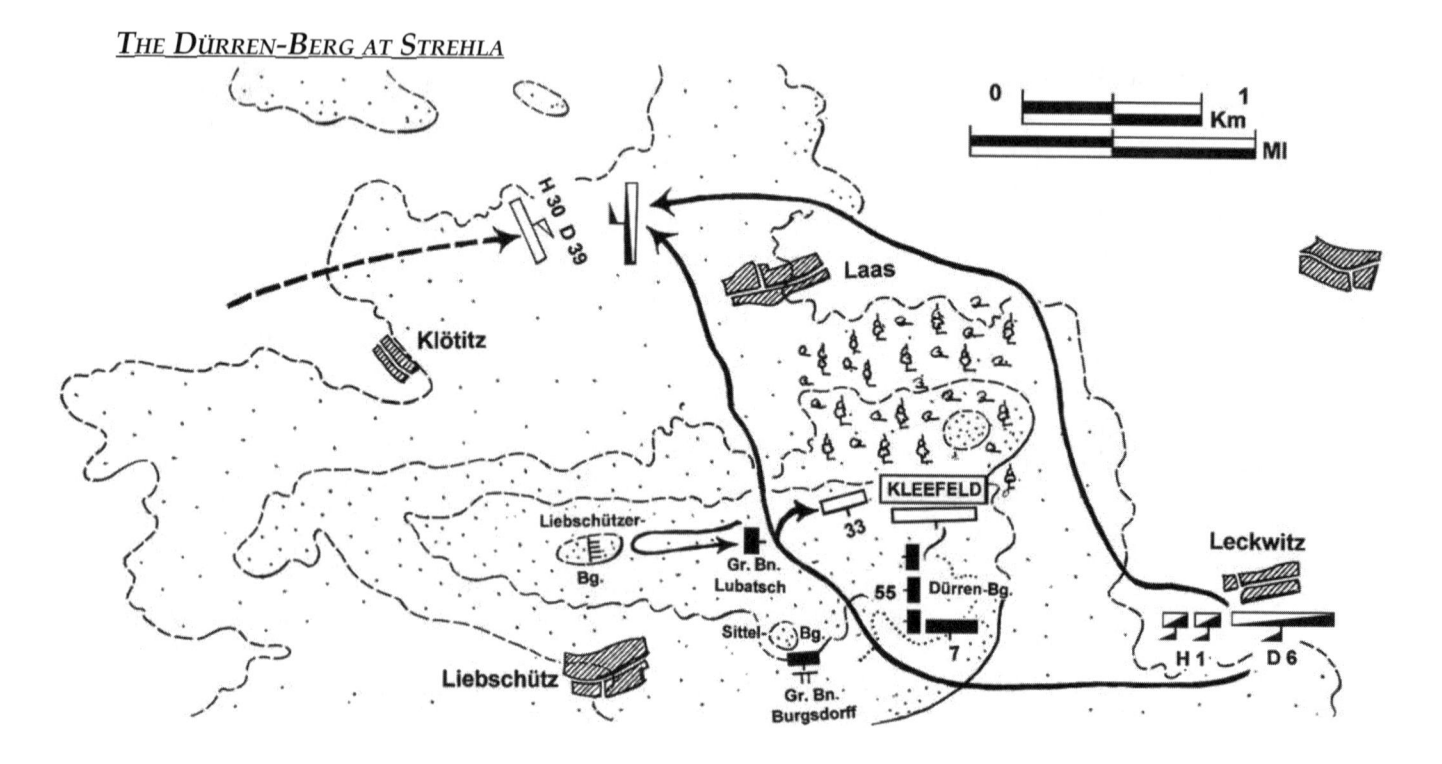

THE DÜRREN-BERG AT STREHLA

reserve too was hanging back, except for its guns on the Liebschützer-Berg, and the lone regiment of Nikolaus Esterházy [33], which had arrived in support of Kleefeld's command, and was now engaged in a close-range fire fight on the reverse slope of the Dürren-Berg. This was the moment when the Prussian defence took an altogether more active turn, for Hülsen had detached five squadrons of the Schorlemer Dragoons [D6] from their station near Leckwitz, and sent them hastening around the southern side of the Dürren-Berg in time to hit the Esterházy regiment in its right flank. The Prince of Stolberg, as commander of the parent *corps de reserve*, was unaware of what was happening, on account of the intervening hills and thickets, and a wholesale massacre was averted only by Captain Seeger of the Austrian staff, who 'advanced with the Swabian Circle regiment of the Hohenzollern Cuirassiers, forcing the enemy cavalry to cease hacking away, and finally driving them off.'[149]

The Prussian dragoons went in search of easier prey, and found it in the more open country east of Laas, in the shape of the Baranyay Hussars [H30] and the Pfalz-Zweibrücken Chevaulegers [D39], who had been posted there in order to intercept any Prussian retreat. These unfortunates were attacked simultaneously by the remaining three squadrons of the Schorlemer Dragoons and by the light cavalry of 'Green' Kleist. The bold Prussians had time to carry off

Strehla, the Dürren-Berg from the SSW.

Colonel the Prince of Nassau-Usingen and three standards of the chevaulegers before allied reinforcements could arrive.

The allies had fourteen intact squadrons ready to intervene, and the *Reichsarmee* was now advancing against the weakened front of the Prussian position. Hülsen had to recognise that he had stretched his forces and his luck to the limit. He disengaged his troops at one in the afternoon. He had lost 1,062 men from all causes, but he had exacted a total price of 1,800 from the Austrians and the *Reichstruppen*. The Prussians got clean away, and by seven in the evening they were ensconced in a still more celebrated position, that of Torgau.

The delay at Torgau, August - September 1760

Hülsen's position extended along the familiar ridge to the west of Torgau town, and a bridge linked him to a double bridgehead on the right (eastern) side of the Elbe, a facility which enabled him to keep a watch on developments in Brandenburg, as well as to guard the way to Magdeburg downstream.

By standing firm at Torgau, Hülsen was able to check the enemy progress in Saxony for more than a month. Zweibrücken and Hadik were disinclined to risk another assault, after the costly affair at Strehla, and they twice thought of bringing forces to the right bank of the Elbe to test the bridgehead. They probed in that direction in the last week of August, but found that the defences were much stronger than they had expected. The next time they thought of risking a force on the right bank it was to be well downstream of Torgau and in the shape of the two newly-arrived formations, the 8,000-strong auxiliary corps of the eccentric Duke Karl Eugen of Württemberg, and the 6,300 troops of the Austrian lieutenant general Luzinsky.

Hülsen now became too enterprising for his own good. He decided to bring his corps through

The summit of the Dürren-Berg. The Prussian defence probably consolidated around the ancient earthwork shown in the photograph.

276

HÜLSEN IS EVICTED FROM DÖBIEN, 2 OCTOBER 1760

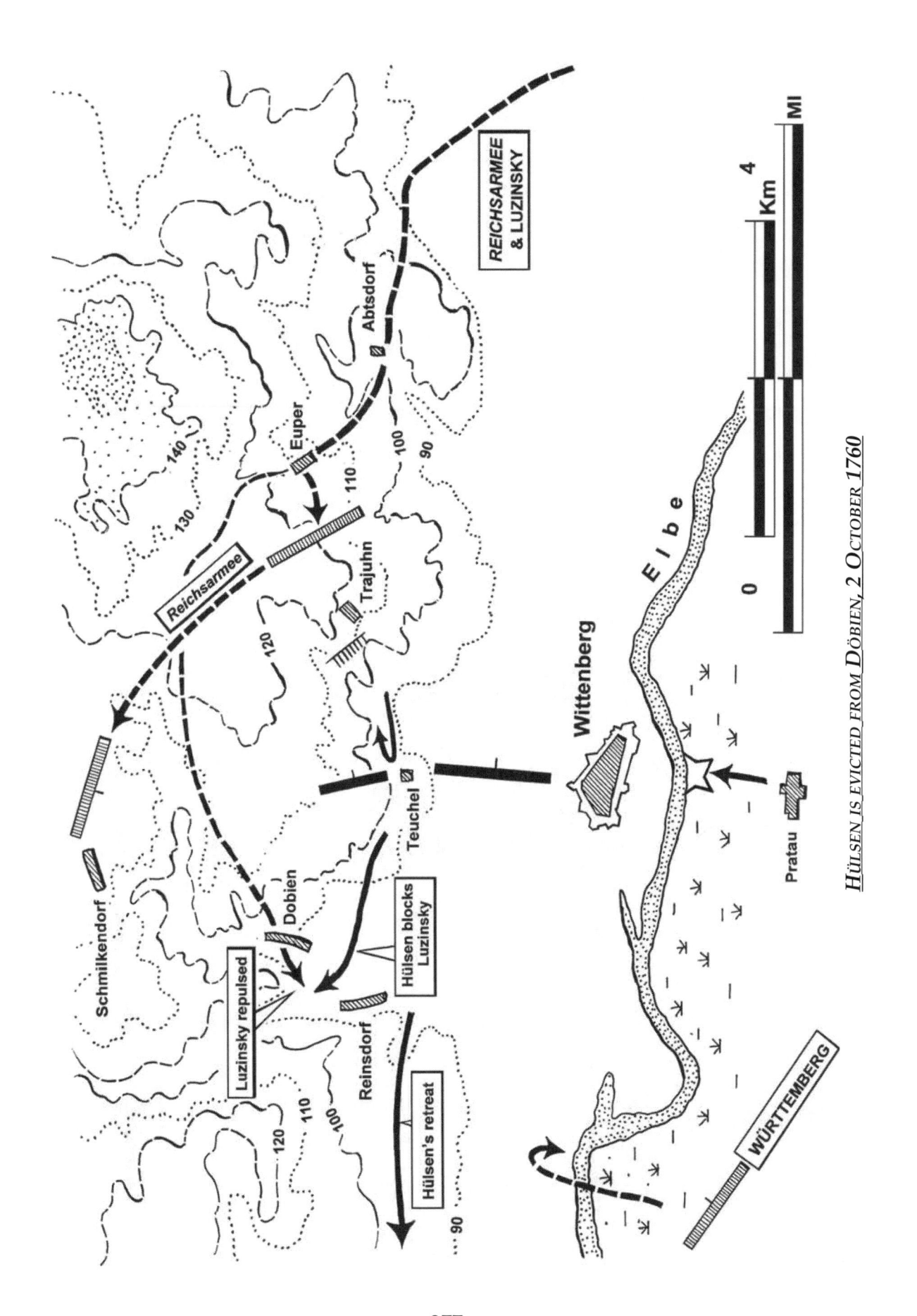

Wittenberg, 10-13 October 1760

Torgau town, over the bridges and strike down the right bank against the forces he supposed to be isolated on that side of the river. He made his move on the night of 26/27 September, but *GFWM*. Kleefeld and Colonel Johann Zedtwitz detected what was afoot and rushed forward from the main army with the nearest forces at hand. Kleefeld's Croats reached the river below Torgau before Hülsen could retrieve his floating bridge, and the Prussians lost forty of their pontoons. To the right, Zedtwitz drove the Prussian rearguard into the town, and brought up howitzers and heavy cannon which caused heavy damage to the wooden spans of the standing bridge.

Hülsen and his main force had reached the right bank of the river, but were now completely cut off from Torgau, where Major Normann and his 1,881 low-grade garrison troops and reconvalescents surrendered later on the 27th. Hülsen did not even have the satisfaction of catching the enemy forces he supposed to be on the right bank, for Luzinsky had re-crossed to Dommitzch, and the Württembergers had not stirred from Pretzch on the left bank. Hülsen at least had a clear path of retreat down the right bank to Wittenberg.

Dobien, 2 October 1760

By 1 October the rival forces had concentrated around the walled town of Wittenberg, which stood on the right bank of the Elbe. Hülsen was preparing defences among the hills and villages which extended in an arc to the north of the town, intending to make a last stand in Saxony just short of Prussian territory.

The *Reichsarmee* and the main force of the Austrians had moved to the right bank, and on the 2nd they went over to the attack. The Austrian Grenadier Corps made the first assault, which carried the village of Teuchel, but was checked among the earthworks, abattis and boggy ground behind. Hadik now hoped to take the Prussians in the rear by a thrust through Dobien. *GFWM*. Vecsey was supposed to lead the way by passing a steep valley above that place, but he unaccountably failed to move, and Hülsen had time to rush up reinforcements in his usual style, and establish himself in strength in Dobien and an ancient earthwork nearby. From these positions he was able to check Luzinsky's Croats and four battalions of fusiliers which came up to support them.

Hülsen was finally unseated by a move on the part of the *Reichsarmee*, which in the course of the afternoon worked around to Schmilkendorf, four miles to the north of Wittenberg, thereby threatening the Prussian communications. Hülsen withdrew his troops from their defences, and at seven in the evening, and only just in time, he fell back down the right bank in the direction of Mühlstadt, as the first stage in his retreat to Brandenburg. 'We must give due justice to the enemy general Hülsen and his corps. He acted as a far-sighted and experienced commander, as shown by the great skill with which he maintained his positions into the night, and exploiting the features of the ground to the full. As for his troops, they put up an obstinate defence of their assigned positions.'[150] Such was Hadik's tribute. Between 300 and 400 men had been lost on each side.

The siege of Wittenberg, 10-13 October 1760

The retreat of Hülsen from the positions outside Wittenberg left the defence of the town entirely in the hands of two Prussian garrison regiments. The walls and bastions were old but strong, and mounted 24-pounder cannon, which were pieces of unusually heavy calibre for such a purpose. On 10 October the Austrians and the *Reichstruppen* opened their first parallel, which embraced the whole of the northern and north-western sides of the town, and at first light on the 13th Major Grumbach opened fire with howitzers and light mortars and three batteries of cannon. The besiegers had the gratification of seeing one of the Prussian pieces dismounted, and two of the fearsome 24-pounders blow up, but their own 12-pounders were too light to breach the walls, and disturbing reports told that large enemy forces were on their way to Saxony.

In such a state of affairs the Prince of Zweibrücken decided, with considerable misgivings, that he must attack the town directly, and he accordingly aimed a number of mortar bombs at one of the towers of the *Schloss*, which was known to contain a powder magazine. Towards noon a great fire broke out in the building, and a violent wind fanned the conflagration towards the town, where the nearby houses were all of wood. Little could be done to save them, for there was no water available inside the town, and the flames spread out of control. Hadik noted as a matter of curiosity that the answering fire from a Prussian howitzer touched off one of the siege mortars without any human intervention.

The blaze extended to the neighbouring church, where the great heretic Luther had nailed his declaration to the door and later was buried (a fact known to Grumbach, who was said to wished to destroy the tomb), and then from tower to tower and along the parapet of the whole of the stretch of wall under attack. The security of Wittenberg was reduced to the wet ditch, and this too was lost at nine at night, when 120 volunteer *Reichstruppen* seized and destroyed the sluices which retained the water. There was no opposition, for the attention of the garrison had been diverted by a demonstration by three battalions against the Elster-Tor. The besiegers were now searching for scaling ladders in the nearby villages, and at eleven at night the defenders beat *chamade*. On 14 October the two regiments marched out with military honours, and laid down their arms as prisoners of war.

BEFORE TORGAU, OCTOBER-NOVEMBER 1760

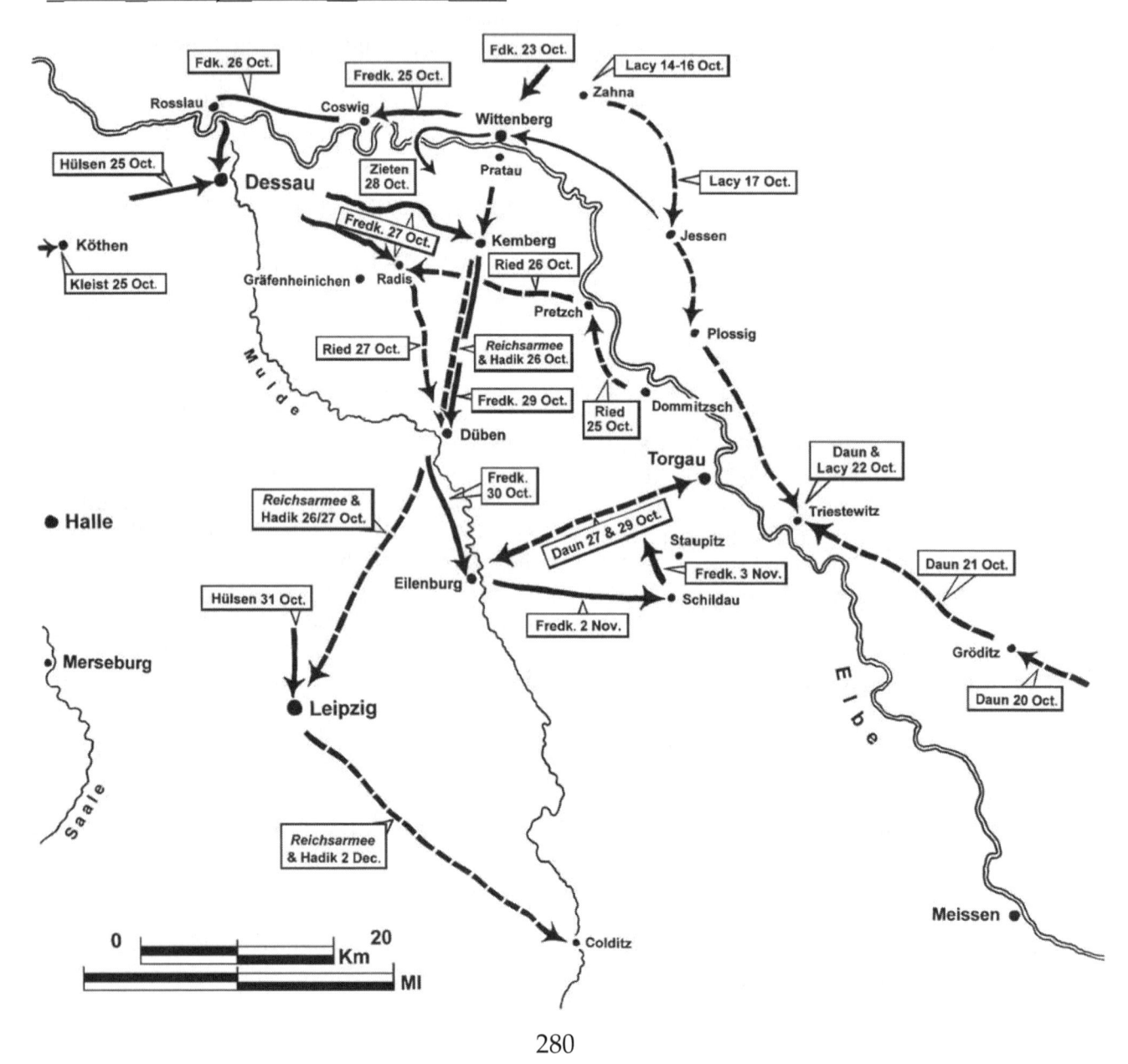

The *Reichsarmee* and the Austrians had lost 43 men killed, 29 missing and 212 wounded, and expended 3,115 rounds of artillery ammunition.

The collapse of the *Reichsarmee*, late October early November 1760

Having ventured so far down the Elbe, the *Reichsarmee* and the supporting Austrians very soon found their position untenable. The joint forces had already been weakened when the Duke of Württemberg left for the Saale on 12 October with his auxiliaries, 'offering as his excuse the fact that the third of the trophies and military equipment (which we hoped to find in Wittenberg) had not been promised to him in advance.'[151] The odds became adverse when the main Prussian and Austrian field armies began to move back towards the Elbe, with the Prussians bringing altogether superior forces to bear on the lower reaches of the river.

The *Reichsarmee* and the supporting Austrians could now hope at best to hold the left bank and so gain time for Daun to come to their help. They wrecked the fortifications of Wittenberg, and evacuated the last of their troops on 23 October. Frederick and his leading forces reached the devastated town later that day, but found the far bank of the river lined with the batteries of the *Reichsarmee*. It was only a stay of execution, for the two corps of Hülsen and Prince Friedrich Eugen of Württemberg (younger brother of Duke Karl Eugen, but a lieutenant general in the Prussian service) were working around their left flank. On 26 October the *Reichstruppen* and the Austrians fell back from the Elbe to Düben, which gave Frederick's leading forces a free passage of the river. The following night was critical for the outcome of the campaign. Zweibrücken needed only to stay at Düben for a few hours more to be able to unite with Daun, who had been with the main Austrian army on the near side of the Elbe for two days now, and was marching to join him.

Instead, the continuing concerns for his left flank induced Zweibrücken to fall back to Leipzig, and then by way of Wechselburg to Colditz on 2 November, where the *Reichsarmee* arrived in a state of collapse. He wrote to Daun that he had good reason to believe that Hülsen's corps was the advance guard of Frederick's army, and that his own retreat was motivated by his concern to cover Daun's western flank and the Erz-Gebirge.

On 3 November the sound of heavy firing carried to Colditz from the direction of Torgau. There followed a courier from Daun, telling Zweibrücken that the Austrian army was retreating after a great battle, and requesting the return of all the Austrian troops with the *Reichsarmee*. Zweibrücken's campaign now effectively was at an end. The 11,500 Austrians took their leave on 4 November, and the 14,000 exhausted and dejected troops of the *Reichsarmee* began an arduous retreat towards the southern hills by way of Chemnitz and Zwickau. Hülsen was in charge of the pursuit. He did not press particularly hard, but he snapped up eighty men of the rearguard in Chemnitz, and proceeded to raise contributions that amounted to a huge 2,491,000 taler in defenceless Saxony.

**TO TORGAU,
30 SEPTEMBER - 2 NOVEMBER 1760**

The turn of September and October found affairs in Silesia in a state of frozen confrontation. On 30 September Daun was aware that Lacy's powerful raiding corps was on its way to Berlin, and on 6 October he received a letter which gave him reason to hope that he was nearing the capital. Conversely Frederick's army showed no signs of stirring from its position, and Daun's headquarters lay under a pall of pessimism. However the niceties demanded that Daun should hold a select dining party on the same 6 October, as the day of the marriage of Archduke Joseph in Vienna to Isabella of Parma. Prince Albert of Sachsen-Teschen and his brother had not been invited and Albert noted in his diary that 'what we learned of the brilliant festivities occasioned by this marriage, made me aware of the striking contrast with our situation here, perpetually exposed to the vicissitudes of the weather, and passing the days splashing about in the mud or fighting. The idle nobility of the capital were putting on a display of the most extraordinary luxury and magnificence on this occasion, and were much more taken up with their entertainments than with our military operations. But it is in just those operations that the honour and glory reside. This matters more than anything else, and I knew that I was much happier amid all our hardships than were those people who sought after diversions in the capital.'[152]

Daylight on 7 October showed that the royal army was at last in full march for the plain of Schweidnitz. There could be little doubt that Frederick was moving to save Berlin. Daun could see little point in following him in that direction, for the Russians (even if they could be trusted) would soon be on their way back east. By swinging into Saxony, on the other hand, Daun could still draw Lacy to himself, and hope to combine with the *Reichsarmee* in that theatre.

Even now Daun hesitated to take the full responsibility of transferring the main weight of the Austrian forces to the Elbe, and as a precaution he believed that he must at least shadow Frederick on his way from Silesia. Daun set his troops in motion in the afternoon of 7 October. The Austrian troops were now distributed as follows:

—Daun and the main force of 25,000 troops were marching to Kunzendorf and Freiburg on the edge of the Silesian plain

—a mobile force of 6,200 troops under *FML*. Beck was following on Frederick's heels

—Loudon remained in Silesia with 38,500 troops, with 3,500 more holding Glatz

—Lacy's corps (18,500) was outside Berlin

—11,500 Austrians were already operating with the *Reichsarmee* in Saxony

Daun's army, taking a generally westerly route, reached Jauer on 8 October, Wiesenthal on the 9th, and Neuland on the 10th, resting there for two days. On the 12th the Austrians arrived at Naumburg-an-der-Queiss. Daun was aware that Frederick's army was in the vicinity of Sagan, which was only two marches distant, and that the king had the choice of continuing on his way to Berlin, turning against the main Russian army on the Oder, or making west for Saxony. In any event Daun was now set firmly on moving to the Elbe. He knew that the Russian raiding force had probably left Berlin already, and that Lacy was now free to take his corps on a course that would converge with that of the his own army.[153]

Daun took up the new direction of march on 12 October, and crossed the Neisse to the Lusatian side at Penzig. The Austrians reached Ullersdorf on the 14th, and there on the next day Daun discovered that the Russians had indeed abandoned Berlin, and that Lacy was on his way to the Elbe. News also came that the *Reichsarmee* had captured Wittenberg, and that the whole stretch of the Saxon Elbe was now in friendly hands.

Daun's further march took him across Lower Lusatia to Milkel beyond the Spree on 16 October, Lieske on the 17th, Arnsdorf on the 19th, to a position between Wainsdorf and the Elsterwerda Canal on the 20th, and finally by way of Gröditz to meet Lacy at Triestewitz on the Elbe 22nd. 'He arrived in a pretty bad state. The cavalry were near collapse. The artillery horses were almost dead, and were being led by the hand in the hope of keeping them alive. His cannon were being drawn by oxen.'[154]

By bringing his disposable forces to Saxony, Daun had anticipated the wishes of Vienna. Kaunitz had been impressed by a memorandum from Count Flemming, the Saxon envoy, who urged the utility of holding all Saxony west of the Elbe, and exploiting the line of 'natural defence' which extended from Eilenburg to Leipzig.[155]

Further cogitations resulted in a detailed instruction which went to Daun in the name of the Empress on 23 October, and may be regarded as the directive which impelled the Austrians to give battle eleven days later. She wrote that it was likely that Frederick would now seek to reoccupy Saxony, and thereby gain the resources in provisions, recruits and money which would enable him to bring a powerful force into the field in 1761, and, by threatening the flank of the French forces in Germany, to compel them to evacuate Hanover. The need for Daun to hold Saxony was therefore something which concerned 'the outcome of the whole war and the subsequent peace, and consequently the present and future welfare of my hereditary house… for this reason I hereby give you the appropriate order to defend the Saxon territories as far as is humanly possible. At the least you must take in the town of Torgau, together with Eilenburg, Leipzig and so on, and you must hold them through the winter, even at the cost of a risky battle, or something else of a decisive nature.'[156]

Probably nothing short of a positive order would have steeled Daun to consider fighting so far down the Elbe. Frederick too had resolved to concentrate his forces in Saxony. He made the necessary arrangements during a (for him) prolonged period of rest and consolidation at Lübben between the 17th and the 20th. He sent Lieutenant General von der Goltz back with 14,000 men to confront Loudon in Silesia, and ordered Hülsen (after his delaying action in Saxony) and Prince Friedrich Eugen of Württemberg to cross the Elbe well downstream at Magdeburg, lever the *Reichsarmee* out of its positions, and wait for him to arrive with his army on the left bank.

On 22 October Daun having met Lacy on the Elbe, brought his army across the river and left Lacy for the time being on the east bank. Daun and Lacy together had more than 55,000 troops at their disposal, and if they had now been joined by the 14,000 men of the *Reichsarmee* and the attached 11,000 Austrians, the total would have reached an impressive 80,000. That was not to be, for Zweibrücken not only abandoned the Elbe, but fell back from Düben on the night of 26/27 October (above). Undisturbed by any enemy action, Frederick brought his army across the river to unite on the left bank with Hülsen and the Prince of Württemberg at Dessau in the course of the 26th. This powerful force marched upriver to Kemberg on the 27th. The king was unaware of the location of the various allied forces, but he had managed to interpose himself between Daun and the *Reichsarmee* and its Austrians, who were recoiling on Leipzig. Their 25,000 troops were now out of the reckoning.

Hardly anybody knew his bearings among the vast tracts of sandy forests, and at four in the morning of 27 October one of Daun's advance detachments, of some 4,000 troops under *GFWM*. Ried, received the very tall order to cover the Elbe from Wittenberg to Coswig, and the Mulde from Düben to Dessau. He was sounding the way to Gräfenheinichen with 400 of the Széchenyi Hussars [H32] and Staff Dragoons when he ran into the Colonel 'Green' Kleist and the advance guard of the Prussian army at **Radis**. It now became a question of 'cutting a way through at sword point.' The Austrians were chased at high speed towards Düben, and before they made their escape they lost 120 men killed and wounded and 165 as prisoners.[157]

Frederick and his 56,000-odd troops were marching almost as blindly, but on a route by way of Kemberg, Düben and Eilenburg which ultimately brought them against the rear of the Austrian army in its position at Torgau. Ried's little corps was keeping only just in front, and on the 29th it once more barely escaped destruction, when Prussians were advancing south from Kemberg. Ried counted on the enemy being delayed by the passage of the Mulde at Düben, for the rearguard under Captain Kovachevish had removed the planks from the bridge, 'but the enemy found such sympathisers there that these "patriots" brought the planks back again and repaired the bridge.'[158] The rearguard was overwhelmed with a loss of one hundred men. Ried himself was once more lucky to escape, and his adventures were still not at an end.

Frederick reached Eilenburg on the 30th, and on 2 November he lunged against Schildau, which he knew to be a favourite position of the Austrians. The enemy were nowhere to be seen, but the day brought him two happy developments. At Staupitz 'Green' Kleist and 2,000 horse caught up with the ten squadrons of the detachment of *GFWM*. Brentano, guarding the Austrian magazines and the communications with Dresden. The Austrians lost 300 men, which was gratifying in itself, and Frederick learned that he had unwittingly arrived in the rear of Daun's army, which was in fact to the north of him just outside Torgau. The Austrians would now have to fight, if they intended to stay in force in Saxony to the west of the Elbe.

As early as 28 October Daun had recognised that it was impossible to comply with Vienna's wishes to cover the river lines of northern Saxony in their entirety. He hoped at least to base himself on Eilenburg, as a central position, and marched there on 27 October. He had to abandon that place too, at the news that the hostile army was on the march from Kemberg, and on the 29th he arrayed his troops in a new camp extending to the west of Torgau. Lacy with the raiding corps from Berlin had already crossed to this side of the Elbe on the 27th, and Daun now had the means of offering a respectable battle. Moreover the position at Torgau was one of the classic defensive sites of northern Saxony, for both Prince Henry of Prussia in 1759 and Lieutenant General Hülsen in the present year had bid defiance from there against greatly superior numbers.

Torgau, The Great Battle, 3 November 1760

a) Austrians
Grand total: c. 55,640
—main army and *corps de reserve*: c. 33,500; 23,546 infantry, c. 10,000 cavalry
—Lacy's corps: 18,449; 11,541 infantry, 6,908 cavalry
—Light corps of Ried: 3,686 assorted troops
—Artillery: 275 pieces: 167 3-pounders, 50 6-pounders, 30 12-pounders, 8 24-pounders, 20 howitzers. Throw weight: 1,343 pounds of shot, 140 pounds (stone weight) of howitzer shells
Losses of the main army and *corps de reserve* 11,499: 1,304 killed, 3,099 wounded, 7,096 missing and prisoners (details from HKRA 1760 XI 1K, Daun to the *Hofkriegsrath*, 14 November). The losses of the Saxon cavalry, the light troops in general, and the two corps of Ried and Lacy brought the total to v. approx. 15,000

b) Prussians: 48,000 (Kessel, lowest), 52,000 (Lindner, highest). Including Zieten's corps of some 18,000 men
Losses: 16,670 (Jany, lowest), 24,700 (Bleckwenn, highest) (N.B. Frederick kept the figures relating to this battle a close secret, and the estimates by the best researchers therefore vary a great deal)

First Dispositions

The position of Torgau extended as a low ridge to the west of the town. The first rise was that of the municipal vineyards (Torgauer Ratsweinberge). The ground dipped to the gentle hollow of Zinna, then rose again to form the heights of Süptitz, standing above the hamlet of the same name. The ground thereabouts was sandy and unproductive, but rich in various kinds of natural obstacles. The southern slopes of the ridge were steep in places, especially above Süptitz, and descended in the south to the Röhr-Graben stream, which rose in the woods to the west, filled a pair of ponds, the 'Sheep Ponds' (Schaf-Teiche), and continued in a double channel by way of Süptitz to the Great Pond (Grosser Teich) which was the misleading name for an extensive lake to the south-west of Torgau. The zone of the Sheep Ponds could be passed only on causeways, and the banks of the stream were marshy and difficult to cross.

Short stretches of open ground separated the open end of the position from the Dommitzscher-Heide, a tract of forest which embraced the ridge in an arc to the west and north-west. It was there that the position was most vulnerable, as Prince Henry had recognised in 1759, when he felled the trees and bushes along the edge of the woods to form an abattis. The ground to the north and east of the ridge descended to an open and level plain, where another of those useful little streams, the Zscheitschken-Graben, rose in the boggy Röhr-Teich, and curved in a gentle anti-clockwise course past Welsau, received the waters of the Strieh-Bach near Neiden and continued to a branch of the Elbe.

On first arriving at the position of Torgau, Daun had deployed the troops of his main army in two lines facing north. The field marshal changed front to the south, when the enemy appeared in the neighbourhood of Schildau, but he held essentially the same ground, which extended for some two miles to the west of Zinna, and took in the tactically strong heights of Süptitz. However a space of one and a half miles, of open and level terrain, separated Zinna from Torgau and the three bridges of boats which spanned the Elbe—those bridges which offered the Austrians their main path of escape of things turned out badly. For that reason Daun entrusted the guarding of this expanse to the corps of Lacy, which amounted to one-third of the total forces available to the Austrians. Lacy arrayed his troops in two thinly-spread lines slantwise from Zinna almost to the northern shore of the Grosser Teich.

Beyond the far, or western end of the ridge, a scattering of detachments guarded the ways through the woods. The much-travelled corps of Ried took up station north of Mockrehna and at Wildenhain. Further north an excellent regiment of Netherlands light horse, the Saint-Ignon Chevaulegers [D31], was posted north of Weidenhain to observe the road from Düben. A similar task fell to Colonel Ferraris, who was standing with the Batthyány Dragoons [D7] and three battalions of grenadiers to the north-west of Elsnig, watching the narrows of Vogelgesang.

The army's *corps de reserve* was a body which had performed great services at Kolin, and was now represented by four regiments of infantry and two of cuirassiers, stationed under the command of *GdC*. Prince Löwenstein on the heights of Grosswig to the W.S.W. of the main position. A fifth regiment of infantry, the Hungarian regiment of Gyulai [51], had been left in garrison in Torgau. The *corps de reserve* was covered on its flank towards the woods by another elite force, namely *GFWM*. d'Ayasasa's twelve companies of carabiniers and mounted grenadiers.

Daun thought it probable that any attack would come from the south, but as a cautious man he counted on detachments just mentioned to give him due warning of any hostile force which might try to reach him by way of the woods. The Austrians (contrary to general repute) were not great diggers on the battlefield, and the field marshal did nothing to prevent his troops from robbing the abattis for firewood. The only other legacy of the Prussian occupation was a useful little redoubt on the hill north of Süptitz.

The Austrians had a superiority in numbers of troops of about 5,000. Frederick was accustomed to going into battle against much greater odds, and now he actually had an advantage in artillery, and especially in the heavier calibres. However the Prussian army was not what it used to be, and the Austrians were in a strong position. A headlong mass frontal assault would not serve, and instead Frederick resolved to divide his forces. He told off General Zieten with 18,000 troops to come at the enemy from the direction they now expected, which was from the south. The rest of the army would divide into three main columns, execute a left-flanking march through the Dommitzscher-Heide, and emerge in the woods in the vicinity of Elsnig and Neiden. From there the king would attack from the north against the rear of the Austrian position, which he envisaged as extending as far to the east as Torgau.

On the cold, dark and wet evening of 2 November Frederick brought his generals together. He was restless and unhappy. '"Gentlemen, there is nothing we can do at the moment. We are waiting for somebody." He was talking about Zieten, who had been delayed, but now came hastening up. 'The king took him by the arm, and led him away a little while from the others. He came back in a cheerful mood and at once gave out the necessary orders.'[159]

Frederick's instructions to Zieten were never written down, though he was probably told to keep the Austrians amused until the main army was ready to deliver its assault from the north, whereupon Zieten would attack from the south, the two elements to meet to the west of Torgau. The written *Disposition* provided for a textbook 'oblique attack,' in this case weighted towards his left wing, which was to evict the Austrians from the vineyards close to Torgau town.

Frederick's approach march

The Prussian army set off into the murk at 6.30 in the morning of 3 November. The force made its way by multiple columns in the direction of Audenhain to the NNW. Just short of the village Zieten turned his corps sharply to the right and began to make his way slowly towards Torgau. He had less than six miles to go. The other three attacking columns, or about 32,000 troops, under the overall command of Frederick, were faced with a clockwise trek of twelve or more miles, taking roughly parallel routes along the forest paths.

The innermost circuit was followed by 15,700 infantry and up to 1,000 hussars. Markgraf Karl of Brandenburg-Schwedt was in nominal charge, but he did little more than manage details, for the king accompanied the column in person.

GFWM. Ried was standing with his light corps in a wood behind Mockrehna, and so for the third time in a matter of days he found himself directly in the way of Frederick. He was also aware that a further column (the second, below) was marching further to the west. Ried made a pretence of a stand, at the same time disengaging his forces by instalments, and finally broke free altogether and took up a new post at Weidenhain. He had won the time for d'Ayasasa's elite cavalry to fall back from there to join the *corps de reserve* at Grosswig. By Ried's account, 'I had scarcely formed up, when the enemy arrayed themselves on the far side of the village [Weidenhain]. Once more we exchanged artillery fire, until I became aware that the enemy were just trying to tie me down, while their infantry were working around my right flank along the edge of the woods by the Dommitzsch road.'[160]

The noise of the cannonades put Daun on the alert. Frederick was therefore losing an important element of surprise, and he suffered a further vexation when the chief forester of the Dommitzscher-Heide directed his column too far to the left, along the Ankerweg, which meant that when he finally emerged from the woods it was too far to the north, near Elsnig instead of Neiden.

Torgau, 3 November 1760, the Prussian approach

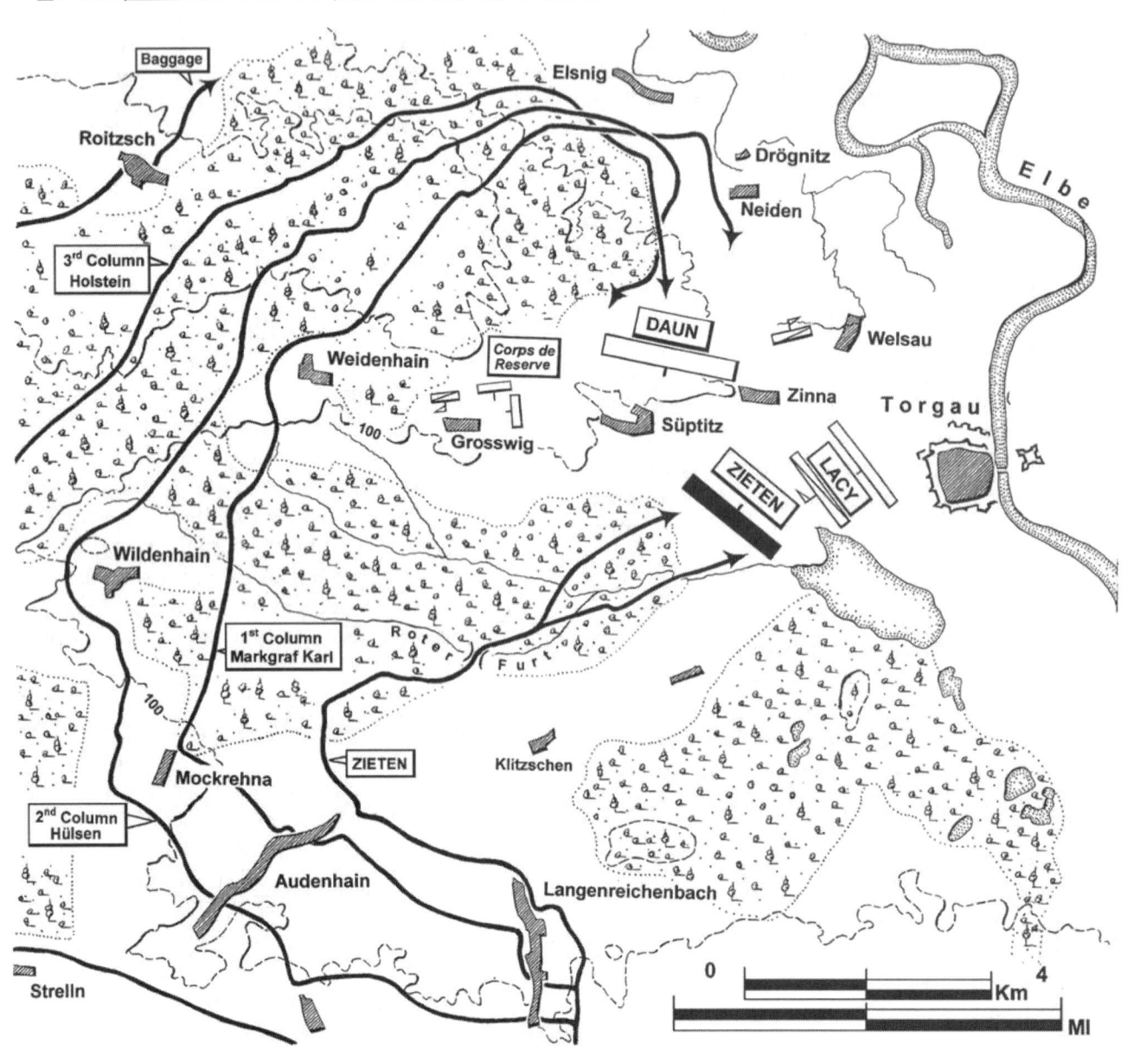

The second, or middle column, that of *GL.* Hülsen, was a smaller affair, of 6,300 infantry but accompanied by a powerful artillery train of 36 heavy 12-pounder *Brummers* and eight howitzers. Hülsen encountered no obstacle until the king's column barged across his route in the way just described. The leading battalions were cut off, and, when the path was clear, they retraced their steps and came up to the former tail which was now in front.

During these complications Frederick learned from prisoners that a body of Austrian horse (the Saint-Ignon Chevaulegers [D31]) was standing somewhere nearby, in fact in a most unenviable position between the two columns. The Zieten Hussars [H2] combed the woods, found the Netherlanders off their guard, and attacked and virtually wiped them out. The grenadiers and dragoons of Colonel Ferraris would have shared the same fate if, by chance, some of the men had not gone in search of water and encountered the enemy. Ferraris gave a few cannon shot, then withdrew to safety across the rain-swollen Strieh-Bach. 'That part of the world was in the rear of our [Austrian] army, and we believed it was so secure that the field marshal's headquarters was due to be transferred to Neiden in the course of the day. From this you may deduce how badly it would have gone for the Austrian army if the enemy had set out from their camp at Langenreichenbach a few hours earlier, and all the columns had arrived at the same time in the neighbourhood of Neiden.'[161]

The third of the Prussian columns was commanded by *GL.* the Prince of Holstein-Gottorp, and consisted entirely of cavalry, apart from a small brigade of infantry and a train of ten 'Austrian' medium 12-pounders. Holstein was assigned the outermost of the three routes, by way of Koberschein and Schöna. He had the furthest to go, and he was delayed by the complications of passing through Schöna and across the bridge over the Mühl-Bach, and by the narrow and sandy paths. He did not arrive within sight of the enemy until after the battle had begun.

Colonel the Prince de Ligne had set out from Lacy's corps to liaise with the main army. 'We found the field marshal issuing the parole [password] to his right wing. Just afterwards we heard the cannon shots from Ried, followed by those of Ferraris by the village of Vogelgesang, and the fire of our [Lacy's] Croats who had just been chased from Klitzschen. This told us that the enemy were coming, and must be close.'[162] Tidings now arrived from the parties in the woods, and in the most detail from d'Ayasasa, which established that the enemy movements out to the west and north were more than a diversion, and 'it was this final report which persuaded the field marshal to reposition our troops.'[163]

Daun reverses front and prepares to meet the enemy

Daun kept his head during these unexpected turns of events, and issued his orders with admirable clarity. The immediate priority was to confront the threat from the north, and Daun ordered the first line of his main army to take itself around and assume the same north-facing deployment as when the Austrians first entered the camp of Torgau. The most speedy procedure would have been for the troops to turn about on the spot and march off, but this would have offended against the principle of seniority, and thus the line executed a countermarch, ensuring that the regiment of Kaiser [1] retained the foremost place of honour on the right, that of Erzherzog Carl [2] the second place, on the far left, and so on.[164] Erzherzog Carl and the companion regiments to its right (Hildburghausen [8] and Baden-Durlach [27]) did not form a geometric extension of the left, but were pivoted back to form a flank which faced west towards the woods, thus closing the gap between the two lines of the army.

GdC. Prince Löwenstein was ordered to bring up the *corps de reserve* from Grosswig, which was sensible enough in itself, but under the pressure of circumstances the infantry components (regiments of Carl Colloredo [40], Tillier [36] and Bayreuth [41]) were stationed beyond the far left of the first line, while the cavalry (Stampach and Serbelloni Cuirassiers [Cs 10, 12]) continued all the way east to Zinna. The mobile reserve had already been weakened when the regiment of Gyulai [51] was detached

Torgau overall, 3 November 1760

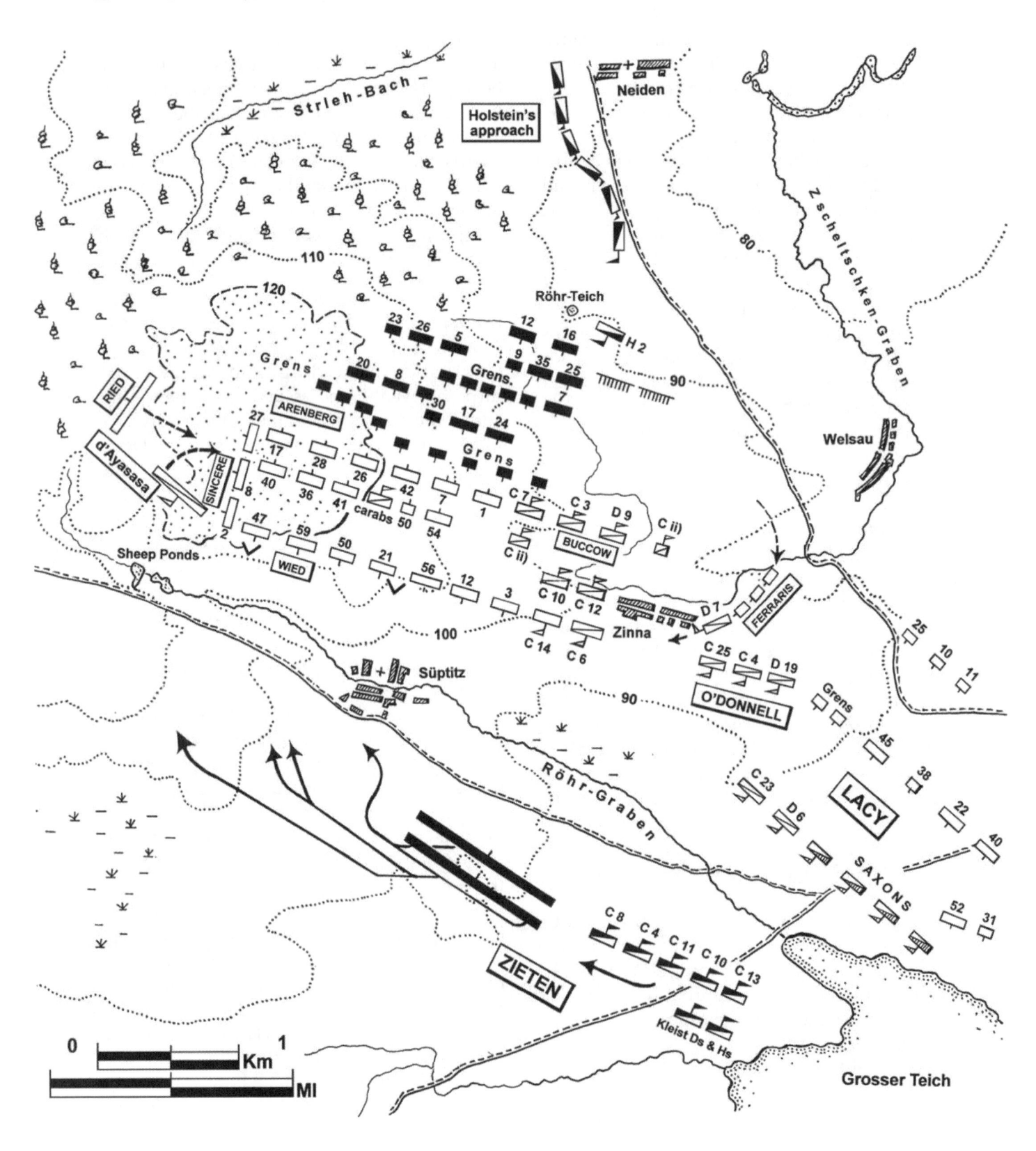

to garrison Torgau town, and now the separation of the infantry and cavalry deprived it of its coherence.

At the same time 'the pieces of artillery were rushed up with all possible speed and unlimbered wherever there were pieces of high ground, and everything generally was placed in high readiness to meet the expected attack. For the same reason the tents and all the baggage without exception were sent across the Elbe, so that there was nothing which could possibly get in the way in the event of battle.'[165]

Daun also identified the continuing threat from the south in the course of the morning, 'and he relied on our general [Lacy] to stop Zieten. He had good reason to fear that Zieten intended to seize the bridges, which would have cut off our retreat if we were beaten.'[166] Lacy was therefore to continue facing south, and this commission was to have an important influence on the later stages of the battle.

The first attacks of the royal army and the massacre of the Prussian infantry

Frederick emerged from the woods opposite Elsnig at about noon. He halted for a while to let the troops of the first two columns close up, then marched south. He had a free passage of the Strieh-Bach, for Daun had withdrawn the command of Ferraris to the main army, instead of stationing it to dispute the crossings, 'which in that marshy neighbourhood could be effected only by means of narrow causeways.'[167]

The advanced season and the low clouds made the span of daylight one of the shortest of the year, and the sense of urgency was heightened when the strong south wind carried what seemed to be the sounds of a major combat on the far side of the ridge. Frederick rode forward with a party of the Zieten Hussars [H2], and a sweep of his telescope told him to his dismay that the Austrian army lay not in front of him, but was heaped up in a strong position

Torgau. The edge of the woods. The right wing of the Prussian grenadiers emerged from the trees and attacked up the slopes to the right.

entirely to the west of Zinna (Lacy's corps being invisible). On the map Frederick would seem to be well placed to advance into the gap between Zinna and Torgau, and then wheel his army to the right to roll up the Austrians from the east. However all his instructions had been predicated on the basis of attacking the Austrian main force where he had originally supposed it to be, and there was no time to issue fresh orders. Moreover there was a threateningly large mass of Austrian cavalry standing on the spur to the west of Zinna, and Frederick still had no horse with him except the Zieten Hussars.

Frederick resolved to manoeuvre his forces into a position from where they could still attack the enemy more or less as planned, which he could do by directing the successive elements to jink to the west. He ordered the battalions already in line to march by ranks to their right, while the rearward battalions took up the new direction by the technically-advanced technique of a diagonal *Deployiren* from column of march. The troops were now marching back through the woods to their right, which ought to have afforded them some cover, but Austrian heavy cannon shot were now tearing into the trees, and the Prussians began to lose men from the falling trunks and branches. Colonel Dieskau contrived to bring up two heavy batteries to the edge of the woods near the Röhr-Teich, but his gunners were overwhelmed by the Austrian fire.

At two in the afternoon ten battalions of Prussian grenadiers emerged from the woods, in echelon towards their left, and Frederick marched them to the attack. It was only a distance of eight hundred paces from the edge of the forest up the gentle slopes to the line of Austrian heavy guns, which at once opened up with appalling effect. 'It was the first rounds which caused the great destruction. This kind of fire is always the most dangerous, for their gunners aim with great accuracy when there is no answering fire, and they are still out of reach of the musketry.'[168] The flames of the Austrian cannon stabbed through the gloom, and Frederick repeatedly exclaimed at the noise, which seemed to him like a battle between two thunderstorms.

For a time the grenadiers absorbed all the punishment, and ten battalions of the first Prussian column, together with the three leading battalions of Hülsen's, were able to approach undisturbed, though 'the thunder of the cannon echoed through the woods in a sinister fashion. The crashing shots assailed the ear like blasts from the trumpets of death.' At three in the afternoon these battalions too strode into the attack, 'and the advancing Prussians... saw before them not a scene of impending triumph, but a slaughter ground full of dead and hideously mangled corpses, which were weltering in their blood.'[169]

The Austrian counterattacks and the first crisis of the battle

It would now have been in the best interests of the Austrians to allow the enemy to continue to come forward. Instead, the first line of infantry was already descending the slopes in the first of a series of counterattacks. *FZM.* the Duke of Arenberg claimed later to Daun that upon the sight of Prussians moving in the forest 'With your agreement I advanced the regiments of Wied [28] and Puebla [26] to prevent the enemy from debouching from the woods. The enemy approached, and when they came within half musket range these two regiments charged with such impetus that they pushed back the enemy beyond their gun lines and as far as the woods.'[170] Franz Count Harrach, colonel of the regiment of Puebla, writes similarly that he advanced his men 'on my own initiative, but with the assent of *GFWM.* Pellegrini.'[171] *GFWM.* Dombasle took the credit for the attack of both this regiment and that of Kollowrat [17],[172] and over to right Colonel Leeuven was proud of having advanced the regiment of Kaiser [1] 'on my own initiative,'[173] a disturbingly familiar phrase. However *GFWM.* Sincère, a stickler for discipline, states specifically that the regiment of Kollowrat advanced contrary to orders,[174] and it is most unlikely that Daun would have consented to allow the precious integrity of his line to be broken in such a dangerous way.

Now it was the Austrians who were exposed on the slopes, and just when the leading regiments of Holstein's cavalry arrived on the scene. An unidentified regiment of Prussian horse broke and scattered the regiment of Baden-Durlach [27] on the Austrian left, and continued on its destructive way against the regiment of Kollowrat, and that of Puebla, where Colonel Harrach had pivoted back the second battalion to form a left flank against the onrushing horse.

The corresponding attack against the Austrian right was led by five squadrons of the crack Bayreuth Dragoons [D5]. At first they made as if to attack Buccow's wing of cavalry, but then wheeled to their right against the regiments of Kaiser [1], Neipperg [7] and Gaisruck [42]. Here *GFWM*. Pellegrini had been trying to form a flank, this time facing east, but at that moment 'a column of enemy cavalry fell on the middle of the brigade to my left. The battalions there had lost heavily under the enemy musketry, and that of the great battery which we had already seized and occupied, and now they were all taken from the rear and scattered. The rout was so great that when, after every effort, the survivors were rallied at Zinna, it was impossible to bring together more than thirty or forty men.'[175]

The Bayreuth Dragoons, the Spaen and Markgraf Friedrich Cuirassiers [Cs12, 5] and the Zieten Hussars [H2] captured altogether twenty-six colours, and were rounding up Austrian infantry by the hundreds as prisoners.

The Prussian cavalry and the re-energised Prussian infantry pressed home their advantage, and for a time looked set to cleave straight through the Austrian army from north to south. Prussian gunners, aiming too high, had already caused execution in the infantry of the south-facing Austrian second line, and especially the regiment of Mercy [56], where more than one hundred officers and men were plucked from the ranks by the roundshot.

At the sight of the Prussian infantry advancing over the ridge, *FML*. O'Kelly, as commander of the infantry of the second line, ordered Mercy and its companion regiments to turn about to face north. There was no stopping the Kollowrat fugitives, who fled through the files, but O'Kelly writes of being able to go over to the counterattack in association with reinforcements which arrived from an unknown quarter. It is impossible to identify the troops in question, but the ones closest at hand were those of the regiments of Jung-Colloredo, Tillier and Bayreuth [40, 36, 41] which were the infantry components of the *corps de reserve*, just inserted between the two lines of the Austrian army. They were launched under the eyes of Daun, and at the suggestion of one of his wing adjutants, Major Franz Neugebauer, and, by his own account 'I came up with them at just the right time, when the regiment of Kinsky [Tillier]

TORGAU, THE FATAL COUNTERATTACK OF ARENBERG'S INFANTRY
(This diagram and the following are schematic, and not to scale)

291

had deployed in half divisions. It advanced at once to within musket range, and through its steadfast behaviour it turned the balance and put the enemy to total flight.'[176]

From about half past three until five in the afternoon the combat surged up and down the northern slopes, as the Prussian infantry and cavalry repeatedly re-formed, renewed the attack, and themselves came under attack from a multitude of directions. It would have taken a substantial part of the present book to describe the episodes in detail, but in outline

—large forces of Austrian cavalry were now deployed in depth against the left (eastern) flank of the Prussian breakthrough

—to the south the Prussian advance was being met head-on by the infantry of the *corps de reserve* and the turned-around regiments of the Austrian second line

—the Prussian right (western) flank was being attacked by d'Ayasasa's elite cavalry and the hard-worked light troops of Ried

From the many available Austrian accounts it can be established that particularly heavy damage was inflicted on the infantry regiments of Goltz [24], Prinz Heinrich [35], Manteuffel [17], Queiss [8], Alt-Stutterheim [30] and Jung-Stutterheim [20], as well as unidentified grenadier battalions, the Bayreuth [D5] and Plettenberg Dragoons [D7], the Spaen Cuirassiers [C12] and the Zieten Hussars [H2]. Even the Gensdarmes [C10] wilted under the fire of Ried's Croats, and left behind three standards.[177]

O'Donnell against Holstein

The only fresh and uncommitted forces available to the Prussians on Frederick's side of the field were the regiments (possibly the Schmettau Cuirassiers [C4], and the Jung-Platen and Württemberg Dragoons [Ds 11, 12]) which were coming up in the rear of the Prince of Holstein's cavalry column. They were still marching generally to the south, and if they had continued on their way they would have arrived on the flank of the great gap between the two

TORGAU, THE COUNTERATTACK AGAINST THE PRUSSIAN BREAKTHROUGH

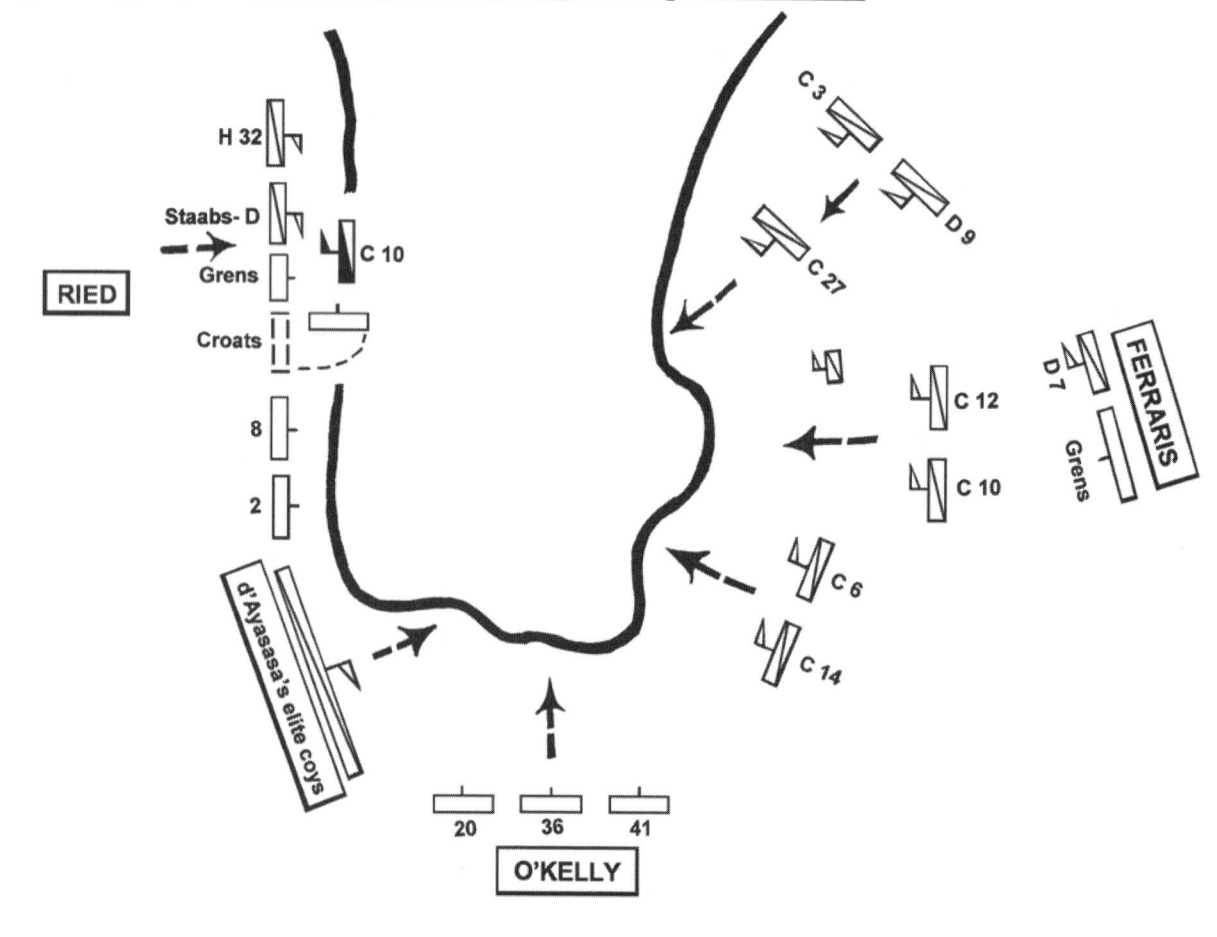

lines of battle on the east wing of the Austrian army. 'This body... would have been a considerable embarrassment to us, and perhaps even have decided the battle. But they were stopped by a small ditch or drain behind which our regiments had been placed, and inconvenienced by some pieces of artillery which we had abandoned, but were now catching them in enfilade. All of this won the time for the cavalry of our second line to form up on the flank.'[178]

The ditch in question was the upper course of the Zscheitschken-Graben, and the cannon were three 3-pounders which were sited by Daun in person. The cavalry belonged to the command of *GdC*. Carl O'Donnell. He had sent two of his cuirassier regiments as reinforcements to the battle in the centre, and he had been standing just to the east of Zinna with his remaining troopers (the Anhalt-Zerbst and Erzherzog Ferdinand Cuirassiers [Cs 25, 4], and the Hessen-Darmstadt Dragoons [D19]) 'and now came that moment when enterprise and a rapid decision gave us the opportunity to deal a weighty and decisive blow.'[179] O'Donnell's cavalry filed across the Zscheitschken-Graben with some difficulty, after which *GFWM*. Stampa and the cuirassiers assailed the Prussians frontally, while *GFWM*. Pettoni and the dragoons fell on the enemy left flank. They pursued the Prussians all the way beyond Neiden, and took a standard and Lieutenant General Finckenstein as trophies. They then had to retire in the face of powerful forces of infantry and cavalry which were rallying in a threatening way.

Daun's wound

Daun had done very well to co-ordinate the scattered elements of the Austrian defence, and he had often been on the spot to take charge in person. He had spent minutes at a time under heavy fire between the Austrian and Prussian lines, and had been standing in front of the

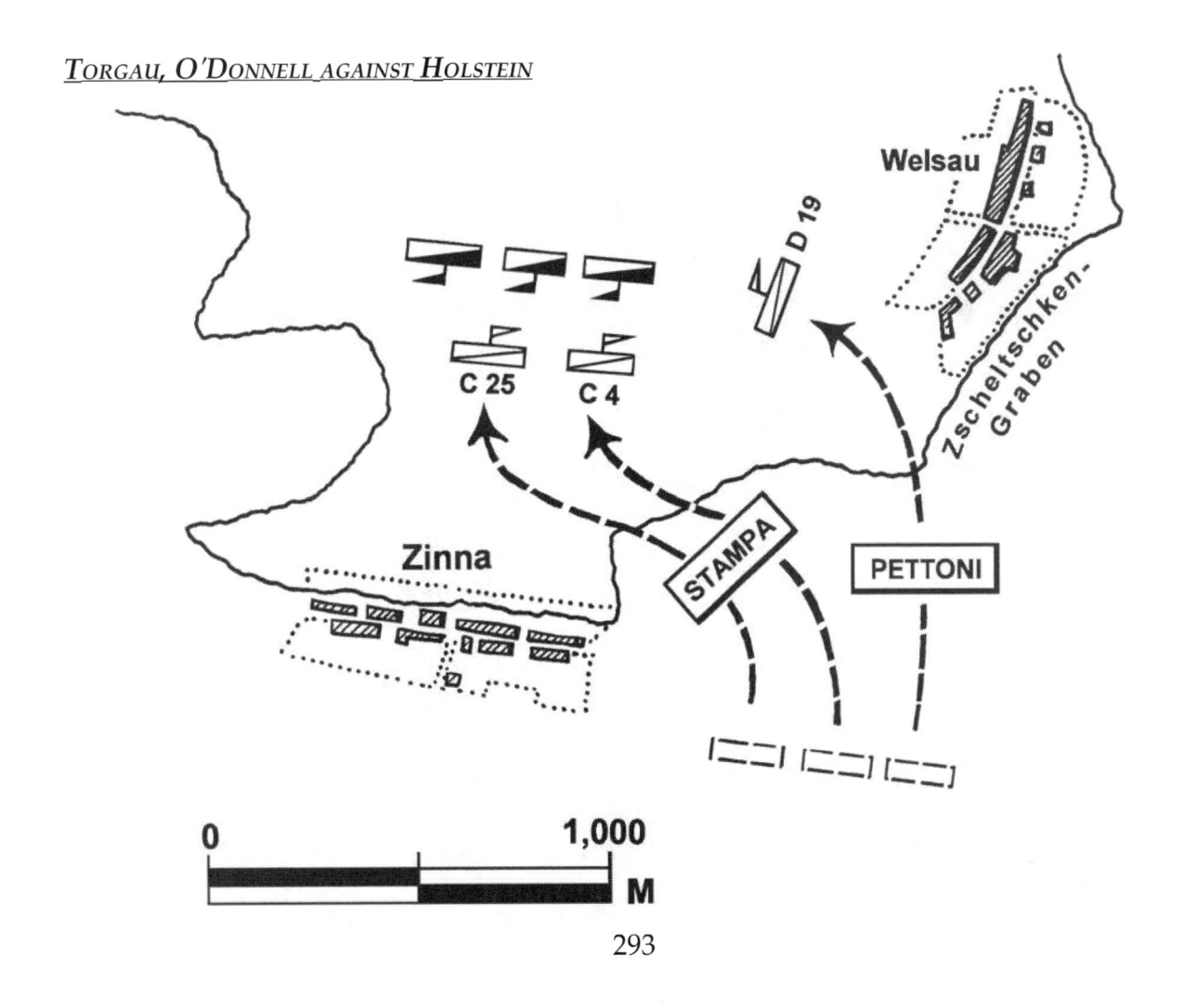

TORGAU, O'DONNELL AGAINST HOLSTEIN

Torgau, Zieten is contained

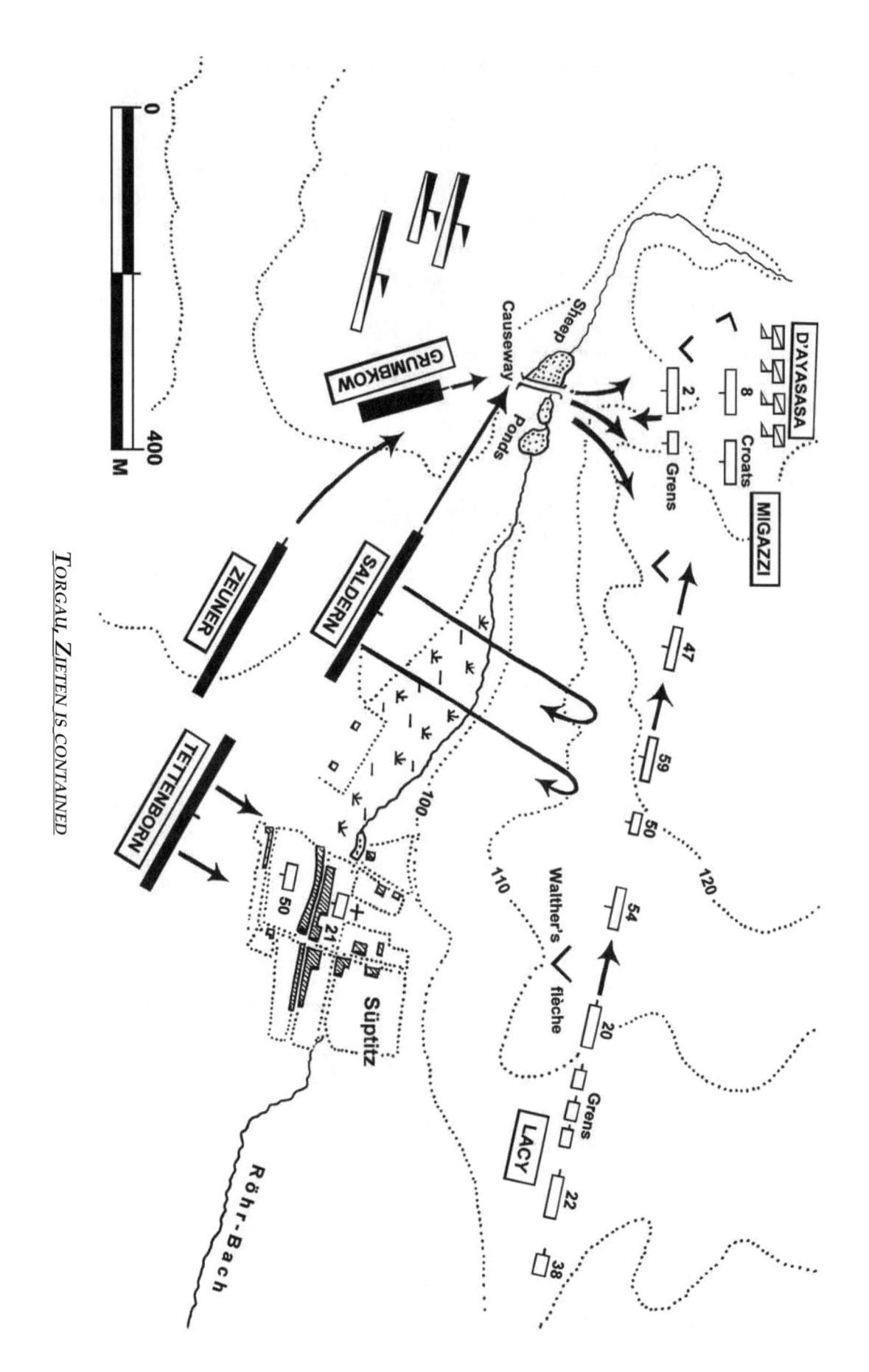

regiment of Tillier [36] when he was wounded in the leg by a musket shot. Just now he had positioned those 3-pounders to hold off Holstein's cavalry. The attaché Montazet was the first to see the blood welling from the boot, '"Why, you are wounded, *monsieur le maréchal!*" "Yes, so I have been aware for two hours," replied the field marshal, 'but don't tell anyone about it.'"[180]

By 5.30 in the afternoon Daun could no longer stay in the saddle, and, having every reason to suppose that he had gained a victory, he had himself carried to Zinna where his suite set him down and cut away the boot. He was still there when heavy firing broke out unaccountably to the west.

Lacy's corps and the second line against Zieten

It is high time to turn to the confrontation of Lacy and Zieten. The Prussian had 18,000 troops under his command, comprising the successive brigades of Zeuner, Saldern, Tettenborn and Grumbkow, the free battalion of Salenmon, 38 squadrons of cuirassiers and dragoons, and Colonel 'Green' Kleist's light corps of sixteen squadrons of hussars and light horse. In all probability his task was to hold the southern-facing Austrian forces fast until the enemy army could be pinched out by two attacks, by Frederick coming from the north, and Zieten himself from the south (above).

Zieten had much less far to march than did the columns under Frederick's command, and so he progressed slowly towards the suspected enemy position to the west of Torgau. On his side Lacy decided to delay the Prussian approach by sending out a number of light troops to make trouble (up to three battalions of the Warasdiner Croats, a company of the Staabs-Jäger and a number of squadrons of the Kaiser Hussars [H2]).

There was a first encounter at the Roter-Furt stream, which forced Zieten to bring up artillery and deploy one of his battalions of regulars. The Warasdiners put up a further fight where there was a high stone bridge which gave onto a clearing. Their business done, they retired towards Lacy's corps. Some of them joined a body of cavalry which had been stationed on the right bank of the Röhr-Graben to receive them, while the rest occupied a wood near the Grosser Teich, from where they continued to skirmish with the enemy.

At the sight of Zieten emerging from the woods, Lacy withdrew all his troops behind the Röhr-Graben, and presented the enemy with an intact front which stretched from Zinna to the north shore of the Grosser Teich. He alerted the cavalry to attack as soon as the Prussian ventured across the stream, but instead Zieten opened a heavy cannonade which caused considerable casualties among the Austrian troopers, who had to leave it to their artillery to reply. One of the Austrian answering shots beheaded a Prussian cuirassier as Zieten was riding past.

On account of the strong southerly wind the sounds of Frederick's combat to the north of the ridge would have been very faint, and it cannot be established for certain what messages might have reached Zieten from the king. The direct way to the north was in any case barred by Lacy, and this in itself would have been enough to persuade Zieten to move over to his left. From about 3.30 in the afternoon Zieten's troops began to work their way up the near bank of the Röhr-Graben, rather in the style of the links of a caterpillar track, for each brigade in turn detached itself from the right of the line, made its way behind the others, and re-inserted itself on the left, very much in the same way as Grant was going to slide his forces across Lee's front in Virginia in 1864.

In response to the threat, the second line of the Austrian army was ordered to face once more to the south, so forming a common front with the corps of Lacy. The sector most directly threatened was around Süptitz. Colonel Poniatowsky and a battalion of the regiment of Harsch [50] accordingly took up station in the lower part of the village, on the southern bank of the Röhr-Graben, while a battalion of the regiment of Arenberg [21] occupied the upper part of the village, which clustered around the church. As a final touch *GFWM*. Ignaz Walther von Waldenau of the artillery (in almost his last act before he was killed) sited three or four medium pieces in the old Prussian earthwork behind the village.

The Austrians at Süptitz were therefore strongly emplaced when the brigade of

Tettenborn advanced to the attack at four in the afternoon. The Prussians cleared the lower village against spirited opposition, but they were checked by the blazing houses and the violent Austrian fire when they tried to ascend through the upper part. They were repulsed with heavy losses, and Tettenborn's right-flanking battalion lost no less than 204 men killed or wounded in the fight.

To the Prussian left, the companion brigade of Saldern then opened an attack across the stream and up the vineyards to the west of Süptitz, which suggests that the Prussian effort on this sector was more than just a demonstration. Seven battalions of the Austrian second line (regiments of Harrach, Leopold Daun and Sincère [47, 59, 54], and one battalion of Harsch [50]) were on the higher ground, and the Austrians were able to throw this attack too back across the Röhr-Graben.

The Prussians sidled once more to their left, and made a further—and this time successful—attempt to reach the ridge. This followed on the discovery that the dam between the upper and lower Sheep Ponds was unoccupied, or at least not guarded sufficiently. The brigade of Saldern was again in action, and was the first to cross the causeway, with that of Grumbkow coming up behind. The brigade of Tettenborn renewed its assault further towards Süptitz, and this time gained the ridge to the west of the village, drove back the regiments of Harrach and Leopold Daun and captured the flèche to the rear. This episode cost the Austrians two of their best generals, Walther von Waldenau of the artillery, who was killed outright, and *FML.* Herberstein who was mortally wounded.

The Austrian second line was unequal to facing the combined attack without further support. Daun at this time was lying stricken at Zinna, but he was able to get word to Lacy to march four of his battalions to Süptitz, with the rest of his corps to follow. In response, Lacy extricated the regiments of Alt-Colloredo and

Torgau. The view from the ridge over the open plain north of Zinna.

Heinrich Daun [20, 45] from his corps and marched them to the west. At Zinna he came across the three grenadier battalions of Colonel Ferraris, and took them with him, and replaced them at that village by the regiment of Heinrich Daun. The rest of the available first-line units of Lacy's infantry—the regiment of Lacy [22] and the battalion of de Ligne [38]—came up behind.

In all of this it is uncertain how far Lacy considered that the most recent order from Daun had superseded his original responsibility, which was to safeguard the communications with Torgau. Physical considerations probably also influenced his judgement, for the light was fading fast, and the path from Saldern's causeway curved up through a little ravine, which must have hidden the Prussian advance on that side for a number of crucial minutes.

Some at least of the Austrian gunners must have detected what was going on, for *GM.* Saldern had two horses killed under him by cannon shot while he was still crossing the causeway. Forceful responses were in any case soon forthcoming from the main Austrian army. From a generally northerly direction the regiments of Erzherzog Carl and Hildburghausen [2 and 8, from the first line of infantry], Captain Kokorchowa's battalion of grenadiers, one battalion and two grenadier companies of Broder Croats, and a number of squadrons of d'Ayasasa's elite cavalry all converged against the Prussians as they appeared on the plateau. These counterattacks were undertaken through the initiatives of d'Ayasasa, Ried and Sincère, and *GFWM.* Migazzi co-ordinated the effort on this side as best he could.

Austrian reinforcements likewise came streaming in from the east along the ridge towards Süptitz, where *GFWM.* Brinken had been rallying the defenders after the loss of the flèche. By chance *GFWM.* Wied had been returning from a mission to Daun, and was now able to organise a general counter-attack from this side against the Prussians emerging from

Torgau. The upper Sheep Pond from the 'Prussian' side.

the zone of the Sheep Ponds. He took the regiments of Leopold Daun and Harrach [59, 47] under his direct command, 'and the Daun regiment did particularly well in this night assault. It kept up a constant fire and drove the enemy further and further back until at last we reached the *Weinhaus* on the hill, at which the soldiers gave vent to spontaneous cries of "*Vivat Maria Theresia!*"'[181] The vintner's house in question was a little rustic affair, standing on the summit of the hill to the north-east of the Sheep Ponds, which indicates how far the Austrian counter-attack had progressed.

After savouring the triumph, Wied renewed the advance, only to hear Prussian voices through the darkness, and receive a volley from the front and on both his flanks, 'whereupon the regiment [Leopold Daun] staggered back thirty paces then rallied. I sent out officers and NCOs to establish who might be ahead and to the sides, but they found nobody but Prussians.'[182] As part of the counter-attack from the north, the regiment of Erzherzog Carl [2] had shared in the brief glory, 'until through some evil turn of fortune an enemy column came up all unsuspected from another side and assailed our regiment in the rear and flank. We found ourselves in action on all sides, and mixed up with the enemy in heavy hand-to-hand fighting.'[183]

The Prussians establish themselves on the plateau

Something altogether unlikely must have happened to have turned the balance of the battle in favour of the Prussians, only a short time after every sign had indicated their total defeat. Zieten had reached, but failed to consolidate himself on the heights above Süptitz and the Sheep Ponds. Frederick had the breath knocked out of him by a spent canister ball which struck him in the chest, and his troops had every appearance of a beaten army. In fact almost all of the Prussian forces had been put through the grinder and had still not managed to capture any key ground.

Frederick ordered Hülsen to prepare for the retreat. That reliable old general set about his work after five in the afternoon. His adjutant Major Gaudi had hardly begun to assemble the troops in the woods when his attention was drawn by a violent outburst of artillery and musketry from the south, where Zieten had opened his attack. Hülsen was sufficiently interested to betake himself to the southern side of the Strieh-Bach, from where the flames of combat and the glow from the blazing village of Süptitz could be seen plainly. Frederick too took on new life, and galloped back to his infantry with the aim of inspiring them to make a new attack.

Fresh troops were at hand, in the shape of the infantry regiments of Alt-Schenckendorff and Dohna [22, 16] which had come up almost unregarded at the tail of Holstein's cavalry column. The reinforcements, together with the men who had been rallied from the first two columns, gave the Prussians enough troops for an initial striking force, and Hülsen (who had been wounded in the foot) planted himself on a cannon at the head of the Alt-Schenckendorff regiment. The Prussians climbed the gentle slopes, the remaining troops from behind the Strieh-Bach followed in succession, and ultimately Hülsen's pushed through to Zieten's forces in the vineyards above Süptitz, bringing together a mass of twenty-five battalions.

Austrian troops were also moving over the heights in the darkness, and they collided repeatedly with the Prussians. The most significant group was put together by *FML.* O'Kelly from three infantry regiments of the second line, namely Mercy, Botta and Carl Lothringen [56, 12, 3]. The commander of the Mercy regiment, Colonel Carl Leopold Stain, mentions that he was now aware that the Prussians were coming at the plateau from two sides, and that he convinced O'Kelly that the attack from the north (the king's) was the more dangerous, for the regiments of the left wing of the Austrian first line were in danger of breaking apart completely.[184]

O'Kelly and his improvised force then marched north through the darkness. Mercy and Botta fell behind, but the Irishman held on his way with Lothringen and arrived at the ground which had been occupied by the regiment of Wied [28] at the beginning of the battle. He came under fire from two howitzers stationed at a salient of the northern woods, and at the same time as he made out cavalry moving in the murk to his right. He sent out patrols, and was rewarded with the news that the horsemen were those of the O'Donnell Cuirassiers [C14]. The infantry and cavalry joined forces and advanced a further 140 or so paces before they heard a violent fire-fight break out four or five hundred paces to their rear. O'Kelly fell back, and contrived to assemble Carl Lothringen, the O'Donnell Cuirassiers, and the regiments of Botta, Mercy, Alt-Colloredo and Lacy on the high ground towards Süptitz, which must have been close to where Hülsen and Zieten were also coming together.

The Austrians abandon the plateau

Lacy was the first of the senior commanders to conclude that the enemy were now established in such strength on the higher ground that the Austrians, in their reduced state, were not equal to evicting them. He went in search of Daun. He met *GdC*. O'Donnell at Zinna, and they rode together to Torgau, where the field marshal was having his wound dressed. By Lacy's own account the tidings left Daun thunderstruck. In his shock Daun could not grasp the implications, for when he had last been in action the royal army had been beaten from the field, and every report from Lacy and other officers indicated that the fighting around Süptitz had also turned out well.

At about eight in the evening Daun told Lacy, O'Donnell, d'Ayasasa and Montazet to go back to the field and report to him again. During their absence the field marshal wrote or dictated a note to Maria Theresa which announced a signal victory. He entrusted the message to his General Adjutant, Colonel Rothschütz, and instructed him to halt just outside Vienna, and get word to Emperor Francis Stephen that a definitive report would follow shortly; for the time being anything which resembled a triumphal entry would be premature. Rothschütz sped into the darkness.

On their way back to the field Lacy and his companions encountered troops and infantry streaming towards them. O'Donnell ordered them back. Nearer Süptitz the party drew enemy fire, and it was clear that the greater part of the position must be in Prussian hands. All the unwounded generals now assembled at Zinna. 'There was talk of attacking the next day, and Lacy offered his corps for this purpose. It had certainly suffered little, and he added that he hoped that the remains of the forces which had

TORGAU, NIGHT, THE PRUSSIAN JUNCTION AND THE AUSTRIAN RETREAT

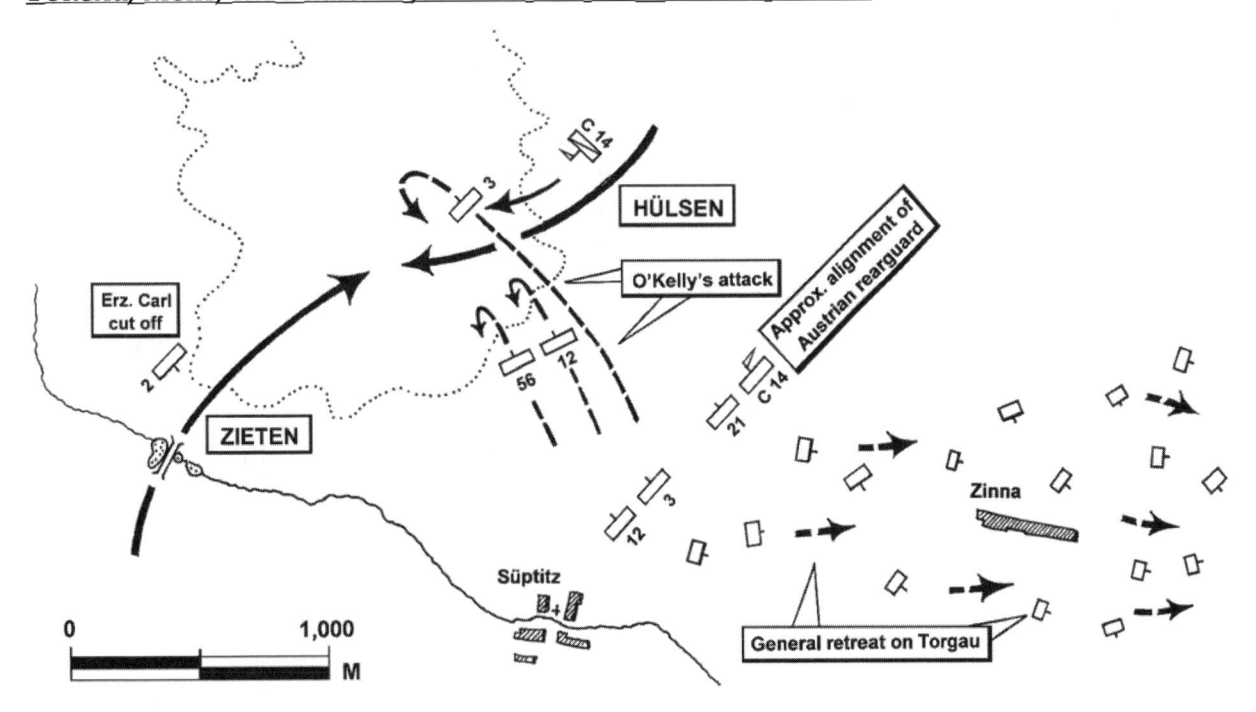

been in combat would be able to join him.'[185]

The generals duly made their reports, and by Lacy's account 'O'Kelly said he knew for certain that only four effective battalions could be formed from his total of eight. General Pellegrini had nothing left out of his ten. Of Brinken's eight battalions there remained just eighty files, which came to about 260 men. Colonel Koch from the *corps de reserve* stated on good authority that the regiment of Bayreuth [41] had been wiped out, and that no more than seventy-odd men were left of his own regiment, that of Tillier [36]. Such were the essentials as far as we could establish, and on this basis O'Donnell and I had no other course than to return to the field marshal to render our report and receive orders. Finally everyone was agreed that there was no more ammunition for either the artillery or the infantry.'[186]

On the last point Prince Albert of Sachsen-Teschen adds that the artillery was indeed out of ammunition, and already making for the bridges at Torgau. As for the infantry, Cogniazzo explains that the troops had not been supplied with enough cartridges to sustain such a long combat. The normal expedient in such cases was to beat in the skins of the drums, so that the drums could be filled from the ammunition waggons, but on this occasion the drums had been left in the rear.[187] Lacy and the others returned to Daun. Even now the field marshal hoped that it might be possible to make a stand nearer Torgau, but nowhere suitable could be found, and so the orders went out to the regiments to retreat. A fast-riding officer was sent to catch up with Colonel Rothschütz before he could announce the 'victory' in Vienna, but Rothschütz most unfortunately got to the capital first.

The fourteen hour-long winter night found many of the troops mingled in confusion. Some of the Prussians threw themselves on the muddy ground in total exhaustion, and lay there until the wet penetrated all their clothing. Others, more active, ran about to keep themselves warm, repeatedly stumbling over dead bodies in the process, or went in search of firewood and joined their Austrian enemies by the fires. A number of soldiers accidentally set fire to straw at Zinna, and burned 1,500 untransportable wounded, who let out piercing shrieks. Out in the darkness 'a host of degenerate beings—soldiers, drivers and women—swarmed over the battlefield on this bloody night, and robbed the living and the dead. The helpless wounded were not allowed to keep even their shirts, and their loud cries were lost in the general thousand-fold lamentations which were being raised to the clouds. Many of the stricken men were murdered by these inhuman creatures out of fear of discovery.'[188]

Lieutenant Colonel Möllendorff of the Prussian Garde unwittingly gave orders to four Austrian hussars in the darkness, and was taken into custody. The enemy repaid the compliment when *GFWM*. Migazzi and Colonel Oross addressed themselves in Austrian accents to units of Prussians. 'Amid all the killing and bloodshed these bizarre misunderstandings gave rise to all kinds of comical episodes, and when the danger was past we could afford to laugh with one another about them.'[189]

A number of Austrian regiments were cut off on the wrong side of the joint forces of Hülsen and Zieten. The regiment of Erzherzog Carl [2] was captured almost whole. The Staff Dragoons of Ried's corps threaded their way through with no great difficulty, but Major Perelli was faced with the task of bringing the Staff Infantry and a battalion of Sclavonian Croats directly through the Prussians and on by way of Mockrehna and Schöna. The Staff regiment (uniquely among the Austrian infantry) wore blue coats, and Perelli told them to do up the buttons to hide the white lining, and give the name of a Prussian free battalion—'Le Noble,' 'Lüderitz' and so on—if challenged. The bluff worked well a couple of times, but it was not easy to explain away the Croats, and the imposture seemed to be at an end when 'one of the generals, more curious and inquisitive than the others, stopped him to ask who might be those men who wore caps and long pants. "In the firelight they look mightily to me like Austrians." The major replied "it's a battalion of Croats, I've just captured them." "But why have you left them their muskets?" continued the general. The major told him "Well, somebody has to carry them. I have removed the locks." "Well then, carry on."'[190]

The gaps in the Prussian forces were closing when Colonel Reischach and forty troopers of the elite cavalry made their bid to escape. They had a brush with a small party on the northern part of the field, but were able to force their way through and even take a number of prisoners back with them. Reischach was unaware of how close he had come to turning the course of the day even at this advanced stage, for the Prussians were those of Frederick's escort, conducting the king to the rear.

FML. O'Kelly was now commissioned by Daun to retrieve all possible troops from the scene of the action, and direct those of the main army to the three bridges of boats so that all would be across the Elbe by six the next morning. Accompanied by his single surviving adjutant and his wounded groom O'Kelly transmitted the orders to all the regiments he could find, and designated those of Carl Lothringen, Botta and Arenberg [3, 12, 21] as the rearguard. All the available generals and officers of the cavalry helped him to conduct a final sweep, and *GFWM.* Carl Joseph Liechstenstein was able to retrieve many pieces of artillery which would otherwise have been left on the field.

O'Kelly reached Torgau at daybreak, and stationed himself with Captain Logier and the last two platoons of Lothringen to protect the remaining artillery, its carts and a number of captured Prussian pieces which were making towards the bridges in grisly confusion. O'Kelly and his band were the last to cross, at eight in the morning, after which the bridges were dismantled and Daun's main army was comfortably out of reach of the enemy. The corps of Lacy was designated to retreat up the left, or western bank of the Elbe. The first regiments to be sent on their way were those of the Saxon cavalry, and the last were the Kaiser Hussars [H2], who left at ten in the morning. The Austrians had broken free, and Frederick was denied a victory of annihilation, but what he had achieved was convincing enough.

Assessments

The Prussians had paid very heavily indeed for their success. Their total losses were in the order of 20,000 of all arms. The heaviest in proportion had been incurred by the main army, and in particular among the grenadiers, where five of the battalions had to be re-formed into a single battalion after the battle, and the remaining ten condensed into five. The Austrians carried away two standards, 43 colours, and eight cannon, and 2,780 or so prisoners, including the lieutenant generals Bülow and Finckenstein, and Lieutenant Colonel Möllendorff of the Garde. In the course of the battle the Austrians had actually taken nearly 8,000 prisoners and more than 50 cannon, but most of these trophies were left behind in the chaos of the night.

The Austrian losses stood at about 15,000, though again we must make allowance for some possibly great variations. Some curious patterns emerge. The senior officers were hit very hard. The highly-regarded *GFWM.* Walther von Waldenau had been killed, and *FML.* Herberstein mortally wounded. Daun survived his wounds, along with the *FZMs.* Buccow, Arenberg and Sincère, the *FMLs.* Angern and Dombasle, and the *GFWMs.* Migazzi and Bibow. The last two fell into the hands of the enemy. It is striking, however, that the Austrians had taken more flags of various descriptions than they had lost (the Prussians claimed only one standard and 29 colours), and that the proportion of dead and wounded among the Prussians amounted to about 89 per cent of their total losses, but only some 37 per cent among the Austrians. The Austrians had therefore struck very hard, which indicates how great their victory would have been if they had remained in possession of the ground, and rounded up all the stray enemy troops and abandoned artillery.

Among the Austrian infantry, the heaviest losses (500 or more) were sustained by the regiments of Erzherzog Carl ([2], 1,061), Gaisruck ([42], 923), Neipperg ([7], 895), Kaiser ([1], 792), Baden-Durlach ([27], 764), Sincère ([54], 697), Harrach ([47], 688), Alt-Colloredo ([20], 629), Bayreuth ([41], 599) and Wied ([28], 544). Kaiser played no further part in any major action in the war, while Erzherzog Carl, Gaisrugg, Neipperg, Alt-Colloredo and Bayreuth, together with Puebla were recommended to be withdrawn to quarters in Bohemia to recover. The hardest-hit cavalry regiments (50 or more) were those of Erzherzog Leopold and Benedict Daun ([Cs 3,

27] 117 each), Savoyen ([D9] 89) and Stampach ([C10] 510).

A pointer to the degree of disintegration in Daun's main army is given by the figures of the officer prisoners regiment by regiment. On this evidence the infantry regiments most affected were those of Neipperg, Kaiser, Gaisrugg and Baden-Durlach (they had received Frederick's initial attack), and that of Erzherzog Carl (cut off towards the end of the action when Hülsen and Zieten converged). By far the greatest proportion among the cavalry was registered among the Saint-Ignon Chevaulegers [D31], who were wiped off the board before the battle. Next, though suffering much less, came the Portugal and O'Donnell Cuirassiers [Cs 6, 14]—companion regiments of Daun's second line, which were in action for most of the combat.

The battle on 3 November 1760 was far from being the last engagement of the Seven Years War—indeed the engagements at Burkersdorf, Reichenbach and Freiberg in 1762 are more interesting technically, and have a much greater strategic importance—but the fighting at Torgau stands as the last great battle of old Europe before the coming of the French Revolution.

In the view of Maria Theresa the risk of battle had been the acceptable cost of denying the resources of Saxony to the Prussians, and securing the flank of the French in Hesse, and 'on the 6th I was inspired with all the greater hope as Field Marshal Daun had sent Baron Rothschütz to me with the joyful news that the king of Prussia had attacked on the 3rd, but been repulsed several times through the excellent measures of my generals and the quite extraordinary courage of my army, and that a magnificent victory was the result. You [she was writing to Lacy] may easily imagine how I was affected by the report which reached me the day immediately following, that on the night of the same 3 November events had taken a drastically different course, and that my army was forced to retreat up both banks of the Elbe.'[191] Centuries of investigation have not dispelled the bafflement.

The reasons for giving battle in the first place were not as evident in the Austrian army as they had been to Maria Theresa, and afterwards Lacy sighed 'this was the most bloody day I have seen in this war; I hope that your heroes in Vienna, who breathe nothing but combat, will be duly pleased with the slaughter.'[192] Daun had always maintained that it was easy enough to liberate Saxony almost as far as the border with Brandenburg, as long as the king of Prussia and his main forces were engaged elsewhere, but impossible to maintain those gains in the long term, for they were distant from Bohemia, and lacked the support of depots and modern strong-points in the locality. 'What would we have gained if we had won?' asked the Prince de Ligne. 'We could not have chased the enemy into those forests, where the pursuers would have fallen into just as much disorder as the pursued. Besides, how could we have held all the ground between the Elbe and the Mulde? Supposing that we wanted to have our right at Torgau, and our left at Leipzig, we would have been condemned to passing a frightful winter under endless alarms.'[193]

Frederick wrote to his brother Prince Henry that on his side he had to fight to secure his winter quarters, and to cover Brandenburg, Pomerania and Silesia. Henry was unconvinced, and many years later he told the Marquis de Toulongeon that the battle made no sense in the king's circumstances at that time. Toulongeon addressed himself on this point to the foreign minister Finckenstein, who replied that '"Prince Henry ought to have added that this was a period when the Russians insisted that we must fight a battle, regardless of the outcome, as the price of their retreat. They were adamant that without such a battle, they would march at once on Berlin, which was defenceless and unguarded." I regret very much [continues Toulongeon] that I cannot explain the political reasoning of the Russians. I asked the minister about it, but he answered that this event was still too recent for him to be allowed to tell me any more.'[194]

As a technical exercise, the battle of Torgau relates to other combats of the war in a number of relevant ways. On the Prussian side it represents an intermediate stage between earlier enterprises like Prague, Leuthen and Zorndorf, where the king sought to move the army in a unitary mass around an enemy flank, and the actions at Burkersdorf and Freiberg in 1762, where the forces were divided into separate columns with specific tasks, in the way pioneered by the Austrians at Hochkirch and Maxen. The plan for Torgau resembles most closely that for Kunersdorf in 1759, where the army was divided into just two elements—a diversionary or supporting force (Finck at Kunersdorf, Zieten at Torgau), and a powerful striking force under Frederick's immediate command. At Torgau the king briefed Zieten by word of mouth, in the old style, but furnished the other generals with a written *Disposition*.

For the Austrians, their experiences on 3 November 1760 matches closely those at Kolin in 1757, at least until darkness enveloped the field at Torgau. In both cases the action opened with a grand assault on the part of the enemy, which the Austrians beat off in a thoroughly convincing style, until some of their infantry broke the cohesion of their own line by sallying forth in a counter-attack. The Prussians struck back so hard that they effected a great breach in the Austrian position, and this salient in turn came under a series of counter-moves which won the battle for the Austrians at Kolin, and very nearly gave them victory at Torgau. The major difference between the two contests was that the Prussian troops at Torgau had a further force in hand, that of Zieten's corps. This too was beaten back, but the Prussians had enough residual energy to re-establish themselves on the key ground in the early hours of the night.

Very soon after the battle of Torgau the Empress put a number of questions to Daun, seeking to establish how something that had started so well had ended so badly. Daun answered the queries point by point. On the decision to retreat, after the heights of Süptitz had been lost, he maintained that any attempt to hold out 'would have brought with it the complete destruction of the army.' The field marshal did not address directly the issue of whether Lacy should have moved the rest of his corps in time to hold the position in question, merely commenting that 'the whole army puts the blame on Lacy. I have no wish to associate myself with this opinion, but it makes him very downcast and has put him in an ill humour.' If the matter were pressed further 'it would only give rise to a witch-hunt, which would only aggravate feelings still more. The damage has been done and cannot be put right. It is my ill fortune which is the root cause of all these evils. I am pursued by a malicious fate which is now so evident that its existence can no longer be doubted. It must be the will of God, otherwise it would not have been possible for events to have ended so badly. God is just.'[195]

Daun was never asked why he had done nothing to prepare the position, and in his letters to Maria Theresa he was able to convey the impression that everything had been going the Austrians' way until he was forced to leave the army. By general consent, the artillery, the foot grenadiers and d'Ayasasa's cavalry had all done well, and deserved fully the place they gained in the official *Relation* and Maria Theresa's good graces.[196]

Persuasive cases have been made for linking the outcome of the battle with failings in the Austrian military culture of the time—an excessive regard for the conservation of the army, as also for the security of communications (in this case with the bridges at Torgau), a defensive mentality, and the lack of anything to set against the dynamism of the Prussians at the lower levels of command.[197]

Such interpretations fail to allow for the workings of chance—the descent of darkness at a crucial stage of the battle, for example, or a fall from a horse which left Lacy in severe pain.[198] When the Austrian conduct of battle is examined in the necessary detail it shows a plenitude of local initiatives. Without inspirations of this kind the Austrians would never have beaten back Zieten to the bluff overlooking the Sheep Ponds. Independent thinking, less happily, led the Austrians to draw heavily on their second line and reserves to fill the gaps on the right wing of their first line, a process which left their forces on the Süptitz heights heavily depleted, and thus enabled Zieten to ascend from the Röhr-Bach in the first place.[199] Whereas Austrian mistakes became a matter of record, the same does not hold true among the Prussians, for, as

Vincent Count Migazzi, captured at Torgau in ridiculous circumstances.
(Military Academy, Wiener Neustadt)

Frederick admitted to Prince Henry, 'there is a great deal which I have suppressed, for not everything is good to say.'[200]

After Torgau—The retreat to Dresden, November 1760

With the Austrian army beaten out of the way, Frederick was free to send off detachments to eliminate a number of nuisances. Good old *GL.* Hülsen turned against the isolated *Reichsarmee*, and before long he forced it over the southern borders of Saxony; *GL.* Prince Friedrich Eugen of Württemberg (the 'Prussian' Württemberg) cleared the Swedes from Prussian Pomerania. Over to the east, the news of Torgau encouraged *GL.* von der Goltz to press back Loudon's Austrians to Bohemia and the County of Glatz (below). As for himself, however, Frederick was aware that only by clearing the Austrians from Dresden and the neighbourhood would he be compensated for the bloodletting at Torgau.

Retreats do not win a war, but they can impose a limit on potential damage, and a well-managed extrication of forces was prized in the eighteenth century as one of the highest proofs of military skill. On this rating the Austrians scored highly after Torgau. Immediately after the battle they divided their forces. The main army passed the Elbe on the night of 3/4 November, dismantled the three bridges of boats behind it, and retreated up the right bank out of reach of the Prussians. Daun was in no state to manage affairs in person, and devolved the command to *GdC.* Carl O'Donnell as the most senior general. The corps of Lacy was to retire up the left (west) bank of the river, and cover the most direct route to Dresden until the Austrians could consolidate in that part of the world.

Lacy's corps was as agile as ever, and in the present emergency it bivouacked every night in the open air, for the train of tents had been sent across the Elbe along with the rest of the Austrian baggage. The corps marched without stopping to reach Strehla on 4 November. The Austrians rested on the heights of Riesa on the night of 5/6 November, and on the following day the first troops of the pursuing Prussians came into view, in the shape of the Möhring Hussars [H3] and three regiments of dragoons under the command of Major General Krockow. There was a brush at the narrows of Gröba, after which Lacy fell back towards **Meissen**, where he would have to descend the valley of the Triebisch, thread his way through the town, and ascend the slope on the far side.

The Austrian rearguard had gone to pieces there on 14 November the year before, and now on 7 November 1760 the battered little command of *GFWM.* Brentano unaccountably missed the road which had been assigned to it, along the side of the Elbe. There was a traffic jam of artillery and troops in the streets, and to compound the confusion the Saxon cavalry got at the barrels of wine in the sutlers' carts. The town gates were shut only in the nick of time in the faces of the Prussians, and the noise of each shot of the enemy cannon, placed on the heights above, reverberated a dozen times along the Triebisch valley. Colonel de Ligne recalls how 'in spite of everything our general [Lacy] encouraged the horses and troops to climb that appalling sunken road, where the stones repeatedly stopped the cannon which we had to haul up. He beat man and beast, where it proved necessary, and urged my soldiers to leave nothing behind… "Count on us, general," they answered, "we are on your side!"'[201]

Towards midnight the last of Lacy's cannon was out of danger, and on 8 November the corps fell back to the vicinity of Dresden, where the main army had just crossed the Augustusbrücke from the east bank of the Elbe. There was panic and confusion, and some of the generals were for abandoning the city, but O'Donnell insisted on retaining 'this patch of Saxony which we still hold.'[202]

It was only on 9 November that the Prussians arrived in force on the heights of Kesselsdorf and Pennrich. The main Austrian army was holding the familiar ridge above the hollow of Plauen. Lacy's corps formed the left wing, and over to the west again Maguire had reached Dippoldiswalde on the 8th with 9,500 troops, being the greater part of the former Austrian contingent with the *Reichsarmee*.

Maria Theresa sent word to O'Donnell that he must hold out at Dresden throughout the winter, whatever the ruinous state of the city and the neighbouring villages. She had learned to her extreme displeasure that many officers had effectively deserted the army, after stealing their soldiers' pay or leave by false pretences, and she ordered they must now be prosecuted with the full rigour of martial law. [203]

The lack of spirit did not extend to the body of the army. Between 13 and 15 December Frederick sent a series of ridiculous summons to the Austrians to surrender Dresden. They were all rejected and 'our troops were still in a high state of enthusiasm… they wanted nothing better than an opportunity to win back from the enemy everything which they had been forced to cede, in spite of their courage.'[204] In fact the king had no intention of putting his army to a further test, and with the arrival of severe weather in the middle of the month the Prussians began to withdraw to winter quarters. In his words, that was 'all the profit we have derived from that risky and bloody battle. I should have known as much. We are being borne down by the weight of our enemies. Scarcely have we beaten one, than we find another who has been queuing up to plague us anew.'[205]

Lacy had done extraordinarily well in the days after the battle. At Meissen he had extricated his troops from one side of the town when the Prussians were literally beating at the gates on the other, and his actions had delayed the enemy long enough to allow the main army to re-cross to the right bank of the Elbe, recover its wits and slide into its impregnable positions by Dresden. But there was no escaping the malice of Lacy's enemies in the army, or among the Viennese *Publicum*—that ill-defined but powerful grouping of ministers, bureaucrats, grandees and coffee-house gossips who kept public affairs under constant review. Ill-wishers of this kind found Lacy's failure to secure the heights of Süptitz all of a piece with the way he was supposed to have let Loudon down at Liegnitz.

Maria Theresa placed Lacy in a vulnerable position when on 7 November she wrote to Daun to tell him to go to Prague to recover, and leave Lacy in acting command. The Empress desired Lacy to view this step as a sign of her continuing confidence in him,[206] but Daun was horrified, for this step would have placed Lacy in charge of O'Donnell, who was not only the most senior of the full generals, but had managed the main army since the battle of Torgau. Daun replied to Maria Theresa to suggest a compromise, whereby O'Donnell would remain in command, but keep Lacy at his side as his principal adviser. 'O'Donnell is an intelligent man, and will be happy to accept Lacy's lead and advice. Lacy on his side will eager and willing to get on with O'Donnell. People of this nation [the Irish] like to stay together, and I have no doubt that these two and Maguire as well will be in perfect agreement.' Of the other full generals, all senior to Lacy, Sincère and Wied were reasonable officers who would fall in with the arrangement. Löwenstein was 'a thoroughly bad individual,' but he had alienated all the others by his malicious tongue, and Lacy's enemies Buccow and Arenberg had removed themselves from the scene by convenient wounds.[207]

Daun here showed himself to be an excellent man-manager. Maria Theresa approved the scheme, and Lacy confided to one of his lady correspondents that he was glad that Daun had rescued him from an embarrassing situation.[208] The field marshal was soon able to report that O'Donnell and Lacy had an excellent working relationship. A personal note from Maria Theresa soothed O'Donnell's ruffled feelings, and she assured Lacy that 'I too take particular pleasure in that restraint which you have shown, and which does you such honour. What has happened has not diminished in the slightest that high regard which I have always harboured for your ability and zeal for the service. On the contrary, I am all the more strengthened in that opinion.' She finally promised him 'a considerable role' in the next campaign.[209]

The enemies of Lacy in Vienna had an interest in elevating the reputation of his supposed enemy, Loudon, yet, when the news of Lacy's initial appointment became known, we find Loudon writing to his protector Kaunitz 'how delighted and happy I am that Her Imperial Majesty has been pleased to give Count Lacy the command of the army… the said count is experienced and knowledgeable in the art of war, and tireless in his application, which convinces me beyond all doubt that he is the best choice which could have been made.'[210]

Loudon in Silesia, October - November 1760

Loudon's generous letter remained private, and there was little which redounded to his own public credit towards the end of the year. When Daun set off from Neuland on 12 October to follow on Frederick's tracks, he had left Loudon with well over 30,000 troops to reduce the isolated Prussian forces in Silesia. Besieging major strongholds was a time-consuming business, and the season was so far advanced that Loudon took up the suggestion of his principal technical adviser, *GFWM*. Gribeauval, to attack the little fortress of Cosel, lying in the far south-eastern corner of Silesia. *FML*. Wolfersdorff remained with 10,200 troops to observe the hostile garrison in Schweidnitz, and cover Bohemia and Glatz, and on 21 October Loudon arrived outside Cosel with a still respectable 21,500 men.

Cosel proved to be a much tougher nut than had been expected. The garrison numbered only 1,500 troops, of mostly low quality, but the commandant *GL*. Lattorf was a determined individual, and he was helped by heavy rains which caused the Oder to flood. Loudon resorted to desperate measures, but a bombardment and two attempts at storming the place failed, and Cosel was still holding out when the Austrians received exaggerated reports of the strength of the Prussian lieutenant general von der Goltz, who was marching to the relief.

On 28 October Loudon abandoned the siege, and on 2 November planted his corps in the position of Kunzendorf in the hills above the plain of Schweidnitz. The great battle of Torgau was fought the next day, and before long it began to exert its influence on events in Silesia. Reinforcements were now being sucked in from Lusatia to help the Austrians in Saxony, which in turn had the effect of teasing out the troops available to Loudon in Silesia. Goltz seized the key position of Landeshut in a bold advance on 18 November. *FML*. Wolfersdorff (who had been facing him) fell back into Bohemia, and over to the east Loudon had to distribute his troops in quarters to cover the entries to the County of Glatz. The enemy actions had been bold and enterprising, while 'Loudon's unusually passive leadership contributed to the Prussian success.'[211]

Thus the campaign of 1760 ended where it had begin, in Glatz, and Loudon's original prize of the fortress and county remained the only tangible Austrian gain by the end of it all. So much had happened in the meantime. In June Loudon had pressed home his advantage by wiping out the corps of Fouqué at Landeshut, and this strike had the effect of drawing the main Austrian and Prussian armies into Silesia. At Liegnitz (15 August) Frederick survived a very dangerous pass when he had been in danger of being taken between the forces of Daun and Loudon. Scarcely less threatening was the crisis in October, when he had lost his capital for a few days, and, more seriously, been faced with the prospect of Austrian, Russian and Swedish forces and *Reichstruppen* uniting in the heart of his state. Timorousness and distrust caused the allies to disperse, and after the battle of Torgau the Austrians retired to the southern hills along the whole theatre of war.

Frederick was free to draw on the riches of Silesia and to plunder Saxony well into the next year, and without the resources of those two lands his state would probably have gone under. But the cost of his efforts was potentially lethal. The king's secretary confessed that 'in the present year Providence in an almost miraculous way has guided us out of what seemed an endless labyrinth. However it is difficult to see what the outcome will be, and I have observed that at the end of each campaign our enemies have remedied their oversights and mistakes, and they come back to wage the next campaign more determined than ever.'[212]

VI
1761

Diplomacy and Strategy for the New Year

Conforming with the seasonal rhythm of war in those times the campaign of 1760 had ended in general exhaustion, after which the diplomatic and military stock-taking extended well into the following spring. Once again the allies, although running out of money, committed themselves to a vigorous prosecution of the war. On 10 December 1760 Kaunitz pointed out to Maria Theresa that the king of Prussia had lost his western provinces to the French, East Prussia to the Russians, and the County of Glatz to the Austrians, but still held Mecklenburg and most of Saxony, which left the alliance with only a marginal advantage if it came to exchanging conquests.'[1]

Only military action could make up the difference. In April 1761 the warring parties agreed to nominate plenipotentiaries to a peace congress to be held in Augsburg in the summer. In the meantime there was to be no cessation of hostilities. On the contrary, as Maria Theresa wrote, 'the general interest demands that in the present campaign the operations must be pressed with more vigour than ever, as the best means of attaining a favourable peace.'[2]

Over this long period of cogitation Kaunitz sought to define Austria's purposes more closely. In October 1760 the Austrians had explored what such a 'favourable' peace might be. On the 31st Kaunitz reported to Maria Theresa that there were five possible outcomes to the war, in descending order of desirability. '1st. The best peace of all would undoubtedly be one whereby Your Majesty acquired the whole of Silesia and Glatz, without having to give an equivalent to France, while at the same time Your Majesty's allies received their due compensations, so that the power of Prussia would be constrained within the tightest bounds.' The next three settlements gave progressively less to Austria and her allies, and 'No. 5. The worst kind of peace would have Your Majesty and her allies going away entirely empty-handed, and our enemy retaining his former strength, in other words a peace on the basis of *uti possidetis*.'[3]

The further paper, which Kaunitz put forward on 10 December 1760 represented Austria's relatively weak position after the disappointing outcome of the last campaign. His ambitions were now more specific and limited, and he recommended 'that as a general rule Your Majesty should formulate our demands step by step, taking all possible care to obtain, if not Upper Silesia, at least the County of Glatz as an essential acquisition and the key to the Kingdom of Bohemia.' Over the long term the foundation of foreign policy must be the connection with France, which must be maintained for at least as long as Prussia remained a danger to the House of Habsburg. Another peril must now be borne in mind, for the health of Empress Elizabeth of Russia gave cause for concern, and the accession of the heir, Grand Prince Peter, might bring Russia into alliance with Frederick, and present a still more comprehensive threat to Austrian interests.[4]

Austria's military aims were being explored at the same time. Maria Theresa asked her leading generals to put forward their ideas on the subject, and at least sixteen of them took up the invitation. The answers presented every conceivable permutation of forces and geography, with the most belligerent coming from Liechtenstein and Lacy, who were breathing fire and slaughter.[5]

In the second of two papers, which he submitted in January 1761, Daun suddenly turned away from any direct co-operation with the French and the Russians, and urged that the allied armies should operate on separate axes just as they saw fit.[6] It was an original notion, and one which, if it had been adopted in earlier years, would have put Frederick in a dilemma, and spared the allies much complication and delay. Unfortunately Daun himself had become an obstacle to rational planning. In August 1760 both the French and the Russian governments had entered protests against his shortcomings, and Daun's enemies in the ministry and in the Viennese *Publicum* continued to mutter against him through the winter. One of Daun's allies, *GFWM.* d'Ayasasa, wrote to him on 29 December that he 'had trembled on reading that we would have Prince Wenzel Liechtenstein in charge for the next campaign, with Serbelloni as his second in command. My fears redoubled when I heard the name of someone else come up in conversation.'[7] The 'someone else' was Prince Charles of Lorraine, whom Maria Theresa thought for a moment of recalling to active command.

Further consideration persuaded the Empress to hold onto Daun, and on 12 February 1761 he accepted the chief command with reluctance. His authority had been compromised, as he must have been aware, and on 28 February a conference decided that he must draw up a new plan of campaign, based on the presence of an army under his own command in Saxony, and a sizeable corps under Loudon's in Silesia. Maria Theresa was advised, on the insistence of Kaunitz, that Loudon was to be allowed full operational freedom.

The emphasis shifted almost entirely to Silesia when, on 7 May, an extraordinarily advanced Russian plan of campaign arrived out of the blue. The Russians had resolved to assemble at least 70,000 combatants at Posen towards the end of the month, and advance on Breslau to unite with the Austrians; the Austrians must reciprocate by reinforcing their troops in Silesia to at least 50,000 men under the leadership of Loudon, and at the same time put provisions and a siege park at the disposal of the Russians. If the Austrian army in Saxony were to fix Frederick on the Elbe theatre, the Russians would in addition send a corps to besiege Colberg on the coast of Pomerania.

After months of fruitless discussion, the essentials of the Austrian plan of campaign were now put together in a matter of hours. Already on 8 May Maria Theresa wrote to Daun that she had fallen in with the Russian proposals, and would build up her troops in Silesia to the desired number, the reinforcements in question inevitably coming from Saxony. The aim of the Austrians in Silesia would not be to besiege fortresses, but to unite with the Russians. Only such forces were to remain in Saxony as were needed to cover Dresden, and the Empress left it to Daun to choose whether to continue in command there, or (an unlikely prospect) take charge in Silesia.

On 10 May came the disturbing news that Frederick had set out from Saxony for Silesia seven days before. A supplementary letter to Daun on the 11th therefore proposed the corps of Austrian reinforcements should not march all the way to Silesia, but turn aside by way of Lusatia to join the Russians on the Oder at Frankfurt, therefore making a powerful diversion in Frederick's rear.[8]

At the outset of the campaign the forces at the disposal of the warring parties stood as follows:

Austrians in Saxony

In May the number of combat effectives available to Daun stood at a nominal 79,695, sinking to 55,925 in September. The last figure was probably more representative of the campaign as a whole. On 9 July Daun complained that on paper he had over 56,000 troops under his command, a number which however included the large force which had to be maintained at Zittau (the way station between the Saxon and Silesian theatres), and 9,233 Croats and hussars. This brought the regulars down to 43,010, many of whom were sickly recruits

Austrians in Silesia

Reinforcements from Saxony and the intermediate corps at Zittau (which was at Loudon's disposal) carried the army to a strength of 58,000 men by 19 May, and to 77,400 by 17 July

Reichsarmee

Commanded by *GdC*. Hadik from his headquarters in Cronach, there were 27,600 troops scattered in quarters along the upper Main, with detachments in exposed positions on the far wide of the Franken-Wald and Thüringer-Wald. Prussian raids had already caused much trouble

French

In 1760, in spite of defeats at Emsdorf and Warburg, the French had established themselves solidly in Hesse-Cassel on the right wing of their operations in Germany. Soubise commanded a companion army of 100,000 on the Main, and if all went well Prince Ferdinand of Brunswick's 70,000 troops would come under threat from two sides

Russians

Not counting the forward detachments, about 70,000 combatants were assembling on the Vistula, and Field Marshal Buturlin was to lead the main force to Silesia

Swedes

In 1760, as in previous years, the little Swedish army had proved itself incapable of offensive operations in depth. The forces quartered in Swedish Pomerania in the spring of 1761 amounted to less than 15,000 men, and scarcely figured in the allied planning

Prussians

Before operations opened in 1761, the 64,000 troops of the king's army were disposed widely in quarters across central and northern Saxony. *GM*. von der Goltz was trying to concentrate the scattered 26,000 troops in Silesia. Prince Friedrich Eugen of Württemberg was facing the Swedes with up to 6,000 troops, and *GM*. Werner and 5,000-odd men had just beaten back the Russian light corps of Major General Totleben. The total of the Prussian field forces amounted to little more than 100,000 troops, and the army as a whole had suffered near-crippling losses in its officer corps and its kernel of native troops. Frederick had never faced a new campaign with greater misgivings.

DAUN IN SAXONY

Early in May the operations in Saxony congealed into the shape they were to retain for the rest of the year. Frederick grasped (quite possibly through treasonable intelligence from the Russian major general Totleben) that the Russians intended to make Silesia the main focus of their efforts, and on the 3rd and 4th he brought 29,000 troops across the Elbe from Torgau and Strehlen, as the first stage of his march to join Goltz in that province.

The depleted Prussian forces remaining in Saxony were commanded by the king's brother Prince Henry, and by 5 May he had deployed them in the fortified position of Schlettau and Katzenhäuser behind the steep valley of the Triebisch. Henry was determined to hold on there at all costs. Long afterwards the Prince de Ligne commented that Prince Henry had a way of making the Seven Years War seem like the Thirty Years War, but on this occasion the methodical Prussian 'Daun' was rightly cautious.

FM. Leopold Daun, the genuine, 'Austrian' Daun, brought his troops out of winter quarters on 8 May, and occupied the familiar positions in front of Dresden, at Boxdorf on the right bank of the Elbe, and at Plauen on the left bank, with the left wing reaching out to Dippoldiswalde. Nowhere in his voluminous correspondence for that campaign do we discern that he ever gave active consideration to any plan to turn Prince Henry out of his position, whether by direct assault or manoeuvre.

It was partly a question of numbers. Daun overestimated Henry's force by at least 5,000 men, (at 40,000 instead of 35,000 at the most), but his own superiority was less than was supposed in Vienna, and in the course of May, June and July his advantage was reduced still further by the demand to feed troops to Loudon in Silesia, and hold the corps at Zittau over and above the permanent guard force on the depot.

On 3 July Maria Theresa wrote to Daun that the forces at Zittau had to be kept at 20,000 combatants, and held at Loudon's disposal. She wished Daun to believe that 'I should very much have liked to have seen the army in Silesia under your experienced command! But what I know of the bizarre behaviour of the Russian generals has deterred me placing you under such an onerous burden.'[9] She was writing only as a matter of form, since it had been known for months that Loudon would be taking command in Silesia.

In Saxony the senior officers were humiliated to see their army relegated to a secondary role, and they were moreover divided among themselves. There was a first hint at the end of March, when Prince Löwenstein insisted he must go to Vienna. Daun would have been glad to be rid of him, but he warned Maria Theresa's secretary that 'Her Majesty will always be pestered and badly served, if she does not once and for all shut her doors to those idle and impatient people who demand access to her. She has become too kind, and they know how to take advantage of Her.'[10]

Matters came to a head in midsummer, when it was a question of finding generals to command the reinforcements for Loudon, the corps at Zittau, and (however unlikely that might be) to take the place of Daun in Saxony. As for the command at Zittau, Daun was of the opinion 'that O'Kelly… is no kind of man to be in charge, nor is Beck. It makes you shudder.'[11] On the matter of the people to go to Silesia, Meyern had ruled himself out of the reckoning, for he was drunk from morning to night. Stampa and Lanthieri believed that the were in fragile health, and were taking spa waters. Campitelli was distrusted by Loudon, and 'Plunkett reports that he would be unacceptable to Loudon, and is therefore unwilling to serve… I think that Loudon would indeed find Plunkett unendurable, as he indicated clearly enough last year by the many complaints he made to me about him. O'Kelly and Buttler are already with the corps at Zittau, and now he would be likely to protest "but they are sending me all the Irishmen!"'[12] Frederick of Prussia would not have tolerated this nonsense in his army for a moment.

Daun was even at odds with Lacy, who was generally regarded as his ally. Daun reported to Maria Theresa that 'Your Majesty can never hope from him more than he is willing to do.' He had refused to take over the command in Saxony, if that fell vacant, declaring whenever the question was raised 'that he would never play second fiddle to Loudon, or become the dupe of Kaunitz.'[13] It was only with an ill grace that Lacy on 19 July accepted the commission to advance a corps of 15,000 troops to Grossenhain, on the eastern side of the Elbe, so as to deny Prince Henry the shortest route to Silesia.

Daun's caution was also rooted in deeply-considered principles, which call for respect, if not necessarily for agreement. 'The course of battles is uncertain, and their outcome still more so. During this unhappy war we have experienced victory and defeat alike, and each time we have had to start from the beginning. The prospects at the present time are no more favourable, and our internal constitution seems to be in a worse state than ever. To reduce this enemy we need double his strength, on account of the fortresses and the other advantages he derives from the nature of this country, not to mention his person and the character of his rule… these are considerations which the cabinet ought to bear in mind. The ministers should not meddle in plans of campaign, and ought to trust their generals instead of criticising them. Certainly, the commanders must be chosen with regard to their suitability, but then they should be supported, and not made the objects of intrigue.'[14]

The conservation of the army in the narrower sense depended on keeping the army fed, and here the bulkiest and most expensive commodities were the raw forage and grain for the horses of the cavalry, the artillery and the supply train. The transport of feed from Bohemia depended exclusively on the navigation of the Elbe. Everything else had to be gathered in (with greater or lesser use of force) by detachments spread over the country under Austrian control north of the border. Lacy had most of Lusatia at his disposal, but in Saxony west of the Elbe the Prussians had seized the nodal point of Freiberg towards the end of the last campaign, and kept the Austrians penned up in the hills towards the Bohemian border. Daun believed that all of this hindered his freedom of action.

By the middle of September the campaigning

season was already far advanced, without the allies having attained any of the successes which might have been expected from their numerical superiority, which Kaunitz put at 120,000. On the 20th he wrote to Maria Theresa that, however unpalatable it might be to the commanding generals, they must abandon the defensive. As for Daun's responsibilities, it would be a scandal if the enemy were left a free hand to plunder Saxony of its resources, 'and it is consequently a matter of pure necessity to drive the enemy from their present position, and thereby win the territory we need to raise supplies in good time, and assemble magazines in Dresden and thereabouts sufficient to see us through the winter.'[15] There were signs that Prince Henry's army, which included a high proportion of the 'free' units, was shaky in morale as well as weak in numbers. A whole battalion had deserted to the *Reichsarmee* on 31 August, and the number of Prussian prisoners and deserters in the neighbourhood of Dresden eventually reached more than 7,000.

The actions were modest in the extreme, even if 'the Vienna *Publicum* advocated and dreamed great battles until deep into November, and had Loudon smashing the king completely out of Silesia, and Daun doing the same to Prince Henry in Saxony.'[16] Daun protested that he must be reinforced from Silesia if he were to undertake the offensive now being demanded of him. By 3 November the left wing of the army around Dippoldiswalde had been built up to 36,700 troops, with the help of the first contingents from Silesia. On the right wing Daun and the advance corps under *GFWM*. Ried had another 23,000 under their command, and action of some kind could no longer be postponed.

The offensive as carried out was limited but well planned, and gained the Austrians the line of the Freiberger Mulde and the Zschopa for the security of their winter quarters. The main effort was on the part of the left wing. On 5 November the free battalion of Le Noble was forced from **Rosswein**, while the companion battalion of Lüderitz was driven over the Mulde by way of Nossen. On the next day the Austrian advance forces exploited to Döbeln.

Ried's corps was expected to do no more than demonstrate against the well-entrenched Prussian main army along the Triebisch, but Colonel Franz Petrovsky took it into his head to attack an earthwork on the **Lerchen-Berg**, just in front of Meissen. On 5 November he led 150 men of his Széchenyi Hussars [H32] up the hill, through the wolf pits and chevaux de frise, and 'in spite of… the violent fire of musketry, and the still more dangerous cannon fire directed from the other works around Meissen, I cut down or captured the garrison of the said work. Gathering new courage, I proceeded to hack down and break the free battalion [of Quintius Icilius] which came hastening up in support.'[17] Petrovsky returned with two cannon and nearly ninety prisoners. It had been a bold stroke, but it should not have been the only action of éclat which Daun's army had to show in 1761.

In the middle of December the Austrian army, 69,000 strong, entered winter quarters across a wide swathe of southern Saxony, from Lusatia in the east to Chemnitz and Zwickau in the west. On 21 December, acting as representative of his sovereigns, Daun presented three Grand Crosses and twenty-three Knights' Crosses to new members of the Military Order of Maria Theresa. 'The ceremonies made a great sensation in Dresden. The field marshal rode across the bridge to the Catholic Church, together with a great train of generals, staff officers and senior officers. The procession was led by several troops of cuirassiers with trumpets and drums, and further troops closed up the rear. After the divine service, the procession made its way to the palace of the Zwinger garden, where the new knights were presented with the insignia, and from there they returned to the field marshal's quarters.'[18]

The *Reichsarmee* in 1760

In this year of the war the operations of the *Reichsarmee* and the main force of the Austrians diverged almost completely. In effect the Germans had been abandoned, and the Austrian presence was confined to a small contingent, which usually consisted of little more than a battalion of Croats, a couple of grenadier companies, a dozen squadrons of hussars and a handful of cannon.

The early months found the fortunes of the army at a low ebb, for it had yielded almost the whole of south-western Saxony in the face of Hülsen's advance at the close of the last campaign. The greater part of the *Reichsarmee* was safe and snug in their quarters to the south of the Franken-Wald and the Thüringer-Wald. However there was nobody else to form the connection between the Austrians towards the Elbe in the east, and the French in Hesse to the west, and the requirement to operate down the Saale left a number of units isolated and exposed beyond the hills. In such a way the Cologne contingent was overwhelmed on 1 April at **Billwitz** and the heights of **Garmsdorf**, and that was the end of 'two of the best battalions of the army.'[19]

Gd.C. Hadik handed over the command of the dispirited army to *FM*. Serbelloni on 9 April. There was still no sign of the German states bringing their contingents up to strength, whether in troops (a nominal 13,000) or basic equipment. Hadik's departure was regretted, and Serbelloni was one of the most disliked officers in the Austrian service, by repute taciturn, sluggish and quirky. The fact that he was going to do better than Daun in the next campaign is evidence either of unsuspected talents in Serbelloni, or of more than usual pessimism in Daun.

Serbelloni's first thoughts were directed to Thuringia, where he could come up on the right flank of the French in Hesse, but he reckoned without the priority which Vienna gave to supporting the Austrians, and on 23 May Emperor Francis Stephen sent him the order to take the *Reichsarmee* to electoral Saxony. The route lay through the Voigtland and the Erz-Gebirge, lands which had been thoroughly eaten-out in 1760, and Serbelloni compared the impending march with the wanderings of the Israelites through the desert, though without the consolation of heavenly manna.

The army reached Hof on 12 June. Serbelloni reported from there two days later that 1,329 men had been lost to desertion in April and May, another 889 between 1 and 12 June, and that more than one hundred had vanished on the 13th alone. He could not bring himself to blame the runaways, for the *Reichsarmee* had received scarcely any help from the Austrians, who had ceased even to forward the customary herds of cattle from Hungary, and provisions of every kind were so scarce along the route that the troops could not possibly provide for themselves.[20]

The main body arrived at Reichenbach on 21 June, and, after nearly a month's delay, reached Ronneburg on 20 July. Advance detachments fanned out north-east to Altenburg and Pennig, and north to Zeitz on the Elster and on to Naumburg, Weissenfels and Merseburg on the Saale. These parties thus controlled a considerable tract of territory, and threatened the right flank of Prince Henry, who was facing the main force of the Austrians under Daun.

Henry was now forced to make some expensive and unwelcome detachments. Colonel 'Green' Kleist mounted a first expedition of 3,500 troops between 25 and 29 July, and another with 4,500 between 1 and 7 August. Finally *GL*. Seydlitz and Kleist put together a force of 7,000 men, and advanced against the centre of all evil at **Ronneburg**. The Prussians circled out to the east, and 4 September we find Seydlitz at Mannichswalde and Kleist probing by way of Vogelgesang. Serbelloni took due note, and reinforced his right wing on the Reuster-Berg.

On 5 September the Prussians advanced by way of Rückersdorf to give battle, but were stopped short by the sight of the Reuster-Berg, now packed with troops and guns, and the prospect of having to make a stiff climb under artillery fire. The enemy called off the attack, and Serbelloni fell back undisturbed to an altogether impregnable position behind the Weisse Elster at Werda. He was aggrieved that during this critical episode Daun's army had made not the slightest effort to help him, even in the form of a diversion.[21]

Serbelloni, of all people, had nevertheless succeeded in frustrating Seydlitz and Kleist, who were among the most enterprising spirits that the Prussian army had to show, and by drawing to himself so many Prussians three times over he had created opportunities which Daun should have been able to exploit. Between 3 and 12 September the detachments from the army of Prince Henry had reduced the troops behind the Triebisch to little more than 20,000 men.

In November the forward movement of the left wing of the Austrian main force, limited and tardy though it was, relieved the *Reichsarmee* of further pressure. When operations closed the Germans went into quarters which extended creditably far north into Thuringia and Saxony, along a line from Erfurt to the Weisse Elster.

LOUDON IN SILESIA

Belated union—Austrians and Russians in Silesia, April - August 1760

When the Austrians went on campaign in Silesia in 1761, they carried with them both the monarchy's hope for the successful outcome of the war and the trust which Kaunitz invested in

LOUDON AND THE RUSSIANS IN SILESIA, 1761

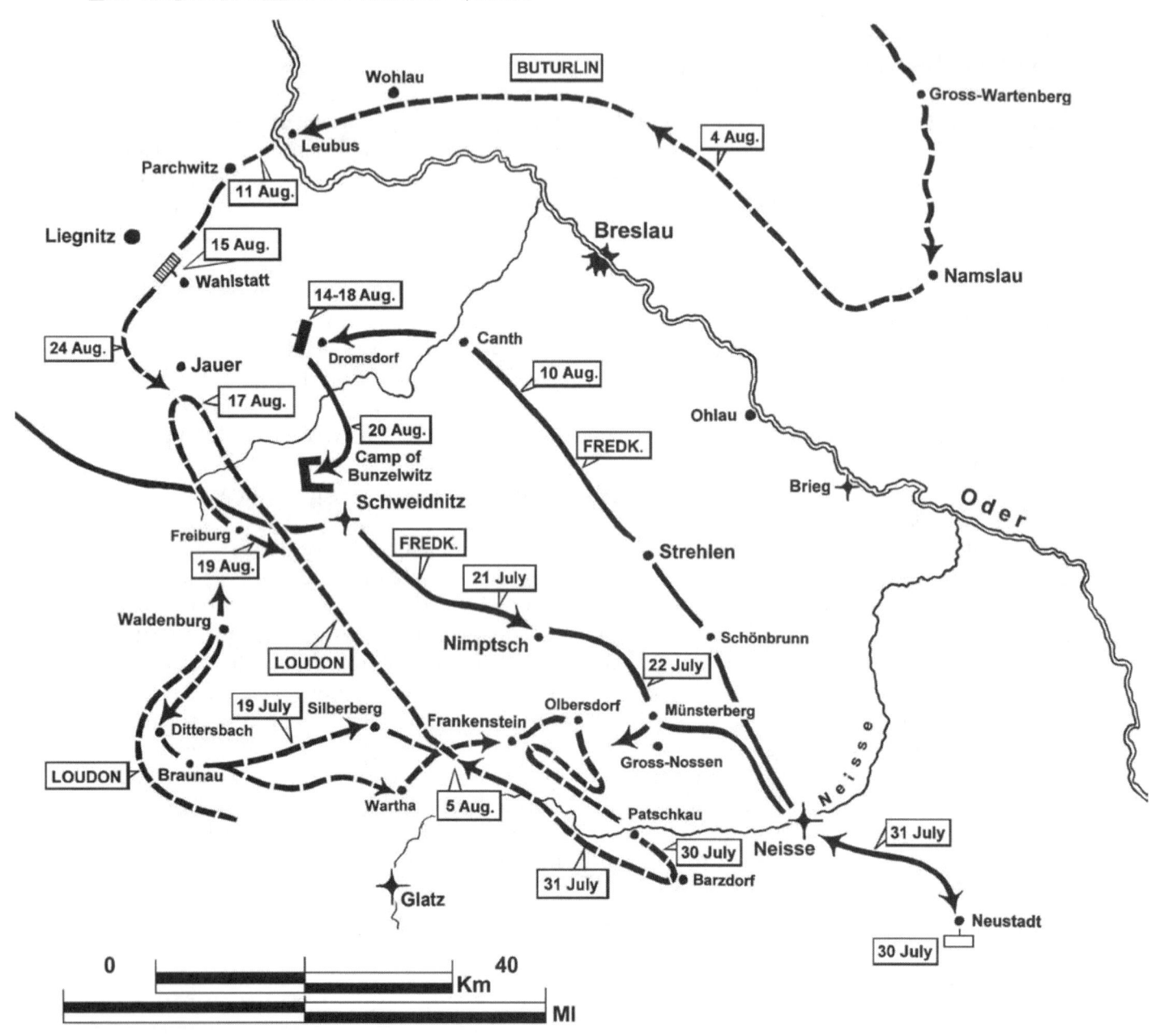

his favourite, Loudon, to prosecute the operations with fiery zeal. Loudon retained the provisional command of the forces on the Bohemian-Silesian borders into the spring, with considerable freedom of action, and he was given the formal command at the end of June.

Kaunitz was aware that his own reputation was at stake, and also the cohesion of the alliance. The Swedish envoy reported to his *Kanslipresident* that the Russian court had taken mortal affront at the maxims of Daun, namely 'to keep aloof from the Russians, and deny them any help, while at the same time exploiting their successes.' If the choice of commander had fallen elsewhere 'there would have been no question of the Russians operating anywhere in Silesia, let alone passing the Oder.' It had therefore been essential for Kaunitz to overcome Maria Theresa's marked preference for Daun,[22] and to insist that all possible troops must be sent to Loudon in Silesia. By 19 May the reinforcements from Saxony and the intermediate corps at Zittau brought his army to a strength of 58,200 men, and by the middle of June to 70,000.

Loudon had exercised independent command in Silesia in 1760, but he was now in charge of more troops than ever, and in his rapid rise from military adventurer he had been promoted not long before to *Feldzeugmeister* (full general), with fewer years of Austrian service under his belt than many others of the same rank. It was against precedent for gentlemen of that kind to be at the behest of a parvenu, and so Daun's army in Saxony became the 'assembly point, almost the dumping-ground' of all the other full generals.'[23] Kaunitz was aware that he was risking his own authority in the process.

Loudon took the initiative in opening hostilities in Silesia by announcing on 19 April that he was abrogating the winter truce. The notice expired on the evening of the 22nd, and the next day some 40,000 Austrians invaded Prussian Silesia from the north-east corner of Bohemia and the from the County of Glatz. This was at a time when the Prussian lieutenant general von der Goltz was in a position to bring together only 12 or 13,000 men, but Loudon supposed the Prussians to be more concentrated than they really were, and so he halted at the edge of the plain.

The pause in operations enabled Goltz to concentrate in front of Freiburg (not to be confused with Freiberg in Saxony). Worse still, Frederick undercut the foundations of the campaign by responding with shocking speed. By 4 May he was in full march from the Elbe with 29,000 men. He had the advantage over the Austrian reinforcements from Saxony and Zittau, which would have to come by way of Bohemia, and he was certain to anticipate by several weeks the arrival of the Russians, who were still gathering on the Vistula.

On the 12th, the day that the king entered Silesia, Loudon took up positions to cover the avenues to Bohemia and Glatz. He had 58,200 troops at his disposal, but no longer enjoyed a clear numerical superiority, for the king had 48,000 troops under his immediate command, and 12,800 more whom he detached under Goltz to guard the Oder against the Russians. In such a way Loudon was forced into a defensive posture when the campaign had scarcely begun.

Loudon, even if he had wished to, could not have advanced in defiance of a *Cabinet-Schreiben* from Vienna of 11 May, which told him not to take the offensive before the Russians arrived in Silesia. Those people set out from their quarters along the Vistula between 26 May and 2 June. They were met on their way by *GFWM*. Caramelli, charged by Loudon to concert the joint operations. He encountered Field Marshal Aleksandr Borisovich Buturlin on 29 May, and discovered in him a man who meant well enough, but who was thin-skinned, obstinate, and anxious not to be led astray by the Austrians, of whom he knew little.

Nothing had yet been settled with the Russians, though a number of projects had been in the air, but on 4 July Loudon received the agreeable news from Caramelli that the allies were well on the way, and that they had held a great council of war in which they resolved to join him with their entire force.

The exclusively Austro-Prussian phase of the campaign came to an end on the night of 6/7 July, when the king abandoned the positions which had kept Loudon penned up in the border hills, and moved to a camp between Pilzen and Reichenbach. He now had direct access to the road network of the Silesian plain, and was better placed to block the union of the Austrians and Russians, which he rightly suspected to be intended for the upper Oder. Both sides were now gathering their forces. Von der Goltz had died from natural causes, and his corps, which now came under the command of General Zieten, was ordered up from Glogau to Breslau, closer to Frederick's main army. Further batches of reinforcements from Zittau were coming to Loudon, which by 17 July put at his disposal 77,400 men and 294 pieces of artillery.

The Russians had reached the Silesian border at Militsch on 15 July, and *GFWM*. Finé, as the permanent Austrian representative at their headquarters, reported 'with considerable pain, that just as in previous years our entry into Silesia has been accompanied with the usual plundering.'[24] The Russians had agreed to join the Austrians up the Oder, but instead of taking the most direct route they hugged the Polish border, which was bound to delay the union. On the 19th Loudon at last left the camp of Dittersbach, and advanced by way of the passes of Silberberg and Wartha into the Silesian plain. He was confident that three further marches would take him to the Oder, and on the next day he reached the heights of Grochau to the south-west of Frankenstein.

Frederick now sought to manoeuvre himself between the converging allied forces. The king set out at three in the morning of 21 July, and executed a forced march of twenty-one miles to reach Siegroth on the Klein Lohe, to the E.S.E of Nimptsch. On that day the Austrians arrived only at Stolz and Leippe, still not far from Frankenstein.

Very early on the rainy morning of 22 July the Prussians were on the move again, for Frederick was making for the high ground near Münsterberg, a direction that would take him close under the Austrian right wing. The tidings from the Austrian detachments were contradictory, and Loudon chose not to believe the report of *GFWM*. Luzinsky, that the Prussians were working around his right flank.

Frederick slipped past the Austrians with no more disturbance than a few distant shot, and planted himself on heights of Gross-Nossen, where Loudon had intended to make his next camp. Loudon feared that he was about to come under attack, and fell back south towards Patschkau. Luzinsky had been in the right, and uttered some bitter comments 'which had no other result than to have him removed a few weeks later to the *Reichsarmee*. Never again did he come under the command of General Loudon.'[25]

After a new and brief confrontation with Frederick in Upper Silesia, Loudon executed a long trek along the north-eastern mountainous fringes of the County of Glatz to his old position south-west of Frankenstein. He had had no news of the Russians for a long time, and he had gained little ground in Silesia. Frederick wrote to Prince Henry that 'Loudon is a very bad general, and as long as Daun and his army do not come to Silesia I will have nothing to fear in these parts.'[26]

News of the debacle of 22 July and its consequences reached Saxony, where Daun and his army had been relegated to a secondary role. Montazet reported 'you can imagine what kind of mood prevails here, and the kind of language which is being applied to Kaunitz's plan of campaign. Without exception the officers senior to Loudon, to begin with the field marshal, are humiliated and outraged by what has happened.'[27] Lacy did not gloat over-much, for it seemed to him that Loudon was just another victim of Kaunitz.

So far Loudon and Frederick had taken it for granted that the Russians were holding to their original intention of crossing the Oder upstream in south-eastern Silesia. On 1 August, and without reference to Loudon, the Russian high command reached the bold decision to take their army down the right bank, by-passing Breslau, and cross the river downstream at Leubus. The Russians set out on the same day, circumvented Breslau on the 4th, and on the 10th the advance guard under the able Lieutenant General Chernyshev reached Leubus and constructed a bridge of boats to the left bank. The main army followed on the next day, and consolidated itself in an entrenched camp at Heydau and Parchwitz, with the Katzbach running across the rear of the position.

On the night of 6/7 August Loudon had his first inkling of the Russian march, and after receiving news he set his troops in motion to his left (west) on the night of 7/8 August. They covered twenty-eight miles in one go, and the main body took up the classic position on the heights of Kunzendorf between Freiburg and Bögendorf, with Brentano's corps at Striegau, as an outpost towards the plain. Loudon was unwilling to venture any further into the open ground, and his thinking was entirely what might have been expected of Daun in the same situation. Loudon had in mind the security of his line of communication, which now described a right-angled turn inside Silesia and ran to the north-west parallel with the Bohemian border. If, as was hoped, Loudon was joined by Buturlin, the Austrians would be responsible for feeding both armies. Loudon was moreover unwilling to lose the tactical protection of the hills, and insisted that the Russians must traverse the plain from the Oder to join him on the high ground, and not the other way around. Buturlin indicated that he was willing to venture only as far as Jauer, and so it was that Frederick was granted all the time he needed to interpose himself anew between the Austrians and the Russians.

A new plea from Loudon, and probably also the imminent exhaustion of their supplies, induced the Russians on the morning of 15 August to march just over four miles from their bridgehead to a position under the dominating plateau-like heights of **Kloster-Wahlstatt**. They were weak in regular cavalry, and now extremely vulnerable in the open plain, and Loudon set out to reinforce them with forty squadrons, of 4,000 or so Austrian cavalrymen, including the elite corps of carabiniers and mounted grenadiers. Loudon's route lay by way of Profen, Hertigswalda and Strachwitz, and took him close by the Prussian army. Frederick was watching the proceedings from the windmill at Mertzdorf, and commissioned *GL.* Lentulus, who was one of his favourites, to chase after them with the Finckenstein Dragoons and three squadrons of the Czettritz Dragoons [Ds 10, 4]. The Austrians were going at a fast trot, but Lentulus caught up with them beyond Strachwitz, which gave rise to a running fight in which, according to Loudon, 'we lost up to sixty men, but took more than thirty of the enemy prisoner, and cut down many others.'[28]

At noon on the same 15th the hard-breathing Austrian cavalry joined Berg's Cossacks on the heights of Wahlstatt, then descended to join the main Russian army. Loudon met Buturlin face to face, and urged him in vain to send just three battalions to secure the plateau while there was still time. According to Cogniazzo, 'the two commanders overwhelmed one another with the customary assurances of mutual trust, and yet each trusted the other not one inch… We were still clinging to our hills five days after the Russians had appeared on this side of the Oder, exposing themselves to being attacked and overwhelmed by the entire force of the enemy.'[29] Lacy too was aware of the risks the Russians were taking.[30] Loudon left the cavalry at the disposal of the Russians, and returned in person to his nearest corps, that of Brentano at Striegau. His main force was still up in the hills, at Freiburg and Hohenfriedeberg.

Frederick took the opportunity to seize the plateau of Kloster-Wahlstatt, but with his 55,000 troops he was still disinclined to attack the Russians in their well-chosen position.

On 17 August Loudon advanced his main force to Jauer, where the hilly country was giving out. The marches by the Russians over the next two days brought them to the Silesian Hochkirch, near Liegnitz, less than five miles from the Austrians. On the 19th Frederick lunged against the Austrian supply line, but Loudon responded so smartly that the king had to call off his enterprise.

It was one thing for Frederick to manoeuvre between two enemies in the open field, but quite another to find himself jammed between them in tactical proximity. The king was now in a sea of foes, and the one resort left to him was to close up to the well-stocked fortress of Schweidnitz. He accordingly abandoned the race for the hills, and entrenched himself in the rolling country to the north-west of the fortress.

The allied commanders now fell to haggling as to how the Russians were to be supplied, and Buturlin refused to move until he could be reassured on that point. The Austrian commissary Grechtler had to apologise to his Russian counterpart General Yakovlev for the musty state of a much-travelled consignment of bread,

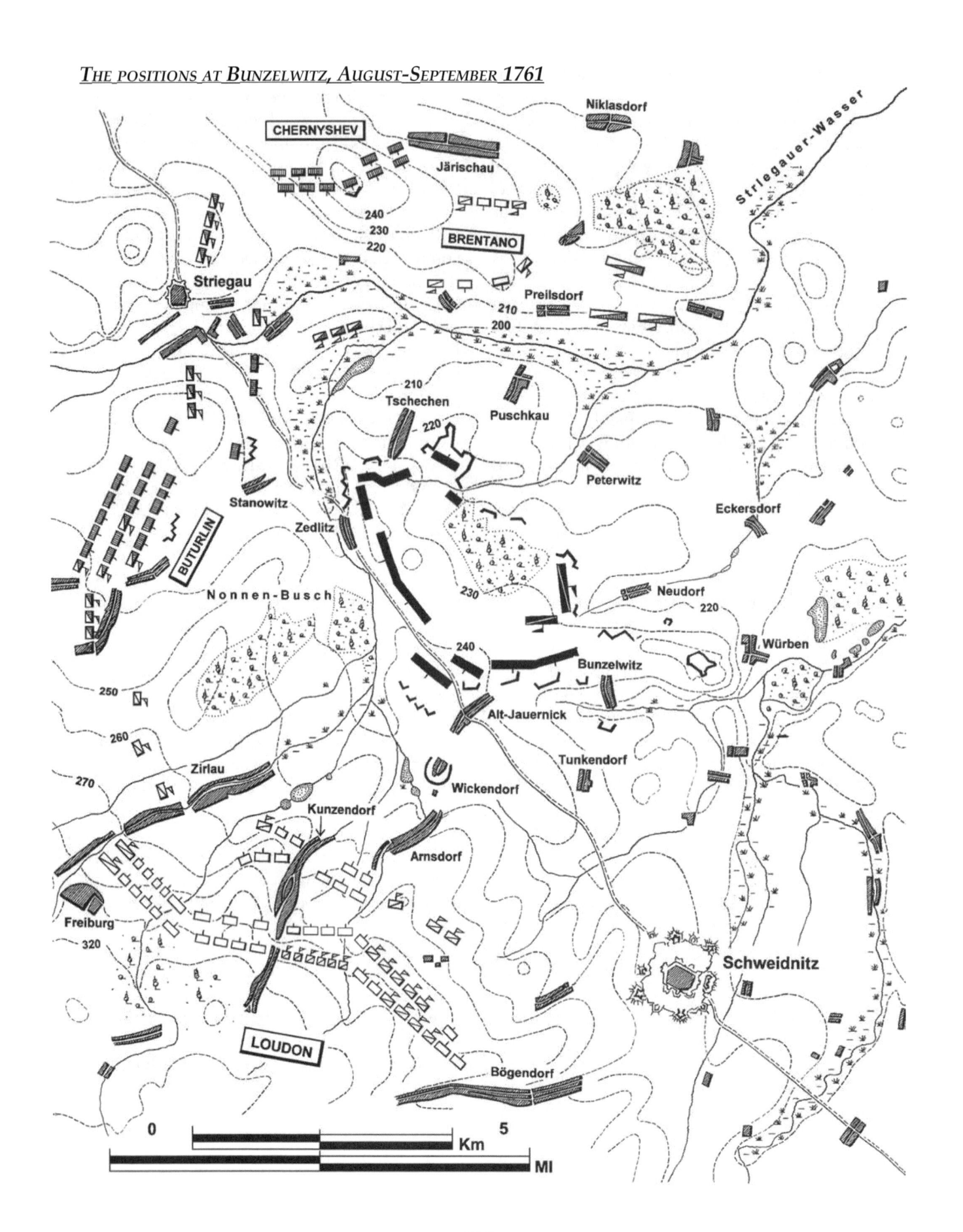

The positions at Bunzelwitz, August–September 1761

while Loudon pledged his word of honour to keep Buturlin supplied with biscuit, flour, oats and other commodities for the better part of two months. The effort absorbed all the capacity of the Austrian transport train, and the requirement for raw forage, which was an extraordinarily bulky commodity, could be met only by requisitions in the Silesian countryside. The Cossacks threw themselves into the work with gusto, and ravaged as far as the Austrian outposts.

Poised in the hills above Schweidnitz, the Austrian awaited the final approach of the Russians, 'who saw fit to take yet another five days. On 20th the enemy the enemy had taken up position at Bunzelwitz, and they put this interlude to excellent use to dig themselves in. As the Russian officers admitted to us quite openly afterwards, those five days were a little revenge on us for the same span of time we left them entirely at the mercy of the enemy after they crossed the Oder.'[31]

At last on 24 August the Russian army marched as far as Jauer. Loudon went to see Buturlin there, and urged that 'if the king remains in his present position we must attack him at once with our united forces.'[32] On the 25th a general movement of the Russian forces to Hohenfriedeberg brought them into immediate contact with the Austrians, and on the next day the two armies descended to the plain and closed in on Frederick's entrenched position, celebrated in military history as the 'Camp of Bunzelwitz.'

Frustration at Bunzelwitz, August - September 1761

Forces at Bunzelwitz
a) Austrians
c. 80,600; c. 70,000 regular infantry and cavalry, c. 10,600 Croats. 290 field pieces
b) Russians:
v. approx. 60,000; 47,000 regular infantry and cavalry, v. approx. 13,000 Cossacks and other light horse.
c) Prussians
54,400; 39,000 infantry, 15,400 cavalry. 148 heavy pieces

Buturlin had offered only a heavily conditional assent to the joint attack, and on 27 August he declared that the Russians needed more time and more assurances from Loudon. The exasperated Loudon replied that Buturlin must bear in mind that with every passing day, indeed every passing hour the king was entrenching himself in more solidly and more elaborately, and that it was impossible to guarantee the success of any military operation with total assurance.[33]

The allies had an overwhelming advantage in terms of numbers (about 141,000 as against 54,200), but the balance was redressed by the cohesion of the Prussian forces, the outstanding quality of the leadership, and the technical skill which made the Camp of Bunzelwitz a marvel of its time. Entrenched positions were a common enough feature of eighteenth-century warfare. They might extend across a sector of a theatre of operations, like the lines which the French constructed in the Netherlands against Marlborough. They might crown a set of heights which overlooked a valley, as in Prince Henry's camp of Katzenhäuser above the Triebisch. What made the position of Bunzelwitz unique was that it was carried out under the personal supervision of Frederick, and formed an all-round defensive position

From the operational aspect, the king settled on the site because it was the only suitable ground from where the army could maintain a lifeline to the fortress of Schweidnitz, with its invaluable stocks of provisions. 'In this location the Prussian army stood on a series of low and mostly gentle eminences, which it utilised in a masterly fashion. While the approaches were by no means physically insurmountable, what rendered them difficult to approach were the little streams, the swampy meadows, and the enfilading and grazing fire from the batteries on every side.'[34] The only daunting heights were the isolated hill above Würben in the southeast, and the ridge above Zedlitz in the northwest, but the site of the camp as a whole was higher-lying than the surrounding country, which enabled Frederick to use his artillery to its full grazing effect.

No less than 182 pieces of the Prussian ordnance, all but ten of them heavy, were emplaced in carefully-sited and mutually-supporting batteries, and Frederick was confident that they would slaughter the enemy cavalry before it could come near. For close-range defence against infantry, the batteries were protected by storm poles, multiple ditches and palisades, with outlying wolf-pits and fougasses. The intervals between the batteries were covered by chevaux de frise and further wolf-pits, but not so firmly barred as to hinder counterattacks, and all but a couple of the batteries were open to the rear, in accordance with the same principle of active defence.

Wickendorf. The Prussians took advantage of the slightly rising ground around the church to build the circular earthwork which was one of the key points of their position at Bunzelwitz. Development has now made this scene unrecognisable.

Most of the construction was the work of the country-people, who were beaten by the Prussians if they refused to labour (and by the Austrians and Russians if they did), but the Prussian soldiers were exposed to the full force of the sun on this near-shelterless plain, and their diet of bread and water gave them scarcely the strength to stand to arms during the nights. The perimeter of the camp extended more than ten miles, and the only sizeable reserve was a mass of fifty-four squadrons (6,900 men) positioned behind the south-eastern angle.

On 26 August Loudon had deployed the main force of Austrians between Zirlau and Bögendorf, which posed a direct threat to the south-western salient at Wickendorf and Alt-Jauernick. The position as a whole was invested two days later, when the Russian army arrived between Striegau and Oels, and the various corps of Lieutenant General Chernyshev, *GFWM*. Brentano and the Russian major general Berg embraced the camp on its northern and north-eastern fronts, all the way from Tschechen to Eckersdorf.

Loudon continued with his reconnaissances, after the first Russian refusal to attack, and on 1 September his chief of staff Giannini submitted a detailed *Disposition*.[35] The plan involved the co-operation, direct or indirect, of the entire allied force, and was composed of three main elements:

1. Buturlin and the main Russian army were to carry out a massive demonstration, by advancing on a broad front through and to the north of the Nonnen-Busch as if to cross the Freiburger-Wasser and attack the camp from the west

2. Chernyshev, Brentano and Berg were to delivery further diversionary attacks across a wide arc from Tschechen in the north and Würben in the east. It is unclear just how far they were supposed to advance. If they came too close, Chernyshev and Berg would have run into strong batteries at Tschechen and Würben respectively. Brentano could have taken advantage of the little valley leading west from Peterwitz, but Frederick had alerted some of his troops to meet an attack from just this direction

3. The main attack was aimed at the southern sector, and involved 58,600 Austrians and 6,200 supporting Russians. It depended crucially on first eliminating the south-western salient at Wickendorf and Jauernick, and this was the business of major generals Brinken and Amadei. The main force would then advance on a wide front to reach the Prussian positions between Jauernick and Bunzelwitz, with *FML*. Luzinsky covering the open right flank with two regiments of hussars

The various columns were to set out for their attacking positions in all possible silence at ten at night on 2 September, and 'the general of the day is to deploy the outposts (consisting of a double complement of picked men, under resolute officers) so as to drive back the enemy outposts along the whole extent of the front before the heads of the columns advance.' The attack proper would open at 3.30 in the morning of the 3rd. Loudon urged the generals to 'help one another out in a comradely fashion,' and 'it would contribute immensely to the happy outcome of this important day if all ranks of the officers would hearten the men (who, as we all know, are of the best will in the world), and make light of our enterprise.'[36]

Loudon had put the new project to Buturlin on 1 September after a meal and a glass of wine. The field marshal gave his full assent, apart from requiring the auxiliary corps of 6,200 Russians to be withdrawn to the main Russian army. This was a not unreasonable request, but left Loudon unprepared for what happened on the morning of the 2nd, when Buturlin told him that the attack had no prospect of success, for the enemy had dug themselves in altogether too strongly. Loudon asked to borrow up to ten Russian battalions, so as to form a third striking column alongside those of Brinken and Amadei. This was denied so emphatically that Loudon believed that he could not even count on the participation of the corps of Chernyshev (12-13,000 regular infantry and horse) which had been assigned to his command under an earlier agreement.

Loudon called off the grand attack which had been intended for the next day, and also had to agree to Buturlin's taking leave of the

Austrians and crossing the Oder, which would leave only Chernyshev with the Austrians. All that he could salvage from the wreck was the reluctant consent on the part of Buturlin to stay a few days beyond 6 September, in the hope that Frederick might even now run out of supplies. 'Thoroughly downcast, he returned to his headquarters, cancelled the arrangements which had already been made for the battle, and fell into the grips of a violent seizure. He had experienced other episodes of the kind, all occasioned by the behaviour of the allies since 1759. A number of his friends used this happening to convince the public that Loudon would have gone ahead with his project on 3 September, with or without the Russians, if only he had not been overcome by his illness, which confined him to bed for nearly forty-eight hours.'[37]

Frederick was certainly exaggerating when he claimed that an assault on the Camp of Bunzelwitz would have been beaten off with a loss of 30,000 men. By any conventional reckoning, however, the Russian high command was right to dissuade Loudon from attacking. There had been no mention of any kind of artillery support, and although the plan had made elaborate provisions for eliminating the salient at Alt-Jauernick in advance, there were no specific arrangements for dealing with the other salient at Bunzelwitz, which was one of the targets of the main army. The Prussians were in any case on high alert, and Frederick's suspicions as to the likely objectives corresponded closely with the targets in the Austrian plan.

By 7 September reports of the imminent departure of the Russians were circulating in Frederick's army, and on the evening of 9 September Buturlin and 35,000 of his troops set out for the Oder, covered by 5,200 Austrian cavalry under *FML*. Beck, 'who was really the most likeable of all our generals… and had won the universal regard of the Russian army.'[38] Frederick soon knocked Buturlin out of the reckoning altogether when he detached *GL*. Platen with 11,000 troops to raid the Russian depots beyond the Oder. Platen destroyed the magazine at Kobylyn on 14 September, and proceeded to wreck an important convoy of provisions at Gostyn the next day. Buturlin was now bent on getting back to his base at Posen, and on 16 September the last division of his army crossed the Oder at Steinau. The news came to Maria Theresa on the 22nd, and she abandoned all hope of any further participation from the Russians.

Loudon still had up to 82,000 Austrian and Russian regular troops under his command (and Frederick 42,000 at the most), but he did not appreciate how severely the Prussians at Bunzelwitz had been depleted by the departure of Platen's raiding corps, and he drew back his infantry to the position among the hills at Kunzendorf, leaving only the cavalry to dispute the plain. A French attaché reported that he believed that Kaunitz was 'most embarrassed in more than one respect. Here we have his strategy for Silesia not only in a state of collapse, but even ridiculed and condemned. Loudon, his hero, is now discredited, while his prime enemy Daun is at the height of his prestige in Vienna… The Empress is now fully entitled to reproach Kaunitz on the following grounds: 1. Because she had always been opposed to his plan. 2. Because she has a genuine liking for Daun, and feels that she has something to make up to him, in view of the bad way has been treated in this affair.'[39]

Loudon had just resigned himself to having to send large numbers of troops back to Daun in Saxony when he learned that Frederick had left the neighbourhood of Schweidnitz. The king had drawn heavily on the stocks of supplies there, and he believed that by moving to the east he could not only replenish his provisions, but make Loudon believe that he was threatening Austrian Silesia and Moravia. He first moved to a camp between Pilzen and Faulbrück. He then drew Loudon's particular attention by a mighty march of thirty kilometres to Siegroth on the 28th, and the next day he reached another favourite position, on the heights of Gross-Nossen south of Münsterberg.

Loudon recognised the move for what it was, no more than a bluff to draw him from his strong position in the hills, 'and so for that reason I was not only content… to stay here, but I aimed to exploit the absence of the king by consolidating my position in these hills. For this purpose I designed to take the fortress of Schweidnitz sword in hand, and I made all the appropriate arrangements for the following night.'[40]

Loudon's triumph—the storm of Schweidnitz, 1 October 1761

a) Allied forces engaged in the assault
16,000: 15,200 Austrians, 800 Russians
Total losses: 1,522
Austrian losses: 1,425; 278 killed, 1,007 wounded, 140 missing
Russian losses: 97; 51 killed, 46 wounded
b) Prussians
very approx. 4,000, of whom 2,426 were on duty in the various works on 30 September.
Losses: Killed, wounded and missing unknown. *GM.* Zastrow captured, along with 3,614 combatants and 163 other personnel. The Austrians found in Schweidnitz 25 colours, 211 cannon, howitzers and mortars, 125 coehorn mortars, 123,077 cannon shot, 5,000 howitzer shells, 18,520 mortar bombs, 1,300,600 musket cartridges and 89,769 carbine cartridges

Victory is a child of many fathers. The storm of Schweidnitz on 1 October 1761 was the most spectacular single Austrian feat of arms in the Seven Years War, and afterwards a number of officers made certain that their contributions were entered on the record. Among these people was Major Heinrich O'Donnell. He knew the fortress only too well, for he had been besieged and finally incarcerated there in 1758, and on 10 August of the present year he approached Loudon with a first project for an assault.

Nothing more was heard of the scheme until Loudon summoned O'Donnell on 28 September and asked for his opinion. Loudon was still not convinced that the place could be taken as swiftly as had been represented, and the other generals raised a multitude of objections, but O'Donnell insisted that the Prussians did not have enough troops to defend all the fortifications adequately, and that out of these works the Galgen-Fort (I) was the most important.[41] In any event the chief of staff Ernst Friedrich Giannini made a decisive contribution by interrogating Pierre Mandelieu, who was a deserter from the regiment of Zastrow [38], and who provided details of the garrison, how it was distributed among the fortifications, and the state of the works.[42]

Loudon made up his mind to go ahead, 'for which purpose I concerted the enterprise most carefully with the Russian lieutenant general Chernyshev. He committed himself entirely to the scheme, and offered all his troops for that purpose, but I did not think that was necessary, and asked for no more than the four companies of grenadiers… which made up 800 men.'[43] On the morning of the 30th the officers of the general staff carried out a detailed reconnaissance. Both Giannini and Amadei afterwards tried to take the credit for the resulting *Disposition*,[44] but fact remains the responsibility for the success or failure of the undertaking rested with Loudon alone.

The Austrians had stormed Schweidnitz once before, on the night of 11/12 November 1757, and yet there were substantial differences in the two operations. The assault in 1757 had been the culmination of a regular siege, in which the Austrians had brought systematic artillery fire to bear on the forts and lunettes, and had worked their way forward by trench attacks. Now there was no artillery preparation of any kind, and Loudon was calling on his troops to advance across open ground. Again the forts and lunettes of 1757 had stood alone, but now they were connected by a continuous palisaded entrenchment. The present commandant was *GM.* Zastrow, a brave veteran who had earned the full trust of his king. Out of his garrison of five battalions 560 troops were assigned to the town rampart, 1,400 were held in reserve to reinforce the outworks, 450 guarded the connecting lines, and the rest garrisoned the forts and lunettes. By all accounts they fought well.

In outline, Loudon intended to take four of the works—the Galgen-Fort (I), the Jauernicker-Fort (II), the Garten-Fort (III) and the Bögen-Fort (IV)—by full-scale storm, while *GFWM.* Jahnus and his Croats waded the Schweidnitzer-Wasser to execute a diversionary attack on the Wasser-Fort (V) to draw the attention of the Prussians to the east. The attacking force comprised twenty battalions of Austrian fusiliers and grenadiers, four squadrons of Austrian dragoons and four large companies of Russian grenadiers, making a total of 16,000 troops. 'The

Loudon storms Schweidnitz, 1 October 1761

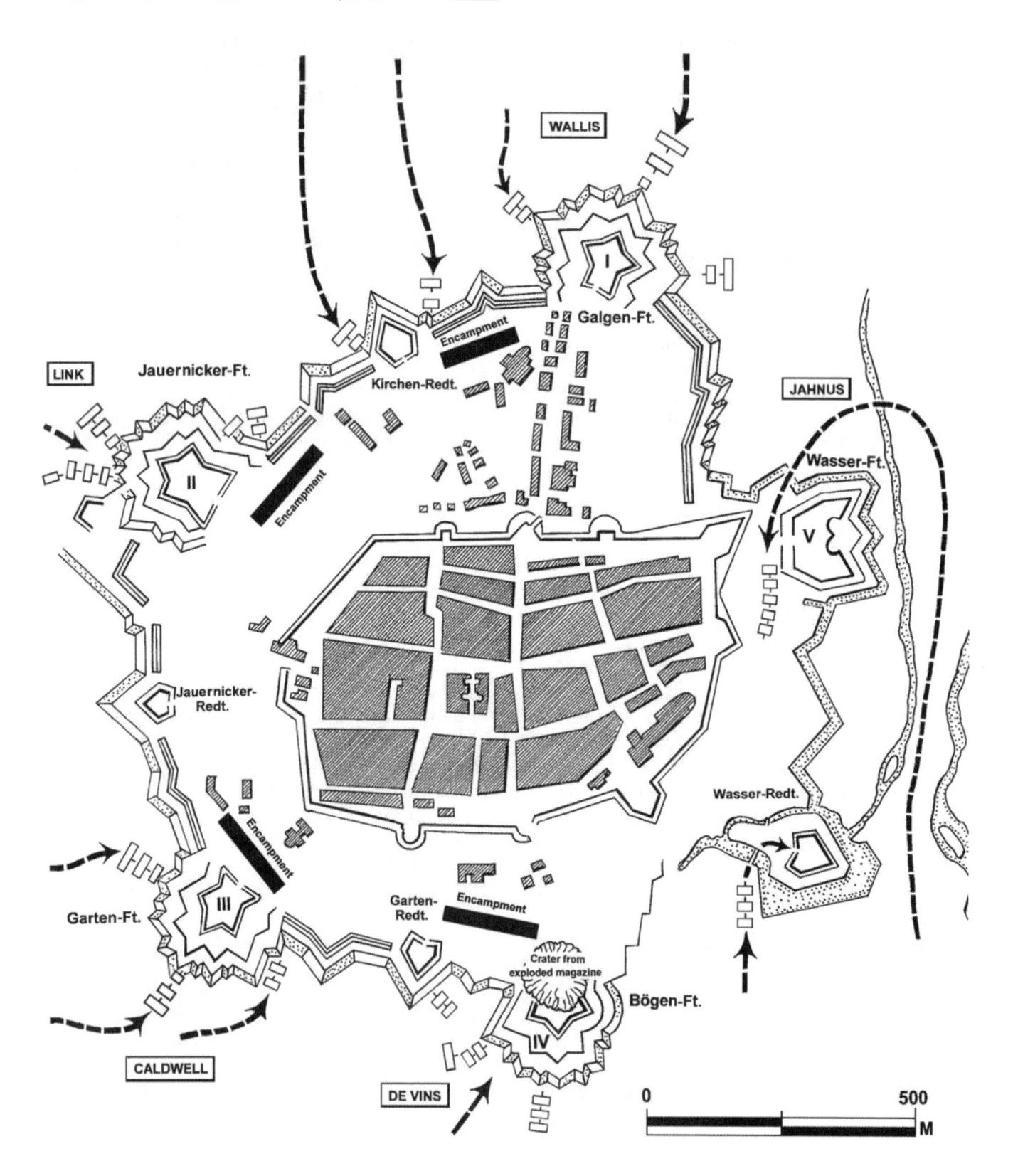

time of the attack is three hours before first light on 1 October, for which purpose the assigned commanders of the four attacks are to synchronise their watches.'[45]

Two major generals of the highest aristocratic houses, Prince Liechtenstein and Count Kinsky, had the unheroic but necessary task of sending troops around the neighbouring villages to collect or construct materials for the escalade. At four in the afternoon of 30 September the ladders were duly delivered to *GFWM*. Amadei, who was forming the four main columns west of Kunzendorf. In addition 'the planks, or rather the large bales of hay or straw which are to be used in their place, are to be distributed to the men so as to cover the wolf-pits around the glacis, so that we may pass the more easily. The troops are to breach the chevaux de frise with all possible speed, and the assigned pioneers are to open up the connecting lines at least widely enough so that we can march through on the frontage of divisions {i.e. two platoons].'[46]

The troops set off into the darkness at nine in the evening of 30 September, and in the earliest morning of 1 October they massed in the vicinity of the villages of Sabischdorf, Schönbrunn and Bögendorf. 'Everything was carried out in the finest order and in total silence, and the columns reached their various rendezvous towards two in the morning without being detected by the enemy.'[47]

The columns had a uniform structure of one small battalion of Austrian or Russian grenadiers, four battalions of Austrian fusiliers, and three squadrons of Austrian dragoons. 'These three squadrons have to make particularly sure that no soldiers (apart from those who are wounded) are left behind, and that all those unwounded men who try to fall back are to be driven into the attack by force.' The grenadiers at the head of the column were to divide, one company hastening around to the rear of the work to seize the drawbridge, while the other escaladed the double rampart. The leading battalion had to support the grenadiers, the next penetrate the connecting line between to one side or another of the work being attacked, while the remaining two battalions and the dragoons acted as a general reserve. The men were issued with sixty cartridges, but 'note well, that as far as possible the enemy are to be driven back with the bayonet, and not by fire. The soldiers are to call out to the enemy to surrender. Those who throw their muskets away are to be spared, but those who offer the slightest resistance are to be cut down without any hesitation.'[48] Colonel Rouvroy assigned a small train of artillery to each column, but the main task of his gunners was to take over the cannon in the captured works and train them around against the town rampart.

In spite of every precaution the attack did not open simultaneously on all sectors. Lieutenant Colonel De Vins commanded the storm on the **Bögen-Fort** (IV) in the south of the perimeter. His column (guided by Major Huyn of the General Staff) moved precisely on time from its assembly area in the hollow south of Bögendorf, but the commander of the fort, Major Ripp, was on full alert, and by lobbing bombs and illuminating shells into the darkness he discovered the advancing troops. This column therefore became the first to draw the enemy fire. De Vins was at the head of the assault with the Russian grenadiers. 'It would have taken altogether too much time to chop down the palisade, and so I gave the lead to my grenadiers by jumping into the covered way. I then climbed the envelope [outer rampart]… and I can say without boasting that I was the first to negotiate the outworks.'[49]

Some of the supporting fusiliers infiltrated along the outer ditch, and the fear of being cut off persuaded the defenders of the envelope to retire to the main rampart. The Russians grenadiers and the Austrian fusiliers now set their ladders against the scarp, and by about 3.30 in the morning they forced their way into the interior of the fort against an obstinate resistance. A number of troops had been told off to attack the rear of the work, and now opened fire against an opening they espied under the drawbridge. By ill fortune it gave onto the powder magazine, which now blew up, wrecking this side of the fort and causing heavy casualties among all parties. De Vins had captured his fort, but his surviving men were so shocked that it took time to round them up and continue the attack against the town.

The outburst of firing from the Bögen-Fort had put the defenders of the other works on their guard, and the illuminating rounds from the Jauernicker-Fort (II) and the Garten-Fort (III) lit up the attacking columns before they could reach the glacis.

Everything now depended on speed. The troops of Major Link, assigned to attack the **Jauernicker-Fort** in the north-west of the fortress complex, ascended the glacis at a run, escaladed both the envelope and the main rampart in rapid succession and overcame the resistance in the interior. The Prussian major Berrenhauer explained afterwards that he had been holding the fort with a typically inadequate garrison of 270 men. 'The night was pitch black, and yet the enemy knew every last detail of the approaches. We shouldn't be surprised, for they had once had Schweidnitz in their possession, and they had plenty of guides—indeed some of them were our own deserters.'[50]

Lieutenant Colonel Caldwell had the mortification of seeing his fusiliers melt away under the fire of the **Garten-Fort** on the south-western perimeter. The attack was sustained only by the grenadiers, and notably by the company of the regiment of Loudon [29] under his fellow Irishman, Captain Wilhelm Lacy, who rallied his men with 'urgent cries,' got them to assault the covered way with its three blockhouses, and finally clamber over the main rampart and take prisoner the Prussian major and what was left of his men.[51] This was Major Siegroth, whose authorised garrison was of 366 men, but now had only 221 under his command. Nearly all these now deserted him, and he was captured after he was clubbed to the ground by a musket butt.,

Over to the east, *GFWM*. Jahnus was splashing across the channels of the Schweidnitzer-Wasser with his Croats (two battalions of Peterwardeiner, one battalion of Gradiscaner, and one grenadier battalion of companies from both regiments). His role was supposed to be a diversionary one, but his target, the **Wasser-Fort** (V) was already filled with Prussian fugitives from the other works, which suggests that he arrived late on the scene.

The grenadiers seem to have attacked the adjacent lunette to the south, while the main body broke through the connecting line to the north of the fort and attacked the work from the rear. The decisive blow was nevertheless dealt by 4-500 Austrian prisoners of war, who burst out of the casemates where they had been confined, overpowered the guard at the gate and lowered the drawbridge to the advancing Croats.

The assault against the rampart of **Schweidnitz town** was already in full swing. Victorious Austrians and Russians were surging towards the enceinte from the captured works and the intervening lines, and Colonel Rouvroy gave such effective support, by traversing the Prussian cannon, that there was hardly any need to employ the accompanying field pieces. Zastrow put up what defence he could with his reserve and the town garrison, but there were stretches of the wall up to sixty paces long with nobody to guard them, and the first of the many escalades was effected by the Russian major Posnikov and two companies of his grenadiers, who led the depleted column of De Vins and climbed the wall next to the Bögen-Tor. The allies overcame the final resistance inside the town, and forced Zastrow and a last small band to surrender.

Fighting was still going on to the north-east of the town for the possession of the **Galgen-Fort** (I) and the adjacent lunette. The assault was commanded by Colonel Oliver Wallis, who had volunteered for this task, bearing in mind that the work was held by the regiment of Tresckow [32], 'the kernel of the garrison… and because the perimeter wall of the town could best be attacked from the direction of this fort, once it was in our possession.'[52] His column consisted of two companies of Russian grenadiers, the grenadier battalion of Heinrich O'Donnell, the fusilier battalions of Carl Lothringen [3, which was attacking the lunette], Waldeck [35] and Gyulai [51], and one squadron only of dragoons. Major Philipp Elmpt gathered the troops in the hollow to the right of Sabischdorf, and 'once they were all drawn up in the shelter of the ground, and were all in ready to attack, I urged the officers and men not to get held up in passing the glacis and the wolf-pits, but to leap the palisades into the covered way. Once there, they would be out of danger.'[53]

Out of all the attacking columns, that of Wallis had the furthest to go. Moreover the fort was held by the regiment of Tresckow, as already indicated, which was alert and determined. The Russians and Austrians were repulsed from the covered way four times over, whereupon, by the account of Wallis, he turned to the troops of a battalion of the regiment of Loudon [29], who were standing in reserve, and 'urged them, brave lads as they were, to save my honour and promote the Imperial service. This they did with uncommon courage, cheerfulness, good orders and resolution under the leadership of Major Baron Engelhard. The captains picked up two ladders among the wolf-pits, carried them into the covered way with their own hands, set them up [i.e. over the envelope], and angled them down into the main ditch. The whole battalion then descended, and finally climbed the main work, in the teeth of a continuous fire from the garrison, which consisted of a lieutenant colonel and 412 men. A large number of our troops spread out to right and left along the rampart, then jumped inside among the enemy, who called out for quarter and surrendered.' [54]

This narrative telescopes the sequence of events. Major Elmpt adds that the ladders which were picked up by the captains had been abandoned during one of the earlier assaults. He claims that the escalades of the envelope and the main rampart might well have failed if he and a small group of regimental pioneers had not also forced their way along the tunnels which led from the covered way to those two works. Lastly he reached the magazine at the rear of the fort, where he discovered 200 barrels of gunpowder, 'and just in time, for our men were actually in the process of beating in the door with their muskets. I put an end to this immediately, and stationed sentries outside.' [55] The action at the Galgen-Fort, the last and the most bitter of the day, was over by six in the morning.

Loudon had promised his troops 100,000 florins if they held back from sacking the town after the assault. However the prospect of loot had probably accounted for much of the eagerness, and Schweidnitz town underwent up to four hours of plundering before the dragoons restored order. The only infantry to stay under control were the regiments of Harrach, Kollowrat, Arenberg and Kónigsegg [47, 17, 21, 16], and the magnificent Russian grenadiers 'who, having accomplished their glorious task, waited calmly in rank and file upon further orders.'[56]

In less than four hours Loudon had deprived Frederick of 3,600 of his troops, 211 pieces of artillery, and the newest and conceivably the most important of his fortresses. The king had never considered for a moment that Schweidnitz might be in danger, and the sound of the artillery fire which carried to him at Gross-Nossen was the first indication that something was amiss. Schweidnitz had fallen 'in a manner which almost defies belief,'[57] and 'after this coup we will have to provide an army for each fortress.'[58]

On 1 October, the day of the conquest, Loudon dispatched Lieutenant Colonel Caldwell to carry the news to Daun in Saxony. He sent a preliminary relation to Maria Theresa on the 3rd, and a more detailed account to Daun the next day. He reflected that it was scarcely possible to overpraise the courage of all ranks of the attacking force, 'and at the same time we must render due credit to the enemy garrison, whose troops fought like real soldiers, and gave way only foot by foot.'[59]

Loudon asked Maria Theresa to promote the *GFWM*s. Liechtenstein, Giannini and Amadei to *FML*s., the lieutenant colonels De Vins and Caldwell to full colonels and the majors Heinrich O'Donnell and Link to lieutenant colonels. He was aware that some of them had been advanced to their present ranks only recently, 'but it is very important for an army to have extraordinary deeds of that kind rewarded in an extraordinary way.'[60] There were special bounties for the troops who had held themselves aloof from the sack of the town.

Kaunitz was repaid in full for the confidence he had placed in Loudon, and in his message of congratulation to Maria Theresa he recalled a war leader of the Old Testament: 'May God preserve Your Majesty's Joshua!'[61]

VII

THE WAR IN THE BALANCE, 1761-2

SILESIA AFTER THE CAPTURE OF SCHWEIDNITZ

Heavy snow set in unseasonably early on 2 October, which showed that Loudon had acted against Schweidnitz just in the nick of time, for the weather now forced the rival armies into cantonments. Loudon used the respite to begin the four months of work which was needed to restore Schweidnitz to a defensible state, but a renewed request to reinforce Daun reached him on 19 October, and two days later he dispatched twenty battalions and twenty grenadier companies on the road to Saxony. In reality he could well afford the sacrifice, for he still had with him 49,900 Austrians and about 16,000 Russians, in addition to the garrison of 5,900 troops in Schweidnitz.

As for the enemy, 'never had the headquarters been afflicted with such anxiety and such trepidations for the future. Everybody was wearing long faces, marked with desperation and gloom… No misfortune in the whole war affected the valiant Prussians more deeply.'[1] The Prussian army fell back to the Oder between Breslau and Brieg, and Frederick took up his quarters in a house in a suburb of Strehlen, where on the night of 29/3 November he was lucky not to be kidnapped and whisked off to the Austrians.

It is a curious story, for the plot was hatched by a Lutheran landowner, Heinrich Gottlob Baron Warkotsch of Schönbrunn, and the scheme was betrayed to the Prussians by his Catholic Bohemian huntsman, Matthias Keppel, 'whose example shows us the workings of virtue even in the humblest of souls.'[2] Warkotsch saved himself by escaping through a window and galloping away on a horse which he kept saddled outside, and in 1762 we find the Austrians paying him a pension and arranging for him to stay in Hungary under the pseudonym of a 'Count Löbenstein.'[3] The evidence suggests that it had been an officially-sanctioned but 'deniable' enterprise, and it was not the last of the kind in the course of this war.

Loudon had substantial gains to set against this disappointment. On 4 December the Austrians went into winter quarters in Silesia, and for the first time in this war they established themselves entirely in Prussian territory, behind a screen of outposts which extended all the way from Hirschberg in the west to Ratibor in Upper Silesia to the east.

Loudon was awarded a diamond-encrusted Grand Cross of the Military Order of Maria Theresa, and a little later the Empress sent him her portrait in miniature, again set in diamonds, with the authority to wear it openly as a sign of her favour. Even now his enemies in Vienna suggested that the storm of Schweidnitz had been just a *Croatenstreich* writ large, and that it did not make up for his total lack of achievement during the summer. Lacy could not bring himself to agree, and indicated to Daun that those few hours had brought a conquest which was 'worthy of the efforts of an entire campaign.'[4]

Prussia on the verge of defeat

It is curious that Loudon had intended his coup against Schweidnitz to be no more than a defensive measure, designed to win him an outer defence to his positions in the hills. The outcome surpassed anything which he could possibly have imagined. The capture of this place gave Maria Theresa and her ministers the courage to continue the war, and their hopes were reinforced by the news that the Prussian coastal fortress of Colberg, having been attacked in vain by the Russians in 1758 and 1760, was starved into surrender on 16 December. The Russians now had a port conveniently close to the line of the Oder, and, instead of withdrawing their troops to the Vistula as before, they now quartered them for the winter in eastern Pomerania and along the Warthe, or about seven marches nearer the Prussian heartland.

Frederick conjured up visions of the Austrians picking off his remaining fortresses in Silesia as they chose, the Russians flooding over Brandenburg and Berlin, and his brother Prince Henry being overwhelmed in Saxony. The king thought it possible that the Turks might be persuaded to act against the allies (below), but the prospect was a distant one, and on 6 January 1762 he wrote to his chief minister Finckenstein that 'our present sad situation signifies that our affairs are beyond remedy, whatever our courage, and whatever we might do with our forces, and that it will not even be in our power to sustain a further campaign. In my ruinous state it seems to me that we must turn to negotiation, as the only means of rescuing from the greed of my enemies something for the benefit of my nephew [Prince Frederick William, his heir].'[5]

It is time to set this remarkable statement in a wider diplomatic and military context. In the midsummer of 1761 nobody could have predicted that the expectations of the alliance would be pitched so highly by the end of the year. In western Germany the French had contrived to unite the armies of the Lower Rhine (70,000) under Soubise and the Upper Rhine (50,000) under Broglie, but their combined forces failed in their two-day battle against Ferdinand of Brunswick at Vellinghausen (15 and 16 July), and after this disappointment they went their separate ways. On 18 July the Swedes crossed into Prussian Pomerania; their commander, Ehrensvärd, was the best horse in their stable, but it was beyond their power to capture more than a couple of magazines. The 15th of the same month had been designated for the opening of a congress of peace at Augsburg, but the day came and went without any meeting of delegates. In neither Saxony nor Silesia had the Austrians attained any success which might have tempted them to come to the conference table, while the Duc de Choiseul on behalf of France was still hoping for a favourable outcome of his separate negotiations with the British.

Within a month the shape and character of the alliance were transformed. William Pitt's days as the British prime minister were numbered, but on 29 July he effectively terminated the talks by insisting that the French must give up all the conquests they had made from Britain's associates, and Prussia in particular, and that they must stand aside from the quarrel between Britain and Spain. Choiseul turned to the Spanish, and on 15 August the representatives of France and Spain signed a Family Compact. With this achievement to his credit, Choiseul resigned in favour of his nephew, the Comte de Choiseul-Praslin, the ambassador to Vienna. The two branches of the House of Bourbon were now allied, and the French ministry was in a more bellicose mood than at any time since the summer of 1757.

In Saxony, as we have seen, the Austrians at last bestirred themselves, and pushed back Prince Henry's Prussians to the constricted area between the Elbe, the Triebisch and the Freiberger Mulde. On 1 October the Prussians lost Schweidnitz in Silesia, and 'so unexpected a disaster seemed to presage the approaching fall of the King himself, which everything announced to be imminent and almost inevitable. Charles the Twelfth's situation after his defeat at Pultowa, was hardly more desperate than that of the King towards the close of 1761. Another campaign, according to all appearances, must have laid him entirely at the mercy of the vast combination which had determined his destruction.'[6] On 16 December the Russians captured Colberg. Six days later the Swedes went unexpectedly over to the attack in Pomerania, and on 2 January 1762 they beat Colonel Belling in an action at Neu-Kalen. When he looked back on that prosperous time Kaunitz reflected that 'we had finally reached a situation when the opening of the new year gave us every possible reason to believe that the great goal of our striving was within our grasp.'[7]

The death of Empress Elizabeth of Russia

Kaunitz had complained of the *Lethargie* which from time to time overtook the Empress Elizabeth, but the more recent reports had been encouraging, and nothing prepared Vienna for the news that this constant friend of the common cause had died on 5 January 1762. The inevitable accession of her nephew and heir Grand Prince Peter of Holstein-Gottorp had been viewed as a distant nightmare, but it was now reality. Peter was a German Lutheran, and in one perspective he was a simple-minded prussophile and military maniac, convinced that 'the sovereign good is to have many troops. He adores the king of Prussia, because he has been told that this prince is very skilled in disciplining and drilling his soldiers.'[8]

Less evidently, the new Emperor Peter III harboured the considered policy of withdrawing Russia from her existing allies, leaguing himself with Frederick, and with this support, and the consent of Britain and Sweden, forcing Denmark to return the Holstein and Schleswig lands which had been lost to his inheritance. On 23 February 1762 Peter declared that in the interests of European peace he would give up everything the Russians had taken from Prussia, if the French and Austrians would return their conquests as well. There was not enough here to enable the Austrians to fathom what Peter might have in mind. At the best he might retreat into neutrality. But he also had it in his power to join forces with Frederick, undermine the authority of the Habsburgs in the *Reich*, and foment unrest in Croatia.

The uncertainty was prolonged by Prince Golitsyn, the Russian ambassador in Vienna, who was slow to execute the instructions he received from St. Petersburg, quite possibly on account of Austrian sympathies. Only in the course of time did the Austrians learn how completely the relations between Prussia and Russia had been transformed. The essential stages were as follows:

1. On 29 January 1762 Frederick learned that Elizabeth had died, and on 3 February he ordered hostilities against the Russians to cease

2. On 16 March an armistice between the two powers was signed at Stargard. All prisoners of war were to be returned, and the corps of Chernyshev retrieved from the Austrians

3. On 5 May a treaty of peace at St. Petersburg provided for the evacuation of the conquered Prussian territories

4. The defection of Russia from the grand alliance left Sweden totally isolated. On 22 May Sweden and Prussia concluded a treaty of peace at Hamburg, and confirmed their boundaries in Pomerania as those which existed before the war

5. In June Prussia and Russia entered into active military partnership, and Peter pledged an auxiliary corps of 18,000 troops to help Frederick to regain all of Silesia and Glatz.

By the last week of May all doubts had been removed as to the hostile nature of Peter's ambitions. Enquiries were now made after the parties of Russian officers who were known to be free in the Habsburg dominions, not excluding the Major Sholabov who was guarding those vineyards in Tokay which, by a bizarre privilege, were regarded as Russian territory.[9] There were wider fears that the common Orthodox religion and 'Illyrian' culture would give the Russians an opening into the hearts and minds of the Croats, and Maria Theresa told Daun to consult Loudon, Brentano and others who understood the Croats and had their sources of information among them, as to the best means to prevent these people from being led astray.[10]

At the same time Maria Theresa and her ministers were debating the fundamental question of war and peace. In his *Votum* of 28 May Kaunitz declared that he could not regret strongly enough that the Austrians no longer had it in their power 'to secure the welfare, elevation and security of the Most Illustrious Hereditary House over the long term through the weakening of its most dangerous enemy.' He concluded, nevertheless, that the war must be continued in the interests of security and prestige.[11] Kaunitz had been writing more specifically about Prussia, but the same thinking informed his policies towards Russia under its new master. Peter was now threatening Maria Theresa with war in case she did not restore all the territory which had been wrested from the Prussians, a condition which both Kaunitz and

Maria Theresa found intolerable. With the monarchy now committed to continuing the war, we must ask how fitted the Austrians were to sustain their struggle.

Distractions—economic

The balance of the rival forces was being adjusted in altogether unfamiliar ways. Frederick retrieved the prisoners which had been taken by the Russians and the Swedes, and he was able to recall the forces which had been facing those two enemies. All of Prussian Pomerania was now open to recruiting, and although it was a slow business to integrate the returned prisoners and the new men in the units, he was able to build up the army in Silesia to 78,000 combatants, and that in Saxony to an ultimate 42,000. The train of artillery was augmented to 650 pieces, of which 362 were heavy cannon and howitzers. Already in 1761 Frederick had begun a *grosse Augmentation* of the effective unit complements, which carried all the regiments of infantry to the high establishment of 1,800 officers and men each, and those of the cuirassiers and dragoons to 1,000. The gifted hussar *GL.* Paul Werner returned from captivity, and the free corps of Colonel Friedrich Wilhelm 'Green Kleist' attained a strength of ten squadrons each of light dragoons and free hussars, and two battalions of Green Croats. In such a way Frederick consolidated the basic stock of his army, while enhancing both its heavy firepower and its mobile elements.

The behaviour of the new British ministry was an annoyance to Frederick rather than a blow to his essentials. William Pitt had resigned on 5 October 1761. The new ministry was headed by Lord Bute as Secretary of State for the Northern Department (the formal title of prime minister) and the Duke of Newcastle as First Lord of the Treasury. Austria had not acceded to the Family Compact, and thus held aloof from the wider conflict between the Bourbons and the British, and Newcastle actually suggested that the Austrians should join the British in a revived 'Old System' against France and Spain. Kaunitz rejected this clumsy demarche, which he regarded as nothing more than an attempt to divide the alliance.

It was not yet possible for Britain to rid itself of the engagement to maintain the army of British, Hanoverians and German associates in western Germany, for that force protected Hanover against the French. The only way to reduce Britain's commitments there was to fail to renew the subsidy of £670,000, which had been made over to Prussia every year since 1758. A new parliamentary grant was to be paid instead, but this too was cancelled, on 20 April 1762. Frederick declared that Bute was 'a man to be broken on the wheel.'

Austria's financial troubles were of a greater order. On 9 December 1760 Kaunitz had declared that the cost of the war was becoming intolerable, and on 17 October 1761 he delivered a most elaborate paper in which he argued that there would be a shortfall of fifteen million florins in the funds available for 1762. Every expedient had been explored and exhausted, except the one of reducing the army, which would claw back eight million. The perceptive Lacy was kept in the dark, and, apart from his protégé Loudon, the only man whom Kaunitz consulted was Daun. The field marshal replied on 23 October. He could protest only in general terms, for he did not have the facts at his disposal to contest Kaunitz's financial arguments. Thus the military case went largely by default, and the programme of cuts went ahead with only minor adjustments.

As they were actually carried out, the economies reduced the *Completter-Stand* of the army from 201,311 troops to 177,497, and the personnel of all kinds, including the supporting civilians, to 186,630. Two companies were struck from the six-company strength of the garrison (depot) battalion of each regiment of infantry, and all the supernumerary officers and men dismissed. The cuirassier regiments were reduced to 850 men and horses each, while the regiments of dragoons and hussars retained 1,000 men but only 850 horses. The Pioneer Corps was to be disbanded, the Staff Dragoon Regiment allowed to waste out, the Artillery Fusilier Regiment was reduced from twenty-four companies to eighteen, the Staff Infantry Regiment from sixteen companies to four, and the new Corps of Sappers from three companies to two.

The economies were a masterpiece of presentation, for to a civilian eye the fighting strength of the army seemed to have been scarcely affected. The damage was nevertheless great. With the reduction in the infantry reserves, the regiments lost useful capacity to make good the wastage in the field. All branches of the cavalry had been weakened, which was going to put the Austrians at a severe disadvantage in the next campaign. The Artillery Fusiliers were devoid of social pretensions, but they had relieved the professional gunners of the back-breaking work of moving the pieces in action. The other technical corps and units were hit at least as hard, and now their work would have to be done by untrained troops, or not done at all.

The economies were also a testimony to the skills of Kaunitz as a careerist. It was typical of his methods to have controlled access to information, and to have created a new circle of decision-making, from which outsiders were not even aware that they had been excluded. He was also paying due regard to where power lay in the Habsburg monarchy. The high living at court and in the great houses had been an affront to dedicated officers in the field, and in his protests on 23 October 1761 Daun had noted that the wealth of the individuals and monasteries had been unaffected by the war. Kaunitz refused to be moved, and in this he showed himself to be the protector of privilege in the state and society. The elements most affected by the economies were young officers, and the technical troops which had been Lacy's creation, which is probably one of the reasons why he was not allowed to be a party to the debate.

It is by no means certain that Kaunitz's arithmetic was correct. He presented his calculations at a time when Russia was an active ally, but somehow Austria contrived to meet the very great sums that were considered necessary to meet the new 'reversal of alliances' in 1762, to confront the largely imaginary danger from Turkey, and (as Maria Theresa wrote to Hadik on 27 October) raise 40,000 recruits and reverse most of the cuts which had been ordered less than a year before. But meanwhile the commanders in the field had to live with the consequences of the damaging reductions.

Distractions—Oriental and fantastic

The king of Prussia had a weakness for charlatanry and the exotic. Both elements came together in his schemes to bring the eastern lands of the Habsburgs under attack by Turks and Tartars. The Austrians first learned of his ambitions when they captured the correspondence of Lieutenant General Fouqué at Landeshut in 1760. In that year Frederick was negotiating with the Turks through the agency of 'Carl Adolph von Rexin,' the pseudonym of the Austrian renegade Gottfried Fabian Haude. This Rexin/Haude reinforced his advances by distributing bribes, giving Nuremberg dolls to the ladies of the harem, and promising to have the Bánát of Temesvár returned to the Ottoman Empire. On 2 April 1761 he was able to conclude a treaty of trade and friendship between Prussia and the Ottomans, the implications of which were much overrated by both Frederick and Kaunitz.

At his camp at Strehlen in 1761 Frederick received a visit from Mustafa Aga, who was the favourite of the semi-independent Khan of the Crimean Tartars. The king made much of him, and sent him back to Batchi Sarai with presents for his master, and in the company of Captain Alexander von der Goltz, who was to work with the Prussian envoy Boscamp to get the Tartars to act against both the Russians and the Austrians. Frederick's affairs deteriorated sharply over the following weeks, which gave a new urgency to his relations with the orientals. Indeed he confided in Finckenstein that he would stop at nothing to get the Turks to act on his behalf. 'In a nutshell, we are lost unless they come to our help.'[12]

Russia ceased to be a target early in 1762, when the good intentions of Peter III were confirmed, and now the king concentrated his attention more narrowly on a particular element of the original plan, whereby a mobile Prussian corps would join 6,000 of the Tartars and push south to the Danube.

The king found an ideal commander in another Austrian renegade, the fanatically

Protestant Hungarian Paul Werner, who was now a lieutenant general in the Prussian service. On 12 April Frederick put him in charge of the raiding force, which was to reach out to the Tartars by way of Upper Silesia to Kaschau in Poland. The Prussians and the Tartars together could wreak some useful devastation, but if the Turks joined in as well, Werner was to ravage as far as the villages around Vienna, which were to be put to the torch.

On 2 June 1762 Werner secured the Jablunka Pass, which was the main passage from Austrian Silesia south-east into Hungary. The Austrians took immediate alarm, and the Hungarian *Hofcanzler* Nicolaus Pálffy convened a meeting on the 8th, when the veteran *GFWM*. Gastheim, who had garrisoned the border passes in 1758, pointed out that in summer time there were altogether eleven passages into Hungary from Austrian Silesia and Moravia which could be negotiated with perfect ease by whole army corps. No great reliance could be placed on the local people, many of whom were not Catholics, and *FML*. d'Ayasasa observed with some bitterness that the notorious reductions in the army had ruled out the possibility of defending the passes by regular troops. It was decided to bring up 600 Croats and 150 hussars from the Banal Military Border and place them under the command of Colonel Schuller, who would received a detailed briefing from Gastheim.[13] On the Moravian side of the border arms were issued to the wild Hanáken people of the north, who had proved their loyalty by their attacks on the Prussians in 1758.

To the east, the security of the exposed principality of Transylvania had been put in the hands of *GdC*. Buccow, 'because it was necessary to find a good excuse to remove him from the army.'[14] He felt duty-bound to forward tales of a massive impending invasion by Tartars and Turks, though he made it clear that most of the reports were 'sheer inventions on the part of informants, who want to earn money.'[15] He was probably referring to Samuel Macedonia, who was a Jewish physician with the Khan's army. Buccow was able to report on 14 August that he had duly raised a *National Miliz* of 12,000-odd men. In Bistritz all the young men of the Saxon Nation had been armed and organised into companies, while the newly-raised Wallachian *Grenz-Dragoner Regiment* and the Szekler *Grenz-Husaren Regiment* took over the guard of the frontier plague cordon from the regular forces. The officers and men of the Wallachian dragoons proved to be of good quality, and early in December they responded enthusiastically to a scheme which Buccow put to them to intercept consignments of Prussian gold which were reported to be on their way to the Tartars by way of Horondencka. The design was countermanded by Vienna, in view of the changing face of political affairs

The defence of the Danube and its tributaries had been compromised by the loss of Belgrade to the Turks in 1739. After more than twenty years of neglect, the new alarms prompted the authorities to put the most threatened of the remaining fortresses in a state of defence. The work began at Arad in February 1762, extended to Raab, Komorn, Leopoldstadt and Trentschin in March, and to Ofen in July. In August a commission sitting under the presidency of *FM*. Lynden initiated works at Munkacz, Szigeth and Huszt.[16] The programme of re-fortification was completed in November with the restoration of the Croatian strongholds of Carlstadt, Klissa, Dubica, Petrinia, Bord and Gradisca.

Meanwhile an augmentation of the cuirassiers (much valued for war against the Turks) was ordered for the regular army, and iron helmets of Thirty Years War vintage were taken out of store to protect the horsemen against scimitars, lances, darts and arrows,

All of this was sustained by the over-heated imaginations of both Frederick and Kaunitz. In June 1762 the king dispatched the Transylvanian-born hussar major Somogy to re-inspire the Tartars with the help of letters of credit to the value of 50,000 ducats. This second mission sustained the alarms in Vienna into the autumn, and in November Kaunitz persuaded himself that the malevolence of the Grand Vizier Ragip Pasha (who was actually sympathetic to the Austrians) could project up to 80,000 Turks into Hungary at short notice. Kaunitz had refused to believe the reassuring reports from the envoy in Constantinople, Joseph Peter Schwachheim, and neither Kaunitz nor the *Hofkriegsrath* were swayed by the doubts expressed by Buccow and Lynden as to the reality of the oriental threat. On 4 December Buccow wrote that every report indicated that the Khan had dispersed his concentration (4,000 Tartars at the most) at Kaschau, and dismissed all the Prussian officers, allegedly 'because the senior among them, a Prussian general, had tried to seduce the Khan's daughter.'[17]

The needless effort and expense (which has never been costed) on the part of the Austrians amounted to a mighty diversion from the war against Prussia. To that extent Frederick gained an indirect reward. He also derived a tangible if unintended benefit from having built up an uncommitted reserve on the eastern flank of the theatre of war in Silesia. The foundation was the raiding corps of *GL*. Werner, originally assigned to co-operate with the Tartars on their great sweep through Hungary towards the Danube. Nothing came of the scheme, and a threat to Werner's communications on the part of the Austrian *FML*. Beck forced the Prussians to fall back to Cosel in Prussia Silesia, which they reached on 17 June. Werner called for help, and on the 24th the Duke of Bevern arrived with reinforcements and took command of what was now a powerful corps, amounting to 21 battalions, 35 squadrons and 36 pieces. In August King Frederick was going to put this body to decisive use.

VIII
1762

CONFRONTING THE NEW REALITIES

As a consequence of the reductions, the establishment of the Austrian forces (excluding the Croats) had fallen to 177,407, and by March of 1762 planning for the new campaign was based on the assumption that 140,000 troops could be deployed in the field, as opposed to an estimated 110,000 of the Prussians. The margin of superiority was not particularly comforting, against an enemy of that calibre, and especially if Frederick were reinforced by the Russians. Lacy was particularly disturbed by the cuts among the chevaulegers and the hussars, and so 'we must pay the closest attention to preventing the Prussians gaining the upper hand in light forces.'[1] He was writing about the light cavalry, but the same applied to the light infantry, for the institutions of the Croatian military border were collapsing under the strain of the war, which gave the advantage to the expendable Prussian free battalions and free companies.

As for the shape of the coming operations, all the Austrian planning had been set at naught by the death of the Empress Elizabeth on 5 January. There was a first and inevitably unsatisfactory meeting of the chief ministers and generals on 20 January. Week followed week, without any clear indication arriving from St. Petersburg as to what course Emperor Peter III intended to take. When a decision could no longer be put off, Maria Theresa invited her foremost generals to submit their thoughts by 21 March.

'In the event of the Russian Emperor making common cause with the king of Prussia, I believe [wrote Loudon] that everyone must be bound in duty and conscience to advise Your Majesty most humbly against undertaking an offensive campaign of any kind. She should prefer peace on any terms to continuing the war.' If, however, Peter stayed aloof, 'it is my opinion that we should do something at least to conserve the County of Glatz, as it appears to me indispensable for the security of Your Majesty's Hereditary Lands.'[2] Lacy too favoured peace over war, and argued that offensive action would push Peter into supporting the enemy, if he had not already decided to do so.[3] D'Ayasasa was almost as pessimistic.

Daun's plan was the one best calculated to keep Austria's options open. He proposed to keep the forces for the time being on the defensive, but poised to take advantage of whatever opportunities might offer in Saxony, and more especially in Silesia, where the Austrians should keep 80,000 troops available for operations in the field, in addition to the 10,000 in garrison in Schweidnitz. *FM.* Neipperg likewise favoured massing in Silesia, 'so as to exploit with all possible energy and speed… the first opening which the king of Prussia might give to us.'[4] The respected *FML.* Beck emphasised that Silesia was, after all, the piece of ground for which the war was being waged.

Maria Theresa and Kaunitz settled on Daun's proposals, and this time there was no dispute concerning the command. On 21 March Loudon disclaimed any ambition on his own behalf, and proposed Daun for the chief place, for the field marshal enjoyed the affection and trust of the army, and had a unique breadth of authority at his disposal, having replaced the senile Joseph Harrach as president on 30 January.

SAXONY BEFORE HADIK'S COMMAND, JANUARY - EARLY SEPTEMBER 1762

The new year found the Austrians and the leading forces of the *Reichsarmee* for once established well inside Saxony. Prince Henry's troops were going hungry and falling sick in their cramped quarters between the Elbe, the

Triebisch and the Freiberger Mulde, while his advance corps under *GL.* Platen suffered a number of reverses at the hands of aggressive Austrian detachments. On 9 February *GFWM.* Lobkowitz pushed him from **Pegau**, and on 12 March *GFWM.* Wartensleben carried out a successful raid on **Merseburg** and destroyed the bridge over the Saale. Thereafter both parties had to consign considerable reinforcements to the Silesian theatre, which left Prince Henry with just 36,000 men, while the Austrians had 44,462 combatants and the *Reichsarmee* 18,900.

A period of slackening tension followed, and *FM.* Serbelloni was able to give free rein to his eccentricities. Up to now in command of the *Reichsarmee* alone, he was appointed to the leadership of the Austrian forces in Saxony on 29 March. It was reasonable to suppose that he would now leave the direction of the *Reichstruppen* to his successor, *FZM.* Maguire, but he instead insisted on trying to exercise total control from Dresden, which proved unworkable, in view of the distances involved.

The Austrian *GFWM.* Zedtwitz commanded the outposts on the far left wing of the Austrian forces, which extended in a cordon along the Mulde from Döbeln downstream to Nossen. He was vulnerable in more than one respect. He had only 2,500 troops with which to hold about twelve miles of river line, and with the high command in a state of paralysis he could gain neither reinforcements nor the permission to concentrate his available forces. Moreover Prince Henry was being spurred on by the king to take the offensive, after a long period of demoralising inactivity, and the Prussians had an overwhelming superiority in light cavalry.

On 12 May Prince Henry opened the campaign with a devastating stroke, when he brought four columns across the Mulde in a converging operation in the Austrian style. The difficulties of co-ordinating the separate attacks allowed most of the Austrians to escape, but this action of **Döbeln** cost them five pieces of artillery and nearly 1,500 men, and Zedtwitz was captured at Littdorf, after leading two counterattacks by his cavalry.

There ensued a period of panic and confusion, in which Serbelloni considered abandoning Dresden and all Saxony west of the Elbe. The main force of the shaken Austrians finally brought itself together in the classic line which extended from Dresden to Dippoldiswalde, but Prince Henry had meanwhile driven a wedge between Serbelloni's troops and the Prince of Stolberg's *Reichsarmee* out to the west. Stolberg was nevertheless able to execute a controlled retreat to Zwickau, and on 21 May the Austrian *FML.* Luzinsky with a mobile corps of Austrians and *Reichstruppen* drove the Prussian major general Bandemer from **Chemnitz** and pursued his disintegrating forces across the Flöha. The total Prussian loss came to seven pieces and nearly 1,000 officers and men.

Emperor Francis Stephen wrote to congratulate Serbelloni, and asked him to pass on his thanks to his generals 'so that they will get it into their heads that the Prussians cannot win always and everywhere, and that by keeping cool and holding firm you can often be more successful than through sheer numbers.'[5] In fact the gratifying little victory at Chemnitz had nothing to do with Serbelloni, and in June the enemy regained the initiative through the help of the brigade-size regiment of the Belling Hussars, which had been set free from Pomerania by the end of hostilities against the Swedes and Russians.

The great superiority of the Prussian light horse enabled the enemy to work around the west flank of the Austrian army, with the result that the *Reichsarmee* had to recoil into Franconia, and Serbelloni began to talk once more about abandoning Saxony. He sent Colonel Fantoni to Vienna to represent the sorry state of his army's supplies. The colonel did his duty, but *GFWM.* Hannig noted that 'whenever he had occasion to talk at court and to the ministers, he represented affairs in their full sorry state. He talked of nothing but disorder, dissatisfaction among the generals, officers and ordinary soldiers, and ill-feeling and confusion. The root cause is the irresolution of the commander in chief, and the rudeness which repels all his subordinates. I have heard in confidence that there has already been a move to recall Serbelloni from the army, but as soon as the question of choosing his replacement arises, everything remains as before.'[6]

Löwenstein's victory at Teplitz, 2 August 1762
a) Austrians
c. 5,200: c. 4,000 infantry, 1,200 cavalry
Losses: c. 700, 137 killed, 530 wounded, missing and prisoners unknown. By far the heaviest unit loss was sustained by the infantry regiment of Gyulai (51), with 92 killed and 193 wounded.
b) Prussians
c. 13,000
Losses: c. 1,100: c. 200 killed, c. 300 wounded, c. 600 deserters

The passes to north-western Bohemia were now open to the Prussians, and on 1 August *GL.* Seydlitz irrupted over the border by way of Brüx and Kommotau, and his partner *GM.* Kleist via Einsiedel. The invading force was about 13,000 strong, and the Prussians proceeded to ravage in their usual style. After the visit of Seydlitz's troops to the castle of Brüx, Captain Cogniazzo saw 'ripped-up hangings, chopped-up woodwork, broken windows and mirrors, and the smashing of costly sofas, chairs and tables. The doors had been split, even though they had been left open for the enemy. A splendid orangery had been left a total ruin—all evidence of malice that would have been worthy of a Kalmyk.'[7]

More significant was the threat to the Austrian magazines in northern Bohemia, for if they were destroyed, the army would indeed have to abandon Saxony. The only body which stood in the way was that of the corps of *GdC.* Christian Prince zu Löwenstein-Wertheim, whom Serbelloni had posted at Teplitz with eight battalions and four regiments of horse.

Löwenstein's corps was typical of the composition of the Austrian forces at this stage of the war. He had none of the Croats or hussars who would have been so useful in the hilly and heavily-wooded terrain, and his regiments of cavalry (the Batthyány Dragoons [D7], and the cuirassier regiments of Carl Pálffy, Stampa and Benedict Daun [Cs 8, 23, 27]) were much below establishment, at a total of only 1,200 men, as well as being unsuited to the ground. He had written to Serbelloni to protest that his forces were nowhere near their supposed strength, but 'Serbelloni answered... that he did not find it necessary to make up the shortfall, which amounted to almost 10,000 men for it was likely that the movements of the... enemy generals were intended mostly to cover the retreat of Prince Henry from Frauenstein and Pretzschendorf, and that they therefore harboured no ambitions against me.'[8]

Löwenstein deployed his troops in an east-facing line on either side of the village of Hundorf. On the night of 1/2 August the Prussians moved to envelop him, with Kleist (six battalions and eighteen squadrons) working around to Löwenstein's east, and Seydlitz (four and a half battalions and another eighteen squadrons) executing the main attack in two columns by way of Osseg-Ullersdorf and Ladowitz, aiming to gain the hills about Kradrob to the south-west of the Austrian position.

Löwenstein stared into the darkness. 'I had the cuirassiers lay aside their breastplates, saddlebags and packs, so that they could go out to reconnoitre the enemy march. But every attempt to penetrate the swarms of enemy light horse was in vain, and I did not have what I needed to make up my mind.'[9] Towards four in the morning of the 2nd he betook himself to the left wing with all the generals and colonels, promoted by a report from the Pálffy Cuirassiers. 'I heard a number of pistol shots not far away, and in the first light of day I saw that some of the enemy were in the process of climbing the hills above our left wing and rear, and that some of them were already on the top.'[10] From a captured captain of the Belling Hussars [H9] he learned on the magnitude of the danger, and Cogniazzo comments that 'perhaps only someone like Prince Löwenstein... would have dared to stand his ground in such a situation.'[11]

The Prussian grenadier battalions of Kalckstein, Lossow and Natalis together with 200 volunteers were approaching the summit of the steep Wacholder-Anhöhe (Juniper Hill) just to the north west of Kradrob, and without waiting for orders *GFWM.* Carl Clemens Pellegrini rushed the two battalions of the regiments of Nicolaus Esterházy [33] and Pallavicini [15] to meet them. The enemy were also about to gain a neighbouring hilltop, and Pellegrini hastened back to tell Samuel Gyulai, the colonel of the Hungarian infantry regiment of the same name, that '"the outcome of the present day depends on you!"'[12] The regiment

Teplitz, 2 August 1762

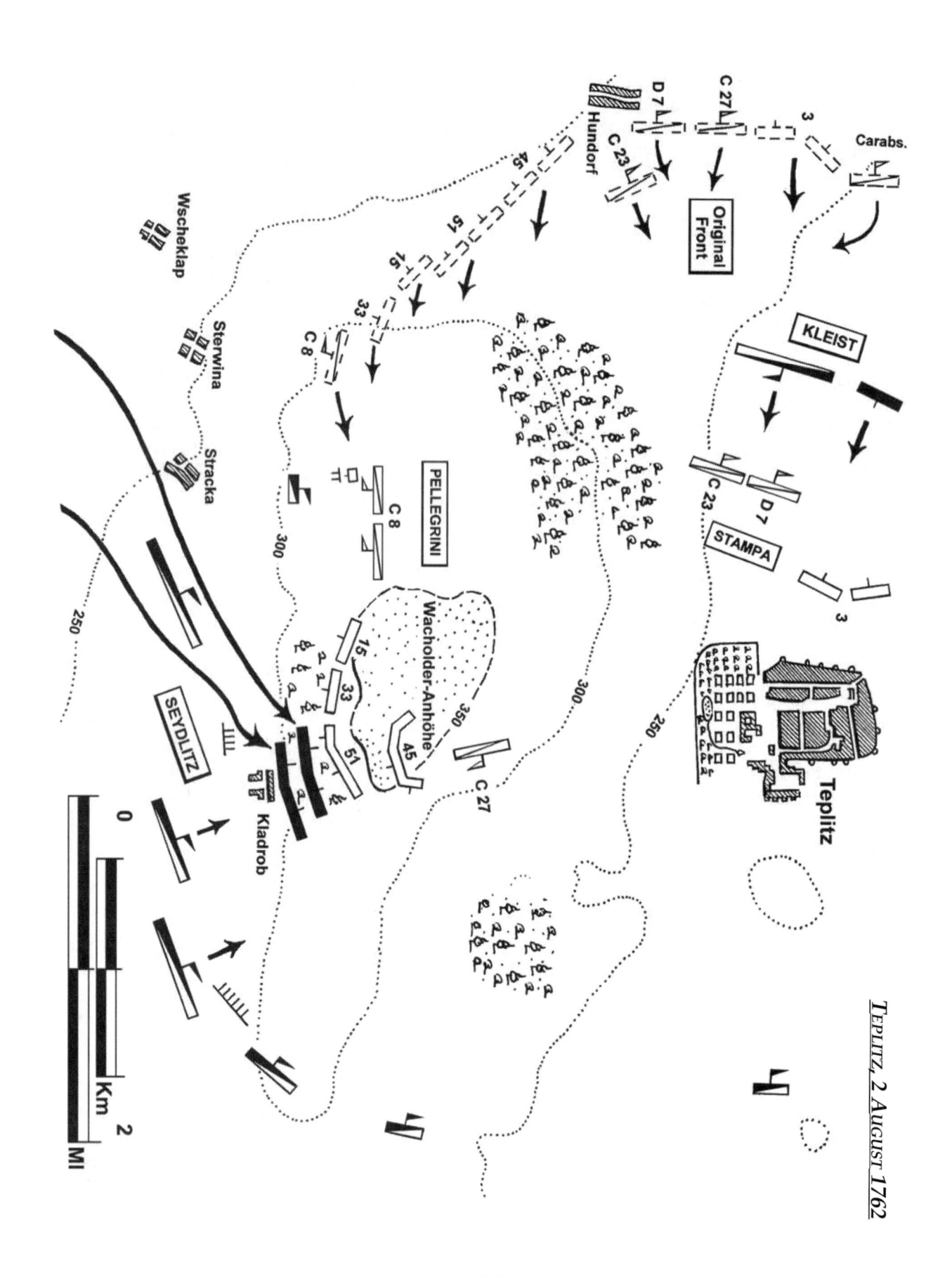

of Gyulai [51] and that of O'Kelly [45] moved directly to counter the threat. Meanwhile the Batthyány Dragoons [D7], the Stampa Cuirassiers [C23] and the regiment of Carl Lothringen [3] fell back east in the face of Kleist's attack, and were able to halt him short of Teplitz.

Up on the hills the Austrians were managing the infantry battle against Seydlitz with considerable skill. Löwenstein rotated the various battalions between the firing line and the reserve, to prevent them from being exhausted, while Gyulai broke his men into platoons so that they could manoeuvre and counterattack effectively on this extensive and difficult terrain. The Prussians began to recoil, and 'the regiment of Gyulai, having shot off all its ammunition, proceeded to sling its muskets, take hold of its sabres, and fall on the enemy in full force, driving the grenadiers back over the hill. In such a way our flank and rear were once more secured. On four occasions the enemy tried to regain this post, but each time our infantry repelled them with loss.'[13]

The Prussians began to retreat, covering themselves by firing from ditches. They made a further stand in the village of Kradrob, but the place became uncomfortable when Löwenstein advanced a howitzer and set one of the houses on fire. Finally Captain Kherer brought the grenadiers of the O'Kelly regiment [45] down the slope at the run and threw the enemy out. The Prussians abandoned three damaged cannon in the village, and by eight in the morning they were in full retreat to Dux. Löwenstein lamented that he had so few mobile forces at his disposal, 'for otherwise, if I had been able to match the enemy in cavalry, I am convinced that with the help of God hardly any of them would have escaped from Bohemia.'[14]

It had nevertheless been an extraordinary success on the part of Löwenstein's greatly outnumbered forces. The Prussians gained a little revenge, when Kleist beat up Löwenstein's outposts on the night of 3/4 August. However the strategic gain was immense and entirely on the Austrian side, and on 5 August the exhausted Löwenstein was able to confirm to Serbelloni that Bohemia was free of the Prussians. His performance had illustrated the strength of the Austrians at the middle levels of command, while Seydlitz, not for the first time, showed himself less than brilliant at managing mixed forces of infantry and cavalry.

A change in the higher Austrian direction could no longer be postponed. The initiative came from the King Augustus of Poland, who claimed that nothing was being done towards the liberation of Saxony, 'which could be ascribed in large part to *FM.* Serbelloni's inactivity and lack of perception.' Serbelloni had a powerful supporter in Emperor Francis Stephen, 'and it is said to Count Serbelloni's credit that he keeps the administration in perfect order, that he maintains strict military discipline, and that he gave proof of personal bravery when under the command of others. But there is reason to doubt that he has the higher judgement required of a commander in chief.'[15]

D'Ayasasa reviewed the state of affairs for the benefit of Daun: 'As for Saxony, I have to tell you that I found things as bad as they could be. If Löwenstein had been beaten it would all have been over. Everyone dreads the future and longs for another commander. I almost believe that Hadik is the man to go there.'[16]

THE LAST CAMPAIGN IN SILESIA

FML. Mercy d'Argenteau had the interim command of the Austrian forces in the area of Lower Silesia north of the hills which had been wrested from the enemy in the previous year. His most urgent concern was with the vipers he might be harbouring in his bosom, in the shape of Lieutenant General Zakhar Chernyshev (an alarmingly intelligent individual) and the auxiliary corps of 16,000 Russians. They were passed the winter in the County of Glatz, which awakened fears that these former allies might seize the passes of Silberberg and Wartha for the king of Prussia. Chernyshev spoke to him with streaming eyes about the change in affairs in Russia, but the Baltic Germans among his officer corps did not conceal their delight.

Mercy learned from his own sources on 20 March that the Russians were about to move. Chernyshev told him so officially on the 22nd, and two days later the troops left their quarters 'for Poland.' Mercy wished that they were already somewhere in the Arctic, and placed his troops on high alert, but on the 25th the last of the Russian units traversed the pass of Wartha. At the beginning of April the Russians crossed the Oder, and continued on their way to new quarters behind the Vistula in Poland. On 2 June Chernyshev and his corps were on the march again for Silesia, this time in support of Frederick of Prussia.

Mercy's troops had taken up cantonments on 28 March along the hills which bordered the plain, and 'there was an unmistakable whiff of scurvy about all those men who had overwintered in Silesia.'[17] Mercy himself was ailing, and *FZM.* Loudon took over the acting command in his place. Arriving at Waldenburg on 5 April he found that more than 5,000 of his men were lying sick in the overcrowded villages.

FM. Daun, as the designated full commander, set out from Vienna on 27 April. His journey took the form of a detailed tour of inspection. On 7 May he viewed the works at Glatz, which were being repaired by Gribeauval, and he continued to the fortified pass of Wartha, among the snowy hills at the exit of the County of Glatz. He was at the neighbouring pass of Silberberg the next day, and on the 9th he reconnoitred the neighbourhood of the Zobten-Berg and Schweidnitz, which was certain to be the scene of major operations before long. Finally on 10 May Daun took over the command at Waldenburg.

On 15 May the troops wound out of their villages and were deployed under canvas in such a way as to guard the passes and offer a forward defence to Schweidnitz. *FML.* Brentano and 7,000 men were positioned on the forward slopes of the isolated Zobten-Berg, rising from the plain. The main army was encamped just behind. Loudon was over to the east at the entrance to the County of Glatz, and the detached corps of *FML.* Beck was covering Austrian Silesia and Moravia (soon to come under threat from Werner).

What considerations weighed with Daun at this time? When operations opened the rival forces were approximately equal in numbers, with 80,000-odd Prussians and Russians facing 76,300 Austrians. Of the whitecoats, however, 10,000 were locked up in the fortress of Schweidnitz, and the detachments just mentioned reduced the forces at the immediate disposal of Daun to 44,000 serviceable troops, and these were falling ill at a rate of two hundred a day. Vienna was trying to reduce the effects of the recent reduction in the army, but in a crude way by a crash programme of recruiting. It was unlikely to do any good, for the depot battalions were so depleted as to be unable to process the raw recruits,[18] and the 'reduced' officers had been mopped up by the Spanish ambassador for service in Spain's new war with Portugal.[19]

Daun had to write to Maria Theresa on 1 June 'unwelcome though it must be, as I can well imagine, it is nevertheless true that only a rapid peace can save the monarchy as its affairs stand just now. We are devoid of magazines, money and any other kind of resource. The infantry are crippled by disease, the cavalry are in a state of collapse, and we have no prospect of doing anything good against an enemy which is double our strength and in a better state than last year, not to mention that one of our most formidable allies is now against us.'[20]

Loudon and Lacy were of the same opinion, and for that reason refused to accept any independent command. Loudon at least was eager to demonstrate his goodwill in other capacities, but Lacy was becoming more sulky by the day, 'and it takes a great effort to draw a single word from him.'[21] Hadik was 'the only one who will turn his hand to everything without reservation and with a good grace, and I can only recommend him once more to Your Majesty's favour. He certainly deserves consideration, for he is both enthusiastic and able.'[22]

Daun's support in Vienna was confined to Maria Theresa and a small circle of confidants. He admitted to the Empress that he felt some jealousy towards Kaunitz, which he was at great pains to counter. 'Whenever I find myself in his presence I make a point of greeting him. I have always spoken of him with regard, and often been to his quarters, but the only time that he is at home is late in the evening, and by then I will have long retired, so as that I can get down to work early the next morning.'[23] *GFWM.* Hannig, who was one of Daun's informants in Vienna, confirmed to him that Kaunitz was the source of the hostile gossip, and much given to sighing *'mon pauvre Loudon.'*[24]

Daun and his senior generals were at least of one mind concerning the conduct of operations. Their forces, although inferior in numbers and enfeebled, were still capable of holding their positions in Austrian Silesia, at Wartha and in the hills south of Schweidnitz.[25] Daun would not willingly abandon his present position, with the Zobten on his right and Hohen-Poseritz on his left, with his headquarters at Kratzkau in between, for that would have endangered Schweidnitz, 'and especially as I have no confidence in the commandant [*FML*. Franz Guasco]. All the same there are objections to replacing him by Gaisruck, as he is totally unfamiliar with the place.'[26]

In her reply on 6 June Maria Theresa naturally asked the question whether it would not be expedient to abandon Schweidnitz altogether, for the 10,000 men of the garrison might be employed more profitably in the open field, and 'it would not be to the credit of our arms if we were reduced to being passive spectators of the siege.'[27] After careful consideration Daun rejected this course, for it would have been physically difficult to evacuate the garrison and destroy the fortifications when the enemy were so close, and Schweidnitz offered an excellent strongpoint as long as the Austrians wished to retain any kind of footing in Silesia.

The rest of June was a time of uncomfortable anticipation. Forces of Austrian cavalry twice ventured out in an attempt to surprise their enemy counterparts, but both times—at **Lampersdorf** (14 June) and **Heidersdorf** (20-21 June) they were routed, and the Prussian haul of prisoners in the first of these actions included *FML*. Draskovich. On the 29th Daun wrote to Maria Theresa that he still could not offer her anything for her comfort. He had been urged to send out foraging parties, 'but it is quite impossible, as we are immobile and facing an overwhelmingly superior enemy.'[28]

The Austrian cavalry was disadvantaged still further by the arrival of the Cossacks, who crossed the Oder ahead of the main Russian force on 25 June. Frederick, his staff, his generals and all his cavalry attached white plumes to their hats, and 'we warned the Cossacks to spare the white plumes.'[29] On the 30th Frederick bedecked himself in addition with the wide blue sash of the Russian Order of St. Andrew to greet Chernyshev when he crossed the Oder with the regulars at Auras. Chernyshev had been in this part of the world before, as an auxiliary of the Austrians, but he was now under strict instructions from his Emperor to conform with Frederick's wishes.

In the period from 1 till 22 July Frederick devoted himself entirely to the ambition of driving Daun so far from Schweidnitz that the Prussians could reduce that fortress undisturbed. The king opened the campaign on 1 July by flooding the plain with the Cossacks and the Prussian hussars and Bosniaken. The swarming light horsemen were supposed to cover a move to anticipate the Austrians on the heights behind Freiburg. However Daun got wind of the scheme from a deserter, and on the following night he marched his army across the Peile to a new position in considerable depth in the hills between Freiburg and Hoch-Giersdorf. The corps of *FML*. Brentano likewise fell back to Burkersdorf, to cover the far right (eastern) flank of the army.

The manoeuvre around Daun's left flank, and Brentano's victory at Adelsbach, 3-9 July 1762

Adelsbach, 6 July 1762

a) Austrians
c. 5,000
Losses: 250; 41 killed, 141 wounded, 68 prisoners or missing. The highest unit losses were in the regiment of Bethlen (52), at 105 from all causes

b) Prussians
c. 21,000, not counting the reinforcements brought up by the king during the action
Losses: 1,352; 88 killed, 602 wounded, 662 prisoners or deserters, 3 colours

On 3 July Frederick's army moved over the Bunzelwitz and occupied much the same position as in the year before, but now in much greater force. To the west, at Striegau, the king had a large fighting advance guard under *GL*. Neuwied, consisting of 24 battalions, 25 squadrons and three heavy batteries, or about 21,000 men in all, including the Cossacks. Neuwied was now to execute an outflanking

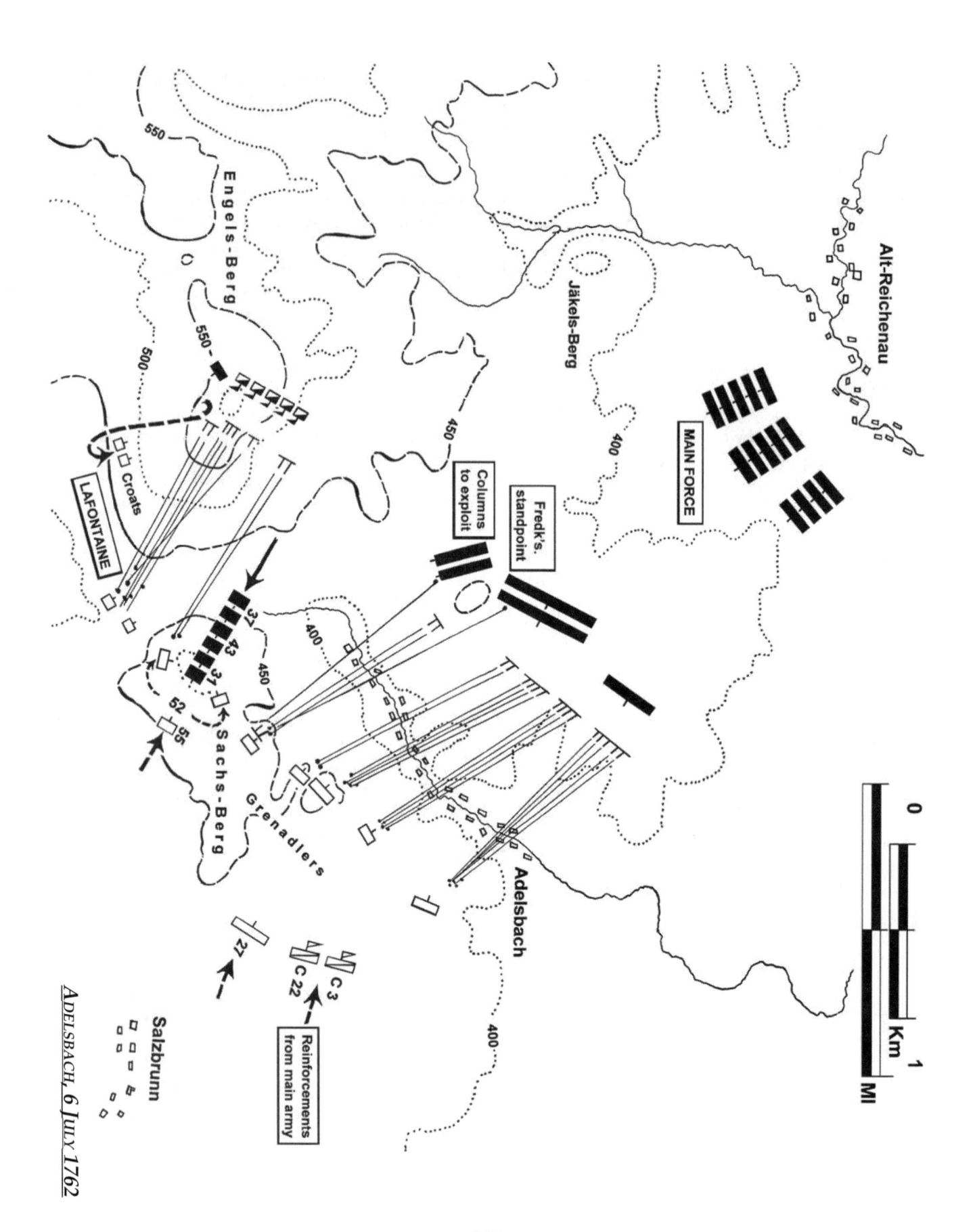

Adelsbach, 6 July 1762

move around Daun's left (west) flank, in an altogether wider sweep than the unsuccessful enterprise on the night of 1 July, namely against the sensitive target of Braunau, just inside Bohemia, where the Austrians had their main depot of provisions.

The roving Prussian light forces were supposed to blind the Austrians, but 'the movements out to our left indicated that the enemy intended to turn us on that side.'[30] Neuwied set out on 3 July, and Daun at once got Brentano's corps to move around the rear of the army to the deep left flank on the heights above Adelsbach.

Very early in the morning on 6 July Neuwied began to drive in Brentano's outposts, and at 3.30 a cannon shot signalled the opening of the action proper. 'Brentano had meanwhile deployed his troops in such a way that he had stuffed the wood which covers the Engels-Berg hill with some of his Croats, while placing the Jäger in Adelsbach, and ranging the rest of his infantry along the height to the left-rear of this village and towards the road which descends the hollow in this direction. The cavalry took up position as a second line behind the infantry, and his batteries were sited as far as possible to bring a cross-fire to bear on those of the enemy. However his forces consisted of only two battalions of Hungarians, one of Walloons, four of Croats, two companies of Jäger, together with two regiments of dragoons and one of hussars, to defend ground which extended almost a German league.'[31]

The Prussians were on the march with potentially overwhelming strength. In addition to Neuwied's corps, Frederick was coming up behind with a supporting body of 22 battalions, 21 squadrons and a gaggle of Bosniaken, all from the main army. That the fighting extended for six and a half hours, and turned to the advantage of the Austrians, was due to the skill with which Brentano had deployed his outnumbered troops in width and depth across the difficult ground. The terrain was typical of upland Silesia, for the valleys, with their little streams and long drawn-out villages, were separated by steep wooded hills, which presented the attackers with successive zones of obstacles if, as in this case, the attack was delivered across the grain of the country.

By this stage in the war the Austrians were weak in cavalry, and by four in the morning the Cossacks and the hussars who spearheaded Neuwied's advance had cleared Alt-Reichenau of the outposts of the Saint-Ignon Chevaulegers [D31], and captured thirty-three of them in the process. The way was now clear for the Prussians to climb the heights which separated the valley of Reichenau from that of Adelsbach to the south, and the bluecoats pushed forward on either side of the path which led to Adelsbach village. To the east, or right (as the Austrians saw it) the defence rested almost entirely on Major Chevalier Collins de Ham with a single battalion of grenadiers and a train of 3- and 6-pounder cannon. The Prussians began to work around his flanks and bring him under a cross-fire from their artillery, but Collins de Ham stood his ground on the broad ridge between the valleys of Reichenau and Adelsbach, and the arrival of two howitzers enabled him to answer the Prussian fire 'with astonishing success.'[32]

The key to the heights to the west of the path was the densely-wooded Engels-Berg, which was held by Major Lafontaine with a battalion of Warasdiner Creutzer. At the sound of the artillery Frederick had turned over the command of the supporting forces to Chernyshev, and made for the scene of the action with 200 Cossacks, 150 Bosniaken, two squadrons of the Lossow Hussars [H5] and the five of the Zastrow Dragoons [D1]. The king orientated himself on the situation, and ordered the free battalion of Wunsch to clear the Engels-Berg of the Croats. The very appearance of these ruffians was enough to persuade Lafontaine and his Croats to abandon their position. The Prussians were now able to bring up a number of 12-pounder cannon and 7-pounder howitzers to the height, and bring an enfilade fire to bear on the grenadiers of Collins de Ham to the east of the path. His position was now untenable, and he brought his troops and artillery in the nick of time down from the hill.

Brentano's entire force was now drawn up on the steep-sided hills behind the second valley, that of Adelsbach. The Prussians cleared parties of Jäger from Nieder-Adelsbach (a repetition of

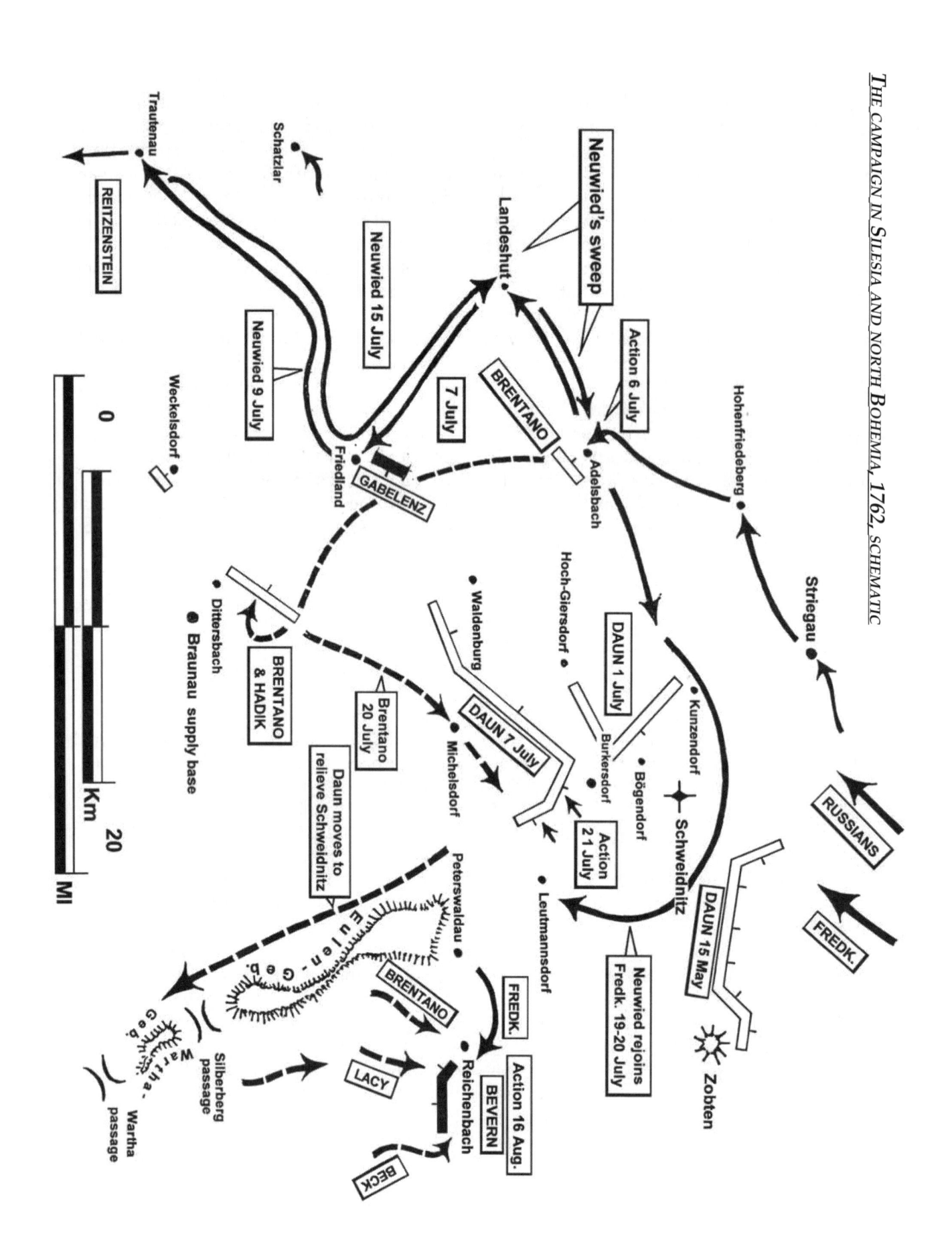

The Campaign in Silesia and North Bohemia, 1762, schematic

their success in the first valley), but they could make little further progress up the further slopes against the Austrian right wing, for Collins de Ham's artillery managed to sustain its fire in the face of a row of fifteen-odd Prussian pieces on the northern side of the valley, and his widely-scattered parties of grenadiers were holding the paths and re-entrants which led up from Nieder-Adelsbach.

To the west, the Austrian left wing was compressed onto the Sachs-Berg, where Brentano concentrated the two battalions of the Hungarian regiment of Bethlen [52], with one battalion of d'Arberg [55] behind, and the two battalions of the Warasdiner Creutzer and St. Georger Croats to the left. The king was eager to dislodge Brentano before the Austrians could be reinforced from their main army, and in his haste he looked to the nearest troops at hand (the free battalion of Wunsch, and the infantry regiments of Lestwitz, Zieten and Braun [31, 43, 37]) and threw them at the Sachs-Berg in a single column. 'The Prussians were marching to the beat of drum. Having sustained the fire of our batteries as far as the foot of the hill, they paused for a moment to take breath and then addressed themselves to the climb.'[33]

The crude attacking formation sacrificed Frederick's advantage in numbers, and he compromised his troops still further when he suddenly ordered the attack to be called off. The reasons are unclear, but perhaps he only now took in the strength of the Austrian position, or perhaps he was dissuaded by the violent rainstorm which now swamped the scene. His standpoint was on a hillock nearly one mile to the north, and it took so long to convey his orders that only the regiment of Braun and the second battalion of that of Zieten actually turned back. The rest of the troops continued on their way up the slippery slopes into the wood, over the summit, and when the head of the column emerged from the trees on the reverse slope the Prussians found that they had unwittingly arrived in the middle of the regiment of Bethlen, under the command of its colonel, Joseph Maximilian Baron Tillier. The two component battalions of Bethlen wheeled inwards, and shot up the enemy from the two sides until their ammunition was exhausted, whereupon the Hungarians slung their muskets and went for the Prussians with their sabres, as did the two battalions of Croats. The enemy were driven from the hilltop, and de Ligne noted how the men of Bethlen were rolling boulders down on the Prussians, which was one of the best things he had seen in his life.[34]

The Prussians tried to rally in a little meadow half-way down the hill, but they were pushed into the valley and up the far side amid scenes of carnage. Frederick himself was in danger, and much shaken by a howitzer shell which had exploded nearby. The Prince de Ligne was up with the pursuit, and 'I saw him just a short distance away; it was certainly him, there could be no doubt.'[35] Thus the action ended in every respect to the advantage of the Austrians.

Frederick through his carelessness, half-heartedness and panics had forfeited his best opportunity of turning the deep left rear of Daun's strategic position in Silesia. In the course of the action Brentano and his officers had staged a fighting retreat across difficult country, and gone over to the counterattack at a critical moment. As at Teplitz, the decisive blow was dealt by a single unit of Hungarian infantry, in this case by the regiment of Bethlen.

When we last saw Daun's army it was overlooking Frederick's camp at Bunzelwitz. The action at Adelsbach had been an Austrian success, and one of the most creditable of the war, but it confirmed to Daun that the greater part of the Prussian forces were now committed in that direction, and on the night of 6/7 July he abandoned the heights of Hoch-Giersdorf and Bögendorf, and swung his army to the left rear, so that the left wing and centre now crowned the hills above the valley of Reussendorf and Dittmannsdorf. The right flank overlooked Burkersdorf, and enabled Daun even now to keep up a connection with Schweidnitz, however tenuous.

The main Austrian concentration was secure for the near future, but it had not been possible to render any immediate help to Brentano, who was left dangling in the air, and the Austrians were still faced with the possibility of losing not just that brave little corps but also the provision depot and bakery at Braunau which fed their army in Silesia.

On 7 July Neuwied lunged once more against Brentano, with a force which the Austrians put at 26 battalions, 34 squadrons of Prussian cavalry and a body of Cossacks. Brentano had fortunately just been authorised to fall back from Adelsbach to a strong position at Friedland, and when Neuwied closed the distance in the middle of the afternoon he saw that the Austrians were holding the heights behind the town. Neuwied consulted his generals, and this pause gave Brentano the opportunity to make for Dittersbach seven miles to the south-west. The Finckenstein Dragoons [D10] and the Gers-dorff Hussars [H7] took up the pursuit, and for a time the salvation of the Austrians depended on their rearguard, which consisted of the Erzherzog Leopold Cuirassiers [C3] under Lieutenant Colonel Haag. This regiment of heavy horse was not mounted, equipped or trained for this kind of work, but it contrived to put up a prolonged and successful rearguard action through the narrows of Johannesberg, and took nearly 300 of the Prussians prisoner.

Brentano was still outnumbered badly, and it was fortunate that Daun still had at his disposal the uncommitted corps of *GdC*. Hadik, who had been guarding the access to the County of Glatz on the far right (eastern) strategic flank. Daun had sent him a warning order as early as 4 July, and on the 8th Hadik arrived at Dittersbach with 10,000 of his troops, which brought the Austrian concentration on this side to 20,000 men. Very early on the morning of 9 July Neuwied fell back by way of Friedland to Rosenau. Lacy testified that the whole army was aware that it was through Brentano's skill that the designs of the king had been 'totally frustrated.'[36] Brentano would in all probability have been remembered as one of Austria's foremost soldiers of the second half of the eighteenth century, if the war had not so soon come to an end, and if he had not died shortly afterwards, of natural causes, on 7 July 1764 at the age of forty-five.

Reitzenstein's raid into Bohemia, 10-18 July 1762

The grand design against Daun's left strategic flank had failed, and it was perpetuated only by a spectacular but inconsequential foray into north-eastern Bohemia. Under the cover of diversions Neuwied took the greater part of his corps to Trautenau and Schatzlar, under the eastern shoulder of the Riesen-Gebirge, and 10 July he dispatched Lieutenant Colonel Reitzenstein with the Finckenstein Dragoons and all the available Bosniaken and Cossacks to ravage the Circle of Königgrätz. Frederick admitted to Neuwied that the expedition had little hope of drawing Daun from Silesia, 'but we can nevertheless wait a couple of days and await the effects of your manoeuvre.'[37]

On 11 July Reitzenstein left most of his force at Smiritz, and continued his progress down the Elbe with just 300 Cossacks. The dignified and important town of Königgrätz should have been in no danger from this rabble, for the Austrian lieutenant colonel Weiss had been stationed there with more than 500 troops, and had enriched himself at the expense of the townspeople. Now, at nine in the morning, he deserted the place at the first wind of Reitzenstein's approach. 'All our unfortunate people complain about him, and with good reason.'[38]

Towards noon the same day, when most of the townspeople were settling down to their lunch, three Cossacks entered the great central market place, looked about them, and rode back to their comrades, who began to arrive by dribs and drabs. Reitzenstein now came in person to demand a contribution of 2,000 ducats, with 100 more as a *douceur* for his men. 'We addressed him in a most submissive and moving manner, pleading the reduced state of our town, but it only made him more and more angry. He threatened us with sack and fire, and declared "I don't want your compliments. I want your money!" In such a way he exacted from us more than 4,000 florins in a variety of coinage, against his assurance that we would be spared from all further harm.'[39]

The Cossacks plundered the town anyway, and set fire to the great hay magazine by the Mautener-Tor. The first batch of visitors rode away at three in the afternoon, but scarcely an hour later fifty further Cossacks, 'all as black as the devil,'[40] wrecked and burned the Jesuit College, and set fire to the whole side of the town from there to the Mautener-Tor, as well as the Mauten suburb and the church of St.

Anthony. Nearly three-quarters of the town was now in flames, and the entire population fled to the woods.

Other parties of Cossacks, totally out of control, ravaged Zipel, Raatsch and Staudenz on the upper Elbe, and some of them raided west towards Prague, where on 12 July the citizens barricaded the gates and hauled cannon onto the ramparts. Daun was unimpressed by this brigandage, and meanwhile stood firm in his position in Silesia, knowing that the expeditions amounted to 'nothing of importance.'[41] The fodder from the magazine at Braunau was already being carted away, which deprived the Prussians of the only target of military worth in Bohemia, and, using the discretion allowed him by Frederick, Neuwied recalled his detachments and returned to the Silesian plain with the greater part of his force on the night of 18/19 July.

The move against Daun's right wing, and the action at Burkersdorf, 13-21 July 1762

The days were long past when Frederick, in a spirit of blind aggression, used to march his army at an enemy, orientate himself on the spot, and fling himself into the attack. His forces were too weary, and the Austrians too experienced and clever, for such simplicities to work any longer. His object in the present case was to complete his reconquest of Silesia by reducing the fortress of Schweidnitz, an undertaking which depended in turn on evicting Daun's army from the heights which overlooked the Silesian plain. The process had begun as early as 3 July, with the launching of Neuwied's expedition around Daun's left flank, which was followed by Reitzenstein's raid into Bohemia. They failed in their immediate objectives, as we have seen, but they succeeded in teasing apart the Austrian forces. From 13 July Frederick tested Daun's right wing, and his operation on this side culminated in the attack at Burkersdorf more than a week later.

At two in the morning of the 13th General Zieten advanced the infantry of the first line of battle to attack the outlying Austrian abattis at Hoch-Giersdorf, while the king circled out to the east with fifteen squadrons of horse to see what he could of the heights on this flank and the great valley of the Weistritz behind Burkersdorf. He noted that the Austrians had half a dozen battalions entrenched in that part of the world, and wrote to Neuwied that he had a new task for him. The Austrians were certainly well dug in, 'but there is a path leading from Leutmannsdorf to Michelsdorf by which this post can be turned. This can enable us not only to get at the rear of the enemy at Burkersdorf, but attack and destroy all their transports on their way from Braunau and the rear.'[42]

The Austrians responded by a cannonade at extreme range, and Daun rode from his headquarters at Tannhausen to give orders to *FML*. Wilhelm O'Kelly, who commanded the forces about Burkersdorf on his right flank—an area which was clearly of interest to the enemy. 'We felt that in order to secure the post at Burkersdorf it was also necessary to occupy the ways from Leutmannsdorf, and so prevent the enemy from turning us on this side and taking us from behind.' So far so good, but now it was a question of finding the forces to cover this flank. Fatally, 'we could not make up our minds to bring back a really significant number of troops from the corps of General Hadik, for that would mean stripping the post at Dittersbach. We still had fears on that side, for there was still an enemy corps at Trautliebersdorf, even though we could not make out its strength.'[43] The force in question amounted to no more than 5,000 troops under *GM*. Gabelentz, who had been left to occupy an extensive camp between Trautliebersdorf and Friedland when Neuwied departed on the king's command on 15 July. The Austrians did not detect the imposture, and so for several days Hadik's command of 21,000 troops was immobilised out to the left rear of the army, which was no longer in danger. As late as the morning of 20 July we find Hadik and Brentano reconnoitring the Prussian camp without being able to determine its full extent,[44] doubtless as a result of the prevailing weakness of the Austrians in light cavalry. Only on the afternoon of that day, as the result of an order from Daun, was Brentano released from Hermsdorf (north of Braunau) with his corps of 9,000 troops.

Meanwhile, in the camp of the main Austrian army, *FZM*. Lacy was writing to a friend. 'We

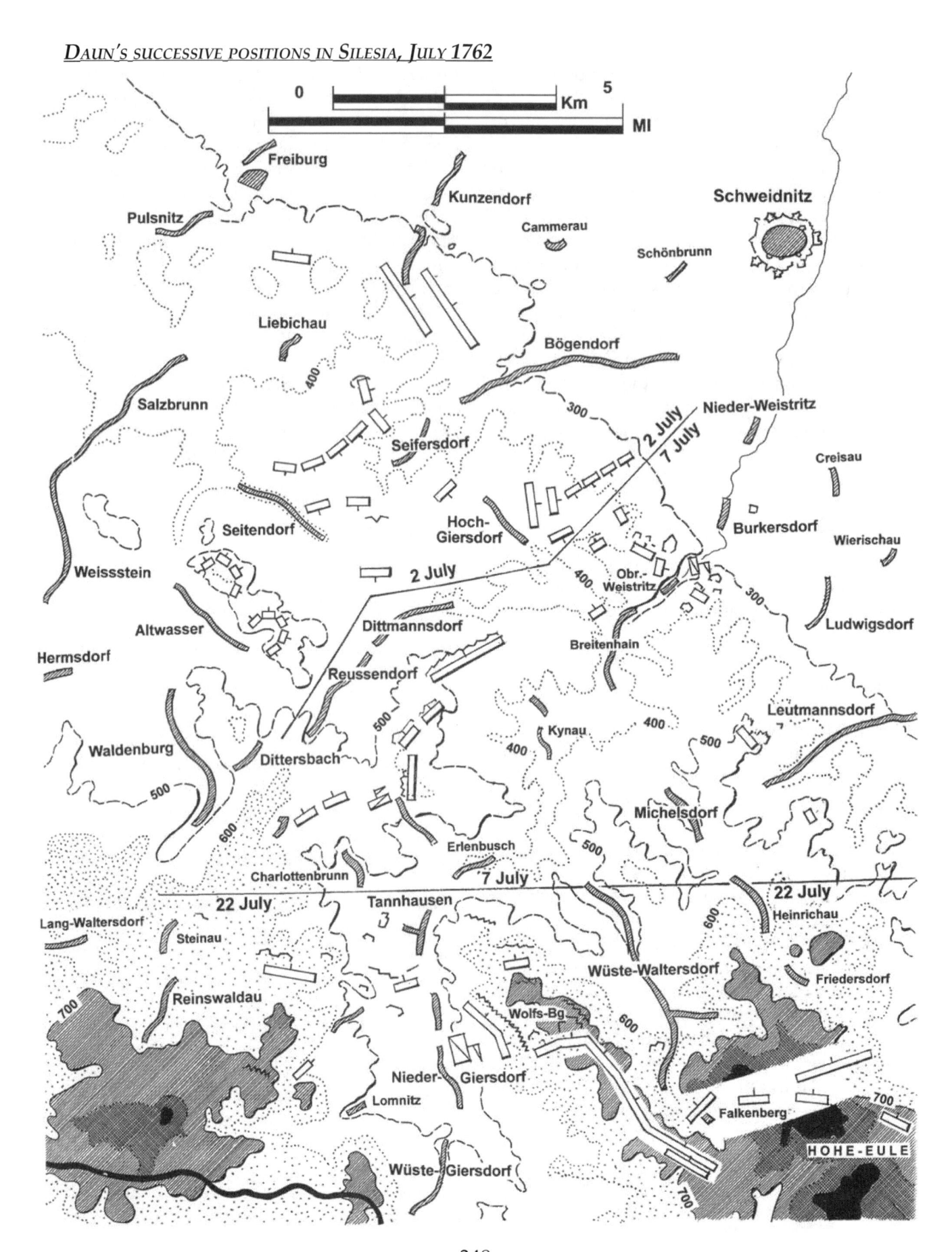

Daun's Successive Positions in Silesia, July 1762

are still… holding out, but in a pretty sad condition, being so inferior in force, lacking fodder and baggage, almost out of food, and desertion rife among our troops. Three days ago there was even a certain major, Count Galler of the regiment of Gaisruck, who deserted quite shamelessly in the full view of the army. What a detestable traitor! But there is nothing I say now which I have not been saying for a long time.'[45]

On 18 July Frederick discovered that the balance of the war was in danger of turning disastrously against the Prussians. In the afternoon Lieutenant General Chernyshev came to him with the appalling news that the Russian Emperor Peter III had been dethroned and was under arrest, and that orders had come to him from the Senate to swear in his troops to his wife Catherine and march them back to Poland. He added that Russian forces had been ordered to reoccupy East Prussia. This had the makings of a grand strategic catastrophe, and it also upset Frederick's immediate plans for throwing the Austrians out of their positions. The news was certain to reach the enemy in the near future, and the king now used all his blandishments to persuade Chernyshev to put off his departure for three days. 'Those three days were important to me,' wrote Frederick in his history of the war. 'I had to put them to good use by some kind of decisive blow. As long as the Russians were present they deterred the Austrians, who were still unaware of the recent revolution. If I did not retake Schweidnitz I would have to fall back to quarters along the Oder, as in the previous year. If this campaign failed to produce results, all the efforts which I had made to reconquer this half of Silesia would have been in vain and the prospects of peace would have vanished like smoke.'[46]

Heavy and continuous rain forced the king to put off his attack, but the delay at least allowed him to move his forces into the best positions for the assault. From his reconnaissances and other information Frederick deduced that the Austrians had weakened their right flank, in order to counter the threat from Neuwied, and in essence he now designed to fix Daun's main force by demonstrations against its left wing and centre, and prise open its right (eastern) flank and rear by meticulously planned penetrations

The demonstrations

The Prussians left their tents standing in their camp, and the eyes of the Austrians were also certain to be caught by the ranks of Chernyshev's corps, which had no active role, but was to be drawn up in an impressive way from Seitendorf to Bögendorf. In front of the Russians, two Prussian brigades would advance threateningly towards Daun's main position—that of **Ramin** by widely-scattered units in two ranks, and that of **Manteuffel** (preceded by the Jäger and the free battalion of Hülsen) skirmishing towards the abattis. When Manteuffel arrived close under the Austrian positions he was to open up with his artillery in support of the main attacking forces over to the east. Altogether only about fifteen battalions were devoted to these diversions, as opposed to more than twice that number to the main attacks.

The assaults

The attacks were to develop in phases from the east. The largest of the striking forces was the corps of GL. **Neuwied**. Coming from the west, it had executed three overnight marches around the rear of the rest of the forces and re-inserted itself on the far left (east) of the Prussian deployment. Neuwied's task was to strike up the Leutmannsdorf valley and open up the right rear of the Austrian position on the hills. The second Prussian formation was that of GM. **Möllendorff**, who was to take the outlying castle of Burkersdorf and establish a great battery that would dominate the entrance of the Weistritz valley by fire. The artillery would open fire at the sound of Neuwied's attack, and when the cannon and howitzers had done their work the infantry would assault the fortifications in and around the valley exit, and gain fresh sites for the artillery. Frederick in person would accompany the brigade of GM. **Knobloch**, the third of the attacking formations. Knobloch was to advance to the right of Möllendorff and assault the fortifications on the Leibel-Berg, a feature which dominated the ground between the Weistritz valley and the triple abattis which wound back towards the position of the main Austrian army.

Daun believed that he was condemned to the defensive, not least because the need to counter the demonstrations of Neuwied and Reitzenstein had reduced the troops at his disposal to 30,000, the equivalent of only half of the force at Frederick's command. Daun's posture was reproduced on the tactical scale in the present position, which extended for seven miles across some very difficult ground. The terrain made for local strength, but the hills, woods and valleys—and especially the great trench of the Weistritz stream—restricted lateral movement. For an effective defence, therefore, the Austrians would have to position their forces where they were going to be the most needed, which depended in turn on identifying the axes of the Prussian attacks in good time.

Daun had first become concerned for his right flank on 13 July. 'His Excellency called me to him [writes *GFWM*. O'Kelly] to tell me of his anxieties about the support available for his posts, and assigned the command to me in the most gracious and flattering terms possible. His Excellency was fully aware of their importance, and of the danger which threatened them.' The sector in question spanned the Weistritz, and Lieutenant Colonel Bechardt and Captain Kohli of the engineers now improved and extended the abattis and the redoubts. The southern side of the valley entrance was defended by a low-lying but strong redoubt, equipped with a palisaded covered way, a deep ditch and a parapet set with storm poles. Smaller works extended up the hill behind, and another very strong redoubt was sited towards the crest. On the northern, or left-hand side of the valley (as the Austrians saw it) O'Kelly devoted his attention to the Leibel-Berg. 'A disagreement arose after I assumed the command, for some people wanted me to abandon the Leibel-Berg and the first abattis. If however, this position fell into the hands of the enemy, it would have been impossible to hold out in the rest of the wood, which it commanded. I therefore ignored the protests and the advice to the contrary and set about fortifying myself there.'[47]

To defend the redoubts of the Weistritz valley and the southern heights, O'Kelly deployed the bulk of the two battalions of the Grenadier Regiment of Green Loudon. The regiments of Waldeck, Angern and Wallis [35, 49, 11], together with Belgiojoso's battalion of combined grenadiers were arranged over the Leibel-Berg and along the abattis towards the main army. The Austrians were short of troops for outpost duty, as was typical of this stage of the war, and the only units standing in front of the line of defence were those of the Nádasdy Hussars [H11] at the entrance of the Weistritz valley, and 150 Croats and 50 of the Green Grenadiers in the isolated castle of Burkersdorf a mile into the plain.

The right rear of the army towards Leutmannsdorf was totally unguarded until 17 July, when Daun deployed *GFWM*. Pfuhl with two battalions (one each of Baden-Baden and Baden-Durlach [23, 27]) to hold two redoubts overlooking Ober-Leutmannsdorf. Early on 20 July the Austrians began to grasp something of the threat which was developing on this side. A column (Knobloch's) moved by way of Hoch-Giersdorf and drew itself up to the west of Nieder-Weistritz. Another column had marched around Schweidnitz during the night, and come into line with the first to the east of the same village. It was that of Möllendorff, but the Austrians mistook it for that of Neuwied. Prince Albert of Sachsen-Teschen observed that 'it was a very odd spectacle, indicating something very rash on the part of the enemy, to see a small corps insert itself in an open plain between a fortress which was stuffed with a large garrison, and a row of heights which was occupied by an army. It pitched camp on either side of Polnisch-[Nieder-] Weistritz, which was almost within range of the cannon of the fortress, and which was certainly with reach of the artillery on the hills.'[48] The Prince de Ligne adds that 'you could not imagine a better chance to punish this temerity on the part of the king: we had assumed that by now he would have known better. Some of our more intelligent officers were for exploiting the opportunity, but the others were in the majority and carried the argument. We did not fight, but we arranged to have ourselves to be beaten on the next day, which duly happened.'[49]

Late on the hot and humid afternoon of the same 20 July the field marshal came to O'Kelly, who had reported the massing of Prussian forces.

In addition to the columns just mentioned, Prussian troops were seen encamped over to the right in the neighbourhood of Gräditz and Faulbrück. The Austrians did not know that these were part of the powerful corps of Neuwied, just arrived after its overnight marches, but Daun was sufficiently alarmed to order a considerable reinforcement of his right flank and rear. *FML.* Brentano set out with his nine battalions and twenty squadrons from distant Hermsdorf to hold the re-entrant at Leutmannsdorf, though 'no matter how speedily he marched, he was able to arrive only during the night, with his troops exhausted by their long and difficult march, and prostrated by the appalling heat.'[50]

Daun in addition detached some forces from his main army to be at O'Kelly's disposal. They consisted of the Württemberg Dragoons [D38] and the two battalions of de Ligne and Mercy [38, 56]. There was nowhere to put them except in the relatively level ground at the entrance of the Weistritz valley, which consequently became very crowded.

Altogether the forces available to the Austrians on their right flank and rear comprised the 4,000 troops under O'Kelly's command on the Weistritz, and the two battalions (1,000 men at most) by Ober-Leutmannsdorf. For both sides the margins of time were eroding very fast. Brentano's troops had halted at 10.30 at night, still short of their destination; Frederick had to precipitate his attack before news of the palace revolution in Russia reached the Austrians.

Burkersdorf, 20/21 July 1762

a) Austrians
c. 15,750.
O'Kelly's corps: 6,500-7,000 overall, but only c. 5,000 in the sectors under attack
Brentano's corps: c. 9,000 (6,500 infantry, 2,500 cavalry)
Losses: c. 1,950: c. 320 killed, c. 420 wounded, c, 1,200 prisoners and missing, 11 cannon, 2 howitzers
b) Prussians
c. 16,000 infantry
Losses: 1,722 from all causes, 1,477 of them from the corps of Neuwied

At about the same time as Brentano's troops threw themselves onto the ground at Michelsdorf, one hundred and thirty Prussian volunteers set out into the darkness to assault the castle of Burkersdorf. It was a massive quadrilateral of two storeys, surrounded by houses, gardens and tall old poplars. The Prussians cleared the Croats from the outbuildings easily enough, but then came under a heavy fire from the Green Grenadiers under Lieutenant Salisch, who were firing from the castle windows. The Prussian canister fire had no effect, but one of the Prussian soldiers had been quartered in the castle in 1761, and with the advantage of local knowledge he was able to cut the cable which supported the drawbridge. The way was now clear for the cannon to smash the barricade which the Austrians had built inside the gateway, and the Prussians poured into the courtyard and forced Salisch and his men to surrender.

The Prussians at once set about constructing a breastwork of fascines to the east of the castle, and brought into position a great battery of fifty-five heavy pieces. Frederick arrived on the scene at 3.30 in the morning of 21 July, declared himself satisfied with the progress, and reminded Möllendorff that he must wait upon Neuwied's attack before he opened fire.

The king rode off to Neuwied's corps, where twenty cannon inaugurated an attack on a frontage of two brigades, that of *GM.* Franz of Anhalt-Bernburg on the Prussian left, and of *GM.* Lottum on their right. Anhalt-Bernburg's troops pushed up the valley of Leutmannsdorf, and braved the fire of the Croats which were lurking in the gardens of the straggling village of the same name. Towards the top the Prussians encountered the southernmost of the two earthworks above Ober-Leutmannsdorf, and reached the crest almost at the same time as the four leading battalions of Brentano. The contest was now more equal, for the battalion of Baden-Baden [23] was putting up a brave defence in its little work, while Brentano's troops were the same men who had beaten Neuwied at Adelsbach only fifteen days before. The combat was resolved in favour of the Prussians only when Neuwied sent two battalions to revive the attack.

Brentano deployed the rest of his force in support of the battalion of Baden-Durlach [27] in

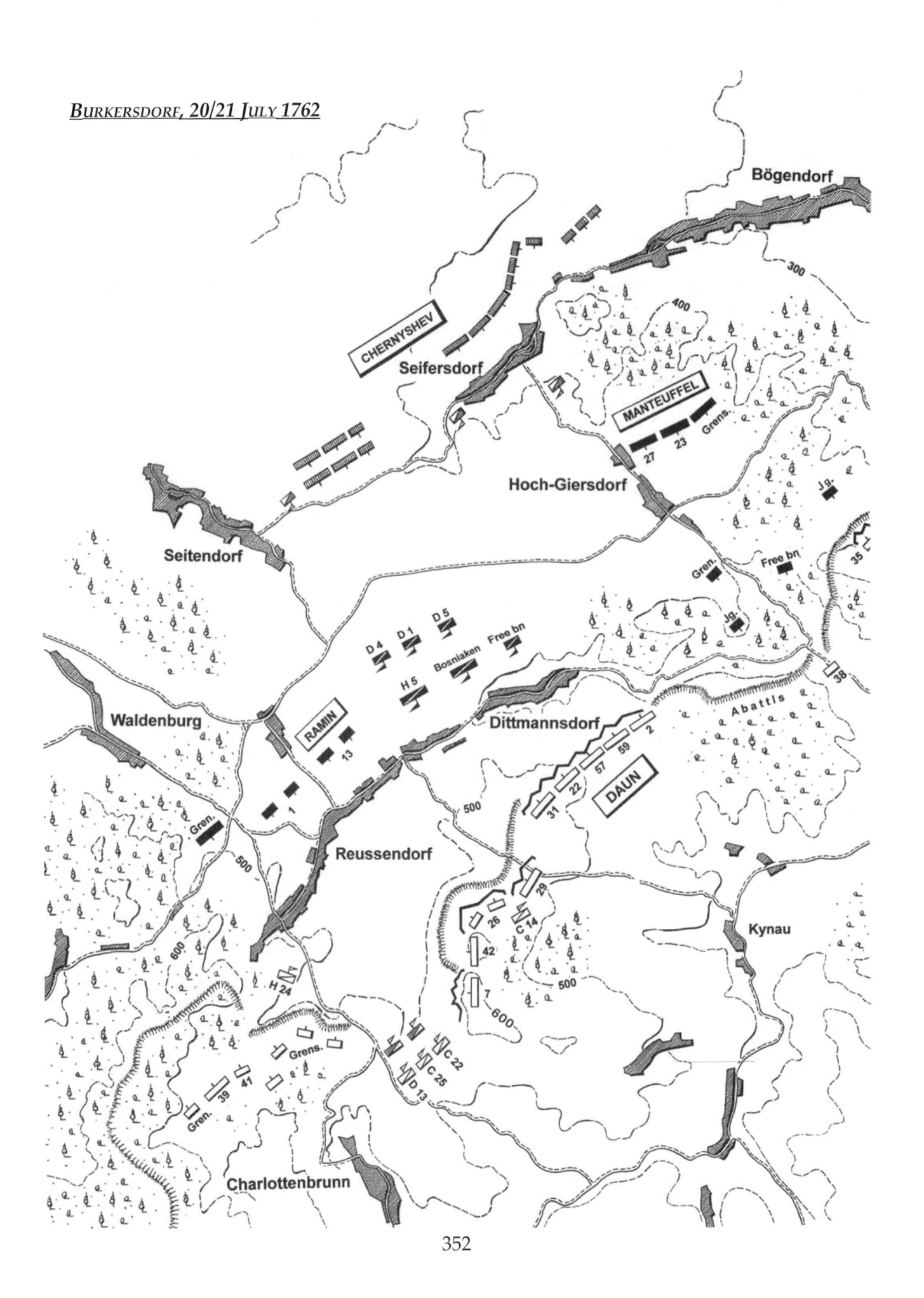

BURKERSDORF, 20/21 JULY 1762

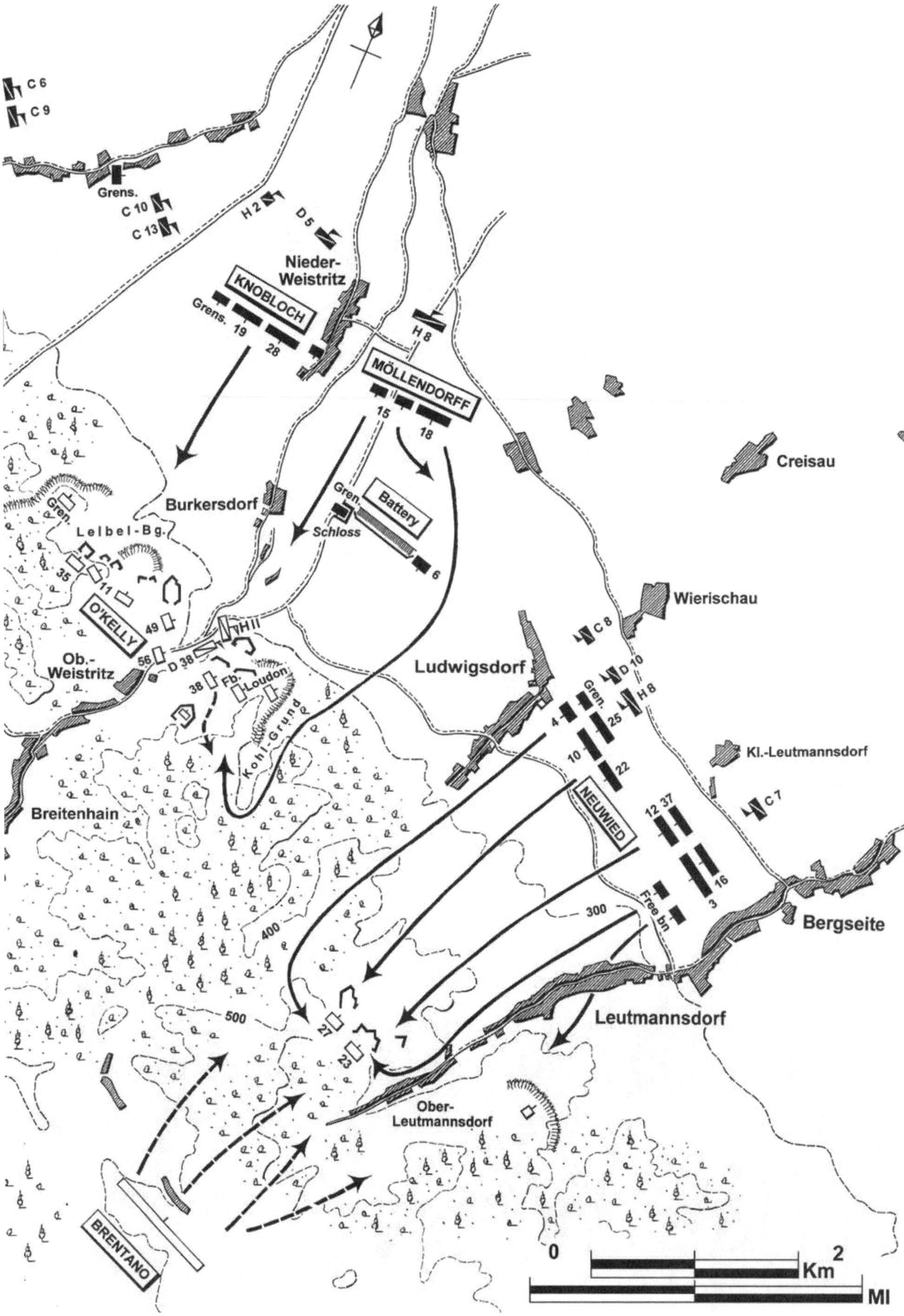
C 6
C 9
Grens.
C 10
C 13
H 2
D 5
Nieder-
Weistritz
KNOBLOCH
Grens.
19
28
H 8
MÖLLENDORFF
15
18
Creisau
Burkersdorf
Gren.
Battery
Schloss
6
Gren.
Leibel-Bg.
35
11
O'KELLY
49
H II
Ob.-
Weistritz
56
D 38
38
Fb.
Loudon
Kohl-Grund
Wierischau
C 8
Ludwigsdorf
D 10
H 8
Gren.
4
25
10
22
Kl.-Leutmannsdorf
NEUWIED
12
37
C 7
Breitenhain
16
3
Free bn
300
400
Bergseite
500
27
23
Leutmannsdorf
Ober-
Leutmannsdorf
BRENTANO
0
2
Km
MI

Burkersdorf.
Above, the Leibel-Berg as seen from the site of the Prussian battery, with the positions of the main Austrian army extending into the haze on the right.

Below, the high ground to the south of the Weistritz. The Austrian positions ran up the hill to the right.

the northern work, now under attack from the brigade of Lottum, ascending from Ludwigsdorf. Frederick was watching the progress of the attack in person, and with this incentive the Pomeranian regiment of Alt-Schenckendorff [22, still usually known by its former name of 'Prinz Moritz'] led the assault by clambering up the steep slopes. Here too the Austrians were putting up a dogged fight, which again forced the Prussians to bring up reinforcements. The regiments of Prinz Moritz and Ramin [25] attacked frontally, while the Westphalian battalion of Mosel advanced up a trackless ravine, and, after suffering heavy casualties, came at the open gorge from the rear. Inside the fortification the Prussians discovered nine cannon and two howitzers, which they trained around to fire at the retreating forces of Brentano. However the battle in this sector had cost Neuwied heavily, and his corps was so depleted and so exhausted that it was unable to exploit its success against the Austrians, who rallied at Michelsdorf.

When daylight came O'Kelly became aware that the Austrian calculations were going badly wrong. In the misty plain to his front a number of Prussian squadrons near Burkersdorf gave way to the side and unmasked the gigantic battery, the existence of which had been unknown to him. From his right he heard cannon fire from the direction of Leutmannsdorf, where he knew that Brentano had still to arrive, 'even though the arrangement had been that he should be there before six [of the previous evening]. My first priority was now to find some means of getting help to him.'[51] He set out on horseback, but before he reached his destination Möllendorff's artillery opened fire.

It was a battery on a truly Napoleonic scale, by far the biggest of any action in the war, and consisted of ten heavy 12-pounder *Brummers*, which were to scour the valley, and forty-five 7- and 10-pounder howitzers, which were aiming at the fortifications. 'The first stroke was terrible, I have seen few openings to compare with it,' remembered the Prince de Ligne. 'The regiments of Württemberg and Nádasdy had been placed in a very bad position to our front. The horses had been unsaddled and were being given fodder, and men were on foot, contrary to the advice I had given to their brigadier to be on their guard, for I had been out to reconnoitre at daybreak and believed I could hear some kind of work going on behind the Prussian cavalry. The shot and shell now had an appalling effect. The horses broke their tethers and ran half a league. The dragoons caught some of them and remounted, which meant that they chased after the loose horses and ended up still further away. The horses of the Nádasdy regiment pretty well disappeared from view.'[52] The horses attached to the limbers and ammunition carts of the artillery also bolted, which prevented the pieces in the fortifications from replying. The Loudon Green Grenadiers and the battalion of Mercy fled up the slopes, which left the battalion of de Ligne isolated for a time in the valley entrance.

The fire of the Prussian artillery scattered O'Kelly's suite and left him alone with Colonel Fabris. With great difficulty they rode up the southern slopes of the Weistritz valley in the hoping of discovering what had happened at Leutmannsdorf. They did not get far before the sound of artillery and musketry (Knobloch's attack) now carried from the Leibel-Berg on the other side of the ravine. The fog lingering in the woods and the hollows made it impossible to make out the events in the direction of Leutmannsdorf, and it now seemed more important to O'Kelly to re-cross the valley to the Leibel-Berg. It proved to be another difficult ride, and this time O'Kelly lost his horse to a cannon shot.

On his way to the Leibel-Berg O'Kelly entrusted the defence of the valley entrance to Colonel the Prince de Ligne. Colonel Kinsky reassembled the Württemberg Dragoons, though the Nádasdy Hussars had disappeared without a trace. The battalion of Mercy re-joined, having made a wide detour to the left. At the same time the Green Grenadiers began to rally under their colonel Richard D'Alton, and extended themselves over the high ground on the southern side of the valley, which now became the target of Möllendorff's assault.

Möllendorff did not relish the prospect, for when the panic among the Austrians subsided it transpired that many of the howitzer shells had burst in the air, and that little real damage had been done to the earthworks, which rose tier upon tier, from the valley entrance to the great redoubt near the crest of the southern heights. In any case the narrow, deep and impassable Kohl-Grund ravine seemed to offer protection against any outflanking movement on this side of the Weistritz valley. To the north of the valley the Austrians were still standing firm on the Leibel-Berg, which was in any case the target of Knobloch's brigade.

In these circumstances Möllendorff leaped at the opportunity which was presented to him by an hussar patrol, which had discovered that the Kohl-Grund could itself be outflanked by an unguarded and practicable path, the 'Schaffstritt' (sheep track). Better still, a woodsman explained that the path led around the head of the Kohlgrund, and could bring the Prussians within attacking distance of the rear of the great redoubt. Möllendorff left the Second Battalion of the Garde [15] at the foot of the hill, to hold the attention of the Austrians. He directed his three remaining battalions over to his left and up the Schaffstritt, probably concealed by the smoke from his great battery at Burkersdorf. Two forces were now converging towards the summit—Möllendorff's Prussians by way of the Schafftstritt, and Colonel de Ligne with 380 assorted Austrian infantry retreating from the valley. De Ligne now found that his forces were being whittled away on the flank by Prussian picquets (detached from Möllendorff's brigade) which were spilling over the hill: 'we killed scarcely anyone, but they were killing a great number of our people.'[53]

O'Kelly sent order upon order to fall back, but de Ligne believed that he must gain a little time if his men were not to go to pieces under the pressure. 'My troops were exhausted from

The flank of one of the Austrian works (probably Captain O'Brady's redoubt) to the south of the Weistritz

all the marching up and down hill, and I let them rest a little. I asked them whether they were happy to start fighting again. They went back to the woods and into action with the best will in the world. I asked them to cry out in as many languages as they could remember, '*tue, tue* for them, *Houdry* as if they were Croats, and whatever foreign expressions came to their minds in Hungarian, German and Czech, and all to make the enemy believe that reinforcements were coming to me.'[54]

The Prussian picquets obligingly disengaged, and de Ligne and his men were able to escape. All the works on this side of the Weistritz valley had now been abandoned, except for the great redoubt towards the summit, which was being held by Captain O'Brady and a force of the Green Grenadiers. This O'Brady was probably a relation of the Jakob Bernard Brady who was about to make a name for himself at Schweidnitz (below), and his troops included many Prussian deserters who were now fighting for their lives. With beating drums the Prussians pushed through a thickets of hazel bushes and oak saplings to attack the rear and right flank of the redoubt. The assault was led by one hundred volunteers of the regiment of Prinz von Preussen [18] under Captain Kuno Friedrich von der Hagen, who was the archetype of the idealistic and determined young Prussian officer. He had already come to the notice of the king, and he now dropped stone dead from a musket ball which took him above the left eye.

The Green Grenadiers beat off this attack and the one which followed, but they were finally compelled to retreat when the surrounding abattis blazed up. It has been supposed either that the tangled branches caught fire from their musketry, or perhaps, as a Prussian account has it, they had been set on fire by a Prussian grenadier, but Prince Albert of Sachsen-Teschen explains that 'the enemy had seized the high ground and almost cut off the retreat, but far from giving up he (O'Brady)

The upper Leutmannsdorf valley. The forces of Brentano and Neuwied clashed on the heights to either side.

kept up his fire until he was completely out of ammunition, whereupon he set light to the palisades and the nearby abattis, after which he retreated under the cover of the dense smoke.'[55] However the rest of the regiment of Prinz von Preussen had cut across the path of retreat behind the redoubt, and O'Brady and his men had to surrender.

The attacks by Neuwied and Möllendorff had lodged the Prussians at the heads of the valleys of Leutmannsdorf, Ludwigsdorf and the Weistritz, and the only intact position remaining to the Austrians on their right flank was to the north of the Weistritz, where the works on the Leibel-Berg and the adjoining abattis were held by Belgiojoso's battalion of grenadiers and four scattered battalions of fusiliers. O'Kelly had devoted particular attention to the fortifications and plan of defence on this sector, which was vital for his communication with the main army, and it now transpired that the Prussian bombardment had even less material effect here than on the other side of the Weistritz.

Frederick betook himself on his little cossack mare to see what Knobloch was making of his attack. The grenadier battalion of Rothenburg and the first battalions of the regiments of Markgraf Karl and Thile [19, 38] began to advance towards the heights, but when the Prussians came closer they could see that the Austrians positions were both strong and strongly held, and Frederick accordingly called off the attack. He knew that if it failed he must call on Möllendorff for support, and that would jeopardise what had been gained on the Weistritz sector. Knobloch's brigade fell back, and the king was content to order Möllendorff to bring his heavy artillery up to the heights to the south of the Weistritz and shoot up O'Kelly's position on the Leibel-Berg in its right flank.

During most of this time the greater part of Daun's army had been immobilised in its extended positions, looking generally north-west at the entertainments which Frederick had arranged for its benefit in the shape of the troops of Chernyshev, Ramin and Manteuffel. By now the progress of Neuwied against Brentano was eroding the right rear of the army, and threatening its communications with the County of Glatz and Braunau, as the king had intended. As a first precaution Daun ordered up reinforcements from both the main army and Hadik's corps to Wüste-Waltersdorf in Brentano's rear, and they arrived in such strength that Neuwied feared that he was going to come under a counterattack. Daun had no such intention, and 'having attended to this important matter, he judged that the army's position as a whole and that of O'Kelly's corps in particular were too vulnerable to be maintained any longer, without risking a reverse that could assume the dimensions of a disaster.'[56]

The retreat was another of Daun's pivoting movements. The left wing rested on Wüste-Giersdorf and Tannhausen as before, while the right wheeled back to Wüste-Waltersdorf. The troops which had the furthest to go were those of O'Kelly on the Leibel-Berg. His heavy artillery consisted of two 12-pounders and four 6-pounders, and in view of the difficulty of bringing them off he sent them in advance at four in the afternoon. Möllendorff's artillery continued to flog the empty battery positions until nine in the evening, and after dark O'Kelly extracted his remaining forces and rejoined the army.

The times had been noted with some exactness by the garrison of Schweidnitz. The opening of the attack had been indicated by heavy artillery fire at 4.45 in the morning. By 6.15 the sounds of artillery from the neighbourhood of Burkersdorf had fallen away somewhat, but that from Ludwigsdorf (Neuwied's attack) continued unabated until 7.45, when the Prussians were seen to be masters of the heights. The diary reads that 'just now the enemy are firing cannon from the hill behind Burkersdorf and seem to be aiming to attack the redoubt on the slopes,' an obvious reference to the combat between O'Brady and von der Hagen. The redoubt was still holding out at 10.45 in the morning, when the Prussian infantry at Nieder-Weistritz (Knobloch's brigade) was advancing towards the Leibel-Berg and coming under Austrian artillery fire.[57]

It is difficult to put a name to the contest on 20/21 July. The fighting was on much too great a scale to be considered a mere action, but the fragmented nature of the combat, in which the

Wilhelm Count O'Kelly von Gallagh und Tywoly.
His spirited conduct helped to save the Austrians from disintegration in the last phase of the battle of Torgau. His wing bore the whole weight of the Prussian assault at Burkersdorf.
(Military Academy, Wiener Neustadt)

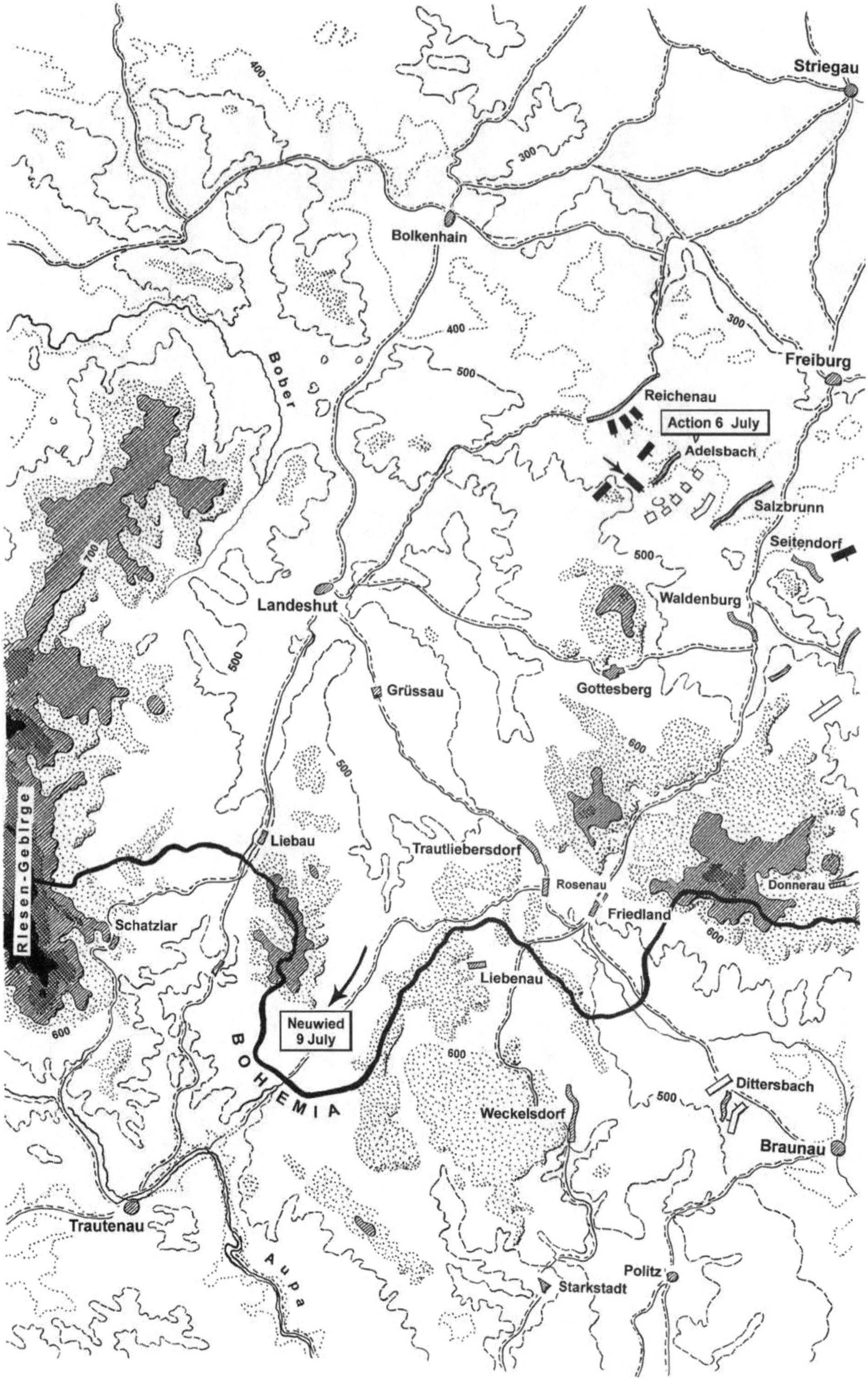

Striegau
Bolkenhain
Freiburg
Reichenau
Action 6 July
Adelsbach
Salzbrunn
Seitendorf
Bober
Landeshut
Waldenburg
Gottesberg
Grüssau
Riesen-Gebirge
Liebau
Trautliebersdorf
Rosenau
Friedland
Donnerau
Schatzlar
Liebenau
Neuwied
9 July
BOHEMIA
Dittersbach
Weckelsdorf
Braunau
Trautenau
Aupa
Politz
Starkstadt
400
300
500
700
600

The scene of operations in Silesia and north Bohemia, 1762

separate Prussian formations had been assigned precise objectives, gives it the character less of battle than an 'operation,' on the pattern first established by the Austrians at Hochkirch in 1758. The Prussians at Burkersdorf showed their mastery of the new techniques, and Frederick launched or held back the individual assaults in such a way that they amounted to a harmonious whole. The Austrians were compromised fatally by the inadequacy of their intelligence, which derived in turn from their lack of light cavalry. They failed to identify Neuwied's corps correctly (supposing it to be that of Möllendorff), and they failed to detect the massive battery which was a-building by Burkersdorf castle.

There can be no doubt as to the wider significance of the combat. It ranked, along with that of Reichenbach twenty-six days after, as one of the two decisive encounters of the campaign in Silesia in 1762, and therefore of the war as a whole.

The action at Reichenbach and the effort to relieve Schweidnitz, 22 July - 24 September 1762

By prising open the right flank of Daun's position above the plain, Frederick had attained the object for which he had been striving since 1 July, which was to push the Austrians far enough into the hills to enable him to lay siege to Schweidnitz. On 22 July Daun recoiled to the heights just short of the Bohemian border, where the positions had been prospected in advance. The left wing now rested at Donnerau and Gross-Giersdorf, the centre overlooked the valley of Tannhausen, and *FZM*. Lacy with the right wing (the troops of O'Kelly and Brentano) extended from the Wolfs-Berg over the Neumannskoppe to Falkenberg. Just in time Lacy was able to send a light force to anticipate Neuwied on the Hoehe-Eule, which was the highest point in Silesia. Two stupendous lines of abattis, one Austrian, the other Prussian, now looped along the mountain ranges, and Daun chose to cling onto this uncomfortable position, from where he retained the freedom to bar the entry to the County of Glatz as well as to northeast Bohemia.

Frederick meanwhile divided his attention between confronting the Austrians among the hills and mountains, where he committed 32,000 troops, and isolating Schweidnitz, which he placed under a tight investment on 4 August. He was disinclined to do anything further for the moment, for Lieutenant General Chernyshev and his Russians, having paid a passive but useful role at Burkersdorf, took their leave on 24 July. Frederick gave Chernyshev a sword with a gold-encrusted hilt, as a sign of his regard. On the same day, too late for his purposes, Daun received firm news that Empress Catherine had taken power in Russia as regent, and that Chernyshev was being recalled from Silesia and Rumyantsev from Pomerania.

What Lacy termed 'those implacable warriors in town' demanded forthright measures,[58] and on 25 July Kaunitz wrote to Daun in flattering but unequivocal terms, to draw his attention to the importance of saving Schweidnitz. Daun, as usual, was unwilling to take the responsibility for decisive action, and asked for the requirement to be put to him in a formal way. Kaunitz, Maria Theresa and Francis Stephen worked together to provide what was needed, and the appropriate instructions were sent to Daun on 10 August.

The first paper emphasised the damage that would follow if Daun stood by and allowed the Prussians to reduce Schweidnitz at their leisure. A battle, even if lost, would show that the Austrians had done everything in their power to save the fortress, and they could then go to the conference table with the honour of their arms intact.[59] The second document provided Daun with a political overview. The deluded Emperor Peter of Russia had indeed been overthrown, but his successor Catherine had disappointed Austrian hopes by holding to the peace with Prussia, and it remained to be seen whether the present feelers being put out by the British on the one side, and the French and the Spanish on the other, might open the way to a settlement acceptable to Austria.

Daun now had to determine how to bring his army to the relief of Schweidnitz. Montazet favoured a series of set-piece assaults directly through the hills, which would play to the Austrian strengths in artillery and regular infantry,[60] but a paper (possibly from Lacy) urged that 'we ought to concentrate the various corps of the army, and emerge from the hills by way of Wartha, Silberberg and Langenbielau, so that we can win the camp of Faulbrück and re-open a secure communication with Schweidnitz. In the avenues of Tannhausen and Wüste-Waltersdorf we should leave behind only the barest minimum of forces necessary for defence.'[61] In other words the Austrians should undertake a wide right-flanking movement down to the County of Glatz, and then swing left by way of the plain of Reichenbach to come at Schweidnitz from the east.

The principle was adopted by Daun, but it was attended with two risks, one recognised at the time, and another which emerged in the course of events. In general terms it was already known that the Austrians were weak in cavalry, which would give the enemy the advantage in mobility and intelligence in wide tracts of open ground which lay on the eastern approaches to Schweidnitz. In the second place Frederick had troops available to frustrate just such a move as the Austrians had in mind, for the wildest of his wild schemes, that of supporting the Turks and Tartars in an advance to the Danube, now bore unexpected fruit.

The light raiding corps of *GL*. Werner had been joined by the corps of the Duke of Bevern at Bauernitz on 24 June. Nothing more had been heard from the Orientals, and for a time the combined force served no purpose than to force the Austrian *FML*. Beck to guard the approaches to Moravia and Austrian Silesia. As early as 28 July Frederick speculated that Daun might try to relieve Schweidnitz by following an anti-clockwise circuit out to the east. For the time being the only force standing in the way was the thirty-eight squadron-strong cavalry corps of Prince Friedrich Eugen of Württemberg, standing at Peterswaldau on the far left of Frederick's array. As the king's suspicions became firmer, and the vision of intervention by Turks and Tartars faded, the forces of Werner and Bevern offered themselves in a providential way as an uncommitted reserve. Frederick needed all the help he could get, for the blockade and siege against Schweidnitz demanded twenty-two battalions and twenty-two squadrons, and he still had to hold the line against Daun's existing positions in the mountains towards the Bohemian border.

As a first instalment Werner brought his nine battalions and fifteen squadrons to join the mass of Württemberg's cavalry, and arrived at Peterswaldau on 11 August. Daun at first interpreted the westward shift of Prussian forces as a threat to the County of Glatz, and in response Beck with his up to 12,000 troops marched by way of Zuckmantel along the foot of the hills to Frankenstein, from where he could join the main army when it emerged by way of the passes of Silberberg and Wartha. It was a creditable march, but it was totally outpaced by Bevern with his remaining 9,000 troops, who set out from Münsterberg at two in the morning of 13 August, and marched an impressive twenty-five miles to arrive at five in the afternoon on the heights to the north of the straggling village of Peilau. He thereby interposed himself neatly between the Austrians and their objective, the beleaguered fortress of Schweidnitz.

Reichenbach, 16 August 1762

a) Austrians
c. 25,000
Losses: 920; 140 killed, 373 wounded, 407 missing or prisoners

b) Prussians
c. 9,000, building up to c. 12,000 in the course of the action, not including the nine battalions coming up from Peterswaldau
Losses: 997 from all causes, of whom c. 500 were taken prisoner

While some 12,000 men of the main Austrian army remained to cover the original positions along the heights of the Silesian/Bohemian border, Daun had been feeding troops out to his right behind the screen of the mountains to the exits of the County of Glatz at Silberberg and Wartha. Early on the morning of the 16th the Austrians descended to the Silesian plain. Their total stood at 45,000 troops, including the corps of Beck, newly-arrived from the east. The route to Schweidnitz by way of Reichenbach was blocked by Bevern, who must now be cleared out of the way before Frederick could bring up reinforcements from the rest of the Prussian army, which was strung out further to the west. The Austrians were taking great risks, and Daun detached Loudon with about 20,000 troops on

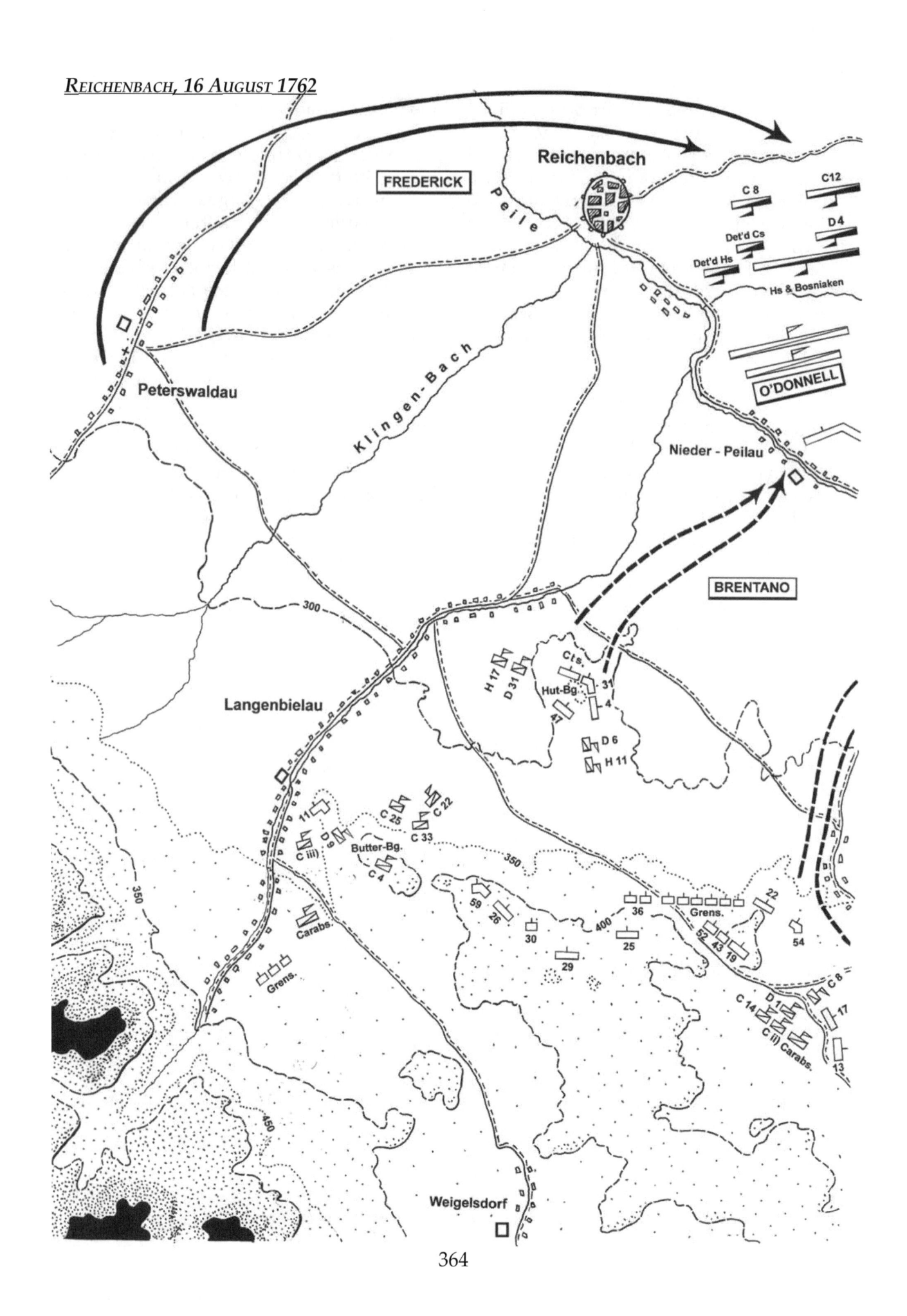

REICHENBACH, 16 AUGUST 1762

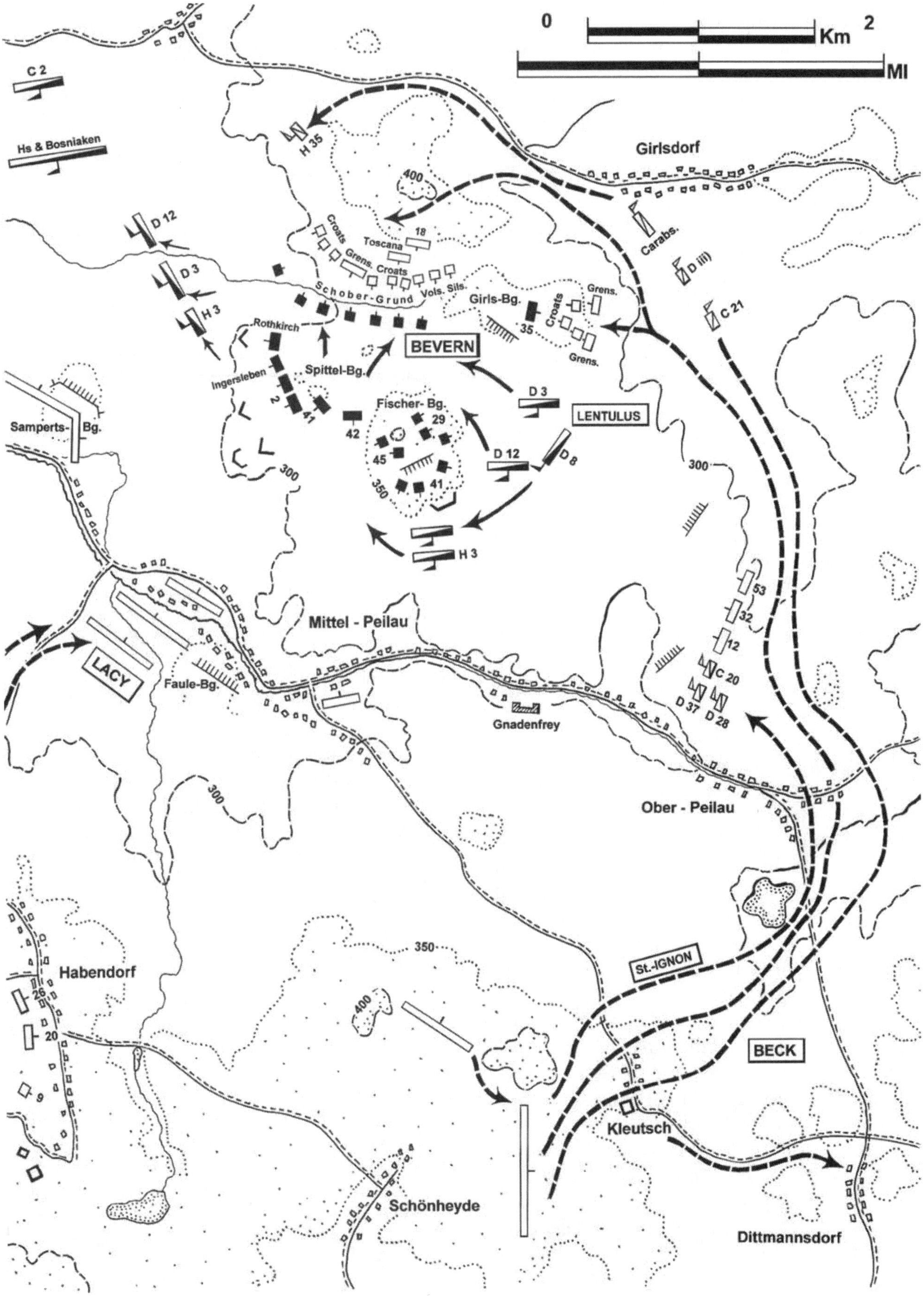

0
2
Km
MI
C 2
Hs & Bosniaken
H 35
Girlsdorf
400
D 12
Croats
Toscana
18
Grens.
Croats
Carabs.
D iii)
D 3
Schober-Grund
Vols. Sils.
Girls-Bg.
Grens.
H 3
Croats
C 21
Rothkirch
35
BEVERN
Grens.
Spittel-Bg.
Ingersleben
2
41
D 3
Fischer- Bg.
LENTULUS
Samperts-
Bg.
42
29
45
D 12
D 8
300
350
41
300
H 3
53
Mittel - Peilau
32
12
C 20
LACY
Faule-Bg.
D 37
D 28
Gnadenfrey
300
Ober - Peilau
350
Habendorf
St.-IGNON
26
400
20
BECK
9
Kleutsch
Schönheyde
Dittmannsdorf

his deep left wing 'who were to cover my rear, and maintain the communication with Wartha.'[62]

The remaining striking force was about 25,000 strong, made up of thirty-three battalions of regulars and Croats, nine regiments of German horse and three of hussars. Daun afterwards summed up the tasks of the component formations as follows: '*FML*. Beck was ordered to attack the rear of the enemy corps with fourteen battalions, four regiments of cavalry and one of hussars. *FML*. Brentano was given eight battalions, two regiments of dragoons and two of hussars to operate against the enemy right flank, while at the same time *FZM*. Count Lacy was to advance directly against the enemy front.'[63] The thinking behind this bare outline was as follows. Two of the columns mentioned by Daun were destined to turn the flanks of the Prussian position: Beck on the Austrian right would work his way around Bevern's left wing and attack the Prussians from the rear; Brentano on the Austrian left was assigned to fall on the Prussian right flank. Lacy, who had the overall command, was meanwhile to fix Bevern's attention by coming at his front and shooting him up with artillery. Bevern was expected to collapse under the multiple threats, whereupon Lacy would push through the disintegrating Prussian forces to the Költschen-Berg, and open the way for the main army to advance to the relief of Schweidnitz.

By venturing thus far into the open ground the Austrians were exposing their left flank to the Prussian horse massed at Peterswaldau, and *GdC*. O'Donnell was to guard this side with the only cavalry which could be spared, making up five feeble regiments.

The enemy, eleven battalions and twenty-five squadrons under the Duke of Bevern, were standing in line on the Spittel-Berg and Fischer-Berg heights north of Mittel-Peilau. Bevern was much inferior in infantry, but his cavalry (typically for the Prussians at this stage of the war) was a respectable force, most of it positioned under *GM*. Lentulus on the left wing. Moreover a consignment of heavy artillery from the king had given Bevern twenty-eight heavy cannon and ten 7-pounder howitzers in addition to his standard complement of battalion pieces.

In the morning of 16 August the Austrians swept forward to their attacking positions. Beck drove the Prussian outposts from Kleutsch and Dittmannsdorf, while Brentano evicted the free battalion of Hordt from Langenbielau after an obstinate resistance.

These preliminary attacks were designed by Lacy to leave the Prussians uncertain as to whether the main blow would fall on Bevern or on the mass of Prussian cavalry at Peterswaldau. As a further refinement, Lacy halted the Austrian advance towards noon, whereupon the cavalry dismounted and the troops of Lacy's column pitched their tents and began to prepare a meal. It was almost unknown for an army to initiate a battle from a standing start in the afternoon, and the king, who had come up with one hundred hussars to view the situation, returned to the cavalry at Peterswaldau, finally convinced that Bevern stood in no further danger for that day.

At 2.30 in the afternoon Beck was on the move again, and by 3.15 the columns of Brentano, Lacy and O'Donnell were in full advance.

Beck's attack

Energy, persistence and *coup d'oeil* combined to make Beck's action the most creditable of the day. He was advancing in three columns, of which the left-hand formation was essentially a screening force, and consisted of three regiments of cavalry [C20, Ds 28, 37] under *GFWM*. Saint-Ignon, and *GFWM*. Simbschen with the Jäger companies and three regiments of infantry [12, 32, 53]. The Jäger established themselves in the churchyard of Ober-Peilau and the adjacent houses, while the fusiliers spread themselves out in front of the cavalry, and two batteries began to shoot up Bevern's left wing in concert with the artillery of Lacy's corps.

This demonstration allowed Beck to slip his main force by two columns around Bevern's left flank, and shortly after five in the afternoon three battalions of his Croats attacked the Girls-Berg, a height in the Prussian rear. After a first repulse the Croats renewed the assault with the support of two battalions of grenadiers, and the combined effort virtually annihilated the second battalion of the regiment of Prinz Heinrich [35].

Beck planted a battery on the captured hill, and opened fire against the rear of the Fischer-Berg, the key to the Prussian position, which Beck had every reason to hope would soon come under attack by Lacy from the opposite side.

Beck then worked his way through the woods which bordered the marshy hollow of the Schober-Grund, hoping to reach firmer ground which would enable him to extend his attack against Bevern's right rear. Beck assumed that the Prussians would now have their hands full with the attacks on the part of Brentano and Lacy, but when he tried to advance from the belt of trees he was thrown smartly back by two battalions of Prussian grenadiers, those of Rothkirch and Ingersleben.

Brentano's march

Brentano had assigned his cavalry to O'Donnell, while his Croats remained for a time in Langenbielau to cover the advance of the main force from the Hutberg to Nieder-Peilau. He progressed little further. The artillery of Bevern's right wing laid down such a heavy fire on the northern exit of Nieder-Peilau that only two of his battalions were able to emerge, and even they had to shelter behind the Samperts-Berg. The only further offensive action on Brentano's part was to advance a battery to the Samperts-Berg, from which the pieces opened a duel with Bevern's pieces.

Lacy's march

Lacy meanwhile advanced his ten battalions and his artillery directly against the Prussian array. He marched by way of Habendorf, and deployed his main force across the Faule-Berg on the near side of Mittel-Peilau. He now opened fire with two powerful batteries against the centre of Bevern's position, and pushed a number of battalions through Mittel-Peilau and formed them on the far side, as if to attack the commanding Fischer-Berg. The advance stopped there, and on this sector too the action was prolonged as a cannonade. The reason was that one of the largest cavalry actions of the war was developing on the far left Austrian flank.

O'Donnell's action

GdC. Carl O'Donnell advanced his five under-strength regiments of horse through Nieder-Peilau at four in the afternoon, and formed them up in the constricted space assigned to him beyond the Peilau stream. Here he was joined by the cavalry element of Brentano's column. His main responsibility, as we have seen, was to cover the left flank of the army against the mass of Prussian cavalry standing under Frederick's command further towards Schweidnitz, but he first had to fight off a determined attack on the part of Bevern's horse, which closed in on his right flank. This consisted of 700 assorted cavalry under Lieutenant Colonel Owstien, and thirteen squadrons which were brought by *GM*. Lentulus from Bevern's left wing. The Swiss-born Lentulus pretended that he was descended from a family of Ancient Rome, and he was rising fast in the esteem of Frederick, who was easily taken in by tall stories. The Erzherzog Joseph Dragoons [D1, originally assigned to Lacy's column] lost three standards in the consequent tussle, but O'Donnell had the support of artillery fire from the main body, and he was able to re-form and drive the enemy back.

After six in the afternoon O'Donnell found that he was facing altogether greater odds, for the king had realised that he had been hoodwinked by the Austrians, and he was coming to Bevern's help from Peterswaldau. The Austrians had to admit that it was a magnificent sight to see the Prussians streaming from Peterswaldau and across the plain to the north of Reichenbach. Frederick, riding the exceptionally fast white Cossack horse *Caesar* was in the lead with the Bosniaken and the Brown Werner Hussars [H6]. Next came Prince Friedrich Eugen of Württemberg with the Czettritz Dragoons [D4], and Captain Philipp Anhalt with a brigade of horse artillery, which galloped through Reichenbach and formed up to the east under the screen of the Bosniaken and the hussars. The 6-pounders of the horse artillery were newcomers to this theatre of war, and they were particularly unwelcome to the Austrians, for they combined the power of medium artillery with something of the mobility of cavalry. The cuirassier regiments of Prinz Heinrich, Spaen and Seydlitz [Cs 2, 12, 8] were pounding up behind, and nine battalions of Prussian infantry were labouring up in the rear.

The 'Peterswaldau' forces were joined by Owstien's troopers, and they assailed O'Donnell's frontally at the same time as Lentulus renewed his attack against the right flank. *GFWM*. Panowski found himself cut off with the Saint-Ignon Chevaulegers [D31] when the enemy were almost upon them. The Netherlanders were strangers to him, and he knew scarcely any French. '"These villains," he said to himself, "like people to speak to them. But what shall I do?" He tried to recall whatever words he might have heard, and with the Bosniaken approaching fast he had to say something before they arrived. An inspiration struck him. "Let's go fuck, by God!" "Oh, oh!" exclaimed the dragoons. "Now that's a brave bugger! So that's what he calls it! He's right, it's just as much fun to fight." Whereupon they fell upon the enemy squadrons like berserkers.'[64]

It was a brave show, but the Austrians were overborne by the mass of Prussian cavalry, and a sequence of attacks and counterattacks ended with the Austrians being driven back towards Nieder-Peilau. The Anhalt-Zerbst Cuirassiers [C25] were nearly sandwiched between the Prussian Brown Hussars and Württemberg Dragoons [D12], and Colonel Johann Lossgallner fell from his horse and had to be rescued by two of his troopers.[65] Panowski was saved in the same way by his adopted Saint-Ignon Chevaulegers. The prolonged ordeal of O'Donnell's wing finally came to a halt when the Prussians were checked by the Austrian infantry firing from the houses and gardens of Nieder-Peilau.

The retreat

Daun was watching events from a hill by Habendorf. Brentano was forming a flank as protection against the swarming Prussian cavalry, a reinforcement of Prussian infantry was likewise approaching from the west, and all of this at a time when Beck's column was still isolated in Bevern's rear. Rather than wait and bring on a full-scale battle, Daun sent word to Beck to retreat. Towards seven in the evening Brentano and Lacy too were ordered to disengage, and the cannonade ceased at 7.30 in the evening. Under the cover of darkness the Austrians resumed the positions they had occupied in the evening.

The losses on the two sides had been roughly even, and it seemed to Frederick that Daun still had it in his power to strike for Schweidnitz, most probably by way of Peterswaldau, and the king accordingly left just two battalions of reinforcements with Bevern, and returned with all the rest of his troops to his original position. With no great conviction both Frederick and Daun discharged *feux de joie* in celebration of their supposed victories; on the Austrian side Daun allowed this honour to the cannon of Beck, 'as it seems to me that this corps is fully entitled to it.'[66]

Daun concluded that there was no further possibility of breaking through to the relief of Schweidnitz. Already on the evening of the action he had sent a message to the fortress, authorising Guasco to negotiate for a surrender on good terms, and on the late evening of 17 August the Austrians fell back on Wartha. On the next day Daun left detachments to cover that pass and the one at Silberberg, with the main force deployed deeper into the County of Glatz and extending as far as the left wing under Hadik, who had been left in the old positions along the Silesian/Bohemian border. The mood among his officers and men was that of a defeated army. Frederick could not understand why the Austrians had given up the contest, and he could only suppose that it was on account of political considerations which were unknown to him, or because the Turks and Tartars had at last come to life.

It was widely believed that the Austrian scheme of 16 August had failed because Lacy and Brentano had not moved to exploit the brilliant operation of Beck against the enemy left flank and rear. In Daun's view Lacy and Brentano had no choice, because the Prussians were arriving in such force from Peterswaldau. Beck was unconvinced, and 'he could not reconcile himself to the fact that we had let slip a victory when it was within our grasp. He passed adverse comments on certain gentlemen who had never been particular friends of his, just as he had never a been a friend to them, which could only be hurtful to the field marshal, for the people in question were the ones he favoured the most.'[67] When Daun ordered Beck's corps to give the *feu de joie* he had intended it to be a sop to its commanders feelings; Beck was not to be appeased, and the opinion in the army was that the salute was a sham.

The Swedish military attaché Major Armfeldt offered an altogether different explanation. The timings for the attacks at Reichenbach cannot be established with any precision, but Armfeldt believed that it had been a basic mistake to stipulate that the assaults were to be made simultaneously. Everything was therefore held back until Beck could arrive in the enemy rear, even though he had much further to go than Lacy and Brentano, which gave time for the king to come to Bevern's rescue. 'If, however, the prince [Bevern] had first been attacked by the generals Lacy and Brentano, his corps would most certainly have been beaten.'[68]

The relief of Schweidnitz is abandoned, 17 August - 24 September 1762

Daun betook himself every now and then to the Wolfs-Berg, and whenever the wet and misty weather permitted he could make out something of the attack and defence of Schweidnitz just over ten miles distant. Contact with the garrison was confined to the nameless heroes who carried messages through the Prussian camps and siege lines. Meanwhile his army was standing idly in the hills.

A large part of the Prussian force was devoted directly to the siege, and the rest (about fifty battalions and ninety squadrons) was strung out in a great arc from Waldenburg to beyond Reichenbach. Loudon and Kaunitz were convinced that something could still be done, and under heavy moral pressure from Vienna Daun finally had to agree to march directly to the relief of Schweidnitz from his present position. He wrote to the commandant Guasco on 12 September that he planned to advance by way of Kunzendorf, and that in any case, if Schweidnitz was about to fall, the garrison must break out, for it was more glorious to be captured in the open field than behind walls.[69] The words were scarcely calculated to give confidence.

Heavy rain put off the enterprise from one day to the next, which gave the Prussians more and more opportunity to anticipate the Austrians on the heights of Kunzendorf and Bögendorf. For once Daun had the support of nearly all his senior commanders. The attaché Montazet, normally so critical of the field marshal, hoped that the rain would continue so long as to put an end to Loudon's madness. Guasco in Schweidnitz believed that the scheme had been hatched directly between his discontented subordinate *GFWM*. Giannini and Loudon, and Loudon himself began to discover difficulties in his project. He was, as Daun observed on 19 September, 'most enthusiastic, but also most inconsistent... We are ready and waiting to go, and he just has to give the word.'[70]

The plan to advance to the relief of Schweidnitz was finally abandoned by 24 September, and Guasco was left to fight on alone.

The Defence of Schweidnitz, 8 August - 9 October 1762

a) Austrians
10,225
Losses: c. 2,980 casualties and missing, all the rest taken prisoner
b) Prussians
Numbers variable
Losses: 3,015 killed and wounded; missing unknown

The fortress-town of Schweidnitz stood in the plain of Silesia. It represented physically and symbolically Austria's claim to that province, and the defence of this place in 1762 became the most sustained Austrian feat of arms in the Seven Years War.

It might seem curious that Vienna had only recently considered that the fortress might have to be abandoned, but one of the reasons was that it demanded an unusually powerful garrison, on account of its perimeter of detached works. When, finally, the decision was taken that Schweidnitz must be held, no less than 10,225 officers and men entered as the new garrison on 9 June. They comprised 23 senior officers, 612 officers and men of the grenadiers, 7,507 of the fusiliers, 130 of the cavalry, and 1,512 of the Croats, together with the 441 personnel of the artillery, artillery fusiliers, engineers and sappers.

Daun was later criticised for having put the garrison together from drafts from almost all the infantry regiments of the army, for officers

The Jauernicker Fort at Schweidnitz, August-October 1762

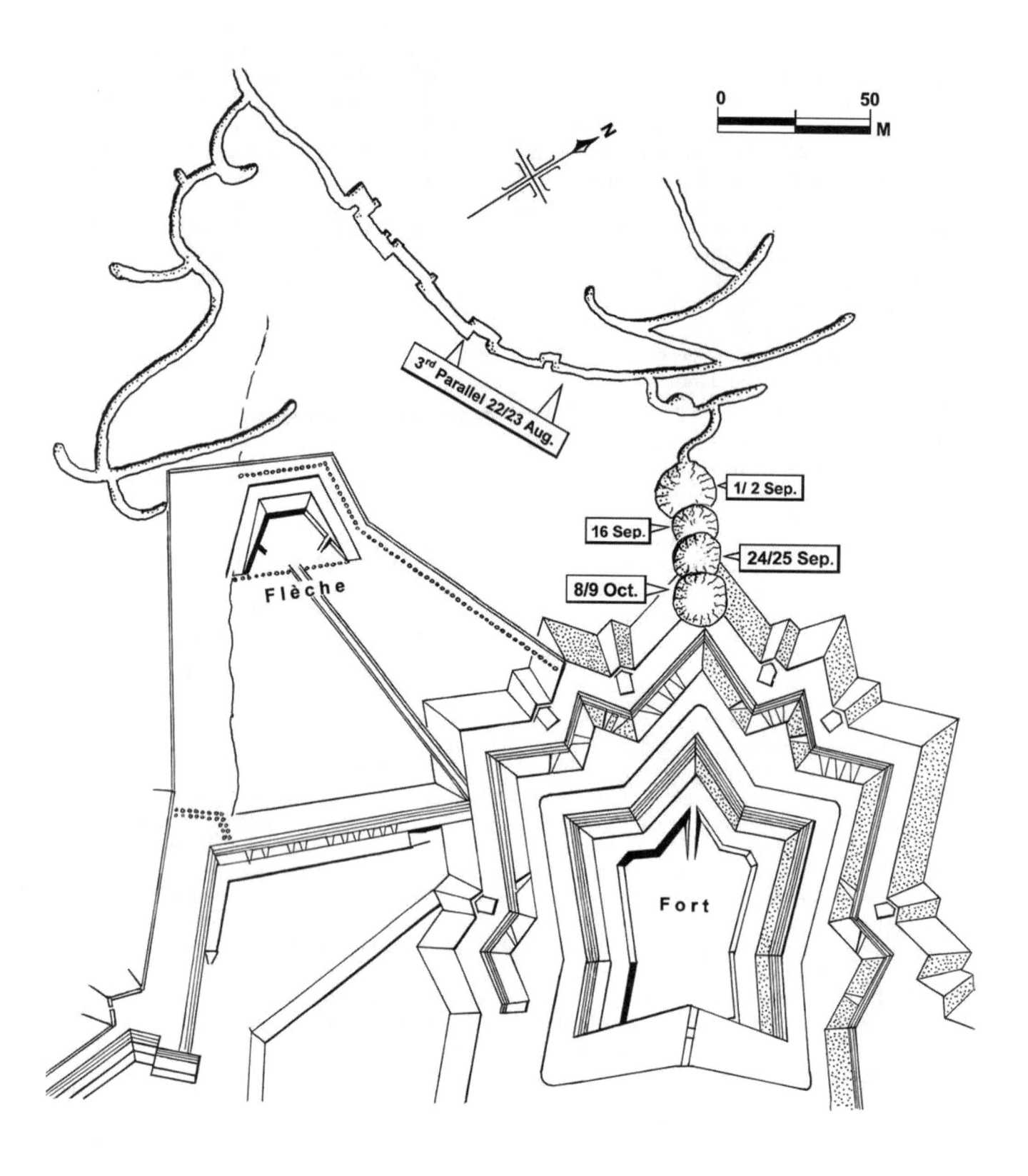

The mine attack against the Jauernicker Fort

Diagram labels: 3rd Parallel 22/23 Aug. | 1/2 Sep. | 16 Sep. | 24/25 Sep. | 8/9 Oct. | Waldhütter's sortie 26/27 Sep. | Outer Ditch | Envelope | Inner Ditch

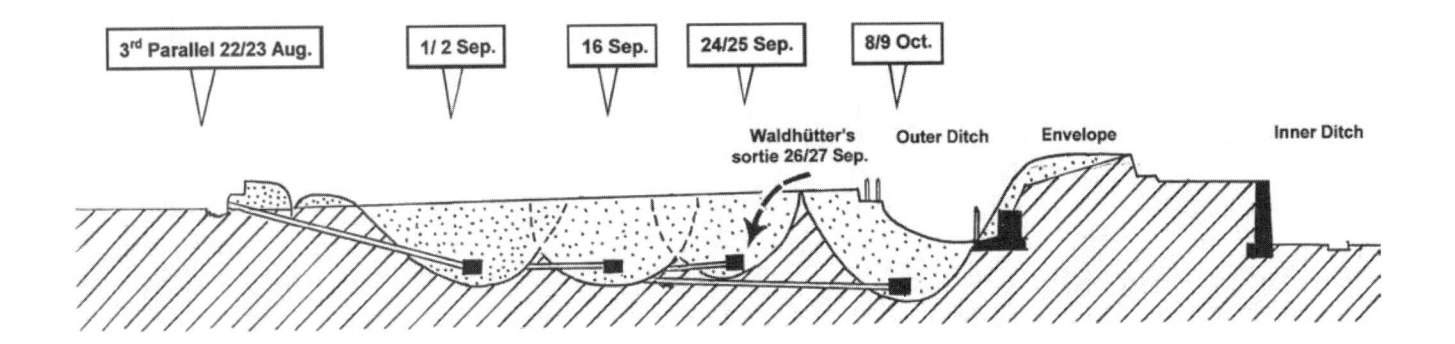

and men rarely knew one another, and often even failed to speak the same language,[71] but the field marshal was only following, perhaps to excess, the well-established principle whereby a force detached on perilous duty (which certainly applied to being besieged in Schweidnitz) must be drawn from a wide diversity of contingents, so as to prevent major units being wiped out completely and perhaps never being reconstituted again.

The commandant was *FML*. Franz Guasco. He did not enjoy Daun's complete trust, and together with his brother Peter Alexander he had the reputation of being something of an adventurer. This was enough in itself to put Guasco at odds with the immediate commander of the troops, *GFWM*. Ernst Friedrich Giannini, a beaky-nosed, absolute and puritanical man, who was an enemy of gambling, and who after the war became a much-feared commandant of the military academy at Wiener Neustadt. In his notes for a confidential history of the siege Guasco reviewed the evidence for Giannini's hostility: 'His malice towards me, as shown even before the siege, by his conversations in Field Marshal Daun's anteroom at Kratzkau, and naturally with the field marshal himself… Many secret investigations he made concerning me. Other harmful comments about me which he made to the Empress.'[72] Giannini in addition had opened a covert channel of communication with Loudon, and therefore with Kaunitz.

Guasco at least had an unconditional supporter in the person of the foremost military technician of the age, Jean-Baptiste Gribeauval de Vaquette, who had been signed over from the French to the Austrian service in 1758 as a *GFWM*., and had the oversight of the artillery, engineers and sappers. He was, in Guasco's words, 'the soul and the great moving force of these three departments.' He directed the main sorties, he played a valued part in the councils of war, 'and altogether it is impossible to overstate the contributions he made… to the long duration of the defence.'[73]

Major Frierenberger (of a famous family of gunners) commanded the artillery, Lieutenant Colonel Steinmetz the engineers, Captain Pabliczek the miners, and Captain Eghels the new Corps of Sappers.

As for the material resources of the defence, Guasco had to fight the Commissariat in order to get the fortress stocked properly with eatables, for 'the term proposed for the total consumption of the provisions was the end of September, by when it was assumed that the coming of peace or some other event would put the fortress out of danger of siege or blockade.'[74] Guasco had to buy 300 oxen from his own cash reserves, but by 9 July he had enough commodities in store to last him in most respects until the end of October.[75]

Guasco was not so well placed with regard to ammunition, for the magazines were filled only 'with what was considered necessary in Vienna, where the opinion was that it was only a third-class fortress, which could hold out under attack for no more than three weeks. Vienna refused to supply howitzers or rampart muskets.'[76]

Guasco at least had the advantage of an intimate knowledge of the works, for he had submitted a detailed memorandum on the subject on 20 November 1761, and concluded that 'the king of Prussia had made no attempt to construct a formal fortress, but only to set out various fortifications around the suburbs to enclose a spacious area for his military depots, and to serve at the same time as a refuge for a beaten army.'[77] It was therefore realistic to consider the 'fortress' as an entrenched camp writ large. The town was defended by nothing more than a low rampart which was set against the medieval wall, and was not designed to give supporting fire to the outworks. The five detached forts and seven redoubts were again not designed for mutual support, and they were in constant danger of escalade, for the envelopes (outer ramparts) were too low. The one significant asset was the existence of a network of countermines. Guasco now extended the countermine galleries by smaller branches, and completed the connecting lines which the Prussians had been building between the detached works.

From 8 July the defenders explored how they might establish visual communication with the army up in the hills to the south. They were fortunate to have at their disposal the tower of the great Jesuit Church, 'from where there is an extensive and beautiful prospect over the wide plains which surround the town to the distant mountains, which look like a wall around the horizon.'[78] A simple numerical code was evolved, and it was found that the best way of drawing the attention of the army was to set fire to a large container of pitch at the top of the tower. An appropriate number of smaller containers were then lit further down the tower, and Major Frierenberger discharged rockets to the same number. Only the most basic messages could be transmitted thereby. Letters were entrusted to daring messengers and Guasco asked Daun 'to send five or six enemy hussar uniforms to me, if at all possible, for I could put them to very good use.'[79]

By 18 July the gunners had succeeded in bowling over a number of the Prussian horsemen who had ventured within range. Guasco lost direct communication with the army on the 20th, and on the next day the observers in the tower watched and timed the progress of the action at Burkersdorf.

At the beginning of August the garrison had reliable news that tough old *GL.* Tauentzien was coming to command the siege, and that a train of heavy artillery was on its way. The Prussians placed Schweidnitz under blockade on 4 August, and on the night of 7/8 August they declared the direction of their attack by opening a first parallel 900 paces from the Jauernicker-Fort and the Jaunericker-Flèche, on the north-western sector of the perimeter of detached works. The besiegers zig-zagged forward in the classic style, and they dug their second parallel on the night of 13/14 August. The garrison responded by sorties on the night of the 7/8, another on the night of the 13/14, and a third on that of 17/18. The Austrians succeeded in filling in a few stretches of trench, but the cost came to a total of 470 officers and men, and the loss of Colonel Tom Caldwell (mortally wounded in the second sortie) was particularly regretted.

One of Caldwell's Irish countrymen, Captain Jakob Bernard Brady or MacBrady, was in command of the Jauernicker-Flèche on the night of 18/19 August. He gained permission to make a small-scale sortie against the two saps which were worming towards the fort. The raid was a success, and Brady returned with three prisoners who told him that the Prussians were massing in their parallel to take the work by storm,

Moments later the Prussians surged forward and lapped around the flèche. Some of them were working around to the rear, while others opened the way for a frontal attack by chopping through the two sets of palisades in the covered way and uprooting the storm poles from the earthen rampart. By the time the enemy were clambering over the parapet Brady had been deserted by all but a lieutenant, a sergeant and two gunners. In this extremity he took up a storm scythe (a long curved blade set on a shaft), 'a magnificent weapon for such an occasion… I was firmly resolved to die… in the defence of my post rather than surrender.'[80] The other four followed his example and slashed about them in a state of desperation, which was heightened when Prussians started to fire down at them from the parapet. Other bluecoats were jammed together in an embrasure, facing the muzzle of a loaded cannon, and when Brady ordered the piece to be fired it produced such carnage and terror that the Prussians on this side of the flèche ran away.

Brady went in search of the rest of his garrison, and found that they were wedged against the barrier at the rear in an attempt to escape. They could not get out, for Brady had locked the gate and kept the key. 'The blade of his scythe had broken off in the fight, but now this dauntless man belaboured the heads of his men with the shaft. He drove them back to the breastwork, and, when they excused themselves by saying that they had run out of ammunition, he ordered them to use their bayonets and musket butts.'[81] The Prussians were still swarming outside the barrier and firing inside, but help was at hand in the shape of forty-two volunteers from the nearby main fort, who crashed through the enemy at bayonet point. Brady opened the barrier to them, and the Prussians gave way on all sides, having lost 33 killed and 101 wounded.

Brady again had the guard of the flèche when the Prussians mounted two assaults on the night of 21/22 August. This time he had grenades at his disposal as well as the storm scythes, and the reserves were quicker to arrive. He was once more victorious, and Guasco and his senior officers testified that 'we could see in Brady that kind of resolution and valour which fills the others with confidence.'[82]

Both parties now took stock. The Austrians were aware that the Prussians were in deadly earnest about their siege, which was certain to last far longer than had been predicted in Vienna. Guasco accordingly sent Colonel Rasp to Tauentzien on 22 August to establish whether the king would allow the garrison to march free in return for giving up the fortress. Frederick had no wish to see Daun reinforced by 10,000 fine troops, and he insisted that the Austrians must surrender as prisoners of war. Guasco had to fight on.

As for the tactics, both the mass assaults of the Prussians and the great sorties of the Austrians were at an end. A new phase of the siege opened on the night of 22/23 August, when the besiegers opened a third parallel against the Jauernicker-Fort, and sank a sixteen-foot deep shaft from which they opened an underground attack. Frederick was putting his trust in the renegade French engineer Simon Deodat Lefèbvre, who had persuaded him that he was a master of the newest device in the mine warfare, the *globe de compression*, which was a super-heavy charge that was guaranteed to cave in the countermines of the defender.

The progress of the Prussian attack could now be measured in terms of the successive and overlapping mine craters which reached towards the salient of the covered way of the Jauernicker Fort. Lefèbvre exploded the first of his charges on the night of 1/2 September, but thereafter his rate of advance was much slower than he had promised. He had failed to allow for the network of permanent countermine galleries, which reached down to the water table, and therefore could not be attacked from underneath. Moreover a zone of filled-in wolf pits extended around the foot of the glacis, and the loose and soggy earth attenuated the force of the Prussian explosions. Most crucially, Lefèbvre met more than his match in Gribeauval and the Bohemian chief miner Joseph Pabliczek, who extended the little branches which led from the permanent galleries, and blew in the sides of the Prussian burrowings with camouflets, which were small and carefully-placed charges which expended the whole of their force underground.

The contest on the surface continued to rage. For days on end the Austrians had been firing their 12-pounder shot at a rate of more than 1,000 rounds every twenty-four hours, but from early September the shortage of ammunition compelled them to retaliate against only the most annoying batteries, and the precious powder was put to more economical use in musketry, and to shower grenades, mortar bombs and pierrier loads into the mine craters.

The Prussian miners meanwhile established lodgements in the craters, and their artillery rained shot, howitzer shells and mortar bombs on the fortifications and the town. The Austrians had no shelter, except in the casemates set into the granite rear walls of the forts, but morale never flagged, being sustained by the remarkable effort which Guasco and Gribeauval put into rewarding the men on the most arduous service by cash, alcohol, extra rations and promotions, and by exalting the achievements of ordinary soldiers in this, the most 'democratic' of the great armies of Europe.

The middle of September found Schweidnitz holding out longer than its expected term, and the possibilities of relief and breakout were being debated both in the garrison and Daun's army. Guasco asked twenty-one of his senior officers for their views, and no less than nineteen of them pronounced against any attempt to break free. Guasco afterwards explained to Daun that it would have taken two marches to arrive at Nimptsch, where the field marshal had suggested that the garrison could establish contact with the main army, and that the troops would be exposed to the greatly superior Prussian cavalry in the open ground on the way, and probably broken up into small parties and destroyed. 'At the very best, chance might favour a few well-mounted individuals on good horses, but the object was to save the whole garrison, or at least a good part of it, and not to lead it to the sacrifice. It deserved something better than that.'[83]

One of the dissenting opinions was from Major Kluck, who commanded one of the forts. The other, which caused much more of a stir, was submitted by Giannini. He proposed a dash by way of Ludwigsdorf and Leutmannsdorf and along the fringes of the Eulen-Gebirge to the County of Glatz, or more desperate still, a march to the north to cross the Oder at Dyherrnfurth, and then to rejoin the army by way of Poland. Guasco noted that 'Count Giannini's true intention was to enhance his reputation. He knew himself that his project was totally unworkable, but he hoped, if it went ahead, that he could save himself on a good horse.'[84]

On the night of 24/25 September the enemy exploded a mine which produced a crater which was nearly twenty-four feet deep, and reached to within six feet of the outer palisade of the Jauernicker Fort. The Austrians could no longer respond by any kind of mine, for a new explosion would have wrecked the palisades, and the defenders had to return to the dangerous expedient of counterattacks.

A party of grenadiers sallied forth on the night of 25/26 September, but the troops shrank from entering the steep-sided crater, because they thought they would never be able to get out again. The next sortie was planned for the night of 26/27 September, and was entrusted to the unlikely command of First Lieutenant Michael Waldhütter of the Hungarian infantry regiment of Erzherzog Ferdinand [2]. He was a Transylvanian Saxon who had joined the regiment nineteen years before, and during his rise to his present rank he had spent some time a sergeant, and not a very effective one. 'Nobody suspected then that he would turn out to be the determined, bold man who would volunteer to hurl himself among the enemy. His reputation was that of that of something of a weakling, over-fond of finery and comfort. His comrades often referred to him jokingly as "Pretty Miss Waldhütter."'[85]

The assaulting detachment consisted of Waldhütter, Sergeant Hayba and thirty fusiliers of his regiment, while the grenadiers of the regiments of Platz, Königsegg, Starhemberg and d'Arberg waited to exploit. To prevent the enemy from rushing up their own reinforcements the miners exploded a countermine against the crater to the rear of the target. They succeeded in burying a large number of men, whereupon the Hungarians 'tore aside the palisades to open their way to the first crater. Waldhütter and his troops jumped inside without hesitation and found the Prussians on their guard. Some of the enemy opened fire, while the others knelt on the floor and raised their muskets, the bayonets fixed to the muzzles. Our men flung themselves blindly among them, sabre in hand; some of them were skewered on the bayonets, but the rest set about the enemy and hacked them to pieces.'[86] They chased the surviving Prussians all the way down the line of craters to the parallel, which enabled Lieutenant Colonel Steinmetz and his men to explore all the galleries leading from the craters and blow them up.

The Austrians had 22 men killed, and Waldhütter and sixty others were wounded, but 'this glorious sortie'[87] gained several days for the defence. A spell of heavy rain from 5 to

7 October retarded the siege still further. Less happily the rain beat down on the shivering Austrians who were sheltering in the roofless houses, and were already showing signs of scurvy.

At one in the afternoon of the fine and cold 8 October a Prussian bomb smashed through one of the beams which covered the connecting line to one side of the Jauernicker-Fort. The comings and goings of the troops had left a trail of gunpowder which led to the interior of the fort, and the flash of the exploding bomb ignited the spilled powder and blew up the fort's magazine, which was set against the rearward face.

The excellent Major Berthold and three companies of troops, amounting to about three hundred officers and men, were killed in the explosion, and this side of the fort was reduced to a ramp of earth and rubble. On the following night the enemy exploded two mines which cast down the first two rows of the triple palisade, and projected a ramp which buried the third and reached to the parapet of the envelope. The grenadier company of the regiment of d'Arberg [55] beat off the assault which followed, and Steinmetz laboured to free the third palisade and seal off the threatened sector by barricades of gabions.

The defence was plainly approaching its term, and the crucial consideration was a review of the ammunition which Major Frierenberger made out on 8 October, and which showed that the powder would run out by the 11th.[88] With the Prussians forming up for a new assault on 9 September, Guasco addressed a note to Tauentzien, and sent Colonel Rasp to negotiate terms, which were reduced to the more or less disagreeable details of surrendering the defenders as prisoners of war.

Thus on 9 October the Prussians gained Schweidnitz at a cost of 63 days of 'open trench,' and 3,015 killed and wounded. One of Guasco's lists puts the loss of the garrison in killed, wounded and missing since 8 August at 2,972.[89] The second list appears to be more complete, and specifies the killed at 589, the wounded at 2,276, and the deserters at 122.[90] In the defence the Austrians had expended 59 howitzer shells, 14,293 mortar bombs, 6,235 pierrier loads of stones and balls, 85,858 roundshot and 3,489 rounds of canister.[91]

GL. Tauentzien, who commanded the siege, was renowned for his hard-headedness even among the Prussian generals, but he was plainly embarrassed to discover in Frederick not an ounce of consideration towards the gallant defenders. Prince Albert of Sachsen-Teschen observed that 'it seems that the king of Prussia was annoyed by the long term of the resistance, and failed to treat Guasco and the other officers with the distinction which their conduct ought to have earned from a generous enemy who could recognise merit when he saw it. He consigned them all to East Prussia, while most of the soldiers were forced to take service with him and distributed among his regiments.'[92]

Only for the private instruction of the incoming Prussian commandant did Frederick uphold the defence as 'a model and example of prudence, courage and vigilance.'[93]

Almost immediately after the fall of Schweidnitz the king's army took refuge in cantonments, and the Austrians soon followed, which put an end to the contest in Silesia. Daun had already written to Maria Theresa 'I fail to see how Your Majesty can continue the war. With matters as they are, there is much reason to fear that the army will not even be able to survive the winter.'[94]

The honour of the campaign in Silesia had resided in the garrison of Schweidnitz. The balance of the war even now hung on events in Saxony, where the Austrians were quite unexpectedly turning affairs to their advantage.

Hadik in Saxony and the Battle of Freiberg, September-November 1762

Hadik's triumphs

On 28 August *GdC.* Andreas Hadik, up to now in charge of the left wing of Daun's army, learned that Maria Theresa desired him to replace *FM.* Serbelloni in Saxony. Daun wrote to him to register his congratulations, and to assure him 'that I associate myself fully with whatever promotes your interests and gives you some pleasure.'[95] He did not envy Hadik his new responsibilities. Prince Henry of Prussia

Hadik's offensive in Saxony, September - October 1762

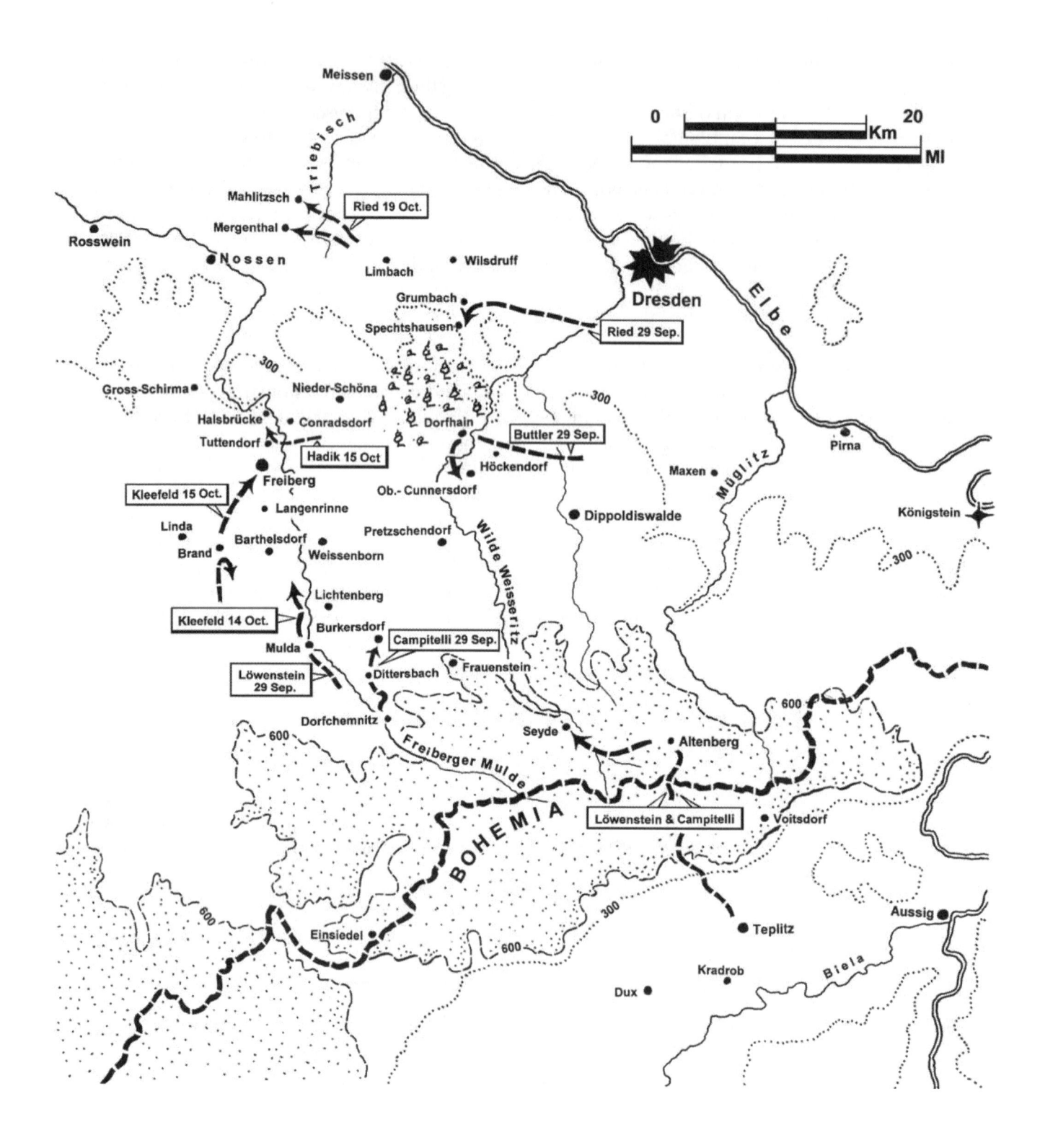

had only about 33,000 under his command in Saxony, but he had pushed back the 60,000 *Reichstruppen* and Austrians so hard that the *Reichsarmee* for a time had recoiled into Franconia, and the Austrians were scarcely clinging onto Dresden and the foothills of the Erz-Gebirge to the west.

Montazet saw Hadik in conversation with Daun on the eve of his departure for Saxony, and wondered 'what Hadik will be able to do, apart from holding out in the prison which has been prepared for him.'[96] The Prussian lieutenant general Hülsen was at Wilsdruff, confronting the Austrians just to the west of Dresden, while Prince Henry's main force was established at Pretzschendorf, from where he could raid almost at will into Bohemia and Franconia. The instructions which came to Hadik from Vienna were less than inspiring, for they asked him to do little more than cover the borders with Bohemia and the *Reich*, and safeguard the Polish-Saxon royal family, which insisted on residing in the exposed city of Dresden.

Hadik reached Dresden on 7 September. On the evening of the following day he learned from the *Hofkriegsrath* that the command in Saxony was to be divided (an ultimately fatal measure). His control was limited to the main body of the Austrian troops in Saxony, and the *Reichsarmee* and the supporting Austrian hussars and Croats were to be under the orders of the *Reichsgeneralfeldzeugmeister* Christian Carl Prince of Stolberg-Gedern, who was physically brave and commendably enthusiastic, although lacking in the experience required for independent command. Although he was only thirty-seven (young for such a post), his health had already been undermined by high living in his earlier years.

Hadik and Stolberg waited on Serbelloni at nine in the morning of 9 September. The field marshal took Hadik to task for having failed to pay his respects on the previous night, and accused him of wanting to bundle him off. Serbelloni added that he was not the kind of man to be hurried, and that he would leave in his own good time. Hadik replied that he had not been in a presentable state to see him, for his baggage had still to arrive, 'and no coach was as yet available, and I could not very well have run on foot from the Altstadt to the Neustadt.'[97] On the next day Hadik and Stolberg learned to their astonishment that Serbelloni had already departed.

Serbelloni had left Hadik no indication whatsoever of what forces were at his disposal or where they were deployed. Hadik had to find out everything for himself, and he undertook a tour of inspection which showed him that in general the Prussian positions faced to the east, and those of the *Reichsarmee* and the Austrians to the west.

Hadik resolved to do a good deal more than what had been expected of him, which had been just to hold his ground. On 21 September he forwarded his plans for an offensive on a broad front. He had explained his scheme to his senior generals; Serbelloni had never drawn them into his confidence in this way, and they now responded well. His communication to the *Hofkriegsrath* emphasised the technical details of the plan.[98] To Maria Theresa he wrote how his *General Disposition* was 'an absolute guarantee of success, for I will manoeuvre to bring the superiority of our arms to bear at the points where it matters. The troops, moreover, are fired with enthusiasm, so that, humanly speaking, we have the best grounds for optimism.'[99] Not since the days of *FM.* Browne had Vienna heard such positive language from a commander in the field.

The operation of 27-29 September 1762

Hadik's strategy was complicated in detail, but in essence he assigned *FZM.* Wied, *GFWM.* Ried and *FML.* Buttler the responsibility of fixing the enemy left and centre by feint attacks north of the Tharandter-Wald and the Wilde Weisseritz, while *GdC.* Löwenstein and *FML.* Campitelli unseated the Prussian right flank by sweeping along the southern Erz-Gebirge.

The Austrians marched on 27 September. Advancing by way of Teplitz and Altenberg, Löwenstein and Campitelli crossed the border ridge from Bohemia, compelled *GM.* Kleist to abandon his posts at Kortenstein and Seyde, and snapped up more than 300 prisoners. Hadik nevertheless feared that the advance in the south was losing momentum, and on 29 September he ordered the forces on the right and centre to

Andreas Count Hadik von Futak. Celebrated for his raid on Berlin in 1757. His successful offensives in Saxony in the late autumn of 1762 revived Austrian hopes even at this late stage of the war. (Military Academy, Wiener Neustadt)

renew their diversionary attacks with new vigour. Up in the north *GFWM*. Ried's Austrians assailed Hülsen's abattis and fortifications between Wilsdruff and the Tharandter-Wald, and evicted the Prussians from the **Lands-Berg**, between Hartha and Spechtshausen.

On the southern flank of the Tharandter-Wald a further Austrian detachment, under *FML*. Buttler, stormed across the Wilde-Weisseritz with altogether too much energy, and established a bridgehead at **Dorfhain** and by **Ober-Cunnersdorf** which in its turn came under a powerful Prussian counterattack. Hadik insisted that the troops must withdraw.

All of this activity had been staged for the benefit of Campitelli and Löwenstein, who were pressing against Prince Henry's extreme right flank, where the detachments of Seydlitz and Kleist were posted at **Dittersbach**, to the west of Frauenstein. The Prussians were dislodged by a violent cannonade, and Löwenstein on the Austrian left was able to reach the Freiberger Mulde and threaten the town of Freiberg itself. Campitelli on the Austrian right advanced to Burkersdorf, just to the north-west of Frauenstein.

The Austrian breakthrough had turned the entire Prussian position. Hadik was fully prepared to renew his offensive on 30 September, but in the course of the morning the enemy abandoned all their posts. Prince Henry fell back to a position just south of Freiberg, while the left wing under Hülsen retreated from Wilsdruff to the familiar camp of the Katzenhäuser behind the Triebisch.

In the fighting between 27 and 29 September the Austrian and Prussian losses had been of the same order, at about 1,000 each, and Hadik was disappointed that Löwenstein and Campitelli's haul of captured artillery amounted to only two 3-pounders. The Austrians had nevertheless turned the Prussians out of all their positions, and Campitelli made bold to congratulate Hadik on 'a masterpiece... in which harmony, courage and firmness were marching in step.'[100]

The operation of 14-15 October 1762

On 6 October Hadik wrote to Daun that 'just now I am directing all my efforts to devise further manoeuvres to force the enemy from Freiberg and thereabouts.'[101] He estimated that Prince Henry had a respectable force of 10,000 infantry there, but that the rest of his troops were strung out between there and the Elbe at Meissen (a distance of more than thirty miles).

Once again Hadik worked out an elaborate programme of diversions and concentrated attacks, this time with the Triebisch and the Freiberger Mulde standing in for the Wilde Weisseritz. The task of *FML*. Ried and the Austrian right wing was to fix Hülsen behind the Triebisch, while *FZM*. Maguire and *FML*. Buttler were to advance in force by way of Nieder-Schöna and Conradsdorf against the Mulde just below Freiberg, thus threatening the left wing of Henry's main concentration, and making him anxious for his communications with Hülsen. The Prince of Stolberg's *Reichsarmee* had played no active role in the first operation, but it was now moved from Pennrich, just outside Dresden, all the way to the left wing to form the bulk of the main striking force, which was to be directed against Henry's positions south of Freiberg. For this purpose Campitelli's corps of Austrians at Dorfchemnitz was placed under Stolberg's orders, which gave the prince a total of 20,000 troops.

The diversions and the attacks developed over two days, as had been the case with the earlier operation. Stolberg's advance was spearheaded by *GFWM*. Kleefeld with a mixed advance guard of Austrians and *Reichstruppen* (Austrians: one battalion of the regiment of Salm [14], a party of Banal Croats and the Baranyay Hussars [H30]; *Reichstruppen*: two battalions of Chur-Mainz, and the regiment of Chur-Mainz Dragoons). On 14 October Kleefeld pushed the corps of Belling from Mönchenfrey to the heights of Erbisdorf, but the Prussians rebounded with such force that Kleefeld had to retreat in order not to be cut off.

On 15 October Hadik came in person to supervise the important diversionary attack just north of Freiberg. From the church tower of Conradsdorf he directed the artillery as it laid down a heavy bombardment of the left wing of Henry's army on the heights of Tuttendorf. Austrian volunteers and grenadiers then swarmed across the Mulde and gained the church in Tuttendorf village. Just to the left,

FREIBERG OVERALL, 29 OCTOBER 1762

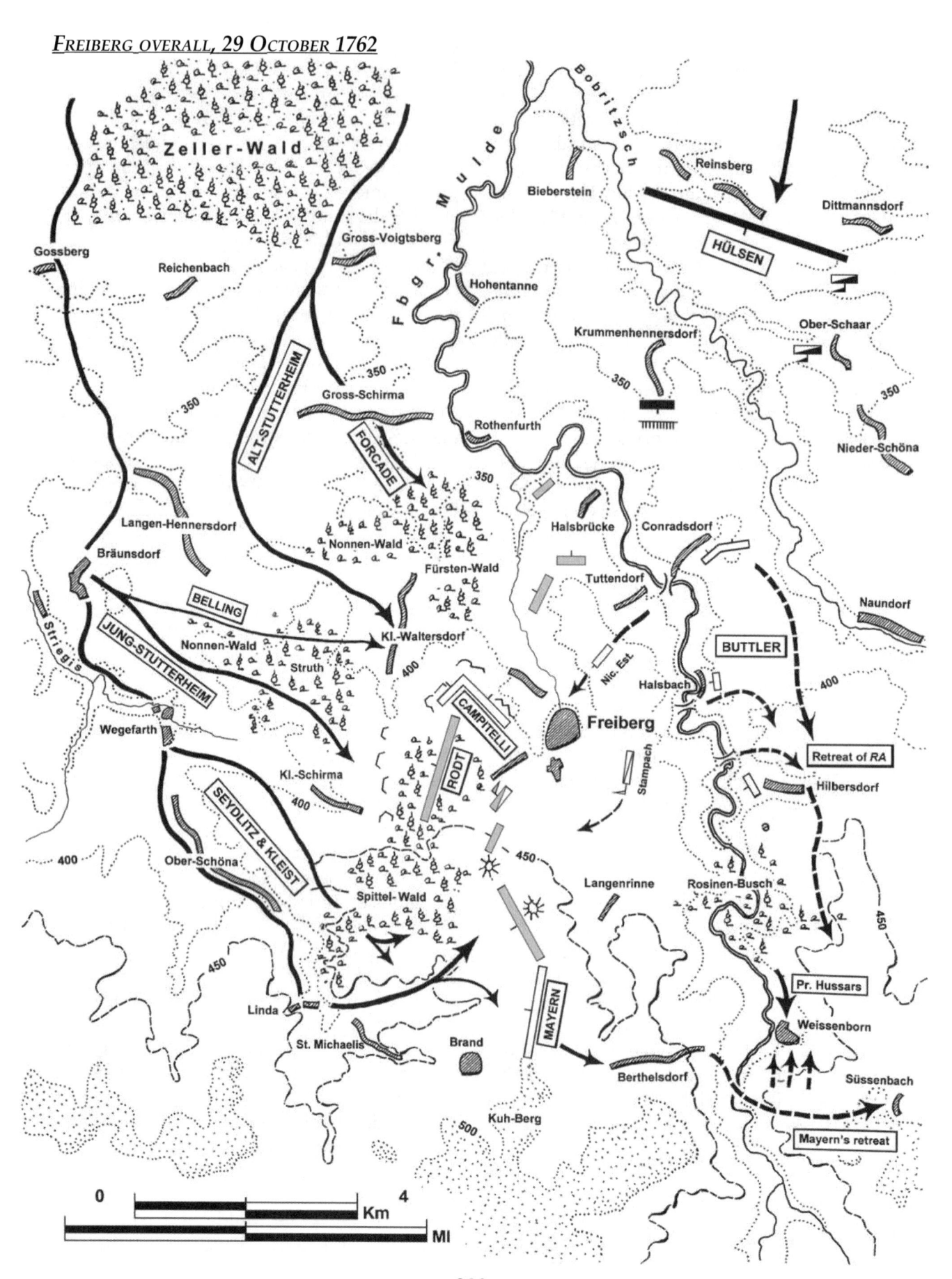

380

GFWM. Luzinsky cannonaded the heights of Weissenborn, which was a particularly useful demonstration as it fixed considerable enemy forces on this side of Erbisdorf.

With this indirect help, Stolberg and Campitelli renewed their attack to the south of Freiberg. Kleefeld was again in the lead, now with the benefit of hard-won knowledge of the ground, and this time the Prussian defence went to pieces amid very atypical confusion.

Prince Henry saw that the Austrians had broken open his right flank, which rendered his position as a whole untenable. Overnight his troops abandoned Freiberg and fell back north to Reichenbach and Gross-Voigtsberg just in front of the Zeller-Wald. The Prussians had been beaten out of their positions, not just out-manoeuvred, and over the two days they had lost ten pieces and more than 2,000 officers and men. Of these, nine cannon and 1,637 officers and men had been lost on the 15th, nearly all of them in the fighting around Freiberg. Hülsen had never come under serious attack, but Henry had been thrown from his positions at Freiberg and the Austrians and the *Reichsarmee* were now masters of the whole of all the northern foothills of the Erz-Gebirge.

Prince Henry plans a revenge, 16-28 October 1762

With the Prussians swept out of immediate contention, the Austrians and the *Reichstruppen* could begin to seek shelter in the little villages. The main forces of the Austrians were to be found in the camps of Wilsdruff and Plauen towards the Elbe, while Stolberg's *Reichsarmee* and the attached Austrians were arranged in the vicinity of Freiberg to the west.

For Stolberg's comfort Hadik wrote to him on 18 October that the Prussians were incapable of undertaking anything beyond reconnaissances in force, 'for now that Prince Henry has been beaten from his position at Freiberg with such heavy loss, and the weather is now so adverse, and the roads so bad, it will be absolutely impossible for him to turn his corps once more around through the Zeller-Wald, and have any intention of attacking the corps under your command.'[102] As further reassurance, Hadik assigned *FML.* Buttler with an initial six battalions, six grenadier companies and the de Ville Cuirassiers to guard the communication between the two blocs of forces, namely the *Reichsarmee* to the west at Freiberg and the Austrians towards Dresden in the east. A further consignment of Austrians (*FML.* Mayern with the two regiments of infantry, and *FML.* Lanthieri with the Stampach Cuirassiers [C10] and two regiments of Saxon chevaulegers) were put at Stolberg's immediate disposal.

Stolberg was anxious lest Hadik should think he was taking fright too easily, and he wrote to him on 22 October that he was establishing himself firmly at Freiberg, 'as I made a good start two days ago on re-fortifying the present camp, and I hope to be finished within a few days. We will then be in a position to offer an excellent defence.'[103] He wrote again on the 24th, and could not longer conceal his anxiety that Prince Henry might receive reinforcements from Silesia and drive him from his position, but Hadik believed that it was neither possible nor necessary to weaken himself any further for the benefit of the *Reichsarmee*.

The campaign in Silesia was at an end, indeed the war in that part of the world was effectively over, and both parties had forces at their disposal to feed to the Saxon theatre of operations. On the Prussian side 20,000 troops came together at Görlitz on 23 September under the command of *GL.* Neuwied and were poised to march to the Elbe, and three days later we find Hadik suddenly writing in all directions in a state of some alarm. He had received accurate information as to the daunting size of the Prussian force, while nearer at hand in Saxony the Prussians were rounding up horses and bringing up artillery and ammunition from Wittenberg, and they had put off the usual winter truce 'evidently because the reinforcement is on its way and will be joining them shortly… all of this gives good reason to suppose that the enemy could undertake an operation of some weight, either against Freiberg, or even against our army and Dresden itself.'[104]

Hadik's choice of words is significant, for he was still uncertain as to where the danger might present itself. There was good reason to believe that the great Prussian reinforcement might arrive on the far bank of the Elbe somewhere just upstream of Dresden, which would threaten his deep right flank. Frederick in fact intended something of the sort, and there was no obvious reason to suppose that Henry, as he actually did, would divert the march on his own authority towards Meissen, well downstream. It must have seemed totally impossible to Hadik that Henry would move before this extremely powerful reinforcement reached him.

The equivalent Austrian reinforcements were commanded by Prince Albert of Sachsen-Teschen, who was not only extremely well connected (being a scion of the Polish-Saxon royal house, and already enamoured of Maria Theresa's favourite daughter, Marie Christine) but an intelligent and active soldier. He had been encamped with a respectable little corps of about 13,000 troops just inside Bohemia at Trautenau, and could have intervened in a very useful way, but his mission was plagued from the start by ambiguous instructions from Daun. The field marshal whisked away more than half his force to meet an imagined threat to Austrian Silesia, and so Albert set out on 18 October with only about 6,000 men. He marched initially along the Bohemian side of the border mountains and hills, then crossed through the ice and snow and emerged into the northern plain on the 24th. Little could be discovered about the whereabouts of the enemy, for the Prussian hussars had an total superiority (a problem familiar to the Austrians at this stage of the war), and Daun repeatedly urged Albert to have an eye to the security of Bohemia, yet he had assigned him to the orders of Hadik, who was now urging him to hurry to the Saxon Elbe near Dresden.

Responding to Hadik's pleas, Albert marched by way of Stolpen to Weissig, on the heights above the Elbe, where his corps arrived on the night of 27/28 October. On the way Albert had turned aside for a few moments to the castle of Stolpen to pay his respects to Countess Mosel, who had been imprisoned there on the orders of her former lover, Albert's grandfather King Augustus II 'The Strong' of Poland-Saxony. She had decided to stay in the castle, even after she had been given her liberty by the new king. 'I found her in a chamber inside one of the round towers of the castle. She was immersed in a military book in folio, Flemming's *Der Vollkommene Teutsche Soldat*. Although she was already eighty, she had a flawlessly white complexion, and her fine dark eyes sparkled with a peculiar fire. She had converted to Judaism, and told me that while she was in prison she had made a study of the various religions, and found this to be the best.'[105]

The 29 October Albert heard sounds of distant artillery fire, carrying from somewhere far to the west. It became too persistent and heavy to be mistaken for anything but a battle, which seemed incomprehensible, for the Prussian reinforcements from Silesia could not possibly have reached Henry, and yet the prince would have been unlikely to have gone into action without them.

Vienna was meanwhile awakening to the magnitude of what Hadik had achieved in his recent operations, just when those gains happened to be most at risk. Kaunitz saw in him a leader of the stamp of Browne or Loudon, and wrote to Hadik that he had not had the honour of meeting him in person. 'In these circumstances I am sure Your Excellency will excuse me if I judge only according to deeds, and more specifically by the planning and conduct of your attack on the enemy, which I regard as a masterpiece of the art of war.'[106]

Prince Henry did not give Hadik the opportunity to savour his glory. Henry, a notoriously systematic and cautious general, was expected to wait for those 20,000 troops under Neuwied to come to him across the Elbe before he embarked on anything so inherently risky as a battle. Instead he defied every reasonable calculation by going over to the attack before he was reinforced.

The body which Henry devoted to his assault was the right wing of his army, or less than 22,000 troops, which comprised an unusually high proportion of light and medium cavalry, and the disreputable men of the free battalions (Frederick hoarded the best troops for himself). The left wing (10,483 men) under *GL*. Hülsen moved up the Triebisch to keep the Austrian intermediate corps under Buttler in awe, and they were to have an important diversionary role, but they were not committed to the main attack. Neuwied was still beyond reach on the far side of the Elbe, and did not cross until the 31st.

The *Reichstruppen* and the Austrians were now the ones who were scattered over the tract of ground between the Elbe and the Freiberger Mulde. The Austrian main force was still held by Hadik in front of Dresden, with *FZM*. Maguire extending his left wing along the Wilde Weisseritz. *FML*. Buttler had the important brief to cover the interval between the two armies (Hadik's and Stolberg's). His force amounted to about 8,000 men, and was made up of eight battalions of regular infantry, twenty-four squadrons and one carabinier company and thirty-four pieces of artillery.

Stolberg's army extended for more than five miles in a bulge to the north-west and west of Freiberg. The rear was covered by the valley of the Mulde, though that obstacle might become a death-trap if Stolberg were forced to retreat in a hurry. The battlefront occupied a broken country of hills, woods and patches of open ground. Major Johann Tobias Seeger of the Austrian General Staff had toured the area with Stolberg, and advised him to hold in strength the outlying woodlands of the Füsten-Wald, the Nonnen-Wald and the Struth, as had been done in 1761, when the Prussians had been deterred from creeping around to the south of the army. He showed the prince the route which the enemy had taken from Ober-Schöna to Linda, and tried to persuade him that they could be stopped again, 'whereupon His Highness was gracious enough to comment that the ground to be occupied would be very extensive, and impossible to hold. I did not contradict him, but hoped that my silence would dissuade him from a major engagement. His Highness had never spoken to me of giving battle, but only to await the enemy, and act according to circumstances.'[107] In the eight days which supervened before the battle only 600 of the 3,000 conscripted labourers turned up, and the fifty regimental pioneers (*Zimmerleuthe*) of the army were not nearly enough to do all the work, and so the work of preparing the existing position was far from complete when the action opened on 29 October.

In the deployment adopted by Stolberg, the greater part of the right wing was formed by *FML*. Campitelli's Austrians, who held the most intact sectors of the earthworks, which extended in a hairpin conformation along the heights above the hollow of Klein-Waltersdorf. Campitelli was under Stolberg's direct orders, and his troops could be considered a tactical part of the *Reichsarmee*.

FML. Rodt's division of the *Reichsarmee* occupied the west-facing centre of the position, where the available defences consisted of a redan between Klein-Waltersdorf and the northern end of the extensive Spittel-Wald, and an incomplete abattis which ran some way through the wood in a southerly direction.

FML. Mayern's corps of Austrians supplied the left wing, which extended from the southern flank of the *Reichsarmee* to the Kuh-Berg near Brand. Mayern had arrived as a recent reinforcement, and he seems to have retained a considerable freedom of action.

Henry's plan was for a fluid 'Hochkirch'-style battle, typical of the later stages of this war. He intended to fix the enemy right wing and centre by a programme of demonstrations and probes, while his main striking force marched across the front of the hostile army as far south as Linda and St. Michaelis, where the Spittel-Wald gave out, from where it was to wheel to its left to reach the more open ground behind the forest, thereby unseating the enemy position from its deep left flank. Prince Henry had rightly supposed the defences, such as they were, to be strongest on the northern sector, but he was unaware of the existence of the corps of Mayern, for it was tucked away to the S.S.E. of the Spittel-Wald.

At 10.30 in the night of 28/29 October Stolberg learned that the Prussians had withdrawn their outposts from Hohentanne and Bieberstein to the left (west) bank of the Mulde, and concluded correctly that the enemy were intending to attack him on the near side. He put his outposts on the alert, and, at least by his account, he ordered Buttler to come from the far right and fall on the enemy flank and rear, and, if necessary, bring the whole of his corps across the Mulde and come to his support. 'At three in the morning,' writes Stolberg, 'an enemy

FREIBERG, THE BATTLE OF THE WOODS

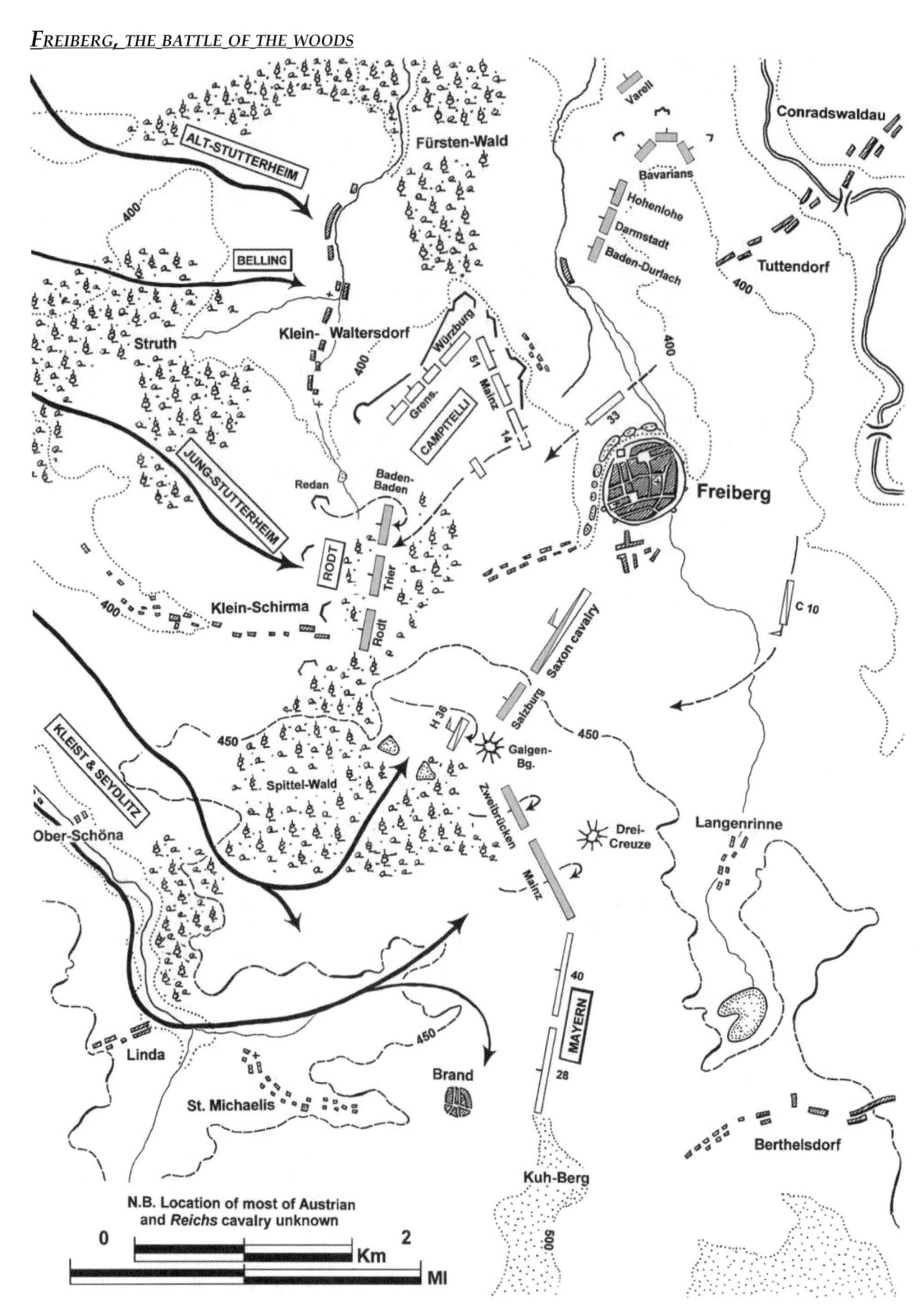

deserter [a Kleist Dragoon] arrived, and said that the entire enemy army had set out at five in the afternoon from its camp behind the Zeller-Wald, passed through the wood, and was now in the process of forming up in battle order on the near side. He added that on the day before Prince Henry had drawn to himself a great number of troops, mainly cavalry, from the Katzenhäuser camp. This was confirmed to be at the same time by a spy. I therefore touched off the three agreed alarm shots, and my army took up arms.'[108]

Freiberg, 29 October 1762

a) *Reichsarmee* and Austrians
Total: c. 27,000; *Reichsarmee* and Campitelli's Austrians c. 21,000; Mayern's Austrians c. 4,000; Buttler's Austrians c 2,000 in action (out of his total c. 8,000)
Losses: unknown (see text below)
b) Prussians
c. 22,000, including Forcade's 3,051 from the left wing of the army. But c. 30,000 counting the support from the rest of the left wing
Losses: c, 1,400; c. 400 killed, c. 1,000 wounded and missing

The diversionary attacks of lieutenant generals Hülsen and Forcade

The two columns of Hülsen consisted of the left wing of the Prussian army, or 10,483 troops, which moved bodily from the camp of the Katzenhäuser on the Triebisch, as if to attack the vital crossings of the Mulde and the Bobritzsch behind the enemy position at Freiberg. Hülsen established his main force between Reinsberg and Dittmannsdorf, and sent parties towards the crossings. Buttler identified a body of infantry and up to eighteen cannon at Krummenhennersdorf, four squadrons towards Ober-Schaar, and up to twelve troops of horse between there and Dittmannsdorf.

On the western side of the Mulde the 3,051 troops of *GL.* Forcade now formed tactically the fourth column of Prince Henry's wing, and advanced by the same route as the third column (below) along the eastern side of the Zeller-Wald before it peeled off towards Gross-Schirma and the Fürsten-Wald. Forcade was to act as the left-hand pivot of Henry's attack, and otherwise 'must… stand motionless, while demonstrating as if to attack the enemy.'[109] He nevertheless got entangled with Campitelli's outposts in the Fürsten-Wald, and the Prussians were 'driven back by our troops, in which Captain Prince Salm of the infantry regiment of Salm [14] did particularly well.'[110]

By themselves Hülsen's troops remaining to the east of the Mulde still had a considerable numerical advantage over Buttler, whose basic task was still to cover the right flank and rear of the army, and its communication with Hadik. He had therefore considered it vital to hold the corridor of land which extended behind Freiberg between the Bobritzsch stream and the Mulde, and to this effect he posted forces to the east of the narrow and winding valley of the Bobritzsch, and east of the Mulde at the vital crossings at Conradsdorf, Halsbach and Hilbersdorf close behind Freiberg.

After the battle Stolberg nevertheless charged Buttler with having failed to fall on the flank and rear of the advancing Prussians, and also with not rendering him direct support. Buttler answered the first accusation by pointing out that it would have taken him a good five hours to arrive at an attacking position, and that Hülsen's corps would have been delighted to have allowed him to cross to the west bank of the Mulde, and then shut the passages in his rear. On the question of the reinforcements, Buttler replied that the only unit in a position to make a night crossing of the Bobritzsch was the regiment of Nicolaus Esterházy [33], which he duly sent across the stream, followed by the regiment of the Saxon Carabiniers Gardes. He himself brought the regiments of Arenberg [21] and O'Kelly [45] across the Bobritzsch at 8.30, but a message from Stolberg told him that he was satisfied with the reinforcements already sent.[111] By then the battle had been developing fast.

The pinning attacks: columns of the major generals Alt-Stutterheim and Jung-Stutterheim

The Prussian brothers Stutterheim, senior and junior, had the initial task of fixing the enemy right wing and centre by preliminary attacks on Klein-Waltersdorf and the northern part of the Spittel-Wald. When, however, the great outflanking movement of the main force was rolling up the hostile army from the south, they were to crash through the defences in all-out assaults.

GM. Alt-Stutterheim commanded the 3,614 troops of the third column, and 'takes with him the four heavy cannon which are drawn by the best teams.'[112] He was supported by *GM.* Belling's detachment of 1,593 grenadiers, cuirassiers, hussars and men of the free battalions.

FML. Campitelli's Austrians and the combined auxiliary regiment of Würzburg were holding the nearly continuous earthworks above Klein-Waltersdorf. *FML.* Rodt of the *Reichsarmee* positioned the Swabian *Creis* regiment of Baden-Baden in the unfinished redan by the north-west angle of the Spittel-Wald, with the regiments of Chur-Trier and Rodt (Swabian) defending the abattis which extended into that forest on the left.

Details of Alt-Stutterheim's attack, like the deployment of the *Reichstruppen* as a whole, are decidedly sketchy, but it appears that the Prussians were content to drive back the enemy outposts, and thereby gain the space for their heavy cannon to deploy and open fire on Klein-Waltersdorf and the nearby defences.

The second column was a more weighty affair of 4,372 troops. Advancing to the right of his elder brother, Jung-Stutterheim approached the Spittel-Wald on the sector between the redan and a track which traversed the forest on its way from Klein-Schirma to Freiberg. For the time being Jung-Stutterheim probably intended to do no more than probe the woods by 300 volunteers under Captain Georg Dietrich Pfuhl. The combat, as elsewhere, developed from eight in the morning, but here assumed an altogether larger dimension than had been foreseen in the plan. *FML.* Rodt's *Reichstruppen* fought back unexpectedly hard, and Jung-Stutterheim had to bring up reinforcements to evict the *Reichs* regiment of Baden-Baden from the redan. The dislodged troops fell back to the regiments of Trier and Rodt, and the three regiments held the

Freiberg, The Spittel-Wald from the south-east. The ground to the front was the scene of the bitter struggle to prevent the Prussians from breaking out of the wood.

abattis until the Prussians, who were being constantly reinforced, drove them back. The defenders were now bolstered in their turn by a battalion of the Austrian regiment of Salm [14], which came up on the right of Trier, and by Prince Stolberg in person who brought a battalion of *Reichs* grenadiers against the enemy right flank, and led a general counterattack, pistol in hand. This action, probably the finest of the *Reichsarmee* in the whole of the war, ended with the Prussians being forced from the wood and all the way back to Klein-Schirma.

The flanking attack: column of *GL*. Seydlitz and *GM*. Kleist

All the demonstrations and lunges so far described had been arranged for the benefit of the first column (9,156 troops), which was directed by the well-tried team of Seydlitz and Kleist and accompanied by Prince Henry in person. The column executed a long trek of a dozen miles, which took it from Marbach, then to the west of the Zeller-Wald, the Struth wood and Klein-Schirma, and finally across the ravine at Linda to reach its attacking position at St. Michaelis and the southern end of the Spittel-Wald. The only encounter along the way had been at seven in the morning, when Kleist and his mixed advance guard drove the Austrian Palatinal Hussars [H36] of Colonel Török from Klein-Schirma.

When the leading troops rounded the southern tip of the Spittel-Wald by St. Michaelis they discovered the Austrian corps of *FML*. Mayern extending across the open ground as far as the Kuh-Berg near Brand. It was a terrible surprise, and a legend, transmitted by the historians, has Mayern already fallen back on the Kuh-Berg, and Prince Henry hesitating to wheel into the gap which had thus been opened between that hill and the Spittel-Wald. Kleist is supposed to have assured Henry that he knew Mayern's character, and that there was nothing to fear. Mayern obligingly allowed himself to be contained by a few battalions and squadrons standing by St. Michaelis, while Prince Henry recovered his confidence and swung through the gap to take the enemy forces in the rear.[113]

In fact the celebrated gap opened only towards the end of the battle, and the Prussian advance was stalled for a considerable time by Mayern's troops at the southern end of the Spittel-Wald. The credit was largely due to Major Seeger of the Austrian staff, who had seen the Prussian column on its way to Linda and St. Michaelis, and at once sent word to Stolberg and Mayern. For one and a half hours Seeger held the end of the wood with one battalion each of the regiments of Chur-Mainz and Wied [28], four squadrons of the Saxon chevaulegers (from the regiments of Curland and Brühl), and Török's Palatinal Hussars, who had retreated through the wood from Klein-Schirma. Forced at last from the Spittel-Wald, the mixed force found the Austrian Zweibrücken Dragoons [D39] standing by the Roter Vorwerk with two 3-pounder cannon and two 6-pounders, and for a time Seeger was able to prevent the Prussians from emerging from the trees.

A prolonged and confused struggle ensued in the open ground behind the forest. In outline, five battalions of Prussian grenadiers now advanced generally north-east against the Drei-Kreuze Hill, with supporting forces (mainly cavalry) extending on either side. Stolberg summoned up all the available cavalry, and testifies that *GM*. Tresckow (not to be confused with the Prussian general of the same name) did wonders with the under-strength *Reichs* Bayreuth Cuirassiers, 'which hewed into the enemy cavalry, put it to total flight, made many prisoners and then re-formed by squadrons thirty paces from the wood to cover my flank; the two squadrons of the Hohenzollern Regiment [of Cuirassiers] had come up to hack into the rear of the same enemy cavalry, and likewise re-formed.'[114]

In contrast some of the Austrian cavalry was performing below its best, and the Batthyány Dragoons [D7] were forced from the Galgen-Berg. Only now did Mayern extract some of his forces (three battalions of infantry, the Zweibrücken Dragoons [D39] and the Stampach Cuirassiers [C10]) from the combat,[115] and concentrated them on the Kuh-Berg to the south. That was when the famous 'gap' came into being.

With fewer and fewer forces opposing them on this sector, the Prussian cavalry proceeded to drive into the backs of the troops still trying to bottle up the Prussian infantry in the Spittel-Wald. Something of the honour of Austrian arms was restored by *GFWM*. Vecsey with the Dessewffy and Baranyay Hussars [Hs 34, 30], which together amounted to scarcely 700 men. He regained the Galgen-Berg by a counterattack, and 'this... unexpected shock, which cost us 80 men, checked the fury of the pursuit for a few moments... and enabled a number of detachments of our horse and foot, which had been surrounded by the enemy, to escape the otherwise inevitable fate of being taken prisoner.'[116]

Breakthrough and exploitation

On the southern sector of the field the now uncontained Prussian infantry burst out of the Spittel-Wald. The grenadiers pushed beyond the Drei-Kreuze Hill, while Seydlitz and Kleist led the cavalry in a chase towards Freiberg. Stolberg explained afterwards that 'most of the pieces of artillery stuck fast in the marshy hollow of the Freiberg suburbs, on account of the poor quality of their teams. If I had really wanted to, I could still have saved some of them by occupying the suburb by infantry, but I preferred to abandon twenty cannons rather than see it burn down. As it turned out, not a single house was destroyed, even through there was heavy and sustained firing all around Freiberg.'[117]

Further north the brothers Stutterheim renewed their attacks, this time bent on effecting a total breakthrough. Alt-Stutterheim sent the grenadier battalion of Lossow and the free battalions of Le Noble and Schach to clear the low-lying village of Klein-Waltersdorf. He then took the earthwork on the hill behind by an enveloping attack, the regiment of Bevern [7] advancing from the south, while the Belling Hussars [H9] and the Schmettau Cuirassiers [C4] closed in from the north. The blow was delivered between ten and eleven in the morning, and with such energy 'that he, General

Freiberg, The ascent to the east of Klein-Waltersdorf. The earthworks defended by the Reichstruppen *and the Austrians extended across the axis of the road.*

Stutterheim himself, was the first to reach the fortification, and severed the hand of an enemy gunner who was about to touch off a cannon. Upon this our grenadiers and further battalions at once threw the enemy line into disorder, and captured all the cannon of their right wing.'[118]

Jung-Stutterheim had hesitated to renew his assault, after his heavy repulse earlier in the morning. He drew fresh courage from the success of his brother on the left, and some inspiring words from Captain Kalckreuth, who came to him with a message from Prince Henry. Jung-Stutterheim now went over to the attack, broke through the abattis and gained the open ground beyond the wood, which brought him close to Freiberg.

The battle as a contest was over by about eleven in the morning. The Hungarian infantry regiment of Nicolaus Esterházy [33], dispatched by Buttler as a reinforcement, arrived to find itself among fugitives, and shared the fate of the abandoned Austrians and *Reichsarmee* infantry. Stolberg's army as a whole was now in an extraordinarily dangerous situation, for the enemy had broken in from both the south and the west, and the only path of retreat would have to describe a vulnerable right angle—first across the Mulde to the north-east and east of Freiberg, and then turning south-east to the next tenable position at Frauenstein ten miles away.

By 12.30 in the afternoon Stolberg had collected his forces in some kind of order at Tuttendorf, and began to send them to the crossings of the Mulde at Conradsdorf, Hasbach and Hilbersdorf. More than 13,500 Prussian troops were poised within striking distance, but Hülsen and Forcade did not think to exceed their orders, and Buttler had made elaborate provision to hold all the approaches and crossings. His artillery now covered the passage of the beaten troops, and his detachments guarded the crossings until all the fugitives were safely across. It took a direct order from Buttler to make Captain Monier of the regiment of O'Kelly [45] fall back from his exposed post at Hilbersdorf. Afterwards the senior officers of the corps testified that 'the dispositions made by *FML*. Buttler were the salvation of the *Reichsarmee*, otherwise few of its troops could have ever passed the Mulde.'[119]

Stolberg had sent an officer to Mayern to tell him that he should now do 'what he thought best.'[120] Mayern's path of retreat lay initially to the east. He had restored his troops to good order, but Prussian hussars had penetrated as far as Weissenborn, and he had to hold them off by parties of infantry until he could reach Süssenbach and regain contact with Stolberg. The joint force retreated overnight by way of Burkersdorf on Frauenstein, with Stolberg's corps forming the rearguard.

Verdicts

The highest Prussian estimate of the losses of the *Reichsarmee* and the Austrians approaches 7,000 men. An official Austrians list puts it at 3,081.[121] On 31 October Stolberg estimated 2,000 at the least, but short of 3,000. By 8 November he concluded that he had exaggerated, 'since many of the missing troops have already found their way back again.'[122] In any event the heaviest losses were undoubtedly incurred by the hard-fighting *Reichs* regiments of Baden-Baden, Trier and Rodt, and by the Austrian regiments of Wied, Gyulai and Nicolaus Esterházy [28, 51, 33], the Esterházy regiment having lost 729 men and been almost wiped out.

When we look at Freiberg as a battle gained, it is clear that Prince Henry had attained his victory by going over to the offensive when it was least expected, by the excellent staff work (and some improvisations) which got the separate columns into their attacking positions, and by the weighting of force towards the right which finally overcame the obstinate resistance in the southern part of the Spittel-Wald.

With the exception of some of the Austrian cavalry regiments, all the units of Stolberg's army had fought well, and some regiments of the *Reichsarmee* remarkably so. Stolberg had been up with the action, and he was able to assure Daun that the entire infantry of the Austrians and the *Reich* behaved with 'true heroism.'[123]

In his reports Stolberg mentioned without comment how the withdrawal of Mayern had created a gap on his left flank. The prince reserved his venom for Buttler, against whom he lodged a written complaint. The accusations lose their force when we take into account the presence of Hülsen and Forcade, of which Stolberg was scarcely aware, but the Viennese public judged Buttler harshly, and Maria Theresa asked Hadik to look into the matter. A little later the Empress wrote to Hadik that there was no point in pursuing the charges, for 'in such cases each puts the blame on the other, and both are usually in the wrong.'[124]

Wise words also come from the attaché Marainville, who believed that the fundamental cause for the defeat was the divided command which Vienna, for political reasons, had imposed on the forces in Saxony: 'I will in no way criticise the goodwill of the Prince of Stolberg, or his activity, but I must say that to command an army requires more service and experience than was at his disposal. He was made major general only at the beginning of this war, and before that he had served only in Holland. Since then he has always been assigned to the *Reichsarmee*, where there was not very much for his instruction. He was therefore in no state to give battle against 30,000 men, on an extensive battlefield where the ground was cut up by woods which helped the enemy to conceal their movements. If Hadik had been in command of the two armies, he would surely have placed himself at Freiberg as the key... but this general could hardly have betaken himself there without offending the Prince of Stolberg.'[125]

The 'when' and 'where' of the battle of Freiberg made it the most important encounter of the war between the Austrians and the Prussians. It came at a time when Maria Theresa had allowed herself to hope that the war could be revived with a good prospect of success, but now, according to Kaunitz, 'it seems to me that we ought to take prudent measures to hastened the process of peace.' Maria Theresa had to agree, and added that her young son Joseph was of the same mind.[126]

After Freiberg

Peace on remotely tolerable terms depended on retaining the corner of Saxony around Dresden, for otherwise the Prussians would hold the entire electorate to ransom in the negotiations. On 31 October *GL*. Neuwied crossed the Elbe at Merschwitz with the 20,000 reinforcements from Silesia, and Prince Henry now had the means of carrying the war into Bohemia as well as penning up the *Reichsarmee* and the Austrians towards the Erz-Gebirge and Dresden. At that time Hadik's main concentration of thirteen battalions was still in the camp of Plauen by the city, with Stolberg at Dippoldiswalde in the Erz-Gebirge, and *FZM*. Maguire strung out between the two along the Wilde Weisseritz.

The initiative lay entirely with the enemy. Between 3 and 7 November *GM*. Kleist raided north-west Bohemia in his accustomed style. The Prussians destroyed the magazine at Saaz, snapped up 500 troops in the rearward depots of the Austrian regiments, and thirty desperadoes under Cornet Stürtzenbecker even ranged as far as the White Mountain above Prague. Hadik was thankful to have saved his main magazine at Leitmeritz by bringing up *FML*. Martigny by forced marches from Reichenberg with two regiments of infantry and two of cavalry.

On 4 November Hadik was forced to report that the *Reichsarmee* had retreated from Frauenstein to Altenberg, close to the border ridge with Bohemia. The main Austrian concentrations were themselves under threat. On 7 November the reinforcements from Silesia made their presence felt when Neuwied advanced from the Katzenhäuser and fell on the detachment of Colonel Dönhoff on the **Lands-Berg** near Spechtshausen. The Austrians lost 509 men and four cannon, and the entire force would have been taken if *GFWM*. Amadei had not hastened to save them. This was the last action of note in Austria's war, and there was no possibility of taking a revenge, for 'reports say that the Katzenhäuser position is more strongly fortified than ever, and protected by an amazing palisade of 16,000 thirty- and eighteen-feet long stakes, taken from the Zeller-Wald. There are two rows, the outer row being made of the shorter stakes.'[127]

On the evening of 8 November 'a reliable man of substance'[128] got news to Hadik that Frederick had reached Meissen at eleven that morning, lunched there, and would be with

Henry the next day. The tidings made a great stir, because 'the enemy become uniquely formidable when the king is present, for he is absolutely despotic and merciless.'[129]

On 13 November all the infantry of the *Reichsarmee* and a number of the attached Austrians fell back into Bohemia and arrived at Teplitz on the next day. *FML.* Martigny covered the nearby border, and *FML.* Campitelli remained at Altenberg with eight battalions, two cavalry regiments and one regiment of hussars.

In its new position the *Reichsarmee* was now covering Hadik's communications with Bohemia. By the same token the *Reich* was left entirely without protection, and now became the target of the most significant Prussian raid of the war. On 17 November *GM.* Kleist struck from Chemnitz with 6,000 troops and invaded Franconia. On his destructive course he proceeded to exact contributions from Bamberg, Fürth, Erlangen, the Bishopric of Fulda and the Principality of Meiningen. He did not care to meet the contingents of Saxon troops which were returning from service with the French, and so he turned about with the great train of cash, hostages and plunder, and reached Leipzig by way of Erfurt on 8 December. The last shots of the Seven Years war on the continent of Europe were probably fired at this time, just as the first had been discharged at Stolpen. For the Germans, the perception of having been left in the lurch was compounded when, on 24 November, Hadik concluded a winter truce with the enemy. It covered the Austrians in Saxony, but made no provision for the *Reich*. Stolberg and his disillusioned officers were full of reproaches, and Hadik protested to them in vain that the Prussians were already well into Franconia by the time the deal was signed.

A few lines in a letter to Francis Stephen indicate that even at this last gasp of the war Hadik had been meditating a stroke which might yet have turned decisively to Austria's advantage. He had a spy in Frederick's entourage, who reported on the king's doings, and thereby opened the possibility of snatching him on his travels. 'I have had to give up all hope for the present time of carrying out the design,' wrote Hadik. 'The reason is that the king's route was changed. Otherwise everything was ready in the so called "Kehl-Busch" on the usual route to Leipzig. The detachment of hussars had been assigned, they had already passed the river, and they would have tried their luck.'[130]

IX

PEACE

Austria's position of diplomatic and military strength had deteriorated significantly over the summer of 1762. Sweden had made peace with the Prussians. Russia, from being the most potent of allies, had become an enemy, and then, under Empress Catherine, had taken up an equivocal neutrality. It was difficult to fathom the intentions of Turkey, and Kaunitz did not discount a new war in the east. The fleets of France and Spain could no longer contest the seas. Those two powers had failed in their invasion of Portugal, and they had seen Martinique, Havana and Manila fall to the British.

By 10 August Maria Theresa was casting about for ways to improve her admittedly poor negotiating position. It had been four years since France had rendered even indirect military help. Maria Theresa was resigned to the inevitability of peace between the Bourbons and the British, and retained a faint hope that the good offices of these powers might promote a tolerable settlement between Austria and Prussia. The issue at stake was 'whether on my side I can retain a substantial gain, like that of the County of Glatz, on account of its situation, or whether I must renounce all conquests and all compensations, whether for me or for Saxony. This last point is the stumbling block, and therefore to forward the process of peace, whether favourable or not, it is essential to bring on a decisive battle for the relief of Schweidnitz, and then waste no time in framing a decision according to the outcome ... as affairs stand at the moment I am unable to make such a resolution, and my peace with Prussia continues to depend on the questionable decisions of the French and British.'[1]

Daun's campaign ended with his army being thrown back to the hills and mountains and the Bohemian border, all his efforts to relieve Schweidnitz frustrated, and the fortress falling to the Prussians on 9 October.

This was the time when the dynamic leadership of Hadik brought altogether unexpected success to the operations of the *Reichsarmee* and the Austrians against Prince Henry. The result was a remarkable revival of confidence in Vienna, and on 27 October we find Maria Theresa writing to Hadik that she was re-building the army, and 'in order that it may appear in strength in the next campaign, not only have 40,000 recruits been enlisted, but every company of cuirassiers will be augmented by thirteen men, the infantry companies by another thirteen each, every regiment of dragoons brought up to its complete establishment, and every hussar regiment put on the strength of 1,200 men. Such a mighty augmentation of my armed forces will naturally inspire the soldiers with new courage, and make its appropriate impact on my foreign friends and foes, which can only be to the good of my service.'[2]

On the 29th Prince Henry defeated the *Reichsarmee* and the supporting Austrians at Freiberg. The Prussians now had the upper hand in Saxony as well as in Silesia, and in her state of disillusion Maria Theresa agreed with Kaunitz on 3 November that they must think seriously about concluding peace.

On the same day the French and British signed preliminary terms, a happening which had long been foreseen in Vienna, and which opened even at this advanced stage the prospect of a new negotiating asset. The French had been acting technically as auxiliaries of Maria Theresa when they had conquered the Prussian Rhineland duchies of Cleve, Mark and Geldern, and Kaunitz now hoped that a timely occupation of these lands by Austrian, Saxon or Württemberg troops would allow Austria to 'inherit' those gains and add them to the other conquest which Austria still had to show, which was the County of Glatz. Most unfortunately such an operation would have required up to 10,000 troops, and the only forces within reach were the four or five thousand men in the Austrian Netherlands, and they could not move without leaving the Netherlands bare. The Prussians were likely to reach their duchies first, and in superior force, since they were gathering together the left-overs of the defunct war in western Germany, and from there they would be able to threaten the Netherlands. The prospect made Maria Theresa shudder, and in the event the Prussian colonel Bawr reached the duchies with 7,957 assorted troops before the end of the year.

Frederick was aware that the Austrians were also open to pressure regarding their sensitivities towards Saxony, for it was nominally on behalf of the electorate that Austria had opened the war. Frederick was the master of the greater part of Saxony, and he now intensified his oppressions to an unprecedented degree, to the point of threatening to devastate the royal forests, and deporting Saxon children to repopulate his states.

With their negotiating assets fast melting away, Kaunitz and Maria Theresa decided to make their first approaches to the enemy through the agency of the Saxons. Augustus III authorised his privy counsellor Karl Thomas Baron Fritsch to address himself to Frederick, nominally to protest at the maltreatment of Saxony, but really to communicate Maria Theresa's desire for a reasonable and fitting peace. Fritsch met the king at Meissen on 29 November, and found that Frederick (later the all-German hero) could not understand his proposals, because they were written in German. He had to make use of a précis in French, and, after having to endure the king's bitter and sarcastic comments, he found that he was open to the idea of negotiation.

The *Hofrat* Heinrich Gabriel Collenbach was nominated as Austria's representative in the tripartite talks, and after some uncertainties the royal Polish-Saxon hunting lodge of Hubertusburg was chosen as the site, 'as being approximately half way between the two headquarters.'[3] Collenbach was instructed to hold out for Austria's retaining the County of Glatz, while Frederick among other concessions was being asked to withdraw his troops from Saxony, guarantee Maria Theresa in possession of her states, and abandon the Hohenzollerns' claim to inherit Ansbach and Bayreuth after the current rulers died. These negotiating positions would in any event have been difficult to sustain, but Kaunitz, Maria Theresa and Collenbach would probably have held to them longer than they did if they had known that on 19 December Frederick received a frightening letter from Empress Catherine of Russia, reminding him that she had sacrificed her conquests for the sake of peace, but that she could have acted otherwise, and that she still had the power to do so.

The talks opened on 30 December, and extended through January 1763, being held up on the question of Glatz, and a number of complicated issues concerning contributions and compensations in Saxony. On 23 January the Prussian representative Hertzberg returned to the charge, and rejected outright Austria's offer to yield up part of Austrian Silesia in return for retaining the disputed county. Frederick was insisting that the Austrians could readily bar the passages from Glatz through the hills and mountains into Bohemia, whereas Glatz in Austrian hands would pose a constant threat to Silesia, and he was actually able to invoke the opinion of Daun in support of his contention. The military logic was questionable, and in any case Daun had no business to undermine Collenbach's negotiating stance in this way.

On 31 January 1763 Collenbach signified that Austria had abandoned its claim on Glatz. The one great obstacle to peace had been removed, and two days later Frederick wrote to Henry 'we are in agreement on everything. The treaty of peace will be signed next week, and put an end to this cruel war which has exacted such a heavy price in blood, anxiety and treasure.'[4]

The preliminaries of the Peace of Hubertusburg were signed on 15 February, and the terms were confirmed when the ratifications were exchanged on 1 March. The most important clauses stipulated that Maria Theresa was to recognise Frederick in possession of all his territories, including the County of Glatz, that Frederick would evacuate the electorate of Saxony, and that all payments due on the enforced military 'contributions' would be cancelled (a great relief to communities in Saxony). Frederick recognised Maria Theresa's right to rule the provinces of German Austria, and undertook to support in due course the claims of the present Archduke Joseph to the symbolic leadership of Germany as represented by the titles of 'King of the Romans' and 'Emperor.' The generosity cost him little, for the authority of the Habsburgs in the *Reich* had been much compromised by the recent campaigns. Kaunitz admitted 'we had to make peace, because we could not make war.'[5]

Central Europe had been visited by far greater devastation in the Thirty Years War, and half a century after the Peace of Hubertusburg it was going to be the scene of some of the bloodiest episodes of the Napoleonic wars. In absolute terms, however, and still more by the standards of the kingly warfare of old Europe, the damage wrought by the Seven Years War was still considerable. Contemporaries were appalled by the vision of 'so many treasuries emptied, so many towns burned, villages destroyed, innocent lives ruined … From the Rhine to the Oder, from the March river to the Baltic, the provinces of Germany were devastated or ravaged to a greater or lesser degree, their pastures stained with the blood of thousands of men and littered with their bodies.'[6]

The best estimates put the mortality at some 500,000 civilians and at least 550,000 soldiers. Prussia alone sustained about 180,000 deaths among its soldiers and 395,000 among its civilians,[7] the latter probably nearly all through starvation and disease. The Austrian civilian deaths must have been much lower than those in the Prussian states, but the Austrian army lost a grand total of 303,595 officers and men from all causes, of whom 41.5 per cent were killed in action or died of wounds or disease.[8] In treasure Austrian expended 260,101,986 florins,[9] and Prussia about 140,000,000 taler from its own resources, and further large sums at the expense of Saxony.

The war had reached into the Austrian states only as far south as the neighbourhoods of Olmütz, Pardubitz, Kolin and Prague. In the latter city the effects of the bombardment of 1757 were still visible in the early 1770s in the form of 'several very large gardens and young orchards, which before that siege were entirely covered with houses, then destroyed, and the people are too poor to rebuild them.'[10] Towards the border with Saxony the Circle of Leitmeritz had still not come to itself, with former arable land overrun with grass and weeds, towns and villages wearing a battered appearance.'[11] It was going to look that way again after the German population was killed or expelled in 1945.

Frederick was confident that all the major powers would recover in the course of time, but then 'ambitious men will generate new wars and case new disasters, for human nature is such that nobody is corrected by example. The lessons of the fathers' mistakes are lost on their children, for every generation must make its own blunders.'[12]

Who had won the war? This simple question does not admit of a simple answer. In territorial terms the balance was even, in that the boundaries remained as they had existed in 1756, with the French yielding up the Westphalian duchies, Frederick evacuating Saxony, and Maria Theresa restoring Glatz.

Sweden and Saxony retreated to the rank of tertiary powers, while, on the contrary, Prusso-German patriots came to view the survival of Prussia as a national epic, and in retrospect as a vital stage in Prussia's gaining the leadership of Germany. Another view is equally tenable, namely that the once opportunistic and aggressive Frederick had been driven permanently onto the defensive, and that the Prussians had to wait until the battle of Königgrätz in 1866 to gain what had slipped from their hands at Kolin in 1757. Frederick doubted towards the end of his reign whether Prussia and the other independent states of Germany would survive in the face of a revivified Austria,[13] and two centuries later a leading

German historian cited the authority of Clausewitz on the matter and concluded that after the war 'Frederick lay triumphant but totally powerless in his camp. Never for the rest of his life did he recover his taste for arbitrary conquests... It is difficult to believe that, without the experience of the Seven Years War, Frederick would have left his victorious sword unsheathed for thirty years. Silesia remained in his possession, but he lost the bold impulse to aggrandise himself at the expense of Austria; that instinct had now been successfully curbed.'[14]

On the other hand Austria had clearly lost the war, if we are to judge the outcome by reference to the aims as they had been set out by Kaunitz, which were to recover Silesia, and deprive Prussia permanently of the power to disturb the public peace. How had it been possible for matters to turn out that way, when the odds had seemed to be piled up so heavily against the king?

Due allowance must be made for the workings of chance. The Seven Years War was one of those contests in which the outcome remained in doubt almost until the end. Frederick put his life and liberty at risk many times over, and he admitted that he would probably have gone under early in 1762 if the Empress of Russia had not died, and the Austrian alliance had not 'gone to the grave with her.'[15]

Frederick retained a number of priceless assets throughout. He inherited a responsive military machine, he had near-total control of all political and military activity, and his lack of scruple allowed him to plunder Saxony at will. In contrast the Austrian management of war was loose and indirect, even when we leave aside considerations like the difficulty of co-ordinating the grand strategy of the alliance, and the bad feeling which existed between the Austrian and Russian commanders. Maria Theresa was disadvantaged by her sex, her family concerns, and the fact that the Habsburg monarchy ruled by the consent of powerful established interests. Kaunitz, for all his brilliant talents, constantly demanded of the Austrian army more than it was capable of performing, and by his search for energetic leadership in the field he sowed divisions among the Austrian generals.

Maria Theresa was moved by passion as well as by policy in her desire to bring Frederick to account, but she and Kaunitz lacked the kind of ruthless concentration which the king brought to his cause. Frederick drew attention to the 'over-refined and minute policy of the court of Vienna, whose principles led it to lay the burden of the most difficult and risky enterprises on its allies, so as to retain by the end of the war an army which was in better state and more complete than that of the other powers.'[16]

Daun, Lacy and Prince Albert of Sachsen-Teschen were all scandalised to discover that the wealth of the great people at home was almost untouched by the war, and Lacy and Albert hinted that the court itself showed unrestrained extravagance. The visitor to the Schönbrunn Palace in Vienna can see the evidence today in the ceiling frescos of the Great Gallery, and the great paintings of the celebrations of the marriage of Archduke Joseph to Isabella of Parma in 1760. Sir James Caldwell of County Fermanagh, who was versed in Austria's economic and political affairs, observed at the close of hostilities that Austria's strength was 'by no means exhausted by the war. She had powerful allies whose interest it was for Germans to cut each other's throats; she did not therefore exert all her strength ... believing, as all the world believed, that the King of Prussia's resources must have failed, that he would have been enfeebled by the violence of his own efforts, and been crushed under a weight he was unable to sustain, his death was also a probable event, and this would at once have established her in her claims.'[17]

Maria Theresa and Kaunitz had recognised in Prussia a new and sinister threat to the European order, and not just a power which was bent on aggrandisement (nothing new in history) but one which was reinforced by a society which was run on military lines, where the authority over the people of a parish lay with the captain of the local garrison. But here we encounter a paradox. The Prussian army was the creation of its kings, and yet for the Habsburgs their army was of greater, literally fundamental importance, as the only institution which represented all the lands of the monarchy in their diversity of peoples, languages, religions and conditions of life. The connections gained in coherence in the 1750s, when the establishment of the Military Order of Maria Theresa and a nobility of merit engendered an ethos of state service. In that sense the Habsburg monarchy was the creation of its army, a fact which was recognised in equal measure by Daun, Archduke Charles and Radetzky.

Daun wrote twice to Maria Theresa on the subject in the summer of 1761. He maintained that in the long perspective 'the greatest of Your Majesty's resources is a large and well-found army.'[18] Again, 'the conservation of Your Majesty's army is to be particularly desired … as it could be employed for Your Majesty's welfare in a future war more effectively than is possible, unfortunately, in the present one.'[19]

Daun set strikingly little store on the conservation of life as such. 'I do not regret the loss of men in the least—20,000 or so are neither here nor there, and especially for the sake of a worthwhile objective. In any case we would only have to maintain them in peacetime.'[20] His devotion was to the army as an institution. Daun knew the army's capabilities and limits better than any other man—how it lacked the recuperative power of the Prussian forces, and how it would be unlikely to survive another 'Leuthen.' Frederick, whose authority in the matter counts for more than any other, concluded that nothing caused him more frustration in the war than Daun's refusal to leave the high ground to give battle, except on the most favourable terms (and then indeed, Daun aimed at the total destruction of the enemy, as at Hochkirch, Maxen and Liegnitz). However such generally cautious proceedings did little to forward the tasks which were set before him by Maria Theresa and Kaunitz, and the central problem of the Austrian campaigning was how to implement an offensive grand strategy without hazarding the army.

Here the mechanics of battle tactics have some relevance. It is clear that from the day of Hochkirch (14 October 1758) onwards the Austrians abandoned the conventional lines of battle for something altogether more fluid and ambitious, whereby their formations operated independently but within an overall design, and attacked in line or column as best suited the objective. Prince Henry of Prussia was quick to grasp the advantages of the concept, and by the end of the war both sides were operating in styles fundamentally different from their first encounters.

Hochkirch was a creditable victory, and yet we find Daun disappointed at the outcome, for he had been aiming to wipe out the enemy. At Liegnitz (1760), another intended battle of annihilation, and Reichenbach (1762) the Austrians failed altogether. What was going wrong? The problem was that military organisation had not kept up with the revolution in grand tactics. Commanders who were accustomed to taking their place in continuous lines of battle were now being expected to operate on their own head, and the challenge was augmented by the practice, common to all armies of the time, that the forces at generals' disposal were shifting collections of units whose order was still determined by feudal notions of precedence. The ultimate solution, as foreseen not only in France, but in Austria by Lacy in 1760 and *GFWM*. Wartensleben in 1762, was to combine commanders and forces in permanent formations that would not only make for greater mechanical efficiency, but enhance identity and cohesion.

It is worth returning to a point which Frederick touched on earlier, which was the 'over-refined' character of Austrian policy. Frederick was highly intelligent and cultured, but he derived his 'principles' of war from the reading of history and the expedients which had stood him in good stead amid 'that kind of chance which presides over the events of war.'[21] In his private tastes he remained faithful to the playful and decorative rococo styles which derived from the French *Régence* and had been in vogue in his younger days. He forbade his gardeners to root up weeds, if they looked like growing up into something of interest, and he was bad a mathematics, spelling and grammar.

Kaunitz in contrast was a self-conscious devotee of the intellectual aspects of what became known as the 'Enlightenment,' and in that respect a man of a later generation than the king. He was bent on purifying and improving the arts, and bringing impersonal calculation to the conduct of policy and strategy, not realising that ultimately 'rationality is not enough' (U.S. Secretary of Defense Robert McNamara on the conduct of the Vietnam War). Thus Kaunitz assembled a coalition of seemingly irresistible numerical weight, the chief foundation being the 'immutable' interests which bound Russia to Austria. Frederick continued to fight on, when by logic he should have gone under, and Russia's interests proved to be less than 'immutable' after Empress Elizabeth died on 5 January 1762.

Frederick survived. His survival was tantamount to victory, and Austria's consequent defeat was that of the scientific by the imponderable.

Kaunitz rests in a chapel by his palace of Austerlitz in Moravia. He is clad not in the robes of a great knightly order, but in the coarse brown woollen habit of a Tertiary Brother of St. Francis. In Vienna a few hundred yards separate Daun from Maria Theresa. Napoleon visited the field marshal's tomb in the Augustinerkirche on 5 October 1809. 'There he lies,' he exclaimed to the generals Ducrot and Rapp. 'Everything is vain, everything vanishes like smoke.'[22]

Maria Theresa died on 29 November 1780, and her coffin was borne in great state to the door of the Kapuzinerkirche, where a herald demanded entrance, reciting her manifold titles one by one. By ancient Habsburg custom the answer came that nobody was known by those names, and the Empress-Queen could be admitted only under the designation of 'a poor sinner.' Maria Theresa and Francis Stephen lie together in a great metal sarcophagus. It is surmounted by their figures, intended to convey their awakening on the day of the Resurrection, though to the Viennese it suggested the companionship of the marriage bed. The panel at the foot depicts the Croats rampaging through the Prussian camp at Hochkirch on 14 October 1758. Well into living memory the last surviving Knight of her Military Order came every year on the anniversary of her death to lay a wreath which was adorned with black and yellow ribbons, and bore the words:

In deepest veneration
Baron Gottfried de Banfield

THE THEATRE OF OPERATIONS

Netze
Landsberg
Warthe
Zorndorf
Cüstrin
Posen
Kunersdorf
Frankfurt/a/O
Paltzig
Züllichau
Crossen
Guben
Bober
Carolath
Oder
Lausitzer Neisse
Sorau
Sagan
Glogau
Queiss
SILESIA
200
Parchwitz
Leubus
Liegnitz
Auras
Katzbach
Görlitz
Hochkirch
Lauban
Moys
Löwenberg
Schmottseiffen
Jauer
Leuthen
Breslau
Zittau
Striegau
Ohlau
Bunzelwitz
Brieg
500
Schweidnitz
Strehlen
Burkersdorf
Reichenbach
Landeshut
Oppeln
Aupa
Frankenstein
Neisse
Iser
Elbe
Silberberg
Münchengrätz
Glatz
Neisse
Gitschin
Nachod
Neustadt
Jung-Bunzlau
Ziegenhals
Jaromiersch
Cosel
Mettau
Königgrätz
Adler
Ratibor
Jägerndorf
Pardubitz
Kolin
Troppau
Mähr.-Ostrau
Kuttenberg
Chrudim
Sazawa
Domstadtl
Mähr.-Trübau
Zwittau
Olmütz
Leipnik
March
Iglau
Brünn

APPENDIX 1

MILITARY GEOGRAPHY

OVERVIEWS

In the course of the Seven Years War we discover the presence of Austrian troops as far to the west as Hanover (Dombasle's corps in support of the French at Hastenbeck in 1757) and as far east as Poland (Loudon's retreat after he separated from the Russians in 1759). However coherent operations by substantial forces were staged across a more restricted theatre which extended for about 250 miles from north to south (from the area of Berlin to that of Brünn in Moravia), and for another 280 miles from west to east (from the Saale in Saxony to Upper Silesia).

The basic structure was simple, because it was formed around two elements:

a transverse range of heights, thrown up by the collision of the Indian tectonic plate with that of Euro-Asia;

two rivers, the Elbe and the Oder, which ran on roughly parallel courses from south-east to north-west.

The Austrians were based to the south of the highlands in their provinces of Bohemia and Moravia, and the Prussians to the north, in their native Brandenburg and adjacent provinces, and in Silesia (conquered and annexed in the 1740s) and the electorate of Saxony (overrun in 1756).

Climate

Operations in this theatre of war were seasonal, in that the Central European winter imposed a halt on anything of consequence. While that season lasted the high passes were blocked by snow, the navigable rivers iced up, and, no less significantly, it was impossible to feed the horses from the resources of the countryside. Life along the outposts was so miserable that the two sides normally agreed upon a winter truce, which could be terminated upon formal notification being given. Snow usually began to fall in the lowlands in December, and on 13 December 1759 Frederick found that there was now an insurmountable barrier between the two armies. The cover might remain knee deep for weeks thereafter, and Bohemia and Moravia could experience treacherous 'returns of winter' in early February, in March and April, and even in the middle of May. The first warm weather actually made things worse, and Major General Guasco reported in 1756 that 'we can hardly open our operations without the danger of being interrupted by the floods caused by the melt water, which usually occur in the lower mountains between the end of March and the middle of April, and which are delayed at higher elevations until towards the middle of May.'[1]

Frederick tested the seasonal limits to the utmost, but even he had to cede victory to the winter. If, for any reason, it became essential to keep the troops ready for combat in the forward positions, the men would have to set up hutments of timber and sods, as in the Austrian positions around Dresden in the bitter winter of 1759/60. Winter quarters proper were established further to the rear by accommodating the troops in towns and the larger villages, while the *Reichsarmee* had to recoil all the way to the upper Main, and the Russians to the upper Vistula. The taking up of 'cantonments' was an intermediate stage, whereby the forces were taken out of winter quarters and billeted in villages closer to the intended theatre of operations. By then the men were usually in a bad physical shape, resulting from poor diet and the diseases which rampaged through their crowded accommodation.

Communications

In the campaigning season (which normally lasted from May until October or November) huge logistic problems were posed by the transport of heavy siege trains and the extraordinarily heavy and bulky commodities which were represented by the barrels and sacks of flour and grain and the bales of hay and straw. Cattle for the slaughter were herded along the roads in their thousands, and individual convoys of carts could reach thousands of vehicles at a time.

The Austrian veteran Lloyd described a 'military road' as one 'where infantry, cavalry, heavy artillery and all kinds of carriages can pass.'[2] The standard measurement of distance was the German *Meile* of 7.5 kilometres (about four and three-quarters English miles), and a normal rate of marching for troops across all but very difficult ground was reckoned at three *Meilen* or less, not counting the rest days which were taken after every few days on the road. The roads in Brandenburg were counted as very bad, those in Silesia as poor, and those in Saxony from adequate to good. As a general rule 'on the far [southern] side of the Erz-Gebirge the inns, roads, post carriages and in fact everything which satisfies the material man, are in splendid condition... As regards physical things Nature has dealt with the two halves of Germany very differently. Saxony, which is counted the best region of northern Germany, cannot begin to compare in natural productivity with Bohemia, Austria, Bavaria or Swabia.'[3]

The very best of the roads in the Austrian territories were represented by the stone-paved *Kaiserstrassen*, so-named after the father of Maria Theresa, the late Emperor Charles VI. There were three main routes in question. The *Kaiserstrasse* from Vienna to Prague passed through south-western Moravia by way of the pretty towns of Iglau and Znaim, touched the upper Elbe at Kolin and continued to the south of the river to Prague, while a branch to the right gave access to Pardubitz and Königgrätz. The landscape on the way to Prague was an agreeable alternation of little hills and valleys, woods and cultivated plains. There were few villages to be seen, but an Austrian officer explained to a tourist that they were not far distant but tucked out of sight, as protection against the robber knights who used to roam the countryside.[4] The total distance from Vienna to Prague amounted to 203 English miles, which represented 30 hours and 45 minutes of continuous travelling-time by post coach, with twenty and a half changes of horses, or alternatively six days by ordinary coach.[5] One of the usual halts was at the inn of *Slati Slunce* on the field of Kolin. Not long afterwards the courtier Khevenhüller-Metsch observed the shattered trees and what he took to be earthworks (actually the site of mass graves), and after the war a German traveller was struck by 'the huge flock of geese which cover the fields. They are driven in countless masses to the capital from the whole kingdom... Together with their drovers they cover between two or three German miles a day.'[6]

A second *Kaiserstrasse*, even more important for Austrian military purposes, ran generally north from Vienna by way of Brünn to Olmütz in Moravia. It was used amongst other things for the transportation of the main siege train, which was held at Vienna until it was moved up to Olmütz in 1760. A third road (from Linz on the Danube up through southern central Bohemia by way of Budweis to Prague) did not come into consideration in the Seven Years War, but caught Frederick's eye later in his reign as a possible means of taking the Prussians to the Danube.

If the quality of the *Kaiserstrassen* told in favour of the Austrians, the direction of these and the other routes worked against them. In general the major roads radiated in star patterns from Vienna, Königgrätz and Prague, which was convenient enough for civilian purposes. What was lacking was a militarily useful lateral communication close to the borders of Saxony and Silesia, the reason being that the highlands on the 'Austrian' side projected in an irregular and lumpy way, which threw the main roads deep into Bohemia and Moravia. The borders could be approached only up isolated and steep-sided valleys, while Bohemia and Moravia were themselves separated by a range of tangled hills.

The Austrians were therefore thrown upon discrete axes of operations, and could scarcely avoid signalling their intentions to the enemy. If they assembled a depot at Königgrätz, for example, Frederick could deduce that they had designs on Glatz and Lower Silesia. Conversely a depot at Olmütz told him that they intended something in Upper Silesia. Preparations at Prague and Leitmeritz indicated that the Austrians were turning their attention to Saxony.

In this respect the advantage lay with the Prussians, for the high ground gave way to Lusatia and the Silesian plain along a continuous and even line. Not far to the north the Prussians could exploit the facility of one of the classic routes of the Old World (in fact a prolongation of the Silk Road), in this case the stretch of highway which ran from Breslau by way of Liegnitz to Görlitz, and from there through Saxon territory by way of Bautzen and Dresden to Leipzig. This highway enabled the Prussians to shift concentrations of force between Silesia and Saxony and back again without detours or obstacles.

Further towards the borders the diverse economy of the Silesian hills had led to the development of another transverse route, namely by way of Neisse, Frankenstein, Schweidnitz, Landeshut and Hirschberg to link up with the highway at Görlitz. The eastern stretch, between Neisse and Schweidnitz, was particularly useful for Frederick's ends, for it enabled him to move his axis of operations between the Moravian and Bohemian theatres without betraying his plans. One of his enemies pointed out that 'all our previous misfortunes derive from the fact that the great advantage of the King of Prussia consists in shuttling to and fro between the Elbe and the Oder.'[7]

Water transport was an invaluable facility for moving forage and heavy ordnance, and here too the Prussians were better placed, since they had all of the navigable Oder and most of the navigable Elbe at their disposal for most of the war.. The Friedrich-Wilhelms Canal, which connected the two rivers, ran entirely through Prussian territory, and remain wholly beyond the reach of the Austrians, except when Hadik blew up some of the locks in 1759.

Fortresses and Positions

If you wished to go on a major campaign you had to establish chains of depots for your provisions and munitions. For this purpose the Prussians used their network of Silesian fortresses in the east, and, for operations up the Elbe, the fortress of Magdeburg and the walled Saxon towns of Wittenberg and Torgau. The Austrians had just one modern fortress (Olmütz) on the entire theatre of war, while Prague and Brünn with their antiquated ramparts stood well back from the borders. Otherwise their magazines were wholly without protection. Their stores were gobbled up wholesale by the Prussians in April 1757, and their depots along the Eger and the lower Bohemian Elbe were raided repeatedly until the end of the war.

Unlike the case in the Netherlands or northern Italy, there were no substantial villages or farm complexes to offer either party any tactical protection. In the plain of the Bohemian Elbe the peasants were treated 'in a wretched manner; they have hovels of the worst sort to live in, little better than those of Westphalia; being loose stones laid on another for the walls, and the crevices filled with mud, and the covering some strong poles with turf spread on them, and a hole at the top in the middle is all the chimney that any of them have.'[8] In the highlands on both sides of the border the villages were affairs of log huts, strung out in a disjointed manner along the valleys of the little streams. Down in the Silesian plain Leuthen was more substantial than most of the villages, but it brought the Prussians to only a temporary halt in the final stages of the great battle on 5 December 1757. Hochkirch in Upper Lusatia was built of timber frames filled in with wattle, and proved highly flammable on 14 October 1758. Here as elsewhere in the Central European theatre of war the only substantial support in such locations was offered by the walled churchyards, which grew higher and higher as successive generations of villagers went to their graves.

Mass formations were characteristic of the tactics of the time, and they demanded space and close control. Heavily wooded or otherwise difficult ground might prove attractive for defensive purposes to the modern eye, but it was well-nigh useless for the Austrian and

Prussian armies in the Seven Years war, which was why Daun did not simply plant his troops on the highest passes, or why Frederick could find nowhere to site his forces on the approaches to Berlin.

The art of the defence at the time depended much more on making the best use of relatively high ground where forces could be deployed in a coherent fashion. Field Marshal Daun equalled Frederick and Prince Henry in this respect, and this option held a particular appeal for him, since it enabled him to site the excellent Austrian artillery to the best advantage, and to cancel the advantage which the Prussians enjoyed in manoeuvre.

This style of tactics presented the two sides with differing operational and strategic dilemmas. For the Austrians, whatever the immediate advantage of staying on the defensive, it was fundamentally irreconcilable with their fundamental need to go forth and regain Silesia. After his defeat at Kolin (1757) Frederick on his side was disinclined to attack the Austrians when they were emplaced so strongly, and had to find some means of fighting them on his own terms, preferably in the plains of Silesia 'where the Court of Vienna, drawn by its insatiable desire to reconquer Silesia, must sooner or later commit its troops. It is then that the power of their ordnance and all the imposing train of their cannon will count for little.'[9]

Modern maps indicate that much of the tactically useful high ground was to be found at about the 300-metre contour, Frederick's low-lying camp at Bunzelwitz in 1761 being a significant exception. Contours were unknown at the time of the Seven Years War, and then as now even the best second-hand topographical data were no substitute for personal observation, 'for in such situations even minor details can prove to be of moment. If a commander wishes to grasp them with the necessary accuracy he must assess them with his own eyes, and even that is not always enough.'[10] That was one reason why individual generals were identified so strongly with particular theatres of war, Hadik or Kleefeld for example with Saxony, or the Prussian lieutenant general Fouqué with Lower Silesia and the County of Glatz.

The Choice of Theatres

Calculations relating to politics, operations and tactical detail all came into play when it was a question of deciding what weight to give to the various theatres of war. Frederick in most campaigns inclined strongly to the offensive. He stole a march on the Austrians by conquering Saxony in 1756, and in the next two years he developed that advantage by carrying the war into Austrian territory. It was easy enough for his forces to gain an initial footing in Bohemia, but the difficulties came when they pressed further into the interior, for they might become ensnarled in difficult country (as around Königgrätz), and they had nowhere secure to plant their depots. In contrast Moravia, to the east, was a highly-developed land which lay on the direct route to Vienna (below). Operations here were certain to command the earnest attention of the Austrians, and after the war they bulked large in Frederick's contingency plans, as a way of forcing the enemy to abandon Bohemia without a fight. Then the king might very well have annexed Prague and the lands of the Bohemian Elbe to his territories.

From the summer of 1758 the Prussians were forced north across the border hills into Silesia and Saxony, and now it was the Austrians' turn to think of offensive operations. Some of the parties to the debates in Vienna could put up a good case for giving priority to campaigning in Saxony, for the military economy of Frederick now depended on the recruits, fodder, cattle and cash which he plundered from that unfortunate land. 'Just look at what happened after the Prussians were defeated at Kolin and Breslau in 1757, at Hochkirch in 1758, and Paltzig, Kunersdorf and Maxen in 1759. Saxony was the place where Frederick came back to vigorous life, and where he was able gather in almost the original strength what he lost in his victories and reverses alike.'[11]

Silesia, the alternative theatre of operations, was a very hard nut to crack. This was due partly to its system of fortifications (of which more later), and partly to the problems of finding a modus operandi with the Russians. Before active operations could begin the relevant Russian army had to march all the way to the

Oder from its winter quarters and supply base in Poland. There were three occasions when it would have been possible for large forces of Austrians and Russians to work together effectively in Silesia—at the time of the campaign of Zorndorf in 1758, again when Daun and Saltykov groped towards one another after the battle of Kunersdorf in 1759, and finally when Loudon and Buturlin actually joined in 1761—but each time the allies broke apart, owing to the difficulty of supplying the Russians, and the distrust which reigned between the two parties.

The only effective co-operation came in the shape of relatively small contingents which contrived to attach themselves to the other army under special arrangements. Such was the case when Loudon's corps reached the Russians in time for the battle of Kunersdorf (12 August 1759), and when an excellent corps of Russian grenadiers accompanied the Austrians in Loudon's storm of Schweidnitz (1 October 1761).

Jacob Cogniazzo therefore had some reason to criticise what he called 'the fundamental principle of state of the House of Austria, which was to be the guideline for our commanders for the entire course of this war, namely *to put as their chief objective the conquest of Silesia, and regard as secondary the liberation of the Electorate of Saxony*—which, it was imagined, would fall by itself.'[12]

On balance the opposite case, for giving the preference to Silesia, was probably stronger still. It was certainly possible for the Austrians and the *Reichstruppen* to recover Saxony as far north as Torgau, Wittenberg and Leipzig, but only if the main Prussian army were absent. Even then it was possible for wily commanders like Hülsen and Prince Henry to win time by skilful fighting retreats, and Magdeburg remained altogether beyond the Austrians' reach without the help of the French, who showed that they had no interest in operating so far to the east. The gains were in any case untenable during the winter, as Daun pointed out, and were certain to be lost as soon as the Prussians returned to Saxony in any strength.

Philipp Levin Beck made the further and basic point that Saxon would have to be restored to the king/elector Augustus at the peace, and that the main army could be deployed more profitably in Silesia, '*the province for which we are fighting the present war.*'[13] A great deal lay behind that simple statement. By winning Silesia Frederick had gained 1,200,000 new subjects and 21,900 square miles, and raised Prussia to the rank of the second power in Germany and to that of the fifth in Europe. Silesia was a natural strategic complement to the heartland of Brandenburg-Prussia, and the skilled Prussian administrators were the people best qualified to develop the rich and diverse economy. Silesia moreover corresponded to what men at the time found attractive in the landscape. Here we are not thinking of the wilder reaches of the Sudetens, which became the haunt of romantic painters and poets, but the vast sweep of the productive plains.

Restored to Austrian sovereignty, Silesia would have given Austria an economic opening to northern Europe and promoted the trade with Britain, which had been promising so well in the 1730s. In that period Silesia had contributed 10 per cent of Austria's military budget, and the Silesian troops were valuable in both numbers and quality. Even at the time of the Seven Years War the Silesians formed a significant element among the NCOs, and Silesians still made up more than 5 per cent of the corps of officers. The interior minister Haugwitz was just one of the Silesian refugees who were influential in Vienna, and the emotional side of Maria Theresa's nature responded to what she was told of the sufferings of her loyalists in that land. In his celebrated memorandum of 24 March 1749 the rising diplomat Wenzel Anton von Kaunitz had written of the loss of Silesia as being intolerable to the House of Habsburg, and that the monarchy must neglect no opportunity to win that land back. These words struck a chord with Maria Theresa, as he knew they would.

THE SCENES OF OPERATIONS

Military geography can be daunting in detail, but the theatres of the Seven Years War can be simplified to a great extent if they are presented in terms of 'corridors,' by which is meant the natural avenues of operations.

The Western Corridor

Prague and North-Western Bohemia

Prague (pop. c. 19,000) stood at the western end of the fertile alluvial plain of the middle Bohemian Elbe, though the river itself passed to the north of the city. Prague had ceded social brilliance to Vienna, but it held a number of magnificent winter palaces of the Bohemian nobility, and was dignified by the cathedral and royal palace complex which rose on the Klein-Seite. The Moldau river ran from north to south through the centre of the city, dividing the Klein-Seite on the left (western) bank from the more extensive Neustadt on the right. The river, though unnavigable, was an impressive 700 paces wide and virtually impossible to ford (as Seydlitz discovered in 1757), which gave a considerable military value to the stone bridge, which was thirty feet wide and ran for 1,580 feet over seventeen arches. 'It is a solid edifice, [but] has nothing of elegance in it; and when a traveller hears that it was a hundred and fifty years a-building, he will suppose it must have been in an age extremely poor, or been undertaken by a prince of little spirit.'[14]

Prague was also important to the Austrians as a military depot which provided ample accommodation of all kinds. It was defensible against raiding parties, but nothing short of an army could enable the city to withstand a formal siege, since the smoky Prague basin was overlooked on all sides, and the town ramparts and the Wischehrad citadel on the right bank were in bad repair and lacked modern outworks.

The lower Bohemian Elbe ran generally north on its way to Saxony, coursing through the fertile Circle of Leitmeritz (the 'garden of Bohemia') then cutting through the Mittel-Gebirge and Elbsandstein-Gebirge. Melnik on the right (eastern) bank was the head of navigation, and therefore the closest to Prague that the Prussians could bring their barges laden with provisions and heavy ordnance. The left bank was the more highly developed and offered the more interesting military geography. Near Budin the river was joined by the Eger, which rose far to the west in the Fichtel-Gebirge, and ran down a highland valley by way of Eger town to Saaz, and thence through Laun to the Elbe almost opposite Leitmeritz.

Roads reached the upper Eger both across the Fichtel-Gebirge from the Upper Palatinate, and across the border range of the Erz-Gebirge (average height 800 metres) from south-western Saxony. The valley therefore offered a convenient back door into Bohemia from the *Reich*, and was exploited as such by both sides. Austrian reinforcements entered by this avenue from the Netherlands early in the war, and it offered the *Reichsarmee* an alternative to the more exposed route by Zwickau and Chemnitz north of the Erz-Gebirge. Conversely Prince Moritz of Anhalt-Dessau came this way by two invading columns in April 1757, marching on parallel routes by way of Annaberg and Marienberg.

The Austrians failed to make defensive use of the right (southern) bank of the Eger, which was higher than the left, as Lloyd pointed out.[15] For operational reasons Field Marshal Browne had to stage his holding action in October 1756 about eight miles to the north at Lobositz, and only in the 1780s did the Austrians provide for the defence of the Eger by building their new fortress of Theresienstadt. By that time the first round of hostilities against Prussia was at an end. Meanwhile north-west Bohemia remained without any fortified protection against the Prussian invasions and raiding parties. The depot at Leitmeritz more than once went up in smoke, and Teplitz would have gone the same way in 1762 if Prince Löwenstein had not staged his brilliant holding action nearby on 2 August.

The northernmost reach of the Bohemian Elbe was straddled by successive ranges of heights. The first, the Mittel-Gebirge, offered an eerie landscape of extinct volcanoes, of which the Lobosch near Lobositz was the most familiar to the warring parties. The river valley opened somewhat at Aussig, where the little Biela entered from the west; low-lying Tetschen opposite was an old fortress of little defence. The valley closed in again on the last stretch to Saxony, being hemmed in by the Elbstandstein-Gebirge, a range which in its way was no less sinister than the Mittel-Gebirge, being formed of great sandstone slabs and basalt intrusions.

The small but strong castle of Schreckenstein was perched on the right bank atop a black cliff which fell near-vertically to the Elbe.

There was no proper road through the heights to the east of the Elbe, and Browne nearly ruined himself and his flying corps when he marched that way in his attempt to relieve the Saxon army in 1756. All the important routes ran to the west of the river, and were prospected by Frederick's chief of intelligence Lieutenant General Winterfeldt, who toured this part of Bohemia in 1754 on the pretext of taking the waters at Carlsbad spa.[16] Two routes from Freiberg and Dippoldiswalde in Saxony crossed the easternmost Erz-Gebirge and converged on Teplitz. The most direct access however lay closer to the Elbe and ran from Berggiesshübel in Saxony by way of Peterswalde, Aussig and the Paschkopole Pass down to Lobositz.

From 1758 the Austrians were operating continuously in Saxony, at the cost of the huge efforts which were needed to draw their supplies across the borders from Bohemia. 'Whenever an army proposes passing from one country into the other, it is absolutely necessary to be masters of the Elbe, because it is because by that

The lower Bohemian Elbe, looking downstream from the right bank below Melnik.

river alone such armies must subsist, the mountains being so high, and the roads so bad, that for many months of the year no carriage could pass.'[17] Even the navigation of the river was interrupted by the winter ice and sometimes also by low water towards the end of summer. In September 1761 Daun sent d'Ayasasa to Vienna to explain that every effort was being made to bring down supplies from Bohemia, 'but there is so little water that the vessels can scarcely accommodate half loads.'[18] Daun could remember one winter that was so hard that the Elbe was unusable from 20 November until 28 February.

Saxony

On the Saxon side of the border the Elbsandstein-Gebirge formed isolated, steep-sided plateaux, some of them very like the mesas of the American West, which represented the original surface of the sandstone before the rest was eroded by water action over millions of years. One such plateau, three hundred feet high, towered above the west bank of the Elbe and was crowned by the spectacular Saxon fortress of Königstein. The castle walls had a circuit of one and a half miles, and the position was extended downriver as the Camp of Pirna, which terminated at its far end at the castle of Pirna and the castle of Sonnenstein, which was built on another high rock. 'It's a wonderful view from here. You can see the river, the hills around Dresden, the terraced vineyards at Meissen, distant Sedlitz… and behind you there is Bohemia. A really good place to spend a good summer evening.'[19]

The Camp of Pirna was naturally strong on all sides except the north-west, and here the Saxon had built three tiers of works and batteries. The position was therefore admirable from a tactical point of view, but in a wider perspective it was also something of a prison, for the Prussians could so easily seal it off by a blockade, as in 1756, when the starving Saxon army was finally compelled to capitulate.

The Bohemian Mittel-Gebirge, looking east from the Paschkopole Pass.

Further towards Dresden the next location of interest was formed by the steep and heavily-wooded valley of the Müglitz stream, which rose in the Erz-Gebirge (literally 'Ore-Mountains') and in time of flood absorbed 'so much iron and tin ore that it runs constantly blood red. No carp can live there, even though it would otherwise suit them magnificently.'[20] The valley was the site of frequent confrontations in the course of the war. The plateau of Maxen on the far side was the scene of the capture of Finck's corps in 1759, while in 1760 the garden palace of Sedlitz on the near bank was the viewpoint of the officers of the *Reichsarmee* when they witnessed the Prussian bombardment of Dresden.

The city of Dresden (pop. c. 40,000) was the capital of Austria's *de facto* ally, the electorate of Saxony (pop. 1,600,000), and was situated in an intensively cultivated basin just below the point where the Elbe left its rocky corridor through the highlands. The Elbe divided the city in much the same way as the Moldau divided Prague, in this case with the Altstadt located on the left (western) bank and the Neustadt on the right bank. Dresden lay at the intersection of the main road from north Germany to Prague and the transverse route from Leipzig to Breslau, which was enough to give the place a certain commercial importance. More significant still was Dresden's standing in European culture, for not long before the city had stood at the peak of its artistic brilliance, a period which endowed the Altstadt with the Catholic Cathedral by the riverside, the tall dome of the Frauenkirche and the royal/electoral palace with its eccentric Zwinger pavilion. The Elbe to the Neustadt was spanned by the nineteen arches of the 540 foot-long Augustusbrücke, which the King/Elector Augustus II had ornamented by a balustrade set with lanterns and stone vases and trophies. 'Even from a distance you can make out at night the broad, still Elbe as it shimmers in the lights of that beautiful bridge.'[21] From there 'the views are entrancing. The Elbe, which to within a short distance had been confined between narrow banks, here broadens out considerably and forms a mighty river which matches the magnificence of the city and the landscape. The highlands towards Lusatia look truly majestic.'[22]

The city was fortified on both banks of the river, and the bastioned ramparts were better maintained and more generously proportioned than those of Prague. However the crowded interior was (like many Saxon towns) highly inflammable, and the field of the defenders' fire to the south was restricted by suburbs and the walled park of the Grosser Garten.

Dresden twice came under direct attack, in 1759 when it was surrendered by the Prussians to the *Reichsarmee* and the supporting Austrians, and again in the following year when Maguire held it successfully against King Frederick. However the wider importance of the place came from its role as a depot and support to the positions in the highland foothills of southern Saxony.

The locations to the east of the river (the post of the Weisser Hirsch Inn, the Camp of Boxdorf and the more distant rock castle of Stolpen) gave access to the routes to Silesia, and formed a natural extension to the defences of the Neustadt. From here Austrian raiding parties could range down the right bank of the Elbe and wreak havoc on the Prussian depots and convoys of barges. Berlin lay only about one hundred miles to the north, but the intervening country was barren and incapable of supporting large forces, and the single road lay by way of Luckau through a great tract of gloomy conifers.

Saxony west of the Elbe was of altogether greater consequence. The first position which figured in the Austrian calculations was the celebrated Camp of Plauen, extending above the valley of the Weisseritz stream from the village of Plauen near Dresden. The Austrians had this ground at their disposal after Zweibrücken and Maguire took Dresden in 1759, and they set about digging themselves in. The Prussian gunner Tempelhof commented that 'it is a well-known fact that the hills which form the landscape here mostly rise up like a wall, and are pretty well inaccessible. Down in the valley flows the Weisseritz, a stream which is not particularly wide or deep, but is difficult for an army to cross when the enemy are only fifty paces away. Moreover there is not enough space in the valley for such an army to form up. The result was that the Austrians stood on the rocky heights as securely as if they had been in a fortress. Not content with this, they laid out fortifications which proved so durable that they defied the elements for twenty years. Thus in 1779 I found a number of the batteries still in excellent condition. Wherever a track led up from the valley bottom you were sure to find it swept by the fire of a battery or closed off by an abbatis.'[23]

The Camp of Plauen was associated in the popular mind with the name of Daun, who in fact doubted whether all the effort was worth while, and he was not the only one. The position was certainly formidable, but it left the Prussians free to plant themselves beyond the valley at Wilsdruff, thus maintaining the threat to Dresden, and also to work around the far left flank of the Austrian position from their base at Freiberg to the west, as Lacy explained in his plan of operations for 1760. 'The Camp of Plauen is certainly very advantageous as regards the actual terrain, but is still defective when we consider its position more widely. The Prussian camp at Freiberg is just as good, and profits them in two further ways: one is that by advancing from there they can turn our position by way of Dippoldiswalde and come at our rear, which means that we must always keep a sizeable corps on that side; the other is that their communication from Freiberg to Wilsdruff is shorter than ours from Dippoldiswalde to Dresden. On top of all that we must always keep an eye on Bohemia, both to secure our communications and to guard against the raids and depredations which the enemy can make by way of Komotau.'[24]

Kaunitz and Maria Theresa nevertheless overrode every objection. In December 1760, when Daun objected to the cost and other practical difficulties of keeping the army at Dresden, the Empress told him that by holding on there 'we are dealing the enemy a painful blow, and undermining the former foundation of their entire system of war.' That system had rested on the facility which Dresden had given them to operate on both banks of the Elbe, concentrate at will in Lusatia, Silesia and the *Reich*, and carry the war into Austrian territory.[25]

This was at a time when the Saxons were protesting at the labour and the materials they were being asked to provide to fortify the suburbs of Dresden. Surely, they argued, it would be better to keep the enemy at a distance by carrying the theatre of war well down the Elbe. Kaunitz urged Maria Theresa not to be dissuaded, and the Saxons were accordingly told that it was essential for their Austrian friends to have a *place d'armes* in southern Saxony, 'and here there is no alternative to Dresden, where the town proper would be too cramped and give rise to all sorts of troubles, unless the suburbs too could be used to accommodate troops and store the war materials.'[26] In such a way Dresden remained the base of the Austrian efforts in Saxony for the rest of the war.

These campaigns were complicated by the need to co-operate with the *Reichsarmee*, which could not be trusted to act without some kind of Austrian support, whether in the shape of an assigned corps or a full-scale army. The Austrian troops most likely to see action were the Croats and hussars, who could work to good effect among the little towns and villages of central Saxony and the winding valleys of the Mulde and the Weisse Elster. In any event Daun would have preferred to operate well away from the Elbe, where the enemy generals knew every inch of the more 'organised' geography and could deploy their outnumbered troops to hold up the advance of the friendly forces.[27]

For the traveller in peacetime the fifteen-mile stretch of the Elbe from Dresden downstream to Meissen offered perhaps 'the most beautiful line of country... in Germany; it is all hill and dale, corn, vines and meadows... a continued picture; the river is everywhere seen to advantage, with the... banks being high and wooded; a more entertaining and picturesque scene can hardly be viewed.'[28]

Austrian military men, on the contrary, were aware that a march down the left bank of the river was certain to be checked by enemy forces holding the 'Camp of Schlettau and the Katzenhäuser.' The position derived its strength from the Triebisch, 'a small rivulet that rises at Klingenberg in the Forest of Tharandt, and falls into the Elbe at Meissen; this rivulet is itself most contemptible, but its banks on both sides are very high and uneven and impracticable in most places. The country behind for nearly two German miles is extremely uneven, cut with deep hollow ways, and by small brooks formed from the neighbouring mountains.'[29]

Meissen town was a miserable little place, but it was overlooked by its celebrated castle-cum-porcelain factory, and the hills round about were set with attractive villas and vineyards. A standing wooden bridge gave convenient access to the right (east) bank of the Elbe, though the passage along the left bank was a slow business for a force of any size, since the troops and the artillery had to thread their way through the walled town and negotiate the steep valley of the Triebisch, where the stream was spanned by a small bridge. Lacy did well to extricate the army from this death trap when the Austrians were retreating after the battle of Torgau.

Riesa, downstream from Meissen, offered the Prussians a convenient depot on their line of communication along the Elbe. Further down again the last foothills of the Erz-Gebirge began to give way to the northern plain, but even here Prussian commanders with a keen eye for the ground, like Prince Henry or Hülsen, were able to extract considerable advantage from the terrain. This side of the Elbe was compartmentalised by little streams (the Döllnitz, the Dahle) and the left flank of the Prussian positions could be covered by the Elbe or the swell of ground at Strehla (which looked like a fortress, even though it was not). The forests of the Dahlener Heide interposed themselves between Strehla and the last of the classic defensive positions of Saxony—namely along the ridge of Siptitz to the east of Torgau. The walled town of Torgau itself gave the Prussians a measure of security for their stores, and the wooden bridge, the lowest on the Saxon Elbe, communicated with a fortified bridgehead on the right bank of the river.

In this northern corner of Saxony the thoughts of all parties turned to securing a trio of walled towns—Torgau just mentioned, Wittenberg on the right bank further downstream, and the commercial city of Leipzig (pop. 30,000) to the south-west. Daun was aware that the Austrians and the *Reichstruppen* were living on no more than borrowed time if they happened to gain any advantage down here, for the Prussians had a forward magazine at Halle (at the head of navigation on the Saale), and the facility of king's mighty depot at Magdeburg, 'a place of great strength, and of equal importance; as he may form there in twenty-four hours such a body of troops as well keep in awe the Saxons on the one side, and Holstein, Mecklenburg and Hanover on the other.'[30] Magdeburg could have been taken only in co-operation with the French, and their assistance was never forthcoming.

The Central Corridor

The Iser Valley, Zittau and the Lusatias

During the invasion of Bohemia in April 1757 the Prussian troops under the Duke of Bevern marched down the Iser valley, joined the column of Field Marshal Schwerin, and continued their advance to reach Frederick in front of Prague. For the rest of the war this axis of operations nevertheless worked wholly in favour of the Austrians. They could feed and quarter their troops to the east of Prague, and march them to a first staging area in the Circle of Bunzlau, which was rich in grain, hay and wood, and could in addition be supported from the fertile districts of Leitmeritz and Gitschin. These advantages had made this region the foundation of Wallenstein's power in the Thirty Years War.

Between the Iser valley and the north German plain extended the Lausitzer-Gebirge and the parallel ridges of the granite Iser-Gebirge. The higher ground itself was impassable to formed bodies of troops, but was traversed by a network of roads which presented the Austrians with an interesting choice of passages. To the west a practicable road (taken by the unfortunate Prince August Wilhelm of Prussia after Kolin in 1757) ran by way of Böhmisch-Leipa and Rumburg to Löbau. Again, from the upper Iser valley a most convenient road gave access by way of Hühnerwasser and the little walled town of Gabel to Zittau in Upper Lusatia. Lastly, roads branching to the north-east could bring the Austrians to the north Bohemian textile town of Reichenberg in its isolated basin, or by Friedland and over the

Iser-Gebirge to the important junction at Löwenberg in Silesia.

Out of all these routes the Austrians made the most use of the one to Zittau. It had begun badly when they bombarded and seized the town on 23 July 1757. A French attaché toured the neighbourhood a few days later and 'I found... all this part of Lusatia... alarmed by what had happened at Zittau and by the misdeeds committed by a number of the detachments. This is augmented by the memory of how the Austrians treated the country in the last war.'[31]

Thereafter Zittau served the Austrians magnificently. The town itself was of little defence, as the Austrians had just shown, but in August they were able to defy Frederick from an excellent position in the hills just to the north, and the town itself enjoyed a degree of protection from being tucked away in a salient of Saxon territory into the border highlands, which helped to preserve the magazine from Prince Henry when he coursed through Lusatia in September 1759. The neighbouring country was thoroughly eaten-out by the comings and goings of the rival armies,[32] but all the time Austrian supplies and reinforcements were able to arrive there in perfect security from central Bohemia.

Above all, by holding Zittau the Austrians gained access to the grand transverse routes not only west to Saxony but east to Silesia, as was emphasised by Major General Franz Guasco as early as 1756. 'If you follow the course of the Neisse from Zittau to Görlitz, and from there in the direction of Naumburg... your whole march will be through a more open country—indeed almost a plain—which continues on your way into Silesia, and which will supply your army in greater abundance.'[33]

From the map it might seem that the Central Corridor would also have put the Austrians in an excellent position to advance straight to Berlin, exploiting their secure line of communication up to Zittau, and using Görlitz and Bautzen as forward bases for a march north-east against the capital.[34] There were no artificial defences to stand in the way, except for the tiny fortress-town of Peitz near Cottbus. But maps can be deceptive if we ignore the nature of the ground. Some clues are given by names like Finsterwalde (signifying gloomy woodlands) or the Schwarze-Elster (which derived its name from its peaty waters), for the terrain in question was the wilderness of Lower Lusatia.

Beyond the Schwarze-Elster extended the twenty-five mile-deep belt of the sandy and woody Fläming waste, and beyond that again the woods, swamps and moors of the Fine-Bruch, Luckenwalde and Baruth. Over to the right, as the Austrians saw it, the young Spree seeped towards Berlin by way of the Spree-Wald, where the river 'divides into more than a hundred small channels, each bearing its own name... this multitude of arms means that the only way to travel from one place in the woods to the other is by water, In fact there are something like 3,000 punts, if we include those at Lübbenau, which the peasants, their wives and even their small children propel with astonishing speed.'[35]

This great tract of land had been shunned by German colonists in the Middle Ages, and was still inhabited by the Sorbs, a Slavonic people who spoke a language related closely to Czech. For present purposes it was incapable of sustaining large-scale operations for any length of time, and it was traversed by the Austrians on just two occasions in the course of the Seven Years War. Hadik came this way with his fast-moving force in October 1757, and lived off the country; Lacy's much larger corps could support itself in October 1760 only by dragging along a cumbersome convoy of provisions. Neither expedition amounted to more than a raid writ large. Proper campaigns against the heartland of Brandenburg-Prussia could be waged only along the axis of the Eastern Corridor, which now commands out attention.

The Eastern Corridor

Königgrätz and north-eastern Bohemia

In all the wars between Austria and Prussia no other location figured more frequently in the calculations of the commanders and their staffs than the neighbourhood of Königgrätz, the principal town of north-eastern Bohemia. Königgrätz boasted a fine Jesuit church and a long drawn-out arcaded market street, but at

THE CENTRAL AND EASTERN BORDER PASSES

the time of the Seven Years War the place itself was unimpressive from the tactical point of view, being defended only by a double circuit of poorish medieval walls. A raiding party of Prussians and Cossacks was able to enter without opposition in 1762.

What endowed Königgrätz with its wider importance was its situation. *Kaiserstrassen* came there both from Prague to the west and Vienna to the south, which made it probably the most significant nodal point of communications within Bohemia. A goodish road, little used in the Seven Years War, ran from Königgrätz northwest by way of Gitschin to the Iser valley at Turnau. More significant at the time were the routes which came from Prussian territory to the north and east and converged on Jaromiersch, which was where the Mettau joined the infant Elbe less than ten miles to the north of Königgrätz.

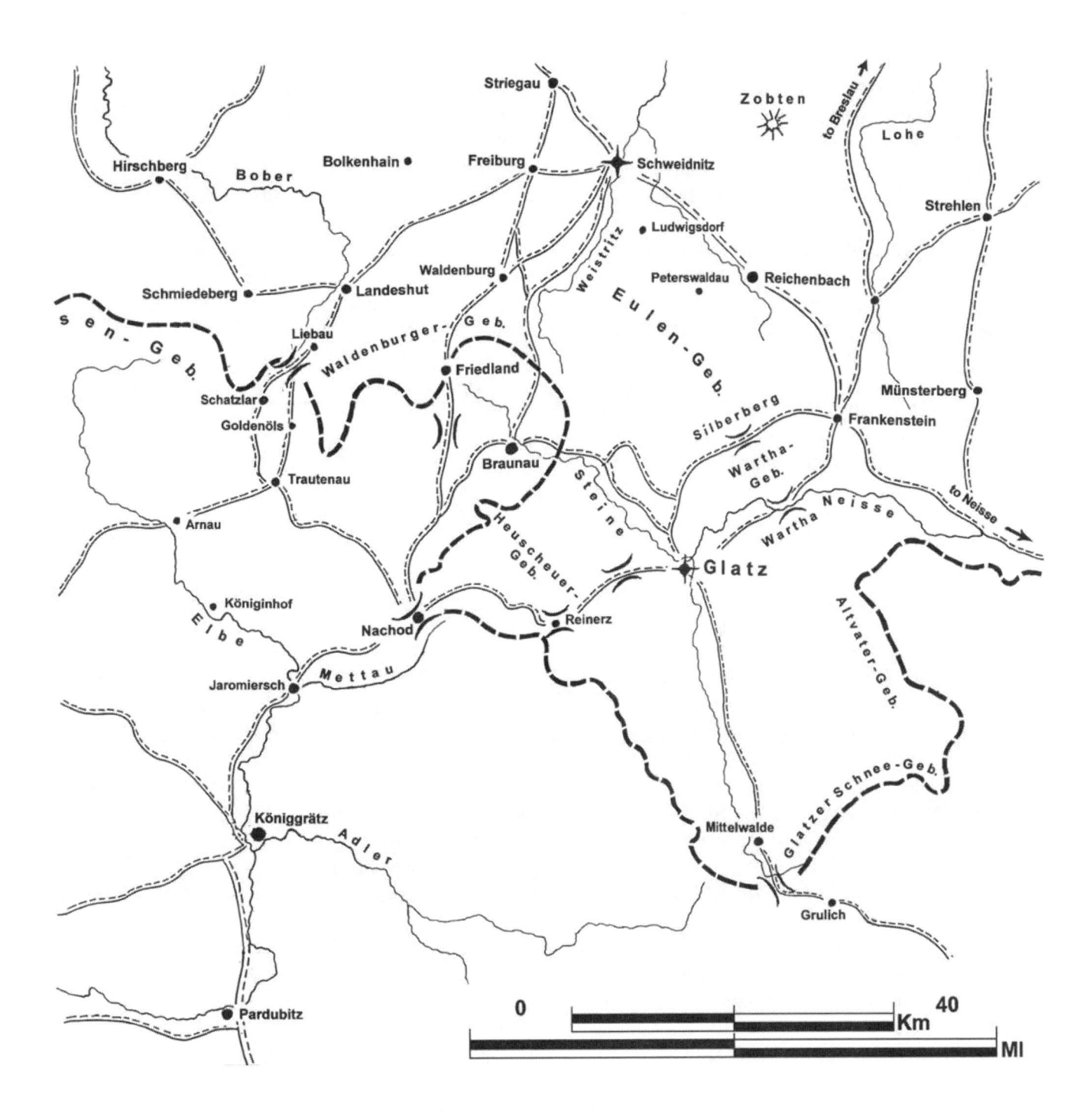

Königgrätz and Pless (Josephstadt) by Jaromiersch were fortified only after the Seven Years War, which yielded the strategic advantage to the Prussians, who had good fortress-depots close at hand. One was Glatz, in the county of the same name, and 'the fortress of Schweidnitz, being another place of arms, supplies them with everything they want; and being so near, enables them to begin their operations much sooner than the Austrians. The mountains are filled with villages, where an army may be put in cantonments [temporary quarters] with safety, if care is taken to occupy the defiles between them and Bohemia, which they can do with ease, being within the Prussian dominions: nothing therefore can hinder them from invading the province on this side... one is amazed to see Her Majesty [Maria Theresa] leave this province entirely defenceless and exposed to the continual ravages of the enemy.'[36]

Out of the passages in question, the avenue of Trautenau stood immediately under the shoulder of the Riesen-Gebirge, a great granite ridge which extended for forty miles to the west, and reached its highest point in the Schneekopf ('Snowy Head,' 1,605 m.). 'The spectator has but to turn his heel,' writes John Quincy Adams, 'and all Silesia, all Saxony and all Bohemia pass in an instant before his view.' The slopes fell in a series of terraces towards Bohemia, but more steeply towards Silesia. 'Just below our feet was the dreadful precipice, at the bottom of which lofty pines, slanting downwards upon the still descending mountain, scarcely appeared to our eyes the height of a lady's needle, while beyond the foot of the mountains our eyes ranged to an almost immeasurable distance, over hills and dales, cornfields and pastures, cities and villages, until they were lost in the grey vapours that bordered the far-extended horizon.'[37] The rains and the melting snow gave rise to a number of clear-running brooks, one of which was identified as the source of the Elbe.

In 1758 a French staff officer noted that 'the Riesen-Gebirge range is impassable to all kinds of mounted troops, being crossed only by steep and very high mountain tracks. The first valley which is practicable for a train of artillery is the one which leads from Landeshut to Trautenau, which is easy enough for wheeled vehicles, but narrow along many stretches and easy to defend.' The Königreich-Wald offered another useful choke point deeper into Bohemia, though (like the Trautenau passage) it was liable to be outflanked from the direction of Nachod to the east. Further defensive possibilities were offered by the course of the Elbe from Königinhof downstream, for the right (western) bank was higher than the left, and by planting themselves in the vicinity of Jaromiersch and Schmirschitz the Austrians could block the way from Nachod as well as that from Trautenau. As a last fall-back position before the more open country the Austrians had at their disposal the plateau of Chlum just to the north-west of Königgrätz, though it was Frederick who derived the greatest benefit from the opportunities thereabouts, in the course of his circuitous retreat from Moravia to Silesia in 1758. The positions were familiar to both parties, and the celebrated Austrian 'lost battery' which fought to the last in the Battle of Königgrätz in 1866 was sited by a Prussian redoubt which dated from the Silesian Wars,

When it was a question of going over to the offensive, the Austrians did not leave the Trautenau route entirely out of consideration, as it was the westernmost and the most direct communication from Bohemia to Silesia. Once inside Prussian territory, however, the Austrians were almost at once confronted by the strong field fortifications which the Prussian lieutenant general Fouqué was constructing in the hills in front of Landeshut, which deterred further progress until Loudon took the position by storm on 23 June 1760. This, together with the difficulties of the passage, was one of the reasons why the main axes of operations between Bohemia and Moravia ran further to the east.

King Frederick's favourite route was probably the one which led from Schweidnitz across the border to Braunau, and thence by way of Politz to Nachod and so to Königgrätz, 'for you have your depots nearby at Schweidnitz, and because, by entering Bohemia on this side you cover the whole of Lower Silesia.'[39] The route also appealed to Daun, coming in the opposite direction, for Braunau gave him a relatively secure base of provisions for his operations in Silesia. The other avenues ran to Bohemia though the County of Glatz, an irregular enclave of Prussian territory, framed by heights, which projected into the borderlands with Bohemia and Moravia.

The County of Glatz

From the fortress-town of Glatz the Prussians could reach north-eastern Bohemia either up the Steine valley and across the border to Braunau, or by way of Reinerz to Nachod, where the two routes joined. The two avenues were separated by the Heuscheuer- ('hay barn') Gebirge, one of those Central European ranges which made such an impact on the dawning Romantic imagination. For a Prussian officer of the time 'the All-Encompassing Power and Greatness of God has always seemed to be to manifest itself far more majestically and masterfully among the heights which disappear into the clouds than in the plains.'[40]

The passes were acceptable by the standards of the theatre of war, but they were objectively bad. Lacy chose the southern route when he travelled in a light open carriage to rejoin the army early in May 1762. 'We were drenched by a cold and piecing rain which did not let up the whole day, and churned up the roads so badly that we could not push on any further than Reinerz... where we arrived only after ten at night, frozen and soaked to the skin... The mountains are still in the grip of ice and snow. There is no sign of the sun, though it beats down so hard in the plains of Vienna that they are complaining of the heat.'[41]

A truly atrocious route, scarcely used in this war, ran across the southernmost salient of the county from Mittelwalde to Grulich in Bohemia. The eastern borders were closed off for all military purposes by the formidable walls of the Glatzer Schnee-Gebirge (1,442 m.) and the Altvater-Gebirge (1,490 m.).

At the heart of the county the already strong fortress complex at Glatz had been reinforced still further by the Prussians during the war. It defied the Austrians until Loudon took the place by his celebrated *coup de main* on 29 July 1760. The Austrians already controlled the passages of Silberberg and Wartha through the low Eulen-Gebirge, and now with the fortress-town of Glatz in their possession they had a usefully wide base for operations into the plain of Lower Silesia.

The mastery of the County of Glatz had wider dimensions which cannot be ignored. Nowhere else in the entire theatre did the Austrian effort have more the character of a war of liberation. The people were largely Catholic, and had suffered grievously under the rule of Lieutenant General Fouqué. 'They all greet one another with a "Praise be to Jesus Christ!" They all, young and old, carry rosaries... everywhere have been set up crucifixes and images of the Madonna and St. Nepomuk. As they returned from Wartha [a place of pilgrimage] many of the country folk came back carrying little candles in their pious way.'[42]

At the close of the campaign of 1762 Glatz was the only piece of Prussian territory which remained in Austrian hands. At the most delicate stage of the peace negotiations early the next year Frederick insisted that he must have the county back, claiming that it was more important to the security of Silesia than that of Bohemia. He succeeded in persuading historians to this effect ever since, and he was able to browbeat the Austrians at the time, though that was probably a measure of the state of their desperation than the validity of his argument. When peace had been under discussion two years earlier Kaunitz had been right to emphasised that 'we must bend every effort to ensure that if not Upper Silesia, at least the County of Glatz must remain to us, as an essential conquest and the key to the Kingdom of Bohemia.'[43]

Lower Silesia

Lower Silesia as a theatre of war existed in a number of important dimensions. Its wealth and its industrious population (1,200,00) made it a prize in its own right, as we have seen. In the southern highlands mining, trading and the manufacture of linen gave rise to a succession of towns, set among 'a continual interchange of hill and dale, exhibiting an endless variety of lovely prospects, frequent considerable villages and country seats; fields covered with luxuriant harvests; oaks rearing their majestic heads to the clouds, and streams meandering through meadows.' Hirschberg was located 'beneath the sublime gloom of the Giant Mountains.'[44] In Landeshut to the east was a square where 'the houses all around... have piazzas before them like those of Covent Garden in London, or the arcades of the Palais Royal at Paris... as the square is the centre of all business, and where all the markets are held, the traveller has always before him an appearance of activity, which makes the town look lively.'[45]

To the south of Landeshut a group of hills gave the Prussians 'a fine position... from whence they may, by an easy march on the left, cover the road that goes from Friedland to Schweidnitz, and sustain effectually any corps they may send to Schmiedeberg and Hirschberg. It was from this camp that Fouqué, with an inconsiderable army, often baffled the attempts made by the Austrians, though much superior, to penetrate that way into Silesia.'[46]

The situation was reversed whenever Frederick arrived on the scene in any strength, which gave rise to a number of classic confrontations later in the war, when we find the king looking for a chance to turn the Austrians out of their positions or to bring them to battle on the more open ground, while Daun clung to his camps on the heights, and was willing to venture into the plain only under the most favourable conditions. The high ground gave way to the plain on a much more even frontage than was the case in Saxony—it might almost have been laid out with a ruler—and the locations of interest ran in a long line from Bolkenhain at the west by way of Freiburg, Dittmannsdorf, Ludwigsdorf and Stein-Seiffersdorf to the exits from the County of Glatz at Silberberg and Wartha.

When operations were staged further into the plain the attention came to focus on road junctions such as those at Jauer, Striegau and nearby Hohenfriedberg, Reichenbach, Peterswaldau, Frankenstein and Münsterberg. As in Saxony, the Prussians enjoyed the facility of good transverse communications, whereas the Austrians could debouch into the lower ground only by isolated passages. In Silesia, moreover, the Prussians owned two fortresses on the immediate theatre of operations.

Over to the east the strengthened and extended fortress of Neisse gave the Prussians a base for operations into Moravia (below), and positioned them on the flank of any Austrian advance into Lower Silesia by way of Glatz. In the Seven Years War the Austrians made only one serious attempt to get rid of the nuisance, which was when Harsch attacked the place in 1758.

To the west, Schweidnitz and its new works lay in a fertile plain hard under the wooded heights of the Waldenburger-Gebirge, 'which look like a wall round the horizon,'[47] The place changed hands four times in the course of the war, which testifies to its importance. As a secure depot, replenished constantly by convoys coming overland from the Oder, Schweidnitz offered the Prussians a springboard for an advance into north-eastern Bohemia before the enemy were in any condition to respond. For the Austrians, Schweidnitz could be supplied securely enough by way of Braunau, and provided them with a much more convenient base for campaigning in Lower Silesia than did distant Zittau to the west. Schweidnitz was in addition of symbolic and practical use to the Austrians as a foothold in the northern plain and a flank support for their field armies.

Tactically advantageous positions were not easy to discover further into Lower Silesia, and the only feature which the Austrians found consistently useful was the isolated granite cone of the Zobten-Berg (730 m.), eight miles to the north-east of Schweidnitz. It was here that Prince Charles and Daun allowed their army its first rest in the headlong retreat from Leuthen in 1757, and the Zobten gave Daun his final support before he recoiled behind Schweidnitz in his last campaign in 1762. Frederick contrived to make something very strong out of the generally low ground nearby at Bunzelwitz in 1761, but that testifies to his tactical genius.

The river system of Silesia was dominated by the Oder, in the same way as the Elbe to the west dominated that of Saxony. Whereas the Austrians could make some use of the Elbe, the advantage of the navigation of the Oder lay wholly with the Prussians, and gave them a vital if not wholly reliable line of supplies. Liable to frequent and sudden flooding in the spring, it could fall so low in the late autumn that on 5 October 1757 Lieutenant General Tauentzien had to write to Frederick that both the river and the Lohe had almost completely dried out.

Unlike the Elbe, the Oder coursed for almost all its length through low country, and 'between great woods which prevent you from making out one bank from the other except for a few places between Breslau and Leubus.'[48] The area to the right (east) of the river was sandy, boggy and difficult of access, and was the scene of major operations only towards the end of the campaign of 1759, when Loudon was stranded among the Russians. The ground to the west was much more highly developed (in which it resembled the Elbe), but compartmentalised by a number of largish streams or little rivers which flowed from the highlands across the plain and met the Oder at right angles. Such were the Lohe, the Schweidnitzer-Wasser (Weistritz), the Katzbach, the Bober and the Queiss (the border river with Lusatia). Of these the most militarily significant was the Katzbach, which was scarcely a stone's-throw across, but ran swiftly in its sunken bed on its way to the Oder near Parchwitz, and bulked large in the manoeuvres before the battles of Leuthen in 1757 and Liegnitz in 1760.

Silesia, then, was a land of one great river. But it was also the site of many strongholds which made the province a very 'strong' country, of which the war 'was a very striking proof, for, undoubtedly, the king owed his preservation to the excellent order all his fortresses were in, and the numerous garrisons they were furnished with.'[49]

Neisse and Schweidnitz stood towards the southern uplands, while all the rest were strung along the Oder. Cosel in Upper Silesia upstream was a small but strong place which held out against Loudon in November 1760. Little Brieg thirty-four miles above Breslau was sunk in decay, but Breslau itself (pop. 40,000) was rivalled only by Dresden and Leipzig as one of the great cities of the scene of war. It lay at the intersection of road systems between eastern and western Europe, and between the Baltic and the Adriatic. It gathered in the linen and other commodities from the industrious highland region of Lower Silesia, and enjoyed the facility of water communication direct to the Baltic, and by means of the Friedrich-Wilhelms Canal, the Spree, the Havel and the Elbe to the North Sea. It was supported by the most agriculturally productive area of Silesia, 'which is another great benefit to the country, always keeping the markets brisk.'[50]

The earthen ramparts and wet ditches of the Breslau fortifications were incapable of withstanding a serious siege, and the city fell to the Austrians easily enough in November 1757. They lost it again soon after the battle of Leuthen, and were never to get it back, even when Loudon arrived outside in 1760.

The last of the fortresses of the Silesian Oder was the strong and agreeably-situated Glogau. It supplied Frederick with the heavy artillery which he put to such good use in the battle of Leuthen. Thereafter it became of interest as lying at the intersection of the Austrian and Russian axes of operations, and for that reason there were 'generally immense magazines and a numerous garrison in this town. It covers the country so effectually that no enterprise of consequence can be undertaken on that side of Silesia until you are master of it.'[51]

After every harvest Frederick took care to bring the grain of the neighbourhood for safekeeping behind the ramparts of Glogau (a practice he followed in relation to Breslau and its countryside), a cunning measure which augmented the supply difficulties of the Russians, who had their nearest magazine sixty miles away on the Warthe, which was itself supplied only with difficulty from the Russian base area along the Vistula (Weichsel) deep inside Poland. The Russians therefore had to apply to the Austrians for help in the matter of provisions, which exacerbated the friction between the respective commanders, confined serious operations to the period between July and October, and rendered any allied successes short-lived. The siege of Glogau was much discussed in the two headquarters, but never put into effect. 'For these reasons all the operations of this [Russian] army were reduced to marching from the Vistula into Silesia, and after fighting and ravaging the country, to the returning again on the Vistula.'[52]

Brandenburg and Berlin

As it continued on its way to the Baltic, the Oder divided the Neumark of Brandenburg to the east from the Kurmark and Berlin to the west. The riverine fortress of Cüstrin with its brick ramparts lay on the direct path of a Russian advance on the capital. 'The situation... is very advantageous, and may be considered as one of the chief keys of Silesia and Brandenburg, particularly the last, whenever an invasion is expected from the Lower Vistula, that is, from

Warsaw to Danzig… This place is small, and not at all strong, yet the Russians who attacked it in 1758 failed in their attempt. It held out till the king came and relieved it, by gaining the battle of Zorndorf.'[53]

The town of Frankfurt twenty miles upstream gave the traveller an impression of prosperity, which did not survive if he turned west towards Berlin. In the heart of Brandenburg the lakes and swamps alternated with unkempt woods and desolate fields where it was possible to see 'scattered spires of wheat, rye, barley and oats shooting from the sand, like the hairs upon a head almost bald.'[54] The typical road was a tract of sand which led through the gloomy forests. The country to the south of Berlin promised little better, for it extended into the wilds of Lower Lusatia.

To the west of Berlin the citadel of Spandau, at the meeting of the Spree and the Havel, offered the Prussian court a final refuge for its personnel and treasures. Potsdam was set amid the lakes of the Havel, but was totally undefended, and Berlin itself was protected by nothing more than an excise barrier. Nowhere in the surrounding country could Frederick identify a tactically coherent defensive position.

On two occasions in the war Berlin was actually occupied by hostile forces, but the Prussian army and monarchy survived intact. The enemy were by definition acting at the limit of long and potentially vulnerable lines of communication, and in such a way Hadik could afford to remain for less than two days in 1757. The Russians and Austrians held Berlin for only a little longer in 1760, and they too had to cut short their stay, and without inflicting essential damage on the Prussian military establishments in the capital.

The Easternmost Corridors

Moravia and the Marchfeld

On no occasion during the Seven Years War did the Austrians venture a substantial invasion of Prussian territory by way of Moravia. It is therefore reasonable to consider this avenue of operations exclusively as a means of bringing Prussian forces into a particularly sensitive area of the Austrian monarchy. No other direction was more likely to trigger alarm among the Austrians, for the ways across the border were the most open in the whole theatre of war, and in a matter of days the Prussians could arrive in the heart of the blooming province of Moravia and be set on the way to Vienna. There is no evidence to suggest that Frederick harboured any serious intention of taking and holding the capital, but he treasured the option of advancing into Moravia as the most potent of possible diversions, which might win him time to deal with other enemies (as he hoped in 1758), or help him to make more serious conquests in Bohemia.

The Prussians were separated from the lowlands of central Moravia only by a rolling plateau. They had an excellent base at Neisse, and the border was accessible from many points in their territory—from Neisse itself due south by way of Zuckmantel and Friedland, for example, or (as Frederick chose in 1758) further to the east by way of Jägerndorf and Troppau. The last town was the capital of Austrian Silesia, which was stranded on the 'wrong' side of the highland zone and therefore indefensible, whatever its symbolic and political value as the sole piece of Silesia left to the Austrians.

The routes converged on the brow of the plateau above Sternberg. From there the view to the south seemed endless, and it was almost possible to imagine oneself already within sight of Vienna. Within six days of crossing the border in 1758 Frederick reached the levels of the upper March (Morava) at Littau. He was now in the Hanna, the immensely fertile region of black earth which extended around Littau, Olmütz, Prerau and Kremsier. Rice was cultivated in the watery levels, flax and grain on the drier ground, and vines on the hillsides. Horses and cattle abounded. The towns were well built and 'not nearly as gloomy and dead as in Bohemia or Silesia. Even the people make a much better impression. They are obliging, and go out of their way to welcome even the foreigners who do not speak their language. A certain refinement and cleanliness adds to the favourable impression. In the spring and autumn the houses in all the villages are refreshed with a new coat of wash.'[55] The Liechtensteins and other great families had seats thereabouts, and Count Kaunitz owned the estate of Austerlitz just outside Brünn.

Frederick calculated that the fortress-town of Olmütz, the guardian of the Hanna, would fall to him within ten days at the most, and meanwhile his light forces sent de Ville's cavalry scampering back towards the ramparts of Brünn (pop. 11,000), the last tenable place on the direct route to Vienna by way of the *Kaiserstrasse*. This too Frederick dismissed as a fortress of little account. Alternatively a push to the left, as the Prussians saw it, could bring them down the flat Marchfeld (the continuation of the Hanna) to the Danube at Pressburg just inside Hungary. There was consternation in Vienna, and the court (though not Maria Theresa) entertained thoughts of abandoning the capital.

Frederick's schemes were overset by a number of unforeseen circumstances. He had underestimated both the strength of the new fortifications at Olmütz and the determination of old Marschall the governor. He had been unaware that Austrians now had a proper general staff, and were able to bring their army speedily and secretly across the rocky and forested hills which separated Bohemia and Moravia. Lastly he had not taken into account the hostility of the Moravian peasants, and the enterprise of commanders like Loudon and Siskovics, who ruined his great convoy at Unter-Gundersdorf and Domstadtl. Frederick made a model retreat, which did much to retrieve his reputation. Olmütz remained to the Austrians, and from 1760 became the home of one of their siege trains, which spared the long transport from Vienna.

The Jablunka

We cannot leave the theatre of war without taking into account the Jablunka Pass, a strategic back door which connected north-western Hungary with the low Moravian Gate and with Upper Silesia. In the crisis of the First Silesian War it had enabled Hungarian irregular forces to cross the Carpathians and reach the scene of operations. This wild and remote passage would have been forgotten in the Seven Years War if the Prussian lieutenant general Werner had not come this way with his light corps in 1762, in the hope of undertaking almost a Protestant-Muslim jihad in concert with Crimean Tartars who were supposed to be coming by way of Poland. The outlandish project came to nothing, but the authorities in Vienna now had to look to the security of the Jablunka and indeed all the other passes on the borders of Hungary and Transylvania.

APPENDIX 2
SOME MILITARY BIOGRAPHIES

These sketches are intended in the main to emphasise the contribution of a number of the lesser ranking commanders. The field ranks are given in the contemporary Austrian style of abbreviations:

GFWM. (*Generalfeldwachtmeister*) = Major General
FML. (*Feldmarschalllieutenant*) = Lieutenant General
FZM. (*Feldzeugmeister*) = full General
GdC (*General der Cavallerie*) = full General
FM. (*Feldmarschall*) = Field Marshal

Arenberg, Charles Marie Raymond, Duke, 1721-78

A son of one of the most distinguished families of Hainault in the Netherlands, he was nevertheless made to learn the military trade from private soldier upwards. *FML.* 1755. In 1757 he took part in the assaults at Gabel and Moys, and commanded the infantry in the siege of Schweidnitz. *FZM.* 22 January 1758. Cogniazzo writes that his natural level of command was that of a line or wing, but the record shows that his capacities were already being over-taxed. Daun was disappointed by his performance on the right wing at Hochkirch. He was defeated in command of a detached corps at Pretzch on 29 October 1759, and was partly responsible for the disastrous counterattack by the regiments of Wied, Puebla, Kaiser and Kollowrat at Torgau.

Amadei, Carl Baron, 1723-96

Lieutenant colonel 1755. Made colonel in recognition of his storm of the Prussian positions on the White Mountain outside Prague on 20 June 1757. Distinguished at Leuthen, and again in the attack on the great redoubt at Hochkirch. *GFWM.* since 27 June 1760, he commanded the storming columns at Schweidnitz in 1761. Amadei had suggested the novel formation in columns for the attack at Hochkirch, and was known as one of the most active and intelligent officers of the army.

d'Ayasasa, Antoine Albert Joseph Count, 1713-79

A distinguished cavalry officer of Netherlands origin. As colonel of the Hessen-Darmstadt Dragoons he won the Small Cross of the Military Order of Maria Theresa for leading a counterattack at Kolin; promoted to *GFWM.* later in 1757. Commanded the first line of elite cavalry at Hochkirch. Distinguished in the action at Kunzendorf 17 September 1760, and made repeated counterattacks with a mixed reserve at Torgau. He was a close confidant of Daun, who employed him on a number of delicate missions to Vienna in the course of the war.

Beck, Philipp Lewin, Baron, c. 1720-68

1755 *GFWM.* and commander of the Warasdin Military Border. It did not take him long to make his name as a commander of light forces in the course of the new war. He carried out a diversionary attack at Brandeis on 1 May 1757 (the day of the battle of Prague), and he was active in the pursuit after Kolin. Captured the Duke of Bevern after the battle of Breslau, but was himself taken prisoner in Breslau after Leuthen, having been denied permission to break out of the city. During his brief captivity before being exchanged he impressed the Prussians as a keen-eyed man who was probably seeing too much. As a *FML.* his remarkable exploits in 1759 included the elimination of Prussian detachments at Cossdorf, Grünberg and Cölln (opposite Meissen). Attached to the main army, he beat off a Prussian lunge at Nieder-Arnsdorf in September 1760. On 16 August 1762 he struck at the rear of Bevern's corps at Reichenbach, but was unsupported by the other forces which were designated for the attack. Beck had a rare talent for independent command, and his operations were characterised by accurate intelligence, the massing of superior forces, and the good order which he maintained in his corps. He did not bother to ingratiate himself with protectors or factions, and never enjoyed the public fame which was attached to Loudon.

Browne de Camus, Maximilian Ulysses Count, 1705-57

FM. 1754. High in the esteem of the court and the troops, Browne commanded the main field army in 1756. His little battle at Lobositz confronted the Prussians for the first time with the greatly-improved Austrian army, and gained him the opportunity to execute a bold if unsuccessful attempt to rescue the beleaguered Saxon army at Pirna. Browne mistakenly discounted the threat of a Prussian invasion in 1757, and had to cede the high command to Prince Charles of Lorraine. The shaken Austrian army was defeated at Prague, and Browne sustained a wound which ultimately proved fatal. He died on 6 July. *(See the references in the main text)*

Brentano-Cimarolli, Joseph, Count, c. 1718-64

Born of a Lombard family, Brentano became one of the most outstanding of the new generation of Austrian commanders which emerged in the Seven Years War. Brentano fought at Prague, and was active in the successful campaigns of the late summer and autumn of 1757. He was captured after Leuthen, but (like Beck) was soon exchanged, and was promoted to *GFWM.* in the summer of 1758. In the following year Brentano commanded the western attack at Maxen, and won high praise from Daun. In 1760 Lacy prized him equally highly for his actions at Lichtenberg and Goldberg and in the course of the raid on Berlin. Brentano's brilliant action at Adelsbach on 6 July 1762 frustrated a daring manoeuvre of Frederick in Silesia. He was then described as being in poor health, which perhaps helps to account for his indifferent performance in the complicated action at Reichenbach. He was nevertheless advanced to *FML.* and awarded the Grand Cross of the Military Order of Maria Theresa. This exceptionally promising career was cut short when Brentano died on 7 July 1764 at the age of forty-five.

Buccow, Adolph Nicolaus. Baron, ? - 1764

A north German who had risen in the Austrian cavalry, Buccow entered on the campaign of 1756 as a *FML.* and one of Browne's most trusted officers. At Leuthen the next year he contrived to hold up the Prussian advance in such a way as to enable the Austrians to make a stand outside Leuthen village. In 1758 Buccow was promoted to *GdC*. He co-ordinated the operations which led to the destruction of the great Prussian convoy at Domstadtl, and after the raising of the siege of Olmütz he made a creditable attempt to block Frederick's escape by way of north-eastern Bohemia. He fought at Hochkirch with distinction, and on 28 January 1760 Daun described him as an admirably active and versatile commander. Buccow nevertheless had the reputation of being something of a soldier of fortune, and he was no friend of Lacy. He directed some important counterattacks at Torgau but suffered a wound which contributed to his removal from active service. In his new post as commanding general in Transylvania he raised a National Militia, and helped to allay some of the panics attending the threat of a Turkish invasion.

Caramelli di Castiglione Fallet, Carl, Count, 1716-88

Caramelli was a Piedmontese nobleman who spent his career in the Austrian cavalry. He saw action as a colonel at Kolin, Breslau and Leuthen, while his performance at Domstadtl, where he was engaged in hand-to-hand combat, earned him promotion to *GFWM.* Caramelli was a brigade commander at Hochkirch, and in 1759 he was established as a trusted member of Loudon's military circle, fighting at Kunersdorf and again at Landeshut, where his pursuit helped to complete the victory. In the early summer Loudon commissioned him to arrange operational plans with the Russians.

Charles-Alexandre de Lorraine et Bar, Prince, 1712-80

Prince Charles of Lorraine owed his standing above all to the fact that he was brother to Emperor Francis Stephen, and thus brother-in-law to Maria Theresa. He was not without genuine ability, as was shown by his performance against the Turks in 1738, and against the French and Bavarians in the earlier campaigns of the War of the Austrian Succession. The Prussians proved to be a more formidable proposition. His reputation never recovered entirely from the beatings he took from the Prussians in 1745, but his self-confidence, together with the favour of Maria Theresa, restored him to high command in the spring of 1757. She continued to offer him her support immediately after the dreadful defeat at Leuthen, but an accumulation of damning evidence induced her on 16 January 1758 to tell him that he must give up the command. After the war Prince Charles became a highly successful governor of the Austrian Netherlands, and he died in that post in 1780. *(See the references in the main text)*

Daun, Leopold Joseph Maria, Count, Prince of Thiano, 1705-66

Son of the famous *FM.* Wirich Philipp Daun, who defended Turin in 1706. *GFWM. 1737; FML. 1739.* One of the leaders of military reform in the late 1740s and early 1750s, being author of the *Daun'sche Reglement* of 1749 and the founder and first director of the Military Academy at Wiener Neustadt. Invested with the Golden Fleece in 1753; *FM. 1754.* Victor at Hochkirch, and commander of the main field army 1758-62. His name became synonymous with the Austrian conduct of war. *(See the references in the main text)*

Esterházy, Emmerich Count, 1726-92

Emmerich was a member of the multi-branched Esterházy family of western Hungary, and was prominent in the Seven Years War as an officer of hussars, rising from colonel to *GFWM.* (1758) and to *FML.* in 1763. He provided a most efficient screen for Daun's march east from Stolpen before the battle of Hochkirch. Two years later he took part in Lacy's raid on Berlin, and seized the opportunity to help himself to valuables in Frederick's palace of Sans Souci.

Esterházy, Nicolaus Joseph, Count (Prince from 1783), 1714-90

GFWM. at the outbreak of the war. He was known mainly as a commander of hussars, but led an infantry brigade with success at Kolin, and was immediately promoted to *FML.* The French attaché Champeaux reported highly on his ability and attachment to the French alliance, but Nicolaus did not share in the further promotions which advanced Lacy, Loudon and others to *FZM.* He is remembered in history as the patron of Haydn.

Esterházy, Paul Anton, Prince, 1711-62

GdC. at the beginning of the war. He was a diplomat as well as a soldier, and politically valuable to the Habsburgs as head of the famous line of Hungarian grandees. He was promoted to *FM.* in 1758, but solely because he was disgruntled at being denied an active command in the cavalry.

Fabris (Tomiotti di Fabris), Dominik, Conte di Cassano, 1725-99

A Venetian nobleman who began the war as a captain in the Austrian service. He made his reputation as a highly accomplished officer in the new General Staff. As a major he persuaded Daun to overcome his doubts and to persist with his advance at Maxen, and he was promoted to lieutenant colonel in the field. Both Daun and Lacy valued his services highly, and later in the war he was distinguished at Torgau (where he was wounded), the storm of Schweidnitz and at Adelsbach. His long and career culminated in 1788 when as *FZM.* he successfully defended Transylvania against the Turks. He was also renowned as a supporter of the arts.

Giannini, Ernst Friedrich Alexander, Count of the Holy Roman Empire, Marchese Carpenato Suavio, 1719-75

Giannini was the son of a Modenese family which had settled in Silesia. As a lieutenant colonel in the regiment of Botta he was wounded and captured on 26 September 1756, very early in the war. After being exchanged he became colonel in the Engineering Corps in April 1757, and in this capacity he was able to get into the besieged fortress of Olmütz in 1758 and take part in the defence. He acted as chief of staff to Loudon from 1759 to 1762, and was promoted to *GFWM.* in 1760. Giannini was a restless and demanding individual, and proved more of a hindrance than a help to his superior Franz Guasco in the defence of Schweidnitz in 1762. After the war he became a celebrated and ferocious director of the Wiener Neustadt Military Academy.

Gribeauval de Vaquette, Jean-Baptiste, 1715-89

Gribeauval came to Vienna in the suite of the French envoy Broglie. In 1758 he was admitted to the Austrian service with the rank of *GFWM.*, and became technical director in the siege of Glatz (1760) and the famous defence of Schweidnitz in 1762. He was promoted to *FML.*, but declined the offer to remain in the Austrian service after the war and returned to France, where he became Director General of Artillery in 1776. His study of the Austrian Artillery System of 1753 inspired him to reform the French ordnance, and he thus laid the foundation of the mighty artillery of Napoleon.

The Brothers Guasco:

Franz, Count, 1711-63

An officer of Piedmontese origin, Franz left the service of Russia for that of Austria in 1752, gaining the rank of *GFWM*. He commanded detachments of grenadiers at Kolin, Moys, Schweidnitz and Breslau in 1757, and in January 1757 was promoted to *FML*. He conducted the negotiations which led to the Prussians surrendering Dresden in 1759, and he helped Maguire to defend that place in the following year. His most signal action was, however, his epic sixty-two day defence of Schweidnitz in 1762. While he was still in captivity he learned that he had been promoted to *FZM.* and awarded the Grand Cross of the Military Order of Maria Theresa. He died at Königsberg on 23 March 1763, a matter of days before he was due to be released.

Peter Alexander, Count, 1714-80

Younger brother of the above, Peter Alexander was a colonel at the start of the Seven Years War, and commanded forces of grenadiers at Kolin, Moys and Breslau. He was taken prisoner after Leuthen, but was very soon exchanged, and saw the campaign of 1758 as *GFWM*. He was promoted to *FML.* in 1759, and to *FZM.* in 1771, in which rank he commanded at Prague in the War of the Bavarian Succession. The brothers Guasco were seen by their enemies as adventurers who were notoriously lucky at cards.

Hadik, Andreas, Count, 1710-90

The youthful Andreas had wished to undergo training as a Jesuit, but was forced into a military career by his father. He devoted himself to his new vocation with enthusiasm, and his energy and meticulous planning were deployed to good effect when as a *FML* he raided Berlin in October 1757. Promoted *GdC.* March 1758. In the high summer of 1759 he was assigned with Loudon to join the Russians, but their two forces became separated and Hadik was unable to take a direct part in the subsequent campaign of Kunersdorf. For most of the war, however, Hadik saw service with the Austrian contingents in Saxony. The success of his schemes did not always correspond with the care which went into their preparation, but Daun knew that he had in him a general who was capable of exercising command at the highest level. In September 1762 Hadik took Serbelloni's place in Saxony, and succeeded so well that Kaunitz allowed himself to hope that triumph in that theatre might make up for Daun's failure in Silesia. Unfortunately the command in Saxony was divided for political reasons, and the isolated forces of the *Reichsarmee* and its supporting Austrians were defeated by Prince Henry at Freiberg. All Saxony except the area around Dresden was lost, and the Austrians were devoid of bargaining assets when they entered into talks for peace. Hadik's reputation survived largely intact. In 1774 he became *FM.* and President of the *Hofkriegsrath*. He commanded the main army in the War of the Bavarian Succession, and would have commanded against the Turks in 1789 if he had not been overtaken by his last illness. *(See the references in the main text)*

Hildburghausen, Joseph Maria Friedrich, Prince, 1702-87

This sovereign prince of the Empire was for a time groomed for the highest command (he married the niece of Prince Eugene of Savoy), and was promoted to *FM.* in 1741. After a brief spell with the army of the opposing Bavarians he returned to the Austrian service, and in the later 1740s he began the reform of the Croatian Military Borders. His active career was terminated by his disastrous experiences as commander of the *Reichsarmee* in 1757. Hildburghausen had some excellent notions for improving that organisation, but he was on the worst possible terms with his own generals and with his French counterpart Soubise. The joint army was routed at Rossbach on 6 November 1757. Still convinced that he had been in the right, he resigned on 26 January 1758 and never again saw active service.

Jahnus von Eberstädt, Franz Maximilian, Baron, 1711-72

Jahnus hailed from a Thuringian family, and studied at the University of Jena before following his father into the Austrian service. As a colonel with the Croats he took an active part in reorganising the Military Borders before the war, and in 1757 we find him roaming Silesia with a force of 4,000 Croats. On 14 August he beat off an attack by the Prussian major general Kreytzen on the Buch-Berg near Landeshut, and was rewarded by promotion to *GFWM.* and by the Little Cross of the Military Order of Maria Theresa. Amongst many other actions he took part in the great ambush at Domstadtl in 1758, and Loudon's storm of Schweidnitz in 1761. He had been promoted to *FML.* in 1760, but he was disinclined to stay in the Austrian service after the war and became Town Commandant of Hamburg.

Kinsky von Chinitz und Tettau, Franz Ulrich, Prince, 1726-92

While still young Franz Ulrich became head of one of the leading noble houses of Bohemia, but he remained dedicated to a military career. His work as an acting colonel at Lobositz earned him promotion to *GFWM.*, and as a brigade commander at Kolin he enabled the regiment of Botta to stay in the battle by commandeering an ammunition cart at pistol point. Kinsky managed a column at Moys and commanded a brigade at Hochkirch, then changed the direction of his career and entered the artillery. He succeeded Liechtenstein as Director General in 1772, but the great day of this distinguished public servant remained that of Kolin, on 18 June 1757.

Kleefeld von Hnogek, Wenzel Matthias, Baron, 1713-79

As commander of the Szluiner Croats on 18 June 1757 Colonel Kleefeld helped to delay the initial Prussian advance. He was promoted to *GFWM.*, and in October he screened the western flank of Hadik's march to Berlin. Thereafter he was constantly active in operations large and small in Saxony, and in helping to calm the increasingly mutinous Croats. He became *FML.* in 1760. The French officer de Guibert visited his household after the war, and was impressed by the simple and old-fashioned German manners which prevailed there.

Lacy, Franz Moritz, Count, 1725-1801

Franz Moritz was the son of an Irish-born Russian field marshal, and a relation of the celebrated *FM.* Browne. As a colonel and acting brigade commander he gained high praise for his conduct at Lobositz, and was promoted to *GFWM.* He had been wounded in that battle, and was wounded again at Prague and Leuthen. Early in 1758 he was made *FML.* and Austria's first proper chief of the General Staff. The operations of the army were now conducted with much greater efficiency, and the victories at Hochkirch and Maxen are to be attributed largely to Lacy's excellent staff work. He was promoted to *FZM.*, but in 1760 he chose to resign his functions as chief of staff and became a corps commander. He repeatedly frustrated the schemes of Frederick, and in October he raided Berlin in association with the Russians. Loudon, his supposed rival, nevertheless stood higher in public opinion, and Lacy's reputation suffered from his disappointing failures at Liegnitz and Torgau in 1760. In 1765 Lacy became *FM.* and succeeded Daun as President of the *Hofkriegsrath*. He worked tirelessly to reform the army, and in 1778 in the War of the Bavarian Succession he succeeded in checking Frederick's advance into Bohemia. Towards the end of his service Lacy again had the experience of being eclipsed by Loudon, whose victorious campaign against the Turks in 1789 stood in contrast with Lacy's failure against those enemies in the previous year. *(See the references in the main text)*

Loudon, Gideon Ernst, Baron, 1716-90

Loudon's early military career was that of a typical soldier of fortune. Having left the Russian army he was rejected for the Prussian service by King Frederick in person, and took service with the Austrians in the notorious 'Pandour' band of Colonel Trenck. He broke with that gentleman in 1745, and in the following year was appointed major with the Liccaner Croats. Loudon's success as a leader of fast-moving detachments gained him rapid promotion in the Seven Years War, becoming colonel and *GFWM.* in 1757, *FML.* in 1758 and *FZM.* in 1759. His military contemporaries were aware of his moodiness and other failings, but he became the darling of the public and he enjoyed the support of Kaunitz. Loudon contributed greatly to the joint Russo-Austrian victory at Kunersdorf. His defeat at Liegnitz was laid at the door of Daun and Lacy, and Loudon went on to repay the Prussians by beating them at Landeshut, then storming the strongholds of Glatz and Schweidnitz. As *FM.* Loudon performed below his best against the Prussians in northern Bohemia in 1778, but he more than fulfilled the hopes which were invested in him when he took Belgrade from the Turks in 1789. This crowning achievement entitles him to dispute with Prince Eugene of Savoy the claim to be Austria's foremost soldier of the eighteenth century. *(See the references in the main text)*

Löwenstein-Wertheim, Christian Philipp Johann Alexander, Prince, 1719-81

Christian Philipp had the advantage of being born to a leading house of Baden, but he made his way in the Austrian service through his genuine talents as an officer of cavalry. As *FML.* he fought at Lobositz and Kolin, and did so well at Breslau that he was chosen to bring the official news of the victory to Vienna. In 1758 Löwenstein pioneered the introduction of *chevaulegers* (light dragoons) in the Austrian service, but Daun began to complain of his penchant for intrigue and malicious gossip. In 1760 Löwenstein gained his long sought-for promotion to *GdC.*, and commanded a mixed reserve at Torgau. At Teplitz in north Bohemia (2 August 1762) he gained a critical victory which safeguarded the supply line of the Austrian army in Saxony.

Lucchesi d'Averna, Joseph, Count, ? - 1757

Lucchesi is described as a hot-blooded Sicilian who was brought up in Spain. He made his reputation as a general adjutant in the 1730s, when he became a firm friend of Maximilian Browne. *FML.* 1745. At Piacenza (1746) he turned the course of the battle by a brilliant counter-charge with his cavalry. *GdC.* 1754. Governor of Brussels 1757. Killed at Leuthen when he tried to emulate his feat at Piacenza.

Maguire von Inniskillin, Johan Sigismund, Count, ? - 1767

Maguire was active in the reform of the Military Border before the war. As *FML.* he was in action at Lobositz and Prague, and commanded the storm of Gabel (14-15 July 1757). Thereafter Maguire's name was associated with operations in Saxony. He captured Sonnenstein in 1758, and besieged and took Dresden the next year, which helped to secure his promotion to *FZM.* He defended that place with success in 1760. In May 1762 Maguire took nominal charge of the *Reichsarmee*, but he resigned that post on finding that Serbelloni was making the exercise of command impossible.

Marschall von Biberstein, Ernst Dietrich, Baron, 1692-1771

Marschall began his career in the service of his native Saxony, and as a very young officer campaigned under Marlborough in the Netherlands. He transferred to the Austrians in 1717, fought in a great variety of theatres, and was made *FZM.* in recognition of his outstanding defence of the fortress of Maastricht in 1748. He commanded on the right wing at Kolin, and gave further proof of his determination and technical skills when he defended Olmütz in 1758. He was promoted to *FM.* and awarded the Grand Cross of the Military Order of Maria Theresa.

Nádasdy auf Fogaras, Franz, Count, 1708-83

In 1756 *GdC.* Nádasdy was kept busy mobilising the *Grenzer* in his capacity as Ban of Croatia. In

1757 he commanded on the right wings at Kolin and Moys. He was then detached to besiege Schweidnitz, and after the capture of that fortress he returned to the main army, and was posted with his corps on the exposed left wing at Leuthen. He became one of the scapegoats for the defeat, and although he was promoted to *FM*. In 1758 he returned to his former responsibilities in Croatia. Nádasdy retained his standing with the people and all ranks of the army, and was recalled to active service in 1778 to command in Galicia.

Nugent-Westmeath, Jacob Robert, Count, 1720-94

Nugent made his name in the early years of the war as a lieutenant colonel in the General Staff. As such he played a major role in the relief of Olmütz in 1758, and directed a column at Hirschfeld in February 1759. As a colonel he was captured in the course of a sortie from Dresden in June 1760, and the loss of this outstanding staff officer was felt all the more severely because Lacy had left the staff to take up a field command (above). Nugent made a deep impression on his Prussian captors, and was appointed ambassador to Berlin in 1764. His good personal relations with Frederick enabled him to allay the king's fears concerning an apparent Austrian mobilisation in 1768. He meanwhile retained military rank, and was promoted *FML*. in 1767. His son Laval became a *FM*. in the next century.

The Brothers O'Donnell

Carl, Count, 1715-71

A *GFWM*. at the outset of the war, Carl was promoted *FML*. for his services at Lobositz. He was captured at Leuthen, but exchanged soon afterwards. He commanded the first column of the main attack at Hochkirch, and as GdC. he exercised the overall tactical command at Maxen. At Torgau he repulsed the attack of Holstein's cavalry and took charge of the army after Daun left the field. At Reichenbach in 1762 he had to contend against greatly superior odds as commander of the cavalry on the exposed left wing of the army. Appointed Inspector General of the cavalry in 1765. Carl was of an amiable disposition, he played the flute, and he enjoyed the company of a young mistress by the name of Augusta. Daun describes him as being something of a showman.

Johann, Count, 1712-84

Johann entered the Austrian cavalry simultaneously with his brother Carl in 1736. He was a *GFWM*. at Leuthen, where he was captured after an epic struggle. He was duly exchanged, and his Jung-Modena Dragoons cleared the whole length of the Maxner-Berg at Maxen, thereby laying open the Prussian position. Promoted *FML*. in 1760.

O'Kelly von Gallagh und Tywoly, Baron, ? - 1767

GFWM. O'Kelly was awarded the Small Cross of the Military Order of Maria Theresa for his work at Breslau, and promoted *FML*. in January 1758. He gave a good account of himself at Hochkirch, Kunzendorf (September 1760) and more particularly at in the later stages of the battle of Torgau. No proper recognition was forthcoming, and in 1762 O'Kelly had the misfortune to command the isolated corps which came under attack by the main Prussian army at Burkersdorf.

Ried, Johann Heinrich, Baron, 1720-79

Ried (a German from the Rhineland) commanded the Gradiscaner Croats as colonel at the beginning of the war. He led the advance guard in Hadik's expedition against Berlin, and was then engaged in numerous actions in Saxony. In 1759 he was broke though to Dresden, then under siege, and was rewarded with the rank of *GFWM*. and the Knight's Cross of the Military Order of Maria Theresa. His speciality then seemed to become running fights against greatly superior Prussian forces—at Arnsdorf and Hoch-Giersdorf on 17 September 1760, and again immediately before Torgau. On the day of the actual battle he did what he could to hold up the Prussian advance through the woods, and then launched counterattacks against the right flank of the enemy breakthrough

Serbelloni, Giovanni Battista, Count, 1697-1778

Serbelloni was an elderly and already high-ranking (*GdC*.) officer at the start of the Seven

Years War. His regiment of cuirassiers was one of the finest in the army, and his wing of cavalry stood firm under artillery fire at Kolin, thus winning valuable time for Daun. His austere virtues were nevertheless offset by objectionable eccentricities which rivalled those of Hildburghausen (q.v.); officers removed themselves from his command if they had the chance, and the attaché Marainville doubted whether he had two friends in the entire army. Serbelloni spent most of the rest of the war in Saxony, and in April 1761 (now *FM.*) he took command of the *Reichsarmee*. That force was in a deplorable state when he finally took his leave on 2 September 1762. He had been sustained by the favour of Emperor Francis Stephen, and by his importance to the Austrians as a representative of one of the great families of the Milanese.

Sincère, Claudius, c. 1696-1769

As a celebrated disciplinarian, Sincère (one of the army's Lorrainers) was regarded as an authority on matters concerning the infantry in general. In spite of his advanced age he took on a new lease of life in the early years of the war, being promoted to *FML.* in 1756, to *FZM.* in January 1757, and having the command of the left wing at Hochkirch. Daun then suspected that Sincère had reached the limit of his competence, for, although being a master of routine, he describes him as going to pieces under pressure.

Siskovics, Joseph, Count, 1719-83

One of the most formidable individuals in the army, Siskovics was colonel commandant of the Hungarian infantry regiment of Erzherzog Carl at the outset of the war. At Kolin his defence of the outlying hamlet of Chozenitz played an important part in disrupting the Prussian scheme of attack. He was awarded the Little Cross of the Military Order of Maria Theresa and promoted to *GFWM*. Loudon blamed him for turning up late for the first attack on the great Prussian convoy north of Olmütz on 28 June 1758, but in fact Siskovics played the greater part in the decisive action at Domstadtl two days later. Siskovics went on to command a grenadier brigade at Hochkirch and again at Maxen. Daun describes him as a soldier through and through, and the Prince de Ligne recalls the experience of being in a mixed brigade which was being manoeuvred by Siskovics in person, and heard him command in French, German, Hungarian and Italian. Siskovics (unlike Sincère) was more than a great drillmaster, and trained his troops in marksmanship against targets.

de Ville de Camon, Charles, Marquis, 1705-92

The influence of Francis Stephen also supported de Ville, a fellow Lorrainer. He was a brigade commander at Hochkirch, and as a *FML.* he conducted a fighting retreat in the face of the Prussian invasion of Moravia in the spring of 1758. He was rewarded by the rank of *GdC.* and by the Knight's Cross of the Military Order of Maria Theresa. In 1759 he wrested the command of a corps from *FZM.* Harsch, his nominal superior, and launched an ill-conceived offensive into Silesia. He had to turn back, and he was lucky not to be destroyed before he reached safety in Bohemia. In 1759 he left Lusatia open to the rampaging Prince Henry of Prussia after the battle of Kunersdorf, and Daun told him to leave the army. Much to his surprise, and that of Francis Stephen, he was given no further responsible command.

Wied (Wied-Runkel), Friedrich Georg Heinrich, Count, 1712-79

At Kolin the mobile reserve under *FML.* Wied was the first formation to move to check the Prussian flanking attack. Wied did well at Moys, and at Breslau he brought up the reserve at an opportune moment and rolled up the enemy defences behind the Lohe. He covered the escape of the beaten army on the night after Leuthen, and as *FZM.* was awarded the Grand Cross of the Military Order of Maria Theresa for his services at Torgau. It was becoming increasingly rare to draw favourable opinions from Daun concerning his generals, but he continued to report on Wied in warm terms. After the war this excellent man became commanding general in Bohemia, where he promoted education and the economy, and mitigated the effects of the famine of 1771-2. He died as *FM.* and commanding general in Lombardy

APPENDIX 3
LIST OF REGIMENTS

The numbers correspond to the numbers entered on our maps, and are those first awarded to the regiments in 1769. At the time of the war the regiments were known exclusively by the name of the *Inhaber* (colonel proprietor), who left the tactical command and the day-to-day running of the regiment to the colonel commandant (*Titular Obrist*). The entry 'Origins of the Rank and File' is based on the best available muster list, and normally confined to 6 per cent and above.

Percentages of detailed local origins in the 'national' regiments relate to that of the relevant nationality (Hungarian, Netherlandish, Italian) and not to the personnel of the regiment as a whole. Silesians had been the backbone of the army before 1740, and the presence of Silesians at this late date usually denotes an element of loyal veterans from the lost province. Prussian Silesia and the small rump of Austrian Silesia are here treated together, as the muster lists did not always distinguish clearly between the two.

'Confession' is only a rough guide to belief in most of the non-Hungarian regiments, as the covert Protestants of Austria, Bohemia and Moravia did not declare their allegiance.

The 'Significant Losses' are derived from the lists compiled immediately after the war, and the average is that of the particular arm of service. The original entries were made as follows: 1. Prisoners of war, 2. Known killed in action (comparatively few), 3. Deaths in hospital from all causes, 4. Deserters, 5. Missing, or Discharged from the Service as Invalids. Losses through enemy action are therefore spread through 3 and 5 as well as the more obvious 1 and 2, while 3, 4 and 5 by themselves may be taken as in indication of the general well-being of the regiment.

INFANTRY REGIMENTS

All but the Hungarian regiments wore a basically identical uniform of white coat, white waistcoat and white breeches, with black field gaiters. Distinguishing colours were confined to the cuffs and lapels; the coat turn-backs were white. All regiments, including the Hungarian, wore the black tricorne hat.

No 1, Kaiser

Proprietor: Francis Stephen, Emperor.

Uniform: White, with red cuffs and lapels.

Record: Lobositz. Prague. Heavy losses at Breslau, and again at Leuthen, where the colonel commandant Leopold Baron von Lagelberg was killed. One battalion at the defence of Olmütz, and the whole regiment at Hochkirch. Distinguished in sorties from Dresden 1760. Almost wiped out at Torgau, and saw no major action for the rest of the war; in July 1761 described as being made up almost entirely of recruits. Daun complained to Maria Theresa on 17 August 1761 that the Emperor had modelled the regiment on the French regiment of Champagne, and that its dirtiness and disorder were a deliberate affront to the discipline which Daun was striving to establish in the rest of the army.

Origins of Rank and File: (4 June 1759) Bohemia 51.0 per cent, Moravia 17.0 per cent, *Reich* 13.8 per cent, Silesia 8.0 per cent, Upper and Lower Austria 5.5 per cent.

Confession: Lutherans 2.0 per cent.

Significant Losses: Total 1.5 per cent above average. Prisoners 19.7 above average, probably resulting from losses at Torgau. Desertion surprisingly low at 23.3 per cent below.

No. 2, Erzherzog Carl, 1762 Erzherzog Ferdinand

Proprietors: Carl Joseph, Archduke (died 1761); passed in 1762 to his brother Archduke Ferdinand.

Uniform: Hungarian-style white coat with yellow cuffs and turn-backs; dark blue waistcoat and pants; yellow barrel sash; sabre

Record: Hungarian national regiment. Distinguished

at Kolin. Breslau, Leuthen, Hochkirch. Heaviest losses of any regiment at Torgau, resulting from its repeated counterattacks. Recuperated in Bohemia. Storm of Schweidnitz 1761, defence of Schweidnitz 1762. An excellent regiment with a remarkable officer corps, which included Joseph Siskovics (colonel commandant in 1756), Joseph von Kökenyesdy de Vettes (colonel commandant in 1757, killed outside Breslau), the commentator Jacob Cogniazzo, and the Lieutenant Waldhütter who became an unlikely hero at Schweidnitz in 1762.

Origins of Rank and File: (18 April 1757) Hungary and Transylvania 90.4 per cent: Transylvania 25.1 per cent (Waldhütter was a Transylvanian Saxon), adjoining County of Bihar 10.3 per cent, and the County of Heves in east-central Hungary 8.1 per cent.

Confession: Calvinists 12.87 per cent, Orthodox 9.2 per cent (both figures reflecting the heavy recruiting in Transylvania), Lutherans 4.7 per cent.

Significant Losses: Total 9.5 per cent above average. Prisoners 90.0 per cent above average. Killed in action 20.7 per cent above, deaths in hospital very low at 57.8 per cent below, but deserters high at 14.8 above.

No. 3, Lothringen (Carl Lothringen)

Proprietor: Lorraine, Charles Alexander, Prince, brother to the Emperor.

Uniform: White, with red cuffs and lapels.

Record: Prague, storm of Gabel. Distinguished in covering retreat at Leuthen, where it suffered the second highest regimental losses in the army. Distinguished Hochkirch. No actions 1759. Did well in O'Kelly's counterattack at Torgau and in covering retreat. Loudon's storm of Schweidnitz. Its service suggests it was the hardest-fighting regiment in the army.

Origins of Rank and File: (19 May 1756) *Reich* 43.5 per cent, Bohemia 25.0 per cent, all rest well below 5 per cent.

Confession: Lutherans 12.6 per cent, Calvinists 4.0 per cent.

Significant Losses: Total 45.1 per cent above average. Killed in action highest in army at 51.6 per cent above average. Missing or invalids very low at 53.9 below.

No. 4, Deutschmeister

Proprietors: Wittelsbach, Clemens August, Prince, Elector of Cologne, as Grand Master (*Hoch-und-Deutschmeister*) of the Teutonic Order; succeeeded as Grand Master in 1761 by Charles Alexander Prince of Lorraine.

Uniform: White, with black cuffs and lapels (unusual, see also No. 14, Salm).

Record: Distinguished at Kolin. Breslau, Leuthen. Stormed the Kirch-Berg at Landeshut. Otherwise of no particular reputation in the war. The crusading days of the Teutonic Order were long past, and Order was chiefly of value to the monarchy from its ability to recruit in its extensive lands in Swabia..

Origins of Rank and File: (12-16 January 1757) *Reich* 27.8 per cent, Bohemia 16.6 per cent, Moravia 14.9 per cent, Upper and Lower Austria 10.7 per cent.

Confession: Lutherans 6.0 per cent.

Significant Losses: Total .4 per cent below average. Very few prisoners or killed in action (43.5 and 46.6 per cent below average). Many deaths in hospital at 20.2 per cent above, and third heaviest desertion in the infantry (142.0 per cent above).

No. 7, Neipperg

Proprietor: Neipperg, Reinhard Wilhelm, Baron (Vice-President of the *Hofkriegsrath*).

Uniform: White, with blue cuffs and lapels

Record: Kolin. Hard-hit at Leuthen. Grenadiers at Hochkirch. Maxen. Regiment ridden down by Bayreuth Dragoons at Torgau, where suffered third-highest regimental losses. Recruited anew in Moravia 1761. Generally unlucky in combat.

Origins of Rank and File: (6 January 1759) Bohemia 39.0 per cent, Moravia 22.4 per cent, Silesia 19.1 per cent (highest in infantry), Upper and Lower Austria 7.2 per cent, *Reich* 5.7 per cent.

Confession: Lutherans 2.5 per cent.

Significant Losses: Total 31.3 per cent above average. Prisoners a startling 152 per cent above average, though identified killed in action 53.3 below.

No. 8, Hildburghausen

Proprietor: Sachsen-Hildburghausen, Joseph Friedrich, Prince.

Uniform: White, with red cuffs and lapels.

Record: Lobositz, Prague, Breslau. Distinguished with heavy casualties at Leuthen. Good record at Hochkirch, Maxen and defence of Dresden. Counterattacked together with regiment of Erherzog Carl (No. 2) at Torgau. Supporting *Reichsarmee* at Freiberg 1762. A consistently good performance.

Origins of Rank and File: (4 January 1763) Bohemia 44.8 per cent, Moravia 18.6 per cent, *Reich* 9.9 per cent, Silesia 7.7 per cent.

Confession: Lutherans 5.8 per cent.

Significant Losses: Total 6.5 per cent below average. Prisoners 41.3 below average, killed in action 48.8 per cent below—strikingly low figures..

No. 9, Los Rios

Proprietor: Frans Los Rios de Gutierez, Marquis.

Uniform: White, with green cuffs and lapels (unusual, see also No. 28, Wied).

Record: Netherlands national regiment. Heavy losses in counterattack at Prague, but did well at Kolin, Breslau and Leuthen. Hochkirch, Kunersdorf. One battalion only in action for rest of war, which probably accounts for the regiment's low cumulative losses (below).

Origins of Rank and File: (6 June 1759) Austrian Netherlands and Liège 94.1 per cent: Brabant and Malines (excluding Brussels) 27.5 per cent, Brussels 21.0 per cent, Luxembourg 16.1 per cent, Flanders 11.7 per cent, Hainault 10.8 per cent, Antwerp 7.1 per cent..

Confession: No recorded Protestants.

Significant Losses: Total 43.5 per cent below average. Prisoners 42.0 per cent below average Killed in action 67.3 per cent below. Desertion very low at 71.7 per cent below.

No. 10, Wolfenbüttel, Jung- (Ludwig, Louis)

Proprietor: Braunschweig-Wolfenbüttel, Ernst Ludwig, Prince.

Uniform: White, with red cuffs and lapels.

Record: Prague, Hochkirch. With Lacy's Berlin raid 1760. Under artillery fire only at Torgau. In unusually high strength of three battalions at Spechtshausen in Saxony 1762, where did well.

Origins of Rank and File: (6 January 1759) Bohemia 48.1 per cent, Moravia 22.7 per cent, *Reich* 11.8 per cent, Silesia 6.3 per cent.

Confession: Lutherans 3.5 per cent.

Significant Losses: Total 13.8 per cent above average. Prisoners 20.9 per cent below average, but killed in action 128.6 per cent above (fifth highest in infantry). Low desertion at 46.8 per below.

No. 11, Wallis

Proprietor: Wallis, Franz Wenzel, Count

Uniform: White, with red cuffs and lapels.

Record: Very old regiment, raised by Wallenstein 1621. Lobositz. Heavy losses at Prague and Breslau, and again at Leuthen (where had highest percentage of prisoners and missing in the army). Distinguished at Hochkirch and Landeshut. Liegnitz.

Origins of Rank and File: (16 May 1759) Bohemia 53.8 per cent, Moravia 11.4 per cent, Silesia 11.6 per cent, Upper and Lower Austria 10.7 per cent, *Reich* 9.4 per cent.

Confession: Lutherans 1.6 per cent.

Significant Losses: Total 15.9 per cent below average. No remarkable variations in the various categories.

No. 12, Botta

Proprietor: Botta d'Adorno, Anton, Marquis.

Uniform: White, with blue cuffs, lapels and (possibly) waistcoat.

Record: At Kolin saved the day for the army by holding the line against the Prussian breakthrough. Storm of Gabel, siege of Schweidnitz, then at Breslau and Leuthen. Large detachment captured at Pretzch. Maxen, Torgau.

Origins of Rank and File: (18-26 May 1756) Bohemia 35.4 per cent, Moravia 27.9 per cent, *Reich* 21. 2 per cent, Silesia 6.0 per cent.

Confession: Lutherans 5.6 per cent.

Significant Losses: Total 4.0 per cent below average. Heavy losses in prisoners and killed in action (19.7 and 44.5 per cent above average), but few deserters (58.8 per cent below), confirming the impression of a very fine regiment.

No. 13, Moltke

Proprietor: Moltke, Philipp Ludwig, Baron.

Uniform: White, with light blue cuffs and lapels.

Record: To the field in the unusual strength of three battalions. Kolin. One battalion lost at surrender of Breslau 1757, another at surrender of Schweidnitz 1758. Under Loudon at Domstadtl and storm of Glatz. Liegnitz. Storm of Schweidnitz 1761, and defence of the place in 1762.

Origins of Rank and File: (25 January 1759) Upper and Lower Austria 29.6 per cent (the highest percentage of Austrians proper in the infantry), *Reich* 19.6 per cent, Moravia 17.4 per cent, Bohemia 13.7 per cent, Styria 6.4 per cent, Silesia 5.5 per cent. A most unusual mix.

Confession: Lutherans 1.5 per cent.

Significant Losses: Total 10.1 per cent above average, mostly due to large numbers of prisoners (41.2 per cent above average).

No. 14, Salm

Proprietor: Salm-Salm, Nicolaus Leopold, Rheingraf.

Uniform: White, with black cuffs and lapels.

Record: Distinguished at Kolin and Moys. Landeshut, Loudon's storm of Glatz. 1761 and 1762 in Saxony, where distinguished at Freiberg.

Origins of Rank and File: (27 November 1754) *Reich* 68.9 per cent (the most 'German' regiment of the army, largely through the influence of the proprietor), Bohemia 8.9 per cent. Probably reverted closer to the norm in the course of the war.

Confession: Lutherans 25.4 per cent, Calvinists 5.3 per cent (both very high).

Significant Losses: Total 7.7 per above average. Killed in action and prisoners very low (56.6 per cent and 51.6 per cent below average). Desertion by far the heaviest in the infantry (a huge 216.1 per cent above), attributed by the regiment to hard outpost duty in Saxony, the recruitment of prisoners and the retention of time-expired *Capitulants* (short-service soldiers).

No. 15, Pallavicini

Proprietor: Pallavicini, Giovanni Luca, Count.
Uniform: White, with red cuffs and lapels.
Record: Prague, Breslau, Leuthen. Maxen. Numerous actions in Saxony 1760. One of the battalions distinguished at Teplitz. The whole regiment at Freiberg. A regiment of middling to low reputation
Origins of Rank and File: (8 February 1759) Bohemia 41.2, *Reich* 15.3 per cent, Silesia 7.6 per cent, Upper and Lower Austria 6.9 per cent, Styria 6.0 per cent, Carniola 5.1 per cent. The representation from Austria's southern-eastern Alpine provinces unusually high.
Confession: Lutherans 4.5 per cent.
Significant Losses: Total a high 52.7 per cent above average. Above average losses in most categories, and deaths in hospital exceptionally high at 86.4 per cent above.

No. 16, Königsegg

Proprietor: Königsegg-Rothenfels, Christian Moritz, Count.
Uniform: White, with dark blue or violet cuffs and lapels.
Record: Heavy losses at Sebastiansberg 1759. Major Count Königsegg dismissed for corruption 1760..
Origins of Rank and File: (24 March 1760) Bohemia 44.8 per cent, *Reich* 23.0 per cent, Upper and Lower Austria 9.2 per cent, Styria 6.5 per cent, Carinthia 5.0 per cent. Such a high representation of Austrians was unusual among the infantry.
Confession: Lutherans 5.3 per cent.
Significant Losses: Total not available, as missing and discharged invalids not listed. Few prisoners (58.2 per cent below average), but many killed in action (137.0 per cent above) and many deaths in hospital (37.7).

No. 17, Kollowrat

Proprietor: Kollowrat-Krakowsky, Cajetan, Count.
Uniform: White, with red cuffs and lapels.
Record: Lobositz, then on Browne's relief expedition to Saxony. Prague, Breslau, Leuthen. Domstadtl. Torgau. One battalion in Loudon's storm of Schweidnitz. A lively history.
Origins of Rank and File: (18 January 1759) Bohemia 54.2 per cent, Upper and Lower Austria 12.4 per cent, Silesia 8.6 per cent, *Reich* 8.2 per cent, Moravia 6.9 per cent.
Confession: Lutherans 1.8 per cent.
Significant Losses: Total 41.1 per cent above average, mainly due to high rates of deaths in hospital (64.5 per cent above average), desertion (38.7 above) and missing and invalids (43.8 per cent above).

No. 18, Marschall

Proprietor: Marschall auf Burgholzhausen, Ernst Friedrich, Baron.
Uniform: White, with red cuffs and lapels.
Record: Notable for its lone stand at Löthain. One battalion at Maxen.
Origins of Rank and File: (13 January 1762) Bohemia 40.5 per cent, Moravia 14.6 per cent, Carniola 11.9 per cent, Upper and Lower Austria 10.3 per cent, Styria 6.6 per cent, Silesia 7.1 per cent.
Confession: Lutherans 2.14 per cent.
Significant Losses: Total 0.78 per cent below average. Prisoners 79.0 per cent below average and identified killed in action 54.1 per cent below, but the other men lost at Löthain probably account for the many listed as missing or discharged as invalids (130.3 per cent above average).

No. 19, Pálffy (Leopold)

Proprietor: Pálffy ab Erdöd, Leopold, Count.
Uniform: Probably the standard 'German' rather than Hungarian style. Light blue cuffs and lapels.
Record: Hungarian national regiment. Distinguished at siege of Schweidnitz 1757 and storm of Schweidnitz 1761. Heavy losses at Torgau.
Origins of Rank and File: (28 January 1763) Hungary and Transylvania 78.2, Poland 13.1 per cent. Recruited mostly from the north central Hungarian counties of Zepes, Saros, Abau, Borsod and Gömer.
Confession: Calvinists 7.3 per cent, Orthodox 6.7 per cent, Lutherans 3.8 per cent.
Significant Losses: Total 17.6 per cent below average. Below average losses in every category except deserters, where 26.5 per cent above.

No. 20, Colloredo, Alt- (Anton)

Proprietor: Colloredo-Waldsee, Anton, Count.
Uniform: White, with dark blue cuffs and lapels.
Record: Prague, Moys, Breslau, but lost at surrender of Breslau December 1757. Raised anew. Distinguished Hochkirch, again Dresden 1760. With Lacy's raid on Berlin, and still in his corps at Torgau. Reichenbach.
Origins of Rank and File: (10 March 1760) Bohemia 49.6 per cent, Moravia 17.3 per cent, *Reich* 7.8 per

cent, Silesia 7.6 per cent, Upper and Lower Austria 6.4 per cent.
Confession: Lutherans 2.4 per cent.
Significant Losses: 10.3 per cent above average, mostly due to the many prisoners (33.3 per cent above average) and deserters (34.2 per cent above).

No. 21, Arenberg

Proprietor: Arenberg, Charles Marie Raymond, Duke.
Uniform: White, with light blue cuffs and lapels.
Record: Adverse inspection report in 1755 noted heavy desertion on account of harsh discipline and strong drink. Kolin, Breslau Leuthen. Hochkirch. Distinguished at Kunersdorf. Excelled at Torgau, where covered retreat together with regiments Carl Lothringen (No.3) and Botta (No. 12). A good fighting regiment.
Origins of Rank and File: A 'German' regiment with a Netherlands proprietor. Bohemia 38.9 per cent, Upper and Lower Austria 26.11 per cent, Moravia 16.6 per cent, *Reich* 10.6 per cent, Silesia 6.7 per cent.
Confession: Lutherans 2.4 per cent.
Significant Losses: Total 9.8 per cent above average. Prisoners high at 56.7 per cent above average, and deserters at 21.2 per cent above.

No. 22, Hagenbach, 1757 Sprecher, 1758 Lacy

Proprietors: Hagenbach, Jacob Ignaz, Baron; 1757 Sprecher von Bernegg, Salomon; 1758 Lacy, Franz Moritz, Count.
Uniform: White, with red cuffs and lapels.
Record: Prague, Breslau. Captured at fall of Breslau December 1757. Raised anew. With Lacy's raid on Berlin. In Saxony 1761.
Origins of Rank and File: (19 March 1760) Bohemia 49.1 per cent, *Reich* 19.1 per cent, Upper and Lower Austria 5.4 per cent, Carniola 5.1 per cent.
Confession: Lutherans 6.9 per cent.
Significant Losses: Total 2.3 per cent below average. Low losses in every category except prisoners, where the surrender of Breslau 1757 helped to bring the total of prisoners to 106.1 per cent above average.

No. 23, Baden-Baden

Proprietors: Baden-Baden, Georg Ludwig, Markgraf; 1761 Baden-Baden, August Georg Simpert, Markgraf.
Uniform: White, with dark blue cuffs and lapels.
Record: Heavy losses at Kunersdorf. Distinguished with fellow-regiment Baden-Durlach at Burkersdorf.
Origins of Rank and File: (19 January 1761) Bohemia 29.8 per cent, Upper and Lower Austria 26.3 per cent, *Reich* 10.9 per cent (surprisingly low, probably on account of losses at Kunersdorf), Moravia 10.5 per cent, Styria 8.1 per cent.

Confession: Lutherans 2.4 per cent.
Significant Losses: Total not available as missing and discharged invalids not listed. Killed in action a very high 197.0 per cent above average.

No. 24, Starhemberg

Proprietor: Starhemberg, Emanuel Michael, Count.
Uniform: White, with dark blue cuffs and lapels.
Record: Reichenberg, Kolin. Domstadtl, Hochkirch. Reduced to single battalion after heavy losses at Liegnitz.
Origins of Rank and File: (8 April 1760) Bohemia 53.0 per cent, Upper and Lower Austria 16.1 per cent, *Reich* 12.5 per cent, Moravia 5.8 per cent.
Confession: Lutherans 2.7 per cent.
Significant Losses: Total 6.0 per cent above average, mostly due to the many prisoners of war (28.0 per cent above average) and the high rate of deaths in hospital at 72.9 per cent above. Many deserters were reported in the summer of 1761, but the cumulative average for the war was low (49.7 per cent below).

No. 25, Piccolomini, 1757 Thürheim

Proprietors: Piccolomini d'Aragona, Ottavio, Prince; 1757 Thürheim, Franz Ludwig, Count.
Uniform: White, with red cuffs and lapels.
Record: Breslau, then distinguished at Leuthen (where a whole battalion and one of the grenadier companies were lost). Distinguished at Hochkirch. With Lacy's raid on Berlin. Torgau. Freiberg.
Origins of Rank and File: (25 February 1760) Bohemia 31.7 per cent, Moravia 18.8 per cent, Upper and Lower Austria 16.9 per cent, Styria 13.3 per cent, *Reich* 6.9 per cent.
Confession: Lutherans and Calvinists both below 1 per cent.
Significant Losses: Total 182.2 per cent below average, mainly on account of a very low rate of deaths in hospital (163.9 per cent below average).

No. 26, Puebla

Proprietor: Puebla, Antonio, Conde de Portugallo.
Uniform: White, with red cuffs and lapels.
Record: Kolin, Breslau, Leuthen. Distinguished at Hochkirch. A battalion was distinguished at Dresden 1760, but the regiment as a whole took part in the disastrous first Austrian counterattack at Torgau. A combative record.
Origins of Rank and File: (4 January 1763) Bohemia 44.3 per cent, *Reich* 11.3 per cent, Moravia 11.2 per cent, Upper and Lower Austria 7.4 per cent, Styria 6.4 per cent, Carinthia 6.2 per cent, Silesia 5.8 per cent.
Confession: Lutherans 3.7 per cent.

Significant Losses: Total .1 per cent above average. Surprisingly low losses in prisoners of war and killed in action, but high rate of missing and discharged invalids (33.3 per cent above average).

No. 27, Baden-Durlach

Proprietor: Baden-Durlach, Christoph, Prince.

Uniform: White, with light blue cuffs and lapels.

Record: Prague, Schweidnitz, Breslau, many captured at Leuthen. Re-constituted. Maxen. Defence of Dresden 1760, Torgau. Storm of Schweidnitz 1761. One battalion distinguished at Burkersdorf 1762, another in Schweidnitz.

Origins of Rank and File: (17-22 May 1761) Bohemia 33.8 per cent, Moravia 32.4 per cent, Upper and Lower Austria 12.2 per cent, Reich 9.7 per cent, Silesia 5.7 per cent.

Confession: Lutherans 2.6 per cent.

Significant Losses: Total percentage not available, as missing and discharged invalids not entered. High outright combat losses (prisoners of war 129.1 per cent above average, killed in action 19.7 per cent above).

No. 28, Wied

Proprietor: Wied-Runkel, Friedrich Georg, Count.

Uniform: White, with green cuffs and lapels (see also No. 9, los Rios).

Record: Distinguished with heavy losses at Prague, captured in Breslau. Raised again 1758. Distinguished at Maxen. Heavy losses at Torgau. A battalion captured at Freiberg.

Origins of Rank and File: (31 March 1760) Bohemia 55.5 per cent, Reich 18.3 per cent, Styria 9.3 per cent, Moravia 6.5 per cent.

Confession: Lutherans 3.3 per cent.

Significant Losses: Total 16.1 per cent above average. Many prisoners of war at 125.6 per cent above average.

No. 29, Wolfenbüttel, Alt- (Carl), 1760 Loudon

Proprietors: Wolfenbüttel, Carl, Duke; 1760 Loudon, Gideon Ernst, Count.

Uniform: White, with light blue cuffs and lapels.

Record: Heavy losses at Leuthen. Prominent at Domstadtl. Very distinguished at Landeshut. Not to be confused with the separate regiment of the Loudon Green Grenadiers.

Origins of Rank and File: (28-29 January 1763) Bohemia 44.0 per cent, Reich 13.8 per cent, Silesia 14.2 per cent, Upper and Lower Austria 6.5 per cent, Moravia 6.5 per cent.

Confession: Lutherans 8.1 per cent.

Significant Losses: Total 2.1 per cent below average. Few prisoners, but many missing or dismissed as invalid (43.0 per cent above average).

No. 30, Sachsen-Gotha

Proprietor: Sachsen-Gotha, Wilhelm, Prince.

Uniform: White coat, with dark blue cuffs and lapels; also dark blue waistcoat.

Record: Netherlands national regiment. Alongside the French as part of Dombasle's contingent at Hastenbeck, 1757. Rest at Kolin, Moys, Leuthen. Hochkirch. Torgau and smaller actions in Saxony in 1760. Distinguished at Loudon's storm of Schweidnitz 1761. A grenadier company destroyed in explosion of magazine at defence of Schweidnitz in 1762.

Origins of Rank and File: (14 January 1759) Austrian Netherlands and Liège 91.8 per cent, Reich 4.8 per cent. Recruited from Luxembourg 45.4 per cent, Flanders 16.4 per cent, Brabant and Malines (excluding Brussels) 10.5 per cent, Hainault and Brussels 6.8 per cent each, Antwerp 6.1 per cent, Limburg 5.8 per cent.

Confession: not recorded.

Significant Losses: Total 4.0 per cent below average. Very low rate of desertion (66.1 per cent below average). High rates of killed in action (177.3 per cent above) and deaths in hospital (34.5 per cent above).

No. 31, Haller

Proprietor: Haller von Hallerstein, Samuel, Baron.

Uniform: Hungarian style. White coat with light blue cuffs; light blue waistcoat and pants.

Record: Hungarian national regiment. Distinguished at Kolin. Breslau. Domstadtl. Maxen.

Origins of Rank and File: (8 January 1759) Hungary and Transylvania 90.1 per cent, Croatia 4.0 per cent, Poland 1.9 per cent. Recruited widely over Hungary, with the largest representations from the counties of Heves (central Hungary, 18.3 per cent) and Eisenburg (6.5 per cent), Translvania 6.2 per cent, and the Hungarian counties of Borsod (5.8 per cent), Bihar (5.6 per cent), Zemplen (5.9 per cent) and Veszprem (5.0 per cent).

Confession: Orthodox 13.5 per cent, Calvinists 11.4 per cent, Lutherans 3.2 per cent.

Significant Losses: Total 11.7 per cent below average due to middling to low combat losses.

No. 32 Forgách

Proprietor: Forgách de Ghyimes, Ignaz, Count

Uniform: Hungarian style. White coat, with blue cuffs and turn-backs. Blue waistcoat and pants.

Record: Hungarian national regiment. Prague, Moys,

Leuthen. A battalion captured at surrender of Schweidnitz 1758. Hochkirch. Maxen. Heavy losses at Torgau. One battalion distinguished at Loudon's storm of Schweidnitz.

Origins of Rank and File: (1 February 1757). Hungary and Transylvania 87.6 per cent, Moravia 3.8 per cent, Upper and Lower Austria 1.6 per cent. Recruited mostly from north-western and western Hungary, where the heaviest representation representations were from the counties of Neutra (15.2 per cent), Pest 11.3 per cent, Pressburg 10.0 per cent, Trentschin (6.6 per cent). Neograd (4.6 per cent) and Komorn (3.1 per cent). 7.8 per cent from Transylvania.

Confession: Calvinists 5.9 per cent, Orthodox 5.3 per cent, Lutherans 3.3 per cent, Unitarians .7 per cent.

Significant Losses: Total 28.5 per cent below average. Low average losses in all categories.

No. 33, Esterházy, Nicolaus

Proprietor: Esterházy de Galantha, Nicolaus, Count (later Prince).

Uniform: Hungarian style. White coat, with dark blue cuffs and turn-backs. Dark blue waistcoat and pants.

Record: Hungarian national regiment. Lobositz. Prague, Schweidnitz, Breslau, lost heavily in missing and prisoners at Leuthen. Distinguished at Hochkirch, where had the second highest regimental losses. Defence of Dresden 1760. At Loudon's storm of Schweidnitz. Actions with *Reichsarmee* in Saxony 1762, and one of battalions distinguished at Teplitz. At hard-fighting regiment.

Origins of Rank and File: (11 June 1759). Hungary and Transylvania 83.5 per cent, Croatia 4.6 per cent, Moravia 4.3 per cent, Upper and Lower Austria 2.6 per cent. Recruited mainly in counties of north-western and western Hungary, reflecting the influence of the house of Esterházy, namely Trentschin (39.8 per cent), Pressburg (8.3 per cent) and Neutra (8.1 per cent). 7.5 per cent from Transylvania.

Confession: Calvinists 4.5 per cent, Orthodox 4.4 per cent, Lutherans 2.6 per cent.

Significant Losses: Total 16.6 per cent above average. High proportion of prisoners (104.0 per cent above average).

No. 34, Batthyány

Proprietor: Batthyány-Strattmann, Adam, Count.

Uniform: Hungarian style. White coat, with yellow cuffs and collar, and grey turn-backs. Blue waistcoat and pants.

Record: Hungarian national regiment. Heavy casualties at Hochkirch and Liegnitz.

Orgins of Rank and File: (3 January 1759) Hungary and Transylvania 79.5 per cent, Croatia 6.6 per cent, Upper and Lower Austria 3.6 per cent. Recruited mainly in counties of western and north-western Hungary, namely Ödenburg (16.9 per cent), Zala (10.7 per cent), Neutra (10.4 per cent), Pressburg (8.2 per cent), Eisenburg (6.9 per cent), Pest (4.7 per cent) and Trentschin (4.9 per cent).

Confession: Lutherans 3.4 per cent, Calvinists 3.2 per cent.

Significant Losses: 30.5 per cent below average. Well below average losses in all categories.

No. 35, Waldeck

Proprietor: Waldeck, Carl August, Prince.

Uniform: White coat, with red cuffs and lapels.

Record: Lobositz. Prague, very heavy losses at Leuthen. The reconstituted regiment at Hochkirch. Kunersdorf. Landeshut and Liegnitz. Burkersdorf.

Origins of Rank and File: (21 January 1759) Bohemia 15.8 per cent, Upper and Lower Austria 15.0 per cent, *Reich* 12.6 per cent, Styria 8.6 per cent, Moravia 5.0 per cent.

Confession: Lutherans 3.7 per cent.

Significant Losses: Total 23.3 per cent above average. High rates of prisoners (47.7 per cent above average), missing or dismissed as invalid.

No. 36, Browne, 1759 Tillier, 1761 Kinsky.

Proprietors: Browne, Ulysses Maximilian, Reichsgraf; 1757 Browne, Joseph; 1759 Tillier, Joseph, Baron; 1761 Kinsky, Franz Ulrich, Prince.

Uniform: White coat, with light blue cuffs and lapels.

Record: Lobositz. Prague, Schweidnitz, Breslau, Leuthen. Distinguished at Hochkirch and Maxen. Kunzendorf (17 September 1760) and distinguished at Torgau.

Origins of Rank and File: (14 April 1760) Bohemia 63.6 per cent (a very high proportion), *Reich* 16.3 per cent.

Confession: Lutherans 3.8 per cent.

Significant Losses: Below average losses in all categories except prisoners (1.7 per cent above) and killed in action (6.8 per cent above).

No. 37, Esterházy, Joseph, 1762 Siskovics

Proprietors: Esterházy de Galantha, Joseph, Count; 1762 Siskovics, Joseph, Baron.

Uniform: Hungrarian style. White coat with red cuffs and turn-backs. Red waistcoat and pants.

Record: Hungarian national regiment. Lobositz, Browne's relief expedition to the Saxons. Prague, Breslau, Leuthen. Ran away at Hochkirch. Maxen. Landeshut, and covered retreat at Liegnitz.

Origins of Rank and File: (29 May 1759). Hungary and

Transylvania 86.8 per cent. Recruited mainly from north-eastern Hungarian counties of Bihar (19.8 per cent), Szatmar (5.4 per cent), Szabolcs (5.0 per cent), Saros (4.3 per cent) and Maramaros (3.8 per cent). Transylvania 12.1 per cent.
Confession: Orthodox 25.6 per cent, Calvinists 20.6 per cent, Lutherans 2.0 per cent.
Significant Losses: Total 8.7 per cent below average. Below average losses in all categories except killed in action (8.9 per cent above average) and missing or dismissed as invalid (47.3 per cent above).

No. 38, de Ligne (Claudius)
Proprietor: Ligne, Claudius Lamoral, Prince.
Uniform: White coat, with cuffs and lapels in rose red (the de Ligne house colours).
Record: Netherlands national regiment. One battalion with Dombasle's contingent at Hastenbeck. Rest of regiment at Kolin, Moys, Breslau and Leuthen. Distinguished at Hochkirch. Maxen. With Lacy's raid on Berlin. Burkersdorf.
Origins of Rank and File: (20 June 1759) Austrian Netherlands and Liège 80.9 per cent, *Reich* 6.0 per cent. Recruited mainly from Luxembourg 45.0 per cent, Flanders 26.5 pr cent, Hainault 11.5 per cent, Limburg 10.6 per cent.
Confession: No Protestants recorded.
Significant Losses: Total very low at 39.7 below average. Low in all categories except desertion, where 23.6 per cent above av..

No. 39, Pálffy, Johann, 1758 Preysach
Proprietors: Pálffy ab Erdöd, Johann, Count; 1758 Preysach, Jacob.
Uniform: Hungarian style. White coat with red cuffs and turn-backs; red waistcoat and pants.
Record: Hungarian national regiment, raised by Johann Pálffy in 1756. Schweidnitz, Breslau, Leuthen. Defence of Olmütz, siege of Neissse. Numerous actions in Bohemia and Saxony 1759. Distinguished at Landeshut, then Liegnitz and Loudon's storm of Glatz. An impressive record.
Origins of Rank and File: (18 December 1760) Hungary and Transylvania 87.5 per cent, Croatia 9.6 per cent. Recruited mainly from the central Hungarian county of Borsod (12.1 per cent), and the south-western and western counties of Baranya (12.7 per cent), Zala (7.2 per cent), Somogy (6.8 per cent). Tolna (6.3 per cent) and Pressburg (6.5 per cent) and the southern county of Bacs (6.7 per cent).
Confession: Orthodox 8.8 per cent, Calvinists 6.6 per cent, Lutherans 2.2 per cent.
Significant Losses: Total 29.1 per cent below average, and all categories below average in spite of numerous combats.

No. 40, Colloredo, Jung- (Carl)
Proprietor: Colloredo, Carl, Count.
Uniform: White coat, with blue cuffs and lapels.
Record: Most distinguished at Lobositz under its then colonel commandant, Franz Moritz Lacy. Prague, Moys, a detachment with Hadik's raid on Berlin. Assigned to *Reichsarmee* 1758. Distinguished at Torgau. Freiberg. Reported to be in bad state in last years of war, and according to Daun (9 July 1761) made up almost entirely of recruits.
Origins of Rank and File: Upper and Lower Austria 30.9 per cent (unusually high), Bohemia 23.5 per cent, *Reich* 18.4 per cent.
Confession: Lutherans 5.8 per cent.
Significant Losses: Total 16.9 per cent below average. Below average losses in all categories except desertion (42.4 per cent above average).

No. 41, Bayreuth
Proprietor: Bayreuth, Friedrich, Markgraf.
Uniform: White coat, with red cuffs and lapels.
Record: Prague. Heavy losses at Moys. Hochkirch. Many captured at Torgau, and the regiment had to be made up by bringing its third (garrison) battalion from Luxembourg.
Origins of Rank and File: (24 May 1756) *Reich* 64.3 per cent (reflecting the territorial base of the Markgraf), Bohemia 11.8 per cent, Upper and Lower Austria 3.9 per cent.
Confession: Lutherans 16.1 per cent, Calvinists 3.9 per cent.
Significant Losses: Not recorded.

No. 42, Gaisruck (Gaisrugg)
Proprietor: Gaisruck, Siegmund Friedrich, Count.
Uniform: White coat, with blue cuffs and lapels.
Record: Very distinguished at Kolin and Breslau. Heavy losses at Leuthen. Distinguished at Hochkirch. Distinguished at defence of Dresden 1760. Second highest regimental losses at Torgau. According to Daun (9 July 1761) made up mostly of recruits. A good record.
Origins of Rank and File: (23 May 1759) Bohemia 45.5 per cent, Moravia 17.8 per cent, *Reich* 14.7 per cent, Styria 10.4 per cent.
Confession: Lutherans 2.0 per cent.
Significant Losses: Total surprisingly low at 8.6 per cent below average. Heavy losses only in missing and men discharged as invalids (31.8 per cent above average), probably resulting from losses at Leuthen and Torgau.

No. 43, Platz

Proprietor: Platz, Joseph Anton, Count.

Uniform: White coat, with red or orange cuffs and lapels.

Record: Heavy losses at Kolin. Distinguished at Landeshut and Liegnitz. On 24 October 1762 colonel commandant Carl Verneda attributed heavy desertion to arduous outpost duty and incorporation of large numbers of foreigners and Prussian deserters.

Origins of Rank and File: (14 November 1754, i.e. well before war) *Reich* 58.6 per cent, Bohemia 12.6 per cent, rest very diverse because made up of very large variety of nationalities with very low individual percentages.

Confession: Lutherans 17.5 per cent, Calvinists 4.7 per cent.

Significant Losses: Total 9.9 per cent below average, but many deaths in hospital (52.4 per cent above average) and huge desertion (201.2 per cent above), exceeded only by Salm (No. 14).

No. 44, Clerici

Proprietor: Clerici, Antonio, Marchese.

Uniform: White coat, with red cuffs and lapels.

Record: Italian national regiment, raised by Clerici at his own cost in 1744. Had a raffish reputation from the outset. Heaviest losses of any regiment at Hochkirch, where beaten off from the churchyard and brutal commandant Colonel Valentiniani mortally wounded. Surprised at Hoyerswerda, 25 September 1759. Heavy desertion reported 1761 and 1762. Proved to be the most loyal of the Milanese regiments in 1859, and many personnel re-engaged with the Austrians after the Milanese was lost to the monarchy.

Origins of Rank and File: (25 March 1760) Non-Austrian Italy 20.6 per cent, Austrian Lombardy 17.8 per cent, Gorizia and Gradisca 16.5 per cent, Tyrol 2.7 per cent.

Confession: No non-Catholics recorded.

Significant Losses: Total a high 51.6 per cent above average. Below average outright combat losses, but high desertion (22.9 per cent above average) and very high numbers of missing and invalids (150.3 per cent above).

No. 45, Daun, Alt- (Heinrich), 1761 O'Kelly

Proprietors: Daun, Heinrich Joseph, Count; 1761 O'Kelly, William, Count.

Uniform: White coat, with light red cuffs and lapels.

Record: Breslau, Leuthen. Hochkirch. With Lacy's raid on Berlin, then distinguished in counterattack at Torgau. Another good counterattack at Teplitz, 2 August 1762. A creditable record, and recruitment and losses (below) indicate solid native stock and excellent internal order.

Origins of Rank and File: (2 June 1759) Bohemia 54.6 per cent, Upper and Lower Austria 17.9 per cent, *Reich* 7.6 per cent, Moravia 7.0 per cent.

Confession: Lutherans 1.1 per cent.

Significant Losses: Total 32.4 per cent below average. All categories below average, with desertion a significant 31.8 per cent below.

No. 46, Maguire (the *Tyroler Land-und Feld Regiment*)

Proprietor: Maguire, Johann Siegmund, Count.

Uniform: White coat, with red cuffs and lapels.

Record: Put into the field with some difficulty, as the regiment had been raised to provide career opportunities for young gentlemen of the Tyrol. Moys, Schweidnitz, Breslau. Defence of Dresden 1760, then covered retreat at Torgau. High proportion of recruits reported 1761, and heavy desertion 1762.

Origins of Rank and File: (24 May 1759, numbers available for three companies only) *Reich* 42.3 per cent, Tyrol 20.0 per cent, Bohemia 10.9 per cent, Breisgau and Vorder-Österreich 10.0 per cent.

Confession: Lutherans 6.6 per cent.

Significant Losses: Total 43.9 per cent below average, and below average in all categories in spite of generally unimpressive record.

No. 47, Harrach

Proprietor: Harrach zu Rohrau, Joseph, Count (a very ancient gentleman, *Inhaber* since 1704).

Uniform: White coat, with blue cuffs and lapels.

Record: Lobositz. Distinguished at Prague; Moys, Breslau, Leuthen. Hochkirch. With the *Reichsarmee* 1760. Distinguished with heavy losses at Torgau. One battalion in storm of Schweidnitz 1761. Reichenbach. A reliable regiment, with record and recruiting similar that of No. 45 (above).

Origins of Rank and File: (3 March 1760) Bohemia 58.4 per cent, Upper and Lower Austria 11.8 per cent, Moravia 9.12 per cent, *Reich* 8.8 per cent.

Confession: Lutherans 1.9 per cent.

Significant Losses: Total 13.2 per cent below average. Below average losses in most categories, though missing and invalids 15.0 per cent above.

No. 48, Luzan

Proprietor: Luzan, Emanuel, Conte.

Uniform: White coat, with green cuffs and lapels.

Record: Italian national regiment. Breslau, Leuthen. Hochkirch. Defence of Dresden 1760. Saxony 1762. Heavy desertion and large numbers of raw recruits 1761 and 1762.

Origins of Rank and File: (12 December 1760) Gorizia and Gradisca 31.9 per cent, Austrian Lombardy 25.0 per cent, non-Austrian Italy 16.6 per cent, Carniola 6.2 per cent, *Reich* 5.3 per cent.
Confession: Lutherans 1.5 per cent.
Significant Losses: Total 11.9 per cent above average. Heavy desertion at 36.1 per cent above average.

No. 49, Kheul, 1758 Angern

Proprietors: Kheul, Carl Gustav, Count; 1758 Angern, Ludwig, Baron.
Uniform: White coat, with red cuffs and lapels.
Record: Lobositz. Distinguished at Prague; Breslau (where Kheul was killed), Leuthen. Hochkirch. Maxen and Meissen. Landeshut. Distinguished at Liegnitz. Loudon's storm of Schweidnitz. Burkersdorf. Good fighting record, though indications of poor internal order (below).
Origins of Rank and File: (10 March 1760) Bohemia 44.7 per cent, *Reich* 12.1 per cent, Moravia 11.0 per cent, Styria 10.1 per cent, Upper and Lower Austria 6.4 per cent, Silesia 7.0 per cent.
Confession: 2.8 per cent.
Significant Losses: Total 24.7 per cent above average, due to high rates of deaths in hospital (68.2 per cent above average), desertion (28.6 per cent above) and missing and discharged invalids (49.6 per cent above).

No. 50, Harsch

Proprietor: Harsch, Ferdinand Philipp, Count.
Uniform: White coat, with red cuffs and lapels; also unique red turn-backs and red Prussian-style ornamental button holes (*Litzen*) on lapels.
Record: The smartest regiment in the army. Its drill and the cut of its uniform were treated as the model for the rest of the infantry before the war. Lobositz. Kolin, Breslau, Leuthen. Hochkirch, Maxen. At defence of Dresden 1760; distinguished at Torgau. In Saxony 1762.
Origins of Rank and File: (20 March 1760) Bohemia 54.9 per cent, *Reich* 25.7 per cent, rest very diverse.
Confession: Lutherans 5.2 per cent, Calvinists 1.0 per cent.
Significant Losses: Total 18.7 per cent above average, mainly on account of very large numbers of missing and discharged invalids (208.8 per cent above).

No. 51, Gyulai

Proprietors: Gyulai, Stephan, Count; 1759 Gyulai, Franz, Count.
Uniform: Hungarian style. White coat, with dark blue cuffs and turn-backs. Dark blue waistcoat and pants.
Record: Hungarian national regiment. Prague. A detachment on Lacy's raid on Berlin. Maxen. Torgau. In Loudon's storm of Schweidnitz 1761. Its outstanding performance decided the action at Teplitz 1762 in favour of the Austrians.
Origins of Rank and File: (various dates, May 1756) Hungary and Transylvania 98.6 per cent.
Confession: Orthodox 34.8 per cent (uniquely high), Calvinists 21.1 per cent, Lutherans 11.5 per cent.
Significant Losses: Total 13.7 per cent below average. All categories well below average except for prisoners (51.5 per cent above average).

No. 52, Bethlen

Proprietor: Bethlen, Wolfgang, Count.
Uniform: Hungarian style. White coat, with light blue cuffs and turn-backs. Light blue waistcoat and pants.
Record: Hungarian national regiment. Distinguished at Breslau (1757), and again at Adelsbach (1762). Reported variously as being one of the best Hungarian regiments, yet difficult to manage.
Origins of Rank and File: (19 January 1762) Hungary and Transylvania 86.9 per cent, of which 43.6 per cent from Transylvania, and the rest recruited over wide areas of Hungary.
Confession: Orthodox 19.1 per cent, Lutherans 7.7 per cent, Calvinists 3.3 per cent.
Significant Losses: Total 30.8 per cent below average. All categories well below average except for prisoners (28.2 per cent above).

No. 53, Simbschen

Proprietor: Simbschen, Joseph Carl, Baron.
Uniform: Hungarian style. White coat, with red cuffs and turn-backs. Red waistcoat and pants.
Record: Set up as a *Panduren-Corps* in 1741, and still recruited largely in Croatia and Sclavonia (below) and therefore not strictly a Hungarian national regiment. Distinguished at defence of Olmütz 1758, and again at Liegnitz 1760.
Origins of Rank and File: (12 March 1760) Croatia and Slavonia 86.6 per cent, Hungary and Transylvania 7.8 per cent.
Confession: Orthodox 32.6 per cent, Calvinists very low at .5 per cent, and Lutherans at .8 per cent.
Significant Losses: Not recorded.

No. 54, Sincère

Proprietor: Sincère, Claudius, Baron.
Uniform: White coat, with red cuffs and lapels.
Record: Reichenberg, Prague, detachment with Hadik's raid on Berlin. Maxen. Sixth highest regimental losses at Torgau, and still unfit for action 1761. Burkersdorf, Reichenbach, detachment

distinguished at defence of Schweidnitz.

Origins of Rank and File: (12 March 1760) Bohemia 33.3 per cent, Moravia 20.2 per cent, Upper and Lower Austria 14.8 per cent, *Reich* 13.6 per cent.

Confession: Lutherans 1.4 per cent.

Significant Losses: Total 3.9 per cent below average. Most categories below average, but killed in action 159.3 per cent above.

No. 55, d'Arberg

Proprietor: d'Arberg, Charles-Antoine, Count.

Uniform: White coat, with red cuffs and lapels.

Record: Netherlands national regiment. First two battalions to Bohemia 1757, and at Prague, Moys, Breslau and Leuthen. Third battalion with Dombasle's corps at Hastenbeck. With main army in Saxony 1759. Landeshut, Liegnitz. Adelsbach, Burkersdorf.

Origins of Rank and File: (22 May, 17 and 20 November 1756) Austrian Netherlands and Liège 76.8 per cent, France 7.3 per cent, *Reich* 6.7 per cent. Recruited from Luxembourg 29.9 per cent, Hainault 24.9 per cent, Brabant and Malines (excluding Brussels) 9.8 per cent, Antwerp 5.9 per cent.

Confession: No recorded Protestants.

Significant Losses: Total 48.0 below average. All categories well below average.

No. 56, Mercy

Proprietor: Mercy d'Argenteau, Antoine, Count.

Uniform: White coat, with dark blue cuffs and lapels.

Record: Reichenberg, Prague, Kolin, Breslau, Leuthen (stood outside Leuthen village, then ran away). Siege of Neisse 1758. Distinguished with heavy loss at Torgau. One battalion at Loudon's storm of Schweidnitz. Whole regiment at Reichenbach.

Origins of Rank and File: (25 January 1762) Bohemia 46.9 per cent, *Reich* 18.3 per cent, Styria 7.0 per cent, Silesia 5.9 per cent, Upper and Lower Austria 5.0 per cent.

Confession: Lutherans 10.1 per cent.

Significant Losses: Total 13.4 per cent above average. Prisoners 29.7 per cent below average, but all other categories above, with heavy desertion (38.4 per cent above) and large numbers of missing and discharged invalids (81.2 per cent above).

No. 57, Andlau

Proprietor: Andlau, Joseph, Baron.

Uniform: White coat, with red cuffs and lapels.

Record: First battalion only in action from 1757 to early in 1759. Prague, Moys, Breslau, heavy losses at Leuthen. Hochkirch. Captured at Sebastiansberg 1759, followed by arrival of second battalion from Italy. Whole reconstituted regiment at Liegnitz. See the memoirs of Gorani for a not unsympathetic description of life in the regiment.

Origins of Rank and File: (8 March 1757) *Reich* 27.8 per cent, Bohemia 24.2 per cent, Upper and Lower Austria 21.4 per cent, Moravia 10.6 per cent.

Confession: Lutherans 8.8 per cent, Calvinists 1.0 per cent.

Significant Losses: Total 7.1 per cent below average. Most categories below average, though killed in action 28.2 per cent above.

No. 59, Daun, Leopold

Proprietor: Daun, Leopold Joseph Count, the field marshal.

Uniform: White coat, with red cuffs and lapels.

Record: Reichenberg, Kolin, Gabel; one battalion with Hadik's raid on Berlin, the other in the storm of Schweidnitz. Both battalions at Breslau and Leuthen. Hochkirch. Maxen. Torgau. Distinguished at defence of Schweidnitz 1762. The losses during the war, detailed below, suggest that it was not a good regiment to be in.

Origins of Rank and File: (31 March 1760) Bohemia 41.1 per cent, Moravia 14.6 per cent, *Reich* 14.2 per cent, Upper and Lower Austria 14.5 per cent.

Confession: Lutherans 3.1 per cent.

Significant Losses: Total 25.1 per cent above average. Deaths in hospital 3.1 per cent below average, but above average losses in all other categories, with heavy desertion (25.2 per cent above) and very many killed in action (134 per cent above)

Newly-Raised Units (*Neu errichtete Corpetti*)

(Each unit was in its way unique, and no comparisons are made with losses with the infantry of the main body of the army)

Loudon-Grenadiere or *Grün-Loudon*

Command: No Proprietor, commanded by d'Alton, Major Richard, Chevalier.

Uniform: Light green coat, with red cuffs and lapels. Light green breeches. Standard tricorne hat.

Record: Raised by Loudon in 1758, mostly from foreigners and Prussian deserters. Kunersdorf. Distinguished at Landeshut, where stormed the Doctor-Berg, then at Liegnitz. Burkersdorf. Reached strength of two battalions. Disbanded 1763. Not to be confused with Loudon's regiment of 'German' infantry, No. 29.

Origins of Rank and File: (28 January 1761) *Reich* 24.8 per cent, Silesia 21.5 per cent, Bohemia 15.8 per cent,

Poland 7.6 per cent, Upper and Lower Austria 5.6 per cent, Moravia 5.2 pr cent, Hungary and Transylvania 5.1 per cent.
Confession: Lutherans 15.7 per cent, Calvinists 1.2 per cent.
Significant Losses: Total 2,211: prisoners 463, killed in action 251, died in hospital, deserted 1,209, missing or discharged as invalids 213.

Volontaires Silésiens or Voluntaires Beck

Command: No Proprietor, and commanded by Montagutti, Major Rochus.
Uniform: Light green coat, with buff cuffs and lapels. Light green waistcoat and breeches. Tricorne hat.
Record: Raised as single battalion in 1759 by Lieutenant General Beck in Silesia. Fought in numerous small-scale actions, then in Beck's corps at Reichenbach; it was better disciplined than Loudon's Green Grenadiers, though shared the same fate of being disbanded in 1763.
Origins of Rank and File: (26 February 1760) Bohemia 28.2 per cent, *Reich* 26.8 per cent, Silesia 18.6 per cent, Poland 6.7 per cent.
Confession: Lutherans 18.9 per cent, Calvinists 1.5 per cent.
Significant Losses: Total 1,477: prisoners 177, killed in action 253, died in hospital 83, deserted 871, missing or discharged as invalids 95.

Deutches Feld-Jäger Corps

Command: No Proprietor, commanded by Richard, Captain Christian, then from 1760 by Enzenberg, Major Carl, Baron.
Uniform: Light blue-grey 'pike-grey' coat, with green cuffs, collar and turn backs. blue-grey waistcoat and breeches. Black leather helmet with stand-up front.
Record: Raised 1757-8 from game-keepers (*Jäger*) volunteered by nobility. Worked closely with the *Pioniers*, and at immediate disposal of General Staff. Distinguished 1760 in defence of Dresden and at Nieder-Arnsdorf and Torgau. Very successful, but paid for association with its Lacy, who was out of favour with the all-powerful Kaunitz. Reduced considerably in 1762 and disbanded 1763.
Origins of Rank and File: (12 December 1760) Tyrol 44.4 per cent, Bohemia 21.0 per cent, *Reich* 8.8 per cent, Upper and Lower Austria 8.5 per cent, Silesia 8.0 per cent. Moravia 5.2 per cent.
Significant Losses: (together with *Pionier-Corps*) Total not available: prisoners 253, killed in action 24, died in hospital 374, deserted 269, missing or discharged as invalids not entered.

Jägercorps Otto

Command: Otto, Major Michael.
Uniform: Light green coat, with black cuffs and lapels. Light green waistcoat and breeches. Tricorne hat.
Record: Raised by Otto in his native Saxony in 1759. Engaged in many actions in association with the *Reichsarmee*. The nearest Austrian equivalent to a Prussian free battalion, and ridden by dissensions and scandals.
Origins of Rank and File, *Confession, Significant Losses*: Not recorded.

Artillerie-Füsiliere

Command: No Proprietor, commanded by Lieutenant Colonel Schroeder..
Uniform: 'Hare-' or 'wolf-brown' coat with red cuffs. Brown waistcoat and breeches. Tricorne hat.
Record: Raised 1758 as three battalions to put semi-skilled labour at the disposal of the field artillery for serving and moving the pieces. Reduced by six companies 1762, and disbanded after war, in spite of having proved utility.
Origins of Rank and File: (29 March 1760) Bohemia 40.3 per cent, Moravia 13.1 per cent, Upper and Lower Austria 10.2 per cent, Styria 7.8 per cent, Silesia 6.8 per cent, Carinthia and the *Reich* 6.7 per cent each.
Confession: Lutherans 2.2 per cent.
Significant Losses: Total 3,715: prisoners 334, killed in action 73, died in hospital 1,951, deserted 1,258, missing or discharged as invalids 99.

Staabs-Infanterie-Regiment

Command: No Proprietor, and commanded by a succession of colonel commandants.
Uniform: Dark blue coat (unique in Austrian infantry), with red cuffs and collar, blue waistcoat, white breeches.
Record: Formed by Lacy as sixteen companies of 2,700 personnel in 1758 to be at the disposal of the new General Staff, essentially to keep the baggage train in order. Caught up in the fighting at Torgau, where its blue coats (resembling those of the Prussians) enabled it to escape largely intact. Reduced to four companies in the winter of 1761/2.
Origins of Rank and File: (8 March 1759) Bohemia 33.1 per cent, Upper and Lower Austria 17.1 per cent, Moravia 12.3 per cent, Silesia 9.8 per cent, *Reich* 9.2 per cent.
Confession: Lutherans 3.0 per cent.
Significant Losses: Total 4,014: prisoners 335, killed in action 104, died in hospital 1,177, deserted 1,607, missing or discharged as invalids 791.

Auxiliary Infantry Units

Mainz
Command: Known as the Mainz regiment of Lamberg, made over to the Austrian service by the Bishop of Mainz in virtue of treaty of 1756.
Uniform: White coat, facings not specified.
Record: Very heavy losses at Prague, and figured little for the rest of the war.
Significant Losses: Total 4,674: prisoners 1,860, killed in action 154, died in hospital 1,571, deserted 1,010, missing or discharged as invalids 79.

Blau-Würzburg and Roth-Würzburg
Command: The two regiments made over to the Austrian service by the Bishop of Würzburg in virtue of treaty of 1756. The Blue Regiment commanded by Moser von Filseck, Colonel Gottfried Wilhelm.
Uniform: The Blue Regiment white coat, with blue cuffs and lapels; the Red Regiment white coat, with red cuffs and lapels.
Record: By far the best of the auxiliary units. The Red Regiment was assigned to the *Reichsarmee*. The Blue served with the Austrians, and as such defended the churchyard at Leuthen with the utmost distinction. On account of losses the two regiments were later combined into one, and served as such in Saxony in 1761 and 1762.
Significant Losses: (the two regiments together) Total 4,757: prisoners 1,187, killed in action 89, died in hospital 1,452, deserted 1,267, missing or discharged invalids 762.

Anhalt-Zerbst Battalion
Command: Raised for the Austrian service by Anhalt-Zerbst, Friedrich August, Prince.
Uniform: Not specified.
Record: Single battalion raised for the Austrian service in 1760. An under-strength unit of under-sized soldiers, and of little military use. However the eccentric Friedrich August was politically valuable as a Protestant prince of northern Germany, and brother of Catherine (later 'the Great,' then wife of the Russian heir Duke Peter of Holstein-Gottorp).
Significant Losses: Only specified losses: prisoners 3, died in hospital 113, deserted 138.

Toscana
Command: Raised in 1758 by Emperor Francis Stephen, in his capacity as Grand Duke of Tuscany.
Uniform: Not specified.
Record: Assigned to Silesia 1760, and Loudon reported very favourably on its performance at Liegnitz.
Significant Losses: Total 3,011: prisoners 62, killed in action 142, died in hospital 1,719, deserted 857, missing or discharged as invalids 231.

Grenzer ('Croatian') Infantry Regiments

Numbered consecutively with the regiments of regular infantry, though some of them had no Proprietors, only Colonel Commandants. The *Significant Losses* are in relation to the Croats as a whole, where all-out desertion was almost unknown, though whole battalions were given to ritual mutiny or marching homewards when term of service expired.

No. 60, Carlstädter Liccaner
Proprietor: Petazzi, Benvenuto Siegmund, Count.
Colonel Commandant: Vela, Franz von; from 1758 Pelican, Max.
Uniform: Red jacket, with pointed green cuffs and yellow lace. Sea-green waistcoat. Red pants. Red and green barrel sash. Black or red cap.
Record: Recruited in area of Lika and Korbavija in the south-east of the Carlstadt general command (*Generalat*) of Croatia. Storm of Tetschen 1756. Prague, Moys. Kunersdorf. Landeshut, Liegnitz. Distinguished at Loudon's storm of Schweidnitz. In 1762 in Saxony and in defence of Schweidnitz.
Significant Losses: Total 65.4 per cent above average, with exceptionally large number of prisoners (92.0 per cent above average). The heaviest overall losses of any 'Croatian' regiment.

No. 61, Carlstädter Ottocaner
Colonel Commandants: Adelsfels, Joseph Dietrich; 1762 Vukassovich, Peter.
Uniform: Red jacket, with pointed blue cuffs and yellow lace. Light blue waistcoat with yellow lace. Red pants. Red and blue barrel sash. Black or red cap.
Record: Recruited in the southern mountainous areas of the Carlstadt general command. Prague. 1758 captured a Prussian battalion at Liebau in Bohemia. Detachment distinguished at Kunersdorf. Landeshut, Liegnitz. One battalion at Loudon's storm of Schweidnitz. With *Reichsarmee* 1762.
Significant Losses: Total 6.8 per cent below average. All categories below average except prisoners (5.3 per cent above average).

No. 62, Carlstädter Oguliner
Colonel Commandants: Losy von Losenau, Anton; 1760 Petzinger, Nicolaus.
Uniform: Blue jacket, with pointed yellow cuffs and yellow lace. Blue waistcoat with yellow lace. Red pants. Red and yellow barrel sash. Black or red cap.
Record: Recruited from the north west of the Carlstadt general command. Lobositz. Some lost with

surrender of Breslau 1757. Kunersdorf, heavy losses at Troppau. One battalion at Landeshut. One battalion at defence of Schweidnitz 1762.

Significant Losses: Total 20.7 per cent below average. All categories below average except missing or discharged as invalids (81.0 per cent above).

No. 63, Carlstädter Szluiner

Colonel Commandants: Kleefeld, Wenzel, Baron; 1758 Vukassovich, Peter; 1761 Kallinich, Peter; 1762 Luzzeni, Joseph, Baron.

Uniform: Blue jacket, with pointed red cuffs and yellow lace. Red waistcoat, with yellow criss-cross embroidery. Blue pants. Blue and yellow barrel sash. Black or red cap.

Record: Recruited n the north east of the Carlstadt general command. 1757 detachments in small actions in Silesia and Bohemia; with Hadik's raid on Berlin. Maxen and other actions in Saxony. In Saxony again in 1760. Wartensleben's battalion distinguished at Pretzschendorf 1762.

Significant Losses: Total 23.0 per cent below average. Generally below average, though prisoners 68.0 pre cent above.

No. 64, Warasdiner Creutzer

Colonel Commandant: Mikassinovich von Schlangenfeld, Michael, Baron.

Uniform: White jacket, with light green round cuffs, collar and turn-backs. Light green waistcoat with white lace and yellow buttons. White pants. White and yellow barrel sash. Black cap.

Record: Recruited from the west of the Warasdin military command. One battalion at Prague, another distinguished at Kolin, whole regiment lost at surrender of Breslau. Reconstituted detachments in Saxony 1758 and 1759. Major Eder's battalion with Lacy's raid on Berlin. Distinguished at Adelsbach 1762; then in action at Burkersdorf and Reichenbach.

Significant Losses: Total 3.2 per cent below average. All categories below average except missing or dismissed as invalids (93.0 per cent above).

No. 65, Warasdiner St. Georger

Colonel Commandants: Brentano-Cimarolli, Joseph, Baron; 1758 Riese, Franz, Baron.

Uniform: White jacket, with round green cuffs, collar and turn-backs. Green waistcoat with white lace. White pants. White and green barrel sash. Black cap.

Record: Recruited from the east of the Warasdin military command. Bohemia 1756. Prague, Moys, Breslau; one battalion lost at surrender of Breslau. Bohemia and Saxony 1758. Maxen, distinguished at Meissen. With Lacy's raid on Berlin. Loudon's storm of Schweidnitz. Adelsbach, Burkersdorf and Reichenbach.

Significant Losses: Total 40.4 per cent below average. Most categories below average, though deserters and missing or discharged as invalids slightly above.

No. 66, Slavonisch Broder

Proprietor: Mercy d'Argenteau, Antoine, Count.

Colonel Commandants: Prodanovich von Ussiczka, Michael; 1761 Dönhoff, Friedrich, Count.

Uniform: Black jacket, with round yellow cuffs and collar. Black waistcoat with yellow lace. Dark blue pants. Yellow and blue barrel sash. Black cap.

Record: Recruited along the lower Sau (Sava) in the Slavonian general command. One battalion distinguished at Brandeis, 1757; one battalion lost at surrender of Breslau. Numerous small actions for rest of war, with second battalion at Torgau 1760.

Significant Losses: Total 39.8 per cent above average (second only to the Carlstädter Liccaner), mostly due to many deaths in hospital (54.0 per cent above average) and missing or discharged as invalids (51.2 per cent above).

No. 67, Slavonisch Gradiscaner

Proprietor: Saint-André, Frédéric Daniel, Baron.

Commandants: Ried, Joseph, Baron; 1758, Liubibratich von Trebinya, Hieronymus.

Uniform: Red jacket, with pointed blue cuffs and collar. Blue waistcoat. Red pants. Yellow barrel sash with blue knots. Black cap.

Record: Recruited in the Slavonian general command. Distinguished at Passberg 1759, and in Loudon's storm of Schweidnitz.

Significant Losses: Total 4 per cent below average. All categories well below average except for deaths in hospital (36.5 per cent above).

No. 68, Slavonisch Peterwardeiner

Proprietors: Helfreich, Christian, Baron; 1757 Lietzen, Friedrich, Baron; 1762 Wulffen, Christian, Baron.

Colonel Commandants: Eberstädt, Franz Joseph; 1758 Lanjus von Wellenburg, Carl, Count.

Uniform: Black jacket, with round red cuffs and collar. Blue waistcoat with red lace. Light blue pants. Red and yellow barrel sash. Black cap.

Record: Distinguished at storm of Schweidnitz 1757. Operations around Olmütz early summer 1758. One battalion at Kunersdorf, another at Maxen. Whole regiment at Landeshut 1760 and Loudon's storm of Schweidnitz 1761. Distinguished at Saubsdorf in Silesia 1762. A lively history.

Significant Losses: Total 46.0 per cent below average, though 'heavy' desertion at 144 individuals (350 per cent above av.).

No. 69, Erstes Banal-Regiment

Proprietor: Nádasdy, Franz, Count.
Colonel Commandants: Zedtwitz, Johann, Baron; 1762 Göhlichich, Friedrich.
Uniform: Blue or dark blue jacket, with pointed red cuffs and yellow lace. Red waistcoat with yellow lace. Red pants. Blue and red barrel sash. Black cap.
Record: Raised by Nádasdy in his capacity as Ban of Croatia from the south-west of the Banal command. Prague, Moys, distinguished at the storm of Schweidntiz. Siege of Neisse 1758. Distinguished at Meissen 1759. Heavily engaged in Saxony 1760. In Saxony and Silesia 1761-2.
Significant Losses: Total 3 per cent above average. All categories below average except prisoners (40.1 per cent above).

No. 70, Zweites Banal-Regiment

Proprietor: Nádasdy, Franz, Count.
Colonel Commandants: Orssich, Christoph, Baron; 1761 Sermage, Peter, Count.
Uniform: Dark blue jacket, with pointed red cuffs. Red waistcoat with yellow lace. Red pants. Red and blue barrel sash. Black cap.
Record: Also raised by Nádasdy. Lobositz. Prague, storm of Schweidnitz. In Saxony 1758 and 1759. Torgau. Numerous small actions in Saxony and Silesia 1761-2.
Significant Losses: Total 10.2 per cent below average. Most categories below average, though prisoners 15.3 per cent above.

Transylvanian Grenzer Regiments

Formed in 1762 to meet the threat of Turkish and Tartar invasion. Wore national dress. Never in action. No losses recorded.

Erstes Székeler Regiment
Zweites Székeler Regiment
Like the first regiment, formed from the ethnically Hungarian population.

Erstes Walachen-Regiment
Formed from the ethnically Wallachian population.

CUIRASSIER REGIMENTS

(Numbered according to the scheme of 1769, which ran through the mounted regiments according to the seniority. Here separated for convenience into cuirassiers, dragoons and hussars, and percentages calculated accordingly. Regiments disbanded before 1769 here designated by roman numerals according to the sequence of their dissolution).

C 3, Erzherzog Leopold

Proprietor: Leopold, Archduke (later Emperor Leopold II, 1780-92).
Uniform: White coat, with red cuffs and turn-backs. White waistcoat. Red breeches.
Record: Prague, in Lucchesi's counterattack at Leuthen; then Breslau. Hochkirch. Saxony 1759. Distinguished at Cossdorf 1760; fourth heaviest cuirassier losses at Torgau. Saxony 1761. Reichenbach. Towards the end of the war it sometimes found itself doing hussar-type service. A good and versatile fighting regiment.
Origins of Rank and File: (29 January 1763) Upper and Lower Austria 32.6 per cent, Bohemia 21.3 per cent, Moravia 20.7 per cent, *Reich* 13.5 per cent, Silesia 8.3 per cent.
Confession: Lutherans 1.0 per cent.
Significant Losses: Total 25.4 per cent above average, entirely due to outright losses in combat—prisoners 148.3 per cent above average, killed in action 16.0 per cent above.

C 4, Erzherzog Ferdinand, 1761 Erzherzog Maximilian

Proprietor: Archduke Ferdinand; 1761 Archduke Maximilian.
Uniform: White coat, with red cuffs and turn-backs. White waistcoat. Red breeches.
Record: The army's most senior mounted regiment. Taken over as a 'Florentine company' in 1619, and on 11 June of the same year rescued an earlier Archduke Ferdinand (later Emperor) from a mob of clamouring Protestant nobles. It thus saved the cause of the Counter-Reformation in Central Europe. It was given (and retained until the collapse of the Austrian monarchy in 1918) the unique privilege of being able to ride without notice into the courtyard of the Hofburg Palace in Vienna. Lobositz. Heavy losses at Prague, Breslau and Leuthen. Distinguished at Hochkirch. Kunersdorf. In O'Donnell's successful counterattack at Torgau. Another good regiment.
Origins of Rank and File: (14 January 1759) Bohemia 48.4 per cent, Moravia 23.6 per cent, Silesia 12.6 per cent, Upper and Lower Austria 8.4 per cent.
Confession: Lutherans .66 per cent.
Significant Losses: Total 37.3 per cent below average. All categories well below average.

C 6 Portugal

Proprietor: Dom Emanuele, Infante of Portugal.
Uniform: White coat, with red cuffs and turn-backs. Red waistcoat. Red breeches.
Record: Distinguished, with heavy losses at Kolin;

one squadron with Hadik's raid on Berlin. Hochkirch. Torgau. Silesia 1761-2. Lacy wrote after Hochkirch that the regiment was being mismanaged by Lieutenant Colonel Kolb.

Origins of Rank and File: (30 January 1759) Moravia 41.1 per cent, Bohemia 19.6 per cent, Silesia 11.7 per cent, *Reich* 7.4 per cent, Upper and Lower Austria 5.6 per cent.

Confession: Lutherans 3.0 per cent.

Significant Losses: Total 35.6 per cent below average. All categories below average, outright combat losses strikingly so (prisoners 55.0 per cent below average, and killed in action 56.0 per cent below).

C 8, Pálffy, Carl Paul

Proprietor: Pálffy ab Erdöd, Carl Paul, Count.

Uniform: White coat, with red cuffs and turn-backs. White waistcoat. Red breeches.

Record: Lobositz. Reichenberg, Prague, Leuthen. In Saxony 1759. Landeshut and Liegnitz. Silesia then Saxony 1761. Teplitz and Freiberg. Loudon reported in March 1761 that it held a large number of recruits, and that it had never had a particularly good reputation.

Origins of Rank and File: (25 January 1760) Bohemia 47.8 per cent, Silesia 18.8 per cent, Moravia 15.7 per cent.

Confession: Lutherans 5.7 per cent (unusually high for a cuirassier regiment; probably due to the representation from Silesia).

Significant Losses: Total .7 per cent below average. Large number of prisoners at 61.7 per cent above average

C 10, Stampach

Proprietor: Stampach (Kager von Stampach), Carl, Baron.

Uniform: White coat, with red cuffs and turn-backs. Red waistcoat. Buff breeches.

Record: Distinguished at Lobositz. Prague, Breslau, Leuthen. Hochkirch. Maxen. Most distinguished at Torgau. An excellent history.

Origins of Rank and File: (22-29 December 1763) Bohemia 52.5 per cent, Upper and Lower Austria 18.8 per cent, Moravia 12.3 per cent, Silesia 9.3 per cent.

Significant Losses: Total 40.1 per cent above average. Only the killed in action below average (78.0 per cent below); prisoners 87.5 per cent above.

C 12, Serbelloni

Proprietor: Serbelloni, Giovanni Battista, Count.

Uniform: White coat, with red cuffs and turn-backs. Red waistcoat. Red breeches.

Record: Distinguished at Lobositz. Destroyed the infantry regiment of Bevern at Kolin; Leuthen. Hochkirch. Maxen. Distinguished at Torgau. Saxony 1761 and 1762, without major actions. A most effective regiment.

Origins of Rank and File: 25 May 1759. Moravia 49.1 per cent, Silesia 16.3 per cent, Bohemia 15.3 per cent, Upper and Lower Austria 13.5 per cent.

Confession: Lutherans 2.9 per cent.

Significant Losses: Total 22.1 per cent below average. Prisoners exactly average, all other categories well below.

C 14, Cordua, 1756 O'Donnell

Proprietor: Cordua, Caspar, Count; late 1756 O'Donnell, Carl Claudius, Count.

Uniform: White coat, with red cuffs and turn backs. White waistcoat. Red breeches.

Record: Distinguished with heavy losses (under name Cordua) at Lobositz. Kolin, Breslau, Leuthen. Distinguished at Hochkirch. Detachment at Maxen. Landeshut, Liegnitz, Torgau. Saxony 1761 and 1762.

Origins of Rank and File: Not available.

Significant Losses: Total 38.7 per cent below average. All categories below average.

C 20, Schmerzing, 1762 d'Ayasasa

Proprietors: Schmerzing, Friedrich Hannibal, Baron; 1762 d'Ayasasa, Joseph, Count.

Uniform: White coat, with red cuffs and turn-backs. White waistcoat. Red breeches.

Record: Reported in 1755 for its repressive regime. Kolin, Breslau, Leuthen. Hochkirch. Distinguished at Maxen and other actions in Saxony 1759. Landeshut, Liegnitz. Saxony 1762. Reichenbach. Lacy noted in 1758 that it had an ineffective commandant in Lieutenant Colonel Siegmund Baron Gabelkoven.

Origins of Rank and File: not available.

Significant Losses: Total 13.5 per cent above average. All categories above average (desertion a heavy 29.9 per cent above average) except for killed in action (58.0 per cent below).

C 21 Trautmannsdorff

Proprietor: Trautmannsdorff, Carl, Count.

Uniform: White coat, with red cuffs and turn-backs. White waistcoat. Red *breeches.*

Record: Lobsitz. Prague, then distinguished at Rossbach. No major actions 1758. Saxony 1759. Distinguished at Landeshut and Liegnitz. Reichenbach.

Origins of Rank and File: (22 January 1759) Bohemia 47.7 per cent, Silesia 12.4 per cent, Upper and Lower Austria 11.9 per cent, *Reich* 10.8 per cent, Moravia

10.5 per cent.

Confession: Lutherans 3.2 per cent.

Significant Losses: Total 13.0 below average, but large proportion of missing and discharged invalids (123.5 per cent above average).

C 22, Kalckreuth, 1760 Albert, Duke/Prince of Sachsen-Teschen

Proprietors: Kalckreuth, Johann Georg, Baron; 1760 Sachsen-Teschen, Albert, Duke/Prince of

Uniform: White coat, with red cuffs and turn-backs. Red waistcoat. Straw breeches.

Record: Kolin, Breslau, Leuthen. Saxony 1758. Distinguished at Landeshut and Liegnitz. Assigned to operate with the Russian army 1761.

Origins of Rank and File: Moravia 51.7 per cent, Bohemia 20.4 per cent, Silesia 10.9 per cent, Upper and Lower Austria 10.8 per cent.

Confession: Lutherans 1.0 per cent.

Significant Losses: Total 2.1 per cent above average. Heavy desertion at 50.0 per cent above average.

C 23, Birkenfeld, 1761 Stampa

Proprietors: Pfalz-Birkenfeld, Wilhelm, Prince; 1761 Stampa, Cajetan, Count.

Uniform: White coat, with red cuffs and turn-backs. White waistcoat. White breeches.

Record: Very distinguished at Kolin. Distinguished at Kunersdorf. With Lacy's raid on Berlin; Torgau. Teplitz.

Origins of Rank and File: (5 April 1760) Silesia 53.1 per cent (the highest proportion of any unit in the army), Bohemia 17.0 per cent, Moravia 14.2 per cent, Upper and Lower Austria 10.4 per cent.

Confession: Lutherans 5.6 per cent, Calvinists 1.0 per cent.

Significant Losses: Total 40.6 per cent above average. All categories well above average.

C 25, Anhalt-Zerbst

Proprietor: Anhalt-Zerbst, Friedrich August, Prince.

Uniform: White coat or jerkin, with red cuffs and turn-backs. Yellow waistcoat with red lower border. Yellow breeches.

Record: Prague, Breslau, Leuthen. Distinguished at Hochkirch. Distinguished again at Maxen. Torgau. Engaged heavily at Reichenbach. A respectable conventional unit, unlike the eccentric prince's battalion of auxiliary infantry.

Origins of Rank and File: (20 January 1759) Bohemia 37.8 per cent, Moravia 30.5 per cent, *Reich* 14.0 per cent, Upper and Lower Austria 9.1 per cent, Silesia 5.6 per cent.

Significant Losses: 32.0 per cent below average. All categories below average.

C 27, Radicati, 1756 Löwenstein, 1758 Daun, Benedict

Proprietors: Radicati, Julius Caesar, Count; late 1756 Löwenstein-Wertheim, Christian, Prince; 1758 Daun, Benedict, Count.

Uniform: White coat, with red cuffs and turn backs. White coat. Red breeches.

Record: Proprietor Radicati killed at Lobositz. Prague, Bresau, Leuthen. Distinguished at Meissen 1759. Distinguished with heavy losses at Torgau, and unfit for duty in 1761. Teplitz. A well turned-out regiment, whose uniform was made the pattern for the cuirassiers before the war.

Origins of Rank and File: (4 January 1759) Upper and Lower Austria 37.8 per cent, Bohemia 24.6 per cent, Moravia 16.0 per cent, Silesia 7.3 per cent.

Confession: Lutherans .6 per cent.

Significant Losses: Total 81.1 per cent above average, mainly owing to large numbers of killed in action (162.9 per cent above average) and deaths in hospital (282.9 per cent above).

C 29 Brettlach (Bretlach)

Proprietor: Brettlach, Carl Ludwig, Baron.

Uniform: White coat, with red cuffs and turn-backs. Straw waistcoat. Straw breeches.

Record: Distinguished at Lobositz. Prague; accompanied the regiment of the Trautmannsdorff Cuirassiers (C 21) in the campaign of Rossbach, and did well in the battle. Principally in Saxony for the rest of the war. Maxen. Distinguished at Freiberg. A good record.

Origins of Rank and File: (29 June 1762) Bohemia 33.9 per cent, Upper and Lower Austria 24.8 per cent, Moravia 15.9 per cent, *Reich* 9.5 per cent, Silesia 9.0 per cent.

Confession: Lutherans 1.8 per cent.

Significant Losses: Total 24.7 per below average. All categories below average except killed in action (92.0 per cent above).

C 33, Anspach (Ansbach)

Proprietor: Brandenburg-Ansbach-Bayreuth, Christian Friedrich, Markgraf.

Uniform: White coat, with red cuffs and turn-backs. White waistcoat. Red breeches.

Record: Distinguished at Lobositz. Prague, Breslau, Leuthen. Hochkirch. Landeshut, then heavy losses at Liegnitz. 1761 attached to Russian army. Silesia 1762. The Markgraf was brother-in-law of Frederick to Prussia, and generally favoured his cause. He

nevertheless maintained his regiment in the Austrian service.
Origins of Rank and File: (1 April 1760) Bohemia 38.9 per cent, Upper and Lower Austria 26.1 per cent, Moravia 13.6 per cent, *Reich* 10.6 per cent, Silesia 6.7 per cent.
Confession: Lutherans 2.4 per cent.
Significant Losses: Total exactly at average. Large numbers of missing and discharged invalids (83.1 per cent above average).

C i) Gelhay, 1759 de Ville

Proprietors: Gelhay, Carl Ludwig, Baron; 1759, de Ville, Charles, Marquis.
Uniform: White coat, with red cuffs and turn-backs. White waistcoat. Red breeches.
Record: Kolin, Breslau, Leuthen. Distinguished at Hochkirch, where sustained the heaviest loss among the regiments of cuirassiers. Silesia 1759. Saxony 1760-2
Origins of Rank and File: (11-18 February 1756) Upper and Lower Austria 36.2 per cent, Moravia 20.3 per cent, Silesia 14.9 per cent, Bohemia 14.0 per cent.
Confession: Lutherans .4 per cent.
Significant Losses: Total 8.4 per cent below average. Large numbers of prisoners (29.6 per cent above average), but all other categories below.

C ii) Lucchesi, 1758 Buccow

Proprietors: Lucchesi d'Averna, Joseph, Count; 1758 Buccow, Adolph Nicolaus, Baron.
Uniform: White coat, with red cuffs and turn-backs. Red waistcoat. Red breeches.
Record: Kolin, Breslau, Leuthen (where the heroic Lucchesi was killed; the new proprietor Buccow was one of the leading cavalry commanders of the service). Hochkirch. Saxony 1759. Distinguished at Torgau. Attached to Russian army 1761. Heavily engaged at Reichenbach. Franz Hrobschitzky von Hrobschütz, Colonel Commandant from 1759, was a noted disciplinarian.
Origins of Rank and File: (27 January 1762) Bohemia 56.9 per cent, Moravia 17.9 per cent, Upper and Lower Austria 15.7 per cent.
Confession: Lutherans .3 per cent.
Significant Losses: Total 20.0 above average, and above average in all categories.

C iii), Modena, Alt-

Proprietor: Modena, Franz III d'Este, Duke.
Uniform: White coat, with unique dark blue cuffs and turn-backs. White waistcoat. Dark blue breeches.
Record: Kolin, with Hadik's raid on Berlin. Distinguished at Maxen. Landeshut, Liegnitz. In Silesia 1761-2.
Origins of Rank and File: (25 January 1763) Moravia 54.4 per cent, Bohemia 26.3 per cent, Upper and Lower Austria 14.6 per cent.
Confession: Lutherans .8 per cent.
Significant Losses: Total 10.2 per cent below average. Few outright combat losses, but heavy desertion (53.4 per cent above average).

Dragoon Regiments

D 1, Erzherzog Joseph

Proprietor: Archduke Joseph (later Emperor Joseph II).
Uniform: Green coat, with red cuffs, lapels and turn-backs. Green waistcoat. Buff breeches.
Record: Lobositz. Prague; distinguished at Breslau and Leuthen. Heavy losses in the campaigns of 1760 (Landeshut and Liegnitz), made up again in 1761 by picked drafts from the rest of the dragoons. Reichenbach.
Origins of Rank and File: (20 March 1760) Bohemia 43.4 per cent, Upper and Lower Austria 30.1 per cent, Moravia 7.1 per cent, Silesia 7.0 per cent.
Confession: Lutherans 1.7 per cent.
Significant Losses: Total 42.9 per cent above average. Prisoners a heavy 90.4 per cent above average.

D 6, Liechtenstein

Proprietor: Liechenstein, Joseph Wenzel, Prince.
Uniform: Dark blue coat, with red cuffs, lapels and turn-backs. Red waistcoat. Red breeches.
Record: Distinguished at Lobositz. Reichenberg, Prague. With the *Reichsarmee* 1758. Kunersdorf. 1760 in Thuringia and Saxony, then with Lacy's raid on Berlin. No major actions 1761. Distinguished against very heavy odds at Reichenbach.
Origins of Rank and File: (16-20 January 1759) Moravia 48.1 per cent, Bohemia 20.6 per cent, Upper and Lower Austria 13.8 per cent, Silesia 7.8 per cent.
Confession: Lutherans .7 per cent.
Significant Losses: Total 23.3 per cent below average. All categories below av..

D 7, Batthyány, Carl

Proprietor: Batthyány, Carl Joseph, Prince.
Uniform: Dark blue coat, with red cuffs, lapels and turn-backs. Dark blue waistcoat. Dark blue breeches.
Record: Reichenberg, Prague (with heavy losses), Breslau, covered retreat at Leuthen. Hochkirch. Distinguished at Torgau. Teplitz and Freiberg.
Origins of Rank and File: (3 and 5 April 1760) Bohemia 55.2 per cent, Upper and Lower Austria 24.6 per cent,

Reich 6.3 per cent, Moravia 6.1 per cent.
Confession: No non-Catholics recorded.
Significant Losses: Total 30.4 per cent above average. Heavy losses in prisoners (33.1 per cent above average), killed in action (73.1 per cent above) and men died in hospital (92.5 per cent above). Few deserters or missing.

D 9, Savoyen (Aspremont-Lynden)
Proprietor: Aspremont-Lynden, Ferdinand, Count.
Uniform: Historic dress of red coat, with black cuffs, lapels and turn-backs. Red waistcoat. Red breeches.
Uniform: Retained the name of its former proprietor, Prince Eugene of Savoy, and the traditions were safeguarded by the current proprietor Aspremont-Lynden. Distinguished at Kolin. With the *Reichsarmee* 1758. Heavy losses in Hesse in 1759. The fourth-heaviest losses among the regiments of cavalry at Torgau. No major actions 1761 or 1762.
Origins of Rank and File: (1 and 3 February 1759) Upper and Lower Austria 26.6 per cent, Silesia 27.6 per cent, Bohemia 20.5 per cent, Moravia 12.7 per cent, *Reich* 6.7 per cent.
Confession: Lutherans .9 per cent.
Significant Losses: Total 29.0 per cent below average, but killed in action 50.0 per cent above.

D 13, Modena, Jung-
Proprietor: Modena, Hercules, Hereditary Prince.
Uniform: Red coat, with light blue cuffs, lapels and turn-backs. Light blue waistcoat. Light blue breeches.
Record: Prague, Kolin (a detachment only), Moys, Breslau, Leuthen. Most distinguished at Maxen. No major actions 1760-2.
Origins of Rank and File: (19 December 1760) Moravia 33.0 per cent, Bohemia 29.5 per cent, Upper and Lower Austria 9.9 per cent, *Reich* 7.8 per cent, Breisgau and Vorder Österreich 6.7 per cent.
Confession: Lutherans .7 per cent.
Significant Losses: Total 2.3 per cent below average, though prisoners 15.4 per cent above average, and missing and discharged invalids 17.2 per cent above.

D 19, Hessen-Darmstadt
Proprietor: Hessen-Darmstadt, Ludwig VIII, Landgraf
Uniform: Red coat, with light green cuffs and turn-backs; no lapels. Light buff waistcoat with green lower border. Light buff breeches.
Record: Distinguished at Kolin; then Moys, Breslau, Leuthen. Distinguished at Hochkirch. Silesia 1759. Third heaviest losses among dragoon regiments at Torgau. Burkersdorf.
Origins of Rank and File: (23 January 1759) Moravia 31.5 per cent, Upper and Lower Austria 28.3 per cent,

Reich 10.8 per cent, Bohemia 9.4 per cent.
Confession: Lutherans 1.1 per cent.
Significant Losses: Total 44.9 per cent below average. All categories below average.

D 28, Sachsen-Gotha
Proprietor: Sachsen-Gotha, Johann August, Duke
Uniform: Red coat, with light blue cuffs, lapels and turn-backs. Light blue waistcoat. Straw breeches.
Record: Distinguished at Kolin and Moys; then Breslau, Leuthen. No major actions 1758 or 1759. 1760 converted temporarily to *chevaulegers* without change of uniform. Landeshut (where cut off Prussian retreat) and Liegnitz. In Silesia 1761. Reichenbach.
Origins of Rank and File: (10 January 1762) Moravia 39.1 per cent, Bohemia 31.3 per cent, Upper and Lower Austria 6.6 per cent, Tyrol and the *Reich* 6.2 per cent each.
Confession: Lutherans 1.2 per cent.
Significant Losses: 6.6 per cent below average. All categories below average except desertion, high at 62.0 per cent above.

D 31, de Ligne, 1757 Benedict Daun, 1758 Löwenstein, 1759 Saint-Ignon
Proprietors: Ligne, Ferdinand, Prince; 1757 Daun, Benedict, Count; 1758 Löwenstein-Wertheim, Christian, Prince; 1759 Saint-Ignon, Joseph, Count.
Uniform: Light green coat, with red cuffs, lapels and turn-backs. Red waistcoat. Straw breeches.
Record: Netherlands national regiment. Ever famous for its attack at Kolin. Captured the silver drums of the Bayreuth Dragoons at Gross-Wisternitz 17 June 1758. Distinguished again at Hochkirch. Kunersdorf, Maxen. 1760 converted to *chevaulegers*; almost wiped out during Prussian approach march at Torgau. Restored 1761. Adelsbach, Burkersdorf, Reichenbach. An eventful career.
Origins of Rank and File: Austrian Netherlands and Liège 92.2 per cent, *Reich* 5.7 per cent. Local recruiting Hainault 28.2 per cent, Luxembourg 22.1 per cent, Brabant and Malines (excluding Brussels) 16.8 per cent, Limburg 8.4 per cent, Namur province and town 4.7 per cent, Brussels 1.0 per cent.
Confession: no non-Catholics recorded.
Significant Losses: Total 58.6 per cent above average. Desertion low at 92.1 per cent below average, all other categories above, led by prisoners at 122.8 per cent above and killed in action at 111.2 per cent above.

D 37, Kollowrat
Proprietor: Kollowrat-Krakowsky, Wenzel, Count.
Uniform: Dark blue coat, with red cuffs, lapels and

turn-backs. Red waistcoat. Red breeches.

Record: Kolin, Breslau, Leuthen. Captured silver drums of Jung-Platen Dragoons at Hochkirch. Kunersdorf. Distinguished at Landeshut and captured ten colours at Liegnitz. 1760 in Saxony without major actions. Reichenbach. One of Austria's most effective regiments of horse.

Origins of Rank and File: Bohemia 65.1 per cent, Moravia 9.1 per cent, Upper and Lower Austria 7.8 per cent, *Reich* 6.7 per cent.

Confession: Lutherans .5 per cent.

Significant Losses: Total 40.9 per cent below average. All categories below average except deaths in hospital (38.5 per cent above).

D 38, Württemberg

Proprietor: Württemberg, Carl Eugen, Duke.

Uniform: Red coat, with black cuffs, lapels and turn-backs. Light buff waistcoat. Light buff breeches.

Record: Distinguished with heavy loss at Kolin; Breslau, Leuthen. Distinguished at Holitz 8 June 1758. Kunersdorf. Landeshut and Liegnitz. Temporarily converted to *chevaulegers* 1760. Hit by preliminary Prussian bombardment at Burkersdorf.

Origins of Rank and File: (date not recorded) Moravia 31.0 per cent, Bohemia 25.4 per cent, Upper and Lower Austria 23.8 per cent, *Reich* 6.8 per cent.

Confession: Lutherans .9 per cent.

Significant Losses: Total 14.0 per cent above average. Few outright combat losses, but all other categories well above average.

D 39, Porporati, 1757 Zweibrücken

Proprietors: Porporati, August, Count; 1757 Zweibrücken, Friedrich Michael, Pfalzgraf.

Uniform: Dark blue coat, with red cuffs, lapels and turn-backs. Dark blue waistcoat. Light buff breeches.

Record: Reichenberg (where Porporati killed), Prague, Kolin, Breslau. Distinguished at Domstadtl; Hochkirch. In Saxony for most of rest of war, with large number of minor actions.

Origins of Rank and File: (20 January 1759) Upper and Lower Austria 38.5 per cent, Moravia 28.6 per cent, Bohemia 18.3 per cent.

Confession: Lutherans .3 per cent.

Significant Losses: Total 20.2 per cent above average. Few deaths in hospital, but all other categories above av., with heavy outright combat losses (prisoners 31.5 per cent above, killed in action 122.4 per cent above).

D iii) Koháry, 1758 Althann

(D iii) because two senior dragoon regiments had been disbanded before the war)

Proprietors: Koháry, Andreas, Count; 1758 Althann, Michael, Count.

Uniform: Unique white coat, with red cuffs, lapels and turn-backs. White waistcoat. White breeches.

Record: In garrison in Vienna 1757. To the field in 1758: Hochkirch. 1759 in Silesia without major actions. Landeshut; heavy losses at Liegnitz. Reichenbach.

Origins of Rank and File: (27 January 1763) Upper and Lower Austria 31.4 per cent; Moravia 28.0 per cent; Bohemia 27.2 per cent.

Confession: Lutherans 1.6 per cent.

Significant Losses: Total 39.9 per cent below average. All categories well below average.

Squadron of *Staabs-Dragoner*

Proprietors: None. Commanded directly by a succession of acting commandants.

Uniform: Dark blue coat, with red cuffs, white turn backs, no lapels. Dark blue waistcoat. Red breeches.

Record: Raised by Lacy 1758 as staff escort. Unlike Staff Infantry the Staff Dragoons were in frequent contact with the enemy. Distinguished at Maxen and in other actions. Disbanded 1762.

Origins of Rank and File: (27 May 1762) Bohemia 30.7 per cent, Moravia 28.6 per cent, Upper and Lower Austria 25.9 per cent, Silesia 8.5 per cent.

Confession: No non-Catholics recorded.

Significant Losses: No direct comparisons to be made with other units of dragoons, though very heavy total losses of 728, made up of 370 prisoners, 43 killed, 141 died in hospital, 136 deserters, 38 missing or discharged as invalids.

Chevauleger (light dragoon) Regiment Clx 18, Löwenstein, Jung-

Proprietor: 1759 Löwenstein-Wertheim, Christian, Prince.

Uniform: Green coat, with red cuffs, lapels and turn-backs. Red waistcoat. Red breeches.

Record: Separated from parent regiment D31 Löwenstein, Alt- in 1758. Distinguished in the same year in actions for the relief of Olmütz; Hochkirch. 1759 became the first of Austria's regiments of *chevaulegers* as an independent unit under Löwenstein. Distinguished at Kunersdorf. Landeshut, Liegnitz. Teplitz, Freiberg.

Origins of Rank and File: (6 January 1763) Upper and Lower Austria 36.6 per cent, Bohemia 21.0 per cent, Moravia 14.6 per cent, *Reich* 9.4 per cent.

Confession: Lutherans .7 per cent.

Significant Losses: Total 21.5 per cent above average. All categories above average except prisoners (30.3 per cent below average).

Hussar Regiments

H 2, *Kaiser Husaren*

Proprietor: Emperor Francis Stephen.
Uniform: Kalpak with dark blue bag. Dark blue pelisse, dolman and pants. Yellow and blue barrel sash. Dark blue sabretache
Record: Raised by the Emperor 1756. Kolin, Moys. Hochkirch. Maxen. Torgau. Reichenberg.
Origins of Rank and File: (11-12 January 1758). Hungary and Transylvania 98.5 per cent. Recruiting heaviest in eastern Hungarian county of Bihar (13.1 per cent), otherwise mainly from western Hungarian counties of Pressburg (12.0 per cent), Neutra (10.4 per cent), Eisenburg (7.9 per cent) and Komorn (7.5 per cent).
Confession: Calvinists 17.2 per cent, Lutherans 2.9 per cent, Orthodox .7 per cent.
Significant Losses: Total 23.0 per cent above average, mainly due to fairly high rates of deaths in hospital (34.4 per cent above average) and desertion (47.4 per cent above).

H 11, Nádasdy

Proprietor: Nádasdy auf Fogaras, Franz Leopold, Count.
Uniform: Kalpak with light green bag. Light green pelisse and dolman with yellow lace. Dark blue pants. Yellow and green barrel sash. Red or brown sabretache.
Record: Kolin, Breslau, Leuthen. Domstadtl. Kunersdorf. Broke Prussian squares at Kunersdorf, and again at Landeshut; Liegnitz. Actions around Bunzelwitz. Burkersdorf, Reichenbach. An old and highly-regarded regiment with an esteemed proprietor.
Origins of Rank and File: (17 January 1759) Hungary and Transylvania 96.3 per cent. Recruited heavily in the far eastern Hungarian county of Bihar (11.4 per cent), otherwise mainly from Ödenburg (12.0 per cent), Fehérvár (10.1 per cent), Zala (7.0 per cent) and other western counties.
Confession: Calvinists 17.4 per cent, Lutherans 1.8 per cent, Orthodox 1.0 per cent.
Significant Losses: Total 30.5 per cent above average. Low desertion (9.6 per cent below average) but heavy outright combat losses (prisoners 40.6 per cent above average, killed in action 137.2 per cent above).

H 16 Károly, 1759 Pálffy, Rudolph

Proprietors: Károly, Franz, Count; 1759 Pálffy, Rudolph.
Uniform: Kalpak with red bag. Mid-blue pelisse, dolman and pants. Red and blue barrel sash. Red sabretache with blue double eagle.
Record: No major actions 1756 or 1757. Hochkirch. Minor actions 1759. Distinguished at Landeshut. Numerous successful encounters 1761.
Origins of Rank and File: (25 May 1759) Hungary and Transylvania 97.2 per cent. Wide recruiting base, with largest individual representations from eastern and central Hungarian counties of Bihar (12.7 per cent), Pest (8.6 per cent), Szatmar (5.2 per cent) and Csongrad (5.2 per cent).
Confession: Calvinists 25.4 per cent, Lutherans 4.8 per cent, Schismatics 2.3 per cent, Orthodox 1.1 per cent.
Significant Losses: Total 15.5 per cent below average. All categories below average, apart from missing or discharged as invalids (34.8 per cent above average).

H 17 Kálnoky, Siebenbürgisches Husaren-Regiment

Proprietor: Kálnoky, Anton, Count.
Uniform: Kalpak with red bag. Light blue pelisse and dolman. Red pants. Yellow and blue barrel sash. Red sabretache with yellow 'K' monogram.
Record: Kolin, Moys. Distinguished in Moravia 1758. Distinguished at Kunersdorf. Burkersdorf, Reichenbach.
Origins of Rank and File: (28 January 1760) Hungary and Transylvania 98.1 per cent. Overwhelming representation from Transylvania (62.0 per cent), with largest Hungarian recruiting in northern counties of Zemplen (4.0 per cent), Borsod (3.8 per cent) and Abau (3.0 per cent).
Confession: Calvinists 24.8 per cent, Orthodox 19.0 per cent, Lutherans 5.1 per cent.
Significant Losses: Total 10.3 per cent below average. All categories below average except deaths in hospital (33.7 per cent above average).

H 24, Esterházy, Paul Anton, 1762 Luzinsky

Proprietors: Esterházy, Paul Anton, Prince; 1762 Luzinsky, Gabriel, Baron.
Uniform: Kalpak with red bag. Light blue pelisse and dolman. Red pants. Unique yellow boots. Yellow and blue barrel sash. Red sabretache with yellow 'E' monogram. Altogether the most colourful of the hussar uniforms.
Record: Prague, Leuthen. Together with H1 screened the Austrian march from Stolpen to Hochkirch, and nearly captured King Frederick. Maxen. With Lacy's raid on Berlin. No major actions 1761 or 1762.
Origins of Rank and File: (6-7 June 1759) Hungary and Transylvania 98.3 per cent. Recruiting reflected the influence of the Esterházy family in Hungary south-

west of the Danube, namely in the counties of Ödenburg (21.1 per cent), Pest (9.4 per cent), Tolna (9.2 per cent), Eisenburg (8.3 per cent) and Zala (7.0 per cent).
Confession: Calvinists 12.1 per cent, Lutherans 4.0 per cent, Orthodox .9 per cent.
Significant Losses: Total 29.4 per cent below average, though fairly large number of killed in action (26.4 per above average).

H 30 Baranyay

Proprietor: Baranyay de Bodorfalva, Joseph, Baron.
Uniform: Kalpak with red bag. Mid-green pelisse and dolman. Light blue pants. Red and yellow barrel sash. Green sabretache with black double eagle.
Record: Lobositz. Prague, Kolin, Moys, with Hadik's raid on Berlin. For rest of war almost wholly in Saxony, with numerous small actions, and engaged in the final battle at Freiberg.
Origins of Rank and File: (31 January 1759) Hungary and Transylvania 98.4 per cent. Recruiting 6.3 per cent from county of Pest, otherwise largest single representations from north-western Hungarian counties of Pressburg (23.3 per cent), Neutra (13.9 per cent), Komorn (7.4 per cent), Raab (5.2 per cent), Veszprem (4.9 per cent) and Eisenburg (4.0 per cent).
Significant Losses: Total 8.2 per cent below average, but many killed in action (42.1 per cent above average).

H 32 Festetics, 1757 Széchenyi

Proprietors: Festetics de Tolna, Joseph, Count; 1757 Széchenyi, Anton, Count.
Uniform: Kalpak with dark blue bag. Dark blue pelisse, pants and dolman. Dark blue sabretache with red 'S'.
Record: Did good work in the campaign of Rossbach. Distinguished at Maxen.
Origins of Rank and File: (2 February 1759) Hungary and Transylvania 96.8 per cent. Recruiting 5.5 per cent from Transylvania, otherwise largest representations from western Hungarian counties of Eisenburg (15.6 per cent), Zala (13.8 per cent) and Ödenburg (5.2 per cent).
Confession: Calvinists 12.8 per cent, Lutherans 4.0 per cent, Orthodox 2.9 per cent.
Significant Losses: Total 19.5 per cent above average. Only missing and discharged invalids below average (17.1 per cent below), all other categories above average with heavy outright combat losses (prisoners 18.6 per cent above, killed in action 74.5 per cent above).

H 34 Dessewffy

Proprietor: Dessewffy, Joseph, Baron.
Uniform: Black mirliton. Mid blue pelisse, dolman and pants. Red sabretache.
Record: Heavily engaged at Leuthen. Distinguished at Hochkirch and Freiberg.
Origins of Rank and File: (10 January 1759) 95.4 per cent from Hungary and Transylvania. Largest representations from the north central Hungarian counties of Abauj (9.5 per cent), Saros (8.4 per cent), the Hajdu towns (8.2 per cent), Pest (7.7 per cent), Borsod (5.5 per cent) and Zemplen (5.4 per cent).
Confession: Calvinists 8.4 per cent, Lutherans 4.8 per cent, Orthodox 2.4 per cent.
Significant Losses: Total 30.6 per cent above average. Prisoners 6.0 per cent below average, but all other categories well above.

H 35 Morocz, 1759 Bethlen

Proprietors: Morocz, Emerich, Baron; 1757 Bethlen, Joseph, Count.
Uniform: Kalpak with red bag. Light blue dolman, pelisse and pants. Red and blue barrel sash.
Record: Distinguished in large number of small actions. Reichenbach.
Origins of Rank and File: (24 January 1759) Hungary and Transylvania 97.2 per cent. Largest representations from west central Hungarian counties of Pest (19.7 per cent), Heves (18.1 per cent) and Neograd (6.1 per cent).
Confession: Calvinists 18.9 per cent, Lutherans 4.6 per cent, Orthodox 1.6 per cent.*Significant Losses*: Total 17.4 per cent above average. Low desertion (21.2 per cent below average), but all other categories above.

H 36 *Jazygier und Kumanen-Regiment*, also known as *Palatinal-Husaren-Regiment*

Proprietor: Batthyány, Ludwig Ernst, Count Palatine.
Uniform: Kalpak with red bag. Light blue dolman and pelisse. Red pants. Red and white barrel sash.
Record: Raised in 1756 by Batthyány in lands of former nomadic peoples. With Hadik's raid on Berlin, and again with Lacy's raid in 1760, otherwise numerous small actions mainly in Saxony. The commandant Colonel Andreas Count Török reported on 1 December 1761 that hard service had reduced the regiment to a poor state. It nevertheless fought with great distinction at Freiberg.
Origins of Rank and File: (2 February 1762) Hungary and Transylvania 100.0 per cent. Recruiting still represented origins in the central Hungarian counties of the Hadju towns (19.0 per cent), Jász-Berérny (16.3

per cent), Gross-Kumanien (13.0 per cent) and Klein-Kumanien (10.5 per cent).
Confession: Calvinists 45.3 per cent, Orthodox 6.1 per cent, Lutherans 4.2 per cent.
Significant Losses: Total 36.7 per cent below average. All categories well below average except for missing and discharged invalids (29.4 per cent above average).

H 47 *Siebenbürgisches Szekler Regiment*
Proprietor: None.
Uniform: Dark blue pelisse and dolman. Red pants.
Record: Raised 1762 from the ethnic Hungarian Szekler population of Transylvania. Intended as security against the Turks, and saw no action.
Origins of Rank and File; Confession: Nothing recorded.

H ii) Splényi, 1762 Esterházy, Emmerich.
Proprietors: Splényi de Miháldy, Gabriel, Baron; 1762 Esterházy, Emmerich, Count.
Uniform: Light green pelisse, dolman and pants. Light green sabretache.
Record: Distinguished at Prague, Rossbach and Maxen.
Origins of Rank and File: (30 March 1762) Hungary and Transylvania 99.2 per cent. Recruited mostly from the northern Hungarian counties of Borsod (18.3 per cent), Neutra (9.8 per cent), Saros (9.1 per cent, Pressburg and Gömer (6.2 per cent each) and Zemplen (5.5 per cent).
Confession: Calvinists 16.0 per cent, Lutherans 7.8 per cent, Orthodox 1.3 per cent.
Significant Losses: Total 42.5 per cent below average. All categories well below average.

H iii) Hadik
Proprietor: Hadik, Andreas, Count.
Uniform: Kalpak with red bag. Dark blue pelisse and dolman. Red pants. Red and yellow barrel sash. Red sabretache with bear device in red.
Record: Lobositz. With Hadik's raid on Berlin. Maxen. Distinguished at Torgau. In Saxony 1761. Reichenbach.
Origins of Rank and File: (25 January 1760) Hungary and Transylvania 97.0 per cent. Largest single representation from the Hungarian county of Pest (18.2 per cent), otherwise mainly recruited from the north-west counties of Neutra (13.0 per cent), Pressburg (7.1 per cent), and Raab, Neograd, Trentschin and Ödenburg (4.4 to 3.3 per cent).
Confession: Calvinists 10.0 per cent, Lutherans 4.3 per cent.
Significant Losses: Total 21.4 per cent above average. Outright combat losses near average, but heavy desertion (37.0 per cent above average).

Hussar Regiments of the Military Borders (Grenz-Husaren-Regimenter)
Raised between 1746 and 1750 along the Military Borders, and numbered here for convenience from 1 to 4. They came under the authority of the local military commands on the Borders, and therefore had no proprietors. There are no records of their local recruiting or religion.
Significant Losses are measured against those for the Border Hussar Regiments alone.

GZ HR 1, *Carlstädter Grenz-Husaren-Regiment*
Commandants: Mittrovsky, Maximilian Joseph, Baron; 1757 Knesevich, Martin.
Uniform: No reliable information.
Record: Lobositz. Prague, Kolin, with Hadik's raid on Berlin. Small actions in Saxony 1759-61. Silesia 1862.
Significant Losses: Total 94.5 per cent above average.

GZ HR 2, *Warasdiner Grenz-Husaren-Regiment*
Commandants: Kukez, Anton; 1762 Schröckinger, Franz.
Uniform: Kalpak with red bag. Red dolman, pelisse and pants. Red and white barrel sash.
Record: In action throughout the war. Distinguished at Maxen and had a good general record.
Significant Losses: Total 89.6 per cent below average.

GZ HR 3, *Banal Grenz-Husaren-Regiment*
Commandants: Skerlecz von Lomnicza, Gabriel; 1762 Voikovich von Voikffy, Siegmund, Count.
Uniform: No reliable information.
Record: In action throughout the war.
Significant Losses: Total 46.1 per cent below average.

GZ HR 4, *Slavonisches Grenz-Husaren-Regiment*
Commandant: Engelshofen, Franz, Baron.
Uniform: No reliable information.
Record: Distinguished in minor actions in Saxony 1760 and 1761. Important for the security of the Military Borders as a whole, as the Slavonian Border was the most exposed to Turkish invasion.
Significant Losses: Total 43.5 per cent above average.

FELD-ARTILLERIE CORPS

Command: Liechtenstein, Joseph Wenzel, Prince, as *Feld-Artillerie-Director*.

Structure: Two brigades of the *Deutsche-Artillerie*, one brigade of the *Niederländische-Artillerie*. (The three battalions of the *Artillerie-Füsiliere* are treated separately under 'Newly-Raised Units,' above).

Origins of the Büchsenmeister (i.e. trained gunners. German and Netherlands artillery treated together): Bohemia 62.6 per cent, Upper and Lower Austria 8.8 per cent, Netherlands and Luxembourg 8.0 per cent, Moravia 8.0 per cent, *Reich* 5.6 per cent.

Significant Losses. (German and Netherlands artillery treated together): Total 4,314. No prisoners recorded, 280 killed in action, 2,198 died in hospital, 941 deserted, 895 missing or discharged as invalids.

Deutsche Artillerie

Uniform: Grey-brown 'hare-' or 'wolf-brown' coat with red cuffs. Grey-brown breeches.

Origins of all Ranks: Predominantly Bohemian. See the detailed Appendix 12 in Volume 1, *Instrument of War*, 2000.

Niederländische Artillerie

Uniform: Grey-brown 'hare-' or 'wolf-brown' coat with red cuffs and lapels. Grey-brown breeches.

Origins of the Büchsenmeister: Austrian Netherlands and Liège 74.3 per cent, *Reich* 16.7 per cent, Prussia 4.4 per cent. Of the representation from the Austrian Netherlands, Luxembourg accounted for 53.3 per cent, Hainault 16.0 per cent, Brabant (excluding Brussels) and Malines 9.4 per cent, Brussels 6.6 per cent, Namur 5.6 per cent, Antwerp 4.2 per cent.

INGENIEUR CORPS

Command: Lorraine, Charles, Prince, as *General-Genie-Director*.

Structure: Four brigades: German, Hungarian, Italian and Netherlandish.

Uniform: Originally white coat. 1761 light blue coat with red lapels, cuffs and turn-backs. Red waistcoat. Red breeches.

Origins and Significant Losses: Details incomplete.

PONTONIERS-CORPS

Command: The *Oberst-Schiffamt* in Vienna.

Uniform: Light blue coat with red lapels, cuffs and turn backs. Light blue waistcoat. Light blue breeches.

Recruitment and Significant Losses: Not available.

SAPPEURS-CORPS

Command: Established 1760 under the authority of the *General-Genie-Director*. Local command by Bechardt, Major Johann, Baron.

Uniform: Originally that of the parent regiments of the individual personnel. Then light blue-grey 'pike-grey' coat with red cuffs and collar. Light blue-greyish or possibly red waistcoat and breeches. Black leather cap with monogram 'MT.'

Origins of Rank and File: (21 June 1760) Bohemia 22.6 per cent, Hungary and Transylvania 19.0 per cent, Upper and Lower Austria 10.4 per cent, Styria 6.7 per cent, Netherlands/Luxembourg and Silesia 6.1 per cent, Moravia 5.5 per cent.

Confession: Lutherans 3.0 per cent.

Significant Losses: Total 65: 20 prisoners, 12 killed in action, 6 died in hospital, 27 deserters.

PIONIER-CORPS

Command: Established 1758, under the local command of the headquarters of the various field armies.

Uniform: Light blue-grey 'pike-grey' coat with green cuffs, collar and turn-backs. White breeches. Plain black leather cap.

Record: Distinguished at Hochkirch, Landeshut and Loudon's storm of Schweidnitz. Reduced heavily towards end of war.

Origins of Rank and File: (8 April 1760) Carniola 37.0 per cent, Upper and Lower Austria 19.5 per cent, Bohemia 15.1 per cent, *Reich* 8.2 per cent, Sytria 5.3 per cent.

Confession: Lutherans 4.6 per cent.

Significant Losses: See *Deutsches Feld-Jäger Corps*, above.

Austrian Regimental Lists
(Regular units only)

Austrian Regiments—Numbers to Names

Infantry Regiments
1. Kaiser
2. Erzherzog Carl, 1761 Erzherzog Ferdinand
3. Lothringen
4. Deutschmeister
7. Neipperg
8. Hildburghausen
9. Los Rios
10. Wolfenbüttel, Jung- (Ludwig, Louis)
11. Wallis
12. Botta
13. Moltke
14. Salm
15. Pallavicini
16. Königsegg
17. Kollowrat
18. Marschall
19. Pálffy, Leopold
20. Colloredo, Alt- (Anton)
21. Arenberg
22. Hagenbach, 1757 Sprecher, 1758 Lacy
23. Baden-Baden
24. Starhemberg
25. Piccolomini, 1757 Thürheim
26. Puebla
27. Baden-Durlach
28. Wied
29. Wolfenbüttel, Alt- (Carl)
30. Sachsen-Gotha
31. Haller
32. Forgách
33. Esterházy, Nicolaus
34. Batthyány
35. Waldeck
36. Browne, 1759 Tillier, 1761 Kinsky
37. Esterházy, Joseph, 1762 Siskovics
38. Ligne
39. Pálffy, Johann, 1758 Preysach
40. Colloredo, Jung- (Carl)
41. Bayreuth
42. Gaisruck (Gaisrugg)
43. Platz
44. Clerici
45. Daun, Alt- (Heinrich), 1761 O'Kelly
46. Maguire
47. Harrach
48. Luzan
49. Kheul, 1758 Angern

Names to Numbers

Infantry Regiments
Andlau, No. 57
Angern, No. 49
d'Arberg, No. 55
Arenberg, No. 21
Baden-Baden, No. 23
Baden-Durlach, No. 27
Batthyány, No. 34
Bayreuth, No. 41
Bethlen, No. 52
Botta, No. 12
Browne, No. 36
Carl, Erzherzog, No. 2
Clerici, No. 44
Colloredo, Alt- (Anton), No. 20
Colloredo, Jung- (Carl), No. 40
Daun, Alt- (Heinrich), No. 45
Daun, Jung- (Leopold), No. 59
Deutschmeister, No. 4
Esterházy, Joseph, No. 37
Esterházy, Nicolaus, No. 33
Ferdinand, Erzherzog, No. 2
Forgách, No. 32
Gaisruck (Gaisrugg), No. 42
Gyulai, No. 51
Hagenbach, No. 22
Haller, No. 31
Harrach, No. 47
Harsch, No. 50
Hildburghausen, No. 8
Kaiser, No. 1
Kheul, No. 49
Kinsky, No. 36
Kollowrat, No. 17
Königsegg, No. 16
Lacy, No. 22
de Ligne, No. 36
Los Rios, No. 9
Lothringen, No. 3
Loudon, No. 29
Luzan, No. 48
Maguire, No. 46
Marschall, No. 18
Mercy, No. 56
Moltke, No. 13
Neipperg, No. 7
O'Kelly, No. 45
Pálffy, Johann, No. 39

452

Austrian Regiments—Numbers to Names **Names to Numbers**

50. Harsch
51. Gyulai
52. Bethlen
53. Simbschen
54. Sincère
55. d'Arberg
56. Mercy
57. Andlau

Pálffy, Leopold, No. 19
Pallavicini, No. 15
Piccolomini, No. 25
Platz, No. 43
Preysach, No. 39
Puebla, No. 26
Sachsen-Gotha, No. 30
Salm, No. 14
Simbschen, No. 53
Sincère, No. 54
Siskovics, No. 37
Sprecher, No. 22
Starhemberg, No. 24
Thürheim, No. 25
Tiller, No. 35
Waldeck, No. 35
Wallis, No. 11
Wied, No. 28
Wolfenbüttel, Alt- (Carl), No. 29
Wolfenbüttel, Jung- (Ludwig, Louis), No. 10

Cuirassier Regiments

C 1. Erzherzog Leopold
C 4. Erzherzog Ferdinand, 1761 Erherzog Maximilian
C 6. Portugal
C 8. Pálffy, Carl Paul
C 10. Stampach
C 12. Serbelloni
C 14. Cordua, 1756 O'Donnell
C 20. Schmerzing, 1762 d'Ayasasa
C 21. Trautmannsdorff
C 22. Kalckreuth, 1760 Albert
C 23. Birkenfeld, 1761 Stampa
C 25. Anhalt-Zerbst
C 27. Radicati, 1757 Löwenstein, 1758 Daun, Benedict
C 29. Brettlach
C 33. Anspach (Ansbach)
C i) Gelhay, 1759 de Ville
C ii) Lucchesi, 1758 Buccow
C iii) Modena, Alt-

Cuirassier Regiments

Albert/ Sachsen-Teschen, C 22
Anhalt-Zerbst, C 25
Anspach (Ansbach), C 33
d'Ayasasa, C 20
Birkenfeld, C 23
Buccow, C ii)
Brettlach, C 29
Cordua, C 14
Daun, Benedict, C 27
Ferdinand, Erzherzog, C 4
Gelhay, C i)
Kalckreuth, C 22
Leopold, Erzherzog, C 3
Löwenstein, C 27
Lucchesi, C ii)
Maxmimilian, Erzherzog, C 4
Modena, Alt-, C iii)
O'Donnell, C 14
Pálffy, Carl, C 8
Portugal, C 6
Radicati, C 27
Schmerzing, C 20
Serbelloni, C 11
Stampa, C 23
Stampach, C 10
Trautmannsdorff, C 21
de Ville, C i)

Austrian Regiments—Numbers to Names

Dragoon Regiments
D 1. Erzherzog Joseph
D 6. Liechtenstein
D 7. Batthyány
D 9. Savoyen (Aspremont-Lynden)
D 13. Modena, Jung-
D 19. Hessen-Darmstadt
D 28. Sachsen-Gotha
D 31. Ligne, 1757 Daun, Benedict, 1758 Löwenstein, 1759 Saint-Ignon
D 37. Kollowrat
D 38. Württemberg
D 39. Porporati, 1757 Zweibrücken
D iii) Koháry, 1758 Althann

Chevauleger *Regiment*
Clx 18. 1759 Löwenstein, Jung-

Hussar Regiments
H 2. Kaiser
H 11. Nádasdy
H 16. Károly, 1759 Pálffy, Rudolph
H 17. Kálnoky
H 24. Esterházy, Paul Anton, 1762 Luzinsky
H 30. Baranyay
H 32. Festetics, 1757 Széchenyi
H 34. Dessewffy
H 35. Morocz, 1759 Bethlen
H 36. Palatinal
H ii) Splényi, 1762 Esterházy, Emerich
H iii) Hadik

Names to Numbers

Dragoon Regiments
Althann, D iii)
Aspremont-Lynden (Savoyen), D 9
Batthyány, D 7
Daun, Benedict, D 31
Hessen-Darmstadt, D 19
Joseph, Erzherzog, D 1
Koháry, D iii)
Kollowrat, D 37
Liechtenstein, D 6
de Ligne, D 31
Löwenstein, D 31
Modena, Jung-, D 13
Porporati, D 30
Sachsen-Gotha, D 28
Saint-Ignon, D 31
Savoyen (Aspremont-Lynden), D 9
Württemberg, D 38

Hussar Regiments
Baranyay, H 30
Bethlen, H 35
Dessewffy, H 34
Esterházy, Emerich, H ii)
Esterházy, Paul Anton, H 24
Festetics, H 32
Hadik, H iii)
Kaiser, H 2
Kálnoky, H 17
Károly, H 16
Luzinsky, H 24
Pálffy, Rudolph, H 16
Morocz, H 35
Nádasdy, H 11
Palatinal, H 36
Splényi, H ii)
Széchenyi, H 32

Prussian Regimental Lists—Numbers to Names Only

(Regular units only)

(The asterisks refer to Frederick's rating of the performance of regiments in the Seven Years War. A single * denotes 'good,' and a double ** 'very good.' The rapid turn-over of proprietors is striking).

Infantry Regiments
1, Winterfeldt, 1758 Lattorff, 1760 Zeuner
2, Kanitz *
3, Anhalt, Alt-, 1758 Kahlden, 1759 Anhalt-Bernburg *
4, Kalnein, 1757 Rautter, 1758 Kleist, 1761 Thadden
5, Braunschweig, Alt- *
6, (*Grenadier-Garde Bataillon*) Retzow, 1759 Saldern
7, Braunschweig-Bevern, December 1756 - November 1757 Bevern, Alt-, for rest of war Bevern
8, Amstell, 1757 Geist, 1759 Queiss
9, Quadt, 1756 Kleist, Jung-, 1758 Oldenburg, 1758 Puttkamer, 1759 Schenckendorff, 1760 Schenckendorff, Jung- **
10, Knobloch, 1757 Pannwitz, 1759 Mosel **
11, Below, 1758 Rebentisch
12, Darmstadt, Alt-, 1757 Finck *
13, Itzenplitz, 1760 Syburg, 1762 Kaiser (i.e. Peter III of Russia) **
14, Lehwaldt
15, *Fuss-Garde Regiment*, of which the first battalion was designated the *Bataillon-Garde* or *Leib-Garde-Bataillon*
16, Dohna, Christoph
17, Manteuffel
18, Prinz von Preussen *
19, Markgraf Carl (of Brandenburg-Schwedt)
20, Zastrow, 1757 Bornstedt, 1759 Stutterheim, Jung- *
21, Hülsen
22, Prinz Moritz, 1760 Schenckendorff, Alt-
23, Forcade
24, Schwerin, 1757 Goltz
25, Kalckstein, 1760 Ramin
26, Meyerinck, 1758 Wedel, 1760 Linden
27, Kleist, Alt-, 1757 Asseburg, 1759 Lindstädt *
28, Hautcharmoy, 1758 Münchow, Jung-, 1758 Kreytzen, Jung-, 1759 Kreytzen, 1759 Ramin, 1760 Thile *
29, Schultze, 1758 Wedel, 1758 Knobloch *
30, Blanckensee, 1756 Pritz, 1757 Kannacher, 1759 Stutterheim, 1759 Stutterheim, Alt-
31, Lestwitz *
32, Tresckow
33, La Motte Fusiliers
34, Prinz Ferdinand **
35, Prinz Heinrich Fusiliers **
36, Münchow Fusiliers, 1759 Münchow, Alt-, Fusiliers
37, Kurssell Fusiliers, 1758 Braun Fusiliers
38, Brandes Fusiliers, 1758 Brandes Fusiliers
39, Braunschweig, Alt-, Fusiliers **
40, Kreytzen Fusiliers, 1758 Kreytzen, Alt-, Fusiliers, 1759 Gablentz Fusiliers
41, Wied Fusiliers **
42, Markgraf Heinrich Fusiliers
43, Kalsow Fusiliers, 1758 Kalckreuth Fusiliers, 1758 Bredow Fusiliers, 1760 Zieten Fusiliers
44, Jungkenn Fusiliers, 1759 Hoffmann Fusiliers, 1759 Grant Fusiliers
45, Dossow Fusiliers, 1757 Hessen-Cassel Fusiliers

46, Württemberg, Alt-, Fusiliers, 1757 Bülow Fusiliers
47, Rohr Fusiliers, 1758 Grabow Fusiliers
48, Hessen-Cassel Fusiliers, 1757 Salmuth Fusiliers
49, Pionier-Regiment Sers, 1758 Diericke Fusiliers *

Former Saxon Infantry Regiments
54, Saldern Fusiliers, 1758 Plotho Fusiliers
55, Hauss Fusiliers, 1760 Roebel Fusiliers
56, Loen Fusiliers, 1758 Kalckreuth Fusiliers, 1758 Wietersheim Fusiliers, 1759 Horn Fusiliers

Standing Grenadier Battalions
St GBn 1, Kahlden, 1758 Wangenheim, 1758 Buddenbrock
St GBn 2, Ingersleben, 1758 Unruh
St GBn 3, Gemmingen, 1757 Benckendorff
St GBn 4, Lossow
St GBn 5, Rath, 1760 Koschenbahr, 1761 Hachenberg
St GBn 6, Plötz, 1758 Rohr, 1759 Busche

Garrison Regiments and Battalions
Gar 1, Luck, 1757 Puttkamer
Gar 2, Sydow, 1759 Sydow, Alt-
Gar 3, Grolman
Gar 4, Grape, 1759 Jungkenn, 1760 Plotho
Gar 5, Mützschefahl, 1759 Sydow, Jung-
Gar 6, Lattorff, 1762 Sass
Gar 7, Lange, 1760 Itzenplitz
Gar 8, Nettelhorst, 1757 Quadt
Gar 9, La Motte, 1759 Bonin
Gar 10, Blanckensee
Gar 11, Manteuffel, 1760 Mellin
Gar 12, Kalckreuth

Cuirassier Regiments
C 1, Buddenbrock, 1757 Krockow, 1759 Schlabrendorff
C 2, Prinz von Preussen, 1758 Prinz Heinrich
C 3, *Leibregiment zu Pferde*
C 4, Gessler, 1758 Schmettau
C 5, Prinz Friedrich or Markgraf Friedrich
C 6, Baron Schönaich, 1759 Vasold
C 7, Driesen, 1758 Horn, 1762 Manstein
C 8, Rochow, 1757 Seydlitz **
C 9, Prince Schönaich, 1758 Bredow
C 10, *Regiment Gensd'armes* **
C 11, *Leib-Carabiniers*
C 12, Kyau, 1759 Spaen, 1762 Dalwig **
C 13, Garde du Corps

Dragoon Regiments
D 1, Normann, 1761 Zastrow *
D 2, Blanckensee, 1757 Krockow
D 3, Truchsess, 1757 Meinicke, 1761 Flanss
D 4, Katte, 1757 Czettritz **
D 5, Bayreuth (double-sized, ten squadrons strong)
D 6, Schorlemer, 1760 Meier (double-sized, ten squadrons strong)

D 7,   Plettenberg
D 8,   Langermann, 1757 Platen, 1758 Platen, Alt-
D 9,   Holstein-Gottorp, 1762 Pomeiske
D 10,   Finck von Finckenstein
D 11,   Stechow, 1758 Platen, Jung-
D 12,   Württemberg (Prince Eugen)

Hussar Regiments
H 1,   (Green Hussars or *Preussisches Husaren-Corps*), Székely, 1759 Kleist
H 2,   (Red Hussars or *Leibhusaren-Regiment*), Zieten **
H 3,   Wartenberg, 1757 Warnery, 1758 Möhring
H 4,   (White Hussars), Puttkamer, 1759 Dingelstädt, 1762 Bohlen
H 5,   (Black 'Death's Head' Hussars), Ruesch, 1762 Lossow **
H 6,   (Brown Hussars), Wechmar, 1757 Werner
H 7,   (Yellow Hussars), Malachowski
H 8,   (Red Hussars), Seydlitz, 1759 Gersdorff
H 9,   Belling
        The Corps of *Bosniaken* came under command of H5.

NB. The designation of Prussian hussar regiments was subject to great turbulence in the later years of the war and immediately afterwards. For the present work I have adopted the scheme in Hans Bleckwenn's *Die Friderizianischen Uniformen*, 4 vols, Osnabrück 1984, III, 139-192.

(For more details on the Prussian Army, see the earlier publication, The Army of Frederick the Great, 2nd Edition*)*

NOTES

Abbreviations used in the notes (See Bibliography for details)
Albert = Archduke Albert of Sachsen-Teschen, *Mémoires de ma Vie*. Magyar Országos Levéltár, Budapest
Arneth = Arneth, A., *Geschichte Maria Theresias*, 10 vols, Vienna 1863-79
Forschungen = Forschungen zur brandenburgischen und preussischen Geschichte, Leipzig, Munich and Berlin, 1888 etc
GSPK = Geheimes Staatsarchiv Preussischer Kulturbesitz, Berlin, IV Hauptabteilung, Rep. 15A, Geheimes Civilkabinett, Militaria
HHStA = Haus-, Hof und Staatarchiv, Vienna
HL = Hadik Levéltár, Hadtörténeti Intézet és Múzeum, Budapest
KA = Kriegsarchiv, Vienna
CA = Cabinettsakten
FA = Feldakten
HKRA = Hofkriegsräthsliche Akten
HKR Protocolle = Hofkriegsrathsprotocolle
M.M.T.O. = Depositions of candidates for the Military Order of Maria Theresa
K-M = Aus der Zeit Maria Theresias. Tagebuch des Fürsten Johann Josef Khevenhüller-Metsch, Kaiserlichen Obersthofmeisters 1742-1776, 11 vols. Vienna, 1907-72
PC = *Politische Correspondenz Friedrichs des Grossen*, 46 vols, Berlin, 1879-1939
SHAT A1 = Correspondance générale, Service Historique de l'Armée de Terre, Vincennes

I. 1756

1. Memorandum on a reform plan of Emperor Joseph II in 1766, Schilling, 1994, 262
2. KA HKRA 1756 VII 1, Browne to the Hofkriegsrath, Brünn, 24 June
3. K-M, IV, 42
4. Gorani, 1944, 55
5. Cogniazzo, 1788-91, I, 192
6. *Kopien eines geheimen Vortrags an der Kaiserin-Königin*, Volz and Küntzel, 1899, 380
7. Ibid., clxxix)
8. *Kopien eines geheimen Vortrags*, ibid., 383
9. HHStA Staatskanzlei Vorträge 79, marginal note on Browne's *Pro Memoria*, Kolin, 31 August 1757
10. Archenholtz, 1840, I,15
11. *Anmerckung*, probably by Neipperg or Prince Charles of Lorraine, Arneth, V, 468
12. KA FA Italien 1746 XII 3, *Verhaltungspuncte*, undated
13. Northumberland County Record Office, North Gosforth, 2BU/B3/91, Horace Paul's note to vol. I, p. 243 of the *Extrait des mémoires due feld Marechal Comte Broun de Camus, écrites de sa propre main. Copie de l'original que me pretat son fils ainé ‡ Vienne le 25 Mars 1761.*
14. KA HKRA 1756 VII 1, Browne to the Hofkriegsrath, Kolin, 24 June
15. KA HKRA 1756 IX 46, Browne to the Hofkriegsrath, Kolin, 7 September
16. Aster, 1848, 201
17. SHAT A1 3407, Lameth, Budin, 21 September 1757
18. KA CA 1756 IX 25, Browne to Francis Stephen, Budin, 22 September
19. HHStA Kriegsakten 387, Browne, Relation von der dem 1ten Octobris *zwischen der Kayserl. König. und Königl. Preussischen Armee in dem Königreich Böheim bei Lobositz fürgewesten Bataille*, Budin, 7 October
20. GSPK, Nr. 611, Prince August Wilhelm, *Rélation de la Bataille de Lowositz et de ce, qui la précéda*
21. GSPK, Nr. 611. *Rélation der Bataille bei Lowositz den 1ten Oct. 1756*
22. GSPK, Nr. 611 Prince August Wilhelm, *Rélation de la Bataille de Lowositz tirée d'une lettre du P. de P. écrite au P.H.*, 2 October 1756 (i.e. to Prince Henry)
23. Letter of an NCO of the regiment of Anhalt, Grosser Generalstab, *Urkundliche* Beiträge zur Geschichte des preussischen Heeres, 1901, etc., I, Heft 2, 22
24. GSPK, Nr. 610, *Brief des Generals von Kyau an den Prinzen Moritz von Dessau*, Lobositz, 2 October 1756
25. Bräker, 1789, 147-9
26. GSPK, Nr. 611, Prince August Wilhelm, *Rélation de la Bataille de Lowowitz tirée d'une lettre du P. de P. au P.H.*, 2 October 1756
27. GSPK, Nr. 610, Bericht des Herzogs von Bevern von der am 1. Okt. 1756 vorgefallenen Schlacht von Lowowitz
28. GSPK, Nr. 611, Prince August Wilhelm, Rélation de la Bataille de Lowositz tirée d'une lettre du P. de P. écrite au P.H., 2 October 1756
29. Kalckreuth, 1840, II, 135
30. Ibid., II, 132-3
31. GSPK, Nr. 611, Prince August Wilhelm, *Rélation de la Bataille de Lowositz tirée d'une lettre du P. de P. au P.H.*, 2 October 1756
32. Kalckreuth, 1840, II, 131
33. KA FA 1756 X 36, *Extrait Schreiben vom Kornet B*, 6 October
34. KA FA 1756 X 9, Mohr, *Bataille von Lobositz geliefert am 6. Octobris*
35. Bräker, 1789, 148
36. HHStA Kriegsakten 388, Jean Georg Pradatsch, *Plan d'opérations par la Lusace*, Prague, 4 April 1757
37. HL Personalia 43, *Rélation Ueber die Action der Cavallerie und Hussaren vom linken Flügel bei Lobositz den 1ten. 8br. 1756*
38. Kalckreuth, 1840, II, 129
39. Bräker, 1789, 148-9
40. Grosser Generalstab, *Urkundliche Beiträge*, 1901 etc., I, Heft 2, 9-10
41. Warnery, 1788, 57
42. KA CA 1756 X 3, Browne to Francis Stephen, 4 October
43. GSPK, Nr. 610, Captain Arnim, *Rélation von der Bataille von Lowositz am 1ten Oktober 1756*
44. Bräker, 1789, 150-1
45. Mauvillon, 1794, I, 194
46. Kistenmacher, in Grosser Generalstab, *Urkundliche Beiträge*, 1901, etc. I, Heft 2, 10

47. Archenholtz, 1840, I, 18
48. Letter of an NCO of the regiment of Anhalt, Grosser Generalstab, *Urkundliche Beiträge*, I, Heft 2, 12
49. GSPK, Nr. 611, *Rélation der Bataille bei Lowositz den 1ten Oct. 1756*
50. GSPK, Nr. 611, Prince August Wilhelm, *Rélation de la Bataille de Lowositz et de ce, qui la précéda*
51. GSPK, Nr. 611, *Rélation der Bataille bei Lowositz den 1ten Oct. 1756*
53. Henckel von Donnersmarck, 1859, I, Part 2, 47
54. Retzow, 1802, I, 60-1
55. PC 8,114, Frederick to *GM*. Manstein, Tetschen, 25 September 1756, XIII, 456
56. PC 8,153, Frederick to the Duke of Bevern, undated, October 1756, XIII, 487-8
57. KA FA 1756 X 12, *Marsch-Zettel*, Kamnitz, 10 October
58. Cogniazzo, 1788-91, II, 153-4
59. KA CA 1756 X 21, Browne's relation of the Pirna expedition
60. HL 1756 X 76, *Précis de la Retraite de l'Armée Saxonne de son Camp de Pirna*, undated
61. Ibid.
62. KA CA 1756 X 10, Browne to Francis Stephen, heights of Schandau, 14 October
63. Ibid.
64. HL 1756 X 76, *Précis*
65. Ibid.
66. KA CA 1756 X 10, Browne to Francis Stephen, heights of Schandau, 14 October
67. Kaunitz's *Vortrag* to Francis Stephen, 7 November 1756 K-M, IV, 251. See also HL 1758 XII 332, Colonel Losy von Losenau to Hadik, undated, 1757
68. SHAT A1 3407, Lameth, 15 October 1757
69. KA CA 1756 X 14, Kaunitz to Browne, 23 October
70. Cogniazzo, 1788-91, II, 253
71. HHStA Kriegsakten 413, Browne to Kaunitz, Budin, 20 October 1756
72. KA CA 1756 X 15, Browne to Francis Stephen, 12 October
73. HHStA Kriegsakten 413, Browne to Kaunitz, Budin, 25 October 1756
74. Cogniazzo, 1788-91, II, 229-30
75. KA CA 1756 X 19, Browne to Francis Stephen, 29 October
76. Riksarkivet, Stockholm, Diplomatica Germanica 438, Bark, Vienna, 21 October 1756

II 1757

1. HHStA Kriegsakten 413, Browne to Prince Charles, 9 April 1757
2. KA FA Hauptarmee 1757 III 27, Browne to Prince Charles, Prague, 27 March
3. KA CA 1756 XII 4, Browne to Francis Stephen, 22 December
4. KA FA 1757 XIII 9, Prince Charles *Rélations de ma Campagne de 1757*
5. Szent-Ivány, 1911, 17
6. Wraxall, 1800, I, 17
7. St. Paul, 1914, 194
8. Ibid., 213
9. SHAT A1 3433, Champeaux, 25 June 1757
10. Ibid., c. 23 June 1757
11. K-M, 22 June 1757, IV, 100
12. SHAT A1 3438, Montazet, Zittau, 27 August 1757
13. K-M, 26 June 1757, IV, 103
14. PC 9,184, Frederick to Princess Wilhelmina, 1 July 1757, XV, 201
15. SHAT A1 3435, Montazet, Münchengrätz, 11 July 1757
16. HHStA Kriegsakten 415, Maria Theresa to Prince Charles, 9 July 1757
17. KA M.M.T.O., Maguire
18. Ligne, 1795-1811, XIV, 28-9
19. KA M.M.T.O., Normann
20. ätátny Ústredény Archív, Bratislava, Fond Amade Üchtritz, 101-12-067, XIV, Wöllwarth, *Kurze Beschreibung meiner geleisteten Dienste*
21. SHAT A1 3433, Champeaux, Nimes, 17 July 1757
22. St. Paul, 1914, 261-2
23. Warnery, 1785-91, III, 66
24. SHAT A1 3436, Champeaux, Krotenau, 22 July 1757
25. SHAT A1 3436, Champeaux, Krotenau, 23 July 1757
26. Gorani, 1944, 63
27. Ibid., 65
28. Ligne, 1795-1811, XIV, 33
29. SHAT A1 3437, letter from Zittau, 28 July 1757
30. SHAT A1 3436, Champeaux, Krotenau, 24 (?) July 1757
31. SHAT A1 3438, Montazet, Zittau, 27 August 1757
32. HHStA Kriegsakten 413, Jahnus, *Rélation von der dem 13ten bis 14. Augusti bey Landeshut gefallenen Action*
33. HHStA Kriegsakten 413, Prince Charles to Maria Theresa, 18 August 1757
34. PC 9,272, Frederick to Keith, 11 August 1757, XV, 296
35. Cogniazzo, 1788-91, II, 394
36. Ligne, 1795-1811, XIV, 35-6
37. Ibid., XIV, 366-7
38. Waddington, 1899-1908, I, 559
39. SHAT A1 3439, Champeaux, Ostritz, 2 September 1757
40. St. Paul, 1914, 308
41. KA M.M.T.O., De Piza
42. Ligne, 1795-1811, XIV, 46-7
43. ätátny Ústredeny Archív, Wöllwarth, *Kurze Beschreibung*, see Note. 21. Above
44. Ligne, 1795-1811, XIV, 50
45. KA FA 1757 XIII 467, *Réflexions sur la Campagne de l'Année 1757*
46. Kalckreuth, 1840, IV, 171
47. HHStA Kriegsakten 415, note for the Comte de Stainville, 3 October 1757, in Maria Theresa to Prince Charles, 4 October 1757
48. HL 1757 X 128, *Befehle bevor man in den feindes Land rücket*
49. HHStA Kriegsakten 414, Hadik, *Unterthänigste Relation über die Expedition in die Mark Brandenburg in die Einnahm der Königl. Preussischen Haubt- und Residenz-Stadt Berlin, 19 October 1757*
50. Archenholtz, 1840, I, 93
51. St. Paul, 1914, 357
52. HHStA Kriegsakten 415, Maria Theresa to Prince Charles, 29 September 1757
53. KA M.M.T.O., Rhédy
54. Ligne, 1795-1811, XIV, I, 63-4
55. KA M.M.T.O., Zorn von Plobsheim
56. Württembergische Landesbibliothek, Cod Milit 2 o, Colonel Nicolai, *Bemerkungen zum Feldzug der herzogl. Würtembergsch. Truppen bey der Kayserlichen Armee in Böhmen und Schlesien im Jahr 1757*
57. HHStA Kriegsakten 415, Maria Theresa to Prince Charles, 11 November 1757
58. Cogniazzo, 1788-91, II, 42
59. Ligne, 1795-1811, XIV, 72
60. KA M.M.T.O., Souhay
61. KA FA Hauptarmee 1757 XI 467, anonymous account, Höfchen, 24 November
62. Northumberland County Record Office, Butler (Ewart) Mss, 2BU B2/1
63. KA FA Hauptarmee 1757 XI 467, anonymous account, Höfchen, 24 November

64. K-M, IV, 143
65. Ligne, 1928, I, 208
66. SHAT A1 2329, Champeaux, Löwenberg, 15 September 1757
67. FA 1757 XIII 696E, Colonel Müffling to FM. Seckendorff, Jauer, 22 September
68. HHStA Kriegsakten 412, Franz Joseph Brettlach to *Reichsvizecanler* Colloredo, Bamberg, 22 November 1757
69. Conference of 27 June 1757, K-M, IV, 382
70. Waddington, 1899-1914, I, 532
71. HHStA Kriegsakten 412, Franz Joseph Brettlach to Colloredo, 27 November 1757
72. FA HKR Protocolle 1757 December 467, Széchenyi to the *Hofkriegsrath*, Gotha, 3 December
73. Ibid
74. HHStA Kriegsakten 412, Franz Joseph Brettlach to Colloredo, 27 November 1757
75. SHAT A1 3442, Marainville, Quelques réflexions sur la bataille de Leuthen, December 1757; Cogniazzo, 1788-91, IV, 416
76. K-M, IV, 142
77. Cogniazzo, 1788-91, II, 419
78. HHStA Kriegsakten 414, Prince Charles to Maria Theresa, 3 December 1757
79. HHStA Kriegsakten 414, Maria Theresa to Prince Charles, 28 November 1757
80. Cogniazzo, 1788-91, II, 424
81. KA Kriegsakten 414, Prince Charles to Maria Theresa, Lissa, 4 December 1757
82. Cogniazzo, 1799, 2
83. KA Kriegsakten 414, *Rélation von der…in der gegend von Leuthen vorgefallenen Bataille*
84. Archenholtz, 1840, I, 14
85. KA Hauptarmee 1757 XII 218, Prince Charles, *Rélation de l'affaire arrivé le5e proche du village de Leuthen*. Confirmed in FA Hauptarmee 1757 XII 223 Ω, *Extract Schreiben eines +sterreichischen Officiers Feldlager bey Freyberg in Schlesien d. 15. Dec. 1757*
86. Württembergische Landesbibliothek, Colonel Nicolai, *Bemerkungen*, see Note 57 above
87. KA M.M.T.O., Johann O'Donnell
88. Cogniazzo, 1788-91, II, 431
89. Ligne, 1795-1811, XIV, 89
90. Kriegsakten 414. Prince Charles to Maria Theresa, 10 December 1757; FA Hauptarmee 1757 XII 218, Prince Charles, *Rélation de l'affaire arrivé le 5e proche du village de Leuthen*
91. Cogniazzo, 1788-91, II, 431-3. See also SHAT A1 3442, Marainville, 17 December 1757; SHAT A1 3486, *Mémoire sur les trouppes de Vurtenberg*
92. Winter, 1886, 258
93. Gorani, 1944, 75
94. SHAT A1 3442, Marainville, 17 December 1757. See also Warnery, 1788-91, II, 166
95. KA CA 1758 III 1B, Lieutenant Colonel Rebain, *Réflexions*, 10 March
96. K-M, IV, 141
97. PC 9,571, Eichel to Finckenstein, 9 December 1757, XVI, 79; PC 9,792, Frederick to Queen Ulrike Eleonora of Sweden, undated January 1758, XVI, 184; Warnery, 1788, 150
98. HHStA Kriegsakten 414, Maria Theresa to Prince Charles, 14 December 1757
99. Belach, 1758, 126-7
100. Ligne, 1795-1811, XIV, 90
101. KA M.M.T.O., Buccow
102. Ligne, 1795-1811, I, 90
103. K-M, IV, 137
104. Quoted by the Hanoverian envoy Steinberg, Grosser Generalstab, 1901-14, VII, 3
105. HHStA Kriegsakten 415, Maria Theresa to Prince Charles, 14 December 1757
106. KA HKR Protocolle 1758 March 715, d'Ayme's attestation
107. Ernst Count Lehndorff, in Lehndorff, 1907, 375
108. KA HKR Protocolle 1758 March 715, Sprecher's *Journal*, 21 December 1757
109. PC 9,634, Eichel to Finckenstein, 22 December 1757, XVI, 119
110. KA HKR Protocolle 1758 September 96, *Hofkriegsrath* to the Prince of Zweibrücken, 5 September
111. Gorani, 1944, 78
112. Ibid., 78
113. KA M.M.T.O., Bülow

III 1758

1. _tátny Ústredeny Archív, Wöllwarth, *Kurze Beschreibung*, see Note 21 in previous chapter
2. K-M, IV, 143
3. HHStA Kriegsakten 403, *Etat des Exigences extraordinaires qu'on a fait après la Catastrophe du 5. Décembre 1757. Pour remettre les Armées de Sa Majesté l'Impératrice Reine en état d'opérer l'Année 1758*
4. HHStA Nachlass Lacy, I, 4, Lacy to Koch, 4 December 1761
5. K-M, V, 11
6. Ibid., V, 3-4
7. HHStA Kriegsakten 415, *Projet, couché par ordre exprès de Sa Majesté, pour Ítre écrit de sa main á S.A. le Prince Charles de Lorraine le 16. Janvier 1758*
8. K-M, V, 3-4
9. Cogniazzo, 1788-91, II, 445
10. K-M, II, 32
11. SHAT A1 3475, Boisgelin, Skalitz, 1 May 1758
12. SHAT A1 3475, Marainville, Skalitz, 1 May 1758
13. SHAT A1 3475, Marainville, Skalitz, 30 April 1758
14. SHAT A1 3475, Boisgelin, Skalitz, 26 May 1758
15. HHStA Nachlass Lacy, I, 2
16. SHAT A1 3475, Boisgelin, Gewitsch, 27 May 1758
17. Riksarkivet, Stockholm, Diplomatica Germanica 440, Bark, 16 January 1758
18. HHStA Staatskanzlei Vorträge 82, Kaunitz to Maria Theresa, 28 April 1758
19. HHStA Kriegsakten 389, *Protocol de la Conférence tenue chez Son Altesse Royale le Duc Charles de Lorraine*, 29 January 1758
20. HHStA Staatskanzlei Vorträge 82, Kaunitz to Maria Theresa, 28 April 1758
21. Ibid.
22. Tempelhof, 1783-1801, II, 48
23. K-M, V, 15
24. HHStA Kriegsakten 416, Maria Theresa to Daun, 19 March 1758
25. 9.839, Frederick to Prince Henry, 11 March 1758, XVI, 304
26. KA M.M.T.O., de Ville
26. Ibid.
27. *Circular-…wegen denen von den Königlichen-Preussischen Kriegs-Völckern in dem Königreich Böhmen und dazugehörigen Lande, wider alle Kriegs-Reguln ausgeübten Gewaltthaten,'* Vienna, 1759
28. HHStA Nachlass Lacy, III, 2, Lacy to Franz Liechtenstein, 6 May 1758
29. KA HKRA 1758 VI 18, de Ville to the *Hofkriegsrath*, Brünn, 18 May

30. HHStA Nachlass Lacy, I, 2
31. HHStA Kriegsakten 416, Maria Theresa to Daun, 15 May 1758
32. SHAT A1 3475, Marainville, Gewitsch, 27 May 1758
33. Ligne, 1795-1811, XIV, 104-5
34. Frederick to Moritz of Anhalt-Dessau, 30 May 1758, Orlich 1842, 118
35. PC 10,032, Frederick to Keith, Klein-Latein, 3 June 1758, XVII, 46
36. HL 1758 VI 124A, Loudon to Hadik, Konitz, 9 June
37. SHAT A1 3477, Marainville, 19 June 1758
38. SHAT A1 3477, Montazet, Eywanowitz, 23 June 1758
39. SHAT A1 3477, Montazet, Eywanowitz, 25 June 1758
40. A1 3477, Montazet, Dobromillitz, 28 June 1758
41. Ligne, 1795-1811, XIV, 113
42. HHStA Nachlass Lacy, I, 2
43. KA FA Hauptarmee 1758 VI ad 475 _, *Aufhebung d. preuss. Convoi bei Domstadtl*
44. Catt, 1884, 111
45. KA FA Hauptarmee 1758 VI ad 475 _, *Aufhebung*
46. KA FA Hauptarmee 1758 VI 468B, Loudon to Buccow, Bärn, 28 June
47. KA FA Hauptarmee 1759 VI ad 475 _, *Original-Auszug aus dr. Chronik von Domstadtl*
48. Gorani, 1944, 99
49. KA HKR Protocolle 1760 March 437
50. KA FA Hauptarmee 1758 VI 468B, Loudon to Buccow, Bärn, 28 June
51. Ibid.
52. Cogniazzo, 1788-91, III, 15
53. Ibid., III, 16
54. KA FA Hauptarmee 1758 VI ad 475 _, *Aufhebung*
55. KA M.M.T.O., Sauer
56. HHStA Kriegsakten 389, Loudon to 'Monseigneur,' 1 July 1758
57. FA M.M.T.O., Caldwell
58. HHStA Kriegsakten 389, Loudon to 'Monseigneur,' 1 July 1758
59. KA M.M.T.O., Riesse
60. KA FA Hauptarmee 1758 VI ad 475 _, *Aufhebung*
61. Gorani, 1944, 100
62. Kalckreuth, 1840, iV, 131
63. KA CA 1758 XIII 15, anon. analysis of the siege
64. Ibid.
65. HHStA Kriegsakten 389, protocol of the military conference of 4 January 1758
66. KA CA 1758 V 6A, Rochepine to the engineer general Bohn, 4 January 1758
67. KA M.M.T.O., Alfson, attestation by Marschall
68. KA CA 1758 V 6D, *Copie d'un note donné au Commando Général par Mr. le Général de Rochepine sur Différents points concernang la défense de la forteresse d'Olmütz,'* 3 May
69. 'Diarium,' in Hirtenfeld, 1858, 56
70. KA CA 1758 VII 2, Marschall, *Extract deren Journals die Belagerung von der Haubt- und Gränitz Vestung Olmütz betreffend*, 3 July
71. Kalckreuth, 1840, iV, 132
72. KA M.M.T.O., Huff
73. KA M.M.T.O., Giannini
74. KA CA 1758 VII 2, Marschall, *Extract deren Journals*
75. Catt, 1884, 115
76. GSPK, Nr. 689, Balbi to Frederick, 10 June 1758
77. KA HKRA 1758VI 3B, de Ville to the *Hofkriegsrath*, Wischau, 30 May
78. Ligne, 1795-1811, XIV, 116
79. SHAT A1 3478, Montazet, Gross-Teinitz, 2 July 1758
80. Krigsarkivet, Stockholm, Armfeldt, *Dagbok*
81. Ligne, 1795-1811, XIV, 121
82. KA CA 1758 VII 18, Daun to Maria Theresa, Pardubitz, 17 July
83. Ibid.
84. HHStA Kriegsakten 416, Maria Theresa to Daun, 29 July 1758
85. National Archives, Kew, S.P. Foreign 90/72, Mitchell, 31 July 1758
86. HHStA Nachlass Lacy III, 2, Lacy to Franz Liechtenstein, Sendraschitz, 1 August 1758
87. KA CA 1758 VIII 9, Maria Theresa to Daun, 21 August
88. KA CA 1758 IX 6, Maria Theresa to Daun, 6 September
89. HHStA Kriegsakten 411, Maria Theresa to Zweibrücken, 25 May 1758
90. HHStA Kriegsakten 412, Brettlach to Colloredo, Königsberg, 25 January 1758
91. HHStA Kriegsakten 411, *Suite du journal de l'armée d'exécution combinée avec l'armée impériale et royale*
92. HL 1758 VII 164, Sulkowsky to Serbelloni, Postelberg, 4 July
93. HL 1758 VII 178, attestation by Johann Christian Hähnl
94. HHStA Kriegsakten 411, Zweibrücken to Maria Theresa, Saaz, 4june 1758
95. Ligne, 1795-1811, I, 137
96. Archenholtz, 1840, I, 177
97. KA CA 1758 IX 6, Maria Theresa to Daun, 6 September
98. SHAT A1 3482, Montazet, *Détail de ce qui s'est passé audjourd'hui au Camp de Stolpen 10 Septembre 1758, dans le cabinet du Mr. le maréchal Daun*
99. Ligne, 1795-1811, XIV, 141
100. SHAT A1 3483, Montazet, Stolpen, 19 September 1758
101. KA CA 1758 IX 11D, Daun to Maria Theresa, 12 September
102. KA M.M.T.O., Kiss
103. KA CA 1758 X 5, Daun to Maria Theresa, Seitlitz, 9 October
104. HHStA Staatskanzlei Vorträge 83, Kaunitz to Francis Stephen, 13 October
105. KA CA 1758 X 6, Maria Theresa to Daun, 14 October
106. KA CA 1758 X 178, Daun to Maria Theresa, undated relation
107. KA M.M.T.O., Amadei
108. KA FA Hauptarmee 1758 X 175 11, *General Disposition den Feind in seinem dermahligen Laager anzugreifen*
109. Ligne, 1795-1811, XIV. 161
110. Ibid., XIV, 154-5
111. Archenholtz, 1840, I, 181
112. Küster, 1792, 28
113. Gorani, 1944, 105. Gorani was a subaltern in the regiment of Andlau, but he attached himself to the battalion of Clerici for the action
114. KA FA Hauptarmee 1758 X 175 _, Marainville, *Rélation*
115. Archenholtz, 1840, I, 182
116. Ligne, 1795-1811, XIV, 164-5
117. Ibid., XIV, 168-9
118. Cogniazzo, 1788-91, III, 48
119. Barsewisch, 1863, 69-70
120. Gorani, 1944, 105
121. KA CA 1759 VIII 14, Thomas Ignaz Pöck to Maria Theresa, Vienna, 13 August
122. Tempelhof, 1783-1801, II, 324
123. KA M.M.T.O., Rhédy
124. Cogniazzo, 1788-91, III, 41
125. Küster, 1791, 39
126. KA M.M.T.O., Murray de Melgum
127. KA Fa 1758 X 179 _, Oross, 29 October. Tessedik survived his wound

128. KA M.M.T.O., Graffenstein
129. Barsewisch, 1863, 75
130. KA M.M.T.O., D'Aysasasa
131. Ligne, 1795-1811, XIV, 175
132. KA 1758 175 _, d'Ursel, *Raport détaillé de l'attaque qui m'a été confié*, 16 October
133. KA M.M.T.O., Brockhausen
134. KA M.M.T.O., Brunyan
135. Henckel von Donnersmarck, 1858, II, Part 1, 90-1
136. Archenholtz, 1840, I, 189
137. KA CA 1758 X 7, Daun to Maria Theresa, Kittlitz, 15 October
138. Gorani, 1944, 108
139. Wraxall, 1800, I, 183-4. This account accords closely with Gorani's statement (Gorani, 1944, 108) that Keith had been killed by a musket ball which had entered 'two fingers' below his left nipple. Keith was buried in the church with full military honours on the day after the battle (the present cenotaph, in the form of a white marble urn, was placed in 1776 by Keith's cousin Robert Murray, the British envoy to Vienna). The body was returned to the Prussians in January 1759, and re-interred in the Potsdam Garrison Church on 2 March of that year. The exposed hands and head were found to be in perfect preservation when the field marshal's coffin was opened in the presence of the artist Adolph Menzel in 1873. A shot through the mouth was now clearly visible, and was thought to have disproved the accounts of the wound in the body (Keisch, C., and Riemann-Reyher, M., *Adolph Menzel 1815-1905*, New Haven, 1996, 361-6), though the existence of two wounds is not incompatible.
140. K-M, V, 98. See also Ligne, 1795-1811, X, 107
141. Ligne, 1795-1811, XIV, 173-4
142. Cogniazzo, 1788-91, III, 50
143. HHStA Kriegsakten 389, undated memorandum
144. KA CA 1758 X 7, Daun to Maria Theresa, Kittlitz, 15 October
145. K-M, V, 68
146. Pichler, 1844, I, 22-3
147. K-M, V, 69
148. HHStA Kriegsakten 416, Maria Theresa to Daun, 17 October 1758
149. HHStA Kriegsakten 416, Maria Theresa to Daun, 19 October 1758
150. HHStA Nachlass Lacy III, 2, Lacy to Franz Liechtenstein, undated, October 1758
151. SHAT A1 3485, Montazet, Löbau, 30 October 1758
152. KA CA 1758 X 19, Daun to Harsch, Jauernick, 27 October
153. HHStA Kriegsakten 414, Kaunitz to Daun, 8 November 1758
154. SHAT A1 3494, Choiseul, Vienna, 2 October 1758
155. SHAT A1 3484, Gribeauval, before Neisse, 7 October 1758
156. Cogniazzo, 1788-91, III, 54
157. SHAT A1 3486, Gribeauval, before Neisse, 4 November 1758
158. KA CA 1758 XI 11 G, *Remarques sur la lettre de Mr. Viomenil*, undated
159. Ligne, XIV, 190
160. Mitchell, 1850, I, 459
161. Gorani, 1944, 111-12
162. KA CA 1758 XI 17B, *Extract Schreiben des Königl. Pohlnisch- und Churfürstl. Sächs...Commissarii Zahn*, Sebnitz, 27 November
163. HHStA Nachlass Lacy III 2, Lacy to Franz Liechtenstein, Gottleub, 20 November 1758
164. K-M, V, 71
165. KA CA 1762 III 4, anon., *Patriotisch-...Reflexionen*
166. Stockholm, Riksarkivet, Diplomatica Germanica 400, Bark, 3 November 1758
167. Verri, 1879, I, 35, 70
168. Frederick, *Oeuvres*, 1846-57, 'Oeuvres Historiques,' III, 'Histoire de Mon Temps. Histoire de la Guerre de Sept Ans,' I, 9-10
169. KA CA 1758 XI 11, Daun to Koch, Berggiesshübel, 16 November
170. Haugwitz to Daun, Arneth, 1863-79, V, 535
171. Kaunitz to Daun, Ibid., 535

IV 1759

1. Waddington, 1899-1908, I, 744
2. Arneth, 1863-79, V 383
3. Stockholm, Riksarkivet, Diplomatica Germanica 401, Bark, 8 January 1759
4. HHStA Staatskanzlei Vorträge 83, Kaunitz to Maria Theresa, 6 November 1758
5. Riksarkivet, Stockholm, Diplomatica Germanica 401, Bark, 24 January 1759
6. HHStA Kriegsakten 389, Daun, *Mémoire qui contient le plan des opérations des la campagne prochaine*
7. SHAT A1 3516, Montazet, Vienna, 27 May 1759
8. KA FA 1759 XIII 3, Tillier to Daun, St. Petersburg, 29 January
9. SHAT A1 3516, Montazet, Vienna, 27 May 1759
10. KA FA 1759 XIII 122, Francis Stephen to Prince Charles, 23 March; KA FA 1759 XIII 123, Francis Stephen to Prince Charles, 27 March
11. SHAT A1 3515, Boisgelin, 14 May 1759
12. HHStA Kriegsakten 417, Maria Theresa to Daun, 6 May 1759
13. PC 11,806, Frederick to Fouqué, 14 June 1759, XVIII, 320
14. KA FA 1759 XIII 35, Lacy to Daun, Vienna, 17 June
15. KA CA 1759 VI 28, Maria Theresa to Daun, 21 June
16. KA CA 1759 VI 36, Daun to Maria Theresa, 26 June
17. SHAT A1 3518, Montazet, Görlitzheim, 7 July 1759
18. HL 1759 VI 106, Hadik to Daun, 9 July
19. HL 1759, Hadik's Journal
20. SHAT A1 3519, Montazet, Görlitzheim, 21 July 1759
21. SHAT A1 3529, Choiseul-Praslin, Vienna, 4 August 1759
23. KA CA 1759 VIII 8, Maria Theresa to Daun, 12 August
24. HL 1759 VIII 166, Hadik to Batthyány, Spremberg, 8 August
25. HL 1759 VIII 161, Captain (Rittmeister) Saint-Genois, Spremberg, 7 August
26. HL 1759 VIII 165, Ensign (Fähnrich) Postlob, Spremberg, 8 August
27. HL 1759 VIII 160, Rudolph Palffy's report, Gross Luga, 5 August
28. HHStA Kriegsakten 418, Loudon to Kaunitz, Jägerndorf, 13 April 1760
29. PC 11,310, Frederick to Prince Henry, Markersdorf, 2 August 1759, XVIII, 467
30. KA FA Korps Loudon 1759 VIII ad 13, *Relation*
31. KA M.M.T.O, D'Alton
32. KA CA 1759 VIII 15, Loudon to Daun, 13 August
33. KA M.M.T.O., Rolke
34. KA FA Korps Loudon 1759 VIII 13, *Relation de la bataille gagnée*
35. Podgursky, 1843, II, 267
36. Warnery, 1788, 306
37. KA M.M.T.O., Graffenstein
38. KA M.M.T.O., Bethlen
39. KA FA Korps Loudon 1759 VIII 36, Loudon to Daun, 15

40. August
   KA CA 1759 VIII 15, Daun to Maria Theresa, 18 August; KA CA 1759 VIII 19, Daun to Maria Theresa, Triebel, 20 August
41. KA CA 1759 VIII 13, Maria Theresa to Daun, 15 August
42. HL, Hadik's Jounral, 15 August 1759
43. HL, Hadik's Journal, 14 August 1759
44. KA HKRA 1759 VIII 6, Beck, *Relation von der…Entreprise gegen die Guarnison von Grünberg*, 18 August; KA M.M.T.O., Barco
45. HL 1759 VIII 174, Loudon to Hadik, Leczenau, 19 August
46. HL, Hadik's Journal, 16 August 1759
47. KA Kriegsakten 417, Maria Theresa to Daun, 20 August 1759
48. KA CA 1760 VII ad 26, *Gehorsamst-ohnmassgebliche Meinung wie das Cabinets Schreiben auf die darinn vorkommende Puncten zu beantworten wäre*
49. KA CA1759 VIII 15, Daun to Maria Theresa, 18 August
50. KA CA 1759 VIII 19, Daun to Maria Theresa, Triebel, 20 August
51. SHAT A1 3521, Montalembert, camp of Oberhausen, 31 August 1759
52. HL, Hadik's Journal, 20 August 1759
53. SHAT A1 3421, Choiseul-Praslin, Vienna, 27 August 1759
54. HL, Hadik's Journal, 22 August 1759
55. KA CA 1759 VIII 39, Daun to Maria Theresa, 28 August
56. PC 11,393, Frederick to Prince Henry, Waldow, 1 September 1759, XVIII, 510
57. HL, Hadik's Journal, 3-4 September 1750
58. Massenbach, 1808, 53
59. SHAT A1 3522, Montalembert, Lieberose, 8 September 1759
60. SHAT A1 3522, Montazet, Bautzen, 13 September 1759
61. Ligne, 1795-1811, XV, 40-1
62. Cogniazzo, 1788-91, III, 111. Cogniazzo had come to the army with Campitelli's reinforcement
63. HHStA Kriegsakten 418, Loudon to Kaunitz, Schlichtingheim, 5 October 1759
64. anon., *Zuverlässige Nachrichten von dem traurigen Schicksale der Stadt und Universität Halle*, Amsterdam 1759, 71
65. KA HKR Protocolle 1759 July 212, Zweibrücken to the *Hofkriegsrath*, Arnstadt, 21 July
66. SHAT A1 3520, Marainville, Naumburg, 5 August 1759
67. KA HKR Protocolle 1759 August 212, Zweibrücken to the *Hofkriegsrath*, Leipzig, 10 August 1759
68. SHAT A1 3520, Marainville, near Leipzig, 12 August 1759
69. KA FA 1759 XIII 167, Prussian *Journal des Feldzugs 1759*
70. Ibid.
71. Ibid.
72. KA HKR Protocolle 1759 July 212, Zweibrücken to the *Hofkriegsrath*, Erfurt, 27 July
73. SHAT A1 3520, Marainville, near Leipzig, 12 August 1759
74. HHStA Kriegsakten 417, Maria Theresa to Daun, 7 September 1759
75. KA CA 1759 IX 16. Daun to Maria Theresa, 16 September
76. KA Ca 1759 IX 23, Daun to Maria Theresa, 21 September
77. KA CA 1759 VIII 20, Daun to Maria Theresa, Triebel, 21 August
78. KA HKR Protocolle 1759 August 212, Journal of the *Reichsarmee*
79. SHAT A1 3521, Marainville, near Dresden, 2 September 1759
80. SHAT A1 3522, Marianville, near Dresden, 5 September 1759
81. See Brabant, 1904-31, III, 322-21, for a review of the evidence concerning Schmettau's 'treason'
82. KA FA 1759 XIII 167, *Journal des Feldzugs 1759*
83. KA M.M.T.O., Ried
84. HHStA Staatskanzlei Vorträge 84, Kaunitz to Maria Theresa, 12 September 1759
85. HL 1759 X 215, *Beantwortung*, 10 October
86. HL, Hadik's Journal, 21 September 1759
87. HL, Hadik's *Relation*, 26 September 1759
88. Ibid.
89. KA M.M.T.O., Leubelfing
90. HL 1759 IX 199, Förster, *Befehle. Welche…mir…aufzuführen aufgetragen worden*
91. KA M.M.T.O., Botta d'Adorno; KA M.M.T.O., Ziegesar
92. KA M.M.T.O., Deym von Stritetz
93. Hildebrandt, 1829-35, III, 133-4
94. HL, Hadik's *Relation*, 26 September 1759
95. HL, Hadik's Journal, 22 September 1759
96. HL, Hadik's Journal, 23 September 1759
97. K-M, V, 127
98. KA HKR Protocolle 1759 November 134, Serbelloni to the *Hofkriegsrath*, Friedrichsstadt of Dresden, 3 November
99. HL 1759 X 221, Stampa to Hadik, 14 October
100. Brabant, 1904-31, III, 360
101. HL, Hadik's Journal, 22 November 1759
102. Verri, 1879, I, 65-6
103. Ligne, 1795-1811, XV, 46
104. KA CA 1759 X 31, Daun to Maria Theresa, Belgerin, 21 October
105. KA Ca 1759 X 18, marginal note by Maria Theresa, on Daun to Maria Theresa, 9 October
106. SHAT A1 3524, Choiseul-Praslin to Montazet, Vienna, 24 October 1759
107. Ligne, 1795-1811, XV, 56
108. KA M.M.T.O., Worbeer
109. Ligne, 1795-1811, XV, 63-4
110. KA CA 1759 XI 9, Daun to Maria Theresa, Heynitz, 8 November
111. KA HKR Protocolle 1760 January 161, *Hofkriegsrath* to Daun, 10 January
112. Verri, 1879, I,88
113. KA M.M.T.O., Petrovsky
114. Ligne, 1795-1811, XV, 88
115. KA CA 1759 XI 21, Daun to Koch, 29 November
116. KA FA Hauptarmee 1759 XI 213, O'Donnell, *Marche Disposition des Corps de Reserve*, undated
117. KA FA Hauptarmee 1759 XI 212, *Marche Disposition für das Corps des Gral. Sincère*, undated
118. KA FA Hauptarmee 1759 XI 209, Daun, *Relation der den 20ten 9bris 759 zwischen einen Kayl. Königlichen und ein Königl. Preussischen Corps unter Commando des General-Lieutenant von Finck bey Maxen vorgefallenen Affaire*
119. Ibid.
120. Lotze, 1981, 114
121. Ligne, 1795-1811, XV, 88
122. Verri, 1879, I, 82-3
123. Albert
124. Ibid.
125. KA FA Hauptarmee 1759 XI 209, Daun, *Relation*
126. KA FA Hauptarmee 1759 167, *Journal des Feldzugs 1759*
127. K.A. M.M.T.O., Lossgallner
128. KA FA Hauptarmee 1759 XI 247, Rudolph Pálffy to Daun, 24 November
129. Albert

130. KA FA Hauptarmee 1759 XI 209, Daun, *Relation*
131. Albert
132. Ligne, 1795-1811, XV, 92
133. Verri, 1965, 46
134. KA CA 1759 XI 22, Daun to Maria Theresa, 24 November
135. K-M, V, 138-9
136. Stockholm, Krigsarkivet, Armfeldt, *Dagbok*
137. KA Ca 1759 XI 22, Daun to Maria Theresa, 24 November
138. Tempelhof, 1783-1801, III, 147
139. KA FA 1759 XIII 69, Gribeauval, *Mémoire*
140. HHStA Staatskanzlei Vorträge 85, Brühl to Flemming, Warsaw, 3 November 1759
141. HHStA Staatkanzlei Vorträge 85, Kaunitz to Maria Theresa, 17 November 1759
142. KA CA 1759 XI 22, Daun to Maria Theresa, 24 November
143. HHStA 417, Maria Theresa to Daun, 22 December 1759
144. KA Ca 1759 XI 22, Daun to Maria Theresa, 24 November
145. KA M.M.T.O., Zedtwitz
146. SHAT A1 3520, Choiseul-Praslin, 9 August 1759
147. Cogniazzo, 1788-91, III, 97-8

V 1760
1. Albert
2. HHStA Kriegsakten 390, *Feldzugsplan des Grafen Lacy für 1760*, undated
3. HHStA Kriegsakten 390, Loudon, *Ohnmassgebliche Anmerkung über den letztern Plan des H. Gr. Lacy*, undated. See also HHStA Kriegsakten 418, Loudon to Kaunitz, Brüx, 23 January 1760
4. HHStA Kriegsakten 390, Kaunitz, *Réflexions sur le Plan d'Opérations pour la Campagne de l'anné 1760*, undated
5. HHStA Kriegsakten 390, *Operations-Plan des F.M. Grafen von Daun*, undated
6. KA FA 1760 XIII 127, Lacy to Daun, Vienna, 11 March
7. KA CA 1760 IV 18, Maria Theresa to Daun, 23 April
8. Wraxall, 1800, I, 343
9. Gorani, 1944, 98
10. Gellert, in *Münchner Intelligenzblätter*, Munich, 1790, Nr. 5
11. HHStA Kriegsakten 418, Loudon to Kaunitz, Jägerndorf, 27 March 1760
12. Wraxall, 1800, I, 334, 346-7
13. HHStA Kriegsakten 418, Loudon to Kaunitz, Prossnitz, 7 March 1760
14. HHStA Kriegsakten 418, Loudon to Kaunitz, Zittau, 15 March 1760
15. KA M.M.T.O., de Ville
16. HHStA Nachlass Lacy II, 2, Lacy to Franz Liechtenstein, 1 January 1760
17. HHStA Kriegsakten 390, Liechtenstein to Maria Theresa, Vienna, undated
18. KA FA 1760 XIII 127, Lacy to Daun, Vienna, 11 March
19. KA FA 1760 XIII 132, Daun to Lacy, 27 April
20. KA FA 1760 XIII 127, Lacy to Daun, Veinna, 11 March
21. KA CA 1760 III 14, Daun to Maria Theresa, 14 March
22. Ligne, 1928, I, 168
23. HHStA Kriegsakten 418, Loudon to Kaunitz, 18 May 1760
24. KA CA 1760 V 23, Daun to Maria Theresa, 22 May
25. KA CA 1760 VI 2, Daun to Maria Theresa, 4 June
26. Arneth, 1863-79, VI, 132
27. Marcus, 1927, 50
28. Catt, 1884, 426
29. Ligne, 1795-1811, 149
30. KA CA 1760 VII 5, Daun to Maria Theresa, Leopoldshayn, 7 July

31. HL, Hadik's Journal, 12 July 1760
32. HHStA 419, Maguire's *Diarium*
33. KA M.M.T.O., Amadei
34. HHStA 419, Maguire's *Diarium*
35. Northumberland County Record Office, ZBU/B2/3/51, Horace St. Paul, *Journal du Siège de Dresde*
36. HHStA 419, Maguire's *Diarium*
37. Gellert, ed. Reynolds, 1983-94, III, 53
38. Northumberland County Record Office, ZBU/B2/3/51, Horace St. Paul, *Journal*
39. Ligne, 1795-1811, XV, 170-1
40. HHStA 419, Maguire's *Diarium*
41. FA CA 1760 VIII 3, Montazet to Choiseul-Praslin, 2 August
42. Northumberland County Record Office, ZBU/B2/3/51, Horace St. Paul, *Journal*. See also FA M.M.T.O., Schorlemmer
43. Mitchell, 1850, II, 176
44. Archenholtz, 1840, II, 55
45. Marainville to Prince Xaver of Saxony, 8 August 1760, in *Correspondance inédite de Victor-François Duc de Broglie avec le Prince Xaver de Saxe*, 4 vols, Paris 1903. II, 611
46. HHStA Kriegsakten 419, Maguire's *Diarium*
47. KA CA 1760 VII 16, Maria Theresa to Lacy, 16 July
48. KA CA 1760 VII 19, Lacy to Maria Theresa, Heidenau, 18 July
49. KA CA 1760 VII 20, Maria Theresa to Lacy, 21 July
50. HHStA Kriegsakten 418, Loudon to Kaunitz, Frankenstein, 5 June 1760
51. HHStA Kriegsakten 418, Loudon to Kaunitz, 13 June 1760
52. FA Korps Loudon 1760 VI 68, Loudon's report, Schwarzwaldau, 28 June
53. Cogniazzo, 1788-91, III, 146-7
54. KA M.M.T.O., De Vins
55. KA M.M.T.O., Worbeer
56. KA Korps Loudon 1760 VI 68, Loudon's report, Schwarzwaldau, 28 June
57. KA M.M.T.O., Wilhelm Lacy
58. KA FA Korps Loudon 1760 VI 82, Staabs-Auditor Johann Adam Graff, *Certification*, 25 August
59. KA M.M.T.O., Looz-Coswarem de Nyel, attestation by Lieutenant F. Unzogsky
60. KA M.M.T.O., Wallis
61. KA M.M.T.O., Graffenstein
62. Archenholtz, 1840, II, 42
63. Cogniazzo, 1788-91, III, 154-5
64. Ibid., III, 158-9
65. KA FA Korps Loudon 1760 VI 84A, letter of Major Semsey
66. KA FA Korps Loudon 1760 VI 68, Loudon's report, Schwarzwaldau, 28 June
67. HL, Hadik's Journal
68. KA HKRA 1760 VI 1A, Neipperg to Loudon, 11 June
69. KA HKRA 1760 VI 1F, Loudon to Neipperg, 16 June
70. KA HKRA 1760 VI 1G, Neipperg to Loudon, 20 June
71. HHStA Kriegsakten 418, Loudon to Kaunitz, Eichholtz, 13 July 1760
72. HHStA Kriegsakten 418, Loudon to Kaunitz, Frankenstein, 5 June 1760
73. KA M.M.T.O., Mylius
74. KA M.M.T.O., Theillières, attestation by Major O'Donnell
75. KA HKRA 1761 III 10A, testimony of Philipp Scharff, in Winulph Stahremberg, Linz, 14 March 1761
76. Wachter, 1897, 7
77. KA M.M.T.O., Theillières

78. Ibid., attestation by Henry
79. HHStA Kriegsakten 418, Loudon to Kaunitz, Höfchen, 2 August 1760
80. Cogniazzo, 1788-91, III, 171
81. HHStA Kriegsakten 418, Loudon to Kaunitz, Sackwitz, 6 August 1761
82. Cogniazzo, 1788-91, III, 173
83. Krigsarkivet, Stockholm, Armfeldt, *Dagbok*
84. Cogniazzo, 1788-91, III, 237-8
85. Archenholtz, 1840, II, 64
86. HHStA Kriegsakten 417, Maria Theresa to Daun, 10 August 1760
87. Ligne, XV, 184
88. KA FA Korps Loudon 1760 VIII 52B, *Disposition zur Attaque des Feindes bey Liegnitz auf den 15ten August 1760 mit Anbruch des Tags*
89. Cogniazzo, 1788-91, III, 200
90. Confirmed by Prussian officers in conversation with Cogniazzo, Ibid., III, 201
91. PC 12,238, Frederick to Ferdinand of Brunswick, 24 August 1760, XIX, 558
92. HHStA Kriegsakten 418, Loudon to Kaunitz, Koischwitz, 16 August 1760
93. Barsewisch, 1863, 113
94. Ibid., 115
95. KA FA Korps Loudon 1761 X ad 31, Wippler von Uschitz, undated
96. HHStA Kriegsakten 418, Loudon to Kaunitz, 16 August 1760
97. KA M.M.T.O., Giannini
98. Ligne, 1795-1811, XV, 194
99. Ibid., XV, 186-7
100. Stockholm, Krigsarkivet, Armfeldt, *Dagbok*
101. Cogniazzo, 1788-91, III, 208
102. Albert
103. KA CA 1760 VIII 18, anon. and undated paper, probably by *GFWM*. Pellegrini
104. Ibid.
105. HHStA Kriegsakten 418, Loudon to Kaunitz, Koischwitz, 16 August 1760
106. KA CA 1760 VIII 8, Daun to Maria Theresa, Conradswaldau, 22 August
107. HHStA Kriegsakten 419, Kaunitz to Loudon, 25 August 1760
108. Albert
109. Waddington, 1899-1908, iV, 65-6
110. KA FA Korps Loudon 1761 X ad 31, Major Migazzi, 21 October
111. Cogniazzo, 1788-91, III, 189-92
112. Henckel von Donnersmarck to Prince Henry, 17 August 1760, in Troeger, 1904-5, 45
113. Ligne, 1796-1811, XVI, 7
114. HHStA Kriegsakten 418, Loudon to Kaunitz, Koischwitz, 16 August 1760
115. HHStA Kriegsakten 417, Maria Theresa to Daun, 22 August 1760
116. HHStA Kriegsakten 433, Plunkett to Daun, Caat, 21 August 1760
117. Northumberland County Record Office ZBU/B2/3/51, Horace St. Paul, *Journal*
118. KA CA 1760 IX 24, Daun to Maria Theresa, 25 September
119. Frederick, 1846-57, 'Oeuvres Historiques,' V, 'Histoire de la Guerre de Sept Ans,' II, 139
120. Anon., *Beiträge zu den Anecdoten*, 1788-9, III, 17-18
121. Cogniazzo, 1788-91, III, 250
122. Ligne, 1794-1811, XVI, 30
123. Ibid., III, 33
124. KA CA 1760 IX 24, Daun to Maria Theresa, 25 September
125. Cogniazzo, 1788-91, III, 255
126. PC 12,366, Frederick to Ferdinand of Brunswick, Dittmannsdorf, 18 September 1760, XIX, 583
127. KA CA 1760 IX 21, Daun to Maria Theresa, Striegau, 22 September
128. HHStA Kriegsakten 417, Maria Theresa to Daun, 26 September 1760
129. Riksarkivet, Stockholm, Diplomatica Germanica 442, Bark, 4 October 1760
130. KA CA 1760 IX 28, Daun to Maria Theresa, 28 September
131. KA FA Hauptarmee 1760 X 24, Chernyshev to Lacy, 2 October
132. Ligne, 1795-1811, XVI, 38
133. Ibid., XVI, 41-2
134. HHStA Kriegsakten 417, Lacy's relation, undated
135. KA FA Hauptarmee 1760 X ad19, enclosed in Lacy to Daun, 1 October
136. KA FA Hauptarmee 1760 X 46, Lacy to Daun, Templow, 10 October
137. Ibid.
138. KA HKRA 1760 XI 1, Totleben, *Relation*, undated
139. Ligne, 1795-1811, XVI, 46-7
140. KA HKRA 1760 XI 1, Totleben, *Relation*. See also Archenholtz, 1840, II, 88; Catt, 1884, 44; Waddington, 1899-1908, IV, 101
141. Archenholtz, 1840, II, 88
142. KA FA Hauptarmee 1760 X 56, Lacy to Daun, Schweinitz, 16 October
143. KA FA Hauptarmee 1760 X 49, Emerich Esterházy to Lacy, Potsdam, 11 October
144. KA FA Hauptarmee 1760 X ad 49, F.X. Neffer, Potsdam, 11 October
145. HHStA Kriegsakten 419, Lacy to Maria Theresa, Plossig, 20 October 1760
146. Warnery, 1788, 535
147. HHStA Kriegsakten 419, Maria Theresa to Lacy, 15 October 1760
148. HL, Hadik's Journal, 12 August 1760
149. KA M.M.T.O., Seeger
150. HL, Hadik's Journal, 2 October 1760
151. HL, Hadik's Journal, 12 October 1760
152. Albert
153. KA FA Hauptarmee 1760 X 53, Daun to Lacy, 12 October, in answer to Lacy's of the 10th
154. Ligne, 1795-1811, XV, 55
155. HHStA Staatskanzlei Vorträge 87, Kaunitz to Maria Theresa, 13 October 1760
156. HHStA Kriegsakten 417, Maria Theresa to Daun, 23 October 1760
157. KA FA Hauptarmee 1760 XI 57L, Ried, *Gehorsamstes Relation*, Teplitz, 14 November
158. Ibid.
159. Anon., *Anecdoten und Karakterzüge*, 1787-9, X, 61
160. KA FA Hauptarmee 1760 XI 57 L, Ried, *Gehorsamstes Relation*, Teplitz, 14 November
161. Cogniazzo, 1788-91, III, 27-8
162. Ligne, XVI, 63-4
163. Albert
164. Ligne, XVI, 67
165. KA HKRA 1760 XI 1B, *Relation. Von der- den 3ten Novembris 1760 bey Siptitz ohnweit Torgau…vorgefallene Action*, undated
166. Ligne, XVI, 64-5
167. Cogniazzo, 1788-91, III, 279
168. Warnery, 1788, 429
169. Archenholtz, 1840, II, 107-8

465

170. KA FA Hauptarmee 1760 XI 57D, Arenberg to Daun, Neudorf, 7 November
171. KA M.M.T.O., Harrach
172. KA M.M.T.O., Dombasle
173. KA FA Hauptarmee 1760 XI 60, Leeuven to Daun, 8 November
174. KA FA Hauptarmee 1760 XI 57C, Sincère to Daun, Dresden, 7 November
175. KA M.M.T.O., Pellegrini
176. KA M.M.T.O., Neugebauer
177. KA FA Hauptarmee 1760 XI 57L, Ried, *Gehorsamstes Relation*, Teplitz, 14 November.
178. Albert
179. KA M.M.T.O., Carl O'Donnell
180. Ligne, XVI, 70
181. KA FA Hauptarmee 1760 XI 58A, Wied's relation
182. Ibid.
183. KA FA Hauptarmee 1760 XI 59, Major Paul Oross to Francis Stephen, Aussig, 12 November
184. KA M.M.T.O., Stein. By Sincère's account [KA FA Hauptarmee 1760 XI 57C, Sincère, Dresden, 7 November] he himself was the author to the initiative, having come across the regiment of Mercy in the darkness
185. Ligne, 1795-1811, XVI, 81
186. KA FA Hauptarmee 1760 XI 27, Lacy's personal report to Maria Theresa, undated
187. Albert; Cogniazzo, 1788-91, III, 299
188. Archenholtz, 1840, II,113
189. Cogniazzo, 1788-91, III, 298
190. Ligne, XVI, 78-9
191. HHStA Kriegsakten 419, Maria Theresa to Lacy, 8 November 1760
192. HHStA Nachlass Lacy, III, 2, Lacy to Franz Liechtenstein
193. Ligne, XVI, 80
194. Toulongeon [writing 1786], 1881, 193-4
195. KA CA 1760 XI 14, Daun to Maria Theresa, 13 November. On the dissatisfaction with Lacy see also KA FA Hauptarmee 1860 XI 60 _, Buccow to Daun, Pillnitz, 8 November
196. KA FA Hauptarmee 1760 XI 54, *Relation*; HHStA Staatskanzlei Vorträge 87, Kaunitz to Maria Theresa, 30 November 1760
197. Lindner, 1993, 139
198. HHStA Nachlass Lacy III 2, Lacy to Franz Liechtenstein, Plauen, 11 November 1760
199. Albert; Warnery, 1785-91, III, 347
200. PC 12,505, Frederick to Prince Henry, 15 November 1760, XX, 87
201. Ligne, XVI, 90-1
202. Ibid., XVI, 94
203. KA HKR Protocolle 1760 December 294, Daun to O'Donnell, Loudon and Hadik, 15 December
204. Albert
205. PC 12,511, Frederick to Finckenstein, Unkersdorf, 16 November 1760, XX, 92
206. HHStA Kriegsakten 419, Maria Theresa to Lacy, 8 November 1760
207. Arneth, VI, 458
208. HHStA Nachlass Lacy III 2, Lacy to an unknown correspondent, 18 November 1760
209. HHStA Nachlass Lacy III 1, Maria Theresa to Lacy, 21 November 1760
210. HHStA Kriegsakten 418, Loudon to Kaunitz, Kunzendorf, 13 November 1760
211. Lindner, 1993, 110
212. PC 11,530, Eichel to Finckenstein, 23 November 1760, XX, 107

VI 1761
1. HHStA Staatskanzlei Vorträge 87, Kaunitz, *Kurz zusammengefasstes ohnmasgeblichstes Darfürhalten des Hof- und Staats Kanzlern über 10 Deliberations Punkten*, 10 December 1760
2. KA CA 1761 IV 5, Maria Theresa to Daun, 28 April. See also Riksarkivet, Stockholm, Diplomatica Germanica 443, Bark, 14 May 1761
3. HHStA Staatskanzlei Vorträge 87, Kaunitz to Maria Theresa, 31 October 1760
4. HHStA Staatskanzlei Vorträge 87, Kaunitz, *Kurz zusammengefasstes…Dafürhalten*, 10 December 1760
5. KA CA 1761 XIII 21, Liechtenstein's plan; KA CA 1761 XIII 6, *Plan des Generals Grafen von Lacy*
6. KA CA 1761 XIII 20, Daun's second plan
7. Arneth, 1863-79, VI, 227
8. HHStA Kriegsakten 417, Maria Theresa to Daun, 11 May 1761
9. HHStA Kriegsakten 417, Maria Theresa to Daun, 3 July 1761
10. KA CA 1761 III 2, Daun to Koch, Nettnitz, 29 March
11. KA CA 1761 VI 6, Daun to Maria Theresa, 22 June
12. KA CA 1761 VII 4, Daun to Maria Theresa, 6 July
13. KA CA 1761 VI 11, Daun to Maria Theresa, 29 June
14. KA CA 1761 VIII 7, Daun to Maria Theresa, 14 August
15. HHStA Staatskanzlei Vorträge 88, Kaunitz, *Ohnmassgeblichste Gedancken und Anmerckungen über den gegenwärtigen Stand der Kriegs-Operationen*, 20 September 1761
16. Cogniazzo, 1788-91, IV, 133
17. KA M.M.T.O., Petrowsky
18. Cogniazzo, 1788-91, iV, 138
19. HL 1761 IV 194, Colloredo to Hadik, 8 April
20. KA HKK Protocolle 1761 June 228, Serbelloni to the *Hofkriegsrath*, 8 April
21. Cogniazzo, 1788-91, IV, 151
22. Riksarkivet, Stockholm, Diplomatica Germanica 443, Bark, 4 September 1761
23. Cogniazzo, 1788-91, iV, 26
24. KA HKRA 1761 VIII 2A, Finé to the *Hofkriegsrath*, Tscheschen, 18 July
25. Cogniazzo, 1788-91, IV, 51
26. PC 13,121. Frederick to Prince Henry, Oppersdorf, 3 August 1761, XX, 583-4
27. SHAT A1 3588, Montazet, Dresden, 1 August 1761
28. KA HKRA 1761 XI 2C, Loudon, *Journal*, Freyburg, 20 August
29. Cogniazzo, 1788-91, IV, 71
30. HHStA Nachlass Lacy III, 3, Lacy to Daun, Gross-Dobritz, 21 August 1761
31. Cogniazzo, 1788-91, IV, 76
32. KA FA Korps Loudon 1761 VIII 70, Loudon, *Pro Memoria*, Jauer, 24 August
33. KA FA Korps Loudon 1761 VIII ad72, Loudon, *Pro Memoria*, Freyburg, 27 August
34. Tielke, 1776-86, III, 84
35. HL 1761 IX 395, Giannini, *Disposition*
36. Ibid.
37. Cogniazzo, 1788-91, IV, 87
38. Ibid.., IV, 93
39. Montazet, Dresden, 21 September 1761, Arneth, 1863-79, VI, 41-2
40. KA HKRA 1761 XI 2E, Loudon, *Journal*, Freyburg, 30 September
41. KA M.M.T.O., Heinrich O'Donnell
42. KA M.M.T.O., Giannini; KA FA Korps Loudon 1761 X ad 15A, *Aussag eines Deserteurs vom Regiment Zastrow*,

nahmens Pierre Mandelieu, so heut as der Vöstung Schweidnitz gekommen
43. KA FA Korps Loudon 1761 X 18, Loudon to Daun, 4 October
44. KA FA Korps Loudon 1761 X 15B, *Disposition zur Brousquirung der Vestung Schweidnitz vor Tages am 1ten. October 1761*
45. Ibid.
46. Ibid.
47. KA FA Korps Loudon 1761 X 18, Loudon to Daun, 4 October
48. KA FA Korps Loudon 1761 X 15B, *Disposition zur Brousquiring*
49. KA M.M.T.O., De Vins
50. Wachter, 1897, 122
51. KA M.M.T.O., Wilhelm Lacy
52. KA M.M.T.O., Olivier Wallis
53. KA M.M.T.O., Elmpt
54. KA M.M.T.O., Oliver Wallis
55. KA M.M.T.O., Elmpt
56. Cogniazzo, 1788-91, IV, 107
57. PC 13,195, Frederick to Prince Henry, Gross-Nossen, 3 October 1761, XXI, 6
58. PC 13,208, Frederick to Prince Henry, Strehlen, 8 October 1761, XXI, 15
59. KA FA Korps Loudon 1761 X 18, Loudon to Daun, 4 October
60. KA FA Korps Loudon 1761 X 16, Loudon to Maria Theresa, 3 October
61. Archenholtz, 1840, II, 181

VII The War in the Balance, Winter 1761-2
1. Catt, 1884, 446; Archenholtz, 1840, II, 184
2. Cogniazzo, 1788-91, IV, 125
3. KA HKR Protocolle 1762 December 689/9, Kaunitz to the *Hofkriegsrath*, 23 December
4. HHStA Nachlass Lacy, III, 2, Lacy to Daun, Dallwitz, 11 October 1761
5. PC 13,383, Frederick to Finckenstein, Breslau, 6 January 1762, XXI, 165-6
6. Wraxall, 1800, I, 206
7. HHStA Staatskanzlei Vorträge 90, Kaunitz to Maria Theresa, 25 November 1762
8. Mercy to Francis Stephen, 26 February 1762, Arneth, 1863-79
9. HHStA Staatskanzlei Vorträge 89, Kaunitz to Maria Theresa, 7 June 1762
10. HHStA Kriegsakten 417, Maria Theresa to Daun, 7 June 1762
11. HHStA Staatskanzlei Vorträge 89, Kaunitz, *Votum*, 28 May 1761
12. PC 13,332, Frederick to Finckenstein, 10 December 1761, XXI, 113
13. KA HKRA 1762 VI 2X, Protocol of the council of 8 June 1762
14. Cogniazzo, 1788-91, iV, 150
15. KA HKR Protocolle 1762 December 763, Buccow to the *Hofkriegsrath*, Hermannstadt, 4 December
16. KA HKR Protocolle 1762 September 2, *Protocollum Commissionis mixtae die 19n. Augusti 1762 habitae*, delivered to Maria Theresa, 21 August
17. KA HKR Protocolle 1762 December 763, Buccow to the *Hofkriegsrath*, Hermannstadt, 4 December

VIII 1762
1. KA CA 1762 III 2, Lacy to Maria Theresa, Vienna, 21 March
2. KA CA 1762 III 6, Loudon to Maria Theresa, 21 March
3. KA CA 1762 III 2, Lacy to Maria Theresa, Vienna, 21 March
4. KA CA 1762 III 1, Neipperg to Maria Theresa, Vienna, 21 March
5. KA CA 1762 V 10, Francis Stephen to Serbelloni, 31 May
6. KA FA Hauptarmee 1762 VII 14, Hannig to Daun, 5 July
7. Cogniazzo, 1788-91, iV, 225
8. KA M.M.T.O., Löwenstein
9. HL 1762 VIII 473/A, Löwenstein, *Relation. Über die den 2ten Aug. 1762 bey dem Dorff Gradrob ohnweith Töplitz in Böheimb vorgefallenen Action*
10. KA M.M.T.O., Pellegrini, attestation by Löwenstein
11. Cogniazzo, 1788-91, IV, 236
12. KA M.M.T.O., Giulay
13. KA CA 1762 VIII 3, Partini von Neuhoff to Maria Theresa, Prague, 5 August
14. HL 1652 VIII 473, Löwenstein to Daun, Teplitz, 2 August
15. Riksarkivet, Stockholm, Diplomatica Germanica 444, Bark, 19 August 1762
16. KA CA 1762 VIII 8, D'Ayasasa to Daun, Vienna, 9 August
17. Ligne, XVI, 117
18. KA CA 1762 V 7, Daun to Maria Theresa, 25 May
19. Cogniazzo, 1788-91, IV, 149
20. KA CA 1762 VI 1, Daun to Maria Theresa, 1 June
21. KA CA 1762 V 7, Daun to Maria Theresa, 25 May
22. KA CA 1762 VI 4, Daun to Maria Theresa, 4 June
23. KA CA 1762 V 7, Daun to Maria Theresa, 25 May
24. KA FA Hauptarmee 1762 VII 14, Hannig to Daun, Vienna, 5 July
25. KA CA 1762 VI 2, Daun to Maria Theresa, 1 June
26. KA CA 1762 VI 3, Daun to Maria Theresa, 3 June
27. HHStA Kriegsakten 417, Maria Theresa to Daun, 6 June 1762
28. KA CA 1762 VI 10, Daun to Maria Theresa, 29 June
29. Catt, 1884, 453
30. Albert
31. Ibid.
32. KA M.M.T.O., Collins de Ham
33. Ligne, XVI, 124
34. Ibid., XVI, 125
35. Ibid., XVI, 126. See also HL 1762 VII 470, Hadik to Vicomte Gréaulme, Hauptmannsdorf, 31 July
36. KA M.M.T.O., Brentano, attestation by Lacy
37. PC 13,385, Frederick to Neuwied, Seitendorf, 10 July 1762, XXII, 13
38. KA FA Hauptarmee 1762 VII ad 65, *Primator* Franz Scheider to *Unter Cammerherr* Count Porkorzawa in Prague, Königgrätz, 12 July
39. Ibid.
40. KA FA Hauptarmee 1762 VII 74A, *Arendator* Stenz Christoph Kohaut, *Relationes so mir in Abwesenheit des abgeschickten Herrn Fähndrichs nacher Königgrätz eingeloffen seynd,' Königgrätz, 14 July*
41. KA FA Hauptarmee 1762 VII 57, Daun to Beck, Tannhausen, 12 July
42. PC 13, 846, Frederick to Neuwied, Seitendorf, 13 July 1762, XXII, 27
43. Albert
44. HL 1762 VII 457, Hadik to Daun, 20 July
45. HHStA Nachlass Lacy, III, 23, Lacy to Franz Liechtenstein, 16 July 1762
46. Frederick, 1846-57, 'Oeuvres Historiques,' IV, 'Histoire de Mon Temps. Hist de la Guerre de Sept Ans,' II, 346
47. KA M.M.T.O., O'Kelly
48. Albert

49. Ligne, XVI, 130-1
50. Albert
51. KA M.M.T.O., O'Kelly
52. Ligne, XVI, 132
53. Ibid., XVI, 136
54. Ibid., XVI, 136-7
55. Albert
56. Ibid.
57. KA Ca 1762 VIII 20, nos. 78-82
58. HHStA Nachlass Lacy, III, 2, Lacy to Franz Liechtenstein, Rudliswalde, 10 August 1762
59. KA CA 1762 VIII 5, Maria Theresa to Daun, 10 August
60. KA CA 1762 IX 6, Montazet, 3 September
61. KA CA 1762 VII 13, anon. (probably Lacy) to Daun, Rudliswalde, 27 July
62. KA FA Hauptarmee 1762 VIII 56, Daun to Maria Theresa, 17 August
63. Ibid.
64. Ligne, 1928, II, 2
65. KA M.M.T.O., Lossgallner
66. KA FA Hauptarmee 1762 VIII 56, Daun to Maria Theresa, 17 August
67. Cogniazzo, 1788-91, IV, 179
68. Krigsarkivet, Stockholm, Armfedlt, *Dagbok*
69. KA HKR Mémoires 1762 880/12, Daun to Guasco, 12 September
70. KA CA 1762 IX 7, Daun to Francis Stephen, 12 September
71. Cogniazzo, 1788-91, IV, 200
72. KA HKR Mémoires 1762 880/12, Guasco, *Notes pour le Mémoire sur le Siège de Schweidnitz*
73. KA HKR Mémoires 1762 880/12, *Relation du Siège de Schweidnitz*, 31 October 1762
74. Ibid.
75. KA HKR Mémoires 1762 880/12, *Erfordernis Aufsatz*
76. KA HKR Mémoires 1762 880/12, Guasco, *Notes pour le Mémoire sur le Siège de Schweidnitz*
77. KA Kartensammlung H III E 237, Guasco, *Mémoire sur Schweidnitz*, 20 November 1761
78. John Quincy Adams, 1894, 185
79. KA FA Hauptarmee 1762 VII 2, Guasco to Daun, Schweidnitz, 15 July
80. KA HKR Mémoires 1762 880/12, Brady, undated; KA M.M.T.O., Brady
81. Cogniazzo, 1788-91, IV, 189
82. KA M.M.T.O., Brady, *Certificat* on his behalf by Guasco, Giannini and Gribeauval, 22 August 1762
83. KA HKR Mémoires 1762 880/12, Guasco to Daun, Danzig, 28 October 1762
84. KA HKR Mémooires 1762 880/12, Guasco, *Notes pour le Mémoire sur le Siège de Schweidnitz*
85. Cogniazzo, 1788-91, IV, 190
86. KA HKR Mémoires 1762 880/12, Guasco, *Relation du Siège de Schweidnitz*, 31 October 1762
87. KA FA Hauptarmee 1762 III ad 20, *Journal de qui est passé pendant le Siège de Schweidnitz*
88. KA HKR Mémoires 1762 880/12, Major Frierenberger, *Geh. Aus-zug*, 8 October 1762
89. KA FA Hauptarmee 1762 X 554C. Guasco, *Specification des tués, blessés, égarés depuis le 8 Aout*
90. KA HKR Mémoires 1762 880/12, Guasco, title as above
91. KA HKR Mémoires 1762 880/12, *Was bey der Belagerung der Vestung Schweidnitz verschossen worden*, undated
92. Albert
93. PC 14,180, Frederick to *GM*. Knobloch, 21 October 1762, XXII, 283
94. Daun to Maria Theresa, second half of October 1762, Arneth, 1863-79,. VI, 372
95. HL, Hadik's letter book, Hadik to Daun, 28 August 1762
96. KA CA 1762 IX 6, Montazet, Scharfeneck, 3 September
97. HL 1762 IX 513, Hadik to Daun, 10 September 1762
98. HL 1762 IX 526, Hadik to the *Hofkriegsrath*, 21 September
99. HL 1762 IX 525, Hadik to Maria Theresa, Dresden, 21 September
100. HL 1762 IX 532, Campitelli to Hadik, Purschdorf, 30 September
101. HL 1762 X 541, Hadik to the *Hofkriegsrath* and Daun, 6 October
102. HL 1762 X 560, Hadik to Stolberg, Dresden, 18 October
103. KA FA Reichsarmee und Korps Hadik 1762 X 133T, Stolberg to Hadik, 22 October
104. HL 1762 X 581, Hadik to Francis Stephen, Dresden, 26 October
105. Albert
106. HL 1762 X 601, Kaunitz to Hadik, 30 October
107. KA FA Reichsarmee und Korps Hadik 1762 X 133I, Seeger's relation of Freiberg
108. KA FA Reichsarmee und Korps Hadik 1762 X 133F, Stolberg, *Relation*, Altenberg, 8 November
109. KA FA Reichsarmee und Korps Hadik 1762 X 133M, Prussian *Disposition zur Bataille bey Freyberg in Sachsen d. 28ten Octbr 1762*
110. KA FA Reichsarmee und Korps Hadik 1762 X 133F, Stolberg, *Relation*
111. KA FA Reichsarmee und Korps Hadik 1762 X 133, Buttler, *Promemoire*, 9 November
112. KA FA Reichsarmee und Korps Hadik 1762 X 133M, Prussian *Disposition*
113. Cogniazzo, 1788-91, IV, 261
114. KA FA Reichsarmee und Korps Hadik 1762 133F, Stolberg, *Relation*
115. Ibid.
116. Cogniazzo, 1788-91, IV, 264-5
117. KA FA Reichsarmee und Korps Hadik 1762 133F, Stolberg, *Relation*
118. Barsewisch, 1863
119. KA FA Reichsarmee und Korps Hadik 1762 X 133, Buttler, *Promemoire*
120. KA FA Reichsarmee und Korps Hadik 1762 X 133I, Seeger's relation
121. KA FA Reichsarmee und Korps Hadik 1762 X 133H
122. KA FA Reichsarmee und Korps Hadik 1762 133F, Stolberg, *Relation*
123. KA FA Reichsarmee und Korps Hadik 1762 X 133A, Stolberg to Daun, 31 October
124. HL, Hadik's Journal, Maria Theresa to Hadik, 17 November 1762
125. SHAT A1 3615, Marainville, 31 October 1762
126. HHStA Staatskanzlei Vorträge 90, Kaunitz to Maria Theresa, 2 November 1762, and Maria Theresa's note thereon
127. HL 1762 XI 640, Hadik to the *Hofkriegsrath* and Daun, 12 November
128. HHStA Kriegsakten 417, Hadik to Daun, Dresden, 8 November 1762
129. HL 1762 XI 633, Daun to Hadik, 9 November
130. HL 1762 XI 669, Hadik to Francis Stephen, Dresden, 25 November. Hadik never identified his many sources of covert information by name, but a possible question for the agent in question was a Herr Coppenzeller, a linguist, who in 1758 convinced Francis Stephen and the hard-headed Kaunitz of his determination and ability to become a spy in the immediate circle of the king

IX Peace
1. KA CA 1762 VIII 6, Maria Theresa to Daun, 10 August
2. HL, Hadik's Journal, Maria Theresa to Hadik, 27 October 1762
3. HL 1762 XII 718, Collenbach to Hadik, Wermsdorf near Hubertusburg, 25 December
4. PC 14,417, Frederick to Prince Henry, 2 February 1762, XXII, 497
5. Riksarkivet, Stockholm, Diplomatica Germanica 450, Bark to Count Ekeblad, 11 February 1763
6. Archenholtz, 1840, II, 533; Retzow, 1802, I, 447
7. Kroener, in Kroener (ed), 1989, 51-2
8. KA FA 1756 XIII 379, *Verzeichnus*, 8 October 1763
9. Loehr, 1925, 104; Janetschek, 1959, 115
10. Marshall, 1772, 305
11. Ibid., 303
12. Frederick, 1846-57, 'Oeuvres Historiques,' IV, 'Histoire de Mon Temps. Histoire de la Guerre de Sept Ans,' II, 420
13. Frederick, 'Considérations sur l'état politique de l'Europe,' in *Politischen Testamente*, 1920, 250
14. Kunisch, J., in Kroener (ed.), 1989, 97
15. Frederick, 1846-57, 'Oeuvres Historiques,' IV, 'Histoire de Mon Temps. Historie de la Guerre de Sept Ans.' II, 412
16. Ibid., II, 411
17. John Rylands Library, Manchester, Bagshawe Muniments 3/21/8, Sir James Caldwell, 'A short view of the present state of Prussia and Austria…written in the year 1763'
18. KA CA 1761 VI 11, Daun to Maria Theresa, 29 June
19. KA CA 1761 VIII 7, Daun to Maria Theresa, 14 August
20. Frederick, 1846-57, 'Oeuvres Historiques,' IV, 'Histoire de Mon Temps. Histoire de la Guerre de Sept Ans,' I, 158
21. Thadden, 1967, 471

Appendix 1, Military Geography
1. KA Kartensammlung 1756 III 3 1046, *Rapport ‡ V.M. Impériale sur la Partie de la Bohème, qui est Frontiere de la Silésie*
2. Lloyd, 1781-90, I, xiii
3. Riesebeck, 1784, II, 186-7
4. Ibid., I, 397
5. Dutens, 1793, 152
6. Becker, 1798, 176-7
7. KA CA 1758 VII 8, anonymous memorandum, Frankfurt-am-Main, 6 July. See also Tempelhof, 1783-1801, I, 132, 135-6
8. Marshall, 1772, III, 307
9. Frederick, 'Réflexions sur la Tactique et sur Quelques Parties de la Guerre,' 27 December 1758, Frederick, 1840-57, XVII, 164-5
10. Tempelhof, 1783-1801, I, 130
11. Cogniazzo, 1788-91, III, 316. See also KA Kriegsakten 387, Field Marshal Batthyány's *Plan d'opérations* for 1757; Count Flemming's protest, as recorded in HHStA Staatskanzlei Vorträge, Kaunitz to Maria Theresa, 13 October 1760
12. Cogniazzo, 1788-91, III, 315-6
13. KA CA 1758 III 3, Beck's plan of operations
14. Marshall, 1772, III, 306
15. Lloyd, 1781-90, I, xxiv
16. Janson, 1913, 170
17. Lloyd, 1781-90, I, xx
18. KA CA 1761 IX 11, *Puncta*, Dresden, 22 September
19. Sanders, 1783-4, II, 162-3
20. Ibid., II, 162
21. Ibid., II, 143
22. Riesebeck, 1784, III, 5
23. Tempelhof, 1783-1801, III, 147
24. HHStA Kriegsakten 390, *Feldzugsplan des Grafen Lacy für 1760*
25. HHStA Kriegsakten 417, Maria Theresa to Daun, 27 December 1760
26. HHStA Staatskanzlei Vorträge 85, Kaunitz, *Pro Memoria*, 17 November 1760
27. HHStA Kriegsakten 389, Daun, *Mémoires qui contiennent le plan des opérations de la campagne prochaine 1759*
28. Marshall, 1772, III, 296
29. National Archives (Public Record Office), SP 90/75, Mitchell, Meissen, 24 May 1760
30. Lloyd, 1781-90, I, xxxv
31. Vincennes A1 3436, Champeaux, late July 1757
32. KA CA 1761 IX 11, *Puncta*, Dresden, 22 September
33. KA Kartensammlung 1756 III 3 1046, Major General Guasco, *Rapport à V.M. Impériale*
34. Küttner, 1801, I, 36
35. Herr Cavalceppi, in Bernouilli, 1781-8, I, 224-5
36. Lloyd, 1781-90, I, xvii. See also Cogniazzo, 1788-91, III, 67-8
37. Adams, 1804, 108, 88-9
38. Vincennes A1 3433, de Vault, *Notes sur la partie des Montagnes qui séparent la Bohème de la Silésie*, spring 1758
39. 'Principes Généraux de la Guerre,' 1748, Frederick, 1846-57, XXVIII, 10
40. Barsewisch, 1863, 212
41. HHStA Nachlass Lacy III 2, Lacy to *Cher Prince*, Glatz, 7 May 1762
42. Küttner, 1801, III, 78
43. HHStA Staatskanzlei Vorträge 87, Kaunitz, Kurz und zusammengefasstes *ohnmassgebliche Dafürhaltens… über 10 Deliberations Puncten*, 30 December 1760. See also KA Kartensammlung 1756 III 3 1046, Major General Guasco, *Rapport à V.M. Impériale*. Lloyd, 1781-90, I, xvi
44. Adams, 1804, 44-5
45. Ibid., 146
46. Lloyd, 1781-90, I, xvi-xvii
47. Adams, 1804, 185
48. Vincennes A1 3441, Boisgelin, Lissa, 15 October 1757
49. Marshall, 1772, III, 273. See also KA Kriegsakten 387, Field Marshal Batthyányi's *Plan d'opérations* for 1757; Lloyd, 1781-90, I, xxxii
50. Marshall, 1772, III, 272
51. Lloyd, 1781-90, I, xxx
52. Ibid., I, xxxiii
53. Ibid., I, xxxiii
54. Adams, 1804, 3
55. Becker, 1798, 170

BIBLIOGRAPHY

MANUSCRIPT SOURCES
(in approximate order of degree of usage)

Vienna, Kriegsarchiv

Feldakten: correspondence of commanders and officers in the field

Cabinettsakten: personal correspondence between Maria Theresa and her officers

Archiv des Militär-Maria Theresien-Ordens: depositions of candidates for the order; a gigantic repository of tactical detail

Hofkriegsräthliche Akten: general correspondence of the HKR

Protocols of the HKR: register of all documents sent and received by the HKR

Kartensammlung: map collection

Ausgearbeitete Kriegsgeschichten: manuscript histories, esp. contributions relevant to the Seven Years War by Friedrich Zechenter (Ms. Nr. 55), *FZM*. Browne and Captain Heller; important details on the lesser actions

Vienna, Haus-, Hof und Staatsarchiv

Kriegsakten: esp. for the official letters of Maria Theresa to her commanders in the field

Staatskanzlei Vorträge: the lengthy memoranda of Kaunitz to Maria Theresa on diplomatic and military affairs

Nachlass Lacy: the official and private correspondence of Franz Moritz Lacy

Budapest, Hadtörtenéti Intézet és Múzeum

Hadik Levéltár: the correspondence and diaries relevant to the Seven Years War take up more than forty substantial files of this huge collection

Vincennes, Service Historique de l'Armée de Terre

Series A1 Correspondance générale: for the reports of the French attachés and volunteers; highly relevant, though allowance has to be made for the generally patronising tone towards matters Austrian

Stockholm, Riksarkivet

Diplomatica Germanica 438-444: for the reports of the Swedish envoy Nils Bark. He was on good personal terms with Maria Theresa, with whom he had lengthy conversations, as also with Kaunitz and the French envoys

Budapest, Magyar Országos Levéltár

Albert of Sachsen-Teschen, Duke, *Mémoires de ma Vie*; important for the later campaigns

Stockholm, Krigsarkivet

Major Fromhold Armfeldt, *Remarquer öfn K.K. Osterrikiska Arméen samt Militärisk dagbok*, Stockholm, 27 May 1763, in *Pommerska Kriget 1757-62*, vol 140. Memorandum on the Austrian army and field diary by the Swedish military attaché, 1759-62

Berlin, Geheimes Staatsarchiv Preussischer Kulturbesitz

IV Hauptabteilung, Rep. 15A, Geheimes Civilkabinett, Militaria: for the documentation and other material collected by the Prussian (later German Great) General Staff for the official histories of the wars of Frederick the Great

Bratislava (Slovakia), státny Ústredeny Archív

Fond Pálfi-Daun: stray papers of Field Marshal Daun

C.K. Línia Pálffyovskéhor. Rudolph Pálffy (1719-1768): the papers of a leading commander of hussars

Fond Rod Amade Üchtritz, 101-12-067, XVI, *GdC*. Wöllwarth, *Kurze Beschreibung meiner geleisteten Dienste*, for the campaign of 1757

Northumberland County Record Office, North Gosforth, Great Britain

Butler (Ewart) Mss., ZBU/2 series. For the unpublished papers of the English volunteer Horace St. Paul and his correspondents, especially the French observers Boisgelin and Rutant de Marainville. Supplements the St. Paul papers published in 1914 (below)

Stuttgart, Württembergische Landesbibliothek

Cod Milit c 29, Colonel Friedrich Nicolai, *Bemerkungen zum Feldzug der herzogl. Würtembersch. Truppen bey der Kayserlichen Armee in Böhmen und Schlesien im Jahr 1757*

Kew, National Archives (formerly Public Record Office), Kew, Great Britain

State Papers Foreign 90/69 etc. The unpublished papers of Sir Andrew Mitchell, the British envoy to Frederick; supplements the Mitchell papers published in 1850 (below)

John Rylands Library, Manchester, Great Britain

Bagshawe Muniments 3/21/18, Sir James Caldwell, *A Short view of the Present State of Austria and Prussia, Written in the Year 1763*

Documentary Collections, Memoirs, Letters, Histories and Commentaries of Contemporaries or Near-Contemporaries

Abbreviation: - *Urkundliche Beiträge* = Grosser Generalstab, *Urkundliche Beiträge und Forschungen zur Geschichte des preussischen Heeres*, Berlin 1901 etc

Adams, John Quincy, *Letters on Silesia*, London 1804

Anon., *Zuverlässige Nachrichten von dem traurigen Schicksale der Stadt und Universität Halle*, Amsterdam 1759

Anon., 'Anekdoten vom König Friedrich II.,' *Militärische Monatsschrift*, IV, Berlin 1786

Anon., *Anecdoten und Karakterzüge aus dem Leben Friedrichs des Zweiten*, 12 vols, Berlin 1787-89

Anon., *Beyträge zu den Anecdoten und Karakterzüge aus dem Leben Friedrichs des Zweiten*, 4 vols, Berlin 1788-9

Archenholtz, Johann Wilhelm von, *Geschichte des Siebenjährigen Krieges in Deutschland*, 2 vols, Berlin 1840. He was a subaltern in the regiment of Forcade.

—*Gemälde der preussischen Armee vor und in dem siebenjährigen Kriege*, reprint, Osnabrück 1874

Arneth, Alfred (ed.), 'Die Relationen der Botschafter Venedigs über Österreich im achtzehnten Jahrhundert,' in *Fontes Rerum Austriacarum*, XX, Vienna 1863

Barsewisch, Ernst Friedrich Rudolph, *Meine Kriegs-Erlebnisse während des Siebenjährigen Krieges 1757-1763*, Berlin 1863. Experiences of a young officer in the regiment of Wedel.

Becker, Johann Nikolay, *Fragmente aus dem Tagebuch eines reisenden Neu-Franken*, Frankfurt and Leipzig 1798

Belach, A., *Der Christ im Kriege und in der Belagerung*, Leipzig 1758

Berenhorst, Georg Henrich von, *Betrachtungen über die Kriegskunst*, 3 vols, Leipzig 1798-9

—*Aus dem Nachlasse von Georg Heinrich von Berenhorst*, 2 vols, Dessau 1845-7

Johann Bernouilli's Sammlung kurzer Reisebeschreibungen, 17 vols, Berlin 1781-8

Blumenthal, Louise Johanne, *Lebensbeschreibung Hans Joachims v. Zieten*, Berlin 1797. By the niece of the old hussar general

Boysen, Friedrich-Eberhard, *Eigene Lebensbeschreibung*, 2 vols, Quedlinburg, 1795

Bräker, Ulrich, *Der arme Mann im Tockenburg*, Leipzig 1852

Correspondance inédite de Victor-François Duc de Broglie avec le Prince Xavier de Saxe, 4 vols, Paris 1903

Brunswick, Prince Ferdinand, 'Réflexions et Anecdotes vraies, mais hardies sur la Campagne de 1756,' *Urkundliche Beiträge*, I, Part 4, 1902

Catt, Heinrich, *Unterhaltungen mit Friedrich dem Grossen. Memoiren und Tagebücher von Heinrich de Catt*, Leipzig 1884

Choiseul, *Mémoires du duc de Choiseul* (ed. Guicciardini, J.-P. and Bonnet, P.), Paris 1872

Cogniazzo, Jakob, *Freymüthiger Beytrag zur Geschichte des östreichischen Militairdienstes*, Frankfurt and Leipzig, 1780

—*Geständnisse eines östreichischen Veterans*, 4 vols, Breslau 1788-91. Ranks alongside de Ligne (q.v.) as the most important Austrian memoir of the war. Cogniazzo (his name appears in many variants) was a captain in the infantry regiment of Erzherzog Carl, but was involved unwittingly and marginally in GFWM. Brunyan's treason in 1762, and left the Austrian service voluntarily after a short period of confinement. He took up residence in Prussian territory, and, although he has sometimes been regarded as a hostile source, he presents a mass of detail and opinion which is unavailable elsewhere

Dutens, M.L., *Itinéraire des Routes les plus Fréquentées, ou Journal de plusieurs Voyages aux Villes Principalles de l'Europe, depuis 1768 jusqu'en 1783*, London 1793

Frederick II, King of Prussia
—*Oeuvres de Frédéric de Grand*, 31 vols, Berlin 1846-57
—*Militärische Correspondenz des Königs Friedrichs des Grossen mit dem Prinzen Heinrich von Preussen*, Berlin 1851-4
—*Politische Correspondenz Friedrichs des Grossen*, 46 vols, Berlin 1879-1939
—*Die Politischen Testamente Friedrichs des Grossen*, Berlin 1920

Gellert, C.F., *C.F. Gellerts Briefwechsel* (ed. Reynolds, J.F), 4 vols, Berlin 1983-96

Gorani, Giuseppe, *Mémoires de Gorani*, Paris 1944. By a subaltern in the regiment of Andlau. Gorani had a genuine commitment to the military life, in contrast to his countryman Verri (q.v.)

Guibert, Jacques-Antoine-Hypolite, *Journal d'un Voyage en Allemagne, fait in 1773*, Paris 1803

'Aus der Zeit des Siebenjährigen Krieges. Tagebuchblätter und Briefe der Prinzessin Heinrich und des Königlichen Hauses' (ed. Berner, E., and Volz., G.), *Quellen und Untersuchungen zur Geschichte des Hauses Hohenzollern*, IX, Berlin 1908. Papers of the wife of Prince Henry of Prussia

Militärischer Nachlass des Königlichen Preussischen Generallieutenants Victor Amadeus Grafen Henckel von Donnersmarck, 2 vols, Leipzig 1858

Hülsen, Carl Wilhelm, *Unter Friedrich dem Grossen. Aus den Memoiren des Aeltervaters 1752-1773*, Berlin 1890. Life as a young officer in the regiment of Below

Kalckreuth, Friedrich Adolph, 'Kalckreuth zu seinem Leben und zu seiner Zeit… Erinnerungen des General-Feldmarschalls Grafen von Kalckreuth,' *Minerva*, 1839, IV; 1840, II-IV, Dresden

Kaltenborn, R.W., *Briefe eines Alten preussischen Officiers verschiedene Characterzüge Friedrichs des grossen betreffend*, 2 vols, Hohenzollern 1790-1

Kaunitz, Wenzel Anton, 'Denkschriften des Fürsten Wenzel Kaunitz-Rittberg,' (ed. Beer, A.), *Archiv für Österreichische Geschichte*, XLVIII, Vienna 1872

Khevenhüller-Metsch, Johann Josef, *Aus der Zeit Maria Theresias. Tagebuch des Fürsten Johann Josef Khevenhüller-Metsch, Kaiserlichen Obersthofmeisters 1742-1776*, (ed. Breunlich-Pawlik, M., and Wagner, H.), 11 vols, Vienna 1907-72. By the master of ceremonies of the Imperial court. Highly relevant details and gossip on personalities and public affairs. The editorial apparatus is of a very high standard, and includes lengthy printed documents in the appendices

Kornauth, Friedrich (ed.), *Das Heer Maria Theresias. Faksimile-Ausgabe der Albertina-Handschrift 'Desseins des Uniformes des Troupes I.I. et R.R. de l'année 1762'*, Vienna 1973. Excellent reproduction of the set of uniform illustrations in the Austrian Army Museum, matched by a first-class commentary. See also the comparable edition of the 'Bautzen Manuscript' by Thümmler (below)

Küster, Carl Daniel, *Bruchstück seines Campagnelebens im Siebenjährigen Kriege*, Berlin 1792

—*Charakterzüge des Preussischen General-Lieutenants von Saldern*, Berlin 1795

The fascinating works of a Prussian *Feldprediger*

Küttner, Carl Gottlob, *Reise durch Deutschland, Dänemark, Schweden, Norwegen und einen Theil von Italien in den Jahren 1792, 1798, 1799*, 4 vols, Leizpig 1801

Laukhard, Friedrich Christian, *Magister Friedrich Christian Laukhards Leben und Schicksale*, 2 vols, Stuttgart 1930

Lehndorff, E. (ed. Schmidt-Lötzen, K.E.), *Dreissig Jahre am Hofe Friedrichs des Grossen*, Gotha 1907 - *Nachträge*, 2 vols, Gotha 1910-13.

By an official at the court of Frederick's badly done-by queen Elisabeth Christine. He had conversations with Austrian officer prisoners, and has some interesting comments on military affairs

Lemcke, Jakob H. (ed. Walz. R.), 'Kriegs- und Friedenbilder aus den Jahren 1754-1759. Nach dem Tagebuch des Leutnants Jakob F. von Lemcke,' *Preussische Jahrbücher*, CXXXVIII, Berlin 1909

Ligne, Charles-Joseph, *Mélanges militaires, littéraires et sentimentaires*, 34 vols, Dresden 1795-1811

—*Oeuvres Choisies du Prince de Ligne*, Paris 1883

—*Fragments de l'Histoire de ma Vie*, 2 vols, Paris 1928

This polymath scandalised and entertained Europe throughout his long life. During the Seven Years War he became colonel commandant of his father's regiment of Nethelandish infantry, and remained a close associate of Lacy. His war diary (vols XIV-XVI of the *Mélanges*) is the most important contemporary printed source on the Austrian campaigns

Lloyd, Henry, *The History of the Late War in Germany between the King of Prussia and the Empress of Germany and her Allies*, 2 vols, London 1781-90. Lloyd was a veteran of the Austrian service in the war (and quite possibly a British agent). His history is dry and theoretical in tone, and the additional material provided by Tempelhof in his translation (below) is of considerably greater interest

Loudon, Gideon Ernst (ed. Buchberger, K.), 'Briefe Loudon's. Beiträge zur Geschichte des siebenjährigen Krieges,' *Archiv für Österreichische Geschichte*, XLVIII, Part 1, Vienna 1872

Maria Theresa, *Briefe der Kaiserin Maria Theresia und ihre Kinder und Freunde* (ed. Arneth, A.), 4 vols, Vienna 1881

—*Kaiserin Maria Theresia und Kurfürstin Maria Antonia von Sachsen. Briefwechsel 1747-1772* (ed. Lippert, W.), Leipzig 1908

Marshall, J., *Travels… in the Years 1768, 1769, and 1770*, for vol III (on Central Europe), London 1772

Massenbach, A.L., *Rückerinnerungen an grosse Männer*, 2 vols, Amsterdam 1808

Memoirs and Papers of Sir Andrew Mitchell (ed. Bisset, A.), 2 vols, London 1850. The British envoy Mitchell accompanied Frederick on his campaigns

Mauvillon, J., *Geschichte Ferdinands Herzogs zu Braunschweig-Lüneburg*, 2 vols, Leipzig 1794

Nicolai, F., *Anekdoten von König Friedrich II. von Preussen*, 6 vols, Berlin 1788-92

Ortmann, A.D., *Patriotische Briefe*, Berlin and Potsdam, 1759

Pichler, Caroline, *Denkwürdigkeiten aus meinem Leben*, 2 vols, Vienna 1844

Podgursky, K., *Selbstbiographie des Husaren-Obersten von Öky*, Leipzig 1843. By an officer of the Puttkamer White Hussars

Prittwitz und Gaffron, Christian Wilhelm, *Unter der Fahne des Herzogs von Bevern. Jugenderinnerungen des Christian Wilhelms von Prittwitz und Gaffron*, Berlin 1935

Retzow, F.A., *Charakteristik der wichtigsten Ereignisse des siebenjährigen Krieges*, 2 vols, Berlin 1802

Riesebeck, Kaspar, *Briefe eines reisenden Franzosen über Deutschland*, 2 vols, Leipzig 1784

St. Paul, Horace, *A Journal of the First Two Campaigns of the Seven Years War*, Cambridge 1914. The diary of an English volunteer with the Austrians, together with much material provided by contacts with the French

—*The Journal of Horace St. Paul* (ed. Neil Cogswell), 7 vols, Guisborough 1997-2007. An important new edition, supported by many new maps and topographical sketches

Salmon, T., *The Universal Traveller*, 2 vols London 1752-3

Sanders, H., *Beschreibung seiner Reisen*, Leipzig 1783-4

Schmettau, Friedrich Wilhelm, *Lebensgeschichte des Grafen von Schmettau*, 2 vols, Berlin 1806. The loyalties of the Prussian lieutenant general Karl Christoph Schmettau are still a matter of debate. This is a biography by his son

Sermage, P.T., *Die Briefen des Grafen Sermage aus dem Siebenjährigen Kriege* (ed. Matasovich, J.). Zagreb, 1923

Szent-Ivány, G. (ed. Sommeregger, Colonel), 'Die Schlacht bei Prag im Jahre 1757,' *Mitteilungen des K. u. K. Kriegsarchivs*, 3rd series, VII, Vienna 1911

Tempelhof, Georg Friedrich, *Geschichte des siebenjährigen Krieges in Deutschland*, 6 vols, Berlin 1783-1801. The core of the work is a translation of Lloyd's history (above), but Tempelhof had been a Prussian gunner in the war, and his additions are important in their own right

Tielke, J.G., *Beiträge zur Geschichte des Krieges von 1756 bis 1763*, 6 parts in 3 vols, Freiberg, 1776-86. By an officer of the Saxon staff; especially important for topography

Thielow, *Tagebuch eines preussischen officiers von der Königlichen Armee im Jahre 1760*, Cologne 1781

Thümmler, Lars-Holger, *Die österreichische Armee im Siebenjährigen Krieg. Die Bautzener Bilderhandschrift aus dem Jahre 1762*, Berlin 1993. Commentary and edition of the uniform plates of the 'Bautzen Manscript' of 1762. Together with Kornauth's edition of the 'Albertina Manuscript' of the same year it provides a comprehensive picture of the dress of the Austrian army in the Seven Years War

Toulongeon and Hullin, generals, *Une Mission Militaire en Prusse, en 1786*, Paris 1881

Verri, Pietro, *Lettere e Scritti Inediti di Pietro et di Alessandro Verri*, 2 vols, Milan 1879. A new version with comments by N. Zolezzi was published as *Lettere Inedite di Pietro Verri*, Milan 1965

—*Pietro Verri* (ed. Valeri, N.), Florence 1969

Verri was a captain in the infantry regiment of Clerici, but remained essentially a military tourist who was in search of sensation. He wrote primarily for literary effect, and Gorani (q.v.) is more reliable

Volz, Gustav Bernhard, and Küntzel, Georg, 'Preussische und Österreichische Acten zur Vorgeschichte des Siebenjährigen Krieges,' *Publicationen aus den Preussischen Staatsarchiven*, LXXIV, Leipzig 1899

Volz, Gustav Bernhard, *Friedrich der Grosse im Spiegel seiner Zeit*, 3 vols, Berlin 1926-7

Wachter, F., *Akten des Kriegsgerichts von 1763 wegen der Eroberung von Glatz and Schweidnitz 1761*, Breslau 1897. Depositions of the Prussian courts martial consequent on the loss of these two fortresses to the Austrians. Much useful detail

Warnery, Charles-Emanuel, *Herrn Generalmajor von Warnery sämtliche Schriften*, 9 vols, Hanover 1785-91

—*Campagnes de Frédéric II, Roi de Prusse de 1756 ‡ 1762*, Amsterdam 1788

Yorke, Philip, *The Life and Correspondence of Philip Yorke Earl of Hardwicke*, 3 vols, Cambridge 1913

Zimmermann, Johann Georg, *Fragmente über Friedrich den Grossen*, 3 vols, Leipzig 1790

Secondary Sources

Abbreviation—*Forschungen* = *Forschungen zur Brandenburgischen und Preussischen Geschichte*, Leipzig, Munich and Berlin, 1888 etc

Albert, B., *Was uns der Becher des P. Andreas Faulhaber erzählt*, Glatz 1928

Allmayer-Beck, Johann Christoph, *Das Heer unter dem Doppeladler. Habsburgs Armeen 1718-1848* (with Lessing, E.), Munich 1981

—'Die friderizianische Armee im Spiegel ihrer österreichischen Gegner,' in Militärgeschictliches Forschungsamt, 1987 (below)

Arneth, Alfred, *Geschichte Maria Theresias*, 10 vols, Vienna 1863-79. Still the foundation of all serious studies. A reminder of the strength of European historiography in its classic period from 1860 to 1914

Aster, H., *Beleuchtung der Kriegswirren zwischen Preussen und Sachsen vom Ende August bis Ende October 1756*, Dresden 1848

Bach, A., *Die Graffschaft Glatz unter dem Gouvernement des Generals Heinrich August Freiherrn de la Motte Fouqué*, Habelschwerdt 1885

Bangert, Dieter Ernst, *Die russisch-österreichische militärische Zusammenarbeit im Siebenjährigen Kriege in den Jahren 1758-1759*, Boppard 1971

Baumgart, Peter, and Schmilewsky, Ulrich (eds.), *Kontinuität und Wandel. Schlesien zwischen Österreich und Preussen*, Sigmaringen, 1990

Baumgart, Peter, 'Die militärische Bedeutung Schlesiens und das Scheitern der österreichischen Rückeroberungspläne im Siebenjährigen Krieg,' in Baumgart and Schmilewsky (eds.), 1990 (above)

—'Schlesien im Kalkül König Friedrichs II. von Preussen und die europäischen Implikationen der Eroberung des Landes,' in Baumgart and Schmilewsky (eds.), 1990 (above)

Bayer, Fritz, *Andreas von Hadik und der kleine Krieg,* unpublished thesis, Graz 1977

Beaulieu-Marconnay, Carl, *Der Hubertusburger Friede,* Leipzig 1871

Bernhardi, T., *Friedrich der Grosse als Feldherr,* Berlin 1881

Bertling, M., *Die Kroaten und Panduren in der Mitte des XVIII. Jahrhunderts und ihre Verwendung in den Friderizianischen Kriegen,* Berlin 1912

Boehme, Klaus-Richard, 'Schwedens Teilnahme am Siebenjährigen Krieg: Innen- und aussenpolitische Voraussetzungen und Rückwirkungen,' in Kroener, B.(ed.), 1989 (below)

Brabant, Artur, *Das Heilige Römische Reich teutscher Nation im Kampf mit Friedrich dem Grossen,* 3 vols, Berlin 1904-31. A highly-readable work by a scholar-archivist in the tradition of Arneth. Reprinted Bad Honnef, 1984. Vol II translated and edited by Sharman, Alister, and Cogswell, Neil, as *1758. The Campaign for the Liberation of Saxony,* 2 vols, Buchholz 1998, with maps and additional material in the style of Cogswell's edition of Horace St. Paul (above).

Brinner, Wilhelm, *Geschichte des k.k. Pionier-Regiments in Verbindung mit einer Geschichte des Kriegs-Brückenwesens in Oesterreich,* Vienna 1878

Broucek, Peter, *Der Geburtstag der Monarchie. Die Schlacht bei Kolin,* Vienna 1982. Important

Brüggemann, F., *Der siebenhährige Krieg im Spiegel des zeitgenössischen Literatur,* Leipzig 1935

Buddruss, Eckhard, *Die französische Deutschlandpolitik 1756-1789,* Mainz 1995

Carl, H., 'Les Meilleurs Ennemis du Monde? L'occupation française en Allemagne pendant la Guerre de Sept Ans,' in *Revue Historique des Armées. Mélanges,* I, Vincennes 1996

Daniels, E., *Zur Schlacht von Torgau am 3. November 1760,* Berlin 1885

Dann, U., *Hanover and Great Britain 1740-1760,* Leicester 1991

Decker, C., *Die Schlachten und Hauptgefechte des siebenjährigen Krieges... mit vorherrschender Bezugnahme auf den Gebrauch der Artillerie,* 1837. Good

Dikreiter, Heinrich Georg (ed.), *Altösterreichische Soldatengeschichten aus der Zeit Maria Theresias,* Breslau 1925

Ditfurth, F.W., *Die Historischen Volkslieder des siebenjährigen Krieges,* Berlin 1871

Duffy, Christopher, *The Wild Goose and the Eagle. A Life of Marshal von Browne,* London 1964; augmented trans. by Inge Lehne, *Feldmarschall Browne,* Vienna, 1966

—*The Army of Frederick the Great,* Newton Abbot 1974; augmented trans. by Jochen Peiper, *Friedrich der Grosse und seine Armee,* Stuttgart 1974. Second English-language edition, Chicago 1996

—*The Army of Maria Theresa,* Newton Abbot 1977

—*Russia's Military Way to the West, 1700-1800,* London 1981

—*Frederick the Great. A Military Life,* London 1986; augmented trans by Guy Montag, *Friedrich der Gross. Ein Soldatenleben,* Zürich 1986

—*Instrument of War.* Part 1 of *The Austrian Army in the Seven Years War, 1756-1763,* Chicago 2000; trans by Claudia Reichel-Ham, *Sieben Jahre Krieg 1756-1763,* Vienna 2003

—*Prussia's Glory: Rossbach and Leuthen,* Chicago 2003

Easum, C.V., *Prince Henry of Prussia, Brother of Frederick the Great,* Madison, 1942

Eicken, H., 'Die Reichsarmee im Siebenjährigen Krieg', in Friese, H.-J. (ed.), 1999

Engelmann, J., with illustrations by Dorn, G., *Friedrich der Grosse und seine Generäle,* Friedberg 1899

—Engelmann and Dorn, *Die Schlachten Friedrichs des Grossen... Führung, Verlauf, Gefechts-Szenen, Gliederung,* Friedberg 1991. A most useful compendium

Friese, H.-J., *Die Reichsarmee 1664-1803,* Buchholz-Sprötze, 1999. A useful collection of reprints of not readily-accessible articles.

Gieraths, G., *Die Kampfhandlungen der brandenburgische-preussischen Armee 1626-1807,* Berlin 1954

Grosse, Oscar, *Prinz Xaver von Sachsen und das sächsische Korps bei der französischen Armee 1758-1763,* Leipzig 1907

Grosser Generalstab, *Der Siebenjährige Krieg,* 13 vols, Berlin, 1901-14. The official history by the German Great General Staff. A text of fundamental importance. The outbreak of the First World War put an end to the coverage just short of the battle of Torgau in 1760

Hackl., Othmar, *Die Vorgeschichte, Gründung und frühe Entwicklung der Generalstäbe Österreichs, Bayerns und Preussens,* Osnabrück 1997

Hagen, E., 'Die Fürstlich Würzburgische Hausinfanterie vom Jahre 1759...', in Friese, H.-J. (ed.), 1999

Heeresgeschichtliches Museum, Vienna (ed.), 'Maria Theresia. Beiträge zur Geschichte des Heerwesens ihrer Zeit,' *Schriften des Herresgeschichtlichen Museums./ Militärwissenschaftliches Institut,* III, Graz 1967

Helmes, H., 'Die fränkischen Kreistruppen im Kriegsjahre 1758 und im Frühjahrefeldzug 1759', in Friese, H.-J. (ed.), 1999

Hennebert, Lieutenant Colonel, *Gribeauval*, Paris 1896

Herrmann, O., 'Olmütz,' *Forschungen*, XXIII, 1910

—'Der "Sieger" von Torgau,' *Forschungen*, XXVI, 1913

—'Prinz Ferdinand von Preussen über den Feldzug vom Jahre 1757, *Forschungen*, XXXI, 1918

Hirtenfeld, Jaromir, *Der Militär-Maria Theresien-Orden und seine Mitglieder*, 2 vols, Vienna 1857. A great store of biographical information

—*Vor Hundert Jahren: Erinnerung an Olmütz und seiner ruhmvollen Vertheidiger*, Vienna 1858

Hochedlinger, Michael, *Austria's Wars of Emergence. War, State and Scoiety in the Habsburg Monarchy 1683-1797*, London 2003

Hoen, Max van, 'Die Schlacht bei Prag am 6. Mai 1757, *Streffleurs Militärische Zeitschrift*, Vienna 1909

—'Die Schlacht bei Kolin am 18. Juni 1757, *Streffleurs Militärische Zeitschrift*, Vienna 1911

Hüttemann, V., *Das Erscheinungsbild und die Gefechtsformen der preussischen Artillerie im 7-jährigen Krieg, 1756-63*, Paderborn 1989

Janetschek, Kurt, *Die Finanzierung des Siebenjährigen Krieges*, unpublished thesis, Vienna 1959

Janko, Wilhelm, *Loudon's Leben*, Vienna 1869

Janson, August, *Hans Karl von Winterfeldt. Des Grossen Königs Generalstabschef*, Berlin 1913

Jany, Curt, 'Zum Friedenstag. Das Treffen von Burkersdorf am 21. Juli 1762,' *Beiheft zum Militärwochenblatt*, Berlin 1907

—'Der siebenjährige Krieg. Ein Schlusswort zum Generalstabswerk,' *Forschungen*, XXXV 1923

—*Geschichte der preussischen Armee vom 15. Jahrhundert bis zum Jahre 1914*, 3 vols, Berlin 1928-9. Reprinted Osnabrück 1967. Authoritative and packed with factual detail

—'Einige Bemerkungen zur Schlacht bei Torgau,' *Forschungen*, LIII, 1941

Jihn, Friedrich, 'Der Feldzug 1760 in Sachsen mit besonderer Berücksichtigung der Schlacht bei Torgau,' *Mitthielungen des k.k. Kriegs-Archivs*, Vienna 1882

Kaplan, H.H., *Russia and the Outbreak of the Seven Years War*, Berkeley 1968

Keep, John L., 'Die russische Armee im Siebenjährigen Krieg,' in Kroener, B. (ed), 1989 (below)

Kennett, Lee, *The French Armies in the Seven Years War. A Study in Military Organization and Administration*, Durham (North Carolina), 1967

Kessel, Eberhard, 'Quellen und Untersuchungen zur Geschichte der Schlacht bei Torgau,' *Schriften der Kriegsgeschichtlichen Seminar der Friedrich-Wilhelms Universität Berlin*, Allgemeine Reihe, XVII, Berlin 1937

—'Die Schlacht bei Freiberg am 29. Oktober 1762, *Neues Archiv für Sächsische Geschichte und Altertumskunde*, LX, Dresden 1939

—'Der russisch-österreichische Feldzugsplan 1761,' *Militärgeschichte und Kriegstheorie in neuerer Zeit. Ausgewählte Aufsätze* (ed. Kunisch, J.), *Historische Forschungen*, XXXIII, Berlin 1987

Kloppert, A., *Der Schlesische Feldzug von 1762*, thesis, Bonn, 1980. V. good

Kloosterhuis, Jürgen, 'Donner, Blitz und Bräker. Der Soldatendienst des "armen Mannes im Tockenburg" aus der Sicht des preussischen Militärsystems,' in *Schreibsucht. Autobiografische Schriften des Pietisten Ulrich Bräker (1735-1798)*, (Messerli, Alfred, and Muschg, Adolf, eds.), Göttingen, 2004

Korobkov, N., *Semiletnyaya Voina (Deistviya Rossii v. 1756-1762 gg.)*, Moscow 1940

Koschatzky, Walter, and Krasa, Selma, *Herzog Albert von Sachsen-Teschen 1738-1822. Reichsfeldmarschall und Kunstmäszen*, Vienna 1982

Koser, R., 'Zur Geschichte der Schlacht von Torgau,' *Forschungen*, XIV, 1901

—*Geschichte Friedrichs des Grossen*, 4 vols, Stuttgart and Berlin 1921-5. New edition, Darmstadt 1963. Still holds its place as the standard narrative biography

Kotasek, Edith, *Feldmarschall Graf Lacy. Ein Leben für Österreichs Heer*, Horn 1956. A scholarly and sympathetic treatment

Kroener, Bernhard R., 'Wirtschaft und Rüstung der europäischen Grossmächte im Siebenjährigen Krieg. ‹berlegungen zu einem vergleichbaren Ansatz,' in Militärgeschichtliches Forschungsamt (ed), 1987 (below)

—Kroener (ed.),.'Europa im Zeitalter Friedrichs des Grossen: Wirtschaft, Gesellschaft, Kriege,' Militärgeschichtliches Forschungsamt, *Beiträge zur Militärgeschichte*, XXVI, Munich 1989

—'Die materiellen Grundlagen österreichischer und preussicher Kriegsanstrengungen 1756-1763, in Kroener (ed.), 1989, (above)

Kunisch, Johannes, 'Feldmarschall Loudon: Jugend und erste Kriegsdienste,' *Archiv für Österreichische Geschichte*, CXXVIII, No. 3, Vienna 1972

—*Der kleine Krieg. Studien zum Heerwesen des Absolutismus*, Wiesbaden 1973

—*Das Mirakel des Hauses Brandenburg. Studien zum Verhältnis von Kabinettspolitik und Kriegführung im Zeitalter des Siebenjährigen Krieges*, Munich and Vienna 1978

—*Staatsverfassung und Mächtepolitik: Zur Genese von Staatskonflikten im Zeitalter des Absolutismus*, Berlin 1979

—'Feldmarschall Loudon oder das Soldatenglück,' *Historische Zeitschrift*, CCXXXVI, Munich, 1983

—'Friedensidee und Kriegshandwerk im Zeitalter der Aufklärung, *Der Staat*, XXVII, Berlin 1988

—'Die grosse Allianz der Gegner Preussens im

Siebenjährigen Krieg,' in Kroener (ed.), 1989 (above)

Küntzel, Georg, 'Friedrich der Grosse am Ausgang des siebenjährigen Krieges und sein Bündnis mit Russland,' *Forschungen*, XIII, 1900

—*Fürst Kaunitz-Rittberg als Staatsmann*, Frankfurt am Main 1923

Lehmann, Max, *Friedrich der Grosse und der Ursprung des siebenjährigen Krieges*, Leipzig 1894

Lindner, Thomas, *Die Peripetie des siebenjährigen Krieges. Der Herbstfeldzug 1760 in Sachsen und der Winterfeldzug 1760/61 in Hessen*, Berlin 1993

Loehr, August Octavian, 'Die Finanzierung des Siebenjährigen Krieges,' *Numismatische Zeitschrift*, LVIII, Vienna 1925

Lotz, L., *Kriegsgerichtsprozesse des Siebenjährigen Kriges in Preussen. Untersuchungen zur Beurteilung militärischer Leistungen durch Friedrich II.*, Frankfurt am Main 1981

Marcus, H., *Friedrichs des Grossen literarische Propaganda in England*, Brunswick, Berlin and Hamburg 1927

Masslowski, D., *Der siebenjährige Krieg nach russischer Darstellung*, 3 vols, Berlin 1889-95

Mediger, Walther, *Moskaus Weg nach Europa. Der Aufstieg Russlands zum europäischen Machtstaat im Zeitalter Friedrichs des Grossen*, Brunswick 1952

Militärgeschichtliches Forschungsamt (ed.), 'Friedrich der Grosse und das Militärwesen seiner Zeit,' *Vorträge zur Militärgeschichte*, VIII, Herford and Bonn, 1987

Naude, Albert, 'Aus ungedruckten Memoiren der Brüder Friedrichs des Grossen. Die Entstehung des siebenjährigen Kriges und der General von Winterfeldt,' *Forschungen*, I, 1888

Neuhaus, H., 'Das Reich im Kampf gegen Friedrich den Grossen. Reichsarmee und Reichskriegsführung im Siebenjährigen Krieg,' in Kroener (ed.), 1989, (above)

Orlich, L., *Fürst Moritz von Anhalt-Dessau. Ein Beitrag zur Geschichte des siebenjärigen Krieges*, Berlin 1842

Pesendorfer, Franz, *Feldmarschall Loudon. Der Sieg und sein Preis*, Vienna 1989

Quandt, F., *Die Schlacht bei Lobositz (1 Oktober 1756)*, Charlottenburg 1909

Richter, A.F., *Historische Bemerkungen über den k.k. österreichischen Militärdienst in allen seinen Zweigen*, 2nd ed., Pressburg 1845

Roider, Karl Andrew, *Austria's Eastern Question*, Princeton 1982

Schieder, Theodor, *Friedrich der Grosse. Ein Königtum der Widersprüche*, Frankfurt am Main 1983

Schilling, Lothar, *Kaunitz und das Renversement des Alliances. Studien zur aussenpolitischen Konzeption Wenzel Antons von Kaunitz*, Berlin 1989. Important

Schmidchen, V., 'Der Einfluss der Technik auf die Kriegführung zur Zeit Friedrichs des Grossen,' in Militärgeschichtlichges Forschungsamt (ed.), 1987 (above)

Schmitt, Richard, *Prinz Heinrich von Preussen als Feldherr im siebenjährigen Kriege*, 2 vols, Greifswald 1885

Schnitter, H., 'Die Schlacht bei Torgau 1760,' *Militärgeschichte*, 1979 No. 2, Potsdam

Schwarze, Karl, *Der Siebenjärige Krieg in der zeitgenössischen deutschen Literatur. Kriegserleben und Kriegserlebnis in Schrifttum und Dichtung des 18. Jahrhunderts*, Berlin 1936

Schwerin, Dettlof, *Feldmarschall Schwerin. Ein Lebensbild aus Preussens grosser Zeit*, Berlin 1928

Shanahan, W.O., 'Enlightenment and War. Austro-Prussian Military Practice, 1760-1790,' in Rothenberg, Gunther Erich, and Király, B.K., Sugar, N. (eds.), *East Central European Society and War in the Pre-Revolutionary Eighteenth Century*, New York 1982

Szabo, Franz A., *Kaunitz and Enlightened Absolutism, 1753-1780*, Cambridge 1994

Teuber, Oscar, with illustrations by Ottenfeld, Rudolf, *Die Österreichsiche Armee von 1700 bis 1867*, 2 vols, Vienna 1895, reprinted Graz 1971. Sumptuously illustrated. The text is excellent, despite the lack of scholarly annotation

Thadden, Franz Lorenz, *Feldmarschall Daun. Maria Theresias grösster Feldherr*, Vienna and Munich 1967

Thüna, I., *Die Würzburger Hilfstruppen im Dienste Österreichs 1756-63*, Würzburg 1893, reprinted Buchholz-Sprötze 1996

Troeger, C., 'Die Schlacht bei Liegnitz,' *Mitteilungen des Geschichts- und Altertums-Vereins für die Stadt und das Fürstentum Liegnitz*, Liegnitz, vol for years 1904-5

Voggeneder, Margarete, *Ein tapfer Offizier des 18. Jahrhunderts. Das Lebenshild des Feldzeugmeisters Johann Sigismund Maguire*, thesis, Vienna 1941

Waddington, Richard, *La Guerre de Sept Ans*, 5 vols, Paris 1899-1914. Most important. As strong on the Austrian participation as on the other aspects

Walter, Friedrich, *Männer um Maria Theresia*, Vienna 1951

—'Feldmarschall Leopold Joseph Graf Daun und Feldmarschall Gideon Ernst Freiherr von Laudon,' *Gestalter der Geschicke Österreichs*, Hantsch, Hugo (ed.), Vienna 1962

Wilson, P.H., *German Armies. War and German Politics, 1648-1806*, London 1998

Winter, G., *Hans Joachim von Zieten*, 2 vols, Leizpig 1886. Impressive detail

Wrede, Alfons, completed by Semek, Anton, *Geschichte der k. und k. Wehrmacht. Die Regimenter, Corps, Branchen und Anstalten von 1618 bis Ende des XIX. Jahrhunderts*, 5 vols, Vienna 1898-1905. Indispensable source for details of Austrian regiments and military institutions

INDEX

Adams, John Quincy, 414
Adelsbach, 343, 351
Adelsbach, action 6 July 1762, 341
Albert of Sachsen-Teschen, Prince, 207, 259, 281, 300, 350, 357, 375, 395
Albert of Sachsen-Teschen, Prince, description 382
Alfson, Adolph Nicolaus, Colonel, 115
Alt-Schadow, 69
Altenberg, 390, 391
Althann, Michael Anton, *GFWM*. 37
Altliebe, 109, 111, 113, 117
Altvater-Gebirge, 415
Amadei, Carl, *GFWM*. 73, 131, 225, 321, 323, 325, 327, 390: biographical note, 420
Amelunxen, Lt. Colonel, 236
Andlau, Friedrich Joseph, general, 52
Angern, Johann Ludwig, *FML*. 143, 150, 230, 231, 301
Anhalt-Bernburg, Prussian general, 351
Anhalt-Dessau, Leopold of (the 'old Dessauer'), Prussian general, 66
Anhalt-Dessau, Moritz, Prussian *FM*. 41, 42, 43, 55, 63, 70, 91, 100, 140, 144, 405
Annaberg, 405
Ansbach, 393
Apraksin, Stepan Fedorovich, Russian *FM*. 98
Apsheron, Russian regiment, 170
d'Arberg, Charles Antoine, *FML*. 142, 143, 151
Arenberg, Charles-Marie-Raymond, Duke of, *FZM*. 41, 43, 65, 84, 131, 142, 143, 156, 193, 194, 195, 210, 290, 301: failings at Hochkirch, 145; conduct at Pretzsch, 195; hostile to Lacy, 306; biographical note, 420
Armfeldt, Fromhold, Swedish military attaché, 369
Army of Observation, 97
Asch, action 19 June 1758, 124
Aschersleben, Ebenreich Friedrich, Prussian *GM*. 196
August Wilhelm of Prussia, Prince, Prussian general, 23, 25, 59, 62, 410: disgrace of, 57; plight in 1757, 63
Augustus III, King of Poland, *see Augustus of Saxony*
Augustus of Saxony 18, 35, 339, 393, 404
Aussig, 19, 21, 157, 196, 405, 406
Austerlitz, 419
Austria, 12, 401
AUSTRIAN ARMY, 12, 37: first major test, 22; military reforms affirmed at Lobositz, 31; military reforms, bind Daun to Maria Theresa, 51; Daun enforces discipline, 94; breakdown in discipline late in 1759, 197; 1762 economies in the military establishment, 331, 335; reductions of 1762 create problems in Eastern defence, 333; preservation all-important, 395, 396

Artillery, 11, 12, 14, 15, 48: devastating at Lobositz, 25; Prussian opinion after Lobositz, 29; excels at Kolin, 55; at Leuthen, 86; its immobility blamed for Leuthen, 88; improved in 1758, 95; performs well at Domstadtl in 1759, 113; praise for Maxen, 203, 207, 209; well handled at Landeshut in 1760, 239; performs well at Torgau, 303; Daun's selection of the best positions,403
Cavalry, 12, 15: heavy cavalry horses, 15; Prussian opinion after Lobositz, 29; deployment at Kolin, 52; Hadik's instructions, 69; rebuilt for 1758 campaign, 95; horses, in good shape for 1758, 95; praised in 1758, 101; performs well at Domstadtl 1759, 113; Hadik's praise after Löthain, 190; instructions for Maxen, 199; do well at Torgau, 303; 1762 reductions, 332; in state of collapse 1762, 340; arrival of cossacks yet another disadvantage, 341; weakness shown before Adelsbach, 343; light cavalry, failure at Burkersdorf 1762, 362; weakness hinders relief of Schweidnitz 363; poor performance at Freiberg 1762, 387
Cuirassiers: carabinier companies, 142; 1762 reductions, 331; to be augmented for 1763 campaign, 392
Cuirassier Regiments:
Anhalt-Zerbst Cuirassiers [C25], **444**, 201, 205, 293, 368
Ansbach Cuirassiers [C33], **444**, 26, 142, 179: Carabiniers, 142
d'Ayasasa Cuirassiers [C20], **443**, see also Schmerzing CR
Birkenfeld Cuirassiers [C23], **444**, 14, see also Stampa CR
Brettlach Cuirassiers [C29], **444**, 26, 79, 80, 190, 200
Buccow Cuirassiers [Cii)], **445**, 142; Carabiniers, 142; see also Lucchesi CR
Carl Pálffy Cuirassiers [C8], see Pálffy CR
Cordua Cuirassiers [C14], **443**, 22, 26, 27, 29; see also O'Donnell CR
Daun, Benedict, Cuirassiers [C27], **444**, 189, 301, 337
Erzherzog Ferdinand Cuirassiers [C4], **442**, 293
Erzherzog Leopold Cuirassiers [C3], **442**, 87, 301, 346
Erzherzog Maximilian Cuirassiers [C4], **442**, see also Erherzog Ferdinand CR
Gelhay Cuirassiers [Ci)], **445**, 139, 144 see also de Ville CR
Lucchesi Cuirassiers [Cii)], **445**, 14, see also Buccow CR
Modena, Alt-, Cuirassiers [Ciii)], **445**, 66, 162, 163, 189, 201, 236

O'Donnell Cuirassiers [C14], **443**, 142, 143, 251, 299, 302; Carabiniers, 142
Pálffy Cuirassiers [C8], **443**, 337
Portugal Cuirassiers [C6], **442**, 302
Prinz Albert Cuirassiers [C22], see Sachsen-Teschen CR
Sachsen-Teschen Cuirassiers [C22], **444**, 236, 255
Schmerzing Cuirassiers [C20], **443**, 189, 195, 200, 255, 259, 366; Carabiniers, 190; see also d'Ayasasa CR
Serbelloni Cuirassiers [C12], **443**, 87, 142, 190, 194, 200, 287, 443
Stampa Cuirassiers [C23], **444**, 337, 339; see also Birkenfeld CR
Stampach Cuirassiers [C10], **443**, 22, 25, 26, 201, 287, 302, 381, 387
Trautmannsdorff Cuirassiers [C21], **443**, 79, 80
de Ville Cuirassiers [Ci)] **445**, 381, see also Gelhay Cuirassiers
Dragoons & Chevaulegers, mounted grenadiers, 142, 171; 1762 reductions, 331; reduced strengths in 1762, 335; to be augmented for 1763 campaign, 392; chevaulegers, 425
Dragoon/Chevauleger Regiments:
Althann Dragoons [Diii)], **447**, 236, 251
Batthyány Dragoons [D7], **445**, 285, 337, 339, 387
Darmstadt Dragoons, see Hessen-Darmstadt DR
Erzherzog Joseph Dragoons [D1], **445**, 22, 26, 76, 367
Hessen-Darmstadt Dragoons [D19], **446**, 144, 293, 420
Jung-Modena Dragoons [D13], see Modena, Jung-
Liechtenstein Dragoons [D6], **445**, 43, 170
de Ligne Dragoons [D31], **446**, 55, see also Löwenstein & St-Ignon Dragoons
Löwenstein Dragoons/Chevaulegers [D31]. **446**, 103, 110, 141, 170, 171, 238, 239 see also de Ligne & Saint-Ignon DR
Löwenstein, Jung-, Chevaulegers [Clx18], **447**
Kollowrat Dragoons [D37], **446**, 169, 170, 237, 255, 366
Modena, Jung-, Dragoons [D13], **446**, 86, 200, 203, 204. 426
Pfalz-Zweibrücken Chevaulegers, see Zweibrücken Dragoons
Sachsen-Gotha Dragoons or Chevaulegers [D28], **446**, 66, 86, 238, 239, 366
Saint-Ignon Dragoons or Chevaulegers [D31], **446**, 194, 205, 285, 287, 302, 343, 368
Savoyen Dragoons [D9], **446**, 302
Staff Dragoons (Staabs-Dragoner) **447**, 300: created by Lacy, 95; 1762 reductions, 331
Wallachian Grenz-Dragoner Regiment, 333
Württemberg Dragoons [D38], **447**, 103, 172, 351, 355
Zweibrücken Dragoons [D39], **447**, 110, 142, 144, 275, 387, 447
Hussars, 1762 reductions, 331; reduced strengths in 1762, 335; lack in 1762, 337; to be augmented for 1763, 392
Hussar Regiments:
Banal Grenz Hussars [GZHR3], **450**, 205
Baranyay Hussars [H30], **449**, 22, 275, 379, 388
Bethlen Hussars [H35], **449**, 172, 238, 239

Dessewffy Hussars [H34], **449**, 84, 103, 257, 388
Esterházy, Emmerich, Hussars [Hii)], **450**, see also Splényi Hussars
Esterházy Hussars [H24], **448**,123, 128, 147, 230, 267
Hadik Hussars [Hiii)], **450**, 22, 27, 205
Kaiser Hussars [H2], **448**, 128, 147, 221, 271, 295, 301
Kálnoky Hussars [H17], **448**, 170
Károly Hussars [H16], **448**, see also Pálffy Hussars
Nádasdy Hussars [H11], **448**, 84, 110, 123, 141, 169, 170, 236, 238, 239, 350, 355
Palatinal Hussars [H36], **449**, 188, 387
Pálffy Hussars [H16], **448**, 236, see also Károly Hussars
Splényi Hussars [Hii)], **450**, 78, 80, 124, 200, 205, 239
Széchenyi Hussars [H32], **449**, 79, 80, 180, 189, 197, 200, 257, 283, 312
Sclavonian Hussars [GZHR4], **450**, 205
Szekler Grenz-Husaren Regiment, **450**, 333
Grenadier Corps, 274, 279; impresses observers, 95; praised for Maxen, 209; perform well at Torgau, 303
Generals: Browne's selection of senior officers, 21; Montazet's opinion in 1757, 62; depress Daun, 129; losses not as damaging as the Prussians', 209
General Staff, 2, 424: lack of in 1757, 62; created by Lacy, 95; in action 1758, 101; in action at Maxen, 200, 209; below standard at Liegnitz, 259
Infantry, 11, 12, 15: Prussian opinion after Lobositz, 29; Montazet's opinion in 1757, 62; Hungarian aversion to infantry service, 64; Hadik's instructions, 69; praised in 1758, 101; Hadik's praise after Löthain, 190; 1762 reductions, 331; crippled by disease 1762, 340; to be augmented for 1763 campaign, 392
Infantry Regiments:
Andlau IR [57], **438**, 61, 113, 157, 241, 244, 438
Angern IR [49], **437**, 201, 244, 350, see also Kheul
d'Arberg IR [55] **438**, 345, 374, 375
Arenberg IR [21], **432,** 295, 301, 327, 385
Baden-Baden IR [23], **432**, 87, 167, 171, 350, 351
Baden-Durlach IR [27], **433**, 31, 92, 184, 201, 287, 291, 301, 350, 351
Batthyány IR [34], **434**, 64, 241
Bayreuth IR [41], **435**, 287, 291, 300, 301
Bethlen IR [52], **437**, 345
Botta IR [12], **430**, 55, 195, 298, 301, 366, 422
Browne IR [36], **434**, 31, 133, see also Kinsky & Tillier IRs
Carl Colloredo IR [40], see Colloredo, Jung-, IR
Carl Lothringen IR [3], **429**, 92, 144, 150, 230, 298, 301, 326, 339
Clerici IR [44], **436**, 137, 144, 196, 197, 201
Colloredo, Alt-, IR [20], **431**, 296, 299, 301
Colloredo, Jung- IR [40], **435**, 28, 287, 291
Daun, Heinrich, or Alt-Daun IR [45], **436**, 73, 297, see also O'Kelly IR
Daun, Leopold, IR [59], **438**, 73, 296, 298
Deutschmeister IR [4], **429**, 238
Erzherzog Carl IR [2] **428**, 53, 64, 86, 109, 136, 140, 287, 297, 298, 300, 301, 427
Erzherzog Ferdinand IR [2], **428**, 374, see also Erzherzog Carl IR
Esterházy, Joseph, IR [37], **434**, 28, 76, 137, 211

Esterházy, Nicolaus, IR [33], **434,** 28, 76, 144, 275, 337, 385, 389
Forgách IR [32], **433,** 366
Gaisruck IR [42], **435,** 150, 291, 301, 349
Gyulai IR [51], **437,** 124, 189, 201, 285, 287, 326, 339, 389
Haller IR [31], **433,** 58, 64, 86, 109, 110, 139, 201
Harrach IR [47], **436,** 296, 298, 301, 327
Harsch IR [50], **437,** 201, 295, 296
Heinrich Daun IR [45], see Daun, Heinrich, IR
Hildburghausen IR [8], **429,** 150, 287, 297, 429
Johann Pálffy IR [39], see Pálffy, Johann, IR
Joseph Esterházy IR [37], see Esterházy, Joseph, IR
Jung-Colloredo IR [40], see Colloredo, Jung-, IR
Kaiser IR [1], **428,** 28, 287, 290, 291, 301
Kheul IR [49], **437,** see also Angern IR
Kinsky IR [36], **434,** see also Browne & Tiller IRs
Kollowrat IR [17], **431,** 28, 31, 110, 111, 290, 291, 327
Königsegg IR [16],**431,** 157, 327, 374
Lacy IR [22], **432,** 297, 299
Leopold Daun IR [59], see Daun, Leopold, IR
Leopold Pálffy IR [19], see Pálffy, Leopold, IR
de Ligne IR [38], **435,** 131, 133, 150, 201, 297, 351, 355
Los Rios IR [9], **430,** 137, 140, 236, 430
Lothringen IR [3], *see Carl Lothringen IR*
Loudon IR [29], **433,** 238, 326, 327
Luzan IR [48], **436,** 73
Maguire IR [46], **436,** 86
Marschall IR [18], **431,** 189, 201, 233
Mercy IR [56], **438,** 291, 298, 351, 355
Neipperg IR [7], **429,** 92, 291, 301
Nicolaus Esterházy IR, see Esterházy, Nicolaus, IR
O'Kelly IR [45] **436,** 339, 385, 389, see also Daun, Heinrich, IR
Pálffy, Leopold, IR [19], **431,** 73, 236
Pálffy, Johann IR [39], **435,** 86, see also Preysach IR
Pallavicini IR [15] **431,** 337
Platz IR [43], **436,** 374
Preysach IR [39], **435,** 115, 236, see also Pálffy IR
Puebla IR [26], **432,** 290, 291
Sachsen-Gotha IR [30], **433,** 143
Salm IR [14], **430,** 244, 379, 385, 387
Simbschen IR [53], **437,** 115, 236, 241, 366
Sincère IR [54], **437,** 296, 301
Starhemberg IR [24] **432,** 111, 255, 374
Tillier IR [36], **434,** 201, 203, 263, 287, 291, 295, 300, see also Browne & Kinsky IRs
Waldeck (or Waldegg) IR [35] **434,** 255, 326, 350, 434
Wallis IR [11], **430,** 92, 350
Wied IR [28], **433,** 95, 201, 290, 298, 301, 387, 389
Wolfenbüttel, Alt2- IR [29], **433,** 110, 111, see also Loudon IR
Croatian Infantry, 12, 14, 19, 22: at Lobositz, 24; musketry, 56; success at Landeshut 1757, 63; Hadik's instructions, 69; strike gold at Gundersdorf, 107; possible Russian sympathies, 330; lack in 1762, 337
Grenzer (Croatian) Regiments:
Banal (or Banalist) Croats, **442,** 26, 35, 65, 211, 225, 379
Broder Croats, **441,** 297
Carlstädter Croats, **440,** 31, 35

Gradiscaner Croats, **441,** 426
Liccaner Croats, **440,** 143, 181, 184, 188, 215, 236, 425
Oguliner Croats, **440,** 181, 184, 188, 236
Ottocaner Croats, **440,** 37, 236
Peterwardeiner Croats, **441,** 62
Sclavonian Croats, 300
Szluiner Croats, **441,** 424
Warasdiner Croats, **441,** 110, 115, 188, 295
Warasdiner Creutzer Croats, **441,** 343, 345
Warasdiner St. Georger Croats, **441,** 107, 111, 345
Auxiliary Infantry Units
Anhalt-Zerbst Battalion, **440**
Blau-Würzburg IR, **440,** 80, 162, 163
Mainz IR, **440,** 181
Roth-Würzburg IR, **440,** 84, 86
Toscana IR, **440,** 100, 159, 244, 254
Würzburg IR, **440,** 386; see also Blau- & Roth-Wurzburg IR
Other Infantry Units:
Artillerie-Füsiliere (Artillery Fusiliers), **439**: raised in 1758, 95; 1762 reductions, 331; implications of reductions, 332
Belgiojoso's grenadier battalion, 350
Green Loudon Grenadiers, *see Grün-Loudon*
Grün-Loudon Grenadiers, **438,** 167, 171, 233, 251, 256, 350, 351, 355, 357
Jäger, 343, 366
Jägercorps Otto, 439
Loudon-Grenadiere, *see Grün-Loudon*
O'Donnell grenadier battalion 326
Staabs-Jäger, 295
Staff Infantry (Staabs-Infanterie), **439,** 300, 439: created by Lacy, 95; praised in 1758, 101; 1762 reductions, 331
Volontaires Silésiens, 439
Voluntaires Beck, 439
Other Units
Deutsche Artillerie, **451**
Feld-Artillerie Corps, **451**
Ingenieur Corps, **451**
Niederländische Artillerie, **451**
Pionier-Corps, **451**: raised by Lacy, 95; praised in 1758, 101; disbanded in 1762, 331
Pontoniers-Corps, **451**
Sappeurs-Corps, **451,** 241: 1762 reductions, 332
Officer corps, 13: helpless at Lobositz, 28; compared with Prussian at Lobositz, 28; losses at Breslau 1757; 76; losses replaced by 1759, 209
Troops: respect for Browne, 17; Prussian opinion after Lobositz, 29; Montazet's opinion in 1757, 62; deportment at Breslau in 1757, 76; conduct at Leuthen, 88; unusually high quality in 1759, 157
Austrian Finances, economies in war establishment 1762, 331, 332, 335; reductions of 1762 create problems in Eastern defence, 333
Austrian monarchy, 11
Austrian Netherlands, 13, 38, 39, 393, 420, 422
Austrian Silesia, 99, 157, 393, 418
d'Ayasasa, Joseph Carl, *FML.* 142, 175, 263, 285, 286, 287, 292, 297, 299, 303, 309 333, 335, 339: holds Daun's confidence, 151; portrait, 174; a great cavalryman,

263
d'Aynse, Louis, *FML*. 131, 137, 172, 201

Baboczay, *GFWM*. 70
Baden-Durlach, Christoph, *FZM*. 121, 128, 131, 143, 145, 147: failings at Hochkirch, 145
Balbi, Giovanni, Prussian colonel, 116
Bandemer, Josachim Christian, Prussian general, 336
Bärnkopp, Johann Wenzel, Major, 207
Barschdorf, 67
Barsewisch, Ernest Friedrich, Prussian lieutenant, 137, 141
Baruth, 411
battle tactics, see tactics
Bautzen 63, 129, 149, 177, 221, 247, 402, 411
Bavaria, 13
Bavarian auxiliary troops, 148; at Leuthen, 85
Bavarian Succession, War of, 423, 424
Bawr, Prussian colonel, 393
Bayreuth, 14, 80, 393
Beaulieu de Marconnay, Pierre-Jean, Major, 137, 200, 203
Bechard, Captain, 200
Bechardt, Joseph, Lt, Colonel, 241, 350
Beck, Philipp Levin, *FML*. 59, 75, 76, 81, 85, 89, 93, 151, 156, 171, 172, 173, 177, 196, 210, 219, 220, 238, 239, 250, 256, 282, 334, 335, 340, 366, 367, 368, 404: proposes breakout from Breslau, 90; Daun's opinion in 1761, 311; wins regard of the Russians, 322; biographical note, 420
Beeskow, 173
Belgiojoso, Anton, *GFWM*. 255
Belgrade: loss to Turks in 1739, 333; taken by Loudon in 1789, 425
Belleisle, French Marshal, 155
Belling, Wilhelm Sebastian, Prussian general, 157, 379
Berg, Russian general, 317, 321
Berggiesshübel, 197, 406
Berlin, 69, 175, 177, 267, 403, 408, 417, 418: raided by Hadik in 1757, 67
Bernis, Cardinal, 153
Berrenhauer, Prussian major, 326
Berthold, Major, 375
Bethlen, Joseph Adam, *GFWM*. 170, 171
Bevern, Duke of, Friedrich August, Prussian general 23, 28, 29, 42, 43, 52, 55, 64, 66, 67, 71, 74, 81, 334, 363, 366, 369, 410: abandons Breslau 1757, 76
Bibow, Christoph, *GFWM*. 301
Billwitz, skirmish 1 April 1761, 313
Bober, 417
Bögendorf, 263, 317, 345
Bögendorf, action 17 September 1760, 261
Bohemia, 14, 15, 18, 41, 42, 51, 57, 62, 71, 121, 196, 213, 307, 308, 390, 391, 400, 401, 403, 406, 412, 414, 415, 416, 418: plundered by Cossacks, 347
Böhmisch-Leipa, 410
Bolkenhain, 416
Bosfort, François, Colonel, 69, 194
Bott, Ignat, Captain, 259
Botta, Jacob, Marquis, Colonel, 190, 203, 238
Boxdorf, Camp of, 310, 408

Brady or MacBrady, Jakob Bernard, Captain, 357, 372, 373
Braganza, Johann Carl, Duke of, 161, 191, 213
Brandeis, 43, 46, 47
Brandenburg, 67, 69, 70, 165, 179, 265, 271, 276, 279, 302, 400, 401, 417
Braun, August Wilhelm, Prussian *GM*. 274
Braunau, 42, 343, 345, 347, 358, 414, 416
Brentano, Joseph, *FML*. 93, 182, 183, 188, 194, 195, 196, 197, 199, 201, 215, 230, 267, 268, 283, 305, 317, 321, 330, 340, 341, 343, 345, 347, 351, 358, 362, 366, 367, 368, 369: skill praised in 1762, 346; promising career cut short, 346; biographical note, 421
Breslau, 67, 71, 81, 83, 88, 89, 245, 247, 249, 261, 309, 402, 408, 416, 417: defence in 1757, 88; Siege, 116; Loudon checked there in 1760, 245
Breslau, 1757 Battle, 74, 403
Brettlach, Franz Johann, *GdC*. 79: good conduct at Rossbach, 80
Bretton, Colonel, 255
Brieg, 417
Brinken, Jakob, *GFWM*. 297, 300, 321
Britain, 212: British alliance with Prussia, 13
Broglie, Victor, French marshal, 79, 329, 423
Browne, Maximilian Ulysses, *FM*. 12, 15, 18, 19, 22, 25, 26, 28, 31, 35, 38, 41, 42, 43, 47, 48, 49, 405: character, 17; rapport with troops, 17; health, 21, 33, 41; admired by Frederick at Lobositz, 29; conduct at Lobositz, 31; conduct of Pirna expedition, 36; opinion of Kaunitz, 36; caught off guard, 42, 51; in pitiable state, 46; wounded at Prague, 48; caught up in the action, 49; death, 57; biographical note, 421
Browne, George, Russian general, 220
Browne, Joseph, Colonel,145
Browne, Philipp, *GFWM*. 51, 133
Brühl, Heinrich, Count, 21, 33, 34, 182
Brünn, 241, 401, 402, 419
Brunyan, Conrad Emanuel, Major, 143
Brüx, 42
Buccow, Adolph Nicolaus, *GdC*. 13, 101, 105, 113, 119, 142, 172, 193, 210, 223, 291, 301, 333, 334: reargard after Leuthen, 89; Daun's criticism, 119; picture, 120; hostile to Lacy, 306l biographical note, 421
Buchwalde, action 8 July 1759, 159
Budin, 19, 43, 157, 405
Budweis, 401
Bülow, Ferdinand Friedrich, *GFWM*. 117: defence of Liegnitz, 90
Bülow, Prussian general, 301
Bunzelwitz, camp of, 319, 403, 416: allies frustrated August - September 1761, 319
Bunzlau, 267: Circle of Bunzlau, 410
Burkersdorf. 302, 303, 347, 349, 350, 355, 356, 362
Burkersdorf, Battle 20/21 July 1762. 351
Bute, Lord, British minister, 331
Buttler, *FML*. 377, 379, 381, 382, 383, 385, 389: serving with Loudon in 1761, 311
Buturlin, Aleksandr Borisovich, Russian *FM*. 310, 317, 321, 404: character, 315

Caldwell, Sir James, 395
Caldwell, Tom, Colonel, 110, 221, 255, 259, 326, 327, 372
Campitelli, Joseph, *FML.* 124, 167, 178, 179, 233, 236, 377, 379, 381, 383, 385, 386, 391: distrusted by Loudon, 311
Caraccioli di S. Eramo, Luigi, praised for Hochkirch, 145
Caraffa, Colonel, 171
Caramelli, Carl, *FML.* 237, 241, 315: biographical note, 421
Carlsbad spa, 406
Carolath, 158
Carpathian mountains, 419
Catherine, Empress of Russia, 362, 392, 393: becomes Empress, 349
Champeaux, French attaché, 422
Charles, Archduke, 396
Charles of Lorraine, 12, 41, 46, 47, 49, 51, 56, 58, 59, 61, 64, 65, 67, 71, 74, 77, 81, 83, 85, 86, 87, 88, 90, 95, 117, 309, 416: not up to Browne's standard, 31; detained in Vienna, 41; takes command in Bohemia, 41; leaves the field at Prague, 49; caught off-guard, 51; question of command after Kolin, 56; humiliated by command arrangements, 57; praises the Croats in 1757, 63; provokes Frederick, 63; excuses for Leuthen. 87; blamed for Leuthen, 88; responsible for loss of Breslau, 90; protected by Francis Stephen, 93; biographical note, 421
Charles VI, Emperor, 401
Charlottenburg, 271
Chemnitz, 281, 312, 336, 405
Chernyshev, Zakhar Grigorevich, Russian general, 246, 249, 260, 265, 267, 268, 270, 316, 321, 323, 339, 340, 341, 343, 349, 358, 362: Plunkett's opinion, 220
Chlum, 414
Choiseul-Stainville, François, later Duc de Choiseul, French minister, 153, 155, 212, 329
Choiseul-Praslin, French ambassador, 193, 212, 329
Clam, Count, Major, 259
Clausewitz, 395
Clerici, Antonio Giorgio, *FML.* 49
Cogniazzo, Jacob, Captain, 81, 145, 265, 300, 317, 337, 404
Colberg, 155, 309, 328, 329
Colditz, 281
Collenbach, Heinrich Gabriel, Hofrat, 393
Collins de Ham, Chevalier, Major 343, 345
Colloredo, Carl Anton, FML. 65, 131, 142, 144
Conradsdorf, 379
Conti, Colonel, 177
corps de reserve, see tactics
Cosel, siege 1760, 307
Coswarem de Nyel, Wilhelm, Captain, 237
Cottbus, 273, 411
Crimean Tartars, *see Tartars*
Croatian Military Border, 424: collapsing under strain, 335
Crossen, 162,165
Cumberland, Duke of, British general, 77, 80
Cüstrin, 123, 417
Czestochowa, 180

Czettritz, Ernst Heinrich, Prussian general 219

Dahle stream, 410
Dalburg, Kriegs-Commissarius, 81
d'Alton, Richard, Chevalier, Major, 167, 355
Danube, 419
Danzig, 418
Daun, Leopold Joseph, 11, 12, 41, 51, 52, 53, 55, 59, 61, 62, 63, 71, 74, 81, 85, 86, 87, 88, 90, 99, 100, 101, 103, 113, 119, 123, 125, 126, 128, 129, 131, 144, 145, 147, 149, 151, 153, 155, 156, 157, 158, 159, 161, 162, 165, 171, 172, 175, 176, 177, 178, 179, 180, 183, 187, 191, 195, 196, 197, 199, 200, 203, 207, 209, 210, 213, 215, 216, 219, 220, 221, 223, 225, 228, 231, 240, 246, 247, 248, 249, 255, 256, 257, 258, 259, 260, 261, 265, 273, 281, 282, 283, 285, 287, 290, 291, 293, 296, 299, 300, 301, 302, 303, 305, 306, 308, 310, 312, 314, 317, 322, 328, 330, 331, 332, 335, 340, 341, 343, 345, 347, 349, 350, 351, 358, 362, 363, 366, 368, 369, 371, 373, 374, 375, 377, 382, 392, 393, 395, 396, 397, 403, 404, 407, 409, 414, 416: takes command in 1757, 51; forced to relieve Prague, 52; conduct of Kolin, 55; question of command after Kolin, 56; second in command, 57; responsible for loss of Breslau, 90; promotion to chief command, 93; his background, 94; enforces disicpline, 94; start of 1758 campaign, 98; Montazet's observations, 104; achievements in 1758, 117; accused of inaction,121; first blow to reputation, 127; humane behaviour, 144; conduct of 1758 campaign, 151; generalship, 151; literary style, 151; lethargy after Kunersdorf 1759, 173; drinking habits, 191; his headquarters, 191; loss of confidence in himself, 193; resolution at Maxen, 207; reverts to usual depression, 210; political betrayal of Lacy in 1760, 217; ambitious plan for Liegnitz 1760, 249; reputation harmed by Liegnitz, 258; relies on support of the Empress, 258; wounded at Torgau, 293; becomes an obstacle to rational planning, 309; reasons for his caution in 1761, 311; Russians offended, 315; support limited to Empress, 340; his devotion to the army as an institution, 396; appeal of the high ground, 403; biographical note, 422
Daun, Countess Josepha, promotes her husband's career, 151
De Vins, Lt. Colonel, 73, 167, 233, 325, 326, 327
Denmark, 330
Dessau, 283
Deutsch-Lodnitz, 101
Diericke, Caspar Christoph, Prussian *GM.* 61, 196, 210, 211
Dieringshofen, Prussian colonel, 156
Dieskau, Prussian colonel, 290
Dimic von Papilla, Lt. Colonel, 236
'Diplomatic Revolution', 13
Dippoldiswalde, 197, 310, 312, 390, 406, 409: skirmish 16 November 1759, 196
Dittersbach, skirmish 29 September 1762, 379
Dittmannsdorf, 345, 416
Döbeln, 312: action 2 October 1760, 279; action 12 May 1762, 336

Dohna, Prussian *GL.* 123, 158
Döllnitz stream, 410
Dombasle, Charles-François, *FML.* 201, 203, 290, 301, 400
Dommitzch, 193, 194
Dommitzscher-Heide, 284, 286
Domstadtl ambush, 105, 107, 109, 110, 113, 215, 231, 419
Dönhoff, Friedrich Ludwig, Colonel, 390
Donnerau, 362
Dorfhain, skirmish 29 September 1762, 379
Draskovich, Joseph, *FML.* 65, 116, 180, 216, 240, 241, 341: portrait, 218; condemned by Loudon as unfit for independent command, 219
Dresden, 125, 126, 127, 128, 149, 151, 175, 176, 178, 182, 184, 187, 191, 193, 196, 197, 209, 212, 213, 220, 221, 223, 225, 247, 273, 305, 312, 381, 382, 383, 390, 400, 402, 407, 408, 409: captured August 1759, 182: crisis there in July 1760, 223: Siege, 254
Driesen, Georg Wilhelm, Prussian *GL.* 87, 124: his attack at Leuthen, 170
Düben, 194, 195, 281: action 29 October 1760, 283
Dübener-Heide, 194, 195
Durlach, *see Baden-Durlach*

East Prussia, 211, 212, 308, 349
Eckartsberg, camp of, 62, 63, 64, 67, 84
Eger, 159, 402, 405
Eger river, 19, 21
Eghls, Jacob, Captain, 241
Eilenburg, 195, 282, 283
Elbe, 18, 19, 155, 184, 191, 193, 194, 196, 210, 213, 273, 282, 284, 302, 305, 306, 313, 382, 400, 402, 403, 405, 406, 408, 409, 413, 414
Elbsandstein-Gebirge, 405, 407
Electoral Prince of Saxony,, *see Friedrich Christian*
Elizabeth, Empress of Russia, 13, 38, 155, 308, 335, 397: death, 329, 330; death saves Frederick, 395
Ellrichshausen, Carl, *GFWM.* 233, 236: portrait, 237
Elmpt, Philipp, Major 326
Empire, troops, *see Reichsarmee*
Emsdorf, battle, 310
Engelhard, Baron, Major, 327
Erbach, Lt. Colone, 258
Erbisdorf, 379
Erfurt, 79
Erz-Gebirge, 156, 381, 401, 405, 406, 408, 410
Esterházy, Emmerich, *GFWM.* 119, 128, 271: biographical note, 422
Esterhazy, Nicolaus, Austrian diplomat, 38
Esterházy, Nicolaus, biographical note, 422
Esterházy, Paul, biographical note, 422
d'Estrées, French Marshal, 77, 93, 155
Eugen of Württemberg, Prussian general, *see Württemberg* 143
Eugene of Savoy, Prince, 162, 423, 425
Eulen-Gebirge, 240, 415

de Fabris, Dominik, Colonel, 200, 203, 207, 355: biographical note, 422
Falkenberg, 362
Fantoni, Colonel, 336

Ferdinand of Brunswick, Prussian general 21, 23, 28, 80, 153, 209, 251, 310, 329
de Feretti, Colonel, 197
Fermor, Villim Villimovich, Russian general, 98, 123, 265, 268: superseded in command, 162; affects indifference to Austrian gifts, 173
Ferraris, Joseph, Colonel, 263, 285, 287, 297
Fichtel-Gebirge, 405
Finck, Friedrich August, Prussian general, 158, 166, 169, 170, 176, 187, 188, 193, 194, 195, 196, 197, 199, 200, 201, 205, 209, 303: fine reputation, 199
Finckenstein, Karl Wilhelm, Prussian foreign minister, 302
Finckenstein, Prussian general, 293, 301
Finé, *GFWM.* 316: attaché to Russian army, 179
Fine-Bruch, 411
Finsterwalde, 411
Fläming waste, 411
Flemming, Karl Georg, Count, Saxon envoy, 210, 282
Forcade, Friedrich Wilhelm, Prussian general, 385, 389, 390
Forgách de Ghyimes, Ignaz, *FML.* 131, 136, 151
Forst, 172
Fouqué, Heinrich August, Prussian general, 89, 157, 158, 159, 172, 177, 220, 232, 233, 237, 238, 239, 403, 414, 415, 416: captured, 238; background, 239; captured correspondence, 332
France, 13, 38, 39, 308, 392: alliance under stress in 1758, 97; Kaunitz presses alliance, 97; secret treaties on 31 December 1758, 155; the French, 13, 310, 313; French Artillery, 423
Francis Stephen, Emperor, 12, 13, 14, 41, 57, 64, 87, 99, 147, 156, 157, 209, 210, 217, 258, 299, 313, 336, 339, 362, 391, 397, 421, 427: responsibility for Leuthen, 88; protects Charles of Lorraine, 93; favors de Ville, 99;
Franconia, 182, 391
Frankenstein, 316, 402, 416
Frankfurt-on-Oder, 159, 162, 163, 165, 166, 173, 175, 271, 418
Frauenstein, 389
Frederick II 'the Great', King of Prussia, 12, 13, 14, 18, 21, 22, 24, 25, 27, 31, 38, 41, 42, 43, 46, 49, 51, 52, 53, 55, 57, 59, 63, 64, 70, 71, 77, 79, 81, 83, 84, 85, 88, 89, 90, 99, 100, 101, 104, 105, 114, 115, 116, 118, 119, 121, 123, 125, 126, 127, 128, 129, 132, 143, 144, 147, 148, 151, 153, 156, 157, 158, 161, 162, 163, 165, 166, 167, 169, 170, 171, 172, 175, 176, 177, 178, 179, 180, 182, 183, 187, 191, 195, 196, 207, 209, 210, 212, 213, 215, 219, 220, 221, 225, 230, 231, 240, 245, 246, 247, 248, 250, 251, 256, 257, 259, 260, 261, 263, 265, 271, 273, 281, 282, 283, 285, 289, 290, 295, 298, 301, 302, 305, 306, 308, 309, 310, 315, 316, 317, 319, 322, 327, 328, 329, 331, 334, 341, 343, 345, 347, 349, 350, 351, 358, 362, 367, 369, 373, 382, 393, 394, 395, 397, 400, 401, 402, 403, 404, 408, 410, 414, 415, 416, 417, 418: starts the war, 11; demoralisation at Lobositz, 28; shaken at Lobositz, 29; poor management of Kolin, 55; enterprise in adversity 1758, 117; recovers from Hochkirch, 147; advantages over Daun, 151; Daun's summary of his strengths, 155; errs at Kunersdorf,

171; miracle of 1759, 175; his *General-Principia vom Kriege* captured, 219; Turk and Tartar schemes, 332; carelessness at Adelsbach, 345; stir created by arrival in Saxony November 1762, 390; on defensive after the war, 394; military advantages, 395; above the over-refined Austrian policy 396
Frederick William of Prussia, Prince, 329
Freiberg, 196, 210, 220, 302, 303, 311, 379, 381, 383, 386, 388, 390, 409
Freiberg, Battle 29 October 1762, 385, 392
Freiburg, 416
Freudenthal, Kozchina von. 181
Friedland. 410, 416, 418: action of 28 July 1759, 158
Friedrich August II, Elector of Saxony, *see Augustus of Saxony*
Friedrich Christian, Electoral Prince of Saxony, 41, 42
Friedrich Eugen of Württemberg, Prussian general, see *Württemberg*
Friedrich-Wilhelms Canal, 172, 175, 402, 417
Frierenberger, Joseph, Major, 233, 372, 375
Froideville, Franz, Prussian captain, 219

Gabel, 43, 177, 410: stormed in 1757, 58
Gabelentz, Prussian general, 347
Gabelkoffen, Sigmund, Colonel, 189
Gaisruck, Rudolph Carl, *FML*. 232, 233
Garmsdorf, skirmish 1 April 1761, 313
Gastheim, GFWM. 333
Gaudi, Prussian major, 298
Geissler, Lieutenant, 123
Gellert, Professor, 216
Gemmingen, Reinhard, *FML*. 156, 157, 159, 163, 190, 195: stand at the Pretzsch, 195
George II, King of Britain, 13, 39, 77, 80
Gersdorff, Prussian *GM*. 199, 203
Gessler, Prussian general, 26
Giannini, Ernst Friedrich, GFWM, 116, 239, 256, 321, 323, 327, 369, 374: loss of his staff work at Liegnitz, 259; character, 371; biographical note, 422
Gitschin, 410,412
Glatz, 38, 113, 155, 231, 232, 240, 246, 307, 340, 393, 394, 402, 413, 415: Siege of 1760, 240
Glatz, County of, 240, 305, 307, 308, 315, 316, 335, 339, 340, 346, 358, 362, 363, 368, 392, 393, 394, 403, 414, 416
Glatzer Schnee-Gebirge, 415
Gleim, Johann Wilhelm, poet. 76
Gleina. 221
Glogau. 81, 177, 179, 246, 260, 417
Goes, Major, 107
Goldberg, 248
Goldenöls, action 1 August 1759, 159
Golitsyn, Prince Aleksandr Mikhailovich, Russian general, 166
von der Goltz, Prussian general, 283, 305, 307, 310, 315, 316
Gorani, Lieutenant, 61, 91, 144, 150, 157, 215
Göritz, 165
Görlitz, 64, 148, 149, 178, 221, 247, 402, 411
Gottesberg, action 27 July 1759, 158

Gotzkowsky, Johann Ernst, Berlin merchant, 270
Gourcy, general,189
Graffenstein, Joseph, Major, 141, 170, 236, 238
Grechtler, Johann Georg, commissary, 317
Greiffenberg, action 26 March 1759, 156
Gribeauval de Vaquette, Jean Baptiste, *GFWM*. 148, 149, 210, 241, 307, 340, 373, 374: history, 371; biographical note, 423
Grolman, Georg Arnold, Prussian colonel,150
Gross-Giersdorf, 362
Gross-Jägersdorf, Russian victory, 67, 98
Gross-Nossen, 316
Gross-Sedlitz, 223, 230
Gross-Wisternitz, 103
Grulich, 415
Grumbach, Anton, Major, 279
Grumbkow, Philipp Wilhelm, Prussian general, 295, 296
Grünberg, action 18 August 1759, 172, 173
Guasco, Franz, *FML*. 73, 83, 228, 274, 341, 368, 369, 373, 374, 375, 411: at Dresden 1760, 223: not trusted by Daun, 371; biographical note, 423
Guasco, Peter, *GFWM*.: at Dresden 1760, 223; reputation as an adventurer, 371; biographical note, 423
Guben, 161, 172
Gundersdorf ambush, 105, 109, 419
Gyulai, Samuel, Colonel 337, 339

Habsburg monarchy 12
Hadik, Andreas, *GdC*. 25, 27, 31, 35, 37, 59, 69, 70, 79, 93, 124, 149, 150, 156, 158, 159, 161, 162, 163, 171, 172, 173, 175, 176, 187, 188, 189, 190, 196, 223, 267, 273, 276, 279, 310, 313, 346, 347, 358, 368, 375, 379, 381, 383, 390, 391, 402, 403, 411, 418: as commander of light forces, 67; raids Berlin 1757, 67; conduct of the Berlin raid, 70; plans typically elaborate, 124; accused by Serbelloni, 191; proposed for Saxon theatre, 339; commendable attitude 1762, 340; takes command in Saxony, 375; low expectations for his Saxon campaign, 377; portrait, 378; congratulated for September 1762 offensive, 379; achievement lauded in Vienna, 382; successes revive confidence in Vienna, 392; biographical note, 423
von der Hagen, Hugo, Prussian captain, 357, 358
Halberstadt, Bishopric of, 180
Halle, 18, 180, 181, 410
Haller von Hallerstein, Samuel, Colonel, 195
Hanáken people, 333
Hannig, *GFWM*. 336, 340
Hanover, Electorate of, 13, 77, 97, 153, 155, 212
Harrach, Franz, Count, Colonel, 290, 291
Harsch, Ferdinand Philipp, *FZM*. 93, 100, 119, 121, 128, 147, 148, 156, 158, 159, 161, 172, 416, 427: Daun's criticism, 119; character, 148; lost the confidence of Daun, 158
Hastenbeck, Battle of, 1757, 77
Haude, Gottfried Fabian, Austrian renegade , 332
Haugwitz, Friedrich Wilhelm, interior minister, 127, 404
Hauss, Friedrich Christian, Prussian *GM*. 181
Havel, 417, 418
Haydn, composer, 422

483

Heidersdorf, skirmish 20-21 June 1762, 341
Henry of Prussia, Prince, general, 66, 99, 121, 123, 125, 126, 156, 159, 161, 162, 165, 172, 173, 175, 178, 180, 182, 191, 193, 195, 196, 220, 245, 246, 249, 260, 284, 285, 302, 305, 310, 312, 313, 314, 319, 329, 335, 336, 375, 379, 381, 382, 383, 387, 389, 391, 392, 393, 403, 404, 410, 411: reaction to Kunersdorf, 176; the equal of Daun, 177; successful methods at Freiberg, 389
Herberstein, Johann Jacob, FML. 296, 301
Herrnstadt, bombarded 23 October 1759, 180
Hertzberg, Prussian diplomat, 393
Hesse-Cassel, 310, 313
Heuscheuer-Gebirge, 415
Hildburghausen, Joseph Friedrich, Prince of, 78, 79, 80, 92: character, 78; expendable after Rossbach 80; resigns 1758, 123; comment on Daun, 145; biographical note, 423
Hirschberg, 402, 415, 416
Hirschfeld, 215
Hoch-Giersdorf, action 17 September 1760, 261, 263: heights, 345
Hochkirch, 129, 151, 259, 303, 362, 396: Battle in 1758, 129, 402, 403; skirmish 24 July 1759, 159; imitated by Prince Henry in 1762, 383
Hoehe-Eule, 362
Hofkriegsrath, 14
Hohenfriedberg, 416
Hohenzollern, general, 85
Holitz, 103
Holstein-Gottorp, Prince Georg Ludwig, Prussian GL. 221, 287, 290, 292, 298
Hoyerswerda, action 25 September 1759, 178
Hubertusburg, peace talks, 393; Peace of, 394
Huff, Carl, Captain, 115
Hülsen, Johann Dietrich, Prussian general, 53, 196, 207, 223, 267, 268, 273, 275, 276, 279, 281, 283, 284, 287, 290, 298, 300, 302, 305, 313, 379, 382, 385, 389, 390, 404, 410: praised for Dobien in 1760, 279
Hungarians, aversion for infantry service, 64
Hungary, 13, 15, 419
Huyn, Major, 325

Iglau, 401
Irish, 13; in Austrian service, 220, 306
Isabella of Parma, 281
Iser Valley, 410, 412
Iser-Gebirge, 410
Itzenplitz, August Friedrich, Prussian GL. 149

Jablunka Pass, 333, 419
Jägerndorf, 418
Jahnus, Franz Maximilian, GFWM. 62, 93, 100, 119, 158, 159, 323, 326: Daun's criticism, 119; biographical note, 424
Jaromiersch, 413, 414
Jauer, 317, 416
Jauernicker-Fort, at Schweidnitz, 372, 373, 374, 375
Jaunericker-Flèche, at Schweidnitz, 372
Jekey, Major, 136
Johannesberg, skirmish 7 July 1762, 346

Joseph, Archduke, 281
Joseph II, Emperor, 216, 390, 394

Kaiserstrassen, 401
Kálnoky, FML. 119, 151: Daun's criticism, 119
Kamnitz, 31, 37
Kannacher, Prussian general, 66
Karl Eugen of Württemberg, Duke, 276, 281
Karl of Brandenburg-Schwedt, Prussian general, 107, 121, 285
Katzbach, 67, 81, 83, 246, 247, 248, 250, 251, 256, 257, 316, 417
Katzenhäuser, camp of, 310, 319, 379, 385, 390, 409
Kaunitz, Wenzel Anton, Staatscanzler, 13, 14, 18, 38, 39, 57, 64, 67, 71, 74, 77, 78, 92, 93, 95, 97, 121, 128, 129, 148, 153, 157, 179, 181, 210, 212, 213, 216, 232, 246, 258, 259, 260, 261, 265, 282, 308, 309, 312, 316, 322, 327, 330, 331, 334, 340, 362, 369, 382, 390, 392, 393, 394, 395, 396, 404, 409, 415, 419: aims, 8, 11; character, 12; not interested in military matters, 14; admiration of Browne, 36; visits Bohemian front in 1757, 51; considers Reichsarmee as dispensable, 80; opinion of Daun, 152; supports Loudon, 216, 258; reliance on Loudon in 1761, 315; on cost of the war, 331; as a careerist, 332; over-heated imagination, 333; source of gossip, 340; demands too much of the army, 395; too rational in his policy, 396
Keith, James Francis Edward, Prussian FM. 21, 23, 41, 51, 56, 57, 59, 100, 115, 119, 139, 144
Kemberg, 283
Kheul, Carl Gustav, FZM. 49
Khevenhüller, FM. 94
Khevenhüller-Metsch, Johann Joseph, Count, 88
Kinsky, Franz Ulrich, Prince, 55: biographical note, 424
Kinsky, Joseph, Colonel, 172, 233, 325, 355
Kleefeld, GFWM. 67, 125, 181, 182, 184, 199, 205, 219, 274, 279, 379, 381, 403: biographical note, 424
Klein-Waltersdorf, 385, 388
Kleist, 'Green', Prussian colonel, later GM. 162, 196, 207, 275, 283, 295, 313, 331
Kleist, Prussian general, 267, 268, 337, 377, 379, 387, 388, 390, 391
Kloster Marienstern, 221
Kloster-Wahlstatt, skirmish 15 August 1761, 317
Kloster-Zeven, Convention of, 78, 80
Kluck, Major, 374
Knobelsdorff, Prussian colonel, 244
Knobloch, Karl Gottfried, Prussian GM. 156, 349, 350, 355, 356, 358
Koch, Colonel, 300
Koch, Ignaz, 14, 191
Kokorchowa, Captain, 297
Kolin, 15, 17, 18, 19, 37, 51, 56, 57, 62, 78, 84, 92, 95, 303, 394, 401, 403: consequences, 394
Komotau, 42
Königgrätz, 17, 37, 52, 98, 119, 121, 128, 148, 151, 156, 157, 401, 403, 411, 414: plundered in 1762, 346
Königgrätz, battle of 1866, 394, 414
Königinhof, 414
Königreich-Wald, 414

Königsegg, Colonel, 157
Königsegg, Christian Moritz, *FZM*. 41, 42, 43, 46
Königstein, 18, 33, 34, 35, 407
Korbitz, action 21 September 1759, 187
Kossdorf, action 20 February 1760, 219
Kovatshovitz, Captain, 107
Kranich at Glatz, 241, 242
Krasnoshchekov, Don Cossack brigadier, 176
Kratzkau, 341
Krefeld, Battle, 153
Kremsier, 418
Kreytzen, Prussian general, 62
Krockow, Prussian general, 305
Krosigk, Christian Siegfried, Prussian *GM*. 55
Kunersdorf, 161, 176, 179, 187, 199, 211, 215, 303: Battle 12 August 1759, 165, 173, 403, 404
Kunzendorf, 307, 317: action 17 September 1760, 261, 420
Küster, Prussian chaplain, 132, 139, 140
Kyau, Friedrich Wilhelm, Prussian general, 25, 26

La Fontaine, Colonel, 188
Lacy, Franz Moritz, *FZM*. 21, 28, 37, 75, 83, 92, 99, 100, 101, 103, 119, 127, 131, 132, 142, 144, 145, 147, 151, 155, 157, 162, 173, 193, 200, 207, 209, 213, 220, 221, 223, 230, 247, 248, 250, 254, 255, 257, 258, 265, 267, 268, 270, 271, 281, 282, 284, 289, 295, 296, 299, 300, 301, 302, 305, 308, 316, 331, 332, 335, 340, 346, 347, 362, 366, 367, 368, 369, 395, 409, 410, 411, 415: warns of Fredrick's approach before Leuthen, 81; becomes chief of staff, 93; not ready for chief command, 93; creates a General Staff, 95; admirable staff work, 128; staff work at Hochkirch, 133; praised for Hochkirch, 145; Daun's opinion,177; plans for Maxen, 199; praised for Maxen, 209; supports plan for 1760 campaign, 215; compared to Loudon, 216; picture, 217; poorly for beginning of 1760 campaign, 217; Frederick claims he was relieved when Lacy was no longer chief of staff, 219 performs well in new role of corps commander, 231; baggage restored by Frederick, 248; army feels loss of his staff work, 259; expedition against Berlin 1760, 265; skill in independent command, 267; blame for Torgau, 303; does well in aftermath of Torgau, 306; troublesome attitude in 1761, 311; praises Loudon for Schweidnitz, 328; becoming sulky 1762, 340; biographical note, 424
Lacy, Wilhelm, Captain, 236, 326
Lacys, family, 17
Lafontaine, Major, 343
Lagos, battle 17 August 1759, 211
Lameth, Comte de, French attaché, 21, 36
Lampersdorf, skirmish 14 June 1762, 341
Landeshut, 157, 236, 402, 414, 416: action of 13 August 1757, 62; Battle of 23 June 1760, 221, 232, 246
Landeskrone, 65, 178
Lands-Berg, skirmish of 29 September 1762, 379; skirmish of 7 November 1762, 390
Langen, Simon v., Prussian major, 139, 142
Lanjus, Franz, Colonel, 101, 105, 107, 110, 163

Lanthieri, Friedrich, *FML*. 381: poor health a problem in 1761, 311
Lantingshausen, Swedish general, 212, 271
Laskupich, Captain, 62
Lattorf, Prussian general, 307
Lauban, 157, 162
Lausitzer-Gebirge, 410
Leckwitz, 273
Leeuven, Colonel, 290
Lefèbvre, Simon, Prussian engineer, 373
Lehwaldt, Prussian *FM*. 97
Leipzig, 61, 79, 150, 151, 181, 184, 281, 282, 402, 404, 408, 410: surrenders to Prussians 13 September 1759, 187
Leitmeritz, 21, 29, 157, 159, 390, 402, 405, 410
Leitmeritz, Circle of, 394, 405
Lemède, Major, 230
Lentulus, Rupert Scipio, Prussian *GM*. 317, 366, 367, 368
Leobschütz, skirmish 15 March 1760, 219
Lerchen-Berg, skirmish 5 November 1761, 312
Lessing, Gotthold Ephraim, dramatist, 246
Lestwitz, Johann Georg, Prussian *GL*. 76
Leubelfing, Baron Friedrich Christian, Colonel, 189
Leubus, 316, 416
Leuthen, 89, 90, 92, 97, 302, 396: Battle of 1757, 53, 84, 402, 416, 417; supply, crisis before the battle, 81; musket cartridges blamed for defeat, 88
Leutmannsdorf, 351, 355, 358
Lieberose, 175
Liechstenstein, Carl Joseph, *GFWM*. 301, 308, 327
Liechtenstein, Franz, 217
Liechtenstein, Prince Joseph Wenzel, *FM*. 11, 55, 213, 309, 325: his artillery tested at Lobositz, 31; supports Loudon's 1760 camp 217
Liechtenstein family, 418
Liegnitz, 67, 81, 83, 90, 92, 247, 248, 250, 251, 273, 396, 402, 417: Siege of 1757, 88, 117; Battle 15 August 1760, 114, 251
de Ligne, Charles Joseph, Prince, 66, 75, 76, 88, 116, 131, 133, 140, 145, 150, 194, 195, 203, 204, 207, 219, 221, 260, 270, 271, 287, 302, 305, 310, 345, 350, 355, 356, 427
Lindstedt, Prussian *GM*. 207
line of battle, four ranks changed to three, 85
line of battle, strung out at Leuthen, 88
Link, Major, 326, 327
Linz, 401
Littau, 418
Löbau, 410
Lobkowitz, Prince Joseph, *GFWM*. 25, 26, 189, 190, 209, 336
Lobositz, 21, 28, 31, 95, 157, 405, 406: Battle 1756, 22
Lohe river, 416, 417
Lorrainers, 427
Lossgallner, Johann, Colonel, 205, 368
Losy von Losenau, Anton, *GFWM*. 184, 188
Löthain, action 21 September 1759, 187
Lottum, Prussian general, 351, 355
Loudon, Gideon Ernst, *FZM*. 37, 51, 56, 80, 93, 100, 101, 105, 107, 109, 110, 113, 119, 121, 123, 127, 131, 133, 136, 139, 141, 142, 148, 156, 159, 161, 162, 163, 165,

485

166, 167, 170, 172, 173, 175, 178, 179, 180, 210, 213, 215, 217, 219, 220, 221, 231, 232, 239, 241, 245, 246, 247, 248, 250, 251, 255, 256, 258, 259, 260, 265, 282, 283, 307, 309, 311, 312, 315, 316, 317, 319, 321, 322, 323, 327, 328, 330, 331, 335, 340, 363, 369, 400, 404, 414, 415, 417, 419: good conduct at Rossbach, 80; at Gundersdorf, 105; fashionable reputation after Domstadtl, 113; promoted to *FML.*, 121; disappointing performance, 145; role at Kunersdorf, 171; tied to Russians in 1759, 175; Daun's opinion, 177; problems with the Russians, 179; portrait, 214; background, 215; character, 216; proves army was open to talent, 216; rise owed little to patronage, 216; generosity creates team spirit, 239; adamant on an attempt on Glatz 240; relies on support of Kaunitz, 258; unsuitable for supreme command, 258; style of generalship, 239; shows support for Lacy after Torgau, 306; unusually passive leadership in late 1760, 307; rapid rise, 315; criticised by Frederick, 316; awards for Schweidnitz, 328; eager to demonstrate goodwill, 340; biographical note, 425

Louis of Württemberg, Prince. 161, 191

Louis XV of France, 13, 38, 39, 78, 97, 153

Löwenberg, 177, 411

Löwenstein, Prince Christian Philipp, *GdC.* 18, 26, 75, 131, 143, 61, 285, 287, 311, 337, 339, 377, 379, 405: failings at Hochkirch, 145; 'a thoroughly bad individual', 306; strength of Austrian middle levels of command, 339; biographical note, 425

Lower Lusatia, 411, 418

Lower Silesia, 403, 415, 416, 417

Lübbenau, 411

Lucchesi, *GdC.* 21, 26, 31, 47, 48, 49, 76, 81, 84, 87: his counterattack at Leuthen, 87; blamed for Leuthen, 88; biographical note, 425

Luckau, 268, 408

Luckenwalde, 411

Ludwigsdorf, 358, 416

Lusatia, 62, 63, 119, 161, 215, 311, 312, 402, 408, 409, 411, 417

Luther, Martin, 14, 280

Luzinsky, Gabriel Georg, *FML.* 124, 181, 182, 220, 276, 279, 316, 321, 336, 381

Luzzeni, Johann, Lt. Colonel, 233, 236

Lynden (d'Aspremont-Lyden), Ferdinand Carl, *FM.* 333, 334

Maastricht, siege of 1748, 425

MacElligot, Peter, Colonel, 19, 37, 46

Magdeburg, 18, 276, 283, 402, 404, 410

Maguer, Lt. Colonel, 259

Maguire, Johann Sigismund, *FZM.* 31, 42, 43, 58, 59, 172, 182, 187, 188, 220, 223, 225, 228, 230, 231, 305, 336, 379, 383, 390, 408: description, 223; portrait, 229; rewarded for defence of Dresden, 231; biographical note, 425

Malachowsky, Prussian general, 237

Manstein, Christoph Hermann, Prussian *GM.* 56

Manteuffel, Prussian general, 349, 358

Marainville, attaché, 390, 427

March (Morava) river, 418

Marchfeld, 99, 418, 419

Maria Antonia, Electoral Princess of Saxony 191

Maria Theresa, Empress, 11, 14, 31, 38, 41, 51, 55, 56, 70, 74, 77, 83, 87, 90, 95, 100, 119, 121, 123, 125, 126, 128, 129, 145, 147, 153, 156, 157, 158, 161, 162, 171, 172, 178, 183, 191, 193, 195, 209, 212, 213, 215, 216, 219, 221, 249, 258, 260, 261, 265, 271, 273, 299, 302, 303, 306, 308, 309, 310, 312, 322, 330, 341, 362, 375, 390, 392, 393, 394, 396, 397, 409, 419, 422: her aims, 8, 11; connection with army,12; outraged at bureaucratic inertia, 15; chooses Charles of Lorraine for command, 57; responsibility for Leuthen 88; reaction to Leuthen, 89; changes mind about Charles of Lorraine, 93; requests Charles' resignation, 93; celebration for Hochkirch, 146; military disadvantages, 395; emotional attachment to Silesia, 404;

Marienberg, 405

Marklissa, camp of, 158, 161

Marlborough, Duke of, 162, 425

Marschall, biographical note 425

Marschall, Ernst Dietrich, *FZM.* 67, 93, 104, 115, 116, 117, 419: character, 114; saves Olmütz, 117; biographical note, 425

Martagne, Saxon major, 21

Martigny, *FML.* 390, 391

von der Marwitz, Prussian lieutenant, 139

Materni, *GFWM.* 51

Maxen, 197, 212, 239, 259, 303, 396: Battle 20 November 1759, 197, 403, 408

Mayern, Joseph Friedrich, *FML.* 381, 383, 387, 389

Mecklenburg, 308

Meissen, 125, 187, 188, 196, 212, 220, 231, 239, 247, 273, 305, 306, 312, 409: action 2-3 December 1759, 210; action 7 November 1760, 305

Melnik, 405

Mercy d'Argenteau, Philipp-Louis, *FML.* 339

Merseburg, 336

Mettau river, 413

Meyerinck, Dietrich, Prussian general, 33

Meyern, General, drunkenness, 311

Migazzi, Vincent, *GFWM.* 297, 300, 301: portrait, 304

Military Order of Maria Theresa, 56, 73, 312, 396

Minden, battle 1 August 1759, 211

Mitchell, Sir Andrew, British ambassador, 150, 231

Mittel-Gebirge, 19, 21, 22, 56, 405

Mittelwalde, 415

Modena, 422

Moldau, 405

Möllendorff, Prussian general, 300, 301, 349, 350, 351, 355, 358, 362

Monier, Captain, 389

Montalembert, Marc-René, French attaché, 173, 177, 179, 260

Montazet, Antoine-Marie, French attaché, 62, 104, 117, 127, 142, 147, 156, 177, 197, 213, 295, 299, 316, 362, 369, 377

Moravia, 14, 15, 17, 99, 100, 113, 117, 121, 333, 400, 403, 414, 416, 418

Moritz of Anhalt-Dessau, *see Anhalt-Dessau*

Morocz, Emmerich, *FML.* 59, 84
Mosel, Countess, 382
Mosel, Prussian colonel, 105
Moser, colonel, 162
Moys, 75: action in 1757, 65
Müffling, Christoph Philipp, *FML.* 188, 233
Müglitz stream, 126, 127, 199, 201, 223, 408
Mulde, 283, 302, 336, 383, 409
Müllrose, 165, 172
Münchow, Prussian colonel, 204
Münsterberg, 316, 416
Murray de Melgum, Joseph Jacob, Colonel, 140
Muskau, 176
Mylius, Anton, Lieutenant, 241

Nachod, 414
Nádasdy, Franz Leopold, *GdC.* 52, 53, 64, 65, 66, 71, 74, 75, 85, 87, 98: command at Leuthen, 84; responsibility for Leuthen, scapegoat, 87; conduct at Leuthen, 88; sacrificed, 93; biographical note, 425
Napoleon Bonaparte, 397
Naselli, *GFWM.* 233
Nassau-Usingen, Prince Friedrich August, Colonel, 276
Nauendorff, *FML.* 110, 233, 237, 238, 251, 255
Navarro, Count de, Colonel, 150
Neipperg, Wilhelm Reinhard, *FM.* 14, 41, 71, 116, 157, 210, 240, 335
Neisse, 128, 147, 148, 151, 179, 221, 402, 416, 417, 418
Neisse, Siege of 1758, 148
Nematz, Colonel, 62
Netolitzky, Baron Wenzel Kasimir, 56, 127
Neugebauer, Franz Ludwig, Major, 291
Neumarkt, 83
Neustadt, skirmish 15 March 1760 219
Neuwied, Prussian general, 341, 343, 346, 347, 349, 350, 351, 358, 362, 381, 383, 390
Nicolai, Württemberg Colonel, 86
Nieder-Gurig, 221
Nieder-Mülsen, action 9 April 1760, 219
Nimptsch, 374
Nollendorf, 197
Normann, Ernst, Major, 58, 59, 279
Nostitz, Georg, Saxon general, 83, 84
Nostitz, Countess Josepha, 94
Nugent, Jakob, *GFWM.* 220, 231: new chief of staff 1760, 230; captured outside Dresden, irreplaceable, 231; army feels loss of his staff work, 259; biographical note, 426
Nugent, Laval, *FM.* 426

d'O, Marquis, Prussian colonel, 241, 244
Ober Glogau, skirmish 15 March 1760, 219
Ober-Cunnersdorf, skirmish 29 September 1762, 379
Ober-Gundersdorf, 107
O'Brady, Captain, 357, 358
Oder, 98, 99, 123, 155, 156, 158, 159, 161, 165, 175, 179, 180, 215, 246, 265, 271, 400, 402, 416, 417
O'Donnell, Carl, *GdC.* 127, 131, 133, 136, 142, 143, 194, 195, 197, 200, 210, 213, 271, 293, 299, 305, 306, 366, 367, 368: praise for Hochkirch, 145; conduct at Pretzsch, 195; biographical note, 426
O'Donnell, Johann, *FML.* 86, 203, 204: biographical note, 426
O'Donnell, Heinrich, Major, 244, 323, 327
O'Kelly, Wilhelm, *FML.* 291, 298, 300, 301, 347, 350, 355, 356, 358, 362: Daun's opinion in 1761, 311; portrait, 359; biographical note, 426
Olmütz, 99, 100, 101, 104, 109, 113, 114, 115, 117, 241, 394, 401, 402, 418, 419: Defence in 1759, 114
Oross, Colonel, 140, 300
Osseg, 196
Ostritz, 215

Pabliczek, Joseph, chief miner, 373
Palasty, Colonel, 123
Pálffy, Nicolaus, Hungarian Hofcanzler, 333
Pálffy, Rudolph, *FML.* 163, 172, 199, 205
Paltzig, Battle 23 July 1759, 159, 161, 403
Panin, Petr Ivanovich, Russian general, 268
Panowski, *GFWM.* 368
Parchwitz, 81, 246, 250, 257, 259, 417
Pardubitz, 394, 401
Paschkopole Pass, 406
Paulmy, Marc-Pierre de Boyer de, French war minister, 78
Peace Congress in Augsburg, 308
Peitz, 273, 411: captured 25 August 1758, 123; surrender 27 August 1759, 175
Pellegrini, Carl, *FML.* 211, 213, 258, 290, 291, 300, 337
Pennavaire, Peter Ernst, Prussian general, 75
Perelli, Major, 300
Peter III, Emperor of Russia, 308, 335: new policies, 330; dethroned, 349
Peterswaldau, 416
Peterswalde, 42, 406
Petrovsky, Franz, Colonel, 197, 312
Pettoni, Johann Anton, *GFWM.* 293
Pfuhl, *GFWM.* 350
Piacenza, battle in 1745, 425
Piccolomini, Aeneas Joseph, *FZM.* 17, 37
Pirna 18, 21, 22, 124: Camp of, 126, 407
Pirna Expedition, 18, 31
Pitt, William, British prime minister, 97, 329, 331
de Piza, Franz, Major 65, 75
Platen, Prussian *GM.* 170, 322, 336
Plauen, 223, 310: Camp of, 390, 408, 409
Plauenscher Grund, position outside Dresden, 191, 213
Pless (Josephstadt), 413
Plunkett, Thomas, *FML.* 201, 260, 265: chosen as Austrian attaché to the Russians, 220; unacceptable to Loudon 1761 311
Podstadzty, Franz Carl, *FML.* 190, 233
Politz, 414
Pomerania, 302, 309
Pompadour, Madame de, 13, 78, 153, 220
Poniatowsky, Colonel, 295
Portugal, 392
Posen, 156, 161, 309
Posnikov, Russian major 326
Potsdam, 271, 273, 418

Prague, 41, 43, 46, 49, 51, 52, 55, 56, 57, 302, 347, 390, 394, 401, 402, 403, 405, 410, 412: Battle 1757, 46, 51, 53
Prerau, 109, 418
Pressburg, 419
Pretzch, action 29 October 1759, 194
Prussia, 8, 11, 12, 13, 39, 394
    Prussian Army: cavalry, 26; officers at Lobositz, 28; infantry, cuirassiers, dragoons & artillery augmented in 1762, 331; horse artillery a new development in this war, 367
Prussian Units
Infantry Regiments
Alt-Braunschweig IR [5], 142
Alt-Kleist IR [27], 24, 28
Alt-Schenckendorff IR [22], 298, 355
Anhalt-Bernburg IR [3], 211, 230, 254, 256, 263
Bevern IR [7], 24, 274, 388
Blanckensee IR [30], 24
Bornstedt IR [20], 140
Braun IR [37], 237, 238, 345
Braunschweig-Bevern IR [7], *see Bevern*
Bülow IR [46], 237, 239
Dohna IR [16], 298
Finck, Prussian regiment 204
Fouqué IR [33], 241
Garde IR [15], 140, 256, 257, 356
Goltz IR [24], 292
Grabow IR [47], 200, 203
Hauss IR [55], 211, 274
Hessen-Cassel IR [45], 205
Hülsen IR [21], 28, 205, 207
Itzenplitz IR [13], 25, 28, 139
Kanitz IR [2], 211
Knobloch IR [29], 205, 207
Kreytzen, Jung-, IR [28], 107
Lehwaldt IR [14], 205, 207
Lestwitz IR [31], 345
Manteuffel [17], 24, 65, 292
Markgraf Karl IR [19], 131, 139, 142, 188, 190, 358
Münchow IR [36], 28
Prinz Ferdinand IR [34], 64, 113, 256
Prinz Heinrich IR [35], 76, 263, 292, 366
Prinz Moritz IR [22], 355
Prinz von Preussen IR [18], 140, 357
Queiss IR [8], 292
Ramin IR [25], 355
Rebentisch IR [11], 205
Schenckendorff IR [9], 205, 207
Stutterheim, Alt-, IR [30], 292
Stutterheim, Jung-, IR [20], 292
Thile IR [38], 358
Tresckow IR [32], 65, 326
Wedel IR [26], 254
Wedel IR [29], 140
Zastrow IR [38], 200, 203, 323
Zieten IR [43], 345
Grenadier Battalions
Alt-Billerbeck Grenadiers, 107
Anhalt Grenadiers, 65
Bähr Grenadiers, 61

Benckendorff Grenadiers, 65, 200, 203, 204
Billerbeck Grenadiers, 200, 203
Burgsdorff Grenadiers, 274
Dieringshofen grenadiers, 65
Diezelsky grenadiers, 62
Grenadier-Garde [6], 140
Kalckstein grenadiers, 337
Kleist grenadiers (St.Gb) [43], 203
Kreytzen grenadiers, 62
Lossow Grenadiers, 337, 388
Natalis grenadiers, 337
Nimschöffsky Grenadiers, 241
Rothenburg grenadiers, 358
Stechow Grenadiers, 255
Unruh Grenadiers [2], 143, 241, 244
Willemy grenadiers, 201, 204
Free Battalions
Angelelli free battalion, 75, 128, 131
Below volunteers, 238
Courbière free battalion, 225
Hülsen free battalion, 349
Le Noble free battalion, 64, 101, 312, 388
Lüderitz free battalion, 238, 312
Mellin free battalion, 233
Quintius Icilius free battalion, 312
Salenmon free battalion, 101, 205, 295
Schach free battalion, 388
Verger free battalion, 128, 131
Wunsch free battalion, 196, 343, 345
Cuirassier Regiments
Garde du Corps [C13], 25, 26, 27, 86, 140, 141
Gensd'armes [C10], 25, 86, 141, 292
Kyau Cuirassiers [C12], 99, 111
Leib-Carabiniers [C11], 140
Leibregiment [C3], 254
Markgraf Friedrich Cuirassiers [C5], 254, 291
Prinz Heinrich Cuirassiers [C2], 263, 367
Prinz von Preussen [C2], 25
Rochow (Seydlitz) Cuirassiers, 26, 55, 103
Schmettau Cuirassiers [C4], 111, 219, 292, 388
Schönaich Cuirassiers [C9], 27
Seydlitz Cuirassiers [C8], 254, 256, 263, 367
Spaen Cuirassiers [C12], 291, 292, 367
Dragoon Regiments
Alt-Platen Dragoons [D8], 169, 237
Bayreuth Dragoons [D5], 25, 26, 103, 219, 291, 292
Czettritz Dragoons [D4], 139, 257, 317, 367
Finckenstein Dragoons [D10], 317, 346
Krockow Dragoons [D2], 162, 254, 256
Menicke Dragoons [D3], 169
Normann Dragoons [D1], 139, 257
Jung-Platen Dragoons [D11], 194, 205, 292
Plettenberg Dragoons [D7], 185, 292
Schorlemer Dragoons [D6], 275
Zastrow Dragoons [D1], 343
Hussar Regiments
Belling Hussars [H9], 150, 169, 337, 388
Brown Werner Hussars [H6], *see Werner Hussars*
Bosniaken, 343, 346, 367
Gersdorff Hussars [H7], 195, 201, 203, 205, 346

488

Kleist Hussars [H1], 169
Lossow Hussars [H5], 343
Möhring Hussars [H3], 101, 177, 195, 230, 248, 257, 305
Puttkamer Hussars [H4], 33, 110, 169
Székely Hussars [H1], 27, 37
Werner Hussars [H6], 111, 367, 368
Württemberg Dragoons [D12], 194, 201, 203, 204, 292, 368
Zieten Hussars [H2], 111, 133, 139, 251, 254, 261, 287, 289, 291, 292
Other units
Grolman garrison battalion,182
Jäger, 225, 349
Kleist Freicorps, 169, 196, 295, 331
Land-Battalion of de Rege, 172
Lange garrison regiment [Gar7], 69
Quadt garrison regiment [Gar 8], 240, 244
Puebla, Anton, Count, 14
Puebla, general 52
Puttkamer, Nicolaus Lorenz, Prussian general, 58, 59, 111, 169

Quadt, Prussian colonel, 244
Quebec, capture 18 September 1759, 211
Queiss river, 157, 158, 161, 175, 221, 417
Quiberon, battle 20 November 1759, 211

Radeberg, 221
Radetzky, 396
Radicati, Alois, *FML.* 25
Radis, action 27 October 1760, 283
Ragip Pasha, Turkish grand vizier, 333
Ramin, Prussian general, 349, 358
Rath, Otto Heinrich, Colonel, 113
Ravizza, Anton, Major, 142
Rebentisch, Johann Karl, Prussian general, 109, 188, 190, 193, 194, 199, 207
Rehbach, Maximilain, *GFWM.* 189
Reichenbach, 302, 362, 363, 369, 416: action of 16 August 1762, 363
Reichenberg, 58, 158, 410: action of 21 April 1757, 42
Reichsarmee, 77, 150, 151, 155, 156, 176, 180, 181, 182, 187, 188, 193, 210, 220, 221, 231, 265, 267, 271, 273, 274, 276, 279, 281, 282, 283, 305, 312, 313, 336, 377, 379, 381, 389, 390, 391, 392, 400, 405, 408, 424, 425, 427: creation of, 38; nature of, 78; Kaunitz's opinion, 78; rebuilt in 1758, 123; by convention on the left of the line, 125; failure before Dresden in 1758, 149; quality of troops, 223; finest action of the war at Freiberg, 387, 389; requires Austrian support, 409
***Reichs* Units**
Baden-Baden IR, 386, 389
Bayreuth Cuirassiers, 387
Chur Trier regiment, see Trier IR
Chur-Mainz Dragoons, 379
Chur-Mainz IR, 379, 387
Chur-Trier IR, 386
Cologne contingent, 313
Effern, Palatinate IR, 181
Hessen-Darmstadt battalion, 80, 185
Hohenzollern Cuirassiers, 190, 275, 387
Kur-Bayern auxiliary regiment, 115
Rodt (Swabian) IR, 386, 389
Trier IR, 184, 386, 389
Reichstruppen, 404; fight unexpectedly well at Freiberg, 386
Reinerz, 415
Reinhardt, *GFWM.* 157
Reinharz, 195
Reischach, Colonel, 301
Reitzenstein, Prussian general, 346, 350
Retzow, Prussian general, 128, 129, 131, 143
Reussendorf, 345
von Rexin, Carl Adolph , pseudonym, 332
Rhédy, Colonel Johann, 73, 139
Richelieu, French Marshal, 77, 78, 79
Ried, Joseph Heinrich, *GFWM.* 70, 180, 181, 185, 199, 205, 223, 225, 228, 256, 257, 261, 263, 283, 284, 285, 286, 287, 292, 297, 300, 312, 377, 379: biographical note, 426
Riesa, 410
Riesen-Gebirge, 158, 161, 414
Riesse, Franz Carl, Colonel, 111, 211
Ripke, Ludwig, Major, 238
Ripp, Prussian Major, 325
Riverson, French siege expert, 71
Rochepine, Bechade de, *GFWM.* 114
Rochow, Prussian general, 69, 70, 270
Rodt, Aton Friedrich, *FML.* 383, 386
Romann, Württemberg general, 86
Ronneburg, near-action 5 September 1761, 313
Rossbach, Battle in 1757, 74, 79, 97: Campaign, 77
Rosswein, skirmish 5 November 1761, 312
Rothschütz, Georg Sigmund, Colonel, 299, 300, 302
Rouvroy, Captain, 107, 111
Rouvroy, Johann Theodor, Colonel, 239, 241, 256, 325, 326
Rüdt von Callenberg, Captain, 190
Rumburg, 410
Rummel, Colonel Joseph, 73
Russia, 12, 13, 38, 39, 212, 330, 332, 392: steadfast support in 1759, 155
Russian Army, 13, 157, 158, 161, 211, 213, 219, 220, 246, 249, 265, 302, 309, 310, 316: little regarded in 1758, 98; praised by Maria Theresa for Zorndorf, 123; changes in high command, 161; and Daun in 1759, 173; army hindered by long supply line, 403
Russian Units
Belosersk regiment, 167
Cossacks as Prussian allies, 341, 346: raid Bohemia in 1762, 346
Don Cossacks, 170
Kazan regiment, 170
Nizhegorod regiment, 167
Novgorod regiment, 167
Observation Corps, 166, 167, 171
Perm regiment, 170
Pskov regiment, 170
Rostov regiment, 170

St. Petersburg regiment, 167
Second Grenadier Regiment, 167
Vologda regiment, 170
Vyborg regiment, 170
Rutowsky, Friedrich Augustus, Saxon *FM.* 34, 35

Saale river, 78, 79, 313, 410
Saalfeld, action 26 March 1759, 156
Saaz, 157
Sachsen-Gotha, territory of, 80
Sagan, 159, 161, 176
Saint-André, *GFWM.* 184
Saint-Genois, Baron, Captain, 163
Saint-Germain, French general, 80
Saint-Germain, French light corps, 80
Saint-Ignon, Joseph, *GFWM.* 103, 105, 233, 236, 366: praise for Hochkirch, 145
St. Petersburg, Treaty of, 38
Salburg, Franz Ludwig, 15
Saldern, Friedrich Christoph, Prussian general, 142, 254, 295, 296, 297
Saltykov, Petr Semovich, Russian general, 163, 165, 166, 167, 170, 172, 173, 175, 176, 177, 179, 180, 246, 249, 271, 404: character, 162; role at Kunersdorf, 171; Plunkett's description, 220
Sandershausen, action, 153
Sans Souci, 271
Saxony, 11, 13, 14, 18, 38, 151, 153, 155, 181, 191, 210, 246, 273, 279, 282, 302, 307, 308, 312, 313, 392, 393, 394, 395, 400, 401, 402, 403, 408, 409, 410, 416: importance, 183
Saxon Army, run-down state, 33; troops surrendered, 35; untrustworthy, 36
Saxon Units
Carabiniers Gardes, 385
Chevaulegers, 55, 66, 83, 84, 381, 387
Prinz Karl Chevaulegers, 103, 110
Saxon-Polish Rudnicki Uhlans, 230
Saxon-Polish Uhlans, 103, 267, 271
Schaffgotsch, Catholic Bishop of Breslau, 77
Schallenberg, *FML.* 190
Schandau, 33
Schenckendorff, Prussian general, 237, 238, 239
Schildau, Friedrich August, *GM.* 193
Schlettau, fortified position of, 310
Schmettau, Karl Christoph, Prussian *GL.* 24, 149, 150, 183, 225
Schmiedeberg, 416
Schmirschitz, 414
Schmottseiffen, camp of, 158, 161, 162, 172, 173, 176, 213, 247
Schorlemer, Prussian general, 170
Schreckenstein, 19, 406
Schuller, Colonel, 333
Schurz, Camp of, 157, 161
Schwachheim, Joseph Peter, 333
Schwarze-Elster, 411
Schweidnitz, 63, 71, 89, 97, 113, 260, 261, 307, 317, 319, 322, 328, 329, 340, 341, 345, 358, 362, 363, 368, 371, 374, 375, 392, 402, 413, 414, 416, 417: stormed 1757, 70; Siege 92, 116; loss in 1758, 98; stormed 1 October 1761, 323, 404; defence August-October 1762, 369
Schweidnitzer-Wasser (Weistritz), 83, 417
Schwerin, Prussian *FM.* 31, 37, 42, 43, 46, 47, 48, 53, 66, 410: slain at Prague, 48
Scots in Austrian service, 140
Sebastiansberg, action 31 July 1758, 125; action 15 April 1759, 157; pass of, 196
Sedlitz, palace, 408
Seeger, Captain 275
Seeger, Johann, Major, 275, 383, 387
Semsey, Major, 239
Serbelloni, *FM.* 12, 42, 43, 84, 87, 123, 125, 156, 180, 187, 188, 190, 273, 309, 336, 337: inactivity in 1757, 52; comment on Lucchesi, 88; obstinate, 125; accusations against Hadik, 191; takes command of *Reichsarmee* 1761, 313; wants to abandon Saxony 1762, 336; army command reveals his eccentricity 1762, 336; inactivity, 339; replaced in Saxon command, 375; complains of his treatment, 377; biographical note, 426
Seriman, Paul, Colonel 203
Sers, Prussian general, 74
Seydlitz, Friedrich Wilhelm, Prussian general, 26, 27, 55, 80, 169, 313, 337, 339, 379, 387, 388, 405
Sholabov, Russian major, 330
Shuvalov, Piotr Ivanovich, Russian *FM.* 166
siege warfare, an Austrian weakness, 61; Austrian incompetence at Schweidnitz, 71
Silberberg, 240, 316, 363, 368, 415, 416: pass, 339
Silesia 11, 38, 42, 67, 71, 77, 155, 177, 178, 221, 240, 246, 281, 302, 307, 308, 309, 310, 335, 343, 392, 395, 400, 401, 402, 403, 404, 408, 409, 414, 416, 417, 418, 422
Silesian plain, 316
Simbschen, Joseph Carl, *GFWM.* 366
Simbschen, Major, 116
Sincère, Claudius, *FZM.* 52, 197, 200, 210, 290, 297, 301: character, 199; a reasonable officer, 306; biographical note, 427
Siskovics, Joseph, *GFWM.* 105, 109, 110, 113, 129, 200, 203, 259, 419: description, 109; biographical note, 427
Somogy, Prussian major, 333
Sonnenstein, 124, 125, 126: castle, 407
Soubise, Charles de Rohan, Prince de, French Marshal, 78, 79, 80, 153, 310, 329, 424: character, 78
de Souhay, Philipp, Colonel, 76
Spain, 392
Spallard, Colonel, 75
Spandau, 270, 271, 418: citadel, 70
Spittel-Wald, 385
Sprecher, Salomon, *FML.* 75, 77: defence of Breslau 89, 90; responsibility for loss of Breslau, 90
Spree, 176, 221, 268, 270, 411, 417, 418
Spree-Wald, 67, 70, 411
Spremberg, 163, 177
Springer, Colonel, Russian attaché, 127, 157
Stain, Carl Leopold, Colonel 298
Stainville, Colonel, 103
Stainville, *see Choiseul*
Stampa, Cajetan, *FML.* 191, 293: praise at Hochkirch, 145; poor health a problem in 1761, 311

Stampach Carl, *GdC*. 48, 201, 203, 205
Starhemberg, Count, diplomat, 93
Starhemberg, Ludwig, General, 52, 85
Staupitz, action 2 November 1760, 283
Stein-Seiffersdorf, 416
Steinau, 251
Steinmetz, Lt. Colonel, 374, 375
Steinmetz, Nikolaus, engineer captain, 241
Sternberg, 418
Stettin, 155
Stolberg-Gedern, Christian Carl, Prince, *FML*. 181, 182, 199, 205, 274, 275, 336, 379, 381, 383, 387, 388, 389, 391: character, 377; verdict after Freiberg, 390
Stolpen, 11, 126, 127, 128, 149: castle, 382, 408
Strachwitz, 317
Stralsund, 97
Strasser von Waldegg, Colonel, 167
Strehla, 193, 273, 276, 410: Camp of, 193; Battle 20 August 1760, 274
Striegau, 416
Stutterheim, Alt-, Joachim Friedrich, Prussian *GM*. 385, 388
Stutterheim, Jung-, Otto Ludwig, Prussian *GM*. 220, 265, 385, 389
Sulkowsky, Prince, *GFWM*. 124, 156
Sweden, 13, 38, 39, 392, 394: still committed to alliance in 1759, 155
Swedes, 220, 265, 271, 310, 329: role in 1758, 97: inactivity, 212
Swedish Pomerania, 310
Széchenyi, Anton, *GFWM*. 79: good conduct at Rossbach, 80

tactics: unconventional battle array at Kolin, 52; linear tactics, 55; at Moys in 1757, 65; Prussian, 125; entirely novel at Hochkirch, 131; adapting to the new methods, 145; use of musketry by cavalry, 190; abandonment of traditional linear methods, 199; horse artillery a new development in this war, 367; plan of attack by converging forces, 259; multiple columns in the new Austrian style, 274: **use of the *corps de reserve*.** 52, 55; use at Kolin, 53; committed rashly at Kolin, 55; use at Eckartsberg, 63; at Moys in 1757, 65; brilliantly handled by Wied at Breslau, 76; placement at Leuthen, 84; use at Leuthen, 85; nucleus of strike force at Maxen, 197; at Strehla, 274; position at Torgau, 285
Tartars, 332, 333, 334, 363, 368, 419: Khan, 332
Tauentzien, Prussian general, 245, 372, 373, 375
Tempelhof, 268, 270
Tempelhof, Georg Friedrich, Prussian gunner, 137
Teplitz, 19, 21, 124, 196, 197, 391, 405, 406: action 2 August 1762, 337
Tetschen, 19, 37, 405
Tettenborn, Prussian general, 295, 296
Tharandter-Wald, 207, 220, 379, 409
Theillières, Franz, Baron, 244
Theresienstadt, fortress, 405
Thiennes, Colonel, 141
Thun, Alter Feuerwerker Georg Joseph, 69

Thürheim, *FML*. 98
Tillier, Johann Anton, *FML*. 140, 147, 155, 157, 217: praise for Hochkirch, 145; portrait, 154
Tillier, Joseph Maximilian, Colonel, 225, 345
Tokay, Russian vineyards 330
Torgau, 150, 151, 181, 184, 193, 196, 231, 276, 282, 283, 305, 402, 404, 410: taken by Prussians 30 August 1759, 184; Battle of 8 September 1759, 185; Austrian delay there August 1760, 276; Battle of 3 November 1760, 284; 1760 battle compared to Kolin, 55
Török, Johann Andreas, Colonel, 157, 387
Totleben, Russian general, 170, 247, 265, 267, 268, 270, 310: shady reputation, 267
Toulongeon, Marquis, 302
transport, Austrian, 15
Transylvania, 15, 333, 419, 421, 422
Traun, *FM*. 94
Trautenau, 158, 382, 414
Trebbin, 271
Trenck, 'Pandour', Franz von der, Colonel, 215, 425
Tresckow, Joachim Friedrich, Prussian *GL*. 55, 98, 148
Tresckow, *Reichs* general, 387
Triebel, 173
Triebisch 187, 191, 196, 305, 310, 314, 379, 382, 409, 410
Troppau, 105, 107, 113, 418
Turkey, 392: Turks, 332, 333, 363, 368
Turnau, 412

Ujházy, Ferdinand, Colonel, 69, 70
Upper Lusatia, 161, 402, 410
Upper Silesia, 308, 402, 419
d'Ursel, Charles Albert, *FML*. 131, 142, 143

Valentiniani, Franz, Colonel, 137
Vecsey, *GFWM*. 69, 188, 189, 279, 388
Vela, Franz, Colonel, 31
Vela, Stephan, *GFWM*. 156, 159, 178, 182
Veldner, Baron, captain of Slavonians, 144
Vellinghausen, battle in 1761, 329
Verri, Pietro, Captain, 161, 191, 207
Versailles, First Treaty of, 13, 38, 155
Versailles, Second Treaty of, 38
Vettesz, Major Johann, 53, 55, 57, 207
Vienna, 99, 114, 401, 403, 412, 418, 419
de Ville, Charles, *GdC*. 99, 115, 128, 156, 157, 158, 159, 161, 177, 419: character, 99, 158; retired, 216; biographical note, 427
Vistula, 155, 179, 310, 315, 329, 417
Vitzthum, general, 190
Vogelsang, *GFWM*. 241
Voghera, August, Marchese, 79
Voith von Salzburg, Carl, Colonel, 110, 238

Waldenburg, 261, 369
Waldenburger-Gebirge, 416
Waldhütter, Michael, Lieutenant, 374
Waldow, 176
Wallis, Oliver, Colonel, 238, 326
Walther von Waldenau, *GFWM*. 295, 296, 301
Warburg, battle of, 310

Warkotsch, Heinrich Gottlob, Baron, 328
Warnery, Prussian colonel, 33, 35
Warsaw, 418
Wartensleben, *GFWM.* 145, 336
Wartha, 240, 316, 339, 340, 363, 368, 415, 416
Warthe 417
Wedel, Karl Heinrich, Prussian *GL.* 150, 159, 161, 194, 195, 225
Weidt, Lieutenant, traitor at Liegnitz, 251
Weiss, Gottlieb, Colonel, 137
Weiss, Lt. Colonel, 346
Weisse Elster, 409
Weisseritz stream, 408
Weissig, heights of, 228
Weistritz valley, 349, 351, 355, 356, 358
Werner, Prussian general, 107, 109, 310, 331, 333, 334, 363, 419
Westminster, Convention of, 13
Wied, *FML.* 18, 52, 53, 55, 76, 147, 148, 297, 377: a reasonable officer, 306; biographical note, 427
Wiener Neustadt Military Academy, 371, 422, 423: founded by Daun, 94
Wiese, *GFWM.* 131, 142
Wilde Weisseritz, 379, 383
William of Brunswick, Prince, 141
Wilsdruff, 379, 409
Wind-Berg, 197
Winterfeldt, Hans Karl, Prussian *GL.* 65, 240, 406: wounded at Prague, 48; his poor health cause of poor performance, 59; his evil reputation, 66; death, 66
Wipper von Uschitz, captain lieutenant, 255
Wittenberg, 182, 193, 271, 279, 402, 404, 410: captured by Wunsch 27 August 1759, 184; siege 10-13 October 1760, 279
Wittgendorf, 63
Wobersnow, Moritz Franz, Prussian *GM.* 156
Wolfersdorff, Gotthold Ephraim, *FML.* 75, 77, 90, 159, 233, 236, 250, 307
Wolfersdorff, Prussian colonel, 181, 182, 185
Wöllwarth, *GFWM.* 65, 66, 92
Worbeer, Sigmund, Captain, 195, 233
Wulffen, *GFWM.* 58
Wunsch, Johann Jakob, Prussian *GM.* 157, 176, 183, 184, 187, 191, 193, 194, 199, 201, 205, 207, 209
Württemberg contingent, 71, 74: grenadiers, 73; last to arrive before Leuthen, 83; poor position at Leuthen, 85; blamed for defeat, 87; sent home 92

Württemberg, Friedrich Eugen of, Prussian general, 87, 143, 169, 267, 268, 273, 281, 283, 305, 310, 363, 367
Wusterhausen, 267

Yakovlev, Russian general, 317

Zastrow, Prussian general, 323, 326
Zedtwitz, Johann, *GFWM.* 211, 225, 279, 336
Zeller-Wald, 381, 387
Zeuner, Prussian general, 295
Ziegesar, Colonel, 190
Zieten, Prussian general, 53, 66, 74, 75, 81, 85, 87, 89, 105, 107, 109, 110, 139, 254, 257, 260, 285, 289, 295, 298, 300, 302, 303, 316, 347
Zittau, 42, 58, 59, 62, 63, 71, 121, 128, 156, 157, 177, 178, 310, 311, 315, 410, 416: burned in 1757, 61
Znaim, 401
Zobten-Berg, 261, 340, 416
Zorn von Plobsheim, Colonel Maximilian August, 73
Zorndorf 153, 302, 404
Zorndorf, battle of, 123, 126, 153, 302, 404
Zossen, 268
Zuckmantel, 418
Zweibrücken, Prince, 92, 125, 126, 149, 151, 176, 180, 181, 182, 183, 184, 187, 191, 220, 223, 230, 231, 271, 273, 276, 279, 281, 283, 408: portrait, 122; takes command of *Reichsarmee*, 123
Zwickau, 281, 312, 405

The Austrian bombardment of Wittenberg, 10-13 October 1760, page 279